"This collection represents an important and timely new contribution to our understanding of green and sustainable finance. It brings together chapters by many of the leading scholars in this field and offers new thinking across a range of topics such as regulation, accounting, and reporting, as well as critical issues such as green-washing and the role of the state."

– **Professor Alex Nicholls**, *Professor of Social Entrepreneurship, Said Business School, University of Oxford, and Fellow in Management, Harris Manchester College, University of Oxford, United Kingdom*

"*The Routledge Handbook of Green Finance* successfully combines a collection of insights from international thought leaders. Thus, the handbook is an invaluable resource for understanding current developments through a breadth of diverse perspectives."

– **Aaron Ezroj**, *Former Director of the Office of Climate Risk Initiatives, California Department of Insurance, United States*

"Green finance is growing, whether it will be a rare plant or a sustainable forest is still to be seen. This book is a great platform to observe and theorize these developments, and possibly imagine a better world."

– **Professor Paolo Quattrone**, *Professor of Accounting, Governance and Society and Director of the Centre for the Analysis of Investment Risk, Alliance Manchester Business School, Manchester, United Kingdom*

"The book is a leading authority on green finance, and those interested in ESG research will find this a good reference material."

– **Dr Matthias Nnadi**, *Senior Lecturer in Accounting, Cranfield School of Management, Bedfordshire, United Kingdom*

"The world of finance is fast-moving and the green finance sector moves even faster – and it moves forward. This book takes a good global look at its latest developments in terms of financing instruments, various evolving regulatory efforts, the main reporting platforms as well as certain less discussed green finance sectors. The book offers a good overview of the state of affairs by multiple contributors but a warning is in place; it may be a portal to a desire for deeper insights into the fascinating world of green finance."

– **Eila Kreivi**, *Director, Chief Sustainable Finance Advisor, European Investment Bank, Member of the Platform for Sustainable Finance*

THE ROUTLEDGE HANDBOOK OF GREEN FINANCE

Green finance is heralded in theory and practice as the new panacea – the ideal way to support the green transition of businesses into more sustainable, environmentally responsible forms, by means of incentivized financial investments. This handbook brings together a variety of expert scholars with industry specialists to offer the most authoritative overview of green finance to date, presenting the current situation in the field. It focuses on green finance in a comprehensive way, discussing its characteristics, underlying principles, and mechanisms.

The book carefully illuminates the issues surrounding green finance and delineates its boundaries, mapping out and displaying the disparate voices, traditions, and professional communities engaged in green and sustainable finance activities. Specifically, it examines the "environmental" in the environmental, social, and governance (ESG) measurements, while also discussing the interplay between each measurement. It develops a range of analytic approaches to the subject, both appreciative and critical, and synthesizes new theoretical constructs that make better sense of hybrid financial relationships. Furthermore, the handbook illustrates existing best practices and theories, and critically examines the gaps to derive the necessary future research questions. It highlights the essential issues and debates and provides a robust research agenda. As such, it helps to create an effective market for the various green financing instruments through clarification and standardization.

This handbook will be the standard reference work for a broad audience, encompassing scholars, researchers, and students but also interested professionals, regulators, and policymakers wishing to orient themselves in a rapidly developing and increasingly topical field.

Othmar M. Lehner is the director of the Center for Accounting, Finance and Governance at the Hanken School of Economics, Helsinki.

Theresia Harrer is a postdoctoral researcher in sustainability accounting at the Hanken School of Economics, Helsinki.

Hanna Silvola is an associate professor of accounting at the Hanken School of Economics, Helsinki.

Olaf Weber is a professor at the Schulich School of Business and holds the CIBC Chair in Sustainable Finance.

THE ROUTLEDGE HANDBOOK OF GREEN FINANCE

*Edited by Othmar M. Lehner, Theresia Harrer,
Hanna Silvola and Olaf Weber*

LONDON AND NEW YORK

Designed cover image: wildpixel/Getty Images

First published 2024
by Routledge
4 Park Square, Milton Park, Abingdon, Oxon OX14 4RN

and by Routledge
605 Third Avenue, New York, NY 10158

Routledge is an imprint of the Taylor & Francis Group, an informa business

© 2024 selection and editorial matter, Othmar M. Lehner, Theresia Harrer, Hanna Silvola and Olaf Weber; individual chapters, the contributors

The right of Othmar M. Lehner, Theresia Harrer, Hanna Silvola and Olaf Weber to be identified as the authors of the editorial material, and of the authors for their individual chapters, has been asserted in accordance with sections 77 and 78 of the Copyright, Designs and Patents Act 1988.

All rights reserved. No part of this book may be reprinted or reproduced or utilised in any form or by any electronic, mechanical, or other means, now known or hereafter invented, including photocopying and recording, or in any information storage or retrieval system, without permission in writing from the publishers.

Trademark notice: Product or corporate names may be trademarks or registered trademarks, and are used only for identification and explanation without intent to infringe.

British Library Cataloguing-in-Publication Data
A catalogue record for this book is available from the British Library

Library of Congress Cataloging-in-Publication Data
Names: Lehner, Othmar M., editor. | Harrer, Theresia, editor. |
Silvola, Hanna, editor.
Title: The Routledge handbook of green finance/
edited by Othmar M. Lehner, Theresia Harrer, Hanna Silvola
and Olaf Weber.
Description: 1 Edition. | New York, NY : Routledge, 2024. |
Series: Routledge international handbooks |
Includes bibliographical references
and index.
Identifiers: LCCN 2023018456 (print) | LCCN 2023018457 (ebook) |
ISBN 9781032385297 (hardback) | ISBN 9781032385334 (paperback) |
ISBN 9781003345497 (ebook)
Subjects: LCSH: Investments—Environmental aspects. | Business
enterprises—Environmental aspects. | Sustainable development—Planning.
| Social responsibility of business.
Classification: LCC HG4515.13 .R68 2024 (print) | LCC HG4515.13
(ebook) | DDC 332.6/04—dc23/eng/20230707
LC record available at https://lccn.loc.gov/2023018456
LC ebook record available at https://lccn.loc.gov/2023018457

ISBN: 978-1-032-38529-7 (hbk)
ISBN: 978-1-032-38533-4 (pbk)
ISBN: 978-1-003-34549-7 (ebk)

DOI: 10.4324/9781003345497

Typeset in Bembo
by Deanta Global Publishing Services, Chennai, India

CONTENTS

List of Figures *xi*
List of Tables *xiv*
Contributors *xvii*
Foreword *xxiii*
Acknowledgements *xxv*
Glossary *xxvi*

    Introduction: Setting the Scene for Green Finance 1
    Othmar M Lehner, Theresia Harrer, Hanna Silvola, and Olaf Weber

PART 1
Green Finance Market and Regulatory Environments   5

1 Sustainable Finance Ecosystem: A Case Study from Aotearoa New Zealand   7
   David Hall and Tongyu (Melody) Meng

2 Accounting for a Green Economy: Sustainable Finance and the Harmonisation of Sustainability Reporting   23
   Josef Baumüller and Susanne Leitner-Hanetseder

3 Double Materiality: Why Does It Matter for Sustainability Reporting?   41
   Tia Rebecca Driver and Amr ElAlfy

4 Climate Scenario Analysis for Central Banks   57
   Matteo Bonetti, Dirk Broeders, Marleen Schlooz, and Vincent Streichert

5 Public Financial Institutions and Climate Change   75
   Lina Xie, Bert Scholtens, and Swarnodeep Homroy

6 Internal Carbon Pricing in Research and Practice　　　　　　　　　　87
   Viktor Elliot, Mari Paananen, Manfred Bergqvist, and Philip Jansson

PART 2
Green Finance Instruments and Their Effects　　　　　　　　　　　　101

7 Corporate Environmental Impact: Measurement, Data, and Information　103
   George Serafeim and T. Robert Zochowski

8 Corporate Carbon Management Systems and Carbon Opportunity:
   An International Study　　　　　　　　　　　　　　　　　　　　　129
   Le Luo

9 Beyond Monetary Gain: Motivational Correlates of Sustainable Finance　149
   Klaus Harnack and Sven Moons

10 The Influence of Firms' ESG Initiatives on Firm Value: An Analysis of
   Select European Firms　　　　　　　　　　　　　　　　　　　　　167
   Paolo Saona and Laura Muro

11 The Yields of Green Bank Bonds: Are Banks Perceived as Trustworthy in
   the Green Financial Markets?　　　　　　　　　　　　　　　　　　189
   Nicholas Apergis, Giuseppina Chesini, and Thomas Poufinas

PART 3
Sector- and Country-Specific Aspects　　　　　　　　　　　　　　　213

12 The Quest for Global Green Finance Participation: Developing
   Countries and Barriers to Full Participation　　　　　　　　　　　　215
   George Kapaya and Orthodoxia Kyriacou

13 Accounting as a Mediating Practice between Values and Contexts: A
   Research Agenda on Impact Investment　　　　　　　　　　　　　227
   Luis Emilio Cuenca, Stephanie Rüegger, and Urs Jäger

14 When Do Bank Loans Become Green?　　　　　　　　　　　　　246
   Olga Golubeva

15 Public Policy and Green Finance in China　　　　　　　　　　　　264
   Andrew C. Worthington and Dong Xiang

16 Green Finance in China: System, Practice, and International Role　　　280
   Christoph Nedopil and Mathias Larsen

17 Finance without Unified Measurement Framework: Rise of Collective
    Norm Entrepreneurs in Impact Finance in Japan   300
    Noriaki Okamoto

18 Green Finance Strategies in Africa: A Focus on Capital Market-Based
    Impact Investments in Small and Medium-Sized Enterprises in Ghana   317
    Richmond Odartey Lamptey, Michael Zisuh Ngoasong, and Richard Blundel

19 The United Nations' Principles for Responsible Banking, CSR, and
    Corporate Governance in the Banking Industry   337
    Emilia Vähämaa

PART 4
Critical Perspectives   355

20 Measuring Biodiversity: Mission Impossible?   357
    Theresia Harrer, Hanna Silvola, and Othmar M. Lehner

21 Can Nuclear Attract Green Finance?   374
    Simon Taylor

22 Green, Greener, Not Green Enough?: Institutional Forces Driving the
    European Green Bond Market   391
    Katrina Pichlmayer and Othmar M. Lehner

23 The Hidden Costs of Impact Measurement   416
    Sean Geobey and Tatianna Brierley

PART 5
Building Theory on Green Finance   429

24 Sustainability Reporting of State-Owned Enterprises: Current Practices
    and Implications of the CSR Directive   431
    Dorothea Greiling and Philumena Bauer

25 Assessing the Current State of Research on Climate and Environment-
    Related Financial Risks: What Are We Missing? A Review and Research
    Agenda   446
    Rosella Carè and Olaf Weber

26 A Systematic Literature Review on Financial Stock Performance of
    Sustainable Investments: Bridging the Gap between Empirical Evidence
    and Recent Theoretical Models   463
    Anouck Faverjon, Céleste Hardy, and Marie Lambert

27 Arguing for Urban Climate Change Adaptation Finance – A Bibliometric Study: An Interdisciplinary Systematic Longitudinal Literature Review and Bibliometric Analysis of Urban Adaptation Financing, a Global North Perspective 2010–2021   485
   Stella Whittaker

28 Green Bonds as a Tool of Green Financing   512
   Markus Düringer, Niels Hermes, and Swarnodeep Homroy

29 Building Normativity in Sustainability Reporting: From National to European Union-Level Regulations   526
   Blerita Korca and Ericka Costa

30 Air Pollution and Investors' Behavior: A Review of Recent Literature   542
   Ze Zhang and Shipeng Yan

Index   *563*

FIGURES

2.1	Regulations addressing the transparency of European companies	26
3.1	The outside-in and inside-out relationships of double materiality through the example of climate change	45
3.2	The dynamic nature of sustainability reporting topics	46
4.1	The figure demonstrates the severity of physical and transition risk according to NGFS (2021) scenarios	63
4.2	The figure presents the construction of Transition Vulnerability Factors (TVFs) and Physical Vulnerability Factors (PVFs)	64
4.3	The figure shows the empirical distribution function of TVFs	65
4.4	The figure shows the empirical distribution function of PVFs	65
4.5	The figure presents the construction of Climate Vulnerability Factors (CVFs) under each climate scenario	66
4.6	The figure presents the deposit facility rate (DFR) trajectories under different climate scenarios	67
5.1	Public financial institutions in the financial system	76
5.2	PFIs' role in channeling climate finance to LCR projects	78
5.3	Geographic flows of PFIs' climate finance. Panel A: Public climate finance across regions (2019–2020 annual average); Panel B: MDBs' climate finance commitments across countries (2015–2020 annual average)	80
5.4	Public climate finance by mitigation and adaptation	81
6.1	Internal Carbon Pricing in Microsoft Inc	93
6.2	Internal Carbon Pricing in Volvo Cars AB	93
6.3	A framework of a dynamic internal carbon pricing system (based on Rossing and Rodhe, 2014)	94
7.1	Distribution of environmental intensity (discount rate of 0%)	113
7.2	Distribution of environmental intensity (operating income, discount rate of 0%)	113
7.3	Environmental intensity (sales) by industry	115

7.4	Environmental intensity (scaled by operating income) by industry	116
7.5	SDG targets (0% discount rate)	117
7.6	SDG targets (3% discount rate)	117
7.7	Market pricing and environmental intensity by industry	122
7.8	Dynamic materiality of environmental intensity by industry (Capital markets industry's dynamic materiality coefficient, though not shown in Figure 7.8, is also statistically significant and very negatively influencing the scale of the chart and thereby omitted from the chart. While there are nine industries that have seen significant increase in materiality, there are only two industries exhibiting significant decrease in materiality: health care equipment and supplies, and household durables.)	122
9.1	Distribution of values of retail investors based on the Schwartz theory of universal values	155
9.2	Distribution of regulatory focus of retail investors based on their superordinate motivation of Schwartz theory of universal values	157
9.3	Simplified correlation table for respondent's inter-item responses for specific subcategories. Note: the correlations within one category are marked in red	160
9.4	Percentage of selected subcategories depending on the importance of considering sustainable factors	161
14.1	The balance sheet of a green firm	252
14.2	When do bank loans become green – the suggested framework	259
16.1	Stages of green finance development in China	282
16.2	Overview and relations between bodies governing green finance	283
16.3	Overview of provincial and municipal green finance pilots and initiatives	285
16.4	Annual Chinese green bond issuance, separated by internationally aligned and nonaligned	289
16.5	Chinese government-issued guidance and opinions relevant for greening finance in the Belt and Road Initiative distinguishing between "host country principle" and "international/Chinese standards" for environmental protection	292
16.6	Chinese, developing, and developed country signatories to the PRI and the Equator Principles	294
17.1	Impact investment in the spectrum (this figure is based on Brandstetter and Lehner (2015, p. 89))	303
18.1	Theoretical framework for analyzing green finance within impact investing	319
18.2	Theoretical framework for uncovering explicit and implicit green finance strategies	322
18.3	Data analytic structure	323
19.1	United Nations' Principles for Responsible Banking (United Nations, 2022a)	339
20.1	Global financing needs to protect and restore biodiversity (adapted by the authors based on UNEP, 2022, p. XIII)	359

20.2	Biodiversity finance flows (own depiction by authors based on OECD, 2019, p. 64)	361
20.3	The three key properties of nature (Dasgupta, 2022, p. 31)	362
21.1	Deaths per TWh of electricity produced by electricity generation type (as of 2014)	383
22.1	Green bond market's organisational field	397
22.2	Use of proceeds analysis of data records	402
22.3	Distribution of data records among rating agencies and rating results	404
22.4	Distribution of data records among third-party reviewers	405
23.1	Net benefits of impact measurement to funders, agencies, and beneficiaries. Venn diagram displaying the connection between impact measurement benefits to funders, agencies, and beneficiaries	420
23.2	Net benefits of impact measures in housing. Venn diagram displaying the net benefits of impact measurement in housing. Benefits are displayed relative to funders, agencies, and beneficiaries	422
25.1	Co-occurrence of author keywords	449
25.2	Density visualization	451
25.3	Overlay visualization	451
26.1	Most used words in the abstracts of the selected papers	468
26.2	Research methodology	469
26.3	Number of empirical studies by research fields	474
26.4	Timeline of theoretical and empirical studies per theoretical framework	474
27.1	Flow diagram for the systematic literature review following the PRISMA Statement 2020	488
27.2	Publications by date and discipline for 2010–2020 (NVIVO) (n=257) Note to Figure 27.2: Twenty-six publications were excluded in Figure 27.2, because the majority of these are from the year 2021 (18), this year was only searched up to March 2021, therefore representing an incomplete year of data. Additionally, a very small number of publications (8) were identified earlier than 2010. The 'Other' disciplines included social sciences, energy, and disaster management research fields	491
27.3	Articles by journal (2010–2021) (VOSViewer)	492
27.4	Keyword clusters (80 most frequently used author keywords) (VOSviewer)	493
27.5	Author citation clusters (VOSViewer)	500
27.6	Co-citation clusters (authors) (VOSViewer)	500
27.7	Top researchers by country (VOSViewer)	501
27.8	Visualization of the core literature (adapted from Mortazavi et al., 2021)	501
28.1	Value of green bond issuance in US dollars (in $m)	514
28.2	Number of green bonds issued	514
30.1	Number of relevant studies published in each year	545

TABLES

1.1	Research participants summary	12
2.1	Comparison of main objectives of EU and IFRS sustainability standards	34
4.1	The table exhibits the stylized balance sheet of a central bank	60
4.2	The table exhibits the stylized balance sheet of De Nederlandsche Bank (DNB)	66
4.3	The table illustrates the climate scenario impact on DNB's profit	68
4.4	The table illustrates the climate scenario impact on interest rate risk	68
4.5	The table illustrates the climate scenario impact on credit risk	69
4.6	The table illustrates the climate scenario impact on market risk	71
5.1	Correlation coefficients matrix of MDBs' mitigation finance and adaptation finance, and countries' CO_2 emissions and vulnerability	82
6.1	The three internal carbon pricing methods	91
7.1	Summary statistics of sample	109
7.2	Sources of variation in environmental intensity	114
7.3	Estimates of correlation between environmental intensity and ratings	118
7.4	Market pricing of environmental intensity	120
7.5	Dynamic materiality of environmental intensity	120
7.6	Returns, risk, and environmental intensity	121
8.1	Sample distribution	136
8.2	Descriptive statistics	140
8.3	Correlations	141
8.4	Main regression results	142
8.5	Moderating effects of an ETS and carbon-intensive sector	144
10.1	Descriptive statistics	174
10.2	Correlation matrix	176
10.3	Multivariate analysis for the whole sample	178
10.4	Multivariate analysis by industry	181
10.5	Multivariate analysis by economic sector	183

11.1	Expected influence of bond-specific and macroeconomic variables	197
11.2	Cross-dependence test	198
11.3	Unit root tests	199
11.4	Dynamic panel estimations	200
11.5	Dynamic panel estimations – pandemic period	202
11.6	Dynamic panel estimations – vaccination period	204
13.1	Exploring the hybrid assessment models used by impact investors	233
13.2	Guiding questions for future research	234
15.1	China's green bond market, 2020–2021	267
15.2	Environmental information disclosure framework	268
15.3	Timing of green finance policies in China	273
17.1	Summary of impact measurement frameworks by various organizations	305
17.2	Actors, motives, and mechanisms in the stages of norm diffusion	307
17.3	Actor-centric norm-diffusion process	308
18.1	Capital market-based impact investment funds studied and data collection	324
18.2	Explicit green finance strategies, motivation, and instruments of fund managers	325
18.3	Implicit green finance strategies, motivation, and instruments of fund managers	327
19.1	Descriptive statistics	345
19.2	Correlation matrix	346
19.3	Univariate tests	347
19.4	Regression results	348
20.1	Most relevant financing options for restoring and protecting biodiversity (based on Binnie et al. (2022); adapted by the authors based on OECD (2020))	360
20.2	Biodiversity disclosure initiatives (based on Bang (2023, p. 16), Mair et al. (2021), Cavender-Bares et al. (2022), Almond et al. (2022), and OECD (2020))	362
20.3	Most important biodiversity measurement approaches and indicators (based on Bang (2023, p. 16), Mair et al. (2021), Cavender-Bares et al. (2022), Almond et al. (2022), Darrah et al. (2019), and OECD (2020))	366
20.4	Most relevant databases for biodiversity assessment (non-exhaustive) (based on Bang (2023, p. 16), Mair et al. (2021), Cavender-Bares et al. (2022), Almond et al. (2022), Darrah et al. (2019), Hamilton and Casey (2016), OECD (2020), FAO (2015), Wamelink et al. (2012))	368
21.1	Share of nuclear in total electricity supply, selected nations (2020)	375
21.2	Countries with nuclear reactors under construction	376
21.3	Key nuclear investment risks and their management	379
21.4	New nuclear construction problems in Europe and the United States	379
24.1	Paper allocation	434
25.1	Search strings and query description	448
25.2	Cluster composition	450
26.1	Sample of empirical studies	470

26.2	Descriptive statistics of the sample of empirical studies	476
26.3	Top ten articles by number of citations	478
27.1	Search terms	489
27.2	Top ten article discipline areas	491
27.3	Top ten journals	492
27.4	Keyword clusters: approaches to UA financing in the literature	494
27.5	Top 20 most cited publications (full SLR database)	497
27.6	Top 15 most productive authors and affiliations (WoS)	499
27.7	Key urban adaptation finance research gaps identified in the studied literature	503
29.1	Sustainability reporting in Europe – from national to EU level regulations (adapted from Larrinaga & Senn, 2021)	529
30.1	Number of relevant studies published in each journal	545
30.2	Distribution of research context in each year	546

CONTRIBUTORS

Nicholas Apergis is Professor of Economics at the University of Piraeus. His research areas are macrofinance and energy economics. He has over 260 published papers with a current Scopus H-index=54. He is also Editor of the journal *Environmental Science and Pollution Research* and Member of the Editorial Board of *Energy Economics*.

Philumena Bauer LL.B is a university assistant at the Institute for Management Accounting at Johannes Kepler University, Linz, Austria. Her main research interests are related to the field of sustainability reporting as well as management and control in the public sector, especially at municipal utilities.

Josef Baumüller is a postdoctoral researcher at the Technical University of Vienna and lecturer at the Technical University of Graz, at the Vienna University of Economics and Business, and, amongst others, at the University of Applied Sciences Upper Austria. His research focuses on sustainability reporting.

Manfred Bergqvist is a graduate of MSc Finance at the School of Business Economics and Law at Gothenburg University, Sweden. His thesis, written together with Philip Jansson, focused on the implementation and effects of internal carbon pricing on commercial- and supply-chain operations.

Richard Blundel is Professor of Enterprise and Organisation at the Open University Business School, UK. He researches the intersection of entrepreneurial activity, innovation, and environmental sustainability, and has appeared in journals such as *Business & Society*, *Entrepreneurship & Regional Development*, *Business Strategy and the Environment*, *Enterprise & Society*, and the *Journal of Small Business Management*.

Matteo Bonetti is a risk manager for the Financial Markets Division of De Nederlandsche Bank. He has a PhD in Finance from the School of Business and Economics of Maastricht University, the Netherlands.

Tatianna Brierley is a master's student at the University of Waterloo in the School of Environment, Enterprise, and Development. Her research has focused on impact measurement in affordable housing. Her research interests include social finance, systems theory, and social development.

Contributors

Rosella Carè is Global Marie Skłodowska-Curie Research Fellow at Waterloo University (Canada). Rosella's primary research areas – where she is the author of several works published by outstanding international academic editors and publishers – include social and sustainable finance, alternative finance, impact investing, sustainable banking, ESG, and climate risks.

Giusy Chesini is Associate Professor of Banking and Finance at the University of Verona, Italy. Her main research interests include empirical banking, financial regulation, and financial markets. She has authored about 70 scientific publications, including papers, chapters, and monographs. She has been involved in several national and international research projects.

Ericka Costa (PhD in Business Economics, University of Udine, Italy) is Associate Professor of Accounting, University of Trento, Italy. Her research interests are focused on investigating sustainability accounting and corporate social responsibility for both for-profit and non-profit organizations. She has written a number of chapters in books, and papers for national and international journals.

Luis Emilio Cuenca is Assistant Professor in Management Accounting at INCAE, Costa Rica, and associate researcher at VIVA Idea, Costa Rica. He holds a PhD in Management Accounting from HEC PARIS. Since the beginning of his academic career, Professor Cuenca has worked in the development of projects with positive social impact for communities and businesses.

Tia Rebecca Driver is a doctoral candidate in the School of Environment, Enterprise and Development at the University of Waterloo, Canada. Her current research interests include sustainability reporting and strategic management.

Markus Düringer is a PhD candidate in economics at the University of Groningen, the Netherlands. His research focuses on climate change and corporate governance. In his professional career, he works as an investment analyst for AXA Insurance in Switzerland and is a board member of a small-cap investment company and advisory committee member for various mid-cap European investment funds.

Amr ElAlfy is an assistant professor of sustainability management at the College of Business and Economics at Qatar University. His research focuses on sustainability management and corporate reporting frameworks. Dr ElAlfy has a long managerial history of working in multinational conglomerates, namely Nestlé and 3M, where he led the marketing and sustainability agendas for the Middle East and Africa (MEA) region.

Viktor Elliot is a senior lecturer in business administration and director of the Business IT Lab at the School of Business Economics and Law at Gothenburg University, Sweden, where he also received his PhD. His research focuses on bank management and regulation, sustainable finance, and digitalization.

Anouck Faverjon is a PhD candidate at HEC Liège (ULiège) and at University Paris-Dauphine, France.

Jean Geobey is Assistant Professor of Social Entrepreneurship and Innovation at the University of Waterloo, Canada, in the School of Environment, Enterprise, and Development (SEED) and the Co-Director of the Waterloo Institute for Social Innovation and Resilience (WISIR).

Olga Golubeva is based at Stockholm Business School, Stockholm University. Dr Golubeva's research findings are published in peer-reviewed journals like "Accounting, Auditing &

Accountability Journal", "Corporate Governance", "Journal of Contemporary Accounting and Economics", etc. Olga won an Outstanding paper award in the 2022 Emerald Literati Awards.

Dorothea Greiling is head of the Institute for Management Accounting at the Johannes Kepler University, Linz, Austria. Her main research focuses on public accountability, performance management, sustainability control, sustainability reporting, and SDG activities, mostly but not exclusively of public enterprises and non-profit organizations as well as in regulated industries.

David Hall has a DPhil in Politics from the University of Oxford and currently is Senior Lecturer at the School of Social Sciences and Public Policy, Auckland University of Technology (AUT). His research focus is climate action with a particular focus on the politics of sustainability transitions, climate policy design, sustainable finance, and nature-based solutions.

Céleste Hardy is a PhD candidate at HEC Liège (ULiège).

Theresia Harrer is a postdoctoral researcher in sustainability accounting at the Hanken School of Economics. Her research focuses on how organizations interact with stakeholders, specifically on how sustainability reporting requirements and online communication change those interactions.

Niels Hermes is Full Professor of International Finance and Chair of the Department of Economics, Econometrics and Finance, University of Groningen. He is also Visiting Professor at the Universite Libre de Bruxelles. His research focuses on corporate governance, international finance and microfinance. He is Editor of *Corporate Governance: An International Review*.

Swarnodeep Homroy is an Associate Professor of Finance at the University of Groningen. His research interests are climate change's economic and financial implications, gender inequality in the workplace, corporate social responsibility, and the intersection of corporate finance and political systems.

Philip Jansson is a graduate of the MSc Finance at the School of Business Economics and Law at Gothenburg University, Sweden. His thesis, written together with Manfred Bergqvist, focused on the implementation and effects of internal carbon pricing on commercial- and supply-chain operations.

Urs Jäger is a professor at INCAE Business School where he holds the Chair of Sustainability VIVA Idea Schmidheiny. He is also Executive Director of VIVA Idea, a think-action tank focused on action research projects in sustainable development. He focuses his research on the social inclusion of formal and informal markets.

George Kapaya is Deputy Head of Accounting and Finance at the University of Northampton. He is a qualified and experienced Chartered Accountant (ICAEW) and has extensive practical experience in accounting, taxation, and auditing. His research interests include international accounting, developing countries, FDI, and multinationals.

Blerita Korca (PhD in Economics and Management, University of Trento, Italy) is a Postdoctoral Researcher at the University of Bamberg in Germany. Her research interests are in the field of sustainability accounting and reporting, and she has published both scientific articles and policy briefs in the field.

Orthodoxia Kyriacou is an Associate Professor in Transdisciplinary Developments at Middlesex University where she is primarily involved in the supervision of professional doctoral candidates. Her previous publications include articles focusing on gender and ethnicity issues in the UK accounting profession and the teaching of ethics to accounting students.

Marie Lambert is Full Professor at HEC Liège, Management School of the University of Liège where she holds the Deloitte Chair in Sustainable Finance.

Richmond O. Lamptey has recently been appointed a Lecturer in Entrepreneurship at the University of Greenwich Business School. He previously held the role of a Teaching Fellow at the University of Greenwich Business School. His PhD in Business Studies, obtained in 2020, investigated the influence of bank-based and capital market-based impact investments on SME financing in Ghana. Richmond's work has been published in *Entrepreneurship and Regional Development*.

Mathias Lund Larsen is a dual PhD Fellow at Copenhagen Business School and the University of the Chinese Academy of Sciences (Sino-Danish Center for Education and Research). His research is focused on the political economy of green finance in China from theory to practice, intention to impact, and domestic to overseas.

Othmar M. Lehner is the director of the Center for Accounting, Finance and Governance at the Hanken School of Economics in Helsinki and associate professor of accounting. His research interests are in the intersection of accounting and organizations, particularly on ethics and sustainability. He is well-published, a passionate book author, and a celebrated keynote speaker.

Susanne Leitner-Hanetseder is a lecturer in accounting at the Johannes Kepler University of Linz, guest lecturer at the Hanken School of Economics, and Professor of Accounting at the University of Applied Sciences Upper Austria. Her research focuses on digitalization in accounting as well as IFRS and sustainability accounting.

Le Luo is a senior lecturer in the Department of Accounting and Corporate Governance at Macquarie University. Her research expertise lies primarily in sustainability and carbon accounting. She has published more than 30 academic papers in peer-refereed international journals, including the *European Accounting Review*, *British Accounting Review*, and *Journal of Banking and Finance*.

Melody Meng has a PhD in Management from the University of Auckland and is currently a research fellow at the Auckland University of Technology. She is also a senior analyst at Sustainalytics working on sustainable bonds issuance projects and taxonomy development. She has diversified experience in a range of sectors including sustainable finance, renewable energy market, cross-border e-commerce, consulting, aviation, real estate, media, education, sports, and tourism.

Laura Muro is Professor of Accounting at Saint Louis University Madrid, with scholarly experience in corporate governance and business sustainability, with scientific publications in international high-ranked journals, in the specific areas of board gender diversity, earnings management, and capital structure decisions. Her present research is focused on sustainable finance, impact investments, and financial inclusion.

Christoph Nedopil is Associate Professor of Practice at Fudan University and the Director of the Green Finance & Development Center at FISF Fudan University. His research focuses on sustainable finance, China and the Belt and Road Initiative (BRI), as well as green innovation finance.

Contributors

Michael Ngoasong is a Senior Lecturer in Management and Head of Department for Public Leadership and Social Enterprise at the Open University Business School. His research on entrepreneurial practices has appeared in journals such as *Energy Policy*, *Management and Organisation Review*, *Entrepreneurship & Regional Development*, and the *Journal of Small Business Management*.

Noriaki Okamoto is a professor of accounting at the College of Business at Rikkyo University. He received his PhD from Kobe University in 2006. His research interests lie in the social, political, and institutional aspects of accounting. His current research project is the quantification of social impact. His previous works appeared in journals including *Accounting Forum*, *Critical Perspectives on Accounting*, and the *Journal of Economic Methodology*.

Mari Paananen is Associate Professor of Accounting and co-director of the Business IT Lab at the School of Business Economics and Law at Gothenburg University, Sweden. Her current research involves examining the capital market effect of financial reporting disclosures, in particular environmental information using computerized text analysis.

Katrina Pichlmayr is a Group Controller and a graduate of the Controlling, Accounting and Financial Management master's program at the University of Applied Sciences in Steyr. Her research project was dedicated to analyzing the European green bond market from an institutional perspective.

Thomas Poufinas is Assistant Professor in the Department of Economics of the Democritus University of Thrace. He holds a PhD in Financial Mathematics from The Ohio State University and a bachelor's degree in Mathematics from the University of Athens. His research interests focus on finance, investments, risk management, actuarial science, and their applications.

Stephanie Rüegger holds an MBA from INCAE Business School and a master's in Strategy and International Management from the University of St. Gallen. She works as a research affiliate at INCAE and VIVA Idea, and at the Institute of Technology Management, University of St. Gallen.

Paolo Saona is Professor of Finance. His research fields include international corporate finance, corporate governance, sustainable finance, the banking industry, and financial systems. He is a research fellow at Universidad Pontificia Comillas in Spain and at Universidad Católica de la Santísima Concepción in Chile. He has more than 50 published studies.

Marleen Schlooz is a risk manager for the Financial Markets Division of De Nederlandsche Bank. She has a master's degree in econometrics and economics from Maastricht University.

Bert Scholtens is a Professor of Sustainable Banking and Finance at the University of Groningen. He specializes in banking, socially responsible investing, and environmental economics. Bert has published widely in top-tier finance and general interest journals.

George Serafeim (Harvard Business School, USA) is Chair of the Valuation Technical and Practitional Committee for the International Foundation for Valuing Impacts. From 2019 to 2022, he was the Faculty Chair of the Impact-Weighted Accounts Project and the Charles M. Williams Professor of Business Administration at Harvard Business School. He has taught courses in the MBA, executive education, and doctoral programs.

Hanna Silvola is an Associate Professor of Accounting at the Hanken School of Economics, Finland. Her research interests are in sustainable investing and in measuring, reporting, and assuring ESG information. She has published on a range of topics in accounting journals and has comprehensive experience as a speaker in media and executive education.

Vincent Streichert is a risk manager for the Financial Markets Division of De Nederlandsche Bank. He has a master's degree in financial economics from Erasmus University Rotterdam.

Simon Taylor is a former utilities analyst in the stock market who joined Cambridge University's Judge Business School in 2006 where he is a Research Associate of the Energy Policy Research Group. He has written two books on the British nuclear power industry and teaches a course on infrastructure finance.

Emilia Vähämaa is Wärtsilä Associate Professor at Hanken School of Economics. Her research interests lie in the areas of sustainable finance, corporate governance, and banking. She has published in various journals including the *Journal of Business Ethics*, *Journal of Business Research*, and *Journal of Financial Services Research*.

Olaf Weber is a professor at the Schulich School of Business and holds the CIBC Chair in Sustainable Finance. His research addresses sustainable lending, investment, and impact finance.

Stella Whittaker is a specialist and scholar in the field of climate change and sustainability, working for over 30 years as an executive and in academia in Europe and Australia. Stella's PhD is in climate adaptation finance. Her overarching interest is exploring and understanding government and investor perspectives in relation to the adaptation financing gap – the deficit between the finance required and the amount of finance available.

Andrew C. Worthington is Professor of Finance at Griffith University, Australia. He holds master's degrees from the University of New South Wales and the University of New England and obtained his doctorate from the University of Queensland. His green finance interests include ESG investing, sustainability, and environmental information disclosure.

Dong Xiang is Professor and Associate Dean at Shandong Normal University, China. He holds a master's degree from Massey University and obtained his doctorate from the University of Newcastle. His green finance interests include green credit policies in Chinese banking and small and medium-sized enterprises.

Lina Xie is a PhD scholar at the University of Groningen who specializes in financial intermediation and climate finance. Her thesis is on the climate-related activities of public financial institutions in OECD countries.

Shipeng Yan is a management scholar with an institutional lens, a sociological orientation, and an interest in organizations. In particular, he is keen to study (1) comparative dynamics of institutional arrangements across countries; and (2) the relationship between finance and society, with a focus on environmental, social, and governance (ESG) issues.

Ze Zhang is a doctoral student in the Faculty of Business and Economics at the University of Hong Kong.

T. Robert Zochowski (International Foundation for Valuing Impacts, USA) is the President and CEO of the International Foundation for Valuing Impacts. Formerly, Rob was the Program Director and Senior Researcher for Multi-Faculty Sustainability and Impact Investing Special Projects, including The Impact-Weighted Accounts Project, the Social Impact Collaboratory, and the Project on Impact Investments at Harvard Business School.

FOREWORD

By Michael B. Dorff
Michael & Jessica Downer Chair
Southwestern Law School

The United Nations' latest report on climate change pulled no punches: human activity has "unequivocally" caused global warming of over 1 degree Celsius since 1850.[1] Climate change has caused immeasurable harm to millions of people across the globe, from greater food scarcity to water insecurity to damage from droughts and storms.[2] Hundreds of species have been driven to extinction.[3] These calamities represent only the leading edge of the damage humanity is wreaking on the environment, as our production of greenhouse gases continues to increase, despite efforts to reduce them through international treaties such as the Kyoto Protocol and the Paris Agreement.

Reversing the damage may already be impossible. Even to minimize it, we must act quickly to curtail our emissions of greenhouse gases across industries as diverse as energy, transportation, agriculture, and construction. This is a monumental and daunting task. Success will require massive investments. We must not only convert our energy production to clean and renewable sources but also at the same time increase the supply of electricity dramatically to power cleaner transportation, agriculture, and industry. The International Renewable Energy Agency has estimated that the cost of limiting global warming may amount to $131 trillion by 2050.[4] The economic cost of failing in this task, though, is likely to prove much higher, and the cost of human life and extinct species may be immeasurable.[5]

Finding the resources to fund this transition is therefore critical. The effort will require enormous amounts of capital from governmental, corporate, and philanthropic sources. We need to think carefully about how we raise and spend this money and about how governments should incentivize private capital to participate in the effort to green our economy. In other words, green finance is at the very heart of our efforts to curb climate change. Our success at mobilizing capital is likely to determine our ability to maintain a livable planet for future generations.

For this reason, the publication of this incredible book, *The Routledge Handbook of Green Finance*, could not be more timely or important. Edited by some of the most prominent scholars in sustainable finance, Othmar M Lehner, Theresia Harrer, Hanna Silvola, and Olaf Weber, the book gathers cutting-edge research from leading international researchers in the field to provide an indispensable resource to scholars, students, and practitioners. The book covers the full range of topics related to green finance, including the regulatory environment, green finance instruments, sector- and country-specific aspects, critical perspectives, and theory. Gathering all this learning together in one place will no doubt prove of inestimable value to our efforts to meet what is the central challenge of our time, preserving an environment that is hospitable to human life on Earth.

Notes

1 United Nations, Synthesis Report of the IPCC Sixth Assessment Report at 4 (2023), available at https://report.ipcc.ch/ar6syr/pdf/IPCC_AR6_SYR_SPM.pdf.
2 *Id.* at 5.
3 *Ibid.*
4 Daniel Orton, *How Much Would It Cost to Reduce Global Warming? $131 Trillion is One Answer*, Wall Street Journal, 29 October 2021, available at www.wsj.com/video/series/wsj-explains/how-much-would-it-cost-to-reduce-global-warming-131-trillion-is-one-answer/7CDC8900-9FF0-4DF6-BD69-25A5FF5B02B5 (last viewed 14 April 2023).
5 Pradeep Phillip and Claire Ibrahim, *The Turning Point*, Deloitte, 20 June 2022 (without intervention, climate change could cost the world economy $178 trillion in net present value terms from 2021–2070).

ACKNOWLEDGEMENTS

We thank Routledge for believing in our book and providing the opportunity to discuss the topic of green finance for a global audience. Specifically, we want to thank Kristina Abbotts and Christiana Mandizha for their guidance and tireless support throughout the whole process of writing the book!

We also extend our warmest thanks to the Foundation for Economic Education, which has funded our ESG research project at the Hanken School of Economics during 2020–2023. This financial support not only helped us to put together the latest scientific outcomes on green finance but most notably also to work with Aaron Afzali who has helped us enormously in preparing the book draft.

Part of this research was also financially supported by the EU Horizon programme TC4BE – 101082057 – GAP-101082057 on Pathways for BioDiversity. The European Commission's support for the production of this publication does not constitute an endorsement of the contents, which reflects the views only of the authors, and the Commission cannot be held responsible for any use which may be made of the information contained therein.

We also would like to thank all the authors for their fantastic contributions to the book. Their diverse expertise has enabled us to compile a truly global perspective on green finance.

Finally, thank you to our loved ones who have encouraged and inspired us to write this book.

GLOSSARY

acceleration depreciation scheme (ADS): form of tax incentive.
advocacy coalition framework theory: public policy is the outcome of a policy subsystem composed of different advocacy coalitions, each with its own beliefs, resources, and strategies.
agency theory: deals with the conflict of interests in corporations caused by asymmetric incentives between the different interested parties.
Air Quality Index (AQI): measure air pollution.
Aotearoa Circle: established in October 2018 as a partnership of public and private sector leaders with a common commitment 'to the pursuit of sustainable prosperity and reversing the decline of New Zealand's natural resources'.
Asset-Liability Management (ALM) model: for future profits assessments and interest rate risk calculations.
Availability WAter REmaining (AWARE) model: provides supplemental water monetization factors, allowing us to account for the effect of local water scarcity.
AWARE Factors: conversion factors for the absolute amount of available freshwater remaining in each country in terms of global-equivalent cubic meters, defined as the world average after human and aquatic ecosystem demands have been met.
BBGF (now ABSA Ghana): bank-based impact funds.
Beta *(BETA)*: is defined as firm's systematic risk.
Better Alignment Project: a ground-breaking two-year project to promote better alignment in the corporate reporting environment to make it easier for companies to prepare effective and coherent disclosures that meet the information needs of capital markets and society.
biodiversity: defined as the variability among living organisms from all sources including, inter alia, terrestrial, marine and other aquatic ecosystems and the ecological complexes of which they are part; this includes diversity within species, between species and of ecosystems.
black credit: Is credit where environmental factors, if not ignored, are given far less weight in the credit assessment process.
Bloomberg and Thomson Reuters (ASSET4) Databases: organization-level emissions and water-use data.

Glossary

Bloomberg ESG Index: the set of organizations within the Bloomberg database that has reported some environmental data.

bounded rationality: is the idea that actors can only make rational decisions based on the information that is available to them and identifying and collecting this information is costly.

business ecosystems: ever-evolving cross-sectoral ecosystem.

capital expenditures: are scaled by total assets since they are recognized as assets.

carbon accounting: research field in the domain of environmental accounting.

Carbon Disclosure Project (CDP): is one of the largest data collections on the climate impact of organizations (based on self-reported data).

carbon finance: comprise carbon market trading and financing tools.

carbon footprint: is the total greenhouse gas emissions caused directly and indirectly by an individual, organization, event, or product..

central banks: are systemic authorities with a specific mandate.

CGIR Climate Security Observatory (CSO): is currently being developed. It will provide descriptions and analysis of the pathways via which climate change and variability might act as a threat multiplier to existing vulnerabilities and insecurity.

characterization pathways: scientifically-based methodologies to transform outputs into impacts.

Climate Bond Initiative (CBI): is an international non-profit organization working on gathering and collating market intelligence, developing market standards, and guiding policy and regulation in the market for sustainable financing.

climate change-related risks: It induce disruptions to several layers of the economy via natural disasters and transition shocks, making it a potential source of price and financial instability.

Climate Change Response (Zero-Carbon) Amendment Act 2019 (New Zealand): Net-zero emissions by 2050 goal.

Climate Disclosure Standards Board (CDSB): an international consortium of business and environmental NGOs offering a framework for reporting environment and social related information.

climate finance: is the primary source to mitigate and adapt to climate change.

climate opportunities: defined as potential positive impacts on an organization resulting from efforts to mitigate and adapt to climate change.

climate scenario analysis (CSA): It is used to quantify the potential financial impact of climate-related developments on a central bank's balance sheet.

climate stress test: methodology to gauge how climate risk might propagate through the financial system.

CMBF1: is a climate and impact fund manager, leading the clean energy transition in emerging markets.

CMBF2: is a capital market-based impact fund.

commensuration: It facilitates the comparison of disparate organizations that are the object of quantifiable data.

Community Score *(CommunityScore)*: which measures the company's commitment towards being a good citizen, protecting public health, and respecting business ethics.

complementary fit: refers to the idea that something is missing or should be added to create a whole, becomes important when people want to compensate for their own "sustainable shortcomings."

corporate governance (CG): measures "a company's systems and processes, which ensure that its board members and executives act in the best interests of its long-term shareholders."

Glossary

corporate social responsibility (CSR): commitment of business to contribute to sustainable economic development by working with employees, their families, the local community and society at large to improve their lives in ways that are good for business and development.

corporate sustainability: links business strategy and sustainability via a systems perspective, which maps the relationships between businesses and society.

Corporate Sustainability Reporting Directive (CSRD): is a reporting European Union directive which aimed at all large companies independent of stock exchange listings, provides detailed reporting standards and requires auditing.

CPI: Climate Policy Initiatives.

Credit Value-at-Risk (CVaR) model: for credit risk calculations.

Cross-dependence test: simple average of all pair-wise correlation coefficients of the OLS residuals obtained from standard augmented Dickey-Fuller regressions for each variable in the panel.

CSR Strategy Score *(CSRScore)*: which reflects a company's practices to communicate that it integrates the economic (financial), social, and environmental dimensions into its day-today decision-making processes.

De Nederlandsche Bank (DNB): the central bank of the Netherlands.

deposit facility rate (DFR): is the remuneration rate for the deposits held by commercial banks at DNB.

direct emissions: occur from sources owned or controlled by the company.

Directive 2014/95 (European Union): companies to provide annual reports on environmental, social, and employee matters. It also requires them to disclose anti-corruption and human rights policies as well as any bribery that may have been attempted in the last year. This directive was superseded by the Corporate Sustainability Reporting Directive, which brought with it the European Sustainability Reporting Standard.

disposition effect: this is a psychological phenomenon where investors tend to sell assets that have increased in value but hold onto assets that have decreased in value, contrary to the rational decision expectation..

disruptive innovation theory: the process by which a product or service initially takes root in simple applications at the bottom of a market— typically by being less expensive and more accessible—and then relentlessly moves upmarket, eventually displacing established competitors.

dividends: as payments made by a corporation to its shareholders, usually in the form of cash or additional shares..

double-hybridity: a combination of financial and impact returns on the one hand, and developing and developed countries on the other.

double materiality: It considers the impacts on enterprise value and the impacts of organizational activities on the natural environment and society.

dynamic materiality: recognizes the fluidity of material.

ecosystem: flows of material and energy.

Emission Reduction Score *(EmissionScore)*: which measures a company's commitment and effectiveness toward reducing environmental emission in the production and operational processes.

emission trading systems: Trading of emission rights among business units (BUs) within an organization to reach an internal market price for carbon.

Energy Taxation Directive (ETD): defines the minimum taxation rates for energy products, such as electricity and fuel.

entrepreneurial ecosystem: system of interdependent actors and relations directly or indirectly supporting the creation and growth of new ventures.

Environmental Information Disclosure: guideline to guide how financial institutions should disclose environmental information in a standardized and structured way.

environmental intensity: as environmental impact scaled by sales or operating income.; This provides an estimate for environmental damage per unit of sales or operating income.

environmental performance pillar score (ENV): captures a firm's commitment to and effectiveness and efficiency in using natural resources, reducing environmental emissions, and supporting the research and development of eco-efficient products and services.

Environmental Priority Strategies (EPS) database: provides a publicly available, scientifically-based methodology to transform the direct results of an organization's operations, referred to as outputs, such as emissions, into their impacts, referred to as characterization pathways.; set of monetization factors and "safeguard subjects" to map emission's characteristic pathways to the SDGs.

epistemic community: defined as a network of professionals with recognized expertise and competence in a particular domain and an authoritative claim to policy-relevant knowledge within that domain or issue area.

EU Emission Trading System (EU ETS): a market for emission rights.

EU 'Fit for 55' policy: directive on the deployment of infrastructure based on alternative fuels.

European Financial Reporting Advisory Group (EFRAG): provide the European Commission with the insights needed to develop reporting standards based on European needs and interests.

European Union Business @ Biodiversity Platform: aims to integrate natural capital and biodiversity considerations in business practices. Its three functional workstreams consist of Methods (developing practical guidance and tools), Pioneers (facilitating corporate collaboration), and Mainstreaming (promoting biodiversity-focused business decision making across Europe).

EU taxonomy: is an important tool for financial markets to define which investment targets are green and sustainable, and it aims to help investors to allocate their financing to green activities.

Exiobase: provides a global environmentally extended multi-regional input-output table as a baseline for supply chain analysis and estimates emissions and resource extractions by industry.

expectancy-value theory: achievement motivation becomes stronger when there is a match with personal values.

Finance for Biodiversity Initiative (F4B): aims to increase the materiality of biodiversity in financial decision-making and align global finance with the conservation and restoration of nature.

Finance for Biodiversity Pledge: was launched in 2020. Financial institutions who sign the pledge commit to protecting and restoring biodiversity through their financial activities through knowledge sharing, engagement with companies, assessing their impacts, setting targets, and reporting on these criteria by 2025.

financial goals: making more money out of the given money.

financial system: an arrangement of components–actors, artifacts; and institutions–and their interrelations.

financing gap: defined and measured as the difference between the costs of, and thus the finance required, for meeting a given adaptation target and the amount of finance available to do so.

firm size: measured as the log transformed firm sales.
firm value (*LnFV*): measured with the proxy for Tobin's Q, computed as the sum of the firm's market capitalization and the total liabilities and then divided by the firm's total assets.
fit for investment: is the grade of congruence, the shared characteristics of an individual, and attributes of the environment.
feed-in tariff (FIT): policy that typically guarantees renewable generators specified payments per unit over a fixed period.
Global Biodiversity Information Facility (GBIF): is an international network and data infrastructure, and is aimed at providing anyone, anywhere, open access to data about all types of life on Earth.
Global Climate Risk Index (GCRI): developed and published annually by the nongovernmental organization Germanwatch. Proxy for the overall physical risk faced by a country.
Global Reporting Initiative (GRI): help organizations to identify the most material issues they should disclose in their sustainability report.
global supply chains (GSCs): flow of goods and supplies from the source to the customer.
global value chains (GVCs): value flows from the customer, in the form of demand, to the supplier
green banks: provide improved credit conditions for clean energy projects, the creation of innovative financial products, and market expansion through the dissemination of information about the benefits of clean energy.
green bonds: are fixed-income securities that are identical to non-green bonds except that the proceeds should be addressed entirely to projects with an environmental or climate-related focus.
Green Climate Fund (GCF): a global fund created to support the efforts of developing countries to respond to the challenges of climate change.
green credit: the practice of banks considering not only economic benefit but also environmental factors in the credit issuance process and making appropriate loan decisions on this basis.
green finance: any structured financial activity – a product or service – that's been created to ensure a better environmental outcome. It includes an array of loans, debt mechanisms and investments that are used to encourage the development of green projects or minimize the impact on the climate of more regular projects. Or a combination of both.
greenhouse gases (GHG): as the seven gases covered by the UNFCCC: carbon dioxide (CO_2); methane (CH_4); nitrous oxide (N_2O); hydrofluorocarbons (HFCs); perfluoro carbons (PFCs); sulfur hexafluoride (SF_6), and nitrogen trifluoride (NF_3).
greenium: the market premium to the price of the green bond.
Green Loan Principles (GLPs): promote the integrity of the green loan product.
green loans: is a type of financing where funding goes to projects and investments with environmental benefits. For example, our bank classified loans to finance wind power projects as green loans.
Green (New) Deal: aims to transform the European Union into a competitive economy, free of net emissions of greenhouse gases by 2050.
greenwashing: the practice of making unsubstantiated or misleading claims about the company's environmental commitment.
gross domestic product per capita (GDPPC): a measure of a country's economic output per person, calculated by dividing the gross domestic product by the total population.
growth: measured as one-year annual sales growth in net sales, calculated as the current year's revenues divided by the preceding year's revenues minus 1.

Glossary

Human Rights Category Score *(HRightsScore)*: which measures a company's effectiveness of respecting the fundamental human rights conventions.

IFC Environmental and Social Performance Standards: define the responsibilities of corporations for managing environmental and social risks.

impact: defined as the change in an outcome.

impact measurement: use of metrics by funders, agencies, and beneficiaries is highlighted with a lens focused on their material uses in decision-making and the costs of impact measurement emphasized.

***IndexESG*1:** represents the average of the three scores.

indirect emissions: from the generation of purchased energy including the emissions resulting from the production of grid electricity.

innovation ecosystem: set of actors, artifacts, and institutions that are critical to the innovative performance of actors.

Innovation Score: which reflects a company's capacity to reduce the environmental costs, and creating new market opportunities through new environmental technologies and processes or eco-designed products.

institutional change theory: relates to the overlap between institutions and policy.

institutional voids: the absence or underdevelopment of specialized intermediaries such as database vendors, and quality certification firms, regulatory corporations, and control-enforcing mechanisms.

interdisciplinarity: defined as the purposeful integration of various pieces of disciplinary knowledge.

interest rate risk: is defined as the cumulative losses over the full evaluation horizon under extreme but plausible interest rate trajectories.

internal carbon pricing (ICP): an instrument that captures the external costs of greenhouse gas (GHG) emissions and ties them to their sources through a price, usually in the form of a price on the carbon dioxide (CO_2) emitted.

International Financial Reporting Standards (IFRS): regulates financial reporting in 160 jurisdictions, took steps into the sustainability reporting domain in 2020.

International Organization for Standardization (ISO): a recognized international multi-stakeholder standard-setting organization, 14000 series (environmental management).

International Sustainability Standards Board (ISSB): develop comprehensive IFRS Sustainability Disclosure Standards material for investment decisions for the global financial markets.

Intergovernmental Panel on Climate Change (IPCC): was founded in 1988 and has currently 195 member countries. The organisation aims at providing scientific research on climate change and associated risks and recommends measures to counter negative developments.

IRIS+: impact measurement framework.

IUCN: guidelines provide an approach for developing a corporate-level biodiversity strategic plan. They can be applied to any company, sector, or operational scale and define measurable goals, objectives, and indicators related to biodiversity performance.

IUCN Red List of Threatened Species: a public database developed by the IUCN, which classifies species into one of seven Red List categories to represent their level of extinction threat (ranging from Least Concern to Extinct). It is considered to be the world's most comprehensive inventory of the conservation status of wildlife species and currently has over 142,000 species logged in the database.

LEGAL: represents a country's legal system.

legitimacy theory: predicts how companies disclose ESG information to improve the image and the reputation of the firm and its value (Sharma & Song, 2018), and, consequently, to reduce the perceived risk.
leverage: measured as one minus the ratio of book value of equity over total assets.
lifecycle management theories (LCM): reasoning, sustainability challenges should be addressed by taking into consideration the entire company life cycle.
loan growth: is measured as an annual growth rate of the loans and is calculated as (current year's total loans / last year's total loans − 1) x 100.
logics: are the formal and informal rules of action, interaction and interpretation that guide and constrain decision makers.
Management Score *(ManagementScore)*: which measures a company's commitment and effectiveness towards following best practice corporate governance principles.
Māori leadership: representatives from banks, insurance companies, industry, professional services, civil society, academia, and the government.
materiality: the degree to which a measure is expected to have an impact on how decisions are made within an organization.; It helps corporations select the most relevant reporting criteria to ensure that the organization's disclosure aligns corporate disclosure with the needs of the organization's stakeholders.
middle-ground approach: it is used for investment impact assessment by prioritizing short-term results over long-term goals.
MiFID II amendment: Explanatory Memorandum to the Commission Delegated Regulation Amending MiFID II Delegated Regulation (EU) 2017/565, 2021, are the first of many essential steps to ensure a congruent structure between the individual needs of a client and the financial products provided.
multilevel governance theory: It is a public policy change where actors move between various levels of action and authority disperses across multiple tiers (i.e., national, regional, or local).
natural capital: defined as the stock of natural resources, such as land and water, that provide economic, social, and environmental benefits.
Natural Capital Finance Alliance (NCFA): it is a finance alliance which aims to integrate natural capital considerations into financial products, as well as improving nature-related risk accounting, disclosure, and reporting.
nature: refers to the natural world, with an emphasis on the diversity of living organisms (including people) and their interactions among themselves and with their environment.
net water consumed: water withdrawal minus water discharged.
Network for Greening the Financial System (NGFS): central banks launched NGFS in 2017, it serves as a platform for central banks to share best practices, contribute to the development of environment and climate risk management in the financial sector, and mobilize mainstream finance to support the transition toward a sustainable economy.
Net-Zero Banking Alliance: Alliance has recognized the vital role of banks in supporting the global transition to the real economy to net-zero emissions by 2050.
norm emergence: is the stage where norm entrepreneurs attempt to convince or persuade a critical mass of states (norm leaders) to embrace different norms.
Notre Dame Global Adaptation Initiative (ND-GAIN Country Index Score): it is an index which captures a country's vulnerability to climate disruptions.
NVivo 12: a software tool used for qualitative data analysis.
open market operations (OMOs): actions taken by the central bank to steer interest rates, manage the amount of liquidity in the financial system, and signal its monetary policy stance.

outcome: result of an action or event which is an aspect of social, environmental, or economic well-being.

outputs: direct results of an organization's operations.

Panda–Dragon paradox: the green parts have expanded, the polluting parts have not decreased fast enough.

Partnership for Biodiversity Accounting Financials (PBAF): aims to develop a standard for financial institutions to assess and disclose impacts and dependencies on biodiversity.

path dependence theory: the theory suggests that policymakers often work within a constrained set of assumptions, rarely learning from past experiences, and generally emphasize caution in decision-making.

Physical Vulnerability Factors (PVFs): based on the geographical location(s) of an issuer.

policy diffusion theory: the theory that knowledge about policies, administrative techniques, and institutions can be transferred and adapted from one setting or time to another.

policy entrepreneurs: agents for policy change who possess the knowledge, power, tenacity and luck to be able to exploit key opportunities to advance particular policies and agendas.

policy learning theory: actors and coalitions of actors learn from the experiences of others in formulating public policy.

policy network theory: where diverse groups form an expansive but loosely coupled network that is bound by a collective identity or purpose.

politics of policy change and reform theory: it affects the origins, formulation, and implementation of public policy especially when significant changes are involved.

prevention focus: is aimed at not deteriorating from a given point, so not slipping from point zero to a minus one state.

Principles for Responsible Banking: set of best practices for the banking industry.

probability of default (PD): it is the likelihood that a borrower will default on its debt obligations. The credit spread can be influenced by the PD, among other factors, but they're not the same thing.

Product Responsibility Score (*ProductScore*): which reflects a company's capacity to produce quality goods and services integrating the customer's health and safety, integrity, and data privacy.

promotion focus: describes efforts to improve circumstances from a given point, that is, the motivation to get from a current state (point zero) to a plus one state.

promotion-oriented goals: are generally more related to positive emotions than prevention oriented goals and are associated with values such as self-enhancement.

public financial institutions (PFIs): financial institutions initiated/owned by governments with official missions to serve the public interest as defined by national, regional, or international policy objectives.

punctuated equilibrium theory: it proposes that once an idea gets attention it will expand rapidly and become unstoppable.

RAB (regulated asset base) model: provides for an independent regulator to provide a guaranteed level of revenue in respect of the cumulative investment made by private investors, using the established framework of regulated network utilities in the UK.

R&D expenditures: as a flow variable, are scaled by sales.

REC: is a certificate awarded to certify the generation of one unit of RE.

Red Rocket Holding Ltd: is an integrated renewable energy independent power producer (IPP) constructing, developing and operating over 2.5 GW of utility-scale, grid-connected wind, solar and hydro projects across Sub-Saharan Africa.

Renewable Energy Directive (RED): constitutes a legal framework that defines standardised objectives and promotes investments in green energy systems to encourage the energy transition.

resource-based accountability: the management accounting tools used by international development organizations aim to ensure proper accountability to the donors, rather than improve impact among beneficiaries.

Resource Use Score *(ResourceScore)*: which reflects a company's performance and capacity to reduce the use of materials, energy, or water, and to find more eco-efficient solutions by improving supply chain management.

return on assets (ROA): proxy for a firm's financial performance, is calculated as net income before extraordinary items/preferred dividends divided by total assets.

return on equity (ROE): a measure of a company's profitability that compares net income to shareholders' equity and is calculated as (net income before preferred dividends + ((interest expense on debt − interest capitalized) x (1 − tax rate))/(last year's total assets − last year's customer liabilities on acceptances) x 100).

ROSES: a framework developed by Haddaway & Macura that builds a list of criteria and steps to perform a systematic literature review.

Royal Society for the Protection of Birds (RSPB): an influential charity in the UK.

scenario analysis: is a method for assessing forward-looking vulnerabilities to the possible evolution of one or more risk drivers.

Science-Based Targets Network (SBTN): as part of the Global Commons Alliance, the SBTN aims to develop methods and resources to guide companies in developing science based targets for nature and climate-related action aligned with the SDGs.

Sector Standards: It improve the comparability between organizations within the same industry by outlining a pre-established list of sustainability issues that are typically relevant for organizations operating within a specified industry.

shadow price: predetermined fictitious internal price to evaluate investment alternatives.

Shareholders Score *(ShareholdersScore)*: which measures a company's effectiveness towards equal treatment of shareholders and the use of anti-takeover devices.

sharpe ratio: defined as the average return earned in excess of the risk-free rate per unit of volatility or total risk.

signaling theory: states how companies can take different policies to signal their value to investors.

SIMI: established in 2016 to promote social impact measurement in Japan.

SIMI Global Resource Center (SIMI-GRC): providing its members with resources regarding impact finance, such as translated reports and case studies.

single materiality: disclosing information related to the impact on the organization's financial performance.

social banks: institutions that grant loans to create a social or environmental benefit.

social impact: is the measurable outcomes of material changes experienced by target populations as the result of deliberative organizational action.

social impact bonds (SIBs): are designed to overcome the challenges governments have in investing in prevention and early intervention. They mitigate the risks of failure and bring in impact investors, who want to test innovation and scale successful programs.

Social Innovation and Impact Foundation (SIIF): founded in 2018 to promote social impact measurement.

Social return on investment (SROI): idea of discounted cash is modified and adapted to measure the social value created per unit of investment.

Glossary

sociology of accounting: provides concepts through which we can understand how value is determined in hybrid settings.
SOCO International: multinational energy company.
supplementary fit: refers to the similarity between individual values with characteristics of the context or environment; it mirrors its own values.
supply chain: process of making and selling commercial goods, including every stage from the supply of materials and the manufacture of the goods through to their distribution and sale.
Sustainability Accounting Standards Board (SASB): standards require organizations to communicate any risks and opportunities that impact enterprise value.
sustainability case for business: It help corporations identify the positive and negative impacts of their operations, services, or products on sustainable development.
sustainability challenges: climate change, population growth and inequality, dwindling clean energy supplies, and freshwater availability.
sustainability reporting: sub-discipline of accounting including specific information on environmental or social: matters as part of company reporting.
sustainability reporting standards: to ensure more complete reporting and to enhance the comparability of published information.
sustainable finance ecosystem: an ecosystem comprising financial sector participants, regulators, entrepreneurs, advisors, and investors; organizational actors such as universities, international organizations, and incubators; and factors such as public policies and networks.
Sustainable Finance Forum (SFF): produce the roadmap to redesign the financial systems to enhance resilience to climate-related risks and to align with the SDGs by mobilizing a large sum of private capital.
system: a set of interrelated elements… which is composed of at least two elements and a relation that holds between each of its elements and at least one other element in the set.
systems-building approach: tests and adjusts the investor's theory of change, builds on previous results, and creates a transparent impact database.
TANG: ratio of total (net) property plant and equipment to total assets.
Taskforce on Nature-related Financial Disclosures (TNFD): was launched in 2021 to develop a risk management and disclosure framework for organizations to report and address nature-related risks in alignment with the TCFD.
taxonomies (China): taxonomies in China refer to the China Banking Regulatory Commission's list of green industries on which banks have to file statistics, the PBOC Green Bond Project Endorsed Catalogue, and the NDRC Green Industry Catalogue, and the PBoC, NDRC, and CSRC updated and joint Green Bond Project Endorsed Catalogue.
Technical Readiness Working Group (TRWG): comprised representatives of organisations which represent the world's capital markets and other users as well as voluntary standard-setters.
tendering: is a procurement mechanism by which RE capacity is solicited from sellers, who offer bids at the lowest price that they would be willing to accept.
Thames Tideway Tunnel (TTT): a large sewerage tunnel project in London.
theories of public policy change: referring to modifications (often incremental amendments, sometimes major reforms) in existing institutional or market structures or new and innovative policies.
tipping point: exists between the norm emergence and the norm acceptance stage.
Tobin's Q: a measure of the market value over the replacement value of assets.

Glossary

Toitū Tahua: is Centre for Sustainable Finance, as an independent entity to carry on the work by implementing the recommendations and legacy from the SFF in order to transform the financial system in New Zealand.

top-down approach: refers to a method where high-level concepts or goals are established first, and then details are filled in.

transfer pricing: as a tool for allocating accountability to, and creating coordination between, different units in large divisionalized companies.

Transition Vulnerability Factors (TVFs): Based on the GHG emissions intensity of an issuer.

UNEP-FI: guidance for biodiversity target setting.

UNEP-WCMC: guidance for biodiversity target setting.

unit root test: employed to determine the degree of integration of the respective variables.

universalism: value that emerges with the realization that, to survive as a group, we must treat others who are different from us justly and protect the natural environment and resources on which life depends.

Universal Standards: provide organizations with the foundational knowledge of key terms and concepts the GRI uses in their reporting framework.

Value Reporting Foundation (VRF): a global non-profit organisation which provides different resources including an Integrated Reporting Framework and SASB Standards adopted in over 70 countries.

values: property of being present and noticeable and function as a mental signpost and door-opener.

water discharge: total amount of liquid waste and process water discharged by the organization.

Waterfund dataset: provides two broad sub-categories – water production and delivery, and wastewater treatment – each of which has components of operating expenses, depreciation, and non-operating expenses.

water withdrawal: total amount of water diverted from any source for use by the organization.

Wetland Extent Trend (WET) database: consists of 306 data sources, including scientific literature, gray literature, national wetland inventories, and four global datasets based on national level data of mangroves, peatlands, and rice paddies.

Workforce Score *(WorkforceScore)*: which measures a company's effectiveness in job satisfaction, and maintaining a healthy, safe, and diverse workplace with equal opportunities and development opportunities for its workforce.

World Database on Key Biodiversity Areas: a global database that identifies the locations of Key Biodiversity Areas (KBA).

World Database on Protected Areas: a global database of marine and terrestrial protected areas, which provides downloadable geospatial information that details the boundary and characteristics of each protected area.

World Governance Indicator *(WGI)*: which measures the quality of the governance and policies in a country.

Z-Score: a statistical measure used to determine the likelihood of a company's bankruptcy.

INTRODUCTION

Setting the Scene for Green Finance

Othmar M Lehner, Theresia Harrer, Hanna Silvola, and Olaf Weber

The world is facing an unprecedented challenge – climate change. In the face of mounting scientific evidence of the devastating effects of climate change, it has become clear that urgent action is needed to address the crisis. As the global economy becomes increasingly interconnected, it has become apparent that all sectors of the global economy must work together to mitigate the effects of climate change and to promote climate action, including through green finance.

Green finance is an emerging field that has enormous potential to help us transition to a low-carbon and climate-resilient economy and promote more equitable solutions. Through green finance, investors, financial institutions, and governments can channel funds toward projects and businesses that support the transition to a low-carbon economy, reduce emissions, minimize loss of biodiversity, drive economic growth, and create jobs and well-being in society. For green finance to be effective, it is essential to develop international standards and frameworks, promote public-private collaboration, and ensure that investments are well-targeted and monitored. While there is much work to be done to realize the potential of green finance, there is no doubt that it can be a powerful force for positive climate action. Research is still needed to better understand the opportunities and challenges of green finance, to listen to critical voices, and to explore the possibilities of using green finance to support local communities in achieving climate resilience in a more equitable future. With the right strategies and actions, green finance can be a powerful tool for tackling the climate crisis.

The purpose of this handbook is to provide an overview of the current state of green finance. It aims to explore the various elements of green finance, including the market and regulatory environments, green finance instruments and their effects, sector and country-specific aspects, and critical perspectives. It also seeks to provide a comprehensive review of the current state of green finance research and to suggest possible avenues for future research.

The handbook is organized into five parts. Part 1, "Green Finance Market and Regulatory Environments," explores the various elements of the green finance market and regulatory environments. Green finance is a rapidly growing field, and its potential to support sustainable development and climate change mitigation is significant. To unlock the potential of green finance, it is essential to have a thorough understanding of the green finance market and regulatory environments. As such, this part of the handbook with Chapters 1–6 will focus on the components of green finance, including the sustainable finance ecosystem in Aotearoa New Zealand, the harmonization of sustainability reporting, double materiality and its implications for sustainability reporting, climate scenario analysis for public financial institutions, climate change, and internal carbon pricing in research and practice.

The sustainable finance ecosystem in Aotearoa New Zealand for example is a multipartite system involving financial institutions, investors, regulators, and other stakeholders. It is essential for the sustainable finance ecosystem to function effectively in order for green finance to be successful. In New Zealand, the Financial Markets Authority (FMA) has the responsibility of overseeing the financial markets and promoting the efficient, fair, and transparent operation of the financial markets. The FMA has been actively engaged in the development of the sustainable finance framework, which includes the formulation of rules, guidelines, and principles for sustainable finance. Related to and demanded by such regulations, climate scenario analysis is an important tool for public financial institutions and other stakeholders to assess the risks associated with climate change. Climate scenario analysis consists of assessing different climate-related scenarios and their impacts on financial stability and the economy. This analysis can be used to inform policy decisions and investments in order to mitigate the financial and economic risks associated with climate change.

Part 2 of the handbook, "Green Finance Instruments and their Effects," examines the various green finance instruments and their effects in greater detail. Chapter 7 looks at how corporate environmental impact can be measured and how data can be used to analyze it, while Chapter 8 goes deeper into corporate carbon management systems and how to identify carbon opportunities. Chapters 9 and 10 focus on the motivational factors behind sustainable finance and the correlation between a firm's environmental, social, and governance (ESG) initiatives and its value. Finally, Chapter 11 delves into the yields of green bank bonds and the effects they have on investors. By focusing on the motivation behind sustainable finance for example, the second part is relevant for policymakers and financial market participants, as they can gain insights into how to create a sustainable financial system that meets both economic and environmental goals and overcomes the challenges based on divergent opinions and motivations.

Part 3 of the handbook, "Sector- and Country-Specific Aspects," provides an in-depth analysis and discussion of green finance from sector and country-specific perspectives. Chapter 12 examines the quest for global green finance participation, exploring the motivations, challenges, and solutions for driving the green finance agenda at an international level. Chapter 13 examines accounting as a mediating practice between values and contexts, exploring how financial statements and other accounting information can be used to help drive green finance initiatives. Chapter 14 looks at when bank loans become green, exploring how loan products can be designed to meet environmental goals. Chapter 15 focuses on public policy and green finance in China, exploring the changes that have been made in China to incentivize green finance projects. Chapter 16 looks at green finance in China more broadly, examining the current state of green finance initiatives in the country and the potential for further growth. Chapter 17 examines finance without unified measurement frameworks, exploring how to effectively measure and track the impact of green finance initiatives. Chapter 18 looks at green finance strategies in Africa, exploring the challenges and opportunities for green finance on the continent. Finally, Chapter 19 looks at the United Nations' Principles for Responsible Banking, CSR, and corporate governance in the banking industry, exploring how banks can apply these principles to their operations and use them to drive green finance initiatives.

The United Nations' Principles for Responsible Banking (UNPRB), a salient example for said chapters in Part 3, is an international framework that sets out the responsibilities of banks to align their operations and strategies with the goals of sustainable development and a transition to a low-carbon, climate-resilient economy. The UNPRB is comprised of 26 principles that are intended to provide guidance to the banking industry on how to best support the transition to a sustainable and equitable global economy. The UNPRB was developed in close collaboration with banks, civil society, and other stakeholders to create a framework that is both comprehensive and practical. It is designed to provide structure and guidance to the banking industry, as well as give banks accountability and transparency in their operations. The principles focus on four key areas: environment, climate, social, and governance. Banks are expected to identify and manage risks and opportunities within their portfolios related to the UNPRB's core principles. Banks are also expected to develop and implement strategies that support the achievement of the Sustainable Development Goals and that are in line with the Paris Agreement on climate change. Banks are also expected to disclose their progress in implementing the UNPRB and embed the principles into their decision-making processes.

Part 4 of the book, titled "Critical Perspectives," provides a comprehensive as well as critical evaluation of green finance. In Chapter 20, readers can explore the challenges of measuring biodiversity and its impact on the environment. Chapter 21 examines the potential of nuclear energy to attract green finance. Chapter 22 examines the effectiveness of green bond covenants, while Chapter 23 dives deeper into the hidden costs of impact measurement and how they can be addressed. This part is designed to provide readers with a more critical understanding of green finance so that businesses and organizations can look behind the buzzwords and implement those principles that work in their operations and use them to drive green finance initiatives.

Part 5 of the book, "Building Theory on Green Finance," provides a comprehensive review of the current state of green finance research, as well as some directions for further research. Chapter 24 takes a closer look at how state-owned enterprises incorporate sustainability into their reporting. Chapter 25 investigates how climate and environment-related financial risks can be managed. Chapter 26 provides an in-depth examination of the financial stock performance of sustainable investments. Chapter 27 focuses on urban climate change adaptation finance. Chapter 28 looks at green bonds as a tool for green financing. Chapter 29 examines the role of normativity in sustainability reporting. Finally, Chapter 30 investigates the impact of air pollution on investor behavior and discusses the various ways air pollution can impair investor decision-making, including the impact on stock prices, the risk-return trade-off, and the potential for increased market volatility. Together, these chapters provide an overview of the current state of green finance research and theory, as well as perspectives for further research.

This handbook was compiled to become an invaluable resource for students, academics, practitioners, and policymakers who seek to gain a better understanding of green finance. It provides an in-depth overview of the current state of green finance, including the market and regulatory environment, green finance instruments and their effects, sector and country-specific aspects, and critical perspectives. It also provides a review of the current state of green finance research and suggests possible avenues for future research. For students, this handbook serves as a comprehensive introduction to green finance, allowing them to gain a deeper understanding of the current state of the field and its potential to create a more sustainable financial system. It will also help them to develop the necessary skills to make informed decisions about green finance and its related issues. For academics, this handbook serves as a useful tool to inform their research and widen their understanding of green finance. It provides an overview of the current state of green finance research and suggests possible avenues for future research. It also encourages academics to think critically about the implications of their findings on the industry and their potential impact on the sustainability of the financial system. For practitioners, this handbook serves as an invaluable resource to help them make informed decisions about green finance and its related issues. It provides an overview of the market and regulatory environments, as well as an in-depth analysis of the various elements of green finance and their effects. This information can help practitioners to better understand the potential risks and opportunities associated with green finance investments and to make more informed decisions. For policymakers, this handbook provides scientific evidence on the current stage of green finance and its possibilities and challenges. This information can help policymakers to sharpen their understanding of the green finance landscape and to create useful and harmonized regulations to further solve global problems (such as climate change).

Overall, this handbook provides a comprehensive overview of the current state of green finance and is an invaluable resource for students, academics, practitioners, and policymakers alike. It provides an in-depth overview of the field and its potential to create a more sustainable financial system, as well as suggestions for future research and insight into the implications of green finance investments. As such, it is an essential tool for anyone interested in learning more about green finance and its potential to create a more sustainable financial system, and we hope you find it a worthwhile and enjoyable read.

The editors

PART 1

Green Finance Market and Regulatory Environments

1
SUSTAINABLE FINANCE ECOSYSTEM

A Case Study from Aotearoa New Zealand

David Hall and Tongyu (Melody) Meng

Introduction

Much remains to be done to fulfill international commitments to sustainable and climate-resilient development, and much of what needs to be done needs to be paid for. Consequently, a reorientation of the financial system toward sustainable finance is critical for achieving sustainability transitions (Markard et al., 2012; Schoenmaker & Schramade, 2019). The scale of sustainable finance has increased significantly over the past decade, but supply still does not match the demand for the necessary investments to address global climate change and emission reduction targets (Buchner et al., 2021; Clark et al., 2018). In order to create a sustainable financial system that supports the UN Sustainable Development Goals (SDGs) and each jurisdiction's nationally determined contributions (NDCs), significant reforms are required. To articulate and activate such reforms, many countries have developed and published sustainable finance roadmaps ('the roadmaps') in recent years, including China (2016), India (2016), Argentina (2018), the EU (2018), the UK (2018), Canada (2019), Australia (2020), and New Zealand (2020). These roadmaps set practical recommendations to enhance the financial system's alignment with the SDGs and NDCs, including changes to the practices of financial sector actors, the regulatory regime, and the broader socio-cultural context.

Part of the turn to sustainable finance is a renewed appreciation that not only is the financial system embedded in the environment – as the saying goes, it is a wholly-owned subsidiary of the environment, not the reverse – but it is also embedded in society. This calls for a sustainable finance ecosystem. An ecosystem incorporates individual actors such as financial sector participants, regulators, entrepreneurs, advisors, and investors; organizational actors such as universities, international organizations, and incubators; and factors such as public policies and networks (Spigel, 2020). An ecosystem with the right actors and factors could create momentum for change, create new collaborations around niche technologies, ideas, and markets, and disrupt prevailing socio-technical configurations. One of the functions of roadmap development is that, in some instances, they can bring together often unconnected actors and factors into a more cohesive vision of how to build an enabling environment that will accelerate the progress of sustainable finance.

New Zealand's Climate Change Response (Zero-Carbon) Amendment Act 2019 has enshrined the net-zero emissions by 2050 goal in law, but significant investment is needed to achieve this target. To reorientate the sustainable finance system toward these challenges, the financial sector collaborated with the government on developing a sustainable finance roadmap, published in November 2020, by convening corporate leaders to change mindsets around sustainability and setting priorities for New Zealand's climate action (The Aotearoa Circle, 2020). The roadmap development was initiated by The Aotearoa Circle, a unique partnership of both public and private leadership with a focus on sustainable prosperity (The Aotearoa Circle, 2020). It established the Sustainable Finance Forum (SFF) in January 2019 to produce the roadmap to redesign the financial systems to enhance resilience to climate-related risks and to align with the SDGs by mobilizing a large sum of private capital.

Building an enabling environment to systematically catalyze sustainable finance requires a strong ecosystem. This pivot toward sustainability and climate alignment is a significant economic adjustment (Dyllick & Muff, 2016; Gladwin et al., 1995), which potentially repositions financial institutions as leaders in sustainability transitions by redirecting financial flows towards sustainable practices and influencing the regulation of the financial system. This chapter draws on the literature on sustainable finance (Bernstein & Hoffmann, 2018) and entrepreneurial ecosystems (Acs et al., 2017; Wurth et al., 2021) to identify and analyze the actors and factors in a sustainable finance ecosystem. This chapter addresses the following questions: *who and what are the actors and factors in the sustainable finance ecosystem in New Zealand, and what needs to be done to build a functioning sustainable finance ecosystem?* This line of inquiry is especially salient given that a sustainable finance ecosystem involves a range of public, private sector, and civil society actors with sometimes contradictory incentives embedded in the institutional and cultural context. The ecosystem can play a critical role in building bridges between various actors in order to overcome barriers to systematic changes (Cavallo et al., 2019; Wurth et al., 2021). The Aotearoa Circle's SFF is seen as a climate intermediary, as a go-between that facilitates sustainability transitions in the finance sector by visioning, convening, and coordinating multiple stakeholders (Hall & Meng, n.d.). This case study illustrates how independent financial sector actors overlap, interact with each other, and mutually adjust within a context of overarching rules while building mutual trust (Jordan et al., 2018).

This chapter is organized as follows. We first review the literature on entrepreneurial ecosystems in sustainability transitions to guide and situate our case study in the entrepreneurial ecosystems literature. We then introduce our methodology with an insider-outsider approach. Our findings highlight the actors and factors in the sustainable finance ecosystem and the interdependencies of these actors and factors. SFF plays the role of coordination and facilitation of the actors and factors in a sustainable finance ecosystem by communicating the normative objectives of participating members in the network that could potentially lead to reforms in the finance sector during the sustainability transitions. We then conclude by bringing out some of the gaps in this literature with future research directions.

The Entrepreneurial Ecosystem in Sustainable Finance

It is commonplace to speak of the financial *system*, but what might it mean to speak of a financial *ecosystem*? What is at stake by shifting our language from one to the other?

A system is defined as 'a set of interrelated elements… which is composed of at least two elements and a relation that holds between each of its elements and at least one other element in the set' (Ackoff, 1971, p. 662). It can refer to a very simple set of components – such as a molecule or bathtub – or a more complex arrangement – such as the carbon cycle or global economy. How these components are interrelated also determines how systems 'produce their own pattern of behavior over time' (Meadows, 2008, p. 2). To refer to the financial *system*, in the conventional sense, is to refer to an arrangement of components – actors, artifacts; and institutions – and their interrelations. Actors include commercial banks, insurers, stock exchanges, regulators, central banks, sovereign wealth funds, credit rating agencies, and more. Artifacts can include assets, contracts, IT systems, and money itself. Institutions encompass governance and company structures, the legislation that establishes financial market regulation, and myriad frameworks for auditing, accounting, risk and return analysis, and more. The relations between these components determine how the system behaves, as well as its response to shocks like the 2008 Global Financial Crisis. By highlighting these dynamics, systems thinking helps to anticipate and manage the outcomes of the global financial system, including its resilience to shocks (Hynes et al., 2020).

The word *ecosystem* has its roots in the sciences of ecology (Tansley, 1935). Here the emphasis is on flows of material and energy:

> Connection and flux are the hallmarks of ecosystems... The importance of the ecosystem perspective is not in the individual organisms or even in the individual species within it; it is in the roles that they take in how resources flow along pathways.
> *(Shaw & Allen, 2018, pp. 89–90)*

For instance, certain animals play a vital role in nutrient cycles or occupy an ecological niche when another species loses its dominance. These ideas influenced the literature on *business ecosystems*, which emerged in the 1990s and emphasized that a company should not be understood as independent but as part of an ever-evolving cross-sectoral ecosystem: 'In a business ecosystem, the companies co-evolve capabilities around a new innovation: they work cooperatively and competitively to support new products, satisfy customer needs, and eventually incorporate the next round of innovations' (Moore, 1993, p. 96). A related concept is the *innovation ecosystem*, which focuses on the set of actors, artifacts, and institutions that are critical to the innovative performance of actors (Adner, 2006; Hannah & Eisenhardt, 2018; Rohrbeck et al., 2009). Drawing on the ecological literature, a recent review (Granstrand & Holgersson, 2020) highlights the further importance of activities and relations, especially the collaborative/complementary and competitive/substitute relations that reflect the dynamic nature of innovation. The collaborative qualities of ecosystems, by which individual firms cooperate to provide solutions, are prioritized in the innovation ecosystems literature, but the competitive qualities, where one firm or technology substitutes another (i.e. the Schumpeterian dynamics of creative destruction) are equally important.

It follows, then, that to think of finance as an ecosystem, not merely as a system, is to place greater emphasis on its relational dynamics and its functioning within a wider context. This article investigates the nature and composition of the New Zealand sustainable finance ecosystem and offers new insights into the role of the financial sector leadership in the ecosystem literature. It does this by drawing on yet another related literature on *entrepreneurial ecosystems* (e.g. Acs et al., 2017; Cavallo et al., 2019; Isenberg, 2011; Isenberg, 2016; Spigel, 2020) to analyze financial sector leaders as ecosystem-builders who accelerate the shift toward a self-sustaining sustainable finance ecosystem. Isenberg (2016) has developed a framework of the entrepreneurial ecosystem and its domains, which includes policy, finance, culture, supports, human capital, and markets. These domains relate to the factors (i.e. public policy, culture, network, physical infrastructure, and markets) that encompass an ecosystem (Spigel, 2020). As such, this framework helps to situate entrepreneurial activity within a wider socio-economic context.

This literature has roots in the regional development literature and the strategy literature, investigating the interdependence of actors in a particular community to create value (Acs et al., 2017). The ecosystem approach is interested in the external environment, where the specific context could allow or restrict the development of sustainable finance and various relational elements among multi-actor networks within regions that govern entrepreneurship and value creation (Brown & Mason, 2017; Stam, 2015). An entrepreneurial ecosystem consists of individual and organizational actors such as entrepreneurs, investors, skilled workers, universities, and anchor firms (Feld, 2012; Spigel, 2020). It also consists of factors such as public policy, culture, support organizations, networks, and physical infrastructure (Spigel, 2020). These actors and factors in an ecosystem ensure that resources and innovation can circulate within. The literature on entrepreneurial ecosystems also – as per the ecological analogy – emphasizes the importance of co-evolution and mutual interdependence, as various actors experience emergence, growth, survival, or decline as the result of cooperative and competitive relationships: 'Cooperative relationships emerge among the actors who can achieve complementary benefits by integrating their functional specializations. Competitive relationships emerge as alternative business paths become evident and different entrepreneurs "place their bets on" and pursue alternative paths' (Stam & van de Ven, 2021, p. 812). It is through the accumulation of these cooperative and competitive relations that the ecosystem emerges.

Entrepreneurial ecosystems are a highly variegated, multi-actor, and multi-scalar phenomenon, centripetal agglomerative requiring bespoke policy interventions. In an entrepreneurial ecosystem, actors are inextricably bound together in an ecosystem with close geographic, institutional, and relational proximity (Brown & Mason, 2017). This attribute of proximity is addressed in the stakeholder salience literature as an added attribute in addition to power, legitimacy, and urgency (Mitchell et al., 1997; Neville et al., 2011).

Entrepreneurial ecosystems are an explanatory concept, a way of understanding the 'infrastructure' – institutions, proprietary business activities, market demand, and the supply of knowledge, finance, and labor – that underpins entrepreneurial activity (Van De Ven, 1993). But there is also a normative (or quasi-normative) dimension to the literature insofar as the model of an entrepreneurial ecosystem is treated as a blueprint for how to effectively stimulate entrepreneurial activity. Although it is debated as to whether the literature is mature enough to be policy prescriptive – in particular, to distinguish between necessary and contingent conditions, or to clearly articulate the role of government and other institutions (Stam & van de Ven, 2021, p. 811) – the ideal of the entrepreneurial ecosystem nevertheless holds promise as a way to overcome the shortcomings of incumbent systems in order to facilitate innovation and business creation.

A useful theoretical complement is the sustainability transitions literature, especially for highlighting the potential for entrepreneurial activity to be goal-oriented toward sustainable development (Geels et al., 2017; Markard et al., 2012). Within the context of sustainability transitions, entrepreneurs play a special role in sustainable innovation journeys by initiating experiments, pushing novel technologies and practices from the niche to the mainstream, and discovering creative solutions to the barriers to technological diffusion (Geels et al., 2008). Creating supportive ecosystems for entrepreneurs who are motivated to produce commercializable and scalable solutions to sustainability challenges is one way to overcome the problem of 'carbon lock-in' (Unruh, 2000), which includes the advantages of long-term incumbency. Specifically, the fossil fuel industry enjoys a productivity advantage through decades of improvement (e.g. learning by doing and using, scale economies, and network externalities) and also stabilization by surrounding institutions through favorable standards, regulations, and subsidies; sunk investments in human, social and fixed capital; and support by vested interests and cultures. But establishing a sustainable entrepreneurial ecosystem ought to reduce this disadvantage by providing entrepreneurs with critical resources to develop, commercialize, and scale up new innovations and business models (Acemoglu, 2002; Acemoglu et al., 2012; Mazzucato, 2016).

There is another dimension of important entrepreneurial activity within sustainability transitions: the influence of *policy entrepreneurs*. Policy entrepreneurs have been described as 'the agents for policy change who possess the knowledge, power, tenacity and luck to be able to exploit key opportunities' (Cairney, 2018, p. 201) to advance particular policies and agendas. In that sense, the product is not a specific good or service but rather a policy idea that addresses real or perceived challenges faced by policymakers. Policy entrepreneurs can work from inside or outside of government, facilitating the uptake of innovative ideas into existing institutions, or even creating 'windows of opportunity' where policy innovation can gain a foothold. Unlike business entrepreneurs who respond to market demand, the focus of policy entrepreneurs is to build public or civic demand for policy. In the words of Béland (2005, p. 10): 'Policy entrepreneurs succeed in imposing certain policy ideas partly because they appeal to the public through the mobilization of political symbols ever-present in the shared ideological repertoires available in their society.' Hence the importance of story-telling and persuasion in order to frame (and reframe) policy problems and solutions is apparent (Cairney, 2018).

In the context of sustainable finance, the importance of framing and reframing the issue cannot be understated. One of the greatest leverage points is to change the dominant culture of risk-return thinking embedded in the financial sector – that is, to change the mindsets of the financial industry actors. In order to overcome this institutional lock-in, a critical part of the transition process is 'breaking through these silos and opening up to the views of other groups' (Schoenmaker & Schramade, 2019, p. 361) in order to destabilize the financial risk-return thinking of traditional finance. In this context, sustainable finance roadmaps are an important vehicle for new visions of the financial system, as well as pathways and recommendations to implement them. Such roadmaps, along with policy reports and advice, are among the 'products' that policy entrepreneurs 'sell' to decision-makers and the public in order to drive change.

This chapter applies these theories to the context of Aotearoa New Zealand, specifically the development of a sustainable finance roadmap through The Aotearoa Circle's SFF. This is itself a process of ecosystem-building, of aligning the actors and factors that might facilitate the emergence of new sustainable finance products, practices and technologies. This involves a geographic, institutional and relational proximity, insofar as the process was based in Aotearoa New Zealand, largely in Auckland, drawing on mostly voluntary participation from the financial sector. It is worth noting that although we are building on the entrepreneurial ecosystem literature, the focus is on the ecosystem approach rather than applying conventional entrepreneurship activities in our case study.

Methodology

The Aotearoa Circle's SFF offers a platform for conversations and actionable recommendations for New Zealand's financial sector. We adopted an insider-outsider research perspective throughout our data collection and analysis (Milligan, 2016). The lead author has been part of SFF's Technical Working Group since 2018 with insider perspectives in the case study, which enabled partial observations of the SFF process and participation in internal discussions and decision-making. We have taken ethical considerations throughout the research design and data collection to minimize biases and gain valuable insights enabled by this insider view.[1]

Key contributors in the SFF include Māori leadership, representatives from banks, insurance companies, industry, professional services, civil society, academia, and the government. We conducted 15 in-depth interviews to collect data directly from these contributors in the SFF process from late 2021 to early 2022. These research participants are identified from the SFF's leadership and Technical Working Group, and are approached through the researchers' own networks. An overview of the interviewees is summarized in the below Table 1.1. We are aware of local contextual factors with a sound understanding of the institutional and cultural norms for engaging with Māori. The detailed interview questions can be found in the Appendix.

Table 1.1 Research participants summary.

Contributor No.	Overview
1.	SFF leadership
2.	Government leader
3.	Leader of a professional services firm
4.	Leader of a charity
5.	SFF leadership
6.	Leader of a central bank
7	Leader of a commercial bank
8	Leader of an advisory firm
9	Leader of a commercial bank
10	Māori leader of a commercial bank
11	Leader of government agency
12	Independent consultant
13	Leader of a professional services firm
14	Leader of a foundation/charity
15	SFF leadership

All 15 interviews are audio-recorded and fully transcribed in verbatim style to provide a more complete and precise rendering of the interview data. We did the transcriptions of the interview ourselves. The technique of axial coding was used to construct emergent themes from interview data using NVivo 12 software to support the coding process. Both authors coded the transcripts, which yielded a set of themes with new insights with the benefit of additional temporal distance from the data collection process. These initial codes were later collated into potential themes around sustainable finance ecosystem. We then reviewed and defined the themes with ongoing analysis based on our theoretical focus.

Findings

The Aotearoa Circle was established in October 2018 as a partnership of public and private sector leaders with a common commitment 'to the pursuit of sustainable prosperity and reversing the decline of New Zealand's natural resources' (The Aotearoa Circle, n.d.). It was established to exercise the ideal of leadership with the intention of being a platform for convening and projecting sustainability leadership. In the words of one interviewee, the Aotearoa Circle is 'not an environmental organization, but a leadership organization' [Contributor 1]. The Aotearoa Circle was designed around six key domains: *Sustainable Finance, Land and Soil, Freshwater, Climate Change, Biodiversity,* and *Marine.* The first project was to establish the SFF to develop a sustainable finance roadmap, in order to establish a vision and an implementation pathway for financial system reform. This catalytic role is supported by the multiple actors and factors in the sustainable finance ecosystem. The relationship among these actors and factors is interdependent and goes beyond national boundaries with international relevance. The actors and factors, and the relationships among them, form the characteristics of the sustainable finance ecosystem.

Actors and Factors in the Sustainable Finance Ecosystem

The SFF is a voluntary initiative, and its members conceive of themselves as taking the role of an ecosystem builder. This is illustrated by one of our research participants:

[The SFF] doesn't have any mandate really to do anything, or any sort of power or authority, other than influence. And I'm not putting that down at all. Because… it's an influencer, a communicator… an educator, a convener of various stakeholders across the finance system.

[Contributor 14]

Financial Sector Actors, Government, and Māori Partners

A sustainable finance ecosystem will necessarily involve financial sector actors, which includes banks, insurance companies, credit unions, private equity companies, professional services companies, asset owners, fund/investment managers, and financial sector associations. Many of these actors were directly involved in the SFF Leadership Group, and Technical Working Group or participated in the wider consultation process that contributed to the roadmap development.[2]

SFF was not formally mandated by a regulatory authority, but rather a voluntary initiative. Leadership was one of its main legitimacies to influence other stakeholders with some level of government engagement. This was illustrated by one research participant [Contributor 1]: 'We also had extremely, you know, we had a really credible leadership group with some excellent people on there that got government's attention.' Government officials attended meetings as observers, tending to involve keen young officials rather than senior officials or ministers, and this engagement diminished when the Covid-19 pandemic started. Consequently, the SFF faced challenges in engaging the government on its eventual recommendations, which suggests that the current ecosystem is not hospitable for policy innovation, not least because of the lack of collaborative relations between the public and private sectors. Indeed, The Aotearoa Circle drew lessons from the SFF, which it carries into other domains, including involving government as partners rather than mere observers, and also seeking ministerial support.

The SFF later evolved into Toitū Tahua: the Centre for Sustainable Finance, as an independent entity to carry on the work by implementing the recommendations and legacy from the SFF in order to transform the financial system in New Zealand.

The SFF focused on the leadership of large financial corporations to mobilize large sums of private capital because they had more bandwidth and capacity to participate. With the emphasis on the financial system change, the entrepreneurship aspect of smaller participants such as emerging startups are less involved in the SFF process:

And this was really about probably thinking about the really big pools of capital as opposed to the smaller bits which are… not going to be as impactful as, say, changing how the banks think about how they could keep risk, or capital, or, you know, price, climate risk, or, you know, just those. Those bigger sort of system-wide things as opposed to the smaller Uhm startups. So yeah, now we didn't have a lot of we didn't have a lot of private markets involvement, which is, uh, you know which you could say it was an issue as well. Probably the private NZ market. The private market is. It's probably not as big proportionately as it is in some markets overseas. So that goes to that bit about what's the context locally and how do you, how do you shift the dial locally in terms of the big pools of capital?

[Contributor 13]

The Māori partnership evolved throughout the process. Initially, it fell short of a successful partnership, both from the perspective of Māori participants and The Aotearoa Circle's own ambitions. As one interviewee put it, early Māori engagement was perfunctory and retrospective, rather than genuine co-development:

> Essentially, I mean that was a tick box… I'm speaking frankly here, but it was like, here's all the work that we have done, what do you think so that we can say we've engaged with Māori and you're on board?
>
> *[Contributor 1]*

Nevertheless, the process of roadmap development offered an opportunity for a paradigm shift, for integrating Māori knowledge into the decision-making process. One Māori interviewee noted their involvement: 'what it did for me personally was a mind shift around how there's a way that the finance system can become inclusive to enable Māori principles of sustaining life and land to come to life' [Contributor 10].

This highlights the point that, for a sustainable finance ecosystem to be successful for Māori (and therefore to be successful in the context of Aotearoa New Zealand), it needs to enable successful participation by Māori. This is critical at the level of participation in the financial system where Māori are prospective borrowers, investors, creditors and so on. Moreover, Māori faces systemic disadvantages in accessing finance and participating equally. But it is also critical at the level of system design and decision making, not least because Māori involvement in decision making can help to anticipate and ameliorate the aforementioned disadvantages. Consequently, ensuring that the sustainable finance ecosystem is accessible and inclusive to Māori perspectives is critical, which is also critical for The Aotearoa Circle's SFF. One interviewee [Contributor 10], who identified as Māori, used the metaphor of a forest ecosystem to illustrate the potential of the process:

> So I think… the roadmap, of enabling voices to come together, it's like having a puriri tree and having all these different birds, and they all have their branch, and they have the ability to sing by though all contribute to the puriri tree… So that's kind of how I see the potential for Aotearoa Circle is the ability to be the puriri tree to enable every bird to come to settle. But it's a shared responsibility that whilst we look after the tree, the tree needs to look after us. And that we will thrive if we both have that mandate.

Factors in SFF Processes

The main factors of the ecosystem in the SFF processes include the underlying culture, policy environment, and network.

Sustainability is embedded in the SFF. The idea of natural capital is integral to the purpose of The Aotearoa Circle and its framing of the sustainability issues. In a think piece that accompanied the launch, Porritt argued that decision-makers will realize that all future endeavors to improve people's material standard of living will fail, if we do not secure the physical foundations on which these improvements depend – namely, the natural wealth contained within our ecosystem (Porritt, 2018). The concept of natural capital's alignment with economic value forms the underlying culture in the SFF. A founder of a charitable organization illustrated this [Contributor 5]:

> This initiative was really rooted in natural capital, and the degree to which natural capital wasn't valued. Not only economically, but in policy terms… and so the initiative was aimed at bringing together key business people in particular, but also senior

government people in order to have a greater focus on how natural capital could be invested in and restored, regenerated, built on, made into something that New Zealanders would value more over time, and which would be more economically valuable over time... then that the discussion around finance was a recognition that finance is one of the key drivers both for the degradation of natural capital, but potentially for the positive aspects of development of natural capital.

New Zealand tends to be classified as supportive of innovation. Still, it lacks the support of a more mature entrepreneurial ecosystem with a relatively low level of research and development funding and inadequate scale-up support. Furthermore, the policy environment for sustainable finance is far from proactive. When asked about what could be done differently to the SFF processes, a participant from the government answered that:

We could have a little bit more on Minister Shaw to help us with the other important politicians, senior finance ministers, associate finance, and we should... probably have spent a bit more time thinking about the government interactions... worked a bit more with the Aotearoa Circle to think about that. So... I think it's... always gonna be hard because this is a classic case of the important rather than the urgent, although it is urgent... but yeah, there's so much other stuff that will get in the gate, and the way from a government policy perspective that you've got to have someone who is a real believer... making your case down in Wellington and we probably didn't do enough... on that relationship.

[Contributor 11]

In this sense, The Aotearoa Circle could improve its strategy for policy entrepreneurship by prioritizing key decision-makers, but there is also scope to improve the collaborative relations between the private and public sectors, so that both can respond in a coordinated fashion to the challenges of sustainability transitions.

The SFF provided a safe place for actors to interact and network within and beyond the financial sector. The idea of the network also links to the relationship aspect of the interactions among the actors and factors. A participant from a commercial bank [Contributor 7] elaborated on this networking factor:

I've participated in the working group, but even as an observer, I think that the relationship... was good... there's plenty of engagement, and I've found that it's increased my own personal networks, but also [the affiliated organization's name] 's networks in this space, so there's a lot more external partnerships... I think it also helped the banks get together in a safe environment and talk about something that is a problem for all of us. So I think that was a really positive outcome as well... It was a safe space and... it was great from a networking perspective... so I think it helped provide insight into other parts of the economy and probably challenged our way of thinking.

Interdependencies among the Actors and Factors

The presence of the actors and factors alone does not constitute an ecosystem. The findings also offer some insights on the relationship and interactions of these actors and factors beyond national boundaries.

The SSF itself depends on the relationships among the actors and factors. As one participant from the public sector mentioned [Contributor 6]:

> It's a coalition of the willing built on collaboration, coordination… leveraging of existing relationships, moral suasion… a little bit of peer pressure. It's about developing easy pathways for directors and business leaders, and showing your shining light on those pathways so kind of demystifying… They use the word amplify, but I guess you know, just reinforcing messages, repeat messages to help change mindsets and give business leaders confidence about what needs to be done.

The sustainable finance ecosystem is a trend going on globally with the proliferation of SFRs in many jurisdictions. The SFF had direct and indirect connections to SFR processes elsewhere. The Aotearoa New Zealand initiative ran in parallel with Australia's, with direct engagement and frequent knowledge-sharing between the two. The SFF also drew inspiration from the EU's High-Level Expert Group on sustainable finance, Canada's Expert Panel on Sustainable Finance, the United Kingdom's Green Finance Taskforce, as well as the United Nations Environment Program Finance Initiative. International leakages between the SFF and other countries were illustrated both in the SFF's final report and by our interviewees. The 11 recommendation areas (responsibility, capability, governance, data, disclosure, coordination, account and value, inclusiveness, government leadership, resiliency, standards and pathways) in the final report are aligned with the EU, the UK, and Canada's action plans.

One independent consultant [Contributor 12] elaborated on the international alignment of the development of SFF:

> We captured what was going on overseas. We did the big mapping exercise, what was going on in the UK… Canada… Australia… We also talked to the Australian equivalent regularly. We also went through the UNDP… for their best practice in sustainable finance… so we just took it and applied them to the NZ context. The international work was the building block and cornerstone of the roadmap.

This alignment was reaffirmed by one participant from a commercial bank [Contributor 7]: 'We looked internationally initially, and certainly in the banking or the lenders' actor group… looked a lot at what was happening overseas, so things like the EU taxonomy and the changes in regulation.'

Discussion

We offer some new insights into the actors and factors in a sustainable finance ecosystem based on the SFF case. The actors and factors answer the questions of who and what these actors and factors are in a sustainable finance ecosystem. But all of these actors and factors need to work together to support the self-sustaining of the ecosystem. We also looked into how they work and operate in concert to create an ecosystem that evolves along time in response to internal and external changes.

Key actors in the sustainable finance ecosystem include financial sector actors, government officials, and indigenous communities. These actors in the SFF are leaders of this ecosystem. Financial sector actors have the capacity to influence policymaking (Dordi et al., 2022), and at the same time are affected by government policies that are designed to incentivize sustainable finance reforms (Howells, 2006). Research in entrepreneurship argues that entrepreneurs, rather than the government, are the best leaders of their ecosystem (Feld, 2012). Entrepreneurs are skilled at identifying gaps in the marketplace and marshalling the resources needed to address them. Flexible and agile entrepreneurs can address immediate issues quicker than public agencies that are bound by procedural and budgetary limitations. Financial sector actors in the SFF are very similar to entrepreneurs in this sense. Financial sector actors are embedded within incumbent regimes and institutions, so they are potentially well-positioned to address the common challenges facing their industry. To be sure, the Global Financial Crisis serves as a prominent failure of sectoral self-regulation, but the turn to sustainable finance is partly a commitment to avoiding such instability in the future. The SFF is also entrepreneurial, insofar as its strategies and roadmaps are a kind of 'product' that needs to be sold to public officials and other decision-makers. This connects to the policy entrepreneur literature, which recognizes that institutional change involves entrepreneurial activity through identifying a policy problem (instead of market demand) and then developing a policy (instead of a good or service) to fill that policy (market) gap (Cairney, 2018). A greater engagement with what makes for *effective* policy entrepreneurship might help to improve the impact of these processes.

Regarding indigenous communities, social exclusion is not hard to find in the financial system because profitability is often prioritized above inclusiveness. This leads to further deprivation, as many people in vulnerable situations are not able to access financial products and services or identify support channels. With COVID-19 accelerating the pace of digital transformation, those that are not digitally literate will become further excluded. While social inclusion was recognized as important for sustainable finance, excluded groups and the wider civil society groups were neglected. Therefore community engagement is essential to ensure an equitable transition in the sustainable finance ecosystem.

We also assessed the leadership's influence on the proximity of sustainable finance ecosystem development processes. In alignment with other processes in different countries, SFF demonstrates clear international linkages that go beyond the spatial agglomeration in cluster studies (Brown & Mason, 2017). This shows how the ecosystem approach goes beyond the jurisdiction level and moves to the paradigm and sector level across the financial system. Financial sector actors' involvement supports other stakeholders' behaviors in climate policy formation. The sustainable finance ecosystem demonstrates that an entrepreneurial ecosystem can be industry-specific and is bounded but not confined by the geographical scale, and does not relate to the size of a city or country.

Entrepreneurial ecosystem literature could be extended to capture the sustainable finance field. There are different ways by which this could occur. Firstly, one objective of sustainable finance reform is to create an ecosystem that facilitates new business models that support sustainable finance, such as new accounting practices, financial instruments, and investment decisions. Indeed, in recent years we have seen a proliferation of private sector initiatives that have accelerated sustainable finance issuance, such as green bonds and sustainability-linked bonds, compared to only a few years ago. Regulatory initiatives, such as New Zealand becoming the first country to require mandatory reporting and disclosure of climate-related risks for large companies, further tilt the ecosystem toward sustainable finance. But this relates to the second way in which the entrepreneurial ecosystem literature might apply, especially when linked to the idea of policy entrepreneurs. In our case, by collaborating under The Aotearoa Circle framework to develop strategies and roadmaps, the domain partners from the private and public sectors are operating as policy entrepreneurs, developing policy ideas to respond to environmental challenges. There is a question as to how the ecosystem might enable and facilitate their effectiveness in order to drive the system-level change.

Future Research Avenues and Implications

By analyzing the SFF, this chapter provides insights into how a financial sector leadership initiative supports building a sustainable finance ecosystem and highlights various improvement opportunities. Research on sustainable finance ecosystems is evolving, and this chapter highlighted four fertile avenues for future research with an ecosystem approach. Among them, the first is the idea of 'ecosystem as context.' Ecosystem as context (Wurth et al., 2021) is illustrated in this case study from Aotearoa New Zealand where the government observed the process in the beginning rather than leading or actively participating. This could be contrasted with other jurisdictions. One comparison is China, where the state plays a more engaged role in the SFR process. This line of research also builds on the policy styles literature. Policy styles are exercised within institutional arrangements and signify the patterns in policy processes (Howlett & Tosun, 2021). Different regions and countries have various policy styles that can be national, sectoral, or hybrid (Richardson, 1982). The working hypothesis here is that the prevailing policy style within a specific country or region has a significant influence on the development and formation of entrepreneurial ecosystems as part of sustainable finance transitions.

A second area for future research is the linkages between the entrepreneurial ecosystem and the financial sector. Startups are often ignored in the sustainable finance literature, and this is evident in our case study where the senior corporate managers in the financial sector lead. This transition among the corporate leaders, however, ignores the smaller scale entrepreneurship aspects for a more inclusive transition. The development of sustainable and inclusive finance promotes entrepreneurship and economic growth (Cao & Zhang, 2022). Entrepreneurial activities that address unmet social and environmental needs often lack financing opportunities and face more institutional barriers (Hoogendoorn et al., 2019). To achieve the SDGs, a more dispersed approach could potentially lead to better results by promoting the entrepreneurial ecosystem and creating a conducive environment.

A third area worth further investigation is around the performance and outcome of the entrepreneurial ecosystem and sustainable finance. This directly influences the attractiveness of an ecosystem to make it stronger or weaker. In the entrepreneurial ecosystem literature, this is often measured and benchmarked by the number of high-growth firms and the local economic growth (Brown & Mason, 2017). In the context of this chapter, the level of success could be assessed based on the presence and interactions of the actors and factors, and the implementation of the milestones and actions identified in the SFF roadmap. Further to the actors and factors of an ecosystem, the social values and public knowledge of sustainable finance could also be studied. This is demonstrated in entrepreneurship research, where entrepreneurship promotion is often centered around policies that affect social values and attitudes towards entrepreneurship in order to reduce the stigma of failure and enhance the appreciation of entrepreneurial activity in the society. The research on the entrepreneurial ecosystem could also borrow from the study of entrepreneurial failure, which focuses on the causes and the consequences of failure (Klimas et al., 2021). The performance of a sustainable finance ecosystem could set comparable standards across regions to better develop the ecosystem to benefit more actors involved.

The final research avenue is around the attribute of proximity. Proximity is illustrated in the interdependencies of actors and factors in this chapter, and it also has aspects of intimacy and affinity through interactions (Driscoll & Starik, 2004). Driscoll and Starik's (2004) notion of 'proximity' as a stakeholder salience dimension is to include the natural environment more explicitly as the primordial stakeholder. The exploration of the characteristics of proximity and how it concretizes in the sustainable finance ecosystem could be a fertile area for future research.

Regarding research methodologies, the field of entrepreneurial ecosystem analysis is dominated by qualitative research using case studies with data collection through literature surveys and interviews (Maroufkhani et al., 2018). By bringing this approach to the subject of sustainable finance, this paper contributes to a growing appreciation of the value of qualitative methods in finance (Salmona et al., 2015). However, there is a gap for studying entrepreneurial and innovation ecosystems based on quantitative modelling with survey-based data (e.g. analysis of ecosystem effectiveness), or a longitudinal perspective of the ecosystem evolvement. Such analysis could reduce uncertainty about which combination of actors and factors can precipitate change, especially in the dynamic context of sustainability transitions.

Concluding Remarks

This chapter explored the sustainable finance ecosystem building process in New Zealand, incorporating its unique actors and factors which are both locally and internationally relevant. It contributes to the literature on entrepreneurial ecosystem and sustainable finance. It offers a corporate leadership aspect to the entrepreneurial ecosystem approach in the financial sectors and shows how changes happen in the sustainability field. The case study of SFF fulfills its aim to build a sustainable finance ecosystem through changing mindsets and envisioning an alternative future for New Zealand's financial system.

Notes

1 This chapter uses the same set of data as a forthcoming article on intermediaries: Hall, D. & Meng, T. (forthcoming). Intermediating sustainable finance: A case study of The Aotearoa Circle's Sustainable Finance Forum. *Policy Studies*.
2 The Leadership Group consists of nine members, and the Technical Working Group consists of 23 members.

References

Acemoglu, D. (2002). Directed technical change. *Review of Economic Studies*, *69*(4), 781–809. https://doi.org/10.1111/1467-937X.00226

Acemoglu, D., Aghion, P., Bursztyn, L., & Hemous, D. (2012). The environment and directed technical change. *American Economic Review*, *102*(1), 131–166. https://doi.org/10.1257/aer.102.1.131

Ackoff, R. L. (1971). Towards a system of systems concepts. *Management Science*, *17*(11), 661–671. http://www.jstor.org/stable/2629308

Acs, Z. J., Stam, E., Audretsch, D. B., & O'Connor, A. (2017). The lineages of the entrepreneurial ecosystem approach. *Small Business Economics*, *49*(1), 1–10. http://www.jstor.org/stable/44697209

Adner, R. (2006). Match your innovation strategy to your innovation ecosystem. *Harvard Business Review*, *84*(4), 98–107.

Beland, D. (2005). Ideas and social policy: An institutionalist perspective. *Social Policy and Administration*, *39*(1), 1–18. https://doi.org/10.1111/j.1467-9515.2005.00421.x

Bernstein, S., & Hoffmann, M. (2018). The politics of decarbonization and the catalytic impact of subnational climate experiments. *Policy Sciences*, *51*(2), 189–211. https://doi.org/10.1007/s11077-018-9314-8

Brown, R., & Mason, C. (2017). Looking inside the spiky bits: A critical review andconceptualizationn of entrepreneurial ecosystems. *Small Business Economics*, *49*(1), 11–30. https://doi.org/10.1007/s11187-017-9865-7

Buchner, B., Naran, B., de Fernandes, A. P., Padmanabhi, R., Rosane, P., Solomon, M., Stout, S., Wakaba, G., Zhu, Y., Meattle, C., Guzmán, S., & Strinati, C. (2021). Global landscape of climate finance 2021. In

Climate policy initiative. https://www.climatepolicyinitiative.org/publication/global-landscape-of-climate-finance-2021/

Cairney, P. (2018). Three habits of successful policy entrepreneurs. *Policy and Politics*, 46(2), 199–215. https://doi.org/10.1332/030557318X15230056771696

Cao, G., & Zhang, J. (2022). The entrepreneurial ecosystem of inclusive finance and entrepreneurship: A theoretical and empirical test in China. *International Journal of Finance and Economics*, 27(1), 1547–1568. https://doi.org/10.1002/ijfe.2230

Cavallo, A., Ghezzi, A., & Balocco, R. (2019). Entrepreneurial ecosystem research: Present debates and future directions. *International Entrepreneurship and Management Journal*, 15(4), 1291–1321. https://doi.org/10.1007/s11365-018-0526-3

Clark, R., Reed, J., & Sunderland, T. (2018). Bridging funding gaps for climate and sustainable development: Pitfalls, progress and potential of private finance. *Land Use Policy*, 71, 335–346. https://doi.org/10.1016/j.landusepol.2017.12.013

Dordi, T., Gehricke, S. A., Naef, A., & Weber, O. (2022). Ten financial actors can accelerate a transition away from fossil fuels. *Environmental Innovation and Societal Transitions*, 44, 60–78. https://doi.org/10.1016/j.eist.2022.05.006

Driscoll, C., & Starik, M. (2004). The primordial stakeholder: Advancing the conceptual consideration of stakeholder status for the natural environment. *Journal of Business Ethics*, 49(1), 55–73. https://doi.org/10.1023/B:BUSI.0000013852.62017.0e

Dyllick, T., & Muff, K. (2016). Clarifying the meaning of sustainable business: Introducing a typology from business-as-usual to true business sustainability. *Organization and Environment*, 29(2), 156–174. https://doi.org/10.1177/1086026615575176

Feld, B. (2012). *Startup communities: Building an entrepreneurial ecosystem in your city*. Wiley.

Geels, F. W., Hekkert, M. P., & Jacobsson, S. (2008). The dynamics of sustainable innovation journeys. *Technology Analysis and Strategic Management*, 20(5), 521–536. https://doi.org/10.1080/09537320802292982

Geels, F. W., Sovacool, B. K., Schwanen, T., & Sorrell, S. (2017). The socio-technical dynamics of low-carbon transitions. *Joule*, 1(3), 463–479. https://doi.org/10.1016/j.joule.2017.09.018

Gladwin, T. N., Kennelly, J. J., & Krause, T.-S. (1995). Shifting paradigms for sustainable development: Implications for management theory and research. *Academy of Management Review*, 20(4), 874. https://doi.org/10.2307/258959

Granstrand, O., & Holgersson, M. (2020). Innovation ecosystems: A conceptual review and a new definition. *Technovation*, 90–91, 102098. https://doi.org/10.1016/j.technovation.2019.102098

Hall, D., & Meng, T. (n.d.). Intermediating sustainable finance: A case study of the Aotearoa Circle's sustainable finance forum. *Policy Studies*, 1–21.

Hannah, D. P., & Eisenhardt, K. M. (2018). How firms navigate cooperation and competition in nascent ecosystems. *Strategic Management Journal*, 39(12), 3163–3192. https://doi.org/10.1002/smj.2750

Hoogendoorn, B., van der Zwan, P., & Thurik, R. (2019). Sustainable entrepreneurship: The role of perceived barriers and risk. *Journal of Business Ethics*, 157(4), 1133–1154. https://doi.org/10.1007/s10551-017-3646-8

Howells, J. (2006). Intermediation and the role of intermediaries in innovation. *Research Policy*, 35(5), 715–728. https://doi.org/10.1016/j.respol.2006.03.005

Howlett, M., & Tosun, J. (Eds.). (2021). *The Routledge handbook of policy styles*. Routledge. https://doi.org/10.4324/9780429286322

Hynes, W., Trump, B., Love, P., & Linkov, I. (2020). Bouncing forward: A resilience approach to dealing with COVID-19 and future systemic shocks. *Environment Systems and Decisions*, 40(2), 174–184. https://doi.org/10.1007/s10669-020-09776-x

Isenberg, D. (2011). The entrepreneurship ecosystem strategy as a new paradigm for economic policy: Principles for cultivating entrepreneurship. *Presentation at the Institute of International and European Affairs*, 1(781), 1–13.

Isenberg, D. J. (2016). Applying the ecosystem metaphor to entrepreneurship. *Antitrust Bulletin*, 61(4), 564–573. https://doi.org/10.1177/0003603X16676162

Jordan, A., Huitema, D., Schoenefeld, J., van Asselt, H., & Forster, J. (2018). Governing climate change polycentrically. In A. Jordan, D. Huitema, H. van Asselt, & J. Forster (Eds.), *Governing climate change* (pp. 3–26). Cambridge University Press. https://doi.org/10.1017/9781108284646.002

Klimas, P., Czakon, W., Kraus, S., Kailer, N., & Maalaoui, A. (2021). Entrepreneurial failure: A synthesis and conceptual framework of its effects. *European Management Review*, 18(1), 167–182. https://doi.org/10.1111/emre.12426

Markard, J., Raven, R., & Truffer, B. (2012). Sustainability transitions: An emerging field of research and its prospects. *Research Policy, 41*(6), 955–967. https://doi.org/10.1016/j.respol.2012.02.013

Maroufkhani, P., Wagner, R., & Wan Ismail, W. K. (2018). Entrepreneurial ecosystems: A systematic review. *Journal of Enterprising Communities: People and Places in the Global Economy, 12*(4), 545–564. https://doi.org/10.1108/JEC-03-2017-0025

Mazzucato, M. (2016). From market fixing to market-creating: A new framework for innovation policy. *Industry and Innovation, 23*(2), 140–156. https://doi.org/10.1080/13662716.2016.1146124

Meadows, D. H. (2008). *Thinking in systems: A primer* (D. Wright (Ed.)). Earthscan. https://research.fit.edu/media/site-specific/researchfitedu/coast-climate-adaptation-library/climate-communications/psychology-amp-behavior/Meadows-2008.-Thinking-in-Systems.pdf

Milligan, L. (2016). Insider-outsider-inbetweener? Researcher positioning, participative methods and cross-cultural educational research. *Compare: A Journal of Comparative and International Education, 46*(2), 235–250.

Mitchell, R. K., Agle, B. R., & Wood, D. J. (1997). Toward a theory of stakeholder identification and salience: Defining the principle of who and what really counts. *Academy of Management Review, 22*(4), 853. https://doi.org/10.2307/259247

Moore, J. F. (1993). Predators and prey: A new ecology of competition. *Harvard Business Review, 71*(3), 75–86.

Neville, B. A., Bell, S. J., & Whitwell, G. J. (2011). Stakeholder salience revisited: Refining, redefining, and refueling an underdeveloped conceptual tool. *Journal of Business Ethics, 102*(3), 357–378. https://doi.org/10.1007/s10551-011-0818-9

Porritt, J. (2018). *Natural capital- and why it matters*. The Aotearoa Circle.

Richardson, J. (1982). *Policy styles in Western Europe (Routledge Revivals)*. Routledge. https://doi.org/10.4324/9780203082010

Rohrbeck, R., Hölzle, K., & Gemünden, H. G. (2009). Opening up for competitive advantage - How Deutsche Telekom creates an open innovation ecosystem. *R and D Management, 39*(4), 420–430. https://doi.org/10.1111/j.1467-9310.2009.00568.x

Salmona, M., Kaczynski, D., & Smith, T. (2015). Qualitative theory in finance: Theory into practice. *Australian Journal of Management, 40*(3), 403–413. https://doi.org/10.1177/0312896214536204

Schoenmaker, D., & Schramade, W. (2019). *Principles of sustainable finance*. Oxford University Press.

Shaw, D. R., & Allen, T. (2018). Studying innovation ecosystems using ecology theory. *Technological Forecasting and Social Change, 136*, 88–102. https://doi.org/10.1016/j.techfore.2016.11.030

Spigel, B. (2020). The actors and factors of entrepreneurial ecosystems. In *Entrepreneurial ecosystems* (pp. 46–86). Edward Elgar Publishing. https://doi.org/10.4337/9781788975933

Stam, E. (2015). Entrepreneurial ecosystems and regional policy: A sympathetic critique. *European Planning Studies, 23*(9), 1759–1769. https://doi.org/10.1080/09654313.2015.1061484

Stam, E., & van de Ven, A. (2021). Entrepreneurial ecosystem elements. *Small Business Economics, 56*(2), 809–832. https://doi.org/10.1007/s11187-019-00270-6

Tansley, A. G. (1935). The use and abuse of vegetational concepts and terms. *Ecology, 16*(3), 284–307. https://doi.org/10.2307/1930070

The Aotearoa Circle. (n.d.). *The Aotearoa Circle*. https://www.theaotearoacircle.nz/

The Aotearoa Circle. (2020). *Sustainable finance forum roadmap for action [final report]*.

Unruh, G. C. (2000). Understanding carbon lock-in. *Energy Policy, 28*(12), 817–830. https://doi.org/10.1016/S0301-4215(00)00070-7

Van De Ven, H. (1993). The development of an infrastructure for entrepreneurship. *Journal of Business Venturing, 8*(3), 211–230. https://doi.org/10.1016/0883-9026(93)90028-4

Wurth, B., Stam, E., & Spigel, B. (2021). Toward an entrepreneurial ecosystem research program. *Entrepreneurship: Theory and Practice*, 1–50. https://doi.org/10.1177/1042258721998948

Appendix

Interview Protocol and Guide Questions

Participant Background and Motives/Intention

1. Could you please tell us how sustainable finance contributes to the objectives of your organization?

Objectives and Barriers

2. Think about the barriers to sustainability transitions in Aotearoa, New Zealand. What barriers was the Aotearoa Circle, in general, and the Sustainable Finance Forum in particular, intended to overcome?
3. How do you describe the approach or strategy of the Sustainable Finance Forum?
4. Sustainability transitions involve a combination of destabilizing and stabilizing the status quo. If you think about the Sustainable Finance Forum, what aspects of the current financial sector regime does it stabilize and destabilize?

Stakeholder Interaction

5. How would you characterize the relationship between the Sustainable Finance Forum and financial sector agencies? How do you think that relationship ought ideally to work?
6. How would you characterize the relationship between the Sustainable Finance Forum and the government? How do you think that relationship ought ideally to work?
7. How would you characterize the relationship between the Sustainable Finance Forum and Māori partners? How do you think that relationship ought ideally to work?

Sustainable Finance in New Zealand and Other Countries (Current State)

8. Were there any international models or precedents that had a decisive influence on the design of the Aotearoa Circle and the Sustainable Finance Forum?
9. How would you characterize the current state of sustainable finance in New Zealand compared to other countries?

Other Information

10. Is there anything else you would like to add?
11. And finally, are there any documents might add to what we have just discussed? Is it possible to get a copy? Who are the other potential parties we could approach for future interviews (snowballing)?

Approved by the Auckland University of Technology Ethics Committee on 7th Dec. 2021
 AUTEC Reference number 21/416

Please note that the exact questions are slightly different based on each participant's profile. This list only includes some main topics that are applicable to all participants.

2
ACCOUNTING FOR A GREEN ECONOMY

Sustainable Finance and the Harmonisation of Sustainability Reporting

Josef Baumüller and Susanne Leitner-Hanetseder

Introduction

While sustainability reporting is considered to be a relatively young sub-discipline in accounting, it has gained considerable momentum over the past decade (Baumüller & Sopp, 2022). Actually, there is a long tradition of including specific information on environmental or social matters as part of company reporting. However, the comprehensive concept of sustainability reporting itself is considered to have originated from the formation of the Global Reporting Initiative (GRI) at the end of the 1990s; the formation of this initiative was the result of the efforts of a few pioneering organisations and an increased change in public expectations towards the responsibility of organisations (Larrinanga & Bebbington, 2021). Dispersed actors such as pioneering companies, NGOs and even the financial sector started to embrace this concept and promote its application – although with different interpretations and underlying interests (Brown et al., 2009; Eccles et al., 2020). The lack of a clearly conceptualised understanding of the nature and scope of the term sustainability and its elements contributed to a diversity in practice that showed to be hindering the advancement of the entire discipline (Purvis et al., 2018). So, even after some time, the question was raised in the literature as to what extent sustainability reporting should just be considered "a fad" (Burritt & Schaltegger, 2010).

Then, however, the turning point of the last decade also marked a change in the approach towards sustainability reporting. In the aftermath of the financial crisis, the relevance of promoting sustainable behaviour by companies – in order to fight "short-termism" – and the extent to which this should be promoted by regulatory requirements was reassessed (Kinderman, 2020). This led to an important push for the still-developing sustainability reporting movement. As a consequence, the 2010s saw the formation of the Sustainability Accounting Standards Board (SASB), the International Integrated Reporting Council (IICR) and the elaboration of the EU's Non-Financial Reporting Directive (NFRD), amongst other initiatives. The quote by Peter Bakker, CEO of the World Business Council for Sustainable Development (WBCSD), that "accountants will save the world" (Bakker, 2013) became somewhat symbolic of the observable momentum.

Several years later, the idea that indeed "Sustainability Reporting Can Help Save The Planet" (Eltobgy & Walter, 2021) seems to have become widely accepted. The regulatory dynamics have reached a never-before-seen climax, driven by European ambitions under the Green (New) Deal, but increasingly also followed by other jurisdictions and international actors. Improved Transparency on sustainability-related matters is considered a key mechanism to change the global economy and shift it towards more sustainable business practices (World Economic Forum, 2022). The effectiveness of this mechanism relates to its role in a broader political agenda that has been pushed forward under the title of sustainable finance – and that ties capital market incentives to the sustainability performance companies can demonstrate via their reporting.

There are different understandings of the nature and aims of sustainable finance (Dyllick & Muff, 2016). This chapter focuses on the European approach that was worked out by the action plan on "Financing Sustainable Growth" from 2018 (Migliorelli, 2021). Based on the aims that were formulated, the pivotal role of sustainability reporting is outlined. In the past years, this European sustainability movement has gained considerable attention from other jurisdictions that followed up by similar initiatives. However, also different understandings of how these mechanisms should unfold and what type of company reporting is necessary for those purposes have emerged on a global level. As a result, the European view on sustainability reporting moved in a different direction than another initiative that has emerged as well and has absorbed many existing initiatives: the International Financial Reporting Standards (IFRS) Foundation's project to establish a set of globally applicable standards for sustainability reporting. So, the debate has moved to the question of which type of sustainability reporting can help save the planet.

The chapter is structured as follows: firstly, the role and importance of sustainability reporting for sustainable finance are outlined. Then, the two most important initiatives in the field of sustainability reporting are discussed and compared. This comparison leads to several implications and calls for action that have to be addressed in order to make sure that (future) reporting practices are able to fulfil their purpose – both in the context of sustainable finance and of the ultimate goal of sustainable development that is pursued in the end. Finally, the chapter ends with a conclusion on the main findings.

The Role of Sustainability Reporting for Sustainable Finance

> This imperative of sustainable finance is nothing new; what is new is the momentum behind its implementation. The twin adoption of the 2030 Agenda for Sustainable Development and the Paris Agreement in 2015/16 has re-ignited discussions – and the impetus for action has been building since then.
>
> *(HLEG, 2018, p. 3)*

The idea of promoting sustainable development via the means of the global finance system played an important role at the Paris climate conference 2015. Article 2.1c of the Paris Agreement puts forward the aim to make finance flows consistent with a pathway towards low greenhouse gas emissions and climate-resilient development. This addresses public finance as well as private finance and requires those decisions to take into consideration associated effects on climate (Rydge, 2020). Private-sector-led initiatives such as the Task Force on Climate-related Financial Disclosures (TCFD) were initiated as a consequence of this call. The Paris Agreement is considered to be one of the most recent and relevant cornerstones of sustainable finance (UNFCCC, 2022).

For the EU, the action plan on "Financing Sustainable Growth" from 2018 was an immediate result of its commitment to the Paris Agreement. The action plan contained ten actions which ultimately aimed at (1) reorienting capital flows towards a more sustainable economy; (2)

improving the management of financial risks stemming from climate change, resource depletion, environmental degradation and social issues; and (3) fostering transparency and long-termism in financial and economic activity. European capital markets and the mechanisms directing financing and investment decisions were at the heart of every measure that was formulated in order to arrive at these aims. Regulations such as the EU Taxonomy Regulation or the Sustainable Finance Disclosure Regulation (SFDR) originated in this action plan. But to support these and similar provisions, also the importance of increased accountability of corporations for their environmental and social impact was stressed.

"Disclosure and accounting" was one of the most extensive chapters in that action plan, comprising several measures that should promote the aims of the legal initiative: "Corporate reporting on sustainability issues enables investors and stakeholders to assess companies' long-term value creation and their sustainability risk exposure" (EU Commission, 2018a, p. 9). This directly relates to both aim (1) and aim (2) of the action plan. Subsequently, the EU Commission refers to Directive 2014/95/EU (NFRD), which entered into force at the end of 2016; its provisions on sustainability reporting obligations within the EU should be evaluated for improvements and additional measures undertaken (such as the formation of a European Corporate Reporting Lab or the issuance of new non-binding guidelines for the application of the NFRD). This also made the NFRD one important element of all future consideration with regard to sustainable finance – an idea that was not that firmly included in the text of the NFRD itself at the time of its passing.

The EU Commission followed up on these initial reasonings soon via its Green (New) Deal in 2019. To promote the increased ambitions towards fighting climate change, improved efforts in the field of sustainable finance were one key element of this programme. An investment plan amounting to 1 trillion euro was part of the proposals, half of that being mobilised via private actors, especially the financial sector. Accountability of European companies thus was again an important part of the programme: "companies and financial institutions will need to increase their disclosure on climate and environmental data so that investors are fully informed about the sustainability of their investments" (EU Commission, 2019, p. 17). As the evaluation of the NFRD conducted by the EU Commission in the previous two years has shown that criticism prevailed on its effectiveness (EU Commission, 2018b), a fundamental review of the Directive was amongst the aims formulated in the Green (New) Deal.

Work on that review started in early 2020 and ultimately led to the EU Commission's proposal of a Corporate Sustainability Reporting Directive (CSRD). Here, the idea of sustainable finance already is one of the fundaments of the initiative, as it states:

> This proposal builds on and revises the sustainability reporting requirements set out in the NFRD, in order to make sustainability reporting requirements more consistent with the broader sustainable finance legal framework, including the SFDR and the Taxonomy Regulation, and to tie in with the objectives of the European Green Deal.
>
> *(EU Commission, 2021, pp. 4–5)*

Beyond that, further endeavours should be undertaken to strengthen the reporting obligations via inclusion in the European framework for corporate governance. As a result, those pieces of legislation that are stressed in this sustainable finance context serve as a framework for accountability mechanisms that should provide the information basis for capital allocation on European capital markets. Figure 2.1 illustrates the connection between those mechanisms at the heart of the European sustainable finance initiative.

Common understanding of sustainable economic activities

```
                         EU Taxonomy

   Supplements                                    Supplements
   and amends                                     and amends

                            provides
 Sustainable Finance Disclosure   data   Non-Financial Reporting Directive (NFRD)
      Regulation (SFDR)                  Corporate Sustainability Reporting
                                                 Directive (CSRD)

                                          Sustainable Corporate Governance
                                                      Initiative

 Transparency of financial products       Transparency + governance of companies
    (Re-)Allocation of investments
```

Figure 2.1 Regulations addressing the transparency of European companies. Source: adapted from Baumüller and Grbenic (2021), p. 372.

One of the key features of the proposed new directive was the introduction of sustainability reporting standards which have to be used on a mandatory basis – in order to ensure more complete reporting and to enhance the comparability of published information. Both of these aims reflect demands by the financial sector so that it can include the relevant information in its capital allocation mechanisms. However, the question of which standards could meet this objective best and if these standards should be European or global soon became a major discussion point. While the CSRD contains that the European Financial Reporting Advisory Group (EFRAG) develops specific European Sustainability Reporting Standards (ESRS) that consider the specific European regulatory environment, it also took notice of already existing standards – and of the newly initiated project of the IFRS Foundation to develop globally accepted sustainability reporting standards on its own. Also from European companies, a demand for a global solution was formulated given the relevance of international markets and investors for the European industry (World Economic Forum, 2021). Nevertheless, the final version of the CSRD published in December 2022 did not incorporate this demand and finally introduced the ESRS into European accounting law.

The Sustainability Reporting Initiatives of the IFRS Foundation and EU

The Case for Harmonised Standards for Sustainability Reporting

Over the last few years, there have been a lot of national legal obligations for sustainability-related reporting, often including the flexibility to use any existing voluntary framework or standards to fulfil the obligations (Biondi et al., 2020). Such frameworks and standards were also developed in abundance, however with differences in matters covered and the main audience for the information published. Even if voluntary reporting frameworks and guidance lead innovation and action in the disclosure of sustainability-related information through that time, the resulting fragmentation of practices around the globe has increased complexity which is costly, inefficient and confusing for users and preparers (EU Parliament, 2021; IFRS Foundation, 2020).

However, developing a de facto framework or standard requires that private standard-setters need a powerful collation of actors including key jurisdictions adopting the frameworks and/or standards (Biondi et al., 2020). Having a look into the past, the worldwide standardisation of financial reporting based on the IFRS is closely related to the decision of the IOSCO to support the adaption of these standards on the global capital markets (Zeff, 2012). Subsequently, due to Regulation 1606/2002 ("IAS Regulation"), consolidated financial statements of EU-listed companies have to be prepared in accordance with the IFRS. This adoption of the IFRS by a key jurisdiction such as the EU has undoubtedly contributed to the success of the International Financial Reporting Standards (Giner & Luque-Vílchez, 2022). As the IFRS are developed by the private standard setter the International Accounting Standards Board (IASB), the IAS Regulation included an endorsement process under the responsibility of the European Commission (Pope & McLeay, 2011).

In the past 20 years, capital markets increasingly started to look beyond financial figures and include environmental and social matters in their reasoning as well – a development that was mainly driven by the sustainable finance agenda in Europe and other jurisdictions. This has also driven the demand for a similar de facto standard for reporting on sustainability matters as the IFRS established them for financial matters: the coherence of the frameworks and standards will be relevant to reduce complexity and costs. Ultimately, this raises the question of which principles are being pursued and on the basis of which standards they are being implemented, or to what extent an international harmonisation of sustainability-related disclosures can be achieved that still meets different sets of interests.

The International Sustainability Standards Board – A New Player on the Market

Institutional Background

In response to the perceived growing and urgent demands for stakeholders (including investors, preparers, central banks, regulators, auditing firms, and other service providers) to adopt a comparable and consistent set of sustainability reporting standards, the IFRS Foundation decided to take the role of sustainability standard setter (IFRS Foundation, 2020). Therefore, it acted reactively due to the demands of capital market (Giner & Luque-Vílchez, 2022) and published in November 2021 a revised IFRS Foundation Constitution to accommodate an International Sustainability Standards Board (ISSB). The objective of the ISSB is to develop comprehensive IFRS Sustainability Disclosure Standards material for investment decisions for the global financial markets (IFRS Foundation, 2022a).

Aiming at a running start of the ISSB, the IFRS Foundation Trustees commissioned a Technical Readiness Working Group (TRWG) with the purpose of providing technical recommendations. To meet the information needs of the users of sustainability disclosure reporting worldwide, the TRWG comprised representatives of organisations which represent the world's capital markets and other users as well as voluntary standard-setters (IFRS Foundation, 2021b).

In addition to the formation of the ISSB, a merger with two voluntary standard-setting initiatives was announced, with Value Reporting Foundation (VRF), a global non-profit organisation which provides different resources including an Integrated Reporting Framework and SASB Standards adopted in over 70 countries; and the Climate Disclosure Standards Board (CDSB), an international consortium of business and environmental NGOs offering a framework for reporting environment and social related information adopted in more than 14,000 organisations worldwide (Littan, 2022). This merger enables the ISSB to build on existing technical standards and frameworks (Giner & Luque-Vílchez, 2022) and, of course, also brings intellectual property and capacities for standard-setting. Furthermore, it signalled the momentum behind the initiative, with reactions calling it "The Biggest Change In Corporate Reporting Since The 1930s" (Forbes, 2021).

At first sight, it is astonishing that the Global Sustainability Standards Board (GSSB), developing the GRI Standards, and one of the acclaimed sustainability reporting standard-setting bodies and pioneers of developing voluntary sustainability reporting standards (Carungu et al., 2022), was not part of the merger (Villiers et al., 2022). This might be explained by the different understandings of relevant information that companies should disclose based on the respective standards. However, in March 2022, the IFRS Foundation and the GRI announced in a Memorandum of Understanding (MoU) to work together to coordinate their work programmes and standard-setting activities (IFRS Foundation, 2022c). This collaboration of the IFRS Foundation and GRI provides two pillars of international sustainability reporting. Pillar I consists of investor-oriented capital market sustainability reporting standards developed by the ISSB. Pillar II is compatible with Pillar I and represents GRI multistakeholder-oriented standards developed by the GSSB (Fass, 2022).

Approach towards Sustainability Reporting

Already in November 2021, the TRWG published two deliverables: prototypes for Climate-related Disclosures (Climate Prototype) and General Requirements for Disclosure of Sustainability-related Financial Information (General Requirements Prototype) (Littan, 2022). After reviewing the deliverables, the ISSB published the first two standards in June 2023. IFRS S1 General Requirements for Disclosure of Sustainability-related Financial Information provides the overall requirements for an entity's sustainability-related financial information disclosure not specifically addressed by another IFRS Sustainability Disclosure Standard and addresses information about entities' sustainability-related governance, strategy and risk management, related metrics and targets (IFRS Foundation, 2023a).

In line with the IFRS financial reporting standards, IFRS Sustainability Disclosure Standards (IFRS S) focus on the needs of primary users of general purpose financial reports (IFRS Foundation, 2023a). The purpose of sustainability-related information is highlighted in paragraph 1 of IFRS S1. Thus, an entity should disclose "sustainability-related risks and opportunities that useful to the primary users of general-purpose financial reports in making decisions relating to providing resources to the entity." (IFRS Foundation, 2023a). Vice versa all other sustainability-related information is out of the scope of IFRS S. Also according to IFRS S1 par. 60, an entity is required to disclose sustainability-related information as part of the general-purpose financial reporting (IFRS Foundation, 2023a). This makes it clear that IFRS S standards only focus on information that impacts financial performance and sustainability-related information should be provided that is material for investment decisions.

Beyond that, the IFRS S1 contains general requirements for the disclosure of sustainability-related financial information along the entire value chain of an entity and is based on IAS 1 Presentation of Financial Statements. IFRS S1, in general, requires yearly sustainability-related disclosures but does not preclude that for some companies, interim reporting may also be deemed necessary (IFRS Foundation, 2023a).

Due to the urgent need for better information about climate-related matters, the IFRS Foundation prioritises this topic. Therefore, the ISSB focused its efforts and published IFRS S2, the ISSB's first topical standard that contains regulations on climate-related disclosures. It requires entities to report, among other things, the impact of significant climate-related risks and opportunities on the entity's value and the entity's response and ability to adapt to those risks and opportunities (IFRS Foundation, 2023a).

Although the ISSB and future sustainability reporting standards are a response to the need for comparable and consistent sustainability reporting standards, it is also seen as an attempt by the IFRS Foundation to link sustainability information and financial accounting and reporting (Villiers et al., 2022). The linkage between the two fields of reporting within IFRS could be possible by using the IFRS Practise Statement 1 Management Commentary, whose Exposure Draft had been issued in 2021 (Giner & Luque-Vílchez, 2022). The aim of the Management Commentary is to complement information from the financial statements and provide insights into facts that might impact an entity's value or future cash flows from capital provider's point of view (IFRS Foundation, 2023a). Therefore, including sustainability reporting within the Management Commentary might be a chance to connect financial reporting and sustainability reporting (Giner & Luque-Vílchez, 2022).

The IFRS Foundation points out that standard-setters working together from key jurisdictions is vital to providing a globally consistent and comparable sustainability reporting baseline, including the flexibility and possibility to capture wider sustainability impacts than an investor-oriented focus (IFRS Foundation, 2021c). This would reduce the existing complexity and help with achieving global comparability. Adding to that, the purpose of IFRS S standards is to establish a "building blocks" (Abela, 2022; IFRS Foundation, 2020) approach that provides an international baseline supplemented by other standard-setters.

Initiatives by the EU and the Development of Sustainability Reporting Standards by the EFRAG

Regulatory Background

Already in the past two decades, there were numerous attempts to establish sustainability-related reporting obligations for companies within the EU. Since the adaption of the EU Directive 2003/51/EC ("Modernisation Directive"), the annual reports of large corporations have to include non-financial key performance indicators (KPI) relevant to the particular business, highlighting the need for KPIs relating to environmental and employee matters (EU Parliament and Council, 2003). In the following years, reporting on sustainability matters has steadily increased in relevance (Velte & Stawinoga, 2017; Baumüller & Sopp, 2022). As a consequence, voluntary corporate sustainability reporting became more and more widespread, while increasingly different national regulations on non-financial disclosure obligations (e.g. Sweden, Denmark, France) were established within the EU member states (Kinderman, 2020). All in all, both voluntary and different regulatory efforts lead to insufficient comparability.

In 2011, the EU Commission communicated its new understanding of corporate social responsibility which includes "the responsibilities of enterprise for their impacts on society" (EU Commission, 2011). With the NFRD, the EU presented its aims to harmonise the European sustainability reporting framework and to increase the relevance, consistency and comparability of non-financial information disclosed across the Union. The NFRD represented a minimum standard for the disclosure of non-financial information of large companies which are public-interest entities with more than 500 employees (EU Parliament and Council, 2014). According to the NFRD,

> large undertakings which are public-interest entities exceeding on their balance sheet dates the criterion of the average number of 500 employees during the financial year shall include in the management report a non-financial statement containing information to the extent necessary for an understanding of the undertaking's development,

performance, position and impact of its activity, relating to, as a minimum, environmental, social and employee matters, respect for human rights, anti-corruption and bribery matters [...].

(EU Parliament and Council, 2014)

The NFRD required specific disclosures on environmental, social and employee, human rights, anti-corruption and bribery matters. For these five sustainability-related matters, a description of the company's business model; a description of the policies pursued by the company in relation to those matters, including due diligence processes implemented; the outcome of those policies; the principal risks related to those matters linked to the company's operations including, where relevant and proportionate, its business relationships, products or services, which are likely to cause adverse impacts in those areas, and how the undertaking manages those risks; and non-financial KPIs relevant to the particular business should be provided (EU Parliament and Council, 2014).

Under the NFRD, companies are required to report on two perspectives: they have to distinguish whether sustainability matters affect the performance and development of an entity (outside-in perspective) and the impact of the entity's activities on people and the environment (inside-out perspective). This is also referred to as the materiality principle for sustainability reporting; the mere wording of the NFRD provides a reporting obligation only if both aspects are to be assessed as material (Baumüller & Schaffhauser-Linzatti, 2018). However, this interpretation was not in the interest of the EU legislator and led to further official communications as well as controversial discussions in the literature in the following years (Baumüller & Sopp, 2022).

The NFRD intentionally left flexibility for member states (Fiandrino et al., 2021; Testarmata et al., 2020). With regard to reporting format, the NFRD highlights in Article 19a that the disclosure of non-financial information might be integrated into the management report. On the other hand, it formulates member state options to bundle the non-financial information into a so-called non-financial statement in a separate section of the management report, or a separate non-financial report can be prepared and in case also be published on the company's website no later than six months after the balance sheet date (EU Parliament and Council, 2014). The NFRD also does not provide a specific framework or standards to achieve harmonisation of reporting contents. Rather, it refers to various international standards such as the United Nations (UN) Global Compact; the International Organisation for Standardisation's ISO 26000; the GRI; and other recognised international frameworks (EU Parliament and Council, 2014).

In 2017, the Global Sustainability Standards Board (GSSB) published a document that shows how GRI Standards comply with the NFRD (GSSB, 2017), and the EU Commission added non-binding guidelines with interpretations of the NFRD. In 2019, following the action plan of "Financing Sustainable Growth", non-binding guidelines on climate-related disclosure were published by the EU Commission; these guidelines also referred to the reporting concept of "double materiality" under the NFRD for the first time.

(New) Approach towards Sustainability Reporting

At the beginning of 2020, the European Commission announced that it would be presenting a proposal for a revised Directive replacing the NFRD (EU Commission, 2020). One year later, the proposal of the so-called CSRD was published, and in June 2022, political agreement on the final version of this directive was finally achieved and the final CSRD was published in December 2023. The CSRD extends the scope of the companies covering all large undertakings as well as undertakings which are listed on EU-regulated markets, with the exception of micro-entities.

According to the EU Commission's estimates, compared to the NFRD, the CSRD would lead to approximately 49,000 companies required to report sustainability-related information, which means a fourfold increase in the number of companies (EU Commission, 2022).

The EU regulator also changed the matters covered by the directive. The CSRD no longer restricts itself to the five matters of the NFRD but aims at covering all aspects of ESG (Baumüller & Grbenic, 2021). Therefore, companies within the scope of CSRD have to report on environmental, social and governance matters. However, the CSRD provides a restriction to disclose sustainability-related information only within the management report. In addition, the disclosure has to be in a digital machine-readable format in accordance with the European Single Electronic Format (ESEF) regulation (EU Commission, 2022). With regard to the materiality perspective, the CSRD clarifies that companies must disclose sustainability-related information that is material from both perspectives: impacts that affect the organisation and impacts that arise from the organisation – i.e. the principle of "double materiality" (EU Commission, 2022).

A further new requirement introduced by the CSRD is the general EU-wide mandatory assurance (limited assurance initially) by an external third party for the reported sustainability information, which also allows the EU member states to open up the assurance service to other firms ("independent assurance service") than the statutory auditors or audit firms. The CSRD comprises an extension of reporting requirements for material ESG topics, and in addition to the requirements of the NFRD, the CSRD requires extended reporting contents (aims and strategies); applicable time frames (retrospective and forward-looking information is required); and newly structured and extended reporting matters (governance matters; more focus on value chain) (Baumüller & Grbenic, 2021; EU Commission, 2022).

Furthermore, and which is seen as a new milestone in sustainability-related standard-setting, the CSRD envisages the adoption of EU Sustainability Reporting Standards (EU Commission, 2022) – ESRS. Thus, demands for adequate guidelines that can be assured for compliance are taken up (Baumüller et al., 2022). For that purpose, detailed draft standards are developed by the EFRAG, including proper due process (EU Commission, 2022). The private organisation EFRAG is already involved in the endorsement process of the IFRS by the European Union as an advisory body and plays an important role in ensuring a "true and fair view" under "cost-benefit" aspects (van Hulle, 2004). Formally, the ESRS drafts will be adopted by the European Commission as supplementary secondary legislation, so-called delegated acts, after consulting with the other EU Parliament and Council (Baumüller & Grbenic, 2021).

This also represented the need to realign EFRAG's organisation, which was reflected in the introduction of a new pillar for sustainability reporting, the creation of a new board structure and the addition of new member organisations, among other things (Baumüller et al., 2022). Furthermore, EFRAG has signed agreements to cooperate on the development of the new standards with organisations such as the GRI, Shift or the World Intellectual Capital Initiative (WICI) (EFRAG, 2022a).

The work on the first set of ESRS is ongoing. As EFRAG itself, due to its restructuring process, has not yet been in a position to take over the corresponding work steps, the European Lab was commissioned: in April 2022, draft standards for the first set of ESRS were published. The overall architecture of the ESRS corresponds to the TCFD and ISSB requirements and includes:

- cross-cutting standards covering the general provisions, the strategy and business model in relation to sustainability; the governance and organisation in relation to sustainability; the materiality assessment of its sustainability-related impacts, risks and opportunities; defini-

tions of policies, targets, actions and metrics; and the presentation standard to provide the basis for the presentation of sustainability reporting within the management report
- topical standards covering a specific sustainability topic or sub-topic of the environment (ESRS E), social (ESRS S) and governance (ESRS G) matters from a sector-agnostic perspective and including implementation measures and performance metrics
- sector-specific standards covering the sector classification and ESG sector-specific disclosures (EFRAG, 2022b)

After opening the ESRS drafts for public comment until August 2022, the EFRAG submits the final standards to the EU Commission for endorsement. In July 2023 the EU Commission adopted the first set of ESRS for use by all companies subject to the CSRD..

Comparison of IFRS S and ESRS

After a recent wave of consolidations amongst existing standard-setters, the projects of the EU and of the ISSB seem to have become the two leading initiatives in the field of standardisation of sustainability reporting. These are likely to shape the future of corporate reporting in the next years. However, there are fundamental differences: the EFRAG follows a comprehensive approach to the disclosure of sustainability-related information, meeting the needs of market participants as well as other stakeholders. Contrary to that, the ISSB is based on an capital market approach.

The aim of the standard-setting initiatives of the projects and the EU is to provide comparable reporting on sustainability disclosure (Biondi et al., 2020). However, the ISSB provides sustainability-related information to assess the enterprise value and make investment decisions, which means that the sustainability-related information of the IFRS S is based on the perspective of financial materiality only. Furthermore, the requirements of the IFRS S are supported by concrete formulas and sector-specific guidance that are still to be developed by the ESRS, which are much more flexible.

Different to the IFRS S, the ESRS sustainability-related information is based on the double materiality perspective and in addition to the financial materiality perspective also includes how the activities of the company impact the people (stakeholders) and the environment. However, the EFRAG sees a strong linkage between the two perspectives, as affecting people and the environment can rebound to the business model and impact the value of an entity (EFRAG, 2021). Thus, there seems to be more consensus with regard to the value relevance of information generated to capital markets than it might appear at first glance; still, the EU seems to have a broader understanding of audiences for the reports generated – and for the entire purpose of the reporting, arguably even going beyond the sustainable finance agenda.

Although the Exposure Draft of the Management Commentary of the IFRS Foundation covers the disclosure of ESG matters (IFRS Foundation, 2021a), in the first run the ISSB focused on climate-related reporting and later on other ESG matters (IFRS Foundation, 2020). The EFRAG already had to work on the development of standards for ESG matters as a whole and aims at ensuring comparability with other standard-setters in all these matters (Baumüller & Grbenic, 2021; EU Commission, 2020). In that respect, the EU has taken the lead in the standard-setting process until now.

For European companies, the ESRS are consistent with the political ambition of the EU and with the existing framework for sustainable finance and will cover all ESG matters including climate. In addition, the standards will be aligned with the EU taxonomy: the classification system for identifying sustainable economic activities. The ESRS also take into account the disclosure requirements that are already in place under the SFDR, which requires the financial sector to report on its contribution to the sustainability agenda.

The legitimacy of the IFRS S is based on the structural legitimacy of the IFRS Foundations' global financial standard-setting (Villiers et al., 2022). The IFRS S are part of the general-purpose financial reporting and have to fulfil the qualitative characteristics of the Conceptual Framework, which also means that sustainability-related financial disclosures require consistency with the corresponding financial data and assumptions in the entity's financial statements (IFRS Foundation, 2022b). Therefore, the IFRS S places emphasis on connectivity and consistency between sustainability-related disclosure and financial reports, which, from a capital provider's point of view, is highly relevant.

Both standard-setters fulfil the demand for streamlining and formalising sustainability-related information. Formal commonalities between ESRS and IFRS S exist, such as including sustainability-related information in the management report or providing information in a machine-readable format. Even if the ISSB and EFRAG schemes will differ in their basic features, there should be a common floor of necessary reporting requirements provided from an investor-oriented point of view but also no ceiling to not restrict those jurisdictions that want to provide more information. That could guarantee that European companies do not have to generate two sustainability reports in accordance with the sustainability reporting standards of the EU and those of the IFRS Foundation (Baumüller et al., 2022). Nevertheless, a formal engagement on standard setting between the ISSB and EFRAG would enhance the coherence of the sustainability-related information and corporate reporting.

Implications

Implications for Regulators

The initiation of both projects of harmonised sustainability reporting – the IFRS S and the ESRS – seems to have started a competition between the institutions that stand behind these projects: the IFRS Foundation and the EU. Both projects are embedded in a similar agenda, and at least in Europe, they will be relevant for a similar group of companies. Still, the ambitions behind them and the quantity and purpose of the information that is required differ considerably.

The political dimension that underlies this competition has become obvious in the recent past. EU representatives stated that Europe should take the lead in promoting sustainability (reporting) practices globally (e.g. Dombrovskis, 2021), coming up with the most ambitious set of standards and demanding that European companies live up to the highest – moral – standards. The ISSB promotes its idea of a global baseline, where all jurisdictions around the world relate their work to a core set of disclosure requirements set forth by the IFRS S. This underlines the leading role both actors want to play in the current reporting landscape – and the need for them to work with each other.

From the perspective of sustainable finance, which was the starting point of the current developments, the question arises of which target groups should be addressed by reporting standards. The more extensive the information that is required, the higher the costs involved and the bigger the threat of information overload. The IFRS S focuses on investors in capital markets, which seems in line with the idea of sustainable finance; the ESRS go beyond that, explicitly stating the relevance of other audiences for sustainability reporting as well. However, in the context of the ESRS, it is also stressed that impact-related information (for various stakeholders) might also become financially relevant (for investors in capital markets). This obvious attempt

Table 2.1 Comparison of main objectives of EU and IFRS sustainability reporting standards.

Comparison	ESRS	IFRS S
Standard-setting setting bodies	European Financial Reporting Advisory Group (EFRAG); private organisation and advisory body of the EU Commission	International Sustainability Standards Boards (ISSB), new board of the IFRS Foundation
Most important standards and frameworks on which the new standards shall build on	EU legislative (e.g. Taxonomy Regulation, SFDR), GRI, TCFD	VRF (resulting from the merger of SASB and the International Integrated Reporting Council, IIRC, in 2021), CDSB, TCFD
Focus	Stakeholder-focused	Capital provider-focused
Materiality perspective of sustainability-related information	Double materiality perspective • impact on enterprise value or • impact on people and the environment	Financial materiality perspective • impact on enterprise value
Priorities in standard-setting	Environmental, social and governance standards	First priorities: climate-related disclosure standard
First-time application	Reports published in 2025	Not specified
Legitimacy	Legitimacy by institutional endorsement	Structural legitimacy
Place of publication	Management commentary	General-purpose financial reporting
Format of publication	Digital machine-readable format in accordance with the European Single Electronic Format (ESEF)	Digital machine-readable format based on IFRS Sustainability Disclosures Taxonomy

to bring the ESRS again close to the frame of sustainable finance does not seem convincing (Abhayawansa, 2022) and leads to the call for more clarity by regulators on the mechanisms that should be employed in order to approach the aim of sustainable development. So far, this has become lost in the European context.

One further implication that merits consideration refers to the legal basis of the current initiatives towards the standardisation of sustainability reporting. So far, mandatory reporting requirements are based upon laws and thus are embedded in processes that bear democratic legitimisation. By contrast, the new standards – both IFRS S and ESRS – are developed by private organisations that might have firm governance processes but that ultimately lack this strong legal foundation. Also, an endorsement mechanism as planned in the EU with regard to the ESRS only seems to be a weak substitute, especially given the fact that still it is mainly at the discretion of the EU Commission to decide about the adoption of specific standards. It comes as no surprise, thus, that opposition is arising, questioning the proposed overall framework for standardisation within the EU (Hommelhoff, 2021; Nettesheim, 2022). With regard to the standards' role for sustainable finance, this also raises the question of to what extent such a fundamental reshaping of an entire economic system should be left almost entirely to private (market) mechanisms or should be led by democratic institutions – with all the advantages and disadvantages of the respective approaches.

Implications for European Companies

For European companies, the standardisation of sustainability reporting leads to extended obligations. While the overall architecture of sustainable finance is developing further and the financial sector is increasingly including environmental and social measures in its decision-making, the new projects on standards for sustainability reporting further increase pressure on their reporting practices. However, those projects also address several deficits from the current reporting regime and provide more guidance on how to draw up compliant sustainability reports. Communication with stakeholders improves and the multitude of different demands with regard to sustainability information may also be channelled by the new standards. Furthermore, in the context of audits that are performed or enforcement activities, this can prove to be helpful.

Obviously, the outcome and especially the strains that companies will have to face depend inter alia on two things: the time that is granted to these companies to adopt the new standards and the gap between the new reporting requirements and the current reporting practices. With regard to the former, the EU Commission follows an ambitious and demanding path – and the proposed requirements by the ESRS also show that many companies will be challenged to provide disclosures in the short time they will be granted. This implies considerable pressure on and costs for companies – and ultimately adds to the demand for more focused reporting obligations as provided by the IFRS S. In any case, European companies will be well-advised to start with their preparations for the upcoming reporting requirements as soon as possible.

Furthermore, from the perspective of European companies, the question of how to link both initiatives is of high relevance and urgency. The notion of the "global baseline" as promoted by the ISSB might be one way forward – and is in line with the concept of a "building-block approach" that was proposed by representatives from practice (IFAC, 2021). Within Europe in particular, companies are increasingly demanding more effort and, thus, a closer alignment between the projects of the ISSB and the EU. The cooperation of both the EFRAG and the ISSB with the GRI might serve as an important element in this alignment.

However, irrespective of the unclear perspective on the future and alignment of the two projects, it is worth mentioning that most likely, the IFRS S and the ESRS will emerge as two co-existing standards that shape the landscape of sustainability reporting. On an international or supranational level, they already led to a consolidation of existing standards. They might be followed by jurisdictions that are still in an early phase of mandatory reporting requirements and thus might prevent any further fragmentation on a national level (e.g. Latham & Watkins LLP, 2022). So, ultimately one major benefit of the current standardisation of sustainability reporting on a company level seems at hand: the formation of a few points of reference that harmonise reporting practices, mainly differing based on their respective understanding of what sustainability means (Howitt, 2022). From the perspective of sustainable finance as well, that seems to be a major step forward from the heterogeneous situation in the past.

Implications for Research

> Academic research has played a vital role in the evolution of financial reporting standard-setting, and there is potential for it to have a similar impact on sustainability reporting standard-setting.
>
> *(Giner & Luque-Vílchez, 2022, p. 1300)*

The different approaches towards materiality and consequently towards the reporting contents and audiences of both projects, in particular, have received considerable attention in literature

(Adams & Mueller, 2022). Conceptually, different views and arguments supporting either financial or impact materiality as core principles of sustainability reporting standards have been put forward, with each side seeing better arguments on their respective approach. There will be a need for expanded theoretical and, especially, empirical evidence, a need to better identify what information is material, and a need to state what should be reported and what not, also in the light of greenwashing concerns. Also, a more thorough analysis of costs and benefits associated with different approaches towards standardisation will be necessary.

Another specific issue that has already drawn some attention refers to criticism that all current projects on standardisation have to face: whether more regulated disclosure requirements are really more informative; if comparability is for sustainability reporting of equal importance as for financial reporting; or if the resulting threat of "checkbox ticking" brings along the risk that the most important aspect of sustainability reporting is missed out – analysing the business model of a specific company and the relationships to its stakeholders, its main impacts and contributions to sustainable development (Adams & Abhayawansa, 2022). So, whether the new standards indeed promote sustainable behaviour and positive impacts on society is open to question.

With regard to research methods that might be applied to investigate sustainable finance and the harmonisation of sustainability reporting in the future, the abundance of data that will be generated will offer ample opportunities for quantitative studies – at least in the long run. However, at the same time, the complexity involved with the application of the new reporting requirements and of the changes these reporting requirements trigger in companies and their economic activities calls for in-depth qualitative analyses as well. For the upcoming transition phase towards the new reporting requirements in particular, case study research and interviews may prove to be helpful for gaining insights into the intended and possibly also unintended consequences of the ongoing changes.

Ultimately, sustainability reporting, just like the entire sustainable finance agenda, is just a means to an end – which is to change the behaviour of companies in order to contribute to sustainable development. The actual impacts of (obligatory) sustainability reporting on decision-making within companies is thus an important field of future research that will reflect back to the work of standard-setters and many of the fundamental questions they have addressed so far.

Outlook

The concept of sustainability reporting has been around for decades; however, only with regard to the role it has started to play in sustainable finance has it achieved its current momentum. The two projects by the ISSB and the EU to establish new sets of sustainability reporting standards are a culmination point that triggered a consolidation of the heterogeneous landscape of existing standard-setters, in the interest of capital markets, companies and their audiences. However, they also illustrate that there are different understandings and directions for the concrete design of reporting requirements on sustainability matters. And at least in the case of the ESRS, these new standards also show that sustainability reporting might have grown beyond the boundaries of the sustainable finance agenda.

With regard to the future development of sustainability reporting, this chapter has raised several questions that need to be addressed. At their core stands the question of how reporting requirements have to be designed in order to promote sustainable development – being embedded in a coherent regulatory framework and finding a balance between the aim of complete and comparable information that is required and the necessity to avoid information overload or a checkbox mentality. Also, the workload that companies have to face because of the respective reporting requirements has to be considered critically from a cost-benefit perspective. Providing more data – especially for the finance sector – is a means and not an end, and the obvious need for openly discussing the question of priorities between stakeholders from the finance sector and other groups of stakeholders might finally lead to the question of whether sustainable finance is enough to save the planet.

The upcoming years in the new standardisation environment for sustainability reporting will put many of these questions to a practical test. European companies in particular will be challenged to comply with these new requirements, while regulators will push their agendas forward and will have to react to their first experiences. Research, finally, is required to contribute data and an open debate to all the crucial points and underlying assumptions of the new sustainability reporting standards and their impacts. Whether this will ultimately strengthen the sustainable finance agenda or lead to new approaches to and understandings of how to motivate companies to take actions towards sustainable development remains to be seen.

Acknowledgement

This chapter is an outcome of the FINCOM project, which is financed by research subsidies granted by the government of Upper Austria (www.land-oberösterreich.gv.at/12854.htm).

References

Abela, M. (2022). "A new direction? The "mainstreaming" of sustainability reporting". *Sustainability Accounting, Management and Policy Journal*, 13(6), 1261–1283. https://doi.org/10.1108/SAMPJ-06-2021-0201

Abhayawansa, S. (2022). Swimming against the tide: Back to single materiality for sustainability reporting. *Sustainability Accounting, Management and Policy Journal*, 13(6), 1361–1385. https://doi.org/10.1108/SAMPJ-07-2022-0378

Adams, C. A., & Mueller, F. (2022). Academics and policymakers at odds: The case of the IFRS Foundation Trustees' consultation paper on sustainability reporting. *Sustainability Accounting, Management and Policy Journal*, 13(6), 1310–1333. https://doi.org/10.1108/SAMPJ-10-2021-0436

Adams, C., & Abhayawansa, S. (2022). Connecting the COVID-19 pandemic, environmental, social and governance (ESG) investing and calls for 'harmonisation' of sustainability reporting. *Critical Perspectives on Accounting*, 82, 102309. https://doi.org/10.1016/j.cpa.2021.102309

Bakker, P. (2013). *Accountants will save the world*. https://hbr.org/2013/03/accountants-will-save-the-world

Baumüller, J., & Grbenic, S. (2021). Moving from non-financial to sustainability reporting: Analyzing the EU Commission's proposal for a corporate sustainability reporting directive (CSRD). *Facta Universitatis, Series: Economics and Organization*, 18(4), 369–381. https://doi.org/10.22190/FUEO210817026B

Baumüller, J., Haring, N., & Merl, S. (2022). Ausblick auf die europäischen Standards für die Nachhaltigkeitsberichterstattung: Die Arbeitspapiere vom Januar 2022. *Zeitschrift für Internationale Rechnungslegung*, 17(3), 125–132.

Baumüller, J., & Schaffhauser-Linzatti, M.-M. (2018). In search of materiality for nonfinancial information—Reporting requirements of the directive 2014/95/EU. *Sustainability Management Forum*, 26(1–4), 101–111. https://doi.org/10.1007/s00550-018-0473-z

Baumüller, J., & Sopp, K. (2022). Double materiality and the shift from non-financial to European sustainability reporting: Review, outlook and implications. *Journal of Applied Accounting Research*, 23(1), 8–28. https://doi.org/10.1108/JAAR-04-2021-0114

Biondi, L., Dumay, J., & Monciardini, D. (2020). Using the international integrated reporting framework to comply with EU directive 2014/95/EU: Can we afford another reporting façade? *Meditari Accountancy Research*, 28(5), 889–914. https://doi.org/10.1108/MEDAR-01-2020-0695

Brown, H. S., de Jong, M., & Lessidrenska, T. (2009). The rise of the global reporting initiative: A case of institutional entrepreneurship. *Environmental Policies*, 18(2), 182–200. https://doi.org/10.1080/09644010802682551

Burritt, R. L., & Schaltegger, S. (2010). Sustainability accounting and reporting: Fad or trend? *Accounting, Auditing and Accountability Journal*, 23(7), 829–846. https://doi.org/10.1108/09513571011080144

Carungu, J., Molinari, M., Nicolò, G., Pigatto, G., & Sottoriva, C. (2022). The impact of mandatory non-financial reporting on corporate governance mechanisms: Insight from an Italian global player. In L. Cinquini & F. De Luca (Eds.), *Non-financial disclosure and integrated reporting* (pp. 61–84). Springer.

de Villiers, C., La Torre, M., & Molinari, M. (2022). The global reporting initiative's (GRI) past, present and future: Critical reflections and a research agenda on sustainability reporting (standard-setting). *Pacific Accounting Review, 34*(5), 728–747. https://doi.org/10.1108/PAR-02-2022-0034

Dombrovskis, V. (2021). *Remarks by executive vice-president Dombrovskis at the press conference on the new sustainable finance strategy and a European green bond standard.* https://ec.europa.eu/commission/presscorner/detail/en/speech_21_3506

Dyllick, T., & Muff, K. (2016). Clarifying the meaning of sustainable business: Introducing a typology from business-as-usual to true business sustainability. *Organization and Environment, 29*(2), 156–174. https://doi.org/10.1177/1086026615575176

Eccles, R. G., Lee, L.-E., & Stroehle, J. C. (2020). The social origins of ESG: An analysis of Innovest and KLD. *Organization and Environment, 33*(4), 575–596. https://doi.org/10.1177/1086026619888994

EFRAG (2021). *Proposal for a relevant and dynamic EU sustainability reporting standard setting (final reporting).* https://ec.europa.eu/info/sites/default/files/business_economy_euro/banking_and_finance/documents/210308-report-efrag-sustainability-reporting-standard-setting_en.pdf

EFRAG (2022a). *Sustainability reporting standards interim draft.* https://www.efrag.org/Activities/2105191406363055/Sustainability-reporting-standards-interim-draft

EFRAG (2022b). *Draft European sustainability reporting standards (April 2022): Cover note for public consultation.* https://www.efrag.org/Assets/Download?assetUrl=%2Fsites%2Fwebpublishing%2FSiteAssets%2FESRS_CN.pdf

Eltobgy, M., & Walter, J. (2021). *What gets measured gets managed: How sustainability reporting can help save the planet.* https://www.forbes.com/sites/worldeconomicforum/2021/01/26/what-gets-measured-gets-managed-how-sustainability-reporting-can-help-save-the-planet/

EU Commission (2011). *A renewed EU strategy 2011–14 for corporate social responsibility.* https://eur-lex.europa.eu/LexUriServ/LexUriServ.do?uri=COM:2011:0681:FIN:EN:PDF

EU Commission (2018a). *Action plan: Financing sustainable growth, COM(2018), 97 final.* https://eur-lex.europa.eu/legal-content/EN/TXT/PDF/?uri=CELEX:52018DC0097&from=EN

EU Commission (2018b). *Summary report of the public consultation on the fitness check on the EU framework for public reporting by companies, 21 March 2018–31 July 2018. Ref. Ares(2018)5582266-31/10/201.* https://ec.europa.eu/info/sites/default/files/business_economy_euro/banking_and_finance/documents/2018-companies-public-reporting-feedback-statement_en.pdf

EU Commission (2019). *The European green deal, COM(2019), 640 final.* https://eur-lex.europa.eu/resource.html?uri=cellar:b828d165-1c22-11ea-8c1f-01aa75ed71a1.0002.02/DOC_1&format=PDF

EU Commission (2020). *Commission work programme 2020 - A union that strives for more, COM(2020), 37 final.* https://eur-lex.europa.eu/resource.html?uri=cellar:7ae642ea-4340-11ea-b81b-01aa75ed71a1.0002.02/DOC_1&format=PDF

EU Commission (2021). *Proposal for a directive of the European parliament and of the council amending directive 2013/34/EU, directive 2004/109/EC, directive 2006/43/EC and regulation (EU) No 537/2014, as regards corporate sustainability reporting. Brussels, 21.4.2021, COM(2021) 189 final.* https://eur-lex.europa.eu/legal-content/EN/TXT/HTML/?uri=CELEX:52021PC0189&from=EN

EU Commission (2022). *Directive 2022/2464/EU of the European Parliament and of the Council of 14 December 2022 amending Regulation (EU) No 537/2014, Directive 2004/109/EC, Directive 2006/43/EC and Directive 2013/34/EU, as regards corporate sustainability reporting. Text with EEA relevance. OJ L 322/15.*

EU Parliament (2021). *Improving corporate sustainability reporting: Impact assessment (SWD(2021) 150, SWD(2021) 151 (summary)) accompanying a European commission proposal for a directive of the European parliament and of the council amending directive 2013/34/EU, directive 2004/109/EC, directive 2006/43/EC and regulation (EU) no 537/2014, as regards corporate sustainability reporting, COM(2021), 189.* https://www.europarl.europa.eu/RegData/etudes/BRIE/2021/694219/EPRS_BRI(2021)694219_EN.pdf

EU Parliament and Council (2003). *Directive (2003/51)/EC of the European Parliament and of the council of 18 June 2003 amending directives 78/660/EEC, 83/349/EEC, 86/635/EEC and 91/674/EEC on the annual and consolidated accounts of certain types of companies, banks and other financial institutions and insurance undertakings.* https://eur-lex.europa.eu/LexUriServ/LexUriServ.do?uri=OJ:L:2003:178:0016:0022:EN:PDF

EU Parliament and Council (2014). *Directive (2014/95)/EU of the European Parliament and of the council of 22 October 2014 amending directive 2013/34/EU as regards disclosure of non-financial and diversity information by certain large undertakings and groups.* https://eur-lex.europa.eu/legal-content/EN/TXT/HTML/?uri=CELEX:32014L0095&from=EN

Fass, N. (2022). IFRS foundation and GRI to align standards. *Strategic Finance, 103*(11), 11.

Fiandrino, S., Di Trana, M. G., Tonelli, A., & Lucchese, A. (2021). The multi-faceted dimensions for the disclosure quality of non-financial information in revising directive 2014/95/EU. *Journal of Applied Accounting Research, 23*(1), 274–300. https://doi.org/10.1108/JAAR-04-2021-0118

Forbes (2021). *The biggest change in corporate reporting since the 1930s: How to read IFRS prototype sustainability and climate standards.* https://www.forbes.com/sites/bhaktimirchandani/2021/11/04/the-biggest-change-in-corporate-reporting-since-the-1930s-how-to-read-ifrs-prototype-sustainability-and-climate-standards/?sh=54eefb5a7327

Giner, B., & Luque-Vílchez, M. (2022). A commentary on the "new" institutional actors in sustainability reporting standard-setting: A European perspective. *Sustainability Accounting, Management and Policy Journal, 13*(6), 1284–1309. https://doi.org/10.1108/SAMPJ-06-2021-0222

Global Sustainability Standards Board. (2017). *Linking GRI standards and European directive on non-financial and diversity disclosure.* https://www.globalreporting.org/media/mwydx52n/linking-gri-standards-and-european-directive-on-non-financial-and-diversity-disclosure.pdf

HLEG (2018). *Financing a sustainable European economy* [Final report]. https://ec.europa.eu/info/sites/info/files/180131-sustainable-finance-final-report_en.pdf

Hommelhoff, P. (2021). Primärrechtlich begründete Mängel im CSRD-Vorschlag und deren Beseitigung. *Der Betrieb, 74*(42), 2437–2447.

Howitt, R. (2022). *How European and global sustainability standards for corporate reporting can and will converge.* https://www.reutersevents.com/sustainability/how-european-and-global-sustainability-standards-corporate-reporting-can-and-will-converge

IFAC (2021). *Enhancing corporate reporting: Sustainability building blocks.* https://www.ifac.org/knowledge-gateway/contributing-global-economy/publications/enhancing-corporate-reporting-sustainability-building-blocks

IFRS Foundation (2020). *Consultation paper on sustainability reporting.* https://www.ifrs.org/content/dam/ifrs/project/sustainability-reporting/consultation-paper-on-sustainability-reporting.pdf

IFRS Foundation (2021a). *Exposure draft ED/2021/6 "management commentary".* http://www.ifrs.org/content/dam/ifrs/project/management-commentary/ed-2021-6-management-commentary.pdf

IFRS Foundation (2021b). *IFRS foundation trustees announce strategic direction and further steps based on feedback to sustainability reporting consultation.* https://www.ifrs.org/news-and-events/news/2021/03/trustees-announce-strategic-direction-based-on-feedback-to-sustainability-reporting-consultation/

IFRS Foundation (2021c). *Summary of the technical readiness working group's programme of work.* https://www.ifrs.org/content/dam/ifrs/groups/trwg/summary-of-the-trwg-work-programme.pdf

IFRS Foundation (2022a). *Exposure draft IFRS S2 climate-related disclosures.* https://www.ifrs.org/projects/work-plan/climate-related-disclosures/exposure-draft-and-comment-letters/

IFRS Foundation (2022b). *Exposure draft on IFRS S1 general requirements for disclosure of sustainability-related financial information.* https://www.ifrs.org/content/dam/ifrs/project/general-sustainability-related-disclosures/exposure-draft-ifrs-s1-general-requirements-for-disclosure-of-sustainability-related-financial-information.pdf

IFRS Foundation (2022c). *IFRS foundation and GRI to align capital marekt and multi-stakeholder standards to create an interconnected approach for sustainability disclosures.* https://www.ifrs.org/news-and-events/news/2022/03/ifrs-foundation-signs-agreement-with-gri/

IFRS Foundation (2023a). *IFRS S1: General Requirements for Disclosure of Sustainability-related Financial Information, London 2023*

IFRS Foundation (2023b). *IFRS S2: Climate-related Disclosures, London 2023.*

Kinderman, D. (2020). The challenges of upward regulatory harmonization: The case of sustainability reporting in the European Union. *Regulation and Governance, 14*(4), 674–697. https://doi.org/10.1111/rego.12240

Larrinaga, C., & Bebbington, J. (2021). The pre-history of sustainability reporting: A constructivist reading. *Accounting, Auditing and Accountability Journal, 34*(9), 162–181. https://doi.org/10.1108/AAAJ-03-2017-2872

Latham & Watkins LLP. (2022). *China to introduce its first ESG disclosure standard.* https://www.jdsupra.com/legalnews/china-to-introduce-its-first-esg-3361000/

Littan, S. (2022). The future of responsible reporting. *Strategic Finance, 103*(8), 19–20.

Migliorelli, M. (2021). What do we mean by sustainable finance? Assessing existing frameworks and policy risks. *Sustainability, 13*(2), 975. https://doi.org/10.3390/su13020975

Nettesheim, M. (2022). *Nachhaltigkeitsberichterstattung: Zur Unionsrechtskonformität des CSRD-Standardsetzungsverfahrens.* https://www.familienunternehmen.de/media/public/pdf/publikationen-studien/studien/Nachhaltigkeitsberichterstattung-Unionsrechtskonformitaet-CSRD-Standardsetzungsverfahrens_Studie_Stiftung-Familienunternehmen.pdf

Pope, P. F., & McLeay, S. J. (2011). The European IFRS experiment: Objectives, research challenges and some early evidence. *Accounting and Business Research, 41*(3), 233–266. https://doi.org/10.1080/00014788.2011.575002

Purvis, B., Mao, Y., & Robinson, D. (2018). Three pillars of sustainability: In search of conceptual origins. *Sustainability Science, 14*(3), 681–695. https://doi.org/10.1007/s11625-018-0627-5

Rydge, J. (2020). *Aligning finance with the Paris agreement.* Policy Insight. https://www.lse.ac.uk/granthaminstitute/wp-content/uploads/2020/12/Aligning-finance-with-the-Paris-Agreement-3.pdf

Testarmata, S., Ciaburri, M., Fortuna, F., & Sergiacomi, S. (2020). Harmonization of non-financial reporting regulation in Europe: A study of the transposition of the directive 2014/95/EU. In S. Brunelli & E. Di Carlo (Eds.), *Accountability, ethics and sustainability of organizations*, 67–88, Springer.

UNFCCC (2022). *Introduction to climate finance.* https://unfccc.int/topics/climate-finance/the-big-picture/introduction-to-climate-finance

van Hulle, K. (2004). From accounting directives to international accounting standards. In C. Leuz, D. Pfaff, & A. Hopwood (Eds.), *The economics and politics of accounting*, 349–375, Oxford University Press Inc., New York.

Velte, P., & Stawinoga, M. (2017). Integrated reporting: The current state of empirical research, limitations and future research implications. *Journal of Management Control, 28*(3), 275–320. https://doi.org/10.1007/s00187-016-0235-4

World Economic Forum (2021). *60 organizations release open letter for EU to act on ESG.* https://www.weforum.org/agenda/2021/10/57-organizations-release-open-letter-for-eu-to-act-on-esg/

World Economic Forum (2022). *Get the reporting right and sustainability will follow.* https://www.weforum.org/agenda/2022/06/sustainability-reporting-why-important/

Zeff, S. A. (2012). The evolution of the IASC into the IASB, and the challenges it faces. *Accounting Review, 87*(3), 807–837. https://doi.org/10.2308/accr-10246

3
DOUBLE MATERIALITY
Why Does It Matter for Sustainability Reporting?

Tia Rebecca Driver and Amr ElAlfy

Introduction

The role of corporations in achieving sustainable development has a long and manifested history in academic literature and practice. The tragic events of the Deepwater Horizon and Rana Plaza and more recent claims of greenwashing against HSBC underline the necessity of more transparent and open communication from businesses with their stakeholders regarding corporate sustainability practices (Burritt & Schaltegger, 2010; Higgins et al., 2020; Torelli et al., 2020). In response to adverse environmental and social problems like those previously mentioned, regulators and reporting bodies have been working on developing and standardizing sustainability reporting to address concerns about the adverse effects of corporate operations on society and the environment.

Theoretically, Drucker's (1984) concept of corporate sustainability altered how businesses approach their operations and their impacts on society and the environment. Prior to this, corporate sustainability had been seen as an addition to a company's main line of business. Scholars have emphasized the tensions and trade-offs between corporate sustainability and financial performance. Nevertheless, according to Drucker, strategic corporate sustainability can help businesses compete more effectively by tackling societal and environmental challenges. As a result, they focus on issues in their reporting that are related to their primary business to gain legitimacy and enhance their stakeholders' relationships.

Additionally, corporate sustainability has been influenced by two critical concepts: corporate sustainability and the sustainable case of business. Corporate sustainability links business strategy and sustainability via a systems perspective, which maps the relationships between businesses and society (Bansal & Song, 2017; ElAlfy et al., 2020).

The sustainability case for business seeks to help corporations identify the positive and negative impacts of their operations, services, or products on sustainable development (Weber & Feltmate, 2016). Businesses can leverage or develop processes that generate financial returns and positive sustainable outcomes (Weber & Feltmate, 2016). Both corporate sustainability and the sustainability case for business focus on connecting sustainability reporting to the strategic management of an organization. Fundamentally, sustainability reporting is a medium through which corporations disclose their financial and non-financial (e.g., social and environmental issues) performance to gain legitimacy and bolster corporate reputation by demonstrating superiority over their competitors (Herzig & Schaltegger, 2006; Setia et al., 2022).

It is important to note that sustainability reporting provides opportunities for organizations to share their sustainability performance with the public, but adopting sustainability reporting does not always result in improved corporate sustainability. For example, the European Union (EU) established a non-financial reporting directive in 2014, which is being updated (European Union Commission, 2014, 2021). The intention behind the directive is to facilitate the adoption of sustainability reporting by mandating sustainability disclosure (European Union Commission, 2017). However, this policy did not result in more informative reports by Italian-listed companies (Agostini et al., 2022). The current approach to implementing the directive allows companies to omit potentially relevant sustainability information from their reports, resulting in less detailed reporting of social impacts (Pizzi et al., 2021). Furthermore, mandatory reporting enacted through the Lima Stock Exchange resulted in fewer submissions of third-party assurance (Loza Adaui, 2020).

Given the scale of corporate operations, a challenge for corporations is comprehensively disclosing such information that satisfies diverse stakeholders' expectations (Abhayawansa, 2022; Bradford et al., 2017; Calabrese et al., 2016). To address such a challenge, several reporting institutions and frameworks have been working on developing reporting guidelines and standards to help organizations to structure their sustainability report (e.g., GRI (2022c) and SASB (2022a)).

In September 2020, the five most prominent reporting frameworks, namely Carbon Disclosure Project (CDP), Global Reporting Initiative (GRI), Sustainability Accounting Standards Board (SASB), the International Integrated Reporting Council (IIRC), and the Climate Disclosure Standards Board (CDSB) issued a statement of collaboration toward the standardization of sustainability reporting (Impact Management Project, 2020). Following this statement, the International Financial Reporting Standards (IFRS), which regulates financial reporting in 160 jurisdictions, intervened in 2020 in the sustainability reporting domain by establishing the International Sustainability Standards Board (ISSB) on November 3, 2021 (International Financial Reporting Standards Foundation, 2022a). The ISSB aims to develop a comprehensive global baseline for sustainability disclosure standards (International Financial Reporting Standards Foundation, 2022a). The IFRS has also brought SASB and the IIRC under its management umbrella (International Financial Reporting Standards Foundation, 2022d). The intention for collaboration and moves by the IFRS highlight the complexity and changing landscape of sustainability reporting.

As part of standardizing the reporting frameworks, there has been an increased debate regarding how organizations determine which reporting topics are relevant to them. The concept of materiality assists companies in understanding which topics should be considered in the sustainability report based on stakeholders' interests or reporting needs (Baumüller & Sopp, 2022; Farooq et al., 2021). However, there remain concerns that enterprises cater their sustainability reports to the needs of financial stakeholders (e.g., financial investors) (Adams & Abhayawansa, 2022; Spence, 2009). These concerns have led to the development of three distinct approaches to materiality. Exploring these approaches will allow us to better understand the future trajectory of sustainability reporting.

This chapter contributes to the ongoing discussion of the standardization of sustainability reporting by examining the present landscape of reporting frameworks and their governing organizations. This chapter aims to provide a brief overview of the current approaches and applications of materiality. Additionally, we review the recent efforts of the IFRS and the European Financial Reporting Advisory Group (EFRAG). Ultimately, we argue that organizations should adopt a double materiality concept when reporting on their sustainability performance because this approach provides a comprehensive interpretation of sustainability issues.

This chapter is organized as follows: first, we will introduce the concept of materiality and three different approaches to conceptualizing this concept (i.e., single materiality, double materiality, and dynamic materiality). The subsequent section will provide an overview of the GRI and SASB frameworks, with consideration of how materiality is used within those frameworks. Then we will present our argument favoring the adoption of double materiality. The final section will highlight insights regarding the future of sustainability reporting.

Understanding Materiality

Within the scope of corporate sustainability reporting, materiality is used to determine whether a piece of information should be disclosed (Jebe, 2019). If knowing or not knowing a specific piece of information impacts the decision-making or assessment by stakeholders, then the information would be considered material and needs to be disclosed (Font et al., 2016). Materiality helps corporations select the most relevant reporting criteria to ensure that the organization's disclosure aligns corporate disclosure with the needs of the organization's stakeholders (Ferrero-Ferrero et al., 2021; Whitehead, 2017). Although materiality is easy to understand, there is a point of contention regarding what information needs to be shared and to whom the report is intended. Depending on the selected stakeholders, the types of information disclosed by organizations will vary (Mio et al., 2020), which could result in different interpretations of corporate performance (Jørgensen et al., 2022). Three approaches to materiality have been identified: single materiality, double materiality, and dynamic materiality. Each of these approaches to materiality will be discussed in turn.

Single Materiality

Single materiality established disclosure rationale based on the information relevant to investors *and* stakeholders (Abhayawansa, 2022; Baumüller & Sopp, 2022). Unfortunately, investors and other stakeholders (e.g., governments, employees, consumers, etc.) tend to have different interests, resulting in different disclosure requirements (Jonsdottir et al., 2022; Whitehead, 2017). The work of Reimsbach et al. (2020) found that capital market actors (e.g., financial analysts) and potential employees (e.g., business students) valued the importance of non-financial information (i.e., sustainability topics) differently.

Single materiality has been further refined to only focus on disclosing information related to the impact on the organization's financial performance (Andreou & Besharov, 2022; Chiu, 2022). The focus on financial performance has led to this interpretation of single materiality to be referred to as financial materiality (Puroila & Mäkelä, 2019). It has also been called "outside-in" materiality because it only considers how the external environment (i.e., the economy, society, and the natural environment) impacts firm performance (Remmer & Gilbert, 2019).

The initial intentions of single materiality could help streamline the reporting process for an organization because they would clearly understand the types of information they need to disclose (Abhayawansa, 2022). However, this approach to materiality contradicts the intentions of sustainability reporting due to the focus on financial or economic impacts (Torelli et al., 2020). Sustainability reporting aims to communicate the organization's performance, activities, and risks associated with sustainable (economic, social, and environmental) topics to provide transparency and generate shared value (Calabrese et al., 2016; Christensen et al., 2021; Herzig & Schaltegger, 2006; Stolowy & Paugam, 2018). To adequately communicate across all three dimensions of sustainability, organizations must provide comprehensive disclosure on various topics. Yet, a single materiality approach provides a limited understanding of the organization because disclosure is restricted to only the topics(s) shared by both investors and other stakeholders. Additionally, the adherence to financial materiality presents additional limitations because this interpretation does not consider the possible implications of non-financial topics (i.e., other environmental and social) on an organization's ability to generate value in the long term (Adams & Abhayawansa, 2022). A single materiality perspective, including the focus on financial materiality, could curtail the breadth and depth of an organization's disclosures and hinder future performance.

Double Materiality

In contrast to the single materiality perspective, double materiality considers the impacts on enterprise value and the impacts of organizational activities on the natural environment and society (Adams et al., 2021). The focus on external effects is called impact materiality (European Financial Reporting Advisory Group, 2021). This approach considers information material if financial or other stakeholder groups consider it essential.

Double materiality recognizes that environmental, social, and financial impacts can coincide and interact with each other (European Financial Reporting Advisory Group, 2021). This approach to materiality is more forward-looking than single materiality because it considers issues that have yet to be directly associated with an enterprise value (e.g., climate change) (Adams & Abhayawansa, 2022). As a result, this double materiality has been referred to as a combination of outside-in and inside-out (Abhayawansa, 2022). The inside-out concept considers whether the organization's activities impact the broader environment, society, and economy (Remmer & Gilbert, 2019). The outside-in and inside-out relationships of double materiality are captured in Figure 3.1.

Through the lens of climate change, Figure 3.1 identifies where risks and opportunities arise for the organization and the broader socio-ecology system. The outside-in aspect can be seen in the lower portion of the diagram, where risks for the organization come in the form of actions taken by social actors (e.g., governments, customers, investors, etc.) and as direct implications from climate change itself (e.g., supply chain delays due to natural hazards). The upper portion of the diagram demonstrates the inside-out approach by considering the impacts of the organization on the socio-ecology system and the potential for new opportunities if the organization takes a proactive approach to climate change adaptation.

In terms of stakeholders, investors and other financial stakeholders remain relevant vital players under the double materiality perspective. This approach to materiality acknowledges that there can be numerous stakeholders, each with distinct reporting needs (Abhayawansa, 2022), which can result in different and, at times, contesting material topics (Puroila & Mäkelä, 2019).

The GRI board, scholars, and many sustainability leaders globally have been advocating for the implementation of double materiality for sustainability reporting purposes for several reasons. First, combining financial and impact materiality could help avoid inadvertent greenwashing because financial and sustainable performances are communicated (Chiu, 2022). Second, investment decisions could be better informed by this approach. Double materiality generates a wealth of non-financial information that could highlight potential risks or opportunities that otherwise would have been missed under single materiality (Adams et al., 2021). Third, double materiality could result in more robust stakeholder engagement, given the need for organizations to understand a wide range of reporting needs (Adams et al., 2021; Baumüller & Sopp, 2022).

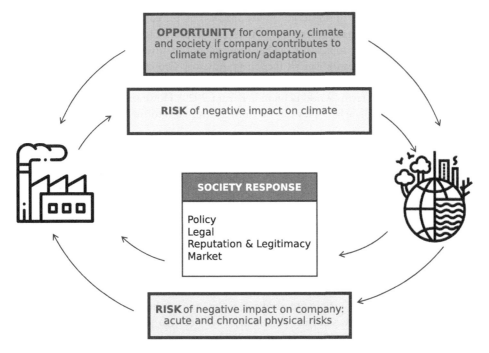

Figure 3.1 The outside-in and inside-out relationships of double materiality through the example of climate change (Source: adapted from European Commission (2019))

Although double materiality provides a more insightful approach to sustainability reporting, there are challenges with this approach. Firstly, given the increased number of potential stakeholders, disclosures might become too complex, or stakeholders might be provided with too much information (Baumüller & Sopp, 2022). Secondly, including the social dimension means new measurements or indicators might be needed to disclose adequately (Chiu, 2022). Thirdly, the target audience for the impact materiality aspect is not clearly defined, thereby creating challenges in isolating relevant stakeholders (Abhayawansa, 2022). Double materiality provides an approach to sustainability reporting, even with the aforementioned challenges, because it is more comprehensive and informative than single materiality.

Dynamic Materiality

Although double materiality offsets some of the limitations of single materiality, both concepts implicitly assume that material issues do not change over time. As Kuh et al. (2020) noted, the accessibility of information through the internet makes it easier for stakeholders to evaluate organizations, meaning organizations have less control over the narrative told about them. The diverse interests of stakeholder groups (Abhayawansa, 2022), coupled with persistent changes in the social, ecological, and economic landscapes, requires expanding upon the double materiality approach to include a specific temporal dimension to materiality. Consequently, the concept of dynamic materiality has been used to capture the temporal nature of material topics (Abhayawansa, 2022; Jørgensen et al., 2022).

In general, dynamic materiality recognizes the fluidity of material topics. One interpretation of dynamic materiality sees the transition from immaterial topics to financially material topics as a result of the interactions or impacts of an organization on the economy, natural environment, and society (European Financial Reporting Advisory Group, 2021; Fiandrino et al., 2022; Kuh et al., 2020). Sustainability topics that can become material are given a provisional classification of "pre-financial" (European Financial Reporting Advisory Group, 2021). These topics would have importance to society or the natural environment and could impact financial performance in the medium to long term (World Economic Forum, 2020). However, it is essential to remember that not all non-financial topics can be easily converted into financial impacts (Adams & Abhayawansa, 2022).

A popular conceptualization of dynamic materiality can be seen in Figure 3.2. The outermost layer represents impact materiality, and the innermost layer signifies financial materiality. The layer in the middle represents topics that could generate or hinder enterprise value generation. The downward-moving arrows indicate the dynamic nature of materiality on the exterior of the layers. Sustainable topics that exist outside of the outermost layer (i.e., immaterial topics) can be drawn into disclosure due to changes in social expectations or because of corporate activities shifting away from acceptable practices (e.g., pharmaceutical companies drastically increasing the cost of medications) (Freiberg et al., 2020).

Dynamic materiality underscores the importance of considering enterprise value creation and social and environmental impacts (Afolabi et al., 2022). This approach has potential pragmatic issues related to collecting and verifying information, which might impose additional challenges for sustainability reporting practitioners even though practitioners are amenable to adopting dynamic materiality (Jørgensen et al., 2022).

This section has shown that single, double, and dynamic materiality are three distinct but interconnected interpretations of materiality. Corporations risk engaging in greenwashing (Chiu, 2022; Ferrero-Ferrero et al., 2021) or failing to provide enough information for stakeholders (Jørgensen et al., 2022) if they only adopt a single materiality perspective. Thus, organizations must understand which materiality approach their selected sustainability reporting framework adopts.

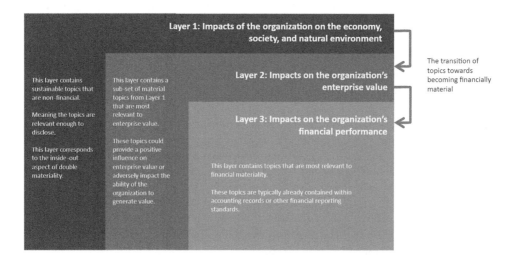

Figure 3.2 The dynamic nature of sustainability reporting topics (Source: adapted from Thinking Ahead Institute (2021) and the World Economic Forum (2020))

Materiality in Practice

Sustainability reporting frameworks guide corporations on how to communicate best their sustainability performance (ElAlfy & Weber, 2019; Herzig & Schaltegger, 2006). However, corporations' stakeholders are not homogeneous. The interests and reporting needs may vary from one stakeholder to the next (Abhayawansa et al., 2019; Reimsbach et al., 2020). The diverse needs of stakeholders have resulted in the development of numerous reporting standards, each with a discrete focus, target audience, and disclosure requirements (Jørgensen et al., 2022; Stolowy & Paugam, 2018).

This section will explore two popular reporting frameworks, GRI and SASB, to understand what stakeholders are considered and how materiality is determined. There will also be a short discussion regarding the IFRS Foundation since it is now an integral part of the SASB reporting standards and the efforts of EFRAG.

The Global Reporting Initiative Framework

The standards outlined by the GRI intend to help organizations identify the most material issues they should disclose in their sustainability report (Global Reporting Initiative, 2022a). Double materiality underpins the GRI's standards (Global Reporting Initiative, 2022h). But, dynamic materiality is seen as a tool to delay the adoption of non-financial topics (Global Reporting Initiative, 2022h). The intended audience of a GRI report would be the organization's investors and other stakeholders interested in understanding the organization's sustainability performance (Global Reporting Initiative, 2022b). The GRI standards are divided into three groupings; Universal Standards, Sector Standards, and Topic Standards (Global Reporting Initiative, 2022a).

All organizations partaking in the GRI framework must ensure they complete the Universal Standards' requirements. The Universal Standards outline the fundamental expectations for a GRI-based sustainability report (GRI 1), disclosure requirements related to the organization's governance and structure (GRI 2), and an explanation of how the organization selected material topics (GRI 3) (Global Reporting Initiative, 2022e, 2022f, 2022d). The Universal Standards provide organizations with the foundational knowledge of key terms and concepts the GRI uses in their reporting framework while ensuring every organization adheres to responsible business practices and considers human rights and good governance principles, as set out by intergovernmental instruments (Global Reporting Initiative, 2022i).

Additionally, the Universal Standards provides a step-by-step materiality assessment process in GRI 3, which assists organizations in identifying the environmental, social, and economic issues that are most relevant for the organization (Global Reporting Initiative, 2022f). GRI's interpretation of materiality requires organizations to consider the direct and potential negative impacts of the organization's operations and activities, including impacts attributed to the organization's business relationships (Global Reporting Initiative, 2022i). The Topics Standards and Sector Standards work with GRI 3 to further identify the sustainability topics that ought to be disclosed (Global Reporting Initiative, 2022f, 2022i).

The GRI developed the Sector Standards to improve the comparability between organizations within the same industry by outlining a pre-established list of sustainability issues that are typically relevant for organizations operating within a specified industry (Global Reporting Initiative, 2022i). It is important to note that the Sector Standards do not provide any guidance on the reporting requirements for the identified sustainability topics; that is the purpose of the Topic Standards (Global Reporting Initiative, 2022i). The GRI stresses that the Sector Standards are not a replacement for the materiality process presented in GRI 3, the Universal Standards (Global Reporting Initiative, 2022i). Topic Standards have been developed for agriculture and aquaculture, coal, oil, and gas sectors (Global Reporting Initiative, 2022g).

The last grouping of standards, the Topic Standards, is the source of disclosure requirements for various sustainability issues (Global Reporting Initiative, 2022f). The GRI has divided the Topic Standards into three broad categories; economic (GRI 200 series), environmental (GRI 300 series), and social (GRI 400 series) (Global Reporting Initiative, 2021). The specific issues explored include, but are not limited to, anti-corporation (GRI 206), indirect economic impacts (GRI 203), waste (GRI 306), emissions (GRI 305), occupational health and safety (GRI 403), and freedom of association and collective bargaining (GRI 407). This short list highlights the range of topics the GRI framework addresses and demonstrates the comprehensiveness a GRI-based report could have.

Even though the GRI framework provides pre-established lists of material topics and a step-by-step guide to conducting a materiality assessment, organizations can omit topics; see requirement five under GRI 1 (Global Reporting Initiative, 2022d). Nonetheless, the GRI framework provides clear guidance on setting the boundaries of materiality for industries, sectors, and firms.

Sustainability Accounting Standards Board

SASB is now part of the IFRS and will eventually be integrated into the IFRS' Sustainability Disclosure Standards (Sustainability Accounting Standards Board, 2022h). The standards require organizations to communicate any risks and opportunities that impact enterprise value (Sustainability Accounting Standards Board, 2022g), suggesting that topics are evaluated based on financial materiality (Sustainability Accounting Standards Board, 2022b). This approach to materiality is sensible, given that the primary audience for SASB standards is investors (Sustainability Accounting Standards Board, 2022d, 2022b). SASB views its approach to materiality as the middle ground between impact materiality and financial reporting (Sustainability Accounting Standards Board, 2022e). SASB recognizes that double and dynamic materiality plays an essential role in the broad scheme of sustainability reporting (Sustainability Accounting Standards Board, 2022i). However, SASB maintains that its standards focus on financial material issues and complement the GRI standards (Sustainability Accounting Standards Board & Global Reporting Initiative, 2021).

Unlike the GRI standards, organizations are not expected to conduct a materiality assessment under the SASB framework. Instead, SASB has developed set lists of material topics for 11 broad sectors, guiding 77 industries (Sustainability Accounting Standards Board, 2022f). SASB has identified 26 General Issue Categories under five dimensions; environment, social capital, human capital, business model and innovation, leadership, and governance (Sustainability Accounting Standards Board, 2022e). Each General Issue Category contains subsequent disclosure topics designed to ensure that the most relevant material topics are being considered by an organization (Sustainability Accounting Standards Board, 2022g). However, like the GRI, SASB allows enterprises to choose which material topics to disclose, so long as a rationale for the omission is provided (Sustainability Accounting Standards Board, 2022c).

The SASB framework provides two metrics to assist organizations in measuring and disclosing material topics. The accounting metrics provide quantitative or qualitative insights into the organizations' performance (Sustainability Accounting Standards Board, 2018). The Activity Metrics are intended to help delineate the scope of the organization's operations and assist in facilitating comparability between organizations (Sustainability Accounting Standards Board,

2022b). Together, these metrics provide clear guidance for organizations to report how sustainability issues impact enterprise value.

The International Financial Reporting Standards Foundation

Before the integration of SASB and the IIRC, the IFRS Foundation primarily focused on establishing standardized financial accounting practices, the premiere reporting standards in many countries worldwide (International Financial Reporting Standards Foundation, 2022b). The creation of the ISSB has allowed the IFRS to enter the sustainability reporting arena (Afolabi et al., 2022). However, there remain doubts regarding the ability of the IFRS to develop adequate sustainability reporting standards given the foundation's financial accounting background (Adams & Abhayawansa, 2022).

In a recent publication, the IFRS stated that it had achieved its commitment to "consult on proposed standards to set the foundations of the global baseline of sustainability-related financial disclosures" (International Financial Reporting Standards Foundation, 2022e). The publication discusses how the primary focus of the ISSB is to support economic and investment decision-making (International Financial Reporting Standards Foundation, 2022e). Thus, any standards developed by the ISSB will be grounded within the financial materiality interpretation. Although the IFRS and GRI have indicated that their frameworks could be coordinated (International Financial Reporting Standards Foundation, 2022c), it remains to be seen how these standard setters will navigate the conceptual tensions between double and financial materiality.

European Financial Reporting Advisory Group

EFRAG was formed to provide the European Commission with the insights needed to develop reporting standards based on European needs and interests (European Financial Reporting Advisory Group, 2022a). To assist in developing financial and sustainable reporting standards, EFRAG develops two thematic boards to provide the association with the necessary technical insights (European Financial Reporting Advisory Group, 2022b). EFRAG has also developed a task force called the Project Task Force on European Sustainability Reporting Standards (PTF-ESRS). The PTF-ESRS intends to explore potential non-financial reporting standards for the EU (European Financial Reporting Advisory Group, 2021). The work by EFRAG has also provided opportunities for consultation and collaboration with GRI and the IFRS (European Financial Reporting Advisory Group, 2022c).

The PTF-ESRS noted that double materiality "is key to sustainability reporting standard-setting in the EU" (European Financial Reporting Advisory Group, 2021, p. 74). This group also supports the adoption of dynamic materiality in conjunction with double materiality (European Financial Reporting Advisory Group, 2021). It is recommended that impact and financial materiality be applied individually and that companies understand the dynamic relationships between these approaches (European Financial Reporting Advisory Group, 2021). This recommendation aligns with the reporting requirements set out within the European Union's newly adopted Corporate Sustainability Reporting Directive (CSRD) (Yakimova, 2022), the existing Non-Financial Reporting Directive (NFRD) (European Union Commission, 2014), and with the approach to materiality used in the GRI standards. Overall, EFRAG's work might strengthen European enterprises' adoption of double and dynamic materiality.

The above sections have highlighted how the three approaches to materiality have been utilized within two reporting frameworks and two standard setters. Both the GRI and SASB frameworks seek to provide clear guidelines for developing their sustainability reports. These frameworks also wish to improve comparability between organizations by outlining materiality instructions. The IFRS and EFRAG wish to establish standardized reporting practices at the international level. The key differences between these organizations are their approaches to materiality. The concept of double materiality is embedded within the GRI standards and EFRAG's reporting recommendations. Alternatively, financial materiality underpins SASB standards and the IFRS's approach to sustainability reporting. Dynamic materiality is not a predominant feature of the GRI and SASB standards but has a role in the EFRAG's recommendations. Overall, each approach to materiality has a place in sustainability reporting, but the question remains whether this should be the case.

The Value of Double Materiality

The last two years have witnessed an unprecedented evolvement in the area of sustainability reporting. In Larry Fink's letter to the CEOs of BlackRock's portfolio companies, he urged them to consider the social and environmental footprints the same as they care about their financial performance (Larry Fink, 2022). There has been a significant increase in the number of sustainability reports issued by firms across all sectors globally since 2020 (KPMG International, 2022). The interest in standardizing sustainability reporting has arisen from a desire to improve the reporting quality (European Union Commission, 2021), consistency, and comparability (International Financial Reporting Standards Foundation, 2021).

Materiality has been a crucial factor in identifying and communicating sustainability-related concerns or impacts, as was evident in the previous section addressing sustainability reporting standards and frameworks. Double, single, and dynamic materiality have been utilized in reporting frameworks to guide organizations in determining the relevance of sustainability topics and what they ought to include in their disclosures. However, single and double materiality cater to different stakeholder reporting needs (Global Reporting Initiative, 2022h; Sustainability Accounting Standards Board, 2022b), resulting in different sustainability focuses. SASB has used financial materiality to appeal to the needs of financial stakeholders (Sustainability Accounting Standards Board & Global Reporting Initiative, 2021). This approach has been further entrenched into the ISSB (International Financial Reporting Standards Foundation, 2022c), which raises concerns about the ability of the IFRS to produce reporting frameworks that fully consider sustainability (Adams & Abhayawansa, 2022; Maechler, 2022). The IFRS has acknowledged that double materiality and the GRI are compatible with SASB standards (International Financial Reporting Standards Foundation, 2022c). However, double materiality already considers financial materiality alongside impact materiality (Adams et al., 2021; EFRAG, 2021). So then, what is the value of producing a global standard based on financial materiality?

The primary issue with relying on a single materiality approach, such as financial materiality, is that it has the potential to reduce the disclosure quality. Corporations already skew their disclosure to the needs of financial stakeholders (Chiu, 2022; Spence, 2009). Combining this practice with a global reporting standard that skews disclosure toward financial stakeholders, enterprises would be hard-pressed to claim that their sustainability reports contain the necessary information for other stakeholder groups to make informed decisions. If corporations solely focus on financial materiality, they risk reducing the quality of their disclosure and alienating key non-financial stakeholders (e.g., their customers).

Therefore, double materiality should be the predominant approach because it considers a broader range of sustainability topics and stakeholders (Adams et al., 2021; Chiu, 2022; European Financial Reporting Advisory Group, 2021). In essence, double materiality provides a more comprehensive final report and ensures that sustainability reporting achieves its purpose of reporting on sustainability.

Conclusion and Future Outlook

Over the past two decades, there has been a significant change in the reporting requirements for sustainability issues: from supplements to improve the decision utility of financial reports, which were formerly little more than a footnote, to a way of tackling comprehensive societal and environmental issues (Cho et al., 2015). Materiality has been crucial in selecting and communicating sustainability-related issues or impacts in sustainability reporting standards and frameworks. Reaching a consensus on materiality has been challenging to do given the competing interpretations (Adams & Abhayawansa, 2022; Afolabi et al., 2022) and the inherent challenges of meeting the disclosure needs of diverse stakeholders (Reimsbach et al., 2020; Whitehead, 2017).

These tensions have resulted in three different but interconnected approaches to materiality. Single and double materiality acts as bookends for the range of reporting topics, while dynamic materiality is a temporal mediator. In practice, single and double materiality appear in two popular reporting frameworks, GRI and SASB (KPMG International, 2022; Sustainability Accounting Standards Board & Global Reporting Initiative, 2021). However, the target audiences for these frameworks are different. SASB's reporting framework supports financial investors (Sustainability Accounting Standards Board, 2022b, 2022d), and the GRI standards provide insights for a broader range of stakeholders (Global Reporting Initiative, 2022b).

Although the financial implications of sustainable topics are valid concerns in sustainability reporting, the focus of sustainability disclosure should not be solely on the needs of financial stakeholders. Sustainability reporting aims to communicate an organization's financial and non-financial performance to stakeholders (Herzig & Schaltegger, 2006; Setia et al., 2022). Yet, the application of single materiality via a financial perspective has resulted in disclosures that favor the interests of financial stakeholders (Adams & Abhayawansa, 2022; Sustainability Accounting Standards Board & Global Reporting Initiative, 2021). The use of financial materiality further moves reporting practices away from the intentions of sustainability reporting (Maechler, 2022). As such, a different interpretation of materiality is needed.

Double materiality requires consideration for financial and non-financial topics (European Financial Reporting Advisory Group, 2021). This approach to materiality allows for more comprehensive disclosure of social, environmental, and economic performances while catering to the interests of a diverse range of stakeholders (Adams et al., 2021). If reporting standards wish to align with the intentions of sustainability reporting, then double materiality should be adopted.

In terms of the future of sustainability reporting and materiality, there are five topical areas that researchers and students should consider. Firstly, the ISSB had its session on December 13, 2022. ISSB officials announced that sustainability is necessary for businesses to maintain their stakeholder relationships and resources (such as financial, human, and natural) required over the short, medium, and long term (International Financial Reporting Standards Foundation, 2022f). The new approach by the ISSB emphasizes that the operating environment for businesses, which would be subject to the new legislation, will become more challenging. Companies need to deal with the rise in stakeholder demand for sustainability information.

Additionally, the ISSB officials shed light on political pressures brought on by efforts of reporting frameworks and governing bodies to enable a transition to more transparent and reliable disclosure (International Financial Reporting Standards Foundation, 2022f). As a result, it is conceivable that companies will be compelled to create new reporting procedures and alter their business management approach towards more integrated reporting because of the new regulations. It will therefore be necessary to pay more attention to the social and environmental costs involved in their operations.

Secondly, the distinction between financial materiality and double materiality is still contested by some practitioners (Afolabi et al., 2022). Double materiality proponents contend that most sustainability issues will eventually have financial repercussions (Global Reporting Initiative, 2022h). The dispute between single and double materiality could be reduced to the considerably simpler issue of which relevant time horizon should be used when making materiality determinations.

Thirdly, there is no apparent enforcement mechanism or verification process for sustainability disclosures (Loza Adaui, 2020). As such, organizations could conceal harmful effects or overstate their successful performance by manipulating the boundaries of what constitutes materiality and taking advantage of gaps in obligatory reporting laws (Ferrero-Ferrero et al., 2021). Any hasty attempt to standardize sustainability reporting could undermine sustainable development by endorsing a viewpoint that naturally favors one aspect of sustainability (i.e., economic consequences) while downplaying the other two aspects (i.e., society and the environment).

In addition, attempts to standardize sustainability reporting at this time might overlook two challenges with existing sustainability reporting data. The first challenge is the lack of detail contained in existing sustainability reports. As highlighted by Agostini et al. (2022), the introduction of mandatory sustainability reporting increased the quantity of corporate disclosure, but the level of detail provided within the reports did not increase. Even if sustainability reporting were to become mandatory under Universal Standards, the level of detail within the reports might not be addressed if financial materiality underpins the reporting framework, which focuses on sustainability information that is only relevant to financial performance (Andreou & Besharov, 2022; Chiu, 2022). The second challenge is the trustworthiness of existing reporting data. As noted by Pizzi et al. (2021), companies might be strategically motivated to omit negative information from their sustainability reports if the reporting framework allows them to do so, which raises questions about the trustworthiness of existing reports. Consequently, any discussion regarding sustainability reporting standardization must provide adequate consideration to the possibility of companies omitting information that provides a negative view of the firm and understand that creating a sustainability report may not result in a more detailed report.

Fourthly, there exists a challenge with the availability and validity of existing sustainability data. Corporations have been known to implement cost-saving measures that reduce the quality or detail of their reporting data (Herzig & Schaltegger, 2006; Pizzi et al., 2021). As a result, this becomes a challenge for sustainability disclosure because the validity of such data is in question, which seems to underpin the broader calls for reporting consistency and comparability (Adams & Abhayawansa, 2022). Furthermore, mandating reporting might result in businesses not seeking third-party assurances (Loza Adaui, 2020). If the data from corporate sustainability reports are not verified, and businesses have leeway to omit information, then standardizing the current reporting practice might further perpetuate these challenges.

Finally, the ISSB and reporting regulators should develop a mechanism that controls sustainability disclosures. For instance, the repercussions of incorrect reporting or greenwashing are still unknown. As a result, identical regulatory frameworks must be put in place for financial reporting. There is a need to move from disclosure to business alignment. To elaborate, the eventual objective of reporting standardization and regulation should be the alignment of reporting companies with sustainability goals, such as climate issues, and ecological and societal goals. For businesses to achieve sustainable development, disclosure is simply the first step.

We also acknowledge that numerous data problems still need to be addressed to develop meaningful sustainability reports. Further studies in sustainability reporting are needed to assist firms in adopting the recently suggested sustainability standards and achieving the desired corporate sustainability.

References

Abhayawansa, S. (2022). Swimming against the tide: Back to single materiality for sustainability reporting. *Sustainability Accounting, Management and Policy Journal, 13*(6), 1361–1385. https://doi.org/10.1108/SAMPJ-07-2022-0378

Abhayawansa, S., Elijido-Ten, E., & Dumay, J. (2019). A practice theoretical analysis of the irrelevance of integrated reporting to mainstream sell-side analysts. *Accounting and Finance, 59*(3), 1615–1647. https://doi.org/10.1111/acfi.12367

Adams, C., & Abhayawansa, S. (2022). Connecting the COVID-19 pandemic, environmental, social and governance (ESG) investing and calls for 'harmonisation' of sustainability reporting. *Critical Perspectives on Accounting, 82*, 102309. https://doi.org/10.1016/j.cpa.2021.102309

Adams, C., Alhamood, A., He, X., Tian, J., Wang, L., & Wang, Y. (2021). *The double materiality concept: Application and issues* [Project Report]. Global Reporting Initiative. https://www.globalreporting.org/media/jrbntbyv/griwhitepaper-publications.pdf

Afolabi, H., Ram, R., & Rimmel, G. (2022). Harmonization of sustainability reporting regulation: Analysis of a contested Arena. *Sustainability, 14*(9), 5517. https://doi.org/10.3390/su14095517

Agostini, M., Costa, E., & Korca, B. (2022). Non-financial disclosure and corporate financial performance under directive 2014/95/EU: Evidence from Italian listed companies. *Accounting in Europe, 19*(1), 78–109. https://doi.org/10.1080/17449480.2021.1979610

Andreou, N., & Besharov, M. (2022). *Rethinking how we measure companies on social and environmental impact*. MIT Sloan Management Review. https://sloanreview.mit.edu/article/rethinking-how-we-measure-companies-on-social-and-environmental-impact/

Bansal, P., & Song, H.-C. (2017). Similar but not the same: Differentiating corporate sustainability from corporate responsibility. *Academy of Management Annals, 11*(1), 105–149. https://doi.org/10.5465/annals.2015.0095

Baumüller, J., & Sopp, K. (2022). Double materiality and the shift from non-financial to European sustainability reporting: Review, outlook and implications. *Journal of Applied Accounting Research, 23*(1), 8–28. https://doi.org/10.1108/JAAR-04-2021-0114

Bradford, M., Earp, J. B., Showalter, D. S., & Williams, P. F. (2017). Corporate sustainability reporting and stakeholder concerns: Is there a disconnect? *Accounting Horizons, 31*(1), 83–102. https://doi.org/10.2308/acch-51639

Burritt, R. L., & Schaltegger, S. (2010). Sustainability accounting and reporting: Fad or trend? *Accounting, Auditing and Accountability Journal, 23*(7), 829–846. https://doi.org/10.1108/09513571011080144

Calabrese, A., Costa, R., Levialdi, N., & Menichini, T. (2016). A fuzzy analytic hierarchy process method to support materiality assessment in sustainability reporting. *Journal of Cleaner Production, 121*, 248–264. https://doi.org/10.1016/j.jclepro.2015.12.005

Chiu, I. H.-Y. (2022). The EU sustainable finance agenda: Developing governance for double materiality in sustainability metrics. *European Business Organization Law Review, 23*(1), 87–123. https://doi.org/10.1007/s40804-021-00229-9

Cho, C. H., Laine, M., Roberts, R. W., & Rodrigue, M. (2015). Organized hypocrisy, organizational façades, and sustainability reporting. *Accounting, Organizations and Society, 40*, 78–94. https://doi.org/10.1016/j.aos.2014.12.003

Christensen, H. B., Hail, L., & Leuz, C. (2021). Mandatory CSR and sustainability reporting: Economic analysis and literature review. *Review of Accounting Studies, 26*(3), 1176–1248. https://doi.org/10.1007/s11142-021-09609-5

Drucker, P. F. (1984). Converting social problems into business opportunities: The new meaning of corporate social responsibility. *California Management Review (Pre-1986), 26*(000002), 53.

ElAlfy, A., Darwish, K. M., & Weber, O. (2020). Corporations and sustainable development goals communication on social media: Corporate social responsibility or just another buzzword? *Sustainable Development, 28*(5), 1418–1430. https://doi.org/10.1002/sd.2095

ElAlfy, A., & Weber, O. (2019). *Corporate sustainability reporting: The case of the banking industry* (No. 38; CIGI Papers). CIGI. https://www.cigionline.org/publications/corporate-sustainability-reporting-case-banking-industry/

European Commission. (2019). *Guidelines on reporting climate-related information* (C(2019) 4490). European Union. https://ec.europa.eu/finance/docs/policy/190618-climate-related-information-reporting-guidelines_en.pdf

European Financial Reporting Advisory Group. (2021). *Final report: Proposals for a relevant and dynamic EU sustainability reporting standard-setting*. https://www.efrag.org/Assets/Download?assetUrl=%2Fsites%2Fwebpublishing%2FSiteAssets%2FEFRAG%2520PTF-NFRS_MAIN_REPORT.pdf

European Financial Reporting Advisory Group. (2022a). *EFRAG facts*. https://www.efrag.org/About/Facts

European Financial Reporting Advisory Group. (2022b). *Governance*. https://www.efrag.org/About/Governance

European Financial Reporting Advisory Group. (2022c). *Sustainability reporting standards interim draft*. https://www.efrag.org/Activities/2105191406363055/Sustainability-reporting-standards-interim-draft#

European Union Commission. (2014). Directive 2014/95/EU of the European parliament and of the council of 22 October 2014-amending directive 2013/34/EU as regards disclosure of non-financial and diversity information by certain large undertakings and groups. *Official Journal of the European Union, L 330*(1). https://eur-lex.europa.eu/legal-content/EN/TXT/PDF/?uri=CELEX:32014L0095&from=EN

European Union Commission. (2017). Communication from the commission—Guidelines on non-financial reporting (methodology for reporting non-financial information). *Official Journal of the European Union, C 215*(1). https://eur-lex.europa.eu/legal-content/EN/TXT/?uri=CELEX:52017XC0705(01)

European Union Commission. (2021). Proposal for a directive of the European parliament and of the council—Amending directive 2013/34/EU, directive 2004/109/EC, directive 2006/43/EC and regulation (EU) No 537/2014, as regards corporate sustainability reporting. *Register of Commission Documents, COM(2021), 189*. https://eur-lex.europa.eu/legal-content/EN/TXT/?uri=CELEX%3A52021PC0189

Farooq, M. B., Zaman, R., Sarraj, D., & Khalid, F. (2021). Examining the extent of and drivers for materiality assessment disclosures in sustainability reports. *Sustainability Accounting, Management and Policy Journal, 12*(5), 965–1002. https://doi.org/10.1108/SAMPJ-04-2020-0113

Ferrero-Ferrero, I., León, R., & Muñoz-Torres, M. J. (2021). Sustainability materiality matrices in doubt: May prioritizations of aspects overestimate environmental performance? *Journal of Environmental Planning and Management, 64*(3), 432–463. https://doi.org/10.1080/09640568.2020.1766427

Fiandrino, S., Tonelli, A., & Devalle, A. (2022). Sustainability materiality research: A systematic literature review of methods, theories and academic themes. *Qualitative Research in Accounting and Management, 19*(5), 665–695. https://doi.org/10.1108/QRAM-07-2021-0141

Font, X., Guix, M., & Bonilla-Priego, M. J. (2016). Corporate social responsibility in cruising: Using materiality analysis to create shared value. *Tourism Management, 53*, 175–186. https://doi.org/10.1016/j.tourman.2015.10.007

Freiberg, D., Rogers, J., & Serafeim, G. (2020). *How ESG issues become financially material to corporations and their investors* (Working Paper No. 20-056). Havard Business School. https://www.hbs.edu/faculty/Pages/item.aspx?num=57161

Global Reporting Initiative. (2021). *The GRI standards: A guide for policy makers*. https://www.globalreporting.org/media/nmmnwfsm/gri-policymakers-guide.pdf

Global Reporting Initiative. (2022a). *A short introduction to the GRI standards*. https://www.globalreporting.org/media/wtafl4tw/a-short-introduction-to-the-gri-standards.pdf

Global Reporting Initiative. (2022b). *Consolidated set of the GRI standards*. https://www.globalreporting.org/how-to-use-the-gri-standards/gri-standards-english-language/

Global Reporting Initiative. (2022c). *GRI - Mission & history*. https://www.globalreporting.org/about-gri/mission-history/

Global Reporting Initiative. (2022d). *GRI 1: Foundation 2021*. https://www.globalreporting.org/how-to-use-the-gri-standards/gri-standards-english-language/

Global Reporting Initiative. (2022e). *GRI 2: General disclosures 2021*. https://www.globalreporting.org/how-to-use-the-gri-standards/gri-standards-english-language/

Global Reporting Initiative. (2022f). *GRI 3: Material topics 2021*. https://www.globalreporting.org/how-to-use-the-gri-standards/gri-standards-english-language/

Global Reporting Initiative. (2022g). *Sector program*. https://www.globalreporting.org/standards/sector-program/

Global Reporting Initiative. (2022h, February 22). *The materiality madness: Why definitions matter. The GRI perspective, 3*. https://www.globalreporting.org/media/r2oojx53/gri-perspective-the-materiality-madness.pdf

Global Reporting Initiative. (2022i). *GRI universal standards 2021: Frequently asked questions (FAQs)*. https://www.globalreporting.org/media/zauil2g3/public-faqs-universal-standards.pdf

Herzig, C., & Schaltegger, S. (2006). Chapter 13: Corporate sustainability reporting—An overview. In M. Bennett, S. Schaltegger, & R. Burritt (Eds.), *Sustainability accounting and reporting* (pp. 301–324). Springer.

Higgins, C., Tang, S., & Stubbs, W. (2020). On managing hypocrisy: The transparency of sustainability reports. *Journal of Business Research, 114*, 395–407. https://doi.org/10.1016/j.jbusres.2019.08.041

Impact Management Project. (2020, September 11). *Statement of intention to work together towards comprehensive corporate reporting*. https://impactmanagementproject.com/structured-network/statement-of-intent-to-work-together-towards-comprehensive-corporate-reporting/

International Financial Reporting Standards Foundation. (2021, February 2). *IFRS foundation trustees announce next steps in response to broad demand for global sustainability standards*. IFRS. https://www.ifrs.org/news-and-events/news/2021/02/trustees-announce-next-steps-in-response-to-broad-demand-for-global-sustainability-standards/

International Financial Reporting Standards Foundation. (2022a). *International sustainability standards board*. IFRS. https://www.ifrs.org/groups/international-sustainability-standards-board/

International Financial Reporting Standards Foundation. (2022b). *Who we are*. IFRS. https://www.ifrs.org/about-us/who-we-are/

International Financial Reporting Standards Foundation. (2022c, March 24). *IFRS foundation and GRI to align capital market and multi-stakeholder standards to create an interconnected approach for sustainability disclosures*. IFRS. https://www.ifrs.org/news-and-events/news/2022/03/ifrs-foundation-signs-agreement-with-gri/

International Financial Reporting Standards Foundation. (2022d, August 1). *IFRS foundation completes consolidation with value reporting foundation*. IFRS. https://www.ifrs.org/news-and-events/news/2022/08/ifrs-foundation-completes-consolidation-with-value-reporting-foundation/

International Financial Reporting Standards Foundation. (2022e, November 8). *ISSB at COP27: ISSB makes key announcements towards the implementation of climate-related disclosure standards in 2023*. IFRS. https://www.ifrs.org/news-and-events/news/2022/11/issb-cop27-progress-implementation-climate-related-disclosure-standards-in-2023/

International Financial Reporting Standards Foundation. (2022f, December 14). *ISSB describes the concept of sustainability and its articulation with financial value creation, and announces plans to advance work on natural ecosystems and just transition*. IFRS. https://www.ifrs.org/news-and-events/news/2022/12/issb-describes-the-concept-of-sustainability/

Jebe, R. (2019). The convergence of financial and ESG materiality: Taking sustainability mainstream. *American Business Law Journal, 56*(3), 645–702. https://doi.org/10.1111/ablj.12148

Jonsdottir, B., Sigurjonsson, T. O., Johannsdottir, L., & Wendt, S. (2022). Barriers to using ESG data for investment decisions. *Sustainability, 14*(9), 5157. https://doi.org/10.3390/su14095157

Jørgensen, S., Mjøs, A., & Pedersen, L. J. T. (2022). Sustainability reporting and approaches to materiality: Tensions and potential resolutions. *Sustainability Accounting, Management and Policy Journal, 13*(2), 341–361. https://doi.org/10.1108/SAMPJ-01-2021-0009

KPMG International. (2022). *Big shifts, small steps: Survey of sustainability reporting 2022*. https://home.kpmg/xx/en/home/insights/2022/09/survey-of-sustainability-reporting-2022.html

Kuh, T., Shepley, A., Bala, G., & Flowers, M. (2020). *Dynamic materiality: Measuring what matters*. SSRN. https://doi.org/10.2139/ssrn.3521035

Larry Fink. (2022). *Larry Fink's 2022 letter to CEOs: The power of capitalism*. Black Rock. https://www.blackrock.com/corporate/investor-relations/larry-fink-ceo-letter

Loza Adaui, C. R. (2020). Sustainability reporting quality of Peruvian listed companies and the impact of regulatory requirements of sustainability disclosures. *Sustainability, 12*(3), 1135. https://doi.org/10.3390/su12031135

Maechler, S. (2022). Accounting for whom? The financialisation of the environmental economic transition. *New Political Economy*, 1–17. https://doi.org/10.1080/13563467.2022.2130222

Mio, C., Fasan, M., & Costantini, A. (2020). Materiality in integrated and sustainability reporting: A paradigm shift? *Business Strategy and the Environment, 29*(1), 306–320. https://doi.org/10.1002/bse.2390

Pizzi, S., Venturelli, A., & Caputo, F. (2021). The "comply-or-explain" principle in directive 95/2014/EU. A rhetorical analysis of Italian PIEs. *Sustainability Accounting, Management and Policy Journal, 12*(1), 30–50. https://doi.org/10.1108/SAMPJ-07-2019-0254

Puroila, J., & Mäkelä, H. (2019). Matter of opinion: Exploring the socio-political nature of materiality disclosures in sustainability reporting. *Accounting, Auditing and Accountability Journal, 32*(4), 1043–1072. https://doi.org/10.1108/AAAJ-11-2016-2788

Reimsbach, D., Schiemann, F., Hahn, R., & Schmiedchen, E. (2020). In the eyes of the beholder: Experimental evidence on the contested nature of materiality in sustainability reporting. *Organization and Environment, 33*(4), 624–651. https://doi.org/10.1177/1086026619875436

Remmer, S., & Gilbert, U. (2019). Applying materiality assessment in strategic management: The implicit coating of the materiality lens. In T. Wunder (Ed.), *Rethinking strategic management: Sustainability strategizing for positive impact* (pp. 267–291). Springer.

Setia, N., Abhayawansa, S., & Joshi, M. (2022). In search of a wider corporate reporting framework: A critical evaluation of the international integrated reporting framework. *Accounting in Europe*, 1–26. https://doi.org/10.1080/17449480.2022.2060752

Spence, C. (2009). Social and environmental reporting and the corporate ego. *Business Strategy and the Environment, 18*(4), 254–265. https://doi.org/10.1002/bse.600

Stolowy, H., & Paugam, L. (2018). The expansion of non-financial reporting: An exploratory study. *Accounting and Business Research, 48*(5), 525–548. https://doi.org/10.1080/00014788.2018.1470141

Sustainability Accounting Standards Board. (2018). *E-commerce: Sustainability accounting standard* (No. 2018-10). https://www.sasb.org/standards/download/

Sustainability Accounting Standards Board. (2022a). *About us*. SASB Standards. https://www.sasb.org/about/

Sustainability Accounting Standards Board. (2022b). *Apparel, accessories & footwear*. SASB Standards. https://www.sasb.org/standards/materiality-finder/find/?industry%5b%5d=CG-AA&lang=en-us

Sustainability Accounting Standards Board. (2022c). *Implementation primer*. SASB Standards. https://www.sasb.org/implementation-primer/developing-your-disclosures/

Sustainability Accounting Standards Board. (2022d). *Investor use*. SASB Standards. https://www.sasb.org/investor-use/

Sustainability Accounting Standards Board. (2022e). *Materiality finder*. SASB Standards. https://www.sasb.org/standards/materiality-finder/?lang=en-us

Sustainability Accounting Standards Board. (2022f). *SASB's sustainable industry classification system (SICS)*. SASB Standards. https://www.sasb.org/wp-content/uploads/2018/11/SICS-Industry-List.pdf

Sustainability Accounting Standards Board. (2022g). *Standards*. SASB Standards. https://www.sasb.org/standards/

Sustainability Accounting Standards Board. (2022h, March 22). *What is the future of SASB Standards under the IFRS?* SASB Standards. https://www.sasb.org/blog/whats-the-future-of-sasb-standards-under-the-issb/

Sustainability Accounting Standards Board. (2022i, September 2). *Double and dynamic: Understanding the changing perspectives on materiality*. SASB Standards. https://www.sasb.org/blog/double-and-dynamic-understanding-the-changing-perspectives-on-materiality/

Sustainability Accounting Standards Board & Global Reporting Initiative. (2021). *A practical guide to sustainability reporting using GRI and SASB standards*. https://www.sasb.org/knowledge-hub/practical-guide-to-sustainability-reporting-using-gri-and-sasb-standards/

Thinking Ahead Institute. (2021). *With great power comes great responsibility: Duty of ownership working group paper*. Willis Towers Watson. https://www.thinkingaheadinstitute.org/research-papers/with-great-power-comes-great-responsibility/

Torelli, R., Balluchi, F., & Furlotti, K. (2020). The materiality assessment and stakeholder engagement: A content analysis of sustainability reports. *Corporate Social Responsibility and Environmental Management, 27*(2), 470–484. https://doi.org/10.1002/csr.1813

Weber, O., & Feltmate, B. W. (2016). *Sustainable banking: Managing the social and environmental impact of financial institutions*. University of Toronto Press.

Whitehead, J. (2017). Prioritizing sustainability indicators: Using materiality analysis to guide sustainability assessment and strategy: Prioritising sustainability indicators. *Business Strategy and the Environment, 26*(3), 399–412. https://doi.org/10.1002/bse.1928

World Economic Forum. (2020). *Measuring stakeholder capitalism: Towards common metrics and consistent reporting of sustainable value creation* [White Paper]. World Economic Forum. https://www3.weforum.org/docs/WEF_IBC_Measuring_Stakeholder_Capitalism_Report_2020.pdf

Yakimova, Y. (2022, November 10). *Sustainable economy: Parliament adopts new reporting rules for multinationals*. European Parliament. https://www.europarl.europa.eu/news/en/press-room/20221107IPR49611/sustainable-economy-parliament-adopts-new-reporting-rules-for-multinationals

4
CLIMATE SCENARIO ANALYSIS FOR CENTRAL BANKS

Matteo Bonetti, Dirk Broeders, Marleen Schlooz, and Vincent Streichert

Introduction

Understanding climate change-related risks is key for central banks due to the major consequences these risks may have for the economy and the financial system. Climate change has the potential to induce disruptions to several layers of the economy via natural disasters and transition shocks, making it a potential source of price and financial instability (Bolton et al., 2020; Giglio et al., 2021). Physical risks such as floods, extreme droughts, and forest fires cause supply shocks in commodity markets, for instance, which then lead to increasingly volatile inflation. Transition risks in the form of unexpected carbon pricing shocks affect the stability of the financial system, assuming that they bring about stranded assets of companies and financial institutions exposed to these shocks. In comparison to traditional financial risks, we lack experience in dealing with physical and transition risks. Furthermore, climate change is surrounded by fundamental uncertainty because its future trajectory is characterized by unknown features such as nonlinearities, tipping points, feedback loops, and interactions that may generate a waterfall of effects that physical or transition risks do not capture separately (Broeders & Schlooz, 2021).

Climate change risks also impact a central bank's balance sheet directly.[1] Central bank risk managers, therefore, face the challenge of integrating climate change risks into their regular operations. A good starting point is to define climate risk management principles that describe the core assumptions driving decision-making for identifying, assessing, mitigating, and disclosing climate risks. These climate risk management principles should also highlight the tools that the central bank uses in each of these four steps of the climate risk management cycle. In this chapter, we focus on one important assessment tool to derive the impact of climate risks on a central bank's balance sheet: climate scenario analysis.

Scenario analysis in general is a method for assessing forward-looking vulnerabilities to the possible evolution of one or more risk drivers. The goal of this technique is to reduce uncertainty and enhance the prospects of achieving a preferred outcome. The analysis can be either qualitative or quantitative in nature and is useful in anticipating a response to large shocks such as wars, pandemics, economic transitions, and technological revolutions. Since the Global Financial Crisis of 2008, scenario analysis and stress testing have become standard tools for risk management in the financial sector. The scenarios used in such an analysis can include regular 'business cycle stress' or risk-driver-specific 'tail risks' (Crouhy et al., 2014). Furthermore, effective scenario analysis requires a 'narrative' of how shocks evolve over time. This narrative is important for decision-makers to link the outcome of the scenario analysis to the potential actions that they contemplate.

On that note, we develop a top-down climate scenario analysis to assess the forward-looking vulnerabilities of a central bank's profitability and financial risks. We take an approach that considers different climate scenarios that are likely to materialize depending on particular policy actions and then compute the financial implications for a central bank under each one of these scenarios. This methodology is also useful for other types of financial institutions.

Our top-down methodology comprises four sequential steps and facilitates the simultaneous integration of both transition and physical risks. First, we select climate scenarios from the Network of Central Banks and Supervisors for Greening the Financial System (NGFS). Second, we obtain macroeconomic projections under each scenario from the National Institute Global Econometric Model (NiGEM) provided by the National Institute of Economic and Social Research. Third, we translate the macro-level effects into impacts on the prices of individual securities by generating issuer-specific vulnerability factors. While the vulnerabilities to transition risks are based on an issuer's normalized carbon emissions, the vulnerabilities to physical risks refer to an issuer's geographical location(s). Fourth, we provide estimated impacts on profit projections, interest rate risk, credit risk, and market risk. As a case study, we apply this scenario analysis to the balance sheet of De Nederlandsche Bank (DNB), the central bank of the Netherlands. We show that an orderly transition to a low-carbon economy strongly impacts profitability and interest rate risk in the short term. Further, a disorderly transition or a failure to implement climate policies may lead to a significant increase in credit risk and market risk in the long term.

The remainder of this chapter is structured as follows. First, we provide a short review of the literature on climate risk and climate risk stress testing. Then we describe the role of a central bank in the economy and its balance sheet, followed by the purpose and setup of the climate scenario analysis. After that, we provide an application of the climate scenario analysis, and we conclude in the final section.

Literature

In this section, we discuss the recent developments in the field of climate risk and asset pricing and the first examples of climate risk stress testing by central banks. We cover academic studies as well as publications from central banks in this area.

Climate Risk and Asset Pricing

Climate change is unequivocally driven by human economic activity and poses large risks to the global economy (IPCC, 2021). As fossil fuels are an important production input, economic growth increases greenhouse gas (GHG) emissions. These emissions induce climate change, which has disruptive effects on society through more frequent and extreme natural disasters and higher costs for firms and individuals. The seminal work of Nordhaus (1977) started to integrate climate change into macroeconomic models and to discuss ways to mitigate it.[2] Subsequent studies incorporate uncertainty around climate change to expose the social costs of global warming. They further describe how mitigation policies are affected by this uncertainty (see, e.g., Golosov et al., 2014; Lemoine & Traeger, 2012; Nordhaus, 1994; Weitzman, 2009). Central banks are eager to understand the impact of climate change projections on economic growth and price stability. However, this impact is uncertain and runs in two directions. First, there is uncertainty about the path of climate change as a source of risk for the economy (Wagner & Weitzman, 2015; Weitzman, 2012, 2014). Second, there is also uncertainty about the evolution of the economy, the actual release of GHG emissions, and consequently the evolution of climate change (Nordhaus & Boyer, 2000).

Climate change uncertainty affects discount factors in the economy, which in turn affect asset prices.[3] Today, there is a rapidly emerging stream of literature that investigates the extent to which asset prices incorporate climate risks. This literature indicates that different dimensions of climate risk, most notably levels of carbon intensity, are beginning to be priced in. For example, Bolton and Kacperczyk (2021) note higher equity returns for high-emitting firms and interpret this as compensation for the climate risk exposure associated with holding these stocks. Engle et al. (2020) propose a methodology to dynamically hedge climate risk by constructing a portfolio overweighting stocks that rise in value when negative news about climate change appears, and vice versa. Hong et al. (2019) and Choi et al. (2020) show that stock prices react to climate events such as more frequent droughts or heatwaves. Similarly, there is evidence suggesting that climate risk may also be priced in fixed-income markets (Huynh & Xia, 2021).

In parallel with the literature investigating the implications for asset pricing, researchers, risk managers, and policymakers are also increasing their efforts to analyze climate risks.

Climate Risk Analysis and Stress Testing

The fundamental uncertainty of climate change means that traditional financial risk management tools are not always adequate (Ackerman, 2017; Barnett et al., 2020). Therefore, alternative techniques to identify and assess climate-related risks should be considered (Battiston, 2019; Broeders & Schlooz, 2021).

Battiston et al. (2017) develop a network-based climate stress test methodology to gauge how climate risk might propagate through the financial system. Campiglio et al. (2017) show that stranded assets that originate from the climate transition can generate financial losses via network effects. Roncoroni et al. (2021) introduce a model to describe the interplay between climate policy shocks and market conditions. Their contribution shows a contagion of transition risk to banks and investment funds through common asset holdings. Battiston and Monasterolo (2020) adjust standard financial risk metrics, such as Value-at-Risk and Expected Shortfall, of corporate and sovereign bonds conditional on forward-looking climate transition risk scenarios. These findings provide evidence supporting the usefulness of stress testing to assess the impact of climate change on the financial soundness of individual institutions and on the stability of the financial system as a whole.

Central banks have performed various climate stress tests in recent years. So far, these stress tests have been economy-wide. Vermeulen et al. (2018) assess the impact of the energy transition on Dutch financial institutions by using a top-down stress testing approach. With this approach, the economy and the holdings of financial institutions are stressed by applying different energy transition shocks. The Banque de France (BdF) carried out a pilot stress test on French banks and insurance companies to measure their exposure to transition risks and physical risks and to raise awareness of climate risks (BdF, 2020). The approach employed by the BdF has a bottom-up structure, whereby financial institutions compute the impact of climate risk using their internal models and apply climate pathways and key macroeconomic scenarios that are provided by the BdF. The results are then aggregated by the BdF to compile an overview of the exposure of the French financial sector to climate risk. In addition, between 2019 and 2021, the Bank of England launched similar climate stress tests on the domestic banking and insurance sectors (BoE, 2021).

The European Central Bank (ECB) recently carried out a top-down euro area economy-wide stress test that considers both transition and physical risk (Alogoskoufis et al., 2021).

To conclude, there is a growing body of literature on the impact of climate change on asset pricing and climate stress testing. In this chapter, we extend this literature on climate stress testing by introducing a methodology to perform a climate scenario analysis. This analysis determines the possible impact of climate risk on a central bank's profitability and financial risks. We highlight the effects of the risks that are specific to the way in which central banks operate with both monetary portfolios and non-monetary portfolios. The next section therefore first explains the role of a central bank and the modalities of a central bank's balance sheet.

The Role of a Central Bank and Its Balance Sheet

Central banks are independent, systemic authorities with a specific mandate. This mandate includes issuing fiat money, implementing monetary policy, acting as a lender of last resort vis-à-vis commercial banks, and maintaining a secure payment infrastructure. Often central banks also manage part of the national reserves. A central bank is the sole monetary authority in its jurisdiction. It can however also be part of a monetary union such as the national central banks in the Eurosystem. For the purposes of our climate scenario analysis, a basic understanding of a central bank's balance sheet is necessary.

The asset side consists of monetary and non-monetary portfolios. The monetary portfolios relate to the central bank's monetary policy operations. Among these are open market operations (OMOs), which are used by the central bank to steer interest rates, manage the amount of liquidity in the financial system, and signal its monetary policy stance. During a crisis, a central bank can also provide long-term refinancing to commercial banks or decide to undertake outright asset purchases in financial markets for monetary purposes. Central banks typically also invest in financial markets via non-monetary portfolios containing gold, sovereign bonds, corporate bonds, and, sometimes, equities.

On the liability side, the dominant constituents are deposits held by commercial banks at the central bank, banknotes in circulation, and capital and reserves. Table 4.1 shows a stylized balance sheet of a central bank. A major risk for the central bank is the difference in duration, or the sensitivity to changes in interest rates, between assets and liabilities. The result of this duration gap is commonly referred to as an asset-liability management (ALM) mismatch. Currently, for many central banks, the weighted average duration of the assets exceeds that of the liabilities. Consequently, a central bank's profit becomes vulnerable to sharp interest rate increases that

Table 4.1 The table exhibits the stylized balance sheet of a central bank.

Assets	Liabilities	
Asset purchase programs	Banknotes	
Refinancing operations	Deposits	} ALM mismatch
Non-monetary portfolios		
Gold	Capital and reserves	
	Fixed-rate remuneration	
	Floating rate remuneration	

Source: authors' work.

may occur under certain climate trajectories. In these scenarios, the floating remuneration paid on the deposits of commercial banks increases rapidly, whereas the interest income on the assets increases comparatively less.

Central banks are vulnerable to changes in interest rate and, therefore, to the macroeconomic and external factors driving these changes. In the remainder of this chapter we focus on one of these external factors in particular: climate change.

Objective and Setup of the Climate Scenario Analysis

In this section, we present the outline of the climate scenario analysis (henceforth CSA). First, we elaborate on the specific objective of the CSA. Second, we illustrate the methodology, based on a top-down approach involving four sequential steps from high-level climate scenarios to the possible implications of these scenarios for the profits and financial risks of a central bank.

Key Objective of the Climate Scenario Analysis

The key objective of our CSA is to quantify the potential financial impact of climate-related developments on a central bank's balance sheet. Such an exercise serves multiple functions. First, the outcome of the CSA provides the central bank's decision-making bodies with key management information on institutional vulnerabilities with respect to climate change. This is relevant when considering risk-mitigating actions. Second, the CSA's implications can be disclosed to inform stakeholders, i.e., the bank's shareholder(s) and the public, about the nature and size of the exposures to climate risks. Third, the CSA provides guidance to other financial institutions that also face the challenges of evaluating climate risks. By sharing the methodology, findings, and lessons learned, these institutions are encouraged to perform similar exercises.

The CSA is grounded on the ambition of assessing climate-related risks via direct financial exposures to different types of issuers, including sovereigns, sub-sovereigns, agencies, and financial and non-financial corporations. Furthermore, a central bank's balance sheet is affected by changes in the policy and market interest rates via the asset-liability mismatch. For this purpose, the CSA puts the sensitivity of a central bank's balance sheet to long-term climate scenarios to the test.[4] Specifically, we examine the impact of different climate scenarios on:

- Profit projections, and
- Financial risks: in particular interest rate risk, credit risk, and market risk.

We focus on these two dimensions for a number of reasons. Profits are the main source of capital growth for central banks. Also, adequate risk management is key for central banks to remain sufficiently capitalized and to be perceived as credible and independent systemic authorities (Wessels & Broeders, 2022).

It is good to note upfront that the results of the CSA should not be interpreted as predictions of profitability or risks. Instead, the outcomes measure the sensitivity of the two dimensions to a range of specific scenarios that are severe but plausible. Obviously, a scenario analysis requires making a series of assumptions. The identification of the scenarios necessitates the collaboration of different experts in the field, and the application of the scenarios in financial risk analysis requires the independent work of specialized risk managers. A risk management committee can oversee the full CSA.

Top-Down Method

The top-down approach extrapolates the impact of different climate scenarios on the central bank's balance sheet using sensitivity factors. The methodology involves four sequential steps.

Step 1: Scenario Selection

The CSA starts with the selection of high-level climate scenarios. We use comprehensive climate scenarios provided by the NGFS via its Scenarios Portal.[5] These scenarios build on long-term projections of political, regulatory, economic, technological, and environmental developments, which were designed jointly by the NGFS and an academic consortium of experts in the field. Each scenario is grounded on a distinct narrative regarding the sincerity with which global policymakers and regulatory bodies take action to thwart climate change. Policy assumptions relate to overall ambitions and expected interventions, as well as an indicator of international coordination in terms of regional variation between measures. Another key dimension is technological change, including potential CO_2 removal systems advancements.

All climate scenarios incorporate both physical and transition risks from climate change, with their manifestations varying per scenario. In particular, policy ambitions regarding the limitation of global warming drive the potential severity of the physical risks impact. In contrast, transition risks originate primarily from the uncertain timing and scope of policy and regulatory interventions as well as from the pace of technological change. However, both types of climate-related risks ultimately contribute to the macroeconomic developments in the respective climate scenarios. In the section 'An Application of the CSA', we select three specific climate trajectories considered by the NGFS, as well as a baseline scenario (NGFS Base). The three scenarios are referred to as 'Net Zero 2050', 'Delayed Transition', and 'Current Policies'. The 'Net Zero 2050' scenario comes with a low degree of physical risk, whereas the main risk driver under this scenario is transition risk due to an immediate, strong increase in carbon pricing and fast technological change. Transition risk from technological change, late policy reaction, and the variation between regional policies is also material under the disorderly 'Delayed Transition' scenario. By way of contrast, the physical risk from insufficient policy ambitions to contain global warming, and the associated increase in the likelihood and severity of extreme climate events, is most strongly marked under the 'Current Policies' scenario. Figure 4.1 summarizes the intensity of physical risks and various types of transition risks under the different climate scenarios.

Step 2: Macroeconomic Impact

The NGFS also provides estimates of the potential long-term effects of the climate scenarios on a series of key macroeconomic and financial variables, such as GDP, interest rates, and equity returns. Via the NGFS Scenarios Portal, annual projections of these variables are made available on a country level over the 2021–2050 period. All estimates are generated from NiGEM runs. Projections are presented for an NGFS Base scenario, assuming the absence of both physical and transition risk shocks and thus no climate-related policy interventions, as well as for each of the climate scenarios in terms of deviations from that Base scenario.[6]

From a central bank's perspective, a key variable is the central bank intervention rate (CBIR). The NiGEM integrates the assumption that the monetary policy authority operates primarily through the setting of the short-term nominal interest rate. For Eurozone countries, for instance, the CBIR refers to the ECB's short-term policy interest rates. We furthermore use the projected paths of long-term interest rates on government bonds and equity returns for all major markets around the globe.

Scenario	Physical risk	Transition risk			
	Policy ambition	Policy reaction	Regional policy variation	Technology change	CO₂ removal systems use
Net Zero 2050	1.5°C	Immediate	Medium	Fast	Medium
Delayed Transition	1.8°C	Delayed	High	Slow/Fast	Low
Current Policies	3°C+	None	Low	Slow	Low

The different shades of gray indicate whether the characteristic makes the scenario more or less severe from a macro-financial risk perspective:

Low risk   Moderate risk   High risk

Figure 4.1 The figure demonstrates the severity of physical and transition risk according to NGFS (2021) scenarios. *Notes:* This assessment is based on expert judgment with regard to how changing an assumption affects key drivers of physical and transition risk. For example, higher temperatures are correlated with higher impacts on physical assets and the economy. On the transition risk side, economic and financial impacts increase with a) strong, sudden, and/or divergent policy, b) stronger policy in specific countries and/or regions, c) fast technological change even if carbon price changes are modest, and d) limited availability and use of CO_2 removal systems, implying that the transition must be more abrupt in other parts of the economy. Source: NGFS (2021).

Step 3: Microeconomic Impact

Subsequently, we translate macroeconomic effects into impacts that are specific to the issuers in the portfolios. For this translation, we create vulnerability factors that measure the sensitivity of an asset's price to general market developments under the scenarios. We assume that transition risks typically vary across issuers whereas physical risks vary between geographies (BIS, 2021). Accordingly, we construct issuer-level Transition Vulnerability Factors and Physical Vulnerability Factors.

Transition Vulnerability Factors (TVFs) are based on the GHG emissions intensity of an issuer. For corporations, we use the sum of Scope 1 and 2 GHG emissions (tons of CO_2 equivalents, tCO_2e) relative to their sales as provided by MSCI to determine their GHG emissions intensity. Issuers with a high GHG emissions intensity are subject to comparatively high business transition risks when confronted with the challenge of having to gradually reduce emissions over time. This necessity can arise due to regulatory interventions or as a consequence of an increase in the carbon price over time. For sovereigns, GHG emissions are measured relative to GDP.

Physical Vulnerability Factors (PVFs) are based on the geographical location(s) of an issuer. Issuers that operate in geographical locations that are prone to an increased likelihood and severity of physical hazards are particularly vulnerable. We use the country-specific index provided by the Notre Dame Global Adaptation Initiative (ND-GAIN Country Index Score) that captures a country's vulnerability to climate disruptions. It also assesses a country's readiness to leverage private and public sector investments for adaptive actions. For corporate issuers, we obtain Bloomberg data on the share of revenues generated by a corporation in 2020 in each country in which it operates, if reported. We use this information to calculate a revenues-weighted average of the ND-GAIN Country Index Scores across all countries in which a corporation operates. For corporations that do not provide information on the geographical distribution of revenues, we simply consider the country in which their headquarters are located. For sovereigns, the ND-GAIN Country Index Score is by construction the one for the country issuing the bond. Figure 4.2 summarizes the steps that we take to obtain the TVFs and PVFs.

Figure 4.3 and Figure 4.4 show the empirical distribution functions of the two vulnerability factors for a total of 4,603 issuers that we consider in the CSA case study in the section 'An Application of the CSA'. The vulnerability factors are scaled such that the equally weighted average across all issuers equals one. By construction, the vulnerability factors cannot be negative. Figure 4.3 illustrates that 20% of all issuers have a TVF above 1, and from Figure 4.4 it is easy to observe that 20% of the issuers also have a PVF greater than 1. The skewed distributions reveal that some issuers are particularly vulnerable.

Next, we combine TVFs and PVFs to obtain issuer-specific Climate Vulnerability Factors (CVFs). Here, we assume weighted linear combinations to ensure that transition and physical risks are considered jointly. The CVFs are computed for each scenario, as depicted in Figure 4.5. Net Zero 2050 is geared towards transition risks whereas Current Policies attaches more weight to physical risks. For Delayed Transition, we assume that both risks weigh equally. These weights are derived to reflect the importance that the NGFS assigns to transition and physical risks under each scenario. The CVFs remain constant over the evaluation horizon of the CSA.

	Transition Vulnerability Factors (TVFs)	**Physical Vulnerability Factors (PVFs)**
Data source	MSCI ESG Manager	• Notre Dame Global Adaptation Initiative • Bloomberg
Data granularity	Issuer-specific (Scope 1 + 2 emissions)	Country-specific
Climate risk indicators (corporate issuers)	$GHG\ emissions\ intensity = \dfrac{t\ CO_2 e}{\$m\ Sales}$	ND-GAIN Country Index Score 2019 (based on country of domicile or countries in which a firm generates revenues)
Climate risk indicators (sovereign issuers)	$GHG\ emissions\ intensity = \dfrac{t\ CO_2 e}{\$m\ GDP}$	ND-GAIN Country Index Score 2019
Vulnerability factors	$TVF_i = \dfrac{GHG\ emissions\ intensity_i}{1{,}000}$	$PVF_i = \dfrac{ND\text{-}GAIN\ Country\ Index\ Score_i}{10}$

Figure 4.2 The figure presents the construction of Transition Vulnerability Factors (TVFs) and Physical Vulnerability Factors (PVFs). *Notes*: In this figure, we show the steps taken to compute TVFs and PVFs for each security. Source: authors' work.

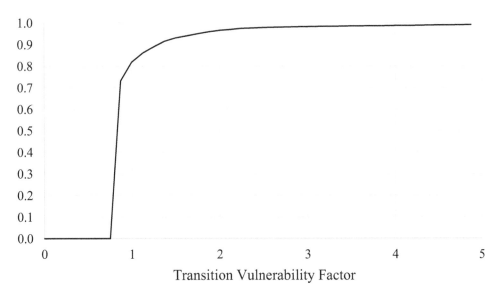

Figure 4.3 The figure shows the empirical distribution function of TVFs. *Notes*: The empirical distribution function refers to a sample of issuers from the CSA case study (N = 4,603). Source: authors' work.

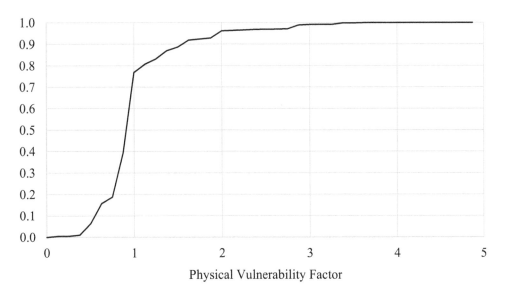

Figure 4.4 The figure shows the empirical distribution function of PVFs. *Notes*: The empirical distribution function refers to a sample of issuers from the CSA case study (N = 4,603). Source: authors' work.

Net Zero 2050 $CVF_i^{Net\ Zero\ 2050} = 0.8 * TVF_i + 0.2 * PVF_i$

Delayed Transition $CVF_i^{Delayed\ Transition} = 0.5 * TVF_i + 0.5 * PVF_i$

Current Policies $CVF_i^{Current\ Policies} = 0.2 * TVF_i + 0.8 * PVF_i$

Figure 4.5 The figure presents the construction of Climate Vulnerability Factors (CVFs) under each climate scenario. *Notes*: In this figure, we show the weights that are assigned to TVFs and to PVFs under each climate scenario to construct the CVFs. The weights are chosen to be consistent with the climate scenario. Under Net Zero 2050, the highest weight is given to transition risks and under Current Policies to physical risks. Source: authors' work.

Step 4: Profit and Risk Assessment

Finally, we provide estimates of the impact of different climate scenarios on profits and financial risks. Typically, existing models can be used for this impact analysis. In the next section, we discuss an application of the CSA to DNB.

An Application of the CSA

In this section, we present an application of the CSA to DNB's profit projections and financial risks in the monetary and non-monetary portfolios. DNB is one of the national central banks in the Eurosystem. Table 4.2 indicates that at the time of the analysis (September 2021), the monetary portfolios mainly consist of instruments bought under the asset purchase programs and refinancing operations to commercial banks. In the non-monetary portfolio, we find sovereign bonds, corporate bonds, and equities from both developed and emerging markets.[7]

Crucial assumptions are that there will be no new monetary policy measures and that the existing unconventional monetary policy measures will be concluded as planned. We distinguish between interest rate risk, credit risk, and market risk. We use projections until 2030 to assess profits and interest rate risk because thereafter the uncertainty about the size of the balance sheet increases significantly, making projections beyond 2030 less insightful. However, we rely on projections until 2050 to compute credit and market risk, and we assume that the size and the composition of the non-monetary portfolios in terms of country, sector, and duration allo-

Table 4.2 The table exhibits the stylized balance sheet of De Nederlandsche Bank (DNB).

Assets		*Liabilities*	
Asset purchase programs	238	Banknotes	81
Refinancing operations	129	Deposits	284
Non-monetary portfolios	12	Other	32
Gold	29	Capital and reserves	11
Total	408	Total	408

Sources: DNB, authors' work.

cations remain constant over time. We use DNB's Asset-Liability Management (ALM) model for future profits assessments and interest rate risk calculations and DNB's Credit Value-at-Risk (CVaR) model for credit risk. In addition to that, we develop a methodology to address the market risk of equity and bond portfolios. The results are presented in this chapter in a qualitative manner for reasons of confidentiality.

Profit Projections

The NGFS scenarios impact DNB's profit projections via the key transmission mechanism of the interest rate channel. DNB's profits are mainly driven by policy and market interest rate developments. The key policy rate affecting future profits is the Eurosystem's deposit facility rate (DFR), which is the remuneration rate for the deposits held by commercial banks at DNB. We assume that the DFR will follow the CBIR in the NGFS scenarios. Figure 4.6 presents the DFR evolution under the different scenarios. Under Net Zero 2050, policy rates will increase in the short term following the sharp increase in carbon pricing that creates inflation. In the Delayed Transition scenario, the DFR will also spike, but only after 2030 (not visible in the figure), indicating a severe and sudden transition. Under Current Policies, the interest rate level is slightly lower than in the NGFS Base scenario from 2024 onwards.

In the short term, higher policy rates reduce DNB's profits due to higher funding costs and given the asset-liability mismatch. In the long term, the profit projections are impacted by the yields on the bonds that the Eurosystem buys under the asset purchase programs.

Table 4.3 illustrates the impact of climate risk on DNB's cumulative profits (from 2021 to 2030) under the different scenarios. The Net Zero 2050 scenario has the most negative impact on DNB's profits because the hike in the DFR starts immediately, at a time when the asset-liability mismatch is large. Under Delayed Transition, the impact of climate change only plays out after 2030 when the size of the balance sheet is much smaller. Therefore, the impact on the cumulative profit projection is limited. The Current Policies scenario predicts slightly lower policy rates in the long term than the Base scenario. These lower policy rates will cause the yields

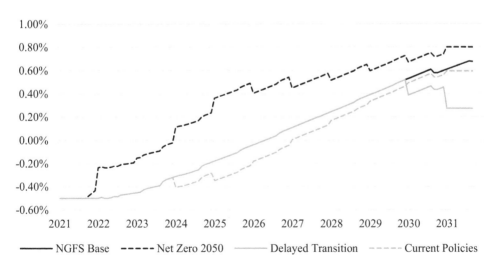

Figure 4.6 The figure presents the deposit facility rate (DFR) trajectories under different climate scenarios.
Notes: DFR trajectories under different scenarios over the 2021–2031 period (in pp). Source: NGFS.

Table 4.3 The table illustrates the climate scenario impact on DNB's profit.

Scenario	Profit impact
Net Zero 2050	High
Delayed Transition	Medium
Current Policies	Low

Source: authors' calculations using NGFS inputs and the ALM model of DNB.

on new asset purchases to drop. This effect is more than evened out by the lower remuneration on bank deposits, however. The impact on DNB's profits is therefore small.

Interest Rate Risk

The transmission of climate-related risks through the interest rate channel also influences DNB's interest rate risk. Interest rate risk is defined here as the cumulative losses over the full evaluation horizon under extreme but plausible interest rate trajectories. To measure interest rate risk, we consider scenario-specific projections of interest rates that are based on the NGFS macro-level data and combined with a DNB-internal expert judgment.[8] Among other factors, all scenarios assume a sharp increase in the DFR of 250 basis points, the timing of which varies per climate scenario. Table 4.4 shows that the interest rate risk is the highest in the Net Zero 2050 scenario as the policy rate hike starts early in this scenario and the balance sheet size is large. The increase of the remuneration on bank deposits leads to higher losses in the first years of the Net Zero 2050 scenario. Over time, the asset purchase programs are presumptively phased out and disappear from the balance sheet. Therefore, the projected policy rate hike after 2030 in the Delayed Transition and Current Policies scenarios has a limited impact on the interest rate risk figures.

Credit Risk

Climate-related risks can also be transmitted through the credit risk channel by means of effects on issuers' creditworthiness. Therefore, we assess the credit risk of the asset purchase programs and the bond portfolios using the CVaR model. We measure credit risk as the Expected Shortfall (ES) at a 99% confidence level over a one-year period. For each scenario, we adjust the credit rating of a corporate bond based on the projected equity index return of the country of the issuer. This is to reflect the fact that an issuer that suffers large equity losses will most likely also experience a deterioration in credit quality. We adjust equity returns as the following product of the equity return of the country in which an issuer is located and the issuer's CVF:

$$r_{i,j,t}^{E,S} = NGFS\ Equity\ return_{j,t}^{S} \star CVF_i^S \qquad (1)$$

Table 4.4 The table illustrates the climate scenario impact on interest rate risk.

Scenario	Impact on interest rate risk
Net Zero 2050	High
Delayed Transition	Low
Current Policies	Low

Source: authors' calculations using NGFS inputs and the ALM model of DNB.

where i is an issuer based in country j, t indicates the reference year, E indicates equities, and S is one of the NGFS scenarios. The returns in Eq. (1) are measured relative to the NGFS Base scenario level of the country index in the same year. Bonds receive a one-notch downgrade (e.g., from A– to BBB+) in year t if the adjusted equity return from Eq. (1) is lower than –10% in that year. If an issuer's adjusted stock price decreases by more than 20%, the rating downgrade is two notches, a 30% decrease results in a downgrade of three notches, etc. For each scenario, we also adjust the rating of a sovereign bond based on the country's equity index return and CVF using Eq. (1). Using these adjusted ratings as input for the CVaR model, we obtain the credit risk per scenario per year. In particular, we assess the credit risk in the following years:

- 2022 because the timely policy actions in the Net Zero 2050 scenario will be reflected in short-term corporate profits and stock market returns.
- 2033 because under the Delayed Transition scenario policy actions will start affecting corporate profits and stock indices mainly after 2030.
- 2050 because we intend to measure the long-term impact of climate shocks in the event of no policy actions under the Current Policies scenario.

Table 4.5 shows the impact of climate change on credit risk under the different scenarios. This impact is small in the short term and more severe after 2030 under Delayed Transition and Current Policies scenarios. Under the Net Zero 2050 scenario, credit risk is similar to the Base scenario in 2022. Under the Delayed Transition scenario, the credit risk increases in 2033 compared to the Base scenario. Similarly, under the Current Policies scenario, the credit risk increases substantially in 2050 relative to the Base scenario.

Market Risk

DNB is further exposed to market risk in the non-monetary portfolios. This risk is driven by the potential price fluctuations of individual stocks and bonds under the different scenarios.[9] We define market risk as the portfolio value in a climate scenario relative to what the portfolio value would have been under the NGFS Base scenario. To translate the climate-driven macroeconomic shock to individual stocks we first apply Eq. (1) again. Next, we take the value-weighted average of the adjusted returns of all stocks included in the portfolio:

$$r_t^{E,S} = \sum_{i=1}^{N} w_i \star r_{i,j,t}^{E,S} \qquad (2)$$

where w_i is the weight of stock i in the equity portfolio. We assume that these weights of the N stocks remain the same over the full evaluation period. In Eq. (2), $r_{i,j,t}^{E,S}$ is the return of each

Table 4.5 The table illustrates the climate scenario impact on credit risk.

Year	Scenario	Net Zero 2050	Delayed Transition	Current Policies
2022		Low	Low	Low
2033		Medium	High	Low
2050		Medium	Low	High

Source: authors' calculations using NGFS inputs and the credit risk model of DNB.

stock i under scenario S relative to the NGFS Base scenario. The value of the equity portfolio under the NGFS Base scenario ($BaseValue_t$) evolves over time following the NGFS Base scenario year-on-year returns $\left(1 + r_t^{BaseYoY}\right)$ on a world equity index. The base value of the equity portfolio is therefore described by the following equation:

$$BaseValue_t = BaseValue_{t-1} \star \left(1 + r_t^{BaseYoY}\right) \tag{3}$$

We then compute the value of the equity portfolio in each year under each of the climate scenarios as follows:

$$PortfolioValue_t^S = \left(1 + r_t^{E,S}\right) \star BaseValue_t \tag{4}$$

We apply a similar approach to assess the market risk of the bond portfolios. Returns on individual bonds are driven by changes in the term structure of risk-free interest rates and changes in the rating-specific credit spread. We assume parallel shifts in the term structure of interest rates in the country of domicile of each issuer. These changes ($\Delta rf_{j,t}^S$) are expressed relative to the NGFS Base scenario and multiplied by the bond portfolio's modified duration to capture the sensitivity of each bond's price to interest rate fluctuations under each scenario. Therefore, the impact of a change in the risk-free interest rate on a bond's return is:

$$rf_{i,j,t}^S\ impact = -\Delta rf_{j,t}^S \star Duration_i \tag{5}$$

for bond i, of an issuer located in country j in year t. Note that the '−' sign captures the inverse relation between interest rate changes and price.

Next, we turn to the impact of changes in the rating-specific credit spread. We calculate credit spread changes per bond, given that more vulnerable issuers will likely experience a larger increase in credit risk compared to less vulnerable issuers with comparable ratings. The credit spread changes depend on the rating of a bond. These ratings are modified on a year-scenario basis using Eq. (1) to get adjusted stock returns. If the adjusted return leads to a downgrade, then the bond receives the probability of default (PD) that corresponds to the new rating. This approach allows us to find the 'stressed PD'. The stressed PD can be seen as the impact on the credit spread of a bond, and consequently, a change in the credit spread will influence the price change. We call the impact of a PD change on the bond's price 'credit impact'. This credit impact is computed as follows:

$$CR_{i,z,t} impact = -PD_{i,z,t} \star Duration_i \tag{6}$$

for bond i, with rating z in year t. $PD_{i,z,t}$ is the stressed one-year PD.

The total change in price of a bond under a stressed scenario is driven by a combination of risk-free interest rate and credit impacts. It is computed as follows:

$$r_{i,j,t}^{B,S} = rf_{i,j,t}\ impact + CR_{i,z,t}\ impact + \left(rf_{i,j,t}\ impact \star CR_{i,z,t}\ impact\right). \tag{7}$$

The interaction term $\left(rf_{i,j,t}\ impact \star CR_{i,z,t}\ impact\right)$ captures the cross-duration-credit impact. Namely, bonds with a longer duration experience larger price effects. Using the change in each bond's price ($r_{i,j,t}^{B,S}$), we can derive the change in the bond portfolio's value analogous to Eq. (2). Note that $r_{i,j,t}^{B,S}$ is again the percentage difference of a bond price relative to its value under the

Table 4.6 The table illustrates the climate scenario impact on market risk.

Scenario	Corporate bonds		Equities	
Horizon	Short term	Long term	Short term	Long term
Net Zero 2050	Medium	Medium	Medium	Medium
Delayed Transition	Low	High	Low	High
Current Policies	Low	High	Low	High

Source: authors' calculations using NGFS inputs and holdings of DNB in equity and bond portfolios.

NGFS Base scenario. Similar to equity, we compare the value of the bond portfolios under each scenario relative to the NGFS Base scenario.

Table 4.6 presents the relative impact of the three climate scenarios on the market risk of DNB's bond and equity portfolios, both in the short and in the long term. The Net Zero 2050 scenario has a medium impact on market risk because of the moderate reaction of financial markets to new policies. The Delayed Transition and Current Policies scenarios have a high impact on the market risk of both asset classes in the long term due to the vulnerability of many issuers to transition and physical risks in the further future.

Evaluation and Outlook

Summarizing the outcome of the CSA for DNB we observe the following. In the Net Zero 2050 scenario, the climate risk is almost entirely driven by transition risk. The swift increase in carbon prices leads to inflation, which also causes interest rates to rise sharply in this scenario. This sudden rise in interest rates negatively impacts DNB's profit and interest rate risk. Under this scenario, however, credit risk and market risk remain moderate due to the relatively smooth financial market reaction to climate policies. Under the Delayed Transition and Current Policies scenarios, the macroeconomic variables are mostly affected by the climate change impact after 2030. In line with the assumption that the monetary portfolios on DNB's balance sheet will have decreased significantly by then, these two scenarios do not have any sizable impact on interest rate risk. However, greater credit risk and market risk start to materialize in the long term. This observation originates from the vulnerability of the corporate sector to climate risks in these scenarios.

Still, there are important points to consider when interpreting the results of the CSA. The first notable characteristic is that the Delayed Transition and Current Policies scenarios present the most uncertainty as their impacts emerge further downstream. Second, the effects presented only describe the effects on DNB's balance sheet. Accordingly, any implications must be distinguished from the effect of climate scenarios on the financial stability of the economic system as a whole.

From a central banking perspective, regular climate stress testing of the Eurosystem balance sheet is anticipated to be introduced in 2023–2024. This proposition is in line with the ECB's comprehensive climate change-related action plan released in July 2021, following the review of its monetary policy strategy. Beyond that, our CSA approach is closely related to ongoing developments and regulations in the financial sector. Climate stress testing exercises will become more prominent tools to assess climate-related risks on financial institutions' balance sheets over the years to come. At present, no standardized frameworks exist for such exercises, mainly due to challenges related to data availability and a multitude of measurement methodologies to identify and quantify climate risks. Nevertheless, the importance of this risk type is emphasized by the ECB's 2022 climate risk stress test on significant supervised entities in the Eurosystem (ECB, 2022). While being regarded as a learning exercise, results are evaluated qualitatively against the supervisory expectations set out by the ECB in 2020. The recent stress test results do not have a direct impact on capital requirements, but credit risk effects, possible loan losses, and financial stability implications of specific climate scenarios are considered relevant for future regulatory advancements.

Looking ahead, in light of this increasing demand for analyzing climate risks, future research can extend the work presented in this chapter by scrutinizing supplementary climate scenarios. An example of such a scenario is the impact of a (regional) flood on the balance sheet of a financial institution. The main difference with our CSA approach is that a flood is a scenario with primarily short-term impact. Furthermore, the CSA presented can be enhanced by adding more geographic granularity to the analysis.

Conclusion

Climate change can have a significant financial impact on central banks. As a risk factor, climate change is characterized by fundamental uncertainty. as its unfolding and ramifications come with many unknown features. In this chapter, we present a tool to generate a forward-looking assessment of the vulnerability of central banks to climate change. Our top-down methodology for climate scenario analysis involves four sequential steps and allows the integration of both transition and physical risks. Depending on the climate scenarios selected, the impact on a central bank's profitability and distinct types of financial risks can vary substantially. Scenarios in which transition risks are assumed to materialize with greater magnitude in the near future have a negative effect on profits and interest rate risk in the short term, whereas scenarios in which physical risks are more pronounced have a substantial impact on credit risk and market risk in the long term. These results depend on the specific balance sheet structure of the central bank, however.

The top-down approach presented in this chapter provides key information that both central banks and other financial institutions can use in their further decision-making on managing climate-related risks and disclosing them to their stakeholders. If institutions deploy comprehensive and openly available climate scenario data such as that provided by the NGFS, results may ultimately be compared. Given the non-standard nature of climate scenario analysis, central banks should, however, disclose any model assumptions which can have major financial implications.

Notes

1. The many hurdles observed by central banks in addressing climate change are discussed in detail by Hansen (2022).
2. From an economic perspective, pricing is an effective means of mitigating carbon emissions. An adequate carbon price equals the present discounted value of future damages resulting from an additional metric ton of carbon emissions today.
3. Assets with a high payoff when climate change has severe consequences have a low discount rate, and vice versa.
4. A separate kind of assessment could measure the impact of abrupt shocks to the balance sheet.
5. The portal's URL is: www.ngfs.net/ngfs-scenarios-portal/.
6. In the section 'An Application of the CSA', we use the macroeconomic variables from the REMIND MAgPIE 2.1-4.2 integrated assessment model.
7. Out of scope are the liquidity-providing refinancing operations that are part of the Eurosystem's open market operations (OMOs) because these are fully collateralized and therefore present limited risks. Gold is also excluded, as the risks are covered by a large revaluation account.

8 The interest rate risk scenario is, therefore, scenario-nested in each climate scenario.
9 Price losses partially also capture an increase in the credit risk of the bond portfolio. Nevertheless, we measure both market losses and credit risk because the former are not only driven by credit risk changes but also by changes in market interest rates.

References

Ackerman, F. (2017). *Worst-case economics: Extreme events in climate and finance*. Anthem Press.
Alogoskoufis, S., Dunz, N., Emambakhsh, T., Hennig, T., Kaijser, M., Kouratzoglou, C., Muñoz, M. A., Parisi, L., & Salleo, C. (2021). *ECB economy-wide climate stress test: Methodology and results* (ECB Occasional Paper No. 281). European Central Bank. https://doi.org/10.2866/460490
Barnett, M., Brock, W., & Hansen, L. P. (2020). Pricing uncertainty induced by climate change. *Review of Financial Studies*, *33*(3), 1024–1066. https://doi.org/10.1093/rfs/hhz144
Battiston, S. (2019). The importance of being forward-looking: Managing financial stability in the face of climate risk. *Financial Stability Review*, *23*, 39–48. https://publications.banque-france.fr/sites/default/files/media/2019/08/27/financial_stability_review_23.pdf
Battiston, S., Mandel, A., Monasterolo, I., Schütze, F., & Visentin, G. (2017). A climate stress-test of the financial system. *Nature Climate Change*, *7*(4), 283–288. https://doi.org/10.1038/nclimate3255
Battiston, S., & Monasterolo, I. (2020). *The climate spread of corporate and sovereign bonds* [Working paper]. SSRN 3376218. https://doi.org/10.2139/ssrn.3376218
BdF. (2020). *A first assessment of financial risks stemming from climate change: The main results of the 2020 climate pilot exercise* (Analyses et Synthesess No. 122-2021). Banque de France, Autorité de Contrôle Prudentiel et de Résolution. https://acpr.banque-france.fr/sites/default/files/medias/documents/20210602_as_exercice_pilote_english.pdf
BIS. (2021). *Climate-related financial risks — Measurement methodologies*. Bank for International Settlements, Basel Committee on Banking Supervision. https://www.bis.org/bcbs/publ/d518.pdf
BoE. (2021). *Stress testing the UK banking system: 2021 solvency stress test results*. Bank of England. https://www.bankofengland.co.uk/stress-testing/2021/bank-of-england-stress-testing-results
Bolton, P., Despres, M., Pereira da Silva, L. A., Samama, F., & Svartzman, R. (2020). *The green swan: Central banking and financial stability in the age of climate change*. Bank for International Settlements.
Bolton, P., & Kacperczyk, M. (2021). Do investors care about carbon risk? *Journal of Financial Economics*, *142*(2), 517–549. https://doi.org/10.1016/j.jfineco.2021.05.008
Broeders, D., & Schlooz, M. (2021). Climate change uncertainty and central bank risk management. *Journal of Risk Management in Financial Institutions*, *14*(2), 121–130. https://ideas.repec.org/a/aza/rmfi00/y2021v14i2p121-130.html
Campiglio, E., Godin, A., & Kemp-Benedict, E. (2017). *Networks of stranded assets: A case for a balance sheet approach* (AFD Research Paper No. 2017-54). Agence Française de Développement. https://www.afd.fr/sites/afd/files/2017-10/pr_54_Networks%20of%20stranded%20assets_Campiglio_Godin_Kemp-Benedict_0.pdf
Choi, D., Gao, Z., & Jiang, W. (2020). Attention to global warming. *Review of Financial Studies*, *33*(3), 1112–1145. https://doi.org/10.1093/rfs/hhz086
Crouhy, M., Galai, D., & Mark, R. (2014). *The essentials of risk management* (2nd ed.). McGraw-Hill Education.
ECB. (2022). *2022 climate risk stress test*. European Central Bank, Banking Supervision. https://www.bankingsupervision.europa.eu/ecb/pub/pdf/ssm.climate_stress_test_report.20220708~2e3cc0999f.en.pdf
Engle, R. F., Giglio, S., Kelly, B., Lee, H., & Stroebel, J. (2020). Hedging climate change news. *Review of Financial Studies*, *33*(3), 1184–1216. https://doi.org/10.1093/rfs/hhz072
Giglio, S., Kelly, B., & Stroebel, J. (2021). Climate finance. *Annual Review of Financial Economics*, *13*(1), 15–36. https://doi.org/10.1146/annurev-financial-102620-103311
Golosov, M., Hassler, J., Krusell, P., & Tsyvinski, A. (2014). Optimal taxes on fossil fuel in general equilibrium. *Econometrica*, *82*(1), 41–88. https://doi.org/10.3982/ECTA10217
Hansen, L. P. (2022). Central banking challenges posed by uncertain climate change and natural disasters. *Journal of Monetary Economics*, *125*, 1–15. https://doi.org/10.1016/j.jmoneco.2021.09.010
Hong, H., Li, F. W., & Xu, J. (2019). Climate risks and market efficiency. *Journal of Econometrics*, *208*(1), 265–281. https://doi.org/10.1016/j.jeconom.2018.09.015
Huynh, T. D., & Xia, Y. (2021). Climate change news risk and corporate bond returns. *Journal of Financial and Quantitative Analysis*, *56*(6), 1985–2009. https://doi.org/10.1017/S0022109020000757

IPCC. (2021). *Climate change 2021: The physical science basis* (Working Group I Contribution to the Sixth Assessment Report). Intergovernmental Panel on Climate Change. https://report.ipcc.ch/ar6/wg1/IPCC_AR6_WGI_FullReport.pdf

Lemoine, D. M., & Traeger, C. P. (2012). *Tipping points and ambiguity in the economics of climate change* (NBER Working Paper No. 18230). National Bureau of Economic Research. https://doi.org/10.3386/w18230

NGFS. (2021). *NGFS climate scenarios for central banks and supervisors*. Network of central banks and supervisors for greening the financial system. https://www.ngfs.net/sites/default/files/media/2021/08/27/ngfs_climate_scenarios_phase2_june2021.pdf

Nordhaus, W. D. (1977). Economic growth and climate: The carbon dioxide problem. *American Economic Review*, *67*(1), 341–346. https://www.jstor.org/stable/1815926

Nordhaus, W. D. (1994). *Managing the global commons: The economics of climate change*. MIT Press.

Nordhaus, W. D., & Boyer, J. (2000). *Warming the world: Economic models of global warming*. MIT Press.

Roncoroni, A., Battiston, S., Escobar-Farfán, L. O. L., & Martinez-Jaramillo, S. (2021). Climate risk and financial stability in the network of banks and investment funds. *Journal of Financial Stability*, *54*, Article 100870. https://doi.org/10.1016/j.jfs.2021.100870

Vermeulen, R., Schets, E., Lohuis, M., Kölbl, B., Jansen, D.-J., & Heeringa, W. (2018). *An energy transition risk stress test for the financial system of the Netherlands* (DNB Occasional Studies No. 16/07). De Nederlandsche Bank. https://www.dnb.nl/media/pdnpdalc/201810_nr-_7_-2018-_an_energy_transition_risk_stress_test_for_the_financial_system_of_the_netherlands.pdf

Wagner, G., & Weitzman, M. L. (2015). *Climate shock: The economic consequences of a hotter planet*. Princeton University Press.

Weitzman, M. L. (2009). On modeling and interpreting the economics of catastrophic climate change. *Review of Economics and Statistics*, *91*(1), 1–19. https://doi.org/10.1162/rest.91.1.1

Weitzman, M. L. (2012). GHG targets as insurance against catastrophic climate damages. *Journal of Public Economic Theory*, *14*(2), 221–244. https://doi.org/10.1111/j.1467-9779.2011.01539.x

Weitzman, M. L. (2014). Fat tails and the social cost of carbon. *American Economic Review*, *104*(5), 544–546. https://doi.org/10.1257/aer.104.5.544

Wessels, P., & Broeders, D. (2022). *On the capitalisation of central banks* (DNB Occasional Studies No. 20/04). De Nederlandsche Bank. https://www.dnb.nl/media/5sdmsgld/74393_dnb_os-capitalisation-of-central-banks_web.pdf

5
PUBLIC FINANCIAL INSTITUTIONS AND CLIMATE CHANGE

Lina Xie, Bert Scholtens, and Swarnodeep Homroy

Introduction

Climate finance is at the heart of addressing climate change. To limit the temperature rise to 1.5 degrees Celsius, more than 4 billion USD of climate finance is required annually by 2030 (see Climate Policy Initiative, 2021). Raising such amounts is challenging given the already high and rapidly increasing levels of public debt in relation to the impact of the Covid-19 pandemic and rising inflation worldwide. The UN Climate Change Conference 2021 (COP26) reinforced the importance of taking climate into account in every financial decision for both public and private financial actors. As significant asset owners, public financial institutions (PFIs) provide similar amounts of international climate finance as private institutions. Their investment allocation (e.g., shifting from carbon-intensive to low-carbon infrastructure) can substantially affect the climate system and emission trajectories (Steffen & Schmidt, 2019). However, those PFIs are underappreciated in the academic debate about their engagement in climate actions. To understand the role and potential of PFIs in addressing climate change, we provide the basics about these institutions and why and how they might help address climate change.

A commonly used definition of PFIs is that they are financial institutions initiated/owned by governments with official missions to serve the public interest as defined by national, regional, or international policy objectives (Cochran et al., 2014; Xu et al., 2021). As such, development-oriented PFIs, for example, multilateral development banks (MDBs) such as the World Bank and the African Development Bank, are the most typical PFIs in the financial system. They have explicit investment mandates to support industrial development, structural change, regional development, and innovation (De Aghion, 1999; Fry, 1988; Mazzucato & Penna, 2016). Some PFIs are set up to help achieve specific policies, such as export-import lending and insurance (the EXIM banks), society-wide transition financing, and climate financing (the green banks). Furthermore, they can act as a catalyst in bringing private financial institutions to certain projects (Fleta-Asín & Muñoz, 2021; OECD, 2016). In this chapter, we extend the scope of PFIs to all banks and asset owners in the public sphere (with government ownership), which can be public banks owned by local authorities, public funds, and public insurers. They are on the rise and account for a significant fraction of the financial system with their substantial assets under management (AUMs). More specifically, it shows that the 27 trillion USD AUMs of public pension and sovereign wealth funds make them the third-largest group of asset owners globally (Megginson et al., 2021).

Figure 5.1 illustrates various financial institutions in both the public and private sectors and their involvement in providing climate finance and conventional finance. PFIs are in quadrants II and III. PFIs that focus on facilitating and mobilizing climate finance, such as climate funds and green banks, occupy quadrant II. They are established to provide capital via different financing mechanisms (e.g., in partnership with private investors) for climate change adaptation, mitigation, and capacity-building activities in different sectors and regions (Chaudhury, 2020; Michaelowa et al., 2020a). Adaptation aims to improve the vulnerable country's resilience to climate change and reduce risks of economic damage from climate incidents. Mitigation is to reduce emissions and shift to a low-carbon development path. Capacity-building activities help enhance a country's technical and institutional capacity and ability to respond to climate change. PFIs typically focus on underserved markets, where perceived barriers and lack of private investment slow the adoption of clean energy and related technologies (OECD, 2016, 2017).

The development-oriented PFIs operate in highly diverse fields, such as promoting national and local economic development, small and medium-sized enterprises growth, and addressing societal challenges like climate change. The significant international climate finance providers, MDBs, are committed to increasing their activities' share of climate finance (MDBs, 2019, 2021). More and more national development banks (NDBs) and state investment banks (SIBs) are integrating climate change into their investment decisions and promoting low-carbon and climate-resilient (LCR) development (Geddes et al., 2018). The investment portfolios of those PFIs consist of both climate finance and conventional finance. Therefore, they are positioned in the middle of quadrants II and III.

Furthermore, other public banks and state-owned investors (SOIs, e.g., public pension funds, sovereign wealth funds, and public insurance companies) are more oriented toward providing conventional finance. They take deposits or manage households' retirement plans

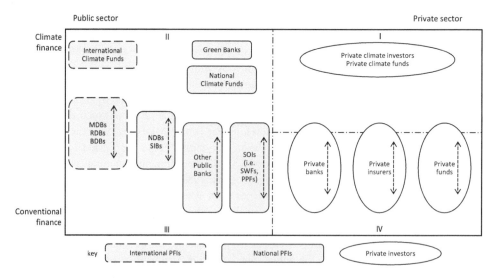

Figure 5.1 Public financial institutions in the financial system. **Note:** MDBs: multilateral development banks; RDBs: regional development banks; BDBs: bilateral development banks, NDBs: national development banks; SIBs: state investment banks; SOIs: state-owned investors; SWFs: sovereign wealth funds; PPFs: public pension funds. Source: authors' construction.

and transform them into loans, equity investments, and other financial vehicles. Given their government ownership, they operate with public interest mandates and stakeholder engagement (DSGV, 2018; Marois, 2021). Regarding climate change, some front runners have started to align their investment portfolios with climate goals and actively promote environmental and climate-related policies in their investee companies (Driouich et al., 2020). For instance, the Environment Agency Pension Fund (UK) targets getting to net zero by 2045, and the California Public Employees' Retirement System (US) actively engages its portfolio companies to encourage them to consider climate-related factors in their operations. However, the majority of them are less proactively engaged in providing climate finance. This suggests the substantial potential for the public financial sector to address climate change.

Private investors are positioned in quadrants I and IV of Figure 5.1. Here, climate funds are initiated by the private sectors in quadrant I and are purely focused on providing climate finance. For example, Bloomberg New Energy Finance (2022) tracked 2.8 billion USD in capital raised by climate-focused venture capital and private equity funds between December 2021 and February 2022. In addition, private banks and asset owners are raising their awareness of climate change, assessing and managing climate risks, and integrating climate into their financial decisions (e.g., participating in climate-related initiatives such as Principles for Responsible Investment, Principles for Responsible Banking, and Climate Action 100+).

In the societal and academic debate, many studies focus on private investors in terms of their motivations for considering climate factors and related impact on financial performance (Bolton & Kacperczyk, 2021; Hartzmark & Sussman, 2019; Mazzucato & Semieniuk, 2018; Reboredo & Otero, 2021; Riedl & Smeets, 2017; Trinks et al., 2018). Though private investors pursue the maximization of shareholder value, they also can collaborate with PFIs to fund low-carbon technology and innovation and to help turn the billions of public climate finance into trillions of total climate investments. It is because, here, private and social interests align.

The Role of PFIs in Addressing Climate Change

PFIs play a crucial role in meeting the urgent need for upscaling global climate finance, given their public features and climate-related market failures. They facilitate climate finance in two ways: by providing their own resources and by mobilizing climate finance from private investors (see Figure 5.2) (Migliorelli & Dessertine, 2019; NRDC, 2016). Left to the market alone, there will be underinvestment in LCR projects. Market failures, presented with the externalities of climate change, information asymmetry, and structural barriers in green innovation financing, decrease the attractiveness of climate projects (Polzin, 2017). Especially private investors and corporations with short planning horizons and prioritizing financial profits are reluctant to bear related risks and engage in LCR investments (Egli et al., 2018; Le et al., 2020; Schmidt, 2014).

Government ownership allows PFIs to primarily pursue their policy objectives while trying to break even financially, which sets them apart from private investors. The explicit or implicit government guarantee enables PFIs to raise a substantial volume of stable capital and transfer it to LCR projects at a lower cost (see Figure 5.2, capital provision), especially for projects which are not able to access capital from the private sector (Mazzucato & Penna, 2016; Steffen & Schmidt, 2017). The basic funding means include concessional loans, intermediated loans, equity investments, guarantees, etc. Yet, given the already high public debt and the scope of LCR investments in need, it is difficult for PFIs to provide sufficient climate finance on their own. Therefore, mobilizing capital from private investors becomes the other important role for PFIs in addressing climate change (OECD, 2016).

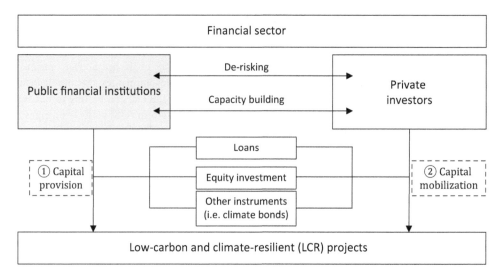

Figure 5.2 PFIs' role in channeling climate finance to LCR projects. Source: authors' construction

Mobilizing private climate finance can be achieved through two channels. First, the involvement of PFIs in LCR projects performs a de-risking role, namely decreasing the downside risk of LCR projects (OECD, 2021; Schmidt, 2014). The relatively high risks and financing costs of LCR projects form significant barriers to accessing capital from private investors. PFIs' involvement brings explicit or implicit risk insurance or guarantees (that cover potential losses) that make LCR projects financially attractive for private investors. PFIs signal to the market that those projects are commercially viable and, in turn, leverage private climate finance to LCR investments (Geddes et al., 2018). In addition, with specific financing structures and arrangements, PFIs' involvement either shares or transfers the risk of LCR projects at different stages among investors with different risk-return portfolios and then leverages more private climate finance (Cochran et al., 2014). OECD (2021) analyzed 328 projects funded by institutional investors with public interventions and recorded 19 de-risking instruments (the three most used instruments are co-investment as an equity fund, loan, and stake cornerstone at the fund level).

Meanwhile, the public actors need to be aware of the potential crowding-out effect of public climate finance. PFIs are expected to provide additional finance for climate projects lacking sufficient funds due to market failures. Their investments in already bankable LCR projects compete with private investors and, as such would crowd out private climate finance (Geddes et al., 2018). It seems many institutional investments and public interventions flow to mature technologies (OECD, 2021). PFIs might focus on higher-risk low-carbon technologies and climate-resilience projects to provide additional climate finance.

Secondly, PFIs play a role in providing and building capacity and expertise regarding climate investment. Though the awareness and understanding of climate change and related risks increase among both public and private investors, expertise in LCR investments and assessing and managing climate-related risks are far from mature (Krueger et al., 2020; Stroebel & Wurgler, 2021). Building capacity and fostering expertise become crucial for PFIs to attract additional capital. Technical assistance is one of the typical financing types of development banks for climate-related projects, especially essential for adaptation projects. Such assistance aims to improve the ability of project developers regarding project preparation and strategic planning and strengthen the technical capacity of the capital market so that LCR projects have better access to financing (United Nations, 2020).

PFIs also invest in researching and developing innovative financial tools and standards for climate investments which are public goods that benefit all investors. Relying on the PFIs' platforms and initiatives, climate investment expertise and knowledge are disseminated to more project developers and investors (Driouich et al., 2020). Given the government ownership and stakeholders' engagement, PFIs can also be a bridge between governments and market actors, advocating climate-related policies and regulations and promoting climate-related responsibility. For example, the water bank in the Netherlands (a national promotional bank) set up a water innovation fund to innovate sustainable water-related projects in the pilot phase (NWB Bank, 2022). It also actively funds sustainable energy projects supported by the government, such as projects that received government grants and projects raised from public-private partnerships.

Many LCR projects are funded with traditional forms of loans and equity investments. PFIs also developed many other financial instruments that leverage private climate finance, for instance, mezzanine finance, quasi-equity, and off-balance sheet instruments (Cochran et al., 2014; NRDC, 2016). In the green bond market, public sector actors take the lead. They issued 230 billion USD of green bonds in 2021, which accounted for 40% of the overall amount of this type of bond issue. Issuance by PFIs like development banks and government-backed entities accounted for more than 22% (Climate Bonds Initiative, 2021).

Geographic Dimension of PFIs' Climate Finance

What is the destination of PFIs' climate finance? As of today, an accurate answer is unavailable due to data limitations. On the one hand, there are no consensus and systematic studies identifying PFIs of all countries. An exhaustive database of PFIs worldwide is still missing. Xu et al. (2021) build the first database of over 500 public development banks and development financial institutions worldwide, but many public banks and SOIs are not included. On the other hand, only a few PFIs start tracking and reporting climate finance in their portfolio, and these data are unavailable for most PFIs. Moreover, without a harmonized and jointly agreed accounting and reporting methodology, the data cannot be aggregated and compared across countries (Shishlov & Censkowsky, 2022; Weikmans & Roberts, 2019).

In this chapter, we adopt public climate finance data from Climate Policy Initiatives (CPI) and eight leading MDBs to illustrate the geographic flows of climate finance from the public sector. CPI aggregates international climate finance from all public actors (e.g., PFIs, government budget, and state-owned enterprises) on the regional level (Climate Policy Initiative, 2021). In 2019–2020, more than half of public climate finance (180 billion USD) went to Asia Pacific Region. CPI estimates most public climate finances were concentrated in China because of its strong government involvement in public spending and policies. Western Europe, which consists of developed economies, has sourced 13.8% of global public climate finance (43 billion USD). The other economically advanced regions, namely the United States, Canada, and Oceania, have sourced only 1.3% and 0.3% of all public climate finance. In those regions, climate finance primarily comes from the private sector. Moreover, regions with the most vulnerable countries, such as sub-Saharan Africa, the Middle East, and North Africa, sourced limited public climate finance for their LCR projects (5.5% and 2.9%). Countries in those regions find it difficult to obtain climate finance from the private sector (see Figure 5.3, panel A).

Data from the MDBs enable us to go deeper into the climate finance flows across countries. Eight MDBs[1] developed common principles for finance to mitigate and support adaptation to climate change and reported their climate finance commitments across countries

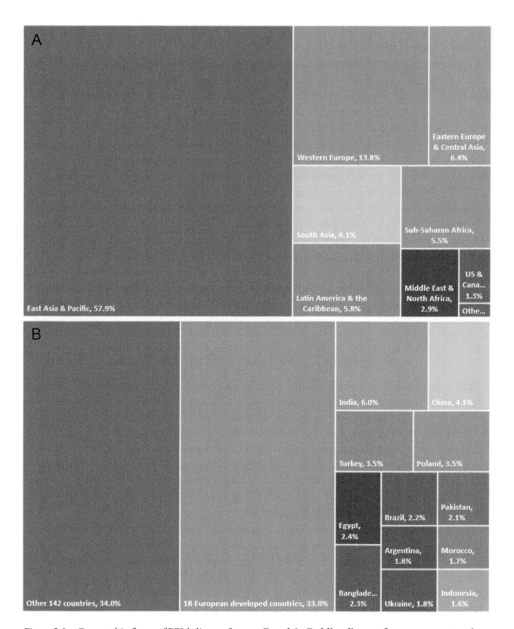

Figure 5.3 Geographic flows of PFIs' climate finance. **Panel A: Public climate finance across regions (2019–2020 annual average); Panel B: MDBs' climate finance commitments across countries (2015–2020 annual average).** Note: transregional public climate finance is not illustrated in this figure. The bottom-right box of Panel A is other Oceania countries, 0.3%. Source: Global Landscape of Climate Finance 2021, Joint Report on Multilateral Development Banks' Climate Finance 2021.

between 2015 and 2020 (MDBs, 2021). MDB climate finance only includes the proportions of project funds that directly contribute to or promote adaptation and/or mitigation. The annual climate finance commitments made by MDBs between 2015 and 2020 were 51.4 billion USD, allocated to 172 countries. The geographic distribution of MDBs' climate finance is highly skewed. For example, EIB provided one-third of the climate finance to 18

European developed countries (17 billion USD per year). Climate finance from EIB constitutes a significant source of public climate finance for Western European countries. The rest was allocated to 154 developing and emerging countries in transition. Among them, the 12 largest recipients and the other 142 countries received a similar proportion (around 33%) of climate finance from MDBs.

PFIs' Climate Finance Priorities: Mitigation Versus Adaptation

PFIs' climate finance is the primary source for developing countries to mitigate and adapt to climate change, while developed countries mainly source funding from the private sector, especially the United States, Canada, and countries in Oceania. The data also confirm the highly skewed distribution of PFIs' climate finance. Moreover, this skew exists not only among countries but also between mitigation and adaptation purposes. Mitigation finance accounted for 86% of all CPI-tracked public climate finance and 75.6% of the eight MDBs' climate finance. Though adaptation projects heavily rely on funding from the public sector, they receive limited funds from PFIs (see Figure 5.4).

Adaptation to climate change that improves economic and social resilience is imperative because of the growing hazardous impacts of climate incidents (e.g., extreme weather events, floods and droughts, and rising sea levels). Even if we achieve net-zero emissions immediately, climate change impacts will last for the next few decades. Adaptation is unavoidable and urgent in the short term, especially for least developed and most vulnerable countries (Klein et al., 2007). Mitigation is to reduce sources or enhance the sinks of greenhouse gases (GHGs), which

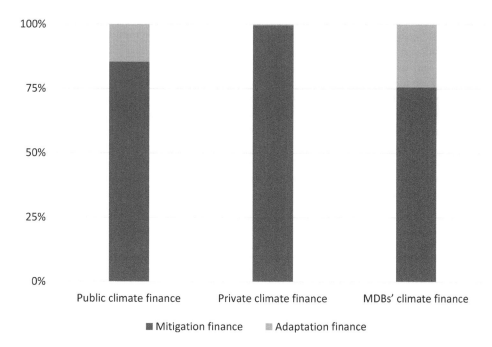

Figure 5.4 Public climate finance by mitigation and adaptation. Source: the two left bars use data from CPI, indicating CPI-tracked climate finance (2019–2020 average) by mitigation and adaptation from public and private actors. The right bar uses data from MDB-reported climate finance from their own resources (2021).

requires significant efforts from major GHG emitters. Mitigation limits the concentration of GHGs in the atmosphere and generates global benefits in the long term. Without mitigation, adaptation will be impossible for some natural systems associated with tremendous social and economic costs. However, because of the long duration of mitigation measures to take effect on the actual climate, this implies that many people have to face increasing climate risks and significant economic damages for a prolonged time. This seeming paradox reflects the real nature of the climate crisis: the urgent need to protect vulnerable societies and ecosystems and the pressure to cut emissions simultaneously.

The Paris Agreement brings the importance of the balance between mitigation and adaptation finance to the table. Article 9 of the Paris Agreement states that the

> provision of scaled-up financial resources should aim to achieve a balance between adaptation and mitigation, and the allocation of climate finance should consider country-driven strategies, and the priorities and needs of developing country Parties, especially those that are particularly vulnerable to the adverse effects of climate change and have significant capacity constraints.
>
> *(United Nations, 2015)*

Whether this Article is implemented in the climate finance allocation, many studies investigate the allocation of international climate funds and MDBs' climate finance.

Garschagen and Doshi (2022) track and analyze the allocation of the World Bank's Green Climate Fund (GCF) and find it allocates its funds largely to vulnerable countries as it aims to prioritize. They observe that the most vulnerable countries with weak institutional governance cannot access project funding. Halimanjaya (2016) connects the recipient country's carbon sink with the mitigation finance allocation and finds discrepancies in the mitigation finance allocation of different donor countries. Michaelowa et al. (2020a) find that mitigation trust funds allocate their funding according to recipients' certified emission reductions, while adaptation trust funds do not prioritize the most vulnerable countries.

We examine the allocation of MDBs' climate finance and connect it to the country's CO_2 emissions and vulnerability to climate risks (Homroy, Xie, and Scholtens, 2021). From project-level data of ADB, EIB,[2] and IDBG, MDBs' mitigation finance and adaptation finance are positively correlated with countries' CO_2 emissions, while their adaptation finance is not positively correlated with countries' vulnerability to climate risks (see Table 5.1). Furthermore, we simulate and predict future emissions and vulnerability under different scenarios of climate finance distribution between mitigation and adaptation. We find that a more evenly balanced allocation

Table 5.1 Correlation coefficients matrix of MDBs' mitigation finance and adaptation finance, and countries' CO_2 emissions and vulnerability

	ADB		EIB		IDBG	
	Mitigation	*Adaptation*	*Mitigation*	*Adaptation*	*Mitigation*	*Adaptation*
CO_2 emissions	0.559***	0.530***	0.172**	0.488***	0.709***	0.326***
Vulnerability	−0.074	−0.044	−0.151**	−0.053	−0.149*	0.056

Source: mitigation and adaptation finance data are drawn from project-level data of ADB, EIB, and IDBG. CO_2 emissions data are the country's total emissions from World Development Indicators. Vulnerability data are the country's vulnerability index from Notre Dame Global Adaptation Index.

between adaptation and mitigation finance (from 30:70 to 60:40) could substantially reduce vulnerability to climate change for around 1.9 billion people.

Adaptation is one of the core topics juxtaposed with *mitigation, collaboration*, and *climate finance* at the UN Climate Change Conference 2021. Adaptation projects face more barriers than mitigation projects to obtain funding from the private sector, therefore rely to a great extent on the public financing source. However, adaptation finance only accounts for a small fraction of the public climate finance portfolio. Studies show that adaptation finance hasn't reached the most vulnerable countries (Garschagen & Doshi, 2022; Michaelowa et al., 2020b). To align its finances with the investment portfolio with Paris Agreement Articles, PFIs must balance mitigation and adaptation finances and take the country's climate priority into account. The COP26 Presidency (2021) also requests developed-country parties to consider doubling adaptation finance to balance mitigation and adaptation.

Conclusion

The transition to a low-carbon and climate-resilient development path is increasingly urgent. The sheer scale and risky funding on mitigation, adaptation, and capacity-building require significant participation from public financial institutions. The public characteristics of PFIs enable them to be used as an atypical climate policy instrument by governments, providing authorities with more policy tools other than conventional regulations, subsidies, emissions trading schemes, and carbon taxes. With implicit or explicit government guarantees, PFIs support specific climate policies with specific financing tasks and fund cheaper than private institutions. They play a crucial role in facilitating sufficient funds for climate projects. Besides traditional development-oriented PFIs, such as MDBs and NDBs, we should also shed light on public banks owned by local authorities and state-owned investors, which have substantial AUMs and great potential to scale up climate finance.

Closing the climate financing gap is challenging for both public and private investors. We have seen an increasing awareness of climate change and the related risks of PFIs. More and more instruments and expertise are developed and accumulated. The balance between mitigation and adaptation finance must be highlighted during this process. Adaptation is not only to protect against negative climate impacts but also to avoid long-term damage to communities and ecosystems and to provide lasting support for climate policies. Similarly, mitigation is important to achieve the objectives of the Paris Agreement. Future emissions will exacerbate vulnerabilities of communities and ecosystems consequently. Therefore, a more balanced allocation between mitigation and adaptation and human health and well-being dimension needs to be considered by PFIs in their investment decisions.

Abbreviations and Acronyms

ADB	Asian Development Bank
AfDB	African Development Bank
AIIB	Asian Infrastructure Investment Bank
AUMs	assets under management
BDBs	bilateral development banks
COP	Conference of the Parties
CPI	Climate Policy Initiative
EBRD	European Bank for Reconstruction and Development

EIB	European Investment Bank
EXIM banks	export-import banks
GCF	Green Climate Fund
GHG	greenhouse gas
IDBG	Inter-American Development Bank Group
IsDB	Islamic Development Bank
LCR	low-carbon and climate-resilient
MDBs	multilateral development banks
NDBs	national development banks
OECD	Organization for Economic Co-operation and Development
PFIs	public financial institutions
RDBs	regional development banks
SIBs	state investment banks
SOIs	state-owned investors
SWFs	sovereign wealth funds
PPFs	public pension funds
UK	United Kingdom
UN	United Nations
US	United States
WBG	World Bank Group

Notes

1 They are Asian Development Bank (ADB), African Development Bank (AfDB), Asian Infrastructure Investment Bank (AIIB), European Bank for Reconstruction and Development (EBRD), European Investment Bank (EIB), Inter-American Development Bank Group (IDBG), Islamic Development Bank (IsDB), and the World Bank Group (WBG).
2 We only include EIB's climate finance to developing and emerging countries here.

References

Bloomberg New Energy Finance. (2022). *Climate funds heat up raising $2.8 billion in three months*. Bloomberg NEF. https://about.bnef.com/blog/climate-funds-heat-up-raising-2-8-billion-in-three-months/
Bolton, P., & Kacperczyk, M. (2021). Do investors care about carbon risk? *Journal of Financial Economics*, 142(2), 517–549. https://doi.org/10.1016/j.jfineco.2021.05.008
Chaudhury, A. (2020). Role of intermediaries in shaping climate finance in developing countries—Lessons from the green climate fund. *Sustainability*, 12(14), 5507. https://doi.org/10.3390/SU12145507
Climate Bonds Initiative. (2021a). *Sustainable debt: Global state of the market 2021*. https://www.climatebonds.net/files/reports/cbi_global_sotm_2021_02h_0.pdf
Climate Policy Initiative. (2021b). *Preview: Global landscape of climate finance 2021*. https://www.climatepolicyinitiative.org/wp-content/uploads/2021/10/Global-Landscape-of-Climate-Finance-2021.pdf
Cochran, I., Hubert, R., Marchal, V., & Youngman, R. (2014). Public financial institutions and the low-carbon transition: Five case studies on low-carbon infrastructure and project investment. OECD Environment Working Papers, No. 72. https://doi.org/10.1787/5jxt3rhpgn9t-en
COP26 Presidency. (2021). *Priorities for public climate finance in the year ahead*. https://ukcop26.org/wp-content/uploads/2021/01/PRIORITIES-FOR-PUBLIC-CLIMATE-FINANCE-IN-THE-YEAR-AHEAD.pdf
De Aghion, B. A. (1999). Development banking. *Journal of Development Economics*, 58(1), 83–100. https://doi.org/10.1016/S0304-3878(98)00104-7
Driouich, R., Ralite, S., Stein, E., & Ghirardi, T. (2020). On the road to Paris? A review of financial institutions' climate-related commitments. In *2 investing initiative (2DII)*. https://2degrees-investing.org/wp-content/uploads/2020/12/On-the-Road-to-Paris.pdf

DSGV. (2018). *Inside the savings banks finance group.* https://www.dsgv.de/bin/servlets/sparkasse/download?path=%2Fcontent%2Fdam%2Fdsgv-de%2Fenglische-inhalte%2FSavings_Banks_Group_2018_EN.pdf&name=Inside the Savings Banks Group.pdf

Egli, F., Steffen, B., & Schmidt, T. S. (2018). A dynamic analysis of financing conditions for renewable energy technologies. *Nature Energy, 3*(12), 1084–1092. https://doi.org/10.1038/s41560-018-0277-y

Fleta-Asín, J., & Muñoz, F. (2021). Renewable energy public–private partnerships in developing countries: Determinants of private investment. *Sustainable Development, 29*(4), 653–670. https://doi.org/10.1002/sd.2165

Fry, M. J. (1988). *Money, interest, and banking in economic development.* Johns Hopkins University Press.

Garschagen, M., & Doshi, D. (2022). Does funds-based adaptation finance reach the most vulnerable countries? *Global Environmental Change, 73,* 102450. https://doi.org/10.1016/j.gloenvcha.2021.102450

Geddes, A., Schmidt, T. S., & Steffen, B. (2018). The multiple roles of state investment banks in low-carbon energy finance: An analysis of Australia, the UK and Germany. *Energy Policy, 115,* 158–170. https://doi.org/10.1016/j.enpol.2018.01.009

Halimanjaya, A. (2016). Allocating climate mitigation finance: A comparative analysis of five major green donors. *Journal of Sustainable Finance and Investment, 6*(3), 161–185. https://doi.org/10.1080/20430795.2016.1201412

Hartzmark, S. M., & Sussman, A. B. (2019). Do investors value sustainability? A natural experiment examining ranking and fund flows. *Journal of Finance, 74*(6), 2789–2837. https://doi.org/10.1111/jofi.12841

Homroy, S., Scholtens, B., & Xie, L. (2021). Climate consequences of rebalancing official climate finance: Analyzing multilateral development banks' allocation practices. Available at SSRN 3972261.

Klein, R., Huq, S., Denton, F., Downing, T., Richels, R., & Robinson, J. (2007). Inter-relationships between adaptation and mitigation. In *Climate change 2007: Impacts, adaptation and vulnerability. contribution of working group II to the fourth assessment report of the intergovernmental panel on climate change* (pp. 745–777). Cambridge University Press. https://www.ipcc.ch/site/assets/uploads/2018/02/ar4-wg2-chapter18-1.pdf

Krueger, P., Sautner, Z., & Starks, L. T. (2020). The importance of climate risks for institutional investors. *Review of Financial Studies, 33*(3), 1067–1111. https://doi.org/10.1093/rfs/hhz137

Le, T. H., Nguyen, C. P., & Park, D. (2020). Financing renewable energy development: Insights from 55 countries. *Energy Research and Social Science, 68,* 101537. https://doi.org/10.1016/j.erss.2020.101537

Marois, T. (2021). *Public banks: Decarbonisation, definancialisation and democratisation.* Cambridge University Press. https://doi.org/10.1017/9781108989381

Mazzucato, M., & Penna, C. C. R. (2016). Beyond market failures: The market creating and shaping roles of state investment banks. *Journal of Economic Policy Reform, 19*(4), 305–326. https://doi.org/10.1080/17487870.2016.1216416

Mazzucato, M., & Semieniuk, G. (2018). Financing renewable energy: Who is financing what and why it matters. *Technological Forecasting and Social Change, 127,* 8–22. https://doi.org/10.1016/j.techfore.2017.05.021

MDBs. (2019). *High level MDB statement.* https://www.adb.org/sites/default/files/page/41117/climate-change-finance-joint-mdb-statement-2019-09-23.pdf

MDBs. (2021). *Joint report on multilateral development banks' climate finance.* 64. https://www.miga.org/sites/default/files/2021-08/2020-Joint-MDB-report-on-climate-finance_Report_final-web.pdf

Megginson, W. L., Lopez, D., & Malik, A. I. (2021). The rise of state-owned investors: Sovereign wealth funds and public pension funds. *Annual Review of Financial Economics, 13*(1), 247–270. https://doi.org/10.1146/annurev-financial-110420-090352

Michaelowa, A., Michaelowa, K., Shishlov, I., & Brescia, D. (2020a). Catalyzing private and public action for climate change mitigation: The World Bank's role in international carbon markets. *Climate Policy, 21*(1), 120–132. https://doi.org/10.1080/14693062.2020.1790334

Michaelowa, K., Michaelowa, A., Reinsberg, B., & Shishlov, I. (2020b). Do multilateral development bank trust funds allocate climate finance efficiently? *Sustainability, 12*(14), 5529.

Migliorelli, M., & Dessertine, P. (2019). *The rise of green finance in Europe.* https://doi.org/10.1007/978-3-030-22510-0_7

NRDC. (2016). *Green & resilience banks.* https://www.nrdc.org/sites/default/files/green-investment-bank-model-emerging-markets-report.pdf

NWB Bank. (2022, December). *The sustainable water bank: NWB Bank.* https://www.nwbbank.com/en/public-finance/sustainable-water-bank

OECD. (2016). *Green investment banks: Scaling up private investment in low-carbon, climate-resilient infrastructure, green finance and investment.* http://doi.org/10.1787/9789264245129-en

OECD. (2017). *Green investment banks: Innovative public Financial Institutions scaling up private, low-carbon investment.* https://newclimateeconomy.report/workingpapers/wp-content/uploads/sites/5/2017/01/Green-Investment-Banks-OECD.pdf

OECD. (2021). *De-risking institutional investment in green infrastructure.* https://doi.org/10.1787/357c027e-en

Polzin, F. (2017). Mobilizing private finance for low-carbon innovation – A systematic review of barriers and solutions. *Renewable and Sustainable Energy Reviews, 77,* 525–535. https://doi.org/10.1016/j.rser.2017.04.007

Reboredo, J. C., & Otero, L. A. (2021). Are investors aware of climate-related transition risks? Evidence from mutual fund flows. *Ecological Economics, 189,* 107148. https://doi.org/10.1016/j.ecolecon.2021.107148

Riedl, A., & Smeets, P. (2017). Why do investors hold socially responsible mutual funds? *Journal of Finance, 72*(6), 2505–2550. https://doi.org/10.1111/jofi.12547

Schmidt, T. S. (2014). Low-carbon investment risks and de-risking. *Nature Climate Change, 4*(4), 237–239. https://doi.org/10.1038/nclimate2112

Shishlov, I., & Censkowsky, P. (2022). Definitions and accounting of climate finance: Between divergence and constructive ambiguity. *Climate Policy, 22*(6), 798–816. https://doi.org/10.1080/14693062.2022.2080634

Steffen, B., & Schmidt, T. S. (2017). The role of public investment & development banks in enabling or constraining new power generation technologies. *International Conference on the European Energy Market, EEM,* 1–6. https://doi.org/10.1109/EEM.2017.7981949

Steffen, B., & Schmidt, T. S. (2019). A quantitative analysis of 10 multilateral development banks' investment in conventional and renewable power-generation technologies from 2006 to 2015. *Nature Energy, 4*(1), 75–82. https://doi.org/10.1038/s41560-018-0280-3

Stroebel, J., & Wurgler, J. (2021). What do you think about climate finance? *Journal of Financial Economics, 142*(2), 487–498. https://doi.org/10.1016/j.jfineco.2021.08.004

Trinks, A., Scholtens, B., Mulder, M., & Dam, L. (2018). Fossil fuel divestment and portfolio performance. *Ecological Economics, 146,* 740–748. https://doi.org/10.1016/j.ecolecon.2017.11.036

United Nations. (2015). *Paris agreement.* https://unfccc.int/sites/default/files/english_paris_agreement.pdf

United Nations. (2020). *Implementation of the framework for capacity-building in developing countries.* https://unfccc.int/documents/210528

Weikmans, R., & Roberts, J. T. (2019). The international climate finance accounting muddle: Is there hope on the horizon? *Climate and Development, 11*(2), 97–111. https://doi.org/10.1080/17565529.2017.1410087

Xu, J., Marodon, R., Ru, X., Ren, X., & Wu, X. (2021). What are public development banks and development financing institutions?—Qualification criteria, stylized facts and development trends. *China Economic Quarterly International, 1*(4), 271–294. https://doi.org/10.1016/j.ceqi.2021.10.001

6

INTERNAL CARBON PRICING IN RESEARCH AND PRACTICE

Viktor Elliot, Mari Paananen, Manfred Bergqvist, and Philip Jansson

Introduction

Today, nearly 50% of the world's 500 largest companies apply some form of internal carbon pricing (ICP) model or intend to do so within two years (World Bank, 2021). Beyond the clear need to reduce global emissions and the extensive policy agenda aimed toward this goal, there are several benefits associated with the use of ICP. These benefits include (i) better tracking of greenhouse gas emissions in preparation for a regulatory future where carbon is priced; (ii) simpler operations across international pricing policies for multinational enterprises (MNEs) in terms of calculating, tracking, and pricing emissions; and (iii) an incentivizing mechanism driving innovation and efficiency improvements (Addicot et al., 2019).

Transfer pricing as a broader phenomenon has long been a fundamental part of many organizations' control systems; however, since the mid-1990s academic and practice-oriented discussions of transfer pricing have gradually shifted toward tax-related issues. Moreover, broader economic trends, such as servicification, and the impact of globalization, digitalization, and economic crises, have created new patterns for internal trade. The issue of carbon pricing adds to the complexity of how to design and use transfer pricing within large MNEs. It also accentuates the need to revisit old models and, based on the knowledge gained, to develop new models to understand which types of transfer pricing systems are suitable in different situations and how these can be adapted to a dynamic world.

This chapter reviews the literature on transfer pricing and ICP for the purpose of developing a bridge between the two fields. Our insights are intended to inform practitioners contemplating the implementation of ICP and offer some suggestions for future research on the topic. The chapter is organized as follows. We first revisit existing work on transfer pricing, focusing on key themes and how the transfer pricing literature has evolved over time. Next, we discuss the burgeoning literature on ICP and how to link it to the transfer pricing literature. We then outline a framework aimed at discussing key research themes and practical implications of ICP models, followed by concluding remarks.

The Antecedents of Transfer Pricing

Transfer pricing dates far back, with studies illustrating the use of internal pricing in the early 1800s, as well as how it was used to determine costs and revenues for various units in the English cotton and textiles industry (Stone, 1973; Mepham, 1988). Although these studies (among others) showed that relatively sophisticated methods of transfer pricing already existed at that time, Emmanuel and Mehafdi (1994) have argued that modern transfer pricing emerged with the divisional corporation in the United States in the mid-20th century. At that time, researchers in economics began to take an interest in transfer pricing issues. This was conveyed mainly via mathematical models, with Hirshleifer (1956) being marked as one of the more significant contributions. The starting point in Hirshleifer's model is that transfer pricing arises because of decentralization and as a tool for allocating accountability to, and creating coordination between, different units in large divisionalized companies. Hirshleifer was one of the first to mathematically show how internal pricing affects both return on invested capital and the incentives for individual units to act in line with the company's goals. More sophisticated models have followed in the footsteps of Hirshleifer, and have gradually developed to include various forms of programming-based optimization problems.

The main problem with these mathematical models is that they are based on simplified assumptions, resulting in limited practical value. Researchers in organizational science started noting this deficiency in the mid-1970s. Watson and Baumler's (1975) seminal paper on transfer pricing built on the notion that a company's organizational form is a result of external conditions; thus, they argued that the degree of decentralization is perhaps the most important starting point when designing an internal pricing structure. Within a decentralized organizational form with business unit accountabilities, the need for the pricing of goods and services among these business units arises. The challenge is then to design the pricing so that it stimulates the business units to maximize performance, without suboptimization. Watson and Baumler's solution is based on the idea of negotiation between business units, where transfer pricing is included as a component in a multifaceted negotiation process between different business unit managers. The authors emphasized the accountant's function as a producer of accounting information, serving as an important starting point in the negotiation process and introducing a form of intraorganizational learning process. Eccles (1985) extended this line of reasoning through his extensive transfer pricing research based on interviews with business leaders in around 50 American companies. He presented a model in which the design and use of transfer pricing are primarily a result of strategy and administrative processes. The model specifically acknowledges the dynamics of transfer pricing, where well-functioning transfer pricing practices can become dysfunctional if the external context changes.

In a more recent attempt to synthesize the dynamics of transfer pricing in an organizational context, Rossing and Rohde (2014) developed a comprehensive framework emphasizing the situational factors impacting the design and use of transfer pricing. They highlighted three types of situational factors: (i) external (such as regulatory or normative pressure), (ii) internal (such as the organizational strategy and structure), and (iii) transfer-related (such as the type of product or service that is being transferred, how frequently it is transferred, and whether it is unique). Depending on the situational factors, different types of transfer pricing mechanisms are more or less suitable for a specific organization. Rossing and Rohde's (2014) framework can also be used to analyze the effectiveness of the transfer pricing system as well as the balance between conflicting objectives. An illustration of such conflicting objectives could be a transfer pricing system designed to meet functional requirements in tax legislation, facilitate internal resource allocation, and have desirable motivational effects on business unit managers. It is the tradeoff between these objectives that makes many transfer pricing systems dysfunctional.

As research increasingly recognized the organizational problems associated with transfer pricing, interest was directed toward the design of transfer pricing systems that enables goal congruence and, simultaneously, provides tools for measuring, evaluating, and rewarding performance at the unit, group, and individual levels. Most of these studies were conceptual or utilized questionnaires to identify different ways of dealing with transfer pricing in different situations. During the same period, another strand of research focusing on various tax-related aspects of transfer pricing was developed. In the early 1980s, questions arose as to whether companies used transfer pricing to take advantage of differences in tax rates between countries. During the 2000s, research on tax-related issues and their relation to transfer pricing was brought to the fore by extensive changes in international tax legislation driven by globalization and the importance of multinational companies for world trade.

A general principle for tax management is that two companies operating under the same financial conditions should pay the same tax regardless of the company form, tax base, and pricing policy (Cools et al., 2008). This creates major challenges for tax authorities in different countries, as they want to avoid double taxation of companies while at the same time preventing illegal tax avoidance. Starting in the mid-1990s, attention to these issues has grown steadily.[1] The increased focus on transfers of products and services between units in different countries can be attributed partly to the increasing volume of intracorporate transactions and partly to increased differences in tax rates between countries (Rossing & Rohde, 2010). Tax authorities engage in extensive collaborations to prevent international companies from taking advantage of these tax rate differences.

To understand what counts as an internal transaction from a taxation perspective, we refer to the OECD's terminology. The OECD (2017) uses the term "associates" to distinguish between internal and external transactions. Two companies are considered associates if either (i) Company A directly or indirectly participates in the management or control, or acts as owner, of Company B; or (ii) the same individuals directly or indirectly participate in the management or control, or act as owners, of both companies. If any of these criteria are met, companies must apply the OECD's framework for transfer pricing for tax purposes. Tax-related transfer pricing is based on the arm's length principle (IRC, Section 482 and related sections in OECD Transfer Pricing Guidelines, 1979, 1995, 1996, 1997, 2017). The principle necessitates that companies, as far as possible, use comparable or verifiable external market prices. In addition, the profit that would arise in a transaction between two external parties should also arise in a similar transaction between two internal parties (OECD, 2017, p. 35).

Abiding by the arm's length principle becomes increasingly difficult in a world of digitalization, where companies can sell products with a minimal physical presence, complicating the determination of the location of a particular activity for tax purposes (Rogers & Oats, 2022). As noted by Löffler (2019), there are tradeoffs related to tax minimization and managerial incentives when determining international transfer prices. These tradeoffs are likely to become increasingly central when large organizations experiment with ICP, a mechanism primarily intended to create managerial incentives for reducing an organization's carbon footprint, but one that might also have tax implications depending on the design of the ICP model.

Internal Carbon Pricing

There is a distinction between carbon pricing and ICP. The former is defined by the World Bank (2021) as "an instrument that captures the external costs of greenhouse gas (GHG) emissions and ties them to their sources through a price, usually in the form of a price on the carbon dioxide (CO_2) emitted." The World Bank (2022) has discerned ICP as a subgroup of carbon pricing and defines it as "a tool an organization uses internally to guide its decision-making process in relation to climate change impacts, risks and opportunities". The difference is that carbon pricing is based on market prices whereas ICP is a voluntary practice that is not necessarily linked to market prices. Gorbach et al. (2022) suggested a broader conceptualization of ICP, defining it as any carbon pricing methodology that is implemented within an organizational context. Their definition is used for the purposes of this chapter.

Prior research has identified three distinct ICP methods: carbon fee, proxy/shadow price, and emission trading systems (ETS) (Gorbach et al., 2022; Ahluwalia, 2017; Harpankar, 2019), although there are also hybrid variants of these methods. In the following two sections, we discuss why and how firms use these methods in practice. Table 6.1 outlines differences between the methods (with transaction-oriented differences shaded gray).

Reasons for Implementing ICP

The Carbon Disclosure Project (CDP, 2021) has revealed that more than 2,000 companies, with a combined market capitalization of more than US $27 trillion, are already using or planning to implement ICP within the next two years. Of the 853 companies that report already implementing ICP, more than 50% utilize a shadow price, followed by a carbon fee (15%) and an ETS (2%). Bento et al. (2021) have argued that there are two main reasons for implementing ICP: (i) to manage regulatory and financial risk and (ii) for signaling reasons. The signaling might be aimed at regulatory bodies, to indicate that no mandatory regulation is needed because the industry is managing the CO_2 problem voluntarily, or for persuading stakeholders of (sometimes negligible) environmental improvements.

Research has shown that organizations make use of ICP for various financial risk-management purposes. Weiss et al. (2015) discussed how ICP is used as means to evaluate potential investments to avoid stranded assets (see also Bhan, 2016; Chang, 2017; Harpankar, 2019). Furthermore, Chang (2017) noted that resources allocated using ICP incentivize low-carbon transition risk and can be used to fund further carbon-reducing investments. Ma and Kuo (2021) discussed the financial impact of ICP on MNEs, describing how companies use ICP as a self-regulatory mechanism to alleviate risks associated with climate change and to achieve sustainable development. Research has also shown that firms use ICP to manage regulatory risk (Harpankar, 2019; Ahluwalia, 2017). One common argument for ICP implementation is risk hedging for future climate-related costs, such as carbon taxes and other environment-related costs (Harpankar, 2019; Ahluwalia, 2017).

Aldy et al. (2021) proposed another potential reason for an organization to implement ICP: to signal to stakeholders and legislators that the firm is at the forefront of the green transition. However, if the ICP system simply serves a symbolic purpose and does not lead to actions, it is in fact a form of greenwashing. Green (2021) followed a similar line of argument, stating that the absence of standardization allows companies to "roam free" and set their own rules. That is, if ICP is used for signaling purposes for policymakers and stakeholders, then the shadow pricing scheme, with its simplistic nature, is a more likely choice. However, the use of shadow pricing does not necessarily mean that the reason for using the method relates to signaling. Shadow pricing is, after all, the most common ICP method used.[2]

How Companies Implement ICP

This section discusses how firms implement the three main ICP methods described in Table 6.1. A carbon fee is determined and allocated to an internal cost center that invests the money in carbon-reducing activities, usually aligned with overarching company goals. Akin to the ETS, a carbon fee system is also based on a predetermined price of carbon, and it results in actual transactions, thereby internalizing the cost of carbon; it does not, however, include the internal trading component (Fawson et al., 2019). The main advantage of the carbon fee method is that it

Table 6.1 The three internal carbon pricing methods

	Carbon Fee	Emission Trading Systems	Shadow Price
Definition	A predetermined price, usually in CO_2/ton, attached to the operational emission of a business unit.	Trading of emission rights among business units (BUs) within an organization to reach an internal market price for carbon.	Predetermined fictitious internal price to evaluate investment alternatives.
Key Objective	Raise capital that is allocated to a cost center to foster change through business activities that reduce emissions by spending the money.	Create a cost incentive to reduce carbon emissions within BUs.	Steer investment decisions toward green initiatives.
Calculation	Arbitrarily set, however, commonly determined by observing current market prices, policies, and regulation.	Supply and demand regulated price. Set by a finite supply of emission rights. Can involve a floor or a ceiling.	Arbitrarily set, though commonly determined by observing current market prices, policies, and regulations.
Observed Price Range, $ (Carbon Disclosure Project, 2021)	18–532	27–71	28–459
Investment and Revenue Allocation	A central department collects the fee and allocates the funds to emission-reducing activities.	Emission rights are traded among the BUs, allowing for trading profits to be made.	–
Key Benefits	Fosters cultural and behavioral change. The funds are directly allocated to impact the carbon footprint of the company.	Fosters cultural and behavioral change. BUs can gain benefits by introducing emission-reducing behavior and investments.	Fosters cultural and behavioral change. Helps prioritize investments in CO_2-reducing projects and serves as preparatory guidance for future carbon prices. Often viewed as a risk-management tool.
Key Challenges	Expensive to implement, requires structural and administrative change. BUs face different challenges and some cannot justify greener methods as these may not align with company interests.	Expensive to implement, requires structural and administrative change. A market price could be non-beneficial for some business units as the emission intensity might differ. Could motivate some BUs to ignore the system.	As the price is fictitious, it might not have the intended guiding effect.

involves transactions—creating a cost and profit incentive—and thus has the potential to change participants' behavior. The disadvantage is its complex and costly implementation. Microsoft Inc. (as described in the example below, see Figures 6.1 and 6.2), Ørsted A/S, Mitsubishi Corporation, Delta, and QANTAS Airways are a few examples of companies using the carbon fee method (Addicot et al., 2019).

Shadow prices (or proxy prices), on the other hand, basically facilitate the incorporation of emission costs into investment decisions, thereby considering the impact of future emissions (Gorbach et al., 2022). Shadow pricing does not result in any real transactions, which makes it easier to manage from an individual project perspective (Barron et al., 2020). The main drawback of the method is that it is used in the context of risk management only and does not result in any cost to the business unit, which means that it is less likely to influence emission-reducing activities (Fawson et al., 2019).

The ETS method involves the firm creating a market environment with a maximum allowed emissions during a specific time period. Emissions certificates that limit carbon emission rights are allocated to each participant (via an internal cost center), and they can choose to use or sell these rights to other participants. Akin to the carbon fee method, the problem with the ETS method is its costly and complex implementation and allocation of emission volumes among participants. Specifically, it is difficult to mimic a market when there are too few participants, which is often the case for internal ETS (Gorbach et al., 2022; Victor & House, 2006).

Research Questions in the Intersection between ICP and Transfer Pricing

There are apparent links between traditional transfer pricing and ICP since both practices serve the purpose of incentivizing efficient resource allocation between business units in an organization. There are, however, important differences that should be accounted for to avoid confusion. The key difference lies in the frequent use of the shadow pricing method for ICP purposes, as it does not involve monetary transactions between business units. In what follows, we build on Rossing and Rohde's (2014) framework for analyzing dynamic transfer pricing systems to highlight differences and similarities between traditional transfer pricing and ICP.

The Rossing and Rohde (2014) framework identifies and describes contextual factors that may influence the design and use of transfer pricing in an organization. Contextual factors can be external (such as requirements from tax authorities or other stakeholders), internal (such as the organization's strategy or structure), or transfer-related. Depending on the transfer-related factors—that is, the type of product or service, how often it is transferred, whether it is unique to the organization (i.e., there is no comparable market price), etc.—different transfer pricing systems may be more or less suitable. Once the situational factors are accounted for, the efficacy and efficiency of the transfer pricing system can be evaluated, considering the system's functional, financial, organizational, and strategic effects on the organization.

Based on the framework in Figure 6.3, we develop a set of research questions in the intersection between ICP and transfer pricing, focusing on the contextual and outcome variables.

The Relationship between Contextual Variables and ICP

Literature focusing on ICP implementation is scarce, and the practical examples available lack generalizability because they involve implementation in a controlled context (e.g., Yale campus buildings; Carattini et al., 2017) and the ETS mechanism being implemented under arbitrary conditions, as discussed above (Victor & House, 2006). The lack of studies on ICP practices could

> **Microsoft Inc.**
> Microsoft Inc. has been using carbon fees since 2012. The company uses a hybrid of the carbon fee and shadow pricing ICP methods, where participants are charged the lion's share based on their emissions, but do not pay the entire cost. The company focuses its scheme on direct emissions (scope 1), such as from company vehicles; purchases of electricity (scope 2); and indirect emissions from supply chain and product use (scope 3).
>
> Initially, the carbon fee focused on scope 1, scope 2, and business air travel. The proceeds from the fee provide funding for carbon-neutral commitments. In 2020, the company began charging internal participants for all scope 3 emissions and, in parallel, worked with suppliers to help them understand their carbon contributions and how to reduce them.
>
> The company aggregates this information and then, each year, charges participants a certain amount in carbon fees. Determining how much is charged is a balancing act, but the fee is enough to encourage meaningful change.
>
> Source: https://cloudblogs.microsoft.com/industry-blog/general/2022/03/24/how-microsoft-is-using-an-internal-carbon-fee-to-reach-its-carbon-negative-goal/

Figure 6.1 Internal Carbon Pricing in Microsoft Inc. (Willmott, 2022)

> **Volvo Cars AB**
> Volvo Cars AB is the first car manufacturer to have implemented an ICP mechanism. While European car manufacturers have been subject to the EU Emissions Trading System for over 15 years (European Commission, 2022), the policy only covers production, which, in the case of Volvo Cars AB, is approximately 3% of emissions.
>
> The reason behind Volvo Cars AB's choice of ICP, which currently most resembles shadow pricing, is that the company recently initiated the process and the approach is the most conservative option at present, prior to the correct pricing level and a proper emission allocation and accounting system being established.

Figure 6.2 Internal Carbon Pricing in Volvo Cars AB (Volvo Cars AB, 2022)

stem from both the relative recency of ICP as a broader phenomenon within organizations and the sensitive nature of the implementation regarding organizational response and stringency. The lack of non-descriptive research means that most ICP studies derive information from official statements (especially the CDP database) (Chang, 2017; Bento & Gianfrate, 2020). This has also led several authors to call for in-depth case studies of ICP. Bento and Gianfrate (2020) have highlighted the need for more research on how ICPs are implemented and the resulting consequences of their adoption, Riedel et al. (2021) have requested a closer focus on the use of ICPs in different sectors, and Chang (2017) has suggested that further research be conducted on how companies use ICP, controlling for firm size and growth. The lack of in-depth research and theory on ICP has led us to propose a set of exploratory, open-ended research questions, rather than testable hypotheses, for future research to consider.

Even though several of the contextual variables are similar for ICP and transfer pricing, little is known about which contextual variables matter for ICP implementation. While there exists a basic understanding of the main reasons why firms are rapidly adopting ICP and how they do it, little is known about how ICP interacts with other control mechanisms, which data, and IT system infrastructure it requires, what type of internal educational activities would foster suc-

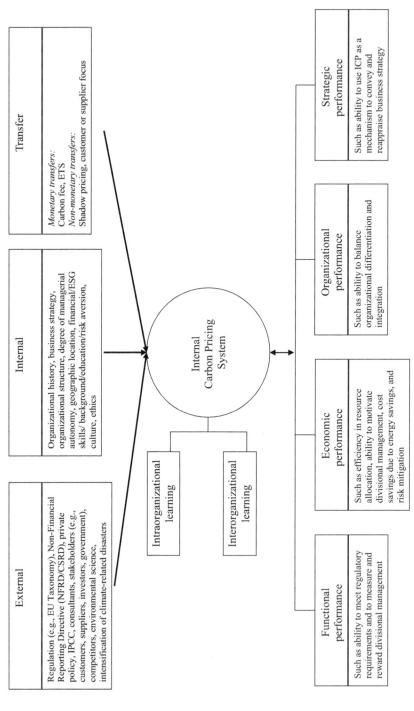

Figure 6.3 A framework of a dynamic internal carbon pricing system (based on Rossing and Rodhe, 2014)

cessful implementation, the extent to which signaling (and perhaps greenwashing) plays a role, and how current regulations and private initiatives feed into the implementation process.

RQ1: How do external, internal, and transfer-related contextual variables interplay and influence the implementation of ICP within organizations?

As ICP continues to gain traction among large corporations, it is worthwhile considering how existing accounting standards and tax legislations impact ICP practices and the extent to which ICP will become integrated into the OECD agenda on transfer pricing. To the best of our knowledge, no existing study has investigated the interlinkages between ICP and either accounting standards or tax legislation.

RQ2: How do tax systems and financial accounting standards affect ICP practices and compliance activities?

In the same vein, the broader literature on ESG reporting has highlighted many challenges associated with data being non-standardized and often self-reported. For example, Kotsantonis and Serafeim (2019) highlighted data inconsistencies, identifying varying definitions of peer groups, ESG data imputation, and differences between ESG data providers as four major limitations to evaluating whether a company performs well. Similar issues exist for companies contemplating the implementation of ICP. Not only does the company need to determine the CO_2 emissions associated with various corporate activities to set a price tag on these activities, but it will also most likely report the results of the program to the CDP. To date, there are no standards or regulatory guidelines on ICP reporting, meaning that the discrepancies commonly identified with ESG ratings (Christensen et al., 2022) are most likely considerably worse with respect to ICP reporting.

RQ3: What are the implications of a lack of standardization in ICP reporting practices?

Implementing carbon fees and ETS implies that the organization should set a price that will not lead to dysfunctional behavior. Just as in the case of transfer pricing, these methods involve transactions between business units and, commonly, across jurisdictions. Thus, the problem is twofold: these schemes attempt to mimic a market with a small number of participants and may incentivize tax planning (tax evasion or tax avoidance); however, the shadow pricing method does not involve any transactions but is still valuable, as it helps to increase organizational awareness of company emissions. This method could be useful as it shifts the perspective from establishing a "fair" price to focusing on increasing the organizational understanding of the importance of reducing carbon emissions.

RQ4: What are the key differences between the implementation of ICP schemes that involve actual monetary transfers and ICP schemes based on shadow prices?

There are clues in the transfer pricing literature on how managerial abilities (such as tax expertise, managerial composition, and professional or educational background) can impact the design and use of transfer pricing systems. However, with regard to ICP, there is no research on similar internal contextual variables. Linkages between the organizations' sustainability agenda and pre-existing sustainability work seem likely to also play a role here.

RQ5: How do managerial characteristics impact ICP decision-making?

Relationship between ICP and Performance

The issue of functional performance is closely linked to both external and internal contextual variables. Presumably, operationalized ICP systems should strengthen firms' ability to meet regulatory requirements, as the firms systematically collect and actively use carbon emission data for internal purposes.

RQ6: How can ICP systems serve as tools for assessing divisional management performance?

However, ICP systems may also lead to earnings management or tax-avoiding behavior. Lo and Wong (2011) found that in a setting where disclosure of carbon prices is voluntary, firms that use transfer pricing for earnings management purposes are less forthcoming with disclosure of transfer pricing methods. In cases where firms use carbon fees or ETS, ICP systems can potentially also be used for earnings management and tax avoidance. However, the fact that these ICP systems involve transactions and are therefore regulated under financial accounting standards (e.g., IAS[3] 12 under IFRS[4] or ASC[5] 740 under U.S. GAAP[6]) should, at least to some extent, deter this behavior. To our knowledge, there is no research on whether ICP systems are used for earnings management and tax avoidance, or on whether there are differences in disclosure quality across ICP models. We, therefore, encourage more research in this area.

RQ7: Are ICP systems used for earnings management and tax avoidance?
RQ8: Is there a difference in disclosure quality across firms with different ICP models?

In terms of research on economic performance, we find two relevant studies. Ma and Kuo (2021) discussed the financial impact of ICP on MNEs. The authors described how ICP is used as an innovative self-regulatory mechanism by companies to mitigate the risks associated with climate change and achieve sustainable development. Using panel data from 132 MNEs from Europe, North America, and Asia, they examined the effect of ICP implementation on the profitability of a given firm (measured by return on assets). Their results showed that implementation of ICP statistically increases return on assets by 1.1%. Furthermore, ICP as a self-regulatory environmental mechanism can improve profitability, primarily through cost reductions.

Similarly, van Emous et al. (2021) examined the relationship between carbon reduction on corporate financial performance to answer the question of whether "it pays to be green." They analyzed a sample of 1,785 firms from more than 53 countries and found that a reduction in carbon emission had a positive impact on short-term performance indicators (return on assets, equity, and sales) but did not influence stock market performance with regard to Tobin's Q and liquidity regarding current ratio (ability to meet short-term obligations).

RQ9: Does ICP lead to efficiency gains? If so, what are they?
RQ10: Are ICP-related efficiency gains reflected in stock market performance?
RQ11: Is there a difference in stock market efficiency gains across different ICP models?

Regarding organizational performance, one key challenge of any transfer pricing system lies in balancing business unit independence and firm integration. In essence, the same is true for ICP, where one major challenge could stem from significant country-specific differences. In countries where demand and the ability and willingness to pay a premium for low-carbon products and services are high, implementing a carbon fee add-on should be unproblematic—and in many cases, may not shift consumer demand. However, in countries where the demand and the ability and willingness to pay are lower, an ICP add-on might significantly impact the attractiveness of the product and service (under the assumption the ICP is set at a fixed rate). This difference could introduce internal conflicts within the organization and reduce the efficiency of the ICP. To alleviate such problems, the organization should consider how the ICP interacts with other control mechanisms, such as target setting, performance evaluations, and bonus schemes, to avoid distortion of firm integration.

RQ12: How does the ICP interact with the organization's overall performance management system?

Finally, from a strategic performance perspective, the rapid growth of ICP among large firms is likely to be closely linked to the speed at which firms announce net-zero targets. While some firms are aligned with the 2050 Paris Agreement, many firms are setting more ambitious targets, with these deadlines quickly approaching. Such targets are increasingly becoming an integral part of the strategy statements of many firms, and, as such, mechanisms such as ICP could be useful to ensure that they reach their targets. However, there is still limited knowledge on the extent to which ICP incentivizes carbon reduction at the firm level, and thus whether it is, in fact, useful in helping organizations reach their targets.

RQ13: Is ICP a useful mechanism to help organizations reach their carbon reduction targets?

Concluding Remarks

This chapter reviews and provides an overview of the literature on transfer pricing and ICP for two purposes: (i) to inform practitioners who consider implementing ICP, and (ii) to identify potentially fruitful areas for future research on the topic. Specifically, we review how the transfer pricing literature has evolved from the 1950s until today, as well as recent research on and examples of the implementation of different ICP systems. We propose a framework representing the dynamics of ICP based on Rossing and Rhode's (2014) model. Finally, based on our proposed framework, we present pursuable research questions linked to the relationship between ICP and contextual variables, and ICP and performance, respectively.

Notes

1 In the mid-1990s, the US Internal Revenue Service issued a document called "Final Regulation Section 482," which deals with tax technical aspects of transfer pricing. This was followed by an update from the OECD, which in 1995 revised its guidelines for international transfer pricing practices. Since then, a number of updates to the rules on transfer pricing have taken place (for an overview, see OECD, 2017), along with a series of regulations added at the national level.
2 CDP Report, 2021 www.google.com/url?sa=t&rct=j&q=&esrc=s&source=web&cd=&cad=rja&uact=8&ved=2ahUKEwiF2eKm2fr3AhVDi8MKHeG8BHUQFnoECAkQAQ&url=https%3A%2F%2Fcdn.cdp.net%2Fcdp-production%2Fcms%2Freports%2Fdocuments%2F000%2F005%2F651%2Foriginal%2FCDP_Global_Carbon_Price_report_2021.pdf%3F1618938446&usg=AOvVaw3gcx7Jz0l-HOzGrL0HBVV6.
3 International Accounting Standards.
4 International Financial Reporting Standards.
5 Accounting Standards Codification.
6 Generally Accepted Accounting Principles.

References

Addicot, E., Badahdah, A., Elder, L., & Tan, W. (2019). *Internal carbon pricing: Policy framework and case studies.* Yale School of Forestry and Environmental Services.

Ahluwalia, M. B. (2017). *The business of pricing carbon: How companies are pricing carbon to mitigate risks and prepare for a low-carbon future.* Center for Climate and Energy Solutions.

Aldy, J. E., Kotchen, M. J., Stavins, R. N., & Stock, J. H. (2021). Keep climate policy focused on the social cost of carbon. *Science, 373*(6557), 850–852. https://doi.org/10.1126/science.abi7813

Barron, A. R., Parker, B. J., Sayre, S. S., Weber, S. S., Weisbord, D. J., Kapuscinski, A. R., & Frumhoff, P. C. (2020). Carbon pricing approaches for climate decisions in US higher education: Proxy carbon prices for deep decarbonization. *Elementa: Science of the Anthropocene, 8*, 1–17. https://doi.org/10.1525/elementa.443

Bento, N., & Gianfrate, G. (2020). Determinants of internal carbon pricing. *Energy Policy, 143*, 111499. https://doi.org/10.1016/j.enpol.2020.111499

Bento, N., Gianfrate, G., & Aldy, J. E. (2021). National climate policies and corporate internal carbon pricing. *Energy Journal, 42*(5), 1–18. https://doi.org/10.5547/01956574.42.5.nben

Bhan, M. (2016, October 21). The business of pricing carbon [Blog post]. Center for Climate and Energy Solutions (C2ES). *Climate Compass Blog.* https://www.c2es.org/blog/bhanm/business-pricing-carbon

Carattini, S., Gillingham, K., & Esty, D. (2017). Lessons from first campus carbon-pricing scheme. *Nature (London), 551*(7678), 27–29. https://www.nature.com/articles/551027a

CDP. (2021). Putting a price on carbon the state of internal carbon pricing by corporations globally. *CDP Worldwide.* https://cdn.cdp.net/cdp-production/cms/reports/documents/000/005/651/original/CDP_Global_Carbon_Price_report_2021.pdf?1618938446

Chang, V. (2017). Private firm incentives to adopt internal carbon pricing. *Journal of Public and International Affairs, 1*, 56–77.

Christensen, D. M., Serafeim, G., & Sikochi, A. (2022). Why is corporate virtue in the eye of the beholder? The case of ESG ratings. *Accounting Review, 97*(1), 147–175. https://doi.org/10.2308/TAR-2019-0506

Cools, M., Emmanuel, C., & Jorissen, A. (2008). Management control in the transfer pricing tax compliant multinational enterprise. *Accounting, Organizations and Society, 33*(6), 603–628. https://doi.org/10.1016/j.aos.2007.05.004

Eccles, R. G. (1985). *The transfer pricing problem: A theory for practice.* Free Press.

Emmanuel, C. R., & Mehafdi, M. (1994). *Transfer pricing.* Academic Press.

European Commission (2022). EU emissions trading system (EU ETS). https://climate.ec.europa.eu/eu-action/eu-emissions-trading-system-eu-ets_en

Fawson, C., Cottle, C., Hubbard, H., & Marshall, M. (2019). Carbon pricing in the US private sector. Working paper AgEcon Search.

Gorbach, O. G., Kost, C., & Pickett, C. (2022). Review of internal carbon pricing and the development of a decision process for the identification of promising internal pricing methods for an organisation. *Renewable and Sustainable Energy Reviews, 154*, 111745. https://doi.org/10.1016/j.rser.2021.111745

Green, J. (2021). Does carbon pricing reduce emissions? A review of ex-post analyses. *Environmental Research Letters, 16*(4), 43004. https://doi.org/10.1088/1748-9326/abdae9

Harpankar, K. (2019). Internal carbon pricing: Rationale, promise and limitations. *Carbon Management, 10*(2), 219–225. https://doi.org/10.1080/17583004.2019.1577178

Hirshleifer, J. (1956). On the economics of transfer pricing. *Journal of Business, 29*(3), 172–184.

Kotsantonis, S., & Serafeim, G. (2019). Four things no one will tell you about ESG data. *Journal of Applied Corporate Finance, 31*(2), 50–58. https://doi.org/10.1111/jacf.12346

Lo, A. W., & Wong, R. M. (2011). An empirical study of voluntary transfer pricing disclosures in China. *Journal of Accounting and Public Policy, 30*(6), 607–628. https://doi.org/10.1016/j.jaccpubpol.2011.08.005

Löffler, C. (2019). Divisionalization and domestic transfer pricing for tax considerations in the multinational enterprise. *Management Accounting Research, 45*, 100646. https://doi.org/10.1016/j.mar.2019.07.003

Ma, J., & Kuo, J. (2021). Environmental self-regulation for sustainable development: Can internal carbon pricing enhance financial performance? *Business Strategy and the Environment, 30*(8), 3517–3527. https://doi.org/10.1002/bse.2817

Mepham, M. J. (1988). The eighteenth-century origins of cost accounting. *Abacus, 24*(1), 55–74. https://doi.org/10.1111/j.1467-6281.1988.tb00203.x

OECD. (2017). *OECD transfer pricing guidelines for multinational enterprises and tax administrations 2017*. OECD Publishing. http://doi.org/10.1787/tpg-2017-en.

Riedel, F., Gorbach, G., & Kost, C. (2021). Barriers to internal carbon pricing in German companies. *Energy Policy*, *159*, 112654.

Rogers, H., & Oats, L. (2022, January). Transfer pricing: Changing views in changing times. *Accounting Forum*, *46*(1), 83–107. https://doi.org/10.1080/01559982.2021.1926778

Rossing, C. P., & Rohde, C. (2010). Overhead cost allocation changes in a transfer pricing tax compliant multinational enterprise. *Management Accounting Research*, *21*(3), 199–216. https://doi.org/10.1016/j.mar.2010.01.002

Rossing, C. P., & Rohde, C. (2014). Transfer pricing: Aligning the research agenda to organizational reality. *Journal of Accounting and Organizational Change*, *10*(3), 266–287. https://doi.org/10.1108/JAOC-03-2012-0017

Stone, W. E. (1973). An early English cotton mill cost accounting system: Charlton Mills, 1810–1889. *Accounting and Business Research*, *4*(13), 71–78. https://doi.org/10.1080/00014788.1973.9729042

van Emous, R., Krušinskas, R., & Westerman, W. (2021). Carbon emissions reduction and corporate financial performance: The influence of country-level characteristics. *Energies (Basel)*, *14*(19), 6029. https://doi.org/10.3390/en14196029

Victor, D. G., & House, J. C. (2006). BP's emissions trading system. *Energy Policy*, *34*(15), 2100–2112. https://doi.org/10.1016/j.enpol.2005.02.014

Volvo Cars AB (2022). Annual Sustainability Report. https://www.media.volvocars.com/global/en-gb/media/pressreleases/309654/volvo-car-ab-publ-publishes-annual-and-sustainability-report-2022

Watson, D. J., & Baumler, J. V. (1975). Transfer pricing: A behavioural context. In *Readings in accounting for management control* (pp. 403–414). Springer. https://doi.org/10.1007/978-1-4899-7138-8_19

Weiss, M., Law, S., Cushing, H., & Clapper, A. (2015). *Putting a price on risk: Carbon pricing in the corporate world*. CDP.

Willmott, E. (2022). "How Microsoft is using an internal carbon fee to reach its carbon negative goal", available at https://www.microsoft.com/en-us/industry/blog/sustainability/2022/03/24/how-microsoft-is-using-an-internal-carbon-fee-to-reach-its-carbon-negative-goal/ accessed, 2022-04-28.

World Bank. (2021). *State and trends of carbon pricing 2021*. https://openknowledge.worldbank.org/handle/10986/35620

World Bank. (2022). *State and trends of carbon pricing 2022*. https://openknowledge.worldbank.org/handle/10986/37455 License: CC BY 3.0 IGO.

PART 2

Green Finance Instruments and Their Effects

7

CORPORATE ENVIRONMENTAL IMPACT

Measurement, Data, and Information

George Serafeim and T. Robert Zochowski

Introduction

As an organization's environmental impact has become a central societal consideration, thereby affecting the industry and organizational competitiveness, interest in measuring and analyzing environmental impact has increased.[1] For example, in recent years an increasing number of regulations seek to limit harmful pollutants, such as tailpipe emissions, that have forced automobile manufacturers to adapt through product development to remain competitive (Lee et al., 2010). Large corporate buyers, such as Walmart, have raised the bar for their suppliers, seeking to reduce carbon emissions in their supply chain, thereby forcing them to innovate (Dauvergne & Lister, 2012). Banks are now offering loans to corporations at preferred rates if they can demonstrate improvements in their environmental impact.

Against this backdrop, an increasing number of companies and investors are measuring and managing their environmental impact, and numerous organizations have emerged to guide various producers and consumers of information, including the Sustainability Accounting Standards Board (SASB), the Global Reporting Initiative (GRI), The Task Force for Climate-related Financial Disclosures (TCFD), and the Corporate Reporting Dialogue (Waddock et al., 2002). These organizations have developed environmental reporting standards for the calculation and disclosure of environmental metrics. Additionally, there has been significant documentation of the process for scoping, gathering data, converting the organization-level results to impacts, and selecting prices by, among others, the Capitals Coalition, ISO 14007 and 14008 Protocols, and the Impact Institute (Tinch et al., 2019).

Despite these numerous efforts, there are still challenges that prevent the full incorporation of environmental data in business decisions. For corporate managers, the main challenge is to understand how different environmental impacts can be measured, compared, and integrated into the decision-making process to allow for better, more seamless management of risk, return, and impact, as well as more efficient, sustainable allocation of resources. From an investor perspective, the challenge lies in measuring environmental impacts across many companies in a transparent, comparable, and reliable way so that the results can be benchmarked and assessed across the market and within industrial classifications.

In this paper, we develop a methodology using several established academic resources that allow us to measure an organization's environmental impact from operations. To achieve this, we use characterization pathways[2] and monetization factors[3] from the Environmental Priority Strategies (EPS) Database, Available WAter REmaining (AWARE) Model, and Waterfund, along with organization-level data of environmental outputs,[4] such as carbon emissions, nitrous oxide, sulfur oxide, VOC, PM 2.5, and water withdrawal and discharge, sourced from Bloomberg and Thomson Reuters. Importantly, given disagreement in the scientific literature, we assess the sensitivity of our measurements to alternative discount rates. We also go to great lengths to reconcile and clean environmental output raw data as we find significant data inconsistencies and errors.

To compare organizations of different sizes, which would reasonably be expected to have different absolute environmental impacts, we scale our calculations for total organizational environmental impact by sales and operating income as proxies for organization size (henceforth defined as *environmental intensity (EI)*). This provides an estimate for environmental damage per unit of sales or operating income.[5] Our key insights are the following. First, we document that the average environmental intensity scaled by sales for our sample, assuming a zero-discount rate, is 11.8%, but the median is only 2.0%. For several industries, such as utilities, construction materials, and airlines, the level of environmental impact is so large that it is equal to more than 25% of revenues. Similarly, we discover that the average environmental intensity scaled by operating income, assuming a zero-discount rate, is 117.4% and the median is 21.5%. A handful of industries have such a high level of environmental impact that it is equivalent to over 150% of their operating income. Pricing of those environmental externalities would lead to significant value erosion for these firms.

Next, we seek to explain what drives variation in environmental intensity across organizations. For the intensity scaled by sales, we find that industry membership explains over 60% of the variation while country effects explain only 5–10%. Including subindustry effects provide additional explanatory power of about 5% over and above industry effects. The environmental intensity scaled by operating income demonstrates a similar trend. About 30% of the variation can be attributed to firm-specific effects suggesting that an organization's unique strategy, asset composition, operations, and competitive positioning are significant factors. For example, the environmental intensity scaled by revenue (operating income) for an airline at the 75th percentile of the distribution is 32% (834%) while an airline at the 25th percentile of the distribution has an environmental intensity of 21% (232%). Therefore, we observe significant differences in their environmental intensity across firms in each industry. Collectively, our evidence suggests that specific industries are poorly positioned if their environmental intensity is priced and therefore exposed to significant levels of regulatory risk. However, within each industry, firms have significantly different profiles, highlighting the importance of divergent strategies.

Further, we use the Environmental Priority Strategies (EPS) database with the set of monetization factors and "safeguard subjects" to map emission's characteristic pathways to the United Nations Sustainable Development Goals (SDGs) (Bexell & Jönsson, 2016). The output of the mapping process shows that, for 0% and 3% discount rates respectively, the vast majority of corporate environmental impact is tied to four main SDG targets: SDG 1.5, which relates to poverty, SDG 2.1 and SDG 2.2, both of which concern ending hunger and malnutrition, and SDG 6, which relates to clean water and sanitation.

We then examine the relationship between environmental intensity and established environmental ratings from data providers. We complement our data with environmental ratings from three of the main data providers, MSCI, RobecoSAM, and Sustainalytics. These data providers are not necessarily measuring impact. Rather, they intend to integrate multiple signals of how well a company is managing environmental-related risks and opportunities. Thus, one would expect somewhat low correlations and should not necessarily be alarmed by the absence of high correlations. We view our results to be informative as to the magnitude of those correlations and whether the ratings can also be interpreted as evidence not only of environmental management but also of environmental impact. The answer is no, as reflected by the relatively low, albeit significant, correlations that range from 0.13 to 0.26. After controlling for industry and country membership, the correlation estimates are reduced by around 65%, suggesting that within an industry, environmental ratings are almost completely uncorrelated with estimates of environmental intensity.

Finally, we ask the question of whether market prices reflect environmental intensity. We estimate the relation between equity valuation multiples, stock returns, volatility, and environmental impact and generate several insights. First, there is a moderate yet significant relationship between environmental intensity and valuation multiples. Second, the environmental intensity has become more material over time. Third, we identify the industries, such as building products, textiles, and apparel, in which the relation between valuation multiples and environmental impact is the strongest and industries such as oil and gas and utilities where the relation has become stronger over time. We infer that environmental impact is a financially material signal across many industries and is becoming increasingly material in recent years.

Overall, our first main conclusion is that measurement of environmental impact from operations is feasible for many companies in the economy with publicly disclosed data. Our paper provides a methodology for how one could go about constructing those impact measurements. Our second main conclusion is that these measurements contain information that is different than that of environmental ratings widely used by investors and other stakeholders, and that this information is value relevant.

The research objectives of this paper are to develop a comparable monetized environmental impact methodology for calculating organization-level environmental outputs, to explore the relation between the calculated EI as a result of the methodology and current commonly used ESG ratings, and to explore the relation of both measures to market valuation. As such, we attempt to address the following research questions. What factors drive variation in EI across organizations? What is the relation between EI and environmental ratings? Do market prices reflect EI?

The remainder of the paper proceeds as follows. The next section describes our data sources. This is followed by a section describing our methodology for calculating environmental impact. The section after this presents the results of our analyses. This is followed by sections that discusses implications of throw results. The final section concludes the paper.

Data Sources

In this section, we describe the data collection process in terms of the required dataset and parameters as input for the EI analysis. We also introduce the databases used to obtain such datasets and the necessary steps of preparing the data along with any assumptions to impute missing values. In particular, we will discuss the datasets obtained from Bloomberg and Thomson Reuters (ASSET4) Databases, Exiobase, The EPS Database, the AWARE model, Waterfund's Global Water Price, and Accounting and Stock Market Data from Worldscope.

Bloomberg and Thomson Reuters (ASSET4) Databases

We acquire organization-level emissions and water-use data from both Bloomberg and Thomson Reuters for the years 2010 to 2019. Specifically, we collect data on four emissions variables and two water-use variables. Total greenhouse gas emissions (GHG total)[6] are the total Scope 1[7] and Scope 2 emissions[8] of an organization in a reporting year for the organization's country of domicile (Sotos, 2015).[9] Nitrogen oxide (NOx), sulfur dioxide (SOx), and volatile organic compounds (VOC) are three additional emissions types collected at the organization level. The two water-use variables include water withdrawal and water discharge.[10] We also collect data on carbon offsets, voluntary purchases of carbon credits, and certificates to compensate for emissions.

Exiobase

While reporting of ESG data has improved significantly over the last decade, particularly data related to environmental variables, data availability is still a concern and a challenge for empirical analysis. When data points are not available from Bloomberg or Thomson Reuters, we impute missing values using data from Exiobase. Exiobase provides a global environmentally extended multi-regional input-output table as a baseline for supply chain analysis and estimates emissions and resource extractions by industry (Schmidt et al., 2014).[11] Specifically, we utilize the factors of production tables from Exiobase. These tables are input-output tables that map inputs and outputs for a given industry in a country. We also use the total industry output table, which provides a total monetary production by industry and by country. Lastly, we use the inter-industry coefficients table, which shows inter-industry purchases to map upstream impacts, such as Scope 2 emissions from power purchases. These imputations could contain large measurement errors as they rely on several assumptions (Kotsantonis & Serafeim, 2019).

The EPS Database

The Environmental Priority Strategies (EPS) database provides a publicly available, scientifically-based methodology to transform the direct results of an organization's operations, referred to as outputs, such as emissions, into their impacts, referred to as characterization pathways. The database also provides a comprehensive set of conversions from impacts denominated in the standard terms of impact, such as quality-adjusted life years, into specific monetary values (usually $/kg emission or input) referred to as monetization factors. The impacts covered are defined as "safeguard subjects" (Steen & Palander, 2016). Each safeguard subject[12] is made up of multiple impact categories and indicators, called state indicators,[13] for measuring the current state of each safeguard subject (Life Cycle Initiative, 2016; Steen & Palander, 2016).[14] Steen and Palander (2016) provide extensive detail on the selection of the safeguard subjects and state indicators. For this paper, we work with eight safeguard subjects: Human Health (Working Capacity), Crop Production Capacity, Meat Production Capacity, Fish Production Capacity, Wood Production Capacity, Drinking Water & Irrigation Water (Water Production Capacity), Abiotic Resources, and Biodiversity.

The EPS database also provides uncertainty estimates,[15] a factor by which the median value may be multiplied or divided to find the values representing one standard deviation higher or lower values in line with guidance from the ISO. The default monetization factor methodology is based on willingness-to-pay[16] (WTP) for one indicator unit, and global variations are captured in the uncertainty factor. Absent an observable market for the good, the methodology uses several approaches including the Contingent Valuation Method[17] (CVM), and hedonic pricing[18] (Steen, 1999). The default discount rate for EPS is 0% given consideration for intergenerational equity. We conduct a sensitivity analysis of this assumption in the results section of this paper by also using a 3% discount rate.

The AWARE Model

The Availability WAter REmaining (AWARE) model provides supplemental water monetization factors, allowing us to account for the effect of local water scarcity. While many environmental impacts may have localized impacts, such as the health implications of PM 2.5 pollution, these impacts can be consistently estimated using the same characterization pathways globally, given that the pathways of impact are dictated by the laws of chemical interactions and their interactions with biological systems such as the human body.[19] However, water scarcity varies significantly among geographical locations based on resource availability, as well as agricultural, industrial, and human needs. Moreover, unlike other commodities with well-defined global markets, inter-regional transfers of water are logistically challenging and expensive.

Water consumption in one area has highly variable implications for human well-being. To better incorporate the nuances of local water scarcity and availability based on various human and ecosystem demands while also enabling comparisons at a corporate level, a more robust model is needed. EPS water monetization factors are on a global level and do not account for local scarcity. Therefore, we incorporate data from the AWARE model, which provides conversion factors for the absolute amount of available freshwater remaining in each country in terms of global-equivalent cubic meters (Lee et al., 2018). In other words, the AWARE factors represent the available water remaining per unit of surface in a given watershed relative to the world average after human and aquatic ecosystem demands have been met.[20] By integrating controls for local water scarcity, the AWARE model provides a more accurate comparison of water use across countries with different levels of water scarcity. The scaling provided by the model also allows for the use of a global price once the local water use is converted to a global-equivalent value by multiplying it with the AWARE factor.

Waterfund's Global Water Price

A key challenge in identifying the price of water is that there is often little correlation between the actual price paid and its availability (Bernick et al., 2017). A global water price is sourced from Waterfund, which has developed a comprehensive measure of water cost for 19 locations globally. The Waterfund dataset provides two broad sub-categories – water production and delivery, and wastewater treatment – each of which has components of operating expenses, depreciation, and non-operating expenses. This helps to provide a key measure of the hidden "economic costs of water," which are not properly incorporated into the price that companies pay for water. Waterfund's data does not provide an estimate for the raw cost of extracting water; however, water itself is viewed as a human right and research on this has been surprisingly sparse.[21] Even absent the raw cost of water, the Waterfund price represents a significantly more economically representative cost of water compared to the current prices in many countries.

Accounting and Stock Market Data

Financial data was collected from Worldscope and converted to USD using year-end exchange rates. In addition to using raw sales data as provided by Worldscope, we calculate return on assets (ROA), return on equity (ROE), Tobin's Q, the price-to-book value of equity, and leverage. All stock market data, such as total investment return, volatility, and market beta are also sourced from Worldscope.

Other Data

We source company name, country of domicile, and Global Industry Classification System (GICS) industries from S&P Global, Inc.

Methodology

Sample Selection

Our sample is derived from the universe of organizations within the Bloomberg ESG Index, the set of organizations within the Bloomberg database that has reported some environmental data. We collect data only for organizations with a market capitalization of greater than 100 million USD, as ESG reporting is most common in larger organizations. This restriction captures the vast majority of the Bloomberg ESG Index and produces a sample of 9,714 unique organizations. We collect data on these 9,714 organizations from 2010 to 2019, resulting in 97,140 organization-year observations. Of these 97,140 observations, only 18,202 have GHG total data from Bloomberg. By adding data from Thomson Reuters's Asset4 ESG database, we expand the quantity of the environmental data in our sample.

We note numerous instances of errors in our collected data, such as incorrectly scaled values or reported values that do not match organizations' sustainability reports. Therefore, we implement a methodology of removing obvious outliers reported by Thomson Reuters and Bloomberg. First, we observe there are a substantial number of organizations with data covered by one provider and not the other. Employing both databases, we collect data from 2010 to 2019, resulting in 24,276 organization-year observations that have data for total greenhouse gas emissions.

To minimize concerns about the quality of the environmental data, we create a methodology to attempt to confirm their accuracy. For all values within our dataset, we attempt to assess the accuracy of a value by comparing it to other values within a specific organization's time series. We hypothesize that the emissions (or water withdrawal/discharge) intensity of an organization is a function of many organization-specific factors (e.g. technology, capital expenditures, etc.) that in the short term are primarily fixed. Therefore, in the absence of mergers and acquisitions or significant changes to the dynamics of organization operations, the year-over-year change in organization emissions intensity should be moderate. We calculate a lagged variable which is the difference between the intensity value in year t and the intensity value in year $t-1$ divided by the intensity value in year $t-1$. We disregard values where year-over-year change is greater than 50% or less than −50%. However, there are reasons intensity values could experience significant year-over-year changes, such as a merger or acquisition, development of new technology, or large changes to organization operations. In order to observe if a change in intensity is sustained into future years, we create a leading value, which is the lagged year-over-year change value calculated for year $t+1$. If the lagged year-over-year variable notes a greater than 50% increase or decrease, but the leading year-over-year variable notes that the increase is sustained in the next year, we assume that some operational or technological change has occurred and, as such, assume the value that experienced a large year-over-year intensity jump or drop to be accurate.

GHG total is deemed the most financially material emission type per the EPS monetization factors. Therefore, we restrict our sample to observations that have reported GHG total data from either Bloomberg or Thomson Reuters. Restricting observations that have GHG total data produces a final sample of 24,276 organization-year observations. Table 7.1 describes summary statistics for this sample.

Table 7.1 Summary statistics of sample

	Obs.	Mean	Median	S.D.	Min	Max
GHG total	24,276	4,009,194	197,780	19,100,000	0	676,000,000
Water withdrawal	16,056	378,000,000	2,380,000	8,990,000,000	0	775,000,000,000
Water discharged	7,226	212,000,000	3,724,955	1,850,000,000	0	70,500,000,000
Water discharged (imputed)	16,263	185,000,000	1,543,031	2,320,000,000	0	215,000,000,000
SOx	6,395	32,284	221	375,625	0	18,600,000
NOx	7,223	29,918	800	344,864	0	10,100,000
VOC	3,716	520,062	330	14,300,000	0	638,000,000
Carbon offsets	2,331	1,117,707	11,000	9,055,419	0	243,000,000

Table 7.1 describes the summary statistics for our sample. All observations have non-missing values for the GHG total. Water discharged contains only data reported by Bloomberg or Thomson Reuters. For observations missing water discharged, we impute values by multiplying water withdrawal by the industry-year median water discharged-water withdrawal ratio. Water discharged (imputed) is the final variable which includes reported water discharged data and the data we impute. All emissions variables have units of metric tons. GHG total and carbon offsets are in CO_2-equivalent metric tons. Water withdrawal, water discharged, and water discharged (imputed) are in cubic meters. Observations are firm-year pairs.

Imputation of Missing Values

Of the 24,276 observations in our sample, 17,053 are missing NOx data, 20,560 are missing VOC data, 17,881 are missing SOx data, 8,220 are missing water withdrawal data, and 17,050 are missing water discharge data. We impute data for these missing values using industry-country emissions data from Exiobase (F Table – Factors of Production).

Global Industry Classification System (GICS) data is sourced from Bloomberg and mapped to our organization's reported emissions data. However, Exiobase uses the Nomenclature of Economic Activities (NACE) industry classification to define industry classifications, requiring a mapping from NACE to GICS codes.[22] To adjust the industry-level values from Exiobase to organization-level values, each Exiobase value is scaled by the ratio of organization revenue in a given year to total industry output in a given year, up to the year 2016, the latest year for Exiobase data.[23] Industry output is sourced from the Exiobase industry output dataset for the organization's domicile country as listed in Bloomberg. As with water, given the lack of information available, the domicile country for the organization is used to select the industry-level information in the Exiobase data.[24] This methodology is an attempt to estimate the missing organization-level emissions by attributing a pro-rata portion of industry totals to an organization. While imperfect, this step is necessary to provide comparability among organizations and industries, and unless otherwise disclosed, we believe it is fair to assume that organizations' production requirements are similar to the standard production requirements of a given industry within a given country.[25]

For 8,830 firm-year observations, water withdrawal data is available but water discharge data is missing. The water withdrawal and consumption data within Exiobase are specifically for companies operating in industries relating to agriculture, livestock, manufacturing, and electricity, but this is far from exhaustive. To ensure that water use is being consistently and comparably measured, we develop a method of imputing the missing data for water discharge when water withdrawal data is available. We first determine the best predictor of water discharge: The correlation of water withdrawal to water discharged is 0.8222 compared to the correlation of 0.0003 between water discharged data and sales. Thus, within a given GICS industry year, we calculate the median ratio of water discharged to water withdrawal using all firms with available water discharge and water withdrawal data. We then impute the missing water discharge for a firm by multiplying its water withdrawal with the industry-year median water discharge-water withdrawal ratio value. Net water consumed is calculated as water withdrawal less water discharged. In order to ensure the imputation process does not produce water discharge data points that create negative net water consumed values, we constrain the maximum imputed water discharge value to be no greater than the firm's water withdrawal value.

Environmental Impact of Water

The environmental impact of water is calculated using Waterfund's global average water price and AWARE factors, as opposed to EPS factors used for monetization of emissions variables. Equation 1 defines the environmental impact of water.

(1) $$\text{Environmental Impact of Water}_{i,t} = \text{Water Production \& Delivery Cost}_{i,t} + \text{Wastewater Treatment Cost}_{i,t}$$

(2) $$\text{Environmental Impact of Water}_{i,t} = \left(\text{Net Water Consumed}_{i,t} \star \text{AWARE Factor}_{j,t} \star \text{Water Production \& Delivery Unit Cost}_j\right) + \left(\text{Net Water Consumed}_{i,t} \star \text{Wastewater Treatment Unit Cost}_j\right)$$

Waterfund posits the best representation of the global average price of water is the sum of all economic costs of supplying water. Therefore, the environmental impact of water is calculated as the sum of two costs: water production and delivery and wastewater treatment. Water production and delivery costs scale by water consumption and by water scarcity. Wastewater treatment costs are not affected by water scarcity and only scale by water consumption. Equation 2 describes the breakdown of these two costs. Water production and delivery costs, for an organization i in year t, are the product of net water consumed, for an organization i in year t, the AWARE factor and the water production and delivery unit cost, both defined for country j (time-invariant factors). The AWARE factor is a measure of water scarcity, relative to a global average. Because both the AWARE factor and water production and delivery unit costs are measured at a country level, an important assumption of our model is that water is withdrawn from an organization's country of domicile. Given that many organizations have operations outside of their country of domicile, our model could be applying incorrect AWARE factors and water unit costs to net water consumption. Increased geographic granularity in water disclosure data would improve the accuracy of our model's calculations. Wastewater treatment costs, for an organization i in year t, are the product of net water consumption and the AWARE factor. Waterfund defines the wastewater processing cost as the sum of expenses incurred by water utilities to both treat the byproduct of water production and to provide specifically recycled water to organizations. Thus, we conclude that this cost component intuitively does not depend on water scarcity, so the AWARE factor is not applied to it.

Environmental Impact Calculation

To calculate the environmental impact of emissions, we multiply EPS monetary coefficients by the reported (or imputed) emissions of an organization. Equation 3 describes the calculation of the environmental impact of emissions for organization i in year t.

(3)
$$\textit{Environmental Impact of Emissions}_{i,t} = \sum \left(\textit{Emissions Volume}_{e,i,t} * \textit{EPS Monetary Coefficient}_{e} \right)$$

The environmental impact of emissions for organization i in year t is the sum of each emissions type e multiplied by the respective EPS monetary coefficient for emissions type e. Specifically, the organization's reported (or imputed) values for GHG,[26] SOx, NOx, and VOC emissions are separately multiplied by the respective EPS monetary coefficients. The resulting four products are summed to produce the environmental impact of emissions.

Finally, we calculate the environmental impact of an organization i in year t as the sum of the environmental impact of emissions and the environmental impact of water.

(4)
$$\textit{Environmental Impact}_{i,t} = \textit{Environmental Impact of Emissions}_{i,t} + \textit{Environmental Impact of Water}_{i,t}$$

Robustness of Imputations

A potential source of error in our calculated value of environmental impact stems from the use of imputed data. To understand the extent of this potential error we conduct a decomposition analysis and determine what proportion of environmental impact is being determined by data reported by Bloomberg or Thomson Reuters and what proportion is based on imputations using Exiobase data. We deconstruct environmental impact into its component pieces – each emissions type (net water consumption) multiplied by the respective EPS monetary coefficients (AWARE factors and Waterfund factors) – and calculate the percent contribution of each component to total environmental impact. Next, we determine the source of data for each environmental impact component, either reported from a data provider (Bloomberg or Thompson Reuters) or imputed using Exiobase data. For example, if VOC data is imputed for an observation, we define that observation's VOC environmental impact component as imputed. The percent contribution of all environmental impact components based on imputed data is the imputed contribution to environmental impact. For example, if VOC and SOx data are imputed and contribute 5% and 7% respectively to environmental impact, the total imputed contribution would be 12%.

To ensure the robustness and reliability of our results, we restrict our sample to observations that have less than 25% imputed contribution to environmental impact. We find the average imputed contribution is less than 10%. This restriction produces a final sample of 14,805 organization-year observations.

Discount Factor Analysis

The EPS methodology assumes a 0% discount rate for purposes of intergenerational equity. There is a strong argument against discounting, given that in the social context, the time component does not represent the creation of wealth but rather involves the re-distribution of resources between generations (Rabl, 1996). Nevertheless, discounting the impacts with a longer impact horizon causes a meaningful change in the cost of these emissions, and thus, it is important to sensitivity test the 0% discount rate.

We apply a uniform discount rate procedure over time; the long-term growth rate of the world from 1913–2012, which is approximately 3% for the sake of conservatism (Piketty & Goldhammer, 2014).[27] A key issue with this discounting methodology, aside from the intergenerational ethics, is that it assumes that impacts are spread evenly throughout the expected impact horizon when in actuality, impacts are likely clustered or more heavily weighted to the end of the horizon when the cumulative effect is highest.

To discount the EPS factors, we first modify the characterization pathway factor to isolate the yearly effect. Each characterization pathway factor is divided by the time horizon estimate. Next, the cumulative cost of the impact with discounting is calculated using a present value calculation of the EPS State Indicator Value ($/unit), the discount rate, and the time horizon. Lastly, the impact value was re-calculated by multiplying the new Environmental Impact Factor by the present value of the Indicator Value.

Results

We conduct statistical analysis of the EI outcome to better compare values across firms and explain the variability between and within different effect levels. We also map the EI results to the UN SDGs targets to better correlate these results with a broadly accepted development framework. We then analyze the correlation between EI and commonly used ESG ratings to measure the magnitude of sensitivity in terms of market, industry, and country fixed effects. Further, we address the question of whether market prices reflect environmental intensity by analyzing the correlation of EI and market pricing measures such as Tobin's Q (a measure of the market value over the replacement value of assets), price-to-book value, Sharpe ratio, stock return, and volatility. These analyses are conducted after controlling for other determinants and by including industry, country, and year-fixed effects.

Environmental Impact Statistics

To make the environmental impact a comparable value across firms, we define *environmental intensity* as environmental impact scaled by sales or operating income. Figure 7.1 shows the distribution of the sample's environmental intensity. The average intensity value scaled by sales, when the discount rate is zero, stands at 11.8%. The median is much lower than the mean at 2.0% and the third quartile of the distribution at 9.4%. This means that a minority of firms have very large values bringing the average up, as depicted in Figure 7.1. As expected, environmental

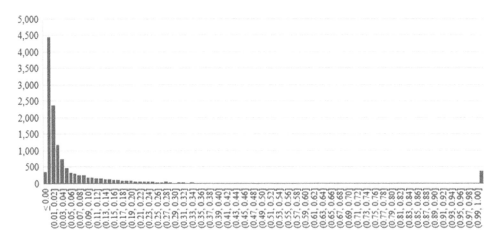

Figure 7.1 Distribution of environmental intensity (sales, discount rate of 0%)

intensity is lower when the discount rate is 3%. The average stands at 5.4% with a median of 0.8% and the third quartile at 4.0%.

The environmental intensity values scaled by operating income demonstrate even greater variability, as demonstrated in Figure 7.2. The average intensity, when the discount rate is zero, is 117.4%, with a median of 21.5% and the third quartile of the distribution at 92.1%. Therefore, similar to the environmental intensity scaled by sales, a small number of firms with large values pull the average up. The environmental intensity scaled by operating income is also lower when the discount rate is 3%. The average stands at 62.2% with the median of 8.8% and the third quartile at 39.2%.

The vertical axis of Figure 7.1 displays the number of firm-year observations that belong to each bin of the histogram. Each bin width is 0.01, representing environmental intensity (scaled by sales) of 1%.

The vertical axis of Figure 7.2 displays the number of firm-year observations that belong to each bin of the histogram. Each bin width is 0.1, representing environmental intensity (scaled by operating income) of 10%

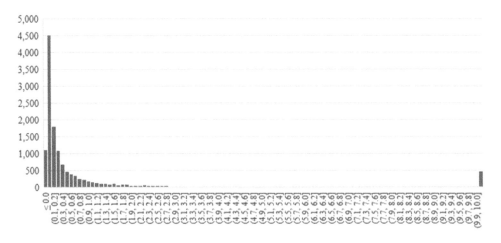

Figure 7.2 Distribution of environmental intensity (operating income, discount rate of 0%)

Table 7.2 Sources of variation in environmental intensity

Environmental Intensity	Year effects	+ Industry Effects	+ Industry, Country Effects	+ Country Effects	+ Subindustry, Country Effects
Env Imp/Sales 0%	0.12%	60.97%	66.52%	11.22%	71.55%
Env Imp/Op Inc 0%	−0.01%	55.74%	61.04%	11.10%	65.92%

Table 7.2 shows the estimated adjusted R-squared, a measure of the explanatory power of the independent variables, from five different models where the environmental intensity is the dependent variable. We discuss only the results for the intensity scaled by sales as scaling by operating income yields similar inferences. The results are practically identical for the 3% discount rate, so for the sake of brevity, we show only the 0% discount rate analysis. The first model only includes year-fixed effects. The explanatory power of the model is less than 1%, suggesting that environmental intensity for the sample has not changed systematically across the years. The second model adds industry effects using the GICS classification. The explanatory power jumps to about 61%, suggesting that industry membership is a major determinant of variation in environmental intensity across companies. Adding in country effects in the third model raises the explanatory power to about 67%, suggesting that country membership also explains some of the variations, but the percentage is small relative to industry membership. The fourth model removes industry effects to understand if the limited explanatory power from country effects is only because we first included industry effects. This is not the case as the explanatory power of the model declines to about 11%, far below that of the industry effects model which stands at roughly 61%. The last model replaces industry with subindustry effects. The explanatory power increases from 67% to 72%, suggesting that even within industries, environmental intensity varies across subindustries, but the increase in power is less pronounced. Moreover, given that we have 155 subindustries (instead of 67 industries), the number of firms within many subindustries is limited, leading some of the subindustry fixed effects to serve a similar function as firm fixed effects. Therefore, for the rest of the paper, we focus our attention on industries rather than subindustries.

Table 7.2 describes the adjusted R-squared of an OLS model that regresses a variety of fixed effects on environmental intensity as the dependent variable. Environmental intensity is created from the 0% discount rate. All models include year-fixed effects. Column 1 only controls for year-fixed effects. Column 2 adds industry effects. Column 3 adds industry and country effects. Column 4 adds only country effects. Column 5 adds subindustry and country effects.

Our findings above, which point to the importance of industry in driving environmental intensity, lead us to further investigate how industry-specific distributions of environmental impact differ. Figure 7.3 helps visualize the average, as well as the ratio between the first and third quartiles for environmental intensity, for each industry. Both axes are log-transformed to aid in visually inspecting the relative positioning of industries given that some industries have orders of magnitude larger environmental intensity than others. Not surprisingly, industries in the utility sector and resources (metals and mining, as well as oil and gas) score very high. Construction materials, airlines, paper, forest products, and chemicals are other industries with very high environmental intensity. Perhaps more surprising is the large variation across companies within the same industry. The differences between first- and third-quartile statistics are informative here. For example, in metals and mining, the firm in the third quartile has an environmental intensity of more than four times the firm in the first quartile. In an industry where asset mix and business lines are even more homogeneous,

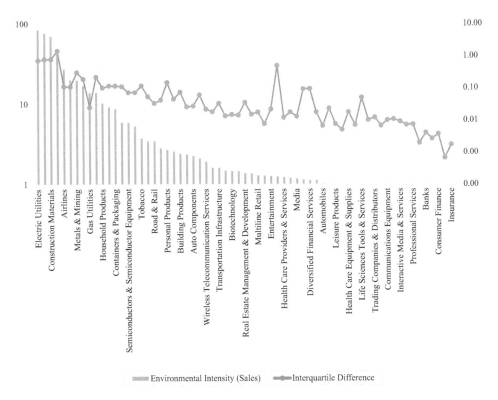

Figure 7.3 Environmental intensity (sales) by industry

such as airlines, we still observe a sizeable spread of 32% versus 21% in the third and first quartiles respectively.[28]

The graphic comparison of industry-specific distributions of median environmental intensity values scaled by sales and operating income points to another interesting note: Figures 7.3 and 7.4 demonstrate which industries tend to have lower profit margins than others, as environmental intensity values scaled by operating income for some industries are affected much more severely than they are when scaled by revenue. For instance, the air freight and logistics industry shows a clear distinction between the two environmental intensity values when it is calculated on a profit basis as opposed to revenue basis. Despite having a relatively low median environmental intensity value of 1.5% when scaled by sales, the median intensity value of the air freight and logistics industry spikes up to 27.6% when scaled by profit. Likewise, other industries with low-profit margins such as construction and engineering, food and staples retailing, and automobiles display an analogous trend.

As expected, in most cases, the distribution of environmental intensity shifts lower when the discount rate is set at 3%. However, the degree of the change is not uniform across industries, as the effect of the discount rate is different across environmental impacts, and therefore, the overall effect depends on the composition of impacts across different industries. In general, industries in which carbon emissions dominate their environmental impact composition would experience a sharper decrease in environmental intensity after applying the 3% discount rate. In contrast, environmental impacts from water withdrawals and other emissions are impacted less as their impacts are both short-term and long-term. Using SOx as an example, the effect on human health from secondary particles and direct exposure is estimated over the next year, while for the climate change pathways, it accumulates over 85 years according to EPS.

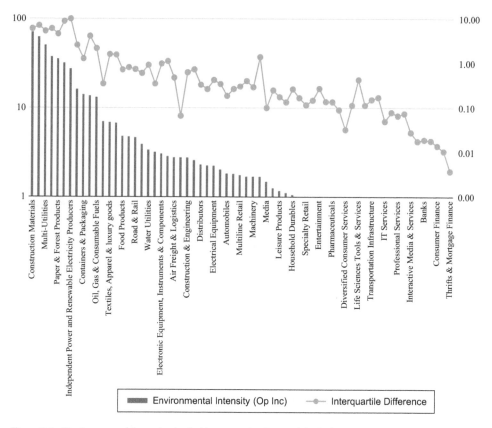

Figure 7.4 Environmental intensity (scaled by operating income) by industry

Figure 7.3 graphs the distribution of environmental intensity by GICS industries. Environmental Intensity (Sales) indicates log-transformed environmental intensity scaled by sales. Interquartile Difference is the log-transformed difference between the third and first quartile of the distribution of environmental intensity across firm-year observations in each industry.

Figure 7.4 graphs the distribution of environmental intensity (scaled by operating income) by GICS industries. Environmental Intensity (Op Inc) indicates log-transformed environmental intensity scaled by operating income. Interquartile Difference highlights the log-transformed difference between the third and first quartile of the distribution of environmental intensity scaled by operating income across firm-year observations in each industry.

Sustainable Development Goals

Utilizing the characterization pathways, safeguard subjects, and monetary conversion factors from the EPS database as previously mentioned, we also delineate each emission's impacts in terms of the United Nations Sustainable Development Goals (SDGs). In total, we map each emission's characterization pathways to 17 relevant SDG targets.[29] Figures 7.5 and 7.6 depict the relative allocation of our sample's environmental impact to each SDG target for 0% and 3% discount rates respectively. We discover that the vast majority of corporate environmental impact is tied to four main SDG targets: SDG 1.5, which relates to poverty, SDG 2.1 and SDG 2.2, both of which concern ending hunger and malnutrition, and SDG 6, which relates to clean

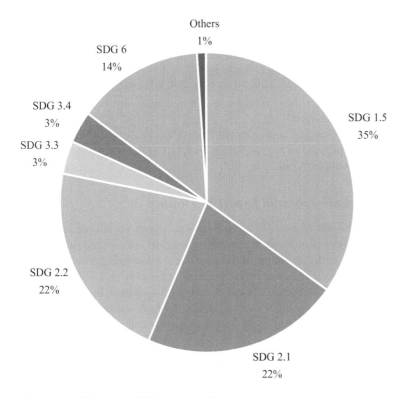

Figure 7.5 SDG targets (0% discount rate)

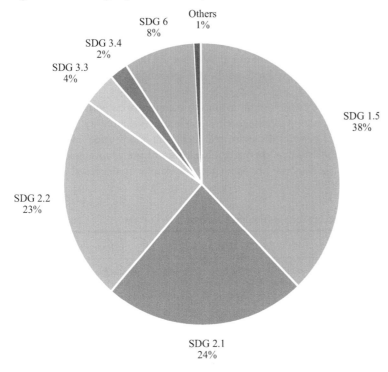

Figure 7.6 SDG targets (3% discount rate)

water and sanitation. As demonstrated by the graphic differences in the relative proportion of impacts that belong to each SDG target under 0% and 3% discount rates, we note once again that discount rates affect each emission's environmental impact differently, thereby resulting in an asymmetrical degree of changes across the SDG targets.

We delineate each emission's impacts in terms of the United Nations Sustainable Development Goals (SDGs). This figure depicts the relative allocation of our sample's environmental impact to each SDG target for 0% discount rates.

We delineate each emission's impacts in terms of the United Nations Sustainable Development Goals (SDGs). This figure depicts the relative allocation of our sample's environmental impact to each SDG target for the 3% discount rate.

Environmental Impact and Ratings

Next, we seek to understand the relationship between our calculated environmental intensity and widely used ratings that intend to measure how well a company is managing environment-related risks and opportunities. To do so, we obtain data from three rating providers: MSCI, RobecoSAM, and Sustainalytics. For Sustainalytics, we have access only to US data, while for the other two providers, our sample includes both US and non-US firms. Given RobecoSAM coverage is more limited than the two providers, we obtain the largest sample for MSCI. The relation between the natural logarithm of environmental intensity and the ratings is negative, consistent with the idea that firms that have greater adverse environmental intensity receive lower ratings.[30] But the correlations are moderate, ranging from −0.13 to −0.26.

Environmental intensity values scaled by sales and operating income calculated using 0% and 3% discount rates have a correlation of 0.98, and as a result, correlations with the environmental ratings are extremely similar. When we examine the univariate correlations separately for each industry, the two environmental intensity estimates under the two discount rate scenarios are very highly correlated. The lowest correlation is 0.80 in the paper and forest products industry. In all other industries, the correlation values are above 0.90, with 57 out of 67 industries above 0.95. Given this finding, for the remainder of our analysis, we use the 0% discount rate estimate and identify any differences in results when using the 3% discount rate to simplify the exposition of the paper.[31]

Given that investors and analysts also use the ratings to compare firms within industries, we are interested in understanding how well ratings reflect environmental intensity (scaled by sales) within each industry. Table 7.3 presents the estimated coefficient and p-value on the environmental rating variable for models where the natural logarithm of the environmental intensity is the dependent variable. The first row presents estimates from a model based on variation

Table 7.3 Estimates of correlation between environmental intensity and ratings

Independent Variable	E Rating M		E Rating RS		E Rating S	
Specification	Coeff.	p-value	Coeff.	p-value	Coeff.	p-value
Across market	−0.151	0.000	−0.071	0.000	−0.328	0.000
Within industry, country	−0.052	0.000	−0.003	0.719	−0.039	0.183
Reduction in coefficient	65%		96%		88%	

across the whole market, while the second model includes industry and country fixed effects, thereby estimating the coefficient based on within-industry and country variation. The coefficients decline sharply, suggesting that the ratings are not differentiating across firms within an industry on the impact dimension. Moreover, they lose statistical significance. The only exception is the MSCI rating, which still exhibits a significant coefficient, but its magnitude has now decreased by 65%.

Table 7.3 describes the OLS results of regressing environmental ratings on environmental intensity scaled by sales for a 0% discount rate. MSCI, RobescoSAM, and Sustainalytics environmental ratings are included as independent variables in separate models. The dependent variable is the natural logarithm of environmental intensity. The second specification introduces controls for industry and country fixed effects. Observations are firm-year pairs for the years 2010–2018.

The results above provide, on average, evidence across many industries. Whether ratings reflect intensity might differ across industries. A few observations are worth highlighting. First, there is a large variation across industries. For example, both MSCI and RobecoSAM ratings exhibit large negative correlations with some industries of the utilities sector. However, for industries such as household durables and real estate development, the correlation is very low or even positive. Second, the industries with the highest correlation differ across rating providers. While for construction materials there is a sizeable negative correlation for Sustainalytics, the correlation is positive for RobecoSAM.[32]

Our overall conclusion is that although ratings may well provide important insights into how different firms attempt to manage environmental risks and opportunities, they are unlikely to provide insights into the impact that an organization has on the environment, and therefore, users should use them with caution in selecting and managing investment products marketed as providing impact.

Financial Materiality of Environmental Intensity

Do market prices reflect environmental intensity? If investors believe that larger environmental intensity might be a risk for the company, because of regulatory, customer, or investor future actions, then all else equal, firms with larger negative environmental intensity would trade at lower valuation multiples. Past literature has provided support to this idea by demonstrating empirical linkage to environmental performance and valuation.[33] Furthermore, even if market prices do not reflect environmental intensity, we are interested in understanding whether our measure provides a financially material signal for financial risk and return. We note that we do not attempt to make a causal claim here that the environmental impact of a firm is necessarily the reason why we observe differences in risk and return. Rather, we are asking the question of whether environmental intensity provides a meaningful signal of corporate valuation.

Table 7.4 shows that the environmental intensity scaled by sales is negatively correlated with both Tobin's Q and the price-to-book value of equity ratios.[34] This is after controlling for other determinants of valuation ratios, such as return on assets, leverage, firm size, capital expenditures, R&D expenditures, and dividends divided by sales.[35] All models include industry, country, and year-fixed effects. Both the dependent variables and the environmental impact variables are log-transformed to mitigate skewness. The estimates suggest that a firm with twice the environmental intensity scaled by sales has 2.4% lower Tobin's Q and 5.2% lower price-to-book value of equity. In terms of the environmental intensity scaled by operating income, a firm with twice the intensity value has 0.3% (2.0%) lower Tobin's Q (price-to-book value of equity).

Table 7.4 Market pricing of environmental intensity

Dependent Variable	Tobin's Q				Price-to-Book Value of Equity			
Parameter	Estimate	p-value	Estimate	p-value	Estimate	p-value	Estimate	p-value
Intercept	0.336	0.005	0.188	0.100	0.048	0.839	−0.191	0.427
Env Imp/Sales 0%	−0.024	0.000			−0.052	0.000		
Env Imp/Op Inc 0%			−0.003	0.500			−0.020	0.021
ROA	4.128	0.000	4.717	0.000	6.172	0.000	6.797	0.000
Leverage	0.119	0.000	0.089	0.006	0.953	0.000	0.959	0.000
CapEx/Sales	0.487	0.000	0.411	0.000	0.882	0.000	0.765	0.000
R&D/Sales	1.688	0.000	1.537	0.000	2.415	0.000	2.100	0.000
Dividend/Sales	0.342	0.000	0.322	0.000	0.767	0.000	0.692	0.000
Sales	−0.016	0.000	−0.009	0.032	−0.003	0.732	0.011	0.195

Table 7.4 describes OLS models that regress the independent variable environmental intensity on dependent variables: Tobin's Q and price-to-book value of equity. Tobin's Q is a measure of market value over the replacement value of assets. ROA is return on assets. All models include year, country, and industry effects. Both dependent variables and the environmental intensity variables are log-transformed. N is the number of observations. Observations are firm-year pairs.

Table 7.5 examines the dynamic materiality of environmental intensity in relation to Tobin's Q and the price-to-book value of equity. We note that the materiality of environmental intensity increases over time, as demonstrated by the negative and significant interaction terms (DM) in relation to both Tobin's Q and the price-to-book value of equity. DM is the interaction term between the environmental intensity and a time trend variable that takes the value of zero in 2010 and increases by one for each subsequent year. In other words, the negative association between environmental intensity and market valuation has become more sizable in recent years.

Table 7.5 Dynamic materiality of environmental intensity

	Tobin's Q				Price-to-Book Value of Equity			
Parameter	Estimate	p-value	Estimate	p-value	Estimate	p-value	Estimate	p-value
Intercept	0.302	0.011	0.188	0.100	−0.013	0.956	−0.192	0.424
Env Imp/Sales 0%	−0.006	0.434			−0.019	0.219		
DM (Env Imp/Sales)	−0.003	0.000			−0.006	0.000		
Env Imp/Op Inc 0%			0.011	0.033			0.003	0.779
DM (Env Imp/Op Inc)			−0.003	0.000			−0.004	0.000
ROA	4.129	0.000	4.726	0.000	6.174	0.000	6.814	0.000
Leverage	0.120	0.000	0.088	0.006	0.955	0.000	0.959	0.000
CapEx/Assets	0.478	0.000	0.402	0.000	0.866	0.000	0.751	0.000
R&D/Sales	1.685	0.000	1.541	0.000	2.410	0.000	2.105	0.000
Dividend/Sales	0.340	0.000	0.311	0.000	0.764	0.000	0.674	0.000
Sales	−0.016	0.000	−0.009	0.026	−0.003	0.708	0.010	0.221

Table 7.6 Returns, risk, and environmental intensity

Dependent Variable	Sharpe Ratio		Stock Return		Volatility	
Parameter	Estimate	p-value	Estimate	p-value	Estimate	p-value
Panel A						
Intercept	0.230	0.293	20.001	0.003	55.478	0.000
Env Imp/Sales 0%	−0.016	0.234	−0.199	0.636	0.318	0.043
ROA	3.534	0.000	101.533	0.000	−11.536	0.000
Leverage	−0.297	0.000	−6.426	0.007	4.450	0.000
CapEx/Sales	−0.167	0.715	5.273	0.750	6.167	0.017
R&D/Sales	0.333	0.223	12.790	0.430	−4.407	0.188
Dividend/Sales	−0.410	0.029	−33.705	0.000	−22.594	0.000
Sales	0.007	0.383	−0.722	0.004	−1.517	0.000
Panel B						
Intercept	0.267	0.243	22.607	0.001	51.709	0.000
Env Imp/Op Inc 0%	−0.045	0.000	−0.822	0.004	0.613	0.000
ROA	2.807	0.000	84.292	0.000	0.293	0.902
Leverage	−0.247	0.002	−4.362	0.090	3.830	0.000
CapEx/Sales	−0.579	0.031	−12.900	0.182	5.881	0.027
R&D/Sales	0.780	0.043	16.919	0.184	−5.496	0.199
Dividend/Sales	−0.445	0.026	−35.325	0.000	−22.246	0.000
Sales	0.005	0.581	−0.861	0.001	−1.404	0.000

The same conclusion holds true for environmental intensity scaled by operating income as shown by the negative and statistically significant interaction terms.

Table 7.5 describes OLS models that regress independent variables listed in the parameter column on dependent variables: Tobin's Q and price-to-book value of equity. ROA is return on assets. All models include year, country, and industry effects.

Table 7.6 presents estimated coefficients on environmental intensity, examining the intensity value's relation with the Sharpe ratio (i.e. stock return over volatility) and its components. Panel A (B) scales environmental impact by sales (operating income). The key insights are as follows. First, environmental intensity is negatively, yet insignificantly related to the Sharpe ratio. This relation is driven by both the numerator and the denominator. More environmentally intensive firms have lower stock returns and higher volatility. Environmental intensity scaled by operating income is more strongly and significantly associated with these financial characteristics.

Table 7.6 describes OLS models that regress independent variable log-transformed environmental intensity on dependent variables: Sharpe ratio, stock return, and stock price volatility. Sharpe ratio is defined as stock return over the calendar year divided by stock price volatility over the calendar year. All models also include year, industry, and country fixed effects. Specifications for the environmental intensity calculated using a 0% discount rate are included.

Figure 7.7 shows the estimated coefficient on the environmental intensity from industry-specific models.[36] Figure 7.8 explores the dynamic materiality of environmental intensity across industries. We note that both figures are produced using a more comprehensive sample that includes firm-year observations with up to 50% of imputed contribution to environmental impact instead of the usual 25% to increase the number of observations and as a result, the statistical power of the test given these industry-specific models use a much smaller number of observations. We show only the industries for which the coefficient on environmental intensity

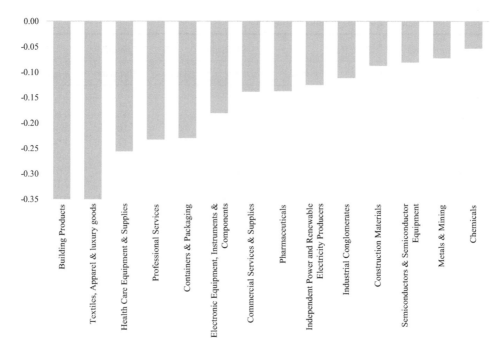

Figure 7.7 Market pricing and environmental intensity by industry

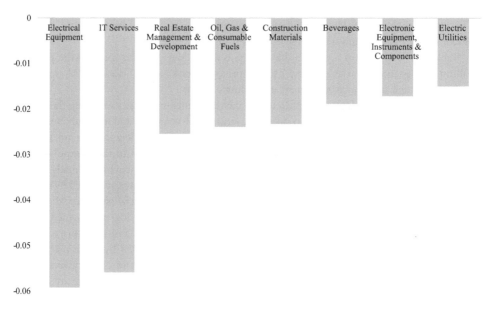

Figure 7.8 Dynamic materiality of environmental intensity by industry (Capital markets industry's dynamic materiality coefficient, though not shown in Figure 7.8, is also statistically significant and very negatively influencing the scale of the chart and thereby omitted from the chart. While there are nine industries that have seen significant increase in materiality, there are only two industries exhibiting significant decrease in materiality: health care equipment and supplies, and household durables.)

is significant. We use Env Impact/Sales 0% variable to represent environmental intensity, in this case, to avoid reporting overload from using all environmental impact estimates, but the results are qualitatively similar using the other variables. We are interested in understanding which industries' prices reflect the environmental impact, as well as how the materiality of environmental intensity has varied over time across industries.

A few interesting observations emerge from this analysis. For most industries, we find that environmental intensity is associated with lower market valuation. However, while environmental intensity is priced in several industries with large environmental impacts such as construction materials or chemicals, it is notably not reflected in some other industries with similarly large and visible environmental impacts, such as those in the utilities sector.[37] A potential explanation is that the industry-level business model is overwhelming any firm-level differences within those industries, leading to no differential pricing of environmental intensity across firms. However, this has changed over time.

Figure 7.8 shows that environmental intensity is becoming increasingly material in recent years for several industries with large environmental impacts including electric utilities, construction materials, and oil industries. Interestingly, however, the materiality of environmental intensity has also noticeably grown in industries that are not traditionally associated with large environmental impacts, such as IT services.

Figure 7.7 shows the estimated coefficient on the environmental intensity from industry-specific models. We show only the industries for which the coefficient on environmental intensity is significant.

Figure 7.8 explores the dynamic materiality of environmental intensity across industries. We show only the industries for which the coefficient on environmental intensity is significant. This shows that environmental intensity is becoming increasingly material in recent years for several industries with large environmental impacts including electric utilities, construction materials, and oil industries. Interestingly, however, the materiality of environmental intensity has also noticeably grown in industries that are not traditionally associated with large environmental impacts, such as IT services.

Discussion

Our paper proposes a methodology whereby investors, companies, or regulators may use established environmental resources, reasonably accessible in the public domain,[38] to measure an organization's environmental impact from operations. We find the median environmental impact as a percentage of an organization's sales (operating income) is close to 2% (22%) and above 10% (100%) in 11 out of 67 industries, suggesting a significant level of 'hidden liabilities' and potential for value erosion if environmental impacts are priced. Our environmental impact monetization methodology differentiates between industry effects and company-specific effects under both a 0% and 3% discount rate. We find that roughly 60% (56%) of the variation in environmental impact scaled by sales (operating income) is driven by industry membership, while approximately 28% (44%) can be attributed to firm-specific factors, with the remaining variation driven by country and more granular industry classifications. The within-industry variation suggests a significant potential to improve environmental impact by diffusing practices from industry leaders to industry laggards.

We further find that our calculated environmental intensity exhibits a negative, yet moderate correlation to the ratings of three widely used environmental ratings providers, consistent with firms that have greater adverse environmental impact receiving lower ratings. However, we find that our estimates of environmental intensity contain information different from that in environmental ratings, especially when comparing firms within industries. This makes sense given that ratings providers are not necessarily measuring impact. Rather, they intend to integrate multiple signals of how well a company is managing environment-related risks and opportunities.

Regarding the question of whether the calculated environmental intensity is reflected in market prices, we find a negative correlation of environmental intensity with both Tobin's Q and price-to-book equity valuation for the full universe of companies examined, consistent with earlier work in the space that examined the correlation between environmental pollution and market valuation (Konar & Cohen, 2001). The estimates suggest that a firm with double the environmental intensity scaled by sales (operating income) has 2.4% (0.3%) lower Tobin's Q and 5.2% (2.0%) lower price-to-book value of equity. Further, we find that environmental intensity has become increasingly financially material over time across industries.

Additionally, regarding the question of whether our environmental intensity measure provides a meaningful signal of financial risk and return, we find that firms with higher environmental intensity have lower stock returns and higher volatility. The results are more prominent and significant when we examine the relationship between environmental intensity scaled by operating income and the financial risk and return measures.

A final interesting finding emerges when we examine the relationship between environmental intensity and market pricing by industry. As expected, environmental intensity is associated with a lower market valuation for several industries with large environmental impacts, such as construction materials and chemicals. However, it is not significantly associated in several industries, suggesting the lack of regulatory or market forces making environmental impact value relevant. We note that the materiality of environmental intensity has increased in industries with large environmental impacts, such as oil, electric utilities, and construction materials.

Conclusion

Several objections may arise from the methodological choices of this study. Best practices for life cycle analysis (LCA) indicate that environmental impacts are highly localized and dependent on local environmental and population dynamics (PricewaterhouseCoopers, 2015). Further, the use of global monetization coefficients ignores local burdens of environmental degradation and disease. In an ideal scenario, investors have complete access to the environmental footprint of an organization and its supply chain, including local resource extraction, emissions, and emission height, which could use leading environmental models to determine the exact populations and resources at risk. However, the realities of corporate disclosure are far from this ideal state.

The second caveat to our results is that we measure only environmental intensity from the operations of the firm. Therefore, we are not measuring any downstream impacts from the use of products and upstream impacts from the organization's supply chain. For example, in the case of GHG, those would be included in Scope 3. There are very few organizations that report Scope 3 emissions. Moreover, there is no consensus currently as to what should and should not be included in Scope 3 emissions. In terms of the other emissions and water data, we are not aware of any that disclose those for upstream and downstream impact. Therefore, extending the scope of measurement for environmental impact in a scalable way that applies to thousands of organizations, as in our study, and is fit for purpose for large-scale statistical analysis, is not feasible at this time.

A final objection relates to reporting and selection bias in the sample in which only companies with better metrics are reporting results. This objection intuitively makes sense, and this is why the methodology proposes to use estimates of industry factors of production rather than simply zeros for those factors to deal with the disclosure problem. As regulations mandate the disclosure of environmental impacts, future research could revisit these estimates.

Notes

1 Impact is defined as a change in one or more dimensions of people's well-being directly or through a change in the condition of the natural environment.
2 Characterization pathways are scientifically-based methodologies to transform outputs into impacts, also referred to in other literature as impact pathways.
3 Provide conversions from impacts denominated in the standard terms of impact, such as quality-adjusted life years, into monetary values (usually $/kg emission or input).
4 Outputs are the direct results of an organization's activities, including products, pathways, services, by-products.
5 A measure of the efficiency of resource use or emissions (e.g. water, energy, materials) needed for the production, processing, and disposal of a unit of good or service, or for the completion of a process or activity; it is expressed in this analysis as a unit under analysis/revenue or operating income.
6 A Bloomberg data point which includes Scope 1 and Scope 2 emissions (see below) of the seven gases covered by the UNFCCC: carbon dioxide (CO_2); methane (CH4); nitrous oxide (N2O); hydrofluorocarbons (HFCs); perfluorocarbons (PFCs); sulfur hexafluoride (SF6), and nitrogen trifluoride (NF3).
7 Defined by the GHG Protocol as direct emissions that occur from sources owned or controlled by the company.
8 Defined by the GHG Protocol indirect emissions from the generation of purchased energy including the emissions resulting from the production of grid electricity.
9 Greenhouse gases are defined by the GHG Protocol as the seven gases covered by the UNFCCC: carbon dioxide (CO_2); methane (CH4); nitrous oxide (N2O); hydrofluorocarbons (HFCs); perfluorocarbons (PFCs); sulfur hexafluoride (SF6), and nitrogen trifluoride (NF3).
10 Water withdrawal is the total amount of water diverted from any source for use by the organization. Water discharge refers to the total amount of liquid waste and process water discharged by the organization. We define net water consumed as water withdrawal minus water discharged.
11 Exiobase provides data from 44 countries and 5 world regions, as well as 164 industries, 417 emission categories, and over 1,000 emission, material, and resources categories. Exiobase tables were accessed through the Pymrio Python Package on Github. Industry factors of production were sourced from the F Table of Exiobase, industry output was sourced from the X Table, and inter-industry coefficients (direct requirements matrix) were sourced from the A Table.
12 Resources that are critical for human health and well-being. Each safeguard subject is made up of multiple impact categories.
13 Indicators which provide a measure of the current state of each safeguard subject.
14 These broadly align with the end-point indicators in the UN Life Cycle Impact Analysis Indicators (UN LCIA) and the International Organization for Standardization (ISO), a recognized international multi-stakeholder standard-setting organization, 14000 series, though there are some differences.
15 A factor by which the median value may be multiplied or divided to find the values representing one standard deviation higher or lower values.
16 A monetary measure for the willingness to restore changes in the safeguard subjects. The WTP in the EPS is measured in today's OECD population and applied to all those who are affected by a change.
17 In contingent valuation, the good to be valued is presented in its entirety (as a bundle of its attributes). The respondents are asked for their WTP to avoid a deterioration in the quality or quantity of the good or to secure an improvement. Alternatively, they are asked for their WTA to tolerate a deterioration or to forgo an improvement. For more information see ISO 14008 Protocol.
18 The starting point for the hedonic pricing method is the observation that market goods have different attributes, each of which influences the price of the good to a greater or lesser extent. The hedonic pricing method uses statistical methods to isolate the implicit "price" of each of these characteristics. For more information see ISO 14008 Protocol.

19 This is not to ignore that some of the impacts, such as the health impact from air-pollution, are very local, however, given the ubiquity of laws of chemistry and the known ranges of biological systems, the same pathway can be used to estimate even local impacts around the world.

20 AWARE Factors are conversion factors for the absolute amount of available freshwater remaining in each country in terms of global-equivalent cubic meters, defined as the world average after human and aquatic ecosystem demands have been met.

21 Turner et al. (2019) estimated the 2017 global price of groundwater to be on average $0.096/m^3, however, this does not include estimates for surface water cost or other high capital costs of the required infrastructure for abstracting, transferring, storing, and treating water. Moreover, the percentages of water sourced from groundwater versus surface water are neither consistent across different water utility agencies nor readily quantified by them.

22 NACE industries are converted to International Standard Industrial Classification Revision 3.1 (ISIC) classifications and then to ISIC 4 using concordance tables from the United Nations, available at https://unstats.un.org/unsd/classifications/econ/ (Schmidt et al. (2014)). These are then mapped to the 2012 North American Industry Classification System (NAICS) using a concordance table from the United States Census Bureau, available at www.census.gov/eos/www/naics/concordances/concordances.html. Lastly, these are mapped to GICS codes from Bloomberg, available at https://sites.google.com/site/alisonweingarden/links/industries. For those that do not match directly, GICS sub-industry codes are hand mapped to NAICS codes.

23 Where the industry revenue was not quantified by Exiobase, as was the case for a small minority of industries given data availability, the above-described pro-rata allocation methodology was not done to the inputs from the Factors of Production table. Instead, the full industry-level factors of production were used, which is equivalent to multiplying by 100% instead of some percentage of company-level revenue to industry output. This occurs in 8,120 out of 71,883 industry-country observations.

24 Review of the Exiobase and economic activity calculation methodology suggests that the challenge of attributing economic activities by domicile is a pervasive issue. The Exiobase uses GDP among its macro inputs for the estimation of economic activity in a region. Guidance from the OECD indicates that foreign subsidiaries of a multi-national organization should be treated as residents in their countries of location rather than in the countries of their parent organization. However, artificial transfer pricing, tax incentives, transfer of intellectual property, consolidated accounting, reporting, and billing practices, among others, can result in a difference between where transactions are reported and where they actually occur (Landefeld et al. 2011). This calls into question the use of the domicile country to select Exiobase industry factors. However, the relatively small contribution of country-level effects, as we document in the paper, indicates that this does not play a substantial role in our sample, given the restriction on the maximum allowable level of the environmental impact valuation derived from the imputation methodology.

25 There are some challenges associated with using organization-level revenue. Organizational revenue can be distorted by complex tax structures that seek to domicile profits in low-tax jurisdictions. Further, this can impact the calculation of national accounts which are used as a key source of reconciling this Exiobase data (Lequiller and Blades 2014).

26 GHG emissions are reduced by carbon offsets.

27 This differs from Rabl's two-part discounting procedure, in which the conventional discount rate is used for the horizon t_{short} (about 30 years) and t_{long} uses the long-term growth rate of the economy, in terms of GNP per capita.

28 The large spread in the airfreight and logistics industry is driven by a few observations having very high water withdrawal numbers while most of the industry has relatively high nitrous oxide, which reduces the global warming potential of the other emissions.

29 More details about SDG targets can also be found on the official UN website: https://sdgs.un.org/goals.

30 We log transform the environmental intensity to decrease the skewness of the distribution that we documented in the Section on Environmental Impact Statistics.

31 The correlation between the environmental ratings are also moderate in the range of 0.31 to 0.46 consistent with the findings of other studies (Christensen, Serafeim, and Sikochi 2019; Berg, Kolbel, and Rigobon 2019).

32 Using the 3% discount rate environmental intensity, we find the following meaningful differences across estimates: we define meaningful as the correlation coefficient moving by more than 0.1 in either direction (the correlation coefficient ranges from −1 to +1). For the MSCI rating, the correlation becomes more negative for automobiles and multi-utilities. For the RobecoSAM rating, the correla-

tion becomes more negative for automobiles and less negative for Equity REITS and Specialty Retail. For the Sustainalytics rating, the correlation becomes more negative for road and rail, and pharmaceuticals, and less negative for banks, independent power producers, and Equity REITS.

33 Matsumura et al. (2014) find that every additional thousand metric tons of carbon emissions decrease the firm value by $212,000 on average pricing of carbon emissions, and Konar and Cohen (2001) find that a 10% reduction in toxic chemical releases added $34.1 million to intangible firm value.

34 Firms with a negative book value of equity are excluded from the model where the price to book value of equity is the dependent variable.

35 Leverage is measured as one minus the ratio of book value of equity over total assets. Firm size is measured as the log transformed firm sales. Capital expenditures are scaled by total assets since they are recognized as assets. R&D expenditures, as a flow variable, are scaled by sales. Dividends, as a flow variable, are scaled by sales.

36 To ensure more robust estimates, we only include estimates for industries that have at least 20 degrees of freedom and are statistically significant.

37 While there are 14 industries that exhibit a negative and significant association between environmental intensity and market valuation, there is only one industry that exhibits a positive and significant association: construction and engineering.

38 Not all resources are free; however, we consider them to be in the public domain given either strong current use among investors (as in the case of Bloomberg and Thomson Reuters) or accessible cost (such as the Environmental Priority Strategies).

References

Berg, F., Koelbel, J. F., & Rigobon, R. (2019, August). *Aggregate confusion: The divergence of ESG ratings* (MIT Sloan Research Paper No. 5822-19). http://doi.org/10.2139/ssrn.3438533

Bernick, L., Bullock, S., Burks, B., Chlebeck, E., Hobson, D., & Tenuta, E. (2017). *Smart water management for business growth: Integrating water risk into business decision making*. Ecolab Water Risk Monetizer. https://about.smartwaternavigator.com/wp-content/uploads/2019/12/2019-WRM-Methodology.12-11.2019.pdf

Bexell, M., & Jönsson, K. (2016). Responsibility and the United Nations' sustainable development goals. *Forum for Development Studies*, 44(1), 13–29. http://doi.org/10.1080/08039410.2016.1252424

Christensen, D. S., Serafeim, G., & Sikochi, A. (2019). Why is corporate virtue in the eye of the beholder? The case of ESG ratings. Harvard Business School (No. 20-084). Working paper.

Dauvergne, P., & Lister, J. (2012). Big brand sustainability: Governance prospects and environmental limits. *Global Environmental Change*, 22(1), 36–45. http://doi.org/10.1016/j.gloenvcha.2011.10.007

Konar, S., & Cohen, M. A. (2001). Does the market value environmental performance? *Review of Economics and Statistics*, 83(2), 281–289. https://doi.org/10.1162/00346530151143815

Kotsantonis, S., & Serafeim, G. (2019). Four things no one will tell you about ESG data. *Journal of Applied Corporate Finance*, 31(2), 50–58. https://doi.org/10.1111/jacf.12346

Landefeld, J. S., Moulton, B., & Whichard, O. (2011). Multinational enterprises and the allocation of output and value-added to national economies. United Nations Economic Commission for Europe. https://unstats.un.org/unsd/trade/events/2014/mexico/documents/session2/UNECE%20-%20Handbook%20on%20Impact%20of%20globalization%20on%20national%20accounts.pdf

Lee, J. S., Lee, M. H., Chun, Y. Y., & Lee, K. M. (2018). Uncertainty analysis of the water scarcity footprint based on the AWARE model considering temporal variations. *Water*, 10(3), 341. https://doi.org/10.3390/w10030341

Lee, J., Veloso, F., Hounshell, D., & Rubin, E. (2010). Forcing technological change: A case of automobile emissions control technology development in the US. *Technovation*, 30(4), 249–264. https://doi.org/10.1016/j.technovation.2009.12.003

Lequiller, F., & Blades, D. (2014). *Understanding national accounts* (2nd ed.). OECD Publishing. https://doi.org/10.1787/9789264214637-en

Life Cycle Initiative. (2016). *Global guidance for life cycle impact assessment indicators*. United Nations Environment Programme. https://www.lifecycleinitiative.org/training-resources/global-guidance-lcia-indicators-v-1/

Matsumura, E. M., Prakash, R., & Vera-Muñoz, S. C. (2014). Firm-value effects of carbon emissions and carbon disclosures. *Accounting Review*, *89*(2), 695–724. http://doi.org/10.2308/accr-50629

Piketty, T., & Goldhammer, A. (2014). *Capital in the twenty-first century*. The Belknap Press of Harvard University Press. https://doi.org/10.4159/9780674369542

PricewaterhouseCoopers. (2015). *Valuing corporate environmental impacts*. https://www.pwc.co.uk/sustainability-climate-change/assets/pdf/pwc-environmental-valuation-methodologies.pdf

Rabl, A. (1996). Discounting of long term costs: What would future generations prefer us to do? *Ecological Economics*, *17*(3), 137–145. https://doi.org/ 10.1016/S0921-8009(96)80002-4

Schmidt, J. H., Merciai, S., Delahaye, R., Vuik, J., Heijungs, R., de Koning, A., & Sahoo, A. (2014). *Recommendation of terminology, classification, framework of waste accounts and MFA, and data collection guideline*. CREEA. https://lca-net.com/files/CREEA_Deliverable_4_1_Report_Task_4.1_Terminology_classification_framework.pdf

Sotos, M. (2015). *GHG protocol Scope 2 guidance. An amendment to the GHG protocol corporate standard*. World Resources Institute. https://ghgprotocol.org/sites/default/files/ghgp/standards/Scope%202%20Guidance_Final_0.pdf

Steen, B. (1999). *A systematic approach to environmental priority strategies in product development (EPS): Version 2000-general system characteristics* (p. 67). Gothenburg, Sweden: Centre for Environmental Assessment of Products and Material Systems.

Steen, B., & Palander, S. (2016). A selection of safeguard subjects and state indicators for sustainability assessments. *International Journal of Life Cycle Assessment*, *21*(6), 861–874. https://doi.org/10.1007/s11367-016-1052-6

Tinch, R., Beaumont, N., Sunderland, T., Ozdemiroglu, E., Barton, D., Bowe, C., … Ziv, G. (2019). Economic valuation of ecosystem goods and services: A review for decision makers. *Journal of Environmental Economics and Policy*, *8*(4), 359–378. http://doi.org/10.1080/21606544.2019.1623083

Turner, S. W., Hejazi, M., Yonkofski, C., Kim, S. H., & Kyle, P. (2019). Influence of groundwater extraction costs and resource depletion limits on simulated global nonrenewable water withdrawals over the twenty-first century. *Earth's Future*, *7*(2), 123–135. https://doi.org/10.1029/2018EF001105

Waddock, S., Bodwell, C., & Graves, S. (2002). Responsibility: The new business imperative. *Academy of Management Perspectives*, *16*(2), 132–148. http://doi.org/10.5465/ame.2002.7173581

Appendix

Exhibit 1   Waterfund Contact Information

The Water Cost Index, produced by Waterfund LLC, is an ever-changing set of rates updated regularly at www.worldswaterfund.com. Please contact Evan Olsen (Phone: +1 (415) 834-5640; Email: evan.olsen@worldswaterfund.com) for current Water Cost Index information.

8
CORPORATE CARBON MANAGEMENT SYSTEMS AND CARBON OPPORTUNITY

An International Study

Le Luo

Introduction

Climate change is a global issue that imposes increasing constraints on firms. These constraints are likely to affect firms' financial performance, either directly by influencing their operations or indirectly by influencing the value chain in which they operate (Busch & Hoffmann, 2007). Gaining better control of greenhouse gas (GHG)[1] emissions is a critical first step in avoiding these adverse impacts, obtaining a competitive advantage, and ultimately finding a solution to this puzzle (Hart, 1995). Many companies worldwide are adopting various carbon management practices to respond to climate change challenges (CDP, 2008). These functional practices for proactively managing carbon are increasingly recognized as the most systematic and integrated mechanisms for achieving the goal of carbon neutrality. Many studies focus on the determinants of the quality of a carbon management system (CMS) or its impact on carbon-related risks, emissions, assurance, or firm value (e.g., Datt et al., 2018; Shrestha et al., 2022; Tang & Luo, 2014). However, no studies have examined the association between the quality of a CMS and carbon opportunity.

Many economists highlight the facts that potential climate change risks may outweigh the costs of mitigating them and that there are significant opportunities to be realized as part of the transition to carbon neutrality. These opportunities include the development of new products or services, access to new markets, resource efficiency and cost savings, and the building of resilience along the supply chain. Lash and Wellington (2007) point out that the climate competitiveness of companies in a low-carbon economy lies in how well they are positioned vis-à-vis climate risk and how they manage climate opportunities. According to the 2018 CDP report, 215 of 500 global companies estimated the potential financial impact of a proportion of their climate risks, reporting some USD 970 billion at risk. However, 225 of these same 500 companies reported climate-related opportunities representing potential financial impacts totaling more than USD 2.1 trillion. This means in addition to avoiding various climate risks, firms should prioritize identifying and exploiting climate opportunities to ultimately achieve the goal of carbon neutrality. Therefore, in this study, I answer a critical research question: do companies with an advanced CMS tend to recognize more carbon opportunities?

I use an international sample of companies that received requests to respond to the CDP climate change survey 2011 to 2020. A wide range of countries/regions and sectors are represented in the sample, which enables a comprehensive global analysis of corporate carbon management practices. Following the framework proposed by Tang and Luo (2014) and Luo and Tang (2016), I identify ten carbon management practices from four perspectives. The data are obtained from responses to the different questions in the CDP annual survey. The descriptive results show that the specific carbon management practices adopted by companies and the overall quality of CMSs vary by year, industry, and country/region.

The regression results reveal a positive association between the quality of a CMS and exposure to carbon opportunities. The findings are consistent with my hypothesis that firms with a higher-quality CMS can quantify climate effects more accurately and reliably, make more efficient carbon investments, access financing more easily, and build more harmonious relationships with stakeholders, which enables them to identify and seize more carbon opportunities. The cross-sectional analysis further shows that a firm's institutional environment plays a significant role in moderating this positive association. More specifically, I find that the positive association is stronger for firms in countries with a national emissions trading scheme (ETS) and for firms that operate in carbon-intensive sectors.

This study contributes to the literature in three ways. First, most carbon studies focus on carbon risks/emissions. For example, a large body of literature examines the capital market effect of carbon emissions or carbon risks (e.g., Balachandran & Nguyen, 2018; Bolton & Kacperczyk, 2021; Chapple et al., 2013; Choi & Luo, 2021; Choi et al., 2021; Clarkson et al., 2015; Ehlers et al., 2022; Griffin et al., 2017; Jung et al., 2018; Luo & Tang, 2014a; Shen et al., 2022). Other studies consider the impact of different firm-, industry-, and country-level factors on firms' exposure to carbon risks and carbon emissions performance (e.g., Haque, 2017; Luo & Tang, 2021, 2022a; Luo & Tang, 2022b). Although climate change represents a major risk, it also poses a significant business opportunity. However, limited studies have explored which or how companies can identify more carbon opportunities (Gasbarro et al., 2017). This study fills this gap by exploring whether firms can capture carbon opportunities via an advanced CMS.

Second, this study adds to the scant literature on CMSs. Although there is a great deal of research on environmental management (e.g., Darnall et al., 2008; Ferreira et al., 2010; Klassen & McLaughlin, 1996; Melnyk et al., 2003; Pérez et al., 2007; Sroufe, 2003), there has been very little empirical academic work on carbon management specifically. Although it is often considered one aspect of an environmental management system, I argue that a CMS has unique features and requires skills, knowledge, and managerial capabilities that are inherently different from general environmental management systems. As He et al. (2022) note, carbon accounting has gradually emerged as a new research field in the domain of environmental accounting that deserves separate investigation. To the best of my knowledge, the present study is the first to investigate the association between a CMS and carbon opportunity. This research extends previous CMS studies by providing insights into the potential benefits of establishing a CMS, which can help firms increase carbon opportunities and thus sustain the net-zero economy.

Third, this study uses an international sample, which sheds valuable light on how interactions between a country's institutional environment and internal carbon management shape a firm's perception of potential carbon opportunities.

The remainder of this paper is organized as follows. The next section provides background and reviews the literature. This is followed by a section that presents the hypothesis development. The research design, including the empirical model and sample selection, is presented next. The empirical results are then reported. A discussion and conclusion are presented in the final section.

Background and Literature Review
Carbon Opportunities

In line with the Task Force on Climate-Related Financial Disclosures (TCFD) framework, climate opportunities are defined as potential positive impacts on an organization resulting from efforts to mitigate and adapt to climate change (CDP Climate Change Reporting Guidance, 2022). Climate opportunities can be broadly classified into two types: physical and transitional. Physical opportunities arise from the physical impacts of climate change (e.g., rising sea levels, changing patterns and amounts of precipitation, changing drought cycles, and extreme weather events). Transitional opportunities are related to the transition to a low-carbon economy (e.g., carbon pricing, changing market demand, and technology). Climate opportunities are dependent on the region, market, and industry in which a company operates.

The CMS Literature

Current carbon management studies can be categorized into three streams. The first stream examines the impact of a CMS on other corporate carbon practices, such as carbon performance and carbon assurance. For example, Tang and Luo (2014) are one of the first to propose a conceptual framework for CMSs that is underpinned by four perspectives: carbon governance, operation, quantification and assurance of carbon emissions data, and external engagement. They then measure CMSs based on ten essential elements: (1) board function (*BOARD*), (2) carbon risk and opportunity assessment (*RISKMANAGE*), (3) staff involvement (*INCENTIVE*), (4) reduction targets (*TARGET*), (5) policy implementation (*PROJECT*), (6) supply chain emissions control (*SUPPLYCHAIN*), (7) GHG accounting (*ACC*), (8) GHG assurance (*AUDIT*), (9) engagement with stakeholders (*POLICYENGAGE*), and (10) external disclosure and communication (*DIS*). Using a sample of 45 Australian firms, they document anecdotally that a better quality CMS is positively associated with carbon mitigation. In addition, concentrating specifically on target setting in carbon management, Ioannou et al. (2016) find that the stringency of carbon reduction targets is positively associated with the percentage of target completion and that this effect is negatively moderated by the provision of monetary incentives. Using an international sample, Datt et al. (2018) document that firms that engage in key CMS practices (i.e., firms with more carbon reduction initiatives, with an environmental committee, with carbon reduction incentives, or with higher carbon disclosure scores) tend to voluntarily obtain carbon assurance to signal their carbon transparency and responsible behaviors. Datt et al. (2020) switch their focus to the choice of assurance provider and reveal that companies that desire to improve their CMS tend to employ consulting firms rather than accounting firms as their assurance providers.

The second stream of studies on carbon management investigates the determinants of carbon management practices (e.g., Bui et al., 2020; Cadez & Guilding, 2017; Jeffrey & Perkins, 2014; Kumarasiri & Gunasekarage, 2017; Moore & McPhail, 2016; Trotman & Trotman, 2015; Yunus et al., 2016) Specifically, Luo and Tang (2016) conduct an international study and find that both external pressures (proxied by the presence of an ETS, competitor pressure, and the nature of the legal system) and internal conditions (proxied by carbon exposure and shareholder/stakeholder orientation) contribute to variation in CMSs across firms.

The third stream of literature focuses on the capital market effects of a firm's adoption of a CMS. In particular, Shrestha et al. (2022) document that having a higher-quality CMS mitigates the adverse association between the level of carbon emissions and firm value. They further suggest that the mitigating effect of a CMS on the negative valuation of carbon emissions occurs only in carbon-intensive, large, mature, and highly profitable firms.

Hypothesis Development

I expect that firms with a high-quality CMS tend to capture more carbon opportunities by designing more proactive carbon strategies, improving operational and investment efficiency, reducing financing costs, and effectively engaging with external stakeholders.

First, climate change is characterized by substantial scientific uncertainty (Luo & Tang, 2022a). A good CMS integrates scenario analysis into the evaluation system, providing companies with a better understanding of their climate impacts and resilience. For example, some companies may use cutting-edge artificial intelligence technologies to develop an interactive, personalized visualization tool. Such a tool can visualize the potential impacts of climate change, such as floods, storms, and wildfires, and provide accessible information regarding the science behind it (e.g., the reasons for frequent extreme weather events and trends). In addition, some countries or industries may implement stringent carbon reduction or reporting regulations. A CMS helps companies swiftly respond to acute climate events and comply or over-comply with these regulations. Meanwhile, companies that are equipped with superior knowledge of carbon-related physical and regulatory effects can better adapt their carbon strategies and implement more robust carbon governance processes and procedures (e.g., establish an environmental committee, set science-based targets, create an interdisciplinary sustainability project team, tie carbon reduction goals to executive pay), which ensures that these companies identify and reap the benefits of more opportunities.

Second, a good CMS enables a well-informed life-cycle cost-benefit analysis for carbon investments and creates opportunities to improve carbon/energy efficiency, increase cost savings, and maximize green revenue through new business models. For example, a company's development or expansion of low-emission goods or services may provide opportunities to reduce direct compliance or operating costs and increase green revenue resulting from increased demand for products and services. In addition, a shift to the use of low-emission energy sources has the potential to substantially reduce reliance on traditional energy sources and save on annual energy costs. According to the 2021 CDP report, as a result of their continual investment in the Green Generation segment (e.g., sustainable energy sources, including wind, hydro, solar, biomass, and waste-to-energy), the earnings before interest, taxes, depreciation, and amortization (EBITDA) of AB Ignitis Group reached EUR 292 million in 2020 and is expected to grow by 4.7–7.5% annually. The Group expects that around 2026 Green Generation assets will make up close to 50% of their total adjusted EBITDA, followed by a further increase in subsequent years as per their corporate strategy. Similarly, AG Barr entered into a power purchase agreement with an energy company to supply 100% renewable electricity across all their sites. As a result of entering into this agreement, since May 2020 AG Barr's electricity has been 100% renewable, resulting in no on-cost versus the supply of standard electricity.

Third, firms with a sophisticated CMS can capture new opportunities through increased access to capital and reduced financing costs. Recent studies show that shareholders discount firms with higher carbon emissions and reward firms that adopt a high-quality CMS (Chapple et al., 2013; Choi & Luo, 2021; Choi et al., 2021; Clarkson et al., 2015; Griffin et al., 2017). Similarly, companies with a strong reputation for superior carbon management can gain and maintain the trust of creditors and thus are favorably assessed when applying for credit (e.g.,

Caragnano et al., 2020; Herbohn et al., 2019; Jung et al., 2018; Shen et al., 2021). Recently there has been rapid growth in green finance, in which the use of proceeds is tied to specific low-carbon projects (e.g., grid connectivity, energy efficiency, low-emission energy production, or transport networks). The increasing prominence of green finance offers new opportunities for companies with a superior CMS and carbon performance to access cheaper financing.

Fourth, prior studies document that firms with a high-quality CMS are willing to reliably communicate their unique carbon profiles via appropriate channels to stakeholders, which results in enhanced transparency and stakeholder relationships (Datt et al., 2018; Luo & Tang, 2014b). This creates or increases opportunities for companies to access new markets through collaboration with stakeholders such as governments, banks, and community groups in developed and developing countries.

Finally, the implementation of a CMS within the firm indicates the firm's commitment to actively measuring, managing, and reporting carbon-related matters. It signals the firm's proactive stance on and attitude toward carbon neutrality and can guide transformative change to corporate infrastructures and carbon management practices. Once these carbon management activities are shaped and institutionalized, a corporate green culture is formed. Staff and managers are then likely to autonomously and actively reduce GHG emissions and identify potential carbon opportunities, such as improving energy efficiency and developing a low-carbon product, which helps companies achieve sustainability and resiliency for the long term (Clarkson et al., 2011; Cramer & Roes, 1993; Dhaliwal et al., 2011; Lawler, 1994). Therefore, I establish the hypothesis as follows:

Hypothesis 1: There is a positive association between the quality of a CMS and carbon opportunity.

Research Design

Research Model

Hypothesis 1 speculates on the effect of the quality of a firm's CMS on the number of the firm's carbon opportunities. Thus, I estimate Equation (1) using an ordinary least squares regression model with robust standard errors:

$$N_{OPPi,t} = \beta_0 + \beta_1 CMS_{it} + \beta_2 SIZE_{it} + \beta_3 ROA_{it} + \beta_4 LEV_{it} + \beta_5 TOBINQ_{it} + \beta_6 GROWTH_{it-1} \\ + \beta_7 TANG_{it-1} + \beta_8 CG_{it-1} + \beta_9 ENV_{it-1} + \beta_{10} BETA_{it} + \beta_{11} ETS_{it} + \beta_{12} GCRI_{it} \\ + \beta_{12} WGI_{it} + \beta_{12} LEGAL_{it} + \beta_{12} GDPPC_{it} + \mu_{it}, \tag{1}$$

where the dependent variable N_OPP is the number of carbon opportunities. The CDP requests that firms report detailed information on drivers of climate opportunities as well as the magnitude and likelihood of their potential financial impact (Gasbarro et al., 2017).[2] To measure carbon opportunity, I count the number of valid carbon opportunity drivers disclosed by companies. A carbon opportunity driver is identified as valid if a company discloses the magnitude and likelihood of its potential financial impact.

Following Luo and Tang (2016), I use two measures of the quality of a CMS. The first measure (*CMS1*) is the average equal-weighted sum of the standardized value of ten CMS elements. The second measure (*CMS2*) is the number of good carbon management practices adopted, where I create a dummy variable for each element mapping the highest commitment to proactive carbon management (e.g., establishing a board-level carbon committee, having a specific risk management process, having higher carbon disclosure scores than the sample median in a particular year).

Following prior studies, I include a set of firm- and country-level control variables (e.g., Berrone & Gomez-Mejia, 2009; Ikram et al., 2019; Karim et al., 2018; Tosi et al., 2000). Larger firms and firms with better financial performance have more resources and funds to explore carbon opportunities. Firm size (*SIZE*) is measured as the natural logarithm of total assets. Return on assets (*ROA*), a proxy for a firm's financial performance, is calculated as net income before extraordinary items/preferred dividends divided by total assets. In addition, firms with a higher leverage ratio are more financially constrained and thus able to invest in fewer carbon opportunities. *LEV* is total debt divided by total assets. Firms with more growth opportunities may focus on economic performance and business expansion and thus be less likely to explore climate opportunities. Tobin's Q (*TOBINQ*) is the total market value of a company based on the year-end price and number of shares outstanding divided by the book value of total assets. *GROWTH* is measured as one-year annual sales growth in net sales, calculated as the current year's revenues divided by the preceding year's revenues minus 1. *TANG* is the ratio of total (net) property plant and equipment to total assets.

Prior research shows that corporate governance plays a significant role in firms' carbon performance and management. Well-governed firms are more likely to design higher-quality CMSs and have greater carbon opportunities. I measure a firm's corporate governance using the corporate governance pillar score (*CG*) from the Refinitiv ESG database. *CG* measures "a company's systems and processes, which ensure that its board members and executives act in the best interests of its long-term shareholders" (Luo & Tang, 2021). I also control in the regression model for the environmental performance pillar score (*ENV*), which captures a firm's commitment to and effectiveness and efficiency in using natural resources, reducing environmental emissions, and supporting the research and development of eco-efficient products and services. Beta (*BETA*), which reflects a firm's systematic risk, is calculated based on between 23 and 35 consecutive month-end price percent changes and their relativity to a local market index (Luo et al., 2012).

Five country-level variables are also included in the regression model to control for a firm's institutional environment (Kanagaretnam et al., 2018; van Essen et al., 2012). First, *ETS* is a dummy variable that takes a value of 1 if the firm operates in a country with a nationwide ETS and 0 otherwise. Second, the Global Climate Risk Index (*GCRI*) is a proxy for the overall physical risk faced by a country. It measures a country's fatality rate and economic losses due to extreme weather events such as storms, floods, and heat waves. This measure reflects a country's physical risks, which may have an impact on firm decisions and performance (e.g., Huang et al., 2017). Third, the World Governance Index (*WGI*) is included in the model (Kaufmann et al., 2010) to control for regulatory governance and legal protection in the country (Choi & Luo, 2021). I expect firms in better-governed countries to create carbon opportunities. Fourth, *LEGAL*, which represents a country's legal system, equals 1 for firms in countries with a common law system and 0 otherwise. Fifth, the country's economic development is measured by its gross domestic product per capita (*GDPPC*). Rich countries have more infrastructure, skilled labor, and sophisticated technology to advance climate goals (Luo et al., 2013). *GDPPC* is calculated as the natural logarithm of the gross domestic product per capita (in constant 2010 U.S. dollars). Finally, I control for sector- and year-fixed effects to address endogeneity due to omitted variables specific to sector and year trends. All continuous variables are winsorized at the 1st and 99th percentiles of their distributions.

Sample

The initial sample includes all companies that responded to the CDP climate change survey 2011 to 2020. Please note that the CDP often requests carbon-related data on a one-year lag, so our sample corresponds to the fiscal years from 2010 to 2019. For example, the targeted firms disclosed their climate change emissions in the 2011 CDP report. Thus, financial data are often on a one-year lag relative to CDP data. The sample period starts in 2011 because, since that time, the CDP has used relatively consistent questionnaires and scoring methodologies, thus making comparisons over these years easy and meaningful. In addition, this sample period reflects the carbon management practices implemented most recently by the largest companies worldwide, thus providing potentially relevant information for regulators and investors for decision-making. Because financial firms differ from other businesses in their special accounting and regulatory requirements, the inclusion of these firms may significantly affect the results. Thus, financial firms are eliminated from the sample. In addition, observations with missing financial data and observations that do not have carbon disclosure or rank scores for constructing the measures of CMS quality are deleted. Finally, firms in countries that have fewer than ten observations are dropped. The final sample comprises 8,839 firm-year observations that meet the selection criteria. The standardization of CMS elements to construct the overall quality of CMSs is based on this sample.

Data on corporate carbon management practices and carbon opportunities are obtained from the CDP database. Corporate governance and environmental pillar scores are collected from the Refinitiv ESG database. Financial data are downloaded from the Refinitiv DataStream database. Data on a country's implementation of an ETS are obtained from the International Carbon Action Partnership (https://icapcarbonaction.com/en). The Global Climate Risk Index is developed and published annually by the nongovernmental organization Germanwatch (https://germanwatch.org/en/cri). Data on legal systems are collected from La Porta et al. (1998). Worldwide Governance Indicators and data on the country-level gross domestic product per capita are sourced from the World Bank.

Empirical Results

Descriptive Analysis of CMSs

Table 8.1 presents the sample distribution and mean values for each of the ten elements for constructing a CMS as well as for the two proxies for the overall quality of a CMS (*CMS1* and *CMS2*) by sector, year, and country/region. The three panels show whether there is significant variation in the adoption of carbon management practices or the overall quality of a CMS between sectors and how firms in each sector implement each of the ten elements.

Panel A of Table 8.1 reports the sample distribution and descriptive statistics by year. Tests for differences in median values across the different years indicate that there is significant variation in the average quality of a CMS (*CMS1* and *CMS2*) over the study period ($p < 0.01$). The results for *AUDIT* demonstrate a substantial increase in the verification/assurance of Scope 1, Scope 2, and Scope 3 emissions. The mean (median) *AUDIT* values of 4.57 in 2010 and 5.177 in 2019 indicate that more and more firms are engaging in external carbon assurance to provide more credible carbon information to stakeholders for decision-making.

Panel B of Table 8.1 presents the descriptive analysis by sector. Consumer discretionary, materials, and consumer staples are the three most represented sectors, accounting for 15.49%, 10.83%, and 10.37% of the sample, respectively. In contrast, telecommunications and real estate have the least firm-year observations. Overall, telecommunications, utilities, and real estate are the three sectors with the highest *CMS1* and *CMS2* (*CMS1*: 0.80, 0.077, and 0.052, respectively; *CMS2*: 6.934, 6.825, and 6.621, respectively). Conversely, healthcare, information technology, and energy are the three sectors with the lowest *CMS1* and *CMS2* (*CMS1*: −0.196, −0.056, and

Table 8.1 Sample distribution

Panel A: Sample distribution by year

Year	N	Percentage	BOARD	RISKMANAGE	INCENTIVE	TARGET	PROJECT	SUPPLYCHAIN	ACC	AUDIT	POLICYENGAGE	DIS	CMS1	CMS2
2010	402	4.55	2.803	1.092	0.796	1.565	6.124	0.789	2.803	4.57	0.923	4.657	−0.016	6.597
2011	457	5.17	2.871	1.037	0.884	1.656	5.538	0.81	2.842	4.906	0.923	5.418	0.075	6.803
2012	619	7	2.864	0.622	0.882	1.693	5.394	0.832	2.872	5.063	0.942	5.483	0.009	6.806
2013	709	8.02	2.855	0.623	0.903	1.663	4.946	0.812	2.879	4.997	0.948	5.893	0.027	6.797
2014	757	8.56	2.869	0.629	0.917	1.728	5.139	0.843	2.889	5.449	0.952	6.822	0.11	7.009
2015	819	9.27	2.905	1.022	0.905	1.805	5.022	0.748	2.846	5.482	0.961	5.98	0.14	6.896
2016	859	9.72	2.923	1.014	0.916	1.757	4.905	0.757	2.844	5.707	0.963	5.687	0.134	6.941
2017	1,172	13.26	2.376	1.009	0.858	1.625	4.292	0.698	2.838	4.125	0.882	4.878	−0.107	6.269
2018	1,417	16.03	2.41	0.977	0.912	1.586	72.19	0.675	2.676	3.404	0.848	5.019	−0.082	6.208
2019	1,628	18.42	2.448	1.029	0.785	1.617	65.579	0.677	2.674	5.177	0.837	5.046	−0.057	6.211
Total	8,839	100												

Panel B: Sample distribution by sector

GICS sector	N	Percentage	BOARD	RISKMANAGE	INCENTIVE	TARGET	PROJECT	SUPPLYCHAIN	ACC	AUDIT	POLICYENGAGE	DIS	CMS1	CMS2
Materials	957	10.83	2.697	0.916	0.885	1.507	29.502	0.816	2.77	4.892	0.937	5.429	0.027	6.576
Consumer Discretionary	1,369	15.49	2.652	0.964	0.888	1.769	33.722	0.66	2.824	4.573	0.905	5.406	0.015	6.578
Consumer Staples	917	10.37	2.662	0.928	0.927	1.703	29.744	0.558	2.823	5.077	0.929	5.709	0.023	6.603
Energy	522	5.91	2.743	0.902	0.912	1.391	21.08	0.805	2.751	4.667	0.929	5.174	−0.01	6.527
Healthcare	530	6	2.553	0.925	0.87	1.566	26.906	0.292	2.743	4.643	0.747	5.302	−0.196	5.836
Industrials	2,210	25	2.692	0.932	0.833	1.6	23.39	0.851	2.8	4.493	0.898	5.351	0.002	6.605
Real Estate	462	5.23	2.703	0.92	0.892	1.613	29.043	0.712	2.805	5.32	0.939	5.749	0.052	6.621
Information Technology	758	8.58	2.483	0.889	0.855	1.796	34.212	0.77	2.736	4.607	0.84	5.173	−0.056	6.335
Telecommunications	456	5.16	2.564	0.914	0.862	1.838	30.217	0.897	2.781	5.763	0.917	5.596	0.08	6.934
Utilities	658	7.44	2.731	0.886	0.859	1.871	9.698	0.884	2.821	5.1	0.971	5.491	0.077	6.825
Total	8,839	100												

Panel C: Sample distribution by country/region

Country/Region	N	Percentage	BOARD	RISKMANAGE	INCENTIVE	TARGET	PROJECT	SUPPLYCHAIN	ACC	AUDIT	POLICYENGAGE	DIS	CMS1	CMS2
Australia	290	3.28	2.762	0.9	0.855	1.224	23.172	0.714	2.769	4.659	0.907	5.155	−0.064	6.362
Austria	44	0.5	2.659	1	0.886	2.045	17.886	0.886	2.909	6.182	1	6.114	0.213	7.205
Belgium	61	0.69	2.279	0.82	0.82	1.492	34.492	0.656	2.639	4.574	0.82	5.082	−0.198	6.082
Brazil	170	1.92	2.588	0.976	0.859	1.429	9.6	0.871	2.876	4.788	0.965	4.994	0.003	6.588
Canada	398	4.5	2.621	0.879	0.844	1.098	16.342	0.673	2.658	2.894	0.907	4.666	−0.216	5.854
Chile	23	0.26	2.565	0.739	0.826	0.652	2.696	0.652	2.696	6.609	0.87	4.609	−0.228	5.783
China	32	0.36	1.719	0.75	0.531	0.781	2.906	0.25	1.656	1.313	0.5	1.219	−1.145	3.063
Colombia	25	0.28	2.6	0.84	0.88	1.24	5.96	0.64	2.52	3.32	0.92	3.84	−0.271	5.84
Denmark	92	1.04	2.728	0.957	0.576	1.674	17.065	0.598	2.728	4.141	0.783	4.891	−0.203	5.739
Finland	137	1.55	2.628	0.927	0.832	1.679	10.993	0.869	2.818	5.781	0.971	5.891	0.08	6.861
France	436	4.93	2.679	0.915	0.927	1.904	28.186	0.807	2.885	6.206	0.933	6.236	0.168	7.222
Germany	301	3.41	2.621	0.86	0.827	1.684	46.957	0.791	2.691	5.538	0.88	5.399	0.001	6.668
Hong Kong	44	0.5	2.886	0.727	0.886	2.136	4.864	0.932	2.864	7.045	0.977	5.864	0.189	7.477
Hungary	12	0.14	2.833	1.083	1	2.333	117	1	2.917	7.167	1	2.167	0.291	7.667
India	178	2.01	2.713	0.904	0.899	1.348	32.219	0.725	2.787	6.14	0.927	5.264	0.025	6.73
Ireland	33	0.37	2.909	1	0.909	1.242	16.909	0.848	2.788	6.424	0.879	5.545	0.085	7
Israel	12	0.14	1.75	1	1	2.083	4.583	0.333	3	3	0.833	6.583	−0.136	5.5
Italy	142	1.61	2.683	0.859	0.901	2.162	20.225	0.908	2.873	6.866	0.944	6.092	0.202	7.472
Japan	1,411	15.96	2.696	0.996	0.929	2.126	39.273	0.856	2.796	4.47	0.941	5.789	0.15	6.839
Jersey	10	0.11	2.9	1.1	0.8	0.8	5.7	1	2.9	3.1	0.9	5.2	−0.032	6.3
Korea	341	3.86	2.645	0.935	0.977	1.944	29.302	0.812	2.845	6.361	0.965	5.408	0.156	6.93
Malaysia	15	0.17	1.667	0.4	0.4	1.067	45.4	0.533	1.533	2.667	0.333	2	−1.131	3.133
Mexico	29	0.33	2.621	0.966	0.966	1.517	9.103	0.586	2.793	4.517	0.862	5.552	−0.05	6.379
New Zealand	59	0.67	2.559	0.983	0.746	1.458	8.102	0.61	2.763	3.797	0.915	5.017	−0.155	5.881
Norway	105	1.19	2.619	1.01	0.895	1.648	16.648	0.762	2.876	5.01	0.914	5.476	0.043	6.524
Poland	10	0.11	0.8	0.8	0.2	0	1.3	0.6	1.6	0	0.3	1.4	−1.475	2
Portugal	43	0.49	2.605	0.837	0.93	1.93	13.953	0.791	2.698	7.395	0.953	6.698	0.153	7.186
Russia	30	0.34	2.533	0.9	0.667	1.5	65.733	0.867	1.967	2	0.833	2.9	−0.399	5.1
Singapore	38	0.43	2.921	1.026	0.842	1.421	9.026	0.658	2.763	4.5	0.895	4.895	−0.047	6.579
South Africa	382	4.32	2.866	0.89	0.832	1.346	11.283	0.634	2.916	4.866	0.898	5.83	−0.014	6.602
Spain	207	2.34	2.671	0.87	0.937	2.217	29.884	0.807	2.894	6.913	0.976	6.309	0.232	7.527

(*Continued*)

Table 8.1 (Continued)

Panel C: Sample distribution by country/region

Country/Region	N	Percentage	BOARD	RISKMANAGE	INCENTIVE	TARGET	PROJECT	SUPPLYCHAIN	ACC	AUDIT	POLICYENGAGE	DIS	CMS1	CMS2
Sweden	218	2.47	2.624	0.876	0.794	1.417	11.735	0.78	2.748	4.041	0.826	5.193	−0.134	6.124
Switzerland	197	2.23	2.574	0.878	0.741	1.69	26.772	0.701	2.746	3.746	0.777	5.178	−0.156	6.086
Thailand	46	0.52	2.87	1.022	0.978	1.696	45.457	0.957	2.957	6.109	1	5.652	0.272	7.5
The Netherlands	102	1.15	2.647	0.951	0.892	1.755	24.284	0.814	2.716	5.265	0.882	5.48	0.032	6.804
Turkey	69	0.78	2.652	1	0.942	1.71	28.029	0.768	2.696	4.652	0.928	5.101	0.023	6.812
United Kingdom	1,034	11.7	2.802	0.928	0.879	1.532	18.539	0.657	2.861	4.805	0.882	5.584	0.001	6.659
United States	2,063	23.34	2.558	0.915	0.858	1.553	31.116	0.681	2.784	4.345	0.888	5.143	−0.07	6.264
Total	8,839	100												

Notes: GICS = Global Industry Classification Standard.

−0.01, respectively; *CMS2*: 5.836, 6.335, and 6.527, respectively). A one-way analysis of variance (results not shown) shows significant variation in the implementation of a CMS (both *CMS1* and *CMS2*) by sector (p < 0.01).

The results in Panel B show that the value of *BOARD* for all sectors exceeds 2, which suggests that on average at least a senior manager or officer has the greatest responsibility for climate change. Especially, 78.88% of the sample firms in the utilities sector have an individual/subset of the board or other committee appointed by the board responsible for climate change issues. For *RISKMANAGE*, although most firms in the healthcare sector (9.62%) have specific climate change risk management processes, many firms in the utilities sector (83.74%) tend to integrate multidisciplinary company-wide risk management processes. For *INCENTIVE*, more than 90% of firms in the consumer staples and energy sectors report that they offer an incentive to reduce the impacts of climate change. For *TARGET*, 69% of firms in the utilities sector have at least an absolute target in place. In contrast, less than half (40%) of firms in the energy sector have an absolute target, and 23.95% have no target. Concerning *PROJECT*, firms in the information technology sector have implemented on average the most initiatives (34), whereas firms in the utilities and energy sectors have the fewest initiatives. With regard to *SUPPLYCHAIN*, an overwhelming majority of firms in the telecommunications sector (89.69%) report that their goods or services directly enable a third party to avoid GHG emissions. In comparison, this percentage is lowest in the healthcare sector, at 29.25%. The mean *ACC* and *AUDIT* for the energy sector are 2.75 and 4.667, respectively. The mean *AUDIT* for telecommunications firms is 5.763, which suggests that a large amount of their carbon emissions have been verified by an external party. For *POLICYENGAGE*, 97.11% of utilities firms have actively engaged with policymakers to negotiate further action on climate change, whereas only 74.72% of firms in the healthcare sector have undertaken active policy engagement. The mean *DIS* in all sectors is above 5. These results show that firms in different sectors may tailor their carbon management practices to cater to their own corporate carbon goals.

Panel C of Table 8.1 reports the sample distribution and descriptive statistics by country/region. The United States, Japan, and the United Kingdom have the most observations, accounting for 23.34%, 15.96%, and 11.7% of the sample, respectively. Hungary, Thailand, and Spain have the highest *CMS1* and *CMS2* scores. Portugal, China, and Malaysia have the lowest scores. A one-way analysis of variance (results not shown) shows significant variation in the implementation of a CMS (both *CMS1* and *CMS2*) by country/region (p < 0.01).

Descriptive Statistics

Table 8.2 reports summary statistics for the variables in the baseline regression model. The mean *N_OPP* is 4.13, which means that the sample firms report an average of four opportunity drivers. The mean *CMS2* is 6.588, which suggests that firms adopt six unique types of high-quality carbon management practices on average. The mean *SIZE* is 16.088, which implies that the study sample consists of relatively large firms. The mean *ROA* is approximately 5.1%, which suggests that on average these firms are moderately profitable.

Univariate Analysis

Table 8.3 reports both parametric and nonparametric correlation coefficients for all variables in Equation (1). Consistent with expectations, both the Pearson and Spearman correlation coefficients for the overall quality of a CMS (*CMS1* and *CMS2*) are high, which

Table 8.2 Descriptive statistics

Variable	N	Mean	SD	Median	P25	P75
N_OPP	8,839	4.13	3.014	3	3	5
lnN_OPP	8,839	1.469	0.605	1.386	1.386	1.792
CMS1	8,839	0.004	0.545	0.126	−0.186	0.341
CMS2	8,839	6.558	1.831	7	6	8
SIZE	8,839	16.088	1.349	16.029	15.164	16.993
ROA	8,839	0.051	0.057	0.045	0.022	0.077
LEV	8,839	0.276	0.158	0.266	0.165	0.379
TOBINQ	8,839	1.123	1.052	0.773	0.463	1.391
GROWTH	8,839	0.038	0.147	0.029	−0.04	0.102
TANG	8,839	0.339	0.243	0.286	0.139	0.495
CG	8,839	60.592	20.473	63.34	45.83	76.9
ENV	8,839	62.955	20.961	66.06	49.88	79.52
BETA	8,839	1	0.463	0.948	0.675	1.268
ETS	8,839	0.39	0.488	0	0	1
GCRI	8,839	51.414	24.4	48	31.5	65.25
WGI	8,839	1.178	0.507	1.278	1.092	1.451
LEGAL	8,839	0.519	0.5	1	0	1
GDPPC	8,839	10.538	0.708	10.687	10.569	10.916

Notes: N = number of observations; SD = standard deviation; P25 and P75 = 25th and 75th percentile of the variables, respectively. Continuous variables are winsorized at the top and bottom 0.01.

shows that they capture the same construct. In addition, the correlations between the two CMS proxies and the carbon opportunity proxies are all positive and significant, which indicates that firms with a more sophisticated CMS tend to identify and exploit more carbon opportunities. These results provide preliminary evidence for the impact of a CMS on carbon opportunity. Overall, cross-correlations between these variables do not suggest problems with multicollinearity. However, this analysis does not control for other compounding effects, so I next conduct a multivariate analysis.

Multivariate Regression

Table 8.4 reports the results of an ordinary least squares regression of the impact of the quality of a CMS on carbon opportunity. The dependent variable in columns (1) and (2) is N_OPP, whereas the dependent variable in columns (3) and (4) is lnN_OPP. The coefficients of CMS1 and CMS2 are all positive and significant at the $p < 0.01$ level, which is consistent with Hypothesis 1. These results confirm that firms that adopt an advanced CMS can identify more beneficial carbon opportunities. With regard to the control variables, I find that the coefficients of TOBINQ and TANG are negative and significant, which suggests that firms with more growth opportunities and greater capital tend to identify fewer carbon opportunities. These results are not surprising, because such firms may prioritize their financial performance and are less likely to identify and explore potential carbon opportunities. In addition, the environmental performance score (ENV) is significantly positively associated with carbon opportunities, with positive coefficients across all four models. Two country-level variables, ETS and WGI, have significant coefficients, which suggests that a firm's institutional environment significantly impacts its carbon opportunities.

Table 8.3 Correlations

Variable	N_OPP	lnN_OPP	CMS1	CMS2	SIZE	ROA	LEV	TOBINQ	GROWTH	TANG	CG	ENV	BETA	ETS	GCRI	WGI	LEGAL	GDPPC
N_OPP	1	1.000***	0.318***	0.343***	0.184***	-0.066***	0.055***	-0.125***	-0.102***	0.074***	0.053***	0.176***	-0.009	0.023**	-0.001	-0.028***	-0.018*	-0.090***
lnN_OPP	0.899***	1	0.318***	0.343***	0.184***	-0.066***	0.055***	-0.125***	-0.102***	0.074***	0.053***	0.176***	-0.009	0.023**	-0.001	-0.028***	-0.018*	-0.090***
CMS1	0.310***	0.457***	1	0.868***	0.361***	-0.053***	0.040***	-0.148***	-0.095***	0.068***	0.136***	0.422***	-0.040***	0.063***	0.035***	-0.061***	-0.182***	-0.147***
CMS2	0.340***	0.456***	0.911***	1	0.315***	-0.043***	0.057***	-0.131***	-0.079***	0.062***	0.114***	0.389***	-0.043***	0.090***	0.048***	-0.056***	-0.126***	-0.136***
SIZE	0.161***	0.194***	0.340***	0.325***	1	-0.141***	0.196***	-0.260***	-0.027**	0.107***	0.215***	0.433***	0.027**	-0.086***	-0.137***	-0.112***	-0.085***	0.084***
ROA	-0.049***	-0.062***	-0.041***	-0.041***	-0.114***	1	-0.272***	0.706***	0.194***	-0.173***	0.039***	-0.021**	-0.155***	-0.023**	-0.069***	0.033**	0.171***	0.102***
LEV	0.029**	0.059***	0.052***	0.061***	0.183***	-0.239***	1	-0.281***	-0.054***	0.254***	0.002	0.022**	-0.043***	-0.018*	-0.074***	-0.127***	0.058***	0.064***
TOBINQ	-0.114***	-0.140***	-0.140***	-0.133***	-0.247***	0.649***	-0.227***	1	0.178***	-0.266***	0.043***	-0.090***	-0.167***	-0.037***	-0.126***	0.083***	0.249***	0.232***
GROWTH	-0.076***	-0.080***	-0.080***	-0.071***	-0.025**	0.181***	-0.043***	0.144***	1	-0.051***	-0.047***	-0.067***	-0.012	-0.049***	-0.032***	-0.021**	0.060***	0.020*
TANG	0.043***	0.054***	0.053***	0.046***	0.095***	-0.145***	0.260***	-0.225***	-0.021*	1	0.001	0.061***	-0.054***	-0.083***	0.015	-0.028***	0.024**	-0.098***
CG	0.054***	0.055***	0.142***	0.129***	0.217***	0.027**	-0.003	0.002	-0.045***	-0.01	1	0.204***	0	-0.056***	-0.061***	0.01	0.100***	0.090***
ENV	0.170***	0.212***	0.426***	0.417***	0.434***	0.002	0.016	-0.070***	-0.070***	0.033***	0.223***	1	0.021**	0.108***	0.040***	-0.047***	-0.180***	-0.063***
BETA	-0.019*	-0.017	-0.036***	-0.043***	0.015	-0.163***	-0.026**	-0.116***	0.011	-0.039***	0.013	0.002	1	-0.029**	-0.053***	0.027**	0.01	0.102***
ETS	0.032***	0.019*	0.037***	0.069***	-0.084***	-0.027**	-0.025**	-0.034***	-0.037***	-0.063***	-0.054***	0.102***	-0.036***	1	0.528***	0.357***	-0.244***	-0.017
GCRI	-0.025**	-0.014	0.016	0.035***	-0.131***	-0.057***	-0.068***	-0.100***	-0.007	-0.004	-0.057***	0.038***	-0.058***	0.503***	1	0.362***	-0.417***	-0.175***
WGI	-0.019*	-0.025**	-0.01	-0.025**	0.021**	-0.027**	-0.079***	0.004	-0.011	-0.044***	0.028**	0.001	0.072***	0.304***	0.192***	1	-0.022**	0.462***
LEGAL	-0.005	-0.014	-0.116***	-0.101***	-0.094***	0.148***	0.059***	0.192***	0.054***	0.081***	0.105***	-0.181***	0.045***	-0.244***	-0.392***	0.001	1	0.333***
GDPPC	-0.038***	-0.048***	-0.028***	-0.046***	0.142***	-0.033***	0.026**	0.008	-0.004	-0.071***	0.048***	0.013	0.102***	0.192***	0.054***	0.853***	0.011	1

Notes: Spearman (Pearson) correlations are presented above (below) the diagonal. N = number of observations. *, **, and *** indicate significance at the 0.1, 0.05, and 0.01 levels, respectively (two-tailed). Continuous variables are winsorized at the top and bottom 0.01.

Table 8.4 Main regression results

VARIABLE	(1) N_OPP	(2) N_OPP	(3) lnN_OPP	(4) lnN_OPP
CMS1	1.364***		0.451***	
	(31.832)		(45.404)	
CMS2		0.435***		0.127***
		(29.616)		(38.197)
SIZE	0.024	0.024	−0.000	0.004
	(0.917)	(0.925)	(−0.099)	(0.755)
ROA	0.051	0.195	0.047	0.108
	(0.081)	(0.312)	(0.350)	(0.795)
LEV	−0.064	−0.131	0.077**	0.061
	(−0.352)	(−0.722)	(2.110)	(1.633)
TOBINQ	−0.090***	−0.097***	−0.024***	−0.028***
	(−2.659)	(−2.857)	(−3.240)	(−3.691)
GROWTH	−0.319	−0.362*	−0.016	−0.031
	(−1.613)	(−1.827)	(−0.435)	(−0.824)
TANG	−0.271*	−0.263*	−0.063**	−0.061**
	(−1.925)	(−1.868)	(−2.173)	(−2.060)
CG	−0.000	0.000	−0.001*	−0.000
	(−0.114)	(0.053)	(−1.926)	(−1.446)
ENV	0.005***	0.004***	0.001**	0.001***
	(3.353)	(2.868)	(2.131)	(2.741)
BETA	−0.095	−0.079	−0.004	−0.002
	(−1.472)	(−1.230)	(−0.312)	(−0.136)
ETS	0.401***	0.321***	0.038***	0.015
	(5.429)	(4.368)	(2.929)	(1.120)
GCRI	−0.002	−0.002	0.000	0.000
	(−1.438)	(−1.518)	(0.802)	(0.716)
WGI	−0.276***	−0.233**	−0.049**	−0.030
	(−2.672)	(−2.265)	(−2.327)	(−1.411)
LEGAL	0.201***	0.162**	0.051***	0.038***
	(2.986)	(2.414)	(4.065)	(2.985)
GDPPC	0.050	0.055	0.006	0.001
	(0.684)	(0.754)	(0.379)	(0.085)
Constant	5.625***	2.742***	1.805***	0.917***
	(7.583)	(3.737)	(12.082)	(6.107)
Observations	8,839	8,839	8,839	8,839
R^2	0.256	0.263	0.344	0.332
Sector-fixed effects	Yes	Yes	Yes	Yes
Year-fixed effects	Yes	Yes	Yes	Yes
Adjusted R^2	0.253	0.260	0.342	0.330
F	103.1	94.54	142.3	118.9

Notes: An ordinary least squares model is used to test the relationship between the quality of a carbon management system and carbon opportunity. *, **, and *** indicate significance at the 0.1, 0.05, and 0.01 levels, respectively (two-tailed). Robust t statistics are in parentheses. Continuous variables are winsorized at the top and bottom 0.01.

Moderating Effects of a Firm's Regulatory Environment

I use two proxies for the regulatory environment around climate change: a firm's operation in a country with a national ETS (*ETS*) and its membership in a carbon-intensive sector (*INTSEC*) (Luo, 2019). *ETS* is a dummy variable that takes a value of 1 if the firm operates in a country with a nationwide ETS and 0 otherwise. *INTSEC* is a dummy variable that takes a value of 1 if the firm operates in a carbon-intensive sector (i.e., energy, materials, or utilities) and 0 otherwise. These two institutional variables are then interacted with the quality of a CMS.

Columns (1) and (2) of Table 8.5 present results for the moderating effect of *ETS* on the relationship, whereas columns (3) and (4) report findings for the moderating effect of *INTSEC*. As shown, the coefficients of all interaction variables (*ETS×CMS1, ETS×CMS2, INTSEC×CMS1,* and *INTSEC×CMS2*) are positive and significant. These results suggest that the positive association between the quality of a CMS and carbon opportunity is stronger for firms that operate in stringent institutional environments (i.e., countries with a national ETS or carbon-intensive sectors). A possible reason for this could be that firms in institutional environments with stringent carbon regulations are motivated to explore various carbon opportunities to gain competitive advantages. In contrast, in countries with lax carbon regulations, this incentive is weaker. These findings highlight a potential bright side of implementing and enforcing carbon regulations.

Discussion and Conclusion

CMSs are relatively new and somewhat innovative carbon management tools that have been adopted by many of the largest companies worldwide, but few studies have systematically explored them. This study contributes to the literature by providing a comprehensive longitudinal analysis of CMSs based on a sample from 2010 to 2019. The results have important implications for standard setters, companies, investors, and government policymakers. First, the descriptive statistics show that firms in different sectors adopt specific carbon management practices. The quality of a CMS does not increase consistently but fluctuates during the sample period. Furthermore, there is a significant variation in the implementation of CMS practices among countries/regions. Firms may struggle to adopt the CMS that best suits them. Thus, standard setters should establish a global standard for firms in different sectors and countries to implement their CMSs and issue certification. Second, the regression results reveal a positive association between the quality of a CMS and exposure to carbon opportunities. They demonstrate that firms that adopt advanced carbon management practices are better able to identify and exploit carbon opportunities. Company executives can use a CMS not only as an effective tool for managing internal carbon costs and risks but also as a useful tool for identifying, exploring, or creating carbon opportunities. This could be an essential benefit for companies that adopt carbon management. Properly designed CMSs provide firms with additional carbon opportunities and leverage over their carbon performance. These companies can consider actively sharing this information with the community and engaging with key stakeholders in their carbon management activities. Ultimately, they can achieve business performance and sustainability goals through the CMS.

A CMS can also be an indicator of a highly innovative company. Innovative companies adopt advanced carbon management practices as part of an overall proactive carbon strategy and good corporate governance. Investors can use such a signal to evaluate a firm's future climate risks and opportunities and incorporate this information into their capital allocation. In countries or sectors with more stringent regulations, these companies tend to enjoy more significant benefits of

Table 8.5 Moderating effects of an ETS and carbon-intensive sector

VARIABLE	(1) N_OPP	(2) N_OPP	(3) N_OPP	(4) N_OPP
ETS×CMS1	0.204*** (2.700)			
ETS×CMS2		0.055** (2.083)		
INTSEC×CMS1			0.469*** (4.431)	
INTSEC×CMS2				0.078** (2.317)
CMS1	1.284*** (24.825)		1.280*** (28.566)	
CMS2		0.413*** (23.339)		0.419*** (26.633)
SIZE	0.022 (0.842)	0.022 (0.851)	0.022 (0.827)	0.022 (0.864)
ROA	0.055 (0.087)	0.204 (0.326)	0.088 (0.141)	0.221 (0.354)
LEV	−0.058 (−0.321)	−0.128 (−0.704)	−0.081 (−0.448)	−0.139 (−0.763)
TOBINQ	−0.091*** (−2.696)	−0.097*** (−2.861)	−0.094*** (−2.782)	−0.099*** (−2.937)
GROWTH	−0.316 (−1.601)	−0.361* (−1.822)	−0.300 (−1.518)	−0.355* (−1.789)
TANG	−0.276* (−1.957)	−0.265* (−1.880)	−0.246* (−1.744)	−0.250* (−1.777)
CG	−0.000 (−0.125)	0.000 (0.037)	−0.000 (−0.085)	0.000 (0.090)
ENV	0.005*** (3.385)	0.004*** (2.901)	0.005*** (3.283)	0.004*** (2.861)
BETA	−0.102 (−1.566)	−0.085 (−1.318)	−0.090 (−1.384)	−0.076 (−1.178)
ETS	0.391*** (5.358)	−0.047 (−0.277)	0.387*** (5.241)	0.314*** (4.266)
GCRI	−0.002 (−1.415)	−0.002 (−1.453)	−0.002 (−1.429)	−0.002 (−1.517)
WGI	−0.253** (−2.435)	−0.212** (−2.057)	−0.263** (−2.549)	−0.222** (−2.167)
LEGAL	0.197*** (2.932)	0.160** (2.388)	0.207*** (3.085)	0.167** (2.491)
GDPPC	0.039 (0.528)	0.044 (0.605)	0.047 (0.651)	0.051 (0.713)
INTSEC			0.336** (2.538)	−0.187 (−0.717)
Constant	5.753*** (7.728)	3.005*** (4.023)	5.326*** (7.129)	2.558*** (3.403)
Observations	8,839	8,839	8,839	8,839
R^2	0.256	0.263	0.257	0.263
Sector-fixed effects	Yes	Yes	Yes	Yes
Year-fixed effects	Yes	Yes	Yes	Yes
Adjusted R^2	0.253	0.260	0.254	0.260
F	100.8	91.95	101.1	92.20

Notes: An ordinary least squares model is used to test moderating effects of the presence of an ETS and membership in a carbon-intensive sector on the relationship between the quality of a carbon management system and carbon opportunity. ETS = emissions trading scheme. *, **, and *** indicate significance at the 0.1, 0.05, and 0.01 levels, respectively (two-tailed). Robust t statistics are in parentheses. Continuous variables are winsorized at the top and bottom 0.01.

adopting a sophisticated CMS in the form of more carbon opportunities. Policymakers can consider how to design policies to better motivate companies to adopt CMSs, which is essential for reduced compliance costs, improved stakeholder management, and better community relations.

Notes

1. The term *greenhouse gas* (GHG) is used in this paper as a generic term that is interchangeable with CO_2, *carbon equivalent* (CO_2-e), and *carbon*.
2. Carbon opportunity drivers are counted based on answers to question CC5.1 in the 2011–2017 CDP questionnaire and question 2.4 in the 2018–2020 CDP questionnaire: CC5.1a C1 – "Please describe your inherent opportunities that are driven by changes in regulation – Risk driver," CC5.1b C1 – "Please describe your inherent opportunities that are driven by changes in physical climate parameters – Risk driver," CC5.1c C1 – "Please describe your inherent opportunities that are driven by changes in other climate-related developments – Risk driver," and C2.4a_C1 – "Provide details of opportunities identified with the potential to have a substantive financial or strategic impact on your business – Identifier."

References

Balachandran, B., & Nguyen, J. H. (2018). Does carbon risk matter in firm dividend policy? Evidence from a quasi-natural experiment in an imputation environment. *Journal of Banking and Finance*, 96, 249–267. https://doi.org/10.1016/j.jbankfin.2018.09.015

Berrone, P., & Gomez-Mejia, L. R. (2009). Environmental performance and executive compensation: An integrated agency-institutional perspective. *Academy of Management Journal*, 52(1), 103–126. https://doi.org/10.5465/amj.2009.36461950

Bolton, P., & Kacperczyk, M. (2021). Do investors care about carbon risk? *Journal of Financial Economics*. https://doi.org/10.1016/j.jfineco.2021.05.008

Bui, B., Chapple, L., & Truong, T. P. (2020). Drivers of tight carbon control in the context of climate change regulation. *Accounting and Finance*, 60(1), 183–226. https://doi.org/10.1111/acfi.12320

Busch, T., & Hoffmann, V. (2007). Emerging carbon constraints for corporate risk management. *Ecological Economics*, 62(3–4), 518–528. https://doi.org/10.1016/j.ecolecon.2006.05.022

Cadez, S., & Guilding, C. (2017). Examining distinct carbon cost structures and climate change abatement strategies in CO2 polluting firms. *Accounting, Auditing and Accountability Journal*, 30(5), 1041–1064. https://doi.org/10.1108/AAAJ-03-2015-2009

Caragnano, A., Mariani, M., Pizzutilo, F., & Zito, M. (2020). Is it worth reducing GHG emissions? Exploring the effect on the cost of debt financing. *Journal of Environmental Management*, 270, 110860. https://doi.org/10.1016/j.jenvman.2020.110860

CDP. (2008). *Making advances in carbon management best practice from the carbon information leaders a joint CDP and IBM study*. https://www.cdproject.net/en-US/Results/Pages/All-Investor-Reports.aspx

CDP. (2022). *Climate change reporting guidance*. https://guidance.cdp.net/en/guidance?cid=30&ctype=theme&idtype=ThemeID&incchild=1&microsite=0&otype=Guidance&tags=TAG-646%2CTAG-604%2CTAG-599

Chapple, L., Clarkson, P. M., & Gold, D. L. (2013). The cost of carbon: Capital market effects of the proposed emission trading scheme (ETS). *Abacus*, 49(1), 1–33. https://doi.org/10.1111/abac.12006

Choi, B., & Luo, L. (2021). Does the market value greenhouse gas emissions? Evidence from multi-country firm data. *British Accounting Review*, 53(1), 1–24. https://doi.org/10.1016/j.bar.2020.100909

Choi, B., Luo, L., & Shrestha, P. (2021). The value relevance of carbon emissions information from Australian-listed companies. *Australian Journal of Management*, 46(1), 3–23. https://doi.org/10.1177/0312896220918642

Clarkson, P. M., Li, Y., Pinnuck, M., & Richardson, G. D. (2015). The valuation relevance of greenhouse gas emissions under the European Union carbon emissions trading scheme. *European Accounting Review*, 24(3), 551–580. https://doi.org/10.1080/09638180.2014.927782

Clarkson, P. M., Li, Y., Richardson, G. D., & Vasvari, F. P. (2011). Does it really pay to be green? Determinants and consequences of proactive environmental strategies. *Journal of Accounting and Public Policy*, 30(2), 122–144. https://doi.org/10.1016/j.jaccpubpol.2010.09.013

Cramer, J., & Roes, B. (1993). Total employee involvement: Measures for success. *Environmental Quality Management*, 3(1), 39–52. https://doi.org/10.1002/tqem.3310030105

Darnall, N., Henriques, I., & Sadorsky, P. (2008). Do environmental management systems improve business performance in an international setting? *Journal of International Management*, 14(4), 364–376. https://doi.org/10.1016/j.intman.2007.09.006

Datt, R., Luo, L., & Tang, Q. (2020). Corporate choice of providers of voluntary carbon assurance. *International Journal of Auditing*, 24(1), 145–162. https://doi.org/10.1111/ijau.12184

Datt, R., Luo, L., Tang, Q., & Mallik, G. (2018). An international study of determinants of voluntary carbon assurance. *Journal of International Accounting Research*, 17(3), 1–20. https://doi.org/10.2308/jiar-52221

Dhaliwal, D. S., Li, O. Z., Tsang, A., & Yang, Y. G. (2011). Voluntary nonfinancial disclosure and the cost of equity capital: The initiation of corporate social responsibility reporting. *Accounting Review*, 86(1), 59. https://doi.org/10.2308/accr.00000005

Ehlers, T., Packer, F., & de Greiff, K. (2022). The pricing of carbon risk in syndicated loans: Which risks are priced and why? *Journal of Banking and Finance*, 136, 106180. https://doi.org/10.1016/j.jbankfin.2021.106180

Ferreira, A., Moulang, C., & Hendro, B. (2010). Environmental management accounting and innovation: An exploratory analysis. *Accounting, Auditing and Accountability Journal*, 23(7), 920–948. https://doi.org/10.1108/09513571011080180

Gasbarro, F., Iraldo, F., & Daddi, T. (2017). The drivers of multinational enterprises' climate change strategies: A quantitative study on climate-related risks and opportunities. *Journal of Cleaner Production*, 160, 8–26. https://doi.org/10.1016/j.jclepro.2017.03.018

Griffin, P. A., Lont, D. H., & Sun, E. Y. (2017). The relevance to investors of greenhouse gas emission disclosures. *Contemporary Accounting Research*, 34(2), 1265–1297. https://doi.org/10.1111/1911-3846.12298

Haque, F. (2017). The effects of board characteristics and sustainable compensation policy on carbon performance of UK firms. *British Accounting Review*, 49(3), 347–364. https://doi.org/10.1016/j.bar.2017.01.001

Hart, S. (1995). A natural-resource-based view of the firm. *Academy of Management Review*, 20(4), 986–1014. https://doi.org/10.2307/258963

He, R., Luo, L., Shamsuddin, A., & Tang, Q. (2022). Corporate carbon accounting: A literature review of carbon accounting research from the Kyoto Protocol to the Paris Agreement. *Accounting & Finance*, 62(1), 261–298.

Herbohn, K., Gao, R., & Clarkson, P. (2019). Evidence on whether banks consider carbon risk in their lending decisions. *Journal of Business Ethics*, 158(1), 155–175. https://doi.org/10.1007/s10551-017-3711-3

Huang, H. H., Kerstein, J., & Wang, C. (2017). The impact of climate risk on firm performance and financing choices: An international comparison. *Journal of International Business Studies*, 49(5), 633–656. https://doi.org/10.1057/s41267-017-0125-5

Ikram, A., Li, Z., & Minor, D. (2019). CSR-contingent executive compensation contracts. *Journal of Banking and Finance*, 105655. https://doi.org/10.1016/j.jbankfin.2019.105655

Ioannou, I., Li, S. X., & Serafeim, G. (2016). The effect of target difficulty on target completion: The case of reducing carbon emissions. *Accounting Review*, 91(5), 1467–1492. https://doi.org/10.2308/accr-51307

Jeffrey, C., & Perkins, J. D. (2014). The relationship between energy taxation and business environmental protection expenditures in the European Union. *International Journal of Accounting*, 49(4), 403–425. https://doi.org/10.1016/j.intacc.2014.10.002

Jung, J., Herbohn, K., & Clarkson, P. (2018). Carbon risk, carbon risk awareness and the cost of debt financing. *Journal of Business Ethics*, 150(4), 1151–1171. https://doi.org/10.1007/s10551-016-3207-6

Kanagaretnam, K., Khokhar, A.-R., & Mawani, A. (2018). Linking societal trust and CEO compensation. *Journal of Business Ethics*, 151(2), 295–317. https://doi.org/10.1007/s10551-016-3211-x

Karim, K., Lee, E., & Suh, S. (2018). Corporate social responsibility and CEO compensation structure. *Advances in Accounting*, 40, 27–41. https://doi.org/10.1016/j.adiac.2017.11.002

Kaufmann, D., Kraay, A., & Mastruzzi, M. (2010). *The worldwide governance indicators: Methodology and analytical issues.* http://info.worldbank.org/governance/wgi/

Klassen, R. D., & McLaughlin, C. P. (1996). The impact of environmental management on firm performance. *Management Science*, 42(8), 1199–1214. https://doi.org/10.1287/mnsc.42.8.1199

Kumarasiri, J., & Gunasekarage, A. (2017). Risk regulation, community pressure and the use of management accounting in managing climate change risk: Australian evidence. *British Accounting Review*, 49(1), 25–38. https://doi.org/10.1016/j.bar.2016.10.009

La Porta, R., Lopez-De-Silanes, F., Shleifer, A., & Vishny, R. W. (1998). Law and finance. *Journal of Political Economy*, *106*(6), 1113–1155. https://doi.org/10.1086/250042

Lash, J., & Wellington, F. (2007). Competitive advantage on a warming planet. *Harvard Business Review*, *85*(3), 94–102. http://courseresources.mit.usf.edu/sgs/geb6930/module_3/read/competative_advantage.pdf

Lawler, E. E. (1994). Total quality management and employee involvement: Are they compatible? *Academy of Management Executive*, *8*(1), 68–76. https://doi.org/10.5465/ame.1994.9411302396

Luo, L. (2019). The influence of institutional contexts on the relationship between voluntary carbon disclosure and carbon emission performance. *Accounting and Finance*, *59*(2), 1235–1264. https://doi.org/10.1111/acfi.12267

Luo, L., Lan, Y. C., & Tang, Q. (2012). Corporate incentives to disclose carbon information: Evidence from the CDP global 500 report. *Journal of International Financial Management and Accounting*, *23*(2), 93–120. https://doi.org/10.1111/j.1467-646X.2012.01055.x

Luo, L., & Tang, Q. (2014a). Carbon tax, corporate carbon profile and financial return. *Pacific Accounting Review*, *26*(3), 351–373. https://doi.org/10.1108/PAR-09-2012-0046

Luo, L., & Tang, Q. (2014b). Does voluntary carbon disclosure reflect underlying carbon performance? *Journal of Contemporary Accounting and Economics*, *10*(3), 191–205. https://doi.org/10.1016/j.jcae.2014.08.003

Luo, L., & Tang, Q. (2016). The determinants of the quality of corporate carbon management systems: An international study. *International Journal of Accounting*, *51*(2), 275–305. https://doi.org/10.1016/j.intacc.2016.04.007

Luo, L., & Tang, Q. (2021). Corporate governance and carbon performance: Role of carbon strategy and awareness of climate risk. *Accounting and Finance*, *61*(2), 2891–2934. https://doi.org/10.1111/acfi.12687

Luo, L., & Tang, Q. (2022a). National culture and corporate carbon performance. *Australian Journal of Management*, *47*(3), 503–538. https://doi.org/10.1177/03128962211038664

Luo, L., & Tang, Q. (2022b). The real effects of ESG reporting and GRI standards on carbon mitigation: International evidence. *Business Strategy and the Environment*. https://doi.org/10.1002/bse.3281

Luo, L., Tang, Q., & Lan, Y. C. (2013). Comparison of propensity for carbon disclosure between developing and developed countries: A resource constraint perspective. *Accounting Research Journal*, *26*(1), 6–34. https://doi.org/10.1108/ARJ-04-2012-0024

Melnyk, S. A., Sroufe, R. P., & Calantone, R. (2003). Assessing the impact of environmental management systems on corporate and environmental performance. *Journal of Operations Management*, *21*(3), 329–351. https://doi.org/10.1016/S0272-6963(02)00109-2

Moore, D. R. J., & McPhail, K. (2016). Strong structuration and carbon accounting: A position-practice perspective of policy development at the macro, industry and organizational levels. *Accounting, Auditing and Accountability Journal*, *29*(7), 1204–1233. https://doi.org/10.1108/AAAJ-08-2015-2203

Pérez, E. A., Ruiz, C. C., & Fenech, F. C. (2007). Environmental management systems as an embedding mechanism: A research note. *Accounting, Auditing and Accountability Journal*, *20*(3), 403–422. https://doi.org/10.1108/09513570710748562

Shen, H., Wu, H., Long, W., & Luo, L. (2021). Environmental performance of firms and access to bank loans. *International Journal of Accounting*, *56*(2), 2150007. https://doi.org/10.1142/s1094406021500074

Shen, H., Yang, Q., Luo, L., & Huang, N. (2022). Market reactions to a cross-border carbon policy: Evidence from listed Chinese companies. *British Accounting Review*, 101116. https://doi.org/10.1016/j.bar.2022.101116

Shrestha, P., Choi, B., & Luo, L. (2022). Does a carbon management system mitigate the consequences of carbon emissions on firm value? An international study. *Journal of International Accounting Research*. https://doi.org/10.2308/jiar-2021-019

Sroufe, R. (2003). Effects of environmental management systems on environmental management practices and operations. *Production and Operations Management*, *12*(3), 416–431. https://doi.org/10.1111/j.1937-5956.2003.tb00212.x

Tang, Q., & Luo, L. (2014). Carbon management systems and carbon mitigation. *Australian Accounting Review*, *24*(1), 84–98. https://doi.org/10.1111/auar.12010

Tosi, H. L., Werner, S., Katz, J. P., & Gomez-Mejia, L. R. (2000). How much does performance matter? A meta-analysis of CEO pay studies. *Journal of Management*, *26*(2), 301–339. https://doi.org/10.1177/014920630002600207

Trotman, A. J., & Trotman, K. T. (2015). Internal audit's role in GHG emissions and energy reporting: Evidence from audit committees, senior accountants, and internal auditors. *Auditing: A Journal of Practice and Theory, 34*(1), 199–230. https://doi.org/10.2308/ajpt-50675

van Essen, M., Heugens, P. P., Otten, J., & van Oosterhout, J. (2012). An institution-based view of executive compensation: A multilevel meta-analytic test. *Journal of International Business Studies, 43*(4), 396–423. https://doi.org/10.1057/jibs.2012.6

Yunus, S., Gillian Vesty, D. S. D. D., Elijido-Ten, E., & Abhayawansa, S. (2016). Determinants of carbon management strategy adoption. *Managerial Auditing Journal, 31*(2), 156–179. https://doi.org/10.1108/maj-09-2014-1087

9
BEYOND MONETARY GAIN
Motivational Correlates of Sustainable Finance

Klaus Harnack and Sven Moons

Introduction

The increasing recognition that money represents power and, therefore, cannot be spent or invested in a value-neutral manner adds a new variable to the equation calculating the fit between a client's needs and a financial product or service. For societies with an emphasis on social and democratic participation, it gives rise to concepts such as sustainable finance and green or impact investing. In societies with a religious emphasis, it fosters faith-based concepts such as Shariah-compliant investing, which is very common in Muslim countries. The trend to include non-monetary aspects in the evaluation of investment products is reflected in current financial legislation such as the Sustainable Finance Disclosure Regulation (Regulation (EU) 2019/2088 of the European Parliament and of the Council of 27 November 2019 on sustainability-related disclosures in the financial services sector, 2019). This requires firms providing investment services to obtain non-financial information from the client, such as sustainability preferences, in addition to the client's financial capacity, financial goals, time horizon, investment knowledge, experience, and risk propensity. We propose that legal requirements such as the MiFID II amendment (Explanatory Memorandum to the Commission Delegated Regulation Amending MiFID II Delegated Regulation (EU) 2017/565, 2021) are the first of many essential steps to ensure a congruent structure between the individual needs of a client and the financial products provided—a step towards a hyper-personalized investment approach to guarantee an overall fit that encompasses financial and non-financial aspects of an investment. To explore and clarify this non-financial variable, the present contribution reviews this variable from a hedonic, motivational, and psychological point of view, supported by recent survey data.

The idea of the clear and calculable objectivity of money has been abandoned following the spread of behavioral theories, such as the prospect theory. This has revealed a clear deviation from the rational approach and shown that maximized expected value is not the sole driver of investment decisions in financial markets. The realization has prevailed that such decisions are driven by more than just monetary gain and that the values and the higher-order goals of individuals need to be incorporated. Financial institutions increasingly respond to this trend, which is reflected by manifold labels such as socially responsible investments (SRI), ethical- or faith-based investments, green finance, and environmental, social, and governance investments (ESG). However, the current debate on this topic generally follows a top-down design and overlooks the human experience of investing, including its hedonic, motivational, and psychological basis. With an increasingly competitive wealth management market, and an ever-tighter corset of legal constraints, a higher sensitivity to an investor's wants and needs will become a real differentiator that leads to better and more distinguishable investment services. Therefore, the present contribution will put the horse before the cart and will overturn the general top-down approaches, such as debates on standardized ESG scoring, and address this topic from a client's psychological perspective. We briefly try to restore the natural order and ask what motivates people to invest their money in financial securities in the first place and unpack the values associated with investing beyond the monetary dimension.

We summarize the current body of empirical research and encourage the financial industry, in the framework of highly regulated markets, to design distinguishable and suitable products to fit investor needs. The claim we make with this contribution is that, instead of nudging people into assumed "better" ESG investments or simply following current trends, financial institutions must look to find the optimal fit between investor needs and values and the investment products and services provided.

Monetary Hedonics as a Starting Point

The first piece of cake gives happiness, the fifth abdominal pain.
The law of diminishing returns

Even if conventional wisdom seems to have a clear opinion—money alone does not make you happy—it seems worthwhile at the beginning of this investigation to outline motivational correlates of sustainable finance to investigate the more basic correlates and to gain a deeper understanding of the motivational forces of money and the interplay of money and individual utility.

In recent years, numerous newspaper headlines have stated that above a certain income, there is no longer any increase in well-being (Killingsworth, 2021). In recent decades, science has found it surprisingly difficult to create a differentiated picture of the connections between money, consumption, and happiness. This debate was curbed (Kim & Oswald, 2021) in a much-cited paper by Brickman and colleagues (Brickman et al., 1978), which concluded that winning the lottery does not significantly affect people's subjective well-being. However, several studies have recently shown that money can increase happiness, but only under the right circumstances and if the money is spent "right" (Dunn et al., 2014).

It is interesting to consider the following example and compare the levels of happiness between fictional lottery winners Peter and Paul. While Peter wins 10,000 euros, Paul pocketed a profit of 10,010 euros. After receiving their prize, both leave the local lottery retailer, and while nothing else unusual happens to Paul, Peter spots a ten euro note on the floor in front of the shop and adds it to the cash bundle of his lottery prize. In total, both have now gained a profit of 10,010 euros; however, Peter is certainly the happier of the two, since he has made two "wins," and the ten additional euros do not vanish in the financial saturation of the first win (cf. Kahneman/Tversky, 1979). By including a social dimension, Peter could further increase his happiness by donating the additionally gained ten euros directly into the tip jar on the counter of the friendly old lady from the lottery shop, which would satisfy his need for social belonging. In summary, monetary utility rises from context, perception, and social relations.

How to Spend Money "Right"

Once we have some money, the question remains of how to spend it. The Canadian social psychologist Elizabeth Dunn offers a good starting point for answering this question with her essay, "If money doesn't make you happy, you aren't spending it right," published in 2011, in which she formulates principles on how we can spend money in ways that will increase our happiness (Dunn et al., 2011). Dunn's first principle states, "Buy experiences instead of things." Unfortunately, the distinction between the constructs of "experience" and "things" is not always clear. For example, if you think of purchasing a bicycle, is the purchase aimed at the experience (bicycle tours and excursions) or at the object itself, the bicycle? Nevertheless, numerous studies show that, regardless of age, gender, or background, purchases that are made with the intention of gaining life experience make people happier than purely material purchases (Van Boven & Gilovich, 2003). In addition, purchased experiences are more likely to alleviate negative feelings such as loneliness, which material purchases are only capable of to a very limited extent (Yang et al., 2021). Purchased experiences make people happier as they address their own identity and strengthen social bonds, a fact that overlaps with the idea of non-financial dimensions of investments. Investments, such as particular stocks or sustainable ETFs can foster an investor's social identity and generate non-monetary added value, provided that the investments are aligned or act congruently with the investor's values.

Dunn's second principle says, "Help others and not yourself," which reflects the entire complex of "prosocial spending" and, in terms of investments, the idea of social and impact investment (Arjaliès et al., 2022; Roundy et al., 2017). Numerous empirical studies indicate that people who spend money on others report more happiness than those who spend money on themselves (Dunn et al., 2014). The happiness created by prosocial spending is not only reflected via self-reports but also through neurophysiological studies (Harbaugh et al., 2007; Weinstein & Ryan, 2010). Furthermore, this effect does not only hold true for money spent on humans but also when we spend money on our pets (White et al., 2021). In a similar vein, matching one's own values with key attributes of a company one invests in can create added value, provided that basic levels of financial security are present.

Dunn's third principle states, "Buy many small pleasures rather than one large." A characteristic of happiness, in general, is that it is related to the frequency rather than the intensity of positive affective experiences (Diener et al., 2009). One reason for this is that stimuli cannot be adapted to as quickly in the case of frequent but smaller happiness impulses, which means that there is no habituation effect and happiness can be preserved. The same effect is seen in leisure and recreation research, with many small vacations found to be more relaxing than one long annual vacation (de Bloom et al., 2012). In the domain of investments, this insight could be used in systematic investment plans that would gain, via repeated value-congruent experiences, a higher non-financial payoff. Another positive effect of this phenomenon is predicted by the expectancy-value theory (Eccles, 1983), which posits that achievement motivation becomes stronger when there is a match with personal values. In other words, people are more likely to initiate and persist in achievement-related behavior if the goal is congruent with their values.

Online Survey

To better understand the motivation, goals, and values of today's retail investors, we conducted an online survey with a panel from an independent fieldwork agency. We interviewed 4,690 potential investors in Belgium, the Netherlands, Denmark, Sweden, and Finland in accordance with the ICC/ESOMAR standards on market research. To qualify, respondents were required to have a financial reserve equivalent to at least six months' net income and indicate their interest or current engagement in investing part of that money in instruments such as stocks, bonds, or funds. We measured several motivational concepts, including financial regulatory focus (Higgins, 2012) or financial goals (Gollwitzer, 1999), individual values (tailored items inspired by the

Schwartz Value Inventory; Schwartz, 1992, 2013), and demographic data (general demographics and financial specifics such as investable assets, income, financial maturity, and risk profile). The data was collected at the end of 2021 as part of a research project on goal-based and value investments. We refer to Moons and Harnack (2021, 2022) for detailed descriptions of the data, further results, and detailed classification. Excerpts from this data will be used to support the ongoing development of hypotheses, and due to scarce direct empirical evidence in this field, we will also draw on scientific knowledge from related areas.

The Importance of Goals

Financial goals of retail investors range from undefined, such as "making more money out of the given money," to abstract, such as "gaining independence," over "saving for the kids' college," and to very concrete goals, such as "finance next year's vacation." Next to the most obvious financial goal most people have (i.e., financial growth and stability), there is a diverse spectrum of superordinate or higher-order goals, such as saving the environment, fostering equal rights, or promoting corporate governance. In this sense, investment goals are similar to everyday goals, for instance, "I want to eat locally produced and thereby do something for the environment." Both exhibit the same compound structure, an individual primary goal, and a collective high-order goal. To arrive at the root of this compound structure, we first examine the configuration of primary goals followed by value-driven superordinate goals.

Primary Goals

Motivational research highlights, in essence, that goal-striving needs to be specific, challenging, and feasible to deliver enhanced task performance (Locke & Latham, 2002). Goals and related contextual information need to be as concrete and SMART, that is, specific, measurable, attainable, relevant, and time-bound (Locke & Latham, 1990) as possible. With respect to the concreteness of goals, the present survey data presents a clear insight that retail investors are not specific about their primary investment goals. From several hundred open answers to the question of which goals investors considered important in their lives, it is evident that people are far less capable of articulating investment goals than they are at choosing them from a predefined list. One out of five respondents from the open-answer version of our survey was rejected from inclusion as they claimed to have no idea or were unable to provide a comprehensible answer to this question.

If the participants had the choice of selecting an investment goal from a predefined list, it assisted in overcoming this problem. When participants were asked if they had a concrete outcome in mind for the number one investment goal chosen from our list, approximately 71% answered, "No, it is more a general goal," only 22% had a specific total amount in mind, and 7% had a return percentage. These figures varied somewhat between countries, generations, and superordinate investment motivations.

Be Concrete

The widespread inability among retail investors to formulate goals is not limited to the finance sector but is deeply rooted in our human cognitive system. Cognition is grounded in the present moment, the here and now, which shapes goal-striving (Barsalou, 2008; Harnack, 2015). Our cognitive hardware has been shaped by evolution to think about urgent rather than important things. However, since financial goals always involve a time lag and a certain amount of uncertainty, the construal level theory (Liberman et al., 2002) is ideal to ease goal-setting and foster concreteness for both primary and superordinate goals. The construal level theory uses the notion of psychological distance to describe a change in thinking and evaluating between the actor bound in space and time and the nature of investments. Psychological distance utilizes four dimensions—spatial, temporal, social, and hypothetical—to describe the space between the planning individual and the representation of a future state, which becomes indistinct and abstract the more distance there is between the person and the desired objective of the goal.

To illustrate the mode of action, imagine going on vacation tomorrow. What is on your mind? It will probably be occupied by concrete things, like how do I get to the airport? Does the neighbor have the mailbox key? Who takes care of the flowers? Are all the passports close at hand? However, when thinking about a vacation a year from now, what is on your mind? No doubt more abstract things dominate your thinking, such as the fact that the trip will be relaxing and that you will have a good time. The psychological distance, consequently, determines the degree of resolution in which we are aware of a future situation. Naturally, this mechanism applies to the financial domain as well. As financial goals by their very nature have a time horizon and can only be viewed by taking uncertainties into consideration, time and uncertainty become the central variables. Both usually have rather abstract representations and are toxic to effective goal-striving and value-congruent investing.

To make financial goal-striving easier and more efficient, psychological distance should be as minimal as possible. This is especially important as the survey revealed that most investors fail to articulate their wishes and desires as investment goals. Regarding the primary investment dimension, most investors had neither a concrete idea of the exact nature of the final goal nor of the exact period. This attitude can be equated with the idea of "do your best" goals, which are always the worst of all goal conditions in goal-striving experiments (Sheeran et al., 2005).

Overcoming Abstraction

A stronger focus on the process rather than on outcomes can assist in forming better plans (Kaftan et al., 2018). Compared to outcomes, the means of goals are psychologically closer and, therefore, more concrete and actionable in themselves. Moreover, a process can be managed and a user experience designed to perform adequately.

One strategy that combines both outcome and process foci is mental contrasting (Oettingen, 2012) combined with implementation intentions (Gollwitzer, 1999), which has been proven to enhance goal-striving behavior. This strategy requires an individual to mentally walk the psychological distance toward their goal and set the starting and endpoint of the path by first imagining a desired future outcome and then contrasting it with the less positive current state (Oettingen & Gollwitzer, 2010). On this mental path, obstacles and needs are identified, implementation intentions are formulated (small if–then plans, e.g., If I receive a salary bonus at the end of the year, then I will buy additional ETFs), and concrete actions are predefined. It is something private bankers intuitively do whenever they sit down with their high net-worth clients, and it can be worked into the process of mass onboarding affluent clients to a digital investment tool. Executing this strategy is not just about asking investors to state their goals but also to describe, contextualize, and add details to sharpen their mental image of this goal. It is important to note that the construal level (psychological closeness vs. distance) must be adjusted based on the context. For instance, when a deadline is distant, a focus on the outcome may distract people from implementing goal-relevant actions; however, if the deadline is near, an outcome focus can revive the importance of the goal and give a final boost to motivation. Extensive research also suggests that goal commitment can be increased by shifting from a process to an outcome focus when the individual has acquired the necessary skills to master the task (Zimmerman & Kitsantas, 1999).

Beyond Monetary Gain: Higher-Value Goals

After investigating primary goals and their underlying motivation mechanisms, we explored superordinate goals and values. Values give meaning to, energize, and regulate behavior. This holds true only if values are cognitively activated and central to the self (Verplanken & Holland, 2002). Therefore, acknowledgment and incorporation of values are central to gaining psychological fit. Two types of values should be considered and are reflected in two emerging trends for sustainability labels, impact investment vs. value investment. While impact investment has an active element and expresses, "I want to do something with my money," value investment is more passive and involves a wish to align with something. In addition, superordinate goals and values can be characterized using different degrees of resolution. For instance, the goal of securing green finance can be broad and abstract (saving nature) as well as very concrete (preventing overfishing). They are shaped by the investor's life experience, current situation in life, and anticipated future states. For example, young investors in Belgium and the Netherlands care more, to some degree, about environmental issues than older investors but also focus markedly more on social issues. A case in point is the issues of board diversity and the gender pay gap in listed companies. Only 6.7% of the Silent Generation and 8.2% of Baby Boomers indicated their concern about this issue, while 16.9% of Millennials and 18.6% of Generation Z respondents indicated that this specific factor would be important to them when considering investments. Young people have only experienced living in a more diverse society and do not want to encounter any of the old glass ceilings in their future careers. Therefore, it is not surprising that they wish to consider these factors when making investment decisions.

Superordinate goals influence the prominence of values; however, only to a certain extent. Respondents to our survey were asked to identify the minimal percentage of their investments that should align with their personal values. Those driven by self-enhancement needs, such as power or achievement, drew the line just under 50%, those driven by conservation needs, such as conformity or security, just over 50%, and only those driven by the very self-transcending universalism motivation crossed the 60% threshold. It is significant to note that this last segment represented less than three percent of the retail investor community in the market that we surveyed.

Describing Values

In our survey, we used the Schwartz theory of universal values (Schwartz, 2007) to capture the wide spectrum of human needs that drive behavior. Assuming values also drive investment behavior, we considered the concept of "value" to be similar to a superordinate goal. The reason for this choice of framework is that it embodies all investment intentions, including the dimension of universalism which is lacking in most models in use by financial institutions today. Universalism is a value that emerges with the realization that, to survive as a group, we must treat others who are different from us justly and protect the natural environment and resources on which life depends. This is, of course, especially important for the entire domain of sustainable finance and all neighboring constructs.

When viewing these superordinate goals arranged along the two bipolar dimensions, some values are clearly in conflict with one another (e.g., benevolence and power), while others are compatible (e.g., conformity and security). As Figure 9.1 illustrates, one dimension contrasts

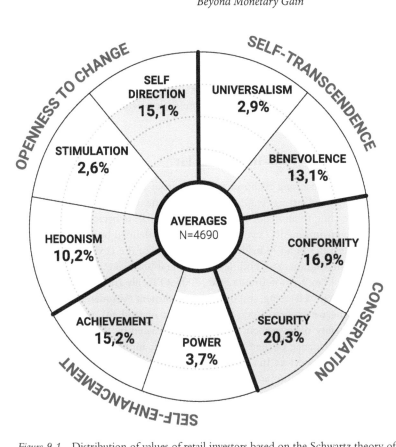

Figure 9.1 Distribution of values of retail investors based on the Schwartz theory of universal values

values of openness to change and conservation. This dimension captures the conflict between values that emphasize independent thought and readiness for change on one hand and conformity and preservation on the other. The second dimension contrasts self-enhancement and self-transcendence, capturing the conflict between values that emphasize concern for the welfare of others and the pursuit of one's own welfare and dominance.

Values Signal Direction

A basic mechanism that enables values to drive behavior is the increased saliency towards an issue. Values have the property of being present and noticeable and function as a mental signpost and door-opener. Whenever we experience a fit of values, mental access is increased, and attention and intellectual accessibility are similarly reduced if one's own values are not represented.

Consider the following example: when analyzing the Schwartz model, it becomes clear that the political representatives of liberal and conservative parties in the United States of America have opposing value structures, especially in the domain of environmental issues where their attitudes are often conflicting. In their research, Feinberg and Willer (2013) showed that the discourse on environmental issues usually centers around moral concerns related to harm to and care of nature, which are core values of the liberals. Meanwhile, the purity of nature is more central to the values of conservatives. Further studies (Feinberg & Willer, 2015) showed that by using the right set of values—that is, the set of values important to the receiver of the message—

it became easier to gain people's attention, and the strength of the argument was increased. In practical terms, when talking to a conservative person about environmental issues, it makes more sense to stress the notion of purity of nature rather than to point out that damage to nature could result from a particular action. Therefore, to present sustainable investments as an appealing alternative and profit from the benefits of superordinate fit, it is crucial to address the set of values compatible with the views of the specific client.

Person–Investment Fit

Psychological theories on fit have a long tradition and result from a long line of research based in organizational and work-related settings (e.g., person–environment fit, person–organizational fit, person–person fit). According to all major fit frameworks, human behavior is a function of both the individual and the environment (Lewin, 1951), and fit is defined by the grade of congruence, the shared characteristics of an individual, and attributes of the environment (P–E fit effect). Results reveal that the alignment of both leads to several positive outcomes (Chatman, 1989; Higgins, 2005; Kristof, 1996; Kristof-Brown et al., 2005; O'Reilly III et al., 1991), including higher motivation, increased well-being, and higher commitment (Verquer et al., 2003).

Building on this tradition, we suggest a person–investment fit (P–I fit) and propose that, analogous to P–E fit, the quality of investment decisions is mediated by the extent to which the investor perceives the congruence of their monetary and non-monetary needs with those attributes of financial products or services. In addition to the fundamental monetary dimensions (financial resources, time horizon, risk propensity, etc.), this includes a regulatory-, superordinate goal- and value-fit, which all contribute to a hyper-personalized approach by financial services providers.

Two types of fit are generally considered—supplementary and complementary. Supplementary fit refers to the similarity between individual values with characteristics of the context or environment; it mirrors its own values. Supplementary fit is more common and has the strongest behavioral implications; for example, similarity drives a trust-establishing mechanism (Brodie & Harnack, 2018). Nevertheless, complementary fit, which refers to the idea that something is missing or should be added to create a whole, becomes important when people want to compensate for their own "sustainable shortcomings" (Hope et al., 2018; Kaklamanou et al., 2015).

Creating Fit

At the beginning of this chapter, we described aspects connecting hedonism and money-spending, but we intentionally left out one crucial element, personality. Although numerous studies explicitly examine relationships between the Big Five personality traits and financial behaviors (Brown & Taylor, 2014; Camgoz et al., 2012; Donnelly et al., 2012), a large-scale field study (Matz et al., 2016) should function as the first blueprint for P–I fit. This study suggested that people individually spend more money on products that match their personalities and report higher life satisfaction if their purchases match their personalities. The experiment rated 59 clusters of products and financial spending based on a standardized Big Five inventory (Gosling et al., 2003) by 100 people. This assigned all potential spending categories a "personality" classification. For instance, art supplies were assigned a high rating for the personality dimension of openness, and paying insurance received a high rating for conscientiousness. These ratings were then matched with participants' identified personality traits and their actual spending using bank transaction records. The results implied that the fit of both dimensions increased the utility of purchase. Therefore, a person scoring high in conscientiousness (efficient, organized, etc.) would become happier buying a book compared to spending the same amount of money at a roulette table, while a person scoring high in extraversion (sociable, cheerful, etc.) would be more likely to derive happiness from purchases for travel, music, and entertainment. In the context of the concept of psychological fit, individual differences determine the "right" type of spending dependent on the personality trait. The authors noted that the effect of right spending was stronger than the effect of individuals' total income or the effect of their total spending (Matz et al., 2016).

Regulatory Fit

If personality attributes like the Big Five should be considered when generating a P–I fit, what other dimensions should also be accounted for? The regulatory focus theory (Higgins, 2012) seems to be a good candidate for a P–I sub-dimension. The theory distinguishes between two basic motivational stances—promotion and prevention focus. Promotion focus describes efforts to improve circumstances from a given point, that is, the motivation to get from a current state (point zero) to a plus one state. In comparison, prevention focus is aimed at not deteriorating from a given point, so not slipping from point zero to a minus one state. Depending on these two basic motivational stances, motivational perception and action is shaped because people direct their attention to information and opportunities aligned with their basic motivation. Promotion-oriented goals are generally more related to positive emotions than prevention-oriented goals and are associated with values such as self-enhancement; this reflects the idea that goals require the right means for goal-striving.

Keller and Kesberg (2017) found that between 75.5% and 83% of participants in their research were predominantly promotion-focused in their general and habitual self-regulatory orientation. Our research corroborates these findings. For instance, depending on the superordinate investment goal, between 68% and 88% of our respondents in Belgium and the Netherlands

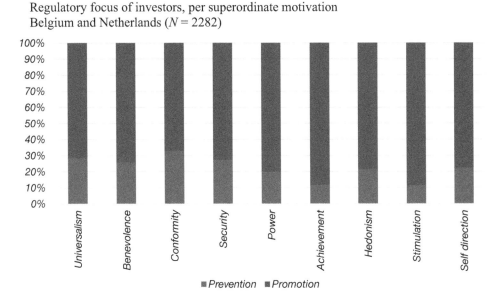

Figure 9.2 Distribution of regulatory focus of retail investors based on their superordinate motivation of Schwartz theory of universal values

were promotion-focused. What is remarkable is that no significant differences were observed between generations or genders. What did result in a difference was investment experience; the focus on promotion was higher (by 6.5% on average) for people who already invested than for those who only had the intention to invest.

Regarding the relationship between human values and basic self-regulatory orientations, our findings parallel those of Keller and Kesberg (2017) and Leikas et al. (2009). We noticed that in investing, the promotion focus was relatively stronger for goals motivated by self-enhancement (achievement, power) than for goals that endorse self-transcendence (universalism). Investment goals reflecting an openness to change (stimulation, hedonism) were also more promotion-focused than those that value conservation (security, conformity). But with an average of 76% of retail investors in the Belgian and Dutch markets being promotion-focused, we conclude there is ample capacity to stir up excitement for positive future outcomes in these markets.

Dating Your Asset?

Since algorithms have found their way into the area in which it is probably most important to have a good fit, dating, it is worth looking at lessons learned from this domain. Independently from the underlying matching algorithm, all online dating apps vary in the degree of individual control from self-selection to preselection by algorithmic involvement. A study by Tong et al. (2016) found that blended systems, using preselection and subsequent self-selection, are most preferred by users. This approach incorporates the "curse of choice," that is, the finding that too much choice has a demotivating effect and that fewer choices lead to greater choice satisfaction (Iyengar & Lepper, 2000). In addition, analysis of dating apps has pinpointed problems that make it difficult to establish a good fit. One problem is that people usually seek sub-dimensions not offered in the given framework (Frost et al., 2008), and even if these attributes are listed, people's stated preferences for an ideal mate do not always align with what they eventually find attractive in a person (Eastwick & Finkel, 2008). With this in mind, practical approaches to gaining P–I fit should, therefore, aim towards a continuous assessment of needs and values instead of a single measure before the consultation and sales process. This should combine an algorithmic preselection with subsequent personal adjustment and ensure that the markers are individual and specific on a pre-selected list.

$E \neq S \neq G$

While the expanded MiFID questionnaires represent current efforts to further prioritize client needs, there is intense debate over the configuration, evaluation, and structuring of ESG ratings. We propose that this debate is partly a product of the neglected bottom-up approach. Although there are some attempts to overcome obvious shortcomings—for instance, using only the governance pillar as a cross-sectoral construct (MSCI ESG Research LLC, 2022)—the current top-down approach generally maintains the idea that there is an objective way of scoring assets. The following example illustrates a potentially major flaw of this assumption.

Peter and Paul have a common friend named John. While Peter values John's qualities as a good listener, Paul has become good friends with John because they share a passion for fishing, a hobby that Peter does not enjoy at all. Although both Peter and Paul have good reasons to be friends with John, their reasons differ depending on the attributes they seek from a friendship with John. Peter and Paul evaluate and utilize John from different angles, and if they were both asked to score John as friend, they would use different sub-dimensions so that their composite score of "John as friend" would not reflect their individual perceptions. It becomes immediately obvious that a general "John as friend" score is a faulty construction. It is exactly this misconception that drives the heated debate over ESG scorings. Whereas some people might perceive companies such as Tesla as a prototypical element of an ESG fund, others are eager to ban Tesla from major indices due to its governance problems. Another reason for the biased perception of a general score relates to the E at the beginning of the acronym ESG, although G is usually the only consistently used factor. Due to the primacy effect, factor E is cognitively the most accessible and creates a bias in the general perception of an overall ESG rating. To conclude, it makes no sense to classify shared friends using a combined "friend rating," and viewed from a psychological needs perspective, there is no such thing as a composite general ESG score. Instead, a well-balanced ESG portfolio could be thought of as a circle of friends, with each friend serving a different need, rather than a set of "average friends."

Just as generalized ESG scores seem to have major flaws on a structural level, a generalized ESG score is also not particularly useful considering the bottom-up approach. One major finding from our survey data was the very weak correlation among the subcategories E, S, and G. From a psychological perspective, a compound ESG score functions on a high construal level. This means that it requires people to think abstractly, look at the bigger picture, and not focus on the details but instead get an overall gist of the matter. Consequently, ESG scores present sustainability goals as a rather abstract concept that is detrimental to goal-commitment and identification. Assuming that investors only consider ESG factors they feel bring added utility when creating their portfolios, and disregard the ones that do not, we proposed the following options to retail investors in our survey:

E. Environmental Considerations

E1 Global warming: reducing carbon emissions, ...
E2 Nature and pollution: toxic emissions, land use, ...
E3 Positive impact: renewable energy, clean technology, ...
E4 Resources used: energy, water, recycling, ...
E5 Controversies: accidents, spills, risky operations, ...

S. Social Considerations

S1 Employee well-being: working conditions, minimum wage, ...
S2 Diversity: gender pay gap, diversity of board members, ...
S3 Social damage: alcohol, weapons, gambling, obesity, ...
S4 Social cohesion: supporting local, regional, national businesses, ...
S5 Social contributions: taxes paid, employment provided, ...

G. Governance Considerations

G1 Shareholder protection: shareholder rights, capital restrictions, ...
G2 Accounting stress: qualified audits, working capital stress, ...
G3 Board composition: independent directors, CEO/chairman, ...
G4 Dividend policy: healthy pay-out ratio, favor dividend payers, ...
G5 Ethical behavior: no controversies, legal disputes, insider dealing, ...

Note: options from the three overarching ESG categories that retail investors could choose from

Variables	E1	E2	S1	S2	G1	G2
E1	—					
E2	.54	—				
E3	.47	.45				
E4	.42	.41				
E5	.29	.37				
S1	.23	.20	—			
S2	.16	.17	.28	—		
S3	.15	.19	.31	.20		
S4	.16	.16	.31	.22		
S5	.15	.15	.34	.17		
G1	.02	.05	.05	.03	—	
G2	.03	.06	.07	.08	.34	—
G3	.02	.06	.06	.06	.28	.34
G4	.00	.04	.05	.03	.34	.35
G5	.05	.08	.10	.05	.35	.36

Figure 9.3 Simplified correlation table for respondent's inter-item responses for specific subcategories. Note: the correlations within one category are marked in red

The matrix in Figure 9.3 shows how ESG preferences correlate for all the respondents in our survey. The main finding here is a moderate to low positive correlation between the choices for subcategories within a general category but not beyond. For example, those who chose E1 (global warming) were moderately inclined to also choose E2 ($r = .54$) or E3 ($r = .47$) but were not inclined to select any of the social factors (with correlation coefficients between .15 and .23) or governance factors (between .00 and .05).

From the number and the type of sustainability preferences our respondents selected, we can conclude that retail investors prefer to be specific when it comes to tailoring their portfolios to suit their values (see Figure 9.4). This is not only the case for investors for whom values are important (18% selected only general ESG categories, and 69% selected specific subcategories) but also for those who consider values unimportant when investing (3% selected only general ESG categories, and 43% selected specific subcategories). The fact that 46% of the latter category of investors nevertheless selected ESG factors from the list, further strengthens our earlier claim that value-fit matters. In fact, only 13.5% of our entire sample stated that considering values is not important to them when investing and refrained from selecting any of the proposed ESG factors.

The tendency to choose subcategories and concentrate choices within a given general category indicates how specific investors are regarding what provides them the utility of value-fit. It could be argued that nudging investors toward a general ESG-themed portfolio is a less-than-optimal tactic because it does not satisfy an investor's desire to consider value choices at a more concrete construal level. This creates needless constraints for portfolio construction that could

Selection of sub-categories to express ESG preferences when investing

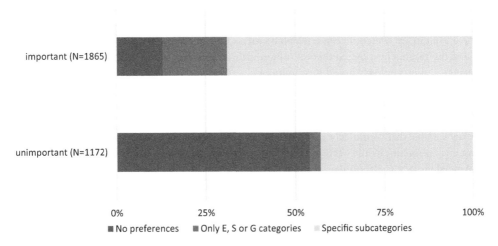

Figure 9.4 Percentage of selected subcategories depending on the importance of considering sustainable factors

negatively affect performance or lessen the chance of reaching a financial goal within a given timeframe. To summarize, a value-fit is not created with an investment portfolio that is 'as ESG-compliant as possible'. It is about allowing investors to consider their choices and create a highly personalized portfolio that simply feels right for them.

Conclusion

The initial Spiderman quote, "with great power comes great responsibility," holds true; based on the empirical research and data provided, people are willing to fall in with this claim (Bauer et al., 2021), taking ESG-dimensions into account while also deriving utility from holding assets with higher sustainability performance (Luz et al., 2022). However, there are several obstacles that need to be overcome to turn this intention into a liberating action. One of these obstacles manifests in the basic understanding of sustainable finance. When browsing the current sustainable finance literature, it becomes obvious that many publications are still concerned with questions like, "Does it pay to be responsible?" This focus on a purely monetary outcome reveals a belief that sustainable finance is composed of a monetary core dimension and some sort of fuzzy, non-pecuniary appendage. We believe this to be a misconception and that sustainable finance should be viewed as an ontologically-driven, coherent concept.

Consider, for instance, the name-letter effect (Nuttin, 1985), a robust empirical finding that describes the propensity to prefer things that are aligned with alphabetical letters in one's name. Knewtson and Sias (2010) showed that this effect holds true for the financial world and that people exhibit this effect when selecting and evaluating financial products (e.g., Adam likes Apple). In a similar vein is the research by Bonnefon et al. (2022), which found that value alignment, rather than impact issues, drives ethical investments. Investors seek to align their investments with their social values.

But why is it so hard to establish a theoretical common ground? One major reason are the disciplinary, epistemological, and terminological boundaries and differences. A possible path from the current transdisciplinary discordant toward a coherent theory is the epistemological concept of consilience (Whewell, 1840). It proposes that evidence unrelated to its sources can converge towards a shared theoretical fundament independent from its epistemological origin. However, this approach requires the willingness to overcome disciplinary vanities. Only when these vanities are overcome can research be carried out that substantially advances the field. It is based on inspired by a shared theoretical foundation that targeted research in the intersection of finance and psychology should be conducted.

Financial Literacy as the Key

A key variable that continually arises is financial education and the practical necessity to translate sustainable intentions into action. Enabling people to participate in the market via increased financial literacy and tools that enable intuitive access is an essential step. This is apparent when considering studies like Anderson and Robinson's (2021), which found that people with pro-environment attitudes are not more likely to hold pro-environment portfolios because this cohort tends toward financial disengagement and is less likely to own stocks. Green financial engagement is stronger only in settings where financial literacy is high. This is analogous to studies illustrating that the likelihood of voting and the possibility to actively impact society increases with the level of education (Hansen & Tyner, 2021). This is because knowledge and understanding enable individual participation, therefore, decreasing informational hurdles and facilitating understanding are essential. This is also supported by the research by de Zwaan et al. (2015), which demonstrates that informative deficits lead to less ESG involvement.

Besides the direct implications, there are manifold other benefits for higher financial literacy, such as increased saliency of the issue—we see what we understand. Higher saliency increases acting possibilities, which is necessary because financial products or services have a low level of construal and are abstract in the mental representation; for example, it is easier to choose a local, organic, or sustainably produced product in the supermarket because it is tangible and concrete. However, better financial education could compensate for this hindrance.

A Financial License

One approach to remedy this deficiency and reform a peculiar practice is to reframe MiFID assessment procedures. Instead of understanding the MiFID assessment as a kind of letter of protection for investors, it could instead be understood as a kind of financial driver's license that determines the scope of financial possibilities and the tools required to pursue personal financial goals. From this analogy, it is easy to see how precarious current practice is. Nobody would take a driving test without having practiced and been instructed beforehand. If you put an untrained person in a car and gave them a driving test, the average person would not get past the controls for the radio, lights, and windshield wipers, resulting in a very restricted driver's license that only allows you to turn the lights on and off. This absurdity reflects the status quo in the area of MiFID assessment, hence the MiFID assessment should be preceded by a phase of education, similar to the training undertaken prior to taking a driving test. In summary, financial literacy and good informational practice is a major prerequisite of financial empowerment (Bethlendi et al., 2022).

Conflicting Goals

Regarding goal-setting, we would like to highlight the presence of a lurking false friend. One must be very careful with direct motivational deductions. Motivation and goal-striving are not unidimensional constructs, goal conflicts are pervasive in our lives (Fishbach et al., 2010), and mixed motives are the rule, not the exception. With different situational circumstances, the saliency and behavioral grounds for goal-striving change. The study by Ciaian et al. (2022) is a good example that no direct conclusions should be immediately drawn. This study deals with the interplay of cryptocurrencies and sustainable investment behavior and reveals that the fact that cryptocurrencies have a large carbon footprint cannot be used to predict that those with a pro-environmental attitude will scorn these markets. On the contrary, they show that people with stronger ESG preferences tend to invest more frequently in crypto-assets than less ESG-conscious investors. It turns out that avoiding carbon emissions is just one factor out of several in a universe of values that shape decision-making for someone with a pro-environmental attitude. In this case, it could be a higher goal and the curiosity and desire for something new that creates this connection. Again, the level of financial education is the key variable that predicts engagement with sustainable-focused products. In summary, no direct conclusions should be drawn from goals, but goal conflict should not be seen as a hindrance. Rather, goal conflict can be productive because it attenuates the robust bias of confirmatory thinking (Kleiman & Hassin, 2013) and supports well-being (Sun et al., 2021).

Person–Investment Fit

In conclusion, we propose a coherent and broader approach to sustainable finance that embraces person–investment fit as a more effective approach to the current and widespread modular view. This approach combines fundamentals, such as individual financial resources, time horizons, and risk propensity, with service needs, goals, and values. Ensuring a good person–investment fit requires solid financial education, continuous needs-congruence evaluation, and attention to an individualized needs assessment. As ESG ratings are inconsistent across sustainability rating providers (Kräussl et al., 2022), using available sub-scores and a more human-centric approach are essential steps. We firmly believe that by considering these issues, we can open the door to further democratizing the financial sector, empower people to activate their hidden intentions, and utilize the huge financial resources of private capital and institutional investors for the implementation of democratic intent.

Acknowledgment

Data collection was funded by InvestSuite and was conducted end of 2021.

References

Anderson, A., & Robinson, D. T. (2021). Financial literacy in the age of green investment. *Review of Finance*, rfab031. https://doi.org/10.1093/rof/rfab031

Arjaliès, D.-L., Chollet, P., Crifo, P., & Mottis, N. (2022). The motivations and practices of impact assessment in socially responsible investing: The French case and its implications for the accounting and impact investing communities. *Social and Environmental Accountability Journal*, 1–29. https://doi.org/10.1080/0969160X.2022.2032239

Barsalou, L. W. (2008). Grounded cognition. *Annual Review of Psychology*, 59, 617–645. https://doi.org/10.1146/annurev.psych.59.103006.093639

Bauer, R., Ruof, T., & Smeets, P. (2021). Get real! Individuals prefer more sustainable investments. *Review of Financial Studies*, 34(8), 3976–4043. https://doi.org/10.1093/rfs/hhab037

Bethlendi, A., Nagy, L., & Póra, A. (2022). Green finance: The neglected consumer demand. *Journal of Sustainable Finance and Investment*, 1–19. https://doi.org/10.1080/20430795.2022.2090311

Bonnefon, J.-F., Landier, A., Sastry, P. R., & Thesmar, D. (2022). *The moral preferences of investors: Experimental evidence* (Working Paper No. 29647). National Bureau of Economic Research. https://doi.org/10.3386/w29647

Brickman, P., Coates, D., & Janoff-Bulman, R. (1978). Lottery winners and accident victims: Is happiness relative? *Journal of Personality and Social Psychology, 36*(8), 917–927. https://doi.org/10.1037/0022-3514.36.8.917

Brodie, H., & Harnack, K. (2018). *The trust mandate* (1st ed.). Harriman House.

Brown, S., & Taylor, K. (2014). Household finances and the 'Big Five' personality traits. *Journal of Economic Psychology, 45*, 197–212. https://doi.org/10.1016/j.joep.2014.10.006

Camgoz, S. M., Karan, M. B., & Ergeneli, A. (2012). Relationship between the Big-Five personality and the financial performance of fund managers. *Diversity, Conflict and Leadership*, 1(13), 137–152.

Chatman, J. A. (1989). Improving interactional organizational research: A model of person-organization fit. *Academy of Management Review, 14*(3), 333–349. https://doi.org/10.5465/amr.1989.4279063

Ciaian, P., Cupak, A., Fessler, P., & Kancs, D. A. (2022). Environmental-social-governance preferences and investments in crypto-assets. *arXiv preprint arXiv:2206.14548*.

de Bloom, J., Geurts, S. A. E., & Kompier, M. A. J. (2012). Effects of short vacations, vacation activities and experiences on employee health and well-being. *Stress and Health, 28*(4), 305–318. https://doi.org/10.1002/smi.1434

de Zwaan, L., Brimble, M., & Stewart, J. (2015). Member perceptions of ESG investing through superannuation. *Sustainability Accounting, Management and Policy Journal, 6*(1), 79–102. https://doi.org/10.1108/SAMPJ-03-2014-0017

Diener, E., Sandvik, E., & Pavot, W. (2009). Happiness is the frequency, not the intensity, of positive versus negative affect. In E. Dinner (Ed.), *Assessing well-being* (pp. 213–231). Springer.

Donnelly, G., Iyer, R., & Howell, R. T. (2012). The Big Five personality traits, material values, and financial well-being of self-described money managers. *Journal of Economic Psychology, 33*(6), 1129–1142. https://doi.org/10.1016/j.joep.2012.08.001

Dunn, E. W., Aknin, L. B., & Norton, M. I. (2014). Prosocial spending and happiness: Using money to benefit others pays off. *Current Directions in Psychological Science, 23*(1), 41–47. https://doi.org/10.1177/0963721413512503

Dunn, E. W., Gilbert, D. T., & Wilson, T. D. (2011). If money doesn't make you happy, then you probably aren't spending it right. *Journal of Consumer Psychology*, 21(2), 115–125.

Eastwick, P. W., & Finkel, E. J. (2008). Sex differences in mate preferences revisited: Do people know what they initially desire in a romantic partner? *Journal of Personality and Social Psychology, 94*(2), 245–264. https://doi.org/10.1037/0022-3514.94.2.245

Eccles, J. (1983). Expectancies, values and academic behaviors. *Achievement and achievement motives.*

Explanatory memorandum to the commission delegated regulation amending MiFID II delegated regulation (EU) 2017/565, Pub. L. No. 2017/565 (2021).

Feinberg, M., & Willer, R. (2013). The moral roots of environmental attitudes. *Psychological Science, 24*(1), 56–62. https://doi.org/10.1177/0956797612449177

Feinberg, M., & Willer, R. (2015). From gulf to bridge: When do moral arguments facilitate political influence? *Personality and Social Psychology Bulletin, 41*(12), 1665–1681. https://doi.org/10.1177/0146167215607842

Fishbach, A., Eyal, T., & Finkelstein, S. R. (2010). How positive and negative feedback motivate goal pursuit. *Social and Personality Psychology Compass*, 4(8), 517–530.

Frost, J. H., Chance, Z., Norton, M. I., & Ariely, D. (2008). People are experience goods: Improving online dating with virtual dates. *Journal of Interactive Marketing, 22*(1), 51–61. https://doi.org/10.1002/dir.20107

Gollwitzer, P. M. (1999). Implementation intentions: Strong effects of simple plans. *American Psychologist, 54*(7), 493–503. https://doi.org/10.1037/0003-066X.54.7.493

Gosling, S. D., Rentfrow, P. J., & Swann Jr., W. B. (2003). A very brief measure of the Big-Five personality domains. *Journal of Research in Personality, 37*(6), 504–528. https://doi.org/10.1016/S0092-6566(03)00046-1

Hansen, E. R., & Tyner, A. (2021). Educational attainment and social norms of voting. *Political Behavior, 43*(2), 711–735. https://doi.org/10.1007/s11109-019-09571-8

Harbaugh, W. T., Mayr, U., & Burghart, D. R. (2007). Neural responses to taxation and voluntary giving reveal motives for charitable donations. *Science, 316*(5831), 1622–1625. https://doi.org/10.1126/science.1140738

Harnack, K. (2015). *Grounded cognition and implementation intentions* (1st ed.). Steinbeis-Edition.

Higgins, E. T. (2005). Value from regulatory fit. *Current Directions in Psychological Science, 14*(4), 209–213. http://www.jstor.org/stable/20183026

Higgins, E. T. (2012). Regulatory focus theory. In P. van Lange, A. Kruglanski, & E. Higgins (Eds.), *Handbook of theories of social psychology* (Vol. 1, pp. 483–504). Sage Publications. https://doi.org/10.4135/9781446249215.n24

Hope, A. L., Jones, C. R., Webb, T. L., Watson, M. T., & Kaklamanou, D. (2018). The role of compensatory beliefs in rationalizing environmentally detrimental behaviors. *Environment and Behavior*, 50(4), 401–425. https://doi.org/10.1177%2F0013916517706730

Iyengar, S. S., & Lepper, M. R. (2000). When choice is demotivating: Can one desire too much of a good thing? *Journal of Personality and Social Psychology*, 79(6), 995–1006. https://psycnet.apa.org/doi/10.1037/0022-3514.79.6.995

Kaftan, O. J., Freund, A. M., Diener, E., Oishi, S., & Tay, L. (2018). *The way is the goal: The role of goal focus for successful goal pursuit and subjective well-being*. https://doi.org/10.5167/uzh-147437

Kaklamanou, D., Jones, C. R., Webb, T. L., & Walker, S. R. (2015). Using public transport can make up for flying abroad on holiday: Compensatory green beliefs and environmentally significant behavior. *Environment and Behavior*, 47(2), 184–204. http://doi.org/10.1177/0013916513488784

Keller, J., & Kesberg, R. (2017). Regulatory focus and human values. *Psihologija*, 50(2), 157–186. https://doi.org/10.2298/PSI160809004K

Killingsworth, M. A. (2021). Experienced well-being rises with income, even above $75,000 per year. *Proceedings of the National Academy of Sciences*, 118(4). https://doi.org/10.1073/pnas.2016976118

Kim, S., & Oswald, A. J. (2021). Happy lottery winners and lottery-ticket bias. *Review of Income and Wealth*, 67(2), 317–333. https://doi.org/10.1111/roiw.12469

Kleiman, T., & Hassin, R. R. (2013). When conflicts are good: Nonconscious goal conflicts reduce confirmatory thinking. *Journal of Personality and Social Psychology*, 105(3), 374–387. https://doi.org/10.1037/a0033608

Knewtson, H. S., & Sias, R. W. (2010). Why Susie owns Starbucks: The name letter effect in security selection. *Journal of Business Research*, 63(12), 1324–1327. https://doi.org/10.1016/j.jbusres.2009.12.003

Kräussl, R., Oladiran, T., & Stefanova, D. (2022). *A review on ESG investing: Investors' expectations, beliefs and perceptions* (SSRN Scholarly Paper No. 4123999). https://doi.org/10.2139/ssrn.4123999

Kristof, A. L. (1996). Person-organization fit: An integrative review of its conceptualizations, measurement, and implications. *Personnel Psychology*, 49(1), 1–49. https://doi.org/10.1111/j.1744-6570.1996.tb01790.x

Kristof-Brown, A. L., Zimmerman, R. D., & Johnson, E. C. (2005). Consequences of individual's fit at work: A meta-analysis of person-job, person-organization, person-group, and person-supervisor fit. *Personnel Psychology*, 58(2), 281–342. https://doi.org/10.1111/j.1744-6570.2005.00672.x

Leikas, S., Lönnqvist, J.-E., Verkasalo, M., & Lindeman, M. (2009). Regulatory focus systems and personal values. *European Journal of Social Psychology*, 39(3), 415–429. https://doi.org/10.1002/ejsp.547

Lewin, K. (1951). *Field theory in social science: Selected theoretical papers* (D. Cartwright, ed.). Harpers.

Liberman, N., Sagristano, M. D., & Trope, Y. (2002). The effect of temporal distance on level of mental construal. *Journal of Experimental Social Psychology*, 38(6), 523–534. https://doi.org/10.1016/S0022-1031(02)00535-8

Locke, E. A., & Latham, G. P. (1990). *A theory of goal setting and task performance*. Prentice-Hall.

Locke, E. A., & Latham, G. P. (2002). Building a practically useful theory of goal setting and task motivation: A 35-year odyssey. *American Psychologist*, 57(9), 705–717. https://psycnet.apa.org/doi/10.1037/0003-066X.57.9.705

Luz, V., Schauer, V., & Viehweger, M. (2022). *Sustainability: Performance, preferences, and beliefs* (SSRN Scholarly Paper No. 4169595). https://doi.org/10.2139/ssrn.4169595

Matz, S. C., Gladstone, J. J., & Stillwell, D. (2016). Money buys happiness when spending fits our personality. *Psychological Science*, 27(5), 715–725. https://doi.org/10.1177/0956797616635200

Moons, S., & Harnack, K. (2021). *The investor's Rubicon: Setting investment goals* [White paper]. InvestSuite.

Moons, S., & Harnack, K. (2022). *The investor's Rubicon: Planning and acting on goals* [White paper]. InvestSuite.

MSCI ESG Research LLC. (2022). *MSCI ESG ratings methodology*. https://www.msci.com/documents/1296102/21901542/ESG-Ratings-Methodology-Exec-Summary.pdf

Nuttin, J. M. (1985). Narcissism beyond Gestalt and awareness: The name letter effect. *European Journal of Social Psychology*, 15(3), 353–361. https://doi.org/10.1002/ejsp.2420150309

Oettingen, G. (2012). Future thought and behavior change. *European Review of Social Psychology*, 23(1), 1–63. https://doi.org/10.1080/10463283.2011.643698

Oettingen, G., & Gollwitzer, P. M. (2010). Strategies of setting and implementing goals: Mental contrasting and implementation intentions. In J. E. Maddux & J. P. Tangney (Eds.), *Social psychological foundations of clinical psychology* (pp. 114–135). Guilford Press.

O'Reilly III, C. A., Chatman, J., & Caldwell, D. F. (1991). People and organizational culture: A profile comparison approach to assessing person-organization fit. *Academy of Management Journal*, *34*(3), 487–516. https://doi.org/10.5465/256404

Regulation (EU) 2019/2088 of the European parliament and of the council of 27 November 2019 on sustainability-related disclosures in the financial services sector, 317. OJ L (2019). http://data.europa.eu/eli/reg/2019/2088/oj/eng

Roundy, P., Holzhauer, H., & Dai, Y. (2017). Finance or philanthropy? Exploring the motivations and criteria of impact investors. *Social Responsibility Journal*, *13*(3), 491–512. https://doi.org/10.1108/SRJ-08-2016-0135

Schwartz, S. (1992). Universals in the content and structure of values: Theoretical advances and empirical tests in 20 countries. *Advances in Experimental Social Psychology*, *25*, 1–65. https://doi.org/10.1016/S0065-2601(08)60281-6

Schwartz, S. (2007). Basic human values: Theory, measurement, and applications. *Revue Française de Sociologie*, *47*(4), 929–968. https://doi.org/10.3917/rfs.474.0929

Schwartz, S. (2013, May). Value priorities and behavior: Applying. In The psychology of values: The Ontario symposium (Vol. 8).

Sheeran, P., Webb, T. L., & Gollwitzer, P. M. (2005). The interplay between goal intentions and implementation intentions. *Personality and Social Psychology Bulletin*, *31*(1), 87–98. https://doi.org/10.1177/0146167204271308

Sun, W., Zheng, Z., Jiang, Y., Tian, L., & Fang, P. (2021). Does goal conflict necessarily undermine wellbeing? A moderated mediating effect of mixed emotion and construal level. *Frontiers in Psychology*, *12*. https://doi.org/10.3389/fpsyg.2021.653512

Tong, S. T., Hancock, J. T., & Slatcher, R. B. (2016). Online dating system design and relational decision making: Choice, algorithms, and control. *Personal Relationships*, *23*(4), 645–662. https://doi.org/10.1111/pere.12158

Van Boven, L., & Gilovich, T. (2003). To do or to have? That is the question. *Journal of Personality and Social Psychology*, *85*(6), 1193–1202. https://psycnet.apa.org/doi/10.1037/0022-3514.85.6.1193

Verplanken, B., & Holland, R. W. (2002). Motivated decision making: Effects of activation and self-centrality of values on choices and behavior. *Journal of Personality and Social Psychology*, *82*(3), 434–447. https://doi.org/10.1037/0022-3514.82.3.434

Verquer, M. L., Beehr, T. A., & Wagner, S. H. (2003). A meta-analysis of relations between person–organization fit and work attitudes. *Journal of Vocational Behavior*, *63*(3), 473–489. https://doi.org/10.1016/S0001-8791(02)00036-2

Weinstein, N., & Ryan, R. M. (2010). When helping helps: Autonomous motivation for prosocial behavior and its influence on well-being for the helper and recipient. *Journal of Personality and Social Psychology*, *98*(2), 222–244. https://psycnet.apa.org/doi/10.1037/a0016984

White, M. W., Khan, N., Deren, J. S., Sim, J. J., & Majka, E. A. (2022). Give a dog a bone: Spending money on pets promotes happiness. *The Journal of Positive Psychology*, *17*(4), 589–595. 10.1080/17439760.2021.1897871

Yang, B., Yu, H., & Yu, Y. (2021). More experience, less loneliness? Exploring the effect of experiential purchases on the alleviation of loneliness. *Frontiers in Psychology*, 581183. https://doi.org/10.3389/fpsyg.2021.581183

Zimmerman, B. J., & Kitsantas, A. (1999). Acquiring writing revision skill: Shifting from process to outcome self-regulatory goals. *Journal of Educational Psychology*, *91*(2), 241–250. https://psycnet.apa.org/doi/10.1037/0022-0663.91.2.241

10

THE INFLUENCE OF FIRMS' ESG INITIATIVES ON FIRM VALUE

An Analysis of Select European Firms

Paolo Saona and Laura Muro

Introduction

It is not an option to do business as usual. The world is facing severe sustainability challenges that must be addressed urgently, such as climate change, population growth and inequality, dwindling clean energy supplies, and freshwater availability, among others (Conard, 2013; Vogt & Weber, 2019). There is a need for cooperation between governments, businesses, and the financial sector in order to rewire the economy for reaching the United Nations Sustainable Development Goals (CISL, 2015, July; updated 2017, November).

The European Union is concerned about these sustainability challenges and has responded to the climate change risk with the ambitious Green Deal,[1] which aims to transform the European Union into a competitive economy, free of net emissions of greenhouse gases by 2050. The plan sets out to boost the green and digital transitions and make Europe's economy fairer, more resilient, and more sustainable for future generations. The European Union has become a leader in international climate strategy (Oberthür & Dupont, 2021) and more specifically in the regulation and harmonization of ESG (environmental, social, and governance) firm disclosure for corporations, which ultimately impacts investors' perceptions of the company and, inevitably, on the firm value. Directive 2014/95 requires companies to provide annual reports on environmental, social, and employee matters. It also requires them to disclose anti-corruption and human rights policies as well as any bribery that may have been attempted in the last year. European Union regulations are in line with the 2030 United Nations Sustainable Development Goals and support the flow of private finance towards sustainable economic activities, making the transition to a carbon-neutral European economy by 2050 possible. As of today, a lingering question is how regulatory changes and sustainable innovations made by companies will impact their market perception and, ultimately, their valuation. This study seeks to shed some light on the answer to that question.

European companies are preparing their sustainability reports as a response not only to these regulation efforts made by the European Union but also to different pressures coming from investors, consumers, constituencies, and other relevant stakeholders (Tura et al., 2019; Wolf, 2014). These reports are based on sustainable business models that take into consideration new concepts of value creation (Bocken et al., 2013; Laukkanen & Tura, 2020); consequently, this

DOI: 10.4324/9781003345497-13

reporting on sustainable initiatives has recently emerged as a new source of value for companies. Indeed, in this respect, Yang et al. (2017) develop a unified perspective for the creation of sustainable business models with embedded economic, environmental, and social cascades of value that are created, delivered, and captured in a value network. Hence, the theory supports an unambiguous relationship between the firm's disclosure of sustainability innovations and its corporate value.

These disclosure processes allow investors to make investment decisions that are better informed, which impact corporate performance and value. Impact investing is gaining momentum with global sustainable funds attracting almost USD 97 billion of net new money in the first quarter of 2022, according to Morningstar (2022). Investors are clearly demanding social and environmental impacts as well as profitability for their investments.

For instance, Taliento et al. (2019) explored the link between ESG and economic performance using a sample of companies listed on major European indices in Belgium, France, Germany, Italy, and Spain. They concluded that ESG responsibilities constitute a new competitive factor for today's corporations, ensuring good economic performance and sustainability concerns, and facilitating the creation of value in a comprehensive sense.

However, despite these suggested relationships, this field remains unexplored for most European corporations. Consequently, the goal of this study is to analyze how ESG disclosure for European firms impacts their perceived value, estimated by Tobin's Q. This study aims to explore the investor's side at the time of evaluating ESG policies, as little is actually known (Lehner, 2021). To the best of our knowledge, our research is the first study to explore how sustainability scores impact environmental, social, and governance innovations. Likewise, we believe it to be the first that investigates how internal corporate policies regarding the use of water, the efficient use of energy, sustainable packaging, and environmental supply chain policies affect valuation. We incorporate data from European countries using econometric models. Additionally, we conduct a comprehensive analysis by considering the differential impact of sustainable initiatives on firm value across multiple industrial sectors.

Our findings show that any of the three pillars of sustainability (environmental, social, and governance), taken individually, are positively associated with firm value. Once the industry effect is considered, the findings show that firms from environmentally friendly industries will see a better response in market perception as a result of improvements in their sustainability scores than companies in less environmentally friendly industries. The second section describes the theoretical framework and research hypotheses. The third section provides details of the methodology and our econometric methods, while the fourth section summarizes the main results. Finally, the study concludes in the fifth section.

Theoretical Framework

Since sustainability is linked to diverse disciplines, there are multiple theories that can be used to explain the relationship between ESG initiatives and their impact on the firm value (Loh et al., 2017). Some of the most remarkable theories in the finance discipline are highlighted in this section.

Agency theory deals with the conflict of interests in corporations caused by asymmetric incentives between the different interested parties (Berle & Means, 1933; Jensen & Meckling, 1976). As corporations become bigger, these potential conflicts may increase, and disclosing more information could reduce agency conflicts and recover otherwise lost company value (Galani et al., 2012). As observed in the empirical literature, ESG disclosure affects the risk, the cost of capital, and the profitability of a company, and therefore is used as a source of value.

Signaling theory states how companies can take different policies to signal their value to investors (Keasey & Short, 1997). Companies disclosing ESG information send signals to the market about their concerns and actions regarding sustainability. Prior research has provided insight into this. For instance, Singhvi and Desai (1971) found evidence of the relationship between an inadequate amount of information and poor firm economic performance. Their research proves how the quality of corporate disclosure influences the quality of financial investment decisions.

Legitimacy theory has become one of the most cited theories when explaining the relationship between ESG and firm performance (Gray et al., 1995). This theory assumes that companies increase their social disclosures as a strategy to alter the public's perception of its legitimacy, with the goal of influencing different stakeholders and ultimately society as a whole (Hooghiemstra, 2000). Legitimacy theory predicts how companies disclose ESG information to improve the image and the reputation of the firm and its value (Sharma & Song, 2018), and, consequently, to reduce the perceived risk (Albuquerque et al., 2019; Cheng et al., 2014; El Ghoul et al., 2011). The research of Lehner et al. (2019) provides insights into the development of strategies to create legitimacy, as there is a need for harmonization and convergence in financial and non-financial disclosures.

Wolf (2014) uses the resource dependence theory to illustrate how companies engage in sustainable supply chain management to eliminate a particular resource dependence problem. For instance, Neste, a traditional oil company from Finland, is taking advantage of a growing social demand for renewable fuel products by reducing its dependence on traditional oil products and focusing instead on sustainable aviation fuels. The company is using a proactive sustainable supply chain management strategy, integrating a long-term sustainability vision of its supply chain as a source of value-creating activity.

More recently, lifecycle management theories (LCM) have started gaining momentum in associating firms' sustainable strategies with firm value (Bianchi et al., 2022). In this line of reasoning, sustainability challenges should be addressed by taking into consideration the entire company life cycle (Buxel et al., 2015; Nilsson–Lindén et al., 2018; Nilsson–Lindén et al., 2019) and circular business models (Galvão et al., 2022). Take for example the case of SOCO International, a multinational energy company. Due to its economic activities in Virunga (the company planned to extract oil from a gorilla sanctuary in the Democratic Republic of Congo), the company experienced significant stakeholder pressure, which caused it to alter its decisions and even change its name.[2] The company performs its economic activities under a new name, Pharos Energy plc, and discloses its sustainability information as part of its new ESG policy disclosure, adopted after the social pressure on its legitimacy.

The empirical literature has found a positive relationship between ESG disclosure and firm value. For instance, Loh et al. (2017) found that in Singapore, the better the quality of the ESG information, the stronger the correlation is with firm value. Bakar and Ameer (2011), with a sample of listed companies from Malaysia, found a relationship between the readability of CSR communication and companies' performance. This finding supports the obfuscation hypothesis that links good financial performance with ease of readability and vice versa. Additionally, Clarkson et al. (2008) conducted a study with firms from the five most polluting industries in the United States and found a positive association between environmental performance and the level of discretionary environmental disclosures and its impact on firm performance. More recently, Chouaibi and Chouaibi (2021), in a sample of companies from France, Denmark, Sweden, Spain, Germany, the UK, and Canada, found that societal and ethical strengths increase firm value with the moderating effect of green innovation. Their research was conducted with a data set of companies from seven different countries headquartered in North America and Western Europe for the period 2005–2019. They show how corporations that integrate socially responsible practices into their strategies create an intangible asset that promotes value generation. Our study adds value to the existent studies in the field, as it deals with an exhaustive sample of 19 European countries with a time period from 2010–2020 and different industry specifications that will be seen later in the chapter.

All these findings support our first hypothesis:

H1: More ESG disclosure will turn into a higher perceived market value.

Regarding contextual variables, the literature has identified that the industry sector in which the company operates plays a critical role in moderating the impact that ESG initiatives have on firm performance (Cai et al., 2012). For instance, the market scrutiny is sharply focused on sensitive industry sectors (or controversial industries as they have also been called), which are characterized by moral debates and political pressures, as well as environmentally irresponsible behavior like that observed in the energy sector, including oil and gas, paper pulp, and mining, among others (Lee & Faff, 2009). In this respect, the disclosure of negative or unfavorable information about a company by the media impacts the company's unsystematic or diversifiable risk which renders a negative impact on the company's valuation and performance (Bansal & Clelland, 2004). These authors use the corporate environmental legitimacy argument to support the notion that companies operating in highly sensitive industries tend to disclose more corporate social and environmental information to increase transparency and ensure legitimacy. By better positioning the corporate legitimacy, the company can isolate market criticism, because the adoption of institutional standards renders less inquiry from external agents (Bansal & Clelland, 2004). One example of this is the choice made by socially responsible funds that use ethical or negative screenings as benchmarks for excluding companies operating in such sectors from their investment portfolios (Zhang et al., 2020).

Hence, according to Sanches Garcia et al. (2017), corporations from environmentally sensitive industries disclose more environmental information than companies from non-environmentally sensitive industries. The environmentally sensitive companies face bigger pressures from their stakeholders related to environmental concerns than those firms operating in industries considered not to be environmentally sensitive (Galani et al., 2012). Consequently, as suggested by Modugu (2020), companies in these sectors are more prone to disclose a larger amount of sustainability information and are subject to heavier regulation, as their activities are supposed to be more environmentally harmful. For instance, Du and Vieira (2012) find a link between business strategy, corporate social responsibility practices, and communication strategies for oil companies as a tool to gain legitimacy in a controverted environment. Although there is evidence suggesting a positive relationship between ESG disclosure and industry sensitivity exists (Kansal et al., 2014; Reverte, 2009), it is not clear how strong such a relation is across different industry sectors. Similarly, Richardson and Welker (2001) indicate that in comparison to companies in non-sensitive industries, those firms operating in sensitive industries have better financial and social disclosure rates, but they exhibit worse financial performance than their counterparts at companies operating in non–controversial sectors. Conversely, however, in the context of BRICS countries, Sanches Garcia et al. (2017) found that companies in sensitive industries present superior environmental performance, even when controlling for firm size and country. Hence, our second hypothesis states the following:

H2: Industry sensitivity will exhibit an asymmetric impact of ESG disclosure on perceived firm value.

Methodology
Source of Information

We are interested in assessing if changes in environmental, social, and governance scores are drivers of firm value, and how such relationship is moderated by the industry sector. Our sample comprised 2,982 firm-year observations from 318 companies in 19 European countries. The sample of companies includes those non-financial listed firms in their corresponding market index of the most traded and liquid firms in each country. Therefore, we included firms from Austria (ATX), Belgium (BE20), the Czech Republic (PX50), Denmark (OMX Copenhagen 20), Finland (OMX Helsinki 25), France (CAC40), Germany (DAX30), Hungary (BUX), Ireland (ISEQ20), Italy (IT40), Luxembourg (LUXX), the Netherlands (NL25), Norway (OMX Oslo 20), Portugal (PSI), Slovenia (SBITOP), Spain (IBEX35), Sweden (OMX Stockholm 30), Switzerland (SMI), and the United Kingdom (FTSE100). The period of analysis ranges from 2010 to 2020, and the sample includes an average of 9.4 continuous observations per company. Financial companies were removed from the sample because the characteristics of their reporting systems could have biased the overall results (Saona & San Martín, 2016). Similarly, companies in technical bankruptcy and those with missing information for the construction of relevant variables were also removed from the sample.

The hypotheses test is made by building panels of companies from Thomson REFINITIV EIKON. This dataset provides financial information and multiple ESG scores per company and year used in the empirical analysis, as well as information regarding the companies' emissions policies and scores related to the efficient use of resources like water, emissions scores, workforce score, the protection of human rights score, and corporate social responsibility score, among other sustainability indicators. In addition to this, country-level Worldwide Governance Indicators concerning accounting standards and legal systems by country were obtained from the updated work of Kaufmann et al. (2011) whose data set is publicly available on the World Bank's web page.[3] Finally, countries' economic freedom index is also used as an independent variable to explain companies' firm value. The economic freedom data is sourced from the Heritage Foundation's Index of Economic Freedom.[4] This is a reliable data set that supplies policy variables under a government's control (Heckelman & Stroup, 2000), which can subsequently impact a firm's performance.

Variables Definition

The dependent variable corresponds to the firm value $(LnFV)$ measured with the proxy for Tobin's Q, computed as the sum of the firm's market capitalization and the total liabilities and then divided by the firm's total assets (Johnson, 2003). The logarithmic transformation of this variable was used to mitigate the risk of a non-normal distribution of the dependent variable. The independent variables used to measure the firm's sustainable scores are the environmental score $(EScore)$, social score $(SScore)$, and government score $(GScore)$. Moreover, *IndexESG1* represents the average of the three scores. In addition, we also used multiple individual scores as metrics of different sustainable aspects of the company such as i) the Resource Use Score $(ResourceScore)$, which reflects a company's performance and capacity to reduce the use of materials, energy, or water, and to find more eco-efficient solutions by improving supply chain management; ii) the Emission Reduction Score $(EmissionScore)$, which measures a company's commitment and effectiveness toward reducing environmental emission in the production and operational processes; iii) the Innovation Score $(InnovationScore)$, which reflects a company's capacity to reduce the environmental costs and burdens for its customers, thereby creating new market opportunities through new environmental technologies and processes or eco-designed products; iv) the Workforce Score $(WorkforceScore)$, which measures a company's effectiveness in job satisfaction, and maintaining a healthy, safe, and diverse workplace with equal opportunities and development opportunities for its workforce; v) the Human Rights Category Score $(HRightsScore)$, which measures a company's effectiveness of respecting the fundamental human rights conventions; vi) the Community Score ($CommunityScore$), which measures the company's commitment towards being a good citizen, protecting public health, and respecting business ethics; vii) the Product Responsibility Score ($ProductScore$), which reflects a company's capacity to produce quality goods and services integrating the customer's health and safety, integrity, and data privacy; viii) the Management Score ($ManagementScore$), which measures a company's commitment and effectiveness towards following best practice corporate governance principles; ix) the Shareholders Score ($ShareholdersScore$), which measures a company's effectiveness towards equal treatment of shareholders and the use of anti-takeover devices; and x) the CSR Strategy Score ($CSRScore$), which reflects a company's practices to communicate that it integrates the economic (financial), social, and environmental dimensions into its day-to-day decision-making processes. In addition to these scores, we also included policy scores like xi) the Policy Water Efficiency Score ($WaterPolicyScore$); xii) the Policy Energy Efficiency Score ($EnergyPolicyScore$), xiii) the Policy Sustainable Packaging Score ($PackagingScore$); and xiv) the Policy Environmental Supply Chain Score ($SupplyChainScore$), which incorporate the various forms of processes, mechanisms, and procedures to improve the use of water, energy, sustainable packaging/reducing the use of packaging for company products, and policies to include its supply chain in the company's effort to lessen its overall environmental impact, respectively. All these scores are provided by Thomson Reuters REFINITIV EIKON and are distributed in a range that goes from 0 to 1 with higher values as the corresponding sustainable score improves. Out of these last 14 scores, we created IndexESG2, which is the ESG index and also goes from 0 to 1.

A number of firm-level and country-level control variables were used. Firm size ($Size$) was computed as the natural logarithm of the firm's total assets, and the return on assets (ROA) was used as a measure of the firm's profitability corresponding to the net income over total assets. We also used the leverage (Lev) computed as the firm's total liabilities over total assets, the capital expenditure ($CAPEX$) calculated as the annual growth in the gross property plant and equipment divided by total assets, and the Altman (1968) Z-Score as a measure of the company's default risk ($ZScore$). This metric is defined as Z-Score. $ZScore = 1.2WK_{it} + 1.4RE_{it} + 3.3EBIT_{it} + 0.6MK_{it} + 0.99S_{it}$, where WK_{it} is the working capital over total assets of the i company in the period t; RE_{it} is the company's retained earnings over total assets; $EBIT_{it}$ is the earnings before interest and taxes divided by total assets; MK_{it} is the market value of the firm's equity over total liabilities; and S_{it} is the sales over total assets. By construction, greater values of this measure imply lower default risk.

At the country level, we also introduced variables in the model to prevent specification problems. For instance, we used *EconFree* to represent the country's economic freedom index. This variable ranges from 0 to 1, with 1 representing greater economic freedom. This index is based on 12 quantitative and qualitative factors, which are grouped into categories of economic freedom in the rule of law, government size, regulatory efficiency, and open markets. The index is intended to measure the prosperity of individuals in a country and their freedom to work, consume and produce, impacting directly on the corporate sector of the economy, and consequently on the performance of companies. Finally, we also included the World Governance Indicator (WGI), which measures the quality of the governance and policies in a country (Kaufmann et al., 2011). This indicator considers six aspects of good governance, such as voice and accountability, the country's political stability and absence of violence/terrorism, government effectiveness, regulatory quality, rule of law, and control of corruption. By construction, the index ranges from 0 to 1 with higher values as the governance in the country is improved.

Consequently, the regression model takes the following form:

$$LnFV_{it} = \beta_0 + \beta_1 ESG_{it} + \sum_{j=1}^{J} \theta_j FLCV_{it} + \sum_{k=1}^{K} \theta_k CLCV_{ct} + \mu_i + \delta_t + \varepsilon_{it} \qquad (1)$$

where $LnFV$ represents the dependent variable corresponding to the firm value, ESG is the variable corresponding to the different ESG scores, $FLCV$ represents the vector of $J = 5$ firm-level control variables included in the analysis (e.g., $Size$, ROA, Lev, $CAPEX$, and $ZScore$), and $CLCV$ corresponds to the $K = 2$ country-level control variables (e.g., $EconFree$ and WGI). The model also includes the individual effect (μ_i), the temporal effect (δ_t), and the stochastic error (ε_{it}).

Interpretation of Results

Descriptive Statistics

The basic statistics exhibited in Table 10.1 highlight that for the companies included in the sample, the average value of the firm value metric (FV) is higher than the unit, indicating that a typical European company has a positive market perception (mean value equals 0.136 in the logarithmic transformation $(LnFV)$ used in the regression analysis).

The scores of the three pillars of Environmental $(EScore)$, Social $(SScore)$, and Governance $(GScore)$ also indicate relatively high average values for our sample in comparison to emerging markets (Azmi et al., 2021). Nevertheless, it is highlighted that the minimum and maximum values of these variables are also very extreme, indicating that there are companies in the sample with very high sustainability standards while other companies exhibit a very low commitment to policies that are environmentally driven. Our composite metric that incorporates the three pillars $(IndexESG1)$ exhibits an average value of 0.638. Almost all the remaining 14 sustainability scores exhibit average numbers higher than 0.5, meaning that a typical European company complies relatively well with the environmental, social, and governance indicators. The only score that remains low is the one associated with the sustainable packaging systems followed by the companies to reduce the use of packaging for products $(PackagingScore)$, which exhibits an average of 0.361 for the companies' sample.

Regarding the control variables, the table shows that for every euro companies have in assets, 5.4 cent in after-tax income is generated (ROA). Additionally, 25.1% of the firm's total portfolio of investments is financed with debt (Lev), while the addition of fixed assets that represent capital expenditure represents 4.80% of total assets. The last control variable used in this study corresponds to the default risk $(ZScore)$, which indicates that average firms are relatively safe and are far away from insolvency.

The country-level variables indicate that the average economic freedom index $(EconFree)$ ranks the countries as mostly free according to the Heritage Foundation, corresponding to the second highest category of economic freedom. Similarly, the World Governance Indicator (WGI) exhibits an average of 0.787, which represents a relatively strong indicator of the governance quality of the countries included in the sample as compared with emerging markets (Saona & San Martín, 2018).

Table 10.2 shows the correlation matrix of the variables used in the analysis. We do not observe significantly high correlations among the right-hand side variables in the model, which

Table 10.1 Descriptive statistics

Variables	Mean	Std. Dev.	Min.	Max.	p25	p50	p75	Kurtosis	Skewness
FV	1.408	1.081	0.073	8.607	0.749	1.068	1.644	12.071	2.600
LnFV	0.136	0.617	−2.613	2.153	−0.289	0.066	0.497	3.569	0.359
EScore	0.647	0.232	0.000	0.986	0.511	0.705	0.827	2.937	−0.843
SScore	0.674	0.208	0.016	0.986	0.548	0.712	0.841	2.843	−0.754
GScore	0.594	0.217	0.024	0.983	0.439	0.623	0.769	2.292	−0.413
IndexESG1	0.638	0.177	0.032	0.943	0.538	0.667	0.772	3.147	−0.741
IndexESG2	0.607	0.167	0.016	0.912	0.512	0.637	0.731	3.156	−0.778
ResourceScore	0.717	0.256	0.000	0.998	0.575	0.794	0.929	3.284	−1.043
EmissionScore	0.709	0.257	0.000	0.998	0.573	0.789	0.915	3.318	−1.069
InnovationScore	0.445	0.336	0.000	0.998	0.074	0.500	0.750	1.603	−0.027
WorkforceScore	0.788	0.194	0.003	0.999	0.692	0.845	0.943	4.099	−1.229
HRightsScore	0.605	0.333	0.000	0.995	0.363	0.715	0.896	2.077	−0.687
CommunityScore	0.638	0.284	0.000	0.998	0.413	0.694	0.892	2.079	−0.521
ProductScore	0.635	0.297	0.000	0.998	0.423	0.718	0.886	2.324	−0.709
ManagementScore	0.605	0.277	0.002	0.999	0.396	0.644	0.849	2.049	−0.418
ShareholderScore	0.545	0.288	0.005	0.999	0.302	0.573	0.798	1.811	−0.181
CSRScore	0.611	0.284	0.000	0.999	0.409	0.696	0.840	2.299	−0.644
WaterPolicyScore	0.532	0.356	0.000	0.942	0.000	0.722	0.786	1.719	−0.767
EnergyPolicyScore	0.631	0.192	0.000	0.967	0.622	0.668	0.720	9.009	−2.585
PackagingScore	0.361	0.417	0.000	0.973	0.000	0.000	0.837	1.162	0.323
SupplyChainScore	0.640	0.301	0.000	0.970	0.680	0.761	0.811	3.656	−1.541
Size	23.090	1.434	17.653	26.914	22.090	23.057	24.142	3.020	−0.116
ROA	0.054	0.059	−0.438	0.285	0.026	0.050	0.080	11.007	−0.708
Lev	0.251	0.142	0.000	0.867	0.152	0.241	0.344	2.920	0.355
CAPEX	0.048	0.034	0.000	0.227	0.024	0.041	0.065	5.371	1.303
ZScore	13.708	12.154	1.976	71.270	5.617	9.689	16.933	7.247	1.997
EconFree	72.724	5.189	58.800	82.500	69.600	73.900	76.400	2.384	−0.448
WGI	0.787	0.062	0.585	0.875	0.754	0.790	0.842	3.010	−0.742

Notes: The table details the descriptive statistics of the variables used in the empirical analysis. The table shows the mean value and standard deviation of the observations, the p25, p50, and p75 values, the minimum and the maximum values, and the skewness and kurtosis measures. Ln FV is measured with the proxy for Tobin's Q, computed as the sum of the firm's market capitalization and the total liabilities, and then divided by the firm's total assets (Johnson, 2003). The logarithmic transformation of this variable was used to mitigate the risk of a non-normal distribution of the dependent variable. The independent variables used to measure the firm's sustainable scores are the environmental score EScore, the social score SScore, and the government score GScore. $IndexESG1$ represents the average of the three scores. Resource Score reflects a company's performance and capacity to reduce the use of materials, energy, or water, and to find more eco-efficient solutions by improving supply chain management. Emission Reduction Score measures a company's commitment and effectiveness toward reducing environmental emissions in the production and operational processes. Innovation Score reflects a company's capacity to reduce the environmental costs and burdens for its customers, thereby creating new market opportunities through new environmental technologies and processes or eco-designed products. Workforce Score measures a company's effectiveness in job satisfaction and maintaining a healthy, safe, and diverse workplace with equal opportunities and development opportunities for its workforce. Human Rights Category Score measures a company's effectiveness in respecting the fundamental human rights conventions. Community Score measures the company's commitment toward being a good citizen, protecting public health, and respecting business ethics. Product Responsibility Score reflects a company's capacity to produce quality goods and services integrating the customer's health and safety, integrity, and data privacy. Management Score measures a company's commitment and effectiveness towards following best practice corporate governance principles. Shareholders Score measures a company's effectiveness towards equal treatment of shareholders and the use of anti-takeover devices. CSR Strategy Score reflects a company's practices to communicate that it integrates the economic (financial), social, and environmental dimensions into its day-to-day decision-making processes. Policy Water Efficiency Score, Policy Energy Efficiency Score, Policy Sustainable Packaging Score, and Policy Environmental Supply Chain Score incorporate the various forms of processes, mechanisms, and procedures to improve the use of water, energy, sustainable packaging/reducing the use of packaging for products by the company, and policies to include its supply chain in the company's effort to lessen its overall environmental impact, respectively. Firm size $(Size)$ was computed as the natural logarithm of the firm's total assets, and the return on assets (ROA) was used as a measure of the firm's profitability corresponding to the net income over total assets. Leverage (Lev) is computed as the firm's total liabilities over total assets. Capital expenditure $(CAPEX)$ is calculated as the annual growth in the gross property plant and equipment divided by total assets, and the Altman (1968) Z-Score was used as a measure of the company's default risk $(ZScore)$.

Table 10.2 Correlation matrix

Variables	1	2	3	4	5	6	7	8	9	10	11	12	13
1 FV	1												
2 LnFV	0.949***	1											
3 EScore	-0.165***	-0.172***	1										
4 SScore	-0.0250	-0.0178	0.668***	1									
5 GScore	-0.0919***	-0.102***	0.374***	0.456***	1								
6 IndexESG1	-0.120***	-0.124***	0.844***	0.858***	0.745***	1							
7 IndexESG2	-0.0800***	-0.0815***	0.853***	0.851***	0.585***	0.936***	1						
8 Size	-0.333***	-0.324***	0.583***	0.559***	0.410***	0.635***	0.627***	1					
9 ROA	0.580***	0.611***	-0.116***	-0.0233	-0.114***	-0.106***	-0.0669***	-0.244***	1				
10 Lev	-0.0532*	-0.0503*	0.0404	0.00741	0.0975***	0.0604**	0.0217	0.227***	-0.230***	1			
11 CAPEX	0.0491*	0.0501*	-0.0367	-0.0431*	-0.0342	-0.0464**	-0.0684**	-0.149***	0.0473*	0.106***	1		
12 ZScore	0.844***	0.810***	-0.206***	-0.0769***	-0.173***	-0.190***	-0.128***	-0.402***	0.596***	-0.417***	0.0723***	1	
13 EconFree	0.220***	0.218***	-0.0707**	-0.0570**	0.0828***	-0.0188	-0.0414	-0.105***	0.153***	0.00494	-0.0318	0.157***	1
14 WGI	0.118***	0.124***	-0.000400	-0.0238	-0.00855	-0.0127	-0.0512*	-0.0590**	0.0942***	-0.0669**	-0.0752***	0.0682**	0.618***

Note: This table presents the bivariate correlations. All variables are defined in Table 10.1.

mitigates any possible autocorrelation problems in the estimations. For space-saving reasons, 14 specific ESG scores have been omitted.

Multivariate Analysis for the Whole Sample

Table 10.3 is split into two panels. Panel A displays the major results that test research hypothesis H1 and considers only the three pillars of the sustainable scores (e.g., *EScore*, *SScore*, and *GScore*) and the two indices of ESG scores (*IndexESG*1 and *IndexESG*2). Panel B, however, just summarizes the findings that were obtained with individual regressions for the other 14 sustainability scores considered in this study. For space-saving reasons, we do not include all the 14 regression outputs but the estimated coefficients of the relevant sustainable score measures only. All regressions satisfy the specification conditions indicated by Arellano and Bond (1991). The GMM estimators are consistent because the z-test denoted as AR (1) reveals the first-order autocorrelation presence, while the AR (2) test rules out the second-order autocorrelation. The Hansen test indicates that the model is instrumentally overidentified. The models use robust variance. Finally, the VIF test supports that the correlations between exogenous regressors do not cause a significant multicollinearity problem.

As observed in Panel A, the three individual sustainability scores (*EScore*, *SScore*, and *GScore*) exhibit coefficients that are positive and statistically significant. This indicates that as any of the three pillars individually increase, they positively impact the firm value. When the three measures are included together in the *IndexESG*1 variable, the results are also positive and statistically significant. Similarly, the aggregated index that considers the 14 individual sustainability scores $\left(IndexESG2\right)$ also exhibits a positive impact on firm value.

For space-saving purposes, we list the 14 sustainability scores and their corresponding coefficients which were obtained in individual regressions in Panel B of Table 10.3. As observed, in most of the cases the impact of the scores on firm value is positive and statistically significant. However, in four of them, the estimated coefficients are negative and statistically significant (i.e., *InnovationScore*, *ShareholdersScore*, *WaterPolicyScore*, and *PackagingScore*). These variables, indeed, are the ones with the lowest mean values as exhibited in descriptive statistics in Table 10.1. These findings could be explained by life cycle assessment theories (Buxel et al., 2015), which aim to consider the entire lifetime of the sustainability policies. Consequently, investments in sustainability require the disposal of today's company's resources hoping to be capitalized in the long run with enhanced firm value in the future. For instance, Lee and Kim (2017) find a curvilinear relationship between corporate innovation and environmental sustainability, indicating how companies suffer trade-off costs between innovation and environmentally sustainable activities up to a certain point in which trade-off costs will be reduced as the firm accumulates a fair level of innovation. Hence, it might be the case in which these identified corporate sustainable innovations will render positive changes in the firm value in the future, even though they exhibit value dilution in the present. We recognize our partial explanations of the observed negative coefficient for some of the identified scores. In this respect, Tura et al. (2019) reveal how there is a lack of a clear fundamental link in many companies between sustainable knowledge and value management and measurement, and highlight the need to understand the entire knowledge use process and its causal links. Our findings open venues for future research agendas focused on exploring the fundamental link between sustainable initiatives and value creation.

Therefore, we find empirical evidence to support research hypothesis H1 that improvements in the sustainability scores are value-creating activities.

Regarding the firm-level control variables, Table 10.3 displays consistent results that larger firms $\left(Size\right)$ are less able to generate value. It seems that small firms are more dynamic and can

Table 10.3 Multivariate analysis for the whole sample

Panel A

Variables	Model 1	Model 2	Model 3	Model 4	Model 5
Size	0.004	−0.011**	−0.011**	−0.010**	−0.009***
	(1.052)	(−2.467)	(−2.085)	(−2.027)	(−5.012)
ROA	1.082***	0.823***	0.897***	0.926***	1.760***
	(20.898)	(18.433)	(22.594)	(25.567)	(196.126)
Lev	1.565***	1.362***	1.702***	1.429***	1.448***
	(66.090)	(54.703)	(78.499)	(62.450)	(148.518)
CAPEX	−1.091***	−1.454***	−1.749***	−1.034***	−1.902***
	(−12.256)	(−12.600)	(−15.358)	(−9.216)	(−32.349)
ZScore	0.046***	0.044***	0.044***	0.043***	0.039***
	(100.331)	(99.787)	(110.445)	(103.045)	(382.498)
EconFree	0.002***	0.003***	0.002***	0.003***	0.000
	(3.126)	(6.388)	(3.377)	(6.134)	(1.029)
WGI	0.500***	0.504***	0.667***	0.469***	0.627***
	(9.963)	(9.026)	(12.174)	(9.225)	(25.748)
EScore	0.052***				
	(4.276)				
SScore		0.072***			
		(6.073)			
GScore			0.049***		
			(6.257)		
IndexESG1				0.154***	
				(11.872)	
IndexESG2					0.296***
					(31.348)
Constant	−1.578***	−1.212***	−1.291***	−1.315***	−1.237***
	(−14.143)	(−10.034)	(−9.094)	(−11.232)	(−35.114)

Panel B

ResourceScore	0.073***	(8.022)
EmissionScore	0.029***	(2.623)
InnovationScore	−0.092***	(−8.754)
WorkforceScore	0.031***	(2.595)
HRightsScore	0.011**	(2.147)
CommunityScore	0.149***	(15.134)
ProductScore	−0.001	(−0.221)
ManagementScore	0.039***	(7.215)
ShareholderScore	−0.016**	(−2.271)
CSRScore	0.071***	(7.944)
WaterPolicyScore	−0.022***	(−5.880)
EnergyPolicyScore	0.196***	(41.904)
PackagingScore	−0.053***	(−174.912)
SupplyChainScore	0.043***	(8.772)

Observations	2,982	2,982	2,982	2,982	2,129
Number of id	318	318	318	318	225
Country/sector/time effect	YES	YES	YES	YES	YES
VIF test	2.47	3.59	5.01	4.31	4.60
Avrg. Obs./Group	9.377	9.377	9.377	9.377	9.462
AR(1)	−3.645***	−3.657***	−3.570***	−3.665***	−4.106***
AR(2)	−0.564	−0.589	−0.700	−0.768	−0.373
Hansen	252.2	258.5	259.9	261.4	210.9
F-test	7,625***	9,146***	5,971***	4,516***	2,556***

Note: Panels A and B show the regression estimates which explain the effect of the different variables used on the econometric model on FirmValue. First- and second-order autocorrelation tests are reported as AR (1) and AR (2).VIF test is used to formally examine the multicollinearity problem. The Hansen contrast is used to test the hypothesis that the instruments are properly chosen. Standard errors are in parentheses. ***, **, and * represent statistical significance at the 1, 5, and 10% levels, respectively.

adapt quickly to changing market conditions that allow them to generate value. Large firms, however, are mature companies less able to find new markets and take advantage of favorable market conditions. On the other hand, profitability (ROA) and leverage (Lev) have been widely recognized as determinants of firm value. More profitable firms have a greater capacity to attract external investors, which increases the market value of the company. Similarly, leverage is used as a mechanism to exponentially increase the operating capacity of the company to enhance value.

The quality of the country's governance systems (WGI) exhibits a consistent pattern in its relationship with the firm's value-creation activities $(LnFV)$. A similar effect is observed with the economic freedom index $(EconFree)$. Therefore, when countries exhibit a sound regulatory and legal system, and when the economic system guarantees freedoms for the development of productive activities, as a whole, a significant positive impact on the value of companies is observed, ceteris paribus (Table 10.3).

Analysis of the Sample of Companies by Industry and Economic Sector

In this part of the analysis, we split the company sample into those industries that a priori have a significant environmental impact given the nature of their operations from those with relatively low environmental impact. Therefore, following Patten (2002), we consider the following industries as more aggressive with the environment: i) basic materials, ii) energy, iii) industrials, and iv) utilities. The industries with relatively lower environmental impact included i) consumer cyclicals, ii) consumer non-cyclicals, iii) the financial sector, iv) healthcare, v) technology, and vi) telecommunication services, according to the industry classification provided by Thomson Reuters Refinitiv Eikon. These two big groups of industries were used to conduct the estimations to assess the asymmetric impact of sustainable decisions on firm value across industrial sectors.

The most important findings are summarized in Tables 10.4 and 10.5. The tables exhibit that the autocorrelation tests confirm the GMM estimators' consistency, while the Hansen test supports the model overidentification. These models used robust variance, and the VIF test supports that multicollinearity does not systematically affect the model specification.

It is observed in all the models reported in Table 10.4 that the estimated coefficients of *EScore*, *SScore*, *GScore*, *IndexESG*1, and *IndexESG*2 variables are lower for the group of firms that operate in environmentally more aggressive industrial sectors (H Impact, for high impact) than for the group of firms operating in the more environmentally friendly industries (L Impact, for low impact). This indicates, therefore, that there is an asymmetric impact of sustainable measures considered by companies on their firm value that are highly dependent on industry sector. In most of cases, the impact of sustainable innovations on firm value is still positive. However, the firm value is more elastic to little changes in sustainable innovations in environmentally friendly industries (L Impact) than in industries, which by their very nature are more aggressive with the environment (H Impact). These findings indicate that investors reward more significantly those companies that operate in industrial sectors with less environmental impact and with better governance indicators than those companies operating in more aggressive sectors and that exhibit poorly governed systems. Indeed, there is only one finding that exhibits the opposite expected relation: *SScore*. In this case, firm value is destroyed as the social score improves for the group of companies operating in sensitive industry sectors.

Additionally, as a way to provide robustness to our findings, we follow a similar approach and split the company sample based on the economic sector in which the company operates, into either the primary sector, secondary sector, or tertiary sector. The findings observed

Table 10.4 Multivariate analysis by industry

Variables	H Impact	L Impact	H Impact	L Impact	H Impact	L Impact	H Impact	L Impact	H Impact	L Impact
Size	−0.029***	−0.009***	−0.025***	−0.021***	−0.025***	−0.016***	−0.030***	−0.054***	0.010	−0.030***
	(−13.553)	(−4.714)	(−11.232)	(−6.795)	(−9.297)	(−6.010)	(−13.533)	(−105.824)	(0.876)	(−13.244)
ROA	0.621***	1.794***	0.409***	1.813***	0.785***	1.211***	0.635***	1.766***	1.394***	2.359***
	(29.444)	(55.425)	(34.811)	(156.955)	(72.333)	(57.324)	(27.772)	(119.695)	(21.129)	(132.974)
Lev	1.587***	1.255***	1.569***	1.121***	1.678***	1.290***	1.535***	1.156***	1.548***	1.105***
	(119.269)	(90.842)	(86.836)	(59.706)	(85.454)	(96.169)	(84.489)	(130.010)	(31.083)	(90.348)
CAPEX	−1.915***	−0.329***	−2.149***	0.369***	−1.541***	−1.128***	−1.657***	−0.556***	−5.038***	−0.034
	(−31.710)	(−6.171)	(−103.189)	(8.800)	(−47.110)	(−48.537)	(−44.418)	(−17.896)	(−23.881)	(−0.982)
ZScore	0.052***	0.035***	0.051***	0.034***	0.047***	0.034***	0.047***	0.033***	0.043***	0.031***
	(243.346)	(181.368)	(232.508)	(233.950)	(230.230)	(187.188)	(131.516)	(255.604)	(34.866)	(380.474)
EconFree	0.003***	0.004***	0.003***	0.004***	0.003***	0.004***	0.004***	0.005***	−0.003**	0.002***
	(11.056)	(15.552)	(9.889)	(70.191)	(14.035)	(50.060)	(20.014)	(31.792)	(−2.089)	(6.114)
WGI	0.418***	0.385***	0.402***	0.442***	0.519***	0.639***	0.412***	0.225***	0.452***	0.483***
	(16.234)	(14.959)	(12.951)	(12.336)	(35.519)	(50.037)	(16.792)	(14.704)	(4.443)	(11.624)
EScore	0.022***	0.057***								
	(3.562)	(11.899)								
SScore			−0.072***	0.157***						
			(−12.446)	(20.435)						
GScore					0.040***	−0.004				
					(13.795)	(−1.288)				
IndexESG1							0.062***	0.123***		
							(9.470)	(40.848)		
IndexESG2									−0.036	0.290***
									(−0.505)	(37.578)
Constant	−0.786***	−1.125***	−0.767***	−0.961***	−0.963***	−1.060***	−0.804***	−0.084***	−0.974***	−0.689***
	(−15.714)	(−22.941)	(−12.651)	(−17.900)	(−18.760)	(−16.200)	(−11.906)	(−14.254)	(−3.668)	(−13.870)
Observations	1,481	1,501	1,481	1,501	1,481	1,501	1,481	1,501	737	1,392
Number of id	154	164	154	164	154	164	154	164	77	148
Country/time effect	YES	YES	YES	YES	YES	YES	YES	YES	YES	YES
VIF test	3.91	4.06	5.19	3.18	4.41	5.09	3.12	4.80	5.01	3.77

Table 10.4 (Continued)

Variables	H Impact	L Impact	H Impact	L Impact	H Impact	L Impact	H Impact	L Impact	H Impact	L Impact
Avrg. Obs. Group	9.617	9.152	9.617	9.152	9.617	9.152	9.617	9.152	9.571	9.405
AR(1)	−2.289**	−3.551***	−2.216**	−3.637*	−2.405***	−3.541***	−2.388***	−3.763	−2.516**	−4.271***
AR(2)	−0.059	−1.398	−0.994	−1.727	−0.325	−0.737	−0.216	−0.334	−0.378	−1.528
Hansen	970.3	154.2	149.2	261.4	146.9	1375	143.2	700.1	69.42	137.7
F-test	2,956***	2,297***	11,326***	46,207***	17,606***	11,807***	69,683***	42,401***	1,006***	19,816***

Note: This table shows the regression results for the whole sample divided into industries with a high and a low significant environmental impact.

Table 10.5 Multivariate analysis by economic sector

Variables	Primary	Secondary	Tertiary	Primary	Secondary	Tertiary
Size	−0.019***	−0.072***	−0.086***	0.001	−0.040***	0.033**
	(−7.710)	(−11.350)	(−25.734)	(0.105)	(−4.768)	(2.407)
ROA	0.929***	3.544***	0.191***	0.965***	3.567***	0.407***
	(26.133)	(37.209)	(12.376)	(10.681)	(30.996)	(4.685)
Lev	1.288***	1.691***	1.495***	1.542***	1.442***	1.607***
	(54.765)	(30.285)	(97.891)	(32.198)	(30.565)	(27.129)
CAPEX	−1.727***	−1.824***	0.005	−4.907***	−3.108***	−0.944***
	(−16.701)	(−10.892)	(0.078)	(−22.215)	(−16.158)	(−6.884)
ZScore	0.049***	0.034***	0.040***	0.044***	0.028***	0.037***
	(211.223)	(144.741)	(211.288)	(38.476)	(75.081)	(37.394)
EconFree	0.003***	−0.003***	−0.000	−0.003*	−0.001	0.009***
	(12.612)	(−2.965)	(−0.461)	(−1.862)	(−1.269)	(12.568)
WGI	0.416***	0.785***	0.883***	0.642***	0.714***	0.279**
	(6.641)	(10.350)	(17.210)	(10.256)	(7.674)	(2.039)
IndexESG1	0.061***	0.261***	0.767***			
	(7.276)	(9.365)	(34.279)			
IndexESG2				−0.006	0.152***	0.021
				(−0.088)	(3.394)	(0.212)
Constant	−0.979***	0.214	0.044	−0.983***	−0.329*	−2.390***
	(−15.259)	(1.237)	(18.224)	(−4.288)	(−1.719)	(−7.696)
Observations	1,265	1,028	689	737	812	580
Number of id	133	107	78	77	86	62
Country/time effect	YES	YES	YES	YES	YES	YES
VIF test	2.96	3.38	3.58	4.26	4.71	3.09
Avrg. Obs./Group	9.511	9.607	8.833	9.571	9.442	9.355
AR(1)	−2.647***	−3.315***	−1.129***	−2.234**	−3.517***	−1.745**
AR(2)	−4.258	0.0722	−2.652	−2.252	0.718	−2.062
Hansen	148.4	101.3	1907	69.82	78.42	53.57
F−test	194,806***	38,194***	20,101***	4,970***	21,591***	1,621***

Note: This table shows the regression results for the whole sample divided into the three economic sectors: primary, secondary, and tertiary.

in Table 10.5 are consistent with our previous findings. For space-saving reasons, it is only reported in the results of *IndexESG1* and *IndexESG2* variables. As observed, the estimated coefficient of *IndexESG1* variable increases as we move from the primary sector to the tertiary sector. This indicates that companies operating in economic activities that are primarily focused on collecting, extracting, exploiting, or harvesting natural resources exhibit the lowest impact on firm value when sustainable actions are taken. These economic activities involve the production of goods that can be consumed without further production processes, such as commodities and products that cannot be consumed without being processed that are eventually part of the secondary economic sector. The primary economic activity is deeply connected to the earth's natural resources, and, consequently, we would expect this to cause a significant environmental impact on land or water like the agriculture, fishing, or mining industries.

The secondary sector is involved in the conversion of raw materials extracted from the primary activities into finished, manufactured products. The environmental impact of companies operating in the secondary sector is in some specific cases also significant. Nevertheless, by definition, the environmental impact of the manufacturer is significantly lower than companies operating in the primary sector.

Finally, firms operating in the tertiary sector are engaged in the transfer and distribution of tangible and mostly intangible goods such as healthcare services and educational services. By their very nature and the characteristics of the operating systems of companies in the tertiary sector, their impact on the environment is significantly lower than in any of the other economic sectors. In all the cases, the coefficients are positive and statistically significant as observed in most of the previous findings. However, the responsiveness of the firm value before changes in the environmental, social, and governance score is comparatively higher for companies in the tertiary sector than in the secondary sector, which in turn is greater than for companies operating in the primary sector. Therefore, once again, we observe that the firm's market value is more sensitive to companies' sustainable initiatives in more environmentally friendly industries.

Similar estimations were conducted when *IndexESG2* was used as the explicative variable. In this case, the regression on the secondary sector exhibited a statistically significant estimated coefficient for *IndexESG2*.

Conclusions

Sustainability matters. Our research sheds light on how ESG disclosures are an important driver of firm value creation. Although we found relatively high scores of ESG disclosure for the majority of European firms, our results also show that there is a significant proportion of companies in the sample of outperformers and underperformers, indicating the need for government policies with a clear focus on the enforcement of non-financial disclosure regulations. The European Union is making some progress on this matter. As of February 2022, the Commission adopted a proposal for a directive on corporate sustainability due diligence with the goal of fostering sustainable and responsible corporate behavior.[5] The directive will provide a harmonized legal framework in the EU, creating legal certainty and corporate legitimacy for sustainability. The proposed directive comes in line with the recommendations of the United Nations Secretary-General, Antonio Guterres, who, in his "Common Agenda,"[6] designs and envisions a plan for the future of global cooperation through an inclusive, networked, and effective multilateralism, with a global code of conduct that promotes integrity in public information. We identify a research avenue in the future implementation of the above-mentioned "Corporate sustainability due diligence," by contrasting and studying if the new rules will effectively ensure that businesses address the adverse impacts of their actions. Different institutional legal contexts in Europe and how they affect the enforcement of the regulation will be an interesting area to explore in future research. Sustainability implementation requires a multi-stakeholder approach in which the public and private sectors join forces to develop technological advances and social innovations (Lehner, 2021, p. 201).

Our primary findings indicate that each of the three pillars of sustainability is individually and positively associated with firm value. This finding is robust under alternative metrics of sustainability based on the created composite indices that include either the three pillars together or the alternative 14 different specific sustainability scores used in this study. European markets are valuating positively companies' efforts in developing sustainable strategies along their value chains and are rewarding these companies as our data shows. Nevertheless, discrepancies among companies exist with respect to non-financial disclosures. We recognize the important moment in which the proposed directive takes place and want to acknowledge the relevance of its coming approval. Once the industry effect is considered, the findings show that firms from environmentally friendly industries will see a better response in market perception as a consequence of improvements in their ESG scores. Likewise, even though the impact for companies operating in sensitive industries, like companies in the primary sector, is not that pronounced, we still observe that ESG disclosure is highly important and a necessary value-creation tool for the business community in support of reaching compliance with the 2030 United Nations Sustainable Development Goals.

Small companies are more agile and can adapt more easily to new market regulations. Big corporations that are more mature and that have more traditional business models will have to use more resources if they want to transition towards more sustainable business models and will have to take on short-term costs that could penalize their value-creation opportunities.

We recommend that policymakers implement measures to help these corporations as they transition to being more sustainable. In particular, resources should be devoted to promoting more sustainable actions in primary economic sectors and those that are known as having more detrimental impacts on the environment. Direct public investment, for instance, could support early research stages by lowering the risk of private financial investments toward more sustainable business models (CISL, 2022).

The European Union is working on regulating and establishing the rules of the game for European corporations in respect of ESG issues. These regulations come because of the necessity of moving from the old model of business as usual into a world where businesses focus on creating and maintaining sustainable business models that protect the planet, people, and corporations. This book chapter shows evidence that supports the work done by the European Union in the promotion of the adoption of ESG disclosure policies at the corporate level as a mechanism of value creation.

We acknowledge that further research is needed to understand the relationship between some of the variables considered in this study and their specific impact on firm value, such as the *InnovationScore*, *ShareholdersScore*, *WaterPolicyScore*, and *PackagingScore*, in which the coefficients were found to be contrary to our expectations. We leave a door open for future research that could bring potential solutions to overcome those challenges and barriers in the business sustainability field. We propose a long-term horizon analysis on the relationship between these variables and firm value creation, as today's investments in sustainability need to be evaluated in a time frame sufficient to estimate the future net cash flows over the life cycle.

We acknowledge that our research is not free of limitations. Our empirical model includes as independent variables, among others, the firm's sustainability scores from the Thomson REFINITIV EIKON data set, which offers a very reliable source of data. Nevertheless, today's approaches to measuring the impact of sustainability are still far from being universally accepted, and as stated by Lehner et al. (2022), the complexity of resolving potentially differing perspectives on key impact measurement issues can generate important avenues for further research.

As our findings evidence, investors reward companies with the best sustainability practices, indicating the beginning of a new way of understanding the way of doing business: creating shared value for the benefit of all stakeholders (Porter & Kramer, 2011).

Notes

1 https://eur-lex.europa.eu/legal-content/EN/TXT/?uri=CELEX:52019DC0640
2 https://virunga.org/
3 https://databank.worldbank.org/source/worldwide-governance-indicators
4 https://www.heritage.org/index/
5 https://ec.europa.eu/info/business-economy-euro/doing-business-eu/corporate-sustainability-due-diligence_en
6 https://www.un.org/en/content/common-agenda-report/#download

References

Albuquerque, R., Koskinen, Y., & Zhang, C. (2019). Corporate social responsibility and firm risk: Theory and empirical evidence. *Management Science, 65*(10), 4451–4469. https://doi.org/10.1287/mnsc.2018.3043

Altman, E. I. (1968). Financial ratios, discriminant analysis and the prediction of corporate bankruptcy. *Journal of Finance, 23*(4), 589–609. https://doi.org/10.2307/2978933

Arellano, M., & Bond, S. (1991). Some tests of specification for panel data: Monte Carlo evidence and an application to employment equations. *Review of Economic Studies, 58*(2), 277–297. https://ezp.slu.edu/login?url=https://search.ebscohost.com/login.aspx?direct=true&db=edsjsr&AN=edsjsr.2297968&site=eds-live

Azmi, W., Hassan, M. K., Houston, R., & Karim, M. S. (2021). ESG activities and banking performance: International evidence from emerging economies. *Journal of International Financial Markets, Institutions and Money, 70*, 101277. https://doi.org/10.1016/j.intfin.2020.101277

Bakar, A., & Ameer, R. (2011). Readability of corporate social responsibility communication in Malaysia. *Corporate Social Responsibility and Environmental Management, 18*(1), 50–60. https://ezp.slu.edu/login?url=https://search.ebscohost.com/login.aspx?direct=true&db=edsbl&AN=RN285860396&site=eds-live

Bansal, P., & Clelland, I. (2004). Talking trash: Legitimacy, impression management, and unsystematic risk in the context of the natural environment. *Academy of Management Journal, 47*(1), 93–103. https://doi.org/10.5465/20159562

Berle, A. A., Jr., & Means, G. C. (1933). *The modern corporation and private property*. Macmillan Co. https://www.routledge.com/The-Modern-Corporation-and-Private-Property/Berle/p/book/9780887388873

Bianchi, G., Testa, F., Boiral, O., & Iraldo, F. (2022). Organizational learning for environmental sustainability: Internalizing lifecycle management. *Organization and Environment, 35*(1), 103–129. https://doi.org/10.1177/1086026621998744

Bocken, N., Short, S., Rana, P., & Evans, S. (2013). A value mapping tool for sustainable business modelling. *Corporate Governance: The International Journal of Effective Board Performance, 13*(5), 482–497. https://doi.org/10.1108/CG-06-2013-0078

Buxel, H., Esenduran, G., & Griffin, S. (2015). Strategic sustainability: Creating business value with life cycle analysis. *Business Horizons, 58*(1), 109–122. https://doi.org/10.1016/j.bushor.2014.09.004

Cai, Y., Jo, H., & Pan, C. (2012). Doing well while doing bad? CSR in controversial industry sectors. *Journal of Business Ethics, 108*(4), 467–480. https://ezp.slu.edu/login?url=https://search.ebscohost.com/login.aspx?direct=true&db=edsjsr&AN=edsjsr.23259285&site=eds-live

Cheng, B., Ioannou, I., & Serafeim, G. (2014). Corporate social responsibility and access to finance. *Strategic Management Journal, 35*(1), 1–23. https://doi.org/10.2307/24037207

Chouaibi, S., & Chouaibi, J. (2021). Social and ethical practices and firm value: The moderating effect of green innovation: Evidence from international ESG data. *International Journal of Ethics and Systems, 37*(3), 442–465. https://doi.org/10.1108/IJOES-12-2020-0203

Clarkson, P. M., Li, Y., Richardson, G. D., & Vasvari, F. P. (2008). Revisiting the relation between environmental performance and environmental disclosure: An empirical analysis. *Accounting, Organizations and Society, 33*(4), 303–327. https://doi.org/10.1016/j.aos.2007.05.003

Conard, B. R. (2013). Some challenges to sustainability. *Sustainability, 5*(8). https://doi.org/10.3390/su5083368

CISL. (2015, July; updated 2017, November). *Rewiring the economy: Ten tasks, ten years*. Cambridge Institute for Sustainability Leadership. https://www.cisl.cam.ac.uk/resources/low-carbon-transformation-publications/rewiring-the-economy-ten-tasks-ten-years

CISL. (2022). Policy and regulation as a lever for sustainable change. In *Course materials from sustainability business management*. University of Cambridge Institute for Sustainability Leadership.

Du, S., & Vieira, E. T. (2012). Striving for legitimacy through corporate social responsibility: Insights from oil companies: JBE. *Journal of Business Ethics, 110*(4), 413–427. https://doi.org/10.1007/s10551-012-1490-4

El Ghoul, S., Guedhami, O., Kwok, C. C. Y., & Mishra, D. R. (2011). Does corporate social responsibility affect the cost of capital? *Journal of Banking and Finance, 35*(9), 2388–2406. https://doi.org/10.1016/j.jbankfin.2011.02.007

Galani, D., Gravas, E., & Stavropoulos, A. (2012). Company characteristics and environmental policy. *Business Strategy and the Environment, 21*(4), 236–247. https://doi.org/10.1002/bse.731

Galvão, G. D. A., Evans, S., Ferrer, P. S. S., & de Carvalho, M. M. (2022). Circular business model: Breaking down barriers towards sustainable development. *Business Strategy and the Environment, 31*(4), 1504–1524. https://doi.org/10.1002/bse.2966

Morningstar. (2022). *Global sustainable fund flows: Q1 2022 in review*. Morningstar. https://www.morningstar.com/lp/global-esg-flows

Gray, R., Kouhy, R., & Lavers, S. (1995). Corporate social and environmental reporting. *Accounting, Auditing and Accountability Journal, 8*(2), 47–77. https://doi.org/10.1108/09513579510146996

Heckelman, J. C., & Stroup, M. D. (2000). Which economic freedoms contribute to growth? *Kyklos, 53*(4). https://ezp.slu.edu/login?url=https://search.ebscohost.com/login.aspx?direct=true&db=edsbig&AN=edsbig.A74982230&site=eds-live

Hooghiemstra, R. (2000). Corporate communication and impression management: New perspectives why companies engage in corporate social reporting. *Journal of Business Ethics, 27*(1/2), 55–68. http://www.jstor.org.ezp.slu.edu/stable/25074363

Jensen, M. C., & Meckling, W. H. (1976). Theory of the firm: Managerial behavior, agency costs and ownership structure. *Journal of Financial Economics, 3*(4), 305–360. https://doi.org/10.1016/0304-405X(76)90026-X

Johnson, S. A. (2003). Debt maturity and the effects of growth opportunities and liquidity risk on leverage. *Review of Financial Studies, 16*(1), 209–236. https://doi.org/10.1093/rfs/16.1.0209

Kansal, M., Joshi, M., & Batra, G. S. (2014). Determinants of corporate social responsibility disclosures: Evidence from India. *Advances in Accounting, Incorporating Advances in International Accounting, 30*(1), 217–229. https://doi.org/10.1016/j.adiac.2014.03.009

Kaufmann, D., Kraay, A., & Mastruzzi, M. (2011). The worldwide governance indicators: Methodology and analytical issues. *Hague Journal on the Rule of Law, 3*(2), 220–246. https://doi.org/10.1017/S1876404511200046

Keasey, K., & Short, H. (1997). Equity retention and initial public offerings: The influence of signalling and entrenchment effects. *Applied Financial Economics, 7*(1), 75–85. https://doi.org/10.1080/096031097333862

Laukkanen, M., & Tura, N. (2020). The potential of sharing economy business models for sustainable value creation. *Journal of Cleaner Production, 253*. https://doi.org/10.1016/j.jclepro.2020.120004

Lee, D. D., & Faff, R. W. (2009). Corporate sustainability performance and idiosyncratic risk: A global perspective. *Financial Review, 44*(2), 213–237. https://doi.org/10.1111/j.1540-6288.2009.00216.x

Lee, J., & Kim, S.-J. (2017). Curvilinear relationship between corporate innovation and environmental sustainability. *Sustainability, 9*(7). https://doi.org/10.3390/su9071267

Lehner, O. M. (2021). *A research agenda for social finance*. Elgar. https://www.e-elgar.com/shop/gbp/a-research-agenda-for-social-finance-9781789907957.html

Lehner, O. M., Harrer, T., & Quast, M. (2019). Building institutional legitimacy in impact investing [periodical]. *Journal of Applied Accounting Research, 20*(4), 416–438. https://doi.org/10.1108/JAAR-01-2018-0001

Lehner, O. M., Nicholls, A., & Kapplmuller, S. B. (2022). Arenas of contestation: A Senian social justice perspective on the nature of materiality in impact measurement. *Journal of Business Ethics, 179*(4), 971–989. https://doi.org/10.1007/s10551-022-05158-2

Loh, L., Thomas, T., & Wang, Y. (2017). Sustainability reporting and firm value: Evidence from Singapore-listed companies. *Sustainability, 9*(11), 2112–2112. https://doi.org/10.3390/su9112112

Modugu, K. P. (2020). Do corporate characteristics improve sustainability disclosure? Evidence from the UAE. *International Journal of Business Performance Management, 21*(1/2), (1–2). https://doi.org/10.1504/IJBPM.2020.106106

Nilsson-Lindén, H., Baumann, H., Rosén, M., & Diedrich, A. (2018). Organizing life cycle management in practice: Challenges of a multinational manufacturing corporation. *International Journal of Life Cycle Assessment, 23*(7), 1368–1382. https://doi.org/10.1007/s11367-014-0818-y

Nilsson-Lindén, H., Rosén, M., & Baumann, H. (2019). Product chain collaboration for sustainability: A business case for life cycle management. *Business Strategy and the Environment, 28*(8), 1619–1631. https://doi.org/10.1002/bse.2388

Oberthür, S., & Dupont, C. (2021). The European Union's international climate leadership: Towards a grand climate strategy? *Journal of European Public Policy, 28*(7), 1095–1114. https://doi.org/10.1080/13501763.2021.1918218

Patten, D. M. (2002). The relation between environmental performance and environmental disclosure: A research note. *Accounting, Organizations and Society, 27*(8), 763–773. https://doi.org/10.1016/S0361-3682(02)00028-4

Porter, M. E., & Kramer, M. R. (2011). Creating shared value: How to reinvent capitalism – And unleash a wave of innovation and growth. *Harvard Business Review, 89*(1–2). https://ezp.slu.edu/login?url=https://search.ebscohost.com/login.aspx?direct=true&db=edsbig&AN=edsbig.A248180390&site=eds-live

Reverte, C. (2009). Determinants of corporate social responsibility disclosure ratings by Spanish listed firms. *Journal of Business Ethics*, *88*(2), 351–366. https://doi.org/10.1007/s10551-008-9968-9

Richardson, A. J., & Welker, M. (2001). Social disclosure, financial disclosure and the cost of equity capital. *Accounting, Organizations and Society*, *26*(7), 597–616. https://doi.org/10.1016/S0361-3682(01)00025-3

Sanches Garcia, A., Mendes-Da-Silva, W., & Orsato, R. J. (2017). Sensitive industries produce better ESG performance: Evidence from emerging markets. *Journal of Cleaner Production*, *150*, 135–147. https://doi.org/10.1016/j.jclepro.2017.02.180

Saona, P., & San Martín, P. (2016). Country level governance variables and ownership concentration as determinants of firm value in Latin America. *International Review of Law and Economics*, *47*, 84–95. https://doi.org/10.1016/j.irle.2016.06.004

Saona, P., & San Martín, P. (2018). Determinants of firm value in Latin America: An analysis of firm attributes and institutional factors [report]. *Review of Managerial Science*, *12*(1), 65. https://doi.org/10.1007/s11846-016-0213-0

Sharma, Z., & Song, L. (2018). Corporate social responsibility (CSR) practices by SIN firms: Evidence from CSR activity and disclosure. *Asian Review of Accounting*, *26*(3), 359–372. https://doi.org/10.1108/ARA-06-2017-0102

Singhvi, S. S., & Desai, H. B. (1971). An empirical analysis of the quality of corporate financial disclosure. *Accounting Review*, *46*(1), 129–138. https://ezp.slu.edu/login?url=https://search.ebscohost.com/login.aspx?direct=true&db=edsjsr&AN=edsjsr.243894&site=eds-live

Taliento, M., Favino, C., & Netti, A. (2019). Impact of environmental, social, and governance information on economic performance: Evidence of a corporate 'sustainability advantage' from Europe. *Sustainability*, *11*(6), 1738–1738. https://doi.org/10.3390/su11061738

Tura, N., Ojanen, V., & Hanski, J. (2019). Innovations for sustainability: Challenges of utilising sustainability-related knowledge. *International Journal of Innovation and Sustainable Development*, *13*(3–4). https://doi.org/10.1504/IJISD.2019.100371

Vogt, M., & Weber, C. (2019). Current challenges to the concept of sustainability. *Global Sustainability*, *2*, Article e4. https://doi.org/10.1017/sus.2019.1

Wolf, J. (2014). The relationship between sustainable supply chain management, stakeholder pressure and corporate sustainability performance. *Journal of Business Ethics*, *119*(3), 317–328. https://doi.org/10.1007/s10551-012-1603-0

Yang, M., Vladimirova, D., & Evans, S. (2017). Creating and capturing value through sustainability: The sustainable value analysis tool. *Research–Technology Management*, *60*(3), 30–37. https://doi.org/10.1080/08956308.2017.1301001

Zhang, F., Qin, X., & Liu, L. (2020). The interaction effect between ESG and green innovation and its impact on firm value from the perspective of information disclosure. *Sustainability*, *12*(5), 1866–1866. https://doi.org/10.3390/su12051866

11
THE YIELDS OF GREEN BANK BONDS

Are Banks Perceived as Trustworthy in the Green Financial Markets?

Nicholas Apergis, Giuseppina Chesini, and Thomas Poufinas

Introduction

Climate change is well recognized as having a strong impact on many aspects of our lives, and from a financial point of view, it is worrisome because it represents even a major challenge to financial stability (Alessi et al., 2021). In response to environmental alarms, even financial investors have recently taken up the challenge and become key actors in the energy and environmental transition. Among the activities and instruments of sustainable finance, green bonds are intended to encourage sustainable activities by financing climate-related or environmentally friendly projects, as well as to raise awareness of environmental risks.

Green bonds represent a vertiginously growing subset of the ESG (Environmental, Social, and Governance) investments universe, also called impact investing (Quirici, 2020; Paranque & Revelli, 2019). Technically, they are fixed-income securities that are identical to non-green bonds except that the proceeds should be addressed entirely to projects with an environmental or climate-related focus. Banks play an active role as issuers in this market. In particular, they are increasingly recognizing that their lending and investment choices have an impact on the health of the planet and take action to decrease funding projects that harm the environment and proactively finance renewable energy or climate-positive projects. By doing this they also respond to a growing preference towards green investments expressed by some of their customers.

Even if the risk of bank lending does not change, because green assets are not necessarily linked to lower risk, the commitment to finance green projects – following the issuance of green bonds – produces a decrease in lending to high-polluting sectors and thus may contribute to reducing environmental and climate-related risks (Lamperti et al., 2021). In addition, the issue of green bonds involves both sides of banks' balance sheets and banks becoming "greener", clearly demonstrating a strong orientation towards environmentally beneficial projects.

Over 300 banks representing almost 50% of banking assets worldwide have now signed "The Principles for Responsible Banking", created in 2019 through a partnership between founding banks and the United Nations (UNEP FI, 2021). In this way signatory banks' strategy and practice align with the vision society has set out for its future in the Paris Climate Agreement of 2015 and in the Sustainable Development Goals established for 2030 by the United Nations.

The green bond market is still tiny compared to the whole market – even if it is playing an important role in financing green projects; however, it is increasing vertiginously, and financial companies are evolving as the most active players in the green bond market, based on the amount issued so far (CBI, 2022; Caramichael and Rapp, 2022). Certainly, besides banks, many corporations issue green bonds to face the challenge of climate change; nevertheless, a significant number of firms, particularly small and medium enterprises (SMEs), do not have access to the bond market and rely mainly on the banking sector as a source of external funding. When banks issue green bonds they can involve SMEs in this virtuous circle by offering them specific loans for pro-environmental projects. Synthetically, banks by issuing green bonds can diversify their portfolios, enabling them to apply environmental standards to their borrowers (Turguttopbaş, 2022).

The green bond market is characterized by some peculiarities; for example, the demand for green bonds has often surpassed the supply due to investors' need to address the ESG and SRI (socially responsible investment) mandates. The shortage of supply and the excess of demand in the green bonds market implies a thin market, and liquidity may become relevant in the pricing (Febi et al., 2018)

Moreover, it is worth mentioning that green bonds are mostly self-labeled (Ma et al., 2020). Consequently, investors, having green preferences, have to detect the existence of a genuine commitment on the part of the issuer to use the proceeds in an environmentally friendly way from mere "greenwashing". Even if since 2018 the European Commission has been working on a European Green Bond Standard (GBS), the risk of greenwashing still exists. So far, some guidance in identifying green bonds is provided by the Green Bond Principles (GBP), voluntary process guidelines put forward by the International Capital Market Association (ICMA, 2021). To avoid information asymmetry between issuers and investors, the birth of green bond issues led to not only regular reporting about the use of proceeds, but around 60% of bonds issued were also certified through an external party in the form of a second-party opinion by a certifying institution (Hachenberg & Schiereck, 2018).

Finally, green bond credit risk profiles are unclear since transparency in the reporting of green projects sometimes is lacking and the rating of green bonds relies heavily on the balance sheets of the issuers instead of the green investment project. Obviously, it would be great to verify that issuers could obtain a lower cost of capital by issuing green bonds because investors believe that being "green" is more important than the return (Renneboog et al., 2008). Consequently, one important issue concerning green bonds is related to their convenience for the issuers in comparison to conventional bonds. Some scholars claim that the disclosure and reporting requirements associated with the issuance of green bonds entail additional costs for the borrowers, which could be compensated by the "greenium", i.e., the market premium to the price of the green bond (Cheong & Choi, 2020). This would suggest also that investors are willing to receive a lower yield for investing in bonds that have an impact on the fight against climate change.

These considerations produce the following main research questions of this study:

1) Does the yield of green bonds issued by banks differ from the yield of non-green bonds?
2) Are banks different from other green bond issuers?
3) Why are bank-issuer results neglected in the previous literature, even if they can reasonably play a relevant role in the fight against climate change?
4) Are the banks that are signatories in the UN's responsible banks group perceived by investors as greener than other issuers?
5) Did green bank bonds exhibit different yields in comparison with conventional bonds during the COVID-19 pandemic?

In order to answer the above research questions, this study investigates the relationship between the yields of green bonds and conventional bonds issued by banks, trying to disentangle the reasons underlying the differences characterizing banks when operating in the green financial market.

The present work contributes to the literature in several dimensions. First, it contributes to the increasing literature investigating the pricing implications of the green label on green bonds, in particular analyzing the primary market. In this context, to the best of our knowledge, no papers have focused their analysis only on this sub-sector of the financial markets – namely, bank issuances. Second, this study aims to highlight the peculiarities of green bank bonds, in comparison with the green bonds issued by other issuers (corporations, governments, and supranational agencies). Indeed, banks constitute a special case of enterprises, as bonds are one of the ordinary instruments they use for collecting money and represent a traditional part of their main business. Third, the recent COVID-19 pandemic outbreak caused significant turmoil in financial markets, and this research aims to identify the reaction of green bond yields in comparison to conventional bonds during the different phases of the spreading of the pandemic. Fourth, banks tend to show their responsibility towards climate change, and we want to understand if this is something that makes banks perceived as more trustworthy in the market. Finally, this study contributes to the growing literature on impact investing, especially investigating the role of banks, which may reasonably be important actors in sustainable finance and play a decisive role in the future of the environment and society.

The study is organized as follows. The second section reviews the relevant literature on green bond premiums and develops several hypotheses. The third section presents our dataset. The fourth section describes the econometric model used in the analysis, and the fifth section illustrates the methodological approach. The sixth section discusses the results. The chapter ends with the conclusions and the related implications in the seventh section.

Literature Review on Green Bond Premium and Hypotheses

Although several studies have focused on green bonds to detect differences in yields with respect to conventional bonds, no unequivocal conclusions have yet been reached on this topic. In fact, in the literature results are mixed, depending on different geographical samples and time periods analyzed, as well as on the type of issuer and financial market, primary or secondary (Sheng et al., 2021).

The issue is relevant since green bonds might provide an ideal financing source for green projects; in fact, besides fulfilling their commitment to the environment, issuers can enjoy lower costs of capital, and at the same time, socially responsible investors might accept a lower yield as the non-financial utility component of green bonds may compensate for a lower financial return.

Among the numerous studies that have examined the premiums in the green bond market, several of these do not find any significant difference for green bonds, confirming that investors are not willing to pay a premium to acquire a green bond at issuance (Shishlov et al., 2016). In this regard, Flammer (2021) demonstrates that the cost of capital argument, according to which companies would issue green bonds to benefit from a cheaper source of financing, is inconsistent. She studies the pricing of corporate green bonds following the methodology used by Larcker and Watts (2020) in the context of municipal green bonds. Specifically, for each green bond, both the papers match an otherwise similar non-green bond by the same issuer. This ensures that the two bonds are as similar as possible, except for the "greenness". When comparing the yields, both papers find that no pricing difference between green and non-green bonds in the market exists. This suggests that investors would not invest in green bonds if the returns were not competitive.

Hyun et al. (2020) compare liquidity–adjusted yield premiums of green bonds versus synthetic conventional bonds and find out that on average there is no robust and significant yield premium or discount on green bonds.

Similarly, Kapraun et al. (2021) find on average no difference in yields at issuance for green bonds. In particular, they do detect the presence of a greenium in the primary and secondary markets but this is negligible on average. In the primary market, they find that the existence and significance of green premiums vary substantially across currencies and issuer types. It is high and significant for bonds issued by official entities such as governments or supra-nationals or for bonds denominated in EUR. For corporate green bonds, however, additional verification of green credentials is required in order to benefit from a greenium. They claim that the most important determinant for the existence of a green premium is the perceived "green credibility" of a bond and its issuer.

Finally, also Lau et al. (2022) unveil that investors and therefore society at large remain quite unwilling to pay for conserving the environment because they perceive that some green bonds may be greenwashed, causing a risk premium that offsets the greenium.

Based on the above literature we want to test the following hypothesis:

H1: Green bank bonds exhibit the same yields as conventional bonds. No green bond premium (greenium) does exist.

On the other hand, it is possible to believe that investors are willing to pay a premium, i.e., a higher price over a comparable plain vanilla bond, for investing in environmental-friendly projects (so they accept a lower yield) because they appreciate the pursuit of certain environmental goals. In this way, the issuers receive a premium in the cost of issuance.

One of the first papers that find the existence of a greenium is the work of Baker et al. (2018), which studies the US corporate and municipal green bond markets. In particular, after-tax yields at issue for green bonds in comparison to ordinary bonds are about 6 basis points below the yields paid by otherwise equivalent bonds.

Gianfrate and Peri (2019) study 121 European green bonds issued between 2013 and 2017 by different issuers (mainly corporates, financial institutions, and sovereign states); they find that green bonds are more financially convenient to issuers than non-green ones, even if they have to spend more money in order to get the green label. In other words, green bonds offer lower returns to investors. This is possible as a consequence of a strong demand for these financial products by investors who are willing to fund green investments.

Fatica et al. (2021) also study the pricing of green bonds in the primary market. They find a premium for green bonds issued by supranational institutions and corporates but no yield differences in the case of issuances by financial institutions. The absence of a greenium for financial issuers could derive from the fact that at the time of issuance, investors may not be able to identify a clear link between the green bond issued by a financial institution and a specific green investment project. In fact, the core lending banking business is inherently based on private information. They find also that institutions that have declared commitment to environmental principles (i.e., those subscribing to the United Nations Environment Program Financial Initiative) issued green bonds at a premium.

By analyzing the secondary market, Zerbib (2019) investigates the bond market to clearly identify the impact of pro-environmental preferences on prices. He uses a matching method whereby he estimates the yield of an equivalent synthetic conventional bond for each of the

110 large, investment-grade green bonds in his sample. Unlike two bonds issued by companies with different environmental performances, green and conventional bonds of the same company are subject to the same financial risk once all their differences have been controlled. Comparing the yield of a green bond and that of a conventional counterfactual thus makes it possible to isolate the impact of pro-environmental preferences on bond prices. He finds a −2 basis point average green bond yield premium. This represents the yield that investors are willing to forego to fund green investments rather than conventional investments with strictly equal risk.

Nanayakkara and Colombage (2019) also find that green corporate bonds are traded at a premium of 63 basis points over a comparable corporate bond issue. They highlight that investors' willingness to pay a premium for investing in green bonds may have favorable effects in increasing the flow of private capital for green investments. Further, the green bond premium reflects investor appetite to acquire bonds with a green label, as they perceived the associated risk of such bonds to be relatively lower than that for conventional bonds.

Löffler et al. (2021) analyze green bonds in primary and secondary markets. They find that green bonds have larger issuer sizes and lower-rated issuers on average. In addition, they demonstrate that the yield of green bonds is lower than the yield of comparable non-green bonds. In particular, the yield on green bonds is on average 15–20 basis points lower than that of conventional bonds, both on primary and secondary markets, thus confirming that a greenium exists. The latter is more pronounced in later sample years, from 2018 to 2019.

More recently, Caramichael and Rapp (2022) analyzed how the greenium is allocated by issuer sector and found a significant greenium for EU banks in 2019 in line with their results on a robust euro greenium for large, investment-grade issuers.

Considering the above literature, we plan to test the following hypothesis:

H2: Green bank bonds give a lower yield than conventional bonds to investors. A positive premium (so-called greenium) does exist for the issuers. Consequently, pro-environmental investors are willing to forego some yield to support bonds with environmental or climate benefits.

Finally, it is possible to believe that investors ask for a higher yield when they invest in green bonds because the underlining green projects are usually innovative and consequently riskier. In this regard, Bachelet et al. (2019) find that green bonds issued by private issuers, in comparison to conventional bonds, exhibit higher yields for investors in the presence of relatively lower liquidity and slightly lower volatility. In particular, private issuers of green bonds without third-party verification have significantly higher yields for investors and lower liquidity than their privately verified counterparts. An explanation of this can be attributed to the lack of transparency and information rules that increase informational asymmetries and overcome investors' doubts about the effective greenness of their projects. Hence, the higher average yields of green bonds mainly reflect exposure to greenwashing risks of green bonds of private issuers non-verified by third parties. Consequently, if bonds are not green certificated, the risk of greenwashing is higher, and investors may require a premium. The private or institutional characteristics of the issuer may also affect the premium in a framework of asymmetric information; usually, an institutional issuer has a higher reputation and is more likely to be believed as effectively using financial resources for green investments.

Similarly, Karpf and Mandel (2018), by analyzing the secondary market of US municipal bonds, find that green bonds pay a higher yield than conventional bonds to investors. In particular, green municipal bonds can be considered an increasingly attractive investment, offering a higher premium than conventional bonds to investors wishing to bridge the climate finance gap for climate mitigation and adaptation or other sustainability purposes.

Based on the above literature we want to test the following hypothesis:

H3: Green bank bonds give a higher yield than conventional bonds to investors. A negative premium does exist for the issuers, and pro-environmental investors perceive higher risk and ask for higher returns.

Another issue concerning banks trying to follow the green trend is the current impossibility of halting the financing of highly polluting fossil fuel industries and the consequent necessity to sometimes alter the wording of climate commitments to make them less restrictive (Hodgson et al., 2021). In addition, in verified cases, banks misled customers by promoting their green initiatives while omitting information about their continued financing of companies with substantial greenhouse emissions (Morris, 2022). The difficulties banks face in conforming to their green commitments while maintaining their profit margins are recognized in many examples. Therefore, banks need to strongly communicate their green commitments to investors. The initiative of the United Nations, which has promoted the UN Principles for Responsible Banking (hereafter referred to also as UN Principles), responds to this need, in addition to accelerating a positive global transition of banks towards the green economy. Banks that sign the Principles signal their commitment to the vision society has set out for its future in the Paris Agreement.

Recently, on April 2021, a new alliance was launched, known as the "Net-Zero Banking Alliance". Many banks that signed the UN principles have joined also this new initiative. The Alliance has recognized the vital role of banks in supporting the global transition to the real economy to net-zero emissions by 2050 (UNEP FI, 2022). Signing these agreements is important for signaling the wish to enter decidedly into the green economy, and the investors should reward these efforts.

Based on the above considerations we want to test the following hypothesis:

H4: Green bank bonds give a lower yield than conventional bonds to investors when the issuer has signed the UN Principles for Responsible Banking. A positive premium does exist for the issuers, and pro-environmental investors perceive a lower risk of greenwashing and ask for lower returns.

Another more recent strand in the literature analyses the impact of crises or exogenous shocks on the yields and volatility of green bonds with respect to conventional bonds. In this regard, Cicchiello et al. (2022) investigate whether corporate green bonds were more resilient relative to conventional bonds during the first year of the COVID-19 pandemic. They use the event study methodology and econometric models to investigate the impact of the pandemic and the announcement of the vaccine's effectiveness on Europe's green bond market. In their research, they follow another paper by Naeem et al. (2021), which analyzes the level of efficiency of green and traditional bond markets before and during the pandemic crisis by examining the presence of asymmetric multifractality.

Cicchiello et al. (2022) find that corporate green bonds in periods of heightened market volatility (from February 24 to March 31, 2020) offer a higher risk premium compared to conventional bonds as compensation for uncertain profitability and a higher risk of default. Conversely, after the announcement of Pfizer-BioNTech's COVID-19 vaccine (from November 9 to December 31, 2020), corporate green bonds pay lower premiums compared to conventional ones. Their results reveal that green bonds performed worse than conventional bonds at the onset of the pandemic, just to rebound with greater force as the fear of the pandemic eased after the vaccine announcement. In practice, there was no comparative convenience for the issuers of green bonds immediately after the onset of the pandemic, but, after the announcement of an effective vaccine, green bond issuers re-found the convenience (i.e., the greenium) in financing their green investments.

Naeem et al. (2021) study the price efficiency dynamics of green bonds and conventional bonds and the impact of COVID-19 on their pricing. They find that the conventional bond market tends to be more efficient than the green bond market because of the larger size and level of maturity of the former. The degree of efficiency changes considerably in both markets over time. In particular, inefficiency increases substantially following the COVID-19 outbreak, although the green bond market seems to exhibit a higher level of efficiency during the pandemic. The authors attribute this to the fact that green bonds attract a special type of investors driven by pro-environmental preferences and, at least partly by non-pecuniary motives, because they want to be part of the transition to a greener economy. These investors perceive green bonds as less risky and tend to adopt a long-term strategy. As a result, green bond prices are less vulnerable to market sentiment during episodes of increased economic uncertainty and market turmoil like the COVID-19 pandemic (Ma et al., 2020). This suggests the potential of green bonds as an effective diversifier against conventional bonds in times of extreme stress. In fact, investors appear interested in this new asset class also due to its low correlations with other financial assets (Mensi et al., 2022; Reboredo, 2018).

Mensi et al. (2022) examine the impact of the COVID-19 pandemic and global risk factors on the upside and downside price spillovers of MSCI global, building, financial, industrial, and utility green bonds. Investors are interested in understanding the dependence and spillover effects among green bonds in different sectors in order to check whether they can build a portfolio composed of different green bond assets. In particular, they find that there are dynamic volatility spillover effects between MSCI global green bonds and MSCI sectoral green bonds. Even if spillover effects intensified during the COVID-19 pandemic crisis for all sub-sectors, the spillover index remains relatively stable only for "financial green bonds". The latter sector proved once again to be an effective diversifier in portfolio building.

Based on the above literature we want to test the following hypothesis:

H5: During the COVID-19 pandemic, green bank bonds offered a higher yield than conventional bonds to investors and a lower yield after the announcement of Pfizer-BioNTech's COVID-19 vaccine.

As just described, the previous studies have focused on different kinds of issuers of green bonds, and their analyses often considered the entire world or large areas – geographically – because of the limited number of green bonds issued overall and of the econometrical need to use large enough samples. These days, a higher number of green bonds have been issued, and the present research aims to better analyze the existence or non-existence of green bond premiums and to find more reliable results for a specific and particular universe of issuers: the Eurozone banks.

In particular, we think that the previous results on this topic are mixed also because each issuer type differs in its target investor base, currency risks, and trading and institutional environment (Baker et al., 2018). In the same direction, Lau et al. (2022) affirm that the greenium of green bonds differs significantly depending on the characteristics of the bonds that subject them to the risk of greenwashing to different extents.

The Dataset

We compiled a dataset of bank bonds from Bloomberg's fixed-income database. In order to make a comparison between green bonds and conventional bonds we selected bonds issued by banks belonging to the following countries, which are the founding (or almost founding) countries of the European Union: Austria, Belgium, France, Finland, Germany, Greece, Italy, Ireland, Luxembourg, the Netherlands, Portugal, and Spain. We also extracted data concerning bank bonds issued by UK banks to make a further comparison considering different currencies.

The data set covers the green bank bonds identified by Bloomberg that were issued from 2015 to March 2022. The first green bank bond in our dataset was issued by the French BPCE Group in 2015. In order to have homogeneous bonds to study, we select only bonds with a fixed coupon and with an issue volume of at least 100 million euro equivalent, because the price of smaller issues might get biased by a liquidity premium charged by the market (Hachenberg & Schiereck, 2018). The dataset is composed of 3,316 conventional bank bonds and 400 green bank bonds complying with the Green Bond Principles indexed by Bloomberg.

We concentrate our analysis on the primary market because green bonds tend to be bought in this market by institutional investors and held until maturity. Consequently, if they are not traded much in the secondary market, their prices in that market could be unreliable (Gianfrate & Peri, 2019). The dependent variable is the yield to maturity at the time of issuance. The independent bond-specific variables used in the model are the following:

- Amount outstanding
- Time measured as years to maturity (maturity date − interest accrual date)
- Payment rank
- Coupon
- Coupon frequency
- Bloomberg Composite Rating
- Currency
- Green bond indicator
- Indicator UN Principles (indicating whether the bank is a signatory of the UN Principles for Responsible Banking)

This is complemented by a series of macroeconomic variables:

- Euribor index
- V2X index
- GDP
- Debt/GDP
- Inflation

The expected impact of the variables on the bond yield is indicated in Table 11.1.

The banks that sign the UN agreement about responsible banks are more than 300, 76 of which belong to the countries analyzed in the paper. Only 55 banks are bond issuers in our dataset. We added this information manually into our dataset in order to check if being a bank signatory of the UN agreement has an impact on the related green bond yield. Although there is no unanimity on the subject, most of the works focusing on the bond market suggest that companies with high environmental performance benefit from a lower cost of capital (Baulkaran, 2019; Tang & Zhang, 2020). We, therefore, expect that banks with high environmental commitment also benefit from a lower cost of debt.

Unfortunately, we face significant data constraints. We do not have data concerning the use of proceeds, i.e., the way that the capital collected from investors will be spent, for each green bond

Table 11.1 Expected influence of bond-specific and macroeconomic variables

Variables	Expected influence
Amount_issue	−
Time	+
Coupon	+
Currency (Euro)	?
Payment rank	?
Sr Non Preferred	
Sr Preferred	
Sr Unsecured	
Secured	
Subordinated	
Bond_Rating	−
Green Bond Indicator	?
Indicator UN Principles	−
Euribor_index	?
V2X_index	?
GDP	−
Debt/GDP	+
Inflation	+

issued. Moreover, the classification of bonds as green is based on the evaluation of Bloomberg. We do not have other certifications or green ratings for each bond in the sample.

The Methodological Approach

In the literature it is possible to find mainly two different methodologies to investigate the pricing implications of the green label: 1) the elaboration of a standard equation for bond yields and the application of panel regression analysis; 2) the preliminary construction of a dataset of conventional bonds that is identical to the dataset of green bonds except for the green label, and the performance of panel regression analyses. This is possible because the green bond label is associated with the funded projects and not with the issuer type. Consequently, it is logically feasible to compare a green bond yield with the yield of a similar conventional bond from the same issuer. In addition, in the second methodology, it is possible to select different bonds in the market, which are comparable to the sample of green bonds, or it is possible to estimate counterfactual bonds (Gianfrate & Peri, 2019). Several papers adopt a propensity-score-matching technique to estimate the counterfactual bonds that are to be compared with green bonds.

As an example of the first methodology, Fatica et al. (2021) use a standard equation for bond yields in which the dependent variable is the yield at issuance of bond b issued by issuer i in time t. The independent variables are a set of bond characteristics that may affect the yield. In this equation, they introduce a dummy variable that equals one if a bond is green, and zero otherwise. In particular, they control for the currency of issuance and the purpose of a bond, through the variable use of proceeds, distinguishing between general corporate purposes, securitization, refinancing, and any other use.

As an example of the second methodology, Zerbib (2019) defines the green bond premium as the yield differential between a green bond and an otherwise identical conventional bond. To do so, he builds a counterfactual conventional bond from the same issuer, having the same maturity, currency, rating, bond structure, seniority, collateral, and coupon type, as well as a limited difference in issue date and size. In the second stage, he controls for the residual difference in liquidity between each green bond and its counterfactual to extract a green premium by performing a fixed-effects panel regression: the green premium is the unobserved specific effect of the regression of the yield differential on the bonds' liquidity differential. He focuses on 135 investment-grade green bonds issued worldwide.

By using different independent variables and focusing only on green bonds issued by banks, we adopt a methodology similar to those presented by Fatica et al. (2021) and Kapraun et al. (2021). Namely,

$$\text{Yields}_{b,i,t} = \beta_0 + \beta_1 \text{Green}_{b,i,t} + \beta_2 X_{b,i,t} + \beta_3 Z_{c,t} + \delta_i + \varphi_t + \varepsilon_{b,i,t} \tag{11.1}$$

where:

- $\text{Yields}_{b,i,t}$ denotes the yield at issuance of bond b issued by issuer i in time t.
- $\text{Green}_{b,i,t}$ is the main variable of interest, which equals one if a bond is green, and zero otherwise.
- $X_{b,i,t}$ is a vector that includes a set of bond characteristics that may affect the yield.
- $Z_{c,t}$ is a vector that includes a set of macroeconomic variables concerning countries that may affect the yield of the bonds.

Empirical Results

The first part of the empirical analysis explores the presence of cross-dependence in our panel data framework. The cross-sectional dependence (CD) statistic by Pesaran (2004) is based on a simple average of all pair-wise correlation coefficients of the OLS residuals obtained from standard augmented Dickey-Fuller regressions for each variable in the panel. Under the null hypothesis of cross-sectional independence, the CD test statistic follows asymptotically a two-tailed standard normal distribution. The results, reported in Table 11.2, uniformly reject the null hypothesis of cross-section independence, providing evidence of cross-sectional dependence across all the panel-type of variables in Equation (2), given the statistical significance of the CD statistics.

Table 11.2 Cross-dependence test

Variables	p-values
Yields	0.00
Amount_issue	0.00
Time	0.00
Coupon	0.00
Currency	0.00
Payment rank	0.00
Bond_Rating	0.00
Green Bond Indicator	0.00
Indicator UN Principles	0.01

The test is based on the sum of correlation coefficient squares among cross-sectional residuals. This test, which is asymptotically standard normal distribution, examines the null hypothesis of cross-sectional independence.

Table 11.3 Unit root tests

	CIPS	
Variables	Levels	1st Differences
Yields	−1.259	−5.863***
Amount_issue	−1.132	−6.109***
Coupon	−1.133	−6.189***
Time	−1.153	−6.194***
Currency	−1.126	−6.258***
Payment rank	−1.168	−5.911***
Bond_Rating	−1.114	−6.105***
Green bond indicator	−1.219	−5.938***
Indicator UN Principles	−1.139	−6.081***
GLS test		
Euribor_index	−1.154	−6.028***
V2X_index	−1.116	−6.178***
GDP	−1.224	−6.117***
Debt/GDP	−1.143	−6.196***
CPI prices	−1.110	−6.527***

A constant is included in the Pesaran (2007) tests. The results are reported under the null hypothesis of stationarity. Critical values for the Pesaran (2007) test: −2.40 at 1%, −2.22 at 5%, and −2.14 at 10%. The results are reported at lag = 3. ★★★: p≤0.01.

Next, a second-generation panel unit root test is employed to determine the degree of integration of the respective variables. The Pesaran (2007) panel unit root test does not require the estimation of factor loading to eliminate cross-sectional dependence. The null hypothesis is a unit root for the Pesaran (2007) test. The results of this test are reported in Table 11.3 and support the presence of a unit root across all panel variables. Moreover, Table 11.3 reports the results of the General Least Squared Dickey-Fuller test recommended by Elliott et al. (1996). The results illustrate the presence of a unit root in the levels across all variables, while in terms of their first differences, the testing procedure indicates the presence of stationarity across all of them.

To avoid the presence of potential endogeneity issues, we estimate the dynamic panel data model using the general method of moments (GMM) estimation recommended by Arellano and Bover (1995) and Blundell and Bond (1998). The presence of endogeneity potentially comes through reverse causality between yield spreads and any of the control variables involved. In this direction, we observe that the literature provides evidence of reverse (or even bi-directional) causality from the bond yields to the stock market volatility (see for example Amata et al. (2016); Beirne et al. (2009); and Jawaid and UI Haq (2012)). Furthermore, the yield curve has been found to be a predictor of GDP growth and economic activity, and thus it could justify a reverse causality from the bond yields to GDP (see for example Bonser-Neal and Morley (1997); Chinn and Kucko (2015); De Pace (2013); and Hvozdenska (2015)).

The empirical results are reported in Table 11.4 with columns (1) and (2) indicating two distinctive specifications. In particular, column (1) displays the estimates without including the time series (macroeconomic) variables, while column (2) shows the estimates of the full model described by Equation (1). The standard errors reported in both specifications have been clustered on both bond yield spreads and time through the methodological approach recommended by Petersen (2009). The results indicate that in both specifications, lagged spreads account for spreads persistence.

Table 11.4 Dynamic panel estimations

Variables	(1)	(2)
Δspread(−1)	4.862***	4.531***
	[0.00]	[0.00]
ΔAmount_issue	−5.779***	−5.382***
	[0.00]	[0.00]
Δtime	9.164***	8.376***
	[0.00]	[0.00]
Δcoupon	5.685***	5.180***
	[0.00]	[0.01]
ΔCurrency	5.562***	5.118**
	[0.01]	[0.02]
ΔPayment rank		
Sr Non Preferred	−4.382**	−3.858**
	[0.03]	[0.05]
Sr Preferred	5.284***	4.769**
	[0.00]	[0.02]
Sr Unsecured	−4.854***	−4.319**
	[0.01]	[0.04]
Secured	6.054***	5.693***
	[0.00]	[0.00]
Subordinated	5.493***	4.837***
	[0.00]	[0.01]
ΔBond_Rating	−8.045***	−7.664***
	[0.00]	[0.01]
ΔGreen Bond Indicator	3.864***	3.348**
	[0.01]	[0.02]
ΔIndicator UN Principles	−4.558***	−4.274***
	[0.00]	[0.01]
ΔEuribor_index		−6.769***
		[0.00]
ΔV2X_index		−7.279***
		[0.00]
ΔGDP		−8.816***
		[0.00]
ΔGDP(−1)		−8.074***
		[0.00]
ΔDebt/GDP		12.193***
		[0.00]
ΔCPI		10.074***
		[0.00]
ΔCPI(−1)		9.138***
		[0.00]
Diagnostics		
R^2-adjusted	0.43	0.75
AR(1)	[0.00]	[0.00]
AR(2)	[0.31]	[0.38]

(*Continued*)

Table 11.4 (Continued)

Variables	(1)	(2)
Hansen test	[0.39]	[0.49]
Difference Hansen test	[0.40]	[0.52]
Bond and time fixed-effects	YES	YES
LM test	[0.00]	[0.00]

Figures in brackets denote p-values. AR(1) is the first-order test for residual autocorrelation. AR(2) is the test for autocorrelation of order 2. Hansen is the test for the overidentification check for the validity of instruments. The difference-in-Hansen test checks the exogeneity of the instruments. LM stands for the Lagrange multiplier test for random effects (Breusch & Pagan, 1980). The number of lags was determined through the Akaike criterion. All estimations were performed with bond and time dummies, while standard errors have been clustered on both bond yield spreads and time through the method by Petersen (2009), and they, therefore, are robust to heteroscedasticity. **: p<0.05; *** p<0.01.

In terms of the determinants of green bond yields, the estimates illustrate that the drivers of Amount_issue, Non Preferred, Unsecured, Bond ratings, Indicator UN Principles, the Euribor_index, the V2X_index, and GDP exert a negative impact on green bond yields. By contrast, the remaining drivers have a positive effect on those yields. The relevant diagnostics are reported at the bottom of Table 11.4. In particular, the findings report the LM test for the appropriateness of the random effects modeling approach. The null hypothesis of no random effects is rejected, indicating that a random effects model is more suitable. Moreover, for the validity of the instruments, the results reject the null hypothesis of difference-in-Hansen tests of the exogeneity of instruments. The difference-in-Hansen test fails to reject the respective null. Thus, the test supports the validity of the instruments used, while the difference-in-Hansen test implies the exogeneity of the instruments employed. In the estimation process, instruments were generated from one lag for levels and differences in the regressors.

The Outbreak of COVID-19 – Period Starting February 24, 2020 (1,334 Bonds–80 Green Bonds)

When the same models are used for the period starting on February 24, 2020, the day that signaled the outbreak of the pandemic, comparable results are found in terms of signs and magnitudes of the coefficients, as well as of the significance levels (with small changes). As a matter of fact, all coefficients dropped in absolute value with the exception of the coefficients of the green bond indicator (Table 11.5).

The Announcement of the Vaccine – Period Starting November 9, 2020 (938 Bonds–80 Green Bonds)

Running our models for the period starting on November 9, 2020, the day on which the launch of vaccination was announced, we observe that the coefficients maintained their signs and magnitudes. Significance levels remained pretty much unchanged (with minor shifts). The coefficients increased compared to the post-pandemic period. The coefficients of the green bond indicator increased even more (Table 11.6).

Table 11.5 Dynamic panel estimations – pandemic period

Variables	(1)	(2)
Δspread(−1)	4.559***	4.181***
	[0.00]	[0.00]
ΔAmount_issue	−5.118***	−4.841**
	[0.01]	[0.02]
Δtime	8.763***	8.091***
	[0.00]	[0.01]
Δcoupon	5.508***	4.983***
	[0.00]	[0.01]
ΔCurrency	4.277**	4.084**
	[0.02]	[0.03]
ΔPayment rank		
Sr Non Preferred	−4.257**	−3.694**
	[0.04]	[0.05]
Sr Preferred	5.047***	4.617**
	[0.00]	[0.03]
Sr Unsecured	−4.641**	−4.196**
	[0.02]	[0.05]
Secured	5.872***	5.347***
	[0.00]	[0.00]
Subordinated	5.236***	4.669***
	[0.00]	[0.01]
ΔBond_Rating	−7.895***	−7.419***
	[0.00]	[0.01]
ΔGreen Bond Indicator	4.147***	3.858***
	[0.00]	[0.01]
ΔIndicator UN Principles	−4.186***	−4.046***
	[0.00]	[0.01]
ΔEuribor_index		−6.448***
		[0.00]
ΔV2X_index		−7.091***
		[0.00]
ΔGDP		−8.647***
		[0.00]
ΔGDP(−1)		−7.658***
		[0.00]
ΔDebt/GDP		11.769***
		[0.00]
ΔCPI		9.685***
		[0.00]
ΔCPI(−1)		8.377***
		[0.00]
Diagnostics		
R^2-adjusted	0.42	0.73
AR(1)	[0.00]	[0.00]

(Continued)

Table 11.5 (Continued)

Variables	(1)	(2)
AR(2)	[0.29]	[0.35]
Hansen test	[0.37]	[0.46]
Difference Hansen test	[0.38]	[0.48]
Bond and time fixed-effects	YES	YES
LM test	[0.00]	[0.00]

Figures in brackets denote p-values. AR(1) is the first-order test for residual autocorrelation. AR(2) is the test for autocorrelation of order 2. Hansen is the test for the overidentification check for the validity of instruments. The difference-in-Hansen test checks the exogeneity of the instruments. LM stands for the Lagrange multiplier test for random effects (Breusch & Pagan, 1980). The number of lags was determined through the Akaike criterion. All estimations were performed with bond and time dummies, while standard errors have been clustered on both bond yield spreads and time through the method by Petersen (2009), and they, therefore, are robust to heteroscedasticity. **: $p<0.05$; *** $p<0.01$.

Discussion

In both model specifications presented in Table 11.4, the signs of the coefficients coincide with the expected ones – in the cases we have noted an expectation as depicted in Table 11.1. More precisely, the bond yield spread is negatively correlated with the outstanding/issued amount at a 1% significance level. This is due to the fact that the bigger the issue, the more creditworthy the issuer and the higher the liquidity probably are, which justifies a smaller spread. In the same direction, the bond yield spread is negatively correlated at the 1% significance level both with credit ratings, as well as the indicator of alignment with the UN Principles. The former is aligned with the dependence on the spread from the credit rating; the higher the credit rating is, the smaller the yield spread turns out to be. The latter shows that subscribing to the UN Principles for responsible investments is perceived by investors as a true commitment on behalf of the issuers, and they thus are satisfied with a lower spread. Even Fatica et al. (2021) find that institutions that have declared commitment to environmental principles established by the United Nations issued green bonds at a premium. Our findings confirm hypothesis H4 as stated in the second section of this chapter.

This does not hold true though with the green bond indicator, with which the spread exhibits a positive and statistically significant correlation at the 1% level. As we did not have any prior expectation for this variable, a potential explanation is that the mere characterization of a bond as green is not accepted by investors as a reason to accept a lower spread. In contrast, they may even expect a higher spread, suspecting a possible greenwashing, especially when the use of proceeds is not disclosed. The positive sign of the coefficient suggests that when the dummy variable becomes 1 from 0 (i.e., the bond is green), the green bond indicator leads to an increase in the yield by the coefficient. Therefore, when a bond is labeled as green, its yield becomes higher than if it was a plain vanilla bond. This is indicative of the attractiveness of the bond to investors – most likely lower than that of non-green bonds. Our results go in the same direction as a few previous studies, for example, the paper of Fatica et al. (2021), which finds no premium for green bonds issued by financial issuers, contrarily to other issuers. The authors claim that financial institutions find difficulties in credibly signaling to the market their engagement in green activities. So investors do not have trust, consider investing in green bonds risky, and therefore ask for a higher yield.

Table 11.6 Dynamic panel estimations – vaccination period

Variables	(1)	(2)
Δspread(−1)	5.563***	5.214***
	[0.00]	[0.00]
ΔAmount_issue	−5.669***	−5.194***
	[0.00]	[0.00]
Δtime	8.962***	8.217***
	[0.00]	[0.00]
Δcoupon	5.811***	5.347***
	[0.00]	[0.00]
ΔCurrency	4.381**	4.117**
	[0.02]	[0.02]
ΔPayment rank		
Sr Non Preferred	−4.511**	−3.842**
	[0.03]	[0.04]
Sr Preferred	5.569***	5.106***
	[0.00]	[0.01]
Sr Unsecured	−4.836**	−4.365**
	[0.02]	[0.03]
Secured	6.125***	5.974***
	[0.00]	[0.00]
Subordinated	5.609***	4.984***
	[0.00]	[0.00]
ΔBond_Rating	−8.251***	−7.885***
	[0.00]	[0.00]
ΔGreen Bond Indicator	4.571***	4.084***
	[0.00]	[0.00]
ΔIndicator UN Principles	−4.316***	−4.109***
	[0.00]	[0.00]
ΔEuribor_index		−6.736***
		[0.00]
ΔV2X_index		−7.684***
		[0.00]
ΔGDP		−8.981***
		[0.00]
ΔGDP(−1)		−7.828***
		[0.00]
ΔDebt/GDP		12.635***
		[0.00]
ΔCPI		9.995***
		[0.00]
ΔCPI(−1)		8.816***
		[0.00]
Diagnostics		
R^2-adjusted	0.45	0.76
AR(1)	[0.00]	[0.00]

(*Continued*)

Table 11.6 (Continued)

Variables	(1)	(2)
AR(2)	[0.33]	[0.42]
Hansen test	[0.39]	[0.50]
Difference Hansen test	[0.41]	[0.53]
Bond and time fixed-effects	YES	YES
LM test	[0.00]	[0.00]

Figures in brackets denote p-values. AR(1) is the first-order test for residual autocorrelation. AR(2) is the test for autocorrelation of order 2. Hansen is the test for the overidentification check for the validity of instruments. The difference-in-Hansen test checks the exogeneity of the instruments. LM stands for the Lagrange multiplier test for random effects (Breusch & Pagan, 1980). The number of lags was determined through the Akaike criterion. All estimations were performed with bond and time dummies, while standard errors have been clustered on both bond yield spreads and time through the method by Petersen (2009), and they, therefore, are robust to heteroscedasticity. **: $p<0.05$; *** $p<0.01$.

Similarly, Alessi et al. (2021) consider that financial institutions are probably not the first issuers that come to mind when thinking of companies that are at the forefront of efforts to reduce emissions. In addition, MacAskill et al. (2021), through a systematic literature review, state that in the primary market, there does not appear to be sufficient evidence that a greenium exists.

Furthermore, the bulk of green bond issues are observed at the same time with a series of exogenous (and in some cases unprecedented) events: the outbreak of the pandemic, the inflationary trends due to the disruption in the logistics chain, and the gradual increase of interest rates that followed. As a result, it could be that the green bond yields increased along with the interest rates. Furthermore, this outcome is in line with the available literature that indicates higher yields for green bonds compared to non-green bonds (Bachelet et al. (2019); Karpf and Mandel (2017, 2018)). Our findings confirm hypothesis H3 as stated in the second section of this chapter.

Furthermore, the time to maturity and the coupon are also aligned with the expectations displayed in Table 11.1 and post a positive and statistically significant correlation at the 1% level with the yield spread (Table 11.4). The former is due to the fact that the longer the time to maturity, the longer the time the investors are exposed to the risk of the issuer, and, thus, the higher the expected compensation for this risk. The latter is a consequence of the realization that a higher coupon is indicative of a higher risk, which in its turn implies a higher yield spread.

The spread is positively correlated with the currency (at the 1% level in the model without the macroeconomic variables and at the 5% level in the model with the macroeconomic variables included). This may imply that investors are not really optimistic about euro-denominated bonds compared to non-euro-denominated bonds and, therefore, are looking forward to a higher yield.

The payment rank also exhibits mixed results in terms of correlation. The senior non-preferred and senior unsecured issues post a negative correlation (at the 1% or 5% significance level, depending on the model specification), whereas the senior preferred, secured, and subordinated post a positive correlation (at the 1% or 5% significance level, depending on the model specification). This probably implies that each payment rank appeals to a different segment of investors, who set their own expectations with regard to the spread, and thus the payment order does not affect the spread in a uniform manner.

Turning to the macroeconomic variables, we realize that the interest rate, the stock market volatility, and the GDP are negatively correlated with the yield at the 1% significance level. The first implies that as interest rates increase, the bond yields tend to drop; this may be explained by assuming that the risk-free part of the bond yield increases as well, and the relevant contribution of the spread to the bond yield diminishes. The second suggests that as the stock market volatility grows, the bond spread decreases; this is probably due to the switch of the investors from equity to less risky assets, such as bonds. The third indicates that as the GDP of the country gets bigger, the bond spreads become lower; this is a potential outcome of the trust that investors have in bigger economies, as a result of which they are willing to accept a lower spread.

In contrast, the debt-to-GDP ratio and the inflation rate are positively correlated with the bond yield spread at the 1% significance level. The former displays the concern of investors for economies that show a high debt-to-GDP ratio and thus anticipate a higher spread in order to invest. The latter reflects the wish of investors to receive higher compensation through a higher spread in higher inflation environments that worsen their purchasing power. As a matter of fact, interest rates, and as such yields, aim to compensate investors for the loss in their purchasing power that is caused by inflation.

Last but not least, the lagged spreads post a positive and statistically significant 1% level correlation with the yield. This confirms that the increase in spreads is depicted by an increase in bond yields.

Turning now to the period of the pandemic, we realize that all coefficients remain of the same sign and pretty much the same magnitude. They are smaller in absolute value than the coefficients of the model when the full sample is used, with one notable exception, the green bond index. The former indicates that the variables under investigation had a smaller impact on the bond yield as an exogenous factor affected the bond yields, the pandemic. Moreover, the pandemic was followed by a purchase program that was launched by the ECB (and the Fed), which potentially prevailed in the shaping of the bond yields and led to a lessening of the effect of the (remaining) variables. The latter, though, increased and remained positive and statistically significant at the 1% level. This means that during the pandemic investors required a higher yield from green bonds, reflecting a (possible) concern (i) about the success of the projects financed by such bonds; (ii) about the capacity of the banks to repay from the proceeds; and (iii) about the commitment to sustain green projects in the midst of the pandemic. As a matter of fact, it unveils a fear that – as economies suffered due to lockdowns, healthcare systems became overburdened, and human lives were lost – member states would not be so committed to pursuing the green (and digital) transition envisaged by the European Commission. Such a laxity would jeopardize the realization of the green projects and thus would put at stake the produced proceeds. In this sense, the first part of hypothesis H5 (as stated in the second section of this chapter) is confirmed. There are some minor changes in the significance levels, namely, the effect of the amount issued in the model with the macroeconomic variables and of currency and senior unsecured bonds in the model without the macroeconomic variables moved to 5% from 1% in the pandemic period. In contrast, the significance of the green bond indicator changes from 5% to 1% in the model with the macroeconomic variables. The fact that the COVID-19 crisis has significantly increased the uncertainty and volatility of financial markets is confirmed by Mensi et al. (2022) and Cicchiello et al. (2022); the latter specifically find out that the COVID-19 pandemic introduced considerable uncertainty about the future of green bonds. In particular, these bonds offered higher risk premiums compared with conventional bonds as compensation for the uncertain profitability and a higher risk of default.

Finally, in the period after the vaccination, we observe that the coefficients rebound to higher levels than during the pandemic, in some cases higher and in some other cases lower (in absolute value) than the pre-pandemic levels. The same holds true for the coefficient of the green bond indicator, which increased even more. This increase in the magnitude of the coefficients is possibly attributed to the hope that the launch of the vaccine generated. Optimism returned – besides the fear of downgrades or defaults – which potentially led to the diminution of the impact of the pandemic and the bond purchase programs, which later were announced to cease by March 2022. However, the increase of the green bond indicator coefficient signals that there are still worries with regard to (i) the success of the green-project financing; (ii) the ability of the banks to repay from proceeds; and (iii) the commitment to ensure greener economies and activities. These worries were amplified by the additional disruption caused in the logistics chain, as well as in the energy front by the geopolitical risks in the European continent. Consequently, the second part of hypothesis H5 (stated in the second section of this chapter) is not confirmed. There are also some minor changes in the significance levels, namely, the effect of the amount issued in the model with the macroeconomic variables moving back to the 1% level in the vaccination period and the same increase being observed in the senior preferred variable. The significance level of currency retreated to the 5% level in the model without the macroeconomic variables.

Conclusions and Policy Implications

Green bonds can be considered one of the most promising innovations in sustainable finance since they can play a key role in the allocation of financial resources needed to build a greener economy.

It would be a greatly beneficial process if the issuers of green bonds, besides fulfilling their commitment to the environment, might enjoy the lower cost of capital in primary markets, satisfy the financial needs of pro-environment investors, and, in this way, accelerate the overall funding of the green economy. In doing so, the green bond market would become an effective flywheel to foster the growth of the green economy. Unfortunately, this occurs for some issuers but not for banks, at least not at the moment.

Banks – as green bond issuers – are not considered by investors to be very trustworthy in relation to environmental issues; generally, they provide a non-credible signal of the company's commitment toward the environment. Since a bank normally collects money for financing firms' needs, it seems that behind their green bond issues, there is nothing new. Of course, this is not the truth: a green bank bond issuance can originate a set of green loans that represent a powerful means for greening the economy, also benefiting SMEs that want to undertake "green" investments. It is evident, however, that banks tend to be unable to offer investors a green project as easily perceivable and controllable as a project of a supranational organization or a large firm. Certainly, at the time of the investment, investors in green bank bonds have a global perception of their green investment, which is that of being less "green" compared to green bonds issued by other entities. As MacAskill et al. (2021) find out, green bond investors are driven by supporting climate-aligned objectives with verified and measurable outcomes. The opacity and asymmetry of information that traditionally has characterized bank business can involve the fear of greenwashing; consequently, investors – perceiving a higher risk – wish to be compensated by a higher premium. To avoid this, banks need to promote their "green" business extensively, making investors understand their effective contribution to the challenge of climate change. This explains also why banks tend to sign alliances and make their commitments known to the public.

Synthetically, it is possible to affirm that from the investors' point of view, in particular retail investors, the concern arises that green bank bonds could be misused in finance greenwashing projects. The effects of the issuer's characteristics on asymmetric information and greenwashing risk are perceived by investors and are therefore reflected in the green bond premium.

Along the same vein, Kapraun et al. (2021) affirm that one of the driving factors for the existence of the green bond premium is the investors' preference for green instruments, which is however based on their trust in the green credentials of the corresponding bond. Investors might have higher preferences for green assets that have a higher environmental impact, demonstrated immediately at issuance, for example in terms of tons of CO_2 equivalents avoided. However, such information is generally not available at the time of issuance by bank issuers. Investors do value bonds with a higher impact but only if this potential impact is credible and verifiable by a third party. Trust is definitely the most important element guiding the preference of investors. If investors do not trust the corresponding issuers that are actually financing green projects with an environmental impact, the price for such bonds will stay below or at most at the level of comparable conventional bonds.

The findings of this study indicate that the unambiguous drivers of the bond yield spread are the bond rating, the outstanding amount, the time to maturity, and the coupon rate. Next to this, an alignment with the UN Principles for responsible investments gives bank issuers the possibility to offer a lower yield to investors.

This indicates that investors are not convinced that green bonds bear less risk compared to non-green bonds. On the contrary, they see higher risks and potential greenwashing. They thus focus on more genuine actions – such as the subscription to the UN Principles. Finally, the market and country macroeconomic variables also contribute to the determination of the spread, which implies that if the green label is expected to reduce the cost of borrowing via a lower spread, then it has to reflect the genuine intention of the issuer beyond any doubt.

Finally, it must be said that the green bond market is maturing, but it is still at an early stage. Our findings may not necessarily extend to the future years. In fact, it might be that green bank bond yields are different in the next few years. As the green bond market expands and the sensitivity for ESG topics grows, it is probable that green bank bond investors may ultimately settle for a lower yield compared to non-green bonds (Flammer, 2021).

Regulators and supervisors can ensure that by overseeing the implementation of a series of principles – that promote transparency, including the establishment of a solid process for the evaluation and selection of the projects that are candidates for financing, the correct management of the proceeds, the reporting, as well as the implementation of audit and external review – the trust of investors is gained. These steps will not only protect investors but will ensure that the assignment of a green label was earned as a result of a diligent review/evaluation process. These actions – provided investors are convinced – may lead to lower spreads for green bank bond issues.

References

Alessi, L., Ossola, E., & Panzica, R. (2021). What greenium matters in the stock market? The role of greenhouse gas emissions and environmental disclosures. *Journal of Financial Stability, 54*, 100869. https://doi.org/10.1016/j.jfs.2021.100869

Amata, E. O., Muturi, W., & Mbewa, M. (2016). Relationship between macro-economic variables, investor herding behaviour and stock market volatility in Kenya. *International Journal of Economics, Commerce and Management, 4*(8), 36–54. http://repository.daystar.ac.ke/xmlui/handle/123456789/3619

Arellano, M., & Bover, O. (1995). Another look at the instrumental variable estimation of error-components models. *Journal of Econometrics, 68*(1), 29–51. https://doi.org/10.1016/0304-4076(94)01642-D

Bachelet, M. J., Becchetti, L., & Manfredonia, S. (2019). The green bonds premium puzzle: The role of issuer characteristics and third-party verification. *Sustainability*, *11*(4), 1098. https://doi.org/10.3390/su11041098

Baker, M., Bergstresser, D., Serafeim, G., & Wurgler, J. (2018). *Financing the response to climate change: The pricing and ownership of US green bonds* (No. w25194). National Bureau of Economic Research. https://doi.org/10.3386/w25194

Baulkaran, V. (2019). Stock market reaction to green bond issuance. *Journal of Asset Management*, *20*(5), 331–340. https://doi.org/10.1057/s41260-018-00105-1

Beirne, J., Caporale, G. M., & Spagnolo, N. (2009). Market, interest rate and exchange rate risk effects on financial stock returns: A GARCH-M approach. *Quantitative and Qualitative Analysis in Social Sciences*, *3*(2), 44–68.

Blundell, R., & Bond, S. (1998). Initial conditions and moment restrictions in dynamic panel data models. *Journal of Econometrics*, *87*(1), 115–143. https://doi.org/10.1016/S0304-4076(98)00009-8

Bonser-Neal, C., & Morley, T. R. (1997). Does the yield spread predict real economic activity? A multi-country analysis. *Economic Review-Federal Reserve Bank of Kansas City*, *82*(3), 37–53. https://econpapers.repec.org/RePEc:fip:fedker:y:1997:i:qiii:p:37-53:n:v.82no.3

Breusch, T. S., & Pagan, A. R. (1980). The Lagrange multiplier test and its applications to model specification in econometrics. *Review of Economic Studies*, *47*(1), 239–253. https://doi.org/10.2307/2297111

Caramichael, J., & Rapp, A. C. (2022). The Green corporate bond issuance premium. *International Finance Discussion Paper* (1346). Board of Governors of the Federal Reserve System. https://doi.org/10.17016/IFDP.2022.1346

CBI (Climate Bonds Initiative). (2022, August). *Sustainable debt market: Summary H1 2022*. https://www.climatebonds.net/resources/reports/sustainable-debt-market-summary-h1-2022

Cheong, C., & Choi, J. (2020). Green bonds: A survey. *Journal of Derivatives and Quantitative Studies*, *28*(4), 175–189. https://doi.org/10.1108/JDQS-09-2020-0024

Chinn, M., & Kucko, K. (2015). The predictive power of the yield curve across countries and time. *International Finance*, *18*(2), 129–156. https://doi.org/10.1111/infi.12064

Cicchiello, A. F., Cotugno, M., Monferrà, S., & Perdichizzi, S. (2022). Credit spreads in the European green bond market: A daily analysis of the COVID-19 pandemic impact. *Journal of International Financial Management and Accounting*, *33*(3), 383–411. https://doi.org/10.1111/jifm.12150

De Pace, P. (2013). Gross domestic product growth predictions through the yield spread: Time-variation and structural breaks. *International Journal of Finance and Economics*, *18*(1), 1–24. https://doi.org/10.1002/ijfe.453

Elliott, G., Rothenberg, T. J., & Stock, J. H. (1996). Efficient tests for an autoregressive unit root. *Econometrica*, *64*(4), 813–836. https://doi.org/10.2307/2171846

Fatica, S., Panzica, R., & Rancan, M. (2021). The pricing of green bonds: Are financial institutions special? *Journal of Financial Stability*, *54*, 100873. https://doi.org/10.1016/j.jfs.2021.100873

Febi, W., Schäfer, D., Stephan, A., & Sun, C. (2018). The impact of liquidity risk on the yield spread of green bonds. *Finance Research Letters*, *27*, 53–59. https://doi.org/10.1016/j.frl.2018.02.025

Flammer, C. (2021). Corporate green bonds. *Journal of Financial Economics*, *142*(2), 499–516. https://doi.org/10.1016/j.jfineco.2021.01.010

Gianfrate, G., & Peri, M. (2019). The green advantage: Exploring the convenience of issuing green bonds. *Journal of Cleaner Production*, *219*, 127–135. https://doi.org/10.1016/j.jclepro.2019.02.022

Hachenberg, B., & Schiereck, D. (2018). Are green bonds priced differently from conventional bonds? *Journal of Asset Management*, *19*(6), 371–383. https://doi.org/10.1057/s41260-018-0088-5

Hodgson, C., Morris, S., Walker, O., & Storbeck, O. (2021, November 3). Banks' green pledges under scrutiny. *Financial Times*. https://www.ft.com/content/0ea3267c-d61f-4120-a976-0b81b60836c5

Hvozdenska, J. (2015). The yield curve as a predictor of gross domestic product growth in Nordic countries. *Procedia Economics and Finance*, *26*, 438–445. https://doi.org/10.1016/S2212-5671(15)00871-0

Hyun, S., Park, D., & Tian, S. (2020). The price of going green: The role of greenness in green bond markets. *Accounting and Finance*, *60*(1), 73–95. https://doi.org/10.1111/acfi.12515

ICMA (International Capital Market Association). (2021, June). *Green bond principles: Voluntary process guidelines for issuing green bonds*. https://www.icmagroup.org/assets/documents/Sustainable-finance/2021-updates/Green-Bond-Principles-June-2021-100621.pdf

Jawaid, S. T., & Ul Haq, A. (2012). Effects of interest rate, exchange rate and their volatilities on stock prices: Evidence from banking industry of Pakistan. *Theoretical and Applied Economics*, *19*(8), 153–166. http://store.ectap.ro/articole/769.pdf

Kapraun, J., Latino, C., Scheins, C., & Schlag, C. (2021, April). (In)-credibly green: Which bonds trade at a green bond premium? In *Proceedings of the Paris December 2019 finance meeting EUROFIDAI-ESSEC*. https://doi.org/10.2139/ssrn.3347337

Karpf, A., & Mandel, A. (2017, February). *Does it pay to be green? A comparative study of the yield term structure of green and brown bonds in the US municipal bonds market* [Unpublished manuscript]. Université Panthéon-Sorbonne Paris, 1. https://doi.org/10.2139/ssrn.2923484

Karpf, A., & Mandel, A. (2018). The changing value of the 'green' label on the US municipal bond market. *Nature Climate Change, 8*, 161–165. https://doi.org/10.1038/s41558-017-0062-0

Lamperti, F., Bosetti, V., Roventini, A., Tavoni, M., & Treibich, T. (2021). Three green financial policies to address climate risks. *Journal of Financial Stability, 54*, 100875. https://doi.org/10.1016/j.jfs.2021.100875

Larcker, D. F., & Watts, E. M. (2020). Where's the greenium? *Journal of Accounting and Economics, 69*(2–3), 101312. https://doi.org/10.1016/j.jacceco.2020.101312

Lau, P. T., Sze, A. K., Wan, W., & Wong, A. Y. (2022). The economics of the greenium: How much is the world willing to pay to save the earth? *Environmental and Resource Economics, 81*(2), 379–408. https://doi.org/10.1007/s10640-021-00630-5

Löffler, K. U., Petreski, A., & Stephan, A. (2021). Drivers of green bond issuance and new evidence on the "greenium". *Eurasian Economic Review, 11*(1), 1–24. https://doi.org/10.1007/s40822-020-00165-y

Ma, C., Schoutens, W., Beirlant, J., De Spiegeleer, J., Höcht, S., & Van Kleeck, R. (2020). *Are green bonds different from ordinary bonds? A statistical and quantitative point of view* (No. 394). NBB working paper. National Bank of Belgium, Brussels. https://www.nbb.be/en/articles/are-green-bonds-different-ordinary-bonds-statistical-and-quantitative-point-view

MacAskill, S., Roca, E., Liu, B., Stewart, R. A., & Sahin, O. (2021). Is there a green premium in the green bond market? Systematic literature review revealing premium determinants. *Journal of Cleaner Production, 280*(Part 2), 124491. https://doi.org/10.1016/j.jclepro.2020.124491

Mensi, W., Rehman, M. U., & Vo, X. V. (2022). Impacts of COVID-19 outbreak, macroeconomic and financial stress factors on price spillovers among green bond. *International Review of Financial Analysis, 81*, 102125. https://doi.org/10.1016/j.irfa.2022.102125

Morris, S. (2022, April 29). HSBC faces greenwashing accusations from the advertising watchdog. *Financial Times*. https://www.ft.com/content/6c08ae5f-214f-4a5f-801e-6c849a3e517d

Naeem, M. A., Farid, S., Ferrer, R., & Shahzad, S. J. H. (2021). Comparative efficiency of green and conventional bonds pre-and during COVID-19: An asymmetric multifractal detrended fluctuation analysis. *Energy Policy, 153*, 112285. https://doi.org/10.1016/ j.enpol.2021.112285

Nanayakkara, M., & Colombage, S. (2019). Do investors in green bond market pay a premium? Global evidence. *Applied Economics, 51*(40), 4425–4437. https://doi.org/10.1080/00036846.2019.1591611

Paranque, B., & Revelli, C. (2019). Ethico-economic analysis of impact finance: The case of green bonds. *Research in International Business and Finance, 47*, 57–66. https://doi.org/10.1016/j.ribaf.2017.12.003

Pesaran, M. H. (2004). General diagnostic tests for cross section dependence in panels. Cambridge working papers in economics, No. 435 and CESifo Working Paper, No. 1229. https://ideas.repec.org/p/cam/camdae/0435.html

Pesaran, M. H. (2007). A simple panel unit root test in the presence of cross-section dependence. *Journal of Applied Econometrics, 22*(2), 265–312. https://doi.org/10.1002/jae.951

Petersen, M. A. (2009). Estimating standard errors in finance panel data sets: Comparing approaches. *Review of Financial Studies, 22*(1), 435–480. https://doi.org/10.1093/rfs/hhn053

Quirici, M. C. (2020). The increasing importance of green bonds as instruments of impact investing: Towards a new European standardisation. In M. La Torre & H. Chiappini (Eds.), *Contemporary issues in sustainable finance* (pp. 177–203). Palgrave Studies in Impact Finance. Palgrave Macmillan. https://doi.org/10.1007/978-3-030-40248-8_8

Reboredo, J. C. (2018). Green bond and financial markets: Co-movement, diversification and price spillover effects. *Energy Economics, 74*, 38–50. https://doi.org/10.1016/j.eneco.2018.05.030

Renneboog, L., Ter Horst, J., & Zhang, C. (2008). Socially responsible investments: Institutional aspects, performance, and investor behavior. *Journal of Banking and Finance, 32*(9), 1723–1742. https://doi.org/10.1016/j.jbankfin.2007.12.039

Sheng, Q., Zheng, X., & Zhong, N. (2021). Financing for sustainability: Empirical analysis of green bond premium and issuer heterogeneity. *Natural Hazards, 107*(3), 2641–2651. https://doi.org/10.1007/s11069-021-04540-z

Shishlov, I., Morel, R., & Cochran, I. (2016). Beyond transparency: Unlocking the full potential of green bonds. *Institute for Climate Economics (I4CE), 2016*, 1–28. https://www.i4ce.org/en/publication/unlocking-the-potential-of-green-bonds/

Tang, D.Y., & Zhang, Y. (2020). Do shareholders benefit from green bonds? *Journal of Corporate Finance, 61*, 101427. https://doi.org/10.1016/j.jcorpfin.2018.12.001

Turguttopbaş, N. (2022). Testing the green bond premium in COVID-19 pandemia. In I.Y. Gok (Ed.), *Handbook of research on global aspects of sustainable finance in times of crises* (pp. 173–193). IGI Global. https://doi.org/10.4018/978-1-7998-8501-6

UNEP FI (United Nations Environment Programme Finance Initiative). (2021, November). *Principles for responsible banking*. Guidance Document: Reporting on the Principles for Responsible Banking. UNEP FI. https://www.unepfi.org/banking/bankingprinciples/

UNEP FI (United Nations Environment Programme Finance Initiative). (2022, April). *A vision for change: The NBZA observes its first anniversary*. https://www.unepfi.org/industries/banking/a-vision-for-change-the-nzba-observes-its-first-anniversary/

Zerbib, O. D. (2019). The effect of pro-environmental preferences on bond prices: Evidence from green bonds. *Journal of Banking and Finance, 98*, 39–60. https://doi.org/10.1016/j.jbankfin.2018.10.012

PART 3

Sector- and Country-Specific Aspects

12

THE QUEST FOR GLOBAL GREEN FINANCE PARTICIPATION

Developing Countries and Barriers to Full Participation

George Kapaya and Orthodoxia Kyriacou

Introduction and Purpose

In our view, the relatively recent international focus on and heightened concern over environmental sustainability is extremely important because it prompts reconsideration of how developed and developing countries can work together on this important issue. Connected with this issue is the extent to which green finance can play a meaningful role in this debate. As a starting point, a considerable body of literature has attempted to define green finance. These definitions have overlaps and similarities, but also differences.

In order to engage in this debate, it is helpful to outline a working definition of the term 'green finance'. According to Cai and Guo (2021), green finance is a relatively new field of finance, and 'economists and international organizations have failed to establish a precise definition of or agree upon one unanimously' (p. 2). They, therefore, suggest a broad working definition which they believe may attract some consensus: 'A sustainable financial system is one which incorporates the development values and aids in dealing with financial assets, so that actual wealth may be used to meet the demands of an ecologically sustainable and inclusive economy over time' (p. 2). On the other hand, the City of London Corporation (2016) defines green finance in terms of what it does: 'Green finance provides a bridge between global environmental priorities and the financial system' (p. 11). In our search for a working definition, we lean towards that proposed by the World Economic Forum (2020), which appears to align closely with our own understanding of green finance:

> 'At its simplest ... any structured financial activity – a product or service – that's been created to ensure a better environmental outcome. It includes an array of loans, debt mechanisms and investments that are used to encourage the development of green projects or minimize the impact on the climate of more regular projects. Or a combination of both'.

As indicated by the wide array of definitions, green finance has attracted considerable research interest in recent years. This research has adopted diverse perspectives, ranging from definitions to attempts to quantify the contribution of green finance to the economies of various countries (for examples, see Cai & Guo, 2021; Khan et al., 2021; Lee & Lee, 2022).

Our contribution to this emergent debate focuses on the position of developing countries, especially those in Africa and Asia. According to the United Nations (2022b), in 2022 'the population of Europe and Northern America combined and that of sub-Saharan Africa were comparable in size, with more than 1.1 and 1.2 billion people respectively', 'and more than half of the projected increase in the global population between 2022 and 2050 is expected to be concentrated in just eight countries: the Democratic Republic of the Congo, Egypt, Ethiopia, India, Nigeria, Pakistan, the Philippines and the United Republic of Tanzania' (pp. 4–5).

These statistics highlight the centrality of Africa and Asia to the climate sustainability debate. In this chapter, we argue that these regions have historically played the role of, or more accurately been relegated to, silent or passive partners in this debate. We believe that a new and genuinely reconsidered approach is necessary. Developing countries should not be mere bystanders in this key area. They should be afforded a chance to participate actively, both in outlining the problems as they see them, and in contributing to the debate on possible solutions. Such an inclusive approach is more likely to lead to more equitable and fairer results. We also believe this to be a necessary step in the fight for our planet's survival. The fight against climate change cannot be won simply by protecting one part of the planet; it is a fight in which all parts must feel they have a stake.

A major part of our argument is that for far too long, human beings through their nation-states have tended to see the world from the perspective of their own country or region. Consistent with this, when faced with serious dangers to our environment, or indeed existence, we have not adopted the global and inclusive perspective so necessary for co-inhabitants of our planet. Most actions, however well-meaning, have tended to be narrowly focused, partisan, and ultimately inadequate. With specific reference to the climate change crisis, we argue that most initiatives aimed at curbing the worst environmental excesses have been characterized by a 'them and us' mentality. They have tended to pit one group of nation-states against another: the rich North against the poor South, and developed against developing countries. We also argue very strongly that, ultimately, the issue of environmental sustainability cannot be separated or divorced from that of economic development and sustainability. This, in turn, is very closely linked with international trade, its financing, and terms of trade around the globe.

Approaches to the fight against climate change have focused on a broad range of measures, including carbon emissions reductions, initiatives for environmental protection, sustainable development strategies, and millennium development goals. These date back several decades, including the Tokyo Accord in 2003, the Paris Accord in 2015, and more recently the COP26 Accord in 2021. The results of these efforts have been far from satisfactory: global warming appears to be accelerating, and net-zero CO_2 emissions targets are off course (Macfarlane, 2021). In 2022 alone, there were devastating floods in Pakistan, South Africa, Nigeria, and Bangladesh (BBC News, 2022) and equally devastating fires in parts of the United States, Canada, and other places around the world. All this points to serious changes and challenges to our environment at a global level. It is no wonder that in his first address to the COP27 summit in Egypt, the UN Secretary-General warned starkly that 'we are on a highway to climate hell with our foot on the accelerator' (United Nations, 2022, November 7). All this is happening against a background of economies at a tipping point in many developing countries, especially in Africa and also in Asia. Even more concerning is the fact that, according to UN projections, the same regions are expected to grow at the fastest rate in the world between 2030 and 2050 (UN, 2022b).

Amongst attempts to find a solution, if there is one, attention has increasingly turned to finance, particularly green finance. This is seen as a critical part of a new initiative to achieve the global net-zero carbon target. Until recently, finance and green finance did not feature prominently in these discussions, but many important international players have now moved green finance strategies to the top of their agendas. These include the UN through its Environment Program Finance Initiative (UNEPF), the EU with its Sustainable Finance Initiative, and the UK in the aftermath of the October 2021 COP26 conference. Many countries in the developed world have devised their own specific initiatives. Most importantly, banks and other key financial institutions have also joined in. We await the outcomes of the UN's 2022 COP27 climate change conference.

Just before the COP26 conference, Mark Carney, former Governor of the Bank of England, revealed that more than 450 firms had agreed to join the Glasgow Financial Alliance for Net Zero, an organization for which he was the UN Special Envoy for Climate Action and Finance. The 450 firms who had joined the alliance held assets valued at up to 130 trillion US dollars (Metcalf & Morales, 2021). Taking up the challenge, the UK government formed a Green Finance Taskforce, with terms of reference that indicate the context, objectives, and ways in which green finance is seen as a critical component in the fight for 'clean growth' and a sustainable environment (UK Government, 2019). The UK government is not alone in this. The UN, the EU, and OECD countries, as well as individual countries such as Canada and the United States, and many others, have formally set up forums or strategies for dealing with the climate emergency and climate sustainability issues. At all these levels there is evidently a clear recognition that green finance must be a key part of the package of tools used to deal with the climate emergency. Green finance (or 'sustainable finance', as the UN calls it) is now recognized as a critical component of any efforts to successfully transform the world's economies and achieve the zero-carbon emissions target by 2050 (United Nations, n.d).

There also seems to be wide acknowledgment, and indeed agreement, that governments alone cannot provide sufficient finance to accomplish this task. They require the support and full participation of the private/corporate finance sector. Indeed, both the UN Climate Action team and the British government's Green Finance Taskforce positively welcome the private sector's full participation (UK Government, n.d.), seeing this as a tremendous opportunity rather than a risk to the financial and banking sector. When asked to identify 'the most exciting climate-related development in private finance', Mark Carney stated that 'the dialogue has shifted from viewing climate change as a risk, to seeing the opportunity, and really translating that into a single objective, which is to move our economies to net zero as quickly as possible' (Carney, 2021).

As serious and well-meaning as these efforts and initiatives may appear to be, there remains a 'stark gap between rhetoric and action' (Concern Worldwide, 2021). With specific reference to this chapter's focus on developing countries and green finance, it can be argued that these initiatives do indeed open up new and potentially profitable opportunities for financial institutions to expand their funding operations and the options they can offer to their corporate clients. However, as far as developing countries are concerned, nothing in what any of the key nations and organizations (including the UN) have said or proposed appears to represent a significant departure from what has gone before. Furthermore, we can see no significant prospect of change, either in terms of participation in the discussions and negotiations leading up to these initiatives or in the economic benefits that are likely to result from them.

In essence, developing countries have faced and continue to face real barriers to meaningful participation in the climate debate and the green finance initiative. Their participation in both has been marginal at best. However, one critical aspect that has, as far as we can tell, escaped serious inclusion in this discussion is the issue of fair terms of international trade. In our view, this topic is intricately linked with finance and is of particular relevance to relationships between developed and developing countries. It is important to explore why developing countries find themselves in a position of helplessness, despite their abundant natural resources. For this purpose, we focus first on global supply chains and global value chains. In the next section, we explore how developed and developing countries, respectively, stand and fare in each of these global chains, and how this connects with the green finance debate.

Global Supply Chains and Global Value Chains

We have argued that many of the problems facing developing countries, especially in Africa and Asia, relate to unfair international trading terms. We expand on this here through the concepts of global supply chains and global value chains. Both go to the heart of our understanding of why many developing countries find themselves stuck on an endless poverty treadmill, despite often having enormous mineral wealth and other natural resources and commodities. Thus far, we have not found this issue appearing on the agendas of any key organizations or senior people driving the green finance initiative.

A repeated explanation for why many developing countries have struggled to achieve meaningful economic development is rampant mismanagement, corruption, and political greed. We have no doubt that these ills do indeed exist to varying degrees; however, they are not, by any means, exclusive to developing countries. We argue that the critical factor is the position of developing countries in Africa, Asia, and Latin America vis-à-vis developed Western countries in global supply chains (GSCs) and global value chains (GVCs). These chains are the global business networks underlying the movement of goods and services between countries, and the values placed on them. Feller et al. (2006, p. 4) offer the following description of supply chains and value chains:

> *Both chains overlay the same network of companies. Both are made up of companies that interact to provide goods and services. When we talk about supply chains, however, we usually talk about a downstream flow of goods and supplies from the source to the customer. Value flows the other way. The customer is the source of value, and value flows from the customer, in the form of demand, to the supplier.*

Developing countries contribute key resources, such as oil, gold, cobalt, copper, zinc, and coltan, which are all critical to building and operating essential modern technologies, as well as a whole range of commodities (BBC News, 2013). They are fundamental to both GSCs and GVCs, yet appear to derive no meaningful benefit from either. Simply stated, currently, and indeed historically, the benefits of these chains are not distributed equitably between developed and developing countries. Indeed, it can be argued that most developed countries have achieved their status at the expense, and indeed through exploitation, of developing countries by exploiting GSC/GSV mechanisms (Jordan et al., 2020).

Grimshaw (2020) defines a supply chain as 'the entire process of making and selling commercial goods, including every stage from the supply of materials and the manufacture of the goods through to their distribution and sale'. Depending on the product, this process may include sourcing raw materials, refining them into basic parts, creating or manufacturing new products by combining different basic parts, fulfilling orders and sales, delivering products, and providing customer support and after-sales services. A supply chain may be national or international (global) in character. The supply chain does not indicate the financial benefit that each participant derives from it; it simply shows what each participant contributes to the chain, and at what stage. GSCs can be graphed as a simple horizontal line: for generations, and indeed centuries, the position of most countries in the developing world has not changed. They have served as the starting point for GSCs, providing raw materials, oil, minerals, and other commodities for others to process, refine, and make into final goods for sale.

On the other hand, GVCs do not appear to have received as much attention as GSCs. However, in our view, they are undoubtedly more consequential, more important, and more relevant, especially in the context of this discussion. GVCs deal with the same entities, businesses, and countries as GSCs but, quite significantly, focus on the 'value' that each participant derives from the network. Shih's (1996) work is widely cited in this context. First, his GVC graph is not a horizontal straight line but is U-shaped, and hence is dubbed the 'smiling curve'. This demonstrates that the level of economic value or benefit achievable by any entity or country in any trade transaction depends on its position in the GVC. The higher up the chain or curve, the higher the benefit it derives. Entities at the bottom of the U, such as countries that simply extract and sell their resources or minerals in raw form without the capability to subject them to any form of processing, refining, or manufacturing derive the least value from the chain in terms of international trade. As long as a country remains at the bottom of the GVC, continuing simply to extract raw materials without adding any further value, the odds of it moving up the value chain are slim. Unless it somehow manages to move up the ladder by doing much more than just extracting minerals for others abroad to process and market, it is unlikely to benefit much from the GSC. As a result, its financial and economic position is unlikely to improve.

Amongst many countries that might be cited as practical illustrations of the significance of differing yet disadvantageous positions in GSCs and GVCs, a few illuminate our point. For example, it has long been suggested that the Democratic Republic of Congo (DRC) is cursed by its natural wealth (BBC News, 2013). It is a large country with a wide range and abundance of minerals and other natural resources. However, these have constantly been exploited by corporations and multinational companies from rich developed countries. The local population has received little or no benefit from this natural wealth, as evidenced by the absence or poor state of basic infrastructure (BBC News, 2013). Similarly, a report by the United Nations (2010) indicates that revenues from mining natural resources appear not to have contributed at all to local people's quality of life, with the serious consequence that their life expectancy is no more than 43 years (Info. Note 5). A report by Greenpeace and the Runnymede Trust (Kapoor et al., 2022) also catalogs examples of exploitative practices in 'the Global South' by multinational corporations from 'the Global North'.

The harsh practical implication of this for many developing countries is clear: a country and its people cannot climb out of poverty nor hope to achieve economic and social development purely by extracting minerals or supplying raw materials. If that were possible, then many countries like the DRC, Tanzania, Zambia, Myanmar, and Brazil, to name but a few, with their abundant natural riches, would top the wealth indices. However, in reality, they are at the very beginning of many supply chains and at the bottom of GVCs, supplying all manner of raw minerals for other countries to convert into everyday items such as mobile phones, computers, motor vehicles, motor vehicle parts, planes, satellites, and even, shockingly, nuclear bombs. These are just a few examples of many developing countries that have found themselves in such economically powerless positions.

From an economic and environmental sustainability perspective, this is an extremely dangerous situation. These countries are at the bottom of the economic scale despite their endowments of minerals and other natural resources. Their populations are already struggling from a lack of employment opportunities, poor housing, education, and health services, and meager life chances, as several economic indices show (United Nations, 2022a). At the current rate, all these minerals and other natural endowments will soon be depleted. What will happen then? This is a frightening scenario that is playing out across much of the developing world. Furthermore, many developing countries in Africa, Asia, and parts of South America have very rich natural and mineral resources, yet despite huge amounts of foreign direct investment (FDI) by multinational companies, for generations they have struggled to provide basic socioeconomic essentials for their populations.

Previous studies in various disciplines have adopted a corporate social reporting (CSR) lens to examine the plight of several African countries, particularly with regard to mining, including Tanzania (Lauwo et al., 2020), Nigeria (Hennchen, 2015), Ghana (Arko, 2013; Ayee et al., 2016), and Zambia (Okafor, 1990; Phiri et al., 2019). These countries are rich in natural resources and minerals, and thus occupy prominent positions in various GSCs but have faced similar fates to the DRC. For example, Tanzania's valuable gemstones, such as tanzanite, are being mined by Western countries and Western companies and then exported in virtually raw form to the West, leaving little monetary gain or value to the country and its local communities. The gemstones' real value is then extracted by the West further along the chain for large monetary gains. Similarly, Nigeria has one of the largest reserves of crude oil deposits in the world and is Africa's largest exporter of crude oil (Cotterill, 2022), with Shell and BP actively undertaking exploration and extraction activities since 1936 (Shell, 2022). However, because the country has very limited oil refinery facilities, Shell has to export a huge proportion of this oil in crude form and thus controls the petroleum supply chain and extracts value further down the chain. Given its large population, Nigeria is also a large importer of refined oil and petroleum products (Oyedeji, 2022), from the Netherlands (43.2%), Belgium (21.3%), Norway (5.6%), France (1.4%), the United States (2%), and India (3.2%). In other words, astoundingly, almost 74% of Nigeria's refined oil is imported from Western developed nations, with 72% coming from European countries.

The operations of GSCs and GVCs present genuine problems for both developed and developing countries in relation to limiting damage to our global environment. For developing countries, faced with poverty, unemployment, poor housing, health systems, educational facilities and opportunities, and transport infrastructure, environmental sustainability concerns must simply rank as one of many difficult challenges. Indeed, some may not even see the debate about environmental sustainability as particularly relevant, nor as more urgent than the other social, economic, and other problems they face. Some probably even consider environmental and net-zero emissions concerns as problems that rich countries created and must therefore solve. According to Macfarlane (2021, p. 4), 'While all countries must take swift action to reduce emissions, it is countries in the Global North that have played a disproportionate role in driving climate breakdown, and are still enjoying the privileges of this position to this day.' He also notes that 'the richest 10% of the world's population were responsible for 52% of the cumulative carbon emissions between 1990 and 2015' (Macfarlane, 2021, p. 5, citing a 2020 Oxfam report). This is the context in which some countries in the developing world may appear to regard their more urgent priority as being to achieve economic prosperity and its associated benefits as quickly as possible, rather than to reduce their carbon emissions.

We argue that this misalignment, resulting from cumulative disadvantage over generations at the aggregate level, sets one country against another, and developing against developed countries. For many developing countries, this is a vicious circle from which it is very difficult to negotiate a way out. Even worse, it is a key breeding ground for other social, economic, financial, and other problems in these countries.

In summary, the examples above illuminate some fundamental structural issues at the heart of this debate as far as developing countries are concerned. As previously intimated, the really concerning aspect of this is that many developing countries are struggling with insufficient finance to provide viable transport infrastructure, schools, hospitals, manufacturing and processing capabilities, and employment and housing for their increasing populations, even while they still have some of their natural resources. Many of their natural resources are wasting assets and are being depleted by GSCs and, specifically, large multinationals, for very little return. What nightmarish scenario awaits the day, month, and generation when the natural resources have been exhausted entirely? Furthermore, these extractive activities by multinational companies leave behind their own issues, such as pollution, soil and landscape damage, and invariably environmental degradation. How will these countries ever be in a position to gain access to finance, let alone green finance, to help them remedy all this?

Thus far in net-zero carbon emissions debates, and in largely enthusiastic discussions about green finance joining the fight for a net-zero carbon 'jackpot', we have not come across any serious discussion of the issues described above, despite their undoubted and compelling urgency and relevance to many developing countries. Given the present and historical circumstances, green finance may not even be viable for developing countries, as many financial institutions have historically been more willing to invest in 'traditional', tried and tested fossil-fuel projects than in projects utilizing newer and less certain technologies. According to Sachs et al. (2019, p. 0), this is 'mainly because there are still several risks associated with these new technologies and they offer a lower rate of return'.

This is a major challenge for both financial institutions and developing countries, although for different reasons. For financial institutions, the challenge is to create financial instruments that are attractive to the investing public and that, in turn, can be used to achieve climate sustainability goals. For developing countries, this may be something that they actually dread, another weapon to beat them up with or exploit them. They may be right to worry, and to wonder how these new products differ from FDI, particularly when, as indicated, they are rarely afforded opportunities to participate effectively in discussing the problems and possible solutions.

Another relevant issue concerns the question of whether green finance is effectively FDI in a different guise. For generations, developing countries have been encouraged, implored, and persuaded into making themselves attractive destinations for FDI. A full discussion of the promise of FDI and the reality of receiving it deserves a separate platform, although anecdotally the results have rarely lived up to the promises. If this were not so, many developing countries would arguably be on very different and positive economic development trajectories by now.

Countries like China, India, Malaysia, and others have accomplished considerable economic development in recent years, arguably enabling themselves to move from the bottom of GVCs to higher levels by investing in and improving their refinery, processing, and manufacturing capabilities and capacities. We doubt very much that their economic success has been a result of FDI. Rather, we suspect that, by and large, this success has been achieved by somehow marshaling their own internally generated finance and resources. Indeed, Jafri (2019) offers some evidence from Pakistan that other approaches such as 'impact investing' and 'shadow banking' may be viable alternatives to FDI. This, in turn, raises another question of whether FDI is perhaps less effective than internally generated financial capacity. Indeed, it is quite legitimate to ask whether any developing country has achieved economic development as a result of an FDI, and if not, whether green finance-related FDI will be any different. This is particularly pertinent since the same or similar multinationals that have presided over the exploitation of these countries' resources for generations are now in control of green finance. These questions remain moot but are very relevant. In the next section, we examine aspects of green finance in more detail and explore whether this may indeed be a game changer for developing countries.

Green Finance: Is It a Game Changer?

Green finance has generally received a positive press, especially in the West, as a new tool in the fight against climate change. In the final analysis, financial institutions will be responsible for devising and providing green financial products and tools that are seen, or at least expected, to provide the global drive for a zero-carbon future. We do not wish to be too critical of an initiative that has not yet had a chance to show its real potential in a practical arena. Some personalities associated with or recruited to champion this initiative have some of the highest credentials and profiles in the business and finance worlds. We are reasonably confident that the green finance initiative will make a positive difference to the net-zero-carbon drive, especially with regard to Western countries as a group. However, we are less certain that green finance will make a similar difference to developing countries, for a number of reasons that we outline below.

The ability of private-sector multinational organizations to deliver results for developing countries is a major concern. At the heart of the green finance initiative is trust (or the notion) that such organizations will spearhead the drive towards net-zero carbon emissions by embracing and adhering to the highest ideals, as outlined in the green finance initiative. They may indeed do so with respect to their operations in developed countries, but we have doubts and concerns in relation to developing countries. This is essentially because we have been here before and the results have not been good, as stated earlier in the case of the DRC. Some of the Western world's largest and most profitable companies have been operating in the DRC and other developing countries for several generations. In most cases, these companies report having brought huge amounts of FDI into the country. Based on all we have seen in the DRC, such FDI, to the extent that it has actually been brought in, appears to have been quite transitory, in the sense that it seems to have resulted in no significant, meaningful, or lasting improvements to countries' economic, health, social, or technological fabric. Rather, it seems that far too often the purported FDI inflow is, in reality, an 'extract and run' operation, whereby supposed FDI inflow is used strategically to source particular materials or minerals at a relatively low price, and these are quickly exported in raw form to the investors' home countries, where their true value is realized. This pattern appears to have been repeated throughout the developing world.

At the heart of the new green finance initiative are, once again, multinational companies. They must comply with and adhere to mandatory auditing and financial reporting standards in relation to their financial performance. In the absence of firm international agreements on many aspects of green finance, companies are likely to face serious challenges in attempting to report adherence to and compliance with environmental sustainability practices alongside their annual audited financial reports. As a result, we identify a number of possible challenges or weaknesses.

The first is professional expertise and experience. It is difficult enough for companies to report on their financial performance, and annual audits are usually carried out by seasoned auditors trained over many years in the field of financial reporting for complex audits. Despite this breadth of experience and expertise in producing audit reports, many have been found to be materially wrong, and several top firms of accountants have faced censure and/or fines as a result (Hattersley, 2022). Effectively auditing multinational companies' reports on their compliance with environmental sustainability standards or requirements is likely to pose even more daunting problems and omissions. Moreover, unlike annual financial reports, we doubt that the same level and depth of experience are available in auditing environment-related aspects of multinational firms as those relating to purely financial operations. If this is so, this is likely to be a source of weakness.

The second potential weakness is the comprehensiveness of reports. In order to be meaningful, any audit report on a company's compliance must cover its operations not only in developed countries but across the supply and value chains. This will require qualified personnel in both developed and developing countries. The third challenge relates to self-certification. There are some suggestions that for the purpose of environmental sustainability reports, multinational companies will be allowed to self-certify their compliance, which may render the reports significantly less than objective. The fourth concern is the lack of local involvement in the reports. So far, we have seen no proposal for any local officials, employees, or government officials to have any input or say in the preparation or content of any multinational's annual environmental sustainability report. Finally, consistent with our previous arguments, we contend that no audit report should be limited to environmental sustainability criteria, but should include other information such as long-term investments and contributions made in the countries in which the company operates, and possibly a declaration of the approximate ultimate monetary values of items sourced from each country, as well as the amount of taxes paid to local governments, among other things.

On the latter point, countries in Africa, and indeed elsewhere in the developing world, have sought or been 'advised' that economic transformation will come through their ability to attract FDI. FDI has come and gone, making no visible difference to many, if not all, of these countries' economic prospects. Indeed, we have struggled to identify a single African country that has achieved economic success by attracting FDI. This, like the climate change issue, should be a matter of concern to both developing and developed countries, and should accordingly be placed on the agenda alongside strategies for cutting CO_2 emissions. A number of avenues offer possibilities for developing countries' further participation. We outline a few that we consider might be helpful in furthering positive outcomes for these countries.

The first is the consideration of zero-emissions targets versus economic/social development targets. This is challenging for both developing and developed countries. While developed countries seem to be focusing on trying to cut their CO_2 emissions to zero, developing countries are unlikely to see this as a priority. Once again, for many, their primary concern is the state of their economies, and their poor health, education, and physical infrastructure. Indeed, many even seem to view the climate debate as a problem created, and therefore to be tackled, by developed countries.

The second avenue is to push for inclusive forums. While perhaps rarely publicly admitted, there is a gap between leaders in the North and South. The President of Ghana recently argued that the structure of global economic organizations has historically 'proved inadequate for developing countries' (United Nations, 2021, September 22). This, he explained, is essentially because countries from the developing world, especially those in Africa, parts of South America and Asia, and the Caribbean have been unrepresented in policy and financial institutions, including the World Bank, the International Monetary Fund, and the World Health Organization. Furthermore, he urged institutions such as these to be more inclusive, with 'diverse leaders at the decision-making table'. This is an important issue that we believe would foster a better understanding of each others' positions and priorities, and in turn produce results that have resonance in both developed and developing countries.

Related to this point, the third avenue is the important result of participation for developing countries. Participation in common forums to tackle problems that confront each side is important in itself, as well as for fostering and nurturing a sense of respect and understanding between the parties. It will also nurture cultural awareness of societies other than one's own (Shah, 2022). This will help to bring leaders of developing countries to decision-making tables where their voices and concerns are heard. We are also mindful that such changes will take time, but in the first instance, the key is visibility and representation.

Finally, although green finance may indeed be the answer to the problem, there is a possibility that it may not be the whole or even partial answer. Our concern with the current debate is that answers, or at least some answers, seem to be advanced before the problems and pressures faced by developing countries have been thoroughly understood, including rising population levels, lack of employment opportunities, and poor housing, health facilities, and educational institutions. Indeed, for many developing countries, while environmental sustainability is a real problem that is likely to affect them, it is only one of many challenges they face. As a result, they may well have very different priorities. Therefore, meaningful dialogue is needed between all parties involved. Many developing countries derive most of their income from the exploitation of minerals, oil, and gas, which are finite resources. These countries' priorities may therefore be to ensure that before these resources run out, they get a fair share of the proceeds of their extraction and exploitation.

Concluding Remarks

In summary, we believe that the green finance initiative is well conceived but that, for the reasons outlined above, on its own and in its present form it is wildly inadequate for the task. Overall, we believe that if the world is serious about our planet's fate, the focus should not be solely on what is happening to our climate as a result of our carbon emissions. We should be equally concerned about the tortuous lives that fellow citizens in the South of our planet are and have been experiencing for generations. We should be committed to improving their lives, not through charity but through fair, equitable, and sensible adjustments to international terms of trade. Doing so would make lives better all round, not in 20 or 30 years, but right now.

As we end this discussion, it is useful to reflect on the practical implications of GSC/GVC misalignment, and on whether or not green finance is the solution. First, if developing countries obtained fair prices for the minerals and commodities that they export raw to developed countries, poverty levels in many of these countries would be drastically reduced, and they would have no need for so-called 'aid'. Second, green finance, as far as we can see, simply seeks to replace conventional FDI or serve as an environmentally sanitized version of FDI. If FDI into developing countries were effective in helping them to transform their economies, given their abundant natural and mineral resources, these countries would not be in the dire situations in which they now find themselves and in which they have languished for generations. They would be centers of economic success and prosperity. Third, the fact that neither of the two previous points is or has been happening means that, in a very real sense and contrary to popular belief, currently and for generations past, 'aid' has been going from developing to developed countries through the application of GSCs and GVCs on a massive scale. Accordingly, we argue that simply substituting conventional FDI with green finance as an instrument to promote economic prosperity around the world, as well as to protect the environment, would be wrong. Rather, we recommend that opportunities are taken to engage in serious and meaningful dialogue on the situation and options going forward. One option might be impact investing and shadow banking, a quite different approach from FDI, which appears to have produced positive results in Pakistan (Jafri, 2019). This should be carried out in genuinely inclusive forums involving both rich and poor countries. Our hope is that the outcome would be a new and fairer international trade landscape, in which a richer and more meaningful green finance initiative would play a key part. The very future of our planet will depend on its success.

It seems appropriate to conclude with the following statement by Laurie Macfarlane (2021) ahead of COP26 in Glasgow (our emphasis added):

Tackling climate breakdown and delivering economic justice must go hand in hand ... The climate crisis is not a distinct crisis – it is irrevocably linked to our unjust economic system that is killing the planet. Unless world leaders confront this head-on at COP26, a vital opportunity to put the planet on a sustainable path will be squandered. **It will be those voices that are least represented in Glasgow that will suffer the most**.

References

Arko, B. (2013). Corporate social responsibility in the large scale mining industry in Ghana. *Journal of Business and Retail Management Research*, 8(1), 81–90. https://jbrmr.com/cdn/article_file/i-17_c-157.pdf

Ayee, J., Soreide, T., Shukla, G. P., & Le, T. M. (2016). *Political economy of the mining sector in Ghana*. World Bank Policy Research Working Paper No. 5730. https://papers.ssrn.com/sol3/papers.cfm?abstract_id=1892670

BBC News. (2022, September 17). China, Europe, US drought: Is 2022 the driest year recorded? *BBC News*. https://www.bbc.co.uk/news/62751110

BBC News. (2013, October 9). DR Congo: Cursed by its natural wealth. *BBC News*. https://www.bbc.co.uk/news/magazine-24396390

Cai, R., & Guo, J. (2021). Finance for the environment: A scientometrics analysis of green finance. *Mathematics*, 9(13), Article 1537. https://doi.org/10.3390/math9131537

Carney, M. (2021). *[Interview]: Investing in net-zero climate solutions creates value and rewards*. United Nations Climate Action. https://www.un.org/en/climatechange/mark-carney-investing-net-zero-climate-solutions-creates-value-and-rewards

City of London Corporation. (2016). *Globalizing green finance: The UK as an international hub*. City of London Corporation. https://www.cbd.int/financial/gcf/uk-hubgreenfinance.pdf

Concern Worldwide. (2021, November 15). *'We are drowning in promises': A look back at COP26*. Concern Worldwide. https://www.concern.org.uk/news/we-are-drowning-promises-look-back-cop26

Cotterill, J. (2022, June 6). Fuel shortages across Africa hit motorists, airlines and radio stations. *Financial Times*. https://www.ft.com/content/5f5e1550-f750-4ca6-8c10-873e3372d73e

Feller, A., Shunk, D., & Callarman, T. (2006). *Value chains versus supply chains*. BP Trends. https://www.bptrends.com/publicationfiles/03-06-ART-ValueChains-SupplyChains-Feller.pdf

Grimshaw, J. (2020, May 17). *What is supply chain? A definitive guide*. SupplyChainDigital. https://supply-chaindigital.com/digital-supply-chain/what-supply-chain-definitive-guide

Hattersley, R. (2022, July 28). *Big firm audit failures rack up £46.5m in fines*. Accounting Web. https://www.accountingweb.co.uk/business/financial-reporting/big-firm-audit-failures-rack-up-ps465m-in-fines

Hennchen, E. (2015). Royal Dutch Shell in Nigeria: Where do responsibilities end? *Journal of Business Ethics*, 129(1), 1–25. https://doi.org/10.1007/s10551-014-2142-7

Jafri, J. (2019). When billions meet trillions: Impact investing and shadow banking in Pakistan. *Review of International Political Economy*, 26(3), 520–544. https://doi.org/10.1080/09692290.2019.1608842

Jordan, L., Ross, A., Howard, E., Heal, A., Wasley, A., Thomas, P., & Milliken, A. (2020, November 25). *Cargill, the company feeding the world by helping to destroy the planet*. Unearthed. https://unearthed.greenpeace.org/2020/11/25/cargill-deforestation-agriculture-history-pollution/

Kapoor, A., Youssef, N., & Hood, S. (2022). *Confronting injustice: Racism and the environmental emergency*. Greenpeace & The Runnymede Trust. https://www.greenpeace.org.uk/wp-content/uploads/2022/09/Confronting-Injustice-2022-web.pdf

Khan, M. A., Riaz, H., Ahmed, M., & Saeed, A. (2021). Does green finance really deliver what is expected? An empirical perspective. *Borsa Istanbul Review*, 22(3), 586–593. http://www.elsevier.com/journals/borsa-istanbul-review/2214-8450

Lauwo, S., Kyriacou, O., & Otusanya, O. J. (2020). When sorry is not an option: CSR reporting and 'face work' in a stigmatized industry: A case study of Barrick (Acacia) gold mine in Tanzania. *Critical Perspectives on Accounting*, 71, Article 102099. https://doi.org/10.1016/j.cpa.2019.102099

Lee, C.-C., & Lee, C.-C. (2022). How does green finance affect total factor productivity? Evidence from China. *Energy Economics*, 107, Article 105863. https://doi.org/10.1016/j.eneco.2022.105863

Macfarlane, L. (2021, October 29). *Tackling climate breakdown and delivering economic justice must go hand in hand*. Opendemocracy. https://www.opendemocracy.net/en/oureconomy/cop26-tackling-climate-breakdown-and-delivering-economic-justice-must-go-hand-in-hand/

Metcalf, T., & Morales, A. (2021, November 2). Carney unveils $130 trillion in climate finance commitments. *Bloomberg UK*. https://www.bloomberg.com/news/articles/2021-11-02/carney-s-climate-alliance-crests-130-trillion-as-pledges-soar

Okafor, F. O. E. (1990). The mining multinationals and the Zambian economy. *African Review, 17*(1), 66–79.

Oyedeji, O. (2022, March 2). *How Nigeria's high petrol importation, dead refineries affect its struggling economy*. Dataphyte. https://www.dataphyte.com/latest-reports/development/how-nigerias-high-petrol-importation-and-dead-refineries-affect-its-struggling-economy/

Phiri, O., Mantzari, E., & Gleadle, P. (2019). Stakeholder interactions and corporate social responsibility (CSR) practices: Evidence from the Zambian copper mining sector. *Accounting, Auditing and Accountability Journal, 32*(1), 26–54. https://doi.org/10.1108/AAAJ-04-2016-2540

Sachs, J. D., Woo, W. T., Yoshino, N., & Taghizadeh-Hesary, F. (2019). *Why is green finance important?* Asian Development Bank Institute Working Paper 917. https://www.adb.org/publications/why-green-finance-important

Shah, A. (2022). *Inclusive and sustainable finance: Leadership, ethics and culture*. Routledge.

Shell (2022). *The history of Shell in Nigeria*. https://www.shell.com.ng/about-us/shell-nigeria-history.html

Shih, S. (1996). *Me-Too is not my style: Challenge difficulties, break through bottlenecks, create values*. The Acer Foundation.

UK Government. (2019). *Transition to a green financial system and mobilizing investment in clean and resilient growth*. Updated 2 July. https://www.gov.uk/guidance/green-finance

UK Government. (n.d.). *Green finance taskforce: Terms of reference*. https://assets.publishing.service.gov.uk/government/uploads/system/uploads/attachment_data/file/675361/Green_Finance_Taskforce_-_terms_of_reference.pdf

United Nations. (2010). *Democratic Republic of the Congo, 1993–2003: Report of the mapping exercise documenting the most serious violations of human rights and international humanitarian law committed within the territory of the Democratic Republic of the Congo between March 1993 and June 2003*. UN Office of the High Commissioner for Human Rights. https://digitallibrary.un.org/record/709895

United Nations. (2021, June 27). *The trillion dollar climate finance challenge (and opportunity)*. UN News: Climate and Environment. https://news.un.org/en/story/2021/06/1094762

United Nations. (2021, September 22). *Developing countries need more financial aid, influence in multilateral institutions to overcome economic devastation from COVID-19, speakers tell General Assembly*. UN press release GA/12366. https://www.un.org/press/en/2021/ga12366.doc.htm

United Nations. (2022, November 7). *'Cooperate or Perish': At COP27 UN chief calls for Climate Solidarity Pact, urges tax on oil companies to finance loss and damage*. UN News. https://news.un.org/en/story/2022/11/1130247

United Nations. (2022a). *Financing for sustainable development report 2022*. United Nations Inter-Agency Task Force on Financing Development. https://developmentfinance.un.org/fsdr2022

United Nations. (2022b). *World population prospects 2022: Summary of results*. United Nations Department of Economic and Social Affairs. https://www.un.org/development/desa/pd/sites/www.un.org.development.desa.pd/files/wpp2022_summary_of_results.pdf

United Nations. (n.d.). *UNEP finance initiative brings together a large network of banks, insurers and investors that collectively catalyzes action across the financial system to deliver more sustainable global economies*. UN Environmental Program, Finance Initiative. https://www.unepfi.org/about/

World Economic Forum (2020, November 9). *What is green finance and why is it important?* World Economic Forum. https://www.weforum.org/agenda/2020/11/what-is-green-finance/

13
ACCOUNTING AS A MEDIATING PRACTICE BETWEEN VALUES AND CONTEXTS
A Research Agenda on Impact Investment

Luis Emilio Cuenca, Stephanie Rüegger, and Urs Jäger

Introduction

"Impact," in the impact investment arena, refers to the potential non-financial value (e.g., environmental, social, or ethical) that an impact investor looks for when assessing potential investees. Impact investment puts impact front and center, explicitly seeking to create non-financial value by deploying financial resources (Busch et al., 2021). On the capital supply side, its actors are as varied as venture philanthropists, impact-oriented private equity funds, and sustainable investment funds. On the demand side, they range from companies with sustainability strategies and financial intermediaries in developing countries to small-medium enterprises (SMEs) and international non-governmental organizations (INGOs). As with traditional investment, impact investment requires an assessment of the investment recipient, as well as accountability regarding both the financial value of the investment and its impact. Adopting the lens of the sociology of accounting (Annisette et al., 2017; Burchell et al., 1985; Chapman et al., 2009; Espeland & Sauder, 2007; Hines, 1988; Hopwood, 1983; Miller et al., 2008; Miller & O'Leary, 2007; Miller & Power, 2013), we can assume that both financial and non-financial value is socially constructed and represented by ideas and instruments that in turn construct realities representing these values (Hines, 1988). Moreover, by having agency in the process of constructing reality, accounting mediates between the different ideas, actors, and agendas that are actively engaged in different fields. For example, in impact investment, accounting mediates between different conceptions of value (e.g., financial, social, environmental, ethical). Furthermore, by creating networks of calculation, accounting mediates between investors in developed countries and investees in developing countries. In this sense, we consider impact investment to be a hybridized field that encompasses accounting, as financial expertise is enmeshed with other types of expertise traditionally positioned outside of accounting and operating in different contexts (Kurunmäki, 2004; Miller et al., 2008, p. 952; Miller & O'Leary, 2007).

While the primary objective of the social finance movement is to address global concerns by providing tools and finances to innovative entrepreneurs, the industry has evolved in several ways. In recent years it has grown in terms of market structures, the actors involved, and the investment vehicles used. This progress has been particularly present in impact investment, which receives exceptional attention in practice and is estimated to reach an overall market of roughly USD 502 billion (GIIN, 2019b). Emerging from ethical investment, where investors aggregate ethical next to financial criteria to their investment decisions (Louche et al., 2012), the term "impact investment" was coined in 2007 by leaders in finance, philanthropy, and development (Mendell & Nogales, 2011). They outlined the methods for establishing a global industry that seeks to assess organizations for potential investments that target a positive social, environmental, and/or ethical impact (Harji & Jackson, 2012; GIIN, 2013). Impact investment, like traditional investing, entails the provision of financial resources in exchange for a financial return. While the purpose of generating a financial return distinguishes impact investment from pure impact vehicles such as grant funding and charity, it is distinguished from traditional investment by its explicit focus on some degree of non-financial value added (Addis et al., 2013; Busch et al., 2021). As a result, impact investment blends social, environmental, and/or ethical goals with traditional financial decisions and establishes itself as a hybrid of financial and impact returns.

However, this marks just one side of the challenges impact investors face when assessing potential investees. The GIIN Annual Impact Investor Survey (2019a) reports that the large majority (78%) of impact investors who invest in developing countries are headquartered in developed ones. Consequently, the assessment methods that impact investors use often mirror those of experts in developed countries, and these methods are then used to analyze organizations in developing countries. This leaves impact investors with the challenge of translating assessments from developing countries to the culturally and structurally distinct contexts of the developed countries where most investment decision-makers are located, thus engaging in a hybrid field between the developed and developing world.

Despite the growing popularity of impact investment in practice, academics have yet to explore the fundamental operational features and methods that explain how impact investment works in what we call double-hybridity—a combination of financial and impact returns on the one hand, and developing and developed countries on the other. The literature on non-financial impact assessment highlights the former challenge; while financial performance assessment methods are an established convention, assessing and comparing impact creation across different, unrelated heterogeneous interventions still appears to be a difficult task (Austin et al., 2006; Dacin et al., 2010; Ryan & Lyne, 2008). Nevertheless, the literature addresses hybridity with respect to one side of the double-hybridity equation, that is, financial and impact returns. We propose that the sociology of accounting (Burchell et al., 1980; Chapman et al., 2009; Hopwood, 1983; Miller & Power, 2013) provides a helpful lens through which to theoretically unite both aspects of the double hybridity of impact investment. Using this lens, we aim to integrate the assessment methods used by impact investors with the challenge of applying these methods between developed and developing contexts. The sociology of accounting provides concepts through which we can understand how value is determined in hybrid settings—in our case, between developed and developing countries—by relying on diverse financial, social, environmental, and ethical assessment methods.

In this chapter, we explore the sociology of accounting as a possible theoretical foundation for impact investment's double hybridity and develop nine corresponding research questions. To do this, we construct a baseline scenario for how hybridity is taking place within the impact investment field. We begin by establishing the hybrid dimensions and fields of assessment methods. On one end of the continuum, we distinguish between financial and impact rationales; on the other, between developed and developing contexts. We argue that there is little knowledge on the challenge of assessing and reporting on finance and impact when impact investors located in developed countries assess organizations located in developing countries and must therefore make decisions based on data from sociocultural contexts that are extremely different from their own. To assess hybridity along these continuums, we turn to the mediating role of accounting to elaborate on how assessment tools like measurement instruments can mediate between the different elements, processes, and practices that combine when the hybridization of rationales and contexts occurs (Kurunmäki, 2004; Miller et al., 2008; Miller and O'Leary, 2007; Miller & Power, 2013). From this, we deduce a series of research questions that can guide further studies to explore the hybridity of assessing potential impact in developing countries.

Accounting as a Mediating Practice

In organizations and institutions, as well as with socioeconomic dynamics, accounting has been theorized as a mediating practice (Power & Miller, 2013). By assigning value to organizations, departments, processes, and persons, accounting can indeed play a mediating role. It provides investors with the data needed to judge an organization's performance, for example. Moreover, investors can use this numerical representation of reality to compare the organizations they might want to invest in. Accounting, as such, facilitates a comparison between a given organization's insights and an outside investor's pipeline. This refers to its ability to adjudicate value (Miller and Power, 2013) and, by doing so, to transform qualities like efficiency or competitiveness into numbers—a characteristic known as commensuration (Espeland and Sauder, 2007; Espeland and Stevens, 1998). By adjudicating value and opening the door to commensuration and comparability, accounting acts as a bridge between diverse actors, agendas, political ideas, scientific approaches, organization processes, institutions, and—in the context of impact investment—values and contexts, all of which renders it a mediating activity (Kurunmäki, 2004; Miller et al., 2008; Miller and O'Leary, 2007; Miller and Power, 2013). Indeed, accounting enables the consolidation of results from different economic entities and the communication of these results to the market, the public, and government agencies. It facilitates the comparison of disparate organizations that are the object of quantifiable data. It also makes it possible to coordinate the actions of distinct agents based on the common narratives of economic growth, market efficiency, technological progress, economic citizenship (Burchell et al., 1985; Mennicken, 2010; Miller, 1991; Miller and O'Leary, 2007), and social, environmental, and/or ethical impact.

Rather than viewing accounting objects and tools as merely functional, technical, and neutral apparatus, the sociology of accounting considers accounting to be a social practice that constructs reality by representing reality (Hines, 1988). Furthermore, by constructing a quantified representation of reality, accounting participates in the construction of individuals as calculative selves (Miller, 1994; Miller & Power, 2013), with a critical eye and the capacity to use different value systems to evaluate any situation in which they might find themselves (Annisette et al., 2017; Annisette and Richardson, 2011). It strengthens a dualistic view of assessment. On the one hand, it evaluates situations (e.g., potential investees) that influence contexts and their value systems. These value systems adapt to the fact that context plays an important role when assessing the value of a certain object or organization. The sociology of accounting thus indicates that, while values tend to emerge from social relations, norms, and principles, the context in which these values are regarded is important to understanding values like financial and impact return. On the other hand, the assessors themselves are cultivated in different contexts, such as developed and developing countries, which in turn form their respective value systems.

For instance, impact investment responds to a global policy agenda, bringing together actors as diverse as governments, international organizations, the private sector, and academia, each identifying with different ways of assessing the value of an investment. To move from ideas to practice, this international agenda is mediated by multiple forms of accounting. Indeed, accounting tools are key to understanding how impact investment is disseminated as both an idea and a financial flow, and how the different circuits that enable this dynamic relate to one another. A potential investee, for example, might have to submit accounting and other information regarding the impact of its business. This information is then fed into the investment portfolio manager's analysis model, which reflects the strategic vision of the investors at both the financial and impact level. When investments are allocated, they enter a portfolio whose existence requires accounting to both manage and report to investors on both financial and impact outcomes. Likewise, these investors are players in a capital market, which in part exists because of the accounting information on the different portfolios in which investor capital is distributed. Moreover, in the case of impact investment, the quantification of the impact presents major challenges in terms of both value attribution and comparability. Finally, impact investment development involves actors from different realities (e.g., developed and developing countries), whose objectives are not necessarily homogenous. The common narrative that unites them largely consists of investing with the aim of creating both financial and non-financial value. Implicit in this narrative, therefore, is the need to establish shared conventions about this value creation. As we see it, impact investment resides in a multi-layered ecosystem that operates in both developed and developing countries. Each of these levels is mediated by accounting and its adjudication capacity.

Mediating the Double Hybridity of Impact Investment

Accounting tools are important to understanding how the different circuits through which impact investment is disseminated as both an idea and a financial flow relate to one another. Accounting takes the mediating role in the two aspects of double hybridity.

Hybridity I—Developed and Developing Contexts

Developed countries are characterized by a high degree of institutionalization and access to quality information. This institutionalization inherits market norms such as tax laws and inflation control mechanisms, which allow participants in financial activities to buy and sell a wide range of financial assets freely and with reasonable regularity and price transparency. Additionally, institutionalization assures a certain standard of public services, supplemented by the third sector. Indeed, in industrialized democratic countries, the relationship between the state and the third sector has been largely collaborative, with the state encouraging civic participation through monetary support and regulatory guidance. Hence, impact investors in developed countries act within a context that enables fluid access to established capital markets through trading investments in secondary markets and are supported through sufficient regulatory measures when seeking to invest in impact. This favorable context is further augmented by reliable and easily-accessible information, such as the level of a given country's IFRS adoption (Horton et al., 2013), the availability of independent credit ratings, and statistical societal measurements.

Developing countries, on the other hand, inherit particular investment risks, mainly with respect to institutional voids, underdeveloped capital markets (Mair et al., 2007), and a lack of reliable and accessible financial information. Institutional voids can be defined as "the absence or underdevelopment of specialized intermediaries such as database vendors, and quality certification firms, regulatory corporations, and control-enforcing mechanisms" (Khanna & Palepu, 2010). Hence, although locations with institutional voids have a greater number of opportunities for social enterprises (Mair et al., 2007), the lack of support systems and property rights makes creating social enterprises in such contexts more challenging. This is a significant issue in impact investment; while a potential investee might look promising on paper, it could be financially risky in practice. Moreover, reliable sources of information are often lacking in developing countries, further undermining the accuracy of estimates. Adding to this complexity, relationships between the state and the third sector are often highly confrontational in developing countries. While this can indeed vary substantially from one country to another, many developing countries tend to tighten restrictions on foreign funding and seek to constrain any domestic operations perceived as threats; hence, developing countries often lack a generic support system, and third-sector organizations must push the state for the necessary backing. Investing in developing countries therefore entails engaging and adapting under conditions of resource scarcity, risk, and uncertainty.

Hybridity II—Financial and Impact Assessment

Assessment methods can rely on financial criteria, impact criteria, or an integration of the two into a hybrid form. Using purely financial accounting criteria is a well-established convention in value-based management systems, entailing the application of specific assessment tools and key frameworks. There are many methodologies through which to assess the financial value and potential of a given organization. Most of these assessment methods use accounting information. Examples can be as simple as sales growth, or as complex as EBITDA, economic value added (EVA), and discounted cash flow (DCF) techniques. Each of these methodologies meets the accepted conventions of economic actors.[1] The resulting measurements are usually regulated on a country-by-country basis, and key indicators are shared among organizations within the same industry. Traditional investors then build on these measurements and invest according to economic risk-return relationships to maximize the economic value of their investments.

Generic impact criteria, on the other hand, have yet to be established. No agreement for a dominant set of frameworks for quantifying the value of an organization's social, environmental, and/or ethical impact has been articulated (Lingane & Olsen, 2004), and impact assessment is substantially less focused on precision—particularly in terms of mathematically reducing all impact variables to common denominators (Lockie, 2001). Hence, many of the guidelines and associated streams of literature have a rather predictive (e.g., Finsterbusch, 1985) and descriptive nature and, thus, are of limited use for measuring and comparing. Nevertheless, measuring and comparing social value creation is an ongoing topic in society, policy, and business. In the academic world, there is a vast body of social impact assessment literature (e.g., Esteves et al., 2012) that targets social impact assessment "as an umbrella or overarching framework that embodies the evaluation of all impacts on humans and on all the ways in which people and communities interact with their sociocultural, economic and biophysical surroundings" (Vanclay, 2003, p. 5). The importance of this topic is particularly significant for organizations and projects that aim to alleviate social, environmental, and/or ethical problems as SMEs, NGOs, and social enterprises do. These organizations frequently rely on monetary and intangible assistance from other parties, such as foundations and government institutions, which are placing increasingly high demands on openness and accountability (Campbell, 2002; Grimes, 2010; Miller & Wesley, 2010). Hence, traditional NGOs and social enterprises mainly build on non-financial value and use a variety of measurement tools to report on their impact.

Double Hybridity—Between Hybridity I and Hybridity II

When taken together, these two aspects result in a double hybridity. To address this dynamic, accounting mediates between multiple value attributions that require the different actors involved to avoid becoming "lost in translation." More precisely, viewing accounting as a mediating practice allows us to understand how assessment tools such as instruments of measure can mediate between the opposing moral values that occur in the hybridization of rationales (financial and impact) and contexts (developed and developing countries) (Annisette et al., 2017). Based on the theoretical lens of accounting as a mediating practice, we therefore outline criteria for exploring the hybrid assessment models used by impact investors in hybridized contexts. On one axis of this double hybridity, assessment methods can only rely on financial criteria, impact criteria, or an integration of the two in a hybrid form. On the other, while some investors from developed countries only invest in specific other developed countries (as can occur between developing-developing countries) and thus operate within country-specific standards, most impact investment flows between regions (see Table 13.1).

Research Questions to Explore Hybridity I

As stated above, a large share of impact investment flows between regions. This is because impact investors are mainly based in developed countries (GIIN, 2019a) and aim to support initiatives in developing countries. They focus on solving society's greatest challenges by directing capital toward scalable solutions in sectors such as financial services, agriculture, energy, education, and information and communication technologies. Hence, there is a need to mediate between developed and developing country standards when applying financial or impact assessment methods. In this section, we explore relevant literature on the fields introduced in Table 13.1 and develop corresponding research questions.

Financial Assessment between Developed and Developing Countries

In developed countries, quantified financial information is readily available for financial actors and creates networks of calculation that are constitutive of financial assessment. In the mortgage industry, for example, credit bureaus produce credit scores (Poon, 2009), which lenders use to assess borrowers and commercial banks rely on to determine their risk provisions. These figures are then used by credit rating agencies to assess the rate of risk for commercial banks. In developing countries, however, while the financial assessment methods are roughly the same, such networks of calculation are nearly inexistent. The gap between IFRS adoption and accounting standards interpretation results in a scarcity of financial information about all potential investees, regardless of which actor in the ecosystem requires it. Thus, there is a necessity for contextualized interpretation of local financial information.

As such, investing in developed countries is significantly different from investing in developing ones. Poorly functioning or underdeveloped institutions reduce information flows to foreign investors, increasing uncertainty and discouraging investment. Institutional voids imply a lack of calculative networks such as those described for developed countries. Company credit scores and industry risk information is unavailable and financial information on small-medium sized enterprises is unreliable. The existing literature acknowledges that institutional voids correspond with a scarcity of market intermediaries that analyze and produce information critical to the decision calculus of foreign investors (Khanna & Palepu, 1997). Given that most impact investors are headquartered in developed countries and that impact investment is more common in developing countries (Höchstädter & Scheck, 2015), impact investors must frequently translate between developed and developing assessment contexts. This raises the question: *(1) How does the institutional difference between developed and developing countries influence the financial assessment methods used by impact investors?*

Table 13.1 Exploring the hybrid assessment models used by impact investors

		Assessment context (Hybridity II)		
		Developed country standards	*Developing country standards*	*Mediating between developed and developing country standards*
Assessment methods (Hybridity I)	Financial			• Social convention • Unified toolbox of assessment methods • No social convention • Heterogeneous assessment methods
	Impact			
	Mediating between financial and impact rationales	• Institutionalized • Sufficient reliable information • Calculative networks	• Institutional voids • Scarce reliable information • Rare construction of calculative networks	Double Hybridity: • Mediating between institutionalization and institutional voids • Mediating between reliable information and a lack thereof • Mediating between social convention and non-convention • Mediating between unified and heterogeneous methods

Table 13.2 Guiding questions for future research

		Assessment context (Hybridity II)		
		Developed country standards	*Developing country standards*	*Mediating between developed and developing country standards*
Assessment methods (Hybridity I)	Financial values			(1) *How does the institutional difference between developed and developing countries influence the financial assessment methods used by impact investors?* (2) *How do the financial standards designed in developed countries influence impact investors perceived reality when assessing potential investees in developing countries?*
	Impact values			(3) *How do the specific contextual differences between developed and developing countries influence the impact assessment methods used by impact investors?* (4) *How do the impact assessment standards used in developed countries influence impact investors' perceived reality when assessing potential investees in developing countries?*
	Mediating between impact and financial values	(5) *How do the specific conventions of developed countries influence the emerging standards that mediate between the financial and impact-related assessment methods used by impact investors?* (6) *How do highly established financial standards and heterogeneous impact assessment methods influence the perception of impact investors located in developed countries when assessing potential investees in developed countries?*	(7) *How do the specific challenges of developing countries influence the emerging standards that mediate between the social and financial assessment methods?* (8) *How do highly established financial standards and heterogeneous impact assessment methods influence the perception of impact investors located in developing countries when assessing potential investees in developing countries?*	(9) *How does the general contextual difference between developed and developing countries influence the standards that mediate between the social and financial assessment methods?* (10) *How does the double hybridity of financial and impact assessment standards influence the perception of impact investors in developed countries when assessing potential investees in developing countries?*

Indeed, assessment methodologies that originate in developed countries are based on the requirement of a positive risk-return ratio. The higher the risk, the higher the return. This idea is reinforced by accounting, as the notion of risk has penetrated the formulation of new accounting standards (Gaynor et al., 2011; Mikes, 2011). Consequently, all liabilities, assets, and income statements of the organizations in which impact investors invest are risk-weighted. This implies a phenomenon of translating local risks into financial figures. To assess these risks, however, investors generally look to the quantified information available to them. Because this information generally comes from risk rating agencies or international bodies that rate corruption risks, environmental risks, etc., quantified representations of macro realities in developing countries permeate the accounting representation and are likely to have an impact on how impact investors perceive these realities. This raises the question: *(2) How do the financial standards designed in developed countries influence impact investors' perceived reality when assessing potential investees in developing countries?*

Impact Assessment between Developed and Developing Countries

In developed countries, impact measurement is mainly concerned with public policy implications and potential (G8, 2014; Nicholls & Tomkinson, 2013) and the measurement and effectiveness of social, environmental, and ethical outcomes (Social Finance, 2009; Saltuk et al., 2013). It is primarily driven by impact investors who hold social organizations accountable for achieving social impact (Ebrahim & Rangan, 2014). These organizations, which include private nonprofits as well as associations, foundations, and other cooperatives, are referred to as the third sector (Corry, 2010). Developed countries are often reticent to establish the necessary policies to protect the investors from the third sector by "balance[ing] between enough regulation to protect legitimate social interests in preventing diversion of charitable assets to private pockets and enough regulation to squelch the qualities our society has most valued in the charitable sector" (Chisolm, 1995, p. 149). Hence, impact investments are strongly regulated, establishing a certain degree of market security. Furthermore, although impact assessment is executed in heterogeneous ways, credible, comparable impact data is established through streamlined measures such as the IRIS+. This is not the case, however, in developing countries, where there is substantial distrust toward official statistics. The measurement of impact creation in these contexts is thus unstandardized and difficult to authenticate (Ormiston & Seymour, 2011).

Acting, as impact investors do, between developed and developing countries makes measuring non-financial outcomes a resource-heavy task, as addressed by the critical debate on whether impact investment research should focus on measuring output or outcomes (Weber, 2016). Executing and reporting on impact assessment is a time-consuming and expensive process. This is especially true when impact investors from developed countries set out to assess the impact of their investments in developing countries, which involves visiting and collecting data from the investees and beneficiaries and analyzing this data with the baseline. It is this comparison to the baseline that the lack of reliable and accessible data in developing countries can render burdensome. This occurs, for example, when impact investors analyze how to quantitatively relate the social, environmental, and ethical outcomes of their investments with the initial impact plan provided by the investee, then explore how to measure and validate the outcomes with the authentication measures (Evans, 2013; Jackson, 2013b). This situation increases the complexity of implementing impact assessment methods based on social statistics, which requires control groups, reliable public statistics, and other factors that tend to be unavailable in these contexts. Because data related to non-financial impact can only be understood when compared with official statistics from the countries in which the recipient organizations operate, outcome measurement in developing countries is a significant hurdle. This raises the question: *(3) How do the specific contextual differences between developed and developing countries influence the impact assessment methods used by impact investors?*

Furthermore, the measurements used to assess impact have not yet been accepted as established conventions. Hence, their role in accountability mechanisms remains controversial. Indeed, accountability researchers have observed that the importance impact investors often place on accountability with respect to impact can leave social organizations with the unreasonable and burdensome demand to produce impact evaluations and reports without access to additional resources, leading them to divert precious time, money, and energy away from serving beneficiaries (Jackson, 2013a; Phillips & Johnson, 2021). This scenario takes on a different hue, however, when the assessment provider understands the context of the assessed and the realities they face in developing countries. Unlike remote impact assessment, which seeks quantified reports that quickly summarize impact, impact assessment by actors who are geographically proximate to the investment site has far greater success in understanding the local context. Thus, the inclusion of non-quantified accounts, which seek to transform life stories, community experiences, and other qualitative data, become important means of understanding impact. This raises the question: *(4) How do the impact assessment standards used in developed countries influence impact investors' perceived reality when assessing potential investees in developing countries?*

Research Questions to Explore Hybridity II

When selecting their investees, traditional venture capital firms are driven by profit expectations (Maxwell et al., 2011). The success of impact investment, in contrast, is intricately tied to the success of the investee in terms of impact (Huybrechts & Nicholls, 2013; Busch et al., 2021), leading to a need for hybrid assessment. Nevertheless, how the purpose of impact influences market perception remains unresolved, indicating the need for additional research that explores mediation between financial and impact rationales.

The Influence of Developing Country Standards on Financial and Impact Rationales

Research on the competition between the social and profit logics shows that the profit logic often prevails (King & Gish, 2015). Similarly, in developed countries, where economic assessment methods are highly established, some researchers have highlighted the need to explore investors' use of traditional financial accounting methods and their adoption of these in the impact investment arena. The capital asset pricing model (CAPM) and discounted cash flows in their various forms, for instance, still serve as a basis for many finance-related instruments and act as the guiding principle for investment-related decisions. Social return on investment (SROI) is one such example, in which the idea of discounted cash is modified and adapted to measure the social value created per unit of investment. The hybridity of assessment methods is also reflected by the willingness of many actors to incorporate impact-related information within accounting norms. An example of this occurred in November 2021, when the IFRS Foundation Trustees created the International Sustainability Standards Board (ISSB)[2] to actively construct such established conventions. Nevertheless, if a financial character is to be assigned to the creation of impact-related value, investors must be able to compare, commensurate, and assign value in order to incorporate non-financial impact into accounting norms as an adjudication practice. In other words, the aim is to generate comparable figures that can facilitate investors' decision-making processes based on the assumption that this will lead to improved market liquidity. This requires a major effort to establish applicable and auditable standards, as the ISSB has already begun to do. Progress in this standardization process is a long-term endeavor that requires the commitment of multiple parties. This raises the question: *(5) How do the specific conventions of developed countries influence the emerging standards that mediate between the financial and impact-related assessment methods used by impact investors?*

Recent work on the decision-making methods of impact investors (Serrano-Cinca & Gutierrez-Nieto 2013) provides some frameworks for understanding how both non-financial and commercial goals affect their prioritization and decision-making processes. However, understanding these processes in terms of both financial and impact-related goals at different stages of due diligence is still at a nascent stage. Impact measurement methodologies respond to a strong demand that investees comply with accountability and performance measures in order to satisfy investors in the developed world. These methodologies are built into the technologies currently being disseminated as a means of ensuring proper accountability for the impact funding that investees receive from actors who are operating in highly institutionalized contexts. That being said, for the time being, "there is no consistent global approach to nonprofit [impact-oriented] financial reporting" (Paterson et al., 2021a). Moreover, the literature on the sociology of accounting has extensively documented the limiting nature of accounting tools to account for complex transformations such as social, environmental, or ethical change (Paterson et al., 2021b, 2021a). Clarkin and Quinn, for example, have found that the management accounting tools used by international development organizations aim to ensure proper accountability to the donors, rather than improve impact among beneficiaries. This is also called "resource-based accountability" (Hug & Jäger, 2014). Given the difficulty of raising funds to generate impact, we assume that the way in which impact measurements are used responds to a scenario that aims to maximize the possibility of obtaining additional resources in the future. This has obvious repercussions on how investors perceive the reality of the contexts in which their investees reside. This raises the question: *(6) How do highly established financial standards and heterogeneous impact assessment methods influence the perception of impact investors located in developed countries when assessing potential investees in developed countries?*

For impact investment organizations, impact evaluation helps legitimize investment decisions to key stakeholders such as their own funders, peers, and other industry networks (Glänzel & Scheuerle, 2016; Urban & George, 2018). For organizations focused on social, environmental, and/or ethical outcomes, impact evaluation helps establish legitimacy with both existing and potential investors to receive future investments (O'Leary & Brennan, 2017). Hence, the extant research on performance measurement with respect to impact investors is mainly concerned with measuring the "impact" of these investments (Bugg-Levine & Emerson, 2011; Nicholls & Pharoah, 2008). However, impact assessment can be done in heterogeneous ways. For example, impact investors use three major methodologies to evaluate their investments (Reeder et al., 2015). The first takes a case-by-case approach, relying on either output or results measurements, depending on the specific circumstances of a given investment portfolio. The second takes a systems-building approach, which tests and adjusts the investor's theory of change, builds on previous results, and creates a transparent impact database. The third takes a middle-ground approach, prioritizing short-term results over long-term goals. However, Pradhan et al. (1998) have shown how such variety in evaluation methods can be riddled with complexity, due to issues surrounding the availability of pre-intervention data, the appropriateness of matched comparison design versus randomized control trials, and the difficulty of identifying valid instruments. Indeed, accounting scholars have pointed out that "assessing impact is not straightforward" and

> the characteristics of the often-formalized accounting systems mobilized in practice […] may overall not well fit the purpose of what is required for the desired impact […]

such accountings may be dysfunctional or counterproductive in relation to the impact that is deemed desirable.

(Paterson et al., 2021b, p. 3)

Hence, particularly for rural education, microfinance, and the bottom-of-the-pyramid sectors, in which a significant gap occurs between the social, environmental, or ethical intervention and the real impact it creates (Jackson, 2013b; Rangan et al., 2011; Serrano-Cinca and Gutierrez-Nieto, 2013), impact is difficult to assess with standardized measures. Similarly, impact investors who work in geographical proximity to their investees have realized that conventional financial assessment methods fail to detect the human motivation (Smart, 1999)—a relevant issue with respect to social enterprises, for which elements of effectuation and empathy (Mair & Nooba, 2006), for example, play a major role. This raises the question: *(7) How do the specific challenges of developing countries influence the emerging standards that mediate between social and financial assessment methods?*

In developing countries, accounting quantification and its aggregation are standardized into macroeconomic figures such as gross domestic product. This is a consequence of the spread of financial accounting around the world. As Suzuki has argued, the internationalization of financial accounting standards is one of the most important phenomena to acknowledge when explaining how economic and financial rationale became ubiquitous in modern societies (Suzuki, 2003a, 2003b). The strength of financial figures is therefore closely linked to the legitimacy of this specific system of quantification. However, when it comes to social statistics and impact measures, legitimacy is less reliable than it is for economic data. For instance, social statistics are more controversial in countries with significant institutional voids and a fragile civil society. Consequently, while developing countries might perceive impact as more important than developed countries do, impact in developing countries is less verifiable. At the same time, impact investees in developing countries have an interest in legitimizing themselves through their ability to account for the social, environmental, and ethical impact they generate. Consequently, in many cases, there may be an incentive to quantify impact more loosely. This raises the question: *(8) How do highly established financial standards and heterogeneous impact assessment methods influence the perception of impact investors located in developing countries when assessing potential investees in developing countries?*

Research Questions for Exploring Double Hybridity

Impact investors often engage in double hybridity, operating across country-specific standards as well as impact- and finance-related targets. However, how they mediate between the different spectrums of context and rationales has not yet been addressed by the academic world. Hence, we propose that accounting as a mediating practice can serve as a theoretical baseline from which to explore how assessment tools such as instruments of measure can mediate between the opposing moral values that occur in the hybridization of contexts (developed and developing) and rationales (financial and impact) (Annisette et al., 2017).

Financial and Impact Assessment among Developed and Developing Country Standards

Impact investors must understand the different risks involved and how each is valued, hedged, and optimized for a given investment. This involves reflecting on various social and financial risks with respect to both the investee and the broader investment portfolio. Furthermore, each country is unique in terms of its pace of development and the characteristics of its capital markets, depending on its specific circumstances, global market conditions, and exogenous events. In developing countries, capital markets are not yet matured and often lack the institutions that would allow for more efficient trade. Potential capital providers and information availability are particularly relevant issues. Conversely, well-functioning institutions in developed countries give rise to specific information flows (Makhija & Stewart, 2002) which, in turn, serve to reduce uncertainty and stimulate investment (North, 1990). Impact investors are therefore more likely to invest in organizations that are legally constituted in developed countries and have operations in developing ones. Nevertheless, research has found that these investors' perception of relevant impact is largely shaped by a combination of their particular values and the regulatory situation of the countries in which they are embedded (Mogapi et al., 2019). A given investor's values are mainly shaped by the developed context in which they are embedded, as most impact investment firms are founded in developed economies and only later open operations in developing economies. For impact investors from developed countries who must assess impact in developing countries, however, the framework changes. This is particularly relevant when impact investors select their methods. Since the source of funding determines the means of accountability and performance assessment, evaluating impact investment in developing countries depends on the reporting requirements of the funder (Clerkin & Quinn, 2021; Paterson et al., 2021a). To further enhance our understanding of impact investment outcomes, scholars have thus called for a focus on the inter-organizational level, specifically on the relationship between investors and their investees (Harji & Hebb 2010; Nicholls & Pharoah 2008). This raises the question: *(9) How does the general contextual difference between developed and developing countries influence the standards that mediate between the social and financial assessment methods?*

In response to the lack of a convention regarding (double) hybrid assessment methods in developed and developing countries, some scholars suggest deriving a single measurement by integrating the impact dimension with the financial return dimension for all countries. Viviani and Maurel (2019), for example, offer a quantitative measurement of multidimensional value creation in impact investment by considering both the financial and impact performance of a social enterprise, which could then be used by impact investors to estimate which investment projects would create the highest value in terms of both impact and return (see also Emerson, 2003). Taking this one step further, some researchers suggest that an impact investment decision-making system should also consider several other key dimensions (e.g., risks and stakeholders), without which impact investments may not achieve their intended results (Serrano-Cinca & Gutierrez-Nieto, 2013; Gregory, 2016; Muñoz & Kimmitt, 2019). Brandstetter and Lehner (2015) present one such econometric model for optimizing impact investment decision-making, which not only incorporates financial and impact returns but also the financial and social risks often caused by the complex conditions of developing countries. Although investment decision-making systems based on quantitative methods help in the sensemaking processes involved with investment decisions by quantifying an investment project's value, ignoring its qualitative aspect places too much emphasis on a quantifiable value, which can result in misguided decisions (King, 2017). This shows how evaluating a given investment project based on quantitative methods alone risks a biased picture and how using both quantitative and qualitative methods can provide a more holistic picture of a project's worth. Indeed, qualitative data about an investment project may reveal some subtle yet significant insights, which usually remain beyond the realm of quantitative evaluation methods (Roundy et al., 2017). This suggests that to increase the chance of optimal investment decision-making, impact investors must use qualitative insights and/or data to supplement investment decision-making systems that are built primarily on quantitative methods. However, quantitative and qualitative data have different interpretations when assessments are carried out by actors who are in geographic proximity to the organization being assessed. The sociology of accounting has studied the adjudication of value as a work in which the perspectives of many stakeholders can be integrated, simplified, or excluded (Ruff et al., 2022). The fact that impact methodologies are heterogeneous and unsettled opens the possibility to integrate the different perspectives held by stakeholders who are in geographic proximity to the recipient organization. This raises the question: *(10) How does the double hybridity of financial and impact assessment standards influence the perception of impact investors in developed countries when assessing potential investees in developing countries?*

Conclusion

Interest in impact investment is growing, as is the number of institutions that are working on it at the national and international levels. This is a substantial opportunity to ensure that capital flows go where they are most needed and has the potential to play a role in resolving the world's most significant social, environmental, and ethical challenges. The risk, however, is that such efforts will merely copy the standards used by developed countries and, thus, limit their impact potential—a trap that much development work has historically fallen into. Research that draws attention to the influence of context on the assessment methods and practices used by impact investors to allocate their capital is urgently needed. However, research should not merely educate. It is our hope that a broad range of researchers will engage in studies that aim toward action, dedicating themselves to a constructive search for models that avoid repeating the mistakes of the past. This chapter is intended to serve as a guide. Because the assessment methods used to allocate capital have a significant accounting foundation, the sociology of accounting can provide a useful theoretical grounding for a dualistic view of assessment. In the sociology of accounting, not only does context affect the assessment method that impact investors' use, but the converse is also true: how impact investors use assessment methods influences their perception of a given context. Based on this dualistic view, we have defined context as a theoretical focal point when analyzing the assessment processes that impact investors undertake. Rather than viewing accounting objects and tools as merely functional, technical, and neutral apparatus, we adhere to a sociology of accounting that indicates that these tools and objectives socially construct reality (Hines, 1988).

Based on this theoretical underpinning, we propose the double hybridity of impact investment as the focal point for future analysis. The primary thread that pervades the impact investment arena is the intent to generate both financial and non-financial benefits by engaging in a multi-layered ecosystem that operates in both developed and developing countries. By building on accounting as a mediating practice, we suggest further research towards understanding how assessment tools such as instruments of measure can mediate between the opposing moral values that occur in the hybridization of rationales (financial and impact) and contexts (developed and developing countries) (Annisette et al., 2017).

In this chapter, we have theorized on the double hybridity of impact investment and the components that occur within it. On one axis of this double hybridity is the fact that the assessment context can be based on developed countries, developing countries, or an integration of the two in a hybrid form. While some investors from developed countries only invest in specific other developed countries (as can occur between developing-developing countries) and thus operate within country-specific standards, most impact investment flows between regions. Nevertheless, scholars have not yet acknowledged the importance of context. In fact, context is mainly regarded on a country or sector-based level (e.g., the focus on Australia in Castellas et al., 2018; the focus on agriculture in Kish & Fairbairn, 2018), rather than a categorization of various countries or sectors. This means that impact investment is often perceived as decoupled from context rather than arising from its embeddedness within a complex system of economic, social, and cultural influences. Thus, we call for context to be a significant component of analysis on impact investment. On the other axis of impact investment's double hybridity is the fact that assessment methods can rely on financial criteria, impact criteria, or an integration of the two in a hybrid form. Using purely financial accounting criteria is a well-established convention in value-based management systems, entailing the application of specific assessment tools and key frameworks. Conversely, generic impact criteria have yet to be established. While academia has engaged in studies concerning this hybridity and has elaborated on how impact investment is a blend of economic rationale (based on values and goals such as efficiency, profit maximization, competition, and value capture) and impact rationale (driven by collaboration, cooperation, and value creation) (Busch et al., 2021), it has not yet addressed how these rationales affect one another. Thus, we call for research that explores how established conventions of the financial rationale influence the criteria, perceptions, and measurements found within the impact rationale.

Impact investment is often viewed as a cutting-edge substitute for conventional investment and philanthropic practices. However, while such practices are founded on a single, dominant rationale, impact investors start from the concept that economic and impact logics can be successfully combined and that doing so results in novel opportunities. Our chapter shows, however, that little of the research that elaborates on impact investment activities has focused on the context level. We hope the agenda introduced here will guide researchers who wish to play an active role in developing urgently needed models for addressing the double hybridity of impact investment.

Notes

1 The sociology of accounting has analyzed the way in which techniques like the DCF originated in the margins of accounting and have become accepted conventions by a wide range of actors (Miller, 1991). From this perspective, indicators such as EVA or DCF are hybrids between accounting forms and economic ideas (Miller et al., 2008). To simplify our argument, however, we do not address this discussion here.
2 See www.ifrs.org/groups/international-sustainability-standards-board/, accessed 18 May 2022.

Sources

Addis, R., McLeod, J., & Raine, A. (2013). *Impact—Australia: Investment for social and economic benefit*. Department of Education, Employment and Workplace Relations.

Annisette, M., & Richardson, A. J. (2011). Justification and accounting: Applying sociology of worth to accounting research. *Accounting, Auditing and Accountability Journal, 24*(2), 229–249. https://doi.org/10.1108/09513571111100690

Annisette, M., Vesty, G., & Amslem, T. (2017). Accounting values, controversies, and compromises in tests of worth. In C. Cloutier, J. P. Gond, & B. Leca (Eds.), *Research in the sociology of organizations* (pp. 209–239). Emerald Publishing Limited. https://doi.org/10.1108/S0733-558X20170000052007

Austin, J., Stevenson, H., & Wei-Skillern, J. (2006). Social and commercial entrepreneurship: Same, different, or both? *Entrepreneurship: Theory and Practice, 30*(1), 1–22. https://doi.org/10.1111/j.1540-6520.2006.00107.x

Brandstetter, L., & Lehner, O. M. (2015). Opening the market for impact investments: The need for adapted portfolio tools. *Entrepreneurship Research Journal, 5*(2), 87–107. https://doi.org/10.4324/9781315772578

Bugg-Levine, A., & Emerson, J. (2011). *Impact investing: Transforming how we make money while making a difference* (1st ed.). Jossey-Bass, a Wiley imprint.

Burchell, S., Clubb, C., & Hopwood, A. G. (1985). Accounting in its social context: Towards a history of value added in the United Kingdom. *Accounting, Organizations and Society, 10*(4), 381–413. https://doi.org/10.1016/0361-3682(85)90002-9

Burchell, S., Clubb, C., Hopwood, A., Hughes, J., & Nahapiet, J. (1980). The roles of accounting in organizations and society. *Accounting, Organizations and Society, 5*(1), 5–27. https://doi.org/10.1016/0361-3682(80)90017-3

Busch, T., Bruce-Clark, P., Derwall, J., Eccles, R., Hebb, T., Hoepner, A., ... & Weber, O. (2021). Impact investments: A call for (re) orientation. *SN Business & Economics, 1*(2), 1–13. https://doi.org/10.1007/s43546-020-00033-6

Campbell, D. (2002). Outcomes assessment and the paradox of nonprofit accountability. *Nonprofit Management and Leadership, 12*(3), 243–259. https://doi.org/10.1002/nml.12303

Castellas, E. I. P., Ormiston, J., & Findlay, S. (2018). Financing social entrepreneurship: The role of impact investment in shaping social enterprise in Australia. *Social Enterprise Journal, 14*(2), 130–155. https://doi.org/10.1108/SEJ-02-2017-0006

Chapman, C., Cooper, D., & Miller, P. (2009). Linking accounting, organizations and institutions. In C. Chapman, D. Cooper, & P. Miller (Eds.), *Accounting, organizations, and institutions* (pp. 1–29). Oxford: OUP.

Chisolm, L. B. (1995). Accountability of nonprofit organizations and those who control them: The legal framework. *Nonprofit Management and Leadership, 6*(2), 141–156. https://doi.org/10.1002/nml.4130060204

Clerkin, B., & Quinn, M. (2021). Institutional agents missing in action? Management accounting at non-governmental organisations. *Critical Perspectives on Accounting, 80*, 102276. https://doi.org/10.1016/j.cpa.2020.102276

Corry, O. (2010). Defining and theorizing the third sector. In R. Taylor (Ed.), *Third sector research*. https://doi.org/10.1007/978-1-4419-5707-8_2

Dacin, P. A., Dacin, M. T., & Matear, M. (2010). Social entrepreneurship: Why we don't need a new theory and how we move forward from here. *Academy of Management Perspectives, 24*(3), 37–57. https://doi.org/10.5465/amp.24.3.37

Ebrahim, A., & Rangan, V. K. (2014). What impact? A framework for measuring the scale and scope of social performance. *California Management Review, 56*(3), 118–141. https://doi.org/10.1525/cmr.2014.56.3.118

Emerson, J. (2003). The blended value proposition: Integrating social and financial returns. *California Management Review*, 45(4), 35–51. https://doi.org/10.2307/41166187

Espeland, W. N., & Sauder, M. (2007). Rankings and reactivity: How public measures recreate social worlds. *American Journal of Sociology, 113*(1), 1–40. https://doi.org/10.1086/517897

Espeland, W. N., & Stevens, M. L. (1998). Commensuration as a social process. *Annual Review of Sociology, 24*(1), 313–343. https://doi.org/10.1146/annurev.soc.24.1.313

Esteves, A. M., Franks, D., & Vanclay, F. (2012). Social impact assessment: The state of the art. *Impact Assessment and Project Appraisal, 30*(1), 34–42. https://doi.org/10.1080/14615517.2012.660356

Evans, M. (2013). Meeting the challenge of impact investing: How can contracting practices secure social impact without sacrificing performance? *Journal of Sustainable Finance and Investment, 3*(2), 138–154. https://doi.org/10.1080/20430795.2013.776260

Finsterbusch, K. (1985). State of the art in social impact assessment. *Environment and Behavior, 17*(2), 193–221. https://doi.org/10.1177/0013916585172002

G8. (2014). Impact investment: The invisible heart of markets [Report]. G8 Social Impact Investment Taskforce, September 15.

Gaynor, L. M., McDaniel, L. and Yohn, T. L.. 2011. Fair value accounting for liabilities: The role of disclosures in unraveling the counterintuitive income statement effect from credit risk changes. *Accounting, Organizations and Society*, 36(3), 125–134. https://doi.org/10.1016/j.aos.2011.03.004

GIIN. (2013). *Perspectives on progress: The impact investor survey*. GIIN and Rockefeller foundation.

GIIN. (2019a). *Annual impact investor survey*. GIIN, June 19.

GIIN. (2019b). *Sizing the impact investment market: Global impact investing network*. New York, US. https://thegiin.org/assets/GIIN_2019%20Annual%20Impact%20Investor%20Survey_webfile.pdf

Glänzel, G., & Scheuerle, T. (2016). Social impact investing in Germany: Current impediments from investors' and social entrepreneurs' perspectives. *Voluntas: International Journal of Voluntary and Nonprofit Organizations, 27*(4), 1638–1668. https://doi.org/10.1007/s11266-015-9621-z

Gregory, N. (2016). De-risking impact investing. *World Economics, 17*(2), 143–158.

Grimes, M. (2010). Strategic sensemaking within funding relationships: The effects of performance measurement on organizational identity in the social sector. *Entrepreneurship: Theory and Practice, 34*(4), 763–783. https://doi.org/10.1111/j.1540-6520.2010.00398.x

Harji, K., & Hebb, T. (2010). Impact investing for social finance. *ANSER conference proceedings, Montreal, Canada* (pp. 1–20). https://carleton.ca/3ci/wp-content/uploads/Impact-Investing-for-Social-Finance-v1.pdf

Harji, K., & Jackson, E. T. (2012). *Accelerating impact: Achievements, challenges and what's next in building the impact investing industry.* The Rockefeller Foundation.

Hines, R. D. (1988). Financial accounting: In communicating reality, we construct reality. *Accounting, Organizations and Society, 13*(3), 251–261. https://doi.org/10.1016/0361-3682(88)90003-7

Höchstädter, A. K., & Scheck, B. (2015). What's in a name: An analysis of impact investing understandings by academics and practitioners. *Journal of Business Ethics, 132*(2), 449–475. https://doi.org/10.1007/s10551-014-2327-0

Hopwood, A. G. (1983). On trying to study accounting in the contexts in which it operates. *Accounting, Organizations and Society, 8*(2–3), 287–305. https://doi.org/10.1016/0361-3682(83)90035-1

Horton, J., Serafeim, G., & Serafeim, I. (2013). Does mandatory IFRS adoption improve the information environment? *Contemporary Accounting Research, 30*(1), 388–423. https://doi.org/10.1111/j.1911-3846.2012.01159.x

Hug, N., & Jäger, U. P. (2014). Resource-based accountability: A case study on multiple accountability relations in an economic development nonprofit. *Voluntas: International Journal of Voluntary and Nonprofit Organizations, 25*(3), 772–796. https://doi.org/10.1007/s11266-013-9362-9

Huybrechts, B., & Nicholls, A. (2013). The role of legitimacy in social enterprise-corporate collaboration. *Social Enterprise Journal, 9*(2), 130–146. https://doi.org/10.1108/SEJ-01-2013-0002

Jackson, E. T. (2013a). Evaluating social impact bonds: Questions, challenges, innovations, and possibilities in measuring outcomes in impact investing. *Community Development, 44*(5), 608–616. https://doi.org/10.1080/15575330.2013.854258

Jackson, E. T. (2013b). Interrogating the theory of change: Evaluating impact investing where it matters most. *Journal of Sustainable Finance and Investment, 3*(2), 95–110. https://doi.org/10.1080/20430795.2013.776257

Khanna, T., & Palepu, K. (1997). Why focused strategies. *Harvard Business Review, 75*(4), 41–51.

Khanna, T., & Palepu, K. G. (2010). *Winning in emerging markets: A road map for strategy and execution.* Harvard Business Press.

King, J. (2017). Using economic methods evaluatively. *American Journal of Evaluation, 38*(1), 101–113. https://doi.org/10.1177/1098214016641211

King, L., & Gish, E. (2015). Marketizing social change: Social shareholder activism and responsible investing. *Sociological Perspectives, 58*(4), 711–730. https://doi.org/10.1177/0731121415576799

Kish, Z., & Fairbairn, M. (2018). Investing for profit, investing for impact: Moral performances in agricultural investment projects. *Environment and Planning a: Economy and Space, 50*(3), 569–588. https://doi.org/10.1177/0308518X1773825

Kurunmäki, L. (2004). A hybrid profession—The acquisition of management accounting expertise by medical professionals. *Accounting, Organizations and Society, 29*(3–4), 327–347. https://doi.org/10.1016/S0361-3682(02)00069-7

Lingane, A., & Olsen, S. (2004). Guidelines for social return on investment. *California Management Review, 46*(3), 116–135. https://doi.org/10.2307/41166224

Lockie, S. (2001). SIA in review: Setting the agenda for impact assessment in the 21st century. *Impact Assessment and Project Appraisal, 19*(4), 277–287. https://doi.org/10.3152/147154601781766952

Louche, C., Arenas, D., Cranenburgh, & Van, K. C. (2012). From preaching to investing: Attitudes of religious organisations towards responsible investment. *Journal of Business. Ethics, 110*(3), 301–320. https://doi.org/10.1007/s10551-011-1155-8

Mair, J., Mart, I., & Canly, K. (2007). Institutional voids as spaces of opportunity. *European Business Forum, 31*, 34–39.

Mair, J., & Noboa, E. (2006). Social entrepreneurship: How intentions to create a social venture are formed. *Social Entrepreneurship.* https://doi.org/10.1057/9780230625655_8

Makhija, M., & Stewart, A. (2002). The effect of national context on perceptions of risk: A comparison of planned versus free market managers. *Journal of International Business Studies, 33*(4), 737–756. https://doi.org/10.1057/palgrave.jibs.8491042

Maxwell, A. L., Jeffrey, S. A., & Levesque, M. (2011). Business angel early-stage decision making. *Journal of Business Venturing, 26*(2), 212–225. https://doi.org/10.1016/j.jbusvent.2009.09.002

Mendell, M., & Nogales, R. (2011). Solidarity finance. Working paper, International Forum on the Social and Solidarity Economy (FIESS), Chantier de l'e´conomie sociale, Canada.

Mennicken, A. (2010). From inspection to auditing: Audit and markets as linked ecologies. *Accounting, Organizations and Society, 35*(3), 334–359. https://doi.org/10.1016/j.aos.2009.07.007

Mikes, A. (2011). From counting risk to making risk count: Boundary-work in risk management. *Accounting, Organizations and Society, 36*(4–5), 226–245. https://doi.org/10.1016/j.aos.2011.03.002

Miller, P. (1991). Accounting innovation beyond the enterprise: Problematizing investment decisions and programming economic growth in the U.K. in the 1960s. *Accounting, Organizations and Society, 16*(8), 733–762. https://doi.org/10.1016/0361-3682(91)90022-7

Miller, P. (1994). Accounting and objectivity: The invention of calculating selves and calculable spaces. In Megill Allan (Ed.), *Rethinking Objectivity* (pp. 239–264). Durham & London: Duke University Press.

Miller, P., Kurunmäki, L., & O'Leary, T. (2008). Accounting, hybrids and the management of risk. *Accounting, Organizations and Society, 33*(7–8), 942–967. https://doi.org/10.1016/j.aos.2007.02.005

Miller, P., & O'Leary, T. (2007). Mediating instruments and making markets: Capital budgeting, science and the economy. *Accounting, Organizations and Society, 32*(7–8), 701–734. https://doi.org/10.1016/j.aos.2007.02.003

Miller, P., & Power, M. (2013). Accounting, organizing, and economizing: Connecting accounting research and organization theory. *Academy of Management Annals, 7*(1), 557–605. https://doi.org/10.1080/19416520.2013.783668

Miller, T. L., & Wesley, C. L. (2010). Assessing mission and resources for social change: An organizational identity perspective on social venture capitalists' decision criteria. *Entrepreneurship: Theory and Practice, 34*(4), 705–733. https://doi.org/10.1111/j.1540-6520.2010.00388.x

Mogapi, E. M., Sutherland, M. M., & Wilson-Prangley, A. (2019). Impact investing in South Africa: Managing tensions between financial returns and social impact. *European Business Review, 31*(3), 397–419. https://doi.org/10.1108/EBR-11-2017-0212

Muñoz, P., & Kimmitt, J. (2019). A diagnostic framework for social impact bonds in emerging economies. *Journal of Business Venturing Insights, 12*, 1–9. https://doi.org/10.1016/j.jbvi.2019.e00141

Nicholls, A., & Pharoah, C. (2008). *The landscape of social investment: A holistic topology of opportunities and challenges.* Skoll Centre for Social Entrepreneurship, Said Business School, University of Oxford.

Nicholls, A., & Tomkinson, E. (2013). *The Peterborough pilot: Social impact bonds.* Said Business School, University of Oxford.

North, D. (1990). *Institutions, institutional change, and economic performance.* Cambridge University Press.

O'Leary, S., & Brennan, A. (2017). Ireland's social finance landscape. *ACRN Oxford Journal of Finance and Risk Perspectives, 6*, 90–112.

Ormiston, J., & Seymour, R. (2011). Understanding value creation in social entrepreneurship: The importance of aligning mission, strategy and impact measurement. *Journal of Social Entrepreneurship, 2*(2), 125–150. https://doi.org/10.1080/19420676.2011.606331

Paterson, A. S., Jackson, W. J., & Haslam, J. (2021a). Critical reflections of accounting and social impact, Part II. *Critical Perspectives on Accounting, SI: Accounting and Social Impact, Part II, 80,* 102342. https://doi.org/10.1016/j.cpa.2021.102342

Paterson, A. S., Jackson, W. J., & Haslam, J. (2021b). Critical reflections of accounting and social impact, Part I. *Critical Perspectives on Accounting, SI: Accounting and Social Impact, Part I, 79,* 102341. https://doi.org/10.1016/j.cpa.2021.102341

Phillips, S. D., & Johnson, B. (2021). Inching to impact: The demand side of social impact investing. *Journal of Business Ethics, 168*(3), 615–629. https://doi.org/10.1007/s10551-019-04241-5

Poon, M. (2009). From new deal institutions to capital markets: Commercial consumer risk scores and the making of subprime mortgage finance. *Accounting, Organizations and Society, 34*(5), 654–674. https://doi.org/10.1016/j.aos.2009.02.003

Pradhan, M., Rawlings, L., & Ridder, G. (1998). The Bolivian Social Investment Fund: An analysis of baseline data for impact evaluation. *World Bank Economic Review, 12*(3), 457–482. https://doi.org/10.1093/wber/12.3.457

Rangan, V. K., Appleby, S., Moon, L., & Schervish, P. G. (2011). The promise of impact investing. *Harvard Business Review* (November), 1–21.

Reeder, N., Colantonio, A., Loder, J., & Rocyn Jones, G. (2015). Measuring impact in impact investing: An analysis of the predominant strength that is also its greatest weakness. *Journal of Sustainable Finance and Investment, 5*(3), 136–154. https://doi.org/10.1080/20430795.2015.1063977

Roundy, P., Holzhauer, H., & Dai, Y. (2017). Finance or philanthropy? Exploring the motivations and criteria of impact investors. *Social Responsibility Journal, 13*(3), 491–512. https://doi.org/10.1108/SRJ-08-2016-0135

Ruff, K., Nappert, P. L., & Graham, C. (2022). Impact valuations in social finance: Emic and polyvocal stakeholder accounts. *Accounting, Auditing and Accountability Journal*. https://doi.org/10.1108/AAAJ-01-2021-5081

Ryan, P. W., & Lyne, I. (2008). Social enterprise and the measurement of social value: Methodological issues with the calculation and application of the social return on investment. *Educations Knowledge and Economy*, 2(3), 223–237. https://doi.org/10.1080/17496890802426253

Saltuk, Y., Bouri, A., Mudaliar, A., & Pease, M. (2013). *Perspectives on progress: The impact investor survey* [Report]. Global Impact Investor Network (GIIN), & Global Social Finance, J.P. Morgan (January 7).

Serrano-Cinca, C., & Gutierrez-Nieto, B. (2013). A decision support system for financial and social investment. *Applied Economics*, 45(28), 4060–4070. https://doi.org/10.1080/00036846.2012.748180

Smart, G. H. (1999) Management assessment methods in venture capital: An empirical analysis of human capital valuation. *Venture Capital*, 1(1), 59–82. DOI: 10.1080/136910699295992.

Social Finance. (2009). *Social impact bonds: Rethinking finance for social outcomes*. Social Finance.

Suzuki, T. (2003a). The accounting figuration of business statistics as a foundation for the spread of economic ideas. *Accounting, Organizations and Society*, 28(1), 65–95. https://doi.org/10.1016/S0361-3682(02)00033-8

Suzuki, T. (2003b). The epistemology of macroeconomic reality: The Keynesian Revolution from an accounting point of view. *Accounting, Organizations and Society*, 28(5), 471–517. https://doi.org/10.1016/S0361-3682(01)00061-7

Urban, B., & George, J. (2018). An empirical study on measures relating to impact investing in South Africa. *International Journal of Sustainable Economy*, 10(1), 61–77.

Vanclay, F. (2003). International principles for social impact assessment. *Impact Assessment and Project Appraisal*, 21(1), 5–12. https://doi.org/10.3152/147154603781766491

Viviani, J-L., & Maurel, C. (2019). Performance of impact investing: A value creation approach. *Research in International Business and Finance*, 47, 31–39. https://doi.org/10.1016/j.ribaf.2018.01.001

Weber, O. (2016). Introducing impact investing. In O. M. Lehner (Ed.), *Routledge handbook of social and sustainable finance*. Routledge, Taylor Francis Group. https://doi.org/10.4324/9781315772578

14
WHEN DO BANK LOANS BECOME GREEN?

Olga Golubeva

Introduction

Since the Industrial Revolution, finance has been a powerful enabler of human progress by allocating the world's savings to innovative and efficient projects requiring liquidity. Being the safe-keepers of the deposits made by private individuals, firms, and organizations, banks have traditionally focused on the lower end of the risk spectrum, providing liquidity only to organizations with solid business models and to firms with well-established technology (Golubeva et al., 2019; Alonso, 2020).

The initiation of green lending started already in the 1990s when a few Swiss banks, the Co-operative Bank in the UK and the ASN Bank in the Netherlands dedicated some financial resources to stimulate developments in society towards sustainability (Bouma et al., 2001). Although the topic of *green loans* has attracted scholars' attention (Ehlers et al., 2021; Khan et al., 2021; Wang et al., 2021), the concept has not yet been defined unambiguously (Tang & Zhang, 2020). Furthermore, despite policymakers, the financial community, and academic scholars agreeing on the importance of green loan developments, the question of which factors can assist in the transition of conventional bank debts to green lending is seldom discussed and analyzed explicitly.

The main purpose of this explorative study is to shed light on the complexity of the development/implementation of green loans. The paper combines a review of the academic literature and policy documents on the subject with insights obtained through 11 interviews that were conducted from 2017 to 2021 at one of the Nordic banks (referred to as the "Nordic Bank" in this study).[1] The chapter contributes to the literature on green finance in its application to the bank loans granted to finance the construction of wind farms in Sweden, a country that is ranked first out of 150 countries, based on environmental, social, and governance (ESG) indicators in the Robeco SAM Country Sustainability Ranking (2020). Ambitious national legislation regulating the platform for sustainable business has contributed to many Swedish corporations and financial institutions already advanced in assuming responsibility for the environment (Torvanger et al., 2021).

Searching for the answer to the question *When do bank loans become green?*, the study suggests a "green loans" framework emphasizing the importance of the following factors: (1) the bank's profitability and sustainability goals; (2) green balance sheet; (3) public policy; (4) market mechanisms; (5) needs of the society; and (6) development of science and technology. Current literature, documentary analysis, and verbatim terms from 11 interviews with managers from the Nordic Bank are used to substantiate the suggestions made in the paper.

The Nordic Bank's experience in issuing debt to wind power projects in Sweden, a type of financing that is commonly classified as green loans by policymakers, might be of interest to the international community searching to facilitate the uptake of green loans for the development of a climate-resilient society.

The chapter is structured as follows. First comes a brief presentation of the green loan term, followed by an overview of the factors/variables that are suggested to impact the development of a green loan concept. The chapter concludes with a presentation of a theoretical framework (see Figure 14.2).

What is a Green Loan?

The intense environmental degradation creates a significant and urgent need to adopt green loans as institutional drivers to reduce harmful environmental footprints (Tang & Zhang, 2020; Khan et al., 2021; Wang et al., 2021). But what is a green loan? Green loans are commonly defined as bank lending designed to support the transition to a net-zero carbon economy through environmentally responsible projects and climate change mitigation (Gilchrist et al., 2021). The IFC (2017) proposed a bottom-up approach to estimate the size of the green loan markets according to different data levels: (1) the project-level data by examining the business nature of a project; (2) the firm-level data by estimating the share of green revenues per company; (3) the industry-level data that implicitly assume that the firms within the same industry conduct similar environmental activities on average.

Additionally, the Green Loan Principles (GLPs) have been developed by representatives from financial institutions to promote the integrity of the green loan product (Loan Market Association, 2018). The GLPs set out a clear framework, enabling all market participants to understand the characteristics of a green loan, based on the following four core components: (1) use of proceeds; (2) process for project evaluation and selection; (3) management of proceeds; and (4) reporting.

Capitalizing on the newly introduced Law "Sustainable finance taxonomy–Regulation (EU) 2020/852", green loans can be defined as debt provided to those borrowers that have revenues generated from green economic activities, as stipulated by the EU legislation. According to Gilchrist et al. (2021), the aggregated green loan market approached 480 billion USD in 2017 and accounted for about 55% of total loans, if the EU taxonomy is applied (p. 8).

Compared to conventional banks, Weber (2016) analyses *social* banks[2] as institutions that grant loans to create a social or environmental benefit. For social banks, business and operations are based on ethical goals, and financial products and services are means to create a positive societal impact. Additionally, Sachs et al. (2019) elaborate on the concept of *green banks*, which advantages include improved credit conditions for clean energy projects, the creation of innovative financial products, and market expansion through the dissemination of information about the benefits of clean energy. However, how far the banks are willing to forgo higher financial returns if the intended social and environmental outcomes can be achieved, remains unclear. A question about differences/similarities between loans issued by social and green banks and green loans provided by conventional banks also belongs to future research agenda.

The definition of green loans provided by the interviewed bankers from the Nordic Bank is closely related to the environmental nature of the financed projects.

> What is a green loan? With a green loan, the business will receive financing for investments that aim to implement sustainable solutions.
>
> Green loans support important environmental needs.
>
> Green loan is a type of financing where funding goes to projects and investments with environmental benefits. For example, our bank classified loans to finance wind power projects as green loans.

At the same time, remaining vagueness in the definition of green loans forced the Nordic Bank to search for clarifications:

> What is a green loan? Due to ambiguity in the definition of green loans, we [the Nordic Bank] have established an overall framework that indicates which activities qualify for green loans, a work that was carried out in collaboration with one of the leading ESG-rating providers. Such a framework removes the uncertainties.
>
> It is beneficial for banks to use an external provider of assurance to assess each loan and issue a green certificate for eligible loans based on objective criteria. Involvement of independent assessment provides clarity and transparency of classification

confirmed a manager.

Therefore, for the Nordic Bank, green financing is those loans that have been structured and disbursed based on the internally approved framework including verification by an external assurance provider. Such a confirmation obtained from an independent ESG-rating company has allowed the Nordic Bank to remove ambiguity associated with the definition of green loans. It seems that further efforts to make a definition of green loans clearer and more accountable within the banking community are required.

Based upon an analysis of 3,506 renewable energy (RE) projects, which are commonly classified as green ones,[3] Alonso (2020) estimated that commercial bank loans represent the vast majority (87.5%) of the total debt capacity afforded to these projects. Therefore, the relationship between the commercial banking sector and the RE industry seems to be successful.

Current literature presents some empirical evidence that the banks have started to assess and price possible risks caused by carbon emissions across a broad range of their clients from different industries. The combination of the syndicated loan data with carbon intensity data (CO_2 emissions relative to revenue) allowed Ehlers et al. (2021) to identify a carbon risk premium of about 3–4 basis points (i.e., a 0.03–0.04% loan rate premium), which is a price for carbon emissions directly caused by the firm (scope 1).[4] The study argues that carbon emissions indirectly caused by production inputs were not priced at the margin, suggesting that the overall carbon footprint of firms (scopes 2 and 3) is less of the bankers' concern.

While there is a huge potential for scaling up green loans, several challenges exist for financiers, including difficulties in accounting for environmental externalities in financial decision-making, information asymmetries caused by a lack of consistency in market terms and standards, and maturity mismatches for long-term projects as many investors seek short-term returns (IFC, 2017).

The Bank's Profitability and Sustainability Goals

Based on the experience of the Nordic Bank, *the bank's profitability and sustainability goals* are suggested to be the first factor that impacts the development of the green loan concept.

The neoclassical economic theory assumes that participants in the capital markets seek to maximize their financial gains. On contrary, green finance should combine traditional profit-maximization goals with green returns that are (presumably) derived from green values (Sachs et al., 2019).[5] For example, if a green project decreases carbon emissions, the reduced volume of emissions will be a green return. In the same vein, although banking is a profit-driven economic activity, green loans provided by the financial industry are expected to achieve some verifiable environmental and social outcomes alongside financial returns (Torvanger et al., 2021).

The business model of the Nordic Bank is based on generating long-term and sustainable value for its owners. Long-term profitability is the underlying premise for the Nordic Bank including financial targets like a return on equity (ROE), a cost-to-income ratio; capital requirements, and a dividend payout ratio. At the same time, ESG factors have become an integrated part of the corporate strategy, and the Bank is in the process of establishing industry-specific ESG guidelines based on the standards prepared by the Sustainability Accounting Standards Board (SASB) and the Principles for Responsible Banking (PRB).

The Nordic Bank is committed to the TCFD (Task Force on Climate-related Financial Disclosures) with a focus on both how climate change affects the environment and what it means for companies' performance and financial stability. Furthermore, the Nordic Bank has created project teams devoted to financing green energy and infrastructure projects. An ambitious strategic target to increase about three times the amount of financing for RE and renewable infrastructure between 2020 and 2025 has been announced at the Nordic Bank.

> I think that green lending goes to a sustainable customer. I believe that initial work on the integration of environmental issues into the "know-your-customer" screening process should be further developed. Our bank's long-term profitability depends on our customers' ability to integrate sustainability into their business models and strategies

explained a top manager.

> The terms and conditions of the green loan facility should be gradually shaped to reflect the importance of the sustainability targets.
>
> The green loan is eventually not a static concept, but a developing term, which reflects the continuing work on sustainability targets which is carried out by the bank together with corporate clients

suggested bankers.

Several managers emphasized the importance of searching for a balance between financial goals and sustainability targets, including the elaboration of the specific pricing mechanisms in connection with green lending (see also Krömer, 2019):

> Green loans should be priced to reflect the benefits of being sustainable, in my view. But what is being sustainable?
>
> As an example, our bank together with other Nordic banks participated in a revolving credit facility, which was a sustainability-linked loan. In a sustainability-linked credit facility, the margin of the loan is linked to the achievement of the defined ESG performance targets. The above-mentioned credit facility's targets encompass some of

the core corporate objectives and include both environmental and social KPIs [Key Performance Indicators].

Most regulators do not mandate banks to disclose green lending, therefore, it is hard to get an accurate number of how big the green loan market is. As pointed out by Tang and Zhang (2020), the only information that can be obtained about green loans is through voluntary disclosure or third-party verifications. The Nordic Bank annually reports on scope 1, scope 2, and several scope 3 Greenhouse Gas Emissions (GHG) categories.

> In financial reporting, loans and commitments are presented according to industry, without specification on sustainability features. Green loans can be found in power, manufacturing, services, buildings, etc.
>
> We should consider increasing transparency in reporting in future

explained managers.

At the same time, there is an indication that the firm's willingness to disclose terms and conditions related to green loans is beneficial for the banks. Jung et al. (2018) examined a sample of firms that voluntarily disclose carbon emissions and documented a positive association between the cost of debt and the number of disclosures.

The tools for future climate reporting should be introduced in the Nordic Banks' credit risk assessment of industries that are particularly vulnerable to climate change in the form of both physical risks (such as extreme weather and flooding) and transition risks (such as new regulatory requirements).

> Climate risk is becoming more and more integrated into our business model. However, more insight into climate risk is needed if we are to achieve quantifiable results.

The work to further develop the ESG risk assessment tool and industry-specific risk assessment tools for corporate customers is however far from being completed. Furthermore, the accumulation of data allowing environmental assessment of clients is an important part of the credit process in the Nordic Bank.

> Development of analytical and decision-making tools and specific assessment criteria for ESG-related risks in various industries is also important. Last year, we conducted more in-depth analyses of climate risk in the energy sector (both qualitative and quantitative), including RE.
>
> Although there is uncertainty associated with data related to greenhouse gas emissions, it is important to include emissions data in the analysis of companies' risk profile, alongside other traditional factors. For power companies, we started to collect the reported CO_2 data. The new KPI – the carbon footprint – measured in terms of carbon intensity, shows a company's greenhouse gas emissions relative to its turnover, which is among the factors that indicate a company's climate risk and impact. The development of new metrics allowing to report and analysis of environmental risks is an important part of credit lending. This is not a short-term engagement but a long-term systematic work that is currently developed in steps, depending on the availability of data.

The key lessons learned from the 2007–2009 financial crisis were that the financial markets lacked transparency, "long-termism", and suitable sustainability metrics, as well as appropriate regulation (KPMG, 2021). Based on our empirical evidence, however, the Nordic Bank seems to be committed to contributing to sustainable performance among financial institutions through actively participating in green lending in Sweden.

Green Balance Sheet

The second factor that is suggested to be included in the framework is referred to as a *green balance sheet*. There is no commonly agreed definition of the term "green"; therefore, various governments, financial institutions, and international organizations have started to develop their approaches to green finance according to underlying motivations (IFC, 2017).

GLPs define green loans as any type of debt instrument made available exclusively to finance eligible green projects (Loan Market Association, 2018). Although green finance is commonly associated with the financing of RE and its efficiency, in its broader definition, the scope of green finance is extended to include clean water, recycling, biodiversity protection, organizational pollution control, and environmental proactivity (Khan et al., 2021).

At the same time, clean coal is treated as a green product and is supported by green financial instruments in China, while not in the EU, eventually due to different public priorities when setting green finance standards (Gilchrist et al., 2021). Additionally, "green" is an evolving concept. To take a recent example, after the Russian invasion of Ukraine in February 2022, Sweden-based Skandinaviska Enskilda Banken AB decided to reverse its policy suggesting defense companies and weapons makers satisfy partially the ESG criteria because of their importance for security reasons (Ballard, 2022).

Due to the remaining ambiguity within the meaning of being green, some providers of funds might indeed avoid participating in green finance markets due to the fare of financial instruments being currently labeled "green" but later would be deemed as "insufficiently green", as stressed by Björkholm & Lehner (2021).

The complex nature of the green concept has been emphasized by several bankers from the Nordic Bank.

> I believe that a green firm should apply various green financial sources [equity, bonds, loans] to fund green assets. Can a firm use a green loan to fund an asset that pollutes and destroys the environment?

> Both sides of the balance sheet must be in balance regarding sustainability requirements.

> It seems that all posts in the balance sheet of a firm must be "green". I am not saying, however, that it is an easy task to achieve this green balance. Different sources of finance may have variations in "how they are green". This is an undiscovered topic for investigation

pointed out several managers.

The fundamental determinant of a green loan, therefore, is the utilization of the loan proceeds for green projects, i.e., the investments should provide clear environmental benefits, which should be feasible, quantified, measured, and reported by the borrower. Additionally, the consistency between the environmental nature of the assets and financial sources, including loans, should be ensured within the balance sheet.

BALANCE SHEET	
Green assets	**Green finance**
	Green equity
	Green bonds
	Green loans

Figure 14.1 The balance sheet of a green firm

Based on interviews, the emphasis on the importance of reviewing the whole balance sheet of the company is suggested, which provides both a breakdown and summation of various accounting items ensuring their green nature (see Figure 14.1).

How to achieve a sustainable equilibrium in a green balance sheet seems to be a forward-looking challenge for the business community, academicians, and policymakers.

Another manager pointed out:

> What will happen with wind turbines after retirement? We do not know... Green lending should probably include a responsible recycling standard for the whole life of assets, in my view. As an example, Nordic banks started to include in the loan agreements clauses on responsible ship recycling. In the same vein, a similar clause can be introduced into debt contracts regulating loans to wind power projects. By 2040, most wind power plants developed before 2015 will have reached their technical life spans. Should analysis of green loans cover the whole life of assets beyond the loan maturity? This question is however not answered yet.

Lenders are commonly assumed to monitor and validate the sustainability information provided by the borrower during the life of the loan, mindful of the need to preserve the integrity of the green loan product (Loan Market Association, 2018). What seems to be forgotten so far is that green lending should assess the environmental nature of projects not only during the loan maturity but throughout the lifetime of the assets. A "green balance sheet" should eventually not only assure consistency between the environmental nature of the assets and finances but also expand the analysis horizons beyond the conventional debt maturity.

Public Policy

Current literature is inconclusive on whether the market mechanisms themselves will be able to allocate funds towards more sustainable drivers of economic growth (Mazzucato & Semieniuk, 2018; Gilchrist et al., 2021). Wang et al. (2021) suggest that green development can be implemented only with the help of *public policies*, including carbon tax policy, government subsidy policy, green bond policy, and green investment policy (see also Taghizadeh-Hesary & Yoshino, 2019; Zhang et al., 2019).

Moreover, current projections of future GHG emissions from numerous countries demonstrate that they would not reach their climate targets without the introduction of additional policies to decarbonize the economy. Hafner et al (2020) report on a policy emission gap for the UK, which corresponds to a shortage of 45–65 TWh low carbon electricity generation out to 2030.

A top executive pointed out:

> The energy sector contains long-term and capital-intensive assets like large hydro-power plants, pipelines, refineries, heavy industrial facilities, and buildings that have technical and economic lifetimes of more than 50 years. During such a long-term period, changes in the macroeconomic environment and, particularly, in the economic cycle might be enormous. Therefore, ensuring stable funding for energy projects is the key success factor for RE developments… Can we achieve stable funding without a stable policy?

Similar to Elie et al. (2021), this study points out that the financing needs of power technologies are commonly associated with the high financial cost spread over the total lifetime of a clean energy project. As banks provide loans only against projects' assets and revenue streams, bank debt might become less available in an environment with higher market risks and a lack of supporting mechanisms.

Public policies have been allocated during this century to promote the deployment of sustainable development, including regulatory instruments and fiscal incentives (Elie et al., 2021). Two main types of supporting public policies can be distinguished: market and non-market instruments. Non-market instruments are command-and-control regulations, including active technology support policies. The purpose of market instruments is to put an explicit price on environmental externalities. These instruments can either directly affect prices, such as taxes (e.g., on GHG emissions) and subsidies (Production Tax Credit (PTC), feed-in tariff (FIT)), or they influence quantities, such as tradable allowance systems (e.g., Renewable Energy Certificates (RECs) and tenders).[6]

Auctions and tenders have become one of the most common market support mechanisms for new wind power projects. In an auction-based support scheme, eligible bidders compete, typically based on their required support level, to obtain support rights for a limited quantity of additional RE capacity that the state authority is procuring (Dukan & Kitzing, 2021). A move by governments to introduce a zero-subsidy principle (often understood as a pure merchant environment without public support) undermines the profitability of new wind projects and sharply increases risk.

> In July 2019, a Swedish energy producer Vattenfall won the second Dutch zero-subsidy offshore wind tender for the project amounting to 760 MW. The zero-subsidy structure means that Vattenfall will only receive the wholesale price of electricity, and no further support mechanisms will be granted. Although this tender indeed proves that the offshore costs have come down through technology innovation, how many energy companies like Vattenfall do we have in Sweden? Being owned by a Swedish state and enjoying a credit rating of A3 by Moody's, Vattenfall is a top player in the European energy sector. There is however a strong need to engage small and medium-sized companies in green finance to achieve sustainability targets… Public policy will play a decisive role to involve these smaller players in the sustainability agenda

mentioned one of the bankers.

Albeit the RE sponsors can indeed finance projects without banks, by employing directly the equity funds, balance sheet financing might be unavailable to smaller sponsors (see also Dukan & Kitzing, 2021).

The Swedish government has set the target of Sweden becoming the world's first fossil-free welfare nation (Government Offices of Sweden, 2020) supported by the required measures. At the same time, several stakeholders expressed concerns regarding the impact of the current energy policies on the competitiveness of both small firms and electricity-intensive industries that are being forced even to turn down expansion plans due to electricity shortages.

> Sweden is the country that emits the least carbon dioxide in relation to GDP, yet it has the highest carbon tax in the world. While Sweden levies a tax of SEK 1200 per ton of carbon dioxide, the global average is SEK 26. It is not reasonable that the country in the Western world that emits the least carbon dioxide per capita should emit even less

argued Rydström (2021, p. 6), a representative of a business community.

A survey conducted by Swedish Television (SVT) among the political parties represented in the parliament at the end of December 2021 showed that all parties agree that to achieve the climate target of zero net GHG emissions, a possible doubling of electricity use by 2045 will be required. However, the answers showed a divided parliament, where parties strongly disagree on how electricity should be produced with the main contradiction issue being the role of nuclear power, according to SVT's survey (Öbrink, 2021).

To sum up, to ensure that green lending will consistently not be falling short of what is needed, a divide between top-down targets and the private sector's ability to deploy financial resources for sustainable projects should be minimized. Public policy measures including current and future international climate agreements seem to impact the development of green loans.

Market Mechanisms

A manager pointed out: "Although policy-makers provide the rules of the game, it is up to the market to decide where and when the production of new energy facilities will take place". We suggest therefore that *market mechanisms* should be included in the framework of green loans.

For all the advances being made by green developments, the year 2021 saw a large rebound both in coal and oil usage and an increase in CO_2 emissions (GWEC, 2020). Price volatility and electricity high picks are likely to remain and even escalate in the next decade as demand for traditional energy sources is increasing while funding of new fossil fuel projects is discouraged by policymakers (Khasawneh et al., 2021). The hike in energy prices experienced during the winter of 2021 by many EU member states is a part of the political agenda of the European leaders (Swedish government, 2021).

From 1 January 2012, Sweden and Norway have had a common electricity certificates (EC) market. Together, the two countries decided to increase renewable electricity production by 46.4 TWh between 2012 and 2030. To make renewable electricity production in Sweden more cost-effective, the EC system has been introduced on 1 May 2003 replacing the earlier public grants and subsidy programs.

The EC system operates in such a way that electricity producers receive one EC unit from the Swedish state for each MWh of electricity that they produce from RE sources. The electricity producers are free to sell their certificates, thus generating extra revenue for their electricity production. Purchasers are Swedish or Norwegian parties that are required to purchase certificates corresponding to a certain proportion of their electricity sales or use, known as their quota obligation. If the purchaser is an electricity supplier, he passes on the cost of certificates as part of the price of electricity charged to his customers (SWEA, 2019a; SEA, 2020; Energimyndigheten, 2021).

One of the managers emphasized:

> There is a common misunderstanding that the state is subsidizing the production of RE in Sweden. This is not the case, however; the system is created with the help of market-based support. Your electricity price includes the cost of electricity certificates. For example, in 2020, the average cost of EC was 1.8 cents (öre) per kilowatt-hour, and when customers pay the electricity bill, they contribute to financing the development of RE. For banks, EC is an inseparable part of lending decisions that are based on cash flow valuation of the particular project.
>
> Renewable electricity producers are allocated electricity certificates by the state for a maximum of 15 years. Demand for the certificates is created by an obligation on electricity suppliers and others to buy and cancel electricity certificates in proportion to their electricity sales (quota obligation)

explained another banker.

The joint target of 46.4 TWh to be achieved in 2030 for Sweden and Norway has been accomplished already in March 2021. New wind power plants represented the largest part of the increase in capacity in both countries (SEA, 2020). The Swedish government suggested that the deadline for allocating new ECs with a so-called *stop mechanism* is set for 31 December 2021 (instead of 2030) (Swedish government, 2020). The principles for closing the system should be simple: new investments will not be granted support. SWEA (2019b) is very critical to the proposal, as the basic principle for the system to work is that there is a balance between supply and demand for ECs. The current stop mechanism will result in a collapse of certificate prices due to their oversupply.

> When the Swedish EC system will be abolished, the financial consequences will follow. Higher uncertainty about future prices will decrease secured revenues and increase off-taker risks. To reduce the negative impacts of the abolishment of the EC system, in my view, the Swedish government will be forced to elaborate the remuneration schemes to stabilize revenues. Without supporting market mechanisms, smaller actors might be removed from the wind power market due to the inability to get finance

concluded a top executive.

Green loans that have been issued by the Nordic Bank so far are based on the additional income received by the wind power projects from the existing EC system, which was introduced in 2003 and extended to include Norway in 2012. According to a proposal of the Swedish government to execute a stop mechanism for the EC system (Swedish government, 2020), the systematic credit risk of wind power project financings in Sweden will deteriorate. As reported by Dukan & Kitzing (2021), credit risk is increased in schemes that expose projects to volatile power prices, decreased levels of secured revenues, and greater revenue volatility.

One of the bankers pointed out:

> Certificates – both in Sweden and Norway – are traded on an open market, with the price being determined by supply and demand. The sizes of quota obligations are set by the Swedish and the Norwegian Act Concerning Electricity Certificates, and create

> the demand for certificates. If no quotas are set by the government, the system will be destroyed due to the absence of demand for certificates

pointed out a banker.

Finally, this contractual structure provides an efficient risk allocation amongst all project participants including contractors, off-takers, and technology suppliers allowing cash flow visibility over the long term with a high level of predictability for all participants. Long-term off-take agreements, called power purchase agreements (PPAs) seem to be a common feature in RE generation projects (Dukan & Kitzing, 2021).

> Banks have to apply market-based mechanisms such as corporate PPAs that have been successfully employed, alongside the Swedish certificates' support schemes. PPAs give the possibility to hedge the risk of price exposure, providing the required long-term revenue stability. Corporate PPAs, on the other hand, are alone insufficient to secure the magnitude of investment required to accelerate wind installations worldwide. The supporting mechanism from the government is also required

emphasized a banker.

The Needs of Society

The needs of society are the next factor that is included in the framework of green loans. This chapter suggests that the concept of green loans is not only related to corporate activities and financial sector actors but has a wider influence on the related infrastructure of the whole society (KPMG, 2021).

Sustainable development requires that society addresses many contradictory targets simultaneously. As an example, the energy sector is responsible for almost 75% of GHG emissions worldwide that have already caused visible impacts on weather and climate extremes (IEA, 2021a). Modern energy, on the other hand, is inseparable from the livelihood of a global population, with rising incomes pushing up the demand for energy services, and many developing economies navigating towards energy- and emissions-intensive periods of urbanization and industrialization. The global population without access to electricity continues to shrink, although 10% of the world's population still lacked electricity access in 2019 (REN21, 2021).

Commodity prices have rallied in 2021 as economic activity picked up recovering from a global pandemic, underlining that the affordability of energy remains a major concern for all stakeholders of society: households, businesses, and policymakers. Swedish consumers (electricity zone 3) with a variable electricity contract paid an average of 10.93 cents/kWh in 2020 and 62.82 cents/kWh in 2021.[7] Such a high pricing pick caused numerous debates in Sweden among various stakeholders on the sustainability of wind power investments from a societal perspective.

A decision-maker pointed out:

> According to statistics, global emissions have already pushed global average temperatures 1.1° C higher since the pre-industrial age. Whether it is sustainable to do a complete transformation of the energy system and how we produce, transport and consume energy in Sweden? Please, do not assume that I am against being careful with the environment and taking care of our planet. It is simply a question of the balance of

targets and costs to be paid [by society] to achieve them. I am not sure that all people have a full picture in mind.

Swedish electricity generation has historically been reliant on nuclear and hydropower and produces very little emissions. Sweden's high share of RE is due to the extensive use of biofuels in the industrial sector and for district heating generation, as well as a large share of electricity generation coming from hydropower. On the other hand, Sweden's electricity consumption is very high at approximately 12,600 kWh/annually per capita on average (WNA, 2021).

> Sweden is well suited for utilization of the RE system, not the least thanks to hydropower and our possibilities for importing when the wind is not blowing… But, being a developed country, Sweden consumes a lot of energy

pointed out a manager.

Although the referendum that took place in Sweden in 1980 decided for nuclear energy to be phased out by 2010, the future of present operating nuclear reactors is unclear. Additionally, in the neighboring countries to which Sweden's electricity system is directly connected, coal, oil, and gas still represent 48% of the electricity generation (SWEA, 2019a). Net-importing electricity strategy from these countries to Sweden might take away the environmental outcomes achieved within the Swedish borders.

It seems that today's investments and financings in society appear to be caught between two worlds: neither strong enough to satisfy current fossil fuel consumption trends nor diversified enough to meet tomorrow's clean energy goals (GWEC, 2020; IEA, 2021a).

Finally, societal priorities are changing. The Russian invasion of Ukraine in February 2022 has shaken up the US government to encourage additional output from shale producers; the UK is reviewing the timelines to phase out its remaining coal power plants; and Germany is considering extending the lifespans of its nuclear plants and several countries to cut petrol taxes (Karadima, 2022). The previously announced strategy toward green lending needs to accommodate the societal demand to wrest the countries free from dependency on Russian oil and natural gas.

In our view, the inclusion of the needs of society as a factor that impacts green lending seems to be motivated.

Development of Science and Technology

The final factor suggested impacting the development of a green loan term is the *development of science and technology*. According to the literature, whether the RE funding is based on public or private sources depends primarily on the maturity level of technologies or sectors (Elie et al., 2021).

Managers suggested that various checking points related to technology should be included in the analysis of the project. These are a few examples: "Is it a proven technology? Have previous projects that employed the technology experienced problems?" "It is important to ensure that the supplier of the equipment has a good track record… and [technical] expertise. If it is, for example, well-known companies like Siemens and Vestas, then the supplier risks are lower".

Wind energy has expanded by leaps and bounds in the last 20 years. It began the century as a niche energy source in Europe and the United States and, due to scientific inventions, ended in 2020 as a mainstream source of clean energy with 651 GW cumulative installed capacity around the world. From being rather expensive two decades ago, wind is today more cost-competitive than new-built coal or gas in about two-thirds of the world (GWEC, 2020). In 2020, the global weighted average cost of electricity from onshore wind power has fallen 56% since 2010 (REN21, 2021). This could make wind power the cheapest power source in the future (SWEA, 2019a; Ortegon et al., 2013).

In Northern Europe, offshore wind has shown the potential to provide significant amounts of clean energy, with generation costs already falling to the range of EUR 55 to EUR 70/MWh (a 65% reduction from 2015) (GWEC, 2020). In addition, turbine costs have decreased by around 30% since 2009 showing great progress in developing the technology. This has led to prices of delivering electricity might go as low as USD 0.04 per kWh (Deloitte, 2017).

> There is an example from September 2019 of procurement of the offshore projects in Great Britain with costs below EUR 45 per MWh, which is comparable to the cost of combined heat and power (CHP) in Sweden. Such an example gives hope for offshore wind power

pointed out a banker.

Although wind power is accounted for as one of the most competitive sources of electricity among all energy sources, three grand challenges in wind energy research should be solved by the scientific community: (1) improved understanding of the physics of atmospheric flow in the critical zone of wind power plant operation, (2) materials and system dynamics of individual wind turbines, and (3) optimization and control of fleets of wind plants comprising hundreds of individual generators working synergistically within the larger electric grid system (Veers et al., 2019).

There is a certain optimism among energy scholars that these fundamental questions will be solved; on the other hand, both the schedule and the amounts of the required funding to provide long-term sustainable solutions in the wind power industry remain to be uncertain.

One of the decision-makers concluded: "Our customers follow regularly the technological developments within the energy sector. Many solutions, like building a hydrogen factory, are yet to be tested to fully exploit the potential of the energy sector".

To sum up, science and technology seem to impact the development of the green loan term, mainly by enhancing the cost-benefit competitiveness of environmentally-friendly technologies.

Conclusion and Presentation of the Framework

This chapter focuses on the *green loan* term and factors that are suggested to impact its implementation/development. In line with previous studies (i.e., Zhang et al., 2019; Gilchrist et al., 2021), the paper defines green loans as bank lending designed to support environmentally responsible projects. Additionally, the loans at the Nordic Bank are accounted as green only after assurance is provided by the independent rating company.

The study demonstrates that environmental targets and considerations are increasingly incorporated into policies and financing agendas within financial institutions in Sweden. The inclusion of green factors in companies' analysis and credit assessment systems as well as improving the disclosure policy (see also Krömer, 2019) are currently happening in the Nordic Bank.

At the same time, the study shows that green loans seem to be a complex term that requires accounting for various factors (Khan et al., 2021). Searching for the answer to the question *When do bank loans become green?*, the chapter suggests a "green loans" framework,

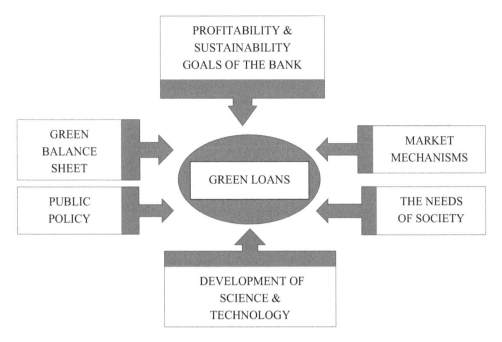

Figure 14.2 When do bank loans become green – the suggested framework

emphasizing the importance of six major factors/variables that have been identified in this study (see Figure 14.2).

Issuing green loans seems to be a complex process that demands long-term commitments from the financial industry to search for acceptable solutions on how to combine *the bank's profitability and sustainability targets*. Green loans are supposed to simultaneously combine the traditional profit-maximization goals with green returns that are (eventually) derived from green values (Sachs et al., 2019). This means that banks will need to take sustainability into account in their green lending strategies, assessment tools, risk management, and reporting. The challenges of definition and measurement of green values and respective returns however await further scientific clarifications.

Second, a green loan provides funding for a green asset (i.e., a bank cannot issue a green loan to finance the construction of an environmentally-unfriendly project). The traditional financial theory is based upon restrictive assumptions regarding capital structure, risks, returns, values, and investment outcomes. The Miller and Modigliani (1959) theorem state that sources of finance (equity or debt) do not impact the valuation of firms. Moreover, in traditional literature, finance commonly takes a passive role in what is being funded (Mazzucato & Semieniuk, 2018). The emergence of the green loan term can eventually impact some of the well-established assumptions in the finance literature. As an example, the bankers argued for the importance of which assets are being financed by the green loans and how to achieve a sustainable equilibrium in a *green balance sheet*.

Moreover, the recently emerged carbon price risk, a new form of political and technological risk, can impact the definition of green assets. Therefore, the loans that are currently classified as green might be assessed differently in the future as a result of the new trends in carbon risk evolution. The collection of narrative empirical data applied by financial institutions on quantitative and qualitative criteria associated with green lending from different countries belongs to the future research agenda.

Third, green loans are commonly related to *public policies* that have been allocated to promote the deployment of green investments, including regulatory instruments and fiscal incentives (Elie et al., 2021). Even if the profitability of wind power projects can be achieved in some environments/for a few sponsors without additional support, other domains need subsidy mechanisms to meet the requirements of the cost-benefit targets. Both in the academic literature and the interviews of the bankers, the lack of stable long-term public policies and supporting mechanisms appeared to be an important barrier deterring banks from funding the RE infrastructure (Hafner et al., 2020).

Fourth, *market mechanisms* are indeed closely related to public policies but still are suggested to be a separate factor that impacts the development of green lending. Due to the proposal of the Swedish government to execute a stop mechanism for the EC market mechanism system on 31 December 2021, the new investments will not be granted any support, and the systematic credit risk of the wind power project financings in Sweden will deteriorate. To meet the climate challenges, financiers must have confidence in the stability of the Swedish market. Additionally, to have competitive wind power, market conditions in Sweden should be similar to those in the other countries around the Baltic Sea, where part of the development and connection costs are state-funded (SWEA, 2019a).

Future research, in our view, should continue the investigation of the role of public policy and market mechanisms in securing the financing terms of green loans, their various risk-sharing arrangements, and possible cooperation schemes between private and public actors (see also Dukan & Kitzing, 2021). For decision-makers, the eventual impacts of policy instruments applied by governments on the amounts of funding that banks would be able to provide under these specific market mechanisms should be taken into consideration.

Fifth, a safe supply and availability of energy to support human lives and business developments are important to consider. Therefore, *the needs of society* are suggested to be enclosed in the proposed framework. Due to the high societal impact, close cooperation of various stakeholders is required to facilitate the uptake of green loans for the development of the climate-resilient energy sector. Assessments of various societal needs and contradictory sustainability targets await the attention of future accounting and finance scholars.

Finally, the real-world transition might involve surprises in terms of research discoveries, technologies, and human behaviors (IEA, 2021b). Although wind power is assessed as one of the most competitive sources of electricity among energy sources, the case study presents several grand challenges remaining in the wind sector (Veers et al., 2019). This chapter, therefore, suggests including *the development of science and technology* as a factor that impacts the development of green lending.

Searching for an answer to the question *When do bank loans become green?*, this chapter suggests six factors that are proposed to impact the implementation of green loans. Notwithstanding the initial stage of the framework's development, it could be a useful departure point for research and policy considerations regarding green loans.

Acknowledgments

The author expresses gratitude to the bankers that participated in interviews and shared their knowledge of green loans. Comments and improvements suggested by Anton Borell, Bino Catasus, Mikael Holmgren, Åsa Plesner, Nathalie Repenning, Andreas Sundström, Olaf Weber, and Niklas Wällstedt were found to be useful and relevant. Finally, the support provided by the editorial team of the "Routledge Handbook of Green Finance" is acknowledged.

Notes

1 The six major Nordic banks include Danske Bank, DNB ASA, Nordea Bank, Skandinaviska Enskilda Banken, Svenska Handelsbanken, and Swedbank. The 11 interviewed bankers are employed by the following departments: (1) project finance; (2) corporate banking; (3) credit and risk management; and (4) sustainability. The duration of interviews lasted between one and one and a half hours. All interviews were transcribed from the notes directly after the interviews had happened.
2 The social banks are defined through their membership in the Global Alliance for Banking on Values (GABV).
3 Despite a prevailing belief, RE is not a synonym for green or environmentally-clean energy, as it consists of non-polluting (e.g., wind, solar, and geothermal) and polluting (e.g., biomass and biofuel) types.
4 Scope 1 includes mandatory reporting on all sources of direct emissions where the organization has operational control. Scope 2 is a mandatory reporting on all indirect emissions where the organization has operational control. Scope 3 is an optional reporting of indirect emissions from the whole value chain.
5 Total Return $_{t+1}$ = (Price $_{t+1}$ − Price $_t$ + Dividend $_{t+1}$) / Price $_t$ + Green Return $_{t+1}$. The total return from a green investment (asset) is the sum of economic return (which is a change in price plus a dividend) plus a green return that derives from the green value (assuming the green value is recognized in advance). Source: Sachs et al., 2019, p. 44.
6 FIT is a policy that typically guarantees renewable generators specified payments per unit over a fixed period. REC is a certificate awarded to certify the generation of one unit of RE. Tendering is a procurement mechanism by which RE capacity is solicited from sellers, who offer bids at the lowest price that they would be willing to accept. Source: REN21, 2021.
7 Source: https://www.fortum.se.

References

Alonso, A. C. (2020). The role of the commercial banks in the financing of the renewable energy industry. In C. W. Donovan (Ed.), *Renewable energy finance: Funding the future of energy* (2nd ed., pp. 217–245). ProQuest Ebook Central.

Ballard, E. (2022, March 2). Sweden's SEB changes course on defense stocks as war tests ESG rules. *Wall Street Journal*. https://www.wsj.com/articles/swedens-seb-changes-course-on-defense-stocks-as-war-tests-esg-rules-11646253384

Björkholm, L., & Lehner, O. M. (2021). Nordic green bond issuers' views on the upcoming EU green bond standard. *ACRN Journal of Finance and Risk Perspectives*, *10*, 222–279. https://www.acrn-journals.eu/resources/jofrp10l.pdf

Bouma, J. J., Jeucken, M., & Klinkers, L. (Eds.). (2001). *Sustainable banking: The greening of finance*. E-book, Taylor & Francis Group.

Deloitte. (2017, August). *A market approach for valuing onshore wind farm assets: Global results* (9th ed.). https://www2.deloitte.com/content/dam/Deloitte/nl/Documents/energy-resources/deloitte-nl-er-valuing-onshore-wind-farm-assets-global-aug2017.pdf

Dukan, M., & Kitzing, L. (2021). The impact of auctions on financing conditions and cost of capital for wind energy projects. *Energy Policy*, *152*, 112197. https://doi.org/10.1016/j.enpol.2021.112197

Ehlers, T., Packer, F., & de Greiff, K. (2021). The pricing of carbon risk in syndicated loans: Which risks are priced and why? *Journal of Banking and Finance*, 136, 106180. https://doi.org/10.1016/j.jbankfin.2021.106180

Elie, L., Granier, C., & Rigot, S. (2021). The different types of renewable energy finance: A bibliometric Analysis. *Energy Economics*, *93*, 104997. https://doi.org/10.1016/j.eneco.2020.104997

Energimyndigheten. (2021). Elkundens bidrag till förnybar elproduktion.

Gilchrist, D., Yu, J., & Zhong, R. (2021). The limits of green finance: A survey of literature in the context of green bonds and green loans. *Sustainability*, *13*(478), 1–12. https://www.mdpi.com/2071-1050/13/2/478

Golubeva, O., Duljic, M., & Keminen, R. (2019). The impact of liquidity risk on bank profitability: Some empirical evidence from the European banks following the introduction of Basel III regulations. *Accounting and Management Information Systems*, *18*(4), 455–485. http://online-cig.ase.ro/jcig/art/18_4_1.pdf

Government Offices of Sweden. (2020). A platform for international sustainable business. Retrieved from https://view.officeapps.live.com/op/view.aspx?src=https%3A%2F%2Fwww.ohchr.org%2Fsites%2Fdefault%2Ffiles%2FDocuments%2FIssues%2FBusiness%2F2020Survey%2FStates%2FSweden.docx&wdOrigin=BROWSELINK

GWEC (Global Wind Energy Council). (2020). Global wind report 2019. Retrieved from https://gwec.net/wp-content/uploads/2020/08/Annual-Wind-Report_2019_digital_final_2r.pdf

Hafner, S., Jones, A., Anger-Kraavi, A., & Pohl, J. (2020). Closing the green finance gap – A systems perspective. *Environmental Innovation and Societal Transitions, 34*, 26–60. https://doi.org/10.1016/j.eist.2019.11.007

IEA. (2021a). World energy outlook 2021. Retrieved from https://www.iea.org/reports/world-energy-outlook-2021

IEA. (2021b). Net zero by 2050. A roadmap for the global energy sector. Retrieved from https://www.iea.org/reports/net-zero-by-2050

IFC. (2017). *Green Finance: A bottom-up approach to track existing flows.* International Finance Corporation, World Bank Group.

Jung, J., Herbohn, K., & Clarkson, P. (2018). Carbon risk, carbon risk awareness and the cost of debt financing. *Journal of Business Ethics, 150*(4), 1151–1171. https://doi.org/10.1007/s10551-016-3207-6

Karadima, S. (2022, March 28). What impact will the Russian invasion of Ukraine have on ESG investing? Report retrieved from https://www.investmentmonitor.ai/special-focus/ukraine-crisis/russian-invasion-ukraine-esg-investing/

Khan, M. A., Riaz, H., Ahmed, M., & Saeed, A. (2021). Does green finance really deliver what is expected? An empirical perspective. *Borsa Istanbul Review*, 22(3), 586–593. https://doi.org/10.1016/j.bir.2021.07.006

Khasawneh, R., Tan, F., & Paul, S. (2021, September 21). *Lack of investment, more demand to drive oil price volatility.* Reuters.

KPMG. (2021). Sustainable finance & responsible banking on top of the agenda. Retrieved January 30, 2021, from https://home.kpmg/se

Krömer, S. (2019). Model risk regarding monthly wind energy production for the valuation of a wind farm investment. *International Journal of Energy Sector Management, 13*(4), 862–884. https://doi.org/10.1108/IJESM-10-2018-0010

Loan Market Association. (2018). Green loan principles. Supporting environmentally sustainable economic activity. Retrieved from https://www.lma.eu.com/sustainable-lending

Mazzucato, M., & Semieniuk, G. (2018). Financing renewable energy: Who is financing what and why it matters. *Technological Forecasting and Social Change, 127*, 8–22. https://doi.org/10.1016/j.techfore.2017.05.021

Modigliani, F., & Miller, M. H. (1959). Cost of capital, corporation finance, and the theory of investment. *American Economic Review, 49*, 655–669. https://www.jstor.org/stable/1809766

Öbrink, A. (2021, December 29). Splittring i elpolitiken – Partierna oense om hur elen ska produceras, SVT Nyheter.

Ortegon, K., Nies, L. F., & Sutherland, J. W. (2013). Preparing for end of service life of wind turbines. *Journal of Cleaner Production, 39*, 191–199. https://doi.org/10.1016/j.jclepro.2012.08.022

REN21. (2021). *Renewables 2021.* Global Status Report. Paris: REN21 Secretariat.

Rydström, A. (2021, December). Miljöpolitiken skadar Sverige till ingen nytta. *Den nya välfärden.*

Sachs, J. D., Woo, W. T., Yoshino, N., & Taghizadeh-Hesary, F. (Eds.). (2019). *Handbook of green finance: Energy security and sustainable development.* Springer. https://link.springer.com/referencework/10.1007/978-981-13-0227-5

SEA (Swedish Energy Agency). (2020). *The Swedish–Norwegian electricity certificate market* [annual report].

SWEA (Swedish Wind Energy Association). (2019a, October). 100 per cent renewable electricity by 2040 wind power: Combating climate change and improving competitiveness.

SWEA (Swedish Wind Energy Association). (2019b, August 20). Swedish government proposes effectless "stop mechanism" in the electricity certificate system [press release].

Swedish Government. (2020, August 13). Elcertifikatssystemet fasas ut. Pressmeddelande från Infrastrukturdepartementet.

Swedish Government. (2021, October 21). Government.se: Covid-19, migration and energy prices on the agenda of the EU Summit.

Taghizadeh-Hesary, F., & Yoshino, N. (2019). The way to induce private participation in green finance and investment. *Finance Research Letters, 31*, 98–103. https://doi.org/10.1016/j.frl.2019.04.016

Tang, D. Y., & Zhang, Y. (2020). Do shareholders benefit from green bonds? *Journal of Corporate Finance*, *61*, 101427. https://doi.org/10.1016/j.jcorpfin.2018.12.001

Torvanger, A., Maltais, A., & Marginean, I. (2021). Green bonds in Sweden and Norway: What are the success factors? *Journal of Cleaner Production*, *324*, 129177. https://doi.org/10.1016/j.jclepro.2021.129177

Veers, P., Dykes, K., Lantz, E., Barth, S., Bottasso, C. L., Carlson, O., Clifton, A., Green, J., Green, P., Holttinen, H., Laird, D., Lehtomäki, V., Lundquist, J. K., Manwell, J., Marquis, M., Meneveau, C., Moriarty, P., Munduate, X., Muskulus, M., Naughton, J., Pao, L., Paquette, J., Peinke, J., Robertson, A., Rodrigo, J. S., Sempreviva, A. M., Smith, J. C., Tuohy, A., & Wise, R. (2019). Renewable energy: Grand challenges in the science of wind energy. *Science*, *366*(6464), eaau2027, 1–9. https://www.science.org/doi/10.1126/science.aau2027

Wang, M., Li, X., & Wang, S. (2021). Discovering research trends and opportunities of green finance and energy policy: A data-driven scientometric analysis. *Energy Policy*, *154*, 112295. https://doi.org/10.1016/j.enpol.2021.112295

Weber, O. (2016). Social banks' mission and finance. In O. M. Lehner (Ed.), *Routledge handbook of social and sustainable finance* (pp. 467–479). Routledge. https://doi.org/10.4324/9781315772578

WNA (World Nuclear Association). (2021). Nuclear power in Sweden. Retrieved from https://www.world-nuclear.org/information-library/country-profiles/countries-o-s/sweden.aspx

Zhang, D., Zhang, Z., & Managi, S. (2019). A bibliometric analysis on green finance: Current status, development, and future directions. *Finance Research Letters*, *29*, 425–430. https://doi.org/10.1016/j.frl.2019.02.003

15
PUBLIC POLICY AND GREEN FINANCE IN CHINA

Andrew C. Worthington and Dong Xiang

Introduction

Green finance is an extremely broad concept in that it includes any finance-related initiative, process, product, or service that is either designed to protect the natural environment or to manage how finance and investment affect the environment (Chartered Banker Institute, 2022). Green finance products and services therefore include those that channel capital to green industry; those that design the product to reward environmentally friendly activity; and those that support the effective management of the physical and transition risks associated with climate change and the low-carbon economy. Green finance also includes knowledge that informs the conduct of green finance, including environmental information disclosure guidelines and mandates regarding company reports, company environmental ratings, and environmental requirements for lending set for banks and other financial institutions set by regulators. Given their nature, the most common green finance industry sectors comprise renewable energy production; distribution and storage; energy efficiency in domestic and industrial buildings; green transport; recycling; pollution prevention; water and biodiversity conservation; and forestation, the sustainable use of natural resources, and land and circular economy initiatives.

Green finance is already growing strongly. For the United Nations, green financing plays an important role in delivering several of its Sustainable Development Goals (SDGs), working with public and private sector organizations to align international financial systems to a sustainable development agenda. As an example, many of the world's largest banks and insurers are members of the United Nations Environment Programme Finance Initiative (UNEP FI) aimed at implementing its Principles for Responsible Banking and Principles for Sustainable Insurance. This mirrors similar green finance initiatives in most countries. In the United Kingdom, for example, since September 2021, more than £18 billion from the sale of green gilts and savings bonds has been raised through National Savings and Investments, a state-owned savings bank, to support projects with clearly defined environmental benefits. In the United States, climate finance mostly aimed at renewable energy production now averages US $74 billion a year, a more than threefold increase since 2014. And the green bond market has grown to over US $100 billion of bonds issued annually, with many countries now beginning to issue sovereign green bonds, the first by Poland in 2016, followed by France, Fiji, Nigeria, Indonesia, and Belgium. Nonetheless, there is much potential for growth remaining, with the World Economic Forum estimating that about US $5.7 trillion is needed to be invested annually in green infrastructure alone in the years ahead, much of which will be in the developing world and by and for the private sector.

Within this, China has very quickly become the world's largest green finance market, with about CN ¥11 trillion (about US $1.8 trillion) in green credit and about CN ¥1 trillion (about US $190 billion) in green bonds, second only to the United States. This well meets the Chinese government's objective for China to achieve carbon neutrality by 2060, which is estimated to require an investment of CN ¥104–487 trillion over the next 30 years, and this has duly placed public policy at the fore of these developments (Moody's Analytics, 2021). However, despite breakneck growth, China needs to build a unified system for green finance and to enhance incentives and disclosure, and this appears important as there are differences in the approach taken to green finance by various departments and inconsistencies with nongovernment developments (International Institute for Sustainable Development, 2015). These particularly contrast with efforts in other countries and the inconsistency in standards. For example, the definition of a green bond in China is only now starting to approximate the definition used in most other countries. It is then unclear whether the approach taken to green finance is only appropriate for it or is also applicable to other countries (Dezan Shira & Associates, 2022).

It is clear to even the casual observer that unlike the bottom-up approach to green finance evident in developed economies, with its emphasis on market innovation, the approach taken in China is very much top-down, with an emphasis on the formulation of public policy and its implementation through a state-controlled bank-centered financial system. Accordingly, the purpose of this chapter is to analyze the evolution of green finance in China from a public policy theory perspective. Aligning the formulation of policy with existing public policy theories will enable us to rigorously evaluate the strengths and weaknesses of the approach taken with the alternative formulations of public policy used in developed and developing countries alike. The remainder of the chapter is structured as follows. The second section briefly reviews the state of play of green finance in China. The third section presents the various public policy theories that can potentially explain the approach taken by China. This is especially important in that while in all economies public policy has played a key role alongside the private sector in moving toward the green financial system, different approaches have been employed with varying emphasis on public or private sector endeavors. The fourth section tracks the evolution of green finance policy in China using the history of specific and actionable policy, and the fifth section seeks to reconcile China's green finance policy with the public policy theories presented earlier. The final section concludes.

Green Finance in China

China's central bank, the People's Bank of China (PBOC) defines green finance as all economic activities used to support environmental improvement, address climate change, and enhance resource conservation and efficient use, that is, energy conservation and environmental protection, clean production, clean energy, ecological environment, infrastructure green upgrade, and green financial services provided in the fields of project investment and financing, project operation, and risk management (Dikau & Volz, 2021). In what follows, we briefly outline the features of the four main green finance segments as they currently exist in China, namely, green credit, green bonds, environmental information disclosure, and carbon finance.

The overarching policy goal for green finance in China has been its objectives to achieve peak carbon emissions by 2030 and carbon neutrality (more precisely, net-zero of all six types of greenhouse gas emissions) by 2060, the so-called "Dual Carbon goals" (Chen, 2021). This in turn rests on "three functions" and "five pillars" supporting the green finance efforts of the

PBOC (2016a, 2016b, 2017, 2018, 2020, 2021a, 2021b) as the primary institution for green policy development and implementation in China (Chen, 2021). The three functions are resource allocation, risk management, and market pricing. First, the PBOC aims to guide financial resources to support low-carbon, green transformation, carbon capture and sequestration, and other green projects by means of monetary, credit, and regulatory policies, mandatory disclosure, green evaluation, industry self-regulation, and product innovation. Second, the PBOC will use tools such as climate-related risk stress testing, environmental and climate risk analysis, and risk weight adjustment of green and other assets to enhance the capability of the financial system to manage climate-related risks. Finally, the PBOC aims to facilitate the building of a national carbon emission exchange market, help develop derivatives such as carbon futures, and price carbon emissions through trading schemes.

For their part, the five pillars of green finance in China are as follows. First, to accelerate the establishment of a green financial standard system. Second, to strengthen information disclosure requirements and financial institution supervision. Third, to improve the incentive and restraint mechanism by guiding financial institutions to increase green asset allocation and strengthen environmental risk management. Fourth, to foster green financial products and the market system through product innovation, issuance, standardized transaction procedures, and better transparency. Finally, to expand international cooperation in green finance using various multilateral and bilateral platforms and cooperation mechanisms to promote exchange and enhance the international community's recognition and participation in green finance policies, standards, products, and markets in China (Chen, 2021).

Green Credit

Green credit (or loans) refers to the practice of banks considering not only economic benefits but also environmental factors in the credit issuance process and making appropriate loan decisions on this basis (Harper Ho, 2018). This contrasts with so-called conventional "black credit" where environmental factors, if not ignored, are given far less weight in the credit assessment process. According to the PBOC, by the end of 2021, the green loan balance in China was CN¥15.9 trillion or some 8.3% of total credit. While only a small share of total credit, but more than 90% of total green finance, green credit in China increased by 33% over the previous five years, exceeding the 21.5% growth rate of total loans. Further, in terms of asset quality, the nonperforming loan ratio of green credit has remained below 0.7% over the past five years, significantly lower than that of ordinary loans.

According to the proportion of credit funds to total investment in green projects, the green credit of China's 21 major banks support the saving of more than 400 million tons of standard coal and the emission of more than 700 million tons of carbon dioxide equivalent each year. Primarily, green credit in China is invested in the green upgrade of infrastructure and clean energy loans, accounting for 46.5% and 26.5% of total green credit respectively by the end of 2021. According to the China Banking and Insurance Regulatory Commission (CBIRC), China's banking and insurance regulator, key sectors for green credits include transportation (37%), emerging industries (21%), renewable energy (20%), and industrial energy-saving (5%) (CBIRC, 2013)

Starting in 2018, financial institutions have been assessed internally by the PBOC based on the amount, percentage, increase, and other criteria for their green credit granted (Harper Ho, 2018). As a result, many Chinese banks have set decarbonization targets for themselves and percentage targets for green credit. In terms of the most recent policy developments, in November 2021 the PBOC rolled out decarbonization support whereby it would provide banks with low-cost loans to cover part of the loans that the bank had granted to borrowers for decarbonization projects, with the PBOC yet to set an upper limit on this subsidized lending. In addition, the PBOC rolled out another targeted re-lending program for the clean and efficient use of coal, currently capped at CN ¥200 billion (Harper Ho, 2018).

Green Bonds

Green bonds are like ordinary bonds expect that the funds raised finance new and existing projects offering climate change and environmental benefits. As shown in Table 15.1, in the first half of 2021, the domestic green bond market in China was on the rise, with 198 new green-labeled bonds issued, with an issuance size of about CN ¥243.1 billion, a year-on-year increase of 118% (Climate Bonds Report, 2021). In terms of green bond issuance types, green debt financing instruments dominate the green bond market, followed by green corporate bonds and green financial bonds. Judging from the number of green bond issuances, clean energy and clean transportation are the main areas where green bond funds are raised. However, green bonds represent only a small part of green finance in China. By the end of June 2021, there were CN ¥1.73 trillion of Chinese green bonds on issue domestically and abroad. Most of these were domestically issued by state-owned enterprises (Climate Bonds Report, 2021).

In the first half of 2021, under the national strategic goals of "carbon peaking, carbon neutrality" and "rural revitalization", regulatory authorities and market institutions in China actively innovated their green bond products and successively launched "carbon-neutral bonds", "green rural revitalization", "green bonds", and "sustainability linked bonds" (being a bond instrument where issuers commit explicitly to future improvements in sustainability outcomes within a pre-defined timeline). As one consequence, from the perspective of regional issuance activity, there are more green bond issuances in richer regions of China and those with strong green bond support policies and where market participation is high.

Of the green bonds issued in 2021, 59% served multiple purposes (such as transportation, energy production, and energy-saving), while 13% were issued specifically for clean energy projects, and 11% were for clean transportation In March 2021, China's National Association of Financial Market Institutional Investors issued a circular on carbon-neutral bonds (Xueqing, 2021, 2022). Carbon-neutral bonds should satisfy requirements on project selection, use of proceeds, and information disclosure. Based on public information, it was found that most of the

Table 15.1 China's green bond market, 2020–2021

Type	Issues (No.)			Value (CN¥ billion)		
	2021	*2020*	*Δ%*	*2021*	*2020*	*Δ%*
Green local government bonds	0	1	−100	0	27	−100
Green financial bonds	13	5	160	394	132	198
Green asset-backed securities	14	12	17	216	129	67
Green financial bonds	16	20	−20	188	226	−17
Green corporate bonds	54	44	23	470	354	33
Green debt financing	101	23	339	1163	247	370
Total	198	105	89	2431	1115	118

carbon-neutral bonds had lower interest rates than other bonds issued around the same time, although that was not a requirement of the circular.

Environmental Information Disclosure

One of the most significant aspects of China's green finance system has been improving green financial standards, with China issuing multiple green finance-related industry standards in recent years. Although not mandatory, these standards serve as guidelines and aim at institutional capacity building for the green finance system. In terms of the most recent developments, in July 2021, the PBOC (2021) released the Financial Institutions Environmental Information Disclosure Guideline to guide how financial institutions should disclose environmental information in a standardized and structured way. Table 15.2 outlines the principal requirements of each element in these guidelines.

Table 15.2 Environmental information disclosure framework

Disclosure method		Specialized Environmental Information Disclosure Report, Annual Social Responsibility Report, Annual Report
Disclosure frequency		At least once a year
Qualitative indicators	Annual overview	Environment-related goals, visions, strategic plans, policies, actions, and key achievements during the reporting year
	Governance structure	At the board level: the status of green finance-related committees and the strategic planning and supervision of environment-related risks and opportunities
	Policy system	Senior management level: the setting of green finance-related management positions or internal institutions, the main responsibilities and reporting routes of the management positions or internal institutions
	Product and service innovation	Professional departments: the situation and results of the implementation of green finance-related work
	Risk management process	Internal management systems related to the environment, especially new policies and measures implemented during the reporting year;
	Green finance innovation and research results	Implement the environmental policies, regulations, and standards of the country and region related to the bank
Quantitative targets	The impact of environmental factors on the organization	Comply with the adoption of bank-related international conventions, frameworks, initiatives, etc. on climate and the environment
	Environmental impacts of investment and financing activities	The basic information of innovative products or services, including name, innovation point, operation scope of operation mode, etc.
	Environmental impact of business activities	Environmental and social benefits of innovative products or services

At the same time, the PBOC released the Environmental Rights Financing Tools, which sets out the general requirements and process of financing based on environmental rights, including the rights to discharge pollutants, emit emissions, and use water and energy. Very recently, in June 2022, the CBIRC issued its Banking and Insurance Sector Green Finance Guidelines. This is the first policy document in China specifically to use the notion of environmental, social, and governance (ESG) and effectively requested that banks and insurance agencies incorporate the concept of ESG into their lending and investing. For example, banks and insurance agencies are required to identify, monitor, and prevent ESG risks, enhance ESG disclosure and stakeholder participation, require their contracts to include terms to elevate the ESG performance of their clients, and conduct ESG due diligence as part of their investment decision-making. The Asset Management Association of China (2018) has also issued green investment guidelines for its members.

Carbon Finance

At present, carbon financial products as part of green finance in China comprise carbon market trading and financing tools. The history of China's participation in carbon emissions control operates across three public policy stages. The first and most important is associated with China's signing of the Paris Agreement in 2016 and its commitment to achieve peak carbon emissions by 2030 and carbon neutrality by 2060. This has since been officially confirmed in a revised 2030 pledge, although it still does not specify the peak date. As discussed, it is China's commitments around its Dual Carbon (or so-called 30–60) goals that provide the policy basis for all green finance in China (Carbon Brief, 2021; Herbert Smith Freehills, 2022).

The second stage of carbon financing in China served to promote carbon trading pilots in some regions and selected industries. However, as some of these pilot programs have been in place since 2013, it therefore predates China's international commitments under the Paris Agreement. In terms of regions, eight provinces and cities including Shenzhen, Beijing, and Shanghai were selected to carry out carbon transactions, covering eight high energy-consuming industries represented by power generation, chemical, and papermaking. In terms of quotas, most of these regions adopted a combination of free allocation and paid bidding. After a successful pilot, China began to prepare for the spot trading of national carbon emission allowances in 2017, which is expected to cover a wider range of regions and industries, with the Chinese national carbon market entering full operation in July 2021

The final and most recent policy stage relates to new forms of climate or carbon finance products being developed. Once again, while most of these changes have been very recent, as early as 2016 the Beijing Green Exchange released contract templates for carbon asset repurchases, swaps, and options for use in the future pilot and national carbon markets. Most recently, in October 2020 five central government departments jointly issued the Guiding Opinions on Promoting the Investment and Financing in Response to Climate Change. This clarified that climate finance was part of green finance and that climate finance should benefit both climate mitigation and climate adaptation activities.

Subsequently, in December 2021, nine central government departments jointly issued the Climate Investment and Financing Pilot Working Program. This encouraged financial institutions in China's climate finance pilot cities (now more than 30 cities), to explore carbon-related financial products and services, including carbon funds, the pledging of carbon assets, and carbon insurance. Pilot cities were also required to limit the development of high carbon emissions emitting industries and enhance carbon accounting and disclosure. As an example of one of the financing tools, under this policy companies can mortgage the carbon allowances they receive to banks to obtain financing. While there are currently no national rules allowing the mortgaging of carbon allowances in China's national carbon market, some rules have been implemented in the local carbon market pilots, including in Guangdong, Shanghai, and Tianjin. Most recently, in April 2022, the China Securities Regulatory Commission (CSRC, 2017) released its carbon financial products, which defined carbon financial products and classified them into carbon market financing, carbon market trading (derivatives), and carbon market support tools.

Theories of Public Policy Change

Political scientists have developed several theories for explaining policy change—referring to modifications (often incremental amendments, sometimes major reforms) in existing institutional or market structures or new and innovative policies. This section briefly reviews the main theoretical approaches to policy change. The purpose is to develop a theoretical background against which we can evaluate the policy changes we discuss in the following section relating to green finance in China in a rigorous way. We discuss the following theories: path dependence, advocacy coalition framework, policy learning, policy diffusion, punctuated equilibrium, institutional change, multilevel governance, policy networks, disruptive innovation, and the politics of change and reform (Cerna, 2013). Of course, it may not be possible to precisely link the theory and practice of public policy as it relates to green finance policy in China, let alone a single theory. Nonetheless, it does offer useful insights from a discipline, including its terminology, not well known among finance researchers and practitioners, and a way to systematically understand how public policy may evolve.

Path dependence theory argues that policy change is difficult because institutions are sticky, and actors within these institutions, however defined, protect the existing model through policy. This implies that policy continuity is much more likely than change and that once a government or government agency sets down a certain policy path, it will require increasingly greater efforts and costs by actors setting out to achieve change. Path dependence suggests that policymakers work within a series of limited assumptions about their world, that they often do not learn from experience, and that they emphasize caution in their decision-making processes. However, this does not suggest that there will be no change, only those changes are slower and smaller than what they would be otherwise. From time to time, critical junctures will appear that allow more substantive and rapid change, but it is not easy to show when and under circumstances these critical junctures will arise. The main contribution of this theory is to show why public policy may change only slowly and predictably, but when it does, unexpectedly.

Advocacy coalition framework theory asserts that public policy is the outcome of a policy sub-system composed of different advocacy coalitions, each with its own beliefs, resources, and strategies. Policy changes then occur through interactions between wide external changes or shocks to the political system and the success of the ideas in these coalitions, which may cause actors in the advocacy coalition to shift coalitions. Stable system parameters influence external system events. But there are also more dynamic factors present within the system, which entail the principal sources of policy change. Both stable and dynamic factors impact the constraints and resources of sub-system actors, and policy brokers are concerned with keeping the level of political conflict within acceptable limits and reaching a reasonable solution to the problem. The main contribution of this theory is that the concept of a policy sub-system serves as a basis for developing a theory of policy change by relating it to the larger political system and viewing coalitions (rather than formal organizations or free-floating actors) as the key units of internal policy structure.

Policy learning theory has a strong connection to some of the other public policy theories, including the advocacy coalition framework. The main premise of this theory is that actors and coalitions of actors learn from the experiences of others in formulating public policy. So, countries, regions, and systems change policies by learning from other countries, regions, and systems. This can involve learning about organizations, learning about programs, and learning about policies. The main contribution is that policy changes occur when individuals, coalitions, and policymakers see policy change elsewhere, and look to implement this change in their own system. For this reason, change will necessarily reflect policy in other contexts, especially internationally.

Like policy learning, *policy diffusion theory* is a process in which policy innovations spread from one government to another. In other words, knowledge about policies, administrative arrangements, and institutions in one time and/or place applies to the development of policies, administrative arrangements, and institutions in another time and/or place. According to Shipan and Volden (2008), there are four mechanisms for policy diffusion: learning from earlier adopters, economic competition, imitation, and coercion. First, policymakers can learn from the experiences of other governments: if an adopted policy elsewhere is successful, then another country/system might also implement it. Second, economic competition results from policymakers considering the economic effects of the adoption or not of policy considering economic spillovers. Third, imitation involves merely copying the policy of the other government. Finally, unlike the other three which are voluntary, policy diffusion can be coercive in that countries can coerce one another into policy change through trade practices or economic sanctions, either directly or through international organizations

Another model of policy change is *punctuated equilibrium theory* which proposes that once an idea gets attention it will expand rapidly and become unstoppable. Many ideas are competing for attention, but then something happens at some point to bring a particular idea to the fore. The process typically comes about from external events that disrupt the political system, particularly those large enough to disrupt or punctuate its equilibrium. So punctuated equilibrium theory is the interaction of beliefs and values concerning policy (termed policy images) with the existing set of political institutions (venues of policy action). It thus explains both prolonged periods of extreme stability and short periods of rapid policy change.

Institutional change theory relates to the overlap between institutions and policy. So, when institutions change, policy will change with them. Within this, there are five distinct types of change: displacement, layering, drift, conversion, and exhaustion. Displacement arises when new institutions and their associated behavioral logics push traditional arrangements to the side. Layering involves the active sponsorship of amendments, additions, or revisions to an existing set of institutions. Drift suggests institutions are subject to erosion or atrophy if they do not adapt to changing political and economic environment. Institutions can also move to new goals, functions, or purposes through conversion. This can be because of new environmental challenges or through changes in power relations or political contestation over what functions and purposes an existing institution should serve. Lastly, exhaustion is a process that leads to breakdown and can happen when the normal working of an institution undermines its external preconditions and there is an erosion of resources.

Multilevel governance theory argues that policymaking becomes increasingly complex where actors move between various levels of action and authority disperses across multiple tiers (i.e., national, regional, or local). Top-down processes mean that policy decisions from the national level pass to lower levels, while bottom-up processes refer to the involvement of the local level in policymaking and its impact on higher levels. In this theory, policy change is usually costly and therefore unusual as it mostly involves reallocating policy functions across various levels of government.

Policy network theory is where diverse groups form an expansive but loosely coupled network that is bound by a collective identity or purpose. For this reason, this theory is useful in highlighting complex interactions between stakeholders (in both the public and private sectors), potentially spanning many actors. This can appear as a coalition, but these networks are more fluid and can develop over time into an institutionalized structure. In fact, it can be difficult to identify a policy network until the policy change manifests itself.

Disruptive innovation theory involves radical policy change and draws on disruptive innovation in products and services as the main driver. Disruptive innovation describes the process by which a product or service initially takes root in simple applications at the bottom of a market—typically by being less expensive and more accessible—and then relentlessly moves upmarket, eventually displacing established competitors. This can have a significant impact on industrial structures and has often led to social change in the process, even if unintended. This provides a powerful explanation for policy change across a wide range of areas as policymakers and others look to catch up with these changes in creating policy, laws, and institutions to regulate and control these innovations.

Finally, the *politics of policy change and reform theory* asserts that politics affects the origins, formulation, and implementation of public policy especially when significant changes are involved. Broad reforms are then only possible when there is sufficient political will and when capable planners and managers design and implement changes to a sector or economy. This is important because politics represents a selection of values that express a particular view of society; policy change and reform have distinct distributional consequences in the allocation of benefits and costs; reform promotes competition among groups that seek to influence consequences; the enactment or non-enactment of reform is often associated with political events or crises, and so reform can have significant consequences for a regime's political stability. Within this, it may be possible for policy change to arise through sheer political will, through serving the desires of diverse groups (interest groups, political parties), or as political survival where governments manipulate policies to ensure the personal political survival or personal interests of political leaders.

The list of these various theories of policy change is not exhaustive. Each theory also has its own strengths and weaknesses, and their applicability differs widely across policy areas, the extent of change, and the chosen time and context. Problematically, the theories seem better able to explain change in the past rather than predict change in the future based on certain conditions. It might simply not be possible for these theories to be applicable across all policy areas, times, and contexts, as different conditions are usually present. Therefore, it seems reasonable to mix and match convincing elements of some if not several of these theories, depending on the policy area and context.

Evolution of Green Finance Policy in China

The notion of "green finance" originated in Western developed economies in the 1970s. However, it was not until the mid-2000s that the practice of green finance began to receive some practical attention and public policy traction in China. And it is only since the early 2010s that the Chinese central government has introduced a range of top-down mechanisms to define green investments and financing, encourage the development of green financial products and services, and create a supervisory and regulatory framework for financial institutions to play a role in implementing green finance policy. These have been guided and controlled by the overarching goals of the central government in its 12th (2011–2013), 13th (2016–2020), and 14th (2102–2025) Five-Year Plans, which at their core entail the promotion of green and low-carbon development, including China's international commitments to addressing climate change. Table 15.3 outlines the main green finance policies implemented in China over this period.

The main impact of these policies was to impose tougher regulatory oversight of China's financial institutions and to specifically instruct due diligence and monitoring of their own and their clients' environmental risk. The primary regulators are the CBIRC as China's bank-

Table 15.3 Timing of green finance policies in China

Year	Policy	Details
Pre-2015	Opinions on Printing and Distributing Environmental Protection Policies and Regulations to Prevent Credit Risks	Ministry of Environment, People's Republic of China (2007)
	Notice on Issuing Green Credit Guidelines	CBRC (2012)
	Opinions on Green Credit Work	CBIRC (2013)
	Common Commitment to Green Credit in China's Banking Industry	Chen (2013)
	Notice on Key Evaluation Indicators of Green Credit Implementation	CBRC (2014)
2015	Overall Plan for Ecological Civilization System Reform	Central Committee of the Communist Party of China (2015)
	Green Bond Issuance Guidelines	National Development and Reform Commission (2015)
2016	Guiding Opinions on Building a Green Financial System	PBOC (2016)
	Green finance included in the 13th Five-Year Plan	–
2017	Financial Industry Standardization System Construction and Development Plan (2016–2020)	PBOC (2017)
	Implementation Plan for Green Bank Evaluation in China's Banking Industry	CBA (2017)
2018	Green Investment Guidelines for Ecological Civilization written into the Constitution	Central People's Government of the People's Republic of China (2018), Hanson (2019)
	Notice on Establishing a Special Statistical System for Green Loans	PBOC (2018)
2019	Green Industry Guidance Catalogue	National Development and Reform Commission (2019)
	Guiding Opinions of the CBIRC on Promoting the High-Quality Development of the Banking and Insurance Industry	China Association of Bank Insurance Regulators (2019)
2020	Guiding Opinions on Promoting Investment and Financing to Address Climate Change	Ministry of Ecology and Environment of the People's Republic of China (2020)
	Guiding Opinions on Building a Modern Environmental Governance System	Central People's Government of the People's Republic of China (2020)
2021	Guiding Opinions on Accelerating the Establishment and Improvement of a Green, Low-Carbon, and Circular Development Economic System	Central People's Government of the People's Republic of China (2021)

ing regulator—and until 2018, its predecessor the China Banking Regulatory Commission (CBRC)—and China's central bank, the PBOC. Until 2018, the regulators also included the National Development and Reform Commission (NDRC) which was responsible for both national development and the Chinese response to climate change. It also implemented policy for energy efficiency credits and green bonds and in partnership with the CBRC and other departments and agencies, especially the Ministry of Environmental Protection (MEP), issued green finance guidance. Subsequently, the Ministry of Ecology and Environment (MEE) as the successor of the MEP assumed responsibility for Chinese climate change policy from the NDRC. In addition, a wide variety of industrial and accounting associations provide guidance and voluntary standards for green finance in business (Ministry of Ecology and Environment and All-China Federation of Industry and Commerce, 2018).

The key mechanism through which this has worked is China's banks. Under a reform schedule starting in the 1990s until 2006, the Chinese banking sector underwent rapid commercialization and capitalization, and heightened exposure to international and domestic competition. There were also significant liberalizations regarding the controls on interest rates and lending. During this time, the five largest state-owned banks all converted to state-owned commercial banks through a partial privatization process, including the taking on of minority foreign ownership, and listing on the Shanghai and Hong Kong stock exchanges. However, the state remains the controlling shareholder for all of China's Big-Five banks, namely, the Bank of China, the Construction Bank of China, the Agricultural Bank of China, the Industrial and Commercial Bank of China, and the Bank of Communications, and controls all but three of the top-tier joint-stock commercial banks through its Ministry of Finance.

Returning to policy, as an early example, in 2005, the ICBC alongside the Shanghai Pudong Development Bank cooperated with the International Finance Corporation (IFC) on several energy efficiency financing projects, introducing the concept of green finance into commercial banks, and the development of green finance in China. Subsequently, in 2007, the State Environmental Protection Agency (SEPA), as the predecessor of the MEE, the CBRC, and the POBC jointly issued the first green policies directed at improving environmental oversight in China's banks. The guidance directed banks to incorporate environmental due diligence into credit management and to ensure compliance with environmental regulations. The guidance also imposed responsibility for violations of the guidance on financial institutions and encouraged them to direct finance to projects with better environmental performance.

Another major development during this pre-2015 phase of green finance policy implementation was in 2012 when the CBRC issued green credit guidelines aiming to encourage all banking institutions to develop green credit and adopt stronger environmental and social risk management. Key provisions included that banks should:

- Effectively identify, measure, monitor, and control environmental and social risks associated with their credit activities; establish environmental and social risk management systems; and improve relevant credit policies and process management.
- Make public their green credit strategies and policies, and fully disclose developments of their green credit business.
- Establish and constantly improve the policies, systems, and processes for environmental and social risk management and identify the directions and priority areas for green credit support.
- Strengthen due diligence in credit granting.
- Perform overall green credit evaluations at least once every two years and submit the self-evaluation reports to competent banking supervisory authorities.

Subsequently, the CBRC introduced the green credit key performance indicators (KPIs) in 2014 to strengthen the monitoring and evaluation of green banking using these guidelines. The then CBRC also introduced its "Green Credit Implementation Key Audit Standards" to guide banks in applying the "Green Credit Guidelines", and while soft standards rather than clear mandates, these allowed the now CBIRC to assess bank compliance and apply to all policy and state-owned and joint-stock commercial banks in China. All these institutions must conduct annual self-audits and submit an annual audit report to the CBIRC, indicating the degree to which they comply with each of the standards.

The next major phase in green finance policy in China came in 2015 when the PBOC in conjunction with the United Nations Environment Programme Finance Initiative—a global partnership between the United Nations Environment Program and the global financial sector—established an initial template for green finance policy in China entitled "Establishing China's Green Financial System". This expanded on the green finance policies first introduced in 2007 to now cover 14 different initiatives, including green credit, green listing, carbon trading, and mandatory green insurance programs, as well as plans to develop or expand green ratings, green indices, and mandatory environmental disclosures for listed firms and bond issuers. Subsequently, in August 2016, the PBOC, together with seven central government ministries and commissions, issued the "Guiding Opinions on Building a Green Financial System", the world's first complete policy framework to support the development of green finance and top-level design for the development of green finance in China. The opinion clearly states that green finance is an economic activity that supports environmental improvement, tackling climate change and resource conservation and efficient use. This concept is widely accepted and used by society, including green credit, green bonds, environmental information disclosure, green investment, green insurance, and carbon finance.

In 2017, the PBOC again took the lead in formulating a corresponding division of labor plan and formulated a timetable and roadmap for the construction and development of China's green financial system. In February 2021, the State Council issued the "Guiding Opinions on Accelerating the Establishment of a Green, Low-Carbon and Circular Development Economic System", which clearly proposed to vigorously develop green finance, promote the convergence of international green finance standards, and promote in an orderly way the two-way opening of the green financial market. In September of the same year, the PBOC and the CSRC issued the "Guiding Opinions on Strengthening Industry-Finance Cooperation to Promote Green Industrial Development", and the fiscal and monetary policies for the development of green finance were gradually implemented, forming an effective positive incentive mechanism.

Reconciling China's Green Finance Policy and Theory

It is clear from the preceding discussion that China has very much taken a top-down approach to green finance policy. And while efforts were evident in policy making and implementation nationally at an early stage, this has been dictated by international factors, especially the Paris Agreement and China's overriding commitment to its 30:60 Dual Carbon goals. These features align with policy diffusion and policy learning. It is also apparent that this policy change has been very rapid, with most of these policy changes being implemented after about 2014. This corresponds with the theory of punctuated equilibrium in public policy change. This also nicely aligns with the appointment of Xi Jinping as general secretary of the Chinese Communist Party in 2013. Schubert and Alpermann (2019) argue that this is because, in contrast to the long pre-2013 period of cycles of Chinese central government decentralization and centralization and the loosening and tightening up of control, Xi Jinping has pursued a sustained effort aimed at recentralization, thereby weakening the influence of the regions and local government, the focusing of the bureaucracy on particular policy challenges, and the removal of close relations between special interest groups and those resistant to reform. For these reasons, Schubert and Alpermann (2019) propose a new "political steering theory" as the most appropriate theoretical approach to understanding contemporary policymaking and implementation in China.

Schubert and Alpermann (2019) argue that the main features of policy setting in Xi Jinping's China are a streamlining of agenda setting and policy formulation at the top, with implementation subjected to stricter control at each level by superior authorities with considerable interference from the center. With this, they distinguish between four steering modes: hard steering, negotiation, competition, and soft steering. Of these, the strongly hierarchical model of hard steering initially appears appropriate to the case of green finance with policy determined solely by the PBOC and CBIRC as the central bank and financial institution regulator, but primarily the PBOC. However, thereafter the steering approach becomes much softer, in that while green finance policy has been determined and relayed at the top, its main impact is as loose guidelines rather than as strictly controlled mandates. At the core is an emphasis on improving environmental information disclosure, especially among banks, a particularly important group in a very bank-focused economy like China.

This improvement in information serves to promote competition, albeit among the small and tightly controlled group of banks and insurance companies, in much the same way as policy diffusion theory. And while some aspects of green finance, such as the carbon market pilot programs, do involve regional and local (mostly large city) governments, the very rapid and widespread rollout of these pilots suggests not so much the evolution of policymaking but an attempt to quickly implement policy where most effective. Subsequently, the carbon trading tools and mechanisms are clearly aimed at reliance on market mechanisms produced by other actors in the political and economic system, including exchanges and associations. This corresponds with some of the mechanisms in policy network theory.

Conclusion

This chapter examines the growth and development of green finance in China from the perspective of public policy. We find that in contrast to the bottom-up approach to green finance found in developed economies, with its focus on market innovation through private sector investment and financing, the approach taken in China is very much top-down, with an emphasis first on the formulation of public policy and then its rapid implementation through a state-controlled and bank-concentrated financial system. The primary impetus for this has been China's agreement and endorsement of the Paris Agreement and its overriding Dual Carbon goals of peak carbon emissions by 2030 and carbon neutrality by 2060. In turn, implementation has been through the PBOC and the three functions of resource allocation, risk management, and market pricing, and the PBOC's pillars of guiding financial resources to support green finance by means of monetary, credit, and regulatory policies (and thereby also the CBIRC), mandatory disclosure, green evaluation, industry self-regulation, and product innovation.

Regarding carbon finance, the PBOC aims to facilitate the building of a national carbon emission exchange market, help develop derivatives such as carbon futures, and price carbon emissions through trading schemes. It is also clear that China is referencing back to international green policymaking by refining its definitions of green finance to better meet international standards and thereby prevent the misallocation of resources through greenwashing and facilitate international capital flows (Reuters, 2022). This is important as the Chinese government is almost certain not to be able to meet its ambitious targets for carbon emissions without significant international and private sector investment (Yao, 2018).

While many existing theories of public policy change work well in explaining some aspects of policy decision-making and implementation in China when it comes to green finance, we argue that political steering theory is the most appropriate theoretical approach to understand most contemporary policymaking and implementation in China. This reflects both the strong hierarchical initiation and setting of green finance policy by the central government and its implementation by the PBOC in conjunction with CBIRC via the state-owned and controlled banks, but also a softer focus on promoting competition among banks through environmental information disclosure. There is also allowance for more market-orientated mechanisms and tools with the eventual creation of carbon trading exchanges, tools, and products.

References

Asset Management Association of China. (2018). *Green investment guidelines.* https://www.amac.org.cn/businessservices_2025/ywfw_esg/esgzc/zczgsc/202007/t20200714_9847.html

Carbon Brief. (2021). *What does China's new Paris agreement pledge mean for climate change?* https://www.carbonbrief.org/qa-what-does-chinas-new-paris-agreement-pledge-mean-for-climate-change/#:~:text=%E2%80%9CChina%20will%20strictly%20control%20coal,(2026%2D2030).%E2%80%9D

Central Committee of the Communist Party of China. (2015). *Overall plan for ecological civilization system reform.* http://www.gov.cn/guowuyuan/2015-09/21/content_2936327.htm

Central People's Government of the People's Republic of China. (2018). *Constitution of People's Republic of China.* http://www.gov.cn/xinwen/2018-03/22/content_5276319.htm

Central People's Government of the People's Republic of China. (2020). *Guiding opinions on building a modern environmental governance system.* http://www.gov.cn/xinwen/2020-03/03/content_5486380.htm

Central People's Government of the People's Republic of China. (2021). *Guiding opinions on accelerating the establishment and improvement of a green, low-carbon, and circular development economic system.* http://www.gov.cn/xinwen/2021-03/25/content_5595541.htm

Cerna, L. (2013). *The nature of policy change and implementation: A review of different theoretical approaches.* Organisation for Economic Cooperation and Development. https://www.oecd.org/education/ceri/The%20Nature%20of%20Policy%20Change%20and%20Implementation.pdf

Chartered Banker Institute. (2022). *The green qualifications workbook.* https://www.charteredbanker.com/static/uploaded/6e89f43e-6a3b-41c7-a2a65d41deeee960.pdf

Chen, Y. (2013). Common commitment to green credit in China's banking industry. *China Securities Journal, 12*, 65. https://www.cs.com.cn/sylm/jsbd/201311/t20131104_4194118.html

Chen, Y. (2021). *Green finance's "three functions" and "five pillars" for realizing "30–60 goals".* People's Bank of China. http://www.pbc.gov.cn/en/3688110/3688175/4205055/index.html

China Association of Bank Insurance Regulators. (2019). *Guiding opinions of the China banking and insurance regulatory commission on promoting the high-quality development of the banking and insurance industry.* http://www.gov.cn/zhengce/zhengceku/2020-03/26/content_5495757.htm

China Banking Association. (2017). *Implementation plan for green bank evaluation in China's banking industry.* https://wenku.baidu.com/view/3d54f72f954bcf84b9d528ea81c758f5f61f2901.html

China Banking and Insurance Regulatory Commission (CBIRC). (2013). *Opinions on green credit work.* http://www.cbirc.gov.cn/cn/view/pages/ItemDetail.html?docId=1054663&itemId=928

China Banking Regulatory Commission (CBRC). (2012). *Notice of CBRC on issuing green credit guidelines.* http://www.gov.cn/gongbao/content/2012/content_2163593.htm

China Banking Regulatory Commission (CBRC). (2014). *Notice on key evaluation indicators of green credit implementation.* http://www.tbankw.com/zcfg/162438.html

China Securities Regulatory Commission (CSRC). (2017). *Guidelines for supporting green bond development.* https://www.greenfinanceplatform.org/policies-and-regulations/green-bond-guidelines-issued-chinas-national-development-and-reform

Climate Bonds Report. (2021). *China green bond market report 2021.* https://www.climatebonds.net/files/reports/cbi_china_sotm_2021_0.pdf

Dezan Shira, & Associates. (2022). *China's green finance market: Policies, incentives, investment opportunities.* https://www.china-briefing.com/news/chinas-green-finance-market-policies-incentives-investment-opportunities/

Dikau, S., & Volz, U. (2021). Out of the window? Green monetary policy in China: Window guidance and the promotion of sustainable lending and investment. *Climate Policy.* https://www.tandfonline.com/doi/full/10.1080/14693062.2021.2012122

Freehills, H. S. (2022). *China's green finance – Key recent developments.* https://hsfnotes.com/fsrandcorpcrime/2022/07/12/chinas-green-finance-key-recent-developments/

Hanson, A. (2019). *Ecological civilization in the People's Republic of China: Values, action, and future needs.* ADB East Asia Working Paper Series, No. 2. https://www.adb.org/sites/default/files/publication/545291/eawp-021-ecological-civilization-prc.pdf

Ho, V. H. (2018). Sustainable finance and China's green credit reforms: A test case for bank monitoring of environmental risk. *Cornell International Law Journal, 51,* 609–681. https://scholarship.law.cornell.edu/cilj/vol51/iss3/3/

International Institute for Sustainable Development. (2015). *Greening China's financial system.* https://www.iisd.org/system/files/publications/greening-chinas-financial-system.pdf

Ministry of Ecology and Environment and All-China Federation of Industry and Commerce. (2018). *Opinions on supporting green development of private enterprises.* https://www.mee.gov.cn/xxgk2018/xxgk/xxgk03/201901/t20190121_690273.html

Ministry of Ecology and Environment of the People's Republic of China. (2020). *Guiding opinions on promoting investment and financing to address climate change.* https://www.mee.gov.cn/xxgk2018/xxgk/xxgk03/202010/t20201026_804792.html

Ministry of Environment, People's Republic of China. (2007). *Opinions on printing and distributing environmental protection policies and regulations to prevent credit risks.* https://www.mee.gov.cn/gkml/zj/wj/200910/t20091022_172469.htm

Moody's Analytics. (2021). *PBC outlines plans for development of green finance in China.* https://www.moodysanalytics.com/regulatory-news/Feb-09-21-PBC-Outlines-Plans-for-Development-of-Green-Finance-in-China

National Development and Reform Commission. (2015). *Green bond issuance guidelines.* https://www.ndrc.gov.cn/xxgk/zcfb/tz/201601/t20160108_963561.html?code=&state=123

National Development and Reform Commission. (2019). *Green industry guidance catalogue.* https://baijiahao.baidu.com/s?id=1627220927477436161&wfr=spider&for=pc

People's Bank of China (PBOC). (2016a). *Guidelines for establishing the green financial system.* https://rccef.cufe.edu.cn/info/1002/1385.htm

People's Bank of China (PBOC). (2016b). *Guiding opinions on building a green financial system.* http://www.scio.gov.cn/32344/32345/35889/36819/xgzc36825/Document/1555348/1555348.htm

People's Bank of China (PBOC). (2017). *Financial industry standardization system construction and development plan (2016–2020).* http://www.pbc.gov.cn/goutongjiaoliu/113456/113469/3322066/index.html

People's Bank of China (PBOC). (2018). *Notice on establishing a special statistical system for green loans.* https://www.vecarbon.com/messageDetail?id=1471834268127742644

People's Bank of China (PBOC). (2020). *Green financial performance evaluation plan of financial institutions.* http://www.pbc.gov.cn/tiaofasi/144941/3581332/4265383/2021061014205828457.pdf

People's Bank of China (PBOC). (2021a). *Guidelines for financial institutions environmental information disclosure.* https://chinadevelopmentbrief.org/wp-content/uploads/2021/08/Guidelines-for-financial-institutions-environmental-information-disclosure.pdf

People's Bank of China (PBOC). (2021b). *Green bond endorsed projects catalogue.* http://www.pbc.gov.cn/goutongjiaoliu/113456/113469/4342400/2021091617180089879.pdf

Report of the Fourth Session of the 12th NPC. (2016). *Outline of the 13th five-year plan for national economic and social development of the People's Republic of China.* http://www.12371.cn/special/sswgh/wen/

Reuters. (2022). *China tightens green bond rules to align them with global norms.* https://www.reuters.com/markets/asia/exclusive-china-tightens-green-bond-rules-align-them-with-global-norms-2022-08-24/#:~:text=Although%20a%20record%20%24109.5%20billion,CBI%2C%20which%20sets%20international%20standards

Schubert, G., & Alpermann, B. (2019). Studying the Chinese policy process in the era of 'top-level design': The contribution of 'political steering' theory. *Journal of Chinese Political Science, 24*(2), 199–224. https://link.springer.com/article/10.1007/s11366-018-09594-8

Shipan, C. R., & Volden, C. (2008). The mechanisms of policy diffusion. *American Journal of Political Science*, *52*(4), 840–857. https://onlinelibrary.wiley.com/doi/10.1111/j.1540-5907.2008.00346.x

Xueqing, J. (2021). China issues first batch of carbon-neutral bonds. *China Daily*. https://global.chinadaily.com.cn/a/202102/09/WS602253c2a31024ad0baa865a.html

Xueqing, J. (2022). China steps up efforts to drive green finance. *China Daily*. https://www.chinadaily.com.cn/a/202201/11/WS61dce214a310cdd39bc804aa.html

Yao, W. (2018). *China's green finance strategy: Much achieved, further to go*. London School of Economics and Political Science. https://www.lse.ac.uk/granthaminstitute/news/chinas-green-finance-strategy-much-achieved-further-to-go/

16
GREEN FINANCE IN CHINA
System, Practice, and International Role

Christoph Nedopil and Mathias Larsen[1]

Introduction

China's green finance development is subject to increasing global attention lying at the intersection of three global trends: first, green ambitions have become a common core policy goal across the world in addressing climate and environmental problems. Second, finance is a major force in shaping economic and social development in an era of increasing financialization and internationalization. Third, the rise of China, with its unique characteristics, is reshaping the world and is consequently drawing increasing attention from all spheres of society. At the nexus of these three global trends, "green finance in China" is a topic that requires the provision of new knowledge to inform the actions of public and private organizations inside and outside China. Developing such knowledge is critical as Chinese green finance is consequential for both individual countries and the global development trajectory (Sachs et al., 2019).

In 2020, China committed to becoming carbon neutral by 2060. To achieve this, new investment of around RMB 138 trillion is needed by 2050 in the energy system alone, equivalent to more than 2.5% of annual GDP (Tsinghua University ICCSD, 2020). Reaching this and other green goals will require a fundamental restructuring of the financial system. Already in 2016, the Chinese government launched an ambitious policy program, after which progress has been impressive in some parts of the financial system and less in others. However, the persistent problem is that while the green parts have expanded, the polluting parts have not decreased fast enough – which we refer to as the "Panda–Dragon paradox." Ultimately, the greening of the Chinese financial system has far to go. What needs to happen is both a rapid scale-up of green financing alongside an equally rapid decrease in fossil financing. For example, China is the world's largest investor in both renewables and fossil fuels domestically (Larsen & Oehler, 2022). Internationally in the "Belt and Road Initiative," China similarly provides financing for both green and non-green infrastructure, particularly in emerging economies (Nedopil, 2022).

This chapter provides an overview of green finance development in China. It does so by applying a mix of qualitative and quantitative methods: qualitative analysis is used to grasp the political economy and institutional environment of green finance by drawing primarily on policy documents and conceptualizations in existing academic literature. Second, descriptive statistics are used to identify trends and dynamics in the financial system based on various data sources. As China's green financial system is too complex to describe in a single chapter, the chapter focuses on some of the most significant developments driving Chinese and global green finance while leaving out other developments (e.g., China's emission trading system).[2] First, it provides an account of how green finance is driven through top-down governance and contrasts this with the situation in Western countries. Second, it goes into detail about the progress made so far across key aspects of the Chinese financial system. Third, an assessment of Chinese international engagement covers both Chinese overseas green finance as well as efforts to coordinate efforts. Fourth, as China is a unique case in green finance, it discusses the need for greater integration with international green finance research as well as how this can be carried out in practice.

Chinese Green Finance System through Top-Down Governance

The development of green finance in China is rooted in China's underlying political economy model. With a strong party-state shaping a capitalist system, China scholars label this model in different ways, such as the "Grand Steerage" of the economy (Naughton, 2020). For green finance, the state takes an active role in providing guidance, regulations, and financial backing. For example, while China had not issued any green bonds by 2015, once support from the government was rolled out, China became the world's largest issuer in 2016. This top-down market-steering approach seen in China (Y. Wang, 2018) can be contrasted with a bottom-up market facilitation approach in the EU (Larsen, 2021b; Nedopil et al., 2021).

In a historical context, green finance in China can be conceptualized into four main stages. First, environmental issues started to be considered in financial system governance in the 1990s when the Chinese central bank, the People's Bank of China, issued guidance to banks on how to include environmental variables in credit decisions (Escalante et al., 2020). Second, preparation for rolling out comprehensive green finance policies started around 2012 with the preparation and launch of the China Banking Regulatory Commission's (CBRC) green credit guidance and statistics system. It further included the establishment of a People's Bank of China (PBOC) and the UN Environment Program (UNEP) task force, which released their report in 2015 (Pan et al., 2015). Based on that report, China entered its third stage in 2016 when the PBOC and six other ministry-level bodies jointly launched Guidelines on green finance, and the Green Finance Committee was established to coordinate implementation. This Guideline is the core document coordinating green finance policies across different regulatory aspects and green finance instruments that includes direct accountability built in through performance targets allocated to each ministry-level body. This enabled initial rapid progress in green finance. However, entering the fourth stage around 2020, green finance progress started stagnating, with green loans and bonds growing at the same pace as the rest of the financial system. This means that despite substantial efforts and increasing environmental and climate ambitions, progress on greening the financial system is not keeping up (Larsen, 2021a).

Governing Green Finance from Central to Local Levels

To coordinate green finance policies in China, the PBOC has taken a central role, with implementation executed by numerous central government ministries and regulators, as shown in Figure 16.1. The key organizations include the National Development and Reform Commission (NDRC), the China Securities Regulatory Commission (CSRC), and the China Banking and Insurance Regulatory Commission (CBIRC), each responsible for greening the part of the financial system related to their mandate. Furthermore, as a venue for discussions between government bodies, financial institutions, and researchers, the China Green Finance Committee

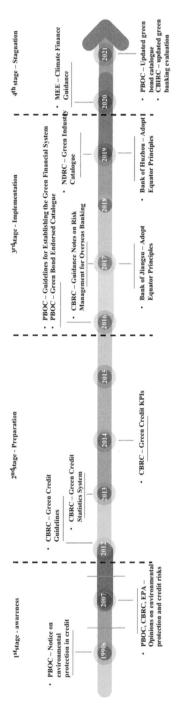

Figure 16.1 Stages of green finance development in China (Source: authors' visualization)

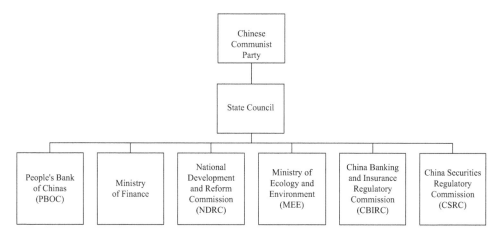

Figure 16.2 Overview and relations between bodies governing green finance (Source: authors' visualization)

plays a key role in the coordination and development of green finance policies. For example, the Ministry of Finance was responsible for establishing the China National Green Development Fund (PBOC, 2016).

Next to the central government's role in green finance development in China, local governments play a key role in turning high-level decisions into green financing in practice. Accordingly, the central ministry level rolls out green finance policies to each sub-governance level, beginning with the provincial level and continuing down to counties and urban districts. For example, provincial-level Development and Reform Commissions (DRCs) are responsible for integrating green finance into economic planning. Simultaneously, pilot projects initiated on local levels and sanctioned by the central level allow for experimentation with green finance policies and instruments that might inform future central green finance applications. Historically, these pilots are rooted in the practice seen in special economic zones set up in the 1980s as part of China's reform policies (Ang, 2016). The goal of these pilots is ultimately to determine the effectiveness of different green finance policies and then implement these at the national and international levels.

For example, in June 2017, the State Council decided to set up pilot zones for green finance reform and innovation in Zhejiang, Jiangxi, Guangdong, Guizhou, and Xinjiang. Next, in 2020, Beijing and Chongqing were added as city-level pilots. This was followed by overall plans with specific goals for each pilot zone jointly released by seven ministry-level government bodies. By establishing these five distinct pilot zones, Chinese central regulators explore different development models for the local green financial system within the diverse provinces that have different economic and social structures, thus offering diverse practical samples for promoting green finance across the country. Furthermore, in response to the national top-level design for green finance, over ten provinces and autonomous regions not covered by the pilot program have voluntarily released policy frameworks on green finance. This shows a bottom-up, natural interest of local governments to be part of China's green finance development. Lastly, supported by national regulatory authorities, several research institutes and large financial institutions have called on local financial institutions to carry out relevant training, exchange, and cooperation and have promoted best practices, exemplary cases, and experiences in developing green finance. Currently, Xinjiang, Guangdong, Zhejiang, and Gansu have all set up their own local "green finance committees," which work as institutions for coordination and discussion on green finance policy and practice.

As part of its top-down governance approach, the Chinese state supports green finance with substantial public capital. Still, according to Ma and Zadek (2016), China's public funds can only make up 15%, while private resources need to make up the rest. It is therefore critical that the public funds have a catalyzing and market-making effect on institutionalizing green finance. As a parallel way of steering private capital and companies, China has included renewable energy targets in its five-year plans since 2001 (NDRC, 2001). Covid-19 provided a litmus test for green commitments across the world as stimulus packages were launched. Discouragingly, China put many times more money into fossil fuels than into renewables in the stimulus package (Vivid Economics 2020), even though renewable energy today makes up the majority of electricity generation investment in China (CEC, 2020). This is arguable because the majority was dispersed through local government, which in many cases has an entrenched interest in fossil fuels, and because with increasingly strict climate targets, now may be the last chance to put money into coal plants (Myllyvirta et al., 2020).

China's Green Financial System in International Comparison

To better understand China's particular approach to green finance in China, the approach can be compared with other efforts to green financial systems. As China and the EU are both early adopters, the most ambitious, and the most influential in financial system development (Barmes & Livingstone, 2021; ICMA, 2021), it is relevant to compare the EU's approach with China's. In summary, China takes a top-down market-steering approach to green finance policy based on its political economy model characterized by party and state intervention and control. On the contrary, the EU takes a bottom-up market-facilitating approach based on its democratic and intergovernmental political system and liberal market economy (Larsen, 2021b). In terms of similar characteristics between China and the EU, in green finance policymaking, they both rely on technical expertise both from inside and outside policymaking bodies and from national and international organizations. This is, for example, seen in the Green Finance Committee in China and the EU's High-Level Expert Group. They also both use expert committees to provide recommendations or draft policies to be launched by authorities. In terms of the chronology of rolling out green finance, there is a striking similarity of first setting up expert groups with a broad representation of stakeholders. Based on input from the groups, the EU and China's governing body mandated with organizing green finance policy have launched financial-system-wide policies, namely the Action Plan (EC, 2018) and the Guidelines (PBOC, 2016).

In terms of different characteristics, the policy approaches diverge substantially despite the similarity across the initial phases of the policy process (Nedopil et al., 2021). First, while the EU takes a bottom-up approach by letting the markets and stakeholders participate or even drive policies, China takes a top-down approach being proactive in advance of green finance activities in the market. Second, while the EU takes a consultative approach, willing to have public dialogue and revise policies based on stakeholder input, China takes a technocratic approach by using experts for technical input rather than opinions and not amending policies substantially after publishing drafts for consultation. This leaves much more room for active lobbying in the EU, as seen with the changes to the taxonomy after the expert group's draft. For example, discussion continues around including gas and nuclear power in the taxonomy (Simon, 2021). On the Chinese side, lobbying and institutional interests surely play a role, but the influence on green finance policy is indirect and instead focuses on avoiding brown penalizing factors. Third, the EU makes public statements at every step in the policy process, even when launch-

Green Finance in China

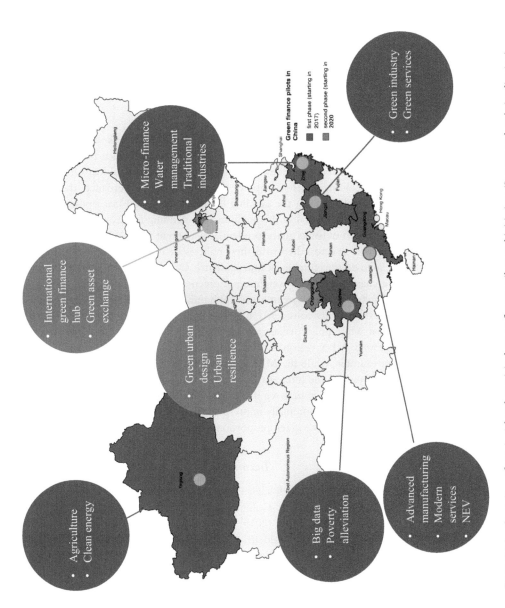

Figure 16.3 Overview of provincial and municipal green finance pilots and initiatives (Source: authors' visualization)

ing closed committees, while China, in many cases, only lets the public know when the policy is launched or when a policy draft is already near completion. Fourth, while the EU is limited by the mandates and independence of financial system regulators, China's government has no mandate limits and is, in that regard, only limited by regulator fragmentation and vested interests.

When contrasting the Chinese green finance approach to that of the United States, even greater differences emerge: as a market-based financial system, the US government and regulators so far have taken a hands-off approach to governing the financial system in a green direction. As such, green finance in the United States had historically developed based on market participants' initiatives (such as ESG funds or privately labeled green bonds). The US market regulator SEC only in 2021 considered issuing policies on environmental information disclosure, with a proposal launched for consultation in early 2022 (SEC, 2022).

China's Green Finance in Practice

Between 2015 and 2020, China made impressive progress in greening its financial system. The below sections provide a run-through of the most important areas of Chinese green finance.

Central Banking

As a key driver of green finance performance in China, the PBOC is ranked by Positive Money as the most advanced in terms of the scope and depth of green finance policies (Barmes & Livingstone, 2021). This difference in risk profiles of green and standard loans has enabled the regulator to justify including green factors for financial system governance: the PBOC has included green industry lending in the standing lending facility (SLF), accepting green bonds at AA rating and above as collateral in the medium-term lending facility (MLF), and including green performance as part of banks' macroprudential assessment (MPA)[3] (Escalante et al., 2020). Compared to central banks across the world, these policies are unique and only possible through policy control as opposed to central bank independence. Over the last few years, there has been a discussion about changing the risk weighting of green assets and reducing the capital reserve requirements for banks with more green loans and bonds (L. Wang & Peng, 2021).

These policy developments considered, together with the stagnating green proportion of lending, suggest that while policymakers are active, their efforts do not adequately turn into practice on the ground. A key reason for this is that the financial materiality of the measures is still limited. For example, while the MPA measures are innovative and ambitious, the influence of banks' greenness and the interest on their reserves is still marginal. As the PBOC plans on increasing this weighting, we may see it translate into further green lending in the future. Overall, while green lending is nominally impressive, the green proportion of all loans is less so. To green the financial system, the green proportion needs to expand significantly faster.

Taxonomies

China was the first country to launch such taxonomies in 2014 and 2015. Key taxonomies include the China Banking Regulatory Commission's (2014) list of green industries on which banks have to file statistics, the PBOC (2015) Green Bond Project Endorsed Catalogue, and the NDRC (2019) Green Industry Catalogue, and the PBoC, NDRC, and CSRC updated and joint Green Bond Project Endorsed Catalogue (2021). Yet, while the taxonomies all come from government bodies, they do not include economic activities but rather differ, for example, on the inclusion of nuclear power, clean coal, or passenger rail. Regarding the contents of the taxonomies, it is worth noting that "green" finance in China both encompasses climate issues and other environmental issues. They include, for example, environmental pollution, natural resource preservation, and biodiversity. The key emphasis of Chinese environmental progress over the last decades has been on air, water, and soil pollution, and these priorities are also reflected in green finance. For example, industrial upgrading, which includes retrofitting chimneys with air filtering equipment, is the main category of outstanding green loans at RMB 7.4 trillion, compared to clean energy at RMB 4.2 trillion (PBOC, 2022b). Furthermore, clean coal and other types of "clean" fossil fuels are included in several of China's green finance taxonomies.

While the technologies included may have a large impact on air pollution, from a climate change perspective, they have limited impact. For example, the type of ultra-supercritical coal-fired power plants with pollution control technology that is included as clean coal in the NDRC's Green Industry Catalogue (2019) can reduce air pollution by more than 90%, though only reducing CO_2 emissions by 10%. Furthermore, though China's latest green bond catalog from 2021 took out coal-fired power plants, it still includes upgrading coal-burning industrial boilers in the "energy efficiency" category (PBoC, 2021). Most international standards exclude all fossil fuels, though the EU's latest version includes gas as a transition fuel. Only in China and Mongolia is coal included. As such, core differences remain when compared to international taxonomies, as discussed below.

Information Disclosure

In terms of environmental information disclosure, the Guidelines and subsequent policies issued a three-step process toward mandatory disclosure by all listed companies. This policy promised full disclosure by the end of 2020, which was postponed due to Covid-19 though uncertainty remains on the scope and requirements. Regulators, in fact, only promise that it will be fully implemented by 2025 (Fitch, 2022b). Alongside this policy rollout process, the Asset Management Association of China has issued ESG investing guidelines to prepare asset managers to better use the information in practice. Furthermore, Hong Kong implemented similar mandatory environmental disclosure in 2020, thus serving as a test site for the policy before its rollout in mainland China. This process shows a gradual rollout giving companies and asset managers time to adjust before being made mandatory. It further shows the importance attributed to expertise by directly involving the Asset Management Association of China (AMAC) to guide the industry. Lastly, this case again shows a clear top-down and proactive approach taken by the Chinese state to institutionalize green finance, as there is very limited bottom-up drive on environmental disclosure. According to AMAC (2020), only 11% of Chinese asset managers surveyed know about ESG factors and use them in practice. This suggests a stark contrast to the bottom-up approach in the EU. In summary, while the initial policies on information disclosure were more ambitious than seen in other countries, the rollout has encountered several challenges, which means that China now lags behind requirements being rolled out elsewhere, for example, in the EU.

Credit Markets

A core characteristic of China's financial system is that it is bank-dominated. Bank loans are the primary financing tools as they make up about 70% of all total social financing (TSF), while securitization and market-based instruments play a smaller role (PBoC, 2022a). Accordingly, the banking sector was the first target of Chinese green finance policies. Already in 1995, the PBOC issued guidance for banks on environmental risks, and in 2007 the CBRC issued guidelines on banks' role in emission reductions. To accelerate green credit, the CBRC issued green credit guidelines in 2012 and a green credit statistics system in 2013, with regular improvements in the systems and reporting (Escalante, Choi, & Larsen, 2020). At the end of 2021, total outstanding green loans totaled RMB 15.9 trillion (PBOC, 2022b), where the share of green loans grew from 8.8% of the total loans market to 10.4% between 2013 and 2019 (Escalante et al., 2020). Since then, however, green credit growth has stagnated and stood at 10.6% at the end of 2021 (CBIN, 2022).

The non-performing loan (NPL) ratio of green loans was only about 0.7%, which was substantially lower than the overall market of 1.7% (Sun, 2022). However, it should be noted that factors other than "greenness" may be influencing the low NPL ratio as well, such as the fact that many green loans are for infrastructure projects, which are already considered a relatively stable asset class. Lastly, as loans are agreements directly between creditors and debtors rather than being traded on the market, only scarce details are released on loan terms, including green characteristics. Consequently, though we know the overarching statistics, the green loan market remains opaque to the degree that it is not possible to measure the impacts (Teer & Larsen, 2019).

Bonds Markets

Green bond policies were rolled out and turned into practice in China at a record pace: from having no green bonds in 2015, China became the world's largest green bond market in 2016, though still smaller than the EU if we considered the EU as a single market (CBI, 2021). The growth was enabled by issuing green bond guidelines and taxonomy in late 2015 and early 2016. The practice allowed for up to 50% of green bond proceeds to be used for non-green purposes. Particularly the beginning of the development of the green bond market was driven by state-owned commercial bank issuance rather than corporate bonds. In fact, considering all Chinese green bonds issued before 2019, state-owned commercial banks make up the majority, with the following categories by size being state-owned enterprises, local governments, and policy banks. Private company issuances only make up 3% of the green bond market (IIGF, 2022). This suggests that also the application of green finance is driven top-down, where the state is able to direct and control the green bond market based on the state's policy goals. Only in recent years have private and lower credit-rated organizations entered the market, potentially as the state has successfully institutionalized the market, making it attractive for issuers on market terms. The need for the state to take such a proactive role in market creation is also seen and argued to be the case for other emerging financial markets (Teer & Larsen, 2019).

A number of aspects of the Chinese green bond market are worth noting. Despite impressive progress, green bonds only make up about 1% of the overall Chinese bond market (IIGF, 2022), suggesting that there is both room and need for further growth. In terms of default rates, there have so far been no defaults amongst green bonds, whereas the default rate for the onshore market as a whole stood at 0.76% in 2021 (Fitch, 2022a). Furthermore, foreign investors only hold about 3.5% of the Chinese bond market, though we cannot tell which proportion of green bonds (Cheng, 2021). Additionally, Chinese green bond standards differ from international standards, resulting in about half of issuances being labeled as nonaligned with international standards. The main differences include that Chinese standards allow up to 50% of funds to be used as working capital and that the taxonomy includes some types of fossil fuels (Escalante et al., 2020).

China's International Role in Green Finance

Beyond China's domestic green finance development, China has become an important partner in influencing global green finance practices. On the one hand, China's overseas engagement

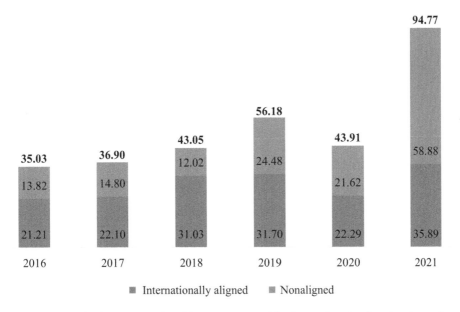

Figure 16.4 Annual Chinese green bond issuance, separated by internationally aligned and nonaligned (Source: S&P Global, 2022)

through its Belt and Road Initiative (BRI) has mobilized about USD 800 billion in investments and construction contracts, particularly in emerging economies, since 2013, which was accompanied by new green finance frameworks for overseas investments, for example through the Green Development Guidance (Nedopil et al., 2020) and the Green Investment Principles (GIP) (Green Finance Leadership Program, 2018), in addition to several green finance and green cooperation government-issued documents (Nedopil, 2021c). At the same time, China has supported global green finance harmonization through engagement in international standard bodies, such as the central banks' Network for Greening the Financial System (NGFS), G20, and the European Union. Contrary to China's support for government-endorsed green finance standards, Chinese public and private financial stakeholders have been slow to engage with sector-led green finance initiatives, such as the Taskforce on Nature-related Financial Disclosure (TNFD), the Taskforce on Climate-Related Financial Disclosure (TCFD), UN Principles for Responsible Investment (PRI), or the Equator Principles.

Green Finance in China's Overseas Activities

Chinese policy banks, commercial banks, and state-owned enterprises are taken together as the largest overseas investors and financiers in the world (X. Ma et al., 2022). Based on China's domestic experience in building infrastructure in transport, energy, and communication technologies, Chinese finance supports particularly the development of infrastructure projects in the over 140 countries of the Belt and Road Initiative (Nedopil, 2022). With its growing clout, Chinese overseas financing is seen as a double-edged sword that could contribute to or impede green development ambitions, and in particular, climate ambitions under the Paris Agreement (J. Ma & Zadek, 2019).

Chinese leaders have verbally confirmed for the BRI, in particular, to be "open, green and clean" while avoiding the "pollute now, clean up later" approach in overseas investments in general (FOCAC, 2021; Xi, 2019). In practice, however, China's green overseas finance policies and its green finance practice have been "more words than action" (Nedopil, 2021c) due to a dominance of fossil fuel investments (Zhou et al., 2018) and a focus on "host country principles" in applying environmental standards (Voituriez et al., 2019) up to 2020. This host country approach was contrary to, e.g., sustainable project finance practices using the Equator Principles that strongly encourage the application of IFC's environmental and social performance standards in countries with weaker institutional environments (Equator Principles Association & International Finance Corporation, 2020). In 2020, however, China's approach to greening finance in the BRI changed, possibly due to increasing stranded asset risks, particularly in coal-fired power plant investments (Myllyvirta et al., 2020; Nedopil, 2021b). Based on international collaboration practices, such as the Belt and Road Initiative International Green Development Coalition (BRIGC) under the Ministry of Ecology and Environment (Nedopil Wang, 2020), China issued the Green Development Guidance Baseline Study with the "Traffic Light System" labeling all fossil fuel-related engagement as "red" (Y. Wang & Nedopil, 2020). In addition, the Ministry of Ecology and Environment, together with five other regulators, issued a Climate Finance Guidance stipulating the application of Chinese environmental standards in overseas finance. This policy drive was paired with a change of financial engagement, where, in 2020, renewable energies took a larger share than fossil fuels for the first time (Nedopil, 2021a). Thus, both regulators and financial institutions play an important role in greening finance in China's overseas engagement, and similarly to domestic green finance development, the overseas development of China's green finance is led by policy signals from regulators.

Regulators

For China's overseas investments, the CBIRC's "Green Credit Guidelines" outlined specific projects and industries that are eligible to receive green credits, which can be applied for overseas finance. In 2017, the "Guidelines on Further Guiding and Regulating Overseas Investment" issued jointly by NDRC, MofCom, MOFA, and PBOC provided a differentiated classification of "encouraged, restricted, and prohibited projects." A "host country approach" was used to define which projects should be restricted. However, environmental factors had not been among the top considerations for the "encouraged" list. In October 2020, the MEE, together with the NDRC, PBOC, CBIRC, and CSRC, jointly launched the "Guidance on promoting investment and financing to address climate change." This guidance mentioned that Chinese financial institutions are encouraged to support the low-carbon development in the countries of the Belt and Road Initiative and South–South cooperation and should facilitate the implementation of climate change mitigation/adaptation projects abroad. Financial institutions should also fulfill their social responsibility by effectively preventing and mitigating climate-related risks.

On December 1, 2020, the BRIGC released the "Green Development Guidance for BRI Projects Baseline Study Report." The Guidance includes a Traffic Light System that provides a methodology to evaluate projects and a list of encouraged, neutral and restricted projects based on three environmental criteria: pollution, climate change, and biodiversity. The "Traffic Light System" has been promoted since then by various entities, and the BRIGC, together with Chinese and international partners such as WRI and ClientEarth, has developed an implementation guide (Y. Wang et al., 2021) and a joint report with the GIP for the Belt and Road (Nedopil et al., 2022a) and continues to improve its application (Y. Wang & Liu, 2021).

The Green Development Guidance also served as a basis for three new policy documents issued in 2021 and 2022 that explicitly encouraged the integration of biodiversity, climate, and pollution control throughout all investment phases based on Chinese or international instead of host country standards: the Green Development Guidelines for Foreign Investment and

Cooperation, issued jointly by MOFCOM and MEE in July 2021, the Guidelines for Ecological Environmental Protection of Foreign Investment Cooperation and Construction Projects, also issued by MOFCOM and MEE in January 2022, and the Opinions on the Joint Implementation of Green Development in the Belt and Road Initiative, issued by NDRC, MOFCOM, MEE, and Ministry of Foreign Affairs in March 2022.[4] Figure 16.5 shows how these policies have moved from a "host country" to an "international standards approach" regarding environmental risk management when financing overseas projects.

Financial Institutions

Chinese overseas financing and investments, particularly in the BRI, are carried out by selected financial institutions and investment funds, with participation from state-owned and private enterprises. Among the most important financial institutions are the two policy banks, the China Development Bank (CDB) and the Export-Import Bank for China (China Exim Bank), and the select international financial institutions, including ICBC, Bank of China, and the Agricultural Bank of China. These financial institutions mostly engage in project financing through the provision of loans to local governments or to the project company. The most important funds providing equity include China Investment Corporation (CIC) and the Silk Road Fund – both financed by the Chinese government. In addition, companies engage in equity finance. Finally, Sinosure provides export credits and insurance for Chinese-funded projects that could secure local government guarantees. Most of the financial institutions engaged in overseas finance have increased the usage of the terms "green" and "environment" significantly from 2016 to 2019 in their annual reports (China Development Bank & United Nations Development Programme, 2019). China Exim Bank has established a "pro-environment" system with "Four Nos," mostly focused on the client's performance. It also stipulates compliance with local laws and internal regulations (the latter of which are not clearly specified).

The Chinese ICBC has installed a "green credit veto" system, under which no loans should be issued to borrowers or projects that do not pass an environmental impact test to "ensure compliance, integrity, and legitimacy in terms of energy-saving and environmental protection" (China Development Bank & United Nations Development Programme, 2019). This system, however, is mostly used to ensure the existence of an environmental impact assessment (EIA) for overseas projects rather than the quality of the EIA and would not exclude fossil fuel financing. In 2021, following China's announcement to not build new coal-fired power plants abroad (关于推进共建"一带一路"绿色发展的意见 – Opinions on Promoting the Green Development of "One Belt, One Road," 2022), the Bank of China said it would no longer finance coal-fired power plants abroad.

Financial Institutions' Initiatives

Internationally, greening project finance, particularly in emerging markets, has been supported and driven by the Equator Principles – a standard to encourage environmental risk management, environmental risk disclosure, and environmental risk mitigation for financial institutions. However, only a few Chinese financial institutions have signed up for the Equator Principles, and none of the Chinese financial institutions engaged in overseas financing had signed up as of April 2022.

As a Chinese alternative, the GIP were launched in 2018 as a voluntary set of principles to accelerate green investments in the BRI region by the Green Finance Committee of China Society for Finance and Banking and the City of London's Green Finance Initiative in London. The seven principles included in GIP are rather high-level and, compared to the Equator Principles, lack specificity. By December 2021, the GIP had 41 signatories and 13

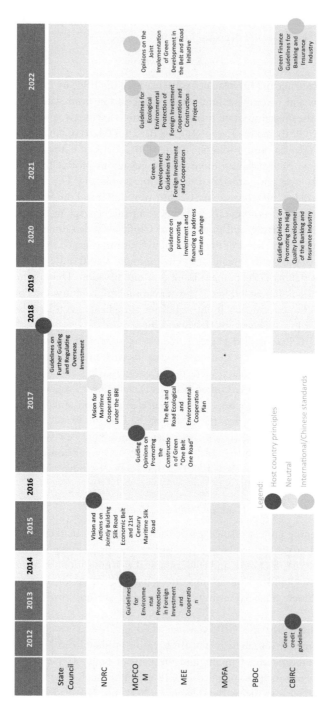

Figure 16.5 Chinese government-issued guidance and opinions relevant for greening finance in the Belt and Road Initiative distinguishing between "host country principle" and "international/Chinese standards" for environmental protection (Source: authors' visualization)

supporters from 15 countries and regions around the world. Nevertheless, the Chinese government has been promoting the GIP internationally as a Chinese-led initiative. For example, President Xi highlighted the GIP at the 2021 Bo'ao Forum (Xi, 2021), and policy documents, such as the 2022 Opinions (see above), emphasize the proliferation and application of the GIP (关于推进共建"一带一路"绿色发展的意见 – Opinions on Promoting the Green Development of "One Belt, One Road," 2022).

International Coordination of Green Finance Development

While China's green financial system is unique due to its top-down approach with the relevance of policy signals over market signals, China has signaled strong interest in coordinating international green finance approaches. This, possibly, has two aims: first, to attract more capital for domestic investment based on harmonized green finance standards (European Investment Bank (EIB) & Green Finance Committee of China Society for Finance and Banking, 2017), for example, through common green taxonomies; and second, to influence global green finance development according to its domestic experience (J. Wang, 2019). At the same time, China's financial markets have sufficient gravity for international partners to be interested in accelerating green finance cooperation with China, and China's domestic green finance development has sufficient signaling power to other countries aiming to learn from the Chinese experience in greening finance (IFC, 2021b).

China's international visibility on green finance was elevated during the G20 in Hangzhou in 2016 (Jiang, 2016) when China initiated green finance to be included as a study group. In 2021, sustainable finance was upgraded to become a standing G20 Working Group. The Sustainable Finance Working Group (SFWG) continues to be led by Chinese support aiming to provide common ambitions, language, and standards across the G20 on green and sustainable finance (MEF Department of Treasury, 2021).

Through the PBOC, China also initiated the Network for Greening the Financial System in 2017, a network of global financial regulators that, by April 2022, had 114 members (Network for Greening the Financial System (NGFS), 2022). Withing the NGFS, particularly macrofinancial risk-based environmental changes are studied. Several of the study groups of the NGFS, such as on biodiversity finance, are led by Chinese institutions. China and the EU, together with relevant authorities from Argentina, Canada, Chile, India, Kenya, and Morocco, also launched the International Platform for Sustainable Finance (IPSF) in October 2019 (European Commission, 2022). The IPSF aims to scale up the mobilization of private capital towards environmentally sustainable investments and to offer a multilateral forum of dialogue between policymakers that are in charge of developing sustainable finance regulatory measures to help investors identify and seize sustainable investment opportunities that truly contribute to climate and environmental objectives. As a product of the IPFS, the European Union and China launched the "common ground taxonomy" (CGT) at COP 26 in November 2021 (Azizuddin, 2020). However, the CGT only provided a comparison of the taxonomies and not a common ground, despite the name, nor did it present proposals to increase compatibility or expand interoperability. Rather, the CGT simply provides a comparison between the green part of the EU taxonomy and the Chinese green bond taxonomy.

Additionally, China cooperates bilaterally on green finance. For example, some of the same Chinese experts from Tsinghua University who led the development of the Chinese green bond catalogue supported the development of the Mongolian green finance taxonomy (IFC, 2021a), while Pakistan aimed to cooperate with China on building an aligned emission trading system (Herekar, et al., 2021). Contrary to government-supported green finance cooperation, however,

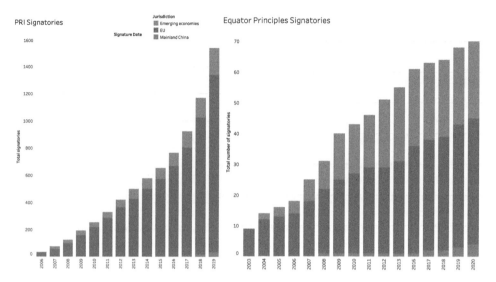

Figure 16.6 Chinese, developing, and developed country signatories to the PRI and the Equator Principles (Source: Nedopil et al., 2021)

Chinese financial stakeholders are underrepresented in sector-driven initiatives. For example, Chinese financial institutions are slow both in signing the PRI and the Equator Principles, also in comparison to other developing economies (see Figure 16.6). Chinese financial institutions are also mostly not disclosing under the TCFD and are not participating in developing the nature-related risk standards of the TNFD. Finally, only one Chinese financial institution, Bin Yuan Capital, signed up for the Glasgow Financial Alliance for Net Zero (GFANZ) at COP26 in Glasgow in 2021 (GFANZ, 2021).

The Need to Integrate China into Global Green Finance Research

In relation to the importance and broadness of the topic of Chinese green finance, academic research on the subject is still evolving. Following China's development trajectory, academic research has changed focus and priorities over the years. As sealed off from the outside world from 1949 to the early 1980s, international academics had a hard time analyzing China, while their Chinese colleagues had limited resources and platforms to do research. As part of China's gradual opening since then, all areas of China studies have proliferated, and Chinese and international academia is increasingly integrated. China's development is increasingly influential to the world and has become too important to ignore: in particular, the last 20 years have seen most social science disciplines develop China-focused literature areas, be it demography, politics, arts, or history. As most related to green finance, academic research about China has also proliferated in economics, politics, finance, and business. However, researching Chinese development forces all academics to reflect on how well their theories can accommodate Chinese realities. Simply put, if a social science theory is not able to the empirical case of China, its relevance will be increasingly questionable and needs to be adjusted. Researchers and practitioners, therefore, need to not only translate from the Chinese language but also to understand the concept that might be related and yet different from more established concepts on green finance. For example, China's distinction between "green enterprises bonds" and "green corporate bonds" or, more broadly, between China's green bond catalogue and green industry catalogue seems easy to ignore (Escalante et al., 2020), but ignorance of the specificities would lead to incomplete and possibly incorrect results. Methodologically speaking, comparative case studies can be a useful tool for comparing China with other countries to see how well existing theories fit with China and identify where gaps may exist. This could be done, for example, with the EU's and China's green bond market and policies.

Equally important, due to the size of China's financial markets, the complexity of its governance between different regulators on the national *and* subnational levels, and its increasingly global footprint, academic research on green finance in China requires very nuanced analyses and theory: we refer to it as the "Panda–Dragon paradox," where China is simultaneously a "Panda" and "Dragon," where it can be a leading economy on green finance and the largest investor in green energies while simultaneously being the biggest emitter of greenhouse gases and the country with the fastest absolute carbon emission growth. Accordingly, future research on Chinese green finance should focus on some of the specific issues of the Chinese top-down financial system and its international footprint driving global harmonization with and without the "Chinese characteristics" of the green financial system. Seeing China as the unit of analysis, intra-unit comparative case studies, comparing, for example, the renewable and fossil energy sectors, could be carried out to identify relations between the "Panda" and the "Dragon."

Furthermore, the de-facto application and efficacy of green financial instruments in China merit more academic research, particularly green credit, green insurance, and emission trading (green bonds seem to receive increasing attention). With its growing clout and stated ambition to deepen capital markets, it is further of interest how the internationalization of its capital markets impacts green finance, including ESG practices and disclosure, as well as ESG harmonization. Additionally, risks and profitability in green finance should be further studied under the assumption of different policy support schemes. This should also include a differentiated view on the political economy of domestic stranded asset risks with a top-down, government-controlled financial and economic system, changing the calculus of transition and, in particular, political risks. Finally, with its diverse provinces and pilot regions, research on China's differentiated approach to green finance and national diffusion could lead to important insights.

Conclusion

Since 2016, China has made impressive progress in greening its financial system. However, China's financial system is simultaneously the largest source of capital for coal assets. In this chapter, we have provided an overview of progress and challenges across key aspects of China's financial system: from central banking, taxonomies, information disclosure, credit, and bond markets to the international role of China through regulators, financial institutions, and coordination initiatives. Across the board, a core feature is apparent. Ongoing efforts have the potential to continue to scale up to a degree where China becomes a driving force in the global green transition. But this is not the case yet, and it is not inevitable that it will happen. Instead, China can today be characterized as a "Panda–Dragon paradox" with an uncertain future. Playing a part in understanding these circumstances and ultimately contributing to its solution, researchers on green finance need to increase their understanding of China's path-dependent development of green finance in regard to the political environment both as a singular case and in comparison with Western countries. Furthermore, China's impact on international green finance development, particularly in emerging markets, remains a large field of research. Finally, the application and effectiveness of various aspects of the green finance system and performance remain a large field of open research, e.g., to understand the interplay between ESG disclosure, carbon emission, green finance instruments, and environmental and financial performance.

Notes

1 Authored with equal contributions.
2 Further information on China's ETS can be found, e.g., in Liu and Nedopil (2021).
3 Considering green performance as part of banks macroprudential assessment means reducing the risk assessment of a bank if it is greener and therefore giving higher interest rates on the banks' mandatory deposits in the central bank (Larsen, 2020).
4 For more information on the latest guidance and opinions, their changing focus, and integration of various environmental dimensions, governance, and target groups, refer to Nedopil et al. (2022b).

References

AMAC. (2020). *China fund industry ESG investment survey report (2019)* (中国证券投资基金业协会: 中国基金业ESG投资专题调查报告(2019)). Asset Management Association of China.
Ang, Y. Y. (2016). *How China escaped the poverty trap*. Cornell University Press.
Azizuddin, K. (2020, October 19). EU and China to co-chair international taskforce on sustainable finance taxonomies [Content]. *Responsible Investor*. https://www.responsible-investor.com/eu-and-china-to-co-chair-international-taskforce-on-sustainable-finance-taxonomies/
Barmes, D., & Livingstone, Z. (2021). *The Green central banking scorecard: How green are G20 central banks and financial supervisors?* Positive Money.
CBI. (2021). *Sustainable debt: Global state of the market 2020*. Climate Bond Initiative.
CBIN. (2022). *21 largest banks' green credit stood at RMB 15.1 trillion at the end of 2021* (中国银行保险报网: 2021年末国内21家主要银行绿色信贷余额达15.1万亿元). China Banking and Insurance News. http://www.cbimc.cn/content/2022-03/24/content_458884.html, 21
CBRC. (2014). *Green credit statistics system* （银监会：绿色信贷统计制度）. China Banking Regulatory Commission.
CEC. (2020). *Power industry statistics 2019*. China Electricity Council. www.http://english.cec.org.cn
Cheng, E. (2021, May 21). *Overseas investors are snapping up mainland Chinese bonds*. CNBC. https://www.cnbc.com/2021/05/21/overseas-investors-buy-up-mainland-chinese-bonds-in-a-search-for-yield.html
China Development Bank, & United Nations Development Programme. (2019). *Harmonizing investment and financing standards towards sustainable development along the Belt and road*. http://www.un.org.cn/uploads/20191108/bbb5cee285b9e35d7de574f4e9e4f6df.pdf
EC. (2018). *Renewed sustainable finance strategy and implementation of the action plan on financing sustainable growth*. European Commission. https://ec.europa.eu/info/publications/sustainable-finance-renewed-strategy_en
Equator Principles Association, & International Finance Corporation. (2020). *Equator principles July 2020*. International Finance Corporation (IFC). www.equator-principles.com
Escalante, D., Choi, J., Chin, N., Cui, Y., & Larsen, M. L. (2020). *The state and effectiveness of the green bond market in China* (p. 29). Climate Policy Initiative.
Escalante, D., Choi, J., & Larsen, M. L. (2020). *Green banking in China – Emerging trends: with a spotlight on the industrial and commercial bank of China (ICBC)*. Climate Policy Initiative.
European Commission. (2022). *International platform on sustainable finance*. European Commission. https://ec.europa.eu/info/business-economy-euro/banking-and-finance/sustainable-finance/international-platform-sustainable-finance_en
European Investment Bank (EIB), & Green Finance Committee of China Society for Finance and Banking. (2017). *The need for A common language in green finance*. European Investment Bank (EIB). https://www.eib.org/attachments/press/white-paper-green-finance-common-language-eib-and-green-finance-committee.pdf
Fitch. (2022a). *China corporate bond default rate set to rise in 2022*. Fitch Ratings. https://www.fitchratings.com/research/corporate-finance/china-corporate-bond-default-rate-set-to-rise-in-2022-27-01-2022

Fitch. (2022b). *Proposed rules may strengthen China's ESG disclosure*. Fitch Ratings. https://www.fitchratings.com/corporate-finance/proposed-rules-may-strengthen-chinas-esg-disclosure-28-10-2021

FOCAC. (2021). *Declaration on China-Africa cooperation on combating climate change (FOCAC)*. Ministry of Foreign Affairs of the People's Republic of China (MFA). http://www.focac.org/eng/zywx_1/zywj/202201/t20220124_10632445.htm

GFANZ. (2021). *Progress report*. Glasgow Financial Alliance for Net Zero. https://www.gfanzero.com/progress-report/

Green Finance Leadership Program. (2018). *Green investment principles (GIP) for the belt and road*. http://www.gflp.org.cn/public/ueditor/php/upload/file/20181201/1543598660333978.pdf

Herekar, Y. et al. (2021, January 28). Comment: China's carbon markets offer Pakistan a big opportunity. The Third Pole. https://www.thethirdpole.net/en/climate/chinas-carbon-markets-offer-pakistan-a-big-opportunity/

ICMA. (2021). *Overview and recommendations for sustainable finance taxonomies*. International Capital Markets Association.

IFC. (2021a). *Mongolia green taxonomy introduction & proposed taxonomy framework*. https://www.ifc.org/wps/wcm/connect/fa534a1e-34a5-49ed-ac09-8fa8e143535f/EN+Framework.+Green+Taxonomy+Mongolia.pdf?MOD=AJPERES&CVID=m.UgfA4

IFC. (2021b). *Sustainable Banking Network (SBN)*. https://www.sbfnetwork.org

IIGF. (2022). *2021 China green bond report (中央财经大学绿色金融国际研究院: 2021年中国绿色债券年报)*. International Institute of Green Finance.

Jiang, Q. (2016). *China's G20 initiative to build-up green finance and incentive mechanism for investment*. https://www.chinadaily.com.cn/business/2016hangzhoug20/2016-10/11/content_27024059.htm

Larsen, M. L. (2020). Green finance international cooperation (绿色金融国际合作). In Y. Wang & H. Xu (Eds.), *China green finance report 2020 (王遥&徐洪峰: 中国绿色金融研究报告2020)*. China Finance Publishing House (中国金融出版社).

Larsen, M. L. (2021a, February 22). How China's green finance slowdown threatens global climate ambitions. *South China Morning Post*. https://www.scmp.com/comment/opinion/article/3122533/how-chinas-green-finance-slowdown-threatens-global-climate

Larsen, M. L. (2021b, July 15). Intersecting interests and coincidental compatibility: How China, the EU, and the United States can coordinate their push for globalizing green finance. *Georgetown Journal of International Affairs*. https://gjia.georgetown.edu/2021/07/15/intersecting-interests-and-coincidental-compatibility-how-china-the-eu-and-the-united-states-can-coordinate-their-push-for-globalizing-green-finance/

Larsen, M. L., & Oehler, L. (2022). Clean at home, polluting abroad: The role of the Chinese financial system's differential treatment of state-owned and private enterprises. *Climate Policy*, 1–14. https://doi.org/10.1080/14693062.2022.2040409

Liu, H., & Nedopil, C. (2021). *Potential harmonisation of emission trading systems (ETS): China and Southeast Asia*. Regional Project Energy Security and Climate Change Asia-Pacific (RECAP). Konrad-Adenauer-Stiftung e.V. https://www.kas.de/en/web/recap/single-title/-/content/potential-harmonisation-of-emission-trading-systems-ets-china-and-southeast-asia

Ma, J., & Zadek, S. (2016). The G20 embraces green finance. *Project Syndicate*, 3.

Ma, J., & Zadek, S. (2019). *Decarbonizing the belt and road—A green finance roadmap*. Tsinghua University. www.vivideconomics.com/publications/decarbonizing-the-belt-and-roadinitiative- a-green-finance-roadmap

Ma, X., Han Springer, C., & Shao, H. (2022). *Outlier or new normal? Trends in China's global energy finance* (GCI Policy Brief No. 11). Boston University Global Development Policy Center. https://www.bu.edu/gdp/files/2022/03/GCI_PB_011_FIN.pdf

MEF Department of Treasury. (2021). *G20 sustainable finance working group*. https://www.dt.mef.gov.it/en/news/2021/g20_working_group.html

Myllyvirta, L., Zhang, S., & Shen, X. (2020, March 24). *Analysis: Will China build hundreds of new coal plants in the 2020s?* Carbon Brief. https://www.carbonbrief.org/analysis-will-china-build-hundreds-of-new-coal-plants-in-the-2020s

Myllyvirta, L., Zhang, S., Shen, X., & Bi, Y. (2020). Political economy of climate and clean energy in China. *Heinrich Böll Foundation & Center for Research on Energy and Clean Air*, 38.

关于推进共建"一带一路"绿色发展的意见—Opinions on promoting the green development of "one belt, one road", 408 (2022). https://www.ndrc.gov.cn/xxgk/jd/jd/202203/t20220324_1320198_ext.html

NDRC, MIIT, NRC, MEE, MoHURD, PBoC, & NEA. (2019). *Green industry guiding catalogue (2019 version)* (国家发展和改革委员会，工业和信息化部，自然资源部，生态环境部，住房城乡建设部，人民银行，国家能源局：绿色产业指导目录（*2019年版*)). National Development and Reform Commission. https://www.ndrc.gov.cn/fggz/hjyzy/stwmjs/201903/W020200217416444788586.pdf

Naughton, B. (2020). Grand steerage. In *Fateful decisions: Choices that will shape China's future* (pp. 51–81). Stanford University Press.

NDRC. (2001). *10th five-year plan regarding development of the national economy and society* 关于国民经济和社会发展第十个五年计划纲要的报告 (p. 18). National Development and Reform Commission.

Nedopil Wang, C. (2020, April 2). Understanding the Belt and road initiative green coalition (BRIGC) – Green Belt and road initiative center. *Green-Bri.Org*. https://green-bri.org/understanding-the-belt-and-road-initiative-green-coalition-brigc

Nedopil, C. (2021a). *China investments in the belt and road initiative (BRI) 2020* [Brief]. IIGF Green BRI Center.

Nedopil, C. (2021b, June 16). Brief: Coal phase-out in the Belt and Road Initiative (BRI): An analysis of Chinese-backed coal power from 2014–2020 – Green finance & development center. *Green BRI Center*. https://greenfdc.org/coal-phase-out-in-the-belt-and-road-initiative-bri-an-analysis-of-chinese-backed-coal-power-from-2014-2020/

Nedopil, C. (2021c). Green finance for soft power: An analysis of China's green policy signals and investments in the Belt and Road Initiative. *Environmental Policy and Governance*. https://doi.org/10.1002/eet.1965

Nedopil, C. (2022). *China Belt and road initiative (BRI) investment report 2021* (FISF Green Finance & Development Center Brief). FISF Green Finance & Development Center. https://doi.org/10.13140/RG.2.2.12834.50887

Nedopil, C., Cheng, L., Chen, Y., Li, P., & Fan, D. (2022a). *Accelerating green BRI investments: Alignment and implementation of the green development guidance for BRI projects (GDG) and the green investment principles for the Belt and road (GIP)*. International Belt and Road Initiative Green Development Coalition (BRIGC). https://doi.10.13140/RG.2.2.23169.53601

Nedopil, C., Dordi, T., & Weber, O. (2021). The nature of global green finance standards—Evolution, differences, and three models. *Sustainability*, *13*(7), 3723. https://doi.org/10.3390/su13073723

Nedopil, C., Wang, Y., Xie, W., DeBoer, D., Liu, S., Chen, X., Li, Y., Zhu, Y., Lan, Y., Li, P., & Zhao, H. (2020). *Green development guidance for BRI projects baseline study report*. International Belt and road initiative green development coalition (BRIGC).

Nedopil, C. et al. (2022b). Understanding China's latest guidelines for greening the belt and road. *China Dialogue*. https://chinadialogue.net/en/business/understanding-chinas-latest-guidelines-for-greening-the-belt-and-road/

Network for Greening the Financial System (NGFS). (2022, April 13). *Network for greening the financial system members*. Network for Greening the Financial System (NGFS). https://www.ngfs.net/en/about-us/membership

Pan, G., Ma, J., & Zadek, S. (2015). *Establishing China's green financial system*. People's Bank of China & UNEP. https://www.unepfi.org/news/establishing-chinas-green-financial-system-report-of-the-green-finance-task-force/

PBoC. (2015). *Green bond endorsed project catalogue*（人民银行：绿色债券支持项目目录）. Peoples' Bank of China.

PBoC. (2016). *Guidelines for establishing the green financial system*. People's Bank of China. http://www.pbc.gov.cn/english/130721/3133045/index.html

PBoC. (2021). *Green bond endorsed project catalogue (*中国人民银行，发展改革委，证监会《绿色债券支持项目目录（*2021年版*)). People's Bank of China, National Development and Reform Commission, and China Banking and Insurance Regulatory Commission. http://www.pbc.gov.cn/goutongjiaoliu/113456/113469/4236341/index.html

PBoC. (2022a). *2021 February social financing statistical report (*中国人民银行：*2021年2月社会融资规模存量统计数据报告*). People's Bank of China. http://www.gov.cn/shuju/2021-03/10/content_5592070.htm

PBoC. (2022b). *2021 Financial institutions loan allocation statistics report*（中国人民银行：*2021年金融机构贷款投向统计报告*). People's Bank of China. http://www.pbc.gov.cn/goutongjiaoliu/113456/113469/4464086/2022013010434016509.pdf

Sachs, J. D., Woo, W. T., Yoshino, N., & Taghizadeh-Hesary, F. (2019). Why is green finance important? *Asian Development Bank Institute*. https://doi.org/10.2139/ssrn.3327149

SEC. (2022). *SEC.gov | SEC proposes rules to enhance and standardize climate-related disclosures for investors*. Securities and Exchange Commission. https://www.sec.gov/news/press-release/2022-46

Simon, F. (2021, January 27). EU green finance advisors asked to clarify "transition" to net-zero climate goal. *Euractiv*. https://www.euractiv.com/section/energy-environment/news/eu-green-finance-advisors-asked-to-clarify-transition-to-net-zero-climate-goal/

S&P Global. (2022). *China green bond issuances set to cross $100B mark in 2022*. S&P Global Market Intelligence. https://www.spglobal.com/marketintelligence/en/news-insights/latest-news-headlines/china-green-bond-issuances-set-to-cross-100b-mark-in-2022-68453272

Sun, C. (2022). Chinese banks see growth in green credit balance in first 9 months. *China Daily*. https://global.chinadaily.com.cn/a/202112/21/WS61c1864fa310cdd39bc7cae1.html

Teer, J., & Larsen, M. L. (2019). *Sustainable finance in Asia: Helping Asian green bond issuers to access global Capital Markets*. International Institute of Green Finance.

Tsinghua University ICCSD. (2020). China's long term low carbon development strategy and transition pathway research (清华大学气候变化与可持续发展研究院: 中国长期低碳发展战略与转型路径研究). *China Polulation, Resources, and Environment (*中国人口，自愿与环境*)*, *30*. ICCSD, 11.

Vivid Economics. (2020). *Greenness of stimulus index*. Vivid Economics & Finance for Biodiversity Initiative, 8.

Voituriez, T., Yao, W., & Larsen, M. L. (2019). Revising the 'host country standard' principle: A step for China to align its overseas investment with the Paris agreement. *Climate Policy*, *19*(10), 1205–1210. https://doi.org/10.1080/14693062.2019.1650702

Wang, J. (2019). *China's governance approach to the belt and road initiative (BRI): Partnership, relations, and law* (SSRN Scholarly Paper ID 3346427). Social Science Research Network. https://papers.ssrn.com/abstract=3346427

Wang, L., & Peng, Q. (2021). Cover story: Taming the "green swan" (王力为&彭骎骎: 封面报道|驯服"绿天鹅"). *Caixin*. http://weekly.caixin.com/2021-02-26/101667412.html

Wang, Y. (2018). China's green finance strategy: Much achieved, further to go. *Grantham Research Institute on Climate Change and the Environment*. https://www.lse.ac.uk/granthaminstitute/news/chinas-green-finance-strategy-much-achieved-further-to-go/

Wang, Y., & Liu, S. (2021). *INSIDER: Can a traffic-light system help China end environmentally harmful overseas investments?* https://www.wri.org/insights/insider-can-traffic-light-system-help-china-end-environmentally-harmful-overseas

Wang, Y., & Nedopil, C. (2020, December 9). *Red-flagging belt and road coal projects can boost China's green ambitions*. South China Morning Post. https://www.scmp.com/comment/opinion/article/3113152/how-red-flagging-coal-can-help-align-belt-and-road-projects-chinas

Wang, Y., Nedopil, C., Xie, W., DeBoer, D., & Liu, S. (2021). *Green development guidance for BRI projects phase II task 1 – Application guide for enterprises and financial institutions*. International Belt and Road Initiative Green Development Coalition (BRIGC).

Xi, J. (2019, April 26). *Opening speech belt and road forum 2019*. Belt and Road Forum. http://www.cpecinfo.com/news/the-complete-text-of-president-xi-jinping-speech-at-the-belt-and-road-forum-for-international-cooperation-2019/NzAwMQ==

Xi, J. (2021, April 20). *Keynote speech by Chinese President Xi Jinping at the opening ceremony of the Bo'ao forum for Asia annual conference 2021*. Xinhua. http://www.xinhuanet.com/english/download/2021-04-20/Fulltext.docx

Zhou, L., Gilbert, S., Wang, Y., Cabré, M. M., & Gallagher, K. P. (2018). Moving the green Belt and road initiative: From words to actions. *World Resources Institute*, 44.

17

FINANCE WITHOUT UNIFIED MEASUREMENT FRAMEWORK

Rise of Collective Norm Entrepreneurs in Impact Finance in Japan

Noriaki Okamoto

Introduction

It has become common for global large corporations to pay close attention to sustainability and corporate social responsibility (CSR) activities. According to KPMG's survey of corporate sustainability reporting, 80% of large global companies reported on sustainability in 2020 compared to 18% in 2002.[1] It reveals that most global corporations have dealt with sustainability or social issues to some extent. However, the term "sustainability" encompasses different meanings, and furthermore, it normally does not connote a direct return to investors but rather a broader return to the wider stakeholders. In the background, there has been a shift in attention from "sustainability" to "impact," as it fits well with investors' increasing awareness and fundraising that contributes to the rapid growth of the environmental, social, and governance (ESG) sectors.[2] Yet, the term "impact" is merely a vague notion despite the rapidly growing awareness of impact in the investment[3] market (Jones et al., 2022). The Global Impact Investing Network (GIIN) estimated that over 3,349 organizations managed $1,164 trillion under impact investing (assets under management) in 2021 (Hand et al., 2022), which has exponentially grown from 2013 ($25.4 billion).

It is interesting to consider what has made this momentum stronger. More importantly, the framework to measure and compare corporate social impact plays a crucial role in the process of impact analysis. Apparently, the existing framework of corporate financial reporting is not sufficient to capture the featured social impact. However, the flourishing modern financial markets could not exist without the current system of financial accounting because accounting can make things (economic knowledge as well as economic phenomena) visible (Hopwood, 1990) through quantification. For instance, the comparable set of financial statements elucidates corporate profitability and financial conditions and thereby supports smooth transactions in the stock market.[4] Having said that, accounting can be and is being changed in the name of discursive developments (Hopwood, 1990, p. 14). The discourse of social impact is now extensively intertwined in economic spheres, and it implies insufficiencies in the traditional accounting framework in line with it (Cohen, 2020).

To investigate the current state of impact finance, it is necessary to consider both the global power struggle of organizations towards a hegemonic position in the field of impact measurement and how local situations are affected by such global politics. Moreover, the kind of impact measurement framework selected by relevant stakeholders or organizations is an interesting matter. In addition to considering the global trend of impact finance/investing, this chapter focuses on impact investment in Japan, where both public and private actors have recently turned their attention to impact finance. By applying a theory of international norm dynamics to the global diffusion of impact finance, the chapter emphasizes the actions of public and private collective norm entrepreneurs in Japan. Although there are epistemic communities[5] and norm entrepreneurs who promote the norm of impact finance in Japan, to reach the norm acceptance or norm internalization stage, norm carriers (consultants, auditors, and professional associations) should play a significant role in the diffusion of the norm. The Japanese public–private partnership seems to reflect legitimacy, reputation, or esteem to some extent that is required to diffuse a specific norm. However, despite the initiatives and declarations towards impact finance in the global trend of "impactization" (Power, 2015),[6] there is no clear consensus as to what kind of impact measurement framework should be used in investment decisions. Although, globally, there are various impact measurement frameworks, at least in Japan, none has achieved legitimacy or reputation yet. This study problematizes the lack of consensus and implies the necessity of a legitimate unification of impact measurement frameworks to promote the norm of impact finance.

This chapter is structured as follows. The next section briefly summarizes the transition of research focus from environmental accounting to impact accounting. The third section discusses the recent global surge of impact finance. It also considers several global organizations' impact measurement frameworks to identify and quantify corporate social impact. The fourth section introduces the theory of international norm diffusion and its application to the diffusion of impact finance. The fifth section consists of a detailed case analysis of impact investment/finance in Japan and is followed by the conclusion section. According to the case analysis, this chapter argues that the collaboration between the public and private sectors in Japan mobilized the diffusion of norm of impact finance that led to the alliance of more than 60 institutions. However, it also highlights the existence of different impact measurement frameworks that reflects Stark's (2009) thesis of multiple evaluative principles.

The Shift from Environmental and Social Accounting to Impact Accounting

Prior to the recent spotlight on corporate social impact, corporate social and environmental accounting had been extensively studied.[7] Put differently, the investigation into corporate social impact is the extension of the general trajectory of accounting for social. Changes in researchers' interests and analyses tend to reflect the shift of central concern in corporate activities.[8] In retrospect, accounting for the environment was in the spotlight to some extent in the 1970s, although the social and environmental accounting literature was underdeveloped before 1980 (Mathews, 1997, p. 484). From the 1980s to 1990s, however, the research about environmental accounting gained momentum, and regulatory agencies in the United States and the United Kingdom established rules to prevent environmentally harmful corporate activities during the period (Mathews, 1997). From the 1990s, environmental accounting became popular as the concern for environmental issues grew. For instance, Macve and Carey (1992) pointed out that the growing pressure on corporate disclosure of environmental performance came from the marketplace and regulatory authorities at that time.

Researchers pivoted from the sphere of environmental accounting to broader social accounting around 2000. This was partly due to the calls for an expansion in research efforts directed towards more comprehensive social responsibility (Parker, 2011). Social and environmental accounting has become a central research agenda in the 2000s, at least in comparison to its former marginalized state in the accounting literature (Parker, 2014).

From that standpoint, in addition to accounting for sustainability and corporate sustainable development goals (SDGs), the pursuit of better accounting for social impact is an emerging contentious topic. The trend was partly spurred by the works of Alex Nicholls (2009 and 2018) who defined impact[9] accounting as "a system that aims to capture the relative importance of outcomes and effects that are not adequately accounted for by the conventions of financial accounting and that cannot be captured in prices in conventional markets" (Nicholls, 2018, p. 150). In other words, social impact accounting is based on the recognition that financial accounting alone does not provide sufficient information for effective decision-making or effective resource allocation to maximize benefits for all stakeholders. Then, how does research on impact accounting differ from environmental or CSR accounting research? Put simply, previous social and environmental accounting research tended to be in the context of CSR or ESG initiatives that typically focused on outputs, rather than impacts, and that focus was on narrow, mainstream, business settings (Nicholls, 2018, p. 132). From a broader practical standpoint, this chapter delineates impact finance/investing and points out challenges faced by researchers.

The Global Pursuit of Impact Finance/Investing and Multiple Measurement Frameworks

Defining Impact Finance/Investing

Although there are several definitions of impact in the context of investment and finance, it is defined as the measure of an action's benefit to people and the planet, and it goes beyond minimizing harmful outcomes to actively enabling good ones, thereby creating positive impact (Cohen, 2020, p. 11).[10] How then does impact investment differ from other common investment methods? Brandstetter and Lehner (2015) located impact investment in the spectrum (Figure 17.1) that ranges from traditional investment, which primarily seeks financial returns, to philanthropy investment, which pursues the solving of social and environmental issues. Brandstetter and Lehner's (2015) classification regards two new paradigmatic investment styles as impact investment. The first one is sustainable investment that pursues competitive return while also seeking opportunities to improve ESG matters. The second one is a visionary investment that focuses on environmental and social impact while putting less emphasis on financial return. Although both of their goals are hybrid, their weight on expected return and focus on impact are slightly different.

Previous Accounting Studies on Social Impact

Although there are some previous accounting studies about social impact, the vague concept of impact has been criticized. For instance, by relying on Bourdieu's notion of symbolic power, Semeen and Islam (2021) revealed that fair trade organizations use social impact disclosures and related rhetorical strategies to perpetuate hegemony by disregarding stakeholders' direct concerns over a lack of measures to improve the lives of farmers or producers in the developing world. In the context of social impact bonds,[11] which rely on a vast array of accounting technologies, Cooper et al. (2016) analyzed an engineered market-based solution to support homeless people in the UK and further indicated that it eliminates from the notion of society

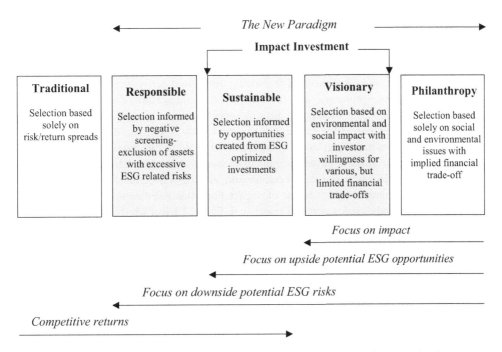

Figure 17.1 Impact investment in the spectrum (this figure is based on Brandstetter and Lehner (2015, p. 89))

everything except calculative aspects of self-interest that suit a market ideology (contracts, profit incentives, risk-taking, and outcome measurement), even if no market exists.

To contradict such criticism, while relying on the acronym of hembig lens (when a concept is hegemonic, ambiguous, and big) developed by Alvesson and Blom (2022), Yang et al. (2021, p. 316) argue that social impact in accounting does not constitute the hembig concept at the moment, as it does not dominate accounting research and practices.[12] Elaborating the concept of "the public interest" from three perspectives (aggregative, processual, and common good), Adams et al. (2021) examined the social impact disclosures of charity organizations. As charities do not have investors or owners per se, accountability to the public interest is the central concern. In terms of aggregative (stakeholders need comparable data to assess which charity produced the highest social returns on investment) and processual (founders and charities can engage with each other) reasons, Australian stakeholders generally agreed on the standardization of social impact disclosures for charity organizations (Adams et al., 2021).

To summarize, as impact finance and accounting is a new type of practice, there are still pros and cons of its diffusion in previous studies. Yet, compared to the rapidly growing interest in impact finance, the accumulation of research on the topic is still scarce. This chapter contributes to reducing this gap in the literature by theoretically analyzing the diffusion of impact finance and investing.

Global Organizations and Various Impact Measurement Frameworks

Although there are pros and cons of capturing the social impact of corporate activities, we should not overlook the growing interest in measuring and managing it. Various methods to quantify social impact currently exist and illustrate a plethora of different methods with mixed success and varying support from different parties (Matthew, 2015). Accordingly, it seems to represent a race toward tyranny of metrics (Muller, 2018). Considering that impact investors and funders usually target more positive (or less negative) social and environmental impact and that the long-lasting acceptance of financial accounting institutions derives from the power of quantified accounting inscriptions (records) (Robson, 1992), quantification of social impact is pivotal. A study of different actors' attempts to quantify social impact would help sharpen the conceptual categories when considering what quantification really is (Berman & Hirschman, 2018, p. 265). Various actors have been so far concerned with making the abstract concept of impact into a concrete instrument of governance in organizations and society at large (Hopwood, 1990, p. 9). As Power (2015) states, the idea of emphasizing impact, or the "impact culture," creeps into different social spheres. In the context of impact financing/investment, how specific impact metrics are selectively used is not well-researched. Table 17.1 lists selected large organizations' attempts to measure corporate social impact to some degree. Although there are other different or similar attempts to measure not only social impact but sustainability or corporate SDGs, this chapter focuses on some of those major impact measurement frameworks.

B Impact Assessment has the longest history among these and is now used by more than 150,000 businesses.[13] By replying to customized questions about governance, workers, community, environment, and customers, an organization receives an impact assessment score. A higher score (above 80 points) can achieve the B Corp Certification, which has symbolic value to stakeholders. GIIN established its impact measurement framework, IRIS+, that makes it easier for investors to translate their impact intentions into real impact results. It consists of regularly updated core metrics sets and is aligned with other principles such as the UN SDGs; it currently has more than 27,000 registered users.[14]

The social value calculation framework established and disseminated by Social Value International (SVI) is a more stakeholder-oriented approach. The SVI has a global network that consists of 25 national and regional organizations working at the forefront of social value and impact management.[15] By focusing on stakeholders' voices and outcomes that anchor the quantification of social value, the estimation of social return on investment is possible. World Benchmarking Alliance (WBA)'s bottom-up approach now involves more than 280 organizations, and the multistakeholder allies share useful data and stories that improve its benchmarks. Finally, the impact-weighted initiative based in Harvard Business School has rapidly gained popularity and is led by leading researchers and an iconic figure of impact finance, Sir Ronald Cohen. Its uniqueness comes from the use of various second-hand market data and the monetization of impact. One of its aims is to achieve an adjacency to the existing financial accounting framework.

Although these five frameworks share the same objective of capturing corporate social impact, the existence of different measurement frameworks causes confusion. The Global Steering Group (GSG) listed nine impact measurement frameworks (Carbon Disclosure Project (CDP), Climate Disclosure Standards Board (CDSB), Chartered Financial Analyst (CFA) ESG Standards, GIIN (IRIS+), Global Reporting Initiative (GRI) standards, International Integrated Reporting Council (IIRC) framework, Sustainability Accounting Standards Board (SASB) standards, SVI standards, and Task Force on Climate-related Financial Disclosures (TCFD)) and stated that the alphabet soup has resulted in no internationally accepted standard and little communication between standard setters (GSG, 2021a, p. 15). Unlike collectively accepted financial reporting systems, there are typically several obstacles in establishing a unified social impact measurement framework. For instance, there is no clear consensus regarding the meaning of "impact," and it is often unclear if an outcome (impact) was the direct result of an organization's intervention (Guter-Sandu, 2022, p. 6). Although the Impact Measurement Project (IMP) was formed in

Table 17.1 Summary of impact measurement frameworks by various organizations

Organization	Headquarters	Established	Impact Measurement Framework	Characteristics
B Lab: Global Impact Investment Rating System (GIIRS)	Rockefeller Foundation	2006	B Impact Assessment Receiving a minimum verified score of 80 points on the assessment is necessary to get the B Corp Certification	Theory of change is applied It is a digital tool that can help measure, manage, and improve positive impact performance for environment, communities, customers, suppliers, employees, and shareholders
Global Impact Investing Network (GIIN)	New York, United States	2009	IRIS is the generally accepted impact accounting system that leading impact investors use to measure, manage, and optimize their impact (e.g., IRIS+)	Four practices define impact investing: intentionality; use evidence and impact data in investment design; manage impact performance; and contribute to the growth of the industry Financial return and asset classes are considered
Social Value International (SVI)	Liverpool, UK It consists of 25 national and regional networks	2011	Social return on investment (SROI) Eight basic principles are: involve stakeholders; understand what changes; value the things that matter; only include what is material; do not overclaim; be transparent; verify the result; and be responsive	A mix of qualitative and quantitative information Stakeholders' changes and outcomes are identified and prioritized Social value is estimated through weighting and anchoring methods
The World Benchmarking Alliance (WBA)	The Netherlands	2018	Benchmarked data sets with scoring and ranking are available to the public: Food and Agriculture Benchmark, Climate and Energy Benchmark, Digital Inclusion Benchmark, Corporate Human Rights Benchmark, and Gender Equality and Empowerment Benchmark	Identified seven systems transformations (social; agriculture and food; nature; digital; urban; decarbonization and energy; and financial) It is based on systems thinking (systems-based approach)

(Continued)

Table 17.1 (Continued)

Organization	Headquarters	Established	Impact Measurement Framework	Characteristics
Impact Weighted Accounts (IWA)	Boston, United States (Harvard Business School)	2019	There are four principles: impact can be measured and compared; impact should be measured within an accounting framework with the aim of harnessing our economy to improve our society and planet; transformational change requires that impact measurement be scalable; to be scalable it needs to be actionable and cost effective	Impacts estimation is classified into products, employees (organizational), and environment It supplements the statement of financial health and performance by reflecting a company's positive and negative impacts on employees, customers, the environment, and the broader society To monetize impact global level secondary market data are used

2016 to provide a forum for building global consensus on measuring, managing, and reporting impacts on sustainability, standardization, and unification of measurement, it is difficult to define such frameworks without different standard-setting organizations' consensus (IMP, 2020).[16]

Two questions need to be addressed regarding the institutionalization of impact finance/investment: 1) how does the global norm of impact finance/investment spread across the world and penetrate local practices? and 2) how does a specific common impact measurement framework become accepted and used by organizations in different countries? To analyze these, this chapter applies a constructivist theory of international dynamics of norms. As investment decisions in impact finance and impact measurement frameworks are inseparable, the analysis below covers both topics. Before turning into an in-depth local case analysis in Japan, the theoretical framework is considered in the next section.

Application of the Dynamics of International Norms

Theory of Life Cycle of Norms from a Constructivist Perspective

As indicated in the previous section, impact finance/investing is a current global trend, rapidly gaining popularity in various countries. This popularity followed the long tradition of diffusion of CSR norms (Bebbington et al., 2012; Dashwood, 2020).[17] The study of norms can shed light on both a "logic of appropriateness" at work in international politics, as well as international actors acting the way they believe is "good" (Peez, 2022). Thus, this viewpoint is useful to examine the phenomena that diffuse globally without explicit clear benefits or by orders of international organizations. In terms of methodology, this norm-centered constructivist perspective is compatible with the interpretive qualitative case-based analysis (Peez, 2022) that unfolds in the next section.

From a social constructivist perspective, the central concern is the process.[18] In other words, a social constructivist study approaches international norms by questioning how they are diffused.

In a global context, international norms are defined as "shared ideas and standards of appropriate behavior" (Finnemore & Sikkink, 1998, p. 191). This chapter regards the movement towards impact finance/investing as a global norm, and its diffusion can be analyzed from this theoretical perspective. Finnemore and Sikkink's seminal study suggests that there are three stages in the life cycle of norms: "norm emergence," "norm acceptance (or norm cascade)," and "norm internalization." An important threshold, known as the "tipping point," exists between the norm emergence and the norm acceptance stage. This is the point at which a critical mass of relevant state actors adopts the emerging norm. Many emergent norms fail to reach the tipping point, and not all norms proceed beyond it (Finnemore & Sikkink, 1998, p. 195).

In the "norm emergence" stage, norm entrepreneurs attempt to convince or persuade a critical mass of states (norm leaders) to embrace different norms. Such norms are actively built by agents who have strong ideas about what is deemed as appropriate or desirable behavior in their community (Finnemore & Sikkink, 1998). Norm entrepreneurs call attention to issues or even "create" issues using language that names, interprets, and dramatizes them (Finnemore & Sikkink, 1998). To achieve norm diffusion, constructing cognitive frames is the basic building block for constructing resonant norms and serves to legitimatize normative orders (Payne, 2001). As shown in Table 17.2, norm entrepreneurs construct such cognitive frames by virtue of altruism, empathy, and ideational commitment. Taken together, they connect with the concept of legitimacy, which provides persuasive reasons why a course of action, rule, or political order is correct and appropriate (Hurrel, 2007).

From this perspective, the diffusion of impact finance is still somewhere between the norm emergence and the norm acceptance stage. In the context of impact finance, norm internalization is not yet achieved, as it occurs when norms acquire a taken-for-granted quality and are no longer a matter of broad public debate (Finnemore & Sikkink, 1998). Impact finance has not even reached the tipping point after which many actors begin to rapidly adopt new norms without domestic pressure for such changes (Finnemore & Sikkink, 1998).

Norms of Accounting for Social Impact

As mentioned above, the introduction of impact investment/finance necessarily entails some degree of accounting mechanism, as investors need to measure the investee's impact performance. Put differently, the diffusion of the norm of impact finance inevitably faces the issue of how to account for impact on stakeholders. Several accounting studies have used the norm-

Table 17.2 Actors, motives, and mechanisms in the stages of norm diffusion[a]

	Norm Emergence	Norm Acceptance	Norm Internalization
Actors	Norm entrepreneurs with organizational platforms	States, international organizations, networks	Law, professions, bureaucracy
Motives	Altruism, empathy, ideational commitment	Legitimacy, reputation, esteem	Conformity
Dominant mechanisms	Persuasion	Socialization, institutionalization, demonstration	Habit, institutionalization

[a] This is based on Table 1 in Finnemore and Sikkink (1998).

Table 17.3 Actor-centric norm-diffusion process[a]

Actors	Epistemic Communities	Norm Entrepreneurs	Carriers	Regulators and Reporters
Roles	Generate ideas	Innovate, translate, or resist ideas	Diffuse practices	Stabilize and enable the inscription of norms
Examples	Academic and experts, think tanks	International initiatives	Consultants, auditors, and professional associations	Government and organizations

[a]This is based on Table 10.3 in Larrinaga and Senn (2021).

diffusion framework in the context of accounting for social factors.[19] For instance, Bebbington et al. (2012) analyzed the production of normativity with respect to environmental reporting in Spain and the UK and considered why some differences existed in those countries from the perspective of the norm-diffusion cycle. Although the authors particularly focused on the tipping point of norm cascade in the process while putting less emphasis on the classification of norm diffusion, three internal conditions were highlighted: the congruence with the underlying values of previous norms, the perceived integration of the rules in a coherent normative framework, and, finally, whether the rule is perceived to provide clarity.

As mentioned above, this chapter specifically focuses on the process of global norm diffusion with respect to impact finance and how different actors are involved in the process. Larrinaga and Senn (2021) theoretically summarize more recent situations and further develop Bebbington et al.'s (2012) study. The authors put emphasis on actors in the process of norm diffusion and a plurality of those actors despite the difficulty in identifying different sources of normativity in environmental reporting (Table 17.3). Although the diffusion process is neither linear nor smooth (Larrinaga & Senn, 2021, p. 142), it normally proceeds from the left (epistemic communities) to the right (regulators and reporters) of the table. At the far right, if regulators set the standards and reporters (or organizations) must comply with them, then norm internalization normally occurs.

As the tipping point, from which norm acceptance or norm cascading happens, is of importance in the context of impact finance, the actions of norm entrepreneurs as well as carriers need to be considered. Based on the theoretical framework, Larrinaga and Bebbington (2021) analyzed the creation of GRI and argued that the combination of relevant actors (such as epistemic communities, carriers, regulators, and reporters) as well as certain conditions (societal context, discourses, analogies, practices, and institutional design) was significant for the path towards corporate sustainability reporting. Although this conclusion sounds understandable, how each actor or factor interacts with each other is still under-researched, and therefore, further investigation in the context of impact finance would be fruitful.

The Rise of Impact Investment in Japan: Public and Private Actions towards Impact Finance

Rapid Development of Impact Investment in Japan[20]

According to the data released in 2020, among the total market volume of global impact investment ($715 billion), the Asian region consisted of only 1.7% ($12.3 billion) (ASEAN-Japan Centre, 2021, p. 36).[21] Almost half of the Asian impact investment ($5.6 billion) was conducted by Japanese organizations, and Japan should lead the development of impact finance trends to solve social issues in this area. Indeed, the Japanese Financial Services Agency recently published the guideline for social bonds (FSA, 2021), as it assumes that issuance of them could be useful to finance projects to address the existing social challenges faced by developing Asian economies (Asian Development Bank, 2021).

Regarding finance and corporate social activities in Japan, it is notable that the first Socially Responsible Investing (SRI)-type mutual fund (Eco Fund) was established in 1999. Subsequently, similar types of investment trusts were introduced that expanded beyond environmental aspects to include social aspects. In the 2000s, social contribution bonds, such as vaccine bonds and microfinance bonds, appeared. In 2010, independent mutual funds that invested in companies contributing to a sustainable society were introduced. In 2011, with the support of the Ministry of Environment, the Principles for Financial Action for the 21st Century were adopted by private sector financial institutions to advance the momentum to promote sustainability from an environmental and financial perspective. In 2015, the Japanese Government Pension Investment Fund signed the Principles for Responsible Investment, which triggered institutional investors in Japan to follow suit. Since then, ESG investment has become increasingly popular in Japan.

Since the latter half of the 2010s, examples of impact investing have emerged. For instance, the Japan International Cooperation Agency signed the International Finance Corporation's[22] Operational Principles to support impact investment from Japan. In 2014, one year after the creation of the GSG (formerly the G8 Impact Investment Task Force) in 2013, a domestic advisory board, known as the GSG-NAB (National Advisory Board), was created. In 2015, Japan's first Social Impact Bond (SIB) was launched as a pilot project by the Nippon Foundation. As an investment model for public–private partnerships, the SIBs have expanded significantly with different social purposes. In 2016, the original body of the Social Impact Measurement Initiative (SIMI)[23] was created to consolidate and disseminate information on impact evaluation and develop human resources. In 2020, the "Study Group on Impact Investment" was launched jointly with the Financial Services Agency. The purpose of this group is to deepen the understanding of financial market participants and the government on impact investment, clarify the significance and challenges of impact investment initiatives to solve social issues in Japan and abroad, and discuss how to promote impact investment to contribute to the sustainable development of the Japanese financial industry.

Collective Norm Entrepreneurs in Impact Finance in Japan

According to the above analysis, impact finance was spotlighted in the late 2010s. In this subsection, a process-tracing method is used in the context of impact finance to investigate what happened chronologically in Japan over the last few years by investigating different materials such as the minutes of meetings from several organizations.

After the announcement of the Social Impact Investment Taskforce by David Cameron (UK Prime Minister at that time) at the G8 Social Impact Investment Forum in June 2013, the GSG became a key global norm entrepreneur, and its national advisory role in Japan was assigned to GSG-NAB Japan. Up until now, GSG-NAB Japan has published many reports and proposals regarding impact investing, held several events, and communicated with other GSG members. As of January 2022, it had held 21 official meetings.

To institutionalize impact finance in Japan, the GSG-NAB Japan had to work with public organizations. In June 2020, the GSG-NAB Japan and Financial Services Agency of Japan co-hosted the first "Impact Investing Roundtable." The roundtable was composed of 35 professionals, executives, and experts mostly in private financial sectors in Japan, including those from major business associations, academics, consultants, and start-ups. The aim of the roundtable was to deepen leaders' understanding of impact investing, as well as the significance and challenges of addressing social issues through impact investing in Japan and beyond. The roundtable held seven meetings through September 2021 and published a report that summarized the results of the discussions at the roundtable's sessions and outlined the challenges to be addressed (GSG, 2021b). However, the report did not clearly mention how actors measure the impact of corporate activities, rather it stated:

> In performing IMM (impact measurement and management), it is important to integrate IMM across the investment/financing process as a whole. However, approaches for performing IMM are still under development. Financial institutions who had worked out their own way to perform IMM offered their practices to the attendees as case studies to share. Some mentioned the importance of performing IMM considering both the level of individual investee companies and the level of the portfolio. Issues raised in relation to the performance of IMM included the need to consider the design of the framework for specific products and/or investees, in addition to the development of in-house systems and human resources, costs, and so forth. There was another opinion that, in order to smoothly perform IMM, it would be important to obtain impact and other non-financial information held by corporations.
>
> *(GSG, 2021b, p. 2)*

As this quotation reveals, the method of IMM had not been discussed thoroughly in the roundtable. Consequently, the roundtable decided to continue the discussion in the second phase in 2022. Although GSG-NAB Japan appears to be a main norm entrepreneur, there are others. The Social Innovation and Impact Foundation (SIIF) was founded in 2018 and set five strategic themes: impact investing, social impact measurement/management, pay-for-success/social impact bonds, progressive philanthropy, and alternative. SIIF was created after the merger between the Institute for the Advancement of Social Innovation (general incorporate foundation) and a social investing promotion office set up within the Nippon Foundation; SIIF has played the general administrative role for both SIMI and the impact-investing roundtable. SIMI was established in 2016 to promote social impact measurement in Japan, and as of June 2023, more than 300 organizations and individuals constitute SIMI.[24] The SIMI Global Resource Center (SIMI-GRC) plays a pivotal role by providing its members with resources regarding impact finance, such as translated reports and case studies. It also holds seminars and workshops regarding social impact measurement and management for a broad range of stakeholders. Previously, a representative director of SIMI shared his opinion of impact finance in one of the impact-investing roundtable meetings.

These three specific organizations (GSG-NAB Japan, SIIF, and SIMI) and the Financial Services Agency in Japan are norm entrepreneurs who have jointly promoted the diffusion of impact finance in Japan. Regarding the impact measurement framework, a working group was organized within GSG-NAB Japan; they met six times in FY2020 and shared global principles, frameworks, and tools of IMM by conducting interviews with foreign professionals who had rich experience in impact measurement. Following that, the working group published a discussion paper that stated they strongly hoped that IMM norms and practices in Japan would not become isolated but rather would follow the front-runner practices in the world and produce best practices from Japan (GSG-NAB, 2021, p. 5). However, the discussion paper repeatedly emphasized that institutional investors should consider the impact measurement framework themselves by working closely with investees on the general steps (Step 1: Investment Strategy,

Step 2: Organization and Structuring, Step 3: Monitoring and Engagement, and Step 4: Sell/Exit and Reporting). In other words, the more detailed and systematic measurement frameworks illustrated in Table 17.1 were not mentioned in the discussion paper.

Meanwhile, in November 2021, 20 representative financial institutions in Japan (the signatories) signed the "Japan Impact-Driven Financing Initiative." The signatories of the initiative believe that the fundamental purpose of private financial institutions is to solve environmental and social issues. The initiative also promotes impact-driven finance by measuring and managing the changes in society and the environment ("impact") created by their investments and loans/bonds. The signatories, while very diverse, will work together to promote high-quality impact investment in Japan. This organizational commitment and platform of impact finance were also led by the "Study Group on Impact Investment" that the Japanese Financial Ministry still regularly holds. In that sense, the public–private partnership is effective in promoting the significance of impact finance in Japan. As of August 2023, the number of signatories has increased to over 60. However, how to measure the impact still needs to be discussed.

Discussion

From the above descriptive case analysis, two points deserve close attention in terms of norm-diffusion dynamics. First, in Japan, three organizations (GSG-NAB Japan, SIIF, and SIMI) have been active norm entrepreneurs in promoting the significance of impact finance. From the perspective of the actor-centric norm-diffusion process (Table 17.3) (Larrinaga & Senn, 2021), these organizations consist or are constitutive of the same epistemic community and have been persuading possible carriers, regulators, and reporters of the norm. Therefore, it is notable that the Financial Services Agency, one of the regulators, works with those norm entrepreneurs. Hypothetically, it would be possible to understand that the partnership between the public and the private sector contributes to expediting the norm-diffusion process. Indeed, in terms of embracing the global norm of impact finance, several norm entrepreneurs have been actively working together, and as a result, the FY2021 total amount of impact investment in Japan quadrupled from FY2020 (from 328 billion yen to 1.3 trillion yen) (GSG-NAB, 2022). Unlike a global situation, in which different private organizations have established their own impact measurement frameworks, the norm entrepreneurs in Japan consist of both public and private organizations and quickly created a platform for the diffusion of social impact investment/finance. Assuming that a set of impact measurement frameworks is a public good, combining private sector managerial abilities and proprietary know-how with public sector assets should enable exploitative and explorative learning and lead to knowledge accumulation, innovation, and more efficient forms of the public good (Kivleniece & Quelin, 2012, p. 276). It is interesting to see if this public–private corroboration (the carriers of impact finance norm), as well as more than 60 financial institutions, can further promote impact finance in Japan. In addition, according to a longitudinal study, Japanese actors tend to actively displace local norms and internalized global norms (Cortell & Davis, 2005), and it is reflected to some extent in the case of acceptance of the global norm of impact investing.[25] Although there was no strong external pressure (*gaiatsu* in Japanese)[26] to introduce impact finance, the G8 taskforce's decision and establishment of GSG-NAB was one of the motivational sources of norm entrepreneurs.

Second, at this moment, there was no strong internal opposition (*naiatsu* in Japanese) to the introduction of impact finance. However, although an increasing number of Japanese companies, financial institutions, and other funders have turned their attention to impact finance, the lack of discussion about detailed impact measurement frameworks is notable. As this chapter illustrates (Table 17.1), there are several different impact measurement frameworks globally. Japan has not yet institutionalized independent specific organizational forms or classifications for social enterprises and charities, and therefore, the knowledge and experiences for measuring social impact are insufficient. Put differently, regarding the impact measurement framework, Japanese corporations and investors encounter the use of multiple evaluative frameworks (Stark, 2009). Although the use of those frameworks would bring positive entrepreneurial results, it is doubtful whether the norm of impact finance will reach a tipping point and cross over to norm cascade and norm acceptance without a clear consensus on the common impact measurement framework. Social impact is inherently subjective and multifaceted, and thus a unification of divergent impact measurement frameworks is undoubtedly an arduous task. However, this unification is necessary to facilitate comparability when analyzing corporate impact information. As the pursuit of positive social impact is essentially a public-minded endeavor, this chapter particularly highlights the public–private partnership in Japan. Future studies should delve into other relevant factors (e.g., significant norm carriers or norm entrepreneurs) in a different context.

Conclusion

This chapter focused on the growing trend of impact finance and considered how such an international norm diffuses globally. Some global organizations have commenced measuring and managing corporate social impact, and this international norm has gained attention in Japan. By analyzing the Japanese case from the theoretical perspective of international norm diffusion, this chapter highlighted several norm entrepreneurs that have been actively working to disseminate the norm of impact finance in Japan; these organizations even collaborate with a significant governmental organization (the Financial Services Agency in Japan). However, it is still doubtful whether this international norm will be widely accepted by Japanese companies and how the norm can be further internalized, as more practical impact measurement frameworks have been left untouched.

As this chapter has illustrated, there are various widely known impact measurement frameworks globally. However, if Japanese norm entrepreneurs do not thoroughly discuss and analyze these alternative frameworks, the acceptance and internalization of the norm of impact finance will be difficult to achieve. What stakeholders want to see is a net positive social impact from corporate activities. As Stark (2009) pointed out, the frictions of multiple evaluative frameworks might bring about productive consequences. Studying the quantification of social impact can provide plenty of opportunities to consider whether this hypothesis is adequate. Assuming that further acceptance or internalization of impact finance norm is necessary, it could occur either through a public top-down or private bottom-up approach. The latter approach tends to rely on the users' (or organizations') trial and error and the survival of the fittest. Reviewing the diffusion of global accounting standards, the international accounting standards committee (IASC)'s spontaneous bottom-up approach did not lead to favorable outcomes. Rather, despite arduous twists and turns, the IFRS under the auspices of IASB has been successful with the public top-down approach through the European Union's regulation and the International Organization of Securities Commissions' endorsement. In the context of impact finance, Japanese public–private relationships have expedited the norm-diffusion process to some extent, and more than 60 financial institutions have decided to work together to advance impact finance. However, without a unified impact measurement framework, quantifying comparable social impact is difficult. Not only institutional arrangements but also powerful norm entrepreneurs might be able to achieve the institutionalization of impact finance. More interdisciplinary studies should be done to analyze this issue.

Acknowledgment

This work was supported by MEXT Grant-in-Aid for Scientific Research (C) (Grant Number: JP22K01796).

Notes

1 This is based on a worldwide sample of 5,200 companies that comprise the top 100 companies by revenue in each of the 52 countries and jurisdictions researched by KPMG (2020).
2 PwC China Press Release "How will ESG develop in the Year of the Ox? PwC identifies eight key trends" www.pwccn.com/en/press-room/press-releases/pr-030321.html.
3 Impact investing is also referred to as social impact investing (SII). Additionally, impact investing and impact finance are used interchangeably. As the difference between the two terms is insignificant, this chapter mostly uses impact finance.
4 Furthermore, a statutory corporate audit system is necessary to support the transactions while the auditing itself would not exist without a set of financial statements.
5 Epistemic community is defined as a network of professionals with recognized expertise and competence in a particular domain and an authoritative claim to policy-relevant knowledge within that domain or issue area (Haas, 1992, p. 3).
6 Council (UK Treasury) funding to UK universities is allocated based on the assessment of the impact of research outputs. This is due to the wider "impactization" of global policy thinking, with its focus on demonstrable outcomes and the specific field of UK public science (Power, 2015).
7 As the scope of this chapter is mainly limited to the social impact of corporations, non-governmental organizations (NGOs) and other social organizations such as charities are not considered.
8 For a more direct analysis of how CSR-related norms have evolved, for example, see Dashwood (2020) and Favotto and Kollman (2020). Dashwood (2020, p. 180) argues that global companies, as moral agents, have acted as norm entrepreneurs in the spread of global CSR with the rise of NGO influence.
9 Nicholls (2018) defines "social impact" as the measurable outcomes of material changes experienced by target populations as the result of deliberative organizational action.
10 According to Cohen (2020), "impact investing" was coined as a term to replace "social investment" at the meeting hosted by Rockefeller Foundation in Italy in 2007.
11 According to Social Finance (www.socialfinance.org.uk/what-we-do/social-impact-bonds), social impact bonds (SIBs) are designed to overcome the challenges governments have in investing in prevention and early intervention. They mitigate the risks of failure and bring in impact investors, who want to test innovation and scale successful programs. Investors provide flexible funding to programs that are designed to be responsive to the needs of vulnerable groups to improve their lives.
12 However, Yang et al. (2021) also warn of the risk of not reflectively using the concept of social impact with awareness and care.
13 The information is available at www.bcorporation.net/en-us/programs-and-tools/b-impact-assessment.
14 The information is available at https://iris.thegiin.org/.
15 The information is available at www.socialvalueint.org/networks.
16 Similarly, in 2018, the Corporate Reporting Dialogue (CRD) initiative, convened by the International Integrated Reporting Council (IIRC), launched the Better Alignment Project, a ground-breaking two-year project to promote better alignment in the corporate reporting environment to make it easier for companies to prepare effective and coherent disclosures that meet the information needs of capital markets and society. The representatives from two organizations in Table 17.2 (Social Value International and IWAI at Harvard Business School) jointly considered the commonalities (as well as differences) in their impact monetization framework (e.g., top-down or bottom-up) (Nicholls and Zochowski, 2020).
17 Dashwood (2020, p. 167) argues that CSR achieved global normative status in the late 1990s when a growing number of global companies began to report on their activities affecting the environment, economy, and society. Simultaneously, the author acknowledged there are still some significant variations across sectors, companies, and countries.
18 At a foundational level, the ontological stance of mutual constitution favored by many constructivists—which highlights the interaction of agency and structure—is a processual view of the social world (Checkel, 2018, p. 154).

19 The framework is used in a different area of accounting. For example, Okamoto (2017) argues that norm entrepreneurs' analogical persuasion of others was significant in the diffusion of international financial reporting standards (IFRS) in Japan.
20 The information in this subsection is from the website of GSG-NAB Japan (https://impactinvestment.jp/en/about/gsg-japan.html).
21 Additionally, the United States consists of $266 billion, Australia consists of $15 billion, and the UK consists of $7 billion. Thus, the other $400 billion was expected to be invested in other areas, such as EU countries (ASEAN-Japan Centre, 2021, p. 36).
22 It is part of the World Bank Group and has been at the forefront of impact investing in emerging markets.
23 Note that SIMI changed its name from Social Impact Measurement Initiative to Social Impact Management Initiative in January 2019.
24 The information is available at https://simi.or.jp/en/about.
25 Cortell and Davis (2005, p. 24) analyzed Japanese acceptance of trade liberalization and argued that the collapse of Japan's economic bubble presented domestic actors with opportunities to challenge widely held beliefs in the appropriateness of economic nationalism but did not provide those actors with a new body of ideas toward which to reorient Japanese trade policy. Japan's membership in the central institutions of the global economic system, specifically the GATT/WTO, provided grounds for arguing the legitimacy of a move toward free trade.
26 Tsunogaya and Patel (2020) analyzed the globalization of accounting regulation in Japan from the perspective of the interaction between *gaiatsu* (external pressure) and *naiatsu* (internal pressure).

References

Adams, S., Tweedie, D., & Muir, K. (2021). Social impact reporting in the public interest: The case of accounting standardisation. *Qualitative Research in Accounting and Management, 18*(3), 390–416. https://doi.org/10.1108/QRAM-02-2019-0026

Alvesson, M., & Blom, M. (2022). The hegemonic ambiguity of big concepts in organization studies. *Human Relations, 71*(1), 58–86. https://doi.org/10.1177/0018726720986847

ASEAN-Japan Centre. (2021). *Impact investing towards ASEAN sustainable development goals (SDGs)*. https://www.asean.or.jp/ja/wp-content/uploads/sites/2/FINAL-Impact-Investing-towards-ASEAN-SDGs-1101.pdf

Asian Development Bank. (2021). *Promoting social bonds for impact investments in Asia*. http://doi.org/10.22617/SPR210180-2

Bebbington, J., Kirk, E. A., & Larrinaga, C. (2012). The production of normativity: A comparison of reporting regimes in Spain and the UK. *Accounting, Organizations and Society, 37*(2), 78–94. https://doi.org/10.1016/j.aos.2012.01.001

Berman, E. P., & Hirschman, D. (2018). The sociology of quantification: Where are we now? *Contemporary Sociology, 47*(3), 257–266. https://doi.org/10.1177/0094306118767649

Brandstetter, L., & Lehner, O. M. (2015). Opening the market for impact investments: The need for adapted portfolio tools. *Entrepreneurship Research Journal, 5*(2), 87–107. https://doi.org/10.1515/erj-2015-0003

Checkel, J. T. (2018). Methods in constructivist approaches. In A. Gheciu & W. C. Wohlforth (Eds.), *The Oxford handbook of international security* (pp. 151–166). Oxford University Press. https://doi.org/10.1093/oxfordhb/9780198777854.013.11

Cohen, R. (2020). *Impact: Reshaping capitalism to drive real change*. Ebury Press.

Cooper, C., Graham, C., & Himick, D. (2016). Social impact bonds: The securitization of the homeless. *Accounting, Organizations and Society, 34*(6–7), 755–769. https://doi.org/10.1016/j.aos.2016.10.003

Cortell, A. P., & Davis, J. W. (2005). When norms clash: International norms, domestic practices, and Japan's internalisation of the GATT/WTO. *Review of International Studies, 31*(1), 3–25. https://doi.org/10.1017/S0260210505006273

Dashwood, H. S. (2020). The rise of social responsibility as a global norm informing the practices of economic actors. In H. Hansen-Magnusson & A. Vetterlein (Eds.), *The rise of responsibility in world politics* (pp. 167–187). Cambridge University Press. https://doi.org/10.1017/9781108867047.012

Favotto, A., & Kollman, K. (2020). An expanding conception of social responsibility? Of global norms and changing corporate perceptions. In H. Hansen-Magnusson & A. Vetterlein (Eds.), *The rise of responsibility in world politics* (pp. 188–212). Cambridge University Press. https://doi.org/10.1017/9781108867047.013

Financial Services Agency (FSA) of Japan. (2021). *Social bond guidelines.* https://www.fsa.go.jp/en/news/2021/001.pdf

Finnemore, M., & Sikkink, K. (1998). International norm dynamics and political change. *International Organization, 52*(4), 887–917. https://doi.org/10.1162/002081898550789

Global Steering Group (GSG). (2021a). *Impact measurement & management (IMM): Impact investing's evolving ecosystem.* https://gsgii.org/reports/impact-measurement-management-imm-impact-investings-evolving-ecosystem/

Global Steering Group (GSG). (2021b). *Achievements in the first phase and challenges ahead.* https://impact-investment.jp/user/media/resources-pdf/Achievements_in_the_First_Phase_and_Challenges_Ahead.pdf

Global Steering Group National Advisory Board of Japan (GSG-NAB) (Working Group on Impact Measurement and Management (IMM)). (2021). *Refining the global standard of impact measurement and management –Views from a Japanese working group– (Part 1)* [Discussion Paper]. https://impactinvestment.jp/user/media/resources-pdf/Discussion_Paper.pdf

Global Steering Group National Advisory Board of Japan (GSG-NAB). (2022). *The current state and challenges of impact investing in Japan FY2021 survey* [in Japanese]. https://impactinvestment.jp/resources/report/20220426.html

Guter-Sandu, A. (2022). Accounting infrastructures and the negotiation of social and economic returns under financialization: The case of impact investing. *Competition and Change, 27*(1), 205–223. https://doi.org/10.1177/10245294221085636

Haas, P. M. (1992). Introduction: Epistemic communities and international policy coordination. *International Organization, 46*(1), 1–35. https://doi.org/10.1017/S0020818300001442

Hand, D., Ringel, B., & Danel, A. (2022). *Sizing the Impact Investing Market: 2022.* The Global Impact Investing Network (GIIN). https://thegiin.org/assets/2022-Market%20Sizing%20Report-Final.pdf

Hopwood, A. G. (1990). Accounting and organisation change. *Accounting, Auditing and Accountability Journal, 3*(1), 7–17. https://doi.org/10.1108/09513579010145073

Hurrel, A. (2007). *On global order.* Oxford University Press.

IMP. (2020). *Impact-Financial Integration: A Handbook for Investors.* Impact Frontiers. https://impactfrontiers.org/wp-content/uploads/2021/05/Impact-Frontiers-Impact-Financial-Integration-A-Handbook-for-Investors.pdf

Jones, S., Anstiss, H., & Garcia, C. (2022). *Social impact investing: An Australian perspective.* Routledge.

Kivleniece, I., & Quelin, B. V. (2012). Creating and capturing value in public-private ties: A private actor's perspective. *Academy of Management Review, 37*(2), 272–299. https://doi.org/10.5465/amr.2011.0004

KPMG. (2020). *The time has come: The KPMG survey of sustainability reporting 2020.* https://home.kpmg/xx/en/home/insights/2020/11/the-time-has-come-survey-of-sustainability-reporting.html

Larrinaga, C., & Bebbington, J. (2021). The pre-history of sustainability reporting: A constructivist reading. *Accounting, Auditing and Accountability Journal, 34*(9), 162–181. https://doi.org/10.1108/AAAJ-03-2017-2872

Larrinaga, C., & Senn, J. (2021). Norm development in environmental reporting. In J. Bebbington, C. Larrinaga, B. O'Dwyer & I. Thomson (Eds.), *Routledge handbook of environmental accounting* (pp. 137–150). Routledge. https://doi.org/10.4324/9780367152369

Macve, R., & Carey, A. (Eds.). (1992). *Business, accountancy and the environment: A policy and research agenda.* ICAEW.

Mathews, M. R. (1997). Twenty-five years of social and environmental accounting research: Is there a silver jubilee to celebrate? *Accounting, Auditing, and Accountability Journal, 10*(4), 481–531. https://doi.org/10.1108/EUM0000000004417

Matthew, H. (2015). Quantifying social value. *Risk and regulation, 10*–11. https://www.lse.ac.uk/accounting/assets/CARR/documents/R-R/2015-Winter/Quantifying-social-value.11.pdf

Muller, J. Z. (2018). *The tyranny of metrics.* Princeton University Press.

Nicholls, A. (2009). 'We do good things, don't we?' 'Blended value accounting' in social entrepreneurship. *Accounting, Organizations and Society, 34*(6–7), 755–769. https://doi.org/10.1016/j.aos.2009.04.008

Nicholls, A. (2018). A general theory of social impact accounting: Materiality, uncertainty and empowerment. *Journal of Social Entrepreneurship, 9*(2), 132–153. https://doi.org/10.1080/19420676.2018.1452785

Nicholls, J., & Zochowski, T. R. (2020). *Mutually compatible, yet different: A theoretical framework for reconciling different impact monetization methodologies and frameworks.* https://ssrn.com/abstract=3715451

Okamoto, N. (2017). Norm entrepreneur lobbying and persuasion: A case study involving the IASB's modification of an exposure draft. *Research in Accounting Regulation, 29*(2), 129–138. https://doi.org/10.1016/j.racreg.2017.09.004

Parker, L. D. (2011). Twenty-one years of social and environmental accountability research: A coming of age. *Accounting Forum, 35*(1), 1–10. https://doi.org/10.1016/j.accfor.2010.11.001

Parker, L. D. (2014). Constructing a research field: A reflection on the history of social and environmental accounting. *Social and Environmental Accountability Journal, 34*(2), 87–92. https://doi.org/10.1080/0969160X.2014.938472

Payne, R. A. (2001). Persuasion, frames and norm construction. *European Journal of International Relations, 7*(1), 37–61. https://doi.org/10.1177/1354066101007001002

Peez, A. (2022). Contributions and blind spots of constructivist norms research in international relations, 1980–2018: A systematic evidence and gap analysis. *International Studies Review, 24*(1), 1–33. https://doi.org/10.1093/isr/viab055

Power, M. (2015). How accounting begins: Object formation and the accretion of infrastructure. *Accounting, Organizations and Society, 47*, 43–55. https://doi.org/10.1016/j.aos.2015.10.005

Robson, K. (1992). Accounting numbers as "inscription": Action at a distance and the development of accounting. *Accounting, Organizations and Society, 17*(7), 685–708. https://doi.org/10.1016/0361-3682(92)90019-O

Semeen, H., & Islam, M. A. (2021). Social impact disclosure and symbolic power: Evidence from UK fair trade organizations. *Critical Perspectives on Accounting, 79*, 1–20. https://doi.org/10.1016/j.cpa.2020.102182

Stark, D. (2009). *The sense of dissonance: Accounts of worth in economic life*. Princeton University Press.

Global Impact Investing Network (GIIN) (2020). *Annual impact investors survey 2020* (10th ed.). https://thegiin.org/assets/GIIN%20Annual%20Impact%20Investor%20Survey%202020.pdf

Tsunogaya, K., & Patel, C. (2020). The impact of external pressures (gaiatsu) and internal pressures (naiatsu) on Japan's accounting reforms since the late 1990s. *Accounting, Auditing and Accountability Journal, 33*(4), 857–886. https://doi.org/10.1108/AAAJ-05-2019-4013

Yang, C., O'Leary, S., & Tregidga, H. (2021). Social impact in accounting: Is it at risk of becoming a hembig concept and does this matter? *Qualitative Research in Accounting and Management, 18*(3), 313–331. https://doi.org/10.1108/QRAM-05-2021-0093

18
GREEN FINANCE STRATEGIES IN AFRICA

A Focus on Capital Market-Based Impact Investments in Small and Medium-Sized Enterprises in Ghana

Richmond Odartey Lamptey, Michael Zisuh Ngoasong, and Richard Blundel

Introduction

Green finance is predicated on the premise that effective financing and investment in climate-smart initiatives at global, regional, and national levels is one of the pathways to ameliorate the effects of climate change. Climate change mitigation is one of the most important UN Sustainable Development Goals (SDGs). Equally, climate change mitigation (Bertilsson & Thörn, 2021) has been crucial to key stakeholders, as seen in the setting up of the Task Force on Climate-related Financial Disclosures in 2015, which is likely to have a growing impact on larger companies and the investment community (TCFD, 2017). Leading corporations, institutional investors, development agencies and other key stakeholders are aligning their strategic and operational activities to the SDGs and are including periodic reporting to achieve set objectives. Some scholars have argued that countries must adopt green finance policies to move from "brown" to "green" industries (Deschryver, 2021) and to transition from fossil-fuel investing toward green alternatives (Balakumar, 2021). Many climate-related funds are currently in operation, and others are in different phases to be operationalized. For example, the Green Climate Fund, is estimated to have an average transaction of USD 2.7 million (Afful-Koomson, 2015; Bertilsson & Thörn, 2021), has lower approval of projects from Africa (Fonta, Ayuk, & van Huysen, 2018).

The arguments in support of green finance are particularly relevant to developing economies in sub-Saharan Africa. For example, the Global Impact Investing Network (GIIN) has estimated that USD 6.8 billion in impact investment flowed into West Africa and USD 7.8 billion into East Africa in 2014 (GIIN 2015a, p. 2, 2015b, p. 8). A more recent study found that after 2015, Nigeria received 29% of impact investment while Ghana accounted for 25%, reflecting fluctuation due to economic decline (IIF, 2019), and at least USD 12 billion went to sub-Saharan Africa (GIIN, 2019). Investments in energy generation are one of the key growth areas. For example, countries in West Africa will require USD 70 billion in annual renewable energy investments by 2030 to address their energy security needs and to meet their targets under the Paris Agreement (Ackah & Graham, 2021). The aim of these investments will be to reduce carbon emissions and to tackle other societal problems such as noise and air pollution from diesel generators (Afful-Dadzie et al., 2020) and the unreliability of existing hydropower, wind energy, and geothermal power systems (Kazimierczuk, 2019). More broadly, locating green finance within the impact investment label can provide insights into how investments can be mobilized to support attempts to transition from brown to green industries in Africa (Okereke et al., 2019). Furthermore, there are potential risks and costs to green finance (Rolffs et al., 2015; Walwyn, 2020).

This chapter seeks to contribute new insights to the growing body of evidence on "impact investing" by focusing on green finance strategies in an African context. Recent empirical studies have examined other areas of social impact in developing economies, such as inclusive finance and shadow banking in Pakistan (Jafri, 2019), gendered biases in access to entrepreneurial finance in Cameroon and Ghana (Ngoasong & Lamptey, 2021), and in promoting enterprise within a marginalized community in India (Rajan et al., 2014; Agrawal & Hockerts, 2021). However, there have been very few studies originating from emerging economies, other than China and India (Zhang et al., 2019, p. 427), and relatively little attention has been paid to the ways in which green finance operates in an African context.

By considering impact investing within a green finance lens, this chapter addresses two closely related research questions. (1) What is the nature of supra-organizational patterns of institutional factors, investment strategies, and stakeholders in impact investing? (2) How can we uncover and account for which logics are, or should be, dominant in green finance?

We draw on institutional and stakeholder theories (Castellas et al., 2018; Agrawal & Hockerts, 2021) to analyze the motivations and financial instruments that underpin implicit and explicit environmental, social, and governance (ESG) strategies employed by fund managers to realize environmental impact and financial returns through investing in small and medium-sized enterprises (SMEs). SMEs are important to understanding the green finance strategies of impact investing because of their potential to contribute to net zero CO_2 emissions through commercially viable eco-innovation in established SMEs and green start-up businesses (Blundel & Hampton, 2021a, 2021b). The recent UN Climate Change Conference of the Parties (COP26) in Glasgow, United Kingdom, 31 October–13 November 2021, included panels that debated climate events and the importance of uniting multiple stakeholders (governments, multilateral institutions, development finance institutions, fund managers, private investors, and policymakers) with regard to strategies to eliminate the effects of climate change by developing new paradigms for transition finance (Bowman & Minas, 2019). Studies on the sustainable finance landscape in Africa also call for more research to uncover cases of green finance that can provide insights into this emerging investment landscape (Marbuah, 2020).

Empirically, this chapter combines desk research on impact investments in Africa and an in-depth qualitative analysis of three case studies of capital market-based impact investment funds in Ghana. A case study approach is applied to analyze how fund managers in African countries, specifically Ghana, effectively engage with SMEs to realize environmental impact and financial returns. Data include primary and secondary data sources collected over a five-year period, while interviews and documents were used as data collection techniques. The study further applies Gioia' et al. (2013) methodology, content, and thematic analysis to uncover emerging themes.

The remainder of this chapter is organized as follows. First, the approach to understanding green investment within the impact investing label through integrating institutional and stakeholder perspectives is presented. Second, the methodology used to carry out the study is described. Third, the green practices of impact investment funds in Africa and the findings from three funds in Ghana are offered. Finally, implications for research and practice, along with future research opportunities, are discussed.

Theoretical Motivation

To uncover how gaining an understanding of the investment strategies of impact investments enables a better understanding of the role of impact investing within the green finance landscape, we draw on the institutional logics perspective to generate a fresh theoretical framing that links institutional logics and the pursuit of dual mission by impact investors. This is summarized in Figure 18.1. We begin with Friedland and Alford's (1991) formulation of the institutional logic's perspective, where they define logics as "a set of material practices and symbolic constructions [that] constitute organizing principles" (p. 248) for "preorganization patterns of human activity" (p. 234). Their book chapter specified five distinctive institutions, each with a distinct logic: "capitalist market, bureaucratic state, democracy, nuclear family, and Christian religion." They suggest that as rules, practices, and symbols guide institutions and societal meaning, logics are even more powerful than the institutions they shape. Their argument that logics guide human behavior is related to what has been popularized in institutional theory as the "rules of the game" (North, 1991). The institutional logics perspective (Friedland and Alford, 1991; Gümüsay et al. 2020) offers a useful starting point for understanding multiple stakeholders and logics (left-side boxes in the figure) in relation to impact investments into SMEs (middle boxes) as our theoretical framing of how the embeddedness of logics within the inter-institutional system influences the green finance strategies within impact investing (right-side box).

While for Friedland and Alford (1991) logics were the basis for understanding macro-level societal ordering and organizing, later studies have applied the institutional logic perspective to practices in organizations. Of relevance here are studies on impact investing (Castellas et al., 2018) and commercial microfinance institutions in Bolivia (Battilana & Dorado, 2010). Castellas et al. (2018) investigate the "why" and "how" of actors' roles, motivations, and instruments, and strategies of green finance investors, intermediary fund managers, and SMEs executing projects

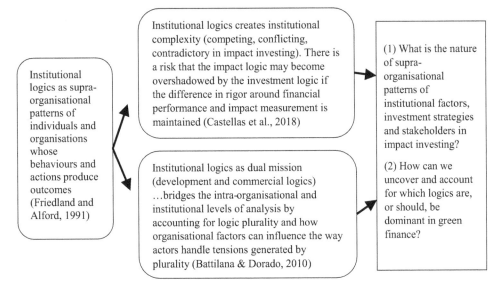

Figure 18.1 Theoretical framework for analyzing green finance within impact investing

including mini-grid clean energy, solar energy, and wind energy. Groups of organizations and individuals with divergent interests, different perspectives, and influences on decision-making create complexity in financing green initiatives/projects towards expected outcomes (Agrawal & Hockerts, 2021). Stakeholders within the impact investing field comprise high-net-worth individual investors, institutional investors, fund managers, governments, and beneficiaries who engage in actions and processes aimed at accomplishing environmental impact and financial returns (Ormiston et al., 2015).

In a study of commercial microfinance in Bolivia, Battilana and Dorado (2010) demonstrated the usefulness of institutional logics by uncovering the existence, or otherwise, of legislative (law) frameworks, clearly defined missions (or orientations), and the organization of the investment activities and key stakeholders (or partnerships). The persistence of competing and potentially conflicted, institutional logics over time represents institutional complexity (Castellas et al., 2018). Impact investments are characterized by institutional complexity because of competing and sometimes conflicted institutional logics: impact logic (social and environmental sustainability) and investment logic (financial returns). From the institutional logic perspective, Castellas et al. (2018) support the view that plural logics can harmonize over the long term. Therefore, to understand institutional logics, the interrelationships between logics, actors (fund managers, investors, and arrangers), and actions/strategies (investment processes, financial instruments) are essential in green finance. Further, Castellas et al. (2018) identified impact investment actors to include local and international social banks, institutional investors, charitable trusts and foundations, and private investors. We focus on the institutional actors of developmental financial institutions and government institutions, and their policymaking concerning green finance, climate adaptation, and impact. Impact investing has emerged over the past decade as a kind of investment that seeks to achieve social and environmental impact alongside financial returns (Höchstädter & Scheck, 2015). Existing academic debates evidence some trade-offs in pursuit of multiple objectives, namely environmental impact and financial returns (Agrawal & Hockerts, 2021).

We now turn to a discussion of existing knowledge about logics in Africa and which ones are most likely dominant, particularly in the context of impact investing. Our focus is reviewing impact investing literature to clarify the logics, focusing on green finance, with a particular emphasis on those relevant to the African context. There is no concurrence in the literature on the definition of logics, and there is a proliferation of types of logics, all of which are considered in our clarification of what we already know about logics in Africa and which ones are most likely dominant, particularly in the context of hybrid investing. According to Roundy (2019, p. 3) logics "are the formal and informal rules of action, interaction and interpretation that guide and constrain decision makers." Henenberger, Mair, and Metz (2019, p. 1695) refer to institutional logics as "a set of material practices and assumptions, values, and beliefs that provides meaning and shapes activity within fields." A related definition emphasizes "organizational field" to refer to contested, dynamic in character, arenas of contradiction and multiple complexities in understanding (Glanzel & Scheurle, 2016, p. 1659), distinct from settled character (Wooten & Hoffman, 2008; Mogapi et al., 2019). Roundy (2019, p. 3) claims that impact investing draws on two logics "market logic, based on values and goals such as efficiency, profit maximization, competition and value capture, with a community logic driven by collaboration, cooperation and value creation." Other scholars within the impact investing field have applied related terminologies to label the logics, for example business and social logics (Mersland et al., 2020); market and civil society logics (Glanzel & Scheurle, 2016); and financial and non-financial impact (Höchstädter & Scheck, 2015).

Thus, the impact investing literature relating to the African context crystallizes around finance-first logic (capital market, commercial or investment logics), impact-first (social/welfare/impact/community or developmental logics), and a hybrid logic that combines finance and impact logics. There is no evidence of a binary, that is, impact-first versus finance-first; rather, it is a degree of hybridity. Studies comparing financial (profit) and impact (social) reveal that finance-first logic dominates, with investors prioritizing financial returns over impacts (King & Gish, 2015). "Finance-first" impact investors/fund managers place a premium on the financial returns with a floor to the social impact (Höchstädter & Scheck, 2015) and seek to achieve market-competitive financial returns from investments that offer the prospect of positive social and environmental impact (Ormiston et al., 2015, p. 355). For example, Watts and Scales (2020) find that impact investment in agriculture in sub-Saharan Africa is largely driven by commercial interests. Impact-first investors seek to maximize social or environmental returns while having minimum-required financial returns (Ormiston et al., 2015). The impact expectation focuses on geographic and multi-sectoral strategies and demographic factors, which vary across communities and investment instruments (Höchstädter & Scheck, 2015; Rajan et al., 2014). The multi-sector strategy of fund managers encompasses sectors (e.g., health education, agribusiness, sanitation, water), relatively smaller deal sizes, and investees located in peri-urban communities, etc.

A hybrid strategy is an investment strategy that positions financial return and social/environmental equally in line with investor expectations, in synergy cases of financial and social returns with no trade-off (Mogapi et al., 2019). Hybrid strategy manifests in diverse forms of strategies. The impact investment literature mentions integrated strategy and adapted portfolio strategy (Brandstetter & Lehner, 2015). An adapted portfolio optimization strategy incorporates social investments' (by extension green investments) specific variables together with financial values into a traditional logic of portfolio optimization premised on a risk-return relationship. Another hybrid strategy is an integrated strategy – an ESG integration portfolio strategy with an explicit environmental impact strategy and broad impacts at the portfolio level (Wood et al., 2013). These strategies are at the center of originating, screening, due diligence, investing, and post-investment decision-making and reporting by fund managers. Mogapi et al. (2019) suggest that impact investing organizations represent arenas of contradiction, presenting a conflict of logics with the dual focus on financial return and impact.

A review of the impact investing literature reveals three areas for locating green finance within the impact investing landscape. The first is green finance as an investment strategy that explicitly targets green projects. Notable examples in the African context are investments in renewable energy finance and the development of green bonds (most developed in South Africa, but also Kenya, Nigeria, Morocco, and Nigeria) (Afful-Koomson, 2015 Page, 2018; Ngwenya & Simatele, 2020). The second is green finance as an investment that seeks to transition from brown (e.g., inefficient and polluting industries) (Deschryver, 2021) or fossil-fuel investing to green investing (Balakumar, 2021). The third is green finance as broadly selective environmental, social, and governance (ESG)-focused investments (Höchstädter & Scheck, 2015). Although some references may be made to the social impact components of the investments, the focus of this chapter is on the environment and governance impacts within the African context. In summary, three institutional logics (finance-first, impact-first, hybrid) influence the investment strategies, stakeholders, and institutional factors that come into play to shape whether, and to what extent, impact investment is viewed as explicit or implicit green finance (figure 18.2). The existence of logic plurality requires a more in-depth study of implicit versus explicit strategy as a way of uncovering the circumstances under which certain

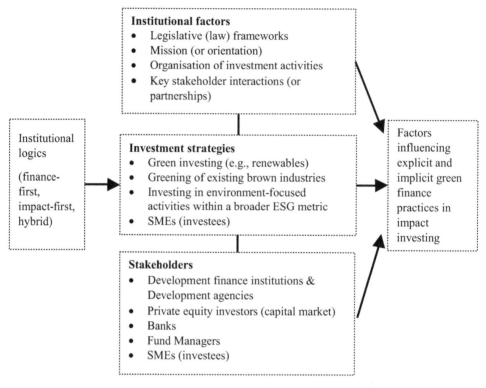

Figure 18.2 Theoretical framework for uncovering explicit and implicit green finance strategies

logic (green finance-related) become dominant in the investment strategies of impact investments.

Research Methodology

The findings reported in this chapter have been obtained by adopting a qualitative approach to understanding green finance in Africa and draw on a variety of sources. The analysis is based on a combination of desk research and interviews and is underpinned by the conceptual framework depicted earlier (Figure 18.2). It is also informed by the lead researcher's previous experience as a financial services practitioner in Ghana, which facilitated access to key informants in this industry sector. The desk research consisted of reviewing annual reports of impact investment funds, policy and technical reports, and independent evaluations and relevant websites. These documents contain narratives outlining the investment strategies, geographic presence within Africa, sector focus, and metrics that are useful and relevant for determining evidence of explicit and implicit strategies of impact investment funds. In analyzing the narratives, the focus was on those targeting women entrepreneurs in African countries, which is significant because some of the impact investing funds also invest in developing countries in Asia and Latin America.

To illustrate the nature of explicit and implicit green finance strategies, this chapter relies on a wider set of data, collected from January 2017 to April 2018 in Ghana (Lamptey, 2020). The International Financial Corporation (IFC) and Ghana's Securities and Exchange Commission (SEC) announced a partnership to facilitate investments in projects that address climate and environmental issues through green bonds. Under the agreement, IFC will assist the SEC to develop guidelines for issuers and investors for green bonds in Ghana (IFC, 2021). The objective is that green bonds will give investors opportunities to finance green buildings, clean transportation, renewable energy, sustainable water management, and other climate-friendly projects in Ghana. Moreover, the green bond initiative will support Ghana's transition to a lower-carbon future.

For the field study, data were gathered through more semi-structured interviews with key informants drawn from three capital market-based impact investment fund managers discussing impact investing in Ghana from the perspective of the informants' organizations and roles. Drawing on Gioia' et al. (2013) methodology of analyzing data, we applied a three-step process to uncover first-order themes (respondent phrases/quotes/statements), second-order concepts, and aggregate dimensions to link theory to empirical data evidenced in the data structure (Figure 18.3).

The case studies are presented in Table 18.1. The perspectives of fund managers matter because of their role in uncovering how the green finance narrative may be embedded in the broader impact of investment fundraising and operationalized in soliciting, screening, and selecting investments in SMEs. Interviews with owner-managers of investee SMEs are significant to understanding how investment strategies are implemented. The three cases also rely on field observations, particularly informal conversations with key stakeholders in Ghana.

Semi-structured interviews were tape-recorded and transcribed, while dialogues and informal discussions were captured as field notes. The three empirical cases were examined in-depth to illustrate green investment strategies in Ghana. The content analysis technique was also applied to analyze the data (Miles et al., 2014), and a narrative analysis was applied for discussing the emergent themes from capital market-based impact investments. Qualitative work of this sort presents limitations as regards extrapolating results from a small set of interviews to the general population (Miles et al., 2014). However, we addressed this limitation through a detailed analysis of secondary data to identify implicit and explicit green finance strategies, from

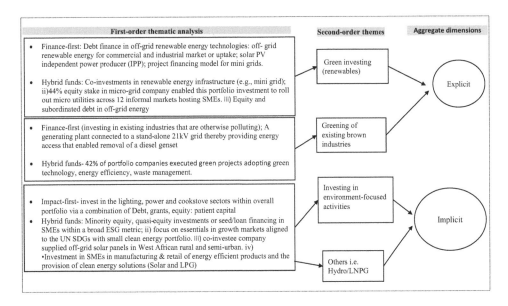

Figure 18.3 Data analytic structure

Table 18.1 Capital market-based impact investment funds studied and data collection

	Case 1	*Case 2*
Capital market-based impact investment fund	CMBF1	CMBF2
Founding year	Over 30 years ago	2002
Key informant interviews	2	3
Position of interviewees	Regional manager – West Africa	1. Fund manager 2. Owner-manager of SME 1 3. Owner-manager of SME 2
Documents analyzed	Company documents, observations (fieldnotes), online documents.	Company reports, observation during meetings between credit managers and entrepreneurs (fieldnotes), online documents.

Source: Authors' fieldwork.

the wider range of impact investment funds in Africa. Therefore, the three case studies serve as qualitative illustrations of green investment strategies of impact investment funds, when viewed in an African context, in this case, Ghana.

Finding

In presenting the empirical findings we detail evidence of (1) explicit green finance strategies reflecting two dimensions of institutional logics (finance-first and hybrid) with explicit green investing (renewables), (2) other explicit green finance strategies with two dimensions of institutional logics focusing greening of existing brown industries (finance-first and hybrid funds), and (3) implicit green finance strategies orientated to impact-first and hybrid institutional logics. This section examines how impact investing within a green finance perspective can be deployed by fund managers in financing small and medium-sized enterprises in Ghana. Different case studies are illustrated before proceeding to the discussion of the emergent themes, elaborating the framework for a better understanding of green finance.

Explicit Green Finance Strategies

Our review of published data on capital market-based fund managers that invest in African countries reveals those fund managers that can be considered as pursuing a green finance strategy (Table 18.2). An illustrative case study developed in Ghana is also presented. In addition to Table 18.3, emerging evidence reflects two unique types of explicit investment strategies aligned to specific institutional logics of finance-first and hybrid.

Finance-First Logic

Emerging evidence from the literature and analysis shows that finance-first investors in the green finance field in Africa are characterized by high-return expectations relative to concessionary lending, large transactions, or deal sizes (e.g., > USD 5 million), anchored mostly by development finance institutions and selective investments or few transactions. Moreover, within

Table 18.2 Explicit green finance strategies, motivation, and instruments of fund managers

Fund managers	Description	African countries	Instruments	Explicit green strategy
Developing World Markets	A fund that has invested or arranged over USD 2.2 billion in financing for more than 200 environmentally and socially positive companies.	Côte d'Ivoire, D.R. Congo, Egypt, Ghana, Kenya, Liberia, Madagascar, Mali, Morocco, Mozambique, Nigeria, Rwanda, Senegal, South Africa, Tanzania.	Debt (85.1%) Equity (12.7%) Subordinated debt (2.2%).	• 200+ socially or environmentally positive companies. • Launched Off-Grid, Renewable Energy and Climate Action (ORCA) Note in 2016 and has since invested in three solar companies and nine IFINs (Inclusive Financial Institutions) with a sum of over USD 325 million via clients for renewable energy and energy efficiency. • Signatory of Net Zero Asset Managers Initiative. • Investments in the off-grid renewable energy sector have resulted in total CO_2 reductions of over 1.3 million metric tons.
Inspired Evolution II	A USD 310 million fund offering development, energy, and resource efficiency growth investments. Investments target utility-scale grid-connected development platforms and projects that generate renewable energy, commercial and industrial market initiatives, mini- and micro-grids, and off-grid solutions.	South Africa, Mauritius, the UK, Côte D'Ivoire, and Kenya.	Third-party co-investment leverage: debt and equity.	• Funded green investment in 14 countries via multiple technologies, grid-tied, distributed, mini-grid, off-grid, and C&I projects. • For example, Resource/Virtus Energy Infrastructure – mini-grids (5 MW+ capacity) in Nigeria adopting technology of hybrid PV solar, batteries, and gensets. • Funded Alten Africa's Energy Infrastructure – grid-connected, 300 MW+ capacity for multiple countries using solar PV technology. • 3.56 TWh clean energy generated to date: current and past investments, 8.90 metric tons of carbon dioxide emission; greenhouse gases avoided as at 2020 Inspired Evolution Annual Report; 1.2 GW; total installed capacity of clean energy investments. • SDG 7: Access to clean energy for all – with 49% equity stake in Alten Africa (solar PV independent power producer (IPP)). 47.1 MWp Hardap Project in Namibia started operations in 2019 and other projects at different stages. An estimated 116.6 GWh in clean energy produced and 107,235 tons of carbon dioxide emissions avoided. • SDG 13 (climate action): equity stake of 7% in Rensource (an off-grid solar solution provider) and a 44% equity stake in Virtus enabled this portfolio investment to roll out micro-utilities across 12 informal markets hosting SMEs in eight provinces in Nigeria.

(Continued)

Table 18.2 (Continued)

Fund managers	Description	African countries	Instruments	Explicit green strategy
Camco Clean Energy	A USD 203 million specialist climate finance fund manager. The fund manager for the Renewable Energy Performance Platform (REPP), develops a thriving and dependable market for the region's small-scale and decentralized renewable energy sector.	Ghana, Mali, Côte D'Ivoire, Sierra Leone, Senegal, Liberia, Nigeria, Chad, Rwanda, Tanzania, Kenya.	Equity, loans (junior, senior, bridging), convertible notes/loans; mezzanine loans.	• Renewable energy and energy efficiency projects. • 17.4 MW renewable energy capacity installed, 26,386 tCo2 avoided. • SDG 7. By investing in innovative renewable energy and energy efficiency solutions in emerging and developing markets, Camco contributes towards access to affordable, reliable, sustainable, and modern energy for al. • SDG 13. Economic growth and carbon emissions, strengthening communities' resilience and adaptive capacity to climate-related hazards and natural disasters, and supporting the implementation of countries' climate policies.
Berkeley Energy	Firm with renewable energy and power engineering, construction, and investment experience focusing on developing markets. Manages the Africa Renewable Energy Fund II (AREF), a ten-year closed-ended renewable energy private equity fund worth USD 300 million.	Ethiopia, Madagascar, Uganda, Zambia.	Debt and equity.	AREF – the Africa Renewable Energy Fund (AREF) invests in small hydro, geothermal, solar, and biomass projects across sub-Saharan Africa, excluding South Africa. A fund size of USD 200 m, nine investments made in six countries.

Table 18.3 Implicit green finance strategies, motivation, and instruments of fund managers

Fund managers	Description	African countries	Instruments	Implicit green strategy
Grofin	A fund manager with USD 540 million assets under management in multiple sectors.	Kenya, Tanzania, Rwanda, Uganda, South Africa, Zambia, Ghana, Nigeria, Senegal, Ivory Coast, Egypt.	Debt and equity.	• Investment in SMEs in manufacturing and retail of energy-efficient products and the provision of clean energy solutions (solar and LPG). • SDG 7. Affordable and clean energy.
Acumen	A fund manager that invests in new, untested markets, backing early-stage, high-risk, high-impact companies serving low-income customers with patient capital in the range of USD 250,000 to 3 million.	Kenya, Uganda, Ghana, Ethiopia, Burundi, Tanzania, South Sudan, Nigeria.	Debt, grants, equity.	• Invested in 20 companies in the lighting and power and cookstove sectors within an overall portfolio. • SGD 7. Affordable and clean energy: 18 million CO_2- and black-carbon emitting kerosene lamps no longer in use.
Vital Capital	A USD 350 million for-profit impact investing fund investing in food, water, healthcare, housing, and off-grid energy.	Ghana, Nigeria, Liberia, Angola, Kenya,	Equity and subordinated debt.	• A focus on essentials in growth markets aligned with the UN SDGs. • Vital contributes to 16 of the 17 SDGs. • SDG 7. Affordable and clean energy; a small portfolio of investments.
Investisseursand Partenaires	An estimated EUR 200 million assets under management for multiple sector financing including renewable energy.	Benin, Burkina Faso, Ivory Coast, Mali, Senegal, Cameroon, Gabon, Uganda, Madagascar.	Minority equity, quasi-equity investments, seed financing, loans.	• 42% of IPAE companies have executed green projects to improve environmental impact (green technology, energy efficiency, waste management).

the green finance field, finance-first investors prioritize large scalable mini-grids. Moreover, the finance-first logic manifests in explicit green finance investment strategies that either focus on green investment (renewables) and/or transforming brown industries into green industries. For example, CMBF1

> Red Rocket Holding Ltd (Red Rocket) is an integrated renewable energy independent power producer (IPP) constructing, developing and operating over 2.5 GW of utility-scale, grid-connected wind, solar and hydro projects across Sub-Saharan Africa. CMBF1 holds a 70% controlling stake. With USD 31.7million capital commitment at end of 2020

Similarly, another explicit investment with a hybrid strategy reflects a finance-first logic initiated based on equity ownership stake of the fund managers as detailed in the excerpts of documents analyzed:

> Construction on the 8.6 MWp Mabuga Project started in 2020 under the lead of EPC (Engineering, Procurement and Construction) contractor, Voltalia. Gigawatt Global will continue to oversee the construction and operation to completion. Evolution II holds a majority shareholding in the project (65.6%) and total fund commitment of USD 7.3 million.

Explicit Green Finance Strategies – Hybrid Institutional Logics

This evidence is another emerging strategy involving the greening of brown industries.

Documents analyzed from CMBF2 reveal the transformation of a community that previously relied on a polluting mini-grid powered by a generator to an environmentally friendly hydro project.

A typical hybrid fund manager with explicit investment strategies acknowledges that:

> "By investing in projects to upgrade and retrofit industries to make them sustainable and resource-use efficient as well as increase the adoption of clean and environmentally sound technologies, CMBF2 is helping to build resilient infrastructure"

Another fund manager explains the motive for hybrid institutional logics emerging from an explicit investment strategy as follows:

> With approximately 75% of Madagascar's power generated from expensive, imported and high-emission heavy fuel oil (HFO) and diesel plants, the government is keen to reduce the country's dependence on fossil fuels and shift towards more sustainable sources.

To this end, the fund manager therefore initiated an investment strategy of greening brown industries through a "hybridized investment with solar PV thanks to a USD 6 million bridge loan from REPP to developer LIDERA Green Power" (Inspired Evolution, 2021).

CMBF1 is a climate and impact fund manager, leading the clean energy transition in emerging markets. As a capital market-based impact fund, it is regulated by the Security Exchange Commission of Ghana as well as the UK Financial Conducts Authority due to access to the global capital market for onward investment in sub-Saharan Africa. Institutional policy frameworks of the country also play a role in financing green initiatives. The fund's explicit green finance narrative is reflected in its mission to be a leading clean energy provider in emerging markets. For example, this is significant to the institutional context with regard to the goals of Ghana's Renewable Energy Master Plan 2019 (Aboagye et al., 2021), which aims to add 200 MWp of distributed solar by 2030 and bring electricity to 1,000 off-grid communities through decentralized electrification options that align with the investment objectives of fund managers. Average project returns on investments in over 200 countries are estimated at 9.3% as of March 2022. When asked to describe the nature of the investment activities in Ghana, the fund manager of CMBF1 responded along the following lines: the flow of funds from investors to SMEs.

> We invest across sectors, project sizes, and geographies to support innovative projects that provide transformative impact to local communities … We have extensive origination and finance networks supported by regional presence, and a team experienced in advice and structuring.
>
> *(Interview, Fund Manager, CMBF1)*

With respect to key stakeholders and the nature of interactions (or partnerships) (REPP, 2021), we see three levels. First, impact investor – the fund manager. The fund manager, CMBFI, raises funds from governments (e.g., the UK government), development finance institutions (e.g., the European Investment Bank), development agencies (e.g., the UN Environment Finance Initiative), and private equity investors (the capital market). Second, the fund manager level. The country fund manager implements and supports developers on various renewable energy projects and engages third-party risk mitigation partners (for project insurance) for risk mitigation. Fund managers have to rely on commercial banks as a catalyst to disburse funds to investee SMEs in Ghana (e.g., PEG (SME1)). For investment strategies or instruments, CMBF1 takes a 49% equity ownership: while in some cases loans.

Third, the fund manager at the SME level. Typically, deals with SMEs are sourced through project proposals received from companies and developers. The fund manager discusses the proposal with the investee company/developer before detailed analyses for consideration by the investment committee (IC). Terms sheets are subsequently agreed between the fund manager and the investee company after the approval of the IC. Know your customer (KYC) and due diligence are conducted prior to the preparation of financing documents detailing the conditions. Final approval is sought and granted, documents signed, and the investee/company fulfills all conditions within the document. Post-disbursement support, monitoring, and evaluation occur in compliance with the policies of the fund manager and reporting to the fund board. It suffices to add that the fund manager is an implementer or a manager of a renewable energy fund:

> In 2018, we participated in PEG's USD 5 million series C equity raise with an equity investment of USD 1.1 million … From 2018 till date, the fund manager has invested in the company using different financing instruments "Lending type: Various and with an estimated funding: USD 3.7 million"
>
> *Lamptey (2020)*

Documents provided by SME1 reveal the environment-focused activities that the business undertakes, which reflect an explicit green finance strategy. Within the ESG metric, CMBF1's allocated USD 200 million plus transactions resulted in 82 Mt CO_2-emission mitigation, 12 renewable energy technologies applied, and eight energy efficiency technologies deployed. The fund is estimated to achieve these targets by 2024, with carbon mitigation (6.9 Mt), a new renewable installed capacity (275 MW), 11 million people to be connected to electricity, and USD 170 million of committed investments. These indicators reflect examples of explicit green finance strategies with a finance-first institutional logic that can contribute to net zero emissions by prioritizing commercially viable SMEs (Blundel & Hampton, 2021a).

At the fund-SME level, governance is critical in pre- and post-investment monitoring and reporting. For example, CMBF1 educate investee companies about sustainable corporate governance through their policy and onboarding processes, as well as stakeholder engagement capacity-building with a specific focus on Environmental and Social Impact Assessment (ESIA) and Environmental and Social Management Systems.

Implicit Green Finance Strategies

Based on the data structure and analyzed data, evidence of impact-first is relatively scarce with semblance emerging from the fund managers with some portfolio allocation under the broad umbrella of ESG (Linnenluecke, 2022). Implicit green finance strategy is where a fund invests in industries as part of a broad set of environment, social, and governance (ESG) measures. An illustrative case study developed in Ghana is also presented.

Hybrid Institutional Logic

CMBF2 is a capital market-based impact fund that has an implicit green finance focus in terms of strategic intent, while for investments at the portfolio level, there is evidence of an explicit green finance focus in investing in renewable energy firms as well as prioritizing SDG 7 within wider ESG metrics. With respect to institutional logic, CMBF2 reflects an implicit hybrid logic investing in environmentally focused sectors as part of an overall portfolio.

To uncover evidence of implicit hybrid green finance strategy and institutional logic, we examine how stakeholders associated with the fund, a fund manager and an investor, respectively, described the fund's focus:

> [We] target African SMEs with financing needs under €3 million, known as the 'missing middle due to a lack of access to long-term financing and a need for strategic and managerial support .... promoting sustainable growth through investment in resource-efficient companies with limited carbon footprints. We believe that our partner companies can play an active role in experiencing and sharing replicable, efficient and renewable energy solutions.
>
> Particularly also around the ESG, you know, we are very much around saying that this is our minimum benchmark of what we require.
>
> *Lamptey (2020)*

Another fund manager emphasized that

> some of our investees are in Manufacturing and retail energy efficient products and the provision of clean energy solutions (solar & LPG). At the portfolio level, USD 10.8 million (3%) disbursement out of a total disbursement portfolio of USD 366 million.
>
> *Lamptey (2020)*

In terms of key stakeholders and the nature of interactions (or partnerships) at the investor-fund manager level, CMBF2 receives funds from three sources. The first is development finance institutions, which include the Dutch Entrepreneurial Development Bank (FMO), the African Development Bank, Proparco, and the European Investment Bank). The second is development agencies (Agence Française de Développement (AFD)). Both these stakeholders provide impact investments and technical assistance facility components of CMBF2. The third is private equity investors (Bank of Africa, CFAO, PhiTrust, BRED, Credit Cooperatif) and foundations and individuals (Wendell), which guarantee access to private investments. This combination of development and private finance requires an investment strategy that is distinct from private wealth-creating SMEs. (Ngoasong et al., 2015). Fund managers, as implementers, must rely on commercial banks as catalysts to disburse funds to investee SMEs. The SMEs range from types labelled as missing-middle (i.e., enterprises which are too big for microfinance funding yet small for private equity and venture capital minimum deal size above USD 1.0 million) and matured SMEs in sectors that include agri-business, microfinance, construction, transport, health, and off-grid energy. With respect to governance, board representation was seen as important for oversight alongside an investment strategy, captured in the below quotation in terms of equity and quasi-equity (Höchstädter & Scheck, 2015).

> The investors appoint a board. We are always the minority investors…. we use a combination of equity and quasi-equity instruments…and it is a function of the size of the company
>
> *Lamptey (2020)*

At the fund manager-SME level, we considered an example of a green finance investment that has been implemented by CMBF2 in Ghana, using equity and/or quasi-equity. We considered SME1, to illustrate a typical example of deal sourcing in-country with regard to green finance, in this case, investment in renewable energy (Marbuah, 2020). The fund manager stated that deal proposals must comply with the investment criteria, after which is proposal screening, lasting two months of the due diligence stage, and initial transactions could reduce from 100% to about 20% to guarantee fit with green finance objectives, alignment with investment strategies, and the outcome of the fund manager. Contract approval and confirmation timesheets for fund disbursement occur after investment committee approval. Then post-investment monitoring ensues to ensure compliance with the timelines set in the contract, and support is provided to investees to facilitate the realization of investment outcomes of environmental impact and financial returns.

Through our review of an investor report by CMBF2, we also considered SME2, an established, top-five Free-Zone pineapple-exporting SME incorporated in 2005. The company was financially exposed to bank-based fund managers totaling GHS 10.5 million (Ghanaian cedi; equivalent to USD 2.6 million) by 2015. CMBF2 and another agri-business impact fund rescued SME2 from near collapse. This case typifies how the multiple stakeholders' missions are aligned through a governance structure for deploying impact investments in environment-focused activity within broader ESG metrics at the fund manager-SME level. Impact investment capital from the fund manager comprised equity of USD 805,000.00 for minority ownership, control, and board representation (fund manager and one independent director). In addition, there was debt capital of USD 2.3 million for repayment of existing obligations and the acquisition of new equipment for growth and expansion.

Technical assistance facility from development agencies supported training and capacity-building, and there was the acquisition of farm management software for operations.

Furthermore, an estimated USD 300,000 was earmarked for an out-grower scheme subject to the realization of key milestones, social impact, and financial returns. The invested impact capital guaranteed USD 1 million in revenue in 2018 and created jobs for more than 100 permanent employees as well as 100 contracted employees. An estimated 1,000 households were impacted by environmental and social factors. The broader ESG focus for SME1 in which the environment, as one of several measures of impact (Ngoasong, 2021), reflects an implicit green finance strategy with a hybrid institutional logic.

Impact-First Institutional Logics

There was relatively little evidence of impact-first institutional logics in line with a green finance strategy. For example, few fund managers allocate portfolio capital (ie long term equity or debt capital together with grant funding) to investees in the lighting, power, and cookstove sectors within an overall portfolio via a combination of debt, grants, and equity: patient capital orientated towards environmentally focused activities. Some have commenced allocating investment capital for investees that supply liquefied natural gas (LNG) to achieve net zero objectives.

Discussion

Implication for Green Finance Research

Drawing on institutional and stakeholder theories and through a qualitative study in Ghana, we have explored a framework for uncovering explicit and implicit green finance strategies of capital market-based impact investment funds. This combined approach has enabled us to examine interactions between the principal stakeholders, probe their motivations, and trace how these are translated into their preferred financial instruments and governance structure. It has also illustrated how impact investment processes are often characterized by competing, and in some instances conflicted, institutional logics of impact (i.e., social and environmental sustainability) and investment (i.e., financial returns and risk) (Castellas et al., 2018). Our study demonstrates how the interplay between three key factors – stakeholders, investment strategies, and governance – can be analyzed in order to determine the extent to which impact investment funds are pursuing explicit and/or implicit green finance strategies. Future research can investigate each of these factors in greater detail by applying both quantitative and qualitative methods to investigate the role that they play in shaping the explicit and implicate green finance strategies, as well as the associated outcomes and real-world impacts.

The contrasting features of explicit and implicit green finance strategies also merit a more detailed examination. As we have demonstrated, an explicit green finance strategy is typified by investment funds, such as Inspired Evolution (fund manager), in which development agencies such as Norfund and Sagemcom participated in a USD 35 million equity investment to establish and finance ESCOTEL in partnership with Orange as a telecoms mobile operator. ESCOTEL provided the installation, operations, and maintenance of decentralized solar and storage hybrid power systems for Orange telecom sites in Sierra Leone and Liberia, thus switching from diesel generators to solar. It is clear from the evidence in this chapter that financial institutions are increasing green lending to SMEs in African countries. Yet, by considering ongoing challenges connected to recovering from the COVID-19 crisis, the long-standing risk of SME lending, and the relatively limited access to SME financing in general, more research is needed to understand how a focus on green finance might shape an already constrained financing environment.

Our analysis suggests that an explicit finance-first institutional logic is dominant in the African context, investing in green (renewables). There is emerging evidence that impact investment funds are taking on transition elements in green finance, requiring the greening of existing brown industries. In view of the struggle to manage the tensions emerging from the institutional logics, some fund managers have adopted hybrid logics as a potential solution to the challenge of merging the logics by some of these fund managers. More research is needed here, building on an institutional logic perspective (Battilana & Dorado, 2010). We found that there are no defined investment instruments under the label of green finance in Ghana's legislation within which impact investors can be evaluated as pursuing a green finance strategy. However, existing research reveals how multilateral agencies, such as the International Finance Corporation, have developed legislative frameworks that have been operationalized for the green bonds market, targeting infrastructure development in several African countries, most notably South Africa, Nigeria, and Morocco (FSDAfrica.org, 2022).

Implications for Policy and Practice

Green finance requires unique sets of financial instruments that must be tailored to the investment needs of companies to realize the anticipated green outcomes. Fund managers need to respond to this challenge by developing appropriate in-house capabilities in deal origination and transaction structuring. Secondly, it is important to develop a modified ecosystem of players/actors/participants to assist companies seeking green finance to be better prepared ("investment-ready"). These actors could include ESG analysts and reporting professionals, training and capacity-building institutions, and green finance intermediaries for exit opportunities for investors. Thirdly, our findings offer practical suggestions for three possible investment strategies that fund managers can pursue when seeking to undertake green finance in SMEs: (1) green investing (e.g., renewables); (2) greening of existing brown industries; and (3) targeted investing in environment-focused activities within a broader ESG metrics.

The development of green bonds in African countries offers useful lessons that could be adopted by the wider impact investment community. This will require a re-allocation of resources to influence institutional stakeholders, especially investors (i.e., through engagement and promotional activities such as road shows and press soirees). Additionally, government policies are needed to develop a green-bond-type instrument by capital market-based investments into specific SMEs that we have studied in the chapter. Fiscal policy instruments such as pay-as-you-go solar, electric utility quota obligation, net metering, and premium payments are examples of policies that have been used to encourage the financial efficiency of green investments in Southern and Eastern African countries (Rolffs et al., 2015). SME owners and management teams in the green investment sector require a deeper engagement with fund managers and other actors in the emerging landscape to explore and understand the investment criteria of these fund managers. The banking system can act as a catalyst to facilitate the disbursement of funds between fund managers and investee SMEs. In addition, as we have seen in the case of bank-based impact funds such as BBGF (now ABSA Ghana) (Lamptey, 2020) that it can also be an important co-investor in projects with the potential to tackle the causes and consequences of climate change. For example, BBGF syndicated funds with some development finance institutions and development agencies to support SMEs using climate-smart technologies in agribusiness in the northern regions of Ghana (Lamptey, 2020).

Conclusion

The growing green finance initiatives in Ghana and Africa, in general, are highly commendable. However, the climate change emergency and the UN's SDG 13 suggest that in order for exponential growth in green finance investment by fund managers and investors, there must be the support of diverse stakeholders and institutions. Multi-faceted problems and issues require substantial development-orientated green financing to realize the anticipated environmental outcomes and financial returns of the key stakeholders. Illustrated examples in this book chapter are noteworthy including policy implications and future research.

References

Aboagye, B., Gyamfi, S., Ofosu, E. A., & Djordjevic, S. (2021). Status of renewable energy resources for electricity supply in Ghana. *Scientific African, 11*, 00660. https://doi.org/10.1016/j.sciaf.2020.e00660p

Ackah, I., & Graham, E. (2021). Meeting the targets of the Paris agreement: An analysis of renewable energy (RE) governance systems in West Africa (WA). *Clean Technologies and Environmental Policy, 23*(2), 501–507.

Afful-Dadzie, A., Mallett, A., & Afful-Dadzie, E. (2020). The challenge of energy transition in the global south: The case of electricity generation planning in Ghana. *Renewable and Sustainable Energy Reviews, 126*, 109830. https://doi.org/10.1016/j.rser.2020.109830

Afful-Koomson, T. (2015). The green climate fund in Africa: What should be different? *Climate and Development, 7*(4), 367–379. https://doi.org/10.1080/17565529.2014.951015

Agrawal, A., & Hockerts, K. (2021). Impact investing: Review and research agenda. *Journal of Small Business & Entrepreneurship, 33*(2), 153–181. https://doi.org/10.1080/08276331.2018.1551457

Balakumar, U. (2021). Fossil-fuel-free investing: Weaving a new investment paradigm. In E. D. M. Sarmento & H. R. Paul (Eds.), *Global handbook of impact investing: Solving global problems via smarter capital markets towards a more sustainable society* (pp. 413–459). Wiley.

Battilana, J., & Dorado, S. (2010). Building sustainable hybrid organizations: The case of commercial microfinance organizations. *Academy of Management Journal, 53*(6), 1419–1440.

Bertilsson, J., & Thörn, H. (2021). Discourses on transformational change and paradigm shift in the green climate fund: The divide over financialization and country ownership. *Environmental Politics, 30*(3), 423–441.

Blundel, R., & Hampton, S. (2021a). How can SMEs contribute to net zero? An evidence review. SOTA Review No 51: July 2021. Enterprise Research Centre. Retrieved May 18, 2022, from https://www.enterpriseresearch.ac.uk/publications/how-can-smes-contribute-to-net-zero-an-evidence-review/

Blundel, R., & Hampton, S. (2021b). Eco-innovation and green start-ups: An evidence review. *Enterprise research centre insight paper*, September 2021. Enterprise Research Centre. Retrieved May 18, 2022, from https://www.enterpriseresearch.ac.uk/publications/eco-innovation-and-green-start-ups-an-evidence-review/

Bowman, M., & Minas, S. (2019). Resilience through interlinkage: The green climate fund and climate finance governance. *Climate Policy, 19*(3), 342–353.

Brandstetter, L., & Lehner, O. M. (2015). Opening the market for impact investments: The need for adapted portfolio tools. *Entrepreneurship Research Journal, 5*(2), 87–107.

Castellas, E. I.-P., Ormiston, J., & Findlay, S. (2018). Financing social entrepreneurship: The role of impact investment in shaping social enterprise in Australia. *Social Enterprise Journal, 14*(2), 130–155. https://doi.org/10.1108/SEJ-02-2017-0006

Deschryver, P. (2021). The role of transition finance instruments in bridging the climate finance gap. In E. D. M. Sarmento & H. R. Paul (Eds.), *Global handbook of impact investing: Solving global problems via smarter Capital Markets towards a more sustainable society* (pp. 461–497). Wiley.

Fonta, W. M., Ayuk, E. T., & van Huysen, T. (2018). Africa and the green climate fund: Current challenges and future opportunities. *Climate Policy, 18*(9), 1210–1225.

Friedland, R., & Alford, R. R. (1991). Bringing society back in: Symbols, practices and institutional contradictions. In W. W. Powell & P. J. DiMaggio (Eds.), *The new institutionalism in organizational analysis* (pp. 232–263). University of Chicago Press.

FSD Africa. (2021). Developing the green bond market in Ghana. Retrieved April 12, 2022, from https://www.fsdafrica.org/event/webinar-developing-the-green-bond-market-in-ghana/

GIIN. (2015a). The landscape for impact investing in West Africa: Understanding the current status, trends, opportunities, and challenges. In *A West Africa regional chapter report by the global impact investing network*

(December). Global Impact Investing Network. https://thegiin.org/assets/160620_GIIN_WestAfrica_full.pdf

GIIN. (2015b). The landscape for impact investing in East Africa. *East Africa full report by the global impact investing network* (August). Global Impact Investing Network.

GIIN. (2019). *Annual impact investor survey.* Global Impact Investing Network. Retrieved May 18, 2022, from https://thegiin.org/assets/GIIN_2019%20Annual%20Impact%20Investor%20Survey_webfile.pdf

Glänzel, G., & Scheuerle, T. (2016). Social impact investing in Germany: Current impediments from investors and social entrepreneurs' perspectives. *Voluntas: International Journal of Voluntary and Nonprofit Organizations, 27*(4), 1638–1668.

Gioia, D.A., Corley, K.G., & Hamilton, A.L. (2013). Seeking qualitative rigor in inductive research: Notes on the Gioia methodology. *Organizational Research Methods, 16*(1), 15–31. https://doi.org/10.1177/1094428112452151

Gümüsay, A. A., Claus, L., & Amis, J. (2020). Engaging with grand challenges: An institutional logics perspective. *Organization Theory, 1*(3), 1–20.

Hehenberger, L., Mair, J., & Metz, A. (2019). The assembly of a field ideology: An idea-centric perspective on systemic power in impact investing. *Academy of Management Journal, 62*(6), 1672–1704.

Höchstädter, A. K., & Scheck, B. (2015). What's in a name: An analysis of impact investing understandings by academics and practitioners. *Journal of Business Ethics, 132*(2), 449–475.

IFC. (2021). The international financial corporation and the Ghana's securities and exchange commission to develop green bonds market. International Finance Corporation. Retrieved May 18, 2022, from https://pressroom.ifc.org/all/pages/PressDetail.aspx?ID=26337

IIF [Impact Investors Foundation]. 2019. Impact Investors' Foundation: Nigeria and Ghana impact investing and policy landscape. https://thegiin.org/research/publication/nigeria-andghana-impact-investing-and-policy-landscape

Jafri, J. (2019). When billions meet trillions: Impact investing and shadow banking in Pakistan. *Review of International Political Economy, 26*(3), 520–544. https://doi.org/10.1080/09692290.2019.1608842

Kazimierczuk, A. H. (2019). Wind energy in Kenya: A status and policy framework review. *Renewable and Sustainable Energy Reviews, 107,* 434–445.

King, L., & Gish, E. (2015). Marketizing social change: Social shareholder activism and responsible investing. *Sociological Perspectives, 58*(4), 711–730.

Lamptey, R. O. (2020). The influence of bank-based and capital market-based impact investments on SME financing in Ghana: Governance, strategy change and impacts [PhD Thesis]. The Open University. Retrieved May 18, 2022, from http://oro.open.ac.uk/69437/

Linnenluecke, M. K. (2022). Environmental, social and governance (ESG) performance in the context of multinational business research. *Multinational Business Review, 30*(1), 1–16. https://doi.org/10.1108/MBR-11-2021-0148

Marbuah, G. (2020). Scoping the sustainable finance landscape in Africa: The case of green bonds, July 2020. Stockholm Sustainable Finance Centre. Retrieved May 18, 2022, from https://www.stockholmsustainablefinance.com/wp-content/uploads/2018/06/SSFC_greenbonds_africa_report.pdf

Mersland, R., Nyarko, S. A., & Sirisena, A. B. (2020). A hybrid approach to international market selection: The case of impact investing organizations. *International Business Review, 29*(1), 101624.

Miles, M. B., Huberman, A. M., & Saldaña, J. (2014). *Qualitative data analysis: A methods sourcebook.* SAGE.

Mogapi, E. M., Sutherland, M. M., & Wilson-Prangley, A. (2019). Impact investing in South Africa: Managing tensions between financial returns and social impact. *European Business Review, 31*(3), 397–419.

Ngoasong, M. Z. (2021). Rethinking a new transition finance paradigm for addressing the climate crisis in Africa. Climate Compatible Growth Programme. https://climatecompatiblegrowth.com/wp-content/uploads/3I-COP26-Policy-Brief.pdf

Ngoasong, M. Z., & Lamptey, R. O. (2021). Gender lens investing in the African context. In E. de M. Sarmento & R. P. Herman (Eds.), *Global handbook of impact investing: Solving global problems via smarter capital markets towards a more sustainable society* (pp. 273–302). Wiley.

Ngoasong, M. Z., Paton, R., & Korda, A. (2015). Impact investing and inclusive business development in Africa: A research agenda. The Open University. https://www.open.ac.uk/ikd/documents/working-papers/ikd-working-paper-76.pdf

Ngwenya, N., & Simatele, M. D. (2020). Unbundling of the green bond market in the economic hubs of Africa: Case study of Kenya, Nigeria and South Africa. *Development Southern Africa, 37*(6), 888–903.

North, D. C. (1991). Institutions. *Journal of Economic Perspectives, 5*(1), 97–112.

Okereke, C., Coke, A., Geebreyesus, M., Ginbo, T., Wakeford, J. J., & Mulugetta, Y. (2019). Governing green industrialisation in Africa: Assessing key parameters for a sustainable socio-technical transition in the context of Ethiopia. *World Development, 11*(5), 279–290.

Ormiston, J., Charlton, K., Donald, M. S., & Seymour, R. G. (2015). Overcoming the challenges of impact investing: Insights from leading investors. *Journal of Social Entrepreneurship, 6*(3), 352–378.

Rajan, T. A., Koserwal, P., & Keerthana, S. (2014). The global epicenter of impact investing: An analysis of social venture investments in India. *Journal of Private Equity, 17*(2), 37–50.

REPP. (2021). *Renewable energy performance platform, report and financial statement, 2020–2021.* Camco Management. https://repp.energy/wp-content/uploads/2021/10/REPP-Report-and-Financial-Statements-2020-2021.pdf

Rolffs, P., Ockwell, D., & Byrne, R. (2015). Beyond technology and finance: Pay-as-you-go sustainable energy access and theories of social change. *Environment and Planning. Part A, 47*(12), 2609–2627.

Roundy, P. T. (2019). Regional differences in impact investment: A theory of impact investing ecosystems. *Social Responsibility Journal, 16*(4), 467–485.

TCFD. (2017). Final report: Recommendations of the task force on climate-related financial disclosures. https://assets.bbhub.io/company/sites/60/2020/10/FINAL-2017-TCFD-Report-11052018.pdf

Walwyn, D. R. (2020). Turning points for sustainability transitions: Institutional destabilization, public finance and the techno-economic dynamics of decarbonization in South Africa. *Energy Research and Social Science, 70*, 101784.

Watts, N., & Scales, I. R. (2020). Social impact investing, agriculture, and the financialisation of development: Insights from sub-Saharan Africa. *World Development, 130*, 104918.

Wood, D., Thornley, B., & Grace, K. (2013). Institutional impact investing: Practice and policy. *Journal of Sustainable Finance and Investment, 3*(2), 75–94.

Wooten, M., & Hoffman, A. J. (2008). Organizational fields: Past, present and future. In R. Greenwood, C. Oliver, K. Sahlin, & R. Suddaby (Eds.), *The SAGE handbook of organizational institutionalism* (pp. 130–147). Sage.

Zhang, D., Zhang, Z., & Managi, S. 2019. A bibliometric analysis on green finance: Current status, development, and future directions. *Finance Research Letters, 29*, 425–430. https://doi.org/10.1016/j.frl.2019.02.003

19
THE UNITED NATIONS' PRINCIPLES FOR RESPONSIBLE BANKING, CSR, AND CORPORATE GOVERNANCE IN THE BANKING INDUSTRY

Emilia Vähämaa

Introduction

Corporate social responsibility (CSR) is commonly accepted as one of the main components of business growth and sustainability. Since the banking industry is largely based on trust, CSR is argued to be a particularly important determinant of bank success. Following the global financial crisis, the banking industry is facing constantly increasing pressure to acknowledge and respond to obligations to society (see e.g., Gill, 2008; Grove et al., 2011; Matten, 2006). Banks have an important role in society since they work as intermediaries between individuals, businesses, and the public sector. Due to this unique role, the banks have the opportunity to influence the environment through their financing decisions (Zimmermann, 2019). Moreover, earlier studies document a positive relationship between bank performance and sustainability (Wu & Shen, 2013; Cornett et al., 2016; Shen et al., 2016; Wu et al., 2017) and indicate that sustainability commitments decrease the bank default risk and that outperformance on sustainability reduces banks' contribution to systemic risk (see e.g., Scholtens & van't Klooster, 2019). Thus, sustainability and responsible business practices should be a high priority for banks.

The importance of green finance has been promoted in public discussions over the past few years, and its role has been highlighted due to the war in Ukraine, general political instability, and the ongoing energy crisis. Green finance refers to any structured financial activity, either a product or a service, that has been created to have a positive environmental impact. Projects that are typically included in the field of green finance focus on goals such as 1) renewable energy and energy efficiency, 2) pollution prevention and control, 3) biodiversity conservation, 4) circular economy initiatives, and 5) sustainable use of natural resources and land (World Economic Forum, 2020). Green finance plays an important role in delivering several of the United Nations' 17 Sustainable Development Goals (United Nations, 2022b) and is also an important tool in fulfilling the United Nations' Principles for Responsible Banking.

To highlight the importance of CSR in the banking industry, The United Nations Environment Programme – Finance Initiative (UNEP FI) launched a set of best practices for the banking industry called the Principles for Responsible Banking for public consultation in November 2018, and the Principles were implemented the following year, on September 22, 2019 (United Nations, 2019). The Principles for Responsible Banking were created by 30 large banks from different countries. Among the creators are important global market leaders such as Barclays, Santander, and Societe Generale.

> The Principles for Responsible Banking are a unique framework for ensuring that signatory banks' strategy and practice align with the vision society has set out for its future in the Sustainable Development Goals and the Paris Climate Agreement.
>
> *United Nations (2022a)*

132 banks that collectively held USD 47 trillion in assets, which corresponds to one-third of the global banking sector, signed the Principles at the implementation. As of August 2023, over 300 banks representing approximately half of the global banking assets have signed the Principles, thereby indicating that a very significant portion of assets globally is held at banks that are committed to responsibility targets. By signing the Principles, banks take actions to align their core strategy and operations with the United Nations Sustainable Development Goals and other international agreements, such as the Paris Climate Agreement.

In this chapter, we introduce the Principles for Responsible Banking in detail and discuss the process of becoming a signatory. Moreover, we study if and how the founding banks and the early signatories of the Principles for Responsible Banking differ from the banking industry in general in terms of their governance. Furthermore, we examine if a higher quality CSR translates into money in terms of better bank performance than that of the peer banks. It is assumed that the social, ethical, and environmental policies of the early adopters of the Principles differ from the general banking population. Thus, it is of interest to examine if these banks that early on committed to the Principles for Responsible Banking either perform or are governed differently compared to the other sample banks.

The reported findings indicate that banks that are committed to the Principles for Responsible Banking underperform compared to the peer banks during the ten years before the launch of the Principles. Moreover, the banks where the board members attend the board meetings more frequently tended to outperform the banks with less active board meeting attendance rates. Finally, *Board experience*, *Board size*, and *Senior executive compensation* are positively associated with firm performance. The reported findings may have important implications for bank supervisors, regulators, depositors, and other stakeholders. Moreover, the findings promote the importance of creating industry-level guidelines for CSR.

Presentation of the Principles

The Principles for Responsible Banking consist of a set of six Principles: 1) aligning the business strategy with society's goals as expressed in the United Nations' sustainable development goals, Paris Climate Agreement, and other frameworks, 2) continuously increasing the bank's positive impacts while reducing its negative impacts, 3) working responsibly with the bank's clients and customers to create shared prosperity for current and future generations, 4) consulting, engaging, and partnering with relevant stakeholders to achieve society's goals, 5) implementing commitments through effective governance and setting targets for the bank's most significant impacts, and 6) committing to transparency and accountability for the bank's positive and negative impacts, and the bank's contribution to society's goals (United Nations, 2022a). These six Principles are listed in the document the banks sign[1] when committing to the Principles for Responsible Banking and summarized in Figure 19.1.

UN Principles and Corporate Governance

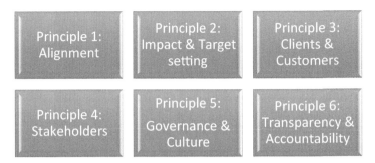

Figure 19.1 United Nations' Principles for Responsible Banking (United Nations, 2022a)

Implementation of the Principles

The Principles themselves are rather general in nature and demand improvement instead of achieving concrete targets. However, the Principles are supported by an implementation framework, which defines clear accountabilities and requires each bank to set, publish and work towards ambitious targets. United Nations (2022a) divides the Principle implementation process into three steps:

1) Impact Analysis
2) Target-Setting and Implementation
3) Public Reporting

To support the banks in the implementation process, the United Nations provides a Members Area on its webpage. This closed platform is aimed at the member banks and those that are in the signatory process. The Members Area includes for example training opportunities and provides peer learning and tools to support the banks in Principle implementation. Next, we will take a closer look at the three steps of the Principle implementation process.

Step 1: Impact Analysis

The first step of the process, Impact Analysis, requires the banks to thoroughly analyze the most significant impact of their products and services from societal, environmental, and economic perspectives. After mapping the impacts, the banks will identify the most significant impacts that are related to them. Focusing on the most significant impacts related to the bank is important as it is very challenging to change many things at once. Thus, prioritization is the key to making progress. Consequently, the banks will focus on supporting the greatest positive impacts and reducing the most significant negative impacts they have on society, the environment, and the economy.

Step 2: Target-Setting and Implementation

After completing the Impact Analysis, the banks move to the next step of the Principle implementation process, Target-Setting and Implementation. In this step, the banks need to set at least two targets that are related to the significant impacts identified in the Impact Analysis step. The set targets need to be SMART, that is,

Specific
Measurable
Achievable
Relevant
Time-bound

In addition, the targets are expected to be ambitious, as well as in line with the United Nations' Sustainable Development Goals and the Paris Climate Agreement. In addition to the final targets defined, the banks are also expected to set intermediate targets and define specific actions that will be taken to achieve the set goals. The United Nations has recently published a guiding FAQ document focusing on the target-setting process (United Nations, 2022c). Moreover, also a series of target-setting guidance documents covering the following areas is available: climate-change mitigation, gender equality, financial health and inclusion, biodiversity, and resource efficiency and circular economy. Each of these documents provides detailed information on the area, as well as good practice for target-setting.

Step 3: Public Reporting

The final stage of the implementation process is Public Reporting. The signatories are expected to include information in their public reporting on how the bank is implementing the Principles for Responsible Banking. The banks are expected to show evidence of how they have progressed in implementing the Principles and to assess if they are meeting the targets set in Step 2 of the implementation process.

Case Nordea. As an example of the required public reporting explained above, we take a look at Nordea Bank, one of the creating members of the Principles. Nordea explains its target-setting and the planned specific actions related to each of the six Principles on its webpages[2] in the following manner:

1. **Alignment.** In 2021 we outlined our 2023 sustainability targets. This meant committing to align our business strategy to be consistent with the goals listed in the Sustainable Development Goals and the Paris Climate Agreement.
2. **Impact.** With our long and solid experience, we will play a leading role through active ownership in our investments and by engaging with our customers to help them accelerate their own transition through our support and offerings. We have also recently updated our policy on the fossil fuel-based industries to reflect this direction.
3. **Clients and customers.** In 2020 we launched our Sustainable Choice symbol, a way for our customers to more easily find our products with a clear sustainable focus. We also created a landing page on all our local home pages where we collected the products with this symbol. For large corporates and institutions, we have instead developed an advisory service.
4. **Stakeholders.** We are proud to engage and partner with relevant stakeholders to achieve society's goals. We are co-founders of the UNEP FI Principles for Responsible Banking and CCCA and founding members of the Net-Zero Asset Owner Alliance, the Net Zero Asset Manager initiative, and other impact-driven investor collaborations.
5. **Governance and target-setting.** We are fully committed to making the financial sector more sustainable. We have set targets for 2023, 2030, and 2050, when our goal is to be a net-zero emission bank.
6. **Transparency and accountability.** An example of this is how we every year present milestones and progress in our Annual Report and in our Sustainability report. We have also joined the Partnership for Carbon Accounting Financials (PCAF) to develop and implement a harmonised approach to measure and disclose emissions from lending and investments.

This reporting example is structured clearly, as it follows the structure of the six Principles. Nordea also provides additional detailed information and specific target documents and supporting material on its webpage. Thus, the supervisor can easily estimate if the bank has improved its behavior as planned.

Supervisory Actions

The progress and reporting of each signatory bank are evaluated yearly. To ascertain that banks are not using a signatory position as a tool for greenwashing or as a publicity stunt with no true advancement towards fulfilling the set goals, United Nations formed a governance body called the Banking Board. The task of the board is to ensure the effective implementation of the commitments. Consequently, a lack of progress could ultimately lead to the non-compliant banks being forced out of the list of Principle signatories. It is also possible for the banks themselves to end their commitment as a signatory.

Earlier academic literature

The World Bank defines that:

> CSR is the commitment of business to contribute to sustainable economic development by working with employees, their families, the local community and society at large to improve their lives in ways that are good for business and development.
> *(Starks, 2009, p. 465)*

Corporate social responsibility has been widely researched in the recent literature. In addition to financial advantages, CSR may also provide strategic gains to companies in the form of competitive advantages (Aguilera et al., 2006; Kolk & Pinkse, 2010). Earlier literature has widely documented that ethical behavior benefits the firm and may matter for shareholder value (see e.g., Gunthorpe, 1997; Fischer & Khoury, 2007; Choi & Jung, 2008; Donker et al., 2008; Blazovich & Smith, 2011). In particular, Blazovich and Smith (2011) suggest that ethical corporate behavior can be considered an intangible asset, which may improve firm value by reducing conflicts and strengthening trust between the main stakeholders of the firm. Based on these findings it can be concluded that companies should invest in promoting and monitoring ethical conduct.

Earlier studies have also documented that board characteristics and other governance attributes may affect the social responsibility of companies. For example, Harjoto and Jo (2011) and Jo and Harjoto (2012) suggest that firms with more independent boards and stronger governance mechanisms may be more likely to participate in social responsibility-related activities. Related to gender diversity, Bear et al. (2010) document that gender diversity on corporate boards is positively associated with social responsibility ratings and with firm reputation. In a similar vein, Garcia-Sanchez et al. (2015) document that firms with larger boards and more gender-diverse boards are more likely to implement ethics codes.

A recent stream of literature focuses on corporate social responsibility in the banking industry. Related to bank performance, the findings related to the relationship between performance and social responsibility are mixed. Simpson and Kohers (2002), Wu and Shen (2013), Cornett et al. (2016), Shen et al. (2016), and Wu et al. (2017) suggest that socially responsible banks tend to outperform their peers, while Chih, Chih, and Chen (2010) find no significant relationship between bank performance and social responsibility.

Grougiou et al. (2014) examine US banks to see if CSR and earnings management are related. Their findings indicate that banks that engage in earnings management practices are also actively involved in CSR, but, interestingly, the reverse relationship is not significant. Finally, related to social responsibility and board characteristics in the financial industry, Jizi et al. (2014) document that board independence and board size are positively related to CSR disclosure in the US banking industry. Interestingly, their findings also suggest that CEO duality impacts CSR disclosure positively.

The corporate board is commonly considered the most important internal governance mechanism within a firm. The role of the board is enhanced in the financial industry since the boards are expected to act not only in the best interests of the shareholders, but the boards also have a fiduciary duty toward other stakeholders of the bank. These are, for example, depositors and bank regulators. According to earlier literature, the board of directors has an important role in the development and implementation of ethics codes and the oversight of the ethical behavior inside the company (see e.g., Singh, 2011; Garcia-Sanchez et al., 2015). Thus, examining board characteristics may help identify the banks with the best ethical practices and, consequently, improve bank performance.

In summary, the existing literature indicates that corporate social responsibility and corporate governance are important determinants of firm performance both in the financial and non-financial sectors. To highlight the importance of CSR in the banking industry, the United Nations has introduced Principles for Responsible Banking as presented in the second section of this chapter. The Principles are designed by a group of founding banks across the world. As only a small portion of the large banks worldwide signed the Principles at launch, it is of interest to examine if and how the founding members and the early signatories of the Principles for Responsible Banking differ from the general banking population. Thus, it is hypothesized:

H1. CSR and bank performance are positively related.
H2. Corporate governance and bank performance are positively related.

Methodology

The relationship between bank performance and corporate social responsibility and governance quality is examined by alternative versions of the following cross-sectional panel regression:

$$Performance_{j,t} = \alpha + \beta_{1-8}\left(Social\ responsibility\ and\ governance\ variables\right)_{j,t}$$
$$+\beta_{9-10}\left(Bank-specific\ controls\right)_{j,t} + \beta_{11-19}\left(Year\ dummies\right)_{j,t} \quad (19.1)$$
$$+\varepsilon_{j,t}$$

where the dependent variable is one of the two alternative performance measures for bank j at time t, i.e., *ROA* or *ROE*. In each of the alternative regressions, we include six different governance variables. Alternative governance variables related to the signatory status of the bank that are employed in different model specifications are (1) *Founder or signer*; (2) *Founder*; and (3) *Signer*. The governance variables included in all the regression specifications are *Board attendance*, *Board diversity*, *Board experience*, *Board size*, and *Senior executive compensation*.[3] The employed bank-specific control variables are *Loan growth* and *Size*. Throughout the regressions, we use robust standard errors which are adjusted for heteroskedasticity.

Performance Measures

Bank performance is estimated by two alternative measures, return on assets (*ROA*) and return on equity (*ROE*). *ROA* is estimated as net income – bottom line + ((interest expense on debt – interest capitalized) x (1 − tax rate)) / average of last year's (total assets − customer liabilities on acceptances) and current year's (total assets − customer liabilities on acceptances) x 100. *ROE* is calculated as (net income before preferred dividends + ((interest expense on debt − interest capitalized) x (1 − tax rate)) / (last year's total assets − last year's customer liabilities on acceptances) x 100.[4]

Social Responsibility and Corporate Governance Variables

The corporate social responsibility activity of the banks is measured by three alternative variables that control for the signatory status of the bank. First, *Founder or signer* is a dummy variable that gets a value of one if the examined bank is one of the founders of the United Nation's Principles for Responsible Banking, or if they signed the Principles at launch in September 2019. Second, *Founder* is a binary variable that is assigned the value of one if the examined bank is one of the 30 banks that together developed the United Nation's Principles for Responsible Banking. Finally, *Signer* is a dummy variable that gets a value of one for the banks that signed the Principles for Responsible Banking when they were launched in September 2019.

Corporate governance is measured by five variables: *Board attendance*, *Board diversity*, *Board experience*, *Board size*, and *Senior executive compensation*. *Board attendance* is measured by the average overall attendance percentage of board meetings, as reported by the company. *Board diversity* is measured as the percentage of women on the board of directors. *Board experience* is calculated as the average number of years each board member has been on the corporate board. *Board size* is the natural logarithm of the total number of board members at the end of the fiscal year. *Senior executive compensation* is calculated as the total compensation paid to all senior executives divided by the total assets of the bank. Thus, the measure of paid compensation takes the size of the company into account.

Control Variables

The most important commonly used control variables are employed to control for other possible factors affecting the performance of the banks. *Loan growth* is measured as an annual growth rate of the loans and is calculated as (current year's total loans / last year's total loans − 1) x 100. Bank *Size* is controlled by the logarithm of total assets. Total assets represent the sum of cash and dues from banks, total investments, net loans, customer liability on acceptances (if included in total assets), investment in unconsolidated subsidiaries, real estate assets, net property, plant, and equipment, and other assets.[5] Finally, the estimations control for potential time-fixed effects with fiscal year dummy variables.

The data consist of the large publicly listed banks across the world. The banks that were either founders of the Principles for Responsible Banking or signed the Principles at launch are included in the sample. In addition, the examined sample includes the 27 major banks that constitute the Nasdaq Global Bank Index and the companies included in the S&P Global 1200 Banks (82 banks). Thus, the sample is considered to consist of all the largest and most significant banks around the world.

Data

The employed data are gathered from Thomson Reuters. The founding member banks and the early committers are identified based on the United Nation's webpage (United Nations, 2019).

The sample covers a ten-year period before the launch of the Principles for Responsible Banking, that is, fiscal years 2009–2018. This sample period is considered relevant since it enables us to examine the situation in the banking sector *prior* to the launch of the Principles. The total sample consists of 698 bank-year observations and 90 individual banks. The summary statistics of the sample are presented in Table 19.1.

Panel A of the table presents the summary statistics for the total sample, whereas Panel B of Table 19.1 denotes the summary statistics for the subsample of banks that were either founders of the Principles for Responsible Banking or signed the Principles at launch in September 2019. As can be seen from the table, 42.5 % of the sample banks are either founders or early signers of the Principles. The mean and median values for *ROA* in the total sample are 0.969 and 1.020 and for *ROE* 9.145 and 10.150, respectively.

The board meeting attendance rates vary from 50 % to 100 % for the total sample and from 75 % to 100 % for the *Founder or signer* subsample. *Board diversity* varies from 0% to 60 %, with the mean value for the total sample being 22.7%. *Board experience* varies from a few months to almost 18 years, whereas the mean value is 6.8 years. The board size goes from 2 to 26 members, with the median board size for the total sample being 14 members. The total executive compensation adjusted by firm size varies from 0 to 3.32 for the total sample and from 0 to 0.845 for the subsample of *Founder or signer* banks.

Regarding the control variables, the mean and median *Loan growth* rates for the total sample are 8.4% and 4.4% and for the *Founder or signer* subsample 10.7% and 3.1%, respectively. In terms of size, the banks in the *Founder or signer* subsample are slightly larger than the sample banks on average (natural logarithm of total assets of 20.709 vs. 20.332).

Pairwise correlations between the employed variables are reported in Table 19.2. As can be seen from the table, the alternative performance measures *ROA* and *ROE* are highly positively correlated (0.83). Moreover, *Founder or signer*, *Founder*, and *Signer* variables have high positive correlations with one another, which is caused by the definitions of the variables. These variables are used in alternative regression models, and, thus, these high positive correlations do not distort the findings.

Interestingly, *Size* and the size-adjusted *Executive compensation* are negatively correlated (−0.45). *Executive compensation* seems to be positively correlated with *Board size*, which is to be expected, as the number of people to be compensated increases with the board size.

Results

First, univariate tests are conducted to examine the social responsibility and governance of the banks. For this purpose, the sample is divided into subsamples based on the banks' commitments to the Principles for Responsible Banking. The first subsample consists of the founders and early signatories of the Principles, while the examined banks that did not commit to the Principles are in the second subsample. We then perform two-tailed t-tests and Wilcoxon rank-sum tests under the null hypothesis that there are no differences in the means and medians between the committed and non-committed banks.

Table 19.3 reports the mean and median values for the examined corporate governance variables of both subsamples and the results of the univariate tests. As can be seen from the table, there are statistically highly significant differences between the two subsamples in terms of *Board attendance*, *Board experience*, and *Senior executive compensation*.

Specifically, as Table 19.3 depicts, the univariate tests indicate that banks that have committed to the Principles for Responsible Banking have better board meeting attendance rates than the non-committed banks. Interestingly, the mean and median tenures of the board members are statistically significantly lower in the committed banks' subsample, which may indicate that they are more prone to update their boards frequently. Alternatively, a high turnover among board members may indicate trouble within the bank. Finally, *Senior executive compensation* is statistically significantly lower in the subsample of banks that are founders or early signers of the Principles.

We continue the empirical analysis by examining the association between bank performance and its corporate governance and social responsibility commitment. The results of these panel regression analyses are reported in Table 19.4.

Table 19.1 Descriptive statistics

Variable	Mean	Median	Std. dev.	Max	Min
Panel A. Summary statistics for the total sample (*n* = 698 obs)					
Performance variables:					
ROA	0.969	1.020	0.695	2.750	−5.780
ROE	9.145	10.150	10.887	37.140	−149.700
Governance variables:					
Founder or signer	0.425	0.000	0.495	1.000	0.000
Founder	0.200	0.000	0.400	1.000	0.000
Signer	0.225	0.000	0.418	1.000	0.000
Board attendance	89.779	94.000	10.471	100.000	50.000
Board diversity	22.733	22.220	11.015	60.000	0.000
Board experience	6.798	6.310	3.083	17.880	0.250
Board size	14.014	14.000	3.584	26.000	2.000
Senior executive compensation	0.095	0.054	0.165	3.320	0.000
Control variables:					
Loan growth	8.382	4.370	62.828	1592.200	−23.940
Size	20.332	20.483	1.569	26.463	15.351
Panel B. Summary statistics for the *Signer or founder* subsample (*n* = 283 obs)					
Performance variables:					
ROA	0.901	0.910	0.791	2.750	−5.780
ROE	7.720	8.180	12.738	37.140	−149.700
Governance variables:					
Founder or signer	1.000	1.000	0.000	1.000	1.000
Founder	0.470	0.000	0.500	1.000	0.000
Signer	0.530	1.000	0.500	1.000	0.000
Board attendance	93.845	95.000	5.687	100.000	75.000
Board diversity	24.122	23.530	12.763	60.000	0.000
Board experience	5.777	5.100	2.704	17.880	0.250
Board size	13.795	13.000	4.040	24.000	2.000
Senior executive compensation	0.067	0.037	0.098	0.845	0.000
Control variables:					
Loan growth	10.691	3.100	95.541	1596.200	−23.940
Size	20.709	20.832	1.320	26.463	15.351

Table 19.1 reports the descriptive statistics for the sample. *ROA* is return on assets and *ROE* denotes return on equity. *Founder or signer* is a dummy variable that gets a value of one if the examined bank is one of the founders of the United Nation's Principles for Responsible Banking or if they signed the Principles at launch in September 2019. *Founder* is a binary variable that is assigned the value of one if the examined bank is one of the 30 banks that together developed the United Nation's Principles for Responsible Banking. *Signer* is a dummy variable that gets a value of one for the banks that signed the Principles for Responsible Banking when they were launched. *Board attendance* is measured by the average overall attendance percentage of board meetings, as reported by the company. *Board diversity* is the percentage of women on the board of directors. *Board experience* is calculated as the average number of years each board member has been on the corporate board. *Board size* is the natural logarithm of the total number of board members at the end of the fiscal year. *Senior executive compensation* is calculated as the total compensation paid to all senior executives divided by the total assets of the bank. *Loan growth* is measured as annual growth rate of the loans. *Size* is controlled by the logarithm of total assets.

Table 19.2 Correlation matrix

	Variable	(1)	(2)	(3)	(4)	(5)	(6)	(7)	(8)	(9)	(10)	(11)
(1)	ROA											
(2)	ROE	0.83										
(3)	Founder or signer	−0.08	−0.11									
(4)	Founder	0.02	0.03	0.58								
(5)	Signer	−0.11	−0.16	0.63	−0.27							
(6)	Board attendance	0.05	0.19	0.33	0.15	0.25						
(7)	Board diversity	0.06	0.14	0.11	−0.01	0.14	0.11					
(8)	Board experience	0.15	0.10	−0.28	−0.14	−0.20	−0.35	0.07				
(9)	Board size	0.04	0.07	−0.05	0.05	−0.11	−0.03	−0.06	−0.03			
(10)	Senior executive compensation	0.07	0.01	−0.14	−0.09	−0.09	−0.28	0.01	0.29	−0.07		
(11)	Loan growth	0.05	0.08	0.03	−0.02	0.06	0.02	−0.03	−0.05	−0.09	0.00	
(12)	Size	0.15	0.28	0.21	0.21	0.05	0.40	0.06	−0.41	0.16	−0.45	0.03

Table 19.2 reports pairwise correlations for the total sample. *ROA* is return on assets and *ROE* denotes return on equity. *Founder or signer* is a dummy variable that gets a value of one if the examined bank is one of the founders of the United Nation's Principles for Responsible Banking or if they signed the Principles at launch in September 2019. *Founder* is a binary variable that is assigned the value of one if the examined bank is one of the 30 banks that together developed the United Nation's Principles for Responsible Banking. *Signer* is a dummy variable that gets a value of one for the banks that signed the Principles for Responsible Banking when they were launched. *Board attendance* is measured by the average overall attendance percentage of board meetings, as reported by the company. *Board diversity* is the percentage of women on the board of directors. *Board experience* is calculated as the average number of years each board member has been on the corporate board. *Board size* is the natural logarithm of the total number of board members at the end of the fiscal year. *Senior executive compensation* is calculated as the total compensation paid to all senior executives divided by the total assets of the bank. *Loan growth* is measured as annual growth rate of the loans. *Size* is controlled by the logarithm of total assets.

Table 19.3 Univariate tests

Variable	Founder or signer Mean	Founder or signer Median	Non-committed bank Mean	Non-committed bank Median	Diff. in means		Diff. in medians	
Board attendance	93.845	95.000	86.775	92.000	7.069	***	3.000	***
Board diversity	24.122	23.530	21.707	21.430	2.415	***	2.100	
Board experience	5.777	5.100	7.552	7.310	−1.775		−2.210	***
Board size	13.795	13.000	14.175	14.000	−0.380		−1.000	
Senior executive compensation	0.067	0.037	0.116	0.072	−0.049	**	−0.035	***

Table 19.3 reports the results of two-tailed t-tests and Wilcoxon rank-sum tests for the null hypothesis that there is no difference in the means and medians between financial institutions who have signed and have not committed to signing the Principles for Responsible Banking. The *Founder or signer* subsample consists of banks that have committed to sign the Principles, whereas the non-committed bank subsample consists of the banks that have not agreed to commit to the Principles for Responsible Banking at their launch. *Board attendance* is measured by the average overall attendance percentage of board meetings, as reported by the company. *Board diversity* is the percentage of women on the board of directors. *Board experience* is calculated as the average number of years each board member has been on the corporate board. *Board size* is the natural logarithm of the total number of board members at the end of the fiscal year. *Senior executive compensation* is calculated as the total compensation paid to all senior executives divided by the total assets of the bank.

Table 19.4 Regression results

Variable	ROA			ROE		
	(1)	(2)	(3)	(4)	(5)	(6)
Governance variables:						
Founder or signer	−0.097 *			−3.675 ***		
	(−0.082)			(−4.584)		
Founder		0.000			−1.227	
		(0.003)			(−1.329)	
Signer			−0.130 **			−3.612 ***
			(−2.021)			(−3.896)
Board attendance	0.005 *	0.004	0.005 *	0.208 ***	0.171 ***	0.196 ***
	(1.850)	(1.495)	(1.863)	(5.136)	(4.252)	(4.848)
Board diversity	−0.002	−0.002	−0.001	0.060 *	0.038	0.060 *
	(−0.663)	(−0.881)	(−0.551)	(1.690)	(1.079)	(1.695)
Board experience	0.051 ***	0.054 ***	0.051 ***	0.815 ***	0.918 ***	0.856 ***
	(5.392)	(5.769)	(5.400)	(5.993)	(6.760)	(6.315)
Board size	0.234 **	0.249 ***	0.224 **	5.282 ***	6.008 ***	5.232 ***
	(2.451)	(2.608)	(2.345)	(3.882)	(4.383)	(3.815)
Senior executive compensation	0.625 ***	0.630 ***	0.616 ***	9.096 ***	9.408 ***	9.001 ***
	(3.604)	(3.625)	(3.553)	(3.715)	(3.790)	(3.659)
Control variables:						
Loan growth	0.001 *	0.001	0.001 *	0.018 ***	0.018 ***	0.019 ***
	(1.863)	(1.840)	(1.922)	(3.125)	(2.998)	(3.244)
Size	0.116 ***	0.115 ***	0.111 ***	2.382 ***	2.383 ***	2.241 ***
	(5.818)	(5.711)	(5.548)	(8.321)	(8.152)	(7.771)
Time FE	Yes	Yes	Yes	Yes	Yes	Yes
N	667	667	667	698	698	698
Adjusted r-squared	0.132	0.128	0.133	0.225	0.203	0.218

Table 19.4 reports the estimates of six alternative versions of Equation 1. The alternative dependent variables in the equation are return on assets (*ROA*) and return on equity (*ROE*). The governance variables are defined as follows: *Founder or signer* is a dummy variable that gets a value of one if the examined bank is one of the founders of the United Nation's Principles for Responsible Banking or if they signed the Principles at launch in September 2019. *Founder* is a binary variable that is assigned the value of one if the examined bank is one of the 30 banks that together developed the United Nation's Principles for Responsible Banking. *Signer* is a dummy variable that gets a value of one for the banks that signed the Principles for Responsible Banking when they were launched. *Board attendance* is measured by the average overall attendance percentage of board meetings, as reported by the company. *Board diversity* is the percentage of women on the board of directors. *Board experience* is calculated as the average number of years each board member has been on the corporate board. *Board size* is the natural logarithm of the total number of board members at the end of the fiscal year. *Senior executive compensation* is calculated as the total compensation paid to all senior executives divided by the total assets of the bank. The control variables are defined as follows: *Loan growth* is measured as annual growth rate of the loans. *Size* is controlled by the logarithm of total assets. The t-statistics (in parentheses) are based on robust standard errors which are adjusted for heteroskedasticity. ***, **, and * denote statistical significance at the 0.01, 0.05, and 0.10 levels, respectively.

Models 1–3 in Table 19.4 employ *ROA* as a dependent variable, whereas models 4–6 use *ROE* as a performance measure. As can be seen from the table, variables *Founder or signer* and *Signer* get negative and statistically significant coefficients, thereby suggesting that banks that are committed to the Principles for Responsible Banking tend to underperform compared to the banks in general during the ten years before the Principles were launched. This finding holds for both performance measures employed. The coefficients for *Founder* are not statistically significant.

Coefficients for *Board attendance* are positive throughout the regression specifications and statistically significant in Models 1 and 3–6, thus indicating that the banks where the board members attend the board meetings more frequently tend to outperform compared to the banks with less active board meeting attendance rates.

Board diversity gets positive and significant coefficients in Models 4 and 6, whereas in the other examined models the coefficients are not significant and vary in sign. The finding indicates that improved board diversity may be positively related to bank performance.

The coefficients for *Board experience* and *Board size* are positive and statistically highly significant throughout the model specifications, thereby indicating that board experience and the size of the board and firm performance are positively associated.

The last employed governance variable *Senior executive compensation* also gets statistically highly significant positive coefficients throughout the model specifications. This finding indicates that the banks with higher bank size-adjusted executive compensation tend to outperform other sample banks.

The employed bank-specific control variables *Loan growth* and *Size* get statistically significant positive coefficients throughout the model specifications, thereby indicating that the banks with higher loan growth rates and larger banks tend to outperform their peers.

Discussion of the Results

As Table 19.4 depicts, interestingly, the banks that are committed to following the Principles for Responsible Banking underperform compared to the total sample of examined banks during the ten years before the launch of Principles for Responsible Banking. This finding may indicate that banks that are not as profitable as they could be are perhaps more willing to invest in social responsibility actions to improve their reputation and, potentially consequently, their performance. Thus, signing the Principles may also be used as a tool to indicate that the bank has good governance practices.

The reported findings further suggest that banks with high board meeting attendance rates tend to outperform the banks with less active board meeting participation. This may suggest that the boards with high attendance rates are more effective monitors than the boards with less active participants, thereby contributing positively to the firm performance.

Board experience and *Board size* are documented to have a statistically highly significant positive relationship with firm performance. Thus, the findings further indicate that an experienced and large board may be beneficial in terms of improved firm performance. Again, it can be argued that larger boards with experienced members can act as more effective monitors and can perhaps also control the risk-taking of the banks in a more efficient manner.

Senior executive compensation also gets statistically highly significant positive coefficients throughout the model specifications. This finding may suggest that executives with higher compensation are more prone to help improve the bank's performance, perhaps because their own wealth is partly tied to the financial performance of the bank in the form of performance-adjusted compensation. However, it should also be kept in mind that the executive teams in the banks may vary in size due to different organizational structures and, thus, the reported total compensation can also consequently vary greatly. For example, larger globally operating banks are prone to have much larger executive teams than smaller domestic banks, and the relative increase in bank performance may be caused by the international aspect of the functions and not by the highly compensated executive team.

To summarize, earlier studies have documented that high-quality CSR practices are associated with better performance in the banking industry, but, interestingly, our findings indicate that the early adopters of the Principles for Responsible Banking underperform before committing to the Principles compared to their peers. In addition, our findings suggest that individual governance attributes are relevant determinants of bank performance. Consequently, we argue that introducing the Principles for Responsible Banking is an important first step that has generally been accepted by the banks globally since close to half of them have signed the Principles. However, the logical next step for the UN would be to invest more into the supervisory process to ascertain that the signatory position is not to be used for greenwashing purposes only but rather for making true improvements on a practical level. Our results may have important implications for bank supervisors, regulators, depositors, and other stakeholders of financial institutions, as we highlight the importance of generally agreed best practices in the banking industry.

Limitations and Suggestions for Future Research

The reported findings should be interpreted with caution due to the following limitations, but, nevertheless, these limitations provide several avenues for future research. First, the sample consists of the founding members and the early signatories of the Principles. Consequently, the sample is limited to rather large banks. It would be interesting to examine how smaller banks are operating both governance- and performance-wise compared to these larger financial institutions.

Second, it can be argued that the Principles for Responsible Banking are designed to wake discussion and encourage banks to initiate a change towards more responsible ways of working within their organizations. Thus, the signatory status may be used for greenwashing purposes and, consequently, the real impact of the Principles can be questioned. This study focuses on examining the period before the launch of the Principles for Responsible Banking. It would also be interesting to study the true possible effects of the Principles on the behavior in the banking sector to see how the early adopters of the Principles differ from the general banking population. However, this type of analysis requires data availability for a longer period than is currently available. Thus, when the Principles have been in use for 5–10 years, for example, it would be useful to perform this type of analysis.

Finally, considering the COVID-19 pandemic, the war in Ukraine, general political instability, and the ongoing energy crisis, the business environment of the banks has changed significantly during the past few years and currently is still very volatile. Thus, it would be interesting to study the effect of these events on the banking sector and its development toward more responsible business practices.

Conclusions

The Principles for Responsible Banking is a voluntary agreement indicating responsibility in the banking industry, and it has been in use since late 2019. The set of Principles consists of six Principles that highlight the importance of responsibility and transparency in the banking industry.

Earlier studies have indicated that corporate commitment to CSR activities plays a role in the financial performance of the company. It is still too early to estimate the usefulness and overall long-term impact of the Principles on responsibility and sustainability in the banking sector. However, it is possible to study how the founding banks and the early signatories of the Principles for Responsible Banking differ from the bank population in general in terms of governance. Moreover, it is of interest if a higher quality CSR translates into money in terms of a better bank performance than that of the peer banks. It is assumed that social, ethical, and environmental policies of the early adopters of the Principles differ from the general banking population, and, thus, it is of interest to examine if these more responsible banks perform or are governed differently compared to the general population of banks.

Interestingly, the findings reported in this chapter indicate that banks that are committed to the Principles for Responsible Banking underperform compared to the banks in general during the ten years before the launch of the Principles. Moreover, the banks where the board members attend the board meetings more frequently tend to outperform the banks with less active board meeting attendance rates. Finally, *Board Experience, Board size, and Senior executive compensation* are positively associated with firm performance.

The reported findings may have important implications for bank supervisors, regulators, depositors, and other stakeholders. Moreover, the findings highlight the role of the corporate board and the benefits of effective monitoring. Finally, this research promotes the importance of creating industry-level guidelines for CSR.

However, it should be kept in mind that signing the Principles is only the first step in the process of becoming and staying a responsible bank. It is sometimes argued that the Principles for Responsible Banking do not press hard enough for action from signatories as the quality of reporting by the banks tends to vary significantly. Now, after the implementation period, it is suggested that the Principles are designed to encourage change rather than demand action. Consequently, the true impact of the Principles is sometimes criticized. However, it can be seen that many banks have improved their processes significantly after becoming a signatory, and thus, the Principles have proved to be valuable. Presumably, the set of Principles is to be developed further in the future to better reflect the needs of the bank stakeholders and regulators in the fast-developing global banking industry.

As explained in the introduction of this chapter, green financing plays a significant role in fulfilling the Principles for Responsible Banking. The importance of green finance has gained significant attention in recent years, and the war in Ukraine, general political instability, and the ongoing energy crisis have highlighted the need for investing in a more sustainable future. Banks have a unique role as agents of change in this development as they decide what kind of projects and businesses get funding. This should eventually lead to the extinction of unsustainable businesses, as they will not be able to attract funding for a reasonable price. This development can be supported by the Principles for Responsible Banking, assuming that the supervisory process is conducted efficiently and that the committed banks truly change their behavior toward more sustainable business practices instead of using the Principles for greenwashing purposes.

Notes

1 The signatory document is available at: https://www.unepfi.org/banking/become-a-signatory/.
2 www.nordea.com/en/news/principles-for-responsible-banking. Further links to specific target documents and supporting material can be found on this webpage.

3 Despite including several governance variables in the model specifications, the estimates should not be affected by multicollinearity. As can be seen from Table 19.2, the correlation coefficients between the governance variables, excluding *Founder or signer*, *Founder*, and *Signer* variables that are not employed simultaneously, are relatively low in magnitude.
4 For both the *ROA* and *ROE*, customer liabilities on acceptances are subtracted only when they are included in total assets.
5 Total assets are adjusted to exclude provision for bad debt or loan losses, treasury stock, and investment in own bonds.

References

Aguilera, R. V., Williams, C. A., Conley, J. M., & Rupp, D. E. (2006). Corporate governance and social responsibility: A comparative analysis of the UK and the US. *Corporate Governance: An International Review*, *14*(3), 147–158. https://doi.org/10.1111/j.1467-8683.2006.00495.x

Bear, S., Rahman, N., & Post, C. (2010). The impact of board diversity and gender composition on corporate social responsibility and firm reputation. *Journal of Business Ethics*, *97*(2), 207–221. https://doi.org/10.1007/s10551-010-0505-2

Blazovich, J. L., & Smith, L. M. (2011). Ethical corporate citizenship: Does it pay? *Research on Professional Responsibility and Ethics in Accounting*, *15*, 127–163. https://doi.org/10.1108/S1574-0765(2011)0000015008

Chih, H., Chih, H., & Chen, T. (2010). On the determinants of corporate social responsibility: International evidence on the financial industry. *Journal of Business Ethics*, *93*(1), 115–135. https://doi.org/10.1007/s10551-009-0186-x

Choi, T. H., & Jung, J. (2008). Ethical commitment, financial performance, and valuation: An empirical investigation of Korean companies. *Journal of Business Ethics*, *81*(2), 447–463. https://doi.org/10.1007/s10551-007-9506-1

Cornett, M. M., Erhemjamts, O., & Tehranian, H. (2016). Greed or good deeds: An examination of the relation between corporate social responsibility and the financial performance of U.S. commercial banks around the financial crisis. *Journal of Banking and Finance*, *30*, 137–159. https://doi.org/10.1016/j.jbankfin.2016.04.024

Donker, H., Poff, D., & Zahir, S. (2008). Corporate values, codes of ethics, and firm performance: A look at the Canadian context. *Journal of Business Ethics*, *82*(3), 527–537. https://doi.org/10.1007/s10551-007-9579-x

Fischer, K., & Khoury, N. (2007). The impact of ethical ratings on Canadian security performance: Portfolio management and corporate governance implications. *Quarterly Review of Economics and Finance*, *47*(1), 40–54. https://doi.org/10.1016/j.qref.2006.02.001

García-Sánchez, I.-M., Rodríguez-Domínguez, L.,. & Frías-Aceituno, J.-V. (2015). Board of directors and ethics codes in different corporate governance systems. *Journal of Business Ethics*, *131*(3), 681–698. https://doi.org/10.1007/s10551-014-2300-y

Gill, A. (2008). Corporate governance as social responsibility: A research agenda. *Berkeley Journal of International Law*, *26*(2), 452–478. https://doi.org/10.15779/Z38MS9P

Grougiou, V., Leventis, S., Dedoulis, E., & Owusu-Ansah, S. (2014). Corporate social responsibility and earnings management in U.S. banks. *Accounting Forum*, *38*(3), 155–169. https://doi.org/10.1016/j.accfor.2014.05.003

Grove, H., Patelli, L., Victoravich, L. M., & Xu, P. (2011). Corporate governance and performance in the wake of the financial crisis: Evidence from US commercial banks. *Corporate Governance: An International Review*, *19*(5), 418–436. https://doi.org/10.1111/j.1467-8683.2011.00882.x

Gunthorpe, D. L. (1997). Business ethics: A quantitative analysis of the impact of unethical behavior by publicly traded corporations. *Journal of Business Ethics*, *16*(5), 537–543. https://doi.org/10.1023/A:1017985519237

Harjoto, M. A., & Jo, H. (2011). Corporate governance and CSR nexus. *Journal of Business Ethics*, *100*(1), 45–67. https://doi.org/10.1007/s10551-011-0772-6

Jizi, M. I., Salama, A., Dixon, R., & Stratling, R. (2014). Corporate governance and corporate social responsibility disclosure: Evidence from the US banking sector. *Journal of Business Ethics*, *125*(4), 601–615. https://doi.org/10.1007/s10551-013-1929-2

Jo, H., & Harjoto, M. A. (2012). The causal effect of corporate governance on corporate social responsibility. *Journal of Business Ethics*, *106*(1), 53–72. https://doi.org/10.1007/s10551-011-1052-1

Kolk, A., & Pinkse, J. (2010). The integration of corporate governance in corporate social responsibility disclosures. *Corporate Social Responsibility and Environmental Management*, *17*(1), 26–150. https://doi.org/10.1002/csr.196

Matten, D. (2006). *Why do companies engage in corporate social responsibility? Background, reasons and basic concepts. The ICCA handbook on corporate social responsibility.* Wiley. https://doi.org/10.1002/9781119202110.ch1

Scholtens, B., & van't Klooster, S. (2019). Sustainability and bank risk. *Palgrave Communications*, *5*(1), Article number: 105. https://doi.org/10.1057/s41599-019-0315-9

Shen, C. H., Wu, M. W., Chen, T. H., & Fang, H. (2016). To engage or not to engage in corporate social responsibility: Empirical evidence from global banking sector. *Economic Modelling*, *55*, 207–225. https://doi.org/10.1016/j.econmod.2016.02.007

Simpson, W. G., & Kohers, T. (2002). The link between corporate social and financial performance: Evidence from the banking industry. *Journal of Business Ethics*, *35*(2), 97–109. https://doi.org/10.1023/A:1013082525900

Singh, J. B. (2011). Determinants of the effectiveness of corporate codes of ethics: An empirical study. *Journal of Business Ethics*, *101*(3), 385–395. https://doi.org/10.1007/s10551-010-0727-3

Starks, L. T. (2009). EFA keynote speech: Corporate governance and corporate social responsibility: What do investors care about? What should investors care about? *Financial Review*, *44*(4), 461–468. https://doi.org/10.1111/j.1540-6288.2009.00225.x

United Nations. (2019). Principles for responsible banking. https://www.unepfi.org/banking/bankingprinciples/

United Nations. (2022a). Principles for responsible banking. https://www.unepfi.org/banking/bankingprinciples/

United Nations. (2022b). Sustainable development goals. https://sdgs.un.org/goals

United Nations. (2022c). Principles for responsible banking: Target setting – Frequently asked questions. https://www.unepfi.org/wordpress/wp-content/uploads/2022/10/17-PRB-target-setting-FAQ-D1.pdf

World Economic Forum. (2020). What is green finance and why is it important? https://www.weforum.org/agenda/2020/11/what-is-green-finance/

Wu, M.-W., & Shen, C.-H. (2013). Corporate social responsibility in the banking industry: Motives and financial performance. *Journal of Banking and Finance*, *37*(9), 3529–3547. https://doi.org/10.1016/j.jbankfin.2013.04.023

Wu, M.-W., Shen, C.-H., & Chen, T. H. (2017). Application of multi-level matching between financial performance and corporate social responsibility in the banking industry. *Review of Quantitative Finance and Accounting*, *49*(1), 29–63. https://doi.org/10.1007/s11156-016-0582-0

Zimmermann, S. (2019). Same same but different: How and why banks approach sustainability. *Sustainability*, *11*(8), 2267. https://doi.org/10.3390/su11082267

PART 4

Critical Perspectives

20
MEASURING BIODIVERSITY
Mission Impossible?

Theresia Harrer, Hanna Silvola, and Othmar M. Lehner

Introduction

The rapid loss of biodiversity, caused by human activities, is one of the most serious environmental threats of our time and can be seen as one of the great challenges to tackle (Dasgupta, 2021; Ferraro et al., 2015). Biodiversity is a complex concept, covering ecosystems and the connections between them, and its importance lies in its ability to sustain life on Earth. The complexity of biodiversity is further compounded by the fact that it is often confused with other concepts such as natural capital. Natural capital is defined as the stock of natural resources, such as land and water, that provide economic, social, and environmental benefits (UNEP, 2023, p. iv). While the two concepts are related, they are distinct. Natural capital is the stock of natural resources that can be used for economic purposes, while biodiversity is the variety of life, including both species and ecosystems, and the connections between them (ibid, but see also Baumgärtner, 2007).

Research and policymakers agree that it is essential to halt or even reverse the loss of biodiversity in order to restore equity among ecosystems. For example, the recently published Dasgupta Report (2022) points out that sustainable engagement with nature is critical to sustaining the livelihood of future generations. Yet, the halting of biodiversity loss can only be achieved by holding industry accountable (O'Dwyer & Unerman, 2020). It not only requires cross-sector collaboration but, particularly, the stepping-up of the financial sector, which is well-positioned to provide financial resources to support the conservation of biodiversity and to bridge the gap between biodiversity and economic development (Arlaud et al., 2018).

However, there is a lack of understanding of how financial instruments can be used to protect biodiversity, due to the complexity of biodiversity and the lack of clear conceptualization, measurement approaches (Bang, 2023), and reliable data. This chapter will first discuss the definition of biodiversity, including its distinction from other concepts such as natural capital. We will then discuss the diversity of measurement approaches and indicators for measuring biodiversity, and the lack of reliable data. For this, we suggest and elaborate on three key challenges in measuring biodiversity and suggest research to address them:

The first challenge is the complexity of biodiversity and the lack of delimitation from other concepts such as natural capital, as it presents a challenge in measuring, managing, and conserving biodiversity. As introduced, biodiversity is a concept that includes the variety of species, their genetic diversity, and their interactions with each other and their environment, making it difficult to clearly define and measure. This is compounded by the fact that concepts such as natural capital, which is the value of natural resources, overlap with biodiversity, making it difficult to separate the two and measure them each independently.

The second challenge in measuring biodiversity is the diversity of measurement approaches and indicators being used. As the concept of biodiversity is complex and encompasses many aspects, there is no single approach or indicator that can accurately measure it. Different approaches and indicators such as species abundance, species richness, and ecosystem services all provide different insights into the biodiversity of an area and must be used together to get a comprehensive view.

Finally, the third challenge is the lack of reliable data, which is also related to measuring biodiversity. Biodiversity data can be difficult to obtain from various, unrelated sources, and the data that is available can often be incomplete, outdated, or unreliable. This makes it difficult to make informed decisions about conservation and management, as the data is not reliable enough to accurately measure and make decisions thereupon.

Biodiversity: The Basis of All Life

The United Nations Convention for Biological Diversity defines biodiversity as "the variability among living organisms from all sources including, inter alia, terrestrial, marine and other aquatic ecosystems and the ecological complexes of which they are part; this includes diversity within species, between species and of ecosystems." (United Nations, 1992). According to this definition, biodiversity captures the health of a variety of ecosystems (e.g., marine, terrestrial, forest, aerial, and social) and in referring to "ecological complexes" also highlights the interdependencies between those ecosystems (Almond et al., 2022, p. 15; Panwar et al., 2022). Since those ecosystems provide food, energy, and raw materials such as oil, and control the climate, air quality, and spread of species (Griscom et al., 2017; Mace et al., 2012), biodiversity is important because it enables and protects virtually all life.

While the importance of biodiversity has been recognized around the globe, recent reports show that biodiversity levels are at an all-time low, with a further downward trajectory. The WWF's Living Planet report (Almond et al., 2022), for instance, suggests that global wildlife populations have declined by almost 70% from 1970 to 2018 and will continue to do so if no action is taken to prevent this. Similarly, the Intergovernmental Science-Policy Platform on Biodiversity and Ecosystem Services (IPBES, 2019) report highlights among other issues that the global abundance of terrestrial species has decreased by at least 20% since 1900, and that over 85% of wetlands were lost globally due to agriculture and farming just between 2010 and 2015 (p. 11). These numbers are alarming. They suggest that many ecosystems are already out of balance, and this may seriously affect the way of living.

Reasons for biodiversity loss are, like biodiversity itself, diverse and complex. In some instances, biodiversity loss stems from natural degradation, changes in habitats, or sea level fluctuations. Yet, most works suggest that a large part of biodiversity loss is driven by human (economic) activity (Dasgupta, 2021). The global food system, for instance, is designed to nourish the ever-growing population. However, it is unfit to deal with the increasing demand for food and thus is often linked to the erosion of forests, land, soil, and water resources (Benton et al., 2021). Such loss in biodiversity also has profound economic effects. Land degradation already reduces the productivity of terrestrial areas by 23%, which in financial terms means a decrease of up to US $577 billion in annual global stock output (IPBES, 2019). The World Economic Forum (2020) furthermore estimates that more than half of global GDP is strongly or fairly strongly dependent on a diverse and prosperous nature and the ecosystem services it provides. As the global population keeps growing, those effects will only be exacerbated (de Silva et al., 2019; Dempsey, 2016).

The above works show that biodiversity and human (including economic) well-being are strongly connected. Coupled with imminent climate change, biodiversity loss therefore poses one of the greatest threats of our time (IPCC, 2022). It requires global efforts to reverse or at least reduce the loss of biodiversity and restore equity among the ecosystems on planet Earth. In the next section, we will outline the central role of the financial system in achieving this.

Biodiversity and the Financial Sector

The financial sector is one of the most important actors in the global quest to limit or reverse biodiversity loss. It not only accounts for approximately 10% of the global GDP (market capitalization of US $8.13 trillion[1]) but also controls more than US $100 trillion of global funds (PwC) via which it directly or indirectly influences the economy. The latter influence on the economy also makes the financial sector a critical actor that can push but also hinder organizations to engage in activities to restore biodiversity (Deutz et al., 2020; Nedopil, 2022).

The United Nations Development Program Biodiversity Finance Initiative (UNDP BIOFIN) estimates the cumulative investment need to protect and restore biodiversity to at least US $9.5 trillion by 2050 (see Figure 20.1 – note that this sum applies in a conservative 2 °C scenario). Research also shows that those funds would be available on the financial market (Dasgupta, 2021; Deutz et al., 2020; Polzin & Sanders, 2020). Yet, while globally the volume of funds made available for biodiversity protection and restoration has already increased to US $143 billion per year, we are far from reaching the needed US $9.5 trillion. To make things worse, the OECD (2020) points out that governments are still funding biodiversity-harmful projects/organizations worth approximately US $500 billion per year (the potentially harmful spending of the private sector is not included in this number).

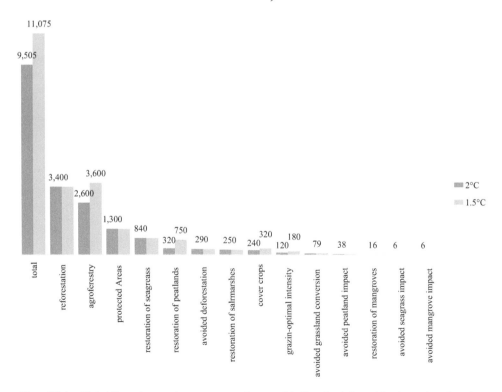

Figure 20.1 Global financing needs to protect and restore biodiversity (adapted by the authors based on UNEP, 2022, p. XIII)

The task to protect and restore biodiversity therefore primarily relates to "leveraging and [...] managing economic incentives, policies, and capital to achieve the long-term well-being of nature and our society" (UNDP BIOFIN). This requires specific funding instruments (Arlaud et al., 2018; Seidl et al., 2020) and decision-making strategies that enable investors and businesses to consider biodiversity risks and opportunities (Nedopil, 2022).

Considerable efforts are already made to develop such financing instruments. The options are diverse, and range from private financing instruments such as green landscape bonds and landscape funds (e.g., the Asia Climate-Smart Landscape Fund in Indonesia), to publicly issued bonds and funds (e.g., the UK-based Clean Growth Fund) (Mazzucato & Semieniuk, 2018), and a mix of public and private funding in so-called nature-based solutions (Bang, 2023; Harrer & Owen, 2022; Toxopeus & Polzin, 2017) (for an overview of the most relevant biodiversity financing instruments see Table 20.1).

Table 20.1 Most relevant financing options for restoring and protecting biodiversity (based on Binnie et al. (2022); adapted by the authors based on OECD (2020))

Instrument	Funding Source	Description	Example(s)
Sovereign sustainability-linked bonds	Public	Linking biodiversity gains to cost of government sovereign debt	Chiles's US $ billion sustainability-linked bonds, Biodiversity conservation bond in France
Debt-for nature swaps	Public	Write-off of debt to preserve natural environment	Ecuador in an attempt to write off debt by committing to protect the Galapagos islands
Blue/green bonds	Private	Linking nature/marine pollution reduction and protection to funding	Philippine BDO Unibank, Common land, Rabobank in the Netherlands, Stora Enso Green Bond Framework, Barito Pacific and Michelin bond for sustainable rubber in Indonesia, DC Water bond for storm-water run-off infrastructure, EIB sustainability awareness bonds
Biodiversity credit (markets)	Public	To promote the establishment of projects that protect or restore ecosystems	Colombia and New Zealand
Finance for nature-based solutions	Mix	Funding of actions to protect, conserve, restore, sustainably use and manage natural or modified terrestrial, freshwater, coastal, and marine ecosystems	Rimba Collective for rethinking long-term conservation project funding in Indonesia
Biodiversity tax	Public	Tax income solely allocated to bolstering nature	Fiji's Environment and Climate Adaption Levy
Strategic nature reserves	Private	Requirement for banks to hold financial buffer for biodiversity risks	Proposal from Pollination
Landscape funds	Mix	Mobilize funding for communities and the conservation and adaption of landscapes to protect and restore biodiversity	Asia Climate-Smart Landscape Fund in Indonesia, OECD or UK Biodiverse Landscape Fund, Legacy Landscapes Fund in Germany, Brazil's Amazon Fund

Overall, the development of the above financing options is a positive development and may be critical in reaching the required US $9.5 trillion to protect and restore biodiversity. However, due to their novelty and rapid development, it is still unclear if the above (and other) financing options work (see Figure 20.2). Measurement approaches and instruments such as indicators are therefore critical to protecting and restoring biodiversity (Gotelli & Colwell, 2001; Harrer & Owen, 2022; Loreau et al., 2021; Nedopil, 2022).

The purpose of the remainder of this chapter is to capture the state of biodiversity measurement approaches and indicators, and outline how biodiversity financing instruments can live up to their promises.

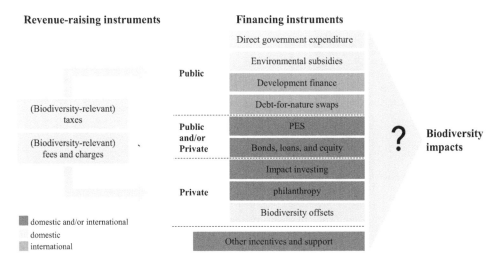

Figure 20.2 Biodiversity finance flows (own depiction by authors based on OECD, 2019, p. 64)

The Challenge of Measuring Biodiversity

A look at the extant literature suggests that the measurement of biodiversity is currently a "mission impossible" because it is fraught with three problems: 1) complexity of biodiversity definitions, 2) diversity of measurement approaches and indicators, and 3) lack of reliable data. Below we outline these problems.

Complexity of Biodiversity Definitions

Measuring biodiversity is difficult, first of all, because biodiversity is a multidimensional concept that is concerned with the linkages between different ecosystems (Ferraro et al., 2015; Panwar et al., 2022). And while most works recognize this complexity, they often conflate biodiversity with similar concepts such as nature and natural capital. Earlier in this chapter we defined biodiversity as "the variability among living organisms from all sources including, inter alia, terrestrial, marine and other aquatic ecosystems and the ecological complexes of which they are part; this includes diversity within species, between species and of ecosystems." (United Nations, 1992, p. 3). In comparison, nature refers to "the natural world, with an emphasis on the diversity of living organisms (including people) and their interactions among themselves and with their environment" (UNEP, 2023). Dasgupta (2022) further suggests that nature has three properties: mobility, invisibility, and silence (see Figure 20.3).

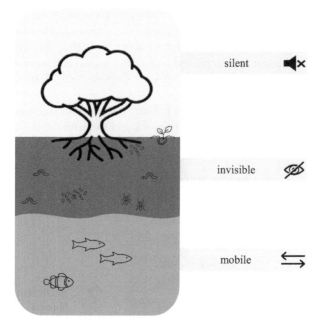

Figure 20.3 The three key properties of nature (Dasgupta, 2022, p. 31)

Comparing the two concepts, biodiversity then essentially describes the health of nature. The ecosystems covered by biodiversity are all relevant to the natural world and as such also have strong interdependencies. Furthermore, all these ecosystems may feature silent, invisible, and mobile properties.

Another concept that is often used synonymously with biodiversity is the concept of natural capital. Natural capital can be defined as "the stock of renewable and non-renewable natural resources (e.g., plants, animals, air, water, soils, minerals) that combine to yield a flow of benefits to people" (UNEP, 2023, p. iv). Such resources are undoubtedly a major part of biodiversity (e.g., soil, air, water, and species are all part of the ecosystems that characterize biodiversity). However, while natural capital primarily refers to the stock of a resource and its productivity (i.e., the flow of economic benefits from land), biodiversity is about the abundance of these resources and whether, taken together, they provide sufficient ecosystem services (e.g., agriculture) (Baumgärtner, 2007). Therefore, while biodiversity includes natural capital, it goes beyond the assessment of the productivity of natural resources.

Diversity of Measurement Approaches and Indicators

Measuring biodiversity is also difficult because the measurement approaches and indicators used to assess and track the state of nature are highly diverse. As a result, it is often unclear which aspect (e.g., ecosystems or natural capital) or dimension (e.g., silent, invisible, or mobile) of nature is measured, and how these aspects and dimensions taken together pose a biodiversity risk (e.g., can a decline in some species lead to a decline in ecosystem health, and if so in which?)

Table 20.2 Biodiversity disclosure initiatives (based on Bang (2023, p. 16), Mair et al. (2021), Cavender-Bares et al. (2022), Almond et al. (2022), and OECD (2020))

Disclosure Initiatives	Description
The EU's sustainability reporting standards (including CSRD, EU taxonomy; and SFRD)	The CSRD will contain a specific standard (ESRS E4) on biodiversity and ecosystems, which requires companies to disclose information on how they integrate biodiversity into their strategy, business implementation process, and performance measures. Biodiversity is also one of the six environmental objectives in defining the EU taxonomy. The EU taxonomy is an important tool for financial markets to define which investment targets are green and sustainable, and it aims to help investors to allocate their financing to green activities. The taxonomy criteria for biodiversity will be completed in 2023. Investors need to apply the taxonomy criteria in conjunction with the SFRD to define funds as dark green (Taxonomy's Article 9), light green (Article 8), and other (Article 6).
International Sustainability Standards Board (ISSB)	The ISSB is developing sustainability reporting standards to be implemented in all companies that now apply International Financial Reporting Standards (IFRS). Those sustainability reporting standards will also include specific guidelines for biodiversity measurement.
Global Reporting Initiative (GRI)	The GRI issues the leading guidelines for sustainability reporting around the globe. It covers various topics and, for each of those outlines, mandatory and voluntary themes of disclosure. Biodiversity has been a key topic in the GRI since 2006; however, a specific standard GRI 304 on biodiversity is to be issued in late 2023.
IFC Environmental and Social Performance Standards (World Bank)	The IFC Performance Standards (PS) on Environmental and Social Sustainability define the responsibilities of corporations for managing environmental and social risks. The importance of conserving biodiversity, maintaining ecosystem services, and sustainably managing natural resources is specifically addressed in PS6: Biodiversity Conservation and Sustainable Management of Natural Resources.
Science-Based Targets for Nature (SBTN): Initial guidance for business	As part of the broader Science-Based Targets Network (SBTN) facilitated by the Global Commons Alliance, the Science-Based Targets for Nature also address goals related to nature. By 2025, the SBTN aims to have widespread adoption of science-based targets for nature by both the public and private sectors.
Taskforce on Nature-related Financial Disclosures (TNFD)	The TNFD was launched in 2021 to develop a risk management and disclosure framework for organizations to report and address nature-related risks in alignment with the TCFD. The first beta version of the framework was released in March 2022. The final framework will be released in late 2023.
UNEP-FI & UNEP-WCMC: Guidance for Biodiversity Target-setting	Designed for signatories of the Principles for Responsible Banking (PRB), the Guidance for Biodiversity Target-setting outlines practical steps towards setting portfolio-wide biodiversity targets.

(Continued)

Table 20.2 (Continued)

Disclosure Initiatives	Description
IUCN: Guidelines for planning and monitoring corporate biodiversity performance	The guidelines provide an approach for developing a corporate-level biodiversity strategic plan. They can be applied to any company, sector, or operational scale and define measurable goals, objectives, and indicators related to biodiversity performance.
Science-Based Targets Network (SBTN)	As part of the Global Commons Alliance, the SBTN aims to develop methods and resources to guide companies in developing science-based targets for nature and climate-related action aligned with the Sustainable Development Goals (SDGs).
Natural Capital Finance Alliance (NCFA)	The NCFA aims to integrate natural capital considerations into financial products, as well as improving nature-related risk accounting, disclosure, and reporting.
European Union Business @ Biodiversity Platform	The EU's B@B platform aims to integrate natural capital and biodiversity considerations in business practices. Its three functional workstreams consist of Methods (developing practical guidance and tools), Pioneers (facilitating corporate collaboration), and Mainstreaming (promoting biodiversity-focused business decision-making across Europe).
Finance for Biodiversity Pledge	The Finance for Biodiversity Pledge was launched in 2020. Financial institutions who sign the pledge commit to protecting and restoring biodiversity through their financial activities through knowledge sharing, engagement with companies, assessing their impacts, setting targets, and reporting on these criteria by 2025.
Partnership for Biodiversity Accounting Financials (PBAF)	The PBAF aims to develop a standard for financial institutions to assess and disclose impacts and dependencies on biodiversity. It is closely aligned with the TNFD and Finance for Biodiversity Pledge. In June 2022, the PBAF launched its first standard describing requirements and recommendations for financial institutions to carry out a biodiversity footprint assessment.
Network for Greening the Financial System (NGFS)	Launched in 2017, the NGFS serves as a platform for central banks to share best practices, contribute to the development of environment and climate risk management in the financial sector, and mobilize mainstream finance to support the transition toward a sustainable economy. Amongst its various work streams is the task force for "biodiversity loss and nature-related risks".
Finance for Biodiversity Initiative (F4B)	The F4B initiative aims to increase the materiality of biodiversity in financial decision-making and align global finance with the conservation and restoration of nature. Established in 2019, it produces research on nature markets, public finance, strategic liabilities, and citizen engagement.

(Ascui & Cojoianu, 2019). Reviewing the literature, three issues contribute most to the above problems in measuring biodiversity.

1) ***Accurate vs. holistic impact measurement***: Current biodiversity measurement frameworks are rooted in a conservative accounting tradition and as such favor methodological accuracy over holistic approaches (e.g., Harrer & Owen, 2022; Michelon et al., 2020). And although accurate metrics and methods may be easier to read, monitor, and trust (Porter, 1996), they tend to reduce big and complex phenomena (e.g., nature) to a few aspects (e.g., CO_2) (Quattrone, 2022). Natural scientists refer to this desire for accuracy as the focus on taxonomic richness (Jihariya et al., 2022; Neige, 2015). Current measurement frameworks therefore risk missing the big picture (related to e.g., biodiversity) for the sake of accuracy (O'Dwyer & Unerman, 2020; Quattrone et al., 2021).
2) ***Long-term impact vs. short-term returns***: The reduction of biodiversity loss and the restoration of biodiversity are long-term issues that require many steps in the right direction, one at a time (Bansal et al., 2018; George et al., 2016). It is therefore critical to imagine how biodiversity and equity should look in different contexts and set the right steps towards this (Gümüsay & Reinecke, 2021). And although contemporary biodiversity measurement frameworks recognize the importance of working towards biodiversity and equity, most of them focus on showing short and medium-term returns instead of forward-looking, transformative accounts (Schoeneborn et al., 2019; Strömmer & Ormiston, 2022).
3) ***Integration of silent stakeholders***: Nature, animals, and indigenous peoples are different across contexts (e.g., Global South vs. Global North). Furthermore, they are all rather silent (e.g., a forest cannot actively voice its opinion) and as such are often unrecognized stakeholders of organizations (including governments and investors). However, the voices of these silent stakeholders are critical to overcoming challenges related to biodiversity loss. Finding a common ground regarding which stakeholders should be prioritized in the metrics for biodiversity restoration and protection, as well as how their voice should be included in decision-making, is therefore difficult at best (e.g., Hehenberger et al., 2019; Lehner et al., 2022; Unerman & Bennett, 2004).

Multiple initiatives have already emerged to resolve the above three issues. On the one hand, they aim to improve transparency related to biodiversity and harmonize the disclosure of biodiversity exposure and risk. The European Union (EU), for example, has recently ratified the Corporate Sustainability Reporting Directive (CSRD), which mandates large organizations (and their subsidiaries) that operate in the EU to issue comprehensive sustainability reports from 2024 onwards. Among many topics (related to e.g., climate change and human rights), the EU defines biodiversity as a central topic in such reports.

On the other hand, the initiatives also aim to harmonize the measurement approaches and indicators. For instance, the SEBI initiative in the EU offers a selection of key indicators to assess and measure biodiversity in Europe. Table 20.3 summarizes the most important measurement approaches and indicators.

Overall, the above initiatives already offer useful insights into a) what to disclose to better understand biodiversity and biodiversity loss, and b) how to assess biodiversity and biodiversity loss. We expect rapid development of these disclosures and measurement approaches in the next five to ten years.

Table 20.3 Most important biodiversity measurement approaches and indicators (based on Bang (2023, p. 16), Mair et al. (2021), Cavender-Bares et al. (2022), Almond et al. (2022), Darrah et al. (2019), and OECD (2020))

Measurement initiatives	Type of measurement	Description
Streamlined European Biodiversity Indicators (SEBI) of the European Environment Agency (EEA)	Quantitative aggregate (European level)	SEBI initiative is a partnership between the European Environment Agency (EEA), its Topic Centre on Biological Diversity (ETC/BD), and DG Environment of the European Commission. It is a central part of the EU's Biodiversity Strategy. It includes indicators such as ecosystem coverage (SEBI 004), livestock genetic diversity (SEBI 006), public awareness of biodiversity (SEBI 026), and relevant metadata.
Species Threat Abatement and Restoration Metric (STAR) – Integrated Biodiversity Assessment Tool (IBAT) Alliance	Quantitative aggregate	The STAR Metric quantifies the potential positive contributions to biodiversity that are made through actions to reduce species extinction risk.
Global Biodiversity Model for Support (GLOBIO) – PBL Netherlands Environmental Assessment Agency	Quantitative aggregate	The GLOBIO model provides a framework to quantify the impacts of six types of human pressures on biodiversity, calculating a "Global Biodiversity Score". Using the mean species abundance (MSA) indicator as a proxy for biodiversity, the model also includes scenario-modeling options for socio-economic development pathways, options to assess ecosystem service values, and covers both terrestrial and aqua ecosystems.
Biodiversity Footprint for Financial Institutions (BFFI) – ASN Bank	Quantitative and qualitative aggregate	Based on a quantitative footprint calculation in combination with a qualitative analysis of sector specificities, the BFFI measures the footprint in the number of hectares in which biodiversity is lost. The impacts of portfolio activities on biodiversity are calculated through a combination of lifecycle assessment data, portfolio company information, and environmental impact indicators.
Exploring Natural Capital Opportunities, Risks and Exposure (ENCORE) – Natural Capital Finance Alliance & UNEWP-WCMC	Quantitative aggregate (on the global industry level)	The ENCORE tool guides financial institutions in understanding natural capital risks through an ecosystem services framework. The tool is tailored to 167 economic sub-industries, all of which depend on a different combination of ecosystem services for production processes.

(Continued)

Table 20.3 (Continued)

Measurement initiatives	Type of measurement	Description
Nature and Biodiversity Benchmark – World Benchmarking Alliance		Driven by a No Net Loss (NNL) or Biodiversity Net Gain (BNG) approach, the benchmark will assess companies under 18 social indicators and 25 nature indicators, including aspects of land-use change, direct resource exploitation, pollution, and climate change.
High Conservation Value (HCV) Approach – Forest Stewardship Council, HCV Network	Qualitative aggregate	The HCV approach was initially developed by the Forest Stewardship Council in 1999 to maintain and enhance six environmental and social values in production landscapes: species diversity (HCV 1), landscape-level ecosystems (HCV 2), rare ecosystems/habitats (HCV 3), critical ecosystem services (HCV 4), community livelihood needs (HCV 5), and cultural values (HCV 6). It offers a methodology to identify and protect high conservation values from the impacts of land-use change.
Remote Sensing including e.g., NatureMetrics	Quantitative and qualitative (visual) aggregate and nuanced	Characterizes the Earth's biophysical environment (incl. variables related to habitat, climate change, and human modification of the Earth system), vegetation composition, function, phenology, physiology, and morphology. It reveals spatial and temporal dimensions of biological diversity through structural, compositional, and functional measurements of ecosystems. Can include environmental DNA surveys (such as those proposed by NatureMetrics) but is not limited to it.
Wetland Extent Trend (WET) Index from the IPBES	Quantitative aggregate	Measures trends in wetland areas over time, enabling the rate of loss of wetland area to be estimated and giving an indication of the status of wetlands globally.

Lack of Reliable Data

The third challenge in measuring biodiversity relates to a lack of standardized data collection approaches and the multiplicity of data types required to adequately assess biodiversity and associated risks. Most of the relevant databases have historical relevance for biology and other natural sciences. Few of them are accessible or usable for business purposes. The question thereby is not only about data and indicators, but more widespread knowledge of biodiversity as a phenomenon and its influence on financial decision-making. Table 20.4 lists the most important databases and platforms.

Table 20.4 Most relevant databases for biodiversity assessment (non-exhaustive) (based on Bang (2023, p. 16), Mair et al. (2021), Cavender-Bares et al. (2022), Almond et al. (2022), Darrah et al. (2019), Hamilton and Casey (2016), OECD (2020), FAO (2015), Wamelink et al. (2012))

Databases & Platforms	Description
IUCN Red List of Threatened Species	A public database developed by the IUCN, which classifies species into one of seven Red List categories to represent their level of extinction threat (ranging from Least Concern to Extinct). The Red List is considered to be the world's most comprehensive inventory of the conservation status of wildlife species and currently has over 142,000 species logged in the database.
World Database on Protected Areas	A global database of marine and terrestrial protected areas, which provides downloadable geospatial information that details the boundary and characteristics of each protected area. The database is the largest assembly of data documenting the world's protected areas, with over 270,000 recorded protected areas.
World Database on Key Biodiversity Areas	A global database that identifies the locations of Key Biodiversity Areas (KBA). Sites are identified based on threatened biodiversity, geographically restricted biodiversity, ecological integrity, biological processes, and irreplaceability. The database has identified over 16,000 KBAs.
Carbon Disclosure Project (CDP)	The CDP is one of the largest data collections on the climate impact of organizations (based on self-reported data). Recently the CDP updated and expanded its survey methodology to questions related to biodiversity.
Global Biodiversity Information Facility (GBIF), based on OECD recommendations	The GBIF is an international network and data infrastructure, and is aimed at providing anyone, anywhere, open access to data about all types of life on Earth. The data comes from many different sources, including everything from museum specimens collected in the 18th and 19th centuries to DNA barcodes and smartphone photos. Through the use of data standards, including Darwin Core, GBIF.org's index of hundreds of millions of species occurrence records is created.
The Taskforce on Nature-Related Financial Disclosures (TNFD) Knowledge Bank	Alongside the development of the TNFD beta framework, the TNFD also develops the Knowledge Bank. This bank features a collection of the latest external resources and market insights on nature-related risks and opportunities. The indicators in the beta framework will also be informed by the data in the Knowledge Bank.
CGIR Climate Security Observatory (CSO)	The CSO is currently being developed. It will provide descriptions and analysis of the pathways via which climate change and variability might act as a threat multiplier to existing vulnerabilities and insecurity. The CSO aims to provide access to high-quality information about and increase awareness of climate security-related issues, focusing primarily, but not exclusively, on the role of water, land, and food systems.
Wetland Extent Trend (WET) database	Consists of 306 data sources, including scientific literature, gray literature, national wetland inventories, and four global datasets based on national-level data of mangroves, peatlands, and rice paddies. It contains 2;130 individual time-series records of change in wetland areas from local sites and aggregated national trends.

Discussion and Ways Forward

Future Research

This chapter aimed to assess if measuring biodiversity is a mission impossible and why. It started by highlighting the central role of the financial sector in combating the current biodiversity crisis and then outlined that biodiversity finance may not yet deliver on its promises because it lacks clear measurement approaches and indicators. The chapter then outlined the three problems of biodiversity measurement as 1) complexity of biodiversity definitions, 2) diversity of measurement approaches and indicators, and 3) lack of reliable data. Overall, while there are many initiatives that already help to assess the impact of the financing options available, biodiversity seems to be approached from a narrow, economic output maximization perspective. As biodiversity requires the restructuring of decision-making (Nedopil, 2022), we outline below the central tenets of that.

Most initiatives do not adopt a "holistic" biodiversity measurement approach (limited to a few ecosystems or features of nature). Future works should therefore explore how to holistically measure biodiversity (e.g., remote sensing) and how this can be operationalized in the financial sector. Since many initiatives are involved in a) reporting requirements, b) measurements, and c) data collection, collaboration (i.e., tele-coupling) on a global level will be critical. Future research should explore how to best do that.

Another question that would deserve more substance is how to effectively involve stakeholders, from both the public and private sectors, in the development of biodiversity metrics and how to ensure their commitment and motivation to adhere to them. In addition, it is important to consider how to develop and use biodiversity metrics, indicators, and reporting frameworks across different sectors and policy areas in order to ensure consistency and comparability of data and to allow for a comprehensive assessment of the impact of different financial interventions on biodiversity.

Finally, further research should explore the potential of biodiversity finance to create incentives for preserving and restoring biodiversity, and to identify who should be responsible for financing these investments, and how. This could include, for example, the development of innovative financial instruments, such as nature-based bonds and green bank loans, and the assessment of their potential to contribute to the conservation of biodiversity and to equitable development.

Practical Implications

At the moment, the valuation of the risks, benefits, and opportunities associated with biodiversity is difficult due to the lack of available tools. Companies can therefore take the following four steps to better understand and assess the impact of their activities on biodiversity:

1. *Identify the risks, benefits, and opportunities related to biodiversity within the scope of their operations;*
2. *Invest in the development and implementation of reliable measurement methods and indicators;*
3. *Estimate the financial effects of their activities on biodiversity; and*
4. *Use this information to inform their decision-making and investments.*

Leading companies have already begun to identify their biodiversity risks and opportunities. However, they do that primarily to increase competitive advantage. There now is growing external pressure for more standardized and transparent disclosure of actual biodiversity impacts. As a result, it can be expected that in the coming years quantitative and even monetary metrics will become increasingly available. In addition, companies should explore how to leverage innovative financial instruments, such as nature-based bonds and green bank loans, to contribute to the conservation of biodiversity while achieving equitable development.

Another practical implication of looking at the above is that better collaboration between different stakeholders is needed. This includes cooperation between the public and private sectors in order to develop reliable measurement approaches and indicators, as well as collaboration across sectors and policy areas to ensure consistency and comparability of data. Furthermore, efforts should be made to engage stakeholders in order to ensure their commitment and motivation to adhere to the established frameworks.

Currently, industry-leading companies and financial institutions organize customized sustainable development training for their key personnel. The loss of nature is identified as a growing theme in these training programs. Companies are willing to invest more in this theme, and they are ready to learn more, but there are few available speakers on the connection between biodiversity and the economy. In any case, continuing education is needed. In particular, small and medium-sized companies (SMEs) and organizations need support, concrete processes, and tools for evaluating biodiversity risks, benefits, and opportunities. The demand for this information for SMEs is increasing due to their supply chains.

The information to be taught must be based on scientific evidence, and multidisciplinary research is therefore essential. Recent studies quite widely demonstrate that ESG factors have financial relevance (e.g., Friede et al., 2015), but we need more scientific evidence on the financial materiality of biodiversity. Financial decisions are as good/bad as the data that we can apply in making these decisions. Therefore, scientific, transparent, and reliable data on this association is a requirement for better-reasoned decisions. One very central shortcoming in the current research environment is the lack of an interdisciplinary approach regarding the association between biodiversity and the economy. The economic dependencies of nature loss have been understood, but their economic consequences have still been estimated very little, even at the international level.

Conclusion

Summing up, the complexity of biodiversity and the lack of clear conceptualization and reliable data, along with the diversity of measurement approaches and indicators, make it difficult to measure and manage biodiversity, and to assess the impact of financial interventions on biodiversity. Quantitative and monetary metrics are becoming increasingly available, and financial instruments such as nature-based bonds and green bank loans have the potential to contribute to the conservation of biodiversity and equitable development. As the great conservationist Aldo Leopold famously said, "To keep every cog and wheel is the first precaution of intelligent tinkering" (Leopold 1966, p. 190); understanding biodiversity and its measurement is the first step to being able to protect and restore it.

Acknowledgement

This research was financially supported by the EU Horizon Programme TC4BE – 101082057 – GAP-101082057 on Pathways for BioDiversity. The European Commission's support for the production of this publication does not constitute an endorsement of the contents, which reflects the views only of the authors, and the Commission cannot be held responsible for any use which may be made of the information contained therein.

Note

1 Market cap as per January 20, 2023, on Fidelity

References

Almond, R. E. A., Grooten, M., Juffe Bignoli, D., & Petersen, T. (2022). *Living planet report: Building a nature-positive society*. WWF, Gland, Switzerland.

Arlaud, M., Cumming, T., Dickie, I., Flores, M., van den Heuvel, O., Meyers, D., Riva, M., Seidl, A., & Trinidad, A. (2018). The biodiversity finance initiative: An approach to identify and implement biodiversity-centered finance solutions for sustainable development. In W. Leal Filho, D. M. Pociovălişteanu, P. R. Borges de Brito, & I. Borges de Lima (Eds.), *Towards a sustainable bioeconomy: Principles, challenges and perspectives* (pp. 77–98). Springer International Publishing.

Ascui, F., & Cojoianu, T. F. (2019). Implementing natural capital credit risk assessment in agricultural lending. *Business Strategy and the Environment, 28*(6), 1234–1249.

Bang, A. H.Y. (2023). *Accounting for biodiversity: Towards measuring and valuing the biodiversity impacts of financial investments*. ADM Capital Foundation.

Bansal, P., Kim, A., & Wood, M. O. (2018). Hidden in plain sight: The importance of scale in organizations' attention to issues. *Academy of Management Review, 43*(2), 217–241.

Baumgärtner, S. (2007). The insurance value of biodiversity in the provision of ecosystem services. *Natural Resource Modeling, 20*(1), 87–127.

Benton, T. G., Bieg, C., Harwatt, H., Pudasaini, R., & Wellesley, L. (2021). *Food system impacts on biodiversity loss: Three levers for food system transformation in support for nature*. Chatham House, London.

Binnie, I., Jessop, S., & Spring, J. (2022). Factbox: Biodiversity finance options grow, but pace of investment still slow. *Reuters*. https://www.reuters.com/business/environment/biodiversity-finance-options-grow-pace-investment-still-slow-2022-12-14/

Cavender-Bares, J., Schneider, F. D., Santos, M. J., Armstrong, A., Carnaval, A., Dahlin, K. M., Fatoyinbo, L., Hurtt, G. C., Schimel, D., Townsend, P. A., Ustin, S. L., Wang, Z., & Wilson, A. M. (2022). Integrating remote sensing with ecology and evolution to advance biodiversity conservation. *Nature Ecology and Evolution, 6*(5), 506–519.

Darrah, S. E., Shennan-Farpón, Y., Loh, J., Davidson, N. C., Finlayson, C. M., Gardner, R. C., & Walpole, M. J. (2019). Improvements to the Wetland Extent Trends (WET) index as a tool for monitoring natural and human-made wetlands. *Ecological Indicators, 99*, 294–298.

Dasgupta, P. (2021). *The economics of biodiversity: The Dasgupta review*. Hm Treasury.

Dasgupta Review. (2022). *The economics of biodiversity*. The Dasgupta Review.

de Silva, G. C., Regan, E. C., Pollard, E. H. B., & Addison, P. F. E. (2019). The evolution of corporate no net loss and net positive impact biodiversity commitments: Understanding appetite and addressing challenges. *Business Strategy and the Environment, 28*(7), 1481–1495.

Dempsey, J. (2016). *Enterprising nature: Economics, markets, and finance in global biodiversity politics*. John Wiley & Sons.

Deutz, A., Heal, G. M., Niu, R., Swanson, E., Townshend, T., Zhu, L., Delmar, A., Meghji, A., Sethi, S. A., & Tobin-de la Puente, J. (2020). *Financing nature: Closing the global biodiversity financing gap*. The Paulson institute, the Nature Conservancy, and the Cornell Atkinson Center for Sustainability.

FAO. (2015). *The state of food insecurity in the world*. https://www.fao.org/3/i4646e/i4646e.pdf

Ferraro, F., Etzion, D., & Gehman, J. (2015). Tackling grand challenges pragmatically: Robust action revisited. *Organization Studies, 36*(3), 363–390.

Friede, G., Busch, T., & Bassen, A. (2015). ESG and financial performance: Aggregated evidence from more than 2000 empirical studies. *Journal of Sustainable Finance and Investment, 5*(4), 210–233.

George, G., Howard-Grenville, J., Joshi, A., & Tihanyi, L. (2016). Understanding and tackling societal grand challenges through management research. *Academy of Management Journal, 59*(6), 1880–1895.

Gotelli, N. J., & Colwell, R. K. (2001). Quantifying biodiversity: Procedures and pitfalls in the measurement and comparison of species richness. *Ecology Letters, 4*(4), 379–391.

Griscom, B. W., Adams, J., Ellis, P. W., Houghton, R. A., Lomax, G., Miteva, D. A., … Fargione, J. (2017). Natural climate solutions. *Proceedings of the National Academy of Sciences, 114*(44), 11645–11650.

Gümüsay, A. A., & Reinecke, J. (2021). Researching for desirable futures: From real utopias to imagining alternatives. *Journal of Management Studies, 59*(1), 236–242.

Hamilton, S. E., & Casey, D. (2016). Creation of a high spatio-temporal resolution global database of continuous mangrove forest cover for the 21st century (CGMFC-21). *Global Ecology and Biogeography*, *25*(6), 729–738.

Harrer, T., & Owen, R. (2022). Reducing early-stage cleantech funding gaps: An exploration of the role of environmental performance indicators. *International Journal of Entrepreneurial Behavior and Research*, *28*(9), 268–288.

Hehenberger, L., Mair, J., & Metz, A. (2019). The assembly of a field ideology: An idea-centric perspective on systemic power in impact investing. *Academy of Management Journal*, *62*(6), 1672–1704.

IPBES. (2019). *Global assessment report on biodiversity and ecosystem services of the intergovernmental science-policy platform on biodiversity and ecosystem services*. Intergovernmental Science-Policy Platform on Biodiversity and Ecosystem Services (IPBES).

IPCC. (2022). *Climate change 2022: Mitigation of climate change*. Intergovernmental Panel on Climate Change (IPCC).

Jihariya, M. K., Meena, R. S., Banerjee, A., & Meena, S. N. (2022). *Natural resources conservation and advances for sustainability*. Elsevier Science.

Lehner, O. M., Nicholls, A., & Kapplmüller, S. B. (2022). Arenas of contestation: A Senian social justice perspective on the nature of materiality in impact measurement. *Journal of Business Ethics*, *179*(4), 971–989.

Leopold, A. (1966). *A sand county almanac with other essays on conservation from round river*. Oxford University Press.

Loreau, M., Barbier, M., Filotas, E., Gravel, D., Isbell, F., Miller, S. J., Montoya, J. M., Wang, S., Aussenac, R., Germain, R., Thompson, P. L., Gonzalez, A., & Dee, L. E. (2021). Biodiversity as insurance: From concept to measurement and application. *Biological Reviews*, *96*(5), 2333–2354.

Mace, G. M., Norris, K., & Fitter, A. H. (2012). Biodiversity and ecosystem services: A multilayered relationship. *Trends in Ecology and Evolution*, *27*(1), 19–26.

Mair, L., Bennun, L. A., Brooks, T. M., Butchart, S. H. M., Bolam, F. C., Burgess, N. D., Ekstrom, J. M. M., Milner-Gulland, E. J., Hoffmann, M., Ma, K., Macfarlane, N. B. W., Raimondo, D. C., Rodrigues, A. S. L., Shen, X., Strassburg, B. B. N., Beatty, C. R., Gómez-Creutzberg, C., Iribarrem, A., Irmadhiany, M., Lacerda, E., Mattos, B. C., Parakkasi, K., Tognelli, M. F., Bennett, E. L., Bryan, C., Carbone, G., Chaudhary, A., Eiselin, M., da Fonseca, G. A. B., Galt, R., Geschke, A., Glew, L., Goedicke, R., Green, J. M. H., Gregory, R. D., Hill, S. L. L., Hole, D. G., Hughes, J., Hutton, J., Keijzer, M. P. W., Navarro, L. M., Lughadha, E. N., Plumptre, A. J., Puydarrieux, P., Possingham, H. P., Rankovic, A., Regan, E. C., Rondinini, C., Schneck, J. D., Siikamäki, J., Sendashonga, C., Seutin, G., Sinclair, S., Skowno, A. L., Soto-Navarro, C. A., Stuart, S. N., Temple, H. J., Vallier, A., Verones, F., Viana, L. R., Watson, J., Bezeng, S., Böhm, M., Burfield, I. J., Clausnitzer, V., Clubbe, C., Cox, N. A., Freyhof, J., Gerber, L. R., Hilton-Taylor, C., Jenkins, R., Joolia, A., Joppa, L. N., Pin Koh, L., Lacher Jr, T. E., Langhammer, P. F., Long, B., Mallon, D., Pacifici, M., Polidoro, B. A., Pollock, C. M., Rivers, M. C., Roach, N. S., Rodríguez, J. P., Smart, J., Young, B. E., Hawkins, F., & McGowan, P. J. K. (2021). A metric for spatially explicit contributions to science-based species targets. *Nature Ecology and Evolution*, *5*(6), 836–844.

Mazzucato, M., & Semieniuk, G. (2018). Financing renewable energy: Who is financing what and why it matters. *Technological Forecasting and Social Change*, *127*, 8–22.

Michelon, G., Rodrigue, M., & Trevisan, E. (2020). The marketization of a social movement: Activists, shareholders and CSR disclosure. *Accounting, Organizations and Society*, *80*, 101074.

Nedopil, C. (2022). Integrating biodiversity into financial decision-making: Challenges and four principles. *Business Strategy and the Environment*, 32(4), 1619–1633.

Neige, P. (2015). *Events of increased biodiversity: Evolutionary radiations in the fossil record*. ISTE Press.

O'Dwyer, B., & Unerman, J. (2020). Shifting the focus of sustainability accounting from impacts to risks and dependencies: Researching the transformative potential of TCFD reporting. *Accounting, Auditing and Accountability Journal*, *33*(5), 1113–1141.

OECD. (2019). *Biodiversity: Finance and the economic and business case for action*. Retrieved from G7 Environment Ministers' Meeting, , 5–6 May 2019, Metz, France. https://www.oecd.org/environment/resources/biodiversity/G7-report-Biodiversity-Finance-and-the-Economic-and-Business-Case-for-Action.pdf

OECD. (2020). *A comprehensive overview of global biodiversity finance*. https://www.oecd.org/environment/resources/biodiversity/report-a-comprehensive-overview-of-global-biodiversity-finance.pdf

Panwar, R., Ober, H., & Pinkse, J. (2022). The uncomfortable relationship between business and biodiversity: Advancing research on business strategies for biodiversity protection. *Business Strategy and the Environment*, 32(5), 2554–2566.

Polzin, F., & Sanders, M. (2020). How to finance the transition to low-carbon energy in Europe? *Energy Policy*, *147*, 111863.

Porter, T. M. (1996). *Trust in numbers*. Princeton University Press, Princeton.

Quattrone, P. (2022). Seeking transparency makes one blind: How to rethink disclosure, account for nature and make corporations sustainable. *Accounting, Auditing and Accountability Journal*, *35*(2), 547–566.

Quattrone, P., Ronzani, M., Jancsary, D., & Höllerer, M. A. (2021). Beyond the visible, the material and the performative: Shifting perspectives on the visual in organization studies. *Organization Studies*, *42*(8), 1197–1218.

Schoeneborn, D., Morsing, M., & Crane, A. (2019). Formative perspectives on the relation between CSR communication and CSR practices: Pathways for walking, talking, and T(w)alking. *Business and Society*, *59*(1), 5–33.

Seidl, A., Mulungu, K., Arlaud, M., van den Heuvel, O., & Riva, M. (2020). Finance for nature: A global estimate of public biodiversity investments. *Ecosystem Services*, *46*, 101216.

Strömmer, K., & Ormiston, J. (2022). Forward-looking impact assessment – An interdisciplinary systematic review and research agenda. *Journal of Cleaner Production*, *377*, 134322.

Toxopeus, H., & Polzin, F. (2017). *Characterizing nature-based solutions from a business model and financing perspective*. Utrecht University. https://dspace.library.uu.nl/handle/1874/370740

UNEP. (2022). *State of finance for nature. Time to act: Doubling investment by 2025 and eliminating nature-negative finance flows*. https://wedocs.unep.org/20.500.11822/41333

UNEP. (2023). *Nature risk profile: A methodology for profiling nature related dependencies and impacts*. Cambridge, United Kingdom.

Unerman, J., & Bennett, M. (2004). Increased stakeholder dialogue and the internet: Towards greater corporate accountability or reinforcing capitalist hegemony? *Accounting, Organizations and Society*, *29*(7), 685–707.

United Nations. (1992). *Convention on biological diversity*. United Nations. https://www.cbd.int/doc/legal/cbd-en.pdf

Wamelink, G. W., van Adrichem, M. H., Van Dobben, H. v., Frissel, J. Y., den Held, M., Joosten, V., Malinowska, A. H., Slim, P. A., & Wegman, R. M. (2012). Vegetation relevés and soil measurements in the Netherlands: The ecological conditions database (EC). *Biodiversity and Ecology*, *4*(17), 125–132.

World Economic Forum. (2020). *Nature risk rising: Why the crisis engulfing nature matters for business and the economy*. https://www3.weforum.org/docs/WEF_New_Nature_Economy_Report_2020.pdf

21
CAN NUCLEAR ATTRACT GREEN FINANCE?

Simon Taylor

Introduction

Nuclear power has been enjoying a modest comeback in the energy policy of several countries. The case for nuclear is that it is a physically concentrated source of reliable, low-carbon electricity. Its contribution to national energy security was given new salience by the Russian invasion of Ukraine. The United States, the UK, France, India and China are all at various stages of building or encouraging new investments in nuclear power. Other countries appear open to the possibility of new nuclear (e.g. Egypt, Poland). Many of these countries hope to raise at least part of the finance from the private sector.

If nuclear is to be funded privately, albeit with government support, the question arises of private capital providers' views. For nuclear to be funded with bank or capital market funds, it must provide both an economic case and also a case on sustainability grounds, at least if it wishes to attract the growing pool of funds that are constrained by investors' preferences for non-financial outcomes.

In short, is nuclear "green"? There is a case on both sides. The outcome matters because it may make the difference between nuclear becoming a workable though expensive part of the energy transition, at least in some countries, and nuclear being either priced out because of a high cost of capital or being unable to mobilise large-scale private funding at any price.

In this chapter, we examine the arguments for whether nuclear is green or not. The answer is important for the future of nuclear power but also relevant to other technologies that may find their future constrained more by investor attitudes than by their intrinsic economic potential.

The second section reviews the status of nuclear power across the world and why the financing of new nuclear matters for decarbonising the energy system.

The third section briefly reviews the technology of nuclear power and the history of its deployment, from the high hopes of the 1960s and 1970s to the collapse in orders in the 1980s and the putative "nuclear renaissance" that began in the 2000s.

The fourth section considers the economic and financial aspects of investing in nuclear. We argue that nuclear usually requires some element of state support, even in purportedly private sector investments.

The fifth section then considers the case for and against nuclear being green, against the rapidly changing field of sustainable and ethical investing, increasingly subsumed in the idea of environmental, social and governance (ESG) criteria.

The sixth section analyses the views of key decision-makers and advisors on the admissibility of nuclear energy to green finance.

The seventh section concludes with some thoughts about whether financial investments in other decarbonisation technologies may also become constrained by investor attitudes to what is or is not green.

Nuclear Power in World Energy Today and Prospects for the Future

Nuclear makes up a small but growing part of global energy, particularly in large developing countries in Asia, and has the potential to become even more widespread depending on the decisions of several other countries in Africa and the Middle East.

In 2020, nuclear energy made up 4% of total primary energy globally and about 10% of electricity generation (BP, 2021). Table 21.1 shows a selection of the countries where nuclear power is a significant share of total electricity supply, or in the case of India and China is planned to be. France is unusual in having such a large share of nuclear, but it is clear that nuclear is a significant part of the electricity system in several advanced economies. Note that Germany is an outlier in planning to completely close its nuclear power stations by the end of 2022, owing to safety concerns (World Nuclear Association, n.d. d).

Table 21.2 shows that there are 13 countries with nuclear reactors currently under construction. Of these countries, Belarus, Bangladesh and Turkey are building reactors for the first time.

Table 21.1 Share of nuclear in total electricity supply, selected nations (2020)

Country	% nuclear power	Policy
France	77	Stable – one EPR under construction; at least eight more planned
Belgium	47	Stable – no new stations planned; phase out originally in 2025 now put back to 2035
Sweden	41	Stable – no new stations planned
Switzerland	38	Stable – no new stations planned
Finland	35	Stable – one EPR close to finishing; additional Russian reactor order now cancelled
Spain	20	Stable – no new stations planned
United States	19	Government support; limited interest in new stations; government supporting life extensions of existing plants
UK	17	Major expansion/replacement planned; one station under construction
Germany	16	Planned phase out nearly complete
Canada	17	Stable – no new stations planned
Japan	4	Gradually restarting but controversial with the general public
South Korea	27	Stable – following a change of government in 2022, which reversed plans for long-term phaseout; four reactors under construction
India	3	Large expansion underway
People's Republic of China	3	Large expansion underway

Source: World Nuclear Association (n.d. f) https://world-nuclear.org/, author's estimates.

Table 21.2 Countries with nuclear reactors under construction

Country	Capacity (MW)
China	15,299
India	6,600
South Korea	4,200
Turkey	3,600
UAE	3,600
UK	3,440
Russia	2,810
United States	2,500
France	1,650
Bangladesh	1,200
Belarus	1,194
Iran	1,057
Slovakia	942

Source: (World Nuclear Association, n.d. f), author's estimates.

Additionally, Egypt and Poland have contracts for new nuclear power stations, Jordan and Uzbekistan have "committed plans" and Thailand, Indonesia, Kazakhstan and Saudi Arabia have "well-developed plans" but have not yet committed to contracts. Nigeria, Kenya, Laos, Morocco, Algeria, Philippines, Ghana, Rwanda and Ethiopia all have "developing plans" for nuclear (World Nuclear Association, n.d. f).

Many countries, including China and India, will finance this new nuclear energy mostly through the state budget, but given the pressures on public spending, finding private finance is also a priority. India plans to use more private finance in future (World Nuclear Association, n.d. e)).

Nuclear is mainly owned by private investor-owned utilities in the United States. In the UK, the government plans to harness private finance with government support (see sixth section). The nuclear sector is in private ownership in Japan.

The availability of private finance for nuclear power is therefore important for at least some countries to achieve their energy decarbonisation goals. Aside from normal commercial considerations such as risk and return, an additional constraint could be whether nuclear is classified as green, sustainable or ethical. To the extent that other forms of energy enjoy a green financial benefit or "greenium" (Caramichael & Rapp, 2022), nuclear would be disadvantaged if it could not access green finance. This would rise nuclear's cost of capital relative to renewable energy but would not be an absolute increase in costs.

More difficult would be if investors, especially equity investors, decided that nuclear is not green or sustainable. The growth of ESG (environmental, social and governance) investment makes this a real possibility. As we show below, there are differing views on whether nuclear is green and whether it fits within an ESG framework. But with forecasts that ESG-related financial assets could rise to a third of the global total by 2025, ESG opinions are likely to become increasingly important, with one estimate being that ESG will account for about a third of total assets under management (Diab & Martin Adams, 2021).

If a majority of ESG investors decide that nuclear is not green, then a large fraction of capital market capacity, especially public markets and retail-based financial institutions, would be unavailable for nuclear investment, regardless of prospective risks and returns. In that case, governments would have to find the funding entirely themselves, putting some of the planned investment in jeopardy.

A Brief History of Nuclear Power
Basic Technology

The advantage of nuclear as a heat source is that a great deal of energy can be extracted from a very small volume of nuclear fuel (US Energy Information Administration, 2021). The essential fuel, uranium, is both plentiful and distributed around the world so its supply should be cheap and reliable (US Energy Information Administration, 2021).

But nuclear fission is dangerous to humans, so it is necessary to build robust protection structures and processes. This means that nuclear power stations are complicated and expensive to build.

Nuclear fission produces dangerous waste products which must be stored safely somewhere. Also, parts of the nuclear power station become contaminated with radiation in the process of operation. When a station is eventually closed and decommissioned, this irradiated material must also be safely stored.

The economics of nuclear follow from these features: a high fixed cost, including a longer construction period than comparable coal or gas power stations; a low variable cost; and a high future cost of managing waste and decommissioning. The economic case for a particular project relative to a fossil fuel alternative will depend on estimates of these costs, plus the rate of interest, since the net present value is very sensitive to the discount rate (Dawson & Sabharwall, 2017).

On the back of the US Atoms for Peace programme in the 1950s, nuclear reactors were successfully sold to US investor-owned utilities (that is, companies owned by private investors and typically listed on the stock exchange) and to some government-owned utilities.

Construction costs often exceeded budgets, especially in the inflationary 1970s, and costs rose owing to increasing safety regulations (Lévêque, 2015 ch.2). What changed and ultimately halted new nuclear construction in the United States, though not in Europe, was the accident at Three Mile Island (TMI) in Pennsylvania in March 1979. Almost overnight, the US public lost its confidence in nuclear safety, partly owing to a lack of credible information about the incident and how much risk the public really faced. No new nuclear reactor was licensed in the United States after TMI until 2012 (Plokhy, 2022).

The official verdict on TMI is that nobody died (Plokhy, 2022 ch.IV). But in 1986 a far more serious accident took place at Chernobyl in the USSR. The radiation released by burning nuclear fuel at Chernobyl spread across much of northern Europe, creating an international dimension to nuclear safety.

Chernobyl had a much greater impact on global public opinion than TMI (Plokhy, 2022 ch.V). Germany and Italy both decided to phase out nuclear power, though Germany's policy was suspended for several years.

In an attempt to rebuild public confidence in nuclear power, power station manufacturers began work on so-called Generation III nuclear designs that would either make an accident impossible or would provide fail-safe methods of dealing with any accident that did arise (Wheeler, 2011).

A Nuclear Renaissance?

Governments' growing emphasis on climate change led to a new consideration of nuclear's proven ability to produce zero-carbon electricity, giving rise to talk of a "nuclear renaissance" (Nuttall, 2022). In the UK, declining North Sea oil and gas output spelt the return of energy imports, giving a further boost to the case for new nuclear on the grounds of energy security (Taylor, 2016a).

India and China's growing nuclear programmes both appeared to be motivated mainly by a combination of mitigating energy import dependence and reducing the use of coal owing to local air pollution (World Nuclear Association, n.d. b).

Just as plans for new nuclear plants were gaining momentum, in 2011 a third major nuclear accident happened when a tsunami overwhelmed the Fukushima Daiichi plant in Japan. The accident led to the revival in Germany of a delayed plan to close all its nuclear plants (Der Spiegel, 2011). But elsewhere, including in the UK and the United States, the effect was only to delay plans for new nuclear plans (Taylor, 2016a).

The key issue for new nuclear plants since Fukushima has been cost, not safety. Renewable electricity costs have fallen rapidly, and faster than most expected, on the back of government support, especially from Germany (solar, onshore wind) and the UK (offshore wind). The manufacturers of Gen III reactors were originally confident that they could compete, at least once they got to the "nth" of a kind, meaning any early troubles had been ironed out (which might be 3, 4, 5 or a higher number).

But while China managed to build every type of reactor, from Russia, Japan, the United States and Europe, more or less on time and budget, the new US and European reactors each suffered from severe delays and budget overruns, with one US project being cancelled after $5 billion of costs had already been incurred (see fourth section).

Energy Security

The invasion of Ukraine by Russia in February 2022 and Russia's role as a major oil and gas exporter led to several countries reappraising their policies on nuclear power, on energy security grounds. Belgium postponed its planned closure of nuclear plants from 2025 to 2035 (World Nuclear News, 2022). Public opinion in Japan appeared to swing back to supporting the opening of plants that had been closed since the Fukushima disaster in 2011 (Japan Times, 2022). In other countries, the energy security argument gave further impetus to a swing towards either extending nuclear (South Korea, United States) or building new reactors (UK, France, United States).

The Financing of New Nuclear

The previous section argued that the economic facts of nuclear included its high fixed costs, amounting to a large construction cost per unit of generation capacity, which is worth incurring if the variable costs are sufficiently low. Then there is the question of risk.

The key risks in a new nuclear project are itemised in Table 21.3, together with ways in which they might be mitigated. Ignoring the ESG aspect of the investment, the key challenge for the investor would be the construction risk, which can only be hedged, if at all, by signing a fixed price contract with a construction company, of the sort that bankrupted the company Westinghouse in 2017 (Hals & Flitter, 2017).

Recent nuclear construction in Europe and the United States has gone very badly (see Table 21.4).

Table 21.4 shows how projects have been delayed and gone over budget for two of the Gen III reactors (in the United States the Westinghouse AP1000 and in Europe the European Pressurized Reactor or EPR). Attracting private finance to bear the construction risk became all but impossible after the Westinghouse bankruptcy, originally American but owned by the Japanese electrical conglomerate Toshiba at the time of its insolvency in 2017, in connection with two US nuclear projects.

Table 21.3 Key nuclear investment risks and their management

Risk type	Comment	Mitigation
Construction risk	Very high (see Table 21.4)	Unhedgeable; state support now essential
Power price risk	High	Power purchase agreement usually available
Fuel cost risk	Minor share of costs	Hedgeable through contracts
Operating risk	Low	Operator needs regulatory approval
Third-party liability risk	Low but potentially catastrophic	Limited by Paris Convention

Source: Author's estimates.

Table 21.4 New nuclear construction problems in Europe and the United States

Project	Country	Status
Olkiluoto 3	Finland	c. 200% over budget; 13 years late
Flamanville 3	France	c. 300% over budget; 12 years late
Vogtle 3 and 4	United States	c. 100% over budget; four years late
Summer 2 and 3	United States	Construction abandoned, $5 bn written off

Source: (World Nuclear Association, n.d. f).

Taylor (2014) argues that, although there is no intrinsic reason why new nuclear could not attract conventional finance, in practice nuclear's recent construction record makes it currently impossible.

The 3,200 MW Hinkley Point C nuclear station under construction since 2016 in the UK appears a successful case of a government managing to get private finance to fully fund the construction of a new nuclear power station. But the two investors in the project are both de facto state-owned enterprises: EDF (two-thirds investor) was 84% owned by the French government at the time (now 100%); and CGN (one-third investor) is a Chinese state-owned company, with a subsidiary listed in Hong Kong (Taylor, 2016a).

In exchange for a 35-year power purchase agreement, indexed to the UK retail price index, these two companies assumed the construction risk of Hinkley Point C. The construction risk was transferred from the UK government to French and Chinese taxpayers instead. It is doubtful that any truly private company would have taken on this risk.

Bearing the construction risk raised the investors' required rate of return, which is reflected in the high price of electricity in the long-term contract (Taylor, 2016b). After widespread criticism of the high price of the Hinkley Point C contract, the UK government sought new ways to attract private finance at a lower cost of capital and therefore lower electricity prices. This is only feasible if the government itself bears some of the risk (or forces electricity customers to bear it). That is what current UK policy now envisages (see below).

If governments want to get nuclear built using private finance, they must mitigate the risk of construction cost overruns. In its consultation on financing a new nuclear project at Sizewell C, the UK government acknowledged the need for "Government protection for investors and consumers against specific remote, low probability but high impact risk events" (UK Government, 2019, p. 4).

The UK government plans to provide insurance[1] against costs exceeding some pre-determined level, equivalent to guaranteeing that investor returns are protected at some minimum level, using the so-called RAB (regulated asset base) model.

The RAB model provides for an independent regulator to provide a guaranteed level of revenue in respect of the cumulative investment made by private investors, using the established framework of regulated network utilities in the UK (Newbery et al., 2019).

The RAB model was used in the Thames Tideway Tunnel (TTT), a large sewerage tunnel project in London. TTT is funded entirely with private sector debt and equity, but the government undertakes to finance any investment over a pre-determined threshold arising from cost overruns. This means that investors have no obligation to put in further investment and removes the risk that the project is left part-built. It provides a de facto floor for investor returns (subject to investors managing the project well in other respects) (Newbery et al., 2019).

TTT's total cost is £4.2 billion (TTT, 2021). The new EPR at Sizewell C would require in the order of £20 billion (EDF Energy, 2020a). It would need private investors to see a new nuclear power station as being similar in financial terms to the TTT. But it also needs those investors to have no opposition on *non-financial* grounds. That is, would nuclear be deemed "non-green" or incompatible with ESG criteria?

There are very few nuclear-linked investments in the UK, so many investors will never have had to ask the question, is nuclear consistent with our ESG criteria? ESG funds are also relatively new, and many investors may simply not have considered nuclear yet in any decision-making. It is also unclear whether the ultimate investors, the ordinary public, have a strong view on this, whether in respect of buying ESG mutual funds or in the way their pension funds are invested.

The next section considers the arguments that these investors and their clients may soon be asked to consider: is nuclear energy green?

Is Nuclear Energy Green?

Previous authors have taken a sceptical view of nuclear's sustainability credentials. In the wake of the Fukushima nuclear accident of 2011, Mez (2012) argues that nuclear, both on grounds of its own CO_2 emissions as well as links to weapon proliferation, could not be considered a fully sustainable source of energy. Verbruggen et al. (2014) broadly agree. Pearce (2012), while emphasising the difficulties, leaves the door open to the possibility of nuclear being seen as sustainable. Muellner et al. (2021) argue that a major expansion of nuclear would not be sustainable because of uranium fuel supplies.

We argue below that few if any energy sources are currently entirely sustainable, so nuclear needs to be judged on a relative basis. We analyse the question of whether nuclear energy is green or not, under five headings: construction; operation; fuel supply; waste disposal and decommissioning; and safety.

Construction and Site Impact

Owing to the need for multiple safety systems and resilience to earthquakes and other hazards, nuclear power plants are among the largest and most complex civil engineering projects undertaken. In particular, they need very large amounts of concrete: each of the two bases at Hinkley Point C used around 49,000 tonnes of concrete (BBC News, 2020).

Since concrete is currently impossible to produce without generating CO_2, a criticism of nuclear is that it is not a sustainable way to produce electricity. But the same charge would apply to many other energy installations, including wind farms (other than floating offshore wind turbines).

Large civil engineering projects involve temporary disruption to the local area and permanent damage to areas that are subsumed in the project. Again, this is not unique to nuclear power. The construction of Sizewell C would potentially harm local wildlife, including rare birds, and is opposed by the Royal Society for the Protection of Birds (RSPB), an influential charity in the UK (Powell, 2022). The project sponsor EDF has argued that by active management of local land, Sizewell C would lead to a net gain in biodiversity (EDF Energy, 2020b).

So large nuclear plants unavoidably have a local environmental impact and use a lot of CO_2-producing concrete. But nuclear energy is not unique in these respects, and opposition to any new nuclear on these grounds would presumably mean opposing any major civil engineering projects that use concrete. Research for the IPPC's fifth working group in 2014 found that median lifetime emissions of nuclear energy per unit of energy were about the same as for wind power and lower than solar (Schlömer et al., 2015).

Operation

Nuclear fission is inherently dangerous, so nuclear power stations are tightly regulated in their operations. In normal operation, a nuclear power station should have a minimal environmental impact. Most obviously, radiation emissions are strictly controlled, both in the wider environment and for workers on site. Nuclear stations also use a lot of water for cooling, and there are regulations governing the temperature and manner of return of any water to the sea or river it was sourced from.

Critics would argue that it is precisely when operations are *abnormal* that concerns arise; see below for an analysis of the safety issue.

Fuel Supply

Nuclear energy is fuelled by uranium, a metal that is relatively plentiful in the Earth's crust (NEA/IAEA, 2020). Since the fuel is finite and could face some physical or economic constraints in future, it can be argued that it is not sustainable (Muellner et al., 2021), in the sense that wind or solar energy is for all practical purposes infinite globally.

But wind and solar PV-generated electricity require minerals in construction that are finite and may face quite severe supply constraints as capacity increases. Low-carbon technologies, particularly solar photovoltaic (PV), wind, and geothermal, are more mineral-intensive relative to fossil fuel technologies (World Bank, 2020, p. 11). Global demand for graphite, lithium and cobalt in 2050 would be more than four times 2018 levels of production in the scenario of increased warming of 2 °C (World Bank, 2020, p. 73).

Aside from the normal impact of mining on the environment, some of these minerals are currently sourced from countries with problematic ESG credentials. For example, in 2016, 54% of the cobalt used in lithium-ion batteries came from the Democratic Republic of the Congo, where there are concerns about human rights in artisanal (small-scale) mining activities (Baumann-Pauly, 2020).

More than half of the rare earths that are needed in electric vehicle manufacturing are currently mined in China (ChinaPower Project, 2020), which also raises questions about the sustainability of supply (Kalantzakos, 2018). China in 2021 proposed to restrict exports of rare earths for strategic reasons (Olander, 2021).

Waste Disposal and Decommissioning

Nuclear energy creates dangerous fission products and irradiates parts of the reactor. Both of these must be stored safely after decommissioning. The policy consensus is that nuclear waste should be stored deep underground in a purpose-built facility. As of 2022, no country had a fully working underground nuclear storage facility, with Finland the closest, where operation is due to start in 2024 (World Nuclear Association, n.d. a). The United States has identified the site for a storage facility in Arizona but faces local opposition (US EPA, 2019): The UK government has yet to identify a site for the construction of such a storage facility but is "working with technical specialists, local communities and regulators to find a safe disposal route for HLW [high-level waste]" (Nuclear Decommissioning Authority, n.d.).

It is difficult to describe nuclear energy as sustainable when it entails producing toxic waste that needs to be stored for thousands of years. But the nuclear industry has always had to account (practically and financially) for this aspect of its operations, precisely because it is so obviously a problem. Other industries, including renewable energy, do not necessarily account for the full life cycle of their operations, even when they also produce long-term waste.

Wind turbines have until recently been designed and built without recycling being a key consideration. Older wind turbine blades currently being decommissioned are typically dumped in landfill. The North America Chief Operating Officer of French environmental services company Veolia is quoted by Bloomberg as saying, "The wind turbine blade will be there, ultimately, forever" (Martin, 2020).

New recyclable wind turbine designs are emerging. The ZEBRA (Zero wastE Blade ReseArch) consortium of wind turbine, materials and construction companies announced in 2022 that it had produced a prototype of a blade that was designed to be fully recyclable, with the goal of being fully validated by the end of 2023 (GE, 2022). So the wind turbine industry may eventually have a path to fuller sustainability.

Solar panels also face difficulties at the end of their life. The US Environmental Protection Agency (EPA) argues for recycling where possible but notes that some elements of solar panels "may be more difficult to recycle" (US EPA, 2021). But in practice, the costs of recycling are high and "there's a real danger that all used solar panels will go straight to landfill" (Atasu et al., 2021). In the United States, only 10% of solar panels are recycled (Crownhart, 2021).

As with wind turbines, there are research projects and commercial ventures aiming to make recycling cheaper, but the solution seems less straightforward with solar panels. In some US states there are now regulations requiring recycling, which adds to the upfront cost of the solar installation. In the EU, legislation requires PV manufacturers to recycle waste panels and recover at least 80% of their mass (Peplow, 2022).

Nuclear waste is intrinsic to the nuclear energy process, whereas the problems of recycling renewable energy (and batteries) are in principle solvable eventually. But the question of whether nuclear in particular should be penalised for its waste problem is arguable.

Safety

Nuclear radiation is dangerous, which is why nuclear power stations are designed to make the release of radiation very unlikely and to protect the environment if it does happen. But there have been three nuclear accidents that show a release of radiation can happen.

According to public research on the outcomes of the three nuclear accidents, deaths per TWh of electricity produced are similar to that of wind and far below fossil fuels (see Figure 21.1).

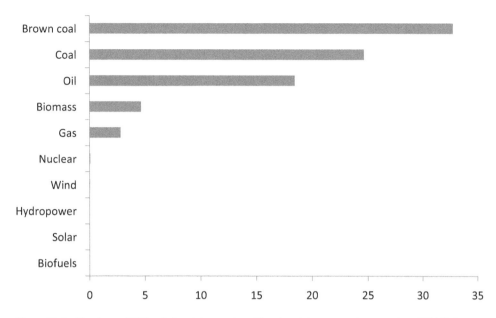

Figure 21.1 Deaths per TWh of electricity produced by electricity generation type (as of 2014). Source: Our World in Data based on Sovacool et al. (2015) and Markandya and Wilkinson (2007).

Of the three civil nuclear accidents,[2] – Three Mile Island (TMI), United States, in 1979; Chernobyl, USSR, in 1986; and Fukushima, Japan, in 2011 – only Chernobyl led to large numbers of deaths. But TMI and Fukushima caused a lot of public anxiety. The evacuation of the Fukushima district led to an estimated 573 deaths, compared with only one from radiation (Ritchie, 2017).

For critics, this is to miss the point that a nuclear accident might cause a very severe loss of life and amenity. At one point during the TMI accident, some experts believed there was a high risk of a hydrogen explosion that would have destroyed the containment vessel and irradiated large parts of the United States (Plokhy, 2022). The fact that they were mistaken doesn't necessarily mean the risk wasn't there, or could be, with this form of technology.

Gen III reactors are designed to be extremely safe, as measured by "core damage frequencies". The EPR documentation submitted to the UK Office of Nuclear Regulation claimed a core damage frequency of 5.62×10^{-7} per reactor year (EDF Energy, 2017); that is, the core would be expected to sustain damage 0.56 times in a million years.

Such claims come close to saying that accidents are all but impossible, but it is human error that has been responsible for the accidents so far. In his recent survey of nuclear accidents, Plokhy quotes another historian of nuclear accidents, James Mahaffey: "Trying to build something that will work perfectly for all time is a noble goal, but it is simply impossible" (Plokhy, 2022).

Against these criteria for assessing nuclear energy's green credentials, different authors and investors can reasonably come to different conclusions.

Opinions on Whether Nuclear Is Green

The question of whether nuclear is green or not can be answered by three groups of people:

i) governments and regulators;
ii) third-party advisors;

iii) investment decision-makers (managing other people's money); and
iv) the ultimate investors.

Systematic evidence on the opinions of categories iii) and iv) is currently limited. We review below the views of advisory organisations or third parties that issue guidelines on green finance.

Governments and Regulators

The most important attempt to define green investments is the EU taxonomy for sustainable activities (hereafter EU taxonomy), in preparation for several years and finalised in February 2022. The EU uses "green", "sustainable" and "ESG" more or less interchangeably.

The goal of the taxonomy is to:

> provide companies, investors and policymakers with appropriate definitions for which economic activities can be considered environmentally sustainable. In this way, it should create security for investors, protect private investors from greenwashing, help companies to become more climate-friendly, mitigate market fragmentation and help shift investments where they are most needed.
>
> *(European Commission, n.d. a)*

The taxonomy is intended to help and guide decision-makers but is not legally binding: investors and companies are free to make their own decisions, subject to other applicable laws and regulations.

The EU taxonomy itself excludes nuclear energy. But, following two expert group reports, the EU issued a Delegated Act (a non-legislative but legally binding act) on nuclear energy (and natural gas) as being classified as sustainable in respect of contributing to the energy transition away from fossil fuel use (European Commission, 2022). Nuclear investments are sustainable if they fall into three categories:

i) Research and development of advanced nuclear technologies, still at pre- commercial stages, with minimal waste from closed fuel cycle or fuel self-breeding (Generation IV);
ii) Construction and operation of new nuclear power plants using the best available technologies (Generation III +) when the permit is issued before 2045;
iii) Renovation and expansion of existing nuclear power plants approved before 2040 (Chaillet et al., 2022).

The long process of reaching this conclusion reflects deep divisions among EU members on the role of nuclear energy. In particular, Germany has closed most of its nuclear power stations, while France gets 75% of its electricity from nuclear energy and plans at least six new nuclear plants (World Nuclear Association, n.d. c).

The UK government, no longer part of the EU, published its own green financing framework in June 2021. Curiously, the framework excludes nuclear: " Recognising that many sustainable investors have exclusionary criteria in place around nuclear energy, the UK Government will not finance any nuclear energy-related expenditures under the Framework." (UK Government, 2021, p. 18).

The US Department of Energy, through its Office of Nuclear Energy, claims that nuclear energy is "clean and sustainable" (Office of Nuclear Energy, 2021).

The OECD Nuclear Energy Agency (NEA) argues

> The analysis of nuclear energy characteristics within a sustainable development framework shows that the approach adopted by the nuclear energy sector is generally consistent with the fundamental sustainable development goal of passing on a range of assets to future generations while minimising environmental impacts.
>
> *(NEA, n.d. b)*

The regulation of financial products claiming to be sustainable, or using the ESG label, is still in its early stages. Regulators have a duty to protect financial consumers from inaccurate or misleading claims, including where the product is not in fact "sustainable". But it is easier to police the process than the substance, given the very lack of agreement as to what sustainable finance means.

Under the Sustainable Finance Disclosures Regulation (SFDR), which came into force in 2021, the EU sets out disclosure obligations on financial products marketed as sustainable (European Commission, n.d. b). Disclosure includes the financial institution's policies, methods of evaluation and data sources. It defines sustainable investment as

> an investment in an economic activity that contributes to an environmental or social objective, or an investment in human capital or economically or socially disadvantaged communities, provided that such investments do not significantly harm any of those objectives and that the investee companies follow good governance practices.
>
> *(European Commission, 2022, p. 10)*

Nothing in the SFDR appears to exclude nuclear energy from sustainable finance.

The US Securities and Exchange Commission (SEC) published proposals in March 2022 for new requirements on registrants (regulated entities) to disclose climate-related risks and impacts, as a way to improve information for investors (SEC, 2022a). The SEC has not proposed a definition of sustainable finance or ESG and is consulting on how the proposed disclosures would work.

In May 2022, the SEC imposed a $1.5 million fine on the US bank BNY Mellon for "misstatements and omissions concerning ESG considerations" (SEC, 2022b). The SEC took no view on the process used by BNY Mellon in its ESG evaluations but fined the bank because it claimed a certain internal ESG evaluation was being applied to all stocks in a portfolio when that was not the case. The fund itself was not marketed as an ESG product. So the regulator in this case was applying the established principle that investors should be entitled to accurate disclosure by providers of funds.

Nothing in the SEC rules or proposals to date appears to limit the inclusion of nuclear energy in a sustainable or ESG fund.

Third Parties Offering Guidelines on Green Finance

A lot of financial activity is, in effect, self-regulated under industry agreements that firms may voluntarily adopt. Two important ones here are the Green Bond Principles and the Green Loan Principles.

The Green Bond Principles are voluntary guidelines for issuers of green bonds, published by the International Capital Markets Association (ICMA). The document gives a long, detailed but not exhaustive list of what counts as green (ICMA, 2021). The Green Loan Principles, published by the Loan Syndications and Trading Association (LSTA), are the equivalent guidance to issuers of loans and closely follow the Green Bond Principles (LSTA, 2021). The word nuclear also does not appear in either document.

Another important quasi-regulator in the field of green finance is the Climate Bond Initiative (CBI), a non-governmental organisation which, among other activities, certifies green bonds for investors. CBI is therefore an unofficial but influential auditor in the world of green bonds.

CBI produces its own climate bond taxonomy (Climate Bonds Initiative, 2021). The taxonomy classifies nuclear energy as compatible with the Paris 2019 agreement but not certifiable, or under consideration for certifiability. There are other isolated examples of activities with this combination, but nuclear appears to be the only type of investment that is completely ruled out from certifiability. The document provides no explanation why.

The World Bank has become a major issuer of green bonds, with $17 billion issued as of 2021 (World Bank, 2022). The Bank used the Norwegian Centre for International Climate Research (CICERO) to validate the green credentials of its green bonds. CICERO Shades of Green claims to be the leading global provider of second opinions on green bonds (CICERO Shades of Green, n.d.). Its "shades of green" framework evaluates how well a green bond aligns with a low-carbon resilient future (CICERO Shades of Green, 2022). The framework doesn't mention nuclear energy.

But in November 2021, CICERO Shades of Green provided a favourable opinion on a green bond issued by the Canadian company Bruce Power, to fund life extensions at existing nuclear power plants. The opinion states "this should not be considered an open door for all nuclear green bonds". (CICERO Shades of Green, 2021).

In conclusion, there is no consensus among governments, regulators or green bond evaluators as to whether nuclear is green or not, with at least some precedents for arguing that nuclear energy is sufficiently aligned with the UN climate change goals that it can be considered eligible for green finance.

Conclusion

Nuclear power may have a significant role to play in decarbonising the electricity system in both advanced and developing economies. The main barrier to attracting private finance has been the very high construction risk in new nuclear projects. If governments can provide insurance against high-cost overruns, there is some reason to think that private investment may be forthcoming.

But a further barrier is that nuclear may not be regarded as green, or ESG-compatible. If a rising share of investor funds is run according to ESG principles, then it matters greatly whether those principles admit nuclear as green, sustainable or ethical.

Currently, there is no consensus on this question. Some governments, the OECD and the EU have kept the door open to nuclear as a form of sustainable investment. Current guidelines on green bonds and loans either ignore nuclear or, in the case of the Climate Bond Initiative, accept that nuclear is consistent with green principles but nonetheless fail to certify it as green. One provider of second opinions has provided a favourable opinion on a green bond for nuclear life extensions.

The ultimate decision-makers are the general public whose savings go into the mutual funds and pension funds that might fund nuclear energy. Amid the confusion about what ESG means, allegations of greenwashing and puzzlement as to how an ESG index can include a tobacco company (Taparia, 2021) but not an electric car company (Kerber & Jin, 2022), the retail investor may well feel somewhat unable to make an informed decision.

The point extends beyond nuclear. The road to decarbonisation is likely to be a long one, and other technologies may emerge that divide opinion on their sustainability credentials, such as methods to remove carbon dioxide, nuclear fusion, climate repair and geoengineering, in roughly ascending order of controversy. Clarifying what investors understand by green or ESG finance will be critical as to whether these technologies can access private finance, either at competitive rates or at all.

While the EU taxonomy is not binding on investors, it probably helps tip the balance for enough funds to consider nuclear to be "green". Given the difficulties in recycling solar and wind energy components, there is little that is completely sustainable in today's energy policy menu. The year 2022 is likely to go down as another year of extreme weather that drew attention to the imminent risks of further climate change. Against that backdrop, the proponents of nuclear have a reasonable case that to exclude a proven source of low-carbon electricity on sustainability grounds is surely the greater evil. Not all investors will agree but it is to be hoped that enough will see nuclear as a worthy candidate for green finance.

Notes

1. Note that nuclear power enjoys state-provided insurance against third-party liability above a certain threshold under the Paris Convention (NEA, n.d. a). Private insurance would not be available for these losses. Without state insurance, private investment in nuclear energy would not be feasible.
2. There have also been two serious nuclear accidents at military installations. Kyshtym in the USSR and Windscale in the UK, both in 1957 (Plokhy, 2022).

Bibliography

Atasu, A., Duran, S., & Wassenhove, L. N.V. (2021, June 18). The dark side of solar power. *Harvard Business Review*. https://hbr.org/2021/06/the-dark-side-of-solar-power

Baumann-Pauly, D. (2020, October 29). *Why cobalt mining in the DRC needs urgent attention*. Council on Foreign Relations. https://www.cfr.org/blog/why-cobalt-mining-drc-needs-urgent-attention

BBC News. (2020, June 1). *Hinkley Point C nuclear reactor concrete base completed*. BBC News. https://www.bbc.com/news/uk-england-somerset-52882999

BP. (2021). *2020 at a glance – Statistical review of world energy 2021*. https://www.bp.com/content/dam/bp/business-sites/en/global/corporate/pdfs/energy-economics/statistical-review/bp-stats-review-2021-at-a-glance.pdf

Caramichael, J., & Rapp, A. (2022). *The green corporate bond issuance premium*. Board of Governors of the Federal Reserve System. https://www.federalreserve.gov/econres/ifdp/the-green-corporate-bond-issuance-premium.htm

Chaillet, G., Honnefelder, S., & Fernandes, L. D. (2022, March). *EU taxonomy: Complementary delegated act covering nuclear and gas*. https://www.europarl.europa.eu/RegData/etudes/BRIE/2022/730459/IPOL_BRI(2022)730459_EN.pdf

ChinaPower Project. (2020, July 17). Does China pose a threat to global rare earth supply chains? ChinaPower Project. https://chinapower.csis.org/china-rare-earths/

CICERO Shades of Green. (n.d.). *CICERO shades of green*. CICERO Shades of Green. Retrieved June 13, 2022, from https://cicero.green

CICERO Shades of Green. (2021, November 18). *CICERO shades of green with second opinion for a nuclear power company*. CICERO Shades of Green. https://cicero.green/latestnews/2021/11/18/cicero-shades-of-green-with-second-opinion-for-a-nuclear-power-company

CICERO Shades of Green. (2022). *Shades of green factsheet, v.6*. https://static1.squarespace.com/static/5bc5b31a7788975c96763ea7/t/627397750c0ba20da0e381b7/1651742582491/CICERO_SHadesofGreen_factsheet_v6_2022-FIN.pdf

Climate Bonds Initiative. (2021, September). *Climate bonds taxonomy*. Climate Bonds Initiative. https://www.climatebonds.net/standard/taxonomy

Crownhart, C. (2021, August 19). *Solar panels are a pain to recycle: These companies are trying to fix that.* MIT Technology Review. https://www.technologyreview.com/2021/08/19/1032215/solar-panels-recycling/
Dawson, K., & Sabharwall, P. (2017). *A review of light water reactor costs and cost drivers* (INL/EXT-17-43273). Idaho National Lab. (INL). https://doi.org/10.2172/1466793
Der Spiegel. (2011, March 14). *Phasing in the phase out: Germany reconsiders reactor lifespan extensions.* Der Spiegel. https://www.spiegel.de/international/germany/phasing-in-the-phase-out-germany-reconsiders-reactor-lifespan-extensions-a-750836.html
Diab, A., & Martin Adams, G. (2021, February 23). ESG assets may hit $53 trillion by 2025, a third of global AUM. *Bloomberg Professional Services.* https://www.bloomberg.com/professional/blog/esg-assets-may-hit-53-trillion-by-2025-a-third-of-global-aum/
EDF Energy. (2017). *Hinkley point C pre-construction safety report 3 public version.* https://www.edfenergy.com/file/3863926/download
EDF Energy. (2020a). *The Sizewell C Project 4.2 funding statement.* https://infrastructure.planninginspectorate.gov.uk/wp-content/ipc/uploads/projects/EN010012/EN010012-001678-SZC_Bk4_4.2_Funding_Statement.pdf
EDF Energy. (2020b, November 25). *How Sizewell C is protecting the environment.* EDF. https://www.edf-energy.com/energy/nuclear-new-build-projects/sizewell-c/news-views/how-sizewell-c-protecting-environment
European Commission. (n.d.a). *EU taxonomy for sustainable activities.* European Commission. https://ec.europa.eu/info/business-economy-euro/banking-and-finance/sustainable-finance/eu-taxonomy-sustainable-activities_en
European Commission. (n.d.b). *Sustainability-related disclosure in the financial services sector.* European Commission. https://ec.europa.eu/info/business-economy-euro/banking-and-finance/sustainable-finance/sustainability-related-disclosure-financial-services-sector_en
European Commission. (2022). *Commission delegated regulation (EU) …/… of 6.4.2022.* https://ec.europa.eu/finance/docs/level-2-measures/C_2022_1931_1_EN_ACT_part1_v6%20(1).pdf
GE. (2022, March 17). *ZEBRA project achieves key milestone with production of the first prototype of its recyclable wind turbine blade.* GE News. https://www.ge.com/news/press-releases/zebra-project-achieves-key-milestone-with-production-of-first-prototype-of-recyclable-wind-turbine-blade
Hals, T., & Flitter, E. (2017, May 2). How two cutting edge U.S. nuclear projects bankrupted Westinghouse. Reuters. https://www.reuters.com/article/us-toshiba-accounting-westinghouse-nucle-idUSKBN17Y0CQ
ICMA. (2021, June). *Green bond principles.* ICMA. https://www.icmagroup.org/sustainable-finance/the-principles-guidelines-and-handbooks/green-bond-principles-gbp/
Japan Times, N. (2022, March 28). *Majority in Japan backs nuclear power for first time since Fukushima.* The Japan Times. https://www.japantimes.co.jp/news/2022/03/28/national/nuke-power-poll/
Kalantzakos, S. (2018). *China and the geopolitics of rare earths.* Oxford University Press.
Kerber, R., & Jin, H. (2022, May 19). *Tesla cut from S&P 500 ESG index, and Elon Musk tweets his fury.* Reuters. https://www.reuters.com/business/sustainable-business/tesla-removed-sp-500-esg-index-autopilot-discrimination-concerns-2022-05-18/
Lévêque, F. (2015). *The economics and uncertainties of nuclear power.* Cambridge University Press.
LSTA. (2021, February). Green loan principles. *LSTA.* https://www.lsta.org/content/green-loan-principles/
Markandya, A., & Wilkinson, P. (2007). Electricity generation and health. *Lancet, 370*(9591), 979–990. https://doi.org/10.1016/S0140-6736(07)61253-7
Martin, C. (2020, February 5). Wind turbine blades can't be recycled, so they're piling up in landfills. *Bloomberg.Com.* https://www.bloomberg.com/news/features/2020-02-05/wind-turbine-blades-can-t-be-recycled-so-they-re-piling-up-in-landfills
Mez, L. (2012). Nuclear energy–Any solution for sustainability and climate protection? *Energy Policy, 48,* 56–63. https://doi.org/10.1016/j.enpol.2012.04.047
Muellner, N., Arnold, N., Gufler, K., Kromp, W., Renneberg, W., & Liebert, W. (2021). Nuclear energy—The solution to climate change? *Energy Policy, 155.* https://doi.org/10.1016/j.enpol.2021.112363.
NEA. (n.d.-a). *Paris convention on third party liability in the field of nuclear energy.* Retrieved November 3, 2022, from https://www.oecd-nea.org/jcms/pl_20196/paris-convention-on-third-party-liability-in-the-field-of-nuclear-energy-paris-convention-or-pc
NEA. (n.d.-b). *Sustainable development and nuclear energy.* Nuclear Energy Agency (NEA). Retrieved June 13, 2022, from https://www.oecd-nea.org/jcms/pl_33568/sustainable-development-and-nuclear-energy

NEA/IAEA. (2020). *Uranium 2020: Resources, production and demand*. OECD Publishing. https://www.oecd-nea.org/upload/docs/application/pdf/2020-12/7555_uranium_-_resources_production_and_demand_2020__web.pdf

Newbery, D., Pollitt, M., Reiner, D., & Taylor, S. (2019, July 25). *Financing low-carbon generation in the UK: The hybrid RAB model EPRG working paper 1926*. Energy Policy Research Group. https://www.eprg.group.cam.ac.uk/eprg-working-paper-1926/

Nuclear Decommissioning Authority. (n.d.). *How do we manage radioactive waste?* UK Radioactive Waste Inventory (UKRWI). Retrieved June 13, 2022, from https://ukinventory.nda.gov.uk/about-radioactive-waste/how-do-we-manage-radioactive-waste/

Nuttall, W. J. (2022). *Nuclear renaissance technologies and policies for the future of nuclear power* (2nd ed.). CRC Press.

Office of Nuclear Energy. (2021, March 31). *3 reasons why nuclear is clean and sustainable*. https://www.energy.gov/ne/articles/3-reasons-why-nuclear-clean-and-sustainable

Olander, E. (2021, January 19). *With the U.S. in its sights, China moves to restrict rare earths exports. Could cobalt be next?* Sup.China. https://supchina.com/2021/01/19/with-the-u-s-in-its-sights-china-moves-to-restrict-rare-earths-exports-could-cobalt-be-next/

Pearce, J. (2012). Limitations of nuclear power as a sustainable energy source. *Sustainability, 4*(6), 1173–1187. https://doi.org/10.3390/su4061173

Peplow, M. (2022). Solar panels face recycling challenge. *ACS Central Science, 8*(3), 299–302. https://doi.org/10.1021/acscentsci.2c00214

Plokhy, S. (2022). *Atoms and ashes. From bikini atoll to Fukushima*. Allen Lane.

Powell, M. (2022, January 27). *RSPB shocked at Sizewell C £100million funding pledge before final decision*. East Anglian Daily Times. https://www.eadt.co.uk/news/business/suffolk-groups-react-to-sizewell-c-100m-8649412

Ritchie, H. (2017, July 24). *What was the death toll from Chernobyl and Fukushima?* Our World in Data. https://ourworldindata.org/what-was-the-death-toll-from-chernobyl-and-fukushima

Schlömer, S., Bruckner, T., Fulton, L., Hertwich, E., McKinnon, A., Perczyk, D., Roy, J., Schaeffer, R., Sims, R., Smith, P., & Wiser, R. (2015). Annex III: Technology-specific cost and performance parameters. In *Climate change 2014: Mitigation of climate change. Contribution of working group III to the fifth assessment report of the intergovernmental panel on climate change*. Cambridge University Press. https://doi.org/10.1017/CBO9781107415416

SEC. (2022a, March 21). *SEC proposes rules to enhance and standardize climate-related disclosures for investors*. https://www.sec.gov/news/press-release/2022-46

SEC. (2022b, May 23). *SEC charges BNY Mellon investment adviser for misstatements and omissions concerning ESG considerations*. https://www.sec.gov/news/press-release/2022-86

Sovacool, B. K., Kryman, M., & Laine, E. (2015). Profiling technological failure and disaster in the energy sector: A comparative analysis of historical energy accidents. *Energy, 90*, 2016–2027. https://doi.org/10.1016/j.energy.2015.07.043

Taparia, H. (2021, July 14). *The world may be better off without ESG investing (SSIR)*. https://ssir.org/articles/entry/the_world_may_be_better_off_without_esg_investing

Taylor, S. (2014, January 15). *Can new nuclear power plants be project financed? EPRG Working Paper 1118*. https://www.eprg.group.cam.ac.uk/eprg-1118/

Taylor, S. (2016a). *The fall and rise of nuclear power in Britain—A history*. UIT.

Taylor, S. (2016b, April 20). *The folly of Hinkley*. Prospect Magazine. https://www.prospectmagazine.co.uk/magazine/the-folly-of-hinkley-point-c

TTT. (2021). *FY2021-22-investor-report-for-the-period-ended-30-september.pdf*. https://www.tideway.london/media/5336/fy2021-22-investor-report-for-the-period-ended-30-september.pdf

UK Government. (2019, July 22). *Regulated asset base (RAB) model for nuclear*. GOV.UK. https://www.gov.uk/government/consultations/regulated-asset-base-rab-model-for-nuclear

UK Government. (2021). *UK government green financing framework*. https://assets.publishing.service.gov.uk/government/uploads/system/uploads/attachment_data/file/1002578/20210630_UK_Government_Green_Financing_Framework.pdf

US Energy Information Administration. (2021, July 2). *Nuclear explained*. https://www.eia.gov/energyexplained/nuclear/nuclear-power-plants.php

US EPA, O. (2019, February 11). *What is the Yucca Mountain repository?* [Overviews and Factsheets]. https://www.epa.gov/radiation/what-yucca-mountain-repository

US EPA, O. (2021, August 23). *Solar panel recycling* [Guidance (OMB)]. https://www.epa.gov/hw/solar-panel-recycling

Verbruggen, A., Laes, E., & Lemmens, S. (2014). Assessment of the actual sustainability of nuclear fission power. *Renewable and Sustainable Energy Reviews, 32*, 16–28. https://doi.org/10.1016/j.rser.2014.01.008

Wheeler, B. (2011, April 6). *Gen III reactor design. Power Engineering.* https://www.power-eng.com/nuclear/gen-iii-reactor-design/

World Nuclear Association. (n.d.-a). *Nuclear energy in Finland.* Finnish Nuclear Power—World Nuclear Association. Retrieved June 13, 2022, from https://world-nuclear.org/information-library/country-profiles/countries-a-f/finland.aspx

World Nuclear Association. (n.d.-b). *Nuclear power in China.* Retrieved June 13, 2022, from https://world-nuclear.org/information-library/country-profiles/countries-a-f/china-nuclear-power.aspx

World Nuclear Association. (n.d.-c). *Nuclear power in France.* French Nuclear Energy—World Nuclear Association. Retrieved June 13, 2022, from https://world-nuclear.org/information-library/country-profiles/countries-a-f/france.aspx

World Nuclear Association. (n.d.-d). *Nuclear power in Germany.* World Nuclear Association. Retrieved December 28, 2022, from https://world-nuclear.org/information-library/country-profiles/countries-g-n/germany.aspx

World Nuclear Association. (n.d.-e). *Nuclear power in India.* Indian Nuclear Energy—World Nuclear Association. Retrieved June 13, 2022, from https://world-nuclear.org/information-library/country-profiles/countries-g-n/india.aspx

World Nuclear Association. (n.d.-f). *World nuclear association.* Retrieved June 13, 2022, from https://world-nuclear.org/

World Bank. (2020). *Minerals for climate action the mineral intensity of the clean energy transition.* https://www.worldbank.org/en/topic/extractiveindustries/brief/climate-smart-mining-minerals-for-climate-action

World Bank. (2022, December). *Green bonds.* World Bank. https://treasury.worldbank.org/en/about/unit/treasury/ibrd/ibrd-green-bonds

World Nuclear News. (2022, March 21). *Extended operation of two Belgian reactors approved.* https://www.world-nuclear-news.org/Articles/Extended-operation-of-two-Belgian-reactors-approve

22
GREEN, GREENER, NOT GREEN ENOUGH?

Institutional Forces Driving the European Green Bond Market

Katrina Pichlmayer and Othmar M. Lehner

Introduction

In response to the urgent demand for regulatory measures to support sustainable finance, the European Commission released an action plan for financing sustainable growth in 2018. This strategy includes three themes: reorienting capital flows towards a sustainable economy, mainstreaming sustainability into risk management, and fostering transparency and long-termism (European Commission, 2018a). Particularly, green bonds have gained popularity and are recognised for their potential to contribute to filling the sustainable finance gap (Flammer, 2021). Green bonds are issued to raise capital for investments; however, their proceeds should be allocated to projects that benefit the environment. Since the first issuance of a green bond in 2007, the green bond market has grown rapidly (Tang & Zhang, 2020). In 2020, global green issuances reached USD 290 bn, resulting in USD 1.1 tn total green database (Harrison & Muething, 2021).

Green bonds have the potential to support the ecological transformation of the economy (Sangiorgi & Schopohl, 2021). Their sustainable impact is broadly discussed (Banga, 2019; Cochu et al., 2016; Immel et al., 2021; Russo et al., 2021), but such discussions often centre on the lack of uniform standards and definitions as well as the lack of obligatory frameworks that transparently guide green bond issuances (Cochu et al., 2016; Fatica et al., 2021). As a result, green bond issuers are often accused of pursuing greenwashing purposes (Cheong & Choi, 2020; Flammer, 2021). To overcome these barriers, the European Union (EU) is currently establishing the European Green Bond Standard (EUGBS). This voluntary standard is part of an action plan embedded in the European Green Deal for financing sustainable growth. The EUGBS aims to standardise the green bond market voluntarily and should hence address the trust barrier of greenwashing (European Commission, 2021a).

This chapter focuses on the European green bond market and elaborates on whether the EU and its institutional settings contribute or ultimately fail to grow a green bond market with an impactful contribution to the achievement of the Paris Agreement objectives. To gain an insight into the factors that influence green bond market development, institutional theory is used to look at coercive, mimetic and normative forces. Based on theoretical and empirical research, propositions are then brought forward.

Background on Green Bonds

Green Bonds

Definition of Green Bonds

Green bonds are in many ways similar to their conventional counterparts. It is a fixed-income instrument that raises debt capital and is repaid after a defined period, including interest. In contrast to conventional bonds, green bond proceeds are to be allocated to green projects (Fatica & Panzica, 2021; Flammer, 2021; Löffler et al., 2021; Tang & Zhang, 2020). The OECD (2015, p. 5) utilises the following definition for green bonds:

> A green bond is differentiated from a regular bond by being 'labelled', i.e. designated as 'green' by the issuer or another entity, whereby a commitment is made to use the proceeds of green bonds (i.e. the principal) in a transparent manner, and exclusively to finance or refinance 'green' projects, assets or business activities with an environmental benefit.

The definition published by the International Capital Market Association (ICMA) (2021, p. 3) agrees with the interpretation of the OECD: Green bonds are 'any type of bond instrument where the proceeds or an equivalent amount will be exclusively applied to finance or re-finance, in part or in full, new and/or existing eligible Green Projects'. The specific dedication of green bond proceeds to green projects differs from the SLB, which aims to finance general corporate purposes and contribute to a sustainable transformation by linking variables, such as the coupon rate, to the achievement of sustainability targets (ICMA, 2020).

According to Pham (2016) and Park (2019), labelled green bonds are specifically issued by entities to support green activities, such as a steel company that builds a wind park. In contrast, unlabelled green bonds are issued by organisations that conduct sustainable business activities, for example, solar energy companies. Hyun et al. (2021) supplement that labelled green bonds are commonly externally reviewed, marked with a green bond certificate or supported in their trustworthiness by a green bond rating.

Green Bond Market Development

Regarding green bond issuances based on the location of the issuers, Europe is the driving force to stimulate green bond market growth. In 2020, Europe accounted for 48% of the total issuances (Harrison & Muething, 2021), though it accounted for 58% of green bond issuances in 2019 (Almeida, 2020).

Subsuming issuer types that show governmental backgrounds, the public purse is the largest issuer of green bonds (Harrison & Muething, 2021). Private non-financial and financial corporates have experienced an over-proportional growth of issuances in recent years. (Almeida, 2020). In 2020, though, private financials and non-financials were confronted with incalculable market dynamics and therefore showed reluctance compared with prior years (Harrison & Muething, 2021).

The use of proceeds describes the utilisation of the collected green funds and constitutes the fundamental for evaluating green bond impacts (OECD, 2015). In 2020, 85% of proceeds gained from green bond issuances were deployed within the energy, transport and buildings sectors. The joint dominance of these three sectors had no significant change from 2014 to 2020, though shares within have changed. A decreasing trend in the energy sector can be observed, whereas the transport and buildings sectors experienced growing attention (Harrison & Muething,

2021). The World Bank analysis of the use of proceeds reveals a similar picture: 36% of funds were allocated to renewable energy and efficiency projects; 27% supported clean transportation; 15% aimed at funding agricultural projects; and 11% were apportioned to water management (World Bank, 2021).

Green Bond Frameworks and Regulations

Defining a green project may become difficult due to subjective assessments concerning sustainability. Thus, standardised characteristics must be defined to provide guidelines for selecting eligible projects (MacAskill et al., 2021). Consequently, voluntary frameworks, such as the GBP, and certification schemes, such as the CBS, were developed (Russo et al., 2021; Tang & Zhang, 2020). The focus on establishing statutory regulations has also increased recently to enhance the reliability and legitimacy of the green bond market (Sangiorgi & Schopohl, 2021; Sartzetakis, 2021).

GREEN BOND PRINCIPLES

A green bond can be labelled by applying the GBP, a framework compiled by ICMA. The guidelines aim to improve transparency by standardising the definition of green bonds. Through consistent disclosure specifications, the credibility of the green bond market should be strengthened (Cheong & Choi, 2020; Chiesa & Barua, 2019). The GBP contain four main principles. First, the bond proceeds must be allocated to green projects with distinct environmental benefits. Second, the issuer must transparently communicate the goals, the valuation process of the project and the risks related to the undertaking. Third, the process by which the management of the proceeds is led must be publicised to the investors. Fourth, issuers must report on the project, the assigned funds and the impacts annually. Material adjustments require information to investors within a narrow time frame. Third-party verification is recommended by ICMA, though not mandatory (ICMA, 2021).

CLIMATE BOND STANDARDS

By providing the CBS, the CBI aims at directing financial flows from conventional to green investments by enhancing trustworthiness. The CBS does not compete with the GBP but exhibits alignment with the GBP, the ASEAN Green Bond Standard and further global standards. The CBS builds on these standards and specifies requirements for the selection of eligible projects, the use and management of proceeds and reporting standards. Its guidelines are categorised into four parts: pre-issuance requirements, post-issuance requirements, project eligibility and certification under the CBS. A key component of the CBS is the provision of a uniform certification scheme that allows a flexible and effective assessment of green projects. In contrast to the GBP, the CBS requires compulsory third-party verification (Climate Bonds Initiative, 2019).

EUROPEAN GREEN BOND STANDARD

To achieve the Paris Agreement goals, the EU established the European Green Deal. The concretisation of financial measures is accomplished within the European taxonomy. The EUGBS is based on the taxonomy and constitutes a voluntary standard that can be applied by issuers globally. The standard adheres to existing frameworks but puts additional emphasis on investor protection and sustainability requirements. The standard should contribute to transparency and increase the trustworthiness of the green capital market.

The proposed framework contains four key elements. First, green bond proceeds must be allocated to environmentally supportive projects that are in line with the taxonomy. Second, detailed reporting on how proceeds are assigned is compulsory. Third, pre- and post-issuance third-party verifications to ensure compliance with the EUGBS and the taxonomy are demanded. Fourth, external reviewers are supervised by the European Securities Markets Authority to ensure high-quality reviews and increase investor protection (European Commission, 2021a).

Barriers to Green Bond Market Growth

Although green debt issuances have rapidly expanded during the last few years, the green financial market is still facing growth barriers. Banga (2019) divides these obstacles into institutional and market barriers. First, institutional barriers are geared towards a lack of knowledge on the implementation, monitoring and assessment of green projects. Moreover, as remarked by Obradovich and Zimmerman (2016), divergent government representatives' attitudes towards sustainable development hinder a trustworthy picture of the green bond market. Fatica et al. (2021) identify the absence of a uniform definition and standardised selection, assessment and reporting processes to depict a material barrier in market development. As existing standards are voluntary and differ in scope, their potential to fill this gap is insufficient. Cochu et al. (2016) also identified these barriers and categorised them into the supply side and demand side. Supply-side barriers include the (1) lack of projects that need financing, (2) insufficient methods to aggregate small projects, (3) lack of standards to identify suitable projects, (4) difficulties in receiving good credit ratings and (5) high (perception of) risk for green investment, whereas demand-side barriers include the (1) lack of green bond characterisation standards, (2) scarce information on green bond impact, (3) lack of mandatory disclosure from issuers, (4) high (perception of) risk for green investments and (5) chance of low-quality second opinions.

Sartzetakis (2021) regards the need for the further development of international guidelines to achieve credibility by reducing greenwashing risk. Nevertheless, cost awareness concerning the issuance, reporting and review of green bonds will be increasingly important to raise attractiveness among market participants. Moreover, enabling small and medium-sized companies to enter the market will be crucial. In its interim report on the planned EUGBS, the Technical Expert Group on Sustainable Finance (TEG, 2019) declares a current imbalance between rising investor demand and insufficient green bond supply. Following other scholars, TEG summarises the main reasons for this condition: (1) lack of a coherent benefit for green bond issuers, (2) issuers' concerns regarding reputational risks and diverging definitions, (3) complicated and potentially expensive review processes, (4) uncertainty on the selection of eligible projects and (5) vague monitoring processes.

Another constraint that may prevent the green bond market from scaling is greenwashing (Immel et al., 2021; Russo et al., 2021; Tuhkanen & Vulturius, 2020). Greenwashing can be defined as misleading stakeholders towards transmitting a distorted image of environmental behaviour by implementing flattering marketing strategies (Berrou et al., 2019). Flammer (2021, p. 500) describes greenwashing as 'the practice of making unsubstantiated or misleading claims about the company's environmental commitment'. Thus, green bonds are misused for sole marketing aims (Cheong & Choi, 2020). Therefore, greenwashing can limit green bond market development by reducing its credibility (Sangiorgi & Schopohl, 2021).

Current Green Bond Literature

Although the green bond market has emerged remarkably during the last decade, its market development maturity has remained in the nascent stage (Tolliver et al., 2020). The number of publications in the green finance research area has increased steadily from 2012 to 2019

(Akomea-Frimpong et al., 2021). This development essentially encourages green finance investments (Taghizadeh-Hesary & Yoshino, 2019). Green bond literature can be divided into different strands: green bond pricing, green bond impacts on the equity market and analyses of the factors that influence the supply side of the market. A brief overview of these strands of literature is provided below.

GREEN BOND PRICING

The first research category deals with the market pricing of green bonds in primary and secondary markets (Cheong & Choi, 2020; Fatica & Panzica, 2021). The literature has particularly focused on the 'greenium', which constitutes a price premium that investors agree to pay compared with conventional 'brown' bonds. The greenium theory argues that investors undertake large green investments in primary markets and accept financial trade-offs in the form of a lower yield. From a pro-environmental investor's perspective, this yield is compensated by offering returns in terms of environmental and societal benefits. In secondary markets, the greenium is reflected in price movements originating from balancing supply and demand (Agliardi & Agliardi, 2019; Cheong & Choi, 2020; Fatica et al., 2021; MacAskill et al., 2021; Russo et al., 2021; Tang & Zhang, 2020; Zerbib, 2019). These investigations have varying outcomes. Certain studies detect a negative premium (e.g. Zerbib, 2019; Gianfrate & Peri, 2019; Wang et al., 2020), confirming that green bonds are traded at a lower yield. Other examinations determine a positive price premium (e.g. Larcker & Watts, 2020; Bachelet et al., 2019). Other studies also provide controversial results, such as Tang and Zhang (2020) and Hachenberg and Schiereck (2018). A selection of studies will be presented subsequently.

STOCK MARKET REACTIONS TO GREEN BONDS

The second strand of green bond literature focuses on the impact of green bond issuances on the stock market. Flammer (2021) examined the stock market reaction after the announcement of green bond issuance and found a positive response. This finding is due to the transmission of a positive signal of the issuing entity to behave environmentally reasonably. Further analyses showed that issuing companies followingly improved their environmental performance. Therefore, Flammer (2021) disagreed with the greenwashing argument and views green bonds as a suitable instrument to mitigate climate change. Tang and Zhang (2020) confirmed that green bond issuance announcements positively influence public attention, expressed in rising Google search volumes. This situation consequently raises the number of potential investors. Wang et al. (2020) analysed reactions in the Chinese market context. On the announcement date, no significant abnormal returns could be ascertained. However, in the following days, abnormal positive stock market returns were noted. This phenomenon confirms that announcements of green bond issuances cause a more positive stock market reaction than those of conventional bonds. Therefore, the pro-environmental behaviour expressed through green bonds creates value for shareholders. Binti Ibrahim et al. (2017) noted an average abnormal return over a market return of 1.17% the day after the announcement. This positive reaction is due to the rising confidence of investors in the future performance of the corporation given their commitment to environmentally friendly behaviour. Binti Ibrahim et al. (2017) also documented a negative cumulative abnormal return over the market return the day before and the day of the announcement. This effect can be attributed to the increasing debt quota and consequently a rising probability of default by the company.

MOTIVATIONAL FACTORS TO PARTICIPATE IN THE GREEN BOND MARKET

The last strand of green bond literature analyses green bond and issuer characteristics that subsequently motivate or prevent the issuance of green bonds. The rapid growth of the market since the first green bond issuance is based on macroeconomic and institutional, which affect all bond markets and on individual drivers that are attributable to the green bond market only (Löffler et al., 2021).

Maltais and Nykvist (2020) determined that increasing the investor base, satisfying investors' expectations to behave environmentally conscious and lowering the cost of capital are key motivators to participate in the green bond market. In terms of financial incentives, the responders mainly referred to the aspiration of securing access to capital by approaching new investors and building trust with existing investors. Non-financial motives, such as reputational effects and legitimacy seeking, risk reduction, creation of new markets and operational efficiency, also play a crucial role (Hockerts, 2015). Another driver that boosts green bond market development is robust Nationally Determined Contributions, which prove commitment to the reduction of CO2 emissions and further efforts to mitigate climate change (Tolliver et al., 2020).

Consumers' and investors' environmental awareness (Agliardi & Agliardi, 2019) and increased competition among corporations essentially influence the decision of an issuer for a green bond (Bagnoli & Watts, 2020). Green bond issuances within a country largely depend on the business culture and attitude of financial institutions towards sustainability. Also, the presence of eligible green projects in the general bond market of a country constitutes a key factor in determining growth potential. Government and institutional focus on sustainability and strengthened impact-reporting activities of sustainable activities enhance information symmetry between investors and issuers and hence can boost the green bond market (Torvanger et al., 2021). According to an analysis of the Vietnamese green bond market, Tu et al. (2020) attribute higher relevance to infrastructural and economic factors of green bonds, such as legal frameworks, national monetary policy and official interest rates, than to cultural, social and political circumstances.

Green Bond Market from an Institutional Perspective

Maltais and Nykvist (2020) conclude that the endeavour to be recognised as legitimate in an institutional environment that strengthens climate protection may have played a crucial role in the Swedish green bond market growth. They find that the main reasons for the integration of sustainable practices are the need for securing legitimacy, demonstrating accountability to sustainable stakeholders and imitating similar organisations to counter uncertainty. Löffler et al. (2021) and Sangiorgi and Schopohl (2021) add that the institutional environment significantly differs at the country level. Institutional aspects positively influence green bond issuance volumes and additionally strengthen the macroeconomic environment. Therefore, direct and indirect positive impacts on green bond market development can be ascertained (Tolliver et al., 2020). This conclusion corresponds to the findings that policy and regulatory measures, such as globally accepted frameworks and national guidelines, coerce and motivate corporations to apply sustainable finance practices, consequently increasing the pressure on counterparts to imitate them (Ng, 2018).

Torvanger et al. (2021) explained the differences between the Swedish and Norwegian green bond market development. The authors emphasised institutional and legitimacy-seeking factors in their analysis. The essential keys for green bond market stimulation are the leadership role of the government and the active engagement of financial institutions in sustainability issues. Moreover, close collaboration between issuers and investors, expressed in transparent communication by means of standardized and reinforced sustainability reporting, is a prerequisite of market stimulation.. Assuming, that strong institutional pressures are present on green bond markets, green bond reporting should be similar due to the development towards homogeneity. Nevertheless, issuers significantly differ in their green bond reporting due to the variance in voluntary green bond frameworks (Tuhkanen & Vulturius, 2020). Banga (2019) evaluated the lack of unified green bond definitions and frameworks as an institutional barrier to market development. Furthermore, a knowledge gap in the specific requirements of green bond issuances is prevalent in emerging countries. Along with conflicting political attitudes towards environmentally friendly projects, the legitimacy of the green bond market in emerging countries is extremely limited.

Scholars acknowledge that institutional theory offers explanations for developments that are not based on the intention to increase efficiency and consequently return (Glover et al., 2014). Studies in the field of CSR (such as Acquah et al., 2021; Baah et al., 2021; Brammer et al., 2012) provide direction for developing a framework that reflects the individual requirements of the green bond market (Maltais & Nykvist, 2020).

Institutional Pressures on the European Green Bond Market

GREEN BONDS' ORGANISATIONAL FIELD

Figure 22.1 displays the organisational field in which green bond agents are embedded. Therefore, the narrow green bond market consists of issuers (supply) and investors (demand). These main characters are influenced by numerous secondary stakeholders.

COERCIVE PRESSURE ON GREEN BOND ISSUERS

Coercive isomorphism results from informal or formal pressure that affects organisations directly or indirectly and is exercised by stakeholders the organisation depends on (DiMaggio & Powell, 1983).

Although the green bond market in Europe is growing rapidly, it remains a voluntary market as growth is based on voluntary guidelines (Tuhkanen & Vulturius, 2020). By imposing

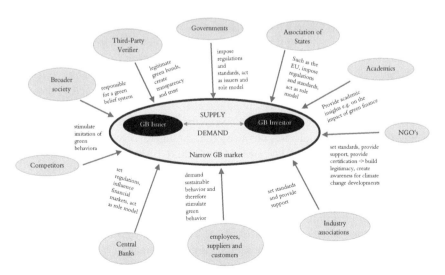

Figure 22.1 Green bond market's organisational field. Source: developed by the authors (based on CBI database and literature review).

regulations, governments and supranational organisations can impose compression on green bond market participants directly and indirectly (Baulkaran, 2019; Flammer, 2021; Sangiorgi & Schopohl, 2021; Tolliver et al., 2020; Weber & ElAlfy, 2019). Examples of a direct, formal exertion of pressure are mandatory green bond guidelines. Such guidelines compel issuers to apply a predetermined framework that regulates key aspects, such as the selection of eligible green projects, intervals and content of disclosures and third-party verification requirements. Mandatory guidelines enable standardisation and transparency and can therefore encounter the risk of greenwashing. Compulsory frameworks reduce the variety of applicable standards, establishing a minimum standard that investors can rely on (author's conclusion based on Banga, 2019; Fatica et al., 2021; Flammer, 2021). Climate change mitigation and adaptation occupy an important role in the EU. By introducing the European Green Deal in 2019, the EU has committed to a sustainable growth strategy for achieving climate neutrality by 2050. Annual investments of EUR 336 bn in energy systems (2.3% of GDP) will be necessary to achieve the intermediate objective by 2030. The EU acknowledges the potential of green bonds to contribute significantly to the closure of the financial gap. Therefore, it decided to establish a green bond standard, that should decrease the growth barriers of lacking transparency, standardisation and therefore credibility of the green bond market. The EUGBS is linked to the EU taxonomy, which provides a classification system for evaluating the sustainability of an activity (European Commission, 2021a). The European Central Bank (ECB) recognises the EUGBS proposal considering that a reliable framework is indispensable for achieving a sustainable transformation. Nevertheless, the voluntariness of the framework is scrutinised critically. Hence, the standard may fail to reduce complexity and increase the trustworthiness of the green bond market. Therefore, the ECB demands the EUGBS be mandatory for newly issued green bonds after a specific transition period (European Central Bank, 2021b). A mandatory EUGBS would create direct, formal coercive pressure on European green bond issuers. As a result, greenwashing risk could decrease, and, consequently, impactful green bond market growth could be strengthened.

Indirect, formal coercive pressure can occur due to tax incentives (Agliardi & Agliardi, 2019; Ng, 2018; Stoian & Iorgulescu, 2019). Tax incentives granted at the issuer or investor level can stimulate green investments, consequently fostering green bond market development. For example, the TEG introduced the acceleration depreciation scheme (ADS) as a form of tax incentive. ADS allows organisations for a higher depreciation of assets in the earlier years of their useful life, resulting in reduced tax liabilities during these years. Tax incentives could positively impact the number of taxonomy-aligned green projects. Although EU-based tax incentives can increase the number of green bond issuances by exerting coercive pressure, their implementation is complicated due to the required unanimity among member states (TEG, 2019). The taxation of unsustainable behaviour also depicts a crucial role in shifting towards an environmentally conscious economy. Thus, the EU emphasises the revision of the Energy Taxation Directive (ETD) and the creation of a Carbon Border Adjustment Mechanism (CBAM) (European Commission, n.d.). The ETD defines the minimum taxation rates for energy products, such as electricity and fuel. Its original version failed to encourage to switch to renewable energy. Therefore, a revision including additional sustainable energy technologies that widen the tax base by increasing the focus on the aviation and maritime industries is essential (KPMG, 2021a).

Based on the EU Emission Trading System (EU ETS), a market for emission rights, the CBAM shall reduce the risk of carbon leakage by substituting imports from countries with low carbon prices or less ambitious carbon reduction objectives. Additionally, the EU 'Fit for 55' policy package also includes initiatives such as a directive on the deployment of infrastructure based on alternative fuels, the definition of performance standards for cars and light commercial vehicles and the amendment of the Renewable Energy Directive (RED). RED constitutes a legal framework that defines standardised objectives and promotes investments in green energy systems to encourage the energy transition (KPMG, 2021b). In addition, the Corporate Sustainability Reporting Directive (CSRD) will considerably increase pressure on corporations to reflect their sustainable behaviour and encourage transformation. The revised directive should provide a broad range of publicly available information to stakeholders regarding environmental risks faced by companies and their impact on the people and environment. The directive is aimed at all large companies independent of stock exchange listings, provides detailed reporting standards and requires auditing. The directive will significantly increase transparency (European Parliament and Council, 2021).

Central banks also play an important role in advancing climate change mitigation (Akomea-Frimpong et al., 2021; Cheong & Choi, 2020; Ng, 2018; Sartzetakis, 2021), as they can exert formal, indirect pressure on green bond issuers. Central banks often perform a reluctant role in supporting change processes as they are expected to act objectively. Active endorsement of central banks is required to achieve sustainability objectives. For example, central banks can channel funds into green projects through quantitative easing programmes or the integration of environmental and social factors into the bank's investment strategy (Sartzetakis, 2021). The ECB has responded to these expectations by presenting an action plan on how to integrate sustainability measures into monetary policy initiatives. The focus will be laid on the integration of climate considerations into monetary policy frameworks, such as the collateral framework, and the integration of climate aspects into statistical modelling and risk assessment or disclosure requirements. Moreover, the decision on corporate sector asset purchases will consider environmental criteria (European Central Bank, 2021a).

Supplementary to pressure resulting from regulatory stakeholders, direct and informal coercive pressure can result from stakeholders that demand sustainable conscious behaviour, such as employees, suppliers and customers (Acquah et al., 2021; Russo et al., 2021). By downgrading or terminating business relationships, customers and suppliers can threaten a corporation's continuity. Employees can leave their employment in favour of a corporation that conforms to their understanding of appropriate operations. The examples above illustrate that these types of stakeholders are crucial to a corporation's long-term survival. Therefore, corporations need to align with the prevalent perception of legitimate behaviour among these stakeholder groups (Baah et al., 2021).

NORMATIVE PRESSURE ON GREEN BOND ISSUERS

Normative pressure is based on values, norms and beliefs embedded in an organisation's environment. These expectations of the 'right' behaviour are taken for granted in society (Fuenfschilling & Truffer, 2014). Thus, to gain legitimacy, organisations should behave according to this informal framework (Deephouse et al., 2016; Fernando & Lawrence, 2014; Glover et al., 2014; Scott, 2014).

The growing awareness of society and increasing pressure of stakeholders concerning environmental protection have created new behavioural requirements for organisations (Martín-de Castro et al., 2020). Relevant actors in shaping a normative environment include the public, media, trade unions, industry associations and NGOs (Chen et al., 2018).

Organisations that raise awareness for environmental transformation play a crucial role in creating supportive, normative conditions for green bond market growth. The IPCC was founded in 1988 by the World Meteorological Organization (WMO), and the UNEP and has currently 195 member countries. The organisation aims at providing scientific research on climate change and associated risks and recommends measures to counter negative developments. Therefore, the IPCC constitutes an important foundation and agent for global environmental strategies (IPCC, n.d.). The UNEP represents another market-shaping actor. By acting within the United Nations system, the organisation aims to set and communicate environmental objectives, elaborate solutions and support member states in implementing the recommended agenda (UNEP, n.d.). International conferences, such as the UN Climate Change Conference, also raise awareness concerning the importance of the topic. Governments that have signed the UNFCCC participate in this conference and discuss how climate change can collaboratively be addressed (United Nations, n.d.a). Moreover, the United Nations has elaborated 17 Sustainable Development Goals (SDG), including no poverty and affordable and clean energy, which constitute guidelines for future development (United Nations, n.d.b). The question of how to accomplish these objectives has drawn attention to the subject of green finance. As sustainable development requires substantial financial resources (Amidjaya & Widagdo, 2020; Sinha et al., 2021; Taghizadeh-Hesary & Yoshino, 2019), the mobilisation of private debt capital to fund green investments is particularly gaining importance (Maltais & Nykvist, 2020).

No uniform definition has been set for green bonds, their eligible projects or their disclosure requirements. Thus, market participants are commonly uncertain about the integrity of the green bond market. Issuers face serious reputational risks if they are accused of greenwashing (Cochu et al., 2016; Fatica & Panzica, 2021; Sartzetakis, 2021). Organisations such as ICMA or the CBI have responded to the call for developing standardised definitions and guidelines. By establishing the GBP, ICMA has published a voluntary framework for green bond issuances that enhances the green bond market's transparency and constitutes a quality assessment for issuances (Pham, 2016). The CBS, elaborated by the CBI, depicts a certification scheme that underlines the adherence to certain issuance criteria by green bond issuers and also pursues to improve credibility (Larcker & Watts, 2020). In addition to these global, voluntary frameworks, regional guidelines are progressively established, including the EUGBS of the TEG (MacAskill et al., 2021). As the European green bond market is characterised by voluntariness, such global and regional standards substantially put normative pressure on green bond issuers to obtain legitimacy. These guidelines form norms and values in green bond issuances and are therefore broadly accepted. However, market developments and the changing awareness of stakeholders can also influence values that consequently provoke the modification of existing standards (Monasterolo, Roventini, & Foxon, 2019).

Another prominent role in creating normative pressure is attributed to central banks and governments by conducting investment and issuance activities. Emphasising central banks' support for the green finance sector not only exerts coercive pressure on market participants but also significantly builds trust in the green bond market's credibility (Sartzetakis, 2021; Torvanger et al., 2021). The banks' support includes greening quantitative easing programmes and revising investment strategies. A visible commitment to sustainability contributes positively to the acceptance of the green debt market, consequently promoting green bond market growth through normative institutionalism (Cochu et al., 2016; Torvanger et al., 2021). Such commitment to sustainability is often expressed in governments' issuance activities.

MIMETIC PRESSURE ON GREEN BOND ISSUERS

Mimetic isomorphism primarily results from confrontation with uncertainty. To cope with uncertain situations, organisations may imitate their counterparts to conform with the disseminated understanding of legitimate behaviour and consequently safeguard their reputation and reduce risk (DiMaggio & Powell, 1983; Galaskiewicz & Wasserman, 1989).

Climate change and its consequences bear different risks that contribute to increasing uncertainty within the organisations' environment. If serious countermeasures are omitted, the impacts of climate change will rigorously affect global socioeconomic systems (Woetzel et al., 2020). Climate change risks are associated with financial risks including physical, transitional and liability risks. Physical risks are 'those risks that arise from the interaction of climate-related hazards with the vulnerability of exposure of human and natural systems' (Batten, Sowerbutts, & Tanaka, 2016, p. 5). Transitional risks result from the transformation to a low-carbon economy, such as rising energy costs. Liability risks arise from organisations' demand for compensation for climate-related damages from parties that are accused of being responsible (The Bank of England, 2015). Transitional risks impact the financial system, though they can be mitigated by instruments that focus on shifting capital from brown to green investments, such as green bonds (Batten et al., 2016).

The successful adoption of corporate environmental activities serves as a positive indicator to stakeholders. By mimicking competitors in introducing a similar environmental management system, organisations aim to attain the same affirmative esteem. Pursuing this strategy of 'being in the same boat' diminishes the perception of uncertainty (Hofer et al., 2012; Yang & Kang, 2020). According to Daddi et al. (2020), compared with coercive forces, mimetic and normative pressures more significantly influence organisations' decisions to adopt climate mitigation strategies. Green bonds provide the required capital for financing climate-supportive investments (Fatica & Panzica, 2021; Flammer, 2021). Therefore, green bond issuance can also be assumed to be influenced by mimetic pressures. The driving force to imitate successful competitors directly acts on organisations as green bonds transmit a credible signal to emphasise climate change mitigation. To avoid reputational disadvantages, corporations may follow their peers and issue green bonds to collect debt capital rather than classic debt instruments (Daddi et al., 2020; Hofer et al., 2012; Maltais & Nykvist, 2020; Russo et al., 2021; Wang et al., 2020). Moreover, mimetic pressures also impact other green bond market actors and their behaviour, indirectly leading to a mimicry-stimulating environment. Non-governmental standard-setters show similarities in their guidelines. Political regulators, such as the EU, also base their regulatory frameworks partly on established voluntary guidelines. This imitating behaviour leads to increasing homogeneity in the rules and recommendations on green bonds, thus strengthening uniformity among issuances (Sartzetakis, 2021). The mimetic pressure on green bond issuers also gains strength due to the advancing engagement of governments in sustainable transformation, specifically in green bond issuances (Banga, 2019; Torvanger et al., 2021). European governments, such as France, Germany, Sweden and the Netherlands, demonstrated their credible efforts to tackle climate change mitigation by issuing debut bonds or providing additional bonds in 2020 (Harrison & Muething, 2021). This action may act as a forerunner role to cope with future uncertainty and influence non-government issuers to mimic the changing issuing behaviour.

Empirical Findings

This section adopts both theoretical and empirical approaches in reflection. For a list of the underlying green bonds, please see Appendix A. The empirical part is divided into an analysis of green and SLB documentation. Along with theoretical outcomes, it enables the derivation of propositions.

Green Bond Data Review

Outcomes of Green and Sustainability-Linked Bond Data Review

USE OF PROCEEDS

The use of proceeds is described in the bond's prospectus and is also included in the bond's terms using brief remarks. The proceeds of usual and SLB are used to finance general corporate purposes (ICMA, 2020), whereas those of green bonds are allocated to green projects (Fatica & Panzica, 2021; Flammer, 2021; Löffler et al., 2021; Tang & Zhang, 2020). The use of proceeds is commonly defined in the prospectus and final terms according to the following scheme:

- The prospectus informs that the proceeds are used to finance general corporate purposes but can also be specifically dedicated to green purposes, if stated in the final terms. Regarding the green use of financial resources, it is referred to the issuer's green finance framework.

In total, 43 out of 44 issuers included a reference to their green finance or sustainability-linked finance framework in their prospectus or final terms and conditions. As the majority of issuers did not include the explicit use of proceeds in the bonds' prospectus or final terms and conditions, the referenced green finance framework should be regarded. Evidently, only a few issuers incorporate detailed projects in their frameworks. Rather, a general description frequently based on the SDG is commonly adopted. Figure 22.2 illustrates the distribution of bonds according to the analysis of the use of proceeds sections.

Further analysis showed that failure to invest green bonds' proceeds in eligible, green projects does not constitute an event of default nor trigger a step-up event that may increase the coupon or redemption basis. The exemplary relevant clarification section of Daimler's prospectus can primarily be found in the risk section.

> While it is the intention of the Issuers and the Guarantor to apply the proceeds of such Green Bonds specifically for a portfolio of eligible green projects (the 'Green Projects') as described in Daimler's Green Finance Framework, there can be no assurance that the relevant project(s) or use(s) (including those the subject of, or related to, any Green Projects) will be capable of being implemented in or substantially in such manner and/or in accordance with any timing schedule and that accordingly such proceeds will be totally or partially disbursed for such project(s) or use(s). Any such event or failure by the Issuer will not constitute an event of default under the terms and conditions of any Green Bond.
>
> *(Daimler AG, 2021, p. 40)*

RISK FACTORS OF GREEN BONDS

The disclosure of specific and material risk factors in the prospectus or another supplement aims to provide investors with the necessary information to make well-informed investment decisions (ESMA, 2019). Green bonds are exposed to the same financial risks as their conventional coun-

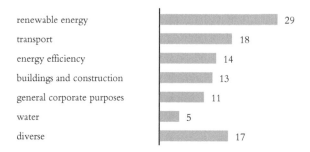

Figure 22.2 Use of proceeds analysis of data records. Source: developed by the authors.

terparts (Agliardi & Agliardi, 2019). This similarity is primarily due to the lack of enforceability of the green purpose (Forsbacka & Vulturius, 2019). Nevertheless, the risk of greenwashing is frequently mentioned along with green bonds (Immel et al., 2021; Russo et al., 2021; Tuhkanen & Vulturius, 2020). The risk of greenwashing is not priced in bond prices but has negative economic consequences in the long term for accused issuers (Forsbacka & Vulturius, 2019).

Moreover, scholars agree that the lack of a unified definition constitutes a limiting factor of the green bond market's legitimacy (Fatica & Panzica, 2021; Sartzetakis, 2021). This weakness is reflected in the green bond issuers' programme prospectus by including part of a section that illustrates the risks relating to green bond instruments. Thirty-nine out of 43 (for one GB, no prospectus could be found) issuers included a risk section about the instrument of green bonds or SLB in their prospectus. Three out of the remaining four issuers that did not include such a risk section are located outside Europe. Although the wording may differ between issuers, the content is similar. The main takeaways are:

- Neither a standardised legal definition nor a common market understanding of what constitutes a 'green' or 'sustainable' project is established. The understanding of these terms differs between individuals, resulting in conflicting interpretations between issuers and investors. Therefore, meeting the expectations of an investor concerning the greenness of the bond cannot be guaranteed. Additionally, an increasing number of the analysed bond issuers (17 out of 44) mention in the risk section the efforts of the EU to create a standardised framework for the definition of green projects. This development may indicate that expectations for the EU to set further regulatory steps are considered necessary for further market development.
- Although issuers tend to apply the proceeds to green projects according to their framework, no assurance is granted that these projects will be implemented according to their specific time frame. Therefore, the proceeds are not guaranteed to be totally or partially disbursed to green projects. A failure will neither constitute an event of default nor trigger a step-up condition.
- A green evaluation conducted by a third party is not part of the prospectus and should be incorporated into the decision-making process as a statement of opinion, not as a statement of fact. Due to a lack of a uniform evaluation process or certain rules, a second-party assessment cannot guarantee to reflect the real sustainable impact of the issuer and the instrument. Investors have no recourse to reviewers, and a negative evaluation or withdrawal of an evaluation will not constitute an event of default. However, the value of the instrument may be affected, which constitutes a risk for the green bond investor.
- A listing on a green segment of an exchange or inclusion in a green index is not guaranteed to meet investor expectations. Moreover, investors must be aware of the diverging admission criteria relevant to these marketplaces or indices. Issuers do not guarantee that such a listing will be obtained or maintained during the bond's lifetime.

This analysis focused on green bond documentation, in addition to a few SLBs. Risks related to the instrument of SLB are similar to those mentioned by green bond issuers. However, they are supplemented by risks related to the defined sustainability performance targets that need to be met to avoid a step-up event. These risks primarily refer to the potential inconsistency of the issuer's intention expressed in KPI with investor requirements and the failure to meet investor expectations after optional recalculations. Such a failure can be triggered by certain events.

The integration of risks related to the instrument of green bonds and SLB is reflected widely in issuers' prospectus. However, ESG risks were incorporated by only 27 out of 44 analysed documents. Nevertheless, the majority of these risk descriptions are limited to a minimum extent. EU disclosure efforts, such as the NFRD and Capital Requirements Regulation (European Banking Authority, 2022), and efforts to rework the prospectus regulation may lead to a change in prospectus design and contribute to addressing greenwashing by supporting the integration of material ESG risks (ESMA, 2022).

RATINGS, EXTERNAL REVIEWS AND REPORTING

Rating, external review and reporting standards provide transparency and verification. Therefore, they contribute to legitimacy creation within the field of green finance (European Commission, 2021a; Flammer, 2021; Hyun et al., 2021).

Thirty-four out of 44 analysed issuers included at least one credit rating in their green bond documentation. Thereof, six issuers remarked that the indicated rating represents the creditworthiness of the issuer, not of the specific bonds. Accordingly, 28 issuers possessed a bond credit rating; 25 issuers (23 bond ratings and two general credit ratings) quoted a second rating, conducted by a different agency; ten additional issuers also included a third bond rating; and one issuer disclosed a fourth rating.

Figure 22.3 presents the distribution of ratings among rating agencies and the rating results.

ESG ratings have gained increasing importance in the measurement of corporate sustainable development, though their validity and effectiveness are discussed controversially by scholars (Tan & Zhu, 2022). ESG ratings in green bond and SLB final terms were not found. Only 4 out of 44 issuers invoked ESG ratings in the associated prospectus, whereas three issuers mentioned that several ESG ratings could be found on the websites of diverse rating agencies.

The EU significantly emphasised the external review of green bonds in elaborating the EUGBS. A bond aligned with the EUGBS will have to undergo pre- and post-issuance review by registered verifiers, which have to comply with the standards of ESMA (European Commission, 2021a). All reviewed green bond frameworks were based on the GBP, except for one issuer. These principles recommend but do not compel issuers to undergo third-party verification (ICMA, 2021), though only one issuer decided not to undergo external review. Frameworks numbering 11, 11, 9 and 5 were reviewed by Cicero, ISS, Sustainalytics and Vigeo Eiris, respectively, whereas the remaining reviews were evenly distributed among nine other reviewers (some issuers show more than one review). The reviewed SLB frameworks are based on the SLB principles published by ICMA, except for one issuer. Those principles demand post-issuance verification and recommend pre-issuance external review (ICMA, 2020). Therefore, if voluntarily applied, these principles exhibit a more stringent character than their green counterparts. Figure 22.4 illustrates the distribution of the entire dataset to the reviewing agencies.

In its GBP, ICMA (2021) requests green bond issuers to report on the usage of proceeds at least annually until full allocation and recommends reporting on the impact generated.

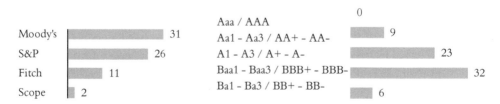

Figure 22.3 Distribution of data records among rating agencies and rating results. Source: developed by the authors.

Figure 22.4 Distribution of data records among third-party reviewers. Source: developed by the authors.

Qualitative and, where possible, quantitative key performance indicators that enable transparently tracking progress are suggested. Thirty-two green bond issuers provided information on intended reporting efforts. They all stated in their green bond frameworks to publish annual allocation reports. Thirty-one quoted to pursue annual impact reporting, and 28 thereof invoked applied qualitative and quantitative indicators in their frameworks. To illustrate how reporting intentions are stated in green finance frameworks, the relevant segment in Covivio's framework was selected:

> Covivio is committed to be as transparent as possible and has published a Sustainable Development Report annually since 2011, which includes the company's Green Bond report (also included in Covivio's annual Reference Document). The issuer will report on the allocation of net proceeds and associated impact metrics within one year from the issuance of the Green bond and annually thereafter until the proceeds have been fully allocated, and as necessary in the event of material development.
>
> *(Covivio, 2019, p. 7)*

Under the EUGBS, issuers are obliged to report annually on the allocation of proceeds to EU taxonomy-aligned projects. In contrast, impact reporting will be necessary only once during the bond's lifetime, though this element will also be mandatory (European Commission, 2021a). The obligatory character of impact reporting in the EUGBS may help to increase transparency and subsequently credibility of the green bond market (Filkova et al., 2019).

Concerning SLB, ICMA (2020) prompts issuers to report at least annually on the performance of the selected KPI to verify the impact and timing of progress relative to the set sustainability performance targets. Issuers also need to publish information that enables investors to monitor target-setting, sustainability strategy updates and ESG information relevant to monitoring KPI progress. The analysis of SLB frameworks shows that its reporting is more diverse than green bonds. The selected issuers include information about the impact of SLBs in their CSR, non-financial, ESG or other reporting documents. This variety in reporting may pose a difficulty for investors to monitor transparently the impact of their investments. To illustrate how reporting intentions are stated in green finance frameworks, the relevant segment in H&M Group's framework was selected:

> In order to provide investors and other stakeholders with adequate information about H&M Group's implementation of our sustainability strategy in general, the progress made on the KPIs, and the achievement or not of the SPTs set out in this Framework and in security specific documentation, H&M Group will provide relevant reporting. The reporting shall be made publicly available on an annual basis in a Sustainability-

Linked Bond Progress Report (SLB Progress Report). The SLB Progress Report shall be published on H&M Group's web page no later than 120 days after each calendar year-end, up to and including the Reporting End Date, which is the date falling 120 days post the Target Observation Date.

(H&M Group, 2021, p. 15)

GREEN TARGETS AND COVENANTS

Green bond proceeds shall be applied to finance green projects, which are often selected according to the criteria defined in the issuer's green finance framework (Fatica & Panzica, 2021; Flammer, 2021; Löffler et al., 2021).

The analysis of the sample showed that 13 out of 32 green bond issuers quoted general corporate sustainability targets in their green finance frameworks. Table 22.1 provides examples that reflect the broad variability in the accuracy and scope of the definition of sustainability targets.

The issuing entities did not state concrete objectives regarding their specific green bond, neither in the final terms, the prospectus nor the green finance framework. Target-setting is limited to the above-mentioned general sustainability targets. Therefore, issuers do not mandatorily achieve predefined impact variables by declaring binding consequences in the case of a failure, such as increased coupon rate or redemption basis.

In contrast, the analysis of SLB contract documents showed such binding elements. The proceeds of such bonds are allocated to general corporate purposes. This finding was also proved in the sample, with only one exemption. However, the bonds' conditions are linked to one or more measurable sustainable targets (ICMA, 2020). Based on the analysed sample, failure to accomplish these goals on an agreed-on observation date lead to either of the following:

- a relative increase in the coupon rate for the residual period
- a relative increase in the final redemption
- payment of a relative or absolute premium

In the selected sample, the occurrence of these events mainly depends on the reduction of scope 1 and 2 greenhouse gas emissions. Moreover, certain issuers also set targets for the collection and use of recycled plastics and other materials or the application of innovative medical therapies to patients. These step-up events are part of the final terms and hence constitute binding contract elements. The process of target-setting is described in the green finance framework, which often incorporates a separate segment for SLBs.

Propositions

The following paragraphs discuss the combination of the theoretical and empirical approaches and consequently allow for the derivation of propositions.

Under the umbrella of the European Green Deal, the European financial market is strongly influenced by the objective of the EU to foster sustainable behaviour and increase its transparency on such behaviour and ESG risks (European Commission, 2018b; European Commission, 2021a; Maltais & Nykvist, 2020). Approaches of the EU that will compel additional organisations to disclose sustainability issues, such as the CSRD (European Parliament and Council, 2021), and measures that support sustainable behaviour, such as tax incentives, the RED and

CBAM, target to support a sustainable transformation by simultaneously creating transparency to tackle the risk of greenwashing (Agliardi & Agliardi, 2019; European Commission, n.d.; KPMG, 2021b; TEG, 2019). These measures may influence indirectly the green bond market development coercively (Agliardi & Agliardi, 2019; Flammer, 2021; Ng, 2018; Sangiorgi & Schopohl, 2021). Regulatory mechanisms that mandatorily, directly influence green bond issuances are currently not discussed, although the ECB would recommend an obligatory EUGBS after a certain transition period (European Central Bank, 2021b). At present, the EUGBS is intended to constitute a voluntary standard that aims at increasing transparency and credibility, consequently ensuring the efficacy of the green bond instrument (European Commission, 2021a). However, the success of the EUGBS largely depends on the legitimacy it will gain among market participants (Monasterolo et al., 2019). The analysis of green bond documents showed that coercive elements in green bond contracts are rare. External regulatory forces stemming from the EU prospectus regulation trigger the integration of risks relative to the green bond instrument (European Parliament and Council, 2017). However, the inclusion of the issuers' ESG risks is brief and not provided by all issuers. Coercive 'green' elements within the contract that would oblige issuers to achieve ESG targets or that lead to consequences in the case of misallocation are not found. In contrast, green bond documents explicitly state that any failure to allocate the proceeds to eligible green projects will not constitute an event of default. These contract elements can be due to the lack of a uniform definition of 'green', missing standardised approaches to ESG risk reporting and impact measurement (Fatica & Panzica, 2021; Sartzetakis, 2021; Williams & Robinson, 2020). The EU taxonomy and other regulatory initiatives may diminish these insecurities and lead to amending the contract design. A standardised categorisation can be a prerequisite to include additional green undertakings or complement existent regulations. The EU intends to provide such a standard by demanding alignment with the EU taxonomy. However, such undertakings increase the issuers' risk and therefore negatively impact investors. As a result, the green bond market growth may be stagnated (Forsbacka & Vulturius, 2019). In contrast, the smaller market of SLBs has shown sustainability target-bound elements. Hence, SLBs transmit a more performative impression than their green counterparts, though their proceeds are used for general corporate purposes. SLB issuers define certain freedom in the recalculation of targets for certain material events, the defined, binding targets put along negative consequences for issuers in the case of failure. Therefore, SLBs have a more mandatory, coercive character than their green counterparts. Green bonds, in contrast, are primarily strongly built on the normative pillar of trustworthiness (Vulturius, Maltais, & Forsbacka, 2022). Accordingly, the following proposition is derived:

I) *The lack of direct coercive pressure on green bond issuers, such as an obligative EUGBS or green undertakings, incentivises issuers to use green bonds as a greenwashing instrument and consequently decreases the instrument's impact*

Mimetic behaviour often results from confrontation with uncertainty. Unforeseen risks, unplanned events and consequently necessary decisions that need to be made without a predefined pathway create an insecure environment (DiMaggio & Powell, 1983; Galaskiewicz & Wasserman, 1989). Humanity nowadays is facing the serious consequences of climate change as well as corporations. The changing natural environment and risks occurring from the adaption to altered framework conditions create precariousness (Woetzel et al., 2020). Organisations that face such an uncertain situation tend to imitate the behaviour of other appreciated organisations (DiMaggio & Powell, 1983). Although this approach may lead to an unreflecting forgery, it transmits the feeling of reducing uncertainty relative to those imitated counterparts (Hofer et al., 2012; Yang & Kang, 2020). Green bond issuance can also be assumed to be influenced by mimetic pressures. The driving force to imitate successful competitors directly motivates organisations as green bonds strongly indicate climate change mitigation. To avoid reputational damage, corporations may follow their peers and issue green bonds to collect debt capital, as this publicly proves the commitment to sustainable objectives (Daddi et al., 2020; Hofer et al., 2012; Maltais & Nykvist, 2020; Russo et al., 2021; Wang et al., 2020). The analysis of green bond documents also revealed mimetic tendencies, which can be attributed to the lack of regulated contract design. Green bond contracts are similar to conventional bond agreements, except for the intention to use the proceeds to finance green projects. This intention to use the proceeds is primarily disclosed with reference to a green bond framework and not as part of the binding agreement. Target-based binding clauses and other green undertakings are not available. Accordingly, issuers significantly emphasise risks arising from the nature of the green bond instrument and preclude investor claims if the requirements of being 'green' are not met. As the green bond contract design has no clear regulation, these resembling elaborations may be attributable to the mimetic behaviour resulting from uncertainty within green bond regulation. The theoretical and empirical analyses concerning mimetic tendencies allow for the derivation of the following proposition:

II) *By providing uniform definitions and regulations, the EU will manage to reduce insecurity for green bond issuers and lead to a higher impact on sustainable transformation achieved through green bonds*

Values, norms and beliefs create a framework of adequate comportment. To gain legitimacy, behaviour according to these principles is necessary (Deephouse et al., 2016; Fernando & Lawrence, 2014; Glover et al., 2014; Scott, 2014). Organisations exist in a societal environment that incorporates the sustainable behaviour they are expected to portray (Martín-de Castro et al., 2020; Yang & Wu, 2016). This development is underpinned and promoted by international organisations, such as the IPCC and UNEP, which inform about climate developments and prompt and support action (IPCC, n.d.; UNEP, n.d.). In green bond market development, organisations such as ICMA or CBI have responded to concerns regarding the non-existence of uniform definitions of terms such as 'green' or 'sustainability' or the lack of legislation concerning green bond issuances (Fatica & Panzica, 2021; Larcker & Watts, 2020; MacAskill et al., 2021; Pham & Nguyen, 2021; Sartzetakis, 2021). The GBP, established by ICMA, play an important role in green bond issuances as the analysis of green bond documentation shows. Except for one issuer, all green bond frameworks were built on the GBP framework, which proves the appreciation of these guidelines and indicates a strongly normative structured green bond environment. The EUGBS adapts the GBP but pursues a more stringent approach to reporting and reviewing procedures (European Commission, 2021a). As the foreseen European 'golden standard' will also have a voluntary character, alignment of issuances will depend on how future green bond issuers assess the potential of the standard to increase transparency, credibility and consequently legitimacy. Moreover, the societal acknowledgement of standards adopted by the EU, such as the EU taxonomy, will also be rated according to their conformity with manifested values, norms and beliefs, hence influencing the societal acceptance of the approach (Tolbert & Zucker, 1999). The green bond document analysis shows that contract design is built on conventional bonds by adding a reference or parts of the green bond framework that aim to provide an overview of the green use of proceeds. In contrast to SLB, committing to green undertakings or target-based objectives that lead to consequences in the case of failure is not included in green bond terms (Vulturius et al., 2022). This aspect underlines that an impactful green bond market development heavily relies on the normative pillars of trustworthiness and credibility. Strengthened reporting requirements and external verification, as emphasised in the EUGBS, aim to increase transparency in the green bond market (European Commission, 2021a). However, whether voluntary frameworks possess sufficient shaping power to counter the risk of greenwashing cannot be determined (Larcker & Watts, 2020). Accordingly, the following proposition has been derived:

III) *Despite its voluntariness, the EUGBS will create an environment that promotes performative green bond market growth by focusing on providing transparency.*

Conclusions

Coercive, normative and mimetic forces have impacts on green bond market participants. Illustrating these governing factors from the issuers' perspective enables drawing conclusions about the key forces that influence the issuing behaviour. An actual-state analysis built on institutional isomorphism demonstrates the interaction between these forces and their capacity to induce institutional change by increasing the contribution of the green bond market to a low-carbon transition. Subsequently, recommendations that induce the reduction of greenwashing risk and consequently ensure performativity in the green bond market can be derived. In the following paragraphs, the propositions and bond documentation analysis will be conflated with the outcomes of the expert interviews. The propositions have been assigned to an institutional force to illustrate the varying degrees of influence on the green bond market.

The green bond market's current voluntary nature is expressed in the lack of mandatory elements in green bond contract design (Forsbacka & Vulturius, 2019; Vulturius et al., 2022). Green bond proceeds are intended to finance green projects (Fatica & Panzica, 2021; Flammer, 2021; Löffler et al., 2021). Green projects are predominantly approached in green bond agreements referencing a green bond framework based on the GBP. Concrete project descriptions in green bond contracts are not available, and green bond frameworks also predominantly include general investment frameworks rather than specific project specifications and aligned targets (bond documentation analysis result). Green bond issuers are obliged to include risks associated with green bonds in their issuance prospectus (European Parliament and Council, 2017), though ESG risks are not incorporated by all issuers and often to a limited extent. ESG risks are highly interrelated to the topic of sustainability. Moreover, green undertakings that compel issuers to achieve certain project-specific or overall sustainable transitional targets are also not part of green bond documentation, in contrast to SLB (Forsbacka & Vulturius, 2019; ICMA, 2020; ICMA, 2021; Vulturius et al., 2022). Policymakers, such as the EU, increasingly emphasise strengthening environmental regulation by establishing a sustainability reporting directive (European Parliament and Council, 2021) and hence enhance coercive pressure on corporations and green bond issuers as a result of the mandatory character of these initiatives. However, the analysis shows that the coercive character of green bond regulation remains ambiguous despite the above-mentioned situation. This voluntariness results from the bottom-up, market-driven development of the green bond market and constitutes a driving force of market growth. Creating stricter regulations for green bond issuances may deter issuers to enter the market. Although it could prevent black sheep market actors from participating, the overall impact of the green bond market may be reduced. Green undertakings represent another coercive instrument in bond documentation (DiMaggio & Powell, 1983; Forsbacka & Vulturius, 2019). Target-based financing is perceived positively, but the target-setting process involves several complex risks verified by market participants. Green covenants, as in SLB, are not required to be added to green bond contracts as these instruments tackle the sustainability topic from a different perspective. In contrast to coercive pressure generated through mandatory regulation or self-obliging green undertakings, investor pressure plays an important role in the green bond market (Maltais & Nykvist, 2020; Torvanger et al., 2021). Investors can directly influence corporates' issuing behaviour by demanding sobriety proven through adherence to standards. Therefore, guidelines receive a mandatory character by being demanded by investors and thus can be significantly influenced by them (outcomes from bond documentation analysis and interviews).

By establishing the EUGBS, the EU can decrease ambiguity in the definition of green finance and foster transparency. Strict third-verification requirements can increase the credibility of the green bond market by reducing greenwashing risk. These positive contributions may increase investor demand for EUGBS-labelled products and therefore enhance coercive pressures from investors. Despite the positive impact, whether the EUGBS can boost impactful market growth cannot be determined, as its strictness may prevent issuers from participating in the market, which will lead to less impact. Furthermore, critical political decisions on regulation design can decrease the legitimacy of the standard and hence its impact on green bond market development. Although the EUGBS focuses on dealing with the current green bond market weaknesses, the topic of strategic alignment is underexplored, though it is important to ensure an impactful green bond market. To reach the agreed-on environmental targets, it is viewed essentially to focus on the sustainable transformation that often does not allow black-and-white thinking. These transitional processes should be emphasised, rather than the final state that is either green or brown, to smooth the path towards a sustainable future. Corporations should be supported in these processes by providing them with green finance tools that can unfold their impact when based on strategic alignment. To boost a low-carbon transition, the rising amounts of green funds must be channelled into the right projects and redirecting is warranted, rather than solely achieving additionality. Therefore, institutional forces should be utilised to set the necessary frameworks and push issuers in the right direction. The analysis of isomorphic influences on green bond issuing and the derived recommendation in this section can be applied by future researchers and policymakers to guide impactful green bond market growth and hence contribute to the necessary ecological transition.

Acknowledgement

This research was financially supported by the EU Horizon programme TC4BE – 101082057 – GAP-101082057 on Pathways for BioDiversity. The European Commission's support for the production of this publication does not constitute an endorsement of the contents, which reflects the views only of the authors, and the Commission cannot be held responsible for any use which may be made of the information contained therein.

References

Acquah, I. S. K., Essel, D., Baah, C., Agyabeng-Mensah, Y., & Afum, E. (2021). Investigating the efficacy of isomorphic pressures on the adoption of green manufacturing practices and its influence on organizational legitimacy and financial performance. *Journal of Manufacturing Technology Management, 32*(7), 1399–1420.

Agliardi, E., & Agliardi, R. (2019). Financing environmentally-sustainable projects with green bonds. *Environment and Development Economics*, 24(6), 608–623.

Akomea-Frimpong, I., Adeabah, D., Ofosu, D., & Tenakwah, E. J. (2021). A review of studies on green finance of banks, research gaps and future directions. *Journal of Sustainable Finance and Investment*, 12, 1–24.

Almeida, M. (2020). *Global green bond state of the market 2019*. Climate Bonds Inititative.

Amidjaya, P. G., & Widagdo, A. K. (2020). Sustainability reporting in Indonesian listed banks. *Journal of Applied Accounting Research*, 21(2), 231–247.

Baah, C., Agyabeng-Mensah, Y., Afum, E., & Mncwango, M. S. (2021). Do green legitimacy and regulatory stakeholder demands stimulate corporate social and environmental responsibilities, environmental and financial performance? Evidence from an emerging economy. *Management of Environmental Quality: An International Journal*, 32(4), 787–803.

Bachelet, M. J., Becchetti, L., & Manfredonia, S. (2019). The green bonds premium puzzle: The role of issuer characteristics and third-party verification. *Sustainability*, 11(4), 1–22.

Bagnoli, M., & Watts, S. G. (2020). On the corporate use of green bonds. *Journal of Economics and Management Strategy*, 29(1), 187–209.

Banga, J. (2019). The green bond market: A potential source of climate finance for developing countries. *Journal of Sustainable Finance and Investment*, 9(1), 17–32.

Batten, S., Sowerbutts, R., & Tanaka, M. (2016). *Let's talk about the weather: The impact of climate change on central banks*. Bank of England.

Baulkaran, V. (2019). Stock market reaction to green bond issuance. *Journal of Asset Management*, 20(5), 331–340.

Berrou, R., Dessertine, P., & Migliorelli, M. (2019). An overview of green finance. In P. Dessertine, M. Migliorelli (Eds.), *Palgrave studies in impact finance: The rise of green finance in Europe, opportunities and challenges for issuers, investors and marketplaces* (pp. 3–29). Springer International Publishing.

Binti Ibrahim, S. A., Mohd Roslen, S. N., & Sin Yee, L. (2017). Green bond and shareholders' wealth: A multi-country event study. *International Journal of Globalisation and Small Business*, 9(1), 61–69.

Brammer, S., Jackson, G., & Matten, D. (2012). Corporate social responsibility and institutional theory: New perspectives on private governance. *Socio-Economic Review*, 10(1), 3–28.

Chen, X., Yi, N., Zhang, L., & Li, D. (2018). Does institutional pressure foster corporate green innovation? Evidence from China's top 100 companies. *Journal of Cleaner Production*, 188, 304–311.

Cheong, C., & Choi, J. (2020). Green bonds: A survey. *Journal of Derivatives and Quantitative Studies*, 28(4), 175–189.

Chiesa, M., & Barua, S. (2019). The surge of impact borrowing: The magnitude and determinants of green bond supply and its heterogeneity across markets. *Journal of Sustainable Finance and Investment*, 9(2), 138–161.

Climate Bonds Initiative. (2019). *Climate bond standard: Version 3.0*. Climate Bonds Initiative, London. https://www.climatebonds.net/files/files/climate-bonds-standard-v3-20191210.pdf

Cochu, A., Glenting, C., Hogg, D., Georgiev, I., Skolina, J., Eisinger, F. et al. (2016). *Study on the potential of green bond finance for resource-efficient investments*. European Commission.

Covivio. (2019). *Covivio green bond framework*. Covivio.

Daddi, T., Bleischwitz, R., Todaro, N. M., Gusmerotti, N. M., & de Giacomo, M. R. (2020). The influence of institutional pressures on climate mitigation and adaptation strategies. *Journal of Cleaner Production*, 244, 1–9.

Daimler, A. G. (2021). *Daimler prospectus of EUR 70,000,000,000 euro medium term note programme*. Daimler A.G.

Deephouse, D. L., Newburry, W., & Soleimani, A. (2016). The effects of institutional development and national culture on cross-national differences in corporate reputation. *Journal of World Business*, 51(3), 463–473.

DiMaggio, P., & Powell, W. W. (1983). The iron cage revisited: Institutional isomorphism and collective rationality in organizational fields. *Journal of Economic Sociology*, 11(1), 34–56.

ESMA. (2019). *Guidelines on risk factors under prospectus regulation*. ESMA (European Securities and Markets Authority).

ESMA. (2022). *Sustainable finance roadmap 2022–2024*. ESMA (European Securities and Markets Authority).

European Banking Authority. (2022). *Final draft implementing technical standards on prudential disclosures on ESG risks in accordance with article, 449a*. CRR.

European Central Bank. (2021a). *ECB presents action plan to include climate change considerations in its monetary policy strategy*. European Central Bank. Retrieved July 19, 2022, from https://www.ecb.europa.eu/press/pr/date/2021/html/ecb.pr210708_1~f104919225.en.html

European Central Bank. (2021b). *Opinion of the European central bank of 5 November 2021 on a proposal for a regulation on European green bonds (CON/2021/30)*.

European Commission. (2018a). *Renewed sustainable finance strategy and implementation of the action plan on financing sustainable growth*. European Commission. Retrieved July 18, 2022, from https://ec.europa.eu/info/publications/sustainable-finance-renewed-strategy_en

European Commission. (2018b). *Technical expert group on sustainable finance (TEG)*. European Commission. Retrieved July 18, 2022, from https://ec.europa.eu/info/publications/sustainable-finance-technical-expert-group_en

European Commission. (2021a). Proposal for a regulation of the European parliament and of the council on European green bonds: 2021/0191.

European Commission. (n.d.). *European green deal: What role can taxation play?* European Commission. Retrieved July 19, 2022, from https://ec.europa.eu/taxation_customs/commission-priorities-2019-24-and-taxation/european-green-deal-what-role-can-taxation-play_en

European Parliament and Council. (2017). Regulation (EU) 2017/1129 of the European parliament and of the council of 14 June 2017 on the prospectus to be published when securities are offered to the public or admitted to trading on a regulated market, and repealing directive 2003/71/EC: 2017/1129.

European Parliament and Council. (2021). Proposal for a directive of the European parliament and of the council amending directive 2013/34/EU, directive 2004/109/EC, directive 2006/43/EC and regulation (EU) no 537/2014, as regards corporate sustainability reporting COM/2021/189 final: 2021/0104.

Fatica, S., & Panzica, R. (2021). Green bonds as a tool against climate change? *Business Strategy and the Environment, 30*(5), 2688–2701.

Fatica, S., Panzica, R., & Rancan, M. (2021). The pricing of green bonds: Are financial institutions special? *Journal of Financial Stability, 54*, 1–20.

Fernando, S., & Lawrence, S. (2014). A theoretical framework for CSR practices: Integrating legitimacy theory, stakeholder theory and institutional theory. *Journal of Theoretical Accounting, 10*(1), 149–178.

Filkova, M., Almeida, M., Tukiainen, K., & Sette, P. (2019). *Post-issuance reporting in the green bond market*. CBI.

Flammer, C. (2021). Corporate green bonds. *Journal of Financial Economics, 142*(2), 499–516.

Forsbacka, K., & Vulturius, G. (2019). A legal analysis of terms and conditions for green bonds: Focus on the financial markets in the Nordics. *Europarättslig Tidskrift, 3*, 397–442.

Fuenfschilling, L., & Truffer, B. (2014). The structuration of socio-technical regimes—Conceptual foundations from institutional theory. *Research Policy, 43*(4), 772–791.

Galaskiewicz, J., & Wasserman, S. (1989). Mimetic processes within an interorganizational field: An empirical test. *Administrative Science Quarterly, 34*(3), 454.

Gianfrate, G., & Peri, M. (2019). The green advantage: Exploring the convenience of issuing green bonds. *Journal of Cleaner Production, 219*, 127–135.

Glover, J. L., Champion, D., Daniels, K. J., & Dainty, A. (2014). An institutional theory perspective on sustainable practices across the dairy supply chain. *International Journal of Production Economics, 152*, 102–111.

H&M Group. (2021). *H&M group: Sustainability-linked bond framework*. H&M Group.

Hachenberg, B., & Schiereck, D. (2018). Are green bonds priced differently from conventional bonds? *Journal of Asset Management, 19*(6), 371–383.

Harrison, C., & Muething, L. (2021). *Sustainable debt global state of the market 2020*. Climate Bonds Inititative.

Hockerts, K. (2015). A cognitive perspective on the business case for corporate sustainability. *Business Strategy and the Environment, 24*(2), 102–122.

Hofer, C., Cantor, D. E., & Dai, J. (2012). The competitive determinants of a firm's environmental management activities: Evidence from US manufacturing industries. *Journal of Operations Management, 30*(1–2), 69–84.

Hyun, S., Park, D., & Tian, S. (2021). Pricing of green labeling: A comparison of labeled and unlabeled green bonds. *Finance Research Letters, 41*, 1–5.

ICMA. (2020). *Sustainability-linked bond principles: Voluntary process guidelines*. ICMA (International Capital Market Association). Paris. https://www.icmagroup.org/assets/documents/Regulatory/Green-Bonds/June-2020/Sustainability-Linked-Bond-Principles-June-2020-171120.pdf

ICMA. (2021). *Green bond principles: Voluntary process of guidelines for issuing green bonds*. ICMA (International Capital Market Association).

Immel, M., Hachenberg, B., Kiesel, F., & Schiereck, D. (2021). Green bonds: Shades of green and brown. *Journal of Asset Management*, *22*(2), 96–109.
IPCC. (n.d.). *About the IPCC*. IPCC. Retrieved July 19, 2022, from https://www.ipcc.ch/about/.
KPMG. (2021a). *Energy taxation directive*. KPMG, London. https://assets.kpmg.com/content/dam/kpmg/xx/pdf/2021/09/energy-taxation-directive.pdf
KPMG. (2021b). *European green deal policy guide: Focus on 'fit for 55 package'*. KPMG.
Larcker, D. F., & Watts, E. M. (2020). Where's the greenium? *Journal of Accounting and Economics*, *69*(2–3), 1–26.
Löffler, K. U., Petreski, A., & Stephan, A. (2021). Drivers of green bond issuance and new evidence on the "greenium". *Eurasian Economic Review*, *11*(1), 1–24.
MacAskill, S., Roca, E., Liu, B., Stewart, R. A., & Sahin, O. (2021). Is there a green premium in the green bond market? Systematic literature review revealing premium determinants. *Journal of Cleaner Production*, *280*, 1–12.
Maltais, A., & Nykvist, B. (2020). Understanding the role of green bonds in advancing sustainability. *Journal of Sustainable Finance and Investment*, 1–20.
Martín-de Castro, G., Amores-Salvadó, J., Navas-López, J. E., & Balarezo-Núñez, R. M. (2020). Corporate environmental reputation: Exploring its definitional landscape. *Business Ethics: A European Review*, *29*(1), 130–142.
Monasterolo, I., Roventini, A., & Foxon, T. J. (2019). Uncertainty of climate policies and implications for economics and finance: An evolutionary economics approach. *Ecological Economics*, *163*, 177–182.
Ng, A. W. (2018). From sustainability accounting to a green financing system: Institutional legitimacy and market heterogeneity in a global financial centre. *Journal of Cleaner Production*, *195*, 585–592.
Obradovich, N., & Zimmerman, B. (2016). African voters indicate lack of support for climate change policies. *Environmental Science and Policy*, *66*, 292–298.
OECD. (2015). *Green bonds: Mobilising the dept capital markets for a low-carbon transition*. OECD Publishing, Paris. https://www.oecd.org/environment/cc/Green%20bonds%20PP%20%5Bf3%5D%20%5Blr%5D.pdf
Park, S. K. (2019). Green bonds and beyond. In B. Sjåfjell & C. M. Bruner (Eds.), *The Cambridge handbook of corporate law, corporate governance and sustainability* (pp. 596–610). Cambridge University Press.
Pham, L. (2016). Is it risky to go green? A volatility analysis of the green bond market. *Journal of Sustainable Finance and Investment*, *6*(4), 263–291.
Pham, L., & Nguyen, C. P. (2021). How do stock, oil, and economic policy uncertainty influence the green bond market? *Finance Research Letters*, 45, 102128.
Russo, A., Mariani, M., & Caragnano, A. (2021). Exploring the determinants of green bond issuance: Going beyond the long-lasting debate on performance consequences. *Business Strategy and the Environment*, *30*(1), 38–59.
Sangiorgi, I., & Schopohl, L. (2021). Why do institutional investors buy green bonds: Evidence from a survey of European asset managers. *International Review of Financial Analysis*, *75*, 1–21.
Sartzetakis, E. S. (2021). Green bonds as an instrument to finance low carbon transition. *Economic Change and Restructuring*, *54*(3), 755–779.
Scott, W. R. (2014). *Institutions and organizations: Ideas, interests and identities*. Sage.
Sinha, A., Mishra, S., Sharif, A., & Yarovaya, L. (2021). Does green financing help to improve environmental & social responsibility? Designing SDG framework through advanced quantile modelling. *Journal of Environmental Management*, *292*, 1–41.
Stoian, A., & Iorgulescu, F. (2019). Sustainable capital market. In M. Zioło & B. S. Sergi (Eds.), *Palgrave studies in impact finance: Financing sustainable development, key challenges and prospects* (pp. 193–226). Cham: Palgrave Macmillan.
Taghizadeh-Hesary, F., & Yoshino, N. (2019). The way to induce private participation in green finance and investment. *Finance Research Letters*, *31*, 98–103.
Tan, Y., & Zhu, Z. (2022). The effect of ESG rating events on corporate green innovation in China: The mediating role of financial constraints and managers' environmental awareness. *Technology in Society*, *68*, 101906.
Tang, D. Y., & Zhang, Y. (2020). Do shareholders benefit from green bonds? *Journal of Corporate Finance*, *61*, 1–18.
TEG. (2019). *Report of the technical expert group (TEG) subgroup on green bond standard: Proposal for an EU green bond standard*. TEG (EU Technical Expert Grop on Sustainable Finance), Brussels.

The Bank of England. (2015). *The impact of climate change on the UK insurance sector: A climate change adaptation report by the prudential regulation authority*. PRA (Prudential Regulation Authority) and Bank of England, London.

Tolbert, P. S., & Zucker, L. G. (1999). The institutionalization of institutional theory. In Stewart R. Clegg & C. Hardy (Eds), *Studying organization: Theory & method* (pp. 169–184). SAGE Publications Ltd.

Tolliver, C., Keeley, A. R., & Managi, S. (2020). Drivers of green bond market growth: The importance of nationally determined contributions to the Paris agreement and implications for sustainability. *Journal of Cleaner Production, 244*, 1–16.

Torvanger, A., Maltais, A., & Marginean, I. (2021). Green bonds in Sweden and Norway: What are the success factors? *Journal of Cleaner Production, 324*, 1–12.

Tu, C. A., Rasoulinezhad, E., & Sarker, T. (2020). Investigating solutions for the development of a green bond market: Evidence from analytic hierarchy process. *Finance Research Letters, 34*, 1–5.

Tuhkanen, H., & Vulturius, G. (2020). Are green bonds funding the transition? Investigating the link between companies' climate targets and green debt financing. *Journal of Sustainable Finance and Investment, 12*, 1–23.

UNEP. (n.d.). *About UN environment programme*. UNEP. Retrieved July 19, 2022, from https://www.unep.org/about-un-environment

United Nations. (n.d.a). *COP26: Together for our planet*. United Nations. Retrieved July 19, 2022, from https://www.un.org/en/climatechange/cop26

United Nations. (n.d.b). *The 17 goals*. United Nations. Retrieved July 19, 2022, from https://sdgs.un.org/goals

Vulturius, G., Maltais, A., & Forsbacka, K. (2022). Sustainability-linked bonds – Their potential to promote issuers' transition to net-zero emissions and future research directions. *Journal of Sustainable Finance and Investment*, 1–12.

Wang, J., Chen, X., Li, X., Yu, J., & Zhong, R. (2020). The market reaction to green bond issuance: Evidence from China. *Pacific-Basin Finance Journal, 60*, 1–19.

Weber, O., & ElAlfy, A. (2019). The development of green finance by sector. In P. Dessertine & M. Migliorelli (Eds.), *Palgrave studies in impact finance. The rise of green finance in Europe. Opportunities and challenges for issuers, investors and marketplaces* (pp. 53–78). Springer International Publishing.

Williams, S., & Robinson, J. (2020). Measuring sustainability: An evaluation framework for sustainability transition experiments. *Environmental Science and Policy, 103*, 58–66.

Woetzel, J., Pinner, D., Samandari, H., Engel, H., Krishnan, M., Boland, B., & Powis, C. (2020). *Climate risk and response: Physical hazards and socioeconomic impacts*. McKinsey Global Institute.

World Bank. (2021). *The world bank impact report: Sustainable development bonds & green bonds*. World Bank, Washington.

Yang, M. G., & Kang, M. (2020). An integrated framework of mimetic pressures, quality and environmental management, and firm performances. *Production Planning and Control, 31*(9), 709–722.

Yang, Y.-K., & Wu, S.-L. (2016). In search of the right fusion recipe: The role of legitimacy in building a social enterprise model. *Business Ethics: A European Review, 25*(3), 327–343.

Zerbib, O. D. (2019). The effect of pro-environmental preferences on bond prices: Evidence from green bonds. *Journal of Banking and Finance, 98*, 39–60.

Appendix

List of Green and Sustainability-Linked Bonds Used in This Study

Table 22.1 provides Green bond and SLB data for review.

Issuer	Example
TenneT Holding B.V.	TenneT has divided its sustainability strategy into three categories: people, planet and profit. Where possible, measurable KPIs have been defined, such as achieving 22% female management hires by 2023 (people), being climate-neutral by 2025 (planet) or achieving a return on capital that exceeds the regulatory determined return on capital (profit) (TenneT Holding B.V., 2020).
Vasakronan	Vasakronan aims to certify 100% of new construction and renovation projects with LEED Platinum. Existing buildings should be certified with LEED Gold. The corporation does not set a concrete time frame (Vasakronan, 2018).

Source: Developed by the authors.

23
THE HIDDEN COSTS OF IMPACT MEASUREMENT

Sean Geobey and Tatianna Brierley

Introduction

When should impact be measured? It is often taken as axiomatic that an impact investment's social and ecological impacts are to be measured, but what is to be measured, why, and for whom are often open questions. Alongside this, the costs of measuring impact often go unacknowledged though operationally they can often be quite substantive. Without measurement, understanding impact becomes an educated guess at best or an exercise in greenwashing. At worst, the resources that could be going towards making an impact are allocated towards data collection and reporting that is of dubious value. We posit that an ethical approach to impact measurement for investing is one that takes into account the economic, social, and environmental costs of that measurement.

To do so, this chapter presents a framework for evaluating when a particular metric or set of metrics should be adopted to monitor an impact investment. The starting point for this framework is centered around two key concepts: the first is that metrics are only beneficial when they have a material impact on an actor's decisions, and the second is that the collection of metrics is always costly. The benefits and costs of metrics are then taken to fall heterogeneously on three broad stakeholder groups: funders, which includes both financiers expecting a financial return and grantors who do not have the same expectations; agencies who produce goods or services expected to have a social impact, often but not always through the sale of these goods and services; and beneficiaries who are expected to receive positive benefits from the goods or services produced by the agency, including but not limited to consumers who purchase the agency's goods and services. As an illustrative example, a set of metrics drawn from the housing sector is used to illustrate the role of impact measurement as a site for the analysis of power in impact investing.

The core research question here asks: *when do the benefits of impact measurement exceed their costs?* Extending this further it is also important to ask: *for whom do the benefits of measurement exceed its costs?* These are fundamental questions for the use of measurement in impact investment. Not only does the answer help address the standing issue in this space of whether or not these investments do any good, but also extends that to ask the corollary question of whether or not these investments *actually* do harm. When does knowing about the impact of an investment undermine the impact of that investment?

To answer these questions, this chapter clarifies that measurements must provide net benefits to key stakeholders to be considered useful metrics. The benefits of measurement come from their material usefulness in decision-making (Lehner et al., 2022) where the relevant decisions involve resources substantial enough to cover the cost of measurement, for which we draw on the concept of bounded rationality (Simon, 1972). However, this is not a straightforward process, as different key stakeholder groups broadly categorized as funders, agencies, and beneficiaries, will have different perceptions of materiality for any particular metric and will take on different burdens attached to the collection of data. Impact investing in housing will be introduced as an illustrative example to demonstrate these heterogeneous interests and how they create a space for complex and often conflictual interactions between key stakeholders. From this, we suggest future research in the impact investing space that can be explored using this framework.

What is Impact Measurement?

In this section, key literature discussing the purpose of impact measurement is outlined. Impact measurement is approached as a tool that is used by different stakeholder groups with overlapping and occasionally conflicting interests rather than as an objective abstraction. The use of metrics by funders, agencies, and beneficiaries is highlighted with a lens focused on their material uses in decision-making and the costs of impact measurement emphasized. These then serve as the foundational pieces for an evaluative framework for the measurement of impact.

The concept of impact measurement has been employed through several different impact measurement approaches including social accounting (Nicholls, 2009), shared value (Porter & Kramer, 2019), social value (Auerswald, 2009; Santos, 2012), social impact assessment (Esteves et al., 2012), or social return or social return on investment (Emerson & Cabaj, 2000; Nicholls et al., 2012). Although each is different, they all attempt to capture the social and environmental value of a project that cannot be typically captured in traditional business performance measures (Bagnoli & Megali, 2009; Emerson, 2003; Nielsen et al., 2021) such as a simple return on investment model (Jahera & Lloyd, 1992). Specific metrics can be developed on an investment-by-investment basis or taken from a set of existing metrics such as the Global Impact Investing Network's (GIIN) Impact Reporting and Investment Standards (ISIS) Measurement Catalog. Implicit in most of these frameworks is that measurement is conducted primarily for funders to determine whether the investments meet their intended non-financial goals, but funders are not the only relevant stakeholders in an impact investment project, and accountability is not the only use of measurement.

Materiality with Heterogeneous Stakeholders

Measuring the results of any project is critical to understanding if intended results match intended goals (Porter & Kramer, 2019), and the absence of measurement processes may lead to the misrepresentation of an investment's impact on its intended beneficiaries (Rawhouser et al., 2017). Beyond strict accountability, measurement ties into learning within a complex social or ecological system, where impact investors can better understand how these systems operate and identify new investment opportunities (Geobey et al., 2012). These complex problem domains are difficult to understand and exploration through experimentation can provide an effective means of better understanding systems (1982). Moreover, once a clear metric or set of impact metrics has been identified, there is a role for metrics in rebalancing impact investment portfolios to make more efficient use of available funds (Geobey & Callahan, 2017).

To make the best use of metrics, the degree to which they will actually be used to make decisions that could change investment fund flows is key. Lehner et al. (2022) apply the concept of materiality to impact measurement in helping understand stakeholder perspective on materiality and how these perspectives can impact the understanding of impact measurement. Materiality can be understood as the degree to which a measure is expected to have an impact on how decisions are made within an organization (Bernstein, 1967). The concept of materiality can then be applied to each decision-making stakeholder tied into an investment (Lehner et al., 2022; Green & Cheng, 2019), though the impact on decision-making does not have to be the same for each. Tied to materiality is the expected value of differing impact decisions that measurements could seed. A measurement that will decide whether 100% of one thousand dollars in funding will be provided or not would have less potential impact than a measurement that will decide whether there will be a 1% increase in funding to a project worth one billion dollars. That said, this centers materiality from a funders' perspective when funders are just one broad class of stakeholders, and here the material interests of agencies and beneficiaries will also be outlined.

Funders and financiers may use impact measurements to compare and assess potential and existing investments and ensure alignment with broader strategic goals. A funder or financier may want to evaluate anticipated or executed results to understand whether the investment was an efficient use of funding (Schiff et al., 2016). Impact measurement can be useful in determining what impacts are anticipated versus those that occur (Bagnoli & Megali, 2009), analyzing the efficiency of funding allocation (Maier et al., 2015; Barman, 2007), improving program results (Esteves et al., 2012), and helping to communicate such benefits to their stakeholders (Hall et al., 2015). Funders can use measured results to direct future funds towards particularly promising investments whose impact they are hoping to scale, or towards new investments that focus on high-impact opportunity spaces that their measurements have helped them identify.

Agencies use impact measurements strategically to revise their programming for greater impact (Berry & Aurum, 2006). When the focus of a project falls outside of the scope of traditional economic measurement tools, such as return on investment analysis (Phillips, 1996), different tools may be employed to understand project results such as social return on investment (Emerson & Cabaj, 2000) or social accounting (Nicholls, 2009). Agencies themselves view measurement as important for benchmarking progress against anticipated results and building a deeper understanding of long-term dynamics in their impact space that can then be used to redesign their programs (Barraket & Yousefpour, 2014).

Social purpose organizations may have an additional need to measure impact. If impact is not being assessed, an organization may assume they are doing well and overlook the negative impacts of a product (Jepson, 2005; Maas & Liket, 2011). Due to the nature of social purpose organizations operating with a goal or mission to achieve additional social or environmental benefits, measuring such impact is an important way of verifying alignment with organizational values (Porter & Kramer, 2019). This has been noted in the literature as the 'measuring impact and mission measurement paradox' where an organization is more focused on growth and is disconnected from the true value of the organization (Ormiston & Seymour, 2011). Material measures for agencies could lead to major program redesigns, changes in staffing, and even cutting entire program areas.

Beneficiaries and consumers can use impact measurements to make more informed decisions on potential programs, services, and products. Impact measurement can help organizations align internal strategy with the shifting priorities of consumers, reflecting a potential desire for increasing environmental and social responsibility (Menichini & Rosati, 2014). A beneficiary of a program or service may use such indicators to determine which program or service to use or promote. For example, a beneficiary may compare available programs to determine which would be more beneficial for the individual, which further promotes their services. For agencies that operate as social enterprises selling goods or services, the measured impact may itself be a key part of their marketing (Rausch et al., 2021). Providing accurate impact measurement information can empower consumer-beneficiaries to make more informed decisions (Akhavannasab et al., 2018). Additionally, to the extent that the measures are of interest to other key stakeholders such as funders and policymakers, savvy beneficiaries may be in a position to use data to self-advocate for changes in policies or services. This self-advocacy can include approaches such as lobbying agencies for changes in their product or service offerings, switching to another service provider, or organizing consumer boycotts.

Measurement Costs and Bounded Rationality

Balanced against the expected benefits of a material measure are the costs of collecting and maintaining data; otherwise, the inclination of impact measurement design would be towards attempting to measure any and all impacts since even marginal issues would have a nonzero chance of being material. Bounded rationality is the idea that actors can only make rational decisions based on the information that is available to them and identifying and collecting this information is costly (Simon, 1972). Applying bounded rationality to impact measurement may provide insight into the cost of selecting measures and evaluating the relative benefits of acquiring additional information. However, the implications of treating measurement as costly are underdeveloped in the impact measurement literature at the moment. An extension of bounded rationality is the recognition that it is impossible to capture all impacts of an investment decision, making measure prioritization a key step in design. Yet this is rarely a specific consideration in SROI studies of housing (Miller et al., 2018; Kraatz & Thomson, 2017; Fulgence Drabo et al., 2021).

The direct cost of impact measurement may fall on the funder, including functions such as data collection, data analysis, and data storage, though many of the costs fall upon agencies. Additional costs may arise from incorporating inaccurate information into funding decisions, suggesting that additional costs come from verifying information coming from other sources (Harris & Tayler, 2019). Evolving technology has helped to decrease the cost of data collection to some extent, such as online platforms providing lower-cost alternatives to in-person interviews (Namey et al., 2020), and cloud storage reducing data storage and management costs (Waibel et al., 2017).

Agencies providing services are often well-positioned to collect on-the-ground data on social impact as well as internal information about resource allocation. For example, an agency will have costs associated with the development of a survey, recruiting participants, facilitating survey responses, analyzing the data, and reporting such data to stakeholders when undertaking a qualitative survey of their intended beneficiaries. In addition to the direct costs of data collection, there are opportunity costs as resources that would have otherwise been expended on mission-aligned activities are diverted to measurement, and the need to hire or develop staff capacity for impact reporting.

Most often overlooked are costs that fall upon intended beneficiaries as these are often amorphous costs like time to respond to information requests, discomfort, or trauma from answering difficult inquiries, and risks associated with confidential information being held insecurely (Cumming, 2009). Additionally, when reporting data back to intended beneficiaries, there are potential costs associated with information overload. For example, providing too much unfiltered information to consumers can lead to decision-making challenges when they try to make ethical purchases (Chen et al., 2009).

General and Differing Costs of Impact Measurement

This section of the chapter will outline the core elements of the framework for measurement selection developed in this chapter. The benefits of impact measurement, focused on their materiality in decision-making for funders, agencies, and beneficiaries, will be outlined as will the costs associated with measurement. Net benefits of a measurement for each stakeholder group will be introduced as a concept, as will the expected consequences when these net benefits differ between funders, agencies, and beneficiaries. The implications of having different interests between these core stakeholder groups will be outlined, including the practical difficulty of administering compensation between stakeholder groups to achieve Pareto-improving efficient solutions.

Bounded rationality forms the core of the framework (Simon, 1972), with the core interpretation of that model being that all information collection that is incorporated into a decision-maker's view of the world is costly to collect (Larson & Sandholm, 2004). Once a measure is adopted, it is assumed that this measure is shared at zero marginal cost between all key stakeholder groups. However, the materiality of this measure and the expected benefit from such materiality will differ between stakeholders, as will the costs of measurement. Consequently, the net benefit to funders, agencies, and beneficiaries will differ. In some cases, the net benefit of a measure for all will be positive, for some the net benefit will be positive for two stakeholders, for some the net benefit will be positive for only one stakeholder, and many measures will have no net benefit for any stakeholder. As a result, all three of these stakeholder groups can be represented with a three-circle Venn diagram (see Figure 23.1 – Net benefits of impact measurements to funders, agencies, and beneficiaries).

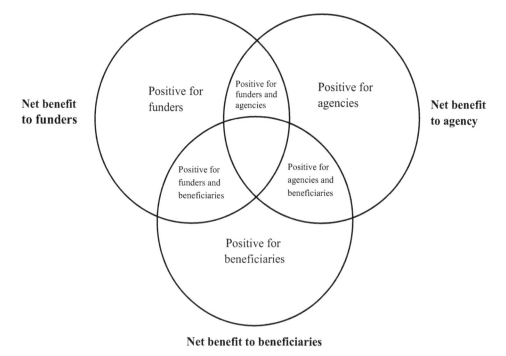

Figure 23.1 Net benefits of impact measurement to funders, agencies, and beneficiaries. Venn diagram displaying the connection between impact measurement benefits to funders, agencies, and beneficiaries.

Finding an optimal selection of metrics in complex problem domains is impossible in practice as an analytical method, but satisficing outcomes are still possible. It would be expected that each stakeholder would be pushing for measures that are of net benefit to them individually, though such a push is not limitless. Having a highly material measure for a stakeholder included in the set of measures makes it less likely that an additional measure will be as materially important. One can expect for any stakeholder that diminishing returns may likely occur from additional measures, and alongside these additional measures would be expected to have increasing marginal costs. For a single stakeholder, this means that there would be a limit to the number of measures they would include if they were designing the measurement systems themselves. However, the ideal measure selection for one stakeholder will enable additional material benefits and impose additional costs on the other stakeholder groups, and while some of those measures may be a net positive for one or both other stakeholder groups, some of those measures will be net negative in their impact on one or both other stakeholder groups.

The result is that measure selection is a site for negotiation. A simple model for measure selection would be to include measures that are a net positive for all three stakeholder groups, and this is a good starting point. However, the measures that are a net benefit to only one or two stakeholder groups are much more contentious. Where those net benefits are high and the net negatives relatively low for the stakeholder groups, it seems straightforward to adopt those measures. Indeed, a case could certainly be made in those circumstances where the benefits may be high enough for the stakeholders that benefit from a measure to compensate those who do not, and if this is possible, it can be an effective solution. However, in practice, both the benefits and the costs of measurement are abstract. It may be difficult to estimate a reasonable compensation plan, and some beneficiaries may be impossible to financially compensate, such as an environmental beneficiary like a wetland. Moreover, it is often the case that the stakeholder for whom a measure is a net negative already faces large systematic barriers, such as non-profit agencies running on thin budgets or beneficiaries from marginalized populations. Even if the net benefit to one stakeholder may be high, if that stakeholder also tends to wield a great deal of power regularly, the centering of their interests in impact measurement may simply compound already existing inequitable distributions of power in a system.

There are also a set of measures where clear communication can avoid risks to one of the key parties involved. There may be a wide range of measures for which one party finds the measure materially important and low cost to collect, while the other party has an ambiguous relationship to the measure. This data may still be collected though it is important for the party with the stronger material interest to ensure that risks are properly managed so that the data does not impose an undue burden on the other. There is also a range of measures where one party faces low materiality and high data collection costs while the other party has an ambiguous relationship with it. While it seems like it would be easy to determine that such data would not be collected, this is not so straightforward. If the party with an ambiguous relationship to the data has a naïve view of the role of metrics, they may overestimate their own material interest in the measure and believe it will impact their decisions when it is unlikely to do so, or they may dismiss the costs that the data collection will impose on their partner. Robust consultation that treats other stakeholders as true partners is critical to mitigating reasonable risks.

Housing Metrics

This section will take the framework developed in this chapter and apply to it impact measurement in the housing sector using an illustrative selection of measures. Background to the housing issue will be provided, focused but not limited to affordable housing as an initial focus on housing studies conducted in Canada. From this, four different measures will be mapped onto the framework: utility cost, household violence rates, indoor air quality, and neighborhood opinion on affordable housing development to demonstrate differing levels of materiality and measurement costs associated with each measure.

To explore the measures in housing as a starting point, SROI analyses of housing are used. It is unclear whether the cost of measurement was considered when determining which metrics of any studies in the housing space were examined (CMHC, 2018; Miller & Offrim, 2016; CHA, 2014), as cost of measurement is not in itself an explicit consideration within the SROI framework (Nicholls, 2009). However, agencies providing housing often face significant resource constraints (Zon et al., 2014; Pomeroy, 2017), so the consideration of measurement costs is of importance to these stakeholders. Figure 23.2 – Net benefits of impact measures in housing – outlines the expected net benefits for funders, agencies, and beneficiaries for utility costs, household violence rates, air quality, and neighborhood opinion on affordable housing development.

Measurements that are net positive for all stakeholder groups are expected to be the easiest ones to adopt. A good example of these metrics is *utility costs* in a housing development (CMHC, 2018). Since utilities have to be paid by tenant-beneficiaries or housing provider agencies anyway, collection costs are minimal since this is administrative information that must be captured anyway. For funders with an interest in environmental sustainability, decreased utility costs usually correlate closely with reduced carbon emissions, and for both funders and housing agencies, lower utility costs improve profitability or allow more funds to be used on programmatic features of a housing program. For the tenants who are also the primary beneficiaries of a housing program, information about utility costs allows them to change their individual tenant behavior

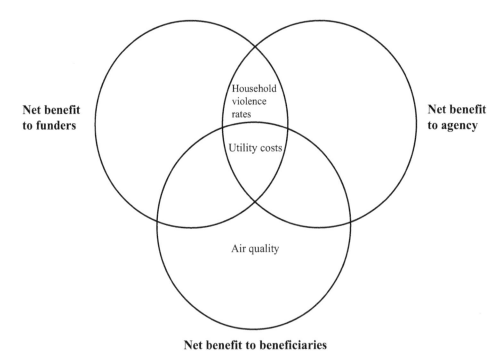

Figure 23.2 Net benefits of impact measures in housing. Venn diagram displaying the net benefits of impact measurement in housing. Benefits are displayed relative to funders, agencies, and beneficiaries.

to reduce utility usage and, when the tenants pay some or all of their utilities directly, put the tenants on stronger financial footing by reducing their own usage.

Changes in *household violence rates* are a more contentious measure, particularly for tenant-beneficiaries. Funders and agencies may both have programmatic goals tied to reducing household violence and the cost of data collection is relatively low for them, likely consisting of surveys or interviews with tenants (CMHC, 2018). However, the cost to the tenant-beneficiary is likely quite significant. If a tenant had experienced domestic violence, they may be retraumatized by having such questions asked. These questions would be low in materiality to the tenant, as it is not relevant for them to disclose information to the agency providing housing since they themselves will be aware of their own experience of domestic violence. Indeed, the disclosure of this information can often be tied to increased perceived or real risk. For example, in a household with small children experiencing domestic violence, a survey respondent may be afraid of alerting child and family service agencies who could remove their children from the household, or in a household where someone has fled an abusive partner the collection of personally identifiable information tied to their home address could put them in danger if data security is compromised. As a result, not only may there be real net costs to tenant-beneficiaries in collecting this information, but the quality of data may also be quite poor because of these costs, as tenants disclose inaccurate information to mitigate their concerns.

In contrast to reduced household violence measures which may be a net negative for beneficiaries but a net positive for funders and agencies, in many circumstances indoor *air quality* may be a measure of net benefit to tenant-beneficiaries and a net negative to funders and agencies. Monitoring indoor air quality requires regular testing at an additional cost to agencies or funders, as would investments to improve indoor air quality such as improved window coverings and clean air ducts (Puri & Smith, 2019), which they may not feel are worth the investment. However, for tenant-beneficiaries living in these housing units, this may be extremely relevant. If indoor air quality is poor, they may be less comfortable in their home. Tenant-beneficiaries may use this information to lobby the housing agency for improvements which if done publicly could raise reputational risks for both agencies and funders. Indeed, if air quality is low enough, they may use this information to justify rent strikes or legal action.

A final measure is included that would often be a net negative to funders, agencies, and beneficiaries, which is neighborhood public opinion of housing development. This is not administrative data that can be collected at a low additional cost, so interviews, surveys, or focus groups would have to be conducted outside the development itself and paid for in time or money by funders or agencies. While there may be some benefit to the funder or agency in trying to make a case to the community about a housing project or to structure it in ways that would mitigate negative public opinion, it is likely that both have already made the decision to acquire or develop a property so any material changes would be minor. However, even trying to collect this data may help neighbors who oppose a housing project mobilize their networks in more formalized opposition to the project. Alongside these, there is little a tenant-beneficiary can use in this data, but mobilized opposition may lead to increased stigma within the community towards tenants of a housing development. Unless the housing project is specifically focused on integration with nearby communities, it is unlikely that this would be measured unless mandated by a public funder or regulator.

Discussion and Future Research

The framework outlined in this chapter focuses on measurement selection when there are at least three different stakeholder groups – funders, agencies, and beneficiaries – who place different values on the materiality of each possible measure and take on different costs from engaging in measurement. This was then applied to the housing sector to demonstrate how some measures are a net positive benefit to all stakeholder groups, such as utility usage, some would be seen as negative by all stakeholder groups such as neighborhood opinion on housing developments, and others are sites of contestation such as indoor air quality and household violence. This section will revisit the implications of having heterogeneous stakeholders with differing interests in impact measures, identify the limitations of this chapter, and, with this, suggest directions for future research.

Bringing different costs associated with metrics into the framework necessarily highlights the role of power in these relationships. Yet power itself does not map onto these relationships in a straightforward way. While it may be reasonable to assume that the general relationship is one in which the funders have more power than agencies and that agencies in turn have more power than beneficiaries, this need not be true. The bringing of resources to an impact investing arrangement is an important source of power, but it is not the only source of power. Agencies with a strong reputation or specialized expertise may be in a strong position to determine terms with funders; for example, high-profile academic research may be in a position to propose impact measures to their funders. Alongside this, a group of beneficiaries that is well-organized outside the channels supported by the funder or agency will be in a much stronger position to self-advocate, as might be the case for a well-organized trade union.

Even this is more complex than it first appears, as this relatively simple framework flattened differences within each stakeholder group. One funder may have a light impact investment orientation and is primarily concerned about financial returns, another may find impact a primary driver, and a third may feel that impact is their primary driver but has different goals than the second investor. In general, the more diverse the interests within any stakeholder group, the more difficult the process of organizing to achieve their goals. Generally, this implies that beneficiaries are often in the weakest position in a traditional philanthropic-charitable program, though this is not universally true.

Furthermore, the framework as outlined is static rather than dynamic. Measure selection at the beginning of an engagement is based more heavily on expectations of both material benefits and costs than observed costs and benefits. As a project shifts from expected outcomes to actual outcomes, it is worth revisiting measures on a regular basis to discontinue measures that are net negative in their impact and add newly identified net positive measures in consultation with key stakeholder groups. Changing measures over time is the operationalization of collective learning that occurs between different stakeholder groups. Yet the key limitation here is that there is often a sunk cost involved in selecting and establishing measurements, which leads to measurement lock-in. A useful heuristic is to rely on relatively few initial measures, possibly with an initial focus on narrative storytelling, until strong net positive measures have been identified.

This leads to a broader set of challenges in trying to optimize measure selection. Even in a static model, it can be difficult to manage the trade-offs between stakeholder groups. Some costs associated with measurement can be estimated, and those who benefit most can and should compensate the stakeholder groups that see little or negative net benefit. For example, a funder could cover the costs of staff time and data storage for an agency collecting survey data as well as providing payment for survey respondents. However, this compensation approach has its limits when the costs and benefits are more abstract. Going back to the example of reduced household violence as a measure, it is difficult to estimate the cost of holding sensitive data that could put a respondent in physical danger. In consultation with stakeholder groups, a useful heuristic here is to identify those measures which are highly costly to a stakeholder early and screen them out, particularly when the negative impacts are ones that may be detrimental to the project's mission.

Better understanding materiality and costs necessarily involves checking assumptions with an investment's key stakeholders.

Applied research to build out practical tools for measure selection would support impact investors in measure selection. Clarity on what measures are material in different sectors is useful and aligns with metric standardization work such as the GIIN's IRIS approach. However, this needs to be coupled with a heuristic such as a decision tree that can be used by funders when developing a set of measures and high-level estimates of the likely fixed and variable costs associated with different impact measures. In particular, those heuristics should be connected directly to how funders, agencies, and beneficiaries will make use of those measures. If they are unlikely to lead directly to different resource allocation, programming, behavioral change, or impactful advocacy, then it is unlikely that a particular measure is of net benefit to a project overall. To this end, improving the materiality of measures is just as important as understanding their costs, and that improved materiality can come from deeper engagement of different stakeholders in decision-making.

To this end a deeper understanding of how measures can be developed and used by beneficiaries is key. Beneficiary empowerment can create added risks to funders and agencies, but in doing so may also open space for better programming. Participatory financing and granting, co-designing prototype programs with beneficiaries, and the mobilization of beneficiaries for system advocacy are all paths worthy of exploration. At its most well-developed, this suggests deeper research into the use of measures by mutual aid organizations, which blur the lines between funders, agencies, and beneficiaries to better understand if there are ways of engaging in impact investment measurement in ways that can center the beneficiaries' self-empowerment as an outcome.

Conclusion

The goal of this chapter was to identify when it is appropriate to use particular measures in a complex problem domain when funders, agencies, and beneficiaries all have different material interests and costs associated with measurement. Measurement is not neutral; in all cases, there are data collection costs, and in many situations, there are additional deeper risks that are tied to data collection and management. It is dangerous to treat measurement as occurring for 'free' – the power of a critical stakeholder group like a funder to request measures without carefully considering the consequences can undermine impact or the quality of the information being requested. When and if to measure an impact are questions that are worthy of critical reflection for those seeking to make changes in the world. Without such reflection, it is far too easy for costly data to get collected and go unused, leaving performance measurement as only performance.

References

Akhavannasab, S., Dantas, D., & Senecal, S. (2018). Consumer empowerment in consumer-firm relationships: Conceptual framework and implications for research. *AMS Review*, 8(3–4), 214–227. https://doi.org/10.1007/s13162-018-0120-4

Auerswald, D. (2009). Creating social value. *Stanford Innovation Review*, 7(2), 51–55. https://doi.org/10.48558/QT6X-TX86

Bagnoli, L., & Megali, C. (2009). Measuring performance in social enterprises. *Nonprofit and Voluntary Sector Quarterly*, 40(1), 149–165. https://doi.org/10.1177/0899764009351111

Barman, E. (2007). What is the bottom line for nonprofit organizations? A history of measurement in the British voluntary sector. *International Journal of Voluntary and Nonprofit Organizations*, 18(2), 101–115. https://doi.org/10.1007/s11266-007-9039-3

Barraket, J., & Yousefpour, N. (2014). Evaluation and social impact measurement among small to medium social enterprises: Process, purpose, and value. *Australian Journal of Public Administration, 72*(4), 447–458. https://doi.org/10.1111/1467-8500.12042

Bernstein, L. (1967). The concept of materiality. *Accounting Review, 42*(1), 86–95.

Berry, M., & Aurum, A. (2006). Measurement and decision making. In S. Biffl, A. Aurum, B. Boehm, H. Erdogmus, & P. Grünbacher (Eds.), *Value-based software engineering*. https://doi.org/10.1007/3-540-29263-2_8

Canada Mortgage and Housing Corporation (CMHC). (2018). *Measures for calculating social return on investment for affordable housing*. Canadian Centre for Economic Analysis, 1–22. https://eppdscrmssa01.blob.core.windows.net/cmhcprodcontainer/sf/project/archive/research_2/measures_for_calculating_sroi_.pdf

Chen, Y., Shang, R., & Kao, C. (2009). The effects of information overload on consumers' subjective state towards buying decisions in the internet shopping environment. *Electronic Commerce Research and Applications, 8*(1), 48–58. https://doi.org/10.1016/j.elerap.2008.09.001

Cumming, A. (2009). Language assessment in education: Tests curricula, and teaching. In B. Spolsky (Ed.), *Language policy and assessment*. Special Issue of Annual Review of Applied Linguistics, *29*, 90–100. https://doi.org/10.1017/S0267190509090084

Cunninghame Housing Association (CHA). (2014). Social return on investment for the Vineburgh regeneration initiative. *Social Value Lab*. https://socialvalueuk.org/wp-content/uploads/2016/03/Vineburgh%20SROI%20Report%20Final%20Assured.pdf

Emerson, J. (2003). The blended value proposition: Integrating social and financial returns. *California Management Review, 45*(4), 35–51. https://doi.org/10.2307/41166187

Emerson, J., & Cabaj, M. (2000). Social return on investment. *Making Waves, 11*(2), 10–14. http://hdl.handle.net/2149/1028

Esteves, A., Franks, D., & Vanclay, F. (2012). Social impact assessment: State of the art. *Impact Assessment and Project Appraisal, 30*(1), 34–42. https://doi.org/10.1080/14615517.2012.660356

Fulgence Drabo, E., Eckel, G., Ross, S., Brozic, M., Carlton, C., Warren, T., Kleb, G., Laird, A., Porter, K. & Pollack, C. (2021). A social-return-on-investment analysis of Bon Secours hospitals 'housing for health' affordable housing program. *Health Affairs, 40*(3), 513–520. https://doi.org/10.1377/hlthaff.2020.00998

Geobey, S., & Callahan, J. (2017). Managing impact portfolios: A conceptual view of scale. *ACRN Oxford Journal of Finance and Risk Perspectives, 6*(4), 17–36.

Geobey, S., Westley, F., & Weber, O. (2012). Enabling social innovation through developmental social finance. *Journal of Social Entrepreneurship, 3*(2), 151–165. https://doi.org/10.1080/19420676.2012.726006

Green, W., & Cheng, M. (2019). Materiality judgements in an integrated reporting setting: The effect of strategic relevance and strategy map. *Accounting, Organizations, and Society, 73*(C), 1–14. https://doi.org/10.1016/j.aos.2018.07.001

Hall, M., Millo, Y., & Barman, E. (2015). Who and what really counts? Stakeholder prioritization and accounting for social value. *Journal of Management Studies, 52*(7), 907–934. https://doi.org/10.1111/joms.12146

Harris, M., & Tayler, B. (2019). Don't let metrics undermine your business. *Harvard Business Review*. https://hbr.org/2019/09/dont-let-metrics-undermine-your-business

Jahera, J., & Lloyd, W. (1992). Additional evidence on the validity of ROI as a measure of business performance. *Mid-Atlantic Journal of Business, 28*(2), 105+.

Jepson, P. (2005). Governance and accountability of environmental NGOs. *Environmental Science and Policy, 8*(5), 515–524. https://doi.org/10.1016/j.envsci.2005.06.006

Kraatz, J., & Thomson, G. (2017). Valuing social housing. Sustainable Built Environment National Research Centre. https://sbenrc.com.au/app/uploads/2015/11/SBEnrc-1.41-Valuing_Social_Housing_FINAL-v10_Digital-170517.pdf

Larson, K., & Sandholm, T. (2004). *Mechanism design for computationally limited agents*. Carnegie Mellon University. https://cs.uwaterloo.ca/~klarson/papers/LarsonThesis.pdf

Lehner, O., Nicholls, A., & Kapplmüller, S. (2022). Arenas of contestation: A Senian social justice perspective on the nature of materiality in impact measurement. *Journal of Business Ethics, 179*(15), 1–19. https://doi.org/10.1007/s10551-022-05158-2

Maas, K., & Liket, K. (2011). Social impact measurement: Classification of methods. In R. Burritt, S. Schaltegger, M. Bennett, T. Pohjola, & M. Csutora (Eds.), *Environmental management accounting and supply chain management: Eco-efficiency in industry and science* (Vol. 27). Springer. https://doi.org/10.1007/978-94-007-1390-1_8

Maier, F., Schober, C., Simsa, R., & Millner, R. (2015). SROI as a method for evaluation research: Understanding merits and limitations. *Voluntas: International Journal of Voluntary and Nonprofit Organizations*, *26*(5), 1805–1830. http://www.jstor.org/stable/43654872

Menichini, T., & Rosati, F. (2014). The strategic impact of CSR consumer-company alignment. *Procedia: Social and Behavioral Sciences*, *109*(8), 360–364. https://doi.org/10.1016/j.sbspro.2013.12.472

Miller, A., & Ofrim, J. (2016). Social return on investment (SROI) of affordable housing development supported through the BC housing community partnership initiative, 1–48. https://www.bchousing.org/publications/Social-Return-On-Investment-Affordable-Housing.pdf

Miller, A., Rosales, A., Mang-Wolley, H., Bolton, C., & Peck, C. (2018). The social and economic value of dedicated-site supportive housing in B.C.: A social return on investment (SROI) analysis. Constellation Consulting Group, 1–52. https://www.toronto.ca/wp-content/uploads/2020/06/9864-SROI-Analysis-Dedicated-Site-Supportive-Housing-002.pdf

Namey, E., Guest, G., O'Regan, A., Godwin, C. L., Taylor, J., & Martinez, A. (2020). How does mode of qualitative data collection affect data and cost? Findings from a quasi-experimental study. *Field Methods*, *32*(1), 58–74. https://doi.org/10.1177/1525822X19886839

Nicholls, A. (2009). 'We do good things, don't we?': 'Blended value accounting' in social entrepreneurship. *Accounting, Organizations and Society*, *34*(6–7), 755–769. https://doi.org/10.1016/j.aos.2009.04.008

Nicholls, J., Lawlor, E., Neitzert, E., & Goodspeed, T. (2012). A guide to Social Return on Investment. The SROI Network (UK), 1–78. http://www.socialvaluelab.org.uk/wp-content/uploads/2016/09/SROI-a-guide-to-social-return-on-investment.pdf

Nielsen, J., Lueg, R., & Liempd, D. V. (2021). Challenges and boundaries in implementing social return on investment: An inquiry into its situational appropriateness. *Nonprofit Management and Leadership*, *31*(3), 413–435. https://doi.org/10.1002/nml.21439

Ormiston, J., & Seymour, R. (2011). Understanding value creation in social entrepreneurship: The importance of aligning mission, strategy and impact measurement. *Journal of Social Entrepreneurship*, *2*(2), 125–150. https://doi.org/10.1080/19420676.2011.606331

Phillips, J. (1996). ROI: The search for best practices. *Training and Development*, *50*(2), 42+.

Pomeroy, S. (2017). Challenges and opportunities in financing affordable housing in Canada. 1–18. http://www.focus-consult.com/wp-content/uploads/Financing-affordable-housing-Mar-2017.pdf

Porter, M., & Kramer, R. (2019). Creating shared value: How to reinvent capitalism – And unleash a wave of innovation and growth. *Harvard Business Review*, *89*, 323–346.

Puri, S., & Smith, K. (2019). Living building challenge: Framework for affordable housing. International Living Future Institute, 1–206. https://responsiblerealestatedevelopment.com/wp-content/uploads/2020/01/Affordable-Housing-Framework-1.pdf

Rausch, T., Baier, D., & Wening, S. (2021). Does sustainability really matter to consumers? Assessing the importance of online shop and apparel product attributes. *Journal of Retailing and Consumer Services*, *63*, 1–16. https://doi.org/10.1016/j.jretconser.2021.102681

Rawhouser, H., Cummings, M., & Newbert, S. (2017). Social impact measurement: Current approaches and future directions for social entrepreneurship research. *Entrepreneurship: Theory and Practice*, *43*(1), 82–115. https://doi.org/10.1177/1042258717727718

Santos, F. M. (2012). A positive theory of social entrepreneurship. *Journal of Business Ethics*, *111*(3), 335–351. https://doi.org/10.1007/s10551-012-1413-4

Schiff, H., Bass, R., & Cohen, A. (2016). The business value of impact measurement. Global Impact Investing Network, 1–26. https://thegiin.org/research/publication/business-value-im/

Simon, H. (1972). Theories of bounded rationality. In McGuire & Radner (Eds.), *Decision and Organization* (pp. 161–176). North Holland.

Waibel, P., Matt, J., Hochreiner, C., Skarlat, O., Hans, R., & Schulte, S. (2017). Cost-optimized redundant data storage in the cloud. *Service Oriented Computing and Applications*, *11*(4), 411–426. https://doi.org/10.1007/s11761-017-0218-9

Zon, N., Molson, M., & Oschinski, M. (2014). Building blocks: The case for federal investment in social and affordable housing in Ontario. Mowat publication, *98*, 1–63.

PART 5

Building Theory on Green Finance

24
SUSTAINABILITY REPORTING OF STATE-OWNED ENTERPRISES

Current Practices and Implications of the CSR Directive

Dorothea Greiling and Philumena Bauer

Introduction

State-owned enterprises (SOEs) are entangled in a dense web of public accountability obligations. In addition to entrepreneurial accountability, many upward mandatory obligations exist, among them political or democratic accountabilities, reporting obligations towards (sector) regulators, and public audit offices (Greiling & Schaefer, 2020). A much more recent trend is that SOEs publish sustainability or integrated reports, mostly voluntarily. Within the European Union, the first step towards mandatory sustainability reporting (SR) was set with the 2014 Directive on disclosure of non-financial and diversity information (2014/95/EU) (European Commission, 2014). The Non-Financial Reporting Directive (NFRD) made it obligatory for certain large public undertakings with an average number of 500 or more employees to publish sustainability information. At least five sustainable matters need to be covered, i.e., environmental, social and employee matters, respect for human rights, anti-corruption, and bribery (Baumüller & Sopp, 2022). The 2014 obligations were a compromise, not least to heavy criticism from big European Union member states such as Germany and the UK, as well as the business sector (Kinderman, 2020). The CSR Directive (CSRD) (European Commission, 2022) puts much more pressure on SOEs to disclose the necessary information to understand the "undertaking's impacts on sustainability matters, and information necessary to understand how sustainability matters affect the undertaking's development, performance and position" (Article 19a CSRD) in their management report. Also, external assurance will be required.

While the 2014 NFRD made sustainability reporting obligatory for 3,000 SOEs, it is estimated that the CSRD will make reporting on sustainability matters, the so-called environmental, social, and governance (ESG) reporting, mandatory for 18,500 large SOEs within the European Union (Schuster, 2022). Till then, only a few countries made SR for SOEs mandatory, and sometimes only in selected fields.

In November 2022, the European Parliament and the Council of the European Union adopted the CSRD (European Commission, 2022). Instead of social factors, the CSRD speaks of social and human rights factors. The CSRD includes the following implementation timelines: the implementers of the NFRD should implement the reporting obligations for the financial year 2024 and the number of enterprises will rise in 2025. Then two of the following three criteria are sufficient to be classified as a large enterprise: 250 employees, a balance sheet total over EUR 20 million, and revenues over EUR 40 million. Capital market-oriented small and medium-sized enterprises will follow later. SOE implementers of the NFRD have to provide a limited assurance audit already for the financial year 2024, and 2025 implementers for 2026. The European Commission must adopt a delegated act for limited assurance until October 2026 and for reasonable assurance until October 2028 (European Commission, 2022). The Sustainability Reporting Board of the European Financial Advisory Board (EFRAG) adopted the first package of sector-agnostic European Sustainability Accounting Standards on 15 November 2022 (EFRAG, 2022). The European Commission has time until 30 June 2023 to adopt the EFRAG's suggestions for European Sustainability Reporting standards. The first package includes general principles, general disclosure requirements, five standards regarding environment disclosure, one on business conduct, and four concerning the social bottom line.

The activities leading to the CSRD happened at a time when the European Union had committed itself to very ambitious climate targets in the wake of the 2015 Paris Agreement. The first step of the European Commission's (EC's) Action Plan was financing sustainability growth (European Commission, 2017). In January 2020, the EC presented a European Green Deal investment plan with a volume of more than EUR 1 trillion of sustainable investments over the next decade. That was followed by the EC's 2030 Climate Target plan in September 2020; which included an increased emission reduction target of 55% by 2030 compared to 1990. This requires even larger investments in green technologies (European Commission, 2020c). In July 2021, the EU strategy for financing the transition to a sustainable economy was published with an updated action plan (European Commission, 2021). The pathway toward CO_2 neutrality in the European Green Deal (European Commission, 2020a) is linked to sustainable finance. The EU taxonomy (European Commission, 2020b), published in June 2020, sets accompanying reporting standards for environmental matters. Companies are asked to provide information on "(i) climate change mitigation; (ii) climate change adaptation; (iii) water and marine resources; (iv) resource use and circular economy; (v) pollution; and (vi) biodiversity and ecosystems" (European Commission, 2020b), which also entails the "do not significantly harm" principle and selected social and human rights obligations. Not only SOEs have to adjust their reporting in line with the EU taxonomy.

Despite the increasing relevance of disclosure on sustainability matters by SOEs, a 2020 literature review by Manes-Rossi and co-authors (Manes-Rossi et al., 2020) shows that within the public sector, more attention has been paid to SR practices of local, regional, or central governments (37.4% out of 91 papers) or higher education institutions (HEIs) (29.7%). Outside the HEIs, the review identified only 13 papers (14%) focusing exclusively on the non-financial reporting of SOEs (Manes-Rossi et. al., 2020).

Against this background, this chapter addresses the following research questions (RQs):

1. What trends and themes can be identified in the existing literature on the SR of SOEs?
2. What are the managerial implications of the CSRD for SOEs?

The remaining part of the paper is structured as follows. The next section provides a theoretical framing for the increasing importance of providing information on sustainability matters by SOEs. To address RQ1, a literature review was performed. The results of the literature review on the SR of SOEs will be presented in the subsequent section. The review presents the main trends of SR by SOEs since the first introduction of an SR standard, back in 2000. The following section will address the potential managerial implications of the CSRD for SOEs (RQ2). The final section includes a discussion and conclusion.

Theoretical Background on the Development of SR of SOEs

SOEs are under constant pressure from multiple stakeholders to be accountable due to their vital role in society and their special public benefit obligations (e.g., Greiling & Grüb, 2014; Stefanescu, 2021). Compared to their private sector counterparts, SOEs have always been confronted with a demand for higher public accountability due to their complex societal mandates, resulting in more than one bottom line. SOEs do not only have to account for their financial performance (financial or entrepreneurial accountability), but also their public mission or public value creation. The democratic accountability obligations of SOEs bring with them complex principal-agent relations with the citizens as the ultimate principal and critical scrutiny by parliamentary bodies, ministries or local governments, and sometimes public audit offices (Greiling & Schaefer, 2020). In line with the new public management reforms, SOEs have to fight an uphill battle against the perception of being inefficient. That politicians, as public owner representatives, sit on the boards of SOEs is also often criticized, first and foremost by the media and neoclassical economists. The ambiguities of public missions and the resulting goal ambiguities lead to many conflicting interpretations by stakeholders of SOEs' mandates. Therefore, what is regarded as debatable or illegitimate behavior of an SOE is a highly contested arena. Legitimacy or reputation management is a much more challenging task for SOEs than it is for for-profit companies.

Theory-wise, the most often referred to theories for analyzing SR practices in SOEs are stakeholder theory, legitimacy theory, and institutional theory. Strategic stakeholder theory suggests that SR is focused on the information requirements of key stakeholders. Such reasoning is in line with the double materiality focus of the CSRD. In recent years, the lines between stakeholder theory and legitimacy theory have become blurred because organizational legitimacy is conferred by important stakeholders (Deephouse et al., 2017). According to Deephouse and co-authors, organizational legitimacy matters for the survival of companies, financial performance, stakeholder support, and strategic choice (Deephouse et al., 2017). The CSRD brings with it new requirements. Therefore, SOEs will have to demonstrate propriety by applying the new standards (gaining phase) (Deephouse et al, 2017). In the maintenance phase, routine monitoring should be established (Deephouse e al., 2017). As organizational legitimacy "is the perceived appropriateness of an organization to social systems according to rules, values norms and definitions" (Deephouse et al., 2017, p. 42), different stakeholders will interpret the CSRD requirements differently, and the quality of ESG reporting will be challenged due to the multiple-stakeholder setting in SOEs. Responding as an approach to maintaining legitimacy would mean that SOEs would establish a "viable bundle of reassurances" (Deephouse et al., 2017, p. 43) for demonstrating appropriateness to key stakeholders which is more than a limited assurance.

Institutional theory stresses the importance of three types of isomorphism, namely coercive, normative, and mimetic isomorphism. The upcoming changes from a mostly voluntary to a mandatory SR will increase coercive pressures (e.g., Ervits, 2021; Manes-Rossi et al., 2021; Nicolò et al., 2020). Legislative pressure will be added once the CSRD is transformed into national law. Applying the three-stage model by Shabana, Buchholtz, and Carroll (2017) on the institutionalization of corporate social responsibility (CSR) reporting, one could argue that the CSRD implementation would lead to some improvements in SR of SOEs, but in a defensive mode (Shabana et al., 2017). In stage one, selective reporting in line with the upcoming sector-agnostic and public sector-specific European Sustainability Reporting Standards (ESRS) will prevail. In the second stage, normative isomorphism is the main driver for SR, leading to proactive reporting where non-compliance becomes normatively sanctioned (Shabana et al., 2017). According to Shabana and co-authors, this is the stage where

CSR reporting will be goal-oriented. This is unlike stage one, where ESG reporting would be used by SOEs to communicate their public mission, their compliance with good governance practices, and the contribution of their business model and strategy towards sustainability matters. In stage three, mimetic isomorphism becomes the dominant driver. ESG reporting will then be a widely accepted practice (Shabana et al., 2017).

Literature Review on SR of SOEs

SR of SOEs

To obtain an overview of the state of the art regarding SR by SOEs, a literature review was carried out. Sixty English-language peer-reviewed articles were identified in the period 2000 to 2022. The year 2000 was chosen because at this time the first Global Reporting Initiative (GRI) guideline came into force.

The first article dealing with SR in SOEs was published in 2001, followed by one in 2008. Since 2012, an increase in publications is evident. Between 2012 and 2017, one to five journal articles were published annually. In 2018 and 2019, one can record between six and ten publications per year. The peak was reached in 2021 with 12 papers. Most of the studies (32) were carried out in Europe, followed by Asia (13) and North America (six). Oceania (four), Africa (three), and South America (two) are the regions with the least research about SR in SOEs.

The 60 journal articles also show a broad spectrum in terms of empirical methods. The most frequently applied methods were content analyses (15 papers), followed by 13 mixed-method studies. *Legitimacy theory* and *stakeholder theory* are the most frequently used theories for framing SR practices of SOEs, being chosen 24 and 20 times, while *institutional theory* was chosen 12 times. The dominance of the three theories does not come as a surprise as they are the most frequently used theories for analyzing SR practices. Overall, four topical clusters emerged from the journal articles. Table 24.1. summarizes these clusters and below we will discuss them in detail.

Table 24.1 Paper allocation

Cluster	Papers	Total Papers
Development of SR of SOEs over time	1; 5; 7; 8; 9; 11; 12; 16; 21; 26; 29; 30; 31; 34; 35; 36; 37; 38; 39; 41; 58; 50; 52; 54; 57, 60	26
Drivers for disclosure	1; 2; 3; 5; 6; 8; 12; 13; 14; 16; 19; 28; 29; 32; 36; 37; 38; 42; 43; 48; 50; 56; 57; 59	24
Status of SR according to GRI and IR	1; 3; 6; 7; 8; 11; 12; 13; 15; 16; 17; 20; 21; 22; 24; 25; 26; 29; 30; 32; 33; 34; 36; 37; 38; 39; 40; 41; 42; 44; 46; 47; 48; 49; 50; 51; 53; 54; 55; 56; 59, 60	42
Sustainable Development Goals (SDGs)	28; 35; 41; 42	4

Development of SR of SOEs over Time

Studies that included *SR practices until 2010* show a very slow start even though GRI issued a public sector supplement in 2005. Larrinaga-González and Pérez-Chamorro (2010) conclude that in the Spanish public water companies that were analyzed, the formal SR is very limited. Kabir (2013) focused on the social dimension and could not find a significant increase in SOEs between 2008 and 2010. Vinnari and Laine (2013) analyzed over 15 years (up to 2010) of environmental disclosure practices of Finnish water utilities, which have declined over time due to internal factors as well as the lack of external pressures (Vinnari & Laine, 2013). In contrast, a study on the environmental disclosure of Brazilian electric utilities and energy and water utilities in Great Britain showed some improvements (Braga et al., 2014; Stray, 2008).

The papers that analyzed SR practices *after 2010* showed some improvement (e.g., Dragomir et al., 2022; Manes-Rossi et al., 2021; Montecalvo et al., 2018;); however, the SR of SOEs could be enhanced (Botica-Redmayne et al., 2022; Manes-Rossi et al., 2020; Masoud & Viij, 2021; Montesinios & Brusca, 2019; Nicolò et al., 2021; Stefanescu, 2021). A study by Domingues and co-authors (2017) revealed how low the starting point really was. It showed that worldwide only 114 public sector organizations (PSO), which also include public agencies and public administrations, had published only one sustainability report adhering to the GRI guidelines in 2014.

Even if SR is mandatory for PSO, there are concerns about the quality and quantity of SR, as two studies focusing on Spain (Andrades Peña & Jorge, 2019; Larrinaga et al., 2018) point out. Spain already made SR obligatory for PSO in 2011. In contrast, a recent study by Leong and Hazelton (2019) concludes that mandatory requirements improve disclosure practices.

The group of studies with a specific sector focus or a focus on disclosure practices of listed companies unites the overall tendency that SOEs are lagging behind in their quantitative guideline compliance and reporting quality (Badia et al., 2020; Chu et al., 2013; De Lima Voss et al., 2013; Slacik & Greiling 2020; Traxler & Greiling, 2018, in contrast: Ervits, 2021). Studies with a focus on public utilities, in general, show some improvement over time (Badia et al., 2020; Greiling & Grüb, 2014; Slacik & Greiling, 2020).

Moving on to the *three triple bottom-line dimensions*, current studies show a slow increase regarding economic performance indicators (Fusco & Ricci, 2019; Orazalin & Mahmood, 2018; Stefanescu, 2021; Zanellato & Tiron-Tudor, 2021). Looking at the environmental performance indicators, there is more room for improvement (e.g., Bae, 2014; De Lima Voss et al., 2013; Fusco & Rico, 2019; Abhishek & Divyashree, 2018; Slacik & Greiling, 2020). Similar to for-profit enterprises, there are very few positive outliers in the social dimensions (Rimmel, 2019; Romolini et al., 2014; Slacik & Greiling, 2020; Traxler & Greiling, 2018), but in general the social dimension is the least reported one (Farneti et al., 2019; Greiling et al., 2015; Slacik & Greiling, 2020; Traxler & Greiling, 2018). The number of studies that address sustainability disclosures by PSOs is significantly lower compared to studies of private sector sustainability disclosure (Larrinaga et al., 2018). Overall, the studies confirm that the SR practices of SOEs are unbalanced (e.g., Clement & Bowery, 2010; Greiling et al., 2015; Kabir, 2013; Nicolò et al., 2021).

Drivers for Disclosure

Firm Characteristics

Some researchers found that size is a very significant variable that affects the disclosure of non-financial information (Alrazi et al., 2016; Andrades Peña & Jorge, 2019; Argento et al., 2019b; Dragomir et al., 2022; Garde Sánchez et al., 2017a; Ruiz-Lozano et al., 2022). The number of years in operation also plays a role (Garde Sánchez et al., 2017a; Orazalin & Mahmood, 2018). Two studies show that the sector in which the SOEs operate is also a driver that significantly affects the disclosure (Garde Sánchez et al., 2017a; Uyar et al., 2021a). Additionally, governance quality is associated with SOEs' SR level (Situ et al., 2021; Uyar et al., 2021b).

Some papers show that internal organizational dynamics are also responsible for the publication of SR in SOEs (Domingues et al., 2017; Garde Sánchez et al., 2017a; Kumasaka et al., 2021; Li & Belal, 2018; Masoud & Vij, 2021). The level of disclosure is also positively associated with the commitment by senior management and sustainability managers as well as leadership styles (Domingues et al., 2017; Dragomir et al., 2022; Ervits, 2021; Garde Sánchez et al., 2017a; Kumasaka et al., 2021; Li & Belal, 2018; Masoud & Vij, 2021). Furthermore, the degree of profitability (Andrades Peña & Jorge, 2019), geographic location (Uyar et al., 2021b), the share of foreign ownership (Orazalin & Mahmood, 2018), and the investor protection obligations and external assurance (Manes-Rossi et al., 2021) are discussed as factors that positively influence the SR by SOEs. Argento and her co-authors (2019b) show that fully state-owned SOEs disclose less sustainability information than partially state-owned SOEs (Argento et al., 2019b).

Isomorphism

Coercive isomorphism. Moving on to the motivations for SR in general, coercive isomorphism plays a very significant role. Across the sectors, important drivers are regulatory requirements based on legal obligations, sector regulations, and pressures from other powerful stakeholders. Stakeholder pressure has a direct influence on the SR disclosure practices of SOEs (De Lima Voss et al., 2013; Garde Sánchez et al., 2017b; Masoud & Vij, 2021). Looking at the role which financial institutions and investors play for SOEs, state-owned banks are also part of the coercive isomorphism pushing for conformity with SR guidelines (De Lima Voss et al., 2013; Ervits, 2021). Legislative pressures are discussed in the context of mandatory reporting in general (Andrades Peña & Jorge, 2019; Evrits, 2021; Larrinaga et al., 2018) and specifically in the context of emission reduction rules (Alrazi et al., 2016; Bae, 2014; De Lima Voss et al., 2013), as well as a consequence of the Directive 95/2014/EU (Manes-Rossi et al., 2021; Nicolò et al., 2020). The Chinese government has created a system of incentives to encourage both state-owned and non-state-owned enterprises to engage in socially responsible behavior and disclosure (Ervits, 2021; Zhao & Pattern, 2016). Coercive pressure comes from industry associations and other quasi-governmental organizations as well as from stock exchanges in the case of listed SOEs (Zhao & Patten, 2016). The reactions of SOEs to coercive pressures are mostly discussed in the context of stakeholder management, legitimation management, or reputation building (Andrades Peña & Jorge, 2019; Argento et al., 2019a; Badia et al., 2020; Braga et al., 2014).

Normative isomorphism. GRI and the Integrated Reporting (IR) standard are seen as sources of normative isomorphism. Some authors argue that IR leads to a more balanced disclosure of material aspects of sustainability and therefore improves SR (e.g., Guthrie et al., 2017; Montecalvo et al., 2018; Nicolò et al., 2021). Other studies show that the adoption of the GRI guideline positively affects the level of disclosure (Manes-Rossi et al., 2021; Traxler & Greiling, 2018; Uyar et al., 2021a; Uyar et al., 2021b; Karman et al., 2021).

Mimetic isomorphism. SOEs attempt to gain national and international reputation by imitating the reporting practices of other actors operating in the same institutional field (Ervits, 2021; Kumasaka et al., 2021; Li & Belal, 2018; Slacik & Greiling, 2020; Uyar et al., 2021b; Zhao & Patten, 2016). SR practices by private sector counterparts and practices by leading multinationals increase mimetic pressures (Li & Belal, 2018; Uyar et al., 2021b).

Status of SR According to GRI and IR

Global Reporting Initiative (GRI) Guidelines

GRI plays a dominant role as a standard for SR in SOEs. In 2005, GRI issued a public sector supplement. From early on, GRI has been qualified by some authors as the accepted global standard for SR practices due to its scope and reputation among stakeholders (Dumay et al., 2010; Guthrie et al., 2010; Larrinaga-González et al., 2018; Lopin et al., 2012; Manes-Rossi et al.,

2021; Massoud & Vij, 2021; Abhishek & Divyashree, 2018; Orazalin & Mahmood, 2018; Slacik & Greiling, 2020; Stefanescu et al., 2016; Traxler & Greiling, 2018). Orazalin and Mahmood (2018) argue that the GRI guidelines will also increase SOEs' shareholder wealth in the long run.

In many studies, the GRI database was used to identify the sample (e.g., Domingues et al., 2017; Greiling et al., 2015; Larrinaga et al., 2018; Pasko et al., 2021; Romolini et al., 2014; Slacik & Greiling, 2020; Traxler & Greiling, 2018; Uyar et al., 2021a; Uyar et al., 2021b). Moreover, some content analyses put a special emphasis on GRI principles (quality, clarity, accuracy, materiality timeliness, stakeholder engagement, comparability, and reliability) leading to mixed outcomes (Badia et al., 2020; Ervits, 2021; Slacik & Greiling, 2020). In addition, GRI principles and categories have been used for constructing SR disclosure indices (Alrazi et al., 2016; Braga et al., 2014; De Lima Voss et al., 2013; Garde Sánchez et al., 2017a; Greiling & Grüb, 2014; Masoud & Vij, 2021; Nicolò et al., 2020; Stefanescu et al., 2016).

Some studies that are using GRI as an evaluation tool have a global sample (Alrazi et al., 2016; Domingues et al., 2017; Dumay et al., 2010) with or without a field focus (Braga et al., 2014; Pasko et al., 2021; Slacik & Greiling, 2020; Traxler & Greiling, 2018; Karman et al., 2021; Slacik & Greiling, 2019). Some studies report findings in the European context (Badia et al., 2020; Nicolò et al., 2021; Slacik & Greiling, 2020; Traxler & Greiling, 2018; Slacik & Greiling, 2019), and other authors are using GRI guidelines to compare a limited number of countries (Greiling & Grüb, 2014; Greiling et al., 2015; Nicolò et al., 2020; Romolini et al., 2014). There are also studies that evaluate the GRI guideline compliance of SOEs in one country or one region (Badia et al., 2020; Braga et al., 2014; Larringa et al., 2018; Masoud & Vij, 2021; Abhishek & Divyashree, 2018; Pasko et al., 2021; Ruiz-Lozano et al., 2022).

The findings show an imbalanced coverage of the *triple bottom-line dimensions*, which is backed up by many studies that use GRI categories for evaluating SR practices (Braga et al., 2014; Garde Sánchez et al., 2017a; Greiling & Grüb, 2014; Greiling et al., 2015; Kabir, 2013; Larringa et al., 2018; Abhishek & Divyashree, 2018; Orazalin & Mahmood, 2018; Rimmel, 2019; Romolini et al., 2014; Slacik & Greiling, 2020; Traxler & Greiling, 2018).

Studies with a focus on reporting quality are far less frequent (Badia et al., 2020; Nicolò et al., 2020; Romolini et al., 2014; Slacik & Greiling, 2020; Stefanescu et al., 2016). Concerning the quality level of social reporting, two studies (Nicolò et al., 2020; Romolini et al., 2014) revealed that Italian SOEs perform better than the analyzed reports of US and Chinese SOEs.

Since 2000, the GRI guidelines have undergone five (major) revisions that resulted in the adoption of the information needed. These revisions are seen as a way of improving the quality of reporting (e.g., Larrinaga-González et al., 2018; Lopin et al., 2012; Orazalin & Mahmood, 2018), despite the associated training and system change costs (Guthrie et al., 2017). The more recent GRI guidelines put a special emphasis on materiality, which is regarded as an advancement (Farneti et al., 2019; Guthrie et al., 2017; Slacik & Greiling, 2020).

Integrated Reporting (IR) Framework

Compared to GRI, fewer studies focus on IR (Argento et al., 2019a; Botica-Redmayne et al., 2022; Guthrie et al., 2017; Li & Belal, 2018; Manes-Rossi et al., 2021; Montesinos & Brusca, 2019; Manes-Rossi, 2019; Montecalvo et al., 2018; Nicolò et al., 2021; Tirado-Valencia et al., 2020) although the IR framework plays an important role in the wake of the NFRD and in the steps towards the CSRD.

The implementation of IR is a process that requires a significant change in organizational structure and processes. Applying IR should lead to a new way of thinking, which is seen by the promotors of IR as a major advantage (Argento et al., 2019a; Guthrie et al., 2017; Manes-Rossi,

2019; Manes-Rossi et al., 2021; Montecalvo et al., 2018; Montesinos & Brusca, 2019; Nicolò et al., 2020; Nicolò et al., 2021; Tirado-Valencia et al., 2020). Compared to GRI, promotors of IR stress that IR can improve the SR of SOEs by documenting public value creation (Manes-Rossi et al., 2021; Montecalvo et al., 2018; Montesinos & Brusca, 2019; Nicolò et al., 2021).

Supporters of IR argue that IR moves away from the "more is better" strategy of the GRI G3 Guidelines to the "more relevant information is better" (Farneti et al., 2019; Guthrie et al., 2017). Concerning social matters, some studies show that IR leads to more relevant information for stakeholders (Farneti et al., 2019; Montecalvo et al., 2018; Nicolò et al., 2021; Zanellato & Tiron-Tudor, 2021). This allows companies to legitimize themselves in a better way (Manes-Rossi et al., 2021; Montecalvo et al., 2018; Nicolò et al., 2021). Increased disclosure about corporate governance, and social and environmental issues, which is neglected in traditional financial reporting, allows SOEs that apply the IR framework to manage stakeholder pressure in a more appropriate way (Farneti et al., 2019; Guthrie et al., 2017; Manes-Rossi et al., 2021; Montecalvo et al., 2018; Nicolò et al., 2021; Grossi et al., 2015).

Sustainable Development Goals (SDGs)

The importance of the 17 SDGs in combination with the United Nations (UN) Agenda 2030 for Sustainable Development has been growing in recent years. Empirical studies on SDG practices of SOEs are a new topic (Kumasaka et al., 2021; Manes-Rossi et al., 2021; Nicolò et al., 2020; Ning et al., 2018). The 2018 paper by Ning and co-authors (2018) focused on SDG 8, analyzing eco-efficiency in state-owned forest enterprises. Nicolò et al. (2020) analyzed 44 integrated reports of SOEs. They found that 50% of the examined companies were disclosing the SDGs or at least mentioned their idea of an SDG contribution (Nicolò et al., 2020). The results of the study by Kumasaka and co-authors (2021), who address the issue of the SDGs by interviewing sustainability managers, revealed that while SDG integration is still at an early stage, it is being strongly pursued in diverse business areas and goals (Kumasaka et al., 2021). Research results from Manes-Rossi and co-authors (2021) show that more than half of the sample of SOEs have started to disclose information on SDGs in their reports since 2016 to show their commitment to the UN 2030 Agenda for Sustainable Development. The SDG reporting is not yet uniform. Some SOEs report on one or more SDGs, while other SOEs include all SDGs in all sections of the report. A few SOEs thus demonstrate that the business model, strategies, and stakeholder engagement process are aligned with the SDGs (Manes-Rossi et al., 2021).

Research Gaps with Respect to the CSRD

The results of the literature review show that SR is not a completely new topic for SOEs. Over the years, the number of studies increased, but most of the findings conclude that there is room for improvement.

CSRD implementation brings major changes in the extent of reporting, as Art. 19a of the CSRD (European Commission, 2019) requires disclosing information about the undertaking's business model and strategy related to sustainable matters, administrative structures, policies, and targets as well as a description of the principal risks of companies related to sustainable matters. Whether that is only symbolically implemented in the ESG reporting of SOEs is something that can be evaluated once the first ESG reports by SOEs are published.

Concerning reporting standards, the CSRD does not favor a specific standard. The CSRD includes references to the IR framework as well as to the GRI. While the NFRD was more in line with IR's stakeholder prioritization, GRI and the IR have to be modified to meet the CSRD requirements.

The focus on double materiality will increase the need for documenting material aspects further. More empirical studies are required to evaluate the quality of SRs by analyzing if SRs are consistent with those indicators that are regarded as highly relevant by important stakeholders. Further research should also analyze how to meet the specific users' needs of SOEs for supporting the development of a sector-specific standard that also embraces accounting for public value creation.

As the literature review has shown, in all three ESG reporting dimensions, the reporting quantity and quality need to be improved. The impact of governance structures so far has only been addressed as a contingency variable. With respect to the EU taxonomy, the most urgent needs arise regarding the six environmental objectives as well as documenting that SOEs act in their economic activities in alignment with the minimum safeguards (European Commission, 2020b). How SOEs can improve their carbon footprint reporting, their greenhouse gas emissions accounting, the scope of the fulfillment of requirements 1–3 of the EU taxonomy, and their reporting on biodiversity impacts will be pressing topics for further research. The coverage of human rights indicators is also a relatively new topic for SOEs and for for-profit companies alike.

The CSRD also changes the assurance from voluntary to obligatory. So far, there is a lack of studies that analyze the SR assurance practices of SOEs and the role of public audit offices and their reporting scope regarding SR practices of SOEs.

Managerial Implications of the CSRD for SOEs

While the 3,000 SOEs that are NFRD implementers have to apply the ESRS in their annual reports for the financial year 2024, another 15,500 SOEs currently envisaged 2025 as their first implementation year. Traditionally, there was a dominance of stand-alone SR of SOEs. With the CSRD in force, the management report must include all the required information on sustainability matters.

Due to the double materiality requirement of the CSRD, many SOEs have to improve their stakeholder engagement processes. However, establishing a real stakeholder dialogue is a challenge that is not solely limited to SOEs. Considering that SOEs are hybrid multi-stakeholder organizations with different, often competing, logics (such as market logic, community logic, and compliance logic), balancing stakeholder demands is particularly difficult. The CSRD implementation also offers a chance for SOEs to improve their reporting on public value creation. It is somewhat ironic that stock-exchange-listed for-profit companies started to systematically document their contributions to society much earlier.

In comparison to the NFRD, the CSRD aims at reducing the discretionary freedom implementers have. It pursues a much more strategic approach toward sustainability matters. Sustainability matters need to be integrated into an SOE's business model, strategy, and risk management. Coming to a consensus about an SOE's sustainability strategy is quite challenging. Most likely as a first step, the interests of the owner's representatives and other resource providers will be considered. It is likely that SOEs also have to show how they contribute to their public owners' sustainability policies. Adapting the business model requires a lot of organizational innovation. The challenges are particularly high for state-owned infrastructure providers (e.g., electric utilities, public transport SOEs, social housing SOEs).

As a consequence of the Green Deal and the European Union's Sustainable Finance Initiatives, regulatory pressure by financial institutions has increased. In some areas, SOEs are currently getting very favorable long-term loans from national and international financial institutions for financing steps towards a green transformation. To be eligible for favorable loans or for issuing green bonds, SOEs must document their contributions towards climate change in line with the EU taxonomy. The tendency shows an increased linkage of public subsidies and grants with the EU's national and supranational sustainability objectives as well as the linkage with public procurement laws. Both developments will affect SOEs directly.

Furthermore, Article 19a of the CSRD also requires that reporting on sustainable matters include information about how an undertaking will contribute to the 1.5 °C reduction mentioned in the Paris Agreement. In order to meet that goal, infrastructure investments are needed as well as changes in SOEs' processes.

Similar to other accounting standards, first implementers have high costs. They have to invest a lot in designing their sustainability strategy, implementing appropriate governance, administrative structures, policies, and procedures, and improving data collection on sustainability matters. Coordinating the compilation of SR is not something that can be handled on top of other tasks, and the existing coordination units for SR will have to be substantially increased. As SR requires multidisciplinary teams, recruiting and forming such teams will not be easy.

Moving on to the indicators needed, the literature review revealed that SOEs still have a lot of homework to do. Improving environmental reporting is the first priority. SOEs can draw from various reporting standards, e.g., the IR stand with its focus on natural capital, various GRI standards dealing with environmental issues, standards for carbon accounting, water accounting, and accounting regulations for biodiversity. Regarding the social bottom line, the CSRD and the EU taxonomy regulation extend the scope. The CSRD calls for a better alignment of the CSRD with international due process requirements along the whole value chain (European Commission, 2022). Furthermore, SOEs must improve their scrutiny of their suppliers until 2024.

In conclusion, implementing the CSRD will require a major change process in SOEs. The managerial implications of the CSRD go far beyond implementing just another set of key performance indicators.

Discussion and Conclusions

The results from the literature review (RQ1) revealed that while SR is not a new subject for SOEs, the identified research gaps show that the state of the literature on SR practices is not yet satisfactory and needs to improve for many reasons. Firstly, in most SOEs, SR has been a voluntary endeavor. Secondly, research on SR practices is much more focused on listed for-profit entities. Thirdly, CSRD implementation and the ESRS will substantially extend the SR requirements.

The section on managerial implications (RQ2) shows that SOEs need to address sustainability matters more strategically. In line with strategic stakeholder theory and organizational legitimacy theory, meeting the expectation of crucial internal and external stakeholders requires much more attention to their specific information needs. For gaining organizational legitimacy under CSRD requirements, SOEs must show that they are fully applying the upcoming ESRS. Initially, ESG reporting will probably be quite selective, especially in the case of first implementers. Such a reactive behavior, triggered by increasing coercive pressures, is suggested by Shabana and co-authors' three-stage model. In that phase, SOEs will be criticized most likely for facade-building and greenwashing. In the maintaining phase, ESG reporting needs to be more elaborated. Changes in stakeholder expectations and regulatory requirements will most likely be a constant challenge for SOEs. Due to their stakeholder heterogeneity, balancing the information needs is much more challenging in SOEs than in their for-profit counterparts. For signaling appropriateness, SOEs will have to invest more in voluntary assurances and therefore go beyond the requirements of the upcoming mandatory limited or reasonable assurances. Existing technical, safety, and quality assurances should be integrated into a strategic approach dealing with assurance.

The envisaged sector-specific ESRS will most likely focus on PSO at large in a later stage. Here SOEs should be active to ensure that a PSO sector standard also meets their information disclosure requirements. Otherwise, the danger exists that public-sector-specific ESRS will be more in line with the reporting obligations that various government levels have. Their reporting requirements are much more on the macro level (e.g., contribution to the EU's climate change agenda, European Pillars of Social Rights, and the EC's whole-of-government approach regarding SDGs). Those SOEs operating in sectors with high sustainability risks should start quite soon with lobbying for sector-specific standards that are in line with their ESG requirements.

Contributing to the highly ambitious European climate change and social inclusion objectives requires much more from SOEs than just adhering to another public accountability obligation. The ESG reporting requirements are attention-directing and are designed in a way that makes purely symbolic compliance not sustainable.

CSRD implementation also offers opportunities for SOEs to move to a more comprehensive reporting on their social and environmental contributions and therefore their public value creation. The Covid-19 pandemic as well as recent re-privatizations have shown how important SOEs are for resilient societies. Not only for securing financial resources but also for attracting employees, communication about sustainability matters is becoming more and more important for SOEs. Stewardship theory would suggest that SOEs should actively position themselves as stewards of public interests. That is much more than improving social bottom-line reporting. To be more transparent, the technical requirements of the CSRD and the upcoming ESRS should be applied in a way that ESG reports of SOEs are easier to understand. Scholars have also proposed an *Integrated Popular Reporting (IPR)* that is concise, easy to understand for citizens, and encompasses the key pillars of public sector prosperity and value creation (Cohen & Karatzimas, 2015; Manes-Rossi, 2019). Under democratic accountability aspects, easy-to-understand information on sustainability matters to citizens would be highly advisable.

References

included in the Literature Review

★[40]Abhishek, N., & Divyashree, M. S. (2018). Global reporting initiatives: A study of environmental accounting practices in Indian electric companies. *Journal of International Business*, *5*(2), 79–92. https://doi.org/10.17492/focus.v5i2.14385

★[1]Alrazi, B., De Villiers, C., & Van Staden, J. C. (2016). The environmental disclosures of the electricity generation industry: A global perspective. *Accounting and Business Research*, *46*(6), 665–701. https://doi.org/10.1080/00014788.2015.1135781

★[2]Andrades Peña, J., & Jorge, M. L. (2019). Examining the amount of mandatory non-financial information disclosed by Spanish state-owned enterprises and its potential influential variables. *Meditari Accountancy Research*, *27*(4), 534–555. https://doi.org/10.1108/MEDAR-05-2018-0343

★[3]Argento, D., Culasso, F., & Truant, E. (2019a). From sustainability to integrated reporting: The legitimizing role of the CSR manager. *Organization and Environment*, *32*(4), 484–507. https://doi.org/10.1177/1086026618769487

★[4]Argento, D., Grossi, G., Persson, K., & Vingren, T. (2019b). Sustainability disclosures of hybrid organizations: Swedish state-owned enterprises. *Meditari Accountancy Research*, *27*(4), 505–533. https://doi.org/10.1108/MEDAR-07-2018-0362

★[6]Badia, F., Bracci, E., & Tallaki, M. (2020). Quality and diffusion of social and sustainability reporting in Italian public utility companies. *Sustainability*, *12*(11), 4525. https://doi.org/10.3390/su12114525

★⁵Bae, H. (2014). Voluntary disclosure of environmental performance: Do publicly and privately owned organizations face different incentives/disincentives? *American Review of Public Administration, 44*(4), 459–476. https://doi.org/10.1177/0275074012468610

Baumüller, J., & Sopp, K. (2022). Double Materiality and the shift from non-financial to European sustainability reporting: Review, outlook and implications. *Journal of Applied Accounting Research, 23*(1), 8–28. https://doi.org/10.1108/JAAR-04-2021-0114

★⁷Botica-Redmayne, N., Vašiček, V., & Čičak, J. (2022). Analysis of nonfinancial reporting and integrated reporting application: The case of state-owned companies in Croatia, Slovenia, and Serbia—Some initial evidence. Eurasian studies in business and economics. In M. Huseyin Bilgin, H. Danis, E. Demir, & A. Zaremba (Eds.), *Eurasian business and economics perspectives* (pp. 285–297). https://doi.org/10.1007/978-3-030-94036-2_16

★⁸Braga, C., Da Silva, P. P., & Dos Santos, A. (2014). Environmental disclosure in the Brazilian electricity sector. *International Journal of Innovation and Sustainable Development, 8*(1), 37–52. https://doi.org/10.1504/IJISD.2014.059221

★⁹Chu, I. C., Chatterjee, B., & Brown, A. (2013). The current status of greenhouse gas reporting by Chinese companies. *Managerial Auditing Journal, 28*(2), 114–139. https://doi.org/10.1108/02686901311284531

★¹⁰Clements, D. M., & Bowrey, D. G. (2010). Corporate social responsibility in public sector supply chains: An insight. *Journal of New Business Ideas and Trends, 8*(2), 1–13.

★¹¹Cohen, S., & Karatzimas, S. (2015). Tracing the future of reporting in the public sector: Introducing integrated popular reporting. *International Journal of Public Sector Management, 28*(6), 449–460. https://doi.org/10.1108/IJPSM-11-2014-0140

★¹²De Lima Voss, B., Pfitscher Dahmer, E., Silvia da Rosa, F., & De Souza Ribeiro, M. (2013). Solid waste environmental disclosures of public companies in brazil of environmentally sensitive industries. *Revista Contabilidade & e Finanças, 24*(62), 125–141. https://doi.org/10.1590/S1519-70772013000200004

Deephouse, L. D., Bundy, J., Leigh Punkett, T., & Suchman, C. M. (2017). Organizational legitimacy: Six key questions. In R. Greenwood, C. Oliver, B. T. Lawrence, & E. R. Meyer (Eds.), *The SAGE handbook of organizational institutionalism* (pp. 27–54). Sage.

★¹³Domingues, R. A., Lozano, R., Ceulemans, K., & Ramos, T. (2017). Sustainability reporting in public sector organisations: Exploring the relation between the reporting process and organisational change management for sustainability. *Journal of Environmental Management, 192*, 202–301. https://doi.org/10.1016/j.jenvman.2017.01.074

★¹⁴Dragomir, V. D., Dumitru, M., & Feleaga, L. (2022). The predictors of non-financial reporting quality in Romanian state-owned enterprises. *Accounting in Europe, 19*(1), 110–151. https://doi.org/10.1080/17449480.2021.2018474

★¹⁵Dumay, J., Guthrie, J., & Farneti, F. (2010). GRI sustainability reporting guidelines for public and third sector organizations, a critical review. *Public Management Review, 12*(4), 531–548. https://doi.org/10.1080/14719037.2010.496266

EFRAG. (2022). *EFRAG's due process procedures: EU sustainability reporting standard setting*. Available at: https://www.efrag.org/Activities/2106151549247651/Due-Process-Procedures-for-Sustainability-Reporting-Standard-Setting-# (accessed 20 July 2023).

★¹⁶Ervits, I. (2021). CSR reporting in China's private and state-owned enterprises: A mixed methods comparative analysis. *Asian Business and Management*. https://doi.org/10.1057/s41291-021-00147-1.

European Commission. (2014). Directive 2014/95/EU of the European parliament and of the council of the European Union of 22 October 2014 amending of directive 2013/34/EU as regards disclosure of non-financial and diversity information by certain large undertakings and groups text with EEA relevance. *Official Journal of the European Union*. Retrieved November 15, 2014, from https://eur-lex.europa.eu/legal-content/DE/TXT/?uri=celex%3A32014L0095

European Commission. (2017). Guidelines on non-financial 2017/C 215/01. *Official Journal of the European Union*. https://eur-lex.europa.eu/legal-content/EN/TXT/PDF/?uri=CELEX:52017XC0705(01)&from=EN

European Commission. (2019). Communication from the commission: Guidelines on non-financial reporting: Supplement on reporting climate-related information. 2019/C 209/01. *Official Journal of the European Union*. Retrieved June 20, 2019, from https://eur-lex.europa.eu/legal-content/EN/TXT/PDF/?uri=CELEX:52019XC0620(01)&from=EN

European Commission. (2020a). *The European green deal*. COM (2019) 640 final. https://eur-lex.europa.eu/resource.html?uri=cellar:b828d165-1c22-11ea-8c1f-01aa75ed71a1.0002.02/DOC_1&format=PDF

European Commission. (2020b). Regulation (EU) 2020/852 of the European parliament and the council of the European Union of 18 June 2020 on the establishment of a framework to facilitate sustainable investment, and amending regulation (EU) 2019/2088. L 198/13. *Official Journal of the European Union*. Retrieved June 22, 2022, from https://eur-lex.europa.eu/legal-content/EN/TXT/PDF/?uri=CELEX:32020R0852&from=EN

European Commission. (2020c). *2030 Climate target plan*. COM (2020) 562 final. https://eur-lex.europa.eu/legal-content/EN/TXT/PDF/?uri=CELEX:52020DC0562&from=EN

European Commission. (2021). *Communication from the commission to the European parliament, the council of the European Union, the European economic and social committee of the regions empty. Strategy for financing the transition to a sustainable economy*. COM (2021) 390 final. https://eur-lex.europa.eu/resource.html?uri=cellar:9f5e7e95-df06-11eb-895a-01aa75ed71a1.0001.02/DOC_1&format=PDF

European Commission. (2022). Directive (EU) 2022/2464 of the European Union and the European parliament of 14 December 2022 amending regulation (EU) No 537/2014, 2013/34/EU, as regards corporate sustainability reporting. *Official Journal of the European Union*. Retrieved December 16, 2022, from https://eur-lex.europa.eu/legal-content/EN/TXT/HTML/?uri=CELEX:32022L2464&from=EN

★[17]Farneti, F., Casonato, F., Montecalvo, M., & Villiers, C. (2019). The influence of integrated reporting and stakeholder information needs on the disclosure of social information in a state-owned enterprise. *Meditari Accountancy Research*, 27(4), 556–579. https://doi.org/10.1108/MEDAR-01-2019-0436

★[18]Fusco, F., & Ricci, P. (2019). What is the stock of the situation? A bibliometric analysis on social and environmental accounting research in public sector. *International Journal of Public Sector Management*, 32(1), 21–41. https://doi.org/10.1108/IJPSM-05-2017-0134

★[19]Garde Sánchez, R., Rodríguez Bolívar, M. P., & López Hernández, A. M. (2017a). Corporate and managerial characteristics as drivers of social responsibility disclosure by state-owned enterprises. *Review of Managerial Science*, 11(3), 633–659. https://doi.org/10.1007/s11846-016-0199-7

★[20]Garde Sánchez, R., Rodríguez Bolívar, M. P., & López Hernández, A. M. (2017b). Perceptions of stakeholder pressure for supply-chain social responsibility and information disclosure by state-owned enterprises. *International Journal of Logistics Management*, 28(4), 1027–1053. https://doi.org/10.1108/IJLM-05-2016-0118

★[21]Greiling, D., & Grüb, B. (2014). Sustainability reporting in Austrian and German local public enterprises. *Journal of Economic Policy Reform*, 17(3), 209–223. https://doi.org/10.1080/17487870.2014.909315

Greiling, D., & Schaefer, C. (2020). Public accountability of stated-owned enterprises: Approaches and research trends. In L. Bernier, M. Florio, & P. Bance (Eds.), *The Routledge handbook of state-owned enterprises* (pp. 460–478). Routledge.

★[22]Greiling, D., Traxler, A. A., & Stötzer, S. (2015). Sustainability reporting in the Austrian, German and Swiss public sector. *International Journal of Public Sector Management*, 28(4/5), 404–428. https://doi.org/10.1108/IJPSM-04-2015-0064

★[23]Grossi, G., Papenfuß, U., & Tremblay, M. (2015). Corporate governance and accountability of state-owned enterprises. *International Journal of Public Sector Management*, 28(4/5), 274–285. https://doi.org/10.1108/IJPSM-09-2015-0166

★[24]Guthrie, J., Ball, A., & Farneti, F. (2010). [Editorial]: Sustainability management of public and not for profit organisations. *Public Management Review*, 12(4), 449–459. https://doi.org/10.1080/14719037.2010.496254

★[25]Guthrie, J., Manes-Rossi, F., & Orelli, R. L. (2017). Integrated reporting and integrated thinking in Italian public sector organisations. *Meditari Accountancy Research*, 25(4), 553–573. https://doi.org/10.1108/MEDAR-06-2017-0155

★[26]Kabir, Md. H. (2013). Corporate social disclosure by public enterprises: Evidence from a less developing African country. *Risk Governance and Control: Financial Markets and Institutions*, 3(3), 76–84. https://doi.org/10.22495/rgcv3i3c1art1

★[27]Karaman, S. A., Orazalin, N., Uyar, A., & Shahbaz, M. (2021). CSR achievement, reporting, and assurance in the energy sector: Does economic development matter? *Energy Policy*, 149(C), 112007. https://doi.org/10.1016/j.enpol.2020.112007

Kinderman, D. (2020). The challenge of upward regulatory harmonization: The case of sustainability reporting in the European Union. *Regulation and Governance*, 14(4), 674–697. https://doi.org/10.1111/rego.12240

★[28]Kumasaka, J. M. V. C., Galleli Dias, B., Henrique, J. S., Cruz Braga, B., & Campigotto Sandri, E. (2021). Sustainability in public organizations: A study in the sustenta Paraná network. *Revista de Administração da UFSM*, 14, 1160–1181. https://doi.org/10.5902/1983465963992

★[29]Larrinaga-Gonzélez, C., Luque-Vilchez, M., & Fernández, R. (2018). Sustainability accounting regulation in Spanish public sector organizations. *Public Money and Management*, 38(5), 345–354. https://doi.org/10.1080/09540962.2018.1477669

★[30]Larrinaga-Gonzélez, C., & Pérez-Chamorro, V. (2010). Sustainability accounting and accountability in public water companies. *Public Money and Management*, 28(6), 337–343. https://doi.org/10.1111/j.1467-9302.2008.00667

★[31]Leong, S., & Hazelton, J. (2019). Under what conditions is mandatory disclosure most likely to cause organisational change? *Accounting, Auditing and Accountability Journal*, 32(3), 811–835. https://doi.org/10.1108/AAAJ-12-2015-2361

★[32]Li, T., & Belal, A. (2018). Authoritarian state, global expansion and corporate social responsibility reporting: The narrative of a Chinese state-owned enterprise. *Accounting Forum*, 42(2), 199–217. https://doi.org/10.1016/j.accfor.2018.05.002

★[33]Lopin, K., Chin-Chen, Y., & Hui-Cheng, Y. (2012). Disclosure of corporate social responsibility and environmental management: Evidence from China. *Corporate Social Responsibility and Environmental Management*, 19(5), 273–287. https://doi.org/10.1002/csr.274

★[34]Manes-Rossi, F. (2019). New development: Alternative reporting formats: A panacea for accountability dilemmas? *Public Money and Management*, 39(7), 528–531. https://doi.org/10.1080/09540962.2019.1578540

★[35]Manes-Rossi, F., Nicolò, G., & Argento, D. (2020). Non-financial reporting formats in public sector organizations: A structured literature review. *Journal of Public Budgeting, Accounting and Financial Management*, 32(4), 639–669. https://doi.org/10.1108/JPBAFM-03-2020-0037

★[36]Manes-Rossi, F., Nicolò, G., Tiron Tudor, A., & Zanellato, G. (2021). Drivers of integrated reporting by state-owned enterprises in Europe: A longitudinal analysis. *Meditari Accountancy Research*, 29(3), 586–616. https://doi.org/10.1108/medar-07-2019-0532

★[37]Masoud, N., & Vij, A. (2021). Factors influencing corporate social responsibility disclosure (CSRD) by Libyan state-owned enterprises (SOEs). *Cogent Business and Management*, 8(1). https://doi.org/10.1080/23311975.2020.18598501859850

★[38]Montecalvo, M., Farneti, F., & Villiers, C. (2018). The potential of integrated reporting to enhance sustainability reporting in the public sector. *Public Money and Management*, 38(5), 365–374. https://doi.org/10.1080/09540962.2018.1477675

★[39]Montesinos, V., & Brusca, I. (2019). Non-financial reporting in the public sector: Alternatives, trends and opportunities. *Revista de Contabilidad*, 22(2), 122–128. https://doi.org/10.6018/rcsar.383071

★[41]Nicolo, G., Zanellato, G., Manes-Rossi, F., & Tiron-Tudor, A. (2021). Corporate reporting metamorphosis: Empirical findings from state-owned enterprises. *Public Money and Management*, 41(2), 138–147. https://doi.org/10.1080/09540962.2020.1719633

★[42]Nicolo, G., Zanellato, G., & Tiron-Tudor, A. (2020). Integrated reporting and European state-owned enterprises: A disclosure analysis pre and post 2014/95/EU. *Sustainability*, 12(5), 1908. https://doi.org/10.3390/su12051908

★[43]Ning, Y., Liu, Z., Ning, Z., & Zhang, H. (2018). Measuring eco-efficiency of state-owned forestry enterprises in Northeast China. *Forests*, 9(8), 455. https://doi.org/10.3390/f9080455

★[44]Orazalin, N., & Mahmood, M. (2018). Economic, environmental, and social performance indicators of sustainability reporting: Evidence from the Russian oil and gas industry. *Energy Policy*, 121, 70–79. https://doi.org/10.1016/j.enpol.2018.06.015

★[45]Pasko, O., Marenych, T., Diachenko, O., Levytska, I., & Balla, I. (2021). Stakeholder engagement in sustainability reporting: The case study of Ukrainian public agricultural companies. *Agricultural and Resource Economics: International Scientific E-Journal*, 7(1), 58–80. https://doi.org/10.51599/are.2021.07.01.04

★[46]Rimmel, G. (2019). Human capital disclosures in Swedish state-owned enterprises - A comparison of integrated reporting versus traditional reporting. In S. Arvidsson (Ed.), *Challenges in managing sustainable business: Reporting, taxation, ethics and governance* (pp. 55–75). Palgrave Macmillan.

★[47]Romolini, A., Gori, E., & Fissi, S. (2014). The disclosure in social reporting of energy sector: Experiences from Italy, the USA and china. *Corporate Ownership and Control*, 11(4), 277–287. https://doi.org/10.22495/cocv11i4c2p5

★[48]Ruiz-Lozano, M., De Vicente-Lama, M., Tirado-Valencia, P., & Cordobés-Madueño, M. (2022). The disclosure of the materiality process in sustainability reporting by Spanish state-owned enterprises. *Accounting, Auditing and Accountability Journal*, 35(2), 385–412. https://doi.org/10.1108/AAAJ-08-2018-3629

Schuster, F. (2022). Sustainable Public Finance: Nachhaltiges Finanzwesen und Auswirkungen auf den öffentlichen Sektor. *Public Governance*, Spring *2022*, 4–10.

Shabana, K., Buchholtz, A. K., & Carroll, A. (2017). The institutionalization of corporate social responsibility reporting. *Business and Society, 56*(8), 1107–1135. https://doi.org/10.1177/000765031662817

★[49]Situ, H., Tilt, C., & Seet, P. (2021). The influence of the Chinese government's political ideology in the field of corporate environmental reporting. *Accounting, Auditing and, Accountability Journal, 34*(9), 1–28. https://doi.org/10.1108/AAAJ-09-2016-2697

Slacik, J., & Greiling, D. (2019). Compliance with materiality in G4-sustainability reports by electric utilities. *International Journal of Energy Sector Management, 14*(3), 583–608.

★[50]Slacik, J., & Greiling, D. (2020). Coverage of G4-indicators in GRI-sustainability reports by electric utilities. *Journal of Public Budgeting, Accounting and Financial Management, 32*(3), 359–378. https://doi.org/10.1108/JPBAFM-06-2019-0100

★[51]Stefanescu, A. C. (2021). Sustainability reporting in the public realm—Trends and patterns in knowledge development. *Sustainability, 13*(8), 4128. https://doi.org/10.3390/su13084128

★[52]Stefanescu, A. C., Oprisor, Z., & Sintejudeanu, A. M. (2016). An original assessment tool for transparency in the public sector based on the integrated reporting approach. *Journal of Accounting and Management Information Systems, 15*(3), 542–564.

★[53]Stray, S. (2008). Environmental reporting: The U.K. water and energy industries: A research note. *Journal of Business Ethics, 80*(4), 697–710. https://doi.org/10.1007/s10551-007-9463-8

★[54]Tirado-Valencia, P., Cordobés-Madueño, M., Ruiz-Lozano, M., & De Vicente-Lama, M. (2020). Integrated thinking in the reporting of public sector enterprises: A proposal of contents. *Meditari Accountancy Research, 28*(3), 435–453. https://doi.org/10.1108/MEDAR-03-2019-0458

★[55]Traxler, A. A., & Greiling, D. (2018). Sustainable public value reporting of electric utilities. *Baltic Journal of Management, 14*(12), 103–121. https://doi.org/10.1108/BJM-10-2017-0337

★[56]Uyar, A., Kuzey, C., & Kilic, M. (2021a). Testing the spillover effects of sustainability reporting: Evidence from the public sector. *International Journal of Public Administration, 44*(3), 231–240. https://doi.org/10.1080/01900692.2019.1677711

★[57]Uyar, A., Karmani, M., Kuzey, C., Kilic, M., & Chadi, Y. (2021b). Does governance quality explain the sustainability reporting tendency of the public sector? Worldwide evidence. *International Journal of Public Administration, 45*(13), 931–947. https://doi.org/10.1080/01900692.2021.1900243

★[58]Vinnari, E., & Laine, M. (2013). Just a passing fad? *Accounting, Auditing and Accountability Journal, 26*(7), 1107–1134. https://doi.org/10.1108/AAAJ-04-2012-01002

★[60]Zanellato, G., & Tiron-Tudor, A. (2021). How cultural dimensions are shaping social expectations: The case of European state-owned enterprises' non financial reporting. *Journal of Applied Accounting Research, 23*(1), 99–121. https://doi.org/10.1108/jaar-04-2021-0116

★[59]Zhao, N., & Patten, D. M. (2016). An exploratory analysis of managerial perceptions of social and environmental reporting in China. *Sustainability Accounting, Management and Policy Journal, 7*(1), 80–98. https://doi.org/10.1108/SAMPJ-10-2014-0063

25
ASSESSING THE CURRENT STATE OF RESEARCH ON CLIMATE AND ENVIRONMENT-RELATED FINANCIAL RISKS

What Are We Missing? A Review and Research Agenda

Rosella Carè and Olaf Weber

Introduction

Climate change has been recently recognized as an increasingly looming source of risk for the financial system (Battiston et al., 2021). The 2030 Agenda for Sustainable Development indicates environmental challenges, including but not limited to climate change, as a major concern for the stability of the global economy (Alexander, 2019). Three broad climate-related financial risks have been identified: (a) physical risks that are linked to the economic damages of climate-related events and can be further classified into event-driven (such as floods and storms) or chronic risks related to long-term climate shifts (such as more frequent heavy precipitation and risk of river flooding); (b) transition risks that have to do with adjustments toward a low carbon economy and include changes in regulation, public policies, technology, and customer sentiment; and (c) liability risks that may emerge if parties who have suffered damage or loss from the effects of climate change seek compensation from those they hold responsible (Baudino & Svoronos, 2021; Capasso et al., 2020; Caselli & Figueira, 2020; Dafermos et al., 2018; Dafermos, 2021; Xepapadeas, 2021). Physical and transition risk drives impact economic activities and consequently the financial system directly through, for example, lower corporate profitability or the devaluation of assets or indirectly through macrofinancial changes (ECB, 2020).

Current risk evaluations have almost exclusively incorporated climate change factors but have paid less attention to natural or environmental sphere threats. The limitation of climate change makes the recognition of the potential impact of these risks very marginal by posing several limitations in the understanding of the relationship between the broad concept of environmental-related risks and financial risks. Overall, climate-related and environmental risks are drivers of existing financial risk categories, such as credit, market, operational, liquidity, and underwriting risks (BIS, 2021, p. 3), and affect all areas of banking activities, including risk management and credit management processes (Weber, 2005; Weber et al., 2008), operational risk management, liquidity risk management, reporting and disclosures, and investment practices.

The potential effects and impacts of climate-related and environmental risks in terms of financial stability (or instability) are increasingly attracting attention at the academic and policy levels. Central banks and financial supervisors started considering climate risks after the famous speech of the Bank of England Governor Mark Carney at Lloyd's that pointed out how the financial system is exposed to climate risks (Carney, 2015). Financial regulators around the world are now formalizing new rules for climate risk management and demanding new stress-test protocols, including the development of methodologies based on forward-looking scenarios (Monnin, 2018). To date, among others, several works have explored the potential impact of environmental risks on corporate financial performance (Bătae et al., 2021; Laguir et al., 2018), the relation between climate risks and financial stability (Battiston, 2019; Battiston et al., 2021; Monasterolo, 2020; Nieto, 2019; Roncoroni et al., 2021), and how central banks should reflect these emerging risks in monetary policy operations and supervision (Bingler et al., 2021; Monnin, 2018, 2020; Schnabel, 2021; Schoenmaker, 2021). Additionally, the contribution of the banking sector to environmental conservation has been explored by many authors (Bouma et al., 2017; Weber, 2005; Weber et al., 2008, 2010).

With the first bibliometric analysis of the climate and environment-related financial risks domain, this paper aims to create an understanding of the core literature and future trends for researchers and practitioners. To accomplish our objectives, we use a bibliometric analysis that, when combined with a co-word analysis, illustrates the structure and central themes of a research area.

The theoretical contribution of this paper lies in its intention to understand the current state of banking and finance research on climate and environment-related financial risks by searching for unexplored and underestimated areas of concern, systematizing the current knowledge, and helping future research on the subject, with an indication of the topics most interesting for the academic world. This might be useful for academics, policymakers, financial institutions, and supervisors who support banks in their understanding of climate and environment-related financial risks.

The next section summarizes the methodological approach used for the study. We then present our findings. Finally, we present a discussion of our findings and draw conclusions by also providing future research directions.

Research Methodology

The aim of this research article is to explore the current stance of academic research on climate- and environment-related financial risks by identifying current gaps and future research directions. The systematic literature review (SLR) and bibliometric analysis (Donthu et al., 2021a, 2021b, 2021c) were identified as the best methodological approaches for this study. More specifically, SLR is based on transparency and rigor and assists researchers in mapping, assessing, and synthesizing different pieces of literature to develop the knowledge base within a field (Tranfield et al., 2003). Bibliometric tools complemented the analysis and were used to systematically evaluate the literature. Moreover, the analysis has been supported by the visualization of similarities technique (van Eck & Waltman, 2010; van Eck & Waltman, 2014). VOSviewer software, an open-access software tool for the analysis of bibliometric networks, was used to process the literature search results and create knowledge maps (van Eck and Waltman, 2010). The following sections describe the approach used.

Data Collection

We started our analysis with a comprehensive search of the Scopus database, which is recognized as the most reliable database for bibliometric studies (Baas et al., 2020; Donthu et al., 2021a; Paul et al., 2021), considering the comprehensiveness of bibliometric information that it provides and its coverage of publications that met stringent requirements for indexing (Kumar et al., 2021). Moreover, compared with other scientific databases, such as Web of Science, Scopus shows high coverage, which leads to its consideration as a more comprehensive yet high-quality data source for review (Boyack et al., 2018). To collect relevant bibliography data, we performed a keyword search in October 2021. Considering their importance and centrality as concepts in our analysis, we used the search keywords "environmental risk*" and "climate risk*". To ensure that relevant studies would not be excluded when querying Scopus, the search strings were tested with several pilot searches and iteratively improved based on a preliminary analysis of the results. The search queries were also tested against a reference collection of relevant articles and refined to minimize the number of irrelevant studies. For these reasons, we added the keyword "financ*" to focus our analysis on studies that explore climate and environmental risks from a financial perspective. Moreover, during our pilot tests, we observed that the vast majority of papers retrieved without any subject area filter were irrelevant and not coherent with the purpose of our study. For these reasons, we added inclusion criteria related to the Scopus subject areas that led us to obtain only articles published in the fields of "Economics, Econometrics and Finance" and "Business, Management and Accounting". The final search queries are summarized in Table 25.1.

After removing duplicates and erroneous entries, two independent researchers scrutinized all the extracted articles to confirm the relevance of each article. Our final sample included 195 articles.

Bibliometric Analysis

After conducting the SLR, we use the bibliometric method to explore the topic of climate- and environment-related financial risks. Science mapping can be described as the spatial representation of how different items (e.g., keywords) are related to one another. In this sense, the objective of this methodology is to show the structural and dynamic aspects of a scientific domain (Börner et al., 2003). The science mapping analysis is constructed using the co-occurrence of keyword analysis (Callon et al., 1983), which allows us to quantify and visualize the thematic evolution of the research field. Using co-word analysis based on the co-occurrence of words

Table 25.1 Search strings and query description

Search String	Description
#1	TITLE-ABS-KEY ("environmental risk*" AND "financ*") AND (LIMIT- TO (DOCTYPE ,"ar") OR LIMIT-TO (DOCTYPE ,"re") OR LIMIT- TO (DOCTYPE ,"sh") AND (LIMIT-TO (SUBJAREA ,"ECON") OR LIMIT- TO (SUBJAREA ,"BUSI")) AND (LIMIT-TO (LANGUAGE ,"English"))
#2	TITLE-ABS-KEY ("climate risk*" AND "financ*") AND (LIMIT- TO (DOCTYPE ,"ar") OR LIMIT-TO (DOCTYPE ,"re") OR LIMIT- TO (DOCTYPE ,"sh") AND (LIMIT-TO (SUBJAREA ,"ECON") OR LIMIT- TO (SUBJAREA ,"BUSI")) AND (LIMIT-TO (LANGUAGE ,"English"))

Source: authors' elaboration.

supports identifying research hotspots in the research field investigated (Gao et al., 2019; Zhou & Song, 2021). The software VOSviewer 1.6.17 was used for data visualization.

Findings

To obtain an extensive view of the results, this section presents a graphical visualization of the co-occurrence of keywords. Co-occurrence means the frequency with which a keyword appears with other keywords by allowing us to detect research gaps and future research areas that might be further explored (Farrukh et al., 2020). We carried out a clustering analysis based on the co-occurrence of keywords to identify research trends by using VOSviewer to obtain the representation of a network of items. The software generates clusters represented by different colors. Each cluster represents a set of closely related nodes, while lines represent the links between the keywords. The size of the circles of each item is proportionate to the relevance of the words shown (van Eck & Waltman, 2014). A smaller distance indicates a stronger relation among the research themes. The map shown in Figure 25.1 involves all keywords and uses a full counting method.

As shown in Figure 25.1, the clusters are all interconnected, while their boundaries are blurred, with borderline keywords that incorporate themes of more than one cluster. Five different clusters have been obtained that define the main research areas and are summarized in Table 25.2 and discussed in the following sections.

The clusters have been labeled by considering the key terms. As shown in Table 25.2, clusters are different regarding the topics they address and the number of keywords they group.

We used both the overlay and density visualization function of VOSviewer to identify the most developed keywords within the field and their evolution over time.

In Figure 25.2, the larger the number of items in the neighborhood of a point and the higher the weights of the neighboring items, the closer the color of the point is to yellow (van Eck & Waltman, 2021).

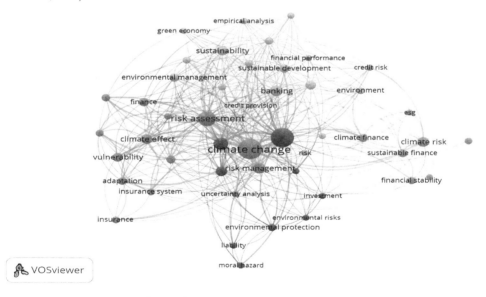

Figure 25.1 Co-occurrence of author keywords. Source: authors' elaboration.
Note: To meet the printing criteria of this chapter, the originally colored figure has been converted into grayscale. The resulting grayscale rendering retains the visual contrasts found in the initial depiction. For additional guidance, consult Table 25.2, which furnishes the compilation of keywords alongside their corresponding cluster colors, serving as a practical aid in deciphering Figure 25.1.

Table 25.2 Cluster composition

Cluster	Keyword	Occurrences	Total link strength
1 (Red)	Adaptation	7	32
1 (Red)	adaptive management	6	28
2 (Green)	Banking	14	63
2 (Green)	China	7	34
1 (Red)	climate change	55	137
1 (Red)	climate effect	12	52
4 (Yellow)	climate finance	8	25
4 (Yellow)	climate risk	13	24
4 (Yellow)	climate stress-test	5	5
2 (Green)	corporate social responsibility	11	37
5 (Purple)	credit provision	5	19
4 (Yellow)	credit risk	5	17
1 (Red)	decision making	7	21
1 (Red)	Economics	5	23
2 (Green)	empirical analysis	5	28
2 (Green)	Environment	6	14
4 (Yellow)	environmental disclosure	6	3
3 (Blue)	environmental economics	20	83
2 (Green)	environmental management	9	35
2 (Green)	environmental performance	5	16
3 (Blue)	environmental policy	12	46
3 (Blue)	environmental protection	7	25
3 (Blue)	environmental risk	48	143
2 (Green)	environmental risk management	7	28
3 (Blue)	environmental risks	5	10
4 (Yellow)	ESG	5	8
2 (Green)	Europe	6	31
1 (Red)	Finance	9	28
3 (Blue)	financial market	5	18
2 (Green)	financial performance	5	14
2 (Green)	financial services	6	23
4 (Yellow)	financial stability	7	14
1 (Red)	financial system	8	37
5 (Purple)	Governance	5	16
5 (Purple)	green economy	5	17
1 (Red)	Insurance	6	13
1 (Red)	insurance system	6	21
3 (Blue)	Investment	5	15
3 (Blue)	Liability	5	12
3 (Blue)	moral hazard	5	10
5 (Purple)	Risk	5	13
1 (Red)	risk assessment	28	114
1 (Red)	risk management	14	58
2 (Green)	Sustainability	12	43
2 (Green)	sustainable development	9	34
4 (Yellow)	sustainable finance	8	14
1 (Red)	uncertainty analysis	5	22
1 (Red)	Vulnerability	10	29

Source: authors' elaboration.

Environment-Related Financial Risks

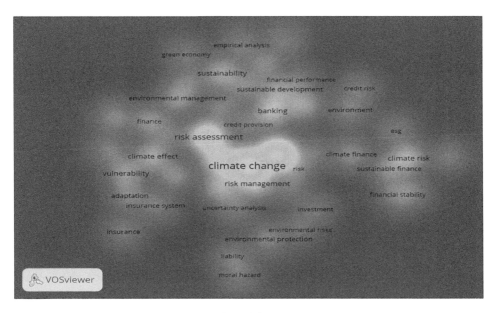

Figure 25.2 Density visualization. Source: authors' elaboration.

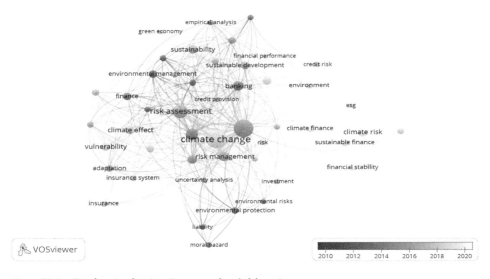

Figure 25.3 Overlay visualization. Source: authors' elaboration.

In Figure 25.2, the central area corresponds to the highest density. In contrast, the peripheral area had the lowest density. The density map shows only three areas in yellow: climate change, risk assessment, and risk management. These keywords are the core of this research field, while the others appear to be characterized by a low density. This aspect can be further analyzed by considering the overlay visualization in Figure 25.3.

In Figure 25.3, a color bar is shown in the bottom right corner of the visualization and indicates how items are mapped to colors. The color of a keyword indicates the average publication year. From Figure 25.3, some keywords are mapped in yellow, which means they have appeared more recently, while the darker ones are the older ones. In this sense, the keywords climate risk, especially financial stability and climate finance, are surely the ones that have been used most recently and can be considered new developments in this research field. In contrast, the keywords moral hazard, liability, and environmental protection have been used since 2010.

The Current State of Research: Clusters Overview

Overall, five different clusters were retrieved by VOSviewer that define the main research topics. The following sections provide an overview of each cluster.

Cluster 1 (Red) – Adaptation Finance, Climate Justice, and Vulnerability Reduction

This cluster includes articles that emphasize the role of adaptation finance as a strategic response to climate change and environmental inequalities. Articles in this cluster often propose theoretical analysis and reflections on the concepts of climate justice, climate debt, and repayment for climate (Khan et al., 2020). The concept of climate justice moves from the idea that less industrialized countries have contributed (also historically) very little to climate change. Nevertheless, they bear a significant proportion of climate change's harmful consequences (Parks and Roberts, 2006; Roberts and Parks, 2007). This phenomenon has been named "double inequity" (Füssel, 2010) based on a reverse distribution of "natural hazard" and "social resilience" and between "risk" (or vulnerability) and "responsibility" (Barrett, 2013; Chang et al., 2021). As clarified by Barrett (2013), research in climate justice focuses on justice principles, allocation criteria, carbon markets, and funding architectures (p. 1819). Cluster 1 also focuses on the role of insurance as a policy tool to address the issue of climate change (Phelan, 2011; Porrini & Schwarze, 2014) or on the potential of risk-sharing agreements in minimizing the social costs of environmentally harmful activities (Liu & Faure, 2018). The reflections on climate change and insurance are not new (Collier et al., 2021) since the insurance industry was one of the earliest sectors to consider climate-related risks and develop models to underwrite natural hazard risks (Andersson & Keskitalo, 2016). However, the increased attention to climate-related risks has also triggered the discussion of how financing for adaptation continues to remain extremely poor (Khan & Munira, 2021), with adaptation finance remaining at one-fifth of total climate finance (Khan et al., 2020).

Publications grouped in this cluster are also showing an increasing interest in the concept of private adaptation finance (Pauw, 2021; Stoll et al., 2021) and discussing barriers to adaptation in general (Biesbroek et al., 2013) and barriers to private investments in adaptation (see, e.g., Adhikari & Safaee Chalkasra, 2021).

Cluster 2 (Green) – The Relationship between Environmental Performance and Financial Performance

Cluster 2 is composed of articles that explore the relationship between environmental performance and financial performance, including environmental risk management practices in the banking industry. Several studies have confirmed that environmental performance and pollution protection and prevention activities are affected by firms' financial status (Andersen, 2017; Tian & Lin, 2019; Zhang et al., 2019; Zhang, 2021). Credit constraints significantly increase pollution emissions, particularly in industries with greater reliance on external credit (Andersen, 2017). The relationship between access to finance and environmental performance confirms that financial institutions can play a pivotal role in removing financing barriers and driving corporate social responsibility activities to promote positive environmental activities (Shen et al., 2021; Zhang, 2021). More specifically, financial institutions' environmental considerations influence the availability of financial support and, consequently, firm environmental performance (Coulson & Monks, 1999). Moreover, the existing relationship between environmental risk and borrowers' failure to fulfill their obligations force banks to incorporate environmental criteria into credit risk management (Zhang, 2021). The cluster also reveals the growing interest in assessing the banking sector's environmental performance (Bătae et al., 2021). Papers in this cluster also analyze the relationship between ESG performance and corporate financial performance or stock performance in the banking sector by showing mixed results (Azmi et al., 2021; Miralles-Quirós et al., 2019; Siueia et al., 2019).

Cluster 3 (Blue) – Growing Environmental Risks, Limited Liability, and Moral Hazard

The cluster is mainly composed of the themes at the intersection between environmental risk (48), environmental protection (7), liability (5), and moral hazard (5). The concept of liability is strictly connected with the concepts of adaptation finance (Khan et al., 2020), insurance (He, 2016; Ross et al., 2007), and climate litigation (Bouwer, 2018; Farber, 2008) located in Cluster 1.

Liability risks can act as a mechanism to transmit climate-related risks from individual market actors, with secondary impacts at portfolio levels and, potentially, tertiary impacts on financial systems (Barker et al., 2021). Requiring operators to hold financial security, such as bonds, insurance, or guarantees, to cover their environmental liabilities offers a potential regulatory instrument to restrict the incentives for environmental irresponsibility derived from the doctrine of limited liability (Mackie, 2014).

Cluster 4 (Yellow) – Credit Risk, Climate Stress Tests, and Financial Stability

The majority of the articles from Cluster 4 focus on the need to estimate the impact of climate risks on the financial system (Battiston et al., 2017) by considering the integration of stress factors from the broader ecological context into the modeling of financial effects (Gramlich, 2018) and the use of network models (Battiston et al., 2017; Monasterolo, 2020).

Climate change can increase the default rate of corporate loans, effecting the banking system's stability (Dafermos et al., 2018). In a recent study, Nieto (2019) emphasized the relevance of exploring prudential policy responses and statistical and reporting frameworks that could contribute to reducing the negative externalities of climate risks. Several studies have been conducted on the potential impact of environmental and climate risks on the financial system in recent years. The question has been recently challenged by central banks (e.g., European Central Bank), financial supervisors, and key international standard setters and framework developers (e.g., Bank of International Settlements). The academic literature in this cluster reveals that climate risks pose a threat to the solvency of the banking system via network effects, that there is a negative correlation between natural catastrophes related to climate change and the resilience of financial markets, and that a higher risk premium is related to environmentally unfriendly infrastructure debt.

In a climate stress-test exercise developed by Battiston et al. (2017), investors are considerably exposed to financial contracts and securities issued by companies with revenues directly or indirectly linked to fossil fuel extraction and combustion. Works in this cluster also focus on the potential use of fiscal, financial, and monetary policies in tackling climate change (see, e.g., Campiglio, 2016; Campiglio et al., 2018; Dafermos et al., 2018; D'Orazio & Popoyan, 2019; Hilmi et al., 2021; Matikainen et al., 2017; McKibbin et al., 2020; Rozenberg et al., 2013; Shobande, 2021) or, more generally, on the role and extent of central bank mandates and financial regulators' powers in supporting a rapid and orderly low-carbon transition (Campiglio et al., 2017; Dikau & Volz, 2021). In this vein, for example, Dafermos et al. (2018) demonstrate how the implementation of a global green quantitative easing (QE) program can reduce climate-induced financial instability, while Dikau and Volz (2021) explained how climate risks can directly affect central banks' traditional core responsibilities by suggesting that all institutions ought to incorporate climate risks into their policy frameworks.

Cluster 5 (Purple) – Credit Provision, Capital Requirements, and Green Policies as Transition Accelerators

Cluster 5 focuses on the role of climate-dependent capital requirements and credit provision/rationing policies as interventions that can facilitate a quicker transition to a more climate-friendly economy due to their ability to channel funding to environmentally friendly activities and to increase the cost of business for carbon-intensive activities (Matikainen et al, 2017; Prudential Regulatory Authority, 2021). Actions such as introducing a global carbon tax and revising the macroprudential banking framework via a green supporting factor have been advocated to align investments with climate targets (Dunz et al., 2021). Dafermos and Nikolaidi (2021) explored the potential impact of the "green supporting factor" and the "dirty penalizing factor" on climate-related financial risks by identifying the transmission channels through which these green differentiated capital requirements can affect credit provision and loan spreads. Among the several instruments that could be implemented, differentiated "green" reserve requirements are drawing particular attention (Campiglio, 2016; D'Orazio & Popoyan, 2019; Rozenberg et al., 2013; Volz, 2017). In a recent study, Lamperti et al. (2021) tested a set of "green" finance policies by highlighting how green capital requirements spur productivity without hampering financial stability and how carbon risk adjustment and green public guarantees mitigate emissions but increase instability. Despite the growing attention toward developing green macroprudential regulation, the possible destabilizing effects for the financial sector remain to be explored.

Discussion of Results

The potential effects and impacts of climate risks in terms of financial stability (or instability) are increasingly attracting attention at the academic and policy levels. This study aimed to disentangle the current stance of scholarly research on climate and environment-related financial risks as it emerges from the keywords used by scholars to address this topic. We adopted a co-word analysis, which is a specific technique developed to better understand the relationships among keywords that emerge as being the most significant in the literature (Callon et al., 1991).

In particular, the co-occurrence of keywords and the cluster analysis led us to identify five main research themes that have been labeled considering the main keywords grouped.

Each of these themes represents an area of interest, and all the themes appear interconnected.

By considering both the overlay map and the composition of our clusters, we can affirm that three main themes can be considered the core of this research field: adaptation finance, environmental credit risk management, and environmental risk/environmental liability. In contrast, the themes related to climate stress testing and credit provision can be considered the two main emerging areas of debate.

What Are We Missing? Future Research Directions and Open Issues

This section provides future research directions based on the review of the five research clusters discussed before. In particular, these future directions attempt to provide a set of guidelines to ensure more comprehensive research efforts in the area of climate- and environment-related financial risks. Research into climate and environment-related financial risks has come a long way from exploring fundamental issues on environmental liability that preoccupied the early literature. Our review has shown that research has started to address complex questions on conceptualizing and measuring the potential impact of climate and environment-related financial risks in terms of financial stability. Despite significant theoretical advancements, notable knowledge gaps remain in a number of areas. The following sections provide some suggestions for future research directions.

Contamination with Other Research Fields: Coproducing Knowledge against Climate Change

The climate- and environment-related financial risk challenges are complex. Complexity also requires interdisciplinary research approaches as well as more cooperation between scientists and nonacademic stakeholders with policymaking expertise. Interdisciplinarity – defined as the purposeful integration of various pieces of disciplinary knowledge (see, e.g., Bergman et al., 2012; Hadorn et al., 2006; Pohl, 2005) – can help researchers from different disciplines collaborate to jointly investigate a research problem to develop new research approaches. For example, current stress-testing exercises miss several variables and are often based on the assumption that future challenges may be replicated as a function of past experiences (assumption of stationarity), but this assumption is more than critical (Gramlich, 2018, p. 174). Future research directions should consider the need to overcome the current data limitations by promoting the integration of different scientific areas (e.g., physics, mathematics, climate scientists).

Moreover, a methodological gap in this area exists. To shed light on the financial implications of climate change, more studies based on methodologies such as network modeling, mathematical financial modeling, agent-based approaches, dynamic evolutionary macroeconomic modeling, and financial econometrics are needed. At the same time, considering the growing pressure from regulatory authorities worldwide, in the coming years, more data will become available because banks will be mandatorily required to collect and disclose them. This is the case, for example, of banks' exposure to pollutant economic sectors. This will lead researchers to explore this field with new lenses and more robust approaches.

New Risk Management Models for Tail Risks and Anthropogenic Hazards: The Need to Not Underestimate Climate Change by Considering It as a "Green Swan"

Future research should address the knowledge gap currently existing in the area of climate/environmental risk management for banks by working on the development of new risk frameworks. Current publications seem to focus on a macro level, for example, by underestimating the need for new accounting and disclosure standards. Going even deeper, to correctly assess the exposure of the banking industry to climate and environmental risks, an assessment of their clients' exposure could be useful even considering the need to develop a risk management approach for all banking activities. Risk matrices able to capture vulnerability to natural events and industry segments should also develop adequate risk management frameworks for the entire financial sector by helping to assess the overall exposure of banks, especially of *global systemically important banks* (G-SIBs).

Emerging Financial Risks: Not Only Climate Change

Environmental breakdown is a more complex set of phenomena than climate change (Kedward et al., 2020). A recent policy paper published by the Bank for International Settlements (BIS) defines environmental risks as those that may arise from exposures to activities that may cause or be affected by environmental degradation, such as pollution (BIS, 2021). The Dasgupta Review (Dasgupta, 2021) – a comprehensive report on the economic explanation behind the current state of global biodiversity aimed at central banks and finance ministries – highlighted that "existing private financial flows that are adversely affecting the biosphere outstrip those that are enhancing natural assets, and there is a need to identify and reduce financial flows that directly harm and deplete natural assets" (p. 474). However, the recent supervisory orientation – including for example, the recent documents published by the BIS and the ECB – focuses mainly on climate change as a source of financial risks and financial instability. More generally, under the umbrella of climate and environment-related risks, the overall planetary boundary framework (Rockström et al., 2009) (which includes climate change, biosphere integrity, land-system change, freshwater use, biochemical flows, ocean acidification, atmospheric aerosol loading, stratospheric ozone depletion, and novel entities) should be considered.

New Shapes of Adaptation and Mitigation Finance

Another aspect that should be considered is the need to switch from event mitigation to adaptation strategies. Adaptation finance represents one of the main research themes identified by our analysis. However, studies in this field seem oriented toward the analysis of current policies and not toward the identification of new strategies. In this sense, future research directions should consider this research gap by focusing on new and alternative funding strategies able to channel private funding. Finally, less has been written about the role of risk mitigation tools (guarantees by third parties, reinsurance, or other forms of protection) and of climate derivatives both as interesting tools for mitigation and adaptation strategies and as a way to hedge against financial losses related to climate risks.

Conclusions and Limitations of the Study

Climate change and environmental challenges are changing policy agendas worldwide. The increased frequency of severe weather events poses severe implications for asset prices, macroeconomic outcomes, credit risks, and the cost and coverage of insurance contracts. At the same time, the transition to a carbon-free economy might increase the risks of economic dislocation and "stranded" assets (Campiglio et al., 2018).

The discussion around the role of the entire banking industry toward climate change questions can be approached from three different perspectives: the first perspective reflects the role of banks in terms of capital provision; the second perspective reflects the need for banks to be "accountable" and "responsible" to their stakeholders; and the third perspective reflects concerns about the potential impact of climate change on banks and thus on financial stability. Regarding this latter perspective, academic literature reveals that climate change can increase the rate of default on corporate loans with effects on the stability of the banking system (Dafermos et al., 2018). The issue has been recently addressed by central banks (e.g., BoE, ECB), financial supervisors, key international standard setters, and organizations (e.g., BIS, ESRB, EBA) that are focusing on two main directions: the development of scenario analysis and of new disclosure frameworks, reflective of how climate-related financial risks are integrated into governance and risk management processes.

Research into climate and environment-related financial risks has come a long way from exploring fundamental issues on environmental liability that preoccupied the early literature. Our review has shown that research has started to address complex questions on conceptualizing and measuring the potential impact of climate and environment-related financial risks in terms of financial stability. Despite significant theoretical advancements, notable knowledge gaps remain in a number of areas. At the theoretical level, the findings emerging from our analysis are essential for knowledge advancement in this research field by depicting the current state of the research and identifying gaps in the literature, which could guide future research directions. We have documented five main research areas with different levels of development and with several interconnections. Some research areas, such as monetary or macroprudential policies and stress testing, have emerged as the most recent research trends. In contrast, those associated with the concept of adaptation finance and environmental liability show an old charm. Exploring how themes and research areas evolved led us to understand how policymaking needs drive research topics. The entire research field appears not too developed from an academic perspective, with a limited number of journal articles published and authors interested. Conversely, gray literature – that despite not being considered in our study cannot be ignored – from the most reputable policymakers (such as the European Commission and the Bank of England) represents the driving force of research in this field, with academia acting as just "follower". Excluding some authors, such as Monasterolo and Battiston, often cited by policy reports, academia appears to be far from contributing to this research area in a groundbreaking way. This can be considered both a theoretical and practical challenge. Without the voices of researchers from academia, this would be a great lost opportunity for cutting-edge research on this topic.

Moreover, a lack of cross-sector collaboration affects the inter- and transdisciplinarity of this field, which in nature should be at the intersection of several scientific areas. This is of particular interest if we think, for example, of the need for more precise forecasts that can also be used for stress testing of new and more effective policies. Integrating different perspectives will likely benefit both practical and theoretical advancement. Finally, for scholars newly interested in this field of research, this study identified "research areas" that may prove to be a good starting point.

This study reveals some interesting results, but several limitations exist. These limitations are widely recognized in the literature, including data sources, data quality, data type, and, more generally, sampling biases and analysis method shortcomings. More specifically, bibliometric data have well-known limitations, including errors and inconsistencies related to the indexing of subjects (Heberger et al., 2010). Moreover, our sample includes only articles from Scopus. Multisource searching and cross-comparison among different databases could be helpful for future wider analysis. Additionally, our inclusion criteria were particularly stringent by excluding books, book chapters, journal articles published in languages other than English, and gray literature, which are a significant part of the literature on climate risks. Future studies should include these further sources of knowledge.

Finally, the results reported in this paper should be considered jointly with the limitations of the co-word technique.

References

Adhikari, B., & Safaee Chalkasra, L. S. (2021). Mobilizing private sector investment for climate action: Enhancing ambition and scaling up implementation. *Journal of Sustainable Finance and Investment*, 1–18. https://doi.org/10.1080/20430795.2021.1917929

Alexander, K. (2019). *Principles of banking regulation*. Cambridge University Press.
Andersen, D. C. (2017). Do credit constraints favor dirty production? Theory and plant-level evidence. *Journal of Environmental Economics and Management*, *84*, 189–208. https://doi.org/10.1016/j.jeem.2017.04.002
Andersson, L. F., & Keskitalo, E. C. H. (2016). Insurance models and climate risk assessments in a historical context. *Financial History Review*, *23*(2), 219–243. https://doi.org/10.1017/S096856501600010X
Azmi, W., Hassan, M. K., Houston, R., & Karim, M. S. (2021). ESG activities and banking performance: International evidence from emerging economies. *Journal of International Financial Markets, Institutions and Money*, *70*, 101277. https://doi.org/10.1016/j.intfin.2020.101277
Baas, J., Schotten, M., Plume, A., Côté, G., & Karimi, R. (2020). Scopus as a curated, high-quality bibliometric data source for academic research in quantitative science studies. *Quantitative Science Studies*, *1*(1), 377–386. https://doi.org/10.1162/qss_a_00019
Bank for International Settlements (BIS). (2021). *Climate and environmental risks – Guide for supervisors – Executive summary*. https://www.bis.org/fsi/fsisummaries/climate_env_risks.pdf
Barker, S., Dellios, J., & Mulholland, E. (2021). *Legal action as a driver and consequence of climate-related physical risk adaptation, Liability risk and adaptation finance*. Minter Ellison and UN Environment Programme and Finance Initiative. https://www.unepfi.org/wordpress/wp-content/uploads/2021/04/UNEPFI-Climate-Change-Litigation-Report-Lowres.pdf
Barrett, S. (2013). Local level climate justice? Adaptation finance and vulnerability reduction. *Global Environmental Change*, *23*(6), 1819–1829. https://doi.org/10.1016/j.gloenvcha.2013.07.015
Bătae, O. M., Dragomir, V. D., & Feleagă, L. (2021). The relationship between environmental, social, and financial performance in the banking sector: A European study. *Journal of Cleaner Production*, *290*, 125791. https://doi.org/10.1016/j.jclepro.2021.125791
Battiston, S. (2019). The importance of being forward-looking: Managing financial stability in the face of climate risk. *Financial Stability Review*, *23*, 39–48. https://econpapers.repec.org/article/bfrfisrev/2019_3a23_3a5.htm
Battiston, S., Dafermos, Y., & Monasterolo, I. (2021). Climate risks and financial stability. *Journal of Financial Stability*, *54*, 100867. https://doi.org/10.1016/j.jfs.2021.100867
Battiston, S., Mandel, A., Monasterolo, I., Schütze, F., & Visentin, G. (2017). A climate stress-test of the financial system. *Nature Climate Change*, *7*(4), 283–288. https://doi.org/10.1038/nclimate3255
Baudino, P., & Svoronos, J.-P. (2021). *Stress-testing banks for climate change: A comparison of practices*. FSI insights on policy implementation no 34, Bank for International Settlements. https://www.bis.org/fsi/publ/insights34.pdf
Bergmann, M., Jahn, T., Knobloch, T., Krohn, W., Pohl, C., & Schramm, E. (2012). *Methods for transdisciplinary research: A primer for practice*. Campus Verlag.
Biesbroek, G. R., Klostermann, J. E., Termeer, C. J., & Kabat, P. (2013). On the nature of barriers to climate change adaptation. *Regional Environmental Change*, *13*(5), 1119–1129. https://doi.org/10.1007/s10113-013-0421-y
Bingler, J. A., Senni, C. C., & Monnin, P. (2021). Uncertainty is not an excuse. Integrating climate risks into monetary policy operations and financial supervision. *SUERF policy briefs*, (72). https://www.suerf.org/docx/f_2047faa23a3afb0518e063b768386764_22935_suerf.pdf
Börner, K., Chen, C., & Boyack, K. W. (2003). Visualizing knowledge domains. *Annual Review of Information Science and Technology*, *37*(1), 179–255. http://nwb.cns.iu.edu/papers/arist02.pdf
Bouma, J. J., Jeucken, M., & Klinkers, L. (Eds.). (2017). *Sustainable banking: The greening of finance*. Routledge.
Bouwer, K. (2018). The unsexy future of climate change litigation. *Journal of Environmental Law*, *30*(3), 483–506. https://doi.org/10.1093/jel/eqy017
Boyack, K. W., van Eck, N. J., Colavizza, G., & Waltman, L. (2018). Characterizing in-text citations in scientific articles: A large-scale analysis. *Journal of Informetrics*, *12*(1), 59–73. https://doi.org/10.1016/j.joi.2017.11.005
Callon, M., Courtial, J. P., & Laville, F. (1991). Coword analysis as a tool for describing the network of interactions between basic and technological research: The case of polymer chemsitry. *Scientometrics*, *22*(1), 155–205. https://doi.org/10.1007/bf02019280
Callon, M., Courtial, J. P., Turner, W. A., & Bauin, S. (1983). From translations to problematic networks: An introduction to coword analysis. *Social Science Information*, *22*(2), 191–235. https://doi.org/10.1177/053901883022002003
Campiglio, E. (2016). Beyond carbon pricing: The role of banking and monetary policy in financing the transition to a low-carbon economy. *Ecological Economics*, *121*, 220–230. https://doi.org/10.1016/j.ecolecon.2015.03.020

Campiglio, E., Dafermos, Y., Monnin, P., Ryan-Collins, J., Schotten, G., & Tanaka, M. (2017). Finance and climate change: What role for central banks and financial regulators. In *CEP-DNB workshop on "central banking and green finance"*, 28–29.

Campiglio, E., Dafermos, Y., Monnin, P., Ryan-Collins, J., Schotten, G., & Tanaka, M. (2018). Climate change challenges for central banks and financial regulators. *Nature Climate Change*, 8(6), 462–468. https://doi.org/10.1038/s41558-018-0175-0

Capasso, G., Gianfrate, G., & Spinelli, M. (2020). Climate change and credit risk. *Journal of Cleaner Production*, 266, 121634. https://doi.org/10.1016/j.jclepro.2020.121634

Carney, M. (2015). Breaking the tragedy of the horizon—Climate change and financial stability speech given at Lloyd's of London. https://www.bankofengland.co.uk/-/media/boe/files/speech/2015/breaking-the-tragedy-of-the-horizon-climate-change-and-financial-stability.pdf

Caselli, G., & Figueira, C. (2020). The impact of climate risks on the insurance and banking industries. In M. Migliorelli & P. Dessertine (Eds.), *Sustainability and financial risks: The impact of climate change, environmental degradation and social inequality on financial markets* (pp. 31–62). Springer International Publishing. https://doi.org/10.1007/978-3-030-54530-7_2

Chang, H.-S., Su, Q., & Chen, Y. S. (2021). Establish an assessment framework for risk and investment under climate change from the perspective of climate justice. *Environmental Science and Pollution Research*, 28(46), 66435–66447. https://doi.org/10.1007/s11356-021-15708-2

Collier, S. J., Elliott, R., & Lehtonen, T. K. (2021). Climate change and insurance. *Economy and Society*, 50(2), 158–172. https://doi.org/10.1080/03085147.2021.1903771

Coulson, A. B., & Monks, V. (1999). Corporate environmental performance considerations within bank lending decisions. *Eco-Management and Auditing: The Journal of Corporate Environmental Management*, 6(1), 1–10. https://doi.org/10.1002/(SICI)1099-0925(199903)6:1<1::AID-EMA93>3.0.CO;2-M

D'Orazio, P., & Popoyan, L. (2019). Fostering green investments and tackling climate-related financial risks: Which role for macroprudential policies? *Ecological Economics*, 160, 25–37. https://doi.org/10.1016/j.ecolecon.2019.01.029

Dafermos, Y. (2021). Climate change, central banking and financial supervision: Beyond the risk exposure approach. In S. Kappes, L.-P. Rochon, & G. Vallet (Eds.), *The future of central banking*. Edward Elgar (Forthcoming). https://eprints.soas.ac.uk/35851/1/WP%20243.pdf

Dafermos, Y., & Nikolaidi, M. (2021). How can green differentiated capital requirements affect climate risks? A dynamic macrofinancial analysis. *Journal of Financial Stability*, 54, 100871. https://doi.org/10.1016/j.jfs.2021.100871

Dafermos, Y., Nikolaidi, M., & Galanis, G. (2018). Climate change, financial stability and monetary policy. *Ecological Economics*, 152, 219–234. https://doi.org/10.1016/j.ecolecon.2018.05.011

Dasgupta, P. (2021). *The economics of biodiversity: The Dasgupta review*. HM Treasury. https://assets.publishing.service.gov.uk/government/uploads/system/uploads/attachment_data/file/962785/The_Economics_of_Biodiversity_The_Dasgupta_Review_Full_Report.pdf

Dikau, S., & Volz, U. (2021). Central Bank mandates, sustainability objectives and the promotion of green finance. *Ecological Economics*, 184, 107022. https://doi.org/10.1016/j.ecolecon.2021.107022

Donthu, N., Kumar, S., Mukherjee, D., Pandey, N., & Lim, W. M. (2021a). How to conduct a bibliometric analysis: An overview and guidelines. *Journal of Business Research*, 133, 285–296. https://doi.org/10.1016/j.jbusres.2021.04.070

Donthu, N., Kumar, S., Pandey, N., & Gupta, P. (2021b). Forty years of the International Journal of Information Management: A bibliometric analysis. *International Journal of Information Management*, 57, 102307. https://doi.org/10.1016/j.ijinfomgt.2020.102307

Donthu, N., Kumar, S., Pandey, N., Pandey, N., & Mishra, A. (2021c). Mapping the electronic word-of-mouth (eWOM) research: A systematic review and bibliometric analysis. *Journal of Business Research*, 135, 758–773. https://doi.org/10.1016/j.jbusres.2021.07.015

Dunz, N., Essenfelder, A. H., Mazzocchetti, A., Monasterolo, I., & Raberto, M. (2021). Compounding COVID-19 and climate risks: The interplay of banks' lending and government's policy in the shock recovery. *Journal of Banking and Finance*, 106306. https://doi.org/10.1016/j.jbankfin.2021.106306

European Central Bank (ECB). (2020). *Guide on climate-related and environmental risks. Supervisory expectations relating to risk management and disclosure*. https://www.bankingsupervision.europa.eu/legalframework/publiccons/pdf/climate-related_risks/ssm.202005_draft_guide_on_climate-related_and_environmental_risks.en.pdf

Farber, D. A. (2008). Tort law in the era of climate change, Katrina, and 9/11: Exploring liability for extraordinary risks. *Valparaiso University Law Review*, 43, 1075. http://doi.org/10.2139/ssrn.1121125

Farrukh, M., Meng, F., Wu, Y., & Nawaz, K. (2020). Twenty-eight years of business strategy and the environment research: A bibliometric analysis. *Business Strategy and the Environment, 29*(6), 2572–2582. https://doi.org/10.1002/bse.2521

Füssel, H. M. (2010). How inequitable is the global distribution of responsibility, capability, and vulnerability to climate change: A comprehensive indicator-based assessment. *Global Environmental Change, 20*(4), 597–611. https://doi.org/10.1016/j.gloenvcha.2010.07.009

Gao, Y., Ge, L., Shi, S., Sun, Y., Liu, M., Wang, B., ... Tian, J. (2019). Global trends and future prospects of e-waste research: A bibliometric analysis. *Environmental Science and Pollution Research, 26*(17), 17809–17820. https://doi.org/10.1007/s11356-019-05071-8

Gramlich, D. (2018). Sustainability stress testing the financial system: Challenges and approaches. In T. Walker, S. D. Kibsey, & R. Crichton (Eds.), *Designing a sustainable financial system: Development goals and socio-ecological responsibility* (pp. 173–197). Palgrave Macmillan. https://doi.org/10.1007/978-3-319-66387-6_7

Hadorn, G. H., Bradley, D., Pohl, C., Rist, S., & Wiesmann, U. (2006). Implications of transdisciplinarity for sustainability research. *Ecological Economics, 60*(1), 119–128. https://doi.org/10.1016/j.ecolecon.2005.12.002

He, Q. (2016). Mitigation of climate change risks and regulation by insurance: A feasible proposal for China. *Boston College Environmental Affairs Law Review, 43*, 319. https://ssrn.com/abstract=2796642

Heberger, A. E., Christie, C. A., & Alkin, M. C. (2010). A bibliometric analysis of the academic influences of and on evaluation theorists' published works. *American Journal of Evaluation, 31*(1), 24–44. https://doi.org/10.1177/1098214009354120

Hilmi, N., Djoundourian, S., Shahin, W., & Safa, A. (2021). Does the ECB policy of quantitative easing impact environmental policy objectives? *Journal of Economic Policy Reform*, 1–13. https://doi.org/10.1080/17487870.2020.1855176

Kedward, K., Ryan-Collins, J., & Chenet, H. (2020). Managing nature-related financial risks: A precautionary policy approach for central banks and financial supervisors. Available at SSRN. http://doi.org/10.2139/ssrn.3726637

Khan, M., Robinson, S. A., Weikmans, R., Ciplet, D., & Roberts, J. T. (2020). Twenty-five years of adaptation finance through a climate justice lens. *Climatic Change, 161*(2), 251–269. https://doi.org/10.1007/s10584-019-02563-x

Khan, M. R., & Munira, S. (2021). Climate change adaptation as a global public good: Implications for financing. *Climatic Change, 167*(3), 1–18. https://doi.org/10.1007/s10584-021-03195-w

Kumar, S., Pandey, N., Lim, W. M., Chatterjee, A. N., & Pandey, N. (2021). What do we know about transfer pricing? Insights from bibliometric analysis. *Journal of Business Research, 134*, 275–287. https://doi.org/10.1016/j.jbusres.2021.05.041

Laguir, I., Marais, M., El Baz, J., & Stekelorum, R. (2018). Reversing the business rationale for environmental commitment in banking: Does financial performance lead to higher environmental performance? *Management Decision, 56*(2), 358–375. https://doi.org/10.1108/MD-12-2016-0890

Lamperti, F., Bosetti, V., Roventini, A., Tavoni, M., & Treibich, T. (2021). Three green financial policies to address climate risks. *Journal of Financial Stability, 54*, 100875. https://doi.org/10.1016/j.jfs.2021.100875

Liu, J., & Faure, M. (2018). Risk-sharing agreements to cover environmental damage: Theory and practice. *International Environmental Agreements: Politics, Law and Economics, 18*(2), 255–273. https://doi.org/10.1007/s10784-018-9386-0

Mackie, C. (2014). The regulatory potential of financial security to reduce environmental risk. *Journal of Environmental Law, 26*(2), 189–214. https://doi.org/10.1093/jel/equ014

Matikainen, S., Campiglio, E., & Zenghelis, D. (2017). The climate impact of quantitative easing. *Policy Paper, Grantham Research Institute on Climate Change and the Environment*. London School of Economics and Political Science. https://www.lse.ac.uk/granthaminstitute/wp-content/uploads/2017/05/ClimateImpactQuantEasing_Matikainen-et-al.pdf

McKibbin, W. J., Morris, A. C., Wilcoxen, P. J., & Panton, A. J. (2020). Climate change and monetary policy: Issues for policy design and modelling. *Oxford Review of Economic Policy, 36*(3), 579–603. https://doi.org/10.1093/oxrep/graa040

Miralles-Quirós, M. M., Miralles-Quirós, J. L., & Redondo Hernández, J. (2019). ESG performance and shareholder value creation in the banking industry: International differences. *Sustainability, 11*(5), 1404. https://doi.org/10.3390/su11051404

Monasterolo, I. (2020). Climate change and the financial system. *Annual Review of Resource Economics, 12*(1), 299–320. https://doi.org/10.1146/annurev-resource-110119-031134

Monnin, P. (2018). Integrating climate risks into credit risk assessment-current methodologies and the case of central banks corporate bond purchases. *Council on Economic Policies, Discussion Note, 2018*(4). http://doi.org/10.2139/ssrn.3350918

Monnin, P. (2020). Shifting gears: Integrating climate risks in monetary policy operations. *CEP Policy Brief, No. 2020/1.* https://www.cepweb.org/wp-content/uploads/2020/01/CEP-Policy-Brief-Integrating-climate-risks-in-monetary-policy-operations.pdf

Nieto, M. J. (2019). Banks, climate risk and financial stability. *Journal of Financial Regulation and Compliance, 27*(2), 243–262. https://doi.org/10.1108/JFRC-03-2018-0043

Parks, B. C., & Roberts, J. T. (2006). Globalization, vulnerability to climate change, and perceived injustice. *Society and Natural Resources, 19*(4), 337–355. https://doi.org/10.1080/08941920500519255

Paul, J., Lim, W. M., O'Cass, A., Hao, A. W., & Bresciani, S. (2021). Scientific procedures and rationales for systematic literature reviews (SPAR-4-SLR). *International Journal of Consumer Studies, 45*(4), O1–O16. https://doi.org/10.1111/ijcs.12695

Pauw, W. P. (2021). The adaptation finance gap can only be closed by limiting the adaptation costs. *One Earth, 4*(10), 1352–1355. https://doi.org/10.1016/j.oneear.2021.09.002

Phelan, L. (2011). Managing climate risk: Extreme weather events and the future of insurance in a climate-changed world. *Australasian Journal of Environmental Management, 18*(4), 223–232. https://doi.org/10.1080/14486563.2011.611486

Pohl, C. (2005). Transdisciplinary collaboration in environmental research. *Futures, 37*(10), 1159–1178. https://doi.org/10.1016/j.futures.2005.02.009

Porrini, D., & Schwarze, R. (2014). Insurance models and European climate change policies: An assessment. *European Journal of Law and Economics, 38*(1), 7–28. https://doi.org/10.1007/s10657-012-9376-6

Prudential Regulatory Authority (PRA). (2021). *Climate-related financial risk management and the role of capital requirements.* Bank of England. https://www.bankofengland.co.uk/-/media/boe/files/prudential-regulation/publication/2021/October/climate-change-adaptation-report-2021.pdf?la=en&hash=FF4A0C618471462E10BC704D4AA58727EC8F8720

Roberts, J. T., & Parks, B. (2007). *A climate of injustice: Global inequality, north-south politics, and climate policy.* MIT Press. https://doi.org/10.1017/S1537592710003634

Rockström, J., Steffen, W., Noone, K., Persson, Å., Chapin III, F. S., Lambin, E., … Foley, J. (2009). Planetary boundaries: Exploring the safe operating space for humanity. *Ecology and Society, 14*(2). https://www.jstor.org/stable/26268316

Roncoroni, A., Battiston, S., Escobar-Farfán, L. O., & Martinez-Jaramillo, S. (2021). Climate risk and financial stability in the network of banks and investment funds. *Journal of Financial Stability, 54*, 100870. https://doi.org/10.1016/j.jfs.2021.100870

Ross, C., Mills, E., & Hecht, S. B. (2007). Limiting liability in the greenhouse: Insurance risk-management strategies in the context of global climate change. *Stanford Journal of International Law, 43*, 251. http://ssrn.com/abstract=987942

Rozenberg, J., Hallegatte, S., Perrissin-Fabert, B., & Hourcade, J. C. (2013). Funding low-carbon investments in the absence of a carbon tax. *Climate Policy, 13*(1), 134–141. https://doi.org/10.1080/14693062.2012.691222

Schnabel, I. (2021). Climate change and monetary policy. *Finance and Development, 0058*(003), A018. https://www.elibrary.imf.org/view/journals/022/0058/003/article-A018-en.xml

Schoenmaker, D. (2021). Greening monetary policy. *Climate Policy, 21*(4), 581–592. https://doi.org/10.1080/14693062.2020.1868392

Shen, H., Wu, H., Long, W., & Luo, L. (2021). Environmental performance of firms and access to bank loans. *International Journal of Accounting, 56*(2), 2150007. https://doi.org/10.1142/S1094406021500074

Shobande, O. A. (2021). Is climate change a monetary phenomenon? Evidence from time series analysis. *International Journal of Sustainable Development and World Ecology*, 1–13. https://doi.org/10.1080/13504509.2021.1920064

Siueia, T. T., Wang, J., & Deladem, T. G. (2019). Corporate social responsibility and financial performance: A comparative study in the Sub-Saharan Africa banking sector. *Journal of Cleaner Production, 226*, 658–668. https://doi.org/10.1016/j.jclepro.2019.04.027

Stoll, P. P., Pauw, W. P., Tohme, F., & Grüning, C. (2021). Mobilizing private adaptation finance: Lessons learned from the green climate fund. *Climatic Change, 167*(3), 1–19. https://doi.org/10.1007/s10584-021-03190-1

Tian, P., & Lin, B. (2019). Impact of financing constraints on firm's environmental performance: Evidence from China with survey data. *Journal of Cleaner Production, 217*, 432–439. https://doi.org/10.1016/j.jclepro.2019.01.209

Tranfield, D., Denyer, D., & Smart, P. (2003). Towards a methodology for developing evidence-informed management knowledge by means of systematic review. *British Journal of Management, 14*(3), 207–222. https://doi.org/10.1111/1467-8551.00375

van Eck, N. J., & Waltman, L. (2010). Software survey: VOSviewer, a computer program for bibliometric mapping. *Scientometrics, 84*(2), 523–538. https://doi.org/10.1007/s11192-009-0146-3

van Eck, N. J., & Waltman, L. (2014). Visualizing bibliometric networks. In Y. Ding, R. Rousseau, & D. Wolfram (Eds.), *Measuring scholarly impact: Methods and practice* (pp. 285–320). Springer. https://doi.org/10.1007/978-3-319-10377-8_13

van Eck, N. J., & Waltman, L. (2021). VOSviewer manual: Manual for VOSviewer version 1.6. 17. Centre for Science and Technology Studies (CWTS) of Leiden University. https://www.vosviewer.com/documentation/Manual_VOSviewer_1.6.17.pdf

Volz, U. (2017). On the role of central banks in enhancing green finance. UN Environment Inquiry Working Paper, 17/01. https://eprints.soas.ac.uk/23817/1/On_the_Role_of_Central_Banks_in_Enhancing_Green_Finance(1).pdf

Weber, O. (2005). Sustainability benchmarking of European banks and financial and financial service organizations. *Corporate Social Responsibility and Environmental Management, 12*(2), 73–87. https://doi.org/10.1002/csr.77

Weber, O., Fenchel, M., & Scholz, R. W. (2008). Empirical analysis of the integration of environmental risks into the credit risk management process of European banks. *Business Strategy and the Environment, 17*(3), 149–159. https://doi.org/10.1002/bse.507

Weber, O., Scholz, R. W., & Michalik, G. (2010). Incorporating sustainability criteria into credit risk management. *Business Strategy and the Environment, 19*(1), 39–50. https://doi.org/10.1002/bse.636

Xepapadeas, A. (2021). Climate change and the financial system: A note. *Journal of Industrial and Business Economics, 48*(1), 5–13. https://doi.org/10.1007/s40812-020-00158-7

Zhang, D. (2021). How environmental performance affects firms' access to credit: Evidence from EU countries. *Journal of Cleaner Production, 315*, 128294. https://doi.org/10.1016/j.jclepro.2021.128294

Zhang, D., Du, W., Zhuge, L., Tong, Z., & Freeman, R. B. (2019). Do financial constraints curb firms' efforts to control pollution? Evidence from Chinese manufacturing firms. *Journal of Cleaner Production, 215*, 1052–1058. https://doi.org/10.1016/j.jclepro.2019.01.112

Zhou, C., & Song, W. (2021). Digitalization as a way forward: A bibliometric analysis of 20 years of servitization research. *Journal of Cleaner Production, 300*, 126943. https://doi.org/10.1016/j.jclepro.2021.126943

26
A SYSTEMATIC LITERATURE REVIEW ON FINANCIAL STOCK PERFORMANCE OF SUSTAINABLE INVESTMENTS

Bridging the Gap between Empirical Evidence and Recent Theoretical Models

Anouck Faverjon, Céleste Hardy, and Marie Lambert

Introduction

Although it has received significant attention, empirical research on the link between firms' environmental, social and governance (ESG) fundamentals and stock returns remains limited in the finance literature. The question was largely under-investigated until the 2010s when the first ESG ratings were commercialized. Without a main theoretical framework, most of the studies have followed an inductive approach and present divergent results. Theoretical frameworks for studying stock returns have only been developed recently. The aim of this article is to provide a systematic review of empirical studies conducted at the firm level and to reconcile this literature with recent theoretical frameworks.

Three main theories exist at the firm or stock level. First, the consideration of ESG-friendly policies might reduce the company systematic risk and therefore lead to lower expected returns (e.g., Hong & Kacperczyk, 2009; Albuquerque et al., 2019; Bolton & Kacperczyk, 2020). Second, investor preferences for sustainable products result in a (price) premium for "greenification" (Pastor et al., 2021; Gibson Brandon et al., 2021), which can also lead to lower returns. Third and finally, some research came to an opposite conclusion – arguing that some indicators, including for instance good governance (Gompers et al., 2003) or high employee engagement and hence their satisfaction (Edmans, 2011), might convey forward-looking information and create an alpha (i.e., abnormal return).

While the first and second claims correspond to an extension of the modern portfolio theory, the latter deviates from it by claiming the existence of an alpha related to ESG. Some authors tried to reconcile these results by theoretically extending the asset pricing models combining investor preferences with the possibility of generating an alpha (Pedersen et al., 2021) or by introducing a measure of disagreement between rating systems – as demonstrated in Berg et al. (2020) and Chatterji et al. (2016) (Avramov et al., 2021; Billio et al., 2021; Gibson Brandon et al., 2021). In particular, Avramov et al. (2021) demonstrate that disagreement distorts the equilibrium model of risk-return by rendering firms with good ESG ratings riskier when there is disagreement in the ratings.

This paper elaborates on a classification of existing empirical work on the relationship between stock financial return and ESG fundamentals with regard to existing theories. Our analysis shows that three recently developed theories can explain previous empirical evidence. We found that articles mobilizing theories linked to demand or risk are more likely to document a negative relationship between sustainability and financial performance, while when articles mobilize the theory of predictability, the relationship is most of the time positive. Articles whose results are consistent with one of the three main theories receive more citations on average. These results are even more pronounced for articles published in top journals.

The remainder of the article is structured as follows. The second section presents the three theoretical models. The third section presents the data collection following the RepOrting Standards for Systematic Evidence Syntheses (ROSES) procedure developed by Haddaway and Macura (2018) as well as the classification of the articles regarding the three theories. The fourth section discusses our results, and the fifth section concludes.

ESG Criteria and Stock Financial Returns: Review of the Theoretical Framework

We identify three different theoretical frameworks to discuss the likely impact on financial performance: (i) stock excess return induced by the predictability of ESG fundamentals, (ii) investor segmentation in terms of ESG preferences, and (iii) ESG as a source of systematic risk.

Predictability of ESG Fundamentals

Firms' involvement in ESG activities is known to have costs and benefits. While some authors view ESG activities as a trade-off against financial performance, the literature has provided evidence that superior environmental and social performance can help to enhance a firm's value. Relying on the "win-win" argument (i.e., doing well by doing good), Bénabou and Tirole (2010) explain that corporate social responsibility (CSR) practices should be seen as a long-term perspective for profit maximization and the creation of value over the long run rather than a short-term perspective where costs related to adverse impacts will be priced. Gregory et al. (2014) argue that firms with a strong ESG profile have a competitive advantage over their peers. This advantage can be linked to more efficient use of resources as well as an improvement of firms' intangible resources such as the better development of human capital, good corporate governance or the enhancement of their reputation. Most dimensions aggregated into the ESG score have been shown to contribute to the greater profitability associated with ESG criteria.

Focusing on the environmental pillar, Porter and Van der Linde (1995) declare that cost savings can be achieved through the implementation of environmental strategies. Better environmental management can contribute to greater productivity by reducing material and energy consumption and avoiding costs associated with environmental liabilities. In addition to this cost savings argument, Klassen and McLaughlin (1996) suggest that strong environmental performance creates market share gains as consumers are showing growing preferences for environmentally friendly products. In the same way, activities focusing on the social dimension have been shown to provide a competitive advantage and thus affect firm profitability. Firms dedicating resources to the implementation of ESG policies, such as providing better health care and retirement benefits or meeting labor union demands, contribute to the improvement of employee productivity (Edmans, 2011). Likewise, Porter and Kramer (2011) speak about "shared value" by suggesting a connection between companies' success and societal improvement. Investment in wellness programs is not only beneficial for society but also for a firm's productivity, as it minimizes employee absences which represent an important cost in the firm's value chain. Analyzing the relation between corporate governance and firm profitability, Gompers et al. (2003) show that firms with strong shareholder rights are more profitable.

In efficient markets, this information conveyed by ESG indicators should be incorporated into prices. An abnormal return might arise if most investors ignore the pricing attached to this information (Pedersen et al., 2021). The markets fail to fully incorporate information related to intangibles, which results in excess returns. The stock return predictability is also consistent with investors' limited attention theory which suggests that investors process information with a delay, leading to a lag in the incorporation of such information into the prices (Green et al., 2019).

ESG and Investor Demand

Theoretical work integrating ESG criteria into investor utility provides an extension to the two-fund separation model from Markowitz (1952). Under the modern portfolio theory, investors are assumed to exhibit utility towards investment products based on their expected return and the risk to deviate from the promised return measured by the asset volatility. As a consequence, they maximize return per unit of risk (i.e., Sharpe ratio) and take holdings in the risk-free asset and the market portfolio in proportions that depend on their level of risk aversion. Current theoretical works extend the two-fund separation model to integrate exposure to an ESG portfolio that captures the return spread between brown and green assets. The excess return on this last portfolio will depend on the investor demand for green assets.

From Two-Fund Separation to Four-Fund Separation

Pastor et al.'s extension to a three-fund separation. Pastor et al. (2021) extend the traditional two-fund separation theorem by assuming that investors receive non-pecuniary benefits from holding green assets and display disutility from holding brown assets. Assuming investors have an exponential utility function with both risk and brown aversion, the model posits a three-fund separation theorem whereby investors hold in various proportions the risk-free asset, the market portfolio and an ESG portfolio. Investors with green (resp. brown) preferences will overweight green assets and underweight brown assets and have positive (resp. negative) exposure to this ESG portfolio.

At the limit, should most investors derive utility from holding green assets, those preferences would be reflected in market prices and the equilibrium of the market portfolio. Moving from two-fund to three-fund separation theorem depends on the investor segmentation in the market and could be a transitory phenomenon.

Perdersen et al.'s four-fund separation. Pedersen et al.'s (2021) model brings together the framework of investor demand with evidence on ESG indicator predictability. They extend the framework of Pastor et al. (2021) by considering – next to traditionally assumed motivated investors who collect non-pecuniary benefits from holding green assets – ESG-aware investors with no preferences for ESG but who are aware of their return predictability, as well as investors who are not aware of the predictive ability of ESG criteria on firm fundamentals. They also consider that investors are aware of the low-volatility anomaly (Frazzini & Pedersen, 2014), i.e., the fact that low-volatility assets exhibit higher Sharpe ratios than high-volatility assets. They deliver a four-fund separation theorem where investors hold the risk-free asset, the market portfolio, the minimum variance portfolio and an ESG portfolio.

The equilibrium will depend on the investor segmentation between the three types of investors. ESG-motivated investors push prices of green assets up and to lower expected returns but could induce short-term benefits in cases of large flow from those investors, while ESG-unaware investors push for mispricing by underreacting to the predictability of fundamentals. As a consequence, the Sharpe ratio follows a hump curve with regard to ESG. ESG-aware investors will achieve a higher Sharpe ratio, while the other two will deviate from the maximum Sharpe ratio to the right and ESG-unaware investors will be below the curve.

The sign of alphas related to greenness will be determined as follows: the ESG portfolio will offer a scaled return should most investors be ESG-motivated or an extra return should they be unaware or short-term motivated (changes in market structure that create a shock in the factor). This framework reconciles conflicting empirical results.

Investor Segmentation

Investor preferences regarding ESG have been shown to differ among retail versus institutional investors. Hong and Kacperczyk (2009) show that institutional investors are subject to social norms which in turn lowers their likelihood of holding sin stocks compared to private investors. In line with this assumption, Nofsinger et al. (2019) show that institutional investors tend to avoid controversial stocks rather than picking ESG ones in order to avoid the risks linked to controversies. Besides, according to Riedl and Smeets (2017), institutional investors focus on economic performance first, while retail investors are more likely to forego economic performance for their social performance. Similarly, Erhemjamts and Huang (2019) postulate that institutional investors are more short-term-minded compared to retail investors, which could explain why they hold fewer ESG assets. Nofsinger et al. (2019) further show that institutional investors are "ESG-aware" meaning that they invest in ESG assets in order to protect themselves from ESG risk, while retail investors tend to be "ESG lovers" meaning that they are driven to ESG investments because of social norms.

These unequal preferences for ESG assets between institutional and retail investors support the investor segmentation pointed out by Pastor et al. (2021) and Pedersen et al. (2021).

The distinction between institutional and retail investors introduced by Hong and Kacperczyk (2009) also has consequences in terms of strategies used. In a study dating from 2018, Amel-Zadeh and Serafeim investigate how institutional investors integrate ESG information in their investment processes. In line with Riedl and Smeets's (2017) assumption, the study reveals that the surveyed investors are motivated by financial reasons rather than ethical ones. As a consequence, active ownership and negative screening are among the most used strategies, while best-in-class strategy ranks last at the time of this study.

Uncertainty around ESG Information

Deviations from the three-fund separation theorem: Uncertainty around ESG. The model of Avramov et al. (2021) builds on the model of Pastor et al. (2021) and also assumes that each investor holds three portfolios: (1) a riskless asset, (2) the maximum Sharpe ratio portfolio in the risk-return space, and (3) the maximum Sharpe ratio portfolio in the risk-ESG space. This is only possible if every agent has access to the same information to build these portfolios. If they do not have access to the same ESG information, and ESG uncertainty exists, the composition of the ESG portfolio will differ and be agent specific. This means that the three-fund model is rejected. In other words, the equilibrium alpha will also vary with the uncertainty around the ESG scores: if the market is green and there is uncertainty, the alpha-ESG relationship is inconclusive. In the case of market green neutrality and uncertainty, a higher market premium is expected as the uncertainty decreases demand for stocks and investors ask for compensation.

ESG and Risk

Lower cost of capital - Reduced investor base. In an equilibrium model considering the price implications of exclusionary ethical investing, Heinkel et al. (2001) show that sustainability reduces firm risk. The model assumes that the financial market is segmented between two types of investors who differ with respect to their preference for green assets. On one hand, "green" investors screen out irresponsible stocks from their investment universe, while on the other hand, "neutral" investors ignore ethical considerations. As a consequence, the return on green and controversial assets can be affected if the fraction of green investors is large enough. The exclusion of polluting firms by green investors leads to reduced risk-sharing opportunities among investors (Merton, 1987). This market segmentation, where firms exhibiting poor corporate social responsibility are held by only a fraction of investors, induces greater systematic risk for these firms. As a result, neutral investors will require a higher rate of return for investing in polluting firms thus increasing the cost of capital of such firms.

Luo and Balvers (2017) extend the Sharpe-Lintner capital asset pricing model (CAPM) by introducing an additional risk factor to compensate unrestricted investors for holding sin stocks "boycotted" by other investors. Similar to Heinkel et al. (2001), they consider a segmentation of the investor base depending on their non-pecuniary preferences. By excluding firms whose activities are morally objectionable from their investment universe, socially responsible investors limit their investment opportunities. As a result, the two groups of investors face different investment opportunity sets and thus choose different portfolios, which violates the key assumption of identical investment opportunities from the CAPM. The reduction of the investor base for boycotted stocks causes unrestricted investors to hold these assets in excess compared to the efficient market weights. This extra risk is compensated by higher returns.

Lower cost of capital – Perceived risk. The lower cost of capital associated with more ESG-related policies can also be explained by the reduction of firms' perceived risk. Focusing on the environmental dimension, Sharfman and Fernando (2008) argue that the implementation of an environmental strategy should be viewed as a risk mitigation tool. Firms with a strong ESG profile face fewer litigation risks, which lowers their systematic risk. Given this reduced risk exposure, investors require a lower rate of return resulting in a lower cost of capital and thereby a higher valuation.

Albuquerque et al. (2019) construct a theoretical model which demonstrates how investment in CSR affects firms' systematic risk. This relationship between ESG criteria and systematic risk has also been proven empirically (Kim et al., 2014; Oikonomou et al., 2012). Their theory suggests that firms can use ESG policies as a product differentiation strategy. As a consequence of this strategy, firms investing in CSR face less-elastic demand – a more loyal customer base – which gives them more pricing power. This ability to charge higher prices and obtain higher profit margins reduces firms' systematic risk and increases their value.

ESG Criteria and Stock Financial Returns: Systematic Review of the Empirical Literature

We conduct a systematic review of the literature following the ROSES approach. ROSES is a framework developed by Haddaway & Macura (2018) that builds a list of criteria and steps to perform a systematic literature review. We followed the checklist provided by the authors to ensure that the performed search is rigorous and representative of the existing literature. Our purpose of analysis is the empirical relationship between issuer ESG scores and their stock financial performance over the period 1970–2022, although the first relevant study dates to 1996.

Article Collection

We first extract articles from the Scopus database (www.scopus.com). We run a query based on abstract, title or keywords that include the terms "csr" or "esg" or "sri" but not "lanka",[1] or "corporate" and "social" and "responsibility" or "environment" and "social" and "governance" or "socially" and "responsible" and "investment". We restrict the search to articles written in English that have been published in an academic journal. This search yielded 7,754 results as of March 20, 2022. We limit our sample to articles that have been published in top ten journals in the Google Scholar citation ranking[2] in the fields of economics, finance, management, business and accounting. This additional screen leads to a sample of 685 articles. The remaining list of articles is screened based on their abstract. We require that the articles have an empirical analysis in the form of an econometrical approach and remove articles that do not investigate the specific link between ESG scores and stock performance, among which were articles related to bonds, funds or banks. Our final sample from the Scopus search contains 164 articles. Figure 26.1 shows the most used words[3] among the abstracts and verifies the quality of our selection.

We complete this sample with articles manually collected. As of March 20, 2022, we collected 362 ESG-related papers thanks to enquiries with colleagues, suggestions at seminars, and informal research. Similar to the query carried out in Scopus, we focus on articles published in the top-ten ranking of Google Scholar, which lead to 127 articles. Of these articles, we retain 54 based on their abstract.

Figure 26.1 Most used words in the abstracts of the selected papers

Financial Stock Performance

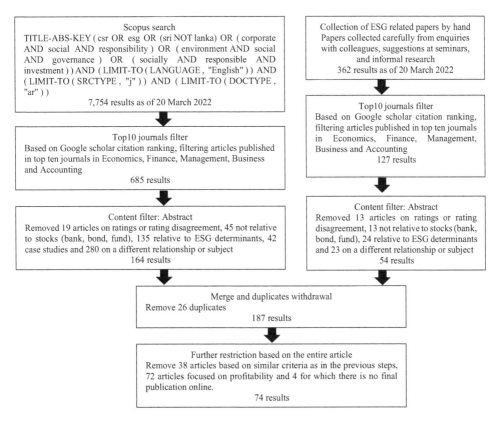

Figure 26.2 Research methodology

After merging these two samples and removing the duplicates, we reached a sample of 187 papers on the relation between ESG and performance. Finally, we focus our analysis on the financial performance of stocks and therefore eliminate the articles analyzing the relation between ESG and firm profitability. The resulting final sample contained 74 articles. The different steps of this search are detailed in Figure 26.2.

Article Classification

Of the 74 empirical works, we classify 68 papers into the three main theories described in the second section. The six remaining papers do not directly relate to one theoretical framework. The classification is realized based on the specific statements that authors most often used in their concluding remarks. Studies whose findings suggest that returns relate to better operating performance were considered to rely on the "predictability of ESG fundamentals" theory. Articles mentioning a heterogeneous pool of investors to support their results are classified under the "ESG and investor demand" category. Finally, the risk category includes all research proposing an extension of the traditional factor models with an additional risk factor. This classification has been cross-checked by the authors.

Table 26.1 provides the results of our classification. Of the 74 included in our sample, 68 could be classified: 29 relate to the framework on the predictability of ESG fundamentals, 24 to

Table 26.1 Sample of empirical studies

Studies	Sample	Dependent variable	Sign of the ESG-return relation
Panel A: Predictability of ESG fundamentals			
Barko et al. (2022)	Geography: World / Period: 2005–2014	Cumulative abnormal returns	+
Dimson et al. (2015)	Geography: United States / Period: 1999–2009	Abnormal returns	+
Ding et al. (2021)	Geography: World / Period: 2020	Stock return	+
Eccles et al. (2014)	Geography: United States / Period: 1993–2010	Excess return	+
Flammer (2015)	Geography: United States / Period: 1997–2012	Abnormal returns	+
Edmans (2011)	Geography: United States / Period: 1984–2009	Excess return	+
Khan et al. (2016)	Geography: United States / Period: 1992–2013	Excess return	+
Green et al. (2019)	Geography: World / Period: 2008–2016	Excess return	+
Gompers et al. (2003)	Geography: United States / Period: 1990–1998	Excess return	+
Klassen and McLaughlin (1996)	Geography: United States / Period: 1985–1991	Abnormal returns	+
Lins et al. (2017)	Geography: United States / Period: 2008–2009	Raw return, abnormal returns	+
Aktas et al. (2011)	Geography: Not specified / Period: 1997–2007	Cumulative abnormal returns	+
Yoon and Welch (2020)	Geography: World / Period: 2011–2018	Excess return	+
Boubaker et al. (2022)	Geography: China / Period: 2020	Cumulative abnormal returns	+
Cellier and Chollet (2016)	Geography: Europe / Period: 2004–2009	Cumulative abnormal return	Conditional
Christensen (2016)	Geography: United States / Period: 1999–2010	Cumulative abnormal returns	+
Deng et al. (2013)	Geography: United States / Period: 1992–2007	Cumulative abnormal returns	+
Humphrey et al. (2012)	Geography: UK / Period: 2002–2010	Excess return	Null
Dhaliwal et al. (2012)	Geography: World / Period: 1994–2007	Earning Forecast Error	+
Hussaini et al. (2021)	Geography: United States / Period: 1992–2014	Takeover premium	+
Shackleton et al. (2022)	Geography: United States / Period: 1991–2015	Return	–
Zhang et al. (2022)	Geography: China / Period: 2020	Raw return, abnormal returns	+
Alexandridis et al. (2022)	Geography: World / Period: 2004–2011	Cumulative abnormal returns	–
Feng et al. (2018)	Geography: United States / Period: 1992–2012	Cumulative abnormal returns	+

(Continued)

Table 26.1 (Continued)

Studies	Sample	Dependent variable	Sign of the ESG-return relation
Gomes and Marsat (2018)	Geography: World Period: 2003–2014	Bid premium	+
Erragragui and Lagoarde-Segot (2016)	Geography: World Period: 2008–2014	Excess return	Null
Jost et al. (2022)	Geography: World Period: 2003–2018	Cumulative abnormal returns	Null
Erhemjamts and Huang (2019)	Geography: United States Period: 2003–2013	Lagged return	Conditional
Verwijmeren and Derwall (2010)	Geography: United States Period: 2001–2005	Credit rating	+
Panel B: Investor demand			
Bansal et al. (2022)	Geography: World Period: 1993–2013	Abnormal returns	–
Bebchuk et al. (2013)	Geography: United States Period: 1990–2008	Excess return	Conditional
Capelle-Blancard and Petit (2019)	Geography: World Period: 2002–2010	Abnormal returns	–
Derwall et al. (2011)	Geography: United States Period: 1992–2008	Excess return	–
Galema et al. (2008)	Geography: United States Period: 1992–2006	Excess return	Null
Serafeim and Yoon (2022)	Geography: United States Period: 2010–2018	Excess return	+
Trinks and Scholtens (2017)	Geography: World Period: 1991–2012	Excess return	–
Becchetti et al. (2012)	Geography: Period: 1990–2004	Excess return	–
Bose et al. (2021)	Geography: World Period: 2006–2018	Acquirer's five-day cumulative abnormal stock returns	–
Bofinger et al. (2022)	Geography: United States Period: 2004–2017	Misvaluation measure (i.e., market cap/true value)	+
Bae et al. (2021)	Geography: United States Period: 2020	Raw return, market-adjusted return	Null
Naughton et al. (2019)	Geography: United States Period: 2002–2010	Abnormal returns	+
Krüger (2015)	Geography: United States Period: 2001–2007	Cumulative abnormal returns	–
Díaz et al. (2021)	Geography: United States Period: 2020	Excess return	Conditional
Dutordoir et al. (2018)	Geography: United States Period: 2004–2013	Cumulative abnormal return	+
Fuenzalida et al. (2013)	Geography: Peru Period: 2007–2010	Excess return	+
Wong and Zhang (2022)	Geography: United States Period: 2007–2018	Excess return	+
Monfort et al. (2021)	Geography: World Period: 1995–2012	Cumulative abnormal returns	Conditional

(Continued)

Table 26.1 (Continued)

Studies	Sample	Dependent variable	Sign of the ESG-return relation
Dhaliwal et al. (2012)	Geography: World Period: 1994–2007	Earning Forecast Error	+
Lee et al. (2022)	Geography: Korea Period: 2020–2021	Excess return	+
Lam et al. (2015)	Geography: United States Period: 1992–2011	Stock return	–
Naffa and Fain (2022)	Geography: World Period: 2015–2019	Excess return	–
Zou and Li (2016)	Geography: China Period: 2001–2011	Excess return	–
Avramov et al. (2021)	Geography: United States Period: 2002–2019	Excess return	Null
Panel C: Risk			
El Ghoul et al. (2011)	Geography: United States Period: 1992–2007	Cost of Equity	–
Bolton and Kacperczyk (2020)	Geography: World Period: 2005–2018	Stock return	–
Chan and Walter (2014)	Geography: United States Period: 1990–2012	Excess return	+
Chava (2014)	Geography: United States Period: 2000–2007	Implied cost of capital	–
Hong and Kacperczyk (2009)	Geography: United States Period: 1962–2006	Excess return	–
Nofsinger et al. (2019)	Geography: United States Period: 2001–2013	Excess return	+
McGuire et al. (1988)	Geography: United States Period: 1982–1984	Risk-adjusted return, alpha, total return	–
Nguyen et al. (2020)	Geography: United States Period: 1991–2009	Excess return	–
Huang et al. (2021)	Geography: United States Period: 2020	Raw return, abnormal returns	–
Lööf et al. (2021)	Geography: World Period: 2018–2020	Value-of-return, conditional Value-of-Return	–
Engle et al. (2020)	Geography: United States Period: 1995–2016	Excess return	+
Ben Hmiden et al. (2022)	Geography: United States Period: 1998–2015	Cost of Equity	–
Brzeszczynski et al. (2021)	Geography: Eastern Europe Period: 2009–2018	Excess return	+
Breuer et al. (2018)	Geography: World Period: 2002–2015	Cost of Equity	–
Luo and Balvers (2017)	Geography: United States Period: 1963–2012	Excess return	–

(*Continued*)

Table 26.1 (Continued)

Studies	Sample	Dependent variable	Sign of the ESG-return relation
Panel D: Not classified			
Masulis and Reza (2015)	Geography: United States Period: 1963–2012	Excess return	–
Erragraguy and Revelli (2015)	Geography: United States Period: 2008–2011	Excess return	Null
Shanaev and Ghimire (2022)	Geography: United States Period: 2016–2021	Risk-adjusted excess return	+
Broadstock et al. (2021)	Geography: China Period: 2015–2020	Excess return	+
Crifo et al. (2015)	Geography: United States Period: Not specified	Firm valuation	+
Ng and Rezaee (2015)	Geography: United States Period: 1991–2013	Cost of equity	–

ESG affecting investor demand, and 15 to systematic risk. For each study, we provide the main characteristics of the sample and the dependent variable used to assess stock performance, and we identify the sign of the relation between ESG and financial return. We document the sign as positive if the article concludes that ESG criteria are associated with higher returns, negative if the article concludes in the opposite direction, null if the article does not find any significant relationship between ESG criteria and stock performance, and conditional if the sign of the relation is conditional to other contextual information (e.g., country, firm characteristics) or if the relationship is non-linear (e.g., U-shape).

As illustrated in Figure 26.3, a large proportion of the empirical articles on the ESG-return relationship are contained within the financial research field. However, this relationship has also been the central focus of various articles in other fields, most of which have been published in top journals.

Discussion

Figure 26.4 provides a timeline illustrating the emergence of empirical studies on the relationship between firm ESG criteria and their financial performance, as well as the main theoretical references. We observed three phases.

The beginning of the sample (1996–2010) corresponds to the appearance of the first empirical studies. In 1996, consistent with the theory of predictability of ESG fundamentals, Klassen and McLaughlin (1996) argue that environmental management positively affects firm financial performance through two specific channels: market gains and cost saving. In addition, a study conducted by McGuire et al. (1988) gives evidence of significant risk reduction as a major benefit of social responsibility. Published about ten years later, a study by Hong and Kacperczyk (2009) pointed out that "sin" stocks are more likely to face litigation risk contributing to the higher return associated with this type of stock. Yet, it is not until 2008 that a study performed by Galema et al. (2008) provides evidence of pricing anomalies resulting from an excess in

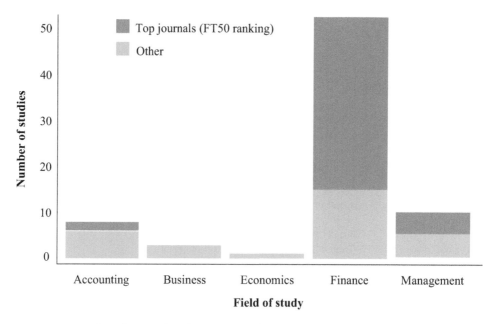

Figure 26.3 Number of empirical studies by research fields

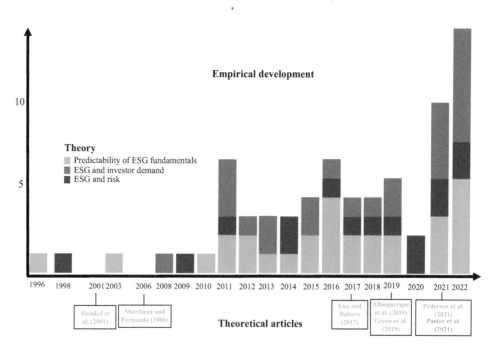

Figure 26.4 Timeline of theoretical and empirical studies per theoretical framework

demand for socially responsible stocks and a shortage of demand for irresponsible stocks. As to the theoretical framework, only the risk theory was formalized during this period (Heinkel et al., 2001; Sharfman & Fernando, 2008).

The ESG-performance relationship remained under-investigated until the 2010s when the first ESG ratings were commercialized.[4] We observe a period of acceleration (2011–2020) with numerous empirical articles studying the ESG-performance relationship. Most of the empirical work in this period can be related to either the theory of predictability (Eccles et al., 2014; Flammer, 2015; Lins et al., 2017) or the implications of heterogeneous investor preferences for asset pricing (Derwall et al., 2011). Applications of the risk framework emerged around the 2010s; among which was the research conducted by El Ghoul et al. (2011).

The theoretical models linked to ESG predictability and investor demand were only released between the end of this second period and the beginning of the third one – recent studies (2021–2022). In particular, Pedersen et al. (2021) built a model on the predictability of ESG fundamentals for firm profitability, describing the mechanism by which it influences stock returns. Furthermore, the literature has extended the classical investor utility function to capture environmental and social aspects impacting the price formation of green or brown assets (Pastor et al., 2021; Pedersen et al., 2021). The number of empirical works supporting these two theories has largely expanded over the past two years. In the same period, empirical papers supporting the risk theory have shown special attention to the reduction in perceived risk, presenting sustainability as an insurance mechanism against risk (Engle et al., 2020).

Table 26.2 provides descriptive statistics on the sample of empirical studies. Empirical research related to the predictability of ESG fundamentals mainly provides evidence of a positive relationship between ESG fundamentals and abnormal returns. This positive effect shows that some ESG criteria such as employee satisfaction (Edmans, 2011; Green et al., 2019) have an impact on stock returns. The work establishing this positive relation has been widely cited in the literature, especially those published in the first part of the sample (1996–2010) and articles published in A+ journals.[5]

When looking at the ESG-financial performance relationship due to investor segmentation, the results are mixed. We observe about the same number of studies supporting respectively a positive or negative relation. Although no consensus can be drawn when considering the entire sample, evidence from studies published in A+ journals seems consistent with existing theories that command an ex-ante negative relation between ESG and stock return due to investor demand.

Among the empirical papers in our sample, two distinguish between institutional and retail investors. Hong and Kacperczyk (2009) show that since institutional investors are norm-constrained, "sin" stocks are neglected by a large part of investors, which creates a premium for these stocks. Lee et al. (2022) also document an ESG premium during the Covid-19 crisis and explain it through the liquidation of brown stocks from institutional investors in order to reduce the risk of their portfolio. Erhemjamts and Huang (2019) distinguish between institutional investors with long-term views and those with short-term views. They show that since ESG criteria have a long-term effect on stock return, the effect of ESG criteria on stock returns depends on the proportion of each type of investor. Consistent with Lee et al. (2022), Nofsinger et al. (2019) further discuss the difference between institutional and retail investors by showing that when institutional investors hold ESG assets, they do it in order to reduce the risk linked to a controversy rather than for their ESG impact.

Recent evidence provides an attempt to reconcile these a priori conflicting research results between empirical evidence and theory. Ardia et al. (2022) and Pastor et al. (2021) demonstrate that although the ex-ante relationship between sustainability and performance is negative, some

Table 26.2 Descriptive statistics of the sample of empirical studies

			Predictability of ESG fundamentals				ESG and investor demand				ESG and risk				Not classified				Total
			Pos	Neg	Null	Conditional	Pos	Neg	Null	Conditional	Pos	Neg	Null	Conditional	Pos	Neg	Null	Conditional	
Entire sample 1996–2022	A+	Number of articles	15	0	0	0	2	5	1	1	1	4	0	0	0	1	0	0	30
		Average number of citations	668	–	–	–	12	361	2	111	49	1,410	–	–	–	220	–	–	596
	Other	Number of articles	6	2	3	3	6	5	2	2	3	6	1	0	3	1	1	0	44
		Average number of citations	41	0	34	12	26	40	178	12	23	536	84	–	–	108	16	–	108
Beginning of the A+ sample 1996–2010		Number of articles	2	0	0	0	0	0	0	0	0	2	0	0	0	0	0	0	4
		Average number of citations	2,547	–	–	–	–	–	–	–	–	2,686	–	–	–	–	–	–	2,617
	Other	Number of articles	1	0	0	0	0	0	1	0	0	0	0	0	0	0	0	0	2
		Average number of citations	112	–	–	–	–	–	309	–	–	–	–	–	–	–	–	–	210
Period of acceleration: 2011–2020	A+	Number of articles	11	0	0	0	1	4	0	1	1	2	0	0	0	1	0	0	21
		Average number of citations	440	–	–	–	23	451	–	111	49	134	–	–	–	220	–	–	348

Other	Number of articles	3	0	2	2	3	3	0	0	2	3	1	0	1	1	1	0	22
	Average number of citations	61	–	51	18	49	65	–	–	32	1,068	84	–	42	108	16	–	184
Recent studies 2021–2022	A+ Number of articles	2	0	0	0	1	1	1	0	0	0	0	0	0	0	0	0	5
	Average number of citations	41	–	–	–	1	1	2	–	–	–	–	–	–	–	–	–	17
	Other Number of articles	2	2	1	1	3	2	1	2	1	3	0	0	2	0	0	0	20
	Average number of citations	1	0	1	1	2	3	48	12	3	4	–	–	41	–	–	–	9
Total number of studies		21	2	3	3	8	10	3	3	4	10	1	0	3	2	1	0	74

Caption: Number of studies published and average number of citations (as of May 13, 2022) relative to the relationship between ESG criteria and stock returns by category. The articles are classified as "A+" following the *Financial Times* ranking for academic journals (last update 2016): www.ft.com/content/3405a512-5cbb-11e1-8f1f-00144feabdc0. The articles classified as "Pos" are the ones for which the relationship between ESG and stock returns is positive, "Neg" when the relationship is negative, "Null" when the relationship is non-significant and "conditional" when the sign of the relationship is conditional to other parameters. The average number of citations corresponds to the sum of citations of the articles in a specific category over the number of articles in the same category.

events conveying climate concerns might affect investors' investing decisions and be responsible for temporary positive returns ex-post. Bansal et al. (2022) show that investor demand for constituting a conscious portfolio increases in good economic times and is responsible for abnormal returns for high-rated socially responsible stocks.

Finally, publications pointing out a negative relationship between ESG and stock performance are predominant among the studies based on the risk framework. These studies also received many more citations.

Table 26.3 shows the ten most cited articles in our sample. The three theoretical frameworks are represented in the subsample, with four articles linked to the risk theory, five articles related to the predictability of ESG ratings theory and only one related to the recent investor demand

Table 26.3 Top ten articles by number of citations

Reference	Journal	Theory	Sign of ESG-return relation	Field	Number of citations
Eccles et al. (2014)	Management Science	Predictability of ESG fundamentals	Positive	Management	664
Gompers et al. (2003)	Quarterly Journal of Economics	Predictability of ESG fundamentals	Positive	Economics	3,568
Klassen and McLaughlin (1996)	Management Science	Predictability of ESG fundamentals	Positive	Management	1,527
Lins et al. (2017)	Journal of Finance	Predictability of ESG fundamentals	Positive	Accounting	660
Dhaliwal et al. (2012)	Accounting Review	Predictability of ESG fundamentals	Positive	Finance	690
Dhaliwal et al. (2011)	Accounting Review	ESG and investor demand	Negative	Accounting	1,360
El Ghoul et al. (2011)	Journal of Banking and Finance	ESG and risk	Negative	Finance	2,443
Breuer et al. (2018)	Journal of Banking and Finance	ESG and risk	Negative	Finance	703
Hong and Kacperczyk (2009)	Journal of Financial Economics	ESG and risk	Negative	Finance	725
McGuire et al. (1988)	Academy of Management Journal	ESG and risk	Negative	Management	4,648

Caption: Top ten articles with the highest number of citations (as of May 13, 2022). The sign of ESG-return relation is defined as "Positive" when the article displays a positive relationship between ESG and stock returns and "Negative" when the article displays a negative relationship. "Field" corresponds to the field of research and is defined based on the journal classification used by Google Scholar.

theory. All ten articles display results that support the associated theories – i.e., a positive relationship between ESG and stock performance for the predictability theory and a negative effect for risk and demand theories. Most cited works are thus in line with the theories.

Concluding Remarks

Research establishing a relationship between the performance of environmental, social or governance criteria of firm policies and their financial returns is recent. The first empirical work dates to 1996, and the number of empirical works started to increase after 2010. In the absence of a main theoretical framework, previous works have mostly followed an inductive approach and led to diverging results. Our paper reconciles the main conclusions brought by both the empirical and theoretical literature. We relied on a systematic approach to review the literature published in top academic journals in the fields of economics, finance, management, business and accounting, and provide a classification of 68 empirical works with regard to three main theoretical frameworks.

The first research providing a theoretical framework for the link between sustainability and stock performance was introduced in the 2000s and relies on the risk associated with green versus brown investment. This theory suggests a decrease in the cost of capital for sustainable firms that is either explained by the reduced investor base for "sin" stocks or the reduced perceived risk associated with firms with a strong ESG profile. Two other theoretical models emerged more recently; one is linked to the predictability of ESG fundamentals, while the second is based on the segmentation of investors' preferences. The former supports the idea that ESG fundamentals have a predictability power for operating performance that further leads to stock excess return. The latter has also been developed over the past couple of years and relies on the hypothesis that a heterogeneous pool of investors in terms of preferences for green assets affects stock performance. The two main theories that emerged recently (i.e., "predictability" and "investor demand") might support different directions in the studied relationship. It has been shown that both could be reconciled in the case that investors present homogeneous preferences towards sustainability and capture the added value of the ESG assessment of a firm. The ESG-return relationship might therefore be a relatively transitory phenomenon that is about to perish in the future.

These three theories therefore converge to the unique conclusion that ESG should not command any sub-performance or outperformance, as the prices of financial assets should reflect the ESG performance of the issuer. Such long-term equilibrium is however conditional on the homogeneity of investor preferences towards sustainability and the availability of perfect information on the ESG of firms. However, the current short-term disequilibrium is associated with, on one hand, imperfect ESG information and, on the other hand, heterogeneous beliefs or preferences with regard to ESG.

As such, further research may enquire into the heterogeneous preferences of agents with regard to ESG with particular attention to the distinction between institutional investors and private investors. In addition, the current academic evidence at the stock level has direct implications on the performance of sustainable investment practices. The reduction of the investment base induced by the exclusion of "sin" stocks by investment funds may increase the risk of such assets and inflate the risks of such funds. Furthermore, the increase in the number of funds based on a best-in-class strategy may push ESG-leading stock prices up. This overpricing of ESG stocks would lead to abnormal returns in the short term but to scaled returns in the long term along the framework of Pastor et al. (2021). Indeed, there is a negative relationship between industry size and performance (Pastor et al., 2015). The increasing demand for ESG funds may also be explained by their good performance during crises (Pastor & Vorsatz, 2020). However, the strategy consisting of active research of ESG characteristics not yet priced by the market may allow long-term abnormal returns and requires further research.

Notes

1. This step avoids the collection of articles relative to Sri Lanka and reduces the noise in our search.
2. The top ten journals in the Google Scholar citation ranking for which there is at least one paper in our sample: *American Economic Review, Quarterly Journal of Economics, Review of Financial Studies, Journal of Finance, Review of Economic Studies, Economic Journal, Journal of Financial Economics, Journal of Banking & Finance, Journal of Corporate Finance, Finance Research Letters, Journal of Accounting and Economics, Journal of Financial and Quantitative Analysis, Journal of Business Research, Management Science, Journal of Business Ethics, Accounting Review, Journal of Accounting Research, Accounting, Auditing & Accountability Journal, Review of Accounting Studies, British Accounting Review, Accounting and Business Research.*
3. Stopwords and punctuation were removed using the "stopword" package for R available at https://github.com/koheiw/stopwords.
4. Some providers started commercializing their ratings earlier (2002 for Refinitiv, 2003 for Moody's (ex-Vigeo Eiris)), but the coverage and time period remains limited until the 2010s.
5. A+ journals are identified using the *Financial Times* ranking for academic journals (last update 2016): www.ft.com/content/3405a512-5cbb-11e1-8f1f-00144feabdc0.
6. The articles included in the systematic literature review are marked with a ★.

References[6]

★Aktas, N., De Bodt, E., & Cousin, J. G. (2011). Do financial markets care about SRI? Evidence from mergers and acquisitions. *Journal of Banking and Finance, 35*(7), 1753–1761. https://doi.org/10.1016/j.jbankfin.2010.12.006

Albuquerque, R., Koskinen, Y., & Zhang, C. (2019). Corporate social responsibility and firm risk: Theory and empirical evidence. *Management Science, 65*(10), 4451–4469. https://doi.org/10.1287/mnsc.2018.3043

★Alexandridis, G., Hoepner, A. G., Huang, Z., & Oikonomou, I. (2022). Corporate social responsibility culture and international M&As. *British Accounting Review, 54*(1), 101035. https://doi.org/10.1016/j.bar.2021.101035

Ardia, D., Bluteau, K., Boudt, K., & Inghelbrecht, K. (2022). Climate change concerns and the performance of green versus brown stocks. *Management Science*, in press. https://doi.org/10.1287/mnsc.2022.4636

★Avramov, D., Cheng, S., Lioui, A., & Tarelli, A. (2021). Sustainable investing with ESG rating uncertainty. *Journal of Financial Economics, 145*(2), 642–664. https://doi.org/10.1016/j.jfineco.2021.09.009

★Bae, K. H., El Ghoul, S., Gong, Z. J., & Guedhami, O. (2021). Does CSR matter in times of crisis? Evidence from the COVID-19 pandemic. *Journal of Corporate Finance, 67*, 101876. https://doi.org/10.1016/j.jcorpfin.2020.101876

★Bansal, R., Wu, D., & Yaron, A. (2022). Socially responsible investing in good and bad times. *Review of Financial Studies, 35*(4), 2067–2099. https://doi.org/10.1093/rfs/hhab072

★Barko, T., Cremers, M., & Renneboog, L. (2022). Shareholder engagement on environmental, social, and governance performance. *Journal of Business Ethics, 180*(2), 777–812. https://doi.org/10.1007/s10551-021-04850-z

★Bebchuk, L. A., Cohen, A., & Wang, C. C. (2013). Learning and the disappearing association between governance and returns. *Journal of Financial Economics, 108*(2), 323–348. https://doi.org/10.1016/j.jfineco.2012.10.004

★Becchetti, L., Ciciretti, R., Hasan, I., & Kobeissi, N. (2012). Corporate social responsibility and shareholder's value. *Journal of Business Research, 65*(11), 1628–1635. https://doi.org/10.1016/j.jbusres.2011.10.022

Bénabou, R., & Tirole, J. (2010). Individual and corporate social responsibility. *Economica, 77*(305), 1–19. https://doi.org/10.1111/j.1468-0335.2009.00843.x

Berg, F., Koelbel, J. F., & Rigobon, R. (2022). Aggregate confusion: The divergence of ESG ratings. *Review of Finance, 26*(6), 1315–1344.

Billio, M., Costola, M., Hristova, I., Latino, C., & Pelizzon, L. (2021). Inside the ESG Ratings:(Dis) agreement and performance. *Corporate Social Responsibility and Environmental Management, 28*(5), 1426–1445. https://doi.org/10.1002/csr.2177

*Bofinger, Y., Heyden, K. J., & Rock, B. (2022). Corporate social responsibility and market efficiency: Evidence from ESG and misvaluation measures. *Journal of Banking and Finance, 134*, 106322. https://doi.org/10.1016/j.jbankfin.2021.106322

Bolton, P., & Kacperczyk, M. T. (2020). Carbon premium around the world. https://doi.org/10.2139/ssrn.3550233

*Bose, S., Minnick, K., & Shams, S. (2021). Does carbon risk matter for corporate acquisition decisions? *Journal of Corporate Finance, 70*, 102058. https://doi.org/10.1016/j.jcorpfin.2021.102058

*Boubaker, S., Liu, Z., & Zhan, Y. (2022). Customer relationships, corporate social responsibility, and stock price reaction: Lessons from China during health crisis times. *Finance Research Letters*, 102699. https://doi.org/10.1016/j.frl.2022.102699

*Breuer, W., Müller, T., Rosenbach, D., & Salzmann, A. (2018). Corporate social responsibility, investor protection, and cost of equity: A cross-country comparison. *Journal of Banking and Finance, 96*, 34–55. https://doi.org/10.1016/j.jbankfin.2018.07.018

*Broadstock, D. C., Chan, K., Cheng, L. T., & Wang, X. (2021). The role of ESG performance during times of financial crisis: Evidence from COVID-19 in China. *Finance Research Letters, 38*, 101716. https://doi.org/10.1016/j.frl.2020.101716

*Brzeszczyński, J., Gajdka, J., & Schabek, T. (2021). How risky are the socially responsible investment (SRI) stocks? Evidence from the Central and Eastern European (CEE) companies. *Finance Research Letters, 42*, 101939. https://doi.org/10.1016/j.frl.2021.101939

*Capelle-Blancard, G., & Petit, A. (2019). Every little helps? ESG news and stock market reaction. *Journal of Business Ethics, 157*(2), 543–565. https://doi.org/10.1007/s10551-017-3667-3

*Cellier, A., & Chollet, P. (2016). The effects of social ratings on firm value. *Research in International Business and Finance, 36*, 656–683. https://doi.org/10.1016/j.ribaf.2015.05.001

*Chan, P. T., & Walter, T. (2014). Investment performance of "environmentally-friendly" firms and their initial public offers and seasoned equity offers. *Journal of Banking and Finance, 44*, 177–188. https://doi.org/10.1016/j.jbankfin.2014.04.006

Chatterji, A. K., Durand, R., Levine, D. I., & Touboul, S. (2016). Do ratings of firms converge? Implications for managers, investors and strategy researchers. *Strategic Management Journal, 37*(8), 1597–1614.

*Chava, S. (2014). Environmental externalities and cost of capital. *Management Science, 60*(9), 2223–2247. https://doi.org/10.1287/mnsc.2013.1863

*Christensen, D. M. (2016). Corporate accountability reporting and high-profile misconduct. *Accounting Review, 91*(2), 377–399. https://doi.org/10.2308/accr-51200

*Crifo, P., Forget, V. D., & Teyssier, S. (2015). The price of environmental, social and governance practice disclosure: An experiment with professional private equity investors. *Journal of Corporate Finance, 30*, 168–194. http://doi.org/10.1016/j.jcorpfin.2014.12.006

*Deng, X., Kang, J. K., & Low, B. S. (2013). Corporate social responsibility and stakeholder value maximization: Evidence from mergers. *Journal of Financial Economics, 110*(1), 87–109. https://doi.org/10.1016/j.jfineco.2013.04.014

*Derwall, J., Koedijk, K., & Ter Horst, J. (2011). A tale of values-driven and profit-seeking social investors. *Journal of Banking and Finance, 35*(8), 2137–2147. https://doi.org/10.1016/j.jbankfin.2011.01.009

*Dhaliwal, D. S., Li, O. Z., Tsang, A., & Yang, Y. G. (2011). Voluntary nonfinancial disclosure and the cost of equity capital: The initiation of corporate social responsibility reporting. *Accounting Review, 86*(1), 59–100. https://doi.org/10.2308/accr.00000005

*Dhaliwal, D. S., Radhakrishnan, S., Tsang, A., & Yang, Y. G. (2012). Nonfinancial disclosure and analyst forecast accuracy: International evidence on corporate social responsibility disclosure. *Accounting Review, 87*(3), 723–759. https://doi.org/10.2308/accr-10218

*Díaz, V., Ibrushi, D., & Zhao, J. (2021). Reconsidering systematic factors during the COVID-19 pandemic–The rising importance of ESG. *Finance Research Letters, 38*, 101870. https://doi.org/10.1016/j.frl.2020.101870

*Dimson, E., Karakaş, O., & Li, X. (2015). Active ownership. *Review of Financial Studies, 28*(12), 3225–3268. https://doi.org/10.1093/rfs/hhv044

*Ding, W., Levine, R., Lin, C., & Xie, W. (2021). Corporate immunity to the COVID-19 pandemic. *Journal of Financial Economics*, *141*(2), 802–830. https://doi.org/10.1016/j.jfineco.2021.03.005

*Dutordoir, M., Strong, N. C., & Sun, P. (2018). Corporate social responsibility and seasoned equity offerings. *Journal of Corporate Finance*, *50*, 158–179. https://doi.org/10.1016/j.jcorpfin.2018.03.005

*Eccles, R. G., Ioannou, I., & Serafeim, G. (2014). The impact of corporate sustainability on organizational processes and performance. *Management Science*, *60*(11), 2835–2857. https://doi.org/10.1287/mnsc.2014.1984

*Edmans, A. (2011). Does the stock market fully value intangibles? Employee satisfaction and equity prices. *Journal of Financial Economics*, *101*(3), 621–640. https://doi.org/10.1016/j.jfineco.2011.03.021

*El Ghoul, S., Guedhami, O., Kwok, C. C., & Mishra, D. R. (2011). Does corporate social responsibility affect the cost of capital? *Journal of Banking and Finance*, *35*(9), 2388–2406. https://doi.org/10.1016/j.jbankfin.2011.02.007

*Engle, R. F., Giglio, S., Kelly, B., Lee, H., & Stroebel, J. (2020). Hedging climate change news. *Review of Financial Studies*, *33*(3), 1184–1216. https://doi.org/10.1093/rfs/hhz072

*Erhemjamts, O., & Huang, K. (2019). Institutional ownership horizon, corporate social responsibility and shareholder value. *Journal of Business Research*, *105*, 61–79. https://doi.org/10.1016/j.jbusres.2019.05.037

*Erragragui, E., & Lagoarde-Segot, T. (2016). Solving the SRI puzzle? A note on the mainstreaming of ethical investment. *Finance Research Letters*, *18*, 32–42. https://doi.org/10.1016/j.frl.2016.03.018

*Erragraguy, E., & Revelli, C. (2015). Should Islamic investors consider SRI criteria in their investment strategies? *Finance Research Letters*, *14*, 11–19. https://doi.org/10.1016/j.frl.2015.07.003

*Feng, Z. Y., Chen, C. R., & Tseng, Y. J. (2018). Do capital markets value corporate social responsibility? Evidence from seasoned equity offerings. *Journal of Banking and Finance*, *94*, 54–74. https://doi.org/10.1016/j.jbankfin.2018.06.015

*Flammer, C. (2015). Does corporate social responsibility lead to superior financial performance? A regression discontinuity approach. *Management Science*, *61*(11), 2549–2568. https://doi.org/10.1287/mnsc.2014.2038

Frazzini, A., & Pedersen, L. H. (2014). Betting against beta. *Journal of Financial Economics*, *111*(1), 1–25. https://doi.org/10.1016/j.jfineco.2013.10.005

*Fuenzalida, D., Mongrut, S., Arteaga, J. R., & Erausquin, A. (2013). Good corporate governance: Does it pay in Peru? *Journal of Business Research*, *66*(10), 1759–1770. https://doi.org/10.1016/j.jbusres.2013.01.008

*Galema, R., Plantinga, A., & Scholtens, B. (2008). The stocks at stake: Return and risk in socially responsible investment. *Journal of Banking and Finance*, *32*(12), 2646–2654. https://doi.org/10.1016/j.jbankfin.2008.06.002

Gibson Brandon, R., Krueger, P., & Schmidt, P. S. (2021). ESG rating disagreement and stock returns. *Financial Analysts Journal*, *77*(4), 104–127. https://doi.org/10.1080/0015198X.2021.1963186

*Gomes, M., & Marsat, S. (2018). Does CSR impact premiums in M&A transactions? *Finance Research Letters*, *26*, 71–80. https://doi.org/10.1016/j.frl.2017.12.005

*Gompers, P., Ishii, J., & Metrick, A. (2003). Corporate governance and equity prices. *Quarterly Journal of Economics*, *118*(1), 107–156. https://doi.org/10.1162/00335530360535162

*Green, T. C., Huang, R., Wen, Q., & Zhou, D. (2019). Crowdsourced employer reviews and stock returns. *Journal of Financial Economics*, *134*(1), 236–251. https://doi.org/10.1016/j.jfineco.2019.03.012

Gregory, A., Tharyan, R., & Whittaker, J. (2014). Corporate social responsibility and firm value: Disaggregating the effects on cash flow, risk and growth. *Journal of Business Ethics*, *124*(4), 633–657. https://doi.org/10.1007/s10551-013-1898-5

Haddaway, N. R., & Macura, B. (2018). The role of reporting standards in producing robust literature reviews. *Nature Climate Change*, *8*(6), 444–447. https://doi.org/10.1038/s41558-018-0180-3

Heinkel, R., Kraus, A., & Zechner, J. (2001). The effect of green investment on corporate behavior. *Journal of Financial and Quantitative Analysis*, *36*(4), 431–449. https://doi.org/10.2307/2676219

*Hmiden, O. B., Rjiba, H., & Saadi, S. (2022). Competition through environmental CSR engagement and cost of equity capital. *Finance Research Letters*, 102773. https://doi.org/10.1016/j.frl.2022.102773

*Hong, H., & Kacperczyk, M. (2009). The price of sin: The effects of social norms on markets. *Journal of Financial Economics*, *93*(1), 15–36. https://doi.org/10.1016/j.jfineco.2008.09.001

*Huang, Y., Yang, S., & Zhu, Q. (2021). Brand equity and the Covid-19 stock market crash: Evidence from US listed firms. *Finance Research Letters*, *43*, 101941. https://doi.org/10.1016/j.frl.2021.101941

*Humphrey, J. E., Lee, D. D., & Shen, Y. (2012). Does it cost to be sustainable? *Journal of Corporate Finance*, *18*(3), 626–639. https://doi.org/10.1016/j.jcorpfin.2012.03.002

*Hussaini, M., Hussain, N., Nguyen, D. K., & Rigoni, U. (2021). Is corporate social responsibility an agency problem? An empirical note from takeovers. *Finance Research Letters*, *43*, 102007. https://doi.org/10.1016/j.frl.2021.102007

*Jost, S., Erben, S., Ottenstein, P., & Zülch, H. (2022). Does corporate social responsibility impact mergers & acquisition premia? New international evidence. *Finance Research Letters*, *46*, 102237. https://doi.org/10.1016/j.frl.2021.102237

*Khan, M., Serafeim, G., & Yoon, A. (2016). Corporate sustainability: First evidence on materiality. *Accounting Review*, *91*(6), 1697–1724. https://doi.org/10.2308/accr-51383

Kim, Y., Li, H., & Li, S. (2014). Corporate social responsibility and stock price crash risk. *Journal of Banking and Finance*, *43*, 1–13. https://doi.org/10.1016/j.jbankfin.2014.02.013

*Klassen, R. D., & McLaughlin, C. P. (1996). The impact of environmental management on firm performance. *Management Science*, *42*(8), 1199–1214. https://doi.org/10.1287/mnsc.42.8.1199

*Krüger, P. (2015). Corporate goodness and shareholder wealth. *Journal of Financial Economics*, *115*(2), 304–329. https://doi.org/10.1016/j.jfineco.2014.09.008

*Lam, S. S., Zhang, W., & Jacob, G. H. (2015). The mispricing of socially ambiguous grey stocks. *Finance Research Letters*, *13*, 81–89. https://doi.org/10.1016/j.frl.2015.02.010

*Lee, S., Lee, D., Hong, C., & Park, M. H. (2022). Performance of socially responsible firms during the COVID-19 crisis and trading behavior by investor type: Evidence from the Korean stock market. *Finance Research Letters*, *45*, 102660. https://doi.org/10.1016/j.frl.2021.102660

*Lins, K. V., Servaes, H., & Tamayo, A. (2017). Social capital, trust, and firm performance: The value of corporate social responsibility during the financial crisis. *Journal of Finance*, *72*(4), 1785–1824. https://doi.org/10.1111/jofi.12505

*Lööf, H., Sahamkhadam, M., & Stephan, A. (2021). Is corporate social responsibility investing a free lunch? The relationship between ESG, tail risk, and upside potential of stocks before and during the COVID-19 crisis. *Finance Research Letters*, 102499. https://doi.org/10.1016/j.frl.2021.102499

*Luo, H. A., & Balvers, R. J. (2017). Social screens and systematic investor boycott risk. *Journal of Financial and Quantitative Analysis*, *52*(1), 365–399. https://doi.org/10.1017/S0022109016000910

Markowitz, H. M. (1952). portfolio selection. *Journal of Finance*, *7*(1), 77–91.

*Masulis, R. W., & Reza, S. W. (2015). Agency problems of corporate philanthropy. *Review of Financial Studies*, *28*(2), 592–636. https://doi.org/10.1093/rfs/hhu082

*McGuire, J. B., Sundgren, A., & Schneeweis, T. (1988). Corporate social responsibility and firm financial performance. *Academy of Management Journal*, *31*(4), 854–872. https://doi.org/10.2307/256342

Merton, R. C. (1987). A simple model of capital market equilibrium with incomplete information. *Journal of Finance (New York)*, *42*(3), 483–510. https://doi.org/10.1111/j.1540-6261.1987.tb04565.x

*Monfort, A., Villagra, N., & Sánchez, J. (2021). Economic impact of corporate foundations: An event analysis approach. *Journal of Business Research*, *122*, 159–170. https://doi.org/10.1016/j.jbusres.2020.08.046

*Naffa, H., & Fain, M. (2022). A factor approach to the performance of ESG leaders and laggards. *Finance Research Letters*, *44*, 102073. https://doi.org/10.1016/j.frl.2021.102073

*Naughton, J. P., Wang, C., & Yeung, I. (2019). Investor sentiment for corporate social performance. *Accounting Review*, *94*(4), 401–420. https://doi.org/10.2308/accr-52303

*Ng, A. C., & Rezaee, Z. (2015). Business sustainability performance and cost of equity capital. *Journal of Corporate Finance*, *34*, 128–149. https://doi.org/10.1016/j.jcorpfin.2015.08.003

*Nguyen, P. A., Kecskés, A., & Mansi, S. (2020). Does corporate social responsibility create shareholder value? The importance of long-term investors. *Journal of Banking and Finance*, *112*, 105217. https://doi.org/10.1016/j.jbankfin.2017.09.013

*Nofsinger, J. R., Sulaeman, J., & Varma, A. (2019). Institutional investors and corporate social responsibility. *Journal of Corporate Finance*, *58*, 700–725. https://doi.org/10.1016/j.jcorpfin.2019.07.012

Oikonomou, I., Brooks, C., & Pavelin, S. (2012). The impact of corporate social performance on financial risk and utility: A longitudinal analysis. *Financial Management*, *41*(2), 483–515. https://doi.org/10.1111/j.1755-053X.2012.01190.x

Pástor, Ľ., Stambaugh, R. F., & Taylor, L. A. (2015). Scale and skill in active management. *Journal of Financial Economics*, *116*(1), 23–45.

Pastor, Ľ., Stambaugh, R. F., & Taylor, L. A. (2021). Sustainable investing in equilibrium. *Journal of Financial Economics*, *142*(2), 550–571. https://doi.org/10.1016/j.jfineco.2020.12.011

Pastor, Ľ., & Vorsatz, M. B. (2020). Mutual fund performance and flows during the COVID-19 crisis. *Review of Asset Pricing Studies, 10*(4), 791–833. https://doi.org/10.1093/rapstu/raaa015

Pedersen, L. H., Fitzgibbons, S., & Pomorski, L. (2021). Responsible investing: The ESG-efficient frontier. *Journal of Financial Economics, 142*(2), 572–597. https://doi.org/10.1016/j.jfineco.2020.11.001

Porter, M. E., & Kramer, M. R. (2011). Creating shared value: Redefining capitalism and the role of the corporation in society. *Harvard Business Review, 89*(1/2), 62–77.

Porter, M. E., & Van der Linde, C. (1995). Green and competitive: Ending the stalemate. *Harvard Business Review, 73*(5), 120–134.

Riedl, A., & Smeets, P. (2017). Why do investors hold socially responsible mutual funds? *Journal of Finance, 72*(6), 2505–2550. https://doi.org/10.1111/jofi.12547

*Serafeim, G., & Yoon, A. (2022). Stock price reactions to ESG news: The role of ESG ratings and disagreement. *Review of Accounting Studies*, 1–31. https://doi.org/10.1007/s11142-022-09675-3

*Shackleton, M., Yan, J., & Yao, Y. (2022). What drives a firm's ES performance? Evidence from stock returns. *Journal of Banking and Finance, 136*, 106304. https://doi.org/10.1016/j.jbankfin.2021.106304

*Shanaev, S., & Ghimire, B. (2022). When ESG meets AAA: The effect of ESG rating changes on stock returns. *Finance Research Letters, 46*, 102302. https://doi.org/10.1016/j.frl.2021.102302

Sharfman, M. P., & Fernando, C. S. (2008). Environmental risk management and the cost of capital. *Strategic Management Journal, 29*(6), 569–592. https://doi.org/10.1002/smj.678

*Trinks, P. J., & Scholtens, B. (2017). The opportunity cost of negative screening in socially responsible investing. *Journal of Business Ethics, 140*(2), 193–208. https://doi.org/10.1007/s10551-015-2684-3

*Verwijmeren, P., & Derwall, J. (2010). Employee well-being, firm leverage, and bankruptcy risk. *Journal of Banking and Finance, 34*(5), 956–964. https://doi.org/10.1016/j.jbankfin.2009.10.006

*Wong, J. B., & Zhang, Q. (2022). Stock market reactions to adverse ESG disclosure via media channels. *British Accounting Review, 54*(1), 101045. https://doi.org/10.1016/j.bar.2021.101045

Yoon, A., & Welch, K. (2020). Corporate sustainability and stock returns: Evidence from employee buy-in to senior management.

*Zhang, J., Zhang, Y., & Sun, Y. (2022). Restart economy in a resilient way: The value of corporate social responsibility to firms in COVID-19. *Finance Research Letters*, 102683. https://doi.org/10.1016/j.frl.2022.102683

*Zou, P., & Li, G. (2016). How emerging market investors' value competitors' customer equity: Brand crisis spillover in China. *Journal of Business Research, 69*(9), 3765–3771. https://doi.org/10.1016/j.jbusres.2015.12.068

27
ARGUING FOR URBAN CLIMATE CHANGE ADAPTATION FINANCE – A BIBLIOMETRIC STUDY

An Interdisciplinary Systematic Longitudinal Literature Review and Bibliometric Analysis of Urban Adaptation Financing, a Global North Perspective 2010–2021

Stella Whittaker

Introduction

In general, there has been an explosion of interest in the literature on climate change in cities over the decade to 2021 (Dupuis & Biesbroek, 2013). This is perhaps not surprising, as cities and communities in that period were increasingly dealing with the impacts of climatic events (flooding, heatwaves, wildfires, storms, and drought). Low carbon and climate-adapted cities of the future will need multiple funding sources to deal with these challenges, and a fundamental re-direction of financial capital to new technologies and practices will be needed. Scholarly attention to the financing of urban climate change adaptation (hereafter referred to as urban adaptation (UA)) is urgently needed to inform and guide the transition. To date, there is no comprehensive overview of the science relating to the financing of UA; existing reviews and syntheses have often focused on one aspect of the science at a time, e.g., climate finance for climate change mitigation or urban adaptation planning or policy, but not finance for UA.

In this paper climate finance (CF) refers to financial flows that are:

> Resources directed to activities limiting [city-induced] GHG emissions or aiming to address climate related risks faced [by cities,] contributing to low-carbon development or resilience.
>
> *(CCFLA et al., 2021, p.8)*

Finance for climate adaptation is a subset of the broader concept of climate finance. It is known that there is currently a range of problems with the supply and demand of CF both for climate mitigation and adaptation and at all geographical scales (global, regional, and city). While finance is a critical enabler of UA and is present in the literature, it is largely side-lined in the UA literature. In addition, much of the CF literature concerns the creation of new funding vehicles, such as green bonds, and is almost exclusively climate mitigation focused. Although there is a mushrooming of scholarly activity in the field of CF, there is a need to go beyond this prevailing focus. The multifaceted and fragmented nature of the two fields of UA and CF may partly explain why to date at least, research on the intersection of the two fields is rather embryonic.

Although recent papers review the CF literature (e.g., Hu & Wei, 2018), these are limited in scope, as they only focus on mitigation. In addition, Zhang et al. (2019) conduct a bibliometric study on green finance and conclude that whilst is an important and expanding research area, there is a dearth of comprehensive literature reviews. Interdisciplinary and transdisciplinary approaches are highly useful for addressing complex, uncertain, and controversial policy areas such as this. In addition, bibliometric approaches are especially beneficial for extending and integrating the discoveries of previous studies and reviews (see Supplementary File S1 and S2 for a detailed analysis of literature reviews and large-n comparative cases in the field). The author's decision was therefore to undertake an interdisciplinary systematic literature review (SLR) together with a bibliometric analysis across environment, business and management, and economic literature. Different from conventional literature reviews, adding the bibliometric method provides an innovative and objective perspective through reproducible, quantitative, and reliable processes (Persson, 2014). By presenting objective and accurate information regarding the inner structure and advancement of the entire field, an overall picture of the topic is presented here. From this 'portrait', dominant research areas, research gaps, and ideas for future research are exposed. The paper is structured as follows. The next section presents critical background information. The methodology is given in the third section. The fourth section describes the results – examining and visualizing topics and concepts observed in the literature field in the period January 2010 to March 2021. The fifth section discusses and dissects the results (the 'state of play' and 'where do we go from here'). The sixth section presents the conclusions, spelling out key implications and offering recommendations for further empirical and theoretical work.

Background – Arguing for Adaptation

Examining the literature to gain an overall 'portrait of the topic' requires consideration of dominant discourses in the literature on the deficiencies in urban adaptation planning and financing. Much of the academic literature on adaptation describes an adaptation deficit or gap (Haasnoot et al., 2020). There is also a wealth of practitioner literature on the deficit (IPCC, 2018; GCA, 2019; Rosenzweig et al., 2018; UNEP, 2016). The author uses the Urban Climate Change Research Network definition of the 'adaptation deficit':

> Failure to adapt adequately to existing climate risks.
> *(Rosenzweig et al., 2018, p. 775)*

The adaptation financing deficit often referred to as a 'financing gap' is:

> defined and measured as the difference between the costs of, and thus the finance required, for meeting a given adaptation target and the amount of finance available to do so.
> *(UNEP, 2016, p. xii)*

Much of the academic literature on CF describes a climate financing deficit (Fatica & Panzica, 2021). The scale of the financing deficit, drawing upon the data collected largely by international agencies, is described as massive (ADB, 2021; CPI, 2017), but many recognize that assessing it is methodologically a very challenging exercise (Bachner et al., 2019; Chen et al., 2016; Lesnikowski et al., 2016). Any study of UA financing and any exercise arguing for adaptation action and financing requires an appreciation of these pervasive conditions.

Method

The methodological process of this paper includes two main phases. In the first phase, relevant literature is identified in the interdisciplinary systematic literature review (SLR) with a keyword search and publication retrieval. The second phase includes a quantitative bibliometric analysis of the literature to produce a summary of the impacts and dynamics of the literature. The aim of this combined SLR and bibliometric study is fourfold, to (1) obtain a research overview, (2) consolidate existing research, (3) visualize the research field's main topics and concepts, and (4) extract recommendations for future research. Taking a detailed look at the progression in citation patterns in particular can make a key contribution to the literature by examining and visualizing the evolution of the research in such a new scholarly field such as this.

The SLR

This study starts with a longitudinal interdisciplinary systematic literature review (SLR) of existing studies to identify and delineate the literature covering aspects of urban adaptation financing. This includes peer-reviewed research covering UA and CF in the past decade – between January 2010 and March 2021. To provide focus, the review spotlights UA and CF in the Global North and Europe in particular. The review follows the approach and protocols recommended in 'Preferred Reporting Items for Systematic Reviews and Meta-Analyses: The PRISMA Statement 2020' (Moher et al., 2009). The search query also draws on a definition of climate change adaptation[1] used in other recent systematic adaptation studies and hence narrows the framing of the searches undertaken (Biesbroek et al., 2018; Biesbroek & Delaney 2020). This definition emphasizes the wide vertical and horizontal span of adaptation between groups of actors and geographies. In this case, an urban and municipal climate change adaptation focus is taken.

As outlined in Figure 27.1, the systematic literature review approach is using the PRISMA Statement 2020 (Page et al., 2021). A final database is produced of more than 283 publications across the three disciplines and areas of UA (n=168) and CF studies (CF) (n=96) (19 publications are unclassified (n=19)). In addition, practitioner reports (n=75) excluded from the SLR and bibliometric analysis are examined in a separate NVIVO project with consistent coding. The practitioner literature is rich in studies on financing for UA mainly published in the period 2020 to 2021 and provides useful insights. The results are compared with the scholarly findings and are filling some important gaps in the literature. The focus of the SLR and bibliometric analysis is therefore primarily on peer-reviewed academic literature. The main focus is on the UA literature rather than the cities and climate resilience literature, although the very strong interconnections between these scholarly areas are acknowledged. Insurance and UA is a further notable area with strong interconnections that is largely excluded in this study. Preliminary investigation showed this is a very prolific field and that it warrants its own SLR and bibliometric study.

In total, more than 907 potentially relevant publications were initially identified for this study, of which 653 were excluded. In general, most publications are excluded because they

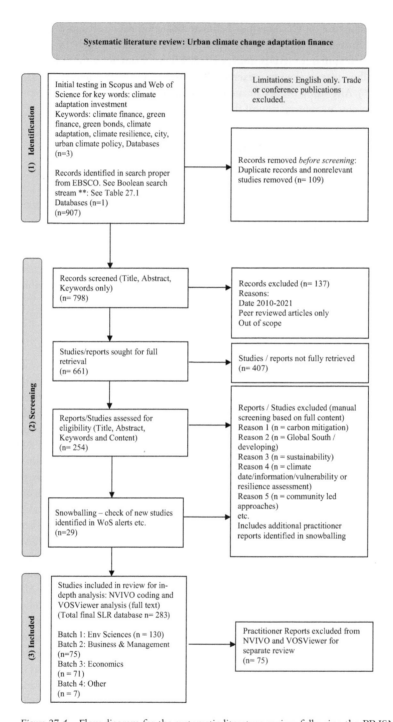

Figure 27.1 Flow diagram for the systematic literature review following the PRISMA Statement 2020

Table 27.1 Search terms

EBSCO search	Boolean search stream	Record results
Search Stream: Step 1: Identification	(i) (Cities OR urban OR "local government" OR municipal* OR "local climate policy" OR "urban planning" OR "municipal planning" OR "municipal government")	1,877,675
	(ii) AND ("climate finance" OR investment* OR "green bonds" OR "green finance" OR "adaptation bonds" OR "climate bonds" OR funding OR "adaptation finance" OR "finance mechanism*" OR "finance sector" OR insurance*)	72,421
	(iii) AND ("climate adaptation*" OR "climate resilience" OR "climate change" OR resilience OR "climate resilient" OR "adaptation planning" OR "dual benefit" OR adaptation OR resilien* OR "adaptive capacity" OR "adaptation planning" OR "dual benefits")	2,136
	(iv) AND (policy OR "policy proportionality" OR "policy under reaction" OR innovation OR "policy innovation" OR "mainstreaming adaptation")	907

do not focus on UA planning, UA implementation, UA financing, and/or climate financing. The approach used several abstract and citation databases, namely EBSCO, Scopus, and Web of Science. The time segment selected for the review was delimited to 2010–2021, primarily to capture the significance of the years post the Paris Conference of Parties (COP) and the United Nations Framework Convention on Climate Change (UNFCCC) in 2015. There has been a very significant increase in scholarly activity on climate change, climate finance, and climate change adaptation since 2015. The full search stream is shown in Table 27.1. A series of iterative literature searches of the databases was undertaken (Table 27.1), starting with abstract-only searches and then fine-tuned manually by performing a manual full-text screening. This was done to narrow the data and to keep the number of publications collected to a manageable size (n=254). Finally, 'snowball sampling' using references and citation tracking tools was undertaken on these publications. A second search for citations based on these now 'in scope' publications resulted in further items. The final database included these new publications, all the data was added to the NVIVO database (n=283) and VOSViewer for analysis and represent the central database of relevant literature for this review. The entire data (n=283 publications) was coded and analyzed in NVIVO for scholarly consensus, controversy, interrelations, influences, and handling of financing themes, to detect gaps within the literature. Combined and separate analyses of the distinct fields were undertaken (UA (n=168) and CF (n=96)) (noting that there was a small number of additional relevant publications (n=19) that were not able to be classified). A deductive and inductive coding strategy was used.

The Bibliometric Analysis

Several tables and data visualizations in VOSViewer were produced to display the distribution of publications by several attributes, such as publication year, journal, author keyword frequency, and citations (van Eck et al., 2010). For data triangulation purposes, citations were also analyzed using WoS and Scopus databases. The VOSViewer software was used to visualize and map the literature, identifying dominant keywords, intellectual structures, and citation clusters, as well as their interconnectedness and scientific relationships. VOS Viewer (Van Eck et al. 2010) is a network analysis software tool that analyses the coupling and co-occurrence of keywords or citations. It quantitatively maps out the relations between variables so that statistical patterns become visible, which helps to better understand the landscape of a research field. Qualitative literature analysis of the publications in the SLR complements this quantitative approach.

Results – Mapping and Visualizing the Scholarly Field

Descriptive Analysis

This paper provides a broad overview of the trends in peer-reviewed UA and CF literature to look at progress in the study of finance for UA needs in cities across distinct disciplines. It is a diverse field with a total of 283 different publications in > 200 different journals and > 740 authors in a very wide range of scholarly fields. Twenty-seven journals feature three or more articles. It is apparent from Figure 27.2 that the field is growing exponentially, and this growth (for the period 2010 to 2020) is in both the UA field (environment science and business/management disciplines) and the CF field (various disciplines). The combined literature has grown considerably, and quickly, since 2017 in particular, by approximately 20% annually. One of the reasons for the steep rise in the research is the increase in activity in the international arena on climate change in the time period.

SLRs are popular in both the UA and the CF research fields. Indeed, 15 SLRs or bibliometric studies were identified. In the period, six SLR studies on green or climate finance and nine in urban adaptation are found (see also Supplementary file S1 for further analysis of these studies). These studies inform the snowball sampling carried out in the SLR. This subset of the literature also shows and corroborates many of the other findings and gaps presented later in this section.

Discipline Distribution

Key journals provide the first indication of the broader scholarly communities in which studies are currently embedded. Table 27.2 illustrates the disciplines, and Table 27.3 and Figure 27.3 illustrate the journals featuring the most articles. This shows that environment-oriented journals dominate especially up to 2015. It is notable that empirical studies of UA effectiveness dictate much of the field to this point and case studies based on single or groups of municipalities are also prominent (29% of the literature). The case studies shed light on the complexity and intricacy of UA planning and the ingredients for success and failure. Of the publications in the final database, 64% are empirical studies of urban adaptation activities or climate financing efforts, 25% are conceptual papers, and 6% are reviews. Conspicuously, the investigation of UA financing is largely missing in all the city-based explorations; a notable example is the study of adaptation planning in 59 cities across the globe, for policy and economic credibility and legitimacy featured in the journal *Landscape and Urban Planning*, an environment-oriented journal (Olazabal & Ruiz De Gopegui, 2021).

In Figure 27.3, the size of the circles represents the number of articles, i.e., the larger a circle, the more featured the articles are, and a smaller distance between two journals suggests a stronger relationship and higher similarity between them. Circles with the same color suggest a similar topic among these journals.

Eleven journals feature largely in the center of Figure 27.3 and account for over one-third of the total literature base. These environment science journals are publishing the majority of the UA articles (64% i.e., 130 of the UA articles (n=202)) included in this review. Environment-

Urban climate change adaptation finance

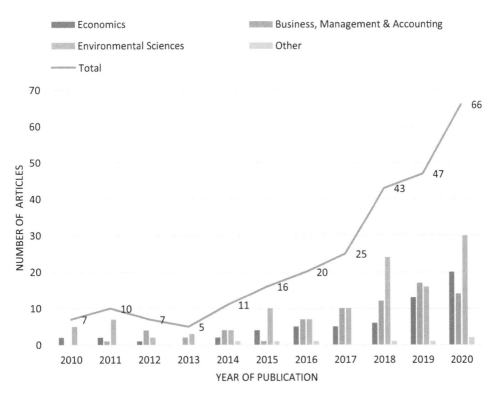

Figure 27.2 Publications by date and discipline for 2010–2020 (NVIVO) (n=257) **Note to Figure 27.2**: Twenty-six publications were excluded in Figure 27.2, because the majority of these are from the year 2021 (18), this year was only searched up to March 2021, therefore representing an incomplete year of data. Additionally, a very small number of publications (8) were identified earlier than 2010. The 'Other' disciplines included social sciences, energy, and disaster management research fields. The disciplines feature in Figure 27.2 left to right are Economics, Environmental Sciences, Business, Management & Accounting and Other).
Source: Author's analysis

Table 27.2 Top ten article discipline areas

Article disciplines	No of articles*	Approximate %*
Environmental Sciences/Environmental Studies	> 105	37
Meteorology Atmospheric Sciences	> 38	12
Green Sustainable Science Technology	34	11
Economics	28	8
Public Administration	26	8
Geography	21	6
Political Science	21	6
Regional Urban Planning	21	6
Development Studies	19	6

(Source: WoS at 23/5/22)
Notes to Table 27.2 and Table 27.3: * WoS discipline categories overlap making it difficult to extract accurate numbers and percentages

Table 27.3 Top ten journals

Journals (n=>130)	Approximate no. of articles*	Approximate %*	Impact Factor (IS) (2020)
Climate Change	16	5	4.743
Environmental Science Policy	12	4	5.52
Mitigation & Adaptation Strategies for Global Change	11	3	3.693
Regional Environmental Change	11	3	3.38
Global Environmental Change: Human and Policy Dimensions	9	3	9.523
Sustainability	8	2	3.251
Journal of Environmental Policy Planning	7	2	3.685
Energy Research Social Science	7	2	6.834
Journal of Cleaner Production	7	2	9.297
Wiley Interdisciplinary Reviews Climate Change	7	2	7.385

(Source: WoS at 23/5/22)

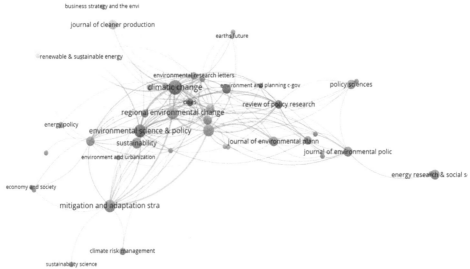

Figure 27.3 Articles by journal (2010–2021) (Author's VOSViewer output)
Note: See Supplementary Files for full color versions of each VOSViewer output https://doi.org/10.5281/zenodo.7614508.

oriented journals account for 45% of the total publication sample. For the CF articles (n=96), the following seven journals feature strongly: *Journal of Cleaner Production, Journal of Sustainable Finance and Investment, Global Environmental Change, Ecological Economics, Climate Policy, Climatic Change,* and *Environmental Innovation and Societal Transition* (accounting for 18% of the total CF articles). An analysis of the journals category shows an emergence of business-oriented journals from 2015. However, in line with the findings of Diaz-Rainey et al. (2017) and Hafner et al. (2020), the interest from economic journals across the period is the least mature, and no articles were found in the elite finance journals (e.g., *Journal of Finance, Journal of Financial Economics,* or

Review of Financial Studies). Overall, the analysis shows a highly fragmented and predominantly environmental science-focused field.

Keywords – Clusters and Connections

Keywords chosen by authors (Figure 27.4) highlight the core focus of publications and indicate research topics. For Figure 27.4, the size of the circles represents the number of occurrences of the keywords, and a smaller distance between two keywords suggests a stronger relationship and similarity (or co-occurrence in the same article). Five major keyword clusters were found in the literature based on the most used author keywords (see also Supplementary file S3 for a detailed analysis of the keyword clusters). Extracting the dominant dates in which each of the keywords occurs in the literature clearly illustrates that the research in keyword cluster 1 on climate finance has grown in importance in the years 2018 to 2021. This work covers authors such as Bhandary et al. (2021); Fatica and Panzica (2021); Hafner et al. (2020); Keenan et al. (2019); Mazzucato and Semieniuk (2018); Zhang et al. (2019) (see Supplementary file S4 for a visualization of author keyword clusters by date).

In Table 27.4, each keyword cluster is also analyzed for the dominant financing type being studied (see Supplementary file S5 for the complete collection of references for each keyword cluster). It was found that publications in cluster 5, climate hazards, are more likely to consider how urban adaptation is financed. Unfortunately, private capital is infrequently featured in this literature, as the focus is on public financing for the majority of the studies in this cluster.

Citation Analysis – Journal, Author, and Article

Citation data on the number of references used by the 283 publications are analyzed in both VOSViewer and the Web of Science database (the author extraction from WoS was made on the 25th of May 2022). Citation analysis permits an objective connection of scholarly clusters or 'schools of thought'; co-citation does this by identifying pairs of references cited together

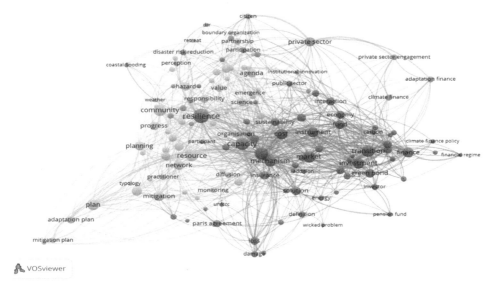

Figure 27.4 Keyword clusters (80 most frequently used author keywords) (Author's VOSViewer output)
Note: See Supplementary Files for full color versions of each VOSViewer output https://doi.org/10.5281/zenodo.7614508.

Table 27.4 Keyword clusters: approaches to UA financing in the literature

Cluster	Keywords and sub-themes	Approaches to financing in the publications in the cluster	Sample reference
(1) Climate finance (renewables/low carbon (green)	Banks, business/private investment, climate finance, capital, markets and investment, climate finance/green finance/green bonds, cost, economy, energy and renewable energy, instruments, investors/pension funds, low carbon economy, market, private sector, transition	• Low carbon and mitigation focused • Private capital markets • New instruments and mechanisms (i.e., Green Bonds) and mechanisms • Investor roles • Market regulation and fiscal policy • Private-sector roles • Low carbon transition	Hafner et al., 2020; Mazzucato & Penna, 2016.
(2) Insurance (light blue)	Insurance, climate transformation, loss and damages, insurance, justice, uncertainty	• Limited or no coverage of adaptation • Insurance mechanisms explored • Investigation of roles for private actors and capital • International climate agreement on loss and damages	Collier & Cox, 2021; Thistlethwaite, 2012.
(3) Urban adaptation planning (purple)	Adaptive capacity, adaptation planning, adaptation strategies, city networks, climate resilience, climate adaptation planning, decision-makers, integration of mitigation and adaptation planning, Paris Agreement, and UNFCCC, private sector	• Urban adaptation focus • Planning efforts and capacity focus • Examination of resource constraints, including funding and finance • Few detailed investigations of finance types, mechanisms, and actors • Predominance of public sector funding	Lesnikowski et al., 2019; Olazabal et al., 2019; Reckien et al., 2018.
(4) Climate Resilience (blue)	Climate resilience, capacity, community, resources for adaptation, sustainability, vulnerability	• Urban climate resilience/adaptation focus • Planning efforts and capacity focus • Examination of resource constraints, including funding and finance • Few detailed investigations of finance types, mechanisms, and actors • Predominance of public sector funding	Collier & Cox, 2021; Stults & Woodruff, 2017.

| (5) | Climate hazards (Yellow) | Actors/authorities, coastal areas, flood/sea level rise, conflict, community, decision-makers, discourse/influence/decision-making, hazard/risk, weather/exposure, disaster risk reduction (DRR), public sector, private sector, responsibility, value, vulnerability | • Climate hazard focus
• Flooding and sea level rise focus
• Planning efforts and capacity focus
• Examination of resource constraints, including funding and finance
• Some investigations of finance types, mechanisms, and actors
• Predominance of public sector funding
• Investigation of roles for private actors and capital
• Few detailed investigations of finance types and mechanisms | Alkhani, 2020; Klein & Juhola, 2018; Tompkins & Eakin, 2012. |

Source: Author's VOSViewer output analysis

(Garfield, 1983). Using WoS data depicted in Table 27.5 and Table 27.6, the author found that each article is cited on average 36.32 times, with a total of > 9,936 citations and > 7,104 citing publications. Further citation analysis is included in Supplementary file S6 and features separate citation analysis for each field of scholarly activity CF and UA.

There were 1,794 citations from 64 publications in 2020 alone and a growing trend in citations each year. In WoS the most cited UA papers are Hanson et al. (2011) (total citations for this article are 375 and on average 31.25 per year) and Eriksen et al. (2015) (Table 27.5). Hanson et al. (2011) conduct an empirical study of future flood losses in major port cities with high exposure to climate extremes, and Eriksen et al. (2015) conduct a conceptual article on adaptation reframing. The Hanson et al. (2011) study is a rare example of academic work found in the SLR that includes a detailed economic analysis of city climate-induced flood risk. The top ten highly cited papers also include several larger-n (larger-n ≥ 20 cases) comparative urban adaptation studies covering European cities (Reckien et al., 2018; Dupuis & Biesbroek, 2013). It is noteworthy that 11 relevant large-n comparative municipal studies were found (see Supplementary file S2) (e.g., Hanson et al., 2011). In WoS, the most cited CF papers are Mazzucato and Semieniuk (2018), Bolton and Foxton (2015), and Mazzucato and Penna (2016); these respectively cover the financing of renewable energy and the role of state banks in financing mitigation (see Supplementary file S6).

The citation maps show how the publications cluster together and clearly illustrate distinct citation assemblages, where each can represent a field of research. The examination of the titles of all individual publications in the citation clusters provides an appropriate label for each. In Figure 27.5, the top seven (7) of the twelve (12) citation clusters are labeled. The many separate citation clusters demonstrate a highly fragmented research field. Some clusters have a single author, and several have a small number (less than five authors). The 'blue' citation cluster of 'climate finance' in Figure 27.5 is clearly separate from all the rest of the other clusters with limited cross-citation. This confirms the separation of the CF field from all the UA research. The two areas are obviously not often researched together. The other citation clusters are more fused, as they represent research on different aspects of urban adaptation. Authors in these citation clusters are clearly working together and citing each other's work.

The co-citation analysis (Figure 27.6) shows a similar pattern and separation of clustering. The co-citation analysis when analyzed with a date overlay again shows that the CF literature is growing in importance in recent years, 2018 to 2020 (see Supplementary file S6 for the co-citation analysis with a date overlay).

Table 27.6 shows the most productive authors in the field. These are predominantly authors and institutions researching urban adaptation and not climate finance. As stated earlier, the CF field is dominated by single publications from less established scholars, with a few exceptions such as authors Mazzucato, M, Semieniuk M, Bolton R, Foxton T J, Hafner S and Penna M. Climate finance publications from these authors are amongst the newest (see Supplementary file S6). Taking the citation and author analysis together (Table 27.5 and 27.6 plus Figure 27.5 and 27.6), it is clear that authors from a small number of institutions and countries dominate the UA field, and as a result case studies of adaptation in cities in these countries also tend to dominate the literature. The top 20 most cited CF publications include Mazzucato and Semieniuk (2018), Mazzucato and Penn (2016), and Bolton and Foxton (2015 (analyzed in WoS). Mazzucato and Semieniuk (2018) have the highest total citation count of 171 and an average of 34.2 per year. The CF publications almost exclusively examine finance for climate mitigation. When UA publications are examined in WoS, the top 20 most cited publications include Hanson et al. (2011) (who have a citation total of 375 and 31.25 per year) and Tompkin and Eakin (2012) (see Supplementary file S6).

Table 27.5 Top 20 most cited publications (full SLR database)

Title	Authors	Source Title	Year	Total	Average per year
A global ranking of port cities with high exposure to climate extremes	Hanson et al.	*Climatic Change*	2011	375	31.25
Reframing adaptation: The political nature of climate change adaptation	Eriksen et al.	*Global Environmental Change: Human and Policy Dimensions*	2015	340	42.5
Governance modes, policy regimes and operational plans	Howlett, Michael★	*Policy Sciences*	2009	299	21.36
Climate change response in Europe: what's the reality? Analysis of adaptation and mitigation plans-200 urban areas	Reckien, et al.★	*Climatic Change*	2014	188	20.89
Local government response to the impacts of climate change: An evaluation of local climate adaptation plans	Baker et al.★	*Landscape And Urban Planning*	2012	181	16.45
How are cities planning to respond to climate change? Assessment of local climate plans from 885 cities in the EU-28	Reckien, et al.★	*Journal Of Cleaner Production*	2018	176	34.2
Financing renewable energy: Who is financing what and why it matters?	Mazzucato, M & Semieniuk, G	*Climatic Change*	2018	171	
Multilevel risk governance and urban adaptation policy	Corfee-Morlot et al.★	*Climatic Change*	2011	158	13.17
An Inconvenient Truth: How Organizations Translate Climate Change Into Business As Usual	Wright, Christopher★; Nyberg, Daniel★	*Academy Of Management Journal*	2017	157	26.17
Will COVID-19 fiscal recovery packages accelerate or retard progress on climate change?	Hepburn et al.★	*Oxford Review Of Economic Policy*	2020	156	52
From the 'old' to the 'new' policy design: design thinking beyond markets and collaborative governance	Howlett, Michael★	*Policy Sciences*	2014	151	16.78
Comparing apples and oranges: Dependent variable problem in comparing/evaluating climate change adaptation policies	Dupuis, Johann; Biesbroek, Robbert	*Global Environmental Change: Human and Policy Dimensions*	2013	147	14.7
Mobilizing Policy (In)Capacity to Fight COVID-19	Capano et al.★	*Policy And Society*	2020	144	48

(*Continued*)

Table 27.5 (Continued)

Title	Authors	Source Title	Year	Total	Average per year
Managing private and public adaptation to climate change	Tompkins, Emma L.; Eakin, Hallie	Global Environmental Change: Human and Policy Dimensions	2012	144	13.09
Climate Change's Role in Disaster Risk Reduction's Future: Beyond Vulnerability and Resilience	Kelman, Ilan; Gaillard, J. C.; Mercer, Jessica	International Journal Of Disaster Risk Science	2015	132	16.5
Innovations in climate policy: the politics of invention, diffusion, and evaluation	Jordan et al.★	Environmental Politics	2014	125	13.89
Climate change adaptation planning in large cities: A systematic global assessment	Aaros et al.★	Environmental Science & Policy	2016	121	17.29
Is adaptation a local responsibility?	Nalau et al.★	Environmental Science & Policy	2015	117	14.63
Why are policy innovations rare and so often negative?	Howlett, Michael	Global Environmental Change: Human and Policy Dimensions	2014	111	12.33
Climate change adaptation in European cities	Carter, Jeremy G.★	Current Opinion In Environmental Sustainability	2011	103	8.58

Source: WoS at 23/5/22
★ These references are included in Supplementary File S8: SLR articles.

Institutions

Publication in terms of affiliations and countries is shown in Table 27.6 and Figure 27.7. According to the WoS dataset, most of the extracted publications are from European countries, especially universities in the Netherlands (41), the UK (28), and Canada (34).

Embryonic Scholarly Focus

By studying the literature closely, the author was able to detect a small 'core' literature examining UA financing issues. Figure 27.8 is a visualization adapted from Mortazavi et al. (2021) which differentiates this 'core' literature from the peripheral literature. Discipline (A) denotes the climate finance literature and discipline (B) the urban adaptation literature. Of the publications (n=83), 29% make up the 'core' literature. A full list of the 'core' literature is listed in Supplementary file S7. The peripheral UA literature includes studies of adaptation where the role of financing is largely absent, and the CF literature includes studies of climate finance where adaptation is largely absent. The author detected that this literature is generating the keyword cluster five on climate hazards (denoted in yellow in Figure 27.4). This literature also includes two literature reviews on urban adaptation financing by Bhandary et al. (2021) and Bisaro et al. (2020). However, the remits for these studies are not the same as this SLR; these SLRs focus on coastal flood risk reduction.

Table 27.6 Top 15 most productive authors and affiliations (WoS at 23 May 2022)

Author	No. of articles	Highest no. of citations	Average citations	H-Index	Country	Affiliation	Type of study (CF or UA)
Berrang-ford L	14	121	(969) 60.7	28	UK	University of Leeds	UA
Biesbroek G R	14	147	(681) 48	28	NL	Wageningen University, Netherlands	UA
Ford JD	12	121	(697) 58.1	53	UK	University of Leeds, UK	UA
Lesnikowski A	11	121	(606) 55.1	16	CA	Concordia University, Canada	UA
Howlett M	9	299	(791) 87.8	49	CA	Simon Fraser University, British Colombia, Canada	UA
Henstra D	8	57	(214) 35.7	14	CA	University of Waterloo, Canada	UA
Olazabal M	7	188	(487) 69.6	15	SP	BC3 – Basque Centre for Climate Change, Spain	UA
Reckein D	6	375	(695) 115.8	11	NL	University of Twente Enschede, Netherlands	UA
Huitema D	6	125	(254) 42.3	17	NL	Vrije Universiteit Amsterdam, Institute Environment Studies IVM, Netherlands	UA
Bouwer L M	5	61	(117) 2 3.4	35	GE	Helmholtz Zentrum Hereon, Germany	UA
Corfee-Morlot J	5	375	(695) 139	14	US	New Climate Economics, Washington, DC, US	UA
Heidrich O	5	188	(505) 101	26	UK	Newcastle University, School Engineering, Newcastle Upon Tyne, UK	UA
Heymann S J	5	97	(337) 75.4	38	US	University of California Los Angeles, Dept. World Policy, Los Angeles, CA, USA	UA
Barerra M	4	97	(285) 71.3	6	US	Loyola University Chicago, Institute Environment Sustainability, Chicago, USA	UA
Bisaro A	4	63	(63) 15.7	12	GE	Global Climate Forum, Berlin, Germany	UA

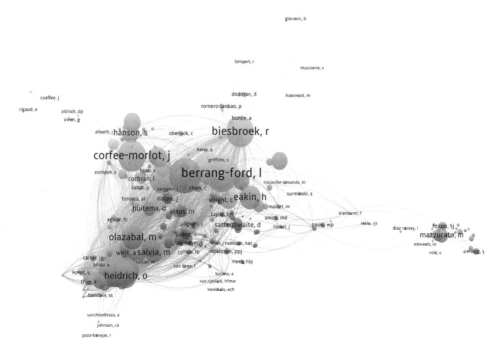

Figure 27.5 Author citation clusters (Author's VOSViewer output)
Note: See Supplementary Files for full color versions of each VOSViewer output https://doi.org/10.5281/zenodo.7614508.

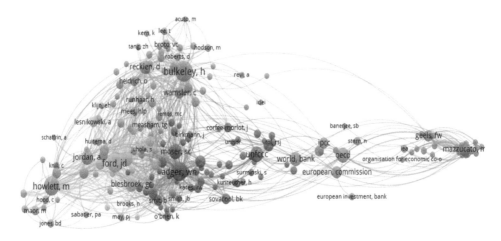

Figure 27.6 Co-citation clusters (authors) (Author's VOSViewer output)
Note: See Supplementary Files for full color versions of each VOSViewer output https://doi.org/10.5281/zenodo.7614508.

The core publications span all three disciplines (environment, business/management; and economic sciences) and are published mainly in the years 2017 to 2022, which is evidence of very recent scholarly activity (e.g., Bachner et al., 2019; Keenan et al. 2019; Moser et al., 2019). The emergence of this scholarly activity may in part be due to the increasing prominence of finance in international climate agreements, most notably the Paris COP21 and the Glasgow COP26 in 2015 and 2021 respectively. This tranche of the literature scrutinizing UA financ-

Urban climate change adaptation finance

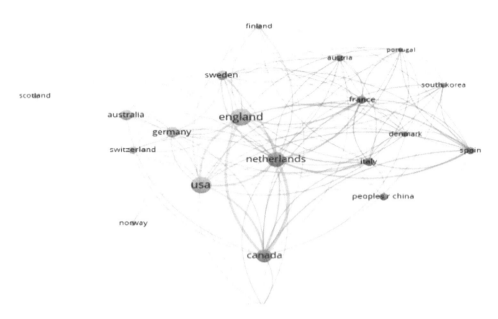

Figure 27.7 Top researchers by country (Author's VOSViewer output)
Note: See Supplementary Files for full color versions of each VOSViewer output https://doi.org/10.5281/zenodo.7614508.

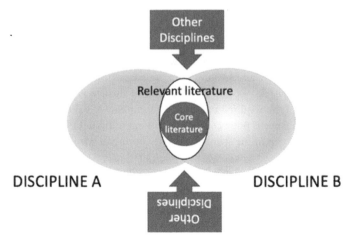

Figure 27.8 Visualization of the core literature (adapted from Mortazavi et al., 2021)

ing is largely empirical city-based studies that focus on sea level rise and inland flood risk. This literature also covers a narrow range of cities where innovative approaches are being progressed, so-called bellwethers of UA, that are already massively exposed to the effects of sea level rise and inland flooding. This literature is not typical so much as it is exemplary of much of the UA and CF literature in its examination of financing approaches for urban adaptation.

Research Gaps

Research gaps in the literature specific to financing UA are also drawn out in this SLR in Table 27.7. The author found seven (7) key themes where scholars identify research gaps relating to UA financing, namely: (i) the adaptation finance gap, (ii) climate finance governance/policies, (iii) finance sector approaches, (iv) private sector and private involvement, (v) finance instruments/mechanisms, (vi) public sector funding, and (vii) disaster risk reduction (DRR) and climate adaptation.

Discussion: State of Play and Where Do We Go from Here?

The State of Play

In this section, the author discusses the results of the SLR literature and bibliometric analysis and the gaps in our knowledge of UA financing. One of the main benefits of an SLR combined with a bibliometric review is the ability to draw conclusions about future research directions by performing statistical analysis of previous and current research (Rey-Martí et al., 2016; Vallaster et al., 2019). Combining the results of a bibliometric analysis with a systematic literature review can produce a sound summary of the past and present research in the field and thereby help create a picture of future research courses (Gast et al., 2015).

Finance Absence in the Urban Adaptation Literature

Much of the UA literature affirms cities will be seriously impacted by a changing climate both now and into the future (Hanson et al., 2011), and to address this there is a need for parity of adaptation with mitigation (Bachner et al., 2019; Biesbroek et al., 2018). Addressing the gap between urban adaptation needs and adaptation efforts needs intensive attention (Abadie et al., 2013; Sovacool & Linnér 2016) and considerable scaling of urban adaptation efforts (Biesbroek et al., 2018; Filho, 2010; Olazabal et al., 2019). The mobilization of finance is critical to this effort, and the private sector is part of the required investment (Tompkins & Eakin, 2012). It is somewhat surprising therefore that finance is not a central component of more UA studies. This study has confirmed this as a research gap in the scholarly activity on urban adaptation.

Adaptation Absence in the Climate Finance Literature

Climate change adaptation (action to address physical climate impacts e.g., sea level rise) in many cases attracts less attention and activity when compared to climate change mitigation (action to reduce greenhouse gas emissions). This is not only from policymakers, politicians, and investors but, as seen in this study, also from scholars (Abadie et al., 2013). This is called the 'mitigation bias' in the literature (Glover & Granberg, 2020). This bias is deeply rooted in international processes such as the United Nations Framework Convention on Climate Change (UNFCCC), which until 2015 promoted mitigation over adaptation. Adaptation was essentially absent from the first two rounds of the UN's scientific advisory body the Intergovernmental Panel on Climate Change (IPCC) assessment reports (IPCC, 2018). Adaptation can be seen by scholars and practitioners alike as an outcome or cost incurred because of a failure to mitigate

Table 27.7 Key urban adaptation finance research gaps identified in the studied literature

Research gap theme	Research gap description	Reference
Adaptation gap	Further research on quantification of a **climate change adaptation gap** at the municipal level.	Chen et al. (2016)
Climate finance policies	The academic literature on **climate finance policies** is limited, where it exists, focus is on North–South climate finance gap or policy analysis based on economic modeling. **Advanced analysis needed of theory/practice in climate finance**.	Bhandary et al. (2021)
	Understanding informal dimensions of **national governing environments** and how they influence local adaptation policy choices.	Lesnikowski et al. (2016)
	More research is needed on the **distributional aspects** of climate change impacts and policies.	Hallegatte et al. (2011)
Finance sector approaches	Knowledge lacking on how **finance sector approaches climate change issues**, research by academics with access to finance professionals.	Diaz-Rainey et al. (2017)
Private sector and private capital	**Modes of governance steering private sector and citizen**s adaptation activities, differences between cities, examine steering between actors, theoretical considerations and practical implications or a stronger involvement of citizens and private sector.	Klein et al. (2018)
	Risks/barriers/opportunities of private investment climate change associated with greater **private investment**.	Adhikari Safaee Chalkasra(2021)
	Patterns of private-sector involvement/governance climate adaptation/mitigation to locate gaps around delivery.	Alkhani (2020)
	How, why and with what – the **governance implications of displacement of public authorities** in coastal flood protection.	Bulkeley and Schroeder (2012)
Finance mechanisms	**Modes of governance steering of private sector and citizen's** adaptation activities, differences between cities, comparing developing/developed country cities, examine steering between actors, relationship between the theoretical considerations and practical implications or a stronger involvement of citizens and private sector.	Olazabal et al. (2019)
	What is **mobilized private finance**? Can actors reach common understanding of private adaptation finance minimizing norms and conflicts in a fragmented climate finance system?	Pauw (2017)
	Economic analysis of flood risk management strategies to inform decision-making.	Der Pol et al. (2017)
	International finance climate change adaptation projects – assessing the within-country variations of different community-focused projects.	Pomme et al. (2020)

(Continued)

Table 27.7 (Continued)

Research gap theme	Research gap description	Reference
	Structural incentives and governance – adaptation **funding/financing mechanisms**.	Keenan et al. (2019)
	Characteristics of available **financial tools** - leverage of value, avoided costs, property values, actuarial risk and resilience metrics.	Woodruff et al. (2020)
	Role of **insurance** as a climate finance mechanism.	Jarzabkowski et al. (2019)
	What sort of collective goods and what kinds of public interventions drawing on the **tools/practices of insurance?** Collective goods interventions and tools/practices insurance.	Collier and Cox (2021)
	Conceptualizations of **self-regulation in private insurance markets.**	Thistlethwaite (2012)
Public sector funding	Comparison of multilevel arrangements across countries, exploring the **performance of public funding arrangements**. Fiscal federalism multilevel governance analysis of public decision-making and fiscal authorities.	Bisaro et al. (2020)
	More **public management research** into climate mitigation and adaptation.	Eckersley et al. (2018)
	Research the implications of insufficient official information on flood events and **disaggregated damage cost estimates** to estimate spatially explicit flood damage. Research reasons/impacts of lack of precise flood modeling in urban areas.	Soto-Montes-de-Oca et al. (2020)
	Who pays for managed retreats? Research on optimum approach to placing the **cost burden** – on the general taxpayer or on the affected communities themselves?	Noy (2020)
	Research on the conditions **weather events** generate for local policy change, insights on local policy actions resulting events.	Giordono et al. (2020)
Disaster risk reduction	**Disaster risk reduction (DRR) and climate change adaptation (CCA) linkages.**	Begum et al. (2014)
	Understanding interrelationships between political economy factors and **distribution of public funds** in Disaster Relief Reduction (DRR).	Islam et al. (2021)
	'Incentivization' disaster mitigation programs such **as insurance, mortgages and loans, tax incentives and credits, grants, regulations, and enhanced building codes.** How to optimize such an incentive scheme.	Song and Wang (2020)

Source: Author's analysis

climate change and is even regarded as being contrary to climate change mitigation. As a result, over time, adaptation has been successively downplayed.

Many of the city case studies (individual and comparative) in the UA literature support the verdict that adaptation effort is the 'Cinderella' response in cities when compared to mitigation and that additional attention is required to attend to this imbalance. This study has also confirmed that this bias is also conspicuous in scholarly activity in the CF literature. Attention is required to address this imbalance in the literature. This review also reveals little theoretical economic research on mobilizing financing for UA (Kotchen & Costello, 2018). CF itself is under-theorized, and there is a lack of finance sector interest in researching climate change generally (Diaz-Rainey et al, 2017). However, it is critical that all areas of climate-related research be given greater attention and prominence in finance journals in order to understand the financing gap (Hong et al., 2020).

The famed 'Holy Grail' of adaptation is being able to measure investment in climate change adaptation and whether this is adequate and proportional to the risks society faces. The task is made difficult because of the fuzziness of adaptation as a policy area (Dupuis & Biesboek, 2013; Lesnikowski et al. 2019) and the limited data and analysis of CF flow at all scales: global, national, and city levels (ADB, 2021; CPI, 2017; Fatica & Panzica, 2021). There is a necessity to address this knowledge gap and accurately measure urban climate finance flows as a prerequisite to understanding the urban adaptation finance gap (Rosenzweig et al., 2018; UNEP, 2016; UNFCCC, 2014). However, scholars stress that the assessment of UA financing needs is methodologically a very challenging exercise:

'adaptation tracking … has numerous challenges and limitations due to, fundamentally, the ambiguity of the concept of adaptation (what can be considered adaptation?) and the lack of comparable, aggregable metrics' (Olazabal & Ruiz De Gopegui, 2021, p. 1).

Where Do We Go from Here?

The review shows that in the five years since 2016, the fields are developing quite remarkably, with a steep rise in the number of papers published, special issues, systematic literature reviews, practitioner literature, and new city and other institutional structures such as the C40 and Cities Climate Finance Leadership Alliance providing financing guidance. The literature abounds with many recommendations for action and policy changes in urban adaptation, but the conditions for financing are not yet clear. There are many research gaps identified in the literature relating to financing UA. Addressing these research gaps is critically important for those seeking to understand or promote UA efforts. The core research identified in this paper seeks to address some of these gaps and is in essence the beginnings of a new research community in UA finance. Interdisciplinary research is needed to address many of these gaps; for instance, there is a need for a coming together of scholars from environmental sciences and economics and from the two areas of UA and CF to collaborate on theoretical considerations and the practical implications of mobilizing greater amounts of finance for UA projects.

By building bridges between scholarly communities and improving conceptual and methodological approaches that cross disciplinary boundaries, as well as building empirical evidence, valuable new insights on effective UA financing will be gained. This will strengthen the UA finance field as a distinct area of research equal to the climate finance field. The issue of financing is an undercurrent in UA research but rarely an upfront consideration as it is here. Both the government (capacity, resources, actors, mechanisms) and market (regulation, capacity, resources, actors, mechanisms) conditions for attracting finance need to become central to UA research. A principal question to be addressed is how the finance regime supports or impedes city and investor engagement in UA. As a first step, the work on barriers and enablers to investment in climate change solutions begun by Hafner et al. (2020) needs to be extended to UA finance to start to unpick the complex issues at play which have led to a UA financing gap. This could be empirical single-city or large-n comparative city cases, as well as empirical and conceptual studies by climate finance scholars focusing on adaptation rather than mitigation.

Given the urgency of this issue [investment in climate change solutions], we call on the academic community to focus more effort in this new and emerging discipline and, in particular, on the need for an independent view on the validity of some of the claims made in these practice-based policy reports.

(Hafner et al., 2020, p. 1)

Limitations

Like any other research, this study has several limits in relation to bibliometric analysis, search, databases, and interpretation. Some of the key limitations include that (i) the SLR and bibliometric analysis is based solely on the selected databases and search streams so results may differ according to this selection, (ii) VOSViewer analysis did not support all of the databases used, (iii) VOSViewer also has requirements on the selection of the minimum number of publications, citations, and keywords occurrences, which influences the results, (iv) citations change over time giving rise to changes in results, (v) citation thresholds in VOSViewer will also influence the results, (vi) the keyword analysis includes only the publications with available author keywords, and (vi) citation analysis is backward-oriented so any projections will be subjective by nature. All of the conclusions presented here should be interpreted within the context of these limitations.

Conclusions

The main aim of the study is to map the field using SLR and bibliometric analysis to understand how this embryonic research is forming. Despite the increasing attention paid to the study of climate finance since 2017, there is a modest understanding of the finance flows being directed at UA. In the literature on UA, the role of financing is largely absent, and in the CF literature climate change adaptation is absent. It is clear that over the years, the major focus in CF is on renewable energy and energy efficiency for carbon reduction and not finance for adaptation. The research fields of UA and CF are also strongly demarcated and fragmented.

Within the core literature delineated in this research, some scholars are studying the financing of UA with a deepness in relation to coastal hazards, retreat, and coastal flooding (Bisaro et al., 2020). This group of scholars could represent the beginnings of a scholarly grouping focusing on the topic. This literature covers a narrow range of cities where innovative approaches are being progressed, so-called bellwethers of UA, that are already massively exposed to the effects of sea level rise and inland flooding, such as Copenhagen, Greater Miami, Helsinki, New Orleans, New York, Randstad, and Rotterdam (e.g., Collier & Cox, 2021; Dabrowski, 2018; Eckersley et al., 2018; Klein & Juhola, 2018; Taylor & Harman, 2016). These cities are grappling with the huge challenge of identifying funding and financing to address these hazards, and they need to look beyond public provisioning to private sources and innovative mechanisms; hence scholarly activity is picking up this shift in focus. These cities are grappling with issues such as the governance and economic complexities in responsibility, trade-offs, equity, and accrual of benefit at the urban level, which will be crucial to mobilizing new private partnerships and financing. Just like the cities themselves, this literature is not typical so much as it is exemplary of much of the UA and CF literature, as these issues do not feature prominently in the majority of the UA nor the CF literature. A coming together of scholars from these two areas may prove very fruitful and provide the much-needed conceptual underpinnings and ideas for future empirical investigations in the intersection of these two fields.

The main contribution of this study is that the author adds to the literature in a couple of ways. The primary outcome is the bringing together of two disparate and separate research strands to present and visualize the interrelated clustering of familiar and frequently cited studies. This enables a quick but comprehensive overview of the main relations within the scholarly field from which ideas for new scholarly fields of research have emerged. Secondly, the different areas of dominance are revealed such that the gaps in the entire field can be identified and addressed, for instance, the dominance in the study of CF of a mitigation focus and a research gap in relation to financing UA.

UA finance flows and needs are largely unquantified and unknown at this stage; however, this should not deter scholars. Rather there is a pressing need to address this knowledge gap and undertake more targeted and detailed urban adaptation financing studies. This could be empirical single-city or large-n comparative city cases. A research focus on cities in the Global North is needed to balance the healthier research attention to date on cities in the Global South (Bhandary et al., 2021). Climate finance scholars could turn their attention towards the empirical studies of suitable financial tools for urban adaptation and the ways to incentivize urban adaptation programs such as insurance, mortgages and loans, tax incentives and credits, grants, regulations, and enhanced building codes (Olazabal et al., 2019). Conceptual and empirical studies are needed on the governance implications of displacing public funding for UA (Bulkeley & Schroeder, 2012), such as avoided costs, impacts on property values, actuarial risk, and distributional and justice implications. Scholars need to extend their work to cover urban adaptation finance to start to disentangle these complex financing issues.

Supplementary Files

Supplementary files and material associated with this article can be found online at: https://doi.org/10.5281/zenodo.7614508. The Supplementary files also include full color graphics for each VOSViewer Figure 27.2 to 27.7.

Note

1 The author uses the following definition of climate change adaptation: "the production of outputs in forms of activities and decisions taken by purposeful public and private actors at different administrative levels and in different sectors, which deals intentionally with climate change impacts, and whose outcomes attempt to substantially impact actor groups, sectors, or geographical areas that are vulnerable to climate change" (Biesbroek et al. 2018 p. 884).

References

Abadie, L. M., Galarraga, I., & Rübbelke, D. (2013). An analysis of the causes of the mitigation bias in international climate finance. *Mitigation and Adaptation Strategies for Global Change*, 18(7), 943–955. https://doi.org/10.1007/s11027-012-9401-7

ADB. (2021). *Catalyzing climate finance: Lessons learned from the Shandong green development fund.* ADB Sustainable Development Working Papers Series, No. 75. http://doi.org/10.22617/WPS210113-2

Adhikari, B., & Safaee Chalkasra, L. S. (2021). Mobilizing private sector investment for climate action: Enhancing ambition and scaling up implementation. *Journal of Sustainable Finance and Investment*, 10, 1–18. https://doi.org/10.1080/20430795.2021.1917929

Alkhani, R. (2020). Understanding private-sector engagement in sustainable urban development and delivering the climate agenda in North-Western Europe—A case study of London and Copenhagen. *Sustainability*, 12(20), 8431. https://doi.org/10.3390/su12208431

Bachner, G., Bednar-Friedl, B., & Knittel, N. (2019). How does climate change adaptation affect public budgets? Development of an assessment framework and a demonstration for Austria. *Mitigation and Adaptation Strategies for Global Change*, 24(7), 1325–1341. https://doi.org/10.1007/s11027-019-9842-3

Begum, A. R., Kabir, S., Hamid, A., & Jacqueline, J. (2014). Toward conceptual frameworks for linking disaster risk reduction and climate change adaptation. *International Journal of Disaster Risk Reduction*, 10, 362–373. https://doi.org/10.1016/j.ijdrr.2014.10.011

Bhandary, R. R., Gallagher, K. S., Zhang, F., Ram, R., & Gallagher, K. S. (2021). Climate finance policy in practice: A review of the evidence. *Climate Policy, 21*(4), 529–545. https://doi.org/10.1080/14693062.2020.1871313

Biesbroek, R., & Delaney, A. (2020). Mapping the evidence of climate change adaptation policy instruments in Europe. *Environmental Research Letter, 15*(8), 083005. https://doi.org/10.1088/1748-9326/ab8fd1

Biesbroek, R., Lesnikowski, A., Ford, J. D., & Berrang-ford, L. (2018). Do administrative traditions matter for climate change adaptation policy? A comparative analysis of 32 high-income countries. *Review of Policy Research, 35*. https://doi.org/10.1080/09644016.2020.1814045

Bisaro, A., de Bel, M., Hinkel, J., Kok, S., Stojanovic, T., & Ware, D. (2020). Multilevel governance of coastal flood risk reduction: A public finance perspective. *Environmental Science and Policy, 112*, 203–212. https://doi.org/10.1016/j.envsci.2020.05.018

Bolton, R., & Foxon, T. J. (2015). A socio-technical perspective on low carbon investment challenges – Insights for UK energy policy. *Environmental Innovation and Societal Transitions, 14*, 165–181. https://doi.org/10.1016/j.eist.2014.07.005

Bulkeley, H., & Schroeder, H. (2012). Beyond state/non-state divides: Global cities and the governing of climate change. *European Journal of International Relations, 18*(4), 743–766. https://doi.org/10.1177/1354066111413308

CCFLA, Negreiros, P., Furio, V., Falconer, A., Richmond, M., Yang, K., Jungman, L., Tonkonogy, B., Novikova, A., & Pearson, M. (2021). *The state of cities climate finance* (Issue June). https://www.climatepolicyinitiative.org/wp-content/uploads/2021/06/SCCF_PART1-FINAL-1.pdf

Chen, C., Doherty, M., Coffee, J., Wong, T., & Hellmann, J. (2016). Measuring the adaptation gap: A framework for evaluating climate hazards and opportunities in urban areas. *Environmental Science and Policy, 66*(2), 403–419. https://doi.org/10.1016/j.envsci.2016.05.007

Collier, S. J., & Cox, S. (2021). Governing urban resilience: Insurance and the problematization of climate change. *Economy and Society, 50*(2), 275–296. https://doi.org/10.1080/03085147.2021.1904621

CPI. (2017). A CPI report global landscape of climate finance 2017. In *Climate policy initiative*. www.climatepolicyinitiative.org

Dąbrowski, M. (2018). Boundary spanning for governance of climate change adaptation in cities: Insights from a Dutch urban region. *Environment and Planning C: Politics and Space, 36*(5), 837–855. https://doi.org/10.1177/2399654417725077

Der Pol, V., van Ierland, E. C., & Gabbert, S. (2017). Economic analysis of adaptive strategies for flood risk management under climate change. *Mitigation and Adaptation Strategies for Global Change, 22*(2), 267–285. https://doi.org/10.1007/s11027-015-9637-0

Diaz-Rainey, I., Robertson, B., & Wilson, C. (2017). Stranded research? Leading finance journals are silent on climate change. *Climatic Change, 143*(1–2), 243–260. https://doi.org/10.1007/s10584-017-1985-1.

Dupuis, J., & Biesbroek, R. (2013). Comparing apples and oranges: The dependent variable problem in comparing and evaluating climate change adaptation policies. *Global Environmental Change, 23*(6), 1476–1487. https://doi.org/10.1016/j.gloenvcha.2013.07.022

Eckersley, P., England, K., & Ferry, L. (2018). Sustainable development in cities: Collaborating to improve urban climate resilience and develop the business case for adaptation. *Public Money and Management, 38*(5), 335–344. https://doi.org/10.1080/09540962.2018.1477642

Eriksen, S. H., Nightingale, A. J., & Eakin, H. (2015). Reframing adaptation: The political nature of climate change adaptation. *Global Environmental Change, 35*, 523–533. https://doi.org/10.1016/j.gloenvcha.2015.09.014

Fatica, S., & Panzica, R. (2021). Green bonds as a tool against climate change? *Business Strategy and the Environment, 30*(5), 2688–2701. https://doi.org/10.1002/bse.2771

Filho, W. (2010). The economic, social and political elements of climate change. In W. Leal Filho (Ed.), Springer. https://doi.org/10.1007/978-3-642-14776-0

Garfield, E. (1983). Mapping science in the Third World. *Science and Public Policy, 10*(3), 112–127.

Gast, J., Filser, M., Gundolf, K., & Kraus, S. (2015). Coopetition research: Towards a better understanding of past trends and future directions. *International Journal of Entrepreneurship and Small Business, 24*(4), 492–452. https://www.researchgate.net/publication/275208637_Coopetition_research_Towards_a_better_understanding_of_past_trends_and_future_directions

Giordono, L., Boudet, H., & Gard-Murray, A. (2020). Local adaptation policy responses to extreme weather events. *Policy Sciences, 53*(4), 609–636. https://doi.org/10.1007/s11077-020-09401-3

Global Commission on Adaptation (GCA). (2019). *Adapt now: A global call for leadership on adaptation*. GCA. www.gca.org
Glover, L., & Granberg, M. (2020). The politics of adapting to climate change. In *The politics of adapting to climate change*. Palgrave Macmillan. https://doi.org/10.1007/978-3-030-46205-5
Haasnoot, M., Biesbroek, R., Lawrence, J., Muccione, V., Lempert, R., & Glavovic, B. (2020). Defining the solution space to accelerate climate change adaptation. *Regional Environmental Change*, 20, 1–5.
Hafner, S., Jones, A., Anger-Kraavi, A., & Pohl, J. (2020). Closing the green finance gap: A systems perspective. *Environmental Innovation and Societal Transitions*, 34, 26–60. https://doi.org/10.1016/j.eist.2019.11.007
Hallegatte, S., Ranger, N., Mestre, O., Dumas, P., Corfee-Morlot, J., Herweijer, C., & Muir Wood, R. (2011). Assessing climate change impacts, sea level rise and storm surge risk in port cities: A case study on Copenhagen. *Climatic Change*, 104(1), 113–137. https://doi.org/10.1007/s10584-010-9978-3
Hanson, S., Nicholls, R., Ranger, N., Hallegatte, S., Corfee-Morlot, J., Herweijer, C., & Chateau, J. (2011). A global ranking of port cities with high exposure to climate extremes. *Climatic Change*, 104(1), 89–111. https://doi.org/10.1007/s10584-010-9977-4
Hong, H., Karolyi, G. A., & Scheinkman, J. A. (2020). Climate finance. *Review of Financial Studies*, 33(3), 1011–1023. https://doi.org/10.1016/j.jeconom.2018.09.015
Hu, F., & Wei, H. (2018). *An empirical study of green finance research through bibliometrics* (pp. 84–106). https://doi.org/10.4018/978-1-5225-7808-6.ch004
IPCC. (2018). *Global warming of 1.5°C*. Intergovernmental Panel on Climate Change. https://www.ipcc.ch/sr15/chapter/chapter-5/
Islam, S., Zobair, K. M., Chu, C., Smart, J. C. R., & Alam, M. S. (2021). Do political economy factors influence funding allocations for disaster risk reduction? *Journal of Risk and Financial Management*, 14(84), 1–20. https://doi.org/10.3390/jrfm14020085
Jarzabkowski, P., Chalkias, K., & Clarke, D. (2019). Insurance for climate adaptation: Opportunities and limitations. *ResearchGate, Global Com*. https://www.researchgate.net/publication/335789060
Keenan, J. M., Chu, E., & Peterson, J. (2019). From funding to financing perspectives shaping a research agenda for investment in urban climate adaptation. *International Journal of Urban Sustainable Development*, 11(3), 297–308. https://doi.org/10.1080/19463138.2019.1565413
Klein, J., & Juhola, S. (2018). The influence of administrative traditions and governance on private involvement in urban climate change adaptation. *Review of Policy Research*, 35(6), 930–952. https://doi.org/10.1111/ropr.12294
Kotchen, M. J., & Costello, C. (2018). Maximizing the impact of climate finance : Funding projects or pilot projects ? *Journal of Environmental Economics and Management*, 92, 270–281. https://doi.org/10.1016/j.jeem.2018.08.009
Lesnikowski, A., Ford, J. D., Berrang-Ford, L., Biesbroek, R., & Berrang-Ford, L. (2019). A policy mixes approach to conceptualizing and measuring climate change adaptation policy. *Climatic Change*, 156(4). https://doi.org/10.1007/s10584-019-02533-3
Lesnikowski, A., Ford, J., Biesbroek, R., Berrang-Ford, L., & Heymann, S. J. (2016). National-level progress on adaptation. *Nature Climate Change*, 6(3), 261–264. https://doi.org/10.1038/nclimate2863
Mazzucato, M., & Penna, C. C. R. (2016). Beyond market failures : The market creating and shaping roles of state investment banks. *Journal of Economic Policy Reform*, 7870, 1–22. https://doi.org/10.1080/17487870.2016.1216416
Mazzucato, M., & Semieniuk, G. (2018). Financing renewable energy : Who is financing what and why it matters ☆. *Technological Forecasting and Social Change*, 127(May 2016), 8–22. https://doi.org/10.1016/j.techfore.2017.05.021
Moher, D., Liberati, A., Tetzlaff, J., & Altman, D. G. (2009). *Preferred reporting items for systematic reviews and meta analyses: The PRISMA statement*. 89(9). http://www.annals.org/cgi/content/ftill/151/4/264
Mortazavi, S., Eslami, M. H., Hajikhani, A., & Väätänen, J. (2021). Mapping inclusive innovation: A bibliometric study and literature review. *Journal of Business Research*, 122(July 2020), 736–750. https://doi.org/10.1016/j.jbusres.2020.07.030
Moser, S. C., Ekstrom, J. A., Kim, J., & Heitsch, S. (2019). Adaptation finance archetypes: Local governments' persistent challenges of funding adaptation to climate change and ways to overcome them. *Ecology and Society*, 24(2). https://doi.org/10.5751/ES-10980-240228
Noy, I. (2020). Paying a price of climate change: Who pays for managed retreats? *Current Climate Change Reports*, 6(1), 17–23. https://doi.org/10.1007/s40641-020-00155-x

Olazabal, M., & Ruiz De Gopegui, M. (2021). Adaptation planning in large cities is unlikely to be effective. *Landscape and Urban Planning, 206*, 103974. https://doi.org/10.1016/j.landurbplan.2020.103974

Olazabal, M., Ruiz De Gopegui, M., Tompkins, E. L., Venner, K., & Smith, R. (2019). A cross-scale worldwide analysis of coastal adaptation planning. *Environmental Research Letters, 14*(12), 124056. https://doi.org/10.1088/1748-9326/ab5532

Page, M. J., McKenzie, J. E., Bossuyt, P. M., Boutron, I., Hoffmann, T. C., Mulrow, C. D., Shamseer, L., Tetzlaff, J. M., Akl, E. A., Brennan, S. E., Chou, R., Glanville, J., Grimshaw, J. M., Hróbjartsson, A., Lalu, M. M., Li, T., Loder, E. W., Mayo-Wilson, E., McDonald, S., … Moher, D. (2021). The PRISMA 2020 statement: An updated guideline for reporting systematic reviews. *BMJ, 372*, n71. https://doi.org/10.1136/bmj.n71

Pauw, W. P. (2017). Mobilising private adaptation finance: Developed country perspectives. *International Environmental Agreements: Politics, Law and Economics, 17*(1), 55–71. https://doi.org/10.1007/s10784-016-9342-9

Persson, P. B. (2014). Downloading-reading-citing? Some thoughts on our bibliometrics. *Acta Physiologica, 211*(2), 249–250. https://doi.org/10.1111/apha.12292

Pomme, O., Biesbroek, R., & Cebotari, V. (2020). What makes internationally financed climate change adaptation projects focus on local communities ? A configurational analysis of 30 Adaptation Fund projects. *Global Environmental Change, 61*(July 2019), 102035. https://doi.org/10.1016/j.gloenvcha.2020.102035

Reckien, D., Salvia, M., Heidrich, O., Church, J. M., Pietrapertosa, F., De Gregorio-Hurtado, S., D'Alonzo, V., Foley, A., Simoes, S. G., Krkoška Lorencová, E., Orru, H., Orru, K., Wejs, A., Flacke, J., Olazabal, M., Geneletti, D., Feliu, E., Vasilie, S., Nador, C., … Dawson, R. (2018). How are cities planning to respond to climate change? Assessment of local climate plans from 885 cities in the EU. *Journal of Cleaner Production, 191*, 207–219. https://doi.org/10.1016/j.jclepro.2018.03.220

Rey-Martí, A., Ribeiro-Soriano, D., & Palacios-Marqués, D. (2016). A bibliometric analysis of social entrepreneurship. *Journal of Business Research, 69*(5), 1651–1655. https://doi.org/10.1016/j.jbusres.2015.10.033

Rosenzweig, C., Solecki, W., Romero-Lankao, P., Mehrotra, S., Dhakal, S., & Ali Ibrahim, S. (Eds.). (2018). *Climate change and cities: Second assessment report of the urban climate change research network*. Cambridge University Press. https://uccrn.ei.columbia.edu/publications

Song, S., & Wang, C. (2020). Incentivizing catastrophe risk sharing. *IISE Transactions, 52*(12), 1358–1385. https://doi.org/10.1080/24725854.2020.1757792

Soto-Montes-de-Oca, G., Bark, R., & González-Arellano, S. (2020). Incorporating the insurance value of peri-urban ecosystem services into natural hazard policies and insurance products: Insights from Mexico. *Ecological Economics, 169*(September 2019), 106510. https://doi.org/10.1016/j.ecolecon.2019.106510

Sovacool, B. K., & Linnér, B.-O. (2016). *The political economy of climate change adaptation* (1st ed.). Palgrave Macmillan UK. https://doi.org/10.1057/9781137496737

Stults, M., & Woodruff, S. C. (2017). Looking under the hood of local adaptation plans: Shedding light on the actions prioritized to build local resilience to climate change. *Mitigation and Adaptation Strategies for Global Change, 22*(8). https://doi.org/10.1007/s11027-016-9725-9

Taylor, B. M., & Harman, B. P. (2016). Governing urban development for climate risk: What role for public – private partnerships? *Environment and Planning C: Government and Policy, 34*(5), 927–944. https://doi.org/10.1177/0263774X15614692

Thistlethwaite, J. (2012). The climatewise principles: Self-regulating climate change risks in the insurance sector. *Business and Society, 51*(1), 121–147. https://doi.org/10.1177/0007650311427595

Tompkins, E. L., & Eakin, H. (2012). Managing private and public adaptation to climate change. *Global Environmental Change, 22*(1), 3–11. https://doi.org/10.1016/j.gloenvcha.2011.09.010

UNEP. (2016). *The adaptation finance gap report*. United Nations Environment Programme. https://wedocs.unep.org/handle/20.500.11822/32865?show=full

UNFCCC. (2014). *Adaptation fund, climate and development, 7*(1), 16–34. https://www.adaptation-fund.org/wp-content/uploads/2015/11/tango-odi-evaluation-of-the-af_annexes.pdf

Vallaster, C., Kraus, S., Merigó Lindahl, J. M., & Nielsen, A. (2019). Ethics and entrepreneurship: A bibliometric study and literature review. *Journal of Business Research, 99*, 226–237. https://doi.org/10.1016/j.jbusres.2019.02.050

Van Eck, N. J., Waltman, L., Dekker, R., & van den Berg, J. (2010). A comparison of two techniques for bibliometric mapping: Multidimensional scaling and VOS. *Journal of the American Society for Information Science and Technology, 61*(12), 2405–2416. https://doi.org/10.1002/asi.21421

Woodruff, S. C., Mullin, M., & Roy, M. (2020). Is coastal adaptation a public good? The financing implications of good characteristics in coastal adaptation. *Journal of Environmental Planning and Management, 63*(12), 2082–2101. https://doi.org/10.1080/09640568.2019.1703656

Zhang, D., Zhang, Z., & Managi, S. (2019). A bibliometric analysis on green finance: Current status, development, and future directions. *Finance Research Letters, 29*, 425–430. https://doi.org/10.1016/j.frl.2019.02.003

28
GREEN BONDS AS A TOOL OF GREEN FINANCING

Markus Düringer, Niels Hermes, and Swarnodeep Homroy

Introduction

Underlying all great stories of innovation in human history is a story of innovative financing. For example, to bring the lightbulb to every household, Thomas Alva Edison needed the (then) innovative concept of a limited liability corporation. The next great challenge for humanity is to mitigate the causes of long-term anthropogenic climate change and adapt to the climate risks soon. Dealing with a multi-dimensional problem like climate change will require large-scale financing. The European Commission estimates that an annual investment of US $376 billion is necessary to address the most urgent climate concerns, such as net-zero greenhouse gas emissions, by 2050. Raising financing of this size will require new financial innovations, both from the private and the public sector. Towards that goal, corporates and business organizations are incorporating sustainability concerns in their business strategies. Some companies have sought to raise capital to (re)finance their green initiatives by taking on a new kind of debt called green bonds.

Green bonds are fixed-income securities committed to using the proceeds for green projects (Climate Bonds Initiative, 2019; ICMA, 2022). The proceeds from these bonds can be deployed to environmental projects consistent with the Paris Agreement's goals to limit global warming to well below two degrees Celsius (and preferably even to one and a half degrees Celsius)[1] To achieve these climate targets in the European Union, the European Commission President Ursula von der Leyen has set a target to raise climate action funds by issuing green bonds. These green bonds will comprise 30 per cent of the €750 billion issued under the Next Generation EU program. In addition, global leaders expressed taking further actions to counter climate change at the recent UN Climate Change Conference 2021 "COP26" (UNFCCC, 2022). This means that more funding focusing on green projects will be necessary in the coming years.

This chapter aims to provide an overview of the *corporate* green bonds market and generate questions for future research related to green bonds. Although also public sector and supranational institutions have issued, and are still issuing, green bonds, we focus on corporate green bonds for three main reasons. First, there has been an intense focus in recent years on the climate impacts of large corporations. Therefore, these organizations are under pressure to generate a new stream of financing for their decarbonization projects. Second, in many cases, public sector green bonds are issued to provide loans to local businesses for their decarbonization projects.

Third, corporate green bonds can be seen as an important instrument to involve the private sector in greening the economy.

In particular, we aim to discuss and synthesize two key questions about corporate green bonds as a tool for financing a greener future. First, we discuss what factors may influence companies to issue green bonds. In that, we focus on factors related to financing needs and company, industry, and country characteristics. Second, we discuss the realized outcomes of green bonds on the company and the environment. In this part, we also focus on the concerns related to greenwashing motives of green bond issuance.

The remainder of this chapter is organized as follows. The second section discusses the nature of green bonds and how they differ from other types of bonds and green finance products. This section also provides a short overview of the trends in issuing green bonds from 2017 to 2020. The third section provides an overview of the research that has investigated the reasons why companies issue green bonds, while the fourth section goes into discussing the outcomes of issuing green bonds both for the issuing company, as well as for the environment. The fifth section provides conclusions as well as some suggestions for future research.

Green Bonds: Concepts and Trends

The growing focus on green bonds as a financing instrument merits a broader understanding of the nature and effectiveness of these bonds. These debt instruments are voluntary capital-raising activities by companies to decarbonize the value creation process. Most green bonds are green "use of proceeds" or asset-linked bonds. Proceeds from these bonds are either earmarked for green projects or used to replace high-emitting assets with greener alternatives. Raising money through green bonds requires that an issuing organization invests or reinvests the proceeds exclusively in projects related to green technology, emission abatement, or adaptation to climate risks, that is, these projects should be geared towards contributing to investments in renewable energy and the energy efficiency sector to combat climate change (European Investment Bank, 2020).

Green bonds usually have the same credit profile as other vanilla bonds from the same issuer, but with an added covenant on environmental outcomes. To obtain the green bond label for the bond issue, an issuer must undergo specific processes as defined for instance by green bond standards by the Climate Bonds Initiative (CBI) and the International Capital Market Association (ICMA). Furthermore, ongoing monitoring of the use of proceeds through independent external parties and appropriate reporting is required for an issuer to maintain the green bond label for the outstanding financing.

The first green bond was issued by the European Investment Bank (EIB) in 2007 (European Investment Bank, 2022a), at this point labeled as the Climate Awareness Bond (CAB). Since this first green bond was issued, several other supranational institutions, such as the World Bank, the European Investment Bank (EIB) and the International Finance Corporation (IFC), but also municipalities, and state-owned banks, and companies have issued similar types of bonds. In some cases, institutions have used different labels, such as Forest Bonds (IFC, 2016), Catastrophe/disaster Bonds (World Bank, 2014), and Green Transition Bonds (European Bank for Reconstruction and Development, 2019) (Schumacher, 2020). In addition, institutions increasingly also issued bonds focusing on other sustainable development goals (SDGs) than climate change, examples being the Sustainability Awareness Bonds (European Investment Bank, 2022b) and the Sustainable Development Bonds (World Bank, 2017), the proceeds of which should be used to fund social projects. (Schumacher, 2020). The most recent development is the issuance of so-called green convertible bonds, which encompass green, social, and sustainable goals. The development of these different types of labels has made the market for green bonds less transparent and has contributed to calls for creating uniform frameworks and standards regarding the definition of green bonds (Schumacher, 2020).

Since the first issue of green bonds in 2007, total annual green bond issuance has increased from less than US $1 billion to over US $250 billion in 2019 (see Figure 28.1), while the number of issues of these bonds has grown from less than 50 in 2010 to around 1,800 in 2019 (Figure 28.2). There is quite some diversity between countries in terms of the values and numbers of green bonds issued. The United States has been clearly leading in terms of total issuance amount (mainly due to bonds issued by municipalities), but China has become an important issuer as well. Within Europe, France is leading the market. In addition, emerging economies such as Mexico, India, and Indonesia have become active issuers of bonds (Weber & Saravade, 2019).

While public sector and supranational issuers have certainly been important drivers of the growth of the green bonds market, companies (including commercial banks) have become important issuers of green bonds as well, showing significant growth rates. In 2019, the total value of corporate green bonds issued was 114.3 billion dollars, a 44 per cent increase over the

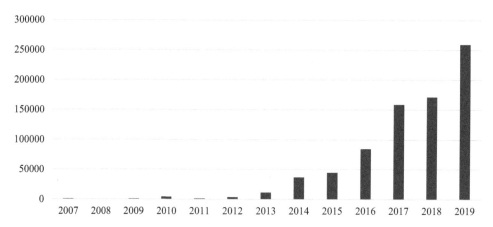

Figure 28.1 Value of green bond issuance in US dollars (in $m). Source: authors' calculation from Climate Bonds Initiative data (2022)

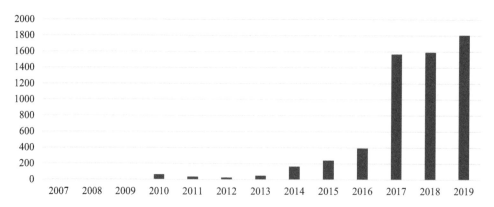

Figure 28.2 Number of green bonds issued. Source: authors' calculation from Climate Bonds Initiative data (2022)

previous year (see Figure 28.2). The supply of green bonds by companies has steadily increased, and the demand for green financial instruments has also grown. These factors yield a price premium compared to conventional bonds (ING, 2021). Again, companies in The United States and, especially China, are most prevalent in issuing green bonds, measured in terms of the value of the issued bonds. In Europe, companies in France, Sweden, and, to a lesser extent, Germany and the Netherlands seem to lead the market in terms of the number of bonds; in terms of value, the Netherlands, France, and Germany are leading. In some emerging markets, such as Mexico, Brazil, India, Taiwan, South Korea, and Singapore, the corporate green bond market seems to have emerged recently as well, although both the number and value of green bond issues remain relatively low (Flammer, 2021).

Despite the growing popularity, there is no universally accepted definition of a green bond nor a global standard for how bonds can be classified as green. The most commonly used classification system is the Climate Bonds Standard of the Climate Bonds Initiative (Climate Bonds Initiative, 2019), hereafter, CBI. CBI is an international non-profit organization working on gathering and collating market intelligence, developing market standards, and guiding policy and regulation in the market for sustainable financing. CBI manually collects data on "green" securities issued by companies, governments, public institutions, and other organizations. CBI has its own criteria to classify a bond as green. Thus, even if a company describes its bonds as green, if the bond characteristics do not satisfy the predetermined criteria and undergo voluntary certification, CBI does not classify it as a green bond in its database.[2]

The lack of a globally accepted verification standard leads to widespread concern about greenwashing motives of issuing green bonds, i.e., the issuance of these debts is merely symbolic without any material impact on the environment. Such concerns plague the green bond market, as issuers are concerned with securitizing verifiable green assets, and investors are concerned about both the returns and the use of proceeds of these bonds. The European Commission aims to solve the current issues arising from the absence of a generally accepted standard by introducing its own standard for green bonds, the European Green Bond Standard (European Union, 2022a). This standard is supposed to embrace the current EU Taxonomy (for sustainable activities) that can be seen as a classification framework for sustainable investments and activities (European Union, 2022b). Further European initiatives, such as the Sustainable Finance Disclosure Regulation (SFDR), which requires certain types of institutional investors to report on their approach towards ESG risks in their portfolios (S&P Global, 2021), will certainly play a role in introducing these standards into common business practice and support the growth of the green bond market.

The introduction of the targets by the European Union and the wider international commitments highlight the importance of green bonds as a financial and public policy tool to address climatic priorities. This increased support is reflected in the sharp increase of the value issued in green bonds recently to US $259 billion in 2019 (Figure 28.1). The growth continued throughout the global pandemic's starting year, leading to a cumulative exposure of US $1,000 trillion since the first green bond issuance in 2007 by early December 2020 (Climate Bonds Initiative, 2022). At present, an ending of the current trend is not foreseeable.

Determinants of Issuing Corporate Green Bonds

In this section, we review the literature that evaluates what factors may influence companies to issue green bonds. We synthesize the academic literature on green bonds with respect to this theme by surveying articles in business, management, economics, finance, sociology, and public policy. Our two main sources for searching for articles are Scopus (for articles published in international peer-reviewed journals) and SSRN (for working papers). In the first phase of the search, we used the following Boolean logic, applied to the abstract, title, and author keywords:

("issuance" OR "issuing" OR "driver" OR "issue" OR "decision" OR "drivers" OR "determinants") AND ("green bond" OR "green bonds")

This resulted in a dataset of 308 articles from Scopus and 184 papers from SSRN. In the second phase of the search, we read the abstracts of these articles and working papers to see to what extent they would fit into a review of the literature on the determinants of green corporate bond issuance. The final dataset consists of 25 articles and papers.

Most of the literature on the determinants of issuing green bonds is of recent date, that is, most publications we use in this review have been published after 2019. Slightly less than half of them (12) have been published as a working paper. The other 13 papers have been published in peer-reviewed journals such as the *Journal of Financial Economics*, *Journal of Business Ethics*, *Business, Society & the Environment*, *Finance Research Letters*, and *Sustainability*.

The literature discusses various reasons explaining why companies decide to issue green bonds. Several papers argue, and show empirical evidence, that issuing green bonds increases access to and reduces the cost of capital (Hadaś-Dyduch et al., 2022; Lin & Su, 2022). Glavas (2022) shows that companies that issue green bonds have significantly higher financial constraints, suggesting that access to finance may be an incentive for companies to engage in the green bond market. Dutordoir et al. (2022) also find some evidence that financial constraints drive green bond issuance.

Investors may find green bonds attractive because they add to improving the "greenness" of their portfolio. Their interest to include green financial instruments in their portfolios can be explained as follows. First, their stakeholders, and in particular their beneficiaries, put pressure on them to include green investments in their portfolios to contribute to reducing climate change. Second, investors are increasingly urged to disclose their strategy with respect to climate change risks and the integration of environmental and social criteria into their investment decisions by their stakeholders. Third, by investing in green financial instruments such as green bonds, investors can reduce the risk of non-green investments because of climate change and other environmental impacts (Weber & Saravade, 2019). The resulting increase in demand for green bonds provides an additional source of finance for companies issuing them and reduces the premium companies must pay when issuing these bonds vis-à-vis the premium for regular (non-green) bonds.

In line with the above arguments, several papers argue that by issuing green bonds companies can signal their commitment to climate-friendly policies, making them attractive for investors who aim at contributing to reducing climate change risks (Kuchin et al., 2019; Daubanes et al., 2021; Flammer, 2021; Sisodia et al., 2022). These papers analyze the signaling effect by looking at how the stock market responds to the issuance of green bonds. Some papers show that the yield for green bonds is lower than that of conventional bonds, suggesting that investors are willing to forego profits for environmentally-friendly projects (Glavas, 2020; Löffler et al., 2021; Zhang et al., 2021; Zhou et al., 2022; Benincasa et al., 2022). The difference in yields between conventional and green bonds is sometimes termed a "greenium". Glavas (2020) shows that the positive market response to the issuance of green bonds increases after the Paris Agreement. He explains this outcome by pointing out that investors apparently expected climate-related regulations following this agreement. For this reason, they find green bonds more attractive as investment targets. Some papers argue that the lower cost of capital only materializes after the repeat issuance of green bonds (Petreski et al., 2022). Zhou et al. (2022) show that the greenium is more pronounced for corporate green bonds with third-party certification. Such a certification informs the market about the green status of a company.

Other papers, however, do not find evidence for the existence of such a greenium. Wang and Li (2020) and Wang et al. (2022) show that investors do not seem to be willing to trade profits in non-green projects for investments in environmentally sustainable projects. Zheng (2021) shows that green bonds differ from regular bonds only when issued by companies in countries that have adopted climate policy by enforcing companies to internalize the cost of emissions through a carbon tax or through introducing an Emissions Trading System (ETS). This latter result is corroborated by Wang et al. (2022), who find that companies that are subject to the ETS are more likely to issue ESG bonds.

These contrasting results may be explained by the fact that different studies focus on different types of green bond issuers and bond issuances in different country contexts. For example, Wang et al. (2022) use a sample of Korean companies; Flammer (2021) has data on corporate green bonds from over 25 countries; and Zheng (2021) uses a sample of corporate green bonds issued in 55 markets around the world. Different types of bond issuers in different country contexts may have different reasons to use green bonds and investors may accordingly respond differently to their use of these bonds. In any case, these mixed findings do question to what extent companies can effectively signal their commitment to climate-friendly policies by issuing green bonds.

A few papers investigate why companies issue green bonds by focusing on the role of specific company characteristics (Bancel & Glavas, 2020). In particular, these papers suggest that the size of companies matters (Bedendo et al., 2022; Wang et al., 2022). They show that larger companies tend to have a higher probability of issuing green bonds. A related finding by Löffler et al. (2021) reveals that green bonds have larger issue sizes as compared to conventional bonds. The argument for these findings may be that issuing green bonds is demanding, as the process of obtaining certification requires funding and expertise. This makes it less likely that smaller companies opt for this type of financing. This corroborates research showing that larger companies tend to be more willing to invest in environmental and social projects as their ESG performance is usually better as compared to smaller companies (Drempetic et al., 2020).

Dutordoir et al. (2022) focus on a few other company-specific characteristics. In their study, they show that companies with lower costs of disclosure, higher reputational gains when investing in green projects, and a stronger focus on innovation have a higher probability of issuing green bonds. These results suggest that companies trade off the costs and benefits of their efforts to commit to environmental efforts when deciding on issuing green bonds. The importance of reputational benefits is also mentioned by Hadaś-Dyduch et al. (2022).

Some papers emphasize the importance of different corporate governance mechanisms, such as ownership structure and board structure composition. Bancel and Glavas (2017) show that state ownership is a primary determinant of green bond issuance and that the role of state ownership in determining the use of green bonds in contexts where institutional frameworks are weak. Their results indicate that the state may be an important stakeholder emphasizing the role companies should play in making contributions to improving the environment, that is, it shows the state as taking up its role as guardian of societal interests. Others emphasize the presence of foreign shareholders (Wang et al., 2022). These foreign shareholders, such as large institutional investors, may have a stronger preference for holding green stocks, leading to a stronger pressure to finance green projects, which among other things, may be achieved by issuing green bonds. Wang and Li (2020) show a related, but different finding. In their study, they find that after a company has issued green bonds, the share of institutional investors increases. Wang and Li (2020) show evidence for reverse causality, that is, their outcomes may indicate that issuing green bonds may make companies more attractive to investors who aim at improving their ESG score.

Wang et al. (2022) find that companies that have established a board committee that focuses on ESG have a higher probability of issuing ESG bonds, including green bonds. Establishing such a committee signals the commitment of a company to sustainability, increasing the willingness to issue green bonds. Cicchiello et al. (2022) show that the independence of boards and board gender diversity are positively related to green bond issuance.

Some papers focus on the environmental and social performance of companies by zooming in on ESG ratings (Dan & Tiron-Tudor, 2021). Higher ESG ratings may signal the company's commitment to contributing to sustainability and reducing climate change. This commitment may show itself by a higher probability of issuing green bonds from companies with higher ESG ratings. This is indeed confirmed in studies by Zheng (2021). Cheng et al. (2022) focus on ESG disclosures, rather than ESG performance, and find similar results. In a related finding, Bedendo et al. (2022) show that commercial banks that have publicly expressed their aim to focus more on contributing to a green transition have a higher probability to issue green bonds.

Corporate Green Bonds and Outcomes

The risk characteristics of a green bond are essentially identical to those of a conventional bond issued by the same company. It is important to note that while the proceeds from the issuance of a green bond are earmarked for environment-linked assets, green bonds are serviced from the cash flows of the entire operations of the issuer – not just the green project. These characteristics are important to evaluate the financial attractiveness of green bonds to issuers and investors. This section focuses on the financial and environmental outcomes for companies that issue green bonds.

Company Outcomes

The primary question on financial outcomes is whether investors are willing to pay a higher price for green-label bonds. If a significant fraction of investors is willing to pay a premium for green bonds, it would be reflected in the issuance price of these bonds. Such demand-and-supply issues can affect bond yield spreads (Collin-Dufrense & Goldstein, 2001; Greenwood & Vayanos, 2014). Investor preference for socially-responsible practices can reduce the cost of debt and lower bond yields (Hasan et al., 2017; Ghouma et al., 2018). Relatively less evidence exists in the specific context of green bonds. As most issuers of green bonds also regularly issue conventional bonds, it is possible to measure the bond yields after accounting for issuer-specific idiosyncratic factors like credit risk.

As was already discussed in the third section, there seems to be no consensus on whether investor preference for green bonds reflects a green premium for these bonds. For example, Ehlers and Packers (2017) and Hachenberg and Schiereck (2018) find a negative premium for green bonds in the primary and secondary markets. Zerbib (2019) finds a negative premium of 2 basis points for green bonds nominated in both euro and USD. In contrast, Karpf and Mandel (2018) control for the bond's liquidity and find a positive premium of 7.8 basis points for green bonds.

Despite the ambiguity about the premium for green bonds, many of the largest institutional investors, asset managers, or owners aim to transform their portfolios towards net-zero emissions by 2050 (UNEPFI, 2022). This raises the demand for securities bound to green purposes. From this perspective, we should expect investors to react positively to the issuance of corporate green bonds. Wang et al. (2020) document positive announcement returns following new issuances of green bonds in China, which they attribute to investors' perception that the environmental engagement of a company will increase its long-term value. Their study thus provides evidence that financial markets seem to associate green bond issuance with the long-term value of an issuer. They suggest issuing companies benefit from higher stock liquidity and higher stock prices around the issuance announcement.

How markets conceive green bond issuances and their underlying projects to be financed mostly depends on the question if the future actions of the issuing company will create or destroy value. If value-enhancing measures are taken, it is reasonable to assume that the financial markets reward the green bond issuance, and stock prices may rise. Likewise, suppose the new business actions reduce risk. In that case, it is reasonable to assume that next to increasing prices, liquidity in these stocks could improve, for instance, by the increased investor base or because of an increase in public attention, as suggested by Tang and Zhang (2020).

In contrast, Lebelle et al. (2020) find evidence for a negative market perception. They show that announcement returns of corporate green bond issuances are negative. They suggest that this may be due to the underlying risks that could arise following changes in the business model. These considerations seem to indicate that value in relation to risks deteriorates.

It is important to answer whether green activities will create long-term value in the discussion about the feasibility of issuing green bonds and the market's reaction. One way to evaluate the financial impact of green bonds is to focus on performance over time because investors may not always hold the bonds until maturity. Therefore, it is important to focus on both the primary and secondary market premia. The green bond indices are a good starting point to examine secondary market premia. Green bond indices contain a diversified portfolio of bonds and provide a good comparison with the performance of other bond indices. Ehlers and Packers (2017) show that the performance of hedged green bond indices is similar to that of global bond indices of comparable credit rating composition.

Environmental Outcomes

Whether corporate green bonds affect the overall environmental impact of their operations depends on the use of proceeds, i.e., what does the company do with the money raised? Currently, no regulations or disclosure norms allow investors to ex-post track the use of proceeds from green bonds. This has led to concern about green bonds being (yet) another avenue of corporate greenwashing.

Greenwashing occurs when entities issue green bonds to improve their reputation or benefit from green bonds by pretending to investors that they are working on projects that help improve the environment, while these bonds are, in fact, not green. Clear standards, certification, and close monitoring are key to the success of green bonds, enabling these bonds to have a true impact on the environment and become an important tool to counter climate change. The green bonds standards, defined by the CBI (Climate Bonds Initiative, 2019) or the ICMA Green Bond Principles (ICMA, 2022), combined with voluntary certification and monitoring, have been established to provide transparency about the funds being adequately used for their green purpose, as defined in the relevant green bond standards. Third parties have started to issue certifications to organizations when their use of proceeds from green bonds qualifies certain requirements. For example, the green bond principle (GBP), the Climate Bond Initiative (CBI), Green Bond Indices, CICERO, and Moody's Green Bond Assessments (Ehlers and Packer, 2017) have all been providing assurance statements for green bonds. However, there is not one general, mandatory certification yet. Certification could help to increase the linkage between green bond proceeds and a company's climate targets and thus close the gap that may arise when issuers face little pressure from stakeholders (Tuhkanen & Vulturius, 2020). Fatica et al. (2021) highlight the importance of external reviews in this regard.

Fatica et al. (2021) compare green bond issuers with conventional bond issuers with similar financial characteristics and environmental ratings. They find that the carbon intensity of a company's assets decreases after issuing green bonds. This decrease is stronger and has a longer-term effect on green bonds that lead to new projects rather than green bonds used for refinancing. Flammer (2021), in her study, finds comparable results. She concludes that, although green bonds as a financing source are still relatively small compared to conventional bonds, her empirical results indicate that green bonds may truly impact the strategies of a company related to environmental issues.

Given the lack of uniform reporting and uniform certification standards, direct causal analysis of the impact of green bonds on environmental outcomes is complicated. The most likely way to evaluate the environmental performance of green bond issuers is to observe whether a company's environmental performance is changing, for instance, in third-party ratings. In many jurisdictions, it is possible to track companies' carbon emissions, waste disposal, and renewable resource management practices. These factors provide circumstantial evidence of whether green bond issuers have materially different environmental impacts. In practice, however, as the underlying projects are often running over the years or even decades in operation, evaluating the impact of green bonds on the environment might face limitations since environmental assessment is a new topic and time-series data is rare. The main concern here is that companies already engaged in sustainable projects may find it easier to issue green bonds since it is not difficult for them to implement these bonds in their strategy. It complicates a causal analysis, but the reinforcing relationship between green bonds and environmental sustainability practices mitigates concerns about greenwashing.

To summarize, it is important to attribute the true marginal contribution of financing projects with green bonds to the environment. The mere assessment of post-issuance improvements on environmental measures of a company might be insufficient and could lead to wrong judgments regarding causality. For example, it can be questioned to what extent the environmental projects for which green bonds are issued would have been financed anyway, using other financing instruments such as conventional bonds, debt, or equity. Concerning this, it is important to assess what implication the potential alternative ways of financing have on the feasibility of the (green) projects when potential benefits of green bonds related to, e.g., financing costs, policy implications, and the availability of financing are absent. Besides that, the costs for companies to issue green bonds also need to be incorporated. Green bond certification, issuance, and monitoring processes may require the company to invest in developing knowledge about these processes.

An underexplored area in the academic literature on green bonds is how these debt instruments affect corporate sustainability initiatives. It is crucial to understand the mechanisms because it sheds light on whether these debt instruments are effective in financing the transition to a low-carbon economy. For example, Flammer (2021) notes that:

> the green bonds themselves are likely too small to bring about significant improvements at the firm level (among public firms, the average green bond issue is $0.26B compared to the average issuer's asset size of $33.5B). Instead, and consistent with the signalling argument, a natural interpretation is that green bonds signal a credible commitment towards the environment. As this commitment materializes in eco-friendly behaviour, companies improve their environmental performance. Some of these improvements – but not necessarily all of them – maybe due to the projects that are financed by the green bond proceeds.

One plausible conjecture about the mechanism through which green bond issuance results in better environmental outcomes may include adopting emission targets. This is because, as green bond issuers attract further scrutiny due to their green label, these companies may be incentivized to engage in activities that will result in tangible and measurable environmental outcomes, such as lower emissions. The signaling motive can also motivate green bond issuers to incur the cost of third-party verification of their carbon emissions. Further, it is plausible that the financial and environmental effects of green bond issuance reflect broader organizational processes and environmental strategies (Walls et al., 2012). For example, companies that consider environmental issues salient will likely have corporate governance systems that facilitate environmental strategies. Board oversight and managerial incentives are two broad channels through which the corporate governance system can impact strategic choices. Green bond issuers may also be more likely to integrate climate change issues into their business strategies (Eccles et al., 2014).

Whilst it is central to understanding the real impacts of green bonds, empirical evidence on the pathways through which proceeds from green bond issuance affect corporate environmental performance is scant. This lack of evidence is primarily due to a lack of transparent and comparable reporting standards for green bond issuers to report the use of proceeds information. The post-issuance disclosure information is often not publicly available in many jurisdictions. Some data vendors, such as the CBI, are increasingly focusing on this aspect (see the Climate Bonds Standard v3.0; Climate Bonds Initiative, 2019), and the data quality is likely to improve in the future.

Discussion and Suggestions for Further Research

Addressing climate change by transitioning to a low-carbon value creation process will take an investment of unprecedented scale. Raising the amount of money available for this transition will, among other things, also take innovations in financing, particularly for companies that must simultaneously optimize profits and their environmental impacts. In this chapter, we provided a review of the antecedents and consequences of one such modern financing tool used by companies to raise money for green technology, that is, green bonds. We focused on discussing the determinants that may explain why companies may want to issue green bonds. Moreover, we discussed whether and how green bond issuance can affect corporate financial and environmental performance. Research on these topics is still in its infancy as green bonds are relatively new financial innovations and, as a consequence, data availability is still fairly limited. As more data become available, future research could provide larger-scale evidence of the reasons why companies may use them as an instrument to finance their environmental efforts, as well as of the long-term implications of corporate green bonds.

In terms of the determinants of green bond issuance by companies, there are various directions future research could explore. In general terms, it would be important to zoom in more systematically on company and country-level differences. In particular, research could focus on the importance of governance mechanisms, such as the role of boards and their individual members in stimulating the issuance of green bonds.

For example, Homroy and Slechten (2019) have looked at the presence of non-executive directors with previous experience in environmental issues and the impact on a firm's ethical and environmental behavior. Chen et al. (2022) find evidence that companies that have appointed directors with executive experience in NGO-type of organizations perform better with respect to ESG. Future research may focus on analyzing whether companies that have appointed directors with a background in environmental issues and/or executive experience in environmental NGOs are also more likely to issue green bonds and whether and to what extent their presence has an impact on the so-called greenium.

Research may also look into the role of executive remuneration and the use of environmental criteria to determine the level of executive pay. Over the last few years, the use of such criteria in executive pay contracts has increased (Cohen et al., 2022). It would therefore be interesting to evaluate to what extent the use of such environmental criteria is also conducive to stimulating the issue of green bonds.

Another area of future research would be to focus on the different ESG profiles of companies and investigate what types of profiles are associated with a higher probability of green bond issuance. For example, do green bonds complement or substitute environmental performance? Is there a difference for the type of environmental performance? Does it substitute or complement social performance? Does governance performance play a role?

Future research could also go deeper into the question of what country-specific features may affect the likelihood of companies issuing green bonds. More specifically, research may focus on differences in environmental policies, macroeconomic conditions, legal institutions, innovation, and cultural traditions and their role in determining the issuance of corporate green bonds. For example, regarding the role of culture, one could focus on how specific cultural settings may have an impact on the extent to which society is committed to taking up environmental challenges. This may also influence the extent to which green bonds may be seen as a potential funding source for companies.

Finally, an important first-order question pertains to the growth and governance of the green bond market. Although this market has been growing rapidly over the past few years, its size is still small in terms of the challenges of climate change it may want to address, as well as compared to the size of traditional bond markets. According to Deschryver and de Mariz (2020), important barriers to its growth are lacking harmonization of global standards, the risk of greenwashing, the (perceived) high costs of issuing green bonds, the low supply of green corporate bonds, and the lack of a well-functioning green bond market infrastructure. These outcomes are at least partly corroborated in a study by Sangiorgi and Schopohl (2021).

To a large extent, the difficulty in drawing conclusive evidence on the role of green bonds in climate financing can be traced back to the current absence of credible systems that govern the issuance and use of the proceeds of green bonds. Companies seek to add credibility to their green bond issuances through third-party certifications. Yet, in the absence of a uniform definition of what constitutes green assets, such certifications are hard to interpret and compare for financial market participants. Future developments in the green bond, such as those proposed by the European Commission's Green Taxonomy, could alleviate some of the issues related to homogeneous disclosure on the use of proceeds from corporate green bonds. We would like to highlight these aspects as exciting avenues for future research.

As a final note, we would like to add that a successful transition to a low-carbon emitting economy also requires actions from governments, next to efforts from businesses. Obviously, the business sector alone will not be able to perform this transition successfully. Companies will need to be incentivized to trigger change. Governments should make way by providing the right policy frameworks, supporting standardization, and providing opportunities for private and public environmental projects to be realized (Magale, 2021). Appropriate measures, such as incentives in the form of governmental support, tax reliefs, or subsidies for environmental activities may help to support the development of green projects and thus allow financing through the green bond market. Restrictive policies, such as those already partly introduced by institutional investors in the form of exclusion lists for non-green business operations, could be another possibility to stimulate change in the economy. Moreover, appropriate international support to countries that are currently lagging behind the green transition can help to reach a balanced worldwide development. In the end, a successful transition to a low-carbon emitting world economy will be based on joint efforts of governments and the business sectors.

Notes

1 More information on the Paris Agreement can be found at: https://unfccc.int/process-and-meetings/the-paris-agreement/the-paris-agreement.
2 A full description of the CBI methodology is available on their website: www.climatebonds.net/cbi/pub/data/bonds.

References

Bancel, F., & Glavas, D. (2017). The role of state ownership as a determinant of green bond issuance. SSRN Electronic Journal. https://www.ssrn.com/abstract_id=3746644

Bancel, F., & Glavas, D. (2020). Why do firms issue green bonds? *Bankers, Markets and Investors*, *160*(1), 51–56. https://www.journaleska.com/index.php/bmi/article/view/11

Bedendo, M., Nocera, G., & Siming, L. (2022). Greening the financial sector: Evidence from bank green bonds. *Journal of Business Ethics*, 1–21. https://doi.org/10.1007/s10551-022-05305-9

Benincasa, E., Fu, J., Mishra, M., & Paranjape, A. (2022). Different shades of green: Estimating the green bond premium using natural language processing. Swiss Finance Institute Research Paper, 22–64. SSRN Electronic Journal. https://www.ssrn.com/abstract_id=4198065

Chen, S., Hermes, N., & Hooghiemstra, R. (2022). Corporate social responsibility and NGO directors on boards. *Journal of Business Ethics*, *175*(3), 625–649. https://doi.org/10.1007/s10551-020-04649-4

Cheng, L. T., Sharma, P., & Broadstock, D. C. (2022). Interactive effects of brand reputation and ESG on green bond issues: A sustainable development perspective. *Business Strategy and the Environment*, 1–17. https://doi.org/10.1002/bse.3161

Cicchiello, A. F., Cotugno, M., Monferrà, S., & Perdichizzi, S. (2022). Which are the factors influencing green bonds issuance? Evidence from the European bonds market. *Finance Research Letters*, *50*, 103190. https://doi.org/10.1016/j.frl.2022.103190

Climate Bonds Initiative. (2019). Climate bonds standard version 3.0. https://www.climatebonds.net/files/files/climate-bonds-standard-v3-20191210.pdf

Climate Bonds Initiative. (2022). Explaining green bonds. https://www.climatebonds.net/market/explaining-green-bonds

Cohen, S., Kadach, I., Ormazabal, G., & Reichelstein, S. (2022). Executive compensation tied to ESG performance: International evidence. European Corporate Governance Institute–Finance Working Paper, 825. SSRN Electronic Journal. https://papers.ssrn.com/sol3/papers.cfm?abstract_id=4097202

Collin-Dufresne, P., & Goldstein, R. S. (2001). Do credit spreads reflect stationary leverage ratios? *Journal of Finance*, *56*(5), 1929–1957. https://doi.org/10.1111/0022-1082.00395

Dan, A., & Tiron-Tudor, A. (2021). The determinants of green bond issuance in the European Union. *Journal of Risk and Financial Management*, *14*(9), 446. https://doi.org/10.3390/jrfm14090446

Daubanes, J. X., Mitali, S. F., & Rochet, J. C. (2021). Why do firms issue green bonds? Swiss Finance Institute Research Paper, 21–97. http://doi.org/10.2139/ssrn.3996238

Deschryver, P., & De Mariz, F. (2020). What future for the green bond market? How can policymakers, companies, and investors unlock the potential of the green bond market? *Journal of Risk and Financial Management*, *13*(3), 61. https://doi.org/10.3390/jrfm13030061

Drempetic, S., Klein, C., & Zwergel, B. (2020). The influence of firm size on the ESG score: Corporate sustainability ratings under review. *Journal of Business Ethics*, *167*(2), 333–360. https://doi.org/10.1007/s10551-019-04164-1

Dutordoir, M., Li, S., & Quariguasi Frota Neto, J. (2022). Determinants of firms' choice between green and conventional bonds: Why is the corporate green bond market still so 'green'? SSRN Electronic Journal. https://www.ssrn.com/abstract_id=4156431

Eccles, R. G., Ioannou, I., & Serafeim, G. (2014). The impact of corporate sustainability on organizational processes and performance. *Management Science*, *60*(11), 2835–2857. https://doi.org/10.1287/mnsc.2014.1984

Ehlers, T., & Packer, F. (2017). Green bond finance and certification. SSRN Electronic Journal. https://www.ssrn.com/abstract=3042378

European Bank for Reconstruction and Development. (2019). EBRD's first green transition bond. https://www.ebrd.com/news/2019/ebrds-first-green-transition-bond.html

European Investment Bank. (2020). Sustainability awareness bonds. https://www.eib.org/en/investor-relations/sab/index.htm

European Investment Bank. (2022a). Climate awareness bonds - The World's first green bond. https://www.eib.org/en/investor-relations/cab/index.htm

European Investment Bank. (2022b). Sustainability awareness bonds - Spanning the full spectrum of sustainability. https://www.eib.org/en/investor-relations/sab/index.htm

European Union. (2022a). European green bond standard. https://ec.europa.eu/info/business-economy-euro/banking-and-finance/sustainable-finance/european-green-bond-standard_en

European Union. (2022b). EU taxonomy for sustainable activities. https://ec.europa.eu/info/business-economy-euro/banking-and-finance/sustainable-finance/eu-taxonomy-sustainable-activities_en

Fatica, S., Panzica, R., & Rancan, M. (2021). The pricing of green bonds: Are financial institutions special? *Journal of Financial Stability*, *54*, 100873. https://doi.org/10.1016/j.jfs.2021.100873

Flammer, C. (2021). Corporate green bonds. *Journal of Financial Economics*, *142*(2), 499–516. https://doi.org/10.1016/j.jfineco.2021.01.010

Ghouma, H., Ben-Nasr, H., & Yan, R. (2018). Corporate governance and cost of debt financing: Empirical evidence from Canada. *Quarterly Review of Economics and Finance*, *67*, 138–148. https://doi.org/10.1016/j.qref.2017.06.004

Glavas, D. (2020). Green regulation and stock price reaction to green bond issuance. *Finance*, *41*(1), 7–51. https://doi.org/10.3917/fina.411.0007

Glavas, D. (2022). Do green bond issuers suffer from financial constraints? *Applied Economics Letters*, 1–4. https://doi.org/10.1080/13504851.2022.2083559

Greenwood, R., & Vayanos, D. (2014). Bond supply and excess bond returns. *Review of Financial Studies*, *27*(3), 663–713. https://doi.org/10.1093/rfs/hht133

Hachenberg, B., & Schiereck, D. (2018). Are green bonds priced differently from conventional bonds? *Journal of Asset Management*, *19*(6), 371–383. https://doi.org/10.1057/s41260-018-0088-5

Hadaś-Dyduch, M., Puszer, B., Czech, M., & Cichy, J. (2022). Green bonds as an instrument for financing ecological investments in the V4 countries. *Sustainability*, *14*(19), 12188. https://doi.org/10.3390/su141912188

Hasan, I., Hoi, C. K., Wu, Q., & Zhang, H. (2017). Social capital and debt contracting: Evidence from bank loans and public bonds. *Journal of Financial and Quantitative Analysis*, *52*(3), 1017–1047. https://doi.org/10.1017/S0022109017000205

Homroy, S., & Slechten, A. (2019). Do board expertise and networked boards affect environmental performance? *Journal of Business Ethics*, *158*(1), 269–292. https://doi.org/10.1007/s10551-017-3769-y

ICMA. (2022). Green bond principles. https://www.icmagroup.org/assets/documents/Sustainable-finance/2021-updates/Green-Bond-Principles-June-2021-140621.pdf

ING. (2021). EU: Easing the green bond shortage. https://think.ing.com/articles/eu-easing-the-green-bond-shortage

IFC. (2016). Forests bond. https://www.ifc.org/wps/wcm/connect/982eb7ef-1daa-49ca-b9c0-e6f3a2d-dcd88/FINAL+Forests+Bond+Factsheet+10-5.pdf?MOD=AJPERES&CVID=nvKDy7K

Karpf, A., & Mandel, A. (2018). The changing value of the 'green' label on the US municipal bond market. *Nature Climate Change*, *8*(2), 161–165. https://doi.org/10.1038/s41558-017-0062-0

Kuchin, I., Baranovsky, G., Dranev, Y., & Chulok, A. (2019). Does green bonds placement create value for firms? Higher School of Economics Research Paper No. WP BRP, 101. SSRN Electronic Journal. https://www.ssrn.com/abstract_id=3477918

Lebelle, M., Lajili Jarjir, S., & Sassi, S. (2020). Corporate green bond issuances: An international evidence. *Journal of Risk and Financial Management*, *13*(2), 25. https://doi.org/10.3390/jrfm13020025

Lin, B., & Su, T. (2022). Green bond vs conventional bond: Outline the rationale behind issuance choices in China. *International Review of Financial Analysis*, *81*, 102063. https://doi.org/10.1016/j.irfa.2022.102063

Löffler, K. U., Petreski, A., & Stephan, A. (2021). Drivers of green bond issuance and new evidence on the "greenium". *Eurasian Economic Review*, *11*(1), 1–24. https://doi.org/10.1007/s40822-020-00165-y

Magale, E. G. (2021). Developing a green bond market in Kenya: Perspectives from practitioners and lessons from developing markets. *Journal of Sustainable Finance and Investment*, 1–18. https://doi.org/10.1080/20430795.2021.1953930

Petreski, A., Schäfer, D., & Stephan, A. (2022). Green bonds' reputation effect and its impact on the financing costs of the real estate sector. SSRN Electronic Journal. https://www.ssrn.com/abstract_id=4248052

S&P Global. (2021). New EU ESG disclosure rules to recast sustainable investment landscape. https://www.spglobal.com/esg/insights/new-eu-esg-disclosure-rules-to-recast-sustainable-investment-landscape

Sangiorgi, I., & Schopohl, L. (2021). Explaining green bond issuance using survey evidence: Beyond the greenium. *British Accounting Review*, 101071. https://doi.org/10.1016/j.bar.2021.101071

Schumacher, K. (2020). Green bonds: The shape of green fixed-income investing to come. *Journal of Environmental Investing*, *10*(1). https://ora.ox.ac.uk/objects/uuid:d6120955-f7d5-4917-b89c-35a1c41681be

Sisodia, G., Joseph, A., & Dominic, J. (2022). Whether corporate green bonds act as armour during crises? Evidence from a natural experiment. *International Journal of Managerial Finance*, 18(4), 701–724. https://doi.org/10.1108/IJMF-10-2021-0501

Tang, D. Y., & Zhang, Y. (2020). Do shareholders benefit from green bonds? *Journal of Corporate Finance*, *61*, 101427. https://doi.org/10.1016/j.jcorpfin.2018.12.001

Tuhkanen, H., & Vulturius, G. (2020). Are green bonds funding the transition? Investigating the link between companies' climate targets and green debt financing. *Journal of Sustainable Finance and Investment*, *12*(4), 1194–1216. https://doi.org/10.1080/20430795.2020.1857634

UNEPFI. (2022). Net zero alliance. https://www.unepfi.org/net-zero-alliance

UNFCCC. (2022). COP 26 outcomes. https://unfccc.int/process-and-meetings/the-paris-agreement/the-glasgow-climate-pact-key-outcomes-from-cop26

Walls, J. L., Berrone, P., & Pan, P. H. (2012). Corporate governance and environmental performance: Is there really a link? *Strategic Management Journal*, *33*(8), 885–913. https://doi.org/10.1002/smj.1952

Wang, B., Lee, J., & Park, H. (2022). Determinants and value implications of corporate ESG bond issuance in Korea. SSRN Electronic Journal. https://www.ssrn.com/abstract_id=4109666

Wang, D., & Li, P. (2020). The benefits of issuing green bonds: Evidence from China green bonds market. SSRN Electronic Journal. https://www.ssrn.com/abstract_id=3710646

Wang, J., Chen, X., Li, X., Yu, J., & Zhong, R. (2020). The market reaction to green bond issuance: Evidence from China. *Pacific-Basin Finance Journal*, *60*, 101294. https://doi.org/10.1016/j.pacfin.2020.101294

Weber, O., & Saravade, V. (2019). Green bonds: Current development and their future. [CIGI Papers], 210. https://www.cigionline.org/publications/green-bonds-current-development-and-their-future

World Bank. (2014). World Bank issues its first ever catastrophe bond linked to natural hazard risks in sixteen Caribbean countries. https://www.worldbank.org/en/news/press-release/2014/06/30/world-bank-issues-its-first-ever-catastrophe-bond-linked-to-natural-hazard-risks-in-sixteen-caribbean-countries

World Bank. (2017). World Bank launches financial instrument to expand funding for sustainable development goals. https://www.worldbank.org/en/news/press-release/2017/03/09/world-bank-launches-financial-instrument-to-expand-funding-for-sustainable-development-goals

Zerbib, O. D. (2019). The effect of pro-environmental preferences on bond prices: Evidence from green bonds. *Journal of Banking and Finance*, *98*, 39–60. https://doi.org/10.1016/j.jbankfin.2018.10.012

Zhang, R., Li, Y., & Liu, Y. (2021). Green bond issuance and corporate cost of capital. *Pacific-Basin Finance Journal*, *69*, 101626. https://doi.org/10.1016/j.pacfin.2021.101626

Zheng, H. (2021). Climate policy and corporate green bonds. https://www.igef.cuhk.edu.hk/igef_media/working-paper/IGEF/IGEF%20Working%20Paper%20No.%2088%20English%20version.pdf

Zhou, G., Li, H., & Luo, S. (2022). Is there a green premium for green bond issuance? Evidence from China. SSRN Electronic Journal. https://www.ssrn.com/abstract_id=3477918

29
BUILDING NORMATIVITY IN SUSTAINABILITY REPORTING

From National to European Union-Level Regulations

Blerita Korca and Ericka Costa

Introduction

Sustainability reporting (SR) represents a way to communicate and be accountable to a broader set of stakeholders, rather than only shareholders, on a range of social and environmental aspects. The extended accountability to a broader group of stakeholders started as an organisation-initiated practice via voluntary SR and later became mandated by law in different jurisdictions worldwide. Currently, mandatory disclosure measures are increasing globally (Carrots & Sticks, 2020; IPSF, 2021). While new measures are developed or developing in different jurisdictions, the European Union (EU) is considered a leader in SR measures. However, the EU agenda towards SR is set at both the EU and the member-state levels. The shifting process from national-level to EU-level regulations has so far characterised SR development in the EU. It started with the Swedish Environmental Code (1998), followed by the Nouvelles Régulations Économiques (NRE) law (no. 2001-420, Article 116) in France (2001), Law 118/2005 in Italy, the Non-Financial Reporting Directive (NFRD) at the EU level (2014) and the proposal for the Corporate Sustainability Reporting Directive (CSRD; April 2021). The latter was announced via the European Commission's (EC's) publication of the European Green Deal (2019). Within this broad framework, the EU adopted a set of regulations to guide financial actors towards proper sustainability strategies. In particular, the Sustainable Finance Disclosure Regulation (SFDR) 2019/2088 requires financial operators to declare their products' positioning on sustainability – ranging from initiatives without sustainability considerations to initiatives with specific and intentional sustainability objectives (Cremasco & Boni, 2022; Schütze & Stede, 2021). The Green Deal and the subsequent regulatory framework on sustainable finance aim to make Europe more sustainable in terms of both environmental and societal impacts. In this regard, the CSRD's and the SFDR's objectives are to strengthen the landscape for more sustainable investments and to engage financial players in environmental and social reporting, in an effort to prevent greenwashing or impact washing phenomena (Torelli et al., 2020). To prevent these manipulative behaviours, the CSRD will require detailed disclosure from entities operating in the EU to enable investors' use disclosed information to make more informed investment decisions (EC, 2021).

The attempts to create SR norms in the EU proceeded from a national level to an EU-level path. While regulatory pressure is considered a significant step towards institutionalising SR, research evidence shows that compliance levels and substantial changes in SR do not always occur (Chauvey et al., 2015; Chelli et al., 2018; Korca et al., 2021). In light of new regulations, previous studies have investigated compliance levels and how reporting quantity or quality has increased or improved, respectively. Chauvey et al. (2015) find that compliance with environmental disclosure regulations in France is low due to the lack of normativity in the regulation itself. Focusing on three different settings (mandatory law in France, stock exchange regime in Canada and voluntary Global Reporting Initiative [GRI] reporting), Chelli et al. (2018) suggest that a combination of both binding requirements (e.g., law) and non-binding ones (e.g., GRI) could result in normativity production in SR.

In their analysis of SR quantity and quality, following the shift from voluntary to mandatory disclosure in the banking sector, Korca et al. (2021) find that the quantity of reporting generally increases after the NFRD, but the quality improves only for specific topics deemed important by the banking group. Therefore, these previous studies clearly point out that normativity production does not arise only from law enforcement *per se*. Rather, it increases as a mix of different mechanisms, such as voluntary reporting experience before the regulation, shared beliefs about what is important to report on within the entity and finally, the regulation mandating such disclosure. Therefore, while previous studies have investigated these different mechanisms separately (Chauvey et al., 2015; Chelli et al., 2018; Korca et al., 2021), it is important to understand their interconnections and how these factors and mechanisms could influence policymakers' decisions to implement and institutionalise norms. The transition from the definition of new binding requirements to its effective application in the entities' daily lives – with the intended purpose – is crucial in the EU sustainability agenda. As highlighted by Cremasco and Boni (2022), there is a need to explore the EU sustainability regulative frameworks in a better way to provide the EU policymakers with specific recommendations for a more effective sustainability agenda.

To fill these gaps in the literature, this chapter builds on previous research on normativity and considers the new regulatory and standard-setting developments in order to offer a thorough reflection on the potential production of normativity in reporting. This chapter argues that normativity production in SR is much more complex than just reporting mandated by binding laws. Accounting for SR dynamics helps uncover the factors that make norms legitimate enough to be internalised (Korca, 2021). In this chapter, the authors use their research experience in the field and take stock of the literature (Larrinaga & Senn, 2021) to formulate the four main messages for policymakers. Therefore, the specific policymaker representations coming from the lessons learned from previous SR experience in both voluntary and mandatory regimes are highlighted in four main directions, as follows: i) "norm" production is not the result of new regulations that come into force but is the outcome of a learning process that starts from voluntary experiences in SR; ii) for small and medium-sized enterprises (SMEs), the challenge to make visible their sustainability practices should consider their dimensions, skills, capabilities and need to learn new reporting mechanisms; iii) stakeholder engagement and the consultation process can enhance a more collaborative and dialogic form of accountability; and iv) in the interplay between normativity and standardisation, both technical and non-technical dimensions should be put into practice, focusing on the process instead of the outcome.

The remaining sections are organised as follows. The second section outlines the emergence of SR regulations in the EU, initially at the national level and subsequently at the EU level. The third section provides a literature review on the first-order and second-order consequences of mandated SR. The fourth section highlights the grand theory in mandatory SR, such as the legitimacy of norms. The fifth section explores the lessons learned from previous SR experiences in the EU and discusses directions for future regulations and norm development. Concluding remarks are presented in the sixth section.

Sustainability Reporting (SR) Regulations – From Country-Specific to European Union (EU) Level

Over the past decades, companies' reporting has changed to reflect other matters that are not necessarily of interest to shareholders. Companies worldwide started to include social and environmental information in their reporting, expanding their accountability to shareholders and the broader set of stakeholders (Gray et al., 1996). Therefore, companies' global attempts to account for social and environmental impacts have increased. The concept of conducting business sustainably is gaining predominance and has proliferated since the publication of the Brundtland Report in 1987 (Bebbington & Larrinaga, 2014). Specifically, in 1992, at the United Nations Conference on Environment and Development in Rio de Janeiro, the need for a sustainable way of conducting business was emphasised. According to the Brundtland report, "Sustainable development is the development that meets the needs of the present without compromising the ability of future generations to meet their own needs" (UNWCED, 1987, p. 43). Therefore, the Brundtland report emphasises humans' role and global impact on the environment. This report does not only highlight the issue but also calls for changes in practices and behaviours that lead to the destruction of resources (Bebbington & Larrinaga, 2014). In the context of sustainable development, businesses are perceived as crucial in responding to global challenges (Hamann, 2003). Companies are increasingly put under the microscope and held responsible for their actions. As a result of the significant attention to companies' actions in society and the environment, the need for sustainability communication has arisen. According to Godemann and Michelsen (2011, p. 6),

> the task of sustainability communication lies in introducing an understanding of the world, that is, of the relationship between humans and their environment, into social discourse, developing a critical awareness of the problems about this relationship and then relating them to social values and norms.

Sustainability communication and financial information reporting got off the ground around the late 1980s and the early 1990s. Therefore, companies started to extend their reporting practices to include information on social and environmental aspects (Milne & Gray, 2010).

SR has been voluntarily exercised for a long time before regulations were drawn to mandate disclosure on sustainability aspects. In previous research, voluntary SR has been criticised and characterised as lacking in quality, standardisation and objectivity (Hibbitt & Collison, 2004; Jeffrey & Perkins, 2013). To increase transparency and enhance information quality, mandatory disclosure measures are increasing globally (IPSF, 2021; Michelon, 2021). A broader set of stakeholders, including the investment community, demands governments' more active and substantive role in the SR field. While SR is currently performed under different regimes (both voluntary and mandatory), it is important to note that SR regulations are not exactly new. In Europe, the SR regulatory landscape has been developing, starting from the national level to the EU level at a later stage. As highlighted by Larrinaga and Senn (2021), many SR laws at the national level were put into force before the recent EU regulation. Table 29.1 presents national and then EU-level SR measures, showing the evolving process from national-level regulations to centralisation at the EU level.

Table 29.1 Sustainability reporting in Europe – from national to EU level regulations (adapted from Larrinaga & Senn, 2021)

Country	Name of the measure	Year	Scope	Disclosure requirements
Sweden	Swedish environmental code	1998	Environmentally sensitive industries	Disclosure of a sustainability report
	Swedish guidelines	2007	State-owned companies (partially or totally)	Disclosure based on the GRI guidelines
United Kingdom	Company Act 2006	2006	Entities exceeding 250 employees and whose turnover and balance sheet exceed a fixed amount	Environmental, social, and governance-related disclosure
	Climate Change Act 2008	2008	Entities exceeding 250 employees and whose turnover and balance sheet exceed a fixed amount	Environmental and social-related disclosure
Denmark	Danish Act (no.1403)	2008	Entities exceeding 250 employees and whose turnover and balance sheet exceed a fixed amount	Human rights disclosure and climate-related issues
Italy	Law 118/2005	2005	Social enterprises	Environmental and social-related disclosure
Spain	Sustainability Economy Law (no 2/2011, article 39)	2011	Entities exceeding 1,000 employees	Disclosure of a sustainability report
France	Law on Energy Transition for Green Growth (no 2015-992, article 225-105)	2015	Entities exceeding 500 employees and whose turnover and balance sheet exceed a fixed amount	Disclosure of financial risks linked to climate change and measures employed to mitigate those risks
	Grenelle 2 law (no 2010-788 article 225)	2010	Entities exceeding 500 employees and whose turnover and balance sheet exceed a fixed amount	Environmental and social-related disclosure

(Continued)

Table 29.1 (Continued)

Country	Name of the measure	Year	Scope	Disclosure requirements
	NRE law (no 2001-420, article 116)	2001	Entities exceeding 500 employees and whose turnover and balance sheet exceed a fixed amount	Environmental and social-related disclosure
Europe	Directive 2003/51/EU	2003	Companies and Groups	A company's development, performance and position could be viewed through the lens of environmental and social aspects. Some EU member states transposed this directive into national laws by requesting disclosure of sustainability aspects in the annual report
	Directive 2014/95/EU or the Non-Financial Reporting Directive (NFRD)	2014	Entities exceeding 500 employees and whose turnover and balance sheet exceed a fixed amount	Disclosure on mainly four aspects: environmental, social and employee, human rights, anti-corruption and bribery matters
	Regulation EU 2019/2088 or the Sustainable Finance Disclosure Regulation (SFDR)	2019	Financial institutions and market participants	Sustainability disclosure both at the entity and product level
	Corporate Sustainability Reporting Directive proposal	Approved in November 2022	All large entities and all listed entities (including SMEs)	Extending disclosure requirements from the NFRD to also include value chain disclosure, sustainability targets, and disclosure on intangibles

SR Regulations at the National Level

In 1998, the Swedish Environmental Code, which replaced the Swedish Environmental Protection Act, issued a regulation that required companies belonging to environmentally sensitive industries to disclose a sustainability report (Larrinaga & Senn, 2021). This was followed by the New Economic Regulations, initially known as the Nouvelles Régulations Économiques (NRE) in French law (2001). The NRE law targeted companies that had 500 employees and met an inevitable turnover and balance sheet threshold (Chelli et al., 2018). Although requiring disclosure of sustainability information, the NRE law does not foresee any penalty for non-compliance. Five years later, the Company Act 2006 was drawn up in the UK, requiring entities with a turnover of more than £36 m to report sustainability information as part of their annual reports (IPSF, 2021). In 2008, new regulations were developed in the UK, Denmark and Italy. The UK's Climate Change Act required listed companies to report information on their greenhouse gas emissions (IPSF, 2021). Denmark's Danish Act required companies with over 250 employees, a balance sheet and a certain turnover threshold to report on climate change and human rights aspects (Larrinaga & Senn, 2021). In Italy, the SR debate dates back to 2005, when Law 118/2005 and subsequently, the 2008 Implementation Decree, introduced compulsory social and environmental reporting (Costa, 2014), targeting only Italian "legal, social enterprises", which applied to the Italian Chamber of Commerce for legal accreditation. After 2010, various new regulations were developed, such as France's Grenelle 2 Law (2010) and Spain's Sustainable Economy Law 2/2011. The latter law mandated companies with over 10,000 employees to publish a sustainability report (Luque-Vílchez & Larrinaga, 2016). This law is considered the precedent of Directive 2014/95/EU (also known as the NFRD) in the EU.

SR Regulations at the EU Level

Since the early 2000s, the EU has actively engaged in drawing its agenda on higher transparency from companies regarding sustainability aspects. The EU published Directive 2003/51/EC, requesting non-financial disclosure from companies and groups. Article 9 of Directive 2003/51/EC highlighted that each company's development, performance and position should also be observed, considering social and environmental aspects (Costa & Agostini, 2016). In some EU countries, this directive was transposed by specifically requesting companies to report information covering social and environmental matters in their annual reports. Spain, France, Portugal, Finland, Sweden and Denmark employed more stringent requirements in the transposition process. However, the research considered Directive 2003/51/EC quite broad, criticising it for not requiring a separate sustainability report with detailed disclosure (Costa & Agostini, 2016).

In contrast to Directive 2003/51/EC, which received several different criticisms, the subsequent Directive 2014/95/EU (NFRD) brought some hope in enhancing corporate transparency. It came into force in 2018, when companies had to comply with it, following the financial year 2017 (EU, 2014). The NFRD required large and listed companies in the EU to publish information on sustainability matters to improve transparency and comparability of information. After a few years, the EC (2020) initiated a revision process for the NFRD by inviting different stakeholders to a public consultation. The revision process shed light on some drawbacks of the NFRD, such as its inability to create comparability and to enhance reporting quality. In light of this process, the EC tabled the CSRD proposal. Proposed in April 2021, the CSRD emerged as part of the EU Green Deal. In the EU Green Deal publication, the EC (2019) announced that the NFRD would be reviewed, with the objective to increase and enhance sustainability disclosure. Announced again in 2021, the CSRD proposal thus emerged from the Sustainable Finance package adopted by the EC in April 2021. This ambitious package contains different measures, aiming to improve the flow of capital towards more sustainable investments. Among the measures introduced, the CSRD will play a crucial role in enabling data availability for investors to make more informed decisions (EC, 2021). The CSRD is expected to introduce significant changes to the mandatory SR landscape in the EU, specifically the scope's expansion to all i) large companies and ii) listed companies operating in the EU (including SMEs). Additionally, the CSRD proposal introduced requirements such as supply chain disclosure, forward-looking and digitalisation of the information.

In contrast to the NFRD, which did not specify one reporting standard for companies to follow, the CSRD foresees the use of the European Sustainability Reporting Standards (ESRS), currently being developed by the European Financial Reporting Advisory Group (EFRAG). Notably, while the NFRD targeted roughly 11,000 companies, the CSRD's scope covers around 50,000 companies. Another EU initiative – the SFDR – targets financial institutions and market participants and requires disclosure of sustainability-related aspects. Since March 2021, the SFDR has required sustainability disclosure at the entity and the product levels of financial institutions and market participants. Therefore, while the NFRD was criticised for several reasons, the EC continues its path towards developing new regulations and overcoming existing regulations' limitations.

First-Order and Second-Order Impacts of EU Regulations

The emergence of different EU-level regulations has increased scholars' interest in gaining a better understanding of the regulations' first-order (e.g., SR) and second-order impacts (e.g., financial performance) (Ottenstein et al., 2021). First, regarding the regulations' impact on SR, a range of studies examined different elements, including the compliance level (Biondi et al., 2020; Matuszak & Różańska, 2017), the quantity or extent (Agostini et al., 2021; Korca et al., 2021) and the quality of information (Cosma et al., 2021; Mion & Adaui, 2019). Matuszak and Różańska (2017) investigated the SR of 150 companies listed on the Warsaw Stock Exchange to better understand their compliance with the NFRD. The authors reported that many companies did not adequately follow the NFRD requirements. Focusing on compliance as well, Biondi et al. (2020) explored whether companies could comply with the NFRD by using *de facto* reporting frameworks. Their results indicate that for reporting frameworks to be widely used, they should be supported by the regulation in place in the respective countries. Other studies examined how the NFRD affected the quantity or extent of information (Agostini et al., 2021; Korca et al., 2021). Korca et al. (2021) explored how the quantity of information improved in an Italian banking group after the NFRD's enforcement. Examining the aspects required by the NFRD, the authors found an increased quantity of information subsequent to the regulation of some disclosure aspects. Focusing on the listed companies in the Italian market, Agostini et al. (2021) reported similar results; the NFRD increased the quantity of information. In contrast, different results showed how the NFRD affected the quality of information.

While some studies noted improvements in the quality of reported information, Mion and Adaui (2019) analysed the NFRD's effect on the quality of the information in Italy and Germany, considering both before and after the introduction of the regulation. The results suggest an increased quality of SR after the NFRD's implementation. Other studies reported the contrary. Cosma et al. (2021) examined the reporting quality before and after the NFRD's implementation (2016 and 2017) and found no improvement, despite the EU's legal intervention.

Second, another research stream explored the NFRD's second-order effects. Agostini et al. (2021) studied the link between mandatory SR and the financial performance of listed companies in Italy. The results suggest a positive relation between the quality of reporting and financial performance, independent of the regulation. However, the SR quality showed no significant relation with the listed firms' financial performance. While studies in different jurisdictions more profoundly explored the mandatory SR's impact on firms' financial performance, in the EU context, studies remain scarce. Conway (2019) investigated the relation between SR using integrated reporting (IR) and the financial performance of firms listed in the African Stock Exchange, considering that reporting is mandatory for South African listed firms. The results indicated that the introduction of mandatory reporting had a significant and negative effect on financial performance (Conway, 2019). Chen et al. (2018) reported similar results when exploring how the SR regulation in China, enacted in 2008, affected the targeted companies' financial performance. The results suggest decreased firm profitability after the regulation's implementation. While many studies have explored the second-order consequences of mandatory SR, in the EU context, there is space for further contributions to the literature in this direction. The EU is considered a leader in developing new SR measures (Carrots & Sticks, 2020); thus, it remains relevant to explore such measures' impacts on second-order aspects, such as firms' financial performance. Analysing both first-order and second-order effects of the EU regulations sheds light on not only the potential benefits of mandatory measures but also their drawbacks, such as higher investment and administrative costs for entities just starting to invest in and report on sustainability.

Legitimacy of Norms

The evolution of SR regulations could be placed in the broad debate about mandatory disclosure when firms comply with legal requirements. However, voluntary mechanisms push firms to satisfy external pressures in order to conform to socially acceptable norms and maintain legitimacy in the SR arena. Therefore, the SR debate has touched on the interplay between voluntary and mandatory provisions for many years. Voluntary disclosure has been criticised for its lack of completeness, accuracy, neutrality and objectivity (Hibbitt & Collision, 2004; Jeffrey & Perkins, 2013), discouraging firms' comparability. Mandatory disclosure is somehow addressed with the "tick-box" approach (La Torre et al., 2018), limiting its transformative aim for societal change. However, a black box beyond the voluntary and the mandatory reporting regimes has been found (Larrinaga & Senn, 2021). Often, formal laws have not been sufficiently impactful in corporate reporting (Chauvey et al., 2015; Korca et al., 2021), while voluntary practices have sometimes shown examples of norm development in SR (Bebbington et al., 2012; Korca et al., 2021). Considering this "grey area" (Larrinaga & Senn, 2021, p. 138) in SR research, the NFRD's normativity production has been questioned over the last few years. The NFRD represents the current regulation mandating SR in the EU, but its success in driving more transparency and high-quality disclosure (EU, 2014) remains under scrutiny.

The notion of normativity relates to how rules are perceived as binding and legitimate (Bebbington et al., 2012) to ensure effective compliance. However, normativity is not only expected by formal laws (e.g., directives) but can also come from informal forms of regulating behaviour (e.g., soft law) (Bebbington et al., 2012; Korca et al., 2021). At times, previous SR experiences might support formal laws and regulations to produce normativity (Korca, 2021; Korca et al., 2021). However, normativity may change over time until the point when it is taken for granted (Bebbington et al., 2012; Chauvey et al., 2015). According to Bebbington et al. (2012), normativity comes through a three-stage process:

> It starts with the emergence of norms, characterised by the innovation of norm entrepreneurs, followed by diffusion leading to a "tipping point" after which the norm cascades to reach a point at the end of the life cycle where norms are internalised and acquire a taken-for-granted quality.
>
> *(p. 79)*

It is important to acknowledge that the emergence of norms in an environment is not isolated from other factors, such as pre-existing SR experiences, non-binding guidelines and other pre-existing or accompanying factors. Some studies have shown that in the SR context, a combination of voluntary and mandatory elements has led to SR internalisation and normativity production (Bebbington et al., 2012; Chelli et al., 2018; Korca et al., 2021; Larrinaga & Senn, 2021). Thus, the diffusion stage, leading to a "tipping point" (Bebbington et al., 2012, p. 79), might combine different elements, such as voluntary disclosure and the emergence of regulatory requirements. Voluntary disclosure is usually a product of soft law – rules that are legally non-binding and influenced by international bodies (i.e., those developing voluntary reporting standards). Instead, mandatory disclosure is characterised by compliance with binding rules and responses to coercive requests (Larrinaga & Senn, 2021). The normativity dynamics are represented linearly, starting from norm emergence to norm diffusion, leading to a tipping point and then to the potential internalisation of the norm (Bebbington et al., 2012). However, the process of norm creation up to norm internalisation is not always straightforward and linear (Korca et al., 2021; Larrinaga & Senn, 2021).

Lessons Learned for Impactful Norms

Considering the potential development of normativity in the EU context, with the NFRD and the lessons learned from the experience of mandatorily reporting sustainability information, this section offers some reflections for policymakers to consider in the next steps of establishing an advanced SR landscape in the EU market. These reflections are built on the authors' extensive research in the field and scoping of the relevant literature. Particularly, the authors take stock of the literature on normativity, following Larrinaga and Senn's (2021) approach. The following lessons learned from studying both voluntary and mandatory SR before and after the recent NFRD are identified:

- Norm production is not the result of a new regulation that comes into force but is the outcome of a learning process that starts from voluntary experiences in SR.
- For SMEs, the challenge to make visible their sustainability practices should consider their dimensions, skills, capabilities and need to learn new reporting mechanisms.
- Stakeholders' engagement and the consultation process can enhance a more collaborative and dialogic form of accountability.
- In the interplay between normativity and standardisation, two main aspects should be considered: i) both technical and non-technical dimensions and ii) the focus on the process instead of the outcome.

In the following subsections, each lesson is argued in detail from a forward-looking perspective.

Mixed Non-Binding and Binding Elements in Driving Norms

Normativity production should be studied by focusing on the underlying factors that grant legitimacy to the norm itself (Bebbington et al., 2012). Binding laws might be legitimate enough to induce normativity, depending on companies' previous practices in reporting information. If the firms' previous experiences are in harmony with the presented norms, normativity might be achieved by regulation alone (Franck, 1990). Previous studies examined how previous voluntary experiences in SR helped entities comply with regulations properly.

Korca et al. (2021) analysed a banking group in Italy that reported information voluntarily before the NFRD came into force. After the NFRD's implementation, reporting sustainability information became mandatory. The results suggest that disclosure topics voluntarily reported by the banking group consequently increased in quantity after the NFRD's implementation. Some disclosure topics had enhanced quality, which the banking group previously reported. Therefore, a combination of both voluntary and mandatory elements successfully drove SR in terms of quantity and quality.

Similarly, analysing the French and Canadian contexts, Chelli et al. (2018) found that an interplay of binding and non-binding elements could help in normativity production. Thus, in SR, normativity can be achieved by combining two or more regimes (Chelli et al., 2018). Voluntary experiences with SR could also be exercised in different jurisdictions worldwide when no mandatory measures exist. For instance, in March 2022, the US Securities and Exchange Commission (SEC) proposed rules to enhance and standardise climate-related disclosure (SEC Press Release, 2022). However, the publicly available SR is still undertaken voluntarily until the rules take effect. The *de facto* approach, involving entities' voluntary reporting using established frameworks (i.e., GRI), should be recognised as an enabler of transparency enhancement (Adams & Abhayawansa, 2022). Despite some researchers' criticism (Hibbitt & Collison, 2004; Jeffrey & Perkins, 2013), voluntary disclosure offers an excellent opportunity for new reporting firms to define the material aspects and consequently report that information. Voluntary disclosure provides the basis for more transparency and can be understood as the transition phase towards mandatory reporting. For normativity to occur in SR, lawful requests are insufficient. Previous experience with reporting, proper definitions of material aspects and clarity of the regulation could drive appropriate reporting by entities (Bebbington et al., 2012; Chelli et al., 2018; Korca et al., 2021; Senn & Giordano-Spring, 2020).

Non-Financial Reporting Directive (NFRD) and Implications for Small and Medium-Sized Enterprises (SMEs)

Delineating how normativity occurred previously in different countries helps create learning effects for upcoming regulations in the EU and in different jurisdictions worldwide. Given the rapid changes in the SR global landscape, with mandatory measures on the rise (IPSF, 2021; Michelon, 2021), it is crucial to move forward by considering the lessons learned from previous regulations. In the EU, the CSRD, besides targeting large entities, will also address the listed SMEs. However, the difference in the CSRD application between large entities and SMEs is that the latter is allowed more time to start complying with the regulation formally. The ESRS for SMEs will be developed based on the proportionality principle, and SMEs must comply with the CSRD beginning in January 2026 (EC, 2021). The time window for listed SMEs' compliance with the CSRD represents their opportunity to exercise reporting on a non-binding basis until it becomes mandatory in 2026. Additionally, the non-listed SMEs in the EU are not subject to CSRD.

Nonetheless, it is important to note that ESRS could help all SMEs be transparent and accountable to stakeholders and be administratively prepared for the future when SR becomes mandatory. The EU is continuously developing its agenda for a sustainable future. Therefore, the development of new measures will increase overall transparency in the market and help entities access sustainable finance. While new regulations could mean more administrative burden for SMEs, it is essential to point out that SMEs represent a substantial fraction of sectors. Thus, their impacts and risks are also significant. In the EU, SMEs represent 99% of businesses. However, the CSRD will target a tiny fraction of them. For instance, the CSRD only covers 30% of economic activities in sectors such as agriculture or land transportation, although they are significant contributors to sustainability-related problems, especially climate change (Bossut et al., 2021).

Despite the CSRD's specific scope, the need to account for sustainability aspects is present in every firm, regardless of its listing status.

Role of Stakeholder Engagement in Producing Norms and Regulations

Stakeholders' and stakeholder-engagement processes are well known in accountability circles; therefore, accountability has been considered a relational concept (Unerman & O'Dwyer, 2006). In the relational approach to accountability, organisations are required to explain their actions to stakeholders and take responsibility for these, thus addressing the "to whom" questions of accountability (Christensen & Ebrahim, 2006; Williams & Taylor, 2012). From a regulatory perspective, stakeholder engagement is crucial in clearly defining stakeholders' needs for SR such that policies can be tailored. Previous regulations have demonstrated the need for stakeholder engagement to understand better which areas could be further improved in a direction that satisfies stakeholders' needs for SR. For instance, the NFRD revision process in 2020 included views from different stakeholders, resulting in comprehensive feedback, which was then addressed by the CSRD proposal in April 2021.

Similarly, different standard setters in SR operating in different regions hold open consultations to receive stakeholders' feedback. The EFRAG has published 13 ESRS drafts, and comments were accepted until August 2022. Similarly, the International Sustainability Standards Board (ISSB) has published two exposure drafts on general and climate-related requirements, respectively. The consultation was open for comments until the end of July 2022. The most recent development comes from the US SEC, enhancing and standardising the climate-related disclosure for investors. Comments were welcome until June 17, 2022. All these recent developments present tools for institutionalising SR. While stakeholder engagement in norm development is necessary, it is also important that stakeholders respond in the same way to different open consultations worldwide. This would allow stakeholders' unified voice in developing specific aspects of SR, indifferent to the region or the jurisdiction in question. As highlighted by Larrinaga et al. (2002), dialogue with stakeholders is needed to ensure a deeper level of accountability rather than simply reporting information without responding to different stakeholders' needs. However, stakeholder dialogue should be initiated early on at the policy development level rather than only at the entity level. This would allow stakeholders' opinions to be considered at the policy (or norm) development stage, which in turn would result in a higher legitimacy of the policy (or norm) itself (Canning & O'Dwyer, 2013). Bebbington et al. (2012) emphasised that norms should be perceived as legitimate for entities' conformance and consequently, proper reporting of information. Therefore, the nature of the norm development process is an important characteristic of the potential normativity creation. Policymakers worldwide should carefully consider different stakeholders' views for a more inclusive and collaborative approach to developing new SR policies, which might induce a more normative internalisation.

Normativity and Standardisation

One of the major questions that still lies in norm production in SR is related to the need to develop a one-size-fits-all standard that could be applied to all organisations or, on the contrary, to promote a more tailored and context-based approach that can take into account sector peculiarities, dimensions, geographic areas and other aspects. By definition, standards are "rules for the many" (Brunsson et al., 2012), which are abstract and general in scope and cannot cater to the idiosyncrasies of the organisations to which they apply (Timmermans & Epstein, 2010). The need for standardised metrics comes from the current neoliberal economics paradigm, which states that the value of a social good may be priced at what a beneficiary or a consumer is willing to pay for it (Nicholls, 2009). However, this evaluation fails to consider situations where there are no comparable goods or services available to the market or conditions in which peculiarities and specific settings do not make information comparable. Three main classifications of standards are provided in the literature (Brunsson et al., 2012): i) technical and non-technical, ii) process and outcome, and iii) *de jure* and *de facto* standards. This discussion aims to bring together all these types of standards in explaining the role of SR standards (e.g., the *de facto* standard GRI) (Etzion & Ferraro, 2010) and their interplay with norm production.

The recent debate in Europe regarding the adoption of SR standards is consistently pursuing a "golden standard" that can be applied to all European companies. Indeed, the NFRD has promoted the adoption of standardised guidelines to develop SR using the GRI guidelines (EU, 2014). With this recommendation, the NFRD aims to achieve standardisation and comparability by suggesting the GRI as a reference framework for SR. Similarly, the EFRAG, which is developing the ESRS, has welcomed the GRI as the co-constructor of the new reporting standards (Giner & Luque-Vilchez, 2022). In this emerging context, it is urgent to investigate the GRI's role and scope and, in general, the process of reporting standardisation.

From a sociological perspective (Brunsson et al., 2012; Timmermans & Epstein, 2010; Etzion & Ferraro, 2010; Brunsson & Jacobsson, 2000), the interplay between the role of standard/standardisation and norm production could be described as the creation of a neoliberal government–industry hybrid of governance (Timmermans & Epstein, 2010). As highlighted by the cited authors, standards are voluntary in principle but can become *de jure* mandatory (e.g., when a European directive promotes its adoption). "National standardising bodies have had cosy relationships with their governments and have been sensitive to policy implications of standards. In most instances, governments partially fund standard-setting organisations and maintain memoranda of understanding with the organisations" (Timmermans & Epstein, 2010, p. 80). In a situation where the EC could not coerce organisations to adopt a specific scheme for SR, standards can fill in the gap to coordinate activities (Brunsson & Jacobsson, 2000). The EU recommendation can be viewed as an alternative way of regulation through social norms and conventions (Brunsson & Jacobsson, 2000), thus considering the GRI standards as social norms based on implicit, shared understandings (Timmermans & Epstein, 2010). However, in this sense, standards (e.g., the GRI) created by NGOs cannot profoundly transform the financial-market orientation and its neoliberal approach. Adapting financial reporting languages and mechanisms (Giner & Luque-Vilchez, 2022; Costa et al., 2022) to SR is likely insufficient to transform companies' behaviours and practices to meet stakeholders' needs. However, accountability and measurement are social activities; thus, measurement criteria are socially constructed (Roberts & Scapens, 1985). If the socially constructed nature of measurement and reporting is acknowledged, it also becomes necessary to adopt a more customised view of reporting standards, where no universal and golden metrics are defined. On the contrary, these metrics and indicators emerge in the context of interactions among specific organisations and stakeholders affected by their activities and output. Together, they enact the provided values.

A possible solution is a better reflection of the interplay among the three types of standards. This paper's authors believe that the EU-level debate suggests adopting the GRI standard as a reference point in its current form. GRI is considered a *de facto* (Etzion & Ferraro, 2010), non-technical (Brunsson et al., 2012) standard focused on the outcome. To become legitimate, the GRI reporting standard and more generally, other SR standards, should be able to face the "adjustment" and "translation" dynamics (Brunsson et al., 2012), which in turn consider the standard's capacity as a result of the process through which those general rules become "translated" into specific organisations. Because this process may involve overcoming potential discrepancies, which in turn may produce tensions between the general nature of the standard and the specifics of the organisation to which it applies, normativity should i) encompass both *technical* and *non-technical* dimensions that are able to promote dialogue at different levels in the organisational setting and ii) focus on the process and only consequently on the outcome – that should not be general and standardised. Combining these different dimensions could enhance the reporting standards' role in norm production to foster sustainable development.

Conclusions

By taking an EU perspective, this chapter conceptualises the process of building normativity in SR over time. How SR developed in the EU is highlighted to show that normativity creation is not a linear process and that a sole regulation might be insufficient to institutionalise it (Bebbington et al., 2012; Chelli et al., 2018; Korca et al., 2021; Larrinaga & Senn, 2021). Specifically, the presented overview of national and EU-level regulations emphasises the SR trajectory in EU member states, from national to EU regulations. While SR started voluntarily in the late 1980s and the early 1990s (Milne & Gray, 2010), recent attempts to mandate this reporting are increasing (IPSF, 2021). Since April 2021, the EC has adopted the Sustainable Finance package, with the aim to improve the flow of capital towards more sustainable investments. In different jurisdictions worldwide, mandatory SR measures are growing. In parallel, the EC (2021) introduced the CSRD as a means to improve the mandatory requirements for non-financial information, enhancing the overall transparency and comparability of EU companies' non-financial information. Therefore, the EU is still considered a leader in SR measures – from national to EU-level regulations. The emergence of the CSRD, first announced in the Green Deal (EC, 2019) and, consequently, the development of ESRS, represent new significant attempts to enhance SR in the EU. However, in its current state, mandated by the NFRD, SR in the EU has not exactly improved. While regulatory pressure is expected to institutionalise SR, research evidence shows that compliance levels and substantial changes in SR do not always occur (Chauvey et al., 2015; Chelli et al., 2018; Korca et al., 2021).

This chapter considers the previous mandatory SR in the EU and highlights four main lessons learned from the process. These reflections could be considered by policymakers in further developing the SR regulatory landscape in the EU. The CSRD is currently at the proposal stage, while the ESRS has published standard drafts, which still need to be finalised. Therefore, the following reflections come from studying both voluntary and mandatory reporting regimes and provide insights into fostering normativity in SR. First, it is important to acknowledge that norm production is not only the result of a binding regulation that comes into force, but it also occurs as a combination of many more elements. This chapter argues that normativity production is the outcome of a learning process that starts from entities experiencing SR on a voluntary basis. Second, in light of recent discussions on mandatory reporting by SMEs, another topic of reflection is how it would best help them consider sustainability impacts, risks and opportunities and consequently report this information. For SMEs, mandatory SR represents administrative burden and extra costs. To facilitate the switch for them, it is important to consider their dimensions, skills, capabilities and most importantly, their needed time to learn new reporting mechanisms. This would allow SMEs to better evaluate and understand SR and institutionalise it in their reporting systems. Third, in developing new regulations and reporting standards, stakeholder engagement and consultation are crucial. To better understand different stakeholders' needs and respond to these, future regulations must establish a more collaborative and dialogic approach, which might induce a more normative internalisation of SR in organisations. Finally, another vital aspect to consider, especially in light of ongoing discussions, is the interplay between normativity and standardisation. The creation of normativity should not only focus on the standardisation design from a technical standard-setting perspective. Instead, it should i) encompass both *technical* and *non-technical* dimensions that enable dialogue at different levels in the organisational setting and ii) focus on the process and only consequently on the outcome – that should not be general and standardised. These four reflections represent lessons learned from the previous SR practice, which did not create normativity. Therefore, future regulations could benefit from a close consideration of these four aspects to further foster SR.

References

Adams, C. A., & Abhayawansa, S. (2022). Connecting the COVID-19 pandemic, environmental, social and governance (ESG) investing and calls for "harmonisation" of sustainability reporting. *Critical Perspectives on Accounting*, *148*, 148–162. https://doi.org/10.1016/j.cpa.2021.102309

Agostini, M., Costa, E., & Korca, B. (2021). Mon-financial disclosure and corporate financial performance under directive 2014/95/EU: Evidence from Italian listed companies. *Accounting in Europe*, *19*(1), 78–109. https://doi.org/10.1080/17449480.2021.1979610

Bebbington, J., Kirk, E. A., & Larrinaga, C. (2012). The production of normativity: A comparison of reporting regimes in Spain and the UK. *Accounting, Organizations and Society*, *37*(2), 78–94. https://doi.org/10.1016/j.aos.2012.01.001

Bebbington, J., & Larrinaga, C. (2014). Accounting and sustainable development: An exploration. *Accounting, Organizations and Society*, *39*(6), 395–413. https://doi.org/10.1016/j.aos.2014.01.003

Biondi, L., Dumay, J., & Monciardini, D. (2020). Using the international integrated reporting framework to comply with EU directive 2014/95/EU: Can we afford another reporting façade? *Meditari Accountancy Research*, *28*(5), 889–914. https://doi.org/10.1108/MEDAR-01-2020-0695

Bossut, M., Jürgens, I., Pioch, T., Schiemann, F., Spandel, T., & Tietmeyer, R. (2021). *What information is relevant for sustainability reporting? The concept of materiality and the EU corporate sustainability reporting directive*. Sustainable Finance Research Platform. Retrieved December 14, 2022, from https://wpsf.de/wp-content/uploads/2021/09/WPSF_PolicyBrief_7-2021_Materiality.pdf

Brunsson, N., & Jacobsson, B. (2000). The contemporary expansion of standardization. In N. Brunsson & B. Jacobsson (Eds.), *A world of standards* (pp. 1–17). Oxford University Press.

Brunsson, N., Rasche, A., & Seidl, D. (2012). The dynamics of standardization: Three perspectives on standards in organization studies. *Organization Studies*, *33*(5–6), 613–632. https://doi.org/10.1177/0170840612450120

Canning, M., & O'Dwyer, B. (2013). The dynamics of a regulatory space realignment: Strategic responses in a local context. *Accounting, Organizations and Society*, *38*(3), 169–194. https://doi.org/10.1016/j.aos.2013.01.002

Carrots, & Sticks. (2020). Sustainability reporting policy: Global trends in disclosure as the ESG agenda goes mainstream. Retrieved December 14, 2022, from https://www.carrotsandsticks.net/

Chauvey, J. N., Giordano-Spring, S., Cho, C. H., & Patten, D. M. (2015). The normativity and legitimacy of CSR disclosure: Evidence from France. *Journal of Business Ethics*, *130*(4), 789–803. https://doi.org/10.1007/s10551-014-2114-y

Chelli, M., Durocher, S., & Fortin, A. (2018). Normativity in environmental reporting: A comparison of three regimes. *Journal of Business Ethics*, *149*(2), 285–311. https://doi.org/10.1007/s10551-016-3128-4

Chen, Y. Ch., Hung, M., & Wang, Y. (2018). The effect of mandatory CSR disclosure on firm profitability and social externalities: Evidence from China. *Journal of Accounting and Economics*, *65*(1), 169–190. https://doi.org/10.1016/j.jacceco.2017.11.009

Christensen, R. A., & Ebrahim, A. (2006). How does accountability affect mission? The case of a nonprofit serving immigrants and refugees. *Nonprofit Management and Leadership*, *17*(2), 195–209. https://doi.org/10.1002/nml.143

Conway, E. (2019). Quantitative impacts of mandatory integrated reporting. *Journal of Financial Reporting and Accounting*, *17*(4), 604–634. https://doi.org/10.1108/JFRA-08-2018-0066

Cosma, S., Leopizzi, R., Pizzi, S., & Turco, M. (2021). The stakeholder engagement in the European banks: Regulation versus governance. What changes after the NF directive? *Corporate Social Responsibility and Environmental Management*, *28*(3), 1091–1103. https://doi.org/10.1002/csr.2108

Costa, E. (2014). Voluntary disclosure in a regulated context: The case of Italian social enterprises. In E. Costa, L. Parker, & M. Andreaus (Eds.), *Accountability and social accounting for social and non-profit organizations* (pp. 223–249). https://doi.org/10.1108/S1041-706020140000017009

Costa, E., & Agostini, M. (2016). Mandatory disclosure about environmental and employee matters in the reports of Italian-listed corporate groups. *Social and Environmental Accounting Journal, 36*(1), 10–33. https://doi.org/10.1080/0969160X.2016.1144519

Costa, E., Pesci, C., Andreaus, M., & Taufer, E. (2022). When a sector-specific standard for non-financial reporting is not enough: Evidence from microfinance institutions in Italy. *Sustainability Accounting, Management and Policy Journal, 13*(6), 1334–1360. https://doi.org/10.1108/SAMPJ-06-2021-0253

Cremasco, C., & Boni, L. (2022). Is the European Union (EU) Sustainable Finance Disclosure Regulation (SFDR) effective in shaping sustainability objectives? An analysis of investment funds' behaviour. *Journal of Sustainable Finance and Investment*. https://doi.org/10.1080/20430795.2022.2124838

Etzion, D., & Ferraro, F. (2010). The role of analogy in the institutionalization of sustainability reporting. *Organization Science, 21*(5), 1092–1107. https://doi.org/10.1287/orsc.1090.0494

EC. (2019). *The European green deal*. Retrieved December 14, 2022, from https://eur-lex.europa.eu/legal-content/EN/TXT/?qid=1576150542719&uri=COM%3A2019%3A640%3AFIN

EC. (2021). *European commission proposal for a directive of the European parliament and of the council amending directive 2013/34/EU, directive 2004/109/EC, directive 2006/43/EC and regulation (EU) no 537/2014, as regards corporate sustainability reporting*. Retrieved December 14, 2022, from https://eur-lex.europa.eu/legal-content/EN/TXT/?uri=CELEX:52021PC0189

EU. (2014). *Directive 2014/95/EU of the European parliament and of the council of 22 October 2014 amending directive 2013/34/EU as regards disclosure of non-financial and diversity information by certain large undertakings and groups*. Retrieved December 14, 2022, from https://eur-lex.europa.eu/legal-content/EN/TXT/?uri=CELEX%3A32014L0095

Franck, T. M. (1990). *The power of legitimacy among nations*. Oxford University Press.

Giner, B., & Luque-Vílchez, M. (2022). A commentary on the "new" institutional actors in sustainability reporting standard-setting: A European perspective. *Sustainability Accounting, Management and Policy Journal, 13*(6), 1284–1309. https://doi.org/10.1108/SAMPJ-06-2021-0222

Godemann, J., & Michelsen, G. (2011). Sustainability communication – An introduction. In J. Godemann & G. Michelsen (Eds.), *Sustainability communication* (pp. 3–11). Springer. https://doi.org/10.1007/978-94-007-1697-1_1

Gray, R., Owen, D., & Adams, C. (1996). *Accounting and accountability: Changes and challenges in corporate social and environmental reporting*. Prentice-Hall.

Hamann, R. (2003). Mining companies' role in sustainable development: The 'why' and 'how' of corporate social responsibility from a business perspective. *Development Southern Africa, 20*(2), 237–254. https://doi.org/10.1080/03768350302957

Hibbitt, C., & Collison, D. (2004). Corporate environmental disclosure and reporting developments in Europe. *Social and Environmental Accountability Journal, 24*(1), 1–11. https://doi.org/10.1080/0969160X.2004.9651708

IPSF. (2021). *State and trends of ESG disclosure policy measures across IPSF jurisdictions, Brazil and the US*. Retrieved December 14, 2022, from https://ec.europa.eu/info/files/international-platform-sustainable-finance-esg-disclosure-report-2021_en

Jeffrey, C., & Perkins, J. D. (2013). Social norms and disclosure policy: Implications from a comparison of financial and corporate social responsibility reporting. *Social and Environmental Accountability Journal, 33*(1), 5–19. https://doi.org/10.1080/0969160X.2012.748468

Korca, B. (2021). Thematic review on the concept of normativity in environmental reporting. *Social and Environmental Accountability Journal, 41*(3), 236–238. https://doi.org/10.1080/0969160X.2021.1955508

Korca, B., Costa, E., & Farneti, F. (2021). From voluntary to mandatory non-financial disclosure following directive 2014/95/EU: An Italian case study. *Accounting in Europe, 18*(3), 353–377. https://doi.org/10.1080/17449480.2021.1933113

La Torre, M., Sabelfeld, S., Blomkvist, M., Tarquino, L., & Dumay, J. (2018). Harmonising non-financial reporting regulation in Europe: Practical forces and projections for future research. *Meditari Accountancy Research, 26*(4), 598–621. https://doi.org/10.1108/MEDAR-02-2018-0290

Larrinaga, C., Carrasco, F., Correa, C., Llena, F., & Moneva, J. (2002). Accountability and accounting regulation: The case of the Spanish environmental disclosure standard. *European Accounting Review, 11*(4), 723–740. https://doi.org/10.1080/0963818022000001000

Larrinaga, C., & Senn, J. (2021). Norm development in environmental reporting. In J. Bebbington, C. Larrinaga, B. O'Dwyer, & I. Thomson (Eds.), *Routledge handbook of environmental accounting* (pp. 137–150). Routledge.

Luque-Vílchez, M., & Larrinaga, C. (2016). Reporting models do not translate well: Failing to regulate CSR reporting in Spain. *Social and Environmental Accountability Journal, 36*(1), 56–75. https://doi.org/10.1080/0969160X.2016.1149301

Matuszak, L., & Rózaszak, E. (2017). CSR disclosure in polish listed companies in the light of directive 2014/95/EU requirements: Empirical evidence. *Sustainability, 9*(12), 2304. https://doi.org/10.3390/su9122304

Michelon, G. (2021). Financial markets and environmental information. In J. Bebbington, C. Larrinaga, B. O'Dwyer, & I. Thomson (Eds.), *Routledge handbook of environmental accounting* (pp. 165–178). Routledge.

Milne, M., & Gray, R. (2010). Future prospects for sustainability reporting. In J. Unerman, J. Bebbington, & B. O'Dwyer (Eds.), *Sustainability accounting and accountability* (pp. 184–207). Routledge.

Mion, G., & Adaui, C. R. L. (2019). Mandatory nonfinancial disclosure and its consequences on the sustainability reporting quality of Italian and German companies. *Sustainability, 11*(17), 4612. https://doi.org/10.3390/su11174612

Nicholls, A. (2009). 'We do good things, don't we?': 'Blended value accounting' in social entrepreneurship. *Accounting, Organizations and Society, 34*(6–7), 755–769. https://doi.org/10.1016/j.aos.2009.04.008

Ottenstein, P., Erben, S., Jost, S., Weuster, C. W., & Zülch, H. (2021). From voluntarism to regulation: Effects of directive 2014/95/EU on sustainability reporting in the EU. *Journal of Applied Accounting Research, 23*(1), 55–98. https://doi.org/10.1108/JAAR-03-2021-0075

Roberts, J., & Scapens, R. (1985). Accounting systems and systems of accountability - Understanding accounting practices in their organisational context. *Accounting, Organizations and Society, 10*(4), 443–456. https://doi.org/10.1016/0361-3682(85)90005-4

Schütze, F., & Stede, J. (2021). The EU sustainable finance taxonomy and its contribution to climate neutrality. *Journal of Sustainable Finance and Investment*, 1–33. https://doi.org/10.1080/20430795.2021.2006129

SEC Press Release. (2022). *SEC proposes rules to enhance and standardize climate-related disclosures for investors.* Retrieved December 14, 2022, from https://www.sec.gov/news/press-release/2022-46

Senn, J., & Giordano-Spring, S. (2020). The limits of environmental accounting disclosure: Enforcement of regulations, standards and interpretative strategies. *Accounting, Auditing and Accountability Journal, 33*(6), 1367–1393. https://doi.org/10.1108/AAAJ-04-2018-3461

Timmermans, S., & Epstein, S. (2010). A world of standards but not a standard world: Toward a sociology of standards and standardization. *Annual Review of Sociology, 36*(1), 69–89. https://doi.org/10.1146/annurev.soc.012809.102629

Torelli, R., Balluchi, F., & Lazzini, A. (2020). Greenwashing and environmental communication: Effects on stakeholders' perceptions. *Business Strategy and the Environment, 29*(2), 407–421. https://doi.org/10.1002/bse.2373

Unerman, J., & O'Dwyer, B. (2006). Theorising accountability for NGO advocacy. *Accounting, Auditing and Accountability Journal, 19*(3), 349–376. https://doi.org/10.1108/09513570610670334

UNWCED. (1987). *Report of the world commission on environment and development: Our common future.* Oxford University Press. Retrieved December 14, 2022, from https://sustainabledevelopment.un.org/content/documents/5987our-common-future.pdf

Williams, A. P., & Taylor, J. A. (2012). Resolving accountability ambiguity in nonprofit organizations. *Voluntas: International Journal of Voluntary and Nonprofit Organizations, 24*(3), 559–580. https://doi.org/10.1007/s11266-012-9266-0

30
AIR POLLUTION AND INVESTORS' BEHAVIOR
A Review of Recent Literature

Ze Zhang and Shipeng Yan

Introduction

Air pollution is broadly recognized as a synthesis of gases and matter that have adverse effects on the health of living beings. These gases include carbon compounds, such as carbon monoxide (CO); nitrogen compounds, such as nitrogen dioxide (NO_2); sulfur compounds, such as sulfur dioxide (SO_2); volatile organic compounds (VOCs); ozone (O_3); and particulate matter (PM), such as 2.5-μm PM ($PM_{2.5}$) and 10-μm PM (PM_{10}) (Brunekreef & Holgate, 2002; Kampa & Castanas, 2008). According to the World Health Organization, air pollution is "the biggest environmental risk to health" (World Health Organization, 2016) and caused seven million deaths globally in 2016 (World Health Organization, 2018).

The social relevance of air pollution has been the subject of extensive research. In the green finance area, numerous research focuses on how investment affects air pollution. Studies have found a linear relationship between investment and air pollution. For example, firm outward foreign direct investment (OFDI) is negatively related to air pollution (Zhou & Li, 2021), while foreign direct investment (FDI) increases air pollution (Huynh & Hoang, 2019; S. Liu & Zhang, 2022; Omri & Bel Hadj, 2020). Green investment can alleviate air pollution through emission reduction (Mngumi et al., 2022), energy conservation (Ren et al., 2022), and reducing the PM 2.5 concentration (Zeng et al., 2022). Scholars have also found a nonlinear relationship between investment and air pollution. For example, urban traffic infrastructure investment decreases air pollution in the short run but increases air pollution in the long run (Sun et al., 2018), and investment in real estate has an inverted-U shape effect on air pollution (Chen & Lee, 2020). Although how investment affects air pollution is well studied, research has paid little attention to the direct effect of air pollution on investments.

Extant research on how air pollution affects investment mainly focuses on three aspects: performance, financial instrument preferences, and willingness to trade.

First, the effects of air pollution on investors' performance have been assessed. Investing is a mentally taxing activity prone to investors' cognitive biases. Numerous studies have found that air pollution impairs people's cognitive functions and leads to depression, anxiety, and other mental disorders (Calderón-Garcidueñas et al., 2008; Hsieh et al., 1991; Lercher et al., 1995; Rautio et al., 2018; Schwarz & Clore, 1983; Weuve et al., 2012). Thus, investors exposed to air pollution may make inferior investment decisions.

Second, the effects of air pollution on investors' financial instrument preferences have been examined. For example, the market value of green bonds has grown substantially, from less than US $10 billion in 2005 to more than US $913.2 billion in 2020 (DBS Bank, 2021). This may be because deterioration in air quality encourages investors' interest in green finance, which aids the development of the green financial market.

Finally, research has also focused on how air pollution affects investors' willingness to trade. One significant factor influencing investors' trading decisions is risk aversion (Cohn et al., 1975; Dow & Werlang, 1992; Eckel & Grossman, 2008). Studies have shown that air pollution increases cortisol concentrations in the body, increasing individuals' levels of risk aversion (Rosenblitt et al., 2001; Tomei et al., 2003). Thus, compared with investors not exposed to air pollution, investors exposed to air pollution may be less likely to make investments due to their increased levels of risk aversion.

Although these studies have focused on how air pollution affects investor behavior, no comprehensive literature review has been conducted. These studies have performed empirical tests on a wide range of financial markets, including the stock market, the bond market, and the poverty market, and have obtained diverse findings. Therefore, there is a need for a review to synthesize these results and provide a coherent framework for future research and implication for the green financial market.

Our review reveals that the relationship between air pollution and investors' performance has been the focus of most studies, which have suggested that air pollution has a significantly negative effect on investor performance. However, studies have obtained mixed results on whether individual investors are more susceptible to the negative effects of air pollution than institutional investors. Similarly, studies of investors' preferences have suggested that air pollution increases investors' holdings of portfolios related to consumption but have obtained mixed results on investors' preferences for green financial instruments. Some studies have argued that air pollution induces investors to invest in green funds and less in polluting firms, while others have found that air pollution has a statistically insignificant effect on investors' preferences for green financial instruments. Studies on the effects of air pollution on investors' willingness to trade have also reported inconclusive results. Studies have generally found that air pollution decreased investors' desire to trade, but some studies have reported that air pollution induces excessive trading by increasing investors' confidence. The findings of our review suggest that since air pollution may to some extent push investors towards green financial instruments, it is important to take air pollution into consideration when promoting green financial instruments to achieve better synergy. In addition, it also implies that investors believe green finance could address environmental issues.

The remainder of this chapter proceeds as follows. The second section discusses the methods used to identify the relevant studies. The third section provides a statistical summary of the studies identified and presents the relevant findings. The chapter ends with a concluding section that offers suggestions for future research.

Methodology

In this section, we detail the approach used to identify the relevant studies. The first part describes the two stages of our search – an initial search and a reference search – and our search criteria. The second part elaborates on the main information we extracted from our search.

Initial Search

Following prior research (Zhang et al., 2019), we searched for studies in Scopus, which can generate highly relevant results and is commonly used for literature reviews in the field of business.

We first used keywords to identify studies, namely "air pollution" and "investor behaviors." To ensure our results were comprehensive, we also used technical terms that describe air pollution, such as "SO2," "NO2," and "PM 2.5," together with several synonyms for air pollution, such as "air quality," "air condition," and "air polluting," as our first batch of keywords.

Carbon dioxide ("CO2") is one of the primary causes of climate change (Solomon et al., 2009) but is not a source of air pollution by definition (Brunekreef & Holgate, 2002; Kampa & Castanas, 2008). We did not include carbon dioxide ("CO2") in this search, as our main focus was on the relationship between air pollution and investor behavior; we used "invest," "investor," "investing," and "investment" as our second batch of keywords.

We searched these keywords in Scopus for an all-time span and filtered the results to include only studies published in peer-reviewed journals in the field of business and economics. This search yielded 466 studies. We examined the titles and abstracts of every study and excluded articles that contained our keywords but whose themes were irrelevant to our topic. For example, some studies contained the keywords "air pollution" and "investment" but investigated "how investment reduced air pollution," which was not our concern. Therefore, we ceded these articles and retained articles closely relevant to our topic. This afforded a set of 23 studies.

Our search code was as follows:

(TITLE-ABS-KEY("air pollution" OR "air condition" OR "air quality" OR "air polluting" OR "polluted air" OR "particulate matter" OR "PM 2.5" OR "PM 10" OR "volatile organic compounds" OR "VOCs" OR "carbon monoxide" OR "ozone" OR "O3" OR "nitrogen dioxide" OR "NO2" OR "sulfur dioxide" OR "SO2") AND TITLE-ABS-KEY("investor" OR "invest" OR "investing" OR "investment")) AND (LIMIT-TO (DOCTYPE, "ar")) AND (LIMIT-TO (SUBJAREA, "BUSI") OR LIMIT-TO (SUBJAREA, "ECON"))

Reference Search

We next checked the reference list of each study selected in our initial search, and other studies that cited each study to identify any omissions. We performed this process iteratively until the results reached saturation.

After these two stages of searching, our final set consisted of 25 studies. We then used a spreadsheet to code their critical information: title, author, year of publication, methods, data source, variables, mechanism, main results, and the publishing journal.

Results

Here, we first provide a basic overview of the literature, such as distributions of publications, the main mechanisms and types of investors examined, and the outcomes. We then synthesized the studies that have focused on how air pollution affects investor performance, their preferences for green financial instruments, and their willingness to trade.

Basic Overview

In this section, we summarize our set of studies and classify them according to their main findings. We provide detailed information for each study in Table A1 in the Appendix.

Time Trend

Figure 30.1 gives the number of studies published each year. The earliest study we identified was published in 2011. The number of published studies has increased since then and reached a

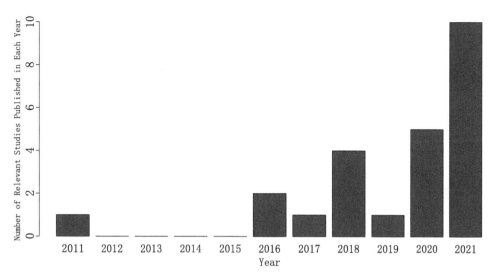

Figure 30.1 Number of relevant studies published in each year

maximum in 2021, which saw ten studies published. This confirms that air pollution has drawn increasing scholarly attention in recent years.

Publishing Journals

We found that the 25 studies were evenly distributed across 19 journals. *Applied Economics* and the *Journal of Cleaner Production* have each published three studies. *Finance Research Letters* and the *Pacific Basin Finance Journal* have each published two studies. Only two studies that have focused

Table 30.1 Number of relevant studies published in each journal

Journal	Count
Applied Economics	3
Journal of Cleaner Production	3
Finance Research Letters	2
Pacific Basin Finance Journal	2
Emerging Markets Review	1
Energy Policy	1
Environmental Science and Pollution Research	1
Frontiers in Public Health	1
International Review of Economics and Finance	1
Journal of Asset Management	1
Journal of Behavioral and Experimental Finance	1
Journal of Economic Psychology	1
Journal of Empirical Finance	1
Journal of Financial Economics	1
Journal of Financial Markets	1
Management Science	1
Real Estate Economics	1
Research in International Business and Finance	1
Sustainability (Switzerland)	1
Total	**25**

Table 30.2 Distribution of research context in each year

Year	China	Italy	United States
2011	0	0	1
2016	1	1	0
2017	1	0	0
2018	4	0	0
2019	1	0	0
2020	5	0	0
2021	9	0	1
Total	21	1	2

on how air pollution affects investors' behavior were from top journals; one was published in the *Journal of Financial Economics* (Li et al., 2021), and the other was published in *Management Science* (Huang et al., 2020).

Research Contexts

Most studies have been based in China; however, two focused on the United States, and one focused on Italy. The first study, from 2011, focused on US investors and air quality in New York City (Levy & Yagil, 2011), and similar studies were then conducted in China and Italy in 2016 (Lepori, 2016; Li & Peng, 2016). From 2017 to 2021, 20 studies focused on China, and only one focused on the United States (Muntifering, 2021). China is a developing country with more severe air pollution than most developed countries and has two exchange centers and numerous active investors in Shanghai and Shenzhen. Thus, China is a suitable context in which to investigate the relationship between air pollution and investors' behavior.

Types of Investors

Institutional and individual investors differ in various aspects. Institutional investors are typically professionals in large organizations such as banks, funds, unions, or insurance companies. Institutional investors generally have more experience and skill than individual investors, and therefore the former may be less affected by air pollution than the latter. However, the findings of studies on this aspect are inconsistent. We next classify the studies according to their main findings.

Measures of Air Pollution

Most studies that have focused on China have used the Air Quality Index (AQI) to measure air pollution. The AQI was initially provided by the Ministry of Environmental Protection of the People's Republic of China (MEPC), which was succeeded by the Ministry of Ecology and Environment of the People's Republic of China (MEEPRC) in 2018. AQI measures air pollution levels in terms of the concentrations of noxious gases, namely CO, O_3, NO_2, and SO_2, and the concentrations of $PM_{2.5}$ and PM_{10}. A grading scale of 0 to 500 is applied, with a higher score representing poorer air quality.

We identified three studies that constructed the national daily AQI of China. Two used provincial AQI data provided by the MEPC and then weighted these data by the number of stock accounts in each province (Liu et al., 2021a) or multiplied these data by the trading ratios of the provincial capitals (Gao et al., 2020). An et al. (2018) calculated the average AQI of major trading cities in China to construct measures of China's national air pollution.

In 12 studies that assessed investors' perceptions, city-level daily AQI data were used to measure the air pollution levels in all Chinese cities. These studies obtained data from the MEPC (Ding et al., 2021; Guo et al., 2021; Huang et al., 2020; Huang & Du, 2022; Li et al., 2021; Teng & He, 2020; Wu et al., 2018a, 2020), city-level environmental protection bureaus (Zhang et al., 2021), the World Air Quality Index website (Jo et al., 2022), the Chinese Air Quality Study Platform website (Wu & Lu, 2020), and all Chinese monitoring stations (Han et al., 2021).

Air pollution in specific Chinese cities was examined in ten studies. These included daily AQI data for Shanghai (He & Liu, 2018; Liu et al., 2021b; Su et al., 2019) and Shenzhen (Jiang et al., 2021) obtained from the MEPC, and hourly AQI data for Beijing obtained from the website of the US Department of State Air Quality Monitoring Program (Zhang et al., 2017). Other studies used daily AQI data for 16 major Chinese cities (those with populations of over eight million) (Li & Peng, 2016) or the maximum daily AQIs of heavily polluted cities each December during the sample period (Wu et al., 2018b) obtained from the MEPC. Some studies measured air pollution levels using the New York City daily AQI data from the US Federal Environmental Protection Agency (EPA) (Muntifering, 2021) or the daily AQI data of the four main US stock exchanges (the New York Stock Exchange (NYSE), the American Stock Exchange (NASDAQ), and the Philadelphia stock exchange (PHLX)) retrieved from AirData websites (Levy & Yagil, 2011). The daily AQI data reported by three monitoring stations were also used to measure the ambient air pollution level in Milan (Lepori, 2016).

The Mechanism by Which Air Pollution Affects Investors

Most of the studies have focused on the psychological or physiological effects of air pollution on investors. Air pollution can have negative psychological effects on investors' moods, leading to depression, anxiety, and negative sentiment. The physiological effects consist of changes to the body's cortisol concentrations.

Psychological effects have been the focus of 15 studies in our set (An et al., 2018; Ding et al., 2021; Gao et al., 2020; Huang et al., 2020; Huang & Du, 2022; Jiang et al., 2021; Jo et al., 2022; Levy & Yagil, 2011; Li et al., 2021; Muntifering, 2021; Teng & He, 2020; Wu et al., 2018a,b; Wu & Lu, 2020; Zhang et al., 2021). One study considered only physiological effects (Guo et al., 2021), and nine examined both physiological and psychological effects (Han et al., 2021; He & Liu, 2018; Lepori, 2016; Li & Peng, 2016; Liu et al., 2021a,b; Su et al., 2019; Wu et al., 2020; Zhang et al., 2017).

Those that considered the psychological effects of air pollution on investor behavior mainly focused on investors' moods and cognitive functions. Research into mental health has suggested that exposure to air pollution can depress mood and impair cognitive function (Calderón-Garcidueñas et al., 2008; Hsieh et al., 1991; Schwarz & Clore, 1983). Psychiatric symptoms such as behavioral bias, cognition decline, and other mental disorders have also been observed (Lercher et al., 1995; Rautio et al., 2018; Weuve et al., 2012). Investing is a mentally taxing activity and requires investors to make complicated decisions, so the negative effect of pollution on their mood and cognitive function can be significant (Huang et al., 2020) and may affect their investing performance and preferences.

Studies that have considered the physiological channel have focused on the effect of air pollution on investors' cortisol concentrations, which will increase their levels of risk aversion. Air pollution is known to increase cortisol concentrations in the body (Tomei et al., 2003), and some studies have suggested that individuals with high cortisol concentrations will be risk-averse (Rosenblitt et al., 2001), which represents a cognitive bias. Air pollution can also inhibit the ability of red blood cells to transfer oxygen to organs, which can also lead to reduced concentration and cause confusion (Kampa & Castanas, 2008). Thus, the negative physiological effect of air pollution can lead to a similarly negative psychological effect, and some studies have therefore considered both effects.

Investor Performance

Most studies have suggested that air pollution has a negative effect on investor performance. That is, compared with investors not exposed to air pollution, investors exposed to air pollution will be more susceptible to the disposition effect, more likely to hold negative sentiments regarding the market, and more likely to misprice assets. However, whether individual investors are more prone to the negative effects of air pollution than institutional investors remains unclear.

Disposition Effect

The disposition effect is the trading behavior of holding "losing stocks" and selling "winning stocks," which is a commonly observed trading abnormality. Specifically, investors sell stocks that are likely to increase in price and retain those that are likely to decrease in price (Shefrin & Statman, 1985).

Air pollution was found to increase the disposition effect through mechanisms such as cognition impairment (Huang et al., 2020) or because investors aim to realize a gain from selling winning stock to offset their depressed moods, which have been caused by air pollution (Li et al., 2021). Huang et al. (2020) used account-level data from 87,054 households from 34 cities in China to examine the effect of air pollution on investor trading performance. The results of their fixed-effect panel regression indicated that air pollution made investors more susceptible to the disposition effect (Huang et al., 2020). Li et al. (2021) considered 773,198 account transactions from a private mutual fund and found that the proportion of disposition effect-related activities by investors was four times greater in areas of high air pollution than in areas of low air pollution. Li et al. (2021) used the Qin Lin Huai River as a boundary when measuring the spatial discontinuity of air pollution in China and used a difference-in-difference (DiD) model to confirm that air pollution negatively affects investors.

Negative Sentiments in the Financial Market

Air pollution may lead to investors holding negative sentiments in terms of their expectations and perceptions of the financial market. Investors' sentiments are closely related to market returns (Brown & Cliff, 2004; Lee et al., 1991; Wright & Bower, 1992), and early studies used the change in the market as a proxy to measure investors' sentiment. This approach was later improved by directly measuring investor sentiment through comments on online forums.

Levy and Yagil (2011) proposed that air pollution leads investors to feel anxious and pessimistic about the market and used market data from the four main stock exchanges in the United States to measure investors' sentiments. The results from their OLS model suggest that the air pollution in New York negatively affected the sentiments of investors on both the NYSE and the PHLX. These results supported their hypothesis that air pollution affects investors located in New York and consequently their trading on the PHLX (Levy & Yagil, 2011). Zhang et al. (2017) obtained similar results by examining the daily data of companies located in Beijing and air quality data to determine the effect of air pollution on the stock market. They hypothesized that air pollution could affect the stock market through the channel of investor mood. They regressed 591,709 observations and found that air pollution worsens investor mood, and their resulting pessimistic sentiments about the market increase its volatility and decrease stock market yields (Zhang et al., 2017). The finds of the empirical study conducted by Wu et al. (2018b) are also consistent with the investor sentiment theory. They developed a regression discontinuity model using the data of heavily polluting Chinese listed enterprises from December 2014 to December 2016 and found that air pollution can induce pessimism in investors about the market, decreasing stock yields (Wu et al., 2018b).

The above studies have not directly measured investor sentiment, but An et al. (2018) built a generalized autoregressive conditional heteroskedasticity (1,1) model to investigate the effect of air pollution on investor sentiment and stock market yield. They examined investor comments from the Snowball website to measure sentiment and used weighted AQI as a proxy for air pollution. They indicated that a high air pollution level led to negative investor sentiment about the market, which ultimately decreased stock market yields and liquidity (An et al., 2018).

Mispricing

Air pollution has also been associated with investors' mispricing of assets. Four main mechanisms have been identified that explain this effect.

First, air pollution can affect the mood of investors and lead them to misprice stocks. Ding et al. (2021) found that this effect can distort investors' perceptions of stock price value, particularly of companies located in the same province as the investors. They built an autoregression model using the data from 1,719 firms located in 221 cities in China and found that air pollution led investors to undervalue stocks, which ultimately decreased their companies' returns. Ding et al. (2021) argued that the undervaluation effect affects local companies more than non-local companies, following research that suggested investors tended to invest 8% more in local firms than the market prediction (Feng & Seasholes, 2004) and that Chinese investors invested more in stocks issued by firms from their province than in those issued by non-local firms (Huang et al., 2016).

However, Zhang et al. (2021) noted that investors' pricing of companies can be distorted as the severe air pollution in some cities can discourage company site visits, thus resulting in an insufficient analysis of the intrinsic value of the companies. Even if investors engage in on-site visits, their decisions may be unreliable due to air pollution, thus leading them to misprice these companies' stock prices. Zhang et al. (2021) used IPO data from the China stock market for 2013–2019 to build a multiple regression model, and the results indicated that the companies' IPO prices significantly decreased if the company was located in a severe air pollution area (Zhang et al., 2021).

Huang and Du (2022) suggested that air pollution can lead investors to produce biased projections and thus misvalue land. That is, investors may assume that air pollution will continue to be a problem, leading them to expect decreased profits from investing in the land market. This will decrease the demand for and the price of land (Huang & Du, 2022).

Huang and Du (2022) also applied the salience theory to explain how air pollution can affect investors' pricing in the land market. This theory holds that investors' decisions are more prone to the most unusual features (Bordalo et al., 2012). They conducted a lottery-based experiment and found that decision-makers pay more attention to lotteries with higher pay-offs than to those with lower pay-offs (Bordalo et al., 2012). In the land market context, investors may focus on air pollution and regard it as a significant risk that will inhibit land market development, and this may reduce their perception of the value of land in the polluted regions (Huang & Du, 2022).

Susceptibility

Although most studies have not distinguished between individual and institutional investors, those that have compared investors' levels of susceptibility to the negative effects of air pollution have reported inconsistent results.

Jiang et al. (2021) argued that air pollution triggers investors to have pessimistic sentiments about the market and that individual investors are more prone to this effect than institutional investors. They noted that the limited experience of individual investors means that they are more susceptible to negative sentiment than institutional investors, and thus the former is more likely than the latter to rush to sell stocks in the market. They used data from the Shenzhen Exchange to construct a quantile regression and confirmed that investors' irrational selling, attributed to air pollution, had a statistically significant and negative effect on market returns (Jiang et al., 2021). Guo et al. (2021) analyzed individual transaction records of Chinese investors from the Snowball database and also found that air pollution had more of an effect on individual rather than institutional investors, in terms of inducing them to sell stocks (Guo et al., 2021).

Han et al. (2021) proposed that air pollution can influence the cognitive bias and emotions of individual investors more than those of institutional investors, as pessimism induced the former to undervalue stock prices. Their multiple regression model suggested that air pollution caused individual investors to submit lower bids than institutional investors on seasoned equity offerings (SEO) by firms and that air pollution had no significant effect on the bids received by firms if they only received them from institutional investors. This suggests that individual investors are more susceptible than institutional investors to the negative effects of air pollution (Han et al., 2021).

However, Wu et al. (2020) revealed that institutional investors were susceptible to the reverse effect of air pollution. They analyzed data from 3,028 open-ended funds and the behavior of 1,493 open-end fund managers in China and used a multiple regression model to establish that air pollution increased institutional investors' levels of risk aversion and ultimately affected their buying and selling decisions. That is, compared with institutional investors in the absence of air pollution, institutional investors in the presence of air pollution were more likely to sell risky assets such as stocks, resulting in a decline in market returns (Wu et al., 2020).

Investor Preferences

Air pollution has also been found to affect investors' preferences for consumption-related financial instruments and portfolios. However, the findings on whether investors prefer green rather than polluting financial instruments when exposed to air pollution are inconsistent. Some studies have argued that evidence of air pollution increases investors' holdings of green stocks and bonds, while others have suggested that investors are indifferent about whether financial instruments are green or polluting.

Preferences for Green Financial Instruments

Studies that have examined whether air pollution encourages investors to apply more green financial instruments have reported inconsistent results.

Su et al. (2019) found that air pollution encouraged investors to hold more green stocks and fewer polluting stocks. In terms of air quality, high levels of air pollution decreased the stock returns of polluting industries such as coal, steel, and thermal power, but those of environmentally positive industries remained high regardless of the air quality. They suggested that this was due to air pollution affecting investors' moods and increasing their levels of risk aversion, thus leading them to negatively evaluate the stocks of polluting industries and positively evaluate those of environment-protecting industries. Investors thus decreased their holdings of polluting stocks and increased their holdings of green stocks, which ultimately decreased the returns of the former and increased those of the latter (Su et al., 2019).

Gao et al. (2020) obtained similar results using aggregate trading data of A-share investors. They built an OLS regression model and used this data to study the relationship between air pollution and investors' preferences. They observed more buyer-initiated trading orders in responsible investment indexes when air pollution was high than it was low. This indicates that air pollution encouraged investors to hold green stocks (Gao et al., 2020). Jo et al. (2022) also found that air pollution increased the flow of green funds. They conducted a DiD test using the enactment of the Chinese Air Pollution Prevention and Control Law and a one-to-one matching sample for green funds and conventional funds. Their results imply that air pollution increased the investor demand for green funds (Jo et al., 2022).

However, some studies have suggested that investors were indifferent to whether financial instruments are green or polluting. Han et al. (2021) analyzed all Chinese uniform-price auction SEOs from 2013 to 2019 and developed a multiple regression model. They found that air pollution led investors to undervalue SEO prices. However, they found no significant differences in the adverse effects on polluting and non-polluting SEO prices, indicating that air pollution did not lead to any significant preference for polluting or non-polluting firms (Han et al., 2021). Liu et al. (2021a) analyzed investor attention and also found that investors were indifferent to whether stocks were from green or polluting companies. They used the Baidu index as a proxy to measure investors' attention towards green or polluting stocks and found that increased air pollution led to an increase in attention towards both types of stocks. Their mediating effect model used data from the China Center for Economic Research (CCER) database, and they found increased investor attention to be positively related to the stock price of a company, no matter whether it was green or polluting (Liu et al., 2021a).

Preferences for Portfolios Related to Consumption

Air pollution can also increase investors' preferences for portfolios related to consumption, and portfolio returns in various categories have been analyzed.

Muntifering (2021) used the fundamental capital asset pricing model and found that the AQI index in New York City has a strong positive relationship with portfolio returns for food products and wholesale. This might have been due to air pollution increasing psychological stress and motivating people to consume more, thus driving up the returns of these portfolios and making them more attractive to investors (Muntifering, 2021).

Investors' Willingness to Trade

Research into whether air pollution affects investors' willingness to trade has obtained inconclusive results. In general, most studies have proposed that air pollution reduces investors' willingness to trade and that environmental awareness increases this negative effect. However, some studies have argued that air pollution stimulates investors to trade by enhancing their overconfidence.

Willingness to Trade

Most studies have found that air pollution discourages investors from trading, although there have been exceptions.

Li and Peng (2016) suggested that air pollution decreased investors' desire to trade. They conducted a causal step regression using the daily money inflow in the Shanghai Stock Exchange and found that air pollution led investors to make pessimistic predictions about the market, which ultimately decreased the demand for the stock.

Lepori (2016) also found a causal relationship between air pollution and investors' reluctance to trade, via a natural experiment in Italy. Based on a previous psychological study, he used the ambient air pollution level of the Milan Stock Exchange (MSE) as the proxy to measure the mood of investors. He hypothesized that air pollution negatively affected investors' moods and thus made them pessimistic about the market, ultimately leading them to buy fewer stocks. May 1994 was applied as the breakpoint, as the specific floor trading technology was retired after that date, such that investors did not need to present in the MSE to trade. The negative effect of air pollution on investors' willingness to trade was found to be significant before 1994 but statistically insignificant after 1994, as after 1994, investors could trade remotely, and thus from places with different levels of air pollution. Thus, a causal relationship was found between air pollution and investors' unwillingness to trade, as investors were only affected by the air pollution in the MSE if they were directly exposed to it (Lepori, 2016).

Wu et al. (2018a) also argued that air pollution inhibited the trading of investors. They designed a local bias test to assess this causal relationship, using data from listed firms on the Shanghai and Shenzhen Stock Exchanges. They found that air pollution depressed the moods of investors, which in turn induced them to trade less on high-pollution days than on low-pollution days. Their results suggested a causal relationship as the stock trading volume only significantly decreased for companies headquartered in highly polluted areas on days when the air quality suddenly deteriorated (Wu et al., 2018a).

Wu and Lu (2020) similarly found that investors had less desire to trade when air quality was bad than when it was good. They used the AQI weighted with the Baidu search volume to assess the moods of investors exposed to air pollution. They found that air pollution negatively affected investors' willingness to trade: investors became less interested in acquiring stock when the air quality worsened, and their trading volume decreased. They also found that individual investors were more prone to the negative effect of air pollution than institutional investors, for whom the effect was insignificant (Wu & Lu, 2020).

However, Huang et al. (2020) suggested that investors exhibited overconfidence on hazy days and thus engaged in excessive trading, which led to their poor trading performance on polluted days. They conducted fixed-effect panel regressions of 87,054 households from 34 cities in China and found that the likelihood of investors making a trade was relatively higher on polluted days than on non-polluted days (Huang et al., 2020).

Environmental Awareness

Environmental awareness in our study context refers to the extent to which investors are aware of the detrimental effects of air pollution (He & Liu, 2018; Teng & He, 2020). A greater level of environmental awareness represents a better understanding of these effects. Environmental awareness has been found to positively moderate the relationship between air pollution and investors' willingness to trade.

He and Liu (2018) suggested that air pollution had an insignificant negative effect on the liquidity of the Chinese stock market by reducing investors' desire to trade in the long run and that their public environmental awareness (PEA) enhanced this effect. They used environmental events to signal the increase in the PEA of Chinese investors and found that the negative effect of air pollution became increasingly significant after these events (He & Liu, 2018). Teng and He

(2020) demonstrated similar results and found that investors' environmental awareness enhanced the negative effect of air pollution on their trading behavior. They use market price volatility, stock turnover rate, and stock illiquidity index on the Shanghai Stock Exchange to directly measure the trading behavior of Chinese investors. They used four significant events in China as a proxy for investors' increased environmental awareness, including the revised "Environmental Protection Law of China" published in 2015, and found that investors' environmental awareness enhanced the negative relationship between air pollution and their willingness to trade, which increased market illiquidity (Teng & He, 2020).

Conclusion

In this chapter, we provide a comprehensive and retrospective review of the emerging topic of how air pollution affects investors' behavior. We summarize the essential information, including the data sources, variables, methods, and main results, presented in 25 studies. Most of these studies used the AQIs obtained from various government websites to measure air pollution and typically applied data from stock and fund markets as indirect measures of investors' behavior. Some studies used account-level data to identify the trading behavior of individual investors, which is a more direct approach than using market-level data.

Two potential mechanisms by which air pollution can affect investor behavior have been suggested. Most of the studies assessed the psychological effects and found that air pollution can affect investors' mental health and thus their behavior. Other studies focused on physiological effects and argued that air pollution affects investors' behavior by increasing their cortisol concentrations.

The 25 studies examined the effects of air pollution on three aspects: investors' performance, financial instrument preferences, and willingness to trade.

First, investors exposed to air pollution have been found to perform poorly, but whether this effect is greater for individual investors than institutional investors remains unclear. Investors have been found to become more susceptible to the disposition effect, lose confidence in the market, and misprice assets when air quality deteriorates. However, some studies found that individual investors are less professional and more prone to the negative effects of air pollution than institutional investors, while other studies argued that institutional investors also suffer from the negative effects of air pollution. That is, institutional investors may misprice stock IPOs, seasoned equity offers, and land when air pollution is severe.

Air pollution has also been found to increase investor preferences for portfolios related to consumption, but it remains unclear whether air pollution increases investor preferences for green financial instruments. Some studies suggested that air pollution induces investors to invest more in green funds and stocks, while others argued that air pollution focuses investors' attention on both green and polluting stocks, and found preferences for green financial instruments to be statistically insignificant.

Finally, research into whether air pollution affects investors' willingness to trade has produced inconclusive results. Some studies suggested that air pollution decreases investors' willingness to trade and that their level of environmental awareness exacerbated this effect. However, other studies determined that investors are overconfident on trading days when pollution levels are high and tend to engage in excessive trading despite insufficient information, leading to a poor trading performance on such days.

Our review also holds implications for broader green financial markets. First, our bibliographic analysis suggests that China is the most studied context of our topic. Research has brought a new perspective to China's green financial market that the natural environment can affect the green financial market through the channel of investors. Given the widely supported results that air pollution has negative effects on investor performance, it is worthwhile for China's policymakers to focus on environmental policies that aim at reducing air pollution to promote sustainable development of the green financial market. Second, studies have shown that air pollution may draw investors' attention to green financial instruments, which deserves further investigation. Extant research explains how air pollution affects investors' preferences for green financial instruments through the mechanisms of risk aversion, which implies that investors perceive green financial instruments as less risky than polluting alternatives in the condition of air pollution. It is suggested that air pollution helps promote green financial instruments to some extent. However, the financial instruments may be riskier than their polluting alternatives due to a limited standard for classifying and labeling relevant risks (Falcone & Sica, 2019). This misalignment of investors' perceived risk and actual risk of green financial instruments requires further attention. It implies that the green financial market should make efforts to improve the risk labeling scheme for green financial instruments to properly guide the investor. Finally, increasing investment in consumption-related portfolios in the condition of air pollution is also relevant for green financial markets. This behavior may increase carbon emissions, which is an important issue that green finance aims to address. The green financial market could focus more on integrating the green perspective with consumption to promote low-carbon consumption, which could alleviate the effects of air pollution.

Furthermore, although the effects of air pollution on investors' behavior have been examined, more extensive investigations could be conducted in future studies.

First, these effects could be assessed under different economic conditions. Although a consensus has been reached in these studies that air pollution is detrimental to investor performance, it may also have a positive effect under certain economic circumstances. For example, if the negative sentiments induced by air pollution coincide with a financial crisis, investors' performance may ultimately increase as they can limit their losses by selling before the market worsens. In addition, the reduction in investors' willingness to trade due to air pollution may also lead to a reduction in losses when exposed to unexpected financial shocks. Future research could therefore assess whether the effects of air pollution on investor performance depend on the state of the economic environment.

Second, the varying effects of air pollution on investors' preferences have not been fully explored. The disclosure of a firm's environmental, social, and governance (ESG) performance may moderate the relationship between air pollution and investor preferences for green financial instruments. Air pollution has been found to increase investors' preferences for green financial instruments, due to their negative sentiments regarding the instruments issued by polluting firms. Thus, if polluting firms comprehensively disclose their ESG activities, such as their promotion of innovative technologies that reduce air pollution, investors' views of these firms may become less negative, and thus their preferences for green financial instruments may decrease. However, if polluting firms have poor levels of ESG activity, investors' views of these firms may become more negative, and thus their preferences for green financial instruments may increase. The most likely of these potential outcomes could therefore be assessed in future studies.

There have also been few studies of investors' levels of environmental awareness. Few studies have focused on whether environmental awareness has a moderating effect on the relationship between air pollution and investors' preference for green financial instruments. In the presence of air pollution and compared with investors with a lower level of environmental awareness, those with a higher level of environmental awareness could be expected to invest more in green financial instruments. However, compared with investors with a lower level of environmental awareness, those with a higher level of environmental awareness may also be more selective and likely to scrutinize the nature of such instruments, and thus the latter may ultimately be less interested than the former in the green financial instruments issued by the firms with poor performance in terms of air pollution. Variations in the moderating effect of investors' environmental awareness on the relationship between air pollution and investors' preferences for green financial instruments should therefore be examined in more detail.

Finally, further systematic comparisons of institutional and individual investors are needed to determine their respective susceptibilities to air pollution. The inconsistent results that have been found may be due to the contexts in which the studies have been performed. Most have concluded that compared with institutional investors, individual investors are more prone to the effects of air pollution and thus perform worse in the stock market. However, further tests of the effect of air pollution on the performance of these two types of investors in various asset categories and market conditions are required. Individual investors may be more resilient to the effects of air pollution than institutional investors in some categories or under specific market conditions. The mechanisms responsible for the differences between these two types of investors in terms of their susceptibility to air pollution remain unclear. Institutional investors may be more experienced than individual investors, thus more resilient to external distractions such as air pollution. Future research could investigate this possibility in more detail by assessing whether experienced individual investors are more resilient to air pollution than inexperienced ones.

References

An, N., Wang, B., Pan, P., Guo, K., & Sun, Y. (2018). Study on the influence mechanism of air quality on stock market yield and volatility: Empirical test from China based on GARCH model. *Finance Research Letters*, *26*, 119–125. https://doi.org/10.1016/j.frl.2017.12.002

Bordalo, P., Gennaioli, N., & Shleifer, A. (2012). Salience theory of choice under risk. *Quarterly Journal of Economics*, *127*(3), 1243–1285. https://doi.org/10.1093/qje/qjs018

Brunekreef, B., & Holgate, S. T. (2002). Air pollution and health. *The Lancet*, *360*(3941), 1233–1242. https://doi.org/10.1016/j.jempfin.2002.12.001

Brown, G. W., & Cliff, M. T. (2004). Investor sentiment and the near-term stock market. *Journal of Empirical Finance*, *11*(1), 1–27. https://doi.org/10.1016/j.jempfin.2002.12.001

Calderón-Garcidueñas, L., Solt, A. C., Henríquez-Roldán, C., Torres-Jardón, R., Nuse, B., Herritt, L., Villarreal-Calderón, R., Osnaya, N., Stone, I., García, R., Brooks, D. M., González-Maciel, A., Reynoso-Robles, R., Delgado-Chávez, R., & Reed, W. (2008). Long-term air pollution exposure is associated with neuroinflammation, an altered innate immune response, disruption of the blood-brain barrier, ultrafine particulate deposition, and accumulation of amyloid β-42 and α-synuclein in children and young adults. *Toxicologic Pathology*, *36*(2), 289–310. https://doi.org/10.1177/0192623307313011

Chen, Y., & Lee, C.-C. (2020). The impact of real estate investment on air quality: Evidence from China. *Environmental Science and Pollution Research*, *27*(18), 22989–23001. https://doi.org/10.1007/s11356-020-08874-2

Cohn, R. A., Lewellen, W. G., Lease, R. C., & Schlarbaum, G. G. (1975). Individual investor risk aversion and investment portfolio composition. *Journal of Finance*, *30*(2), 605–620. https://doi.org/10.1111/j.1540-6261.1975.tb01834.x

DBS Bank. (2021). *Climate investment opportunities: Climate-aligned bonds & issuers 2020*. DBS Bank. https://www.climatebonds.net/files/reports/cbi_climate-aligned_bonds_issuers_2020.pdf

Ding, X., Guo, M., & Yang, T. (2021). Air pollution, local bias, and stock returns. *Finance Research Letters*, *39*, 101576. https://doi.org/10.1016/j.frl.2020.101576

Dow, J., & Werlang, S. R. da C. (1992). Uncertainty aversion, risk aversion, and the optimal choice of portfolio. *Econometrica*, *60*(1), 197–204. https://doi.org/10.2307/2951685

Eckel, C. C., & Grossman, P. J. (2008). Men, women and risk aversion: Experimental evidence. In C. R. Plott & V. L. Smith (Eds.), *Handbook of experimental economics results* (Vol. 1, pp. 1061–1073). Elsevier. https://doi.org/10.1016/S1574-0722(07)00113-8

Falcone, P. M., & Sica, E. (2019). Assessing the opportunities and challenges of green finance in Italy: An analysis of the biomass production sector. *Sustainability*, *11*(2), Article 2. https://doi.org/10.3390/su11020517

Feng, L., & Seasholes, M. S. (2004). Correlated trading and location. *Journal of Finance*, *59*(5), 2117–2144. https://doi.org/10.1111/j.1540-6261.2004.00694.x

Gao, Y., Xiong, X., & Feng, X. (2020). Responsible investment in the Chinese stock market. *Research in International Business and Finance*, *52*, 101173. https://doi.org/10.1016/j.ribaf.2019.101173

Guo, M., Wei, M., & Huang, L. (2021). Does air pollution influence investor trading behavior? Evidence from China. *Emerging Markets Review*, *50*, 100822. https://doi.org/10.1016/j.ememar.2021.100822

Han, L., Cheng, X., Chan, K. C., & Gao, S. (2021). Does air pollution affect seasoned equity offering pricing? Evidence from investor bids. *Journal of Financial Markets*, *59*, 100657. https://doi.org/10.1016/j.finmar.2021.100657

He, X., & Liu, Y. (2018). The public environmental awareness and the air pollution effect in Chinese stock market. *Journal of Cleaner Production*, *185*, 446–454. https://doi.org/10.1016/j.jclepro.2018.02.294

Hsieh, G. C., Sharma, R. P., & Parker, R. D. R. (1991). Hypothalamic-pituitary-adrenocortical axis activity and immune function after oral exposure to benzene and toluene. *Immunopharmacology*, *21*(1), 23–32. https://doi.org/10.1016/0162-3109(91)90004-I

Huang, J., Xu, N., & Yu, H. (2020). Pollution and performance: Do investors make worse trades on hazy days? *Management Science*, *66*(10), 4455–4476. https://doi.org/10.1287/mnsc.2019.3402

Huang, Y., Qiu, H., & Wu, Z. (2016). Local bias in investor attention: Evidence from China's internet stock message boards. *Journal of Empirical Finance*, *38*, 338–354. https://doi.org/10.1016/j.jempfin.2016.07.007

Huang, Z., & Du, X. (2022). Does air pollution affect investor cognition and land valuation? Evidence from the Chinese land market. *Real Estate Economics*, *50*(2), 593–613. https://doi.org/10.1111/1540-6229.12344

Huynh, C. M., & Hoang, H. H. (2019). Foreign direct investment and air pollution in Asian countries: Does institutional quality matter? *Applied Economics Letters*, *26*(17), 1388–1392. https://doi.org/10.1080/13504851.2018.1563668

Jiang, Z., Gupta, R., Subramaniam, S., & Yoon, S.-M. (2021). The effect of air quality and weather on the Chinese stock: Evidence from Shenzhen stock exchange. *Sustainability*, *13*(5), 2931. https://doi.org/10.3390/su13052931

Jo, H., Kim, H.-E., & Sim, M. (2022). Environmental preference, air pollution, and fund flows in China. *Pacific-Basin Finance Journal*, *72*, 101723. https://doi.org/10.1016/j.pacfin.2022.101723

Kampa, M., & Castanas, E. (2008). Human health effects of air pollution. *Environmental Pollution*, *151*(2), 362–367. https://doi.org/10.1016/j.envpol.2007.06.012

Lee, C. M. C., Shleifer, A., & Thaler, R. H. (1991). Investor sentiment and the closed-end fund puzzle. *Journal of Finance*, *46*(1), 75–109. https://doi.org/10.1111/j.1540-6261.1991.tb03746.x

Lepori, G. M. (2016). Air pollution and stock returns: Evidence from a natural experiment. *Journal of Empirical Finance*, *35*, 25–42. https://doi.org/10.1016/j.jempfin.2015.10.008

Lercher, P., Schmitzberger, R., & Kofler, W. (1995). Perceived traffic air pollution, associated behavior and health in an alpine area. *Science of the Total Environment*, *169*(1), 71–74. https://doi.org/10.1016/0048-9697(95)04634-D

Levy, T., & Yagil, J. (2011). Air pollution and stock returns in the US. *Journal of Economic Psychology*, *32*(3), 374–383. https://doi.org/10.1016/j.joep.2011.01.004

Li, J. (Jie), Massa, M., Zhang, H., & Zhang, J. (2021). Air pollution, behavioral bias, and the disposition effect in China. *Journal of Financial Economics*, *142*(2), 641–673. https://doi.org/10.1016/j.jfineco.2019.09.003

Li, Q., & Peng, C. H. (2016). The stock market effect of air pollution: Evidence from China. *Applied Economics*, *48*(36), 3442–3461. https://doi.org/10.1080/00036846.2016.1139679

Liu, F., Kang, Y., Guo, K., & Sun, X. (2021a). The relationship between air pollution, investor attention and stock prices: Evidence from new energy and polluting sectors. *Energy Policy*, *156*, 112430. https://doi.org/10.1016/j.enpol.2021.112430

Liu, L., Wang, K.-H., & Xiao, Y. (2021b). How air quality affect health industry stock returns: New evidence from the quantile-on-quantile regression. *Frontiers in Public Health*, *9*, 789510. https://doi.org/10.3389/fpubh.2021.789510

Liu, S., & Zhang, P. (2022). Foreign direct investment and air pollution in China: Evidence from the global financial crisis. *Developing Economies*, *60*(1), 30–61. https://doi.org/10.1111/deve.12298

Mngumi, F., Shaorong, S., Shair, F., & Waqas, M. (2022). Does green finance mitigate the effects of climate variability: Role of renewable energy investment and infrastructure. *Environmental Science and Pollution Research*, *29*(39), 59287–59299. https://doi.org/10.1007/s11356-022-19839-y

Muntifering, M. (2021). Air pollution, investor sentiment and excessive returns. *Journal of Asset Management*, *22*(2), 110–119. https://doi.org/10.1057/s41260-021-00206-4

Omri, A., & Bel Hadj, T. (2020). Foreign investment and air pollution: Do good governance and technological innovation matter? *Environmental Research*, *185*, 109469. https://doi.org/10.1016/j.envres.2020.109469

Rautio, N., Filatova, S., Lehtiniemi, H., & Miettunen, J. (2018). Living environment and its relationship to depressive mood: A systematic review. *International Journal of Social Psychiatry*, *64*(1), 92–103. https://doi.org/10.1177/0020764017744582

Ren, S., Hao, Y., & Wu, H. (2022). How does green investment affect environmental pollution? Evidence from China. *Environmental and Resource Economics*, *81*(1), 25–51. https://doi.org/10.1007/s10640-021-00615-4

Rosenblitt, J. C., Soler, H., Johnson, S. E., & Quadagno, D. M. (2001). Sensation seeking and hormones in men and women: Exploring the link. *Hormones and Behavior*, *40*(3), 396–402. https://doi.org/10.1006/hbeh.2001.1704

Schwarz, N., & Clore, G. L. (1983). Mood, misattribution, and judgments of well-being: Informative and directive functions of affective states. *Journal of Personality and Social Psychology*, *45*(3), 513–523. https://doi.org/10.1037/0022-3514.45.3.513

Shefrin, H., & Statman, M. (1985). The disposition to sell winners too early and ride losers too long: Theory and evidence. *Journal of Finance*, *40*(3), 777–790. https://doi.org/10.1111/j.1540-6261.1985.tb05002.x

Solomon, S., Plattner, G.-K., Knutti, R., & Friedlingstein, P. (2009). Irreversible climate change due to carbon dioxide emissions. *Proceedings of the National Academy of Sciences*, *106*(6), 1704–1709. https://doi.org/10.1073/pnas.0812721106

Su, C.-W., Wang, K.-H., Tao, R., & Lobonț, O.-R. (2019). The asymmetric effect of air quality on cross-industries' stock returns: Evidence from China. *Environmental Science and Pollution Research*, *26*(30), 31422–31433. https://doi.org/10.1007/s11356-019-06283-8

Sun, C., Luo, Y., & Li, J. (2018). Urban traffic infrastructure investment and air pollution: Evidence from the 83 cities in China. *Journal of Cleaner Production*, *172*, 488–496. https://doi.org/10.1016/j.jclepro.2017.10.194

Teng, M., & He, X. (2020). Air quality levels, environmental awareness and investor trading behavior: Evidence from stock market in China. *Journal of Cleaner Production*, *244*, 118663. https://doi.org/10.1016/j.jclepro.2019.118663

Tomei, F., Rosati, M. V., Ciarrocca, M., Baccolo, T. P., Gaballo, M., Caciari, T., & Tomao, E. (2003). Plasma cortisol levels and workers exposed to urban pollutants. *Industrial Health*, *41*(4), 320–326. https://doi.org/10.2486/indhealth.41.320

Weuve, J., Puett, R. C., Schwartz, J., Yanosky, J. D., Laden, F., & Grodstein, F. (2012). Exposure to particulate air pollution and cognitive decline in older women. *Archives of Internal Medicine*, *172*(3), 219–227. https://doi.org/10.1001/archinternmed.2011.683

World Health Organization. (2016). *Ambient air pollution: A global assessment of exposure and burden of disease*. World Health Organization. https://apps.who.int/iris/bitstream/handle/10665/250141/9789241511353-eng.pdf

World Health Organization. (2018). *World health statistics 2018: Monitoring health for the SDGs, sustainable development goals*. World Health Organization. https://apps.who.int/iris/handle/10665/272596

Wright, W. F., & Bower, G. H. (1992). Mood effects on subjective probability assessment. *Organizational Behavior and Human Decision Processes*, *52*(2), 276–291. https://doi.org/10.1016/0749-5978(92)90039-A

Wu, Q., Chou, R. K., & Lu, J. (2020). How does air pollution-induced fund-manager mood affect stock markets in China? *Journal of Behavioral and Experimental Finance*, *28*, 100399. https://doi.org/10.1016/j.jbef.2020.100399

Wu, Q., Hao, Y., & Lu, J. (2018a). Air pollution, stock returns, and trading activities in China. *Pacific-Basin Finance Journal*, *51*, 342–365. https://doi.org/10.1016/j.pacfin.2018.08.018

Wu, Q., & Lu, J. (2020). Air pollution, individual investors, and stock pricing in China. *International Review of Economics and Finance*, *67*, 267–287. https://doi.org/10.1016/j.iref.2020.02.001

Wu, X., Chen, S., Guo, J., & Gao, G. (2018b). Effect of air pollution on the stock yield of heavy pollution enterprises in China's key control cities. *Journal of Cleaner Production*, *170*, 399–406. https://doi.org/10.1016/j.jclepro.2017.09.154

Zeng, Y., Wang, F., & Wu, J. (2022). The impact of green finance on urban haze pollution in China: A technological innovation perspective. *Energies*, *15*(3), 801. https://doi.org/10.3390/en15030801

Zhang, D., Zhang, Z., & Managi, S. (2019). A bibliometric analysis on green finance: Current status, development, and future directions. *Finance Research Letters*, *29*, 425–430. https://doi.org/10.1016/j.frl.2019.02.003

Zhang, X., Tan, J., & Chan, K. C. (2021). Air pollution and initial public offering underpricing. *Applied Economics*, *53*(39), 4582–4595. https://doi.org/10.1080/00036846.2021.1904123

Zhang, Y., Jiang, Y., & Guo, Y. (2017). The effects of haze pollution on stock performances: Evidence from China. *Applied Economics*, *49*(23), 2226–2237. https://doi.org/10.1080/00036846.2016.1234703

Zhou, A., & Li, J. (2021). Analysis of the spatial effect of outward foreign direct investment on air pollution: Evidence from China. *Environmental Science and Pollution Research*, *28*(37), 50983–51002. https://doi.org/10.1007/s11356-021-13960-0

Appendix

Table A1 Summary table of relevant studies

Studies	Published in	Cited by	Year	Context	Dep variable	Dep variable source	AQI level	AQI frequency	AQI source	Main results	Psychological effect	Physiological effect
Air pollution and stock returns in the US	Journal of Economic Psychology	83	2011	United States	daily data on stock returns	Yahoo Finance	stock exchange	daily	AirData web sites	negative sentiment towards market	Yes	No
The stock market effect of air pollution: Evidence from China	Applied Economics	39	2016	China	demand for stocks (measured by rate of daily money inflow)	Wind Financial Terminal	16 big cities with a population of over 8 million	daily	The Ministry of Environmental Protection of People's Republic of China (MEPC)	negative sentiment towards market	Yes	Yes
Air pollution and stock returns: Evidence from a natural experiment	Journal of Empirical Finance	61	2016	Italy	daily return of Milan Stock Exchange index	World Federation of Exchanges and individual exchange websites	Milan	daily	three monitors in Milan Italian Environmental Protection Agency	reluctant to trade	Yes	No
The effects of haze pollution on stock performances: Evidence from China	Applied Economics	13	2017	China	stock returns and volatilities	Wind database	Beijing	hourly on trading days	website of US Department of State Air Quality Monitoring Program	reluctant to trade	Yes	Yes
Air pollution, stock returns, and trading activities in China	Pacific Basin Finance Journal	19	2018	China	daily stock returns, turnover, illiquidity, and volatility for each firm	Wind database and China Stock Market & Accounting Research (CSMAR) databases	city	daily	The MEPC	reluctant to trade	Yes	No
Study on the influence mechanism of air quality on stock market yield and volatility: Empirical test from China based on GARCH model	Finance Research Letters	13	2018	China	stock market yield; Snowball website comments	Wind database and Snowball website	national (calculated by average AQI of major trading cities)	daily	The MEPC	negative sentiment towards market	Yes	No

(Continued)

Studies	Published in	Cited by	Year	Context	Dep variable	Dep variable source	AQI level	AQI frequency	AQI source	Main results	Psychological effect	Physiological effect
The public environmental awareness and the air pollution effect in Chinese stock market	Journal of Cleaner Production	37	2018	China	Shenzhen Stock Exchange Index	Wind database	exchange center: Shanghai	daily	The MEPC	reluctant to trade	Yes	No
Effect of air pollution on the stock yield of heavy pollution enterprises in China's key control cities	Journal of Cleaner Production	41	2018	China	stock yield	CSMAR database	key cities	maximum daily in December	The MEPC	negative sentiment on market	Yes	Yes
The asymmetric effect of air quality on cross-industries' stock returns: Evidence from China	Environmental Science and Pollution Research	3	2019	China	stock return in nine industries	Shanghai Exchange Index	exchange center: Shanghai	daily	The MEPC	prefer green stocks	No	Yes
How does air pollution-induced fund-manager mood affect stock markets in China?	Journal of Behavioral and Experimental Finance	5	2020	China	stock price; stock liquidity	CSMAR database	city	daily	The MEPC	negative sentiment on market	Yes	No
Pollution and performance: Do investors make worse trades on hazy days?	Management Science	25	2020	China	trading performance, trading behaviors (estimated by return and holding of attention-grabbing stocks)	A large brokerage firm in China	city	daily	The MEPC	disposition effect	Yes	No
Air pollution, individual investors, and stock pricing in China	International Review of Economics and Finance	11	2020	China	individual investor mood (measured by air quality weighted by Baidu search volume)	Wind database and Baidu Search Index	city	daily	website of the Chinese Air Quality Study Platform	negative sentiment on market	Yes	Yes

Title	Journal	Citations	Year	Country	Dependent variable	Data source (financial)	Scope	Frequency	Data source (pollution)	Conclusion	Green	Control variables
Responsible investment in the Chinese stock market	Research in International Business and Finance	5	2020	China	holding preference	Shanghai Stock Exchange	national (measured by trading ratio times AQI of 31 provincial capitals)	daily	China National Environmental Monitoring Center (CNEMC)	preference for green stocks	Yes	No
Air quality levels, environmental awareness and investor trading behavior: Evidence from stock market in China	Journal of Cleaner Production	12	2020	China	variables directly measuring investor trading activities, including price volatility, stock turnover rate, stock illiquidity index, and rate of return	Wind database	city	daily	The MEPC	reluctant to trade	Yes	No
How air quality affect health industry stock returns: New evidence from the Quantile-on-Quantile regression	Frontiers in Public Health	0	2021	China	stock return	Shanghai Stock Exchange	exchange center: Shanghai	daily	The Ministry of Ecology and Environment of the People's Republic of China (MEEPRC)	preference for green stocks	Yes	No
Air pollution, behavioral bias, and the disposition effect in China	Journal of Financial Economics	15	2021	China	difference between the probability of selling winners and probability of selling losers	Center for Research in Security Prices (CRSP)	city	daily	The MEPC	disposition effect	Yes	No
The relationship between air pollution, investor attention and stock prices: Evidence from new energy and polluting sectors	Energy Policy	4	2021	China	stock price	China Center for Economic Research (CCER) and Baidu Search Index	national (by summing the provincial AQIs weighted by the number of stock accounts)	daily	The MEEPRC	no preference for green stocks	Yes	Yes
The effect of air quality and weather on the Chinese stock: Evidence from Shenzhen stock exchange	Sustainability (Switzerland)	2	2021	China	returns of the Shenzhen market	Infomax database	exchange center: Shenzhen	daily	The MEPC	negative sentiment towards market	Yes	No

(Continued)

Studies	Published in	Cited by	Year	Context	Dep variable	Dep variable source	AQI level	AQI frequency	AQI source	Main results	Psychological effect	Physiological effect
Air pollution, investor sentiment and excessive returns	Journal of Asset Management	0	2021	United States	portfolio return	Dr French's personal website	exchange center: NYC	daily	Environmental Protection Agency	more consumptions	Yes	No
Air pollution, local bias, and stock returns	Finance Research Letters	7	2021	China	stock return	CSMAR database	city	daily	The MEPC	mispricing	Yes	Yes
Does air pollution affect seasoned equity offering pricing? Evidence from investor bids	Journal of Financial Markets	1	2021	China	seasonal equity offers discounts	Oriental Fortune website, Wind database, and JiuchaoInformation website	bidder's location	daily (hourly averaged)	all air quality monitoring stations in China	mispricing	Yes	No
Does air pollution influence investor trading behavior? Evidence from China	Emerging Markets Review	4	2021	China	trading behaviors (measured by changes in investor portfolio)	Snowball website and China Stock Market and CSMAR database	city	daily	The MEPC	individual investors are more susceptible to air pollution	Yes	Yes
Air pollution and initial public offering underpricing	Applied Economics	4	2021	China	market-adjusted IPO underpricing	CSMAR database	city	daily	city-level environmental protection bureaus	mispricing	Yes	No
Does air pollution affect investor cognition and land valuation? Evidence from the Chinese land market	Real Estate Economics	1	2021	China	land price premiums	Landchina website	city	daily	The MEPC	mispricing	Yes	Yes
Environmental preference, air pollution, and fund flows in China	Pacific Basin Finance Journal	0	2022	China	fund flow (calculated using a formula)	CSMAR database	city	quarterly	the website of World Air Quality Index	preference for green funds	Yes	Yes

INDEX

Note: Page number in *italics* and **bold** indicates figure and table respectively.

AB Ignitis Group 132
academic research 35–36
acceleration depreciation scheme (ADS) 398
accounting, impact investment 227–240; developed and developing country standards, financial and impact assessment 238–240; developed/developing contexts 230–231; developing country standards on financial/impact rationales, influence of 236–238; double hybridity of impact investment 230–232; financial assessment, developed *vs.* developing countries 232, **233–234**, 235; financial/impact assessment 231; impact assessment, developed *vs.* developing countries 235–236; as mediating practice 229–230; sociology of 228–229, 241n1
actors 7–19, 23–27, 33, 43–44, 78–79
Adams, S. 303
adaptation finance **82**, 82–83, 452
adaptation financing deficit 486–487
adaptation projects **82**, 82–83
Adaui, C. R. L. 532
ADS *see* acceleration depreciation scheme
advocacy coalition framework theory 270
Africa 218, 220; *see also* green finance strategies in Africa
African Development Bank 75
agency theory 168
Agostini, M. 532
Agricultural Bank of China 291
air pollution (study) 542–555; affects investors 547–548; AQI 546–547; disposition effect 548; effects of 542, 547–548; environmental awareness 552–553; FDI 542; green financial instruments, investor preferences for 550–551; green investment 542; individual investors 546; initial search for 543–544; institutional investors 546; investment 542; measures of 546–547; and mispricing of assets (investors') 549–550; negative sentiments in financial market 548–549; OFDI 542; overview 542–543; and performance (investors') 542–543, 548–550; portfolios related to consumption, investor preferences for 551; and preferences (investors') 543, 550–551; psychological effects of 547; publishing journals 545–546, **545–546**; reference search for 544; research contexts 546; social relevance of 542; time trend of studies 544–545, *545*, **559–562**; and willingness to trade (investors') 543, 551–553
Air Quality Index (AQI) 546–547
Albuquerque, R. 467
Aldy, J. E. 90
Alessi, L. 205
Alford, R. R. 319
Alonso, A. C. 248
Alpermann, B. 275–276
Alvesson, M. 303
AMAC *see* Asset Management Association of China
Ameer, R. 169
An, N. 549
Anderson, A. 162
Aotearoa Circle 12–15
AQI *see* Air Quality Index
Arellano, M. 177, 199

563

Index

artifacts 9
ASEAN Green Bond Standard 393
Asia 218
ASSET4 Databases (Bloomberg and Thomson Reuters) 105–106
asset dating 158
Asset Management Association of China (AMAC) 287
assets under management (AUMs) 75–76
Available WAter REmaining (AWARE) Model 104, 107, 110–111, 126n20
Avramov, D. 464, 466

Bachelet, M. J. 193
Bakar, A. 169
Baker, M. 192
Bakker, Peter 23
Balvers, R. J. 467
Bancel, F. 517
Banga, J. 394, 397
Banking and Insurance Sector Green Finance Guidelines (CBIRC) 269
banking industry 337
Bank of China 291
bank size 343
Barerra, M. **499**
Barrett, S. 452
Battilana, J. 320
Baumler, J.V 88
BBGF 333
B Corp Certification 304
Bear, S. 341
Bebbington, J. 308
Bedendo, M. 518
Belt and Road Initiative (BRI), China 280, 289
Belt and Road Initiative International Green Development Coalition (BRIGC) 290
Bénabou, R. 464
Bento, N. 90
Berg, F. 463–464
Berrang-ford, L. **499**
Beta 134
Bhandary, R. R. 493, 498
Biesbroek, G. R. **499**
B Impact Assessment 304
Binti Ibrahim, S. A. 395
biodiversity 357–370; accurate *vs.* holistic impact measurement 365; basis of all life 358–359; databases/platforms for assessment of **368**; definition 357–358, **360**, 361–362; disclosure initiatives **363–366**; finance flows *361*; and financial sector 359, *359*, **360**; future research 367, 369; global financing needs to protect and restore *359*; importance of 358; long-term impact *vs.* short-term returns 365; loss 358–359; of measurement approaches/indicators 365, **366–367**; overview 357–358; practical implications 369–370; properties of nature *362*; reliable data, lack of 367; silent stakeholders, integration of 365
biodiversity credit (markets) **360**
Biodiversity Footprint for Financial Institutions (BFFI) **366**
biodiversity tax **360**
Biondi, L. 532
Bisaro, A. **499**
Bjorkholm, L. 251
Blazovich, J. L. 341
Blom, M. 303
Bloomberg and Thomson Reuters (ASSET4) Databases 105–106
Bloomberg ESG Index 108
Bloomberg New Energy Finance 77
blue/green bonds **360**
Blundell, R. 199
BNY Mellon 385
Bolivia 319; commercial microfinance in 320
Bolton R. 496
Bond, S. 177, 199
bonds markets 288, *289*
Boni, L. 527
Bonnefon, J.-F. 161
Bouwer, L. M. **499**
Bover, O. 199
BP 220
Brandstetter, L. 239, 302
Brazil 219
Brickman, P. 150
business ecosystems 9

Cai, R. 215
California Public Employees' Retirement System (US) 77
Cameron, David 309
Cameroon 318
capital asset pricing model (CAPM) 236, 467
capital expenditures 127n35, 172
Capitals Coalition 103
CAPM *see* capital asset pricing model
Caramichael, J. 193
carbon accounting 130
carbon assurance 131
Carbon Border Adjustment Mechanism (CBAM) 398
carbon dioxide (CO_2) 544
Carbon Disclosure Project (CDP) 42, 90, 129–130, **368**
carbon emissions 72n2
carbon fee 90, **91**, 92
carbon financing in China 269–270
carbon footprint 250
carbon management system (CMS) 129–131; conceptual framework for 131; descriptive

564

analysis of 135, **136–138**, 139; descriptive statistics 139, **140**; discussion on 143, 145; elements 131; firm's regulatory environment, moderating effects of 143, **144**; hypothesis development 132–133; literature 131–132; multivariate regression 140, **142**; research model 133–134; sample 134–135; univariate analysis 139–140, **141**
carbon monoxide (CO) 542
carbon-neutral bonds 267
carbon opportunities 130–131; physical 131; transitional 131
carbon performance 131
carbon tax policy 252
Carey, A. 301
Carney, Mark 447
Castellas, E. I.-P. 320
Catastrophe/disaster Bonds 513
CBAM *see* Carbon Border Adjustment Mechanism
CBI *see* Climate Bond Initiative
CBIRC *see* China Banking and Insurance Regulatory Commission
CBRC *see* China Banking Regulatory Commission
CBS *see* climate bond standards
CDP *see* Carbon Disclosure Project
CDSB *see* Climate Disclosure Standards Board
central banks 399, 447
Centre for International Climate Research (CICERO) 386, 519
CG *see* corporate governance
CGIR Climate Security Observatory (CSO) **368**
CGT *see* common ground taxonomy
Chang, V. 90
characterization pathways 125n2
Chartered Financial Analyst (CFA) ESG Standards 304
Chatterji, A. K. 464
Chauvey, J. N. 527
checkbox ticking 36
Chelli, M. 535
Chen, S. 521
Chen, T. 341
Cheng, L. T. 518
Chernobyl, USSR 377
Chih, H. 341
China 221, 542–555; *see also* air pollution (study)
China Banking and Insurance Regulatory Commission (CBIRC) 266, 275–276, 281
China Banking Regulatory Commission (CBRC) 281, 288
China Development Bank (CDB) 291
China Investment Corporation (CIC) 291
China National Green Development Fund 283
China Securities Regulatory Commission (CSRC) 270, 281

Chinese Air Pollution Prevention and Control Law 551
Chinese green bonds **267**, 267–268
Chouaibi, J. 169
Chouaibi, S. 169
Ciaian, P. 163
Cicchiello, A. F. 194, 206
CICERO *see* Centre for International Climate Research
City of London Corporation 215
Clarkson, P. M. 169
climate and environment-related financial risks 446–457; adaptation finance 456; adaptation finance/climate justice/vulnerability reduction 452; anthropogenic hazards 455–456; bibliometric analysis 448–449; credit provision/capital requirements/green policies as transition accelerators 454; credit risk/climate stress tests/financial stability 453–454; data collection 448; discussion of results 454; emerging financial risks 456; environmental performance and financial performance, relationship between 452–453; environmental risks/limited liability/moral hazard 453; findings *449*, 449–452, **450**, *451*; future research directions 455–456; interdisciplinarity 455; mitigation finance 456; overview 446–447; research methodology 447–449; search strings and query description *448*; tail risks 455–456
Climate Awareness Bond (CAB) 513
Climate Bond Initiative (CBI) 386, 400, 513, 515, 519
climate bond standards (CBS) 393
climate change 1–2, 7, 25, 44–45, *45*, 57–72, 189, 446, 512; asset pricing 58–59; central bank's balance sheet directly, impact on 57, **60**, 60–61; climate finance 75; constraints on firms 129; CSA 2, 57–58, 61–71; environmental-related risks 446–447; evaluation 71–72; event-driven risks 446; financial risks 446–447; green finance for fight against 1–2, 149, 215–216, 222–225; mitigation 317; outlook 71–72; Paris Agreement on 3, 24, 82; physical risks 57; risk analysis 59–60; risk management 57; risks 58–59; stress testing 59–60; transition risks 57; US investment on climate concerns 512
Climate Change Act 2008, UK **529**
Climate Change Response (Zero-Carbon) Amendment Act 2019 (New Zealand) 7–8
Climate Disclosure Standards Board (CDSB) 27–28, 42, 304
climate finance 75–76; financial institutions in 76, *76*; geographic dimension of PFIs' 79–91,

80; market failures 77; MDBs 76, *81*, 81–82, **82**; NDBs 76; PFIs in 75–83, *76*; private investors in *76*, 77–78, *78*; public 78–79; SIBs 76
climate funds 76, 77
climate justice 452
climate opportunities 129–130
Climate Prototype 28
climate scenario analysis (CSA) 2, 57–58, 61–71; application of **66**, 66–71; credit risk **68**, 68–69, 73n9; to DNB's profit projections *67*, 67–68, **68**; interest rate risk 68, 73n8; market risk 69–71, **71**; objective of 61; top-down approach 58, 62–66, *63–66*
climate stress tests 453–454
CMBF1 328–329
CMBF2 330–331
CMS *see* carbon management system
Cochu, A. 394
co-citation analysis 496, **499**, *500*
Cohen, Ronald 304
Colombage, S. 193
commensuration 229
common ground taxonomy (CGT) 293
Community Score (*CommunityScore*) 172
Company Act 2006, UK **529**
complementary fit 156
conflicting goals 162–163
Contingent Valuation Method (CVM) 106
Conway, E. 532
Cooper, C. 302–303
COP26 Accord in 2021 216
Corfee-Morlot, J. **499**
Cornett, M. M. 341
corporate board 342
corporate environmental impact 104; accounting and stock market data 107; AWARE model 107; Bloomberg and Thomson Reuters (ASSET4) Databases 105–106; calculation 111; discount factor analysis 112; discussion 123–124; distribution of 113, *113*; dynamic materiality of **120**, 120–121; environmental ratings 104–105, **118**, 118–119; EPS database 106; Exiobase 106, 126n24; financial materiality of 119–123; GICS industries data 108; imputation of missing values 109–110; by industry *122*, 122–123; market prices 105, 119–120, **120**; operating income by industry 116, *116*; outcome 112–123; overview 103–105; returns/risk 121, **121**; robustness of imputations 111–112; sales by industry 115, *115*; sample selection 108–109, **109**; SDGs 116, *117*, 118; sources of variation in 114, **114**; statistics 112–116; of water 110–111; Waterfund's Global Water Price data 107

corporate governance (CG) 134
corporate governance variables 343
corporate green bonds 192–193; academic literature on 515–518; company outcomes 518–519; credit profile 513; determinants of issuing 515–518; discussion on 521–523; environmental outcomes 519–521; market 512, 514–515; suggestions for further research 521–523; as tool for financing greener future 513–523
corporate green culture 133
Corporate Reporting Dialogue 103
corporate social reporting 220
corporate social responsibility (CSR) 300, 337; in banking industry 337–338, 341–352; control variables 343; and corporate governance variables 343; correlation matrix **346**; data 343–344; definition 341; discussion of results 350–351; limitations 351; outcome 344, 350; performance measures of bank 342–343; Principles for Responsible Banking 337–341; regression results **348–349**; UNEP FI 337–338; univariate tests **347**
corporate sustainability 41–43, 300; materiality in 43–53; and sustainability case for business 41–42; sustainability reporting 41–42
Corporate Sustainability Reporting Directive (CSRD) 25, 30–31, 49, **363**, 365, 399, 431–432, 526, **530**, 531–532
Cosma, S. 532
Costa, E. 532
cost of capital argument 191
credit markets 287–288
credit risk **68**, 68–69, 73n9, 453–454
Cremasco, C. 527
cross-dependence test 198, **198**
crude oil 220
cryptocurrencies 163
CSA *see* climate scenario analysis
CSR *see* corporate social responsibility
CSRC *see* China Securities Regulatory Commission
CSRD *see* Corporate Sustainability Reporting Directive
CSR Strategy Score (*CSRScore*) 172
CVM *see* Contingent Valuation Method

Daddi, T. 401
Dafermos, Y. 454
Danish Act (no.1403) **529**
Dasgupta Report 357
Datt, R. 131
DCF *see* discounted cash flow
debt-for nature swaps **360**
De Mariz, F. 522
Democratic Republic of Congo (DRC) 219, 222

De Nederlandsche Bank (DNB) 58
Desai, H. B. 169
Deschryver, P. 522
Development and Reform Commissions (DRCs) 283
de Zwaan, L. 162
difference-in-difference (DiD) model 548
difference-in-Hansen test 201
Dikau, S. 454
Ding, X. 549
direct emissions 125n7
Directive 2003/51/EC ("Modernisation Directive") 29, **530**
Directive 2014/95/EU (NFRD) 25, 167, **530**, 531–532
discounted cash flow (DCF) 231, 236
dispersed actors 23
disposition effect 548
disruptive innovation theory 272
dividends 127n35
domestic violence 423
Dorado, S. 320
Doshi, D. 82
double-hybridity 228; in developed/developing contexts 230–232; financial assessment 231–232; impact assessment 231–232; of impact investment 230–232
double inequity 452
double materiality 44–45, *45*; for sustainability reporting 44–45, *45*; value of 50–51
DRCs *see* Development and Reform Commissions
Drucker, P. F. 41
Du, S. 170
Du, X. 549
Dual Carbon goals 265–266, 276
Dukan, M. 255
Dunn, Elizabeth 150–151
Dutordoir, M. 516–517
dynamic materiality 45–46, *46*; of environmental intensity **120**, 120–121

Eakin, H. 496
earnings before interest, taxes, depreciation, and amortization (EBITDA) 132, 231
$EBIT_{it}$ 172
Eccles, R. G. 88
EconFree 172
economic value added (EVA) 231
ecosystems 8–9; business 9; collaborative qualities of 9; entrepreneurial 8–11; innovation 9
Edison, Thomas Alva 512
EFRAG *see* European Financial Reporting Advisory Group
Ehlers, T. 248, 518–519
EI *see* environmental intensity
electricity certificates (EC) system 254–256

electricity quota obligation 254
Elie, L. 253
Elliott, G. 199
Emission Reduction Score (*EmissionScore*) 171
emission trading systems (ETS) 90, **91**, 92, 130, 517
Emmanuel, C. R. 88
energy generation, investments in 317–318
Energy Taxation Directive (ETD) 398
entrepreneurial ecosystem in sustainable finance 8–11
Environment Agency Pension Fund (UK) 77
environmental, social, and governance (ESG) investments 149–150, 158–161, *160–161*, 167–185, 463–480; agency theory 168; companies by economic sector, sample analysis of 180, **183**, 183–184; companies by industry, sample analysis of 180, **181–182**; criteria and stock financial returns 467–473; descriptive statistics 173, **174–176**, 177; disclosures 168–185; discussion 473–479; and economic performance 168; empirical studies **470–473**, *474*, **475–478**; on firm performance 170–184; four-fund separation 465–466; fundamentals, predictability of 464–465; and investor demand 465–467; investor segmentation 466; LCM 169; legitimacy theory 169; market value 170; multivariate analysis for whole sample 177, **178–179**, 180; responsibilities 168; and risk 467; signaling theory 169; source of information 170–171; theoretical framework 168–170; three-fund separation 465; uncertainty around 466–467; variables 171–173
environmental accounting 301–302
environmental intensity (EI) 104; accounting and stock market data 107; AWARE model 107; Bloomberg and Thomson Reuters (ASSET4) Databases 105–106; calculation 111; definition 112; discount factor analysis 112; discussion 123–124; distribution of 113, *113*; dynamic materiality of **120**, 120–121; of emissions 111; environmental ratings 104–105, **118**, 118–119; EPS database 106; Exiobase 106, 126n24; financial materiality of 119–123; GICS industries data 108; imputation of missing values 109–110; by industry *122*, 122–123; market prices 105, 119–120, **120**; operating income by industry 116, *116*; outcome 112–123; overview 103–105; returns/risk 121, **121**; robustness of imputations 111–112; sales by industry 115, *115*; sample selection 108–109, **109**; SDGs 116, *117*, 118; sources of variation in 114, **114**; statistics 112–116; of water 110–111; Waterfund's Global Water Price data 107

environmental liabilities 453
environmental outputs 104
environmental performance pillar score (*ENV*) 134
Environmental Priority Strategies (EPS) Database 104, 106
environmental ratings 104–105
Environmental Rights Financing Tools (PBOC) 269
environmental risk 453
environmental score (*EScore*) 171
epistemic community 313n5
Equator Principles 289
Equity REITS 126n32
Eriksen, S. H. 496
Erragraguy, E. 466, 475
ESG-aware 466
ESG lovers 466
ESRS *see* European Sustainability Reporting Standards
ETD *see* Energy Taxation Directive
ethical-/faith-based investments 149
ethical investment 228
ETS *see* emission trading systems
EU *see* European Union
EU Emission Trading System (EU ETS) 398–399
EUGBS *see* European Green Bond Standard
European Central Bank (ECB) 398
European companies 35
European Financial Reporting Advisory Group (EFRAG) 26, 31–32, 42, 49–50
European green bond market: barriers to growth 394; coercive pressure on green bond issuers 397–399; green and sustainability-linked bond data review 401–406; from institutional perspective 396–401; mimetic pressure on green bond issuers 400–401; normative pressure on green bond issuers 399–400; organisational field 397, *397*; propositions 406–409
European green bonds 192
European Green Bond Standard (EUGBS) 391, 393–395; barriers to green bond market growth 394; current green bond literature 394–395; EU taxonomy 398
European Green Deal 393, 526
European Investment Bank (EIB) 513
European Single Electronic Format (ESEF) regulation 31
European Sustainability Reporting Standards (ESRS) 26, 32–33
European Union (EU): Commission 25, 29; CSRD 25, 30–31, **364**, 365, 431–432, 526, **530**; Directive 2003/51/EC ("Modernisation Directive") 29, **530**; Directive 2014/95/EU (NFRD) 25, **530**, 531–532; EUGBS 391, 393–395;

Financing Sustainable Growth, action plan on 24–25; 'Fit for 55' policy 398–399; GBS 190; *vs.* IFRS sustainability standards 32–33, **34**; non-financial reporting directive 23, 29–30, 42, 49, 431–432, 526; regulations 25, *26*; SDGs 167; SFDR 25, **530**; SR measures 526–538; on sustainability challenges 167; Taxonomy Regulation 25, *26*
European Union Business @ Biodiversity Platform **364**
EU Taxonomy Regulation 25
EVA *see* economic value added
EXIM banks 75
Exiobase 106, 126n24
expectancy-value theory 151
experience *vs.* things 151
Exploring Natural Capital Opportunities, Risks and Exposure (ENCORE) **366**
Export-Import Bank for China (China Exim Bank) 291

Fatica, S. 192, 197–198, 203, 394, 493, 520
FDI *see* foreign direct investment
feed-in tariff (FIT) 253, 261n6
Feinberg, M. 155
Feller, A. 218
Fernando, C. S. 467
Final Regulation Section 482, (US) 97n1
finance-first logics 324, **325–327**, 328
Finance for Biodiversity Initiative (F4B) **364**
Finance for Biodiversity Pledge **364**
finance for nature-based solutions **360**
financial goals 152–154; abstraction, overcoming 153–154; concrete 152–153; higher-value 154–156; primary 152; SMART 152
financial license 162
financial literacy 162
Financial Markets Authority (FMA) 2
financial materiality *see* single materiality
financial stability 453–454
financial system 8–9; public financial institutions in 75–83, *76*
financiers 418
financing gap 486–487
Fink, Larry 50
firm outward foreign direct investment (OFDI) 542
firm size 127n35, 134, 172
firm value (*LnFV*) 171
FIT *see* feed-in tariff
'Fit for 55' policy 398–399
fit frameworks 156
Flammer, C. 191, 395, 517, 520
FMA *see* Financial Markets Authority
Ford, J. D. **499**
foreign direct investment (FDI) 220–224, 542

Forest Bonds 513
Foxton T. J. 496
France 527
Friedland, R. 319
Fukushima Daiichi plant, Japan 378
funders 418

GABV *see* Global Alliance for Banking on Values
Gao, Y. 551
García-Sánchez, I.-M. 341
Garschagen, M. 82
GBP *see* Green Bond Principles
GBS *see* Green Bond Standard
gemstones 220
General Least Squared Dickey-Fuller test 199, **199**
general method of moments (GMM) 199
General Requirements Prototype 28
Gen III reactors 378, 383
Ghana 220, 317–334; *see also* green finance strategies in Africa
Ghana's Securities and Exchange Commission (SEC) 322–323
GHG *see* greenhouse gas
Gianfrate, G. 192
GICS *see* Global Industry Classification System
GIIN *see* Global Impact Investing Network
GIIN (IRIS+) 304
GIIN Annual Impact Investor Survey reports 228
Gioia, D. A. 318, 323
Glavas, D. 516–517
Global Alliance for Banking on Values (GABV) 261n2
Global Biodiversity Model for Support (GLOBIO) **366**
Global Climate Risk Index (*GCRI*) 134–135
global economy 1
Global Financial Crisis (2008) 17, 57–58
Global Impact Investing Network (GIIN) 300, 317, 417
Global Industry Classification System (GICS) 108–109
Global Reporting Initiative (GRI) 23, 30, 42, 47–48, 103, **363**, 527; Sector Standards 47–48; Topic Standards 48; Universal Standards 47
Global Reporting Initiative (GRI) standards 304
Global Steering Group (GSG) 304
global supply chains (GSCs) 218–222
Global Sustainability Standards Board (GSSB) 28, 30
global value chains (GVCs) 218–222
global warming 216
Global Water Price data (Waterfund) 107
GLPs *see* Green Loan Principles
GMM *see* general method of moments
goal-striving behavior 153
Godemann, J. 528

Gompers, P. 465
government score (*GScore*) 171
government subsidy policy 252
Green, J. 90
green and sustainability-linked bond data review 401–406; green targets and covenants 406, 415; propositions 406–409; rating, external review and reporting standards *404–405*, 404–406; risk factors *402*, 402–404; use of proceeds 401–402
green balance sheet 251–252, *252*
green banks 247
Green Bond Indices 519
green bond market: barriers to growth 394; coercive pressure on green bond issuers 397–399; from institutional perspective 396–401; mimetic pressure on green bond issuers 400–401; normative pressure on green bond issuers 399–400; organisational field 397, *397*
green bond policy 252
Green Bond Principles (GBP) 190, 385, 393, 519
Green Bond Project Endorsed Catalogue 286–287
green bonds 189–208, 264, 391–410; in China **267**, 267–268, 280–296; climate bond standards 393; concepts 513–515; *vs.* conventional bonds 193–195; corporate 192–193; COVID-19 outbreak 191, 194–195, 201, **202–203**; credit risk profiles 190; cross-dependence test 198, **198**; dataset of 195–197, **197**; definition 392; determinants of issuing corporate 515–518; discussion on 203–207; dynamic panel estimations **200–201**; empirical results 198–203; European 192; frameworks 393; GBP 190, 385, 393; green and sustainability-linked bond data review 401–406; green label on 191; hypotheses 192–195; issuance for 192; and macroeconomic variables 196–197, **197**; market 190–193, 392–393; methodological approach 197–198; motivational factors to participate in market 395–396; peculiarities of 191; policy implications 207–208; premium 191–195, 197–198; pricing 192, 395; by private issuers 193; regulations 393; standard (European) 393–395; stock market reactions to 395; supply/demand 190; *vs.* synthetic conventional bonds premium 192; trends 513–515, **514**; unit root tests 199, **199**; UN Principles for Responsible Banking 194–195; vaccine announcement 194–195, 201, **204–205**; yields 197–198
Green Bond Standard (GBS) 190
Green Climate Fund (GCF) 81–82, 317
green convertible bonds 513

Index

green credit veto system 291
Green Deal 24–25, 167, 526
green development 252
Green Development Guidance 289
green finance 1–2, 149, 215–216, 222–225, 248, 264, 337; in Africa 317–334; building theory on 3; challenges 222–223; in China 265–277; comprehensiveness of reports 223; critical perspectives 3; definitions 215, 251, 265; FDI 221–223; as game changer 222–224; goals 337; industry sectors 264; instruments and their effects 2; market and regulatory environments 1–2; products/services 264; for SDGs 264, 337; sector and country-specific perspectives 2; self-certification 223; in United Kingdom 264; in United States 264
green finance in China 265–277, 280–296; advocacy coalition framework theory 270; in Belt and Road Initiative 289, *292*; bonds markets 288, *289*; carbon finance 269–270; carbon-neutral bonds 267; central banking 286; from central to local levels 281, *282–283*, 283–284; credit markets 287–288; definition 265; disruptive innovation theory 272; environmental information disclosure **268**, 268–269, 287; financial institutions 291–293; five pillars of 266; functions 266; global green finance research 294–295; governing bodies 283, *283*; green bonds **267**, 267–268; green credit/loans 266–267; green rural revitalization 267; guidelines on 274–275, 281; historical context 281; institutional change theory 271; in international comparison 284, *285*, 286; international coordination for 293–294, *294*; international role in 288–294, *289*; market 265; medium-term lending facility 286; MPA 286; multilevel governance theory 271; overseas activities 289–293; overseas regulators 290–291; overview 265–266, 280–281; path dependence theory 270; PBOC aims 266, 281–282; pilot zones 283, *285*; policy 272–276, **273**; policy diffusion theory 271; policy learning theory 271; policy network theory 272; politics of policy change 272; with public capital 284; punctuated equilibrium theory 271; reform theory 272; stages 281, *282*; standing lending facility 286; sustainability linked bonds 267; taxonomies 286–287; theories of public policy change 270–272, 275–276; top-down approach to 265, 281–286; unified system for 265

green finance strategies in Africa 317–334; capital market-based impact investment funds **324**; data analytic structure *323*; energy generation, investments in 317–318; ESG strategies 318, 321, 330; finance-first logic 324, **325–327**, 328; green start-up businesses 318; hybrid institutional logics 321, 328–332; impact-first institutional logics 332; impact investment 317–334; implication for research 332–333; overview 317–319; policy and practice, implication for 333; research methodology 322–324; SMEs 318, 323–333; theoretical motivation *319*, 319–322, *322*
Green Generation segment 132
green gilts 264
greenhouse gas (GHG) 125n9, 129, 250, 254
Green Industry Catalogue 286–287
green investment policy 252
Green Investment Principles (GIP) 289
greenium 190–195, 205, 376, 395, 516–517, 521
Green Loan Principles (GLPs) 247, 385–386
green loans 246–260; bank's profitability/sustainability goals 248–251; characteristics of 247; in China 266–267; definitions 247–248, 251; framework 258–260, *259*; green balance sheet 251–252, *252*; market mechanisms 254–256; needs of society 256–257; overview 247–248; principles 247; public policies 252–254; science and technology development 257–258; size estimation, bottom-up approach to 247; utilization 251
green municipal bonds 193–194
green nuclear 380–386; construction and site impact 380–381; fuel supply 381; governments/regulators opinions on 384–385; green finance, third parties offering guidelines on 385–386; operation 381; opinions on 383–386; safety 382–383, *383*; waste disposal and decommissioning 382
green quantitative easing (QE) program 454
green rural revitalization 267
green start-up businesses 318
Green Transition Bonds 513
greenwashing 193, 394, 515, 519
Gregory, A. 464
Grenelle 2 law (no 2010-788 article 225), France **529**
GRI *see* Global Reporting Initiative
Grimshaw, J. 218
GRI Standards 28
gross domestic product per capita (*GDPPC*) 134
Grougiou, V. 341–342
growth 134
GSCs *see* global supply chains

570

GSG-NAB Japan 309–310
GSSB *see* Global Sustainability Standards Board
Guo, J. 215
Guo, K. 550
Guterres, Antonio 184
GVCs *see* global value chains

Hachenberg, B. 518
Hadaś-Dyduch, M. 517
Haddaway, N. R. 464, 467
Hafner, S. 252, 493, 496
Halimanjaya, A. 82
Han, L. 551
happiness 150–151
Harjoto, M. A. 341
Harnack, K. 152
He, R. 130
He, X. 552–553
hedonic pricing 106, 125n18
Hehenberger, L. 320
Heidrich, O. **499**
Heinkel, R. 467
Henstra, D. **499**
Heymann, S. J. **499**
High Conservation Value (HCV) **367**
higher-value goals 154–156; values 154–155, *155*; values signal direction 155–156
Hinkley Point C nuclear station 379–380
Hirshleifer, J. 88
Homroy, S. 521
Hong, H. 466, 473, 475
household violence rates 423
Howlett, M. **499**
Huang, K. 466, 475
Huang, Z. 548–549, 552
Huitema, D. **499**
human behavior 156
Human Rights Category Score (*HRightsScore*) 171–172
Hyun, S. 192, 392

IASB *see* International Accounting Standards Board
ICMA *see* International Capital Market Association
ICP *see* internal carbon pricing
IFC Environmental and Social Performance Standards (World Bank) **363**
IFRS *see* International Financial Reporting Standards
IFRS Foundation 29, 49
IFRS sustainability (IFRS S) 28, 32–34
IIRC *see* International Integrated Reporting Council
impact 125n1; accounting 301–302; culture 304; materiality 44
Impact Institute 103

impact investment 168, 189, 227–230; assessment 231–232, 235–240; defined 302; in developed/developing countries 230–240; double hybridity of 230–232; financial assessment 231–235; generic impact criteria 231; in Ghana 317; in Nigeria 317; quantification of 230; *see also* green bank bonds
impact investment in Japan 300–312; collective norm entrepreneurs in 309–311; rapid development of 308–309; Social Impact Bond (SIB) 309, 313n9; Social Impact Measurement Initiative (SIMI) 309
impact measurement 417; agencies use 418; beneficiaries and consumers use of 418–419; benefits of 417; bounded rationality to 419; costs 419; discussion 423–425; financiers 418; funders 418; general and differing costs of 420–423; housing metrics 421–423; materiality with heterogeneous stakeholders 417–419; net benefits of 420, *420*, *422*; purpose of 417; social purpose organizations 418
Impact Measurement Project (IMP) 304, 306
Impact Reporting and Investment Standards (ISIS) Measurement Catalog 417
*IndexESG*1 171
Index of Economic Freedom (Heritage Foundation) 171
India 221
indirect emissions 125n8
indoor air quality 423
Industrial and commercial bank of China (ICBC) 291
INGOs *see* international non-governmental organizations
innovation ecosystem 9
Innovation Score (*InnovationScore*) 171
inside-out materiality 44–45, *45*
institutional change theory 271
institutional logics *319*, 319–320; finance-first 320–321, 324, **325–327**, 328; hybrid 321, 328–330; impact-first 320–321
institutional voids 230, 232
institutions 9
interdisciplinarity 455
Intergovernmental Panel on Climate Change (IPCC) 399–400, 502–503
Intergovernmental Science-Policy Platform on Biodiversity and Ecosystem Services (IPBES) 358
internal carbon pricing (ICP) 87, 89–97; benefits 87; carbon fee 90, **91**, 92; contextual variables 92–95, *94*; dynamic, framework of *94*; efficiency gains 96–97; emission trading systems 90, **91**, 92; implementation, reasons for 90; methods 90, **91**, 92; in

Index

Microsoft Inc. *93*; and performance 96–97; as self-regulatory mechanism 90; shadow price 90, **91**, 92; for signaling purposes 90; transfer pricing 92–97; in Volvo Cars AB *93*
International Accounting Standards Board (IASB) 27
International Capital Market Association (ICMA) 190, 400, 513
International Finance Corporation (IFC) 274, 322, 513
International Financial Reporting Standards (IFRS) 24, 27–29, 32–33, **34**, 42
International Integrated Reporting Council (IIRC) 23, 42, 304
International Monetary Fund 223
international non-governmental organizations (INGOs) 227
International Organization for Standardization (ISO) 125n14
International Platform for Sustainable Finance (IPSF) 293
International Standard Industrial Classification Revision 3.1 (ISIC) 126n22
International Sustainability Standards Board (ISSB) 27–29, 42, 52, 236–237, **363**; CDSB 27–28; institutional background 27–28; sustainability reporting, approach towards 28–29; VRF 27
investment goals 152–154; abstraction, overcoming 153–154; concrete 152–153; higher-value 154–156; primary 152
investments 150–151
Ioannou, I. 131
IPBES *see* Intergovernmental Science-Policy Platform on Biodiversity and Ecosystem Services
IPCC *see* Intergovernmental Panel on Climate Change
IRIS+ 304
Islam, M. A. 302
ISO 14007/14008 Protocols 103, 125n17
ISO 26000 30
ISSB *see* International Sustainability Standards Board
IUCN **364**
IUCN Red List of Threatened Species **368**

Jafri, J. 221
Japan International Cooperation Agency 309
Jiang, Z. 550
Jizi, M. I. 342
Jo, H. 341, 551
Jung, J. 250

Kacperczyk, M. 466, 473, 475
Kapraun, J. 192, 198, 208

Karpf, A. 193–194, 518
Kaufmann, D. 171
Keenan, J. M. 493
Keller, J. 157–158
Kesberg, R. 157–158
key performance indicators (KPI) 29
keywords 448–452, *449*, **450**, *451*
Kim, S.-J. 177
Kitzing, L. 255
Klassen, R. D. 464, 473
know your customer (KYC) 329
Kohers, T. 341
Korca, Blerita 532
Kotsantonis, S. 95
KPI *see* key performance indicators
Kramer, M. R. 465
Kuh, T. 45
Kuo, J. 90, 96
KYC *see* know your customer

landscape funds **360**
Larcker, D. F. 191
Larrinaga, C. 308, 528, 534, 536
Lash, J. 129
Latin America 218
Lau, P. T. 192
Law 118/2005, Italy 526, **529**
Law on Energy Transition for Green Growth (no 2015-992, article 225-105), France **529**
LCM *see* lifecycle management theories
Lebelle, M. 519
Lee, J. 177
LEGAL 134
legitimacy theory 169
Lehner, O. 418
Lehner, O. M. 169, 239, 251, 302
Leikas, S. 158
Lepori, G. M. 552
Lesnikowski, A. **499**
LEV 134
leverage 127n35, 172
Levy, T. 548
Li, J. 548
Li, P. 517
Li, Q. 552
lifecycle management theories (LCM) 169
Liu, Y. 551–552
Lo, A. W. 96
loan growth 343
Loffier, C. 89
Loffler, K. U. 193, 396, 517
logics 319–320; finance-first 324, **325–327**, 328; hybrid institutional logics 321, 328–330
Loh, L. 169
low-carbon and climate-resilient (LCR) development 76–77
Lu, J. 552

Index

Luo, H. A. 467
Luo, L. 130–131, 133

Ma, J. 90, 96, 284
Mabuga Project 328
MacAskill, S. 205, 207
Macfarlane, L. 220, 224–225
macroprudential assessment (MPA) 286
Macura, B. 464, 467
Macve, R. 301
Mair, J. 320
Malaysia 221
Maltais, A. 396
Management Score (*ManagementScore*) 172
Mandel, A. 193–194, 518
Māori leadership 11, 13–14
market failures 77
Markowitz, H. M. 465
materiality 42–43, 418; double 44–45, *45*, 50–51; dynamic 45–46, *46*; EFRAG 49–50; future outlook 51–53; in GRI framework 47–48; with heterogeneous stakeholders 417–419; IFRS Foundation 49; impact 44; SASB 48–49; single 43–44; understanding of 43
Matuszak, L. 532
Maurel, C. 239
Mazzucato, M. 493, 496
McLaughlin, C. P. 464, 473
MDBs *see* multilateral development banks
medium-term lending facility (MLF) 286
Mehafdi, M. 88
Memorandum of Understanding (MoU) 28
Mensi, W. 195, 206
Metz, A. 320
Mez, L. 380
Michaelowa, A. 82
Michelsen, G. 528
Microsoft Inc. *93*
middle-ground approach 237
MiFID assessment 162
MiFID II amendment 149
Milan Stock Exchange (MSE) 552
Mion, G. 532
MK_{it} 172
MLF *see* medium-term lending facility
Modugu, K. P. 170
Mogapi, E. M. 321
monetary hedonics 150
monetary utility 150–151
Moody's Green Bond Assessments 519
Moons, S. 152
moral hazard 453
Morningstar 168
Mortazavi, S. 498
mortgage industry 232
MoU *see* Memorandum of Understanding

MPA *see* macroprudential assessment
MSCI 104–105; environmental rating 119; global green bonds 195; sectoral green bonds 195
MSE *see* Milan Stock Exchange
Muellner, N. 380
multilateral development banks (MDBs) 75; climate finance 76, *81*, 81–82; mitigation finance and adaptation finance, and countries' CO_2 emissions and vulnerability **82**
multilevel governance theory 271
municipal green bond 192
Muntifering, M. 551
Myanmar 219

Naeem, M. A. 194–195
Nanayakkara, M. 193
National Development and Reform Commission (NDRC) 274, 281
national development banks (NDBs) 76
National Institute Global Econometric Model (NiGEM) 58
National Institute of Economic and Social Research 58
nationally determined contributions (NDCs) 7
natural capital 357, 362
Natural Capital Finance Alliance (NCFA) **364**
natural hazard 452
Nature and Biodiversity Benchmark **367**
NDBs *see* national development banks
NDCs *see* nationally determined contributions
NDRC *see* National Development and Reform Commission
negotiation process 88
net water consumed 125n10
Network for Greening the Financial System (NGFS) 289, 293, **364**
Net-Zero Banking Alliance 194
net-zero CO_2 emissions 216, 221–223
New Deal *see* Green Deal
New Zealand: Climate Change Response (Zero-Carbon) Amendment Act 2019 7–8; FMA 2; sustainable finance ecosystem, Aotearoa 1–2, 7–19
NFI-Directive 30
NFRD *see* Non-Financial Reporting Directive
Nicholls, Alex 302
NiGEM *see* National Institute Global Econometric Model
Nigeria 220
Nikolaidi, M. 454
Nilsson-Lindén, H. 169
nitrogen dioxide (NO_2) 542
nitrogen oxide (NO_x) 106
Nofsinger, J. R. 466, 475
Nomenclature of Economic Activities (NACE) industry 109

Non-Financial Reporting Directive (NFRD) 23, 29–30, 49, 431–432, 526, 531–532
non-financial value 227
non-performing loan (NPL) ratio 288
Nordic banks 246–249, 261n1; business model of 249; credit risk assessment of industries 250; TCFD, committed to 249
norm entrepreneurs 307
North American Industry Classification System (NAICS) 126n22
Norway 254
Nouvelles Regulations Economiques (NRE) law (no. 2001-420, Article 116) 526, **530**, 530–531
nuclear fission 377, 381
nuclear power 374–387; basic technology 377; brief history 377–378; construction and site impact 380–381; construction problems in Europe and United States **379**; energy security 378; financing of 378–380; fuel supply 381; green 380–386; as heat source 377; investment risks and their management **379**; operation 381; opinions on green nuclear 383–386; private finance for 376; renaissance 377–378; safety 382–383, *383*; waste disposal and decommissioning 382; in world energy (today and future prospects) 375–376, **375–376**
nuclear radiation 382–383
nuclear renaissance 377–378
nuclear waste 382
NVivo 12 software 12
NWB Bank 79
Nykvist, B. 396

Obradovich, N. 394
OFDI *see* firm outward foreign direct investment
Olazabal, M. **499**
OLS model 114, 119–120, **120**
OMOs *see* open market operations
online survey 151–152
open market operations (OMOs) 72n7
outputs 125n4
outside-in materiality *see* single materiality
ozone (O₃) 542

Packer, F. 518–519
Palander, S. 106
Panda–Dragon paradox 280, 295
Panzica, R. 493
Paris Accord in 2015 216
Paris Agreement 3, 24, 82, 269, 317–318
Park, S. K. 392
particulate matter (PM) 542
Partnership for Biodiversity Accounting Financials (PBAF) **364**

Pástor, Ľ. 465–466, 475, 479–480
path dependence theory 270
Patten, D. M. 180
PBOC *see* People's Bank of China
PEA *see* public environmental awareness
Pearce, J. 380
Pedersen, L. H. 465–466, 475
Peng, C. H. 552
Penna, C. C. R. 493, 496
People's Bank of China (PBOC) 265–267, 275–276; Environmental Rights Financing Tools 269; Green Bond Project Endorsed Catalogue 286–287; green finance policies in China 281–282; guidance for banks on environmental risks 287–288; task force 281
Peri, M. 192
person–investment fit (P–I fit) 156–158, 163; complementary 156; creation 156–157; regulatory fit *157*, 157–158; supplementary 156
Pesaran, M. H. 199
Petersen, M. A. 199
PFIs *see* public financial institutions
Pham, L. 392
physical carbon opportunities 131
plural logics 320
policy diffusion theory 271
Policy Energy Efficiency Score (*EnergyPolicyScore*) 172
policy entrepreneurs 10–11
Policy Environmental Supply Chain Score (*SupplyChainScore*) 172
policy learning theory 271
policy network theory 272
Policy Sustainable Packaging Score (*PackagingScore*) 172
Policy Water Efficiency Score (*WaterPolicyScore*) 172
political steering theory 276
Porter, M. E. 464–465
Power, M. 304
power purchase agreements (PPAs) 256
Pradhan, M. 237
PRB *see* Principles for Responsible Banking
premium, green bank bonds 191–195
prevention focus 157
prevention-oriented goals 157
price-to-book value of equity 107, 119–121, **120**, 124
Principles for Responsible Banking (PRB) 249, 337–341, *339*; impact analysis 339; implementation 339–341; public reporting 340–341; supervisory actions 341; target-setting and implementation 339–340
private climate finance 76, 77–78, *78*
Product Responsibility Score (*ProductScore*) 172

Project Task Force on European Sustainability Reporting Standards (PTF-ESRS) 49
promotion focus 157
promotion-oriented goals 157
prosocial spending 151
prospect theory 149
PTF-ESRS *see* Project Task Force on European Sustainability Reporting Standards
public climate finance 78–79
public environmental awareness (PEA) 552–553
public financial institutions (PFIs) in climate change 75–83; climate finance 75–83, *76*; geographic dimension of climate finance 79–81, *80*; governments and market actors, bridge between 79; in LCR projects 77–78; mitigation *vs.* adaptation *81*, 81–83, **82**; in researching and developing innovative financial tools for climate investments 79; role 77–79, *78*; in standards for climate investments 79
public policies 252–254; market instruments 253; non-market instruments 253
punctuated equilibrium theory 271

quota obligation, electricity 254

R&D expenditures 127n35
Rapp, A. C. 193
Reckein, D. **499**
RECs *see* Renewable Energy Certificates
RED *see* Renewable Energy Directive
Red Rocket Holding Ltd 328
Refinitiv DataStream database 135
Refinitiv ESG database 135
reform theory 272
RE funding 257
regulated asset base (RAB) model 380
regulatory fit *157*, 157–158
RE_{it} 172
Remote Sensing **367**
Renewable Energy Certificates (RECs) 253, 261n6
Renewable Energy Directive (RED) 399
renewable energy (RE) projects 248
RepOrting Standards for Systematic Evidence Syntheses (ROSES) 464, 467–468
resource-based accountability 237
resource dependence theory 169
Resource Use Score (*ResourceScore*) 171
return on assets (ROA) 134, 342–343
return on equity (ROE) 342–343
Richardson, A. J. 170
Riedl, A. 466
ROA *see* return on assets
RobecoSAM 104–105; Country Sustainability Ranking 246; environmental rating 119
Robinson, D. T. 162

ROE *see* return on equity
Rohde, C. 88, 92, 97
ROSES *see* RepOrting Standards for Systematic Evidence Syntheses
Rossing, C. P. 88, 92, 97
Roundy, P. T. 320
Royal Society for the Protection of Birds (RSPB) 381
Rózaszak, E. 532
RSPB *see* Royal Society for the Protection of Birds
Russia 378
Rydstrom, A. 254

Sachs, J. D. 221, 247
safeguard subjects 106
sales growth 231
Sanches Garcia, A. 170
Sangiorgi, I. 396, 522
Sartzetakis, E. S. 394
SASB *see* Sustainability Accounting Standards Board
Scales, I. R. 321
Schiereck, D. 518
Schopohl, L. 396, 522
Schubert, G. 275–276
Schwartz theory of universal values 154
Science-Based Targets for Nature (SBTN) **363**
Scopus database 448, 468
SDGs *see* Sustainable Development Goals
Sector Standards, GRI 47–48
Securities and Exchange Commission (SEC) 385
self-enhancement 155
self-transcendence 155
Semeen, H. 302
Semieniuk, M. 496
Senn, J. 308, 528, 534, 536
SEPA *see* State Environmental Protection Agency
Serafeim, G. 95
SFDR *see* Sustainable Finance Disclosure Regulation
SFF *see* Sustainable Finance Forum
shadow price 90, **91**, 92
Shanghai Pudong Development Bank 274
Shareholders Score (*ShareholdersScore*) 172
Sharfman, M. P. 467
sharpe ratio 121
Shell 220
Shen, C.-H. 341
Shipan, C. R. 271
Shrestha, P. 132
SIBs *see* state investment banks
signaling theory 169
SIIF *see* Social Innovation and Impact Foundation
Silk Road Fund 291
SIMI Global Resource Center (SIMI-GRC) 310
Simpson, W. G. 341

Singhvi, S. S. 169
single materiality 43–44
S_{it} 172
Skandinaviska Enskilda Banken AB 251
Slechten, A. 521
SLF *see* standing lending facility
small and medium enterprises (SMEs) 190, 227, 318
SMART 339–340
SMART financial goals 152
Smeets, P. 466
SMEs *see* small and medium enterprises
Smith, L. M. 341
social banks 247, 261n2
social finance movement 227–228
social impact 300–303; accounting 302; bonds 302; disclosures of charity organizations 303; norms of accounting for 307–308, **308**; previous accounting studies on 302–303, *303*
Social Impact Bond (SIB) 309, 313n9
Social Impact Measurement Initiative (SIMI) 309
Social Innovation and Impact Foundation (SIIF) 310
Socially Responsible Investing (SRI)-type mutual fund (Eco Fund) 309
socially responsible investments (SRI) 149
social resilience 452
social return on investment (SROI) 236
social score (*SScore*) 171
Social Value International (SVI) standards 304
SOCO International 169
SOEs *see* state-owned enterprises
SOIs *see* state-owned investors
sovereign sustainability linked bonds **360**
Species Threat Abatement and Restoration Metric (STAR) **366**
SRI *see* socially responsible investments
SROI *see* social return on investment
standing lending facility (SLF) 286
Stark, D. 301, 312
State Environmental Protection Agency (SEPA) 274
state investment banks (SIBs) 76
state-owned enterprises (SOEs) 431–441; CSRD for 431–432, 439–440; discussion on 440–441; sustainability reporting 431, 433–439
state-owned investors (SOIs) 76
Steen, B. 106
strategic nature reserves **360**
Streamlined European Biodiversity Indicators (SEBI) **366**
stress testing 59–60
Su, C.-W 550
sulfur dioxide (SO_2) 106, 542
supplementary fit 156
Sustainability Accounting Standards Board (SASB) 23, 42, 48–49, 103, 249; Activity Metrics 48–49; framework 48–49; General Issue Categories 48; standards 304
sustainability challenges 167
Sustainability Disclosure Standards, IFRS 48
Sustainability Economy Law (no 2/2011, article 39), Spain **529**
sustainability goals 248–251
sustainability linked bonds 267
sustainability reporting 23–37, 526–528, **529–530**; academic research, implications for 35–36; aims 43; double materiality for 44–45, *45*; dynamic materiality for 45–46, *46*; EFRAG, sustainability standards by 24, 29–32; European companies, implications for 35; European initiatives/view on 24, 29–32; EU *vs.* IFRS sustainability standards 32–33, **34**; harmonised standards within 26–27; IFRS S *vs.* ESRS 32–33; ISSB 27–29; legitimacy of norms 533–534; lessons learned for norms 534–538; mixed non-binding/binding elements in driving norms 534–535; NFRD 535–536; normativity 536–538; outlook 36–37; regulations at EU level **529**, 531–533; regulations at national level 530–531; regulators, implications for 33–34; role of 24–26; single materiality for 43–44; SMEs, implications for 535–536; stakeholder-engagement in norms and regulations 536; standardisation 536–538; standards for 24, 26–27
Sustainable Development Bonds 513
Sustainable Development Goals (SDGs) 7, 104, 167; economy for 167; environmental intensity 116, *117*, 118; green finance for 264, 337
Sustainable Finance Disclosure Regulation (SFDR) 25, 149, 385, 515, 526, **530**, 531–532
sustainable finance ecosystem, Aotearoa New Zealand (case study) 1–2, 7–19; actors in 12–16; discussion 16–17; entrepreneurial ecosystem in 8–11; factors in 14–16; financial sector actors in 13; findings 12–16; future research avenues and implications 18–19; government in 13; interdependencies among actors and factors 15–16; interview protocol and guide questions 21–22; Māori partners in 13–14; methodology 11–12; overview 7–8; research participants **12**; roadmap 7–8; scale of 7; SFF in 12–19; sustainability reporting 23–37
Sustainable Finance Forum (SFF) 8, 11–19
Sustainable finance taxonomy–Regulation (EU) 2020/852 247
Sustainalytics 104–105

Sustainalytics environmental rating 119
Suzuki, T. 238
SVI *see* Social Value International
Sweden 254–258
Swedish Environmental Code (1998) 526, **529**
Swedish Wind Energy Association (SWEA) 255
systems-building approach 237

tailpipe emissions 103
Taliento, M. 168
TANG 134
Tang, D. Y. 250, 395, 519
Tang, Q. 130–131, 133
Tanzania 219–220
tanzanite 220
Task Force for Climate-related Financial Disclosures (TCFD) 24, 103, 249, 289, 304, 317
Taskforce on Nature-related Financial Disclosure (TNFD) 289, **363**, **368**
tax-related transfer pricing 89
Taylor, S. 379
TCFD *see* Task Force for Climate-related Financial Disclosures
Technical Readiness Working Group (TRWG) 27
Technical Working Group 11
tendering 253, 261n6
Teng, M. 552–553
Thames Tideway Tunnel (TTT) 380
Three Mile Island (TMI), Pennsylvania 377
tipping point 307
Tirole, J. 464
Tobin's Q (TOBINQ) 96, 112, 119–121, **120**, 134, 168, 171
Toitū Tahua 13
Tokyo Accord in 2003 216
Tompkins, E. L. 496
Tong, S. T. 158
top-down approach of CSA 58, 62–66, 72; macroeconomic impact (step 2) 62–63, *63*; microeconomic impact (step 3) 63–66, *64–66*; profit and risk assessment (step 4) 66; scenario selection (step 1) 62
top-down climate scenario analysis 58
top-down governance, green finance in China 265, 281–286; from central to local levels 281, *282–283*, 283–284; in international comparison 284, *285*, 286
Topic Standards, GRI 48
Torvanger, A. 396
total greenhouse gas emissions (GHG total) 106
transfer pricing 87–89; contextual factors 92; design/use 88; dynamics of 88; ICP 92–97; OECD Guidelines 89; organizational problems with 88–89; situational factors 88; tax-related issues 89
transitional carbon opportunities 131

TRWG *see* Technical Readiness Working Group
TTT *see* Thames Tideway Tunnel
Tura, N. 177

UN Climate Change Conference 2021 (COP26) 75
UNDP BIOFIN *see* United Nations Development Program Biodiversity Finance Initiative
UN Environment Program (UNEP) 281, 400
UNEP *see* UN Environment Program
UNEP FI *see* United Nations Environment Programme Finance Initiative
United Nations Development Program Biodiversity Finance Initiative (UNDP BIOFIN) 359
United Nations Environment Programme Finance Initiative (UNEP FI) 264, 337–338, **363**
United Nations Framework Convention on Climate Change (UNFCCC) 502
United Nations (UN) Global Compact 30
United Nations' Principles for Responsible Banking (UNPRB) 2–3
unit root tests 199, **199**
universalism 154
Universal Standards, GRI 47
UN Life Cycle Impact Analysis Indicators (UN LCIA) 125n14
UNPRB *see* United Nations' Principles for Responsible Banking
UN Principles for Responsible Banking 194
UN Principles for Responsible Investment (PRI) 289
uranium 377, 381
urban climate change adaptation finance (study) 485–507; background 486–487; bibliometric analysis 489–490; citation analysis 493, 496, **497–498**; descriptive analysis 490; discipline distribution 490–493, **491–492**, *491–492*; guidance 505–506; institutions 498, **499**, 500, *500–501*; keywords 493, **494–495**; limitations 506; methodological process of study 487–490; overview 485–486; research gaps 502; state of play 502, **503–504**, 504–505; systematic literature review 487–489, *488*, **489**
US Atoms for Peace programme (1950) 377
US municipal bonds 193–194
utility costs, housing development 422

Value Reporting Foundation (VRF) 27
values 154–155, *155*; signal direction 155–156; universal 154
Van der Linde, C. 464
van Emous, R. 96
Verbruggen, A. 380
Vieira, E. T. 170

577

Vietnamese green bond market 396
Viviani, J-L. 239
volatile organic compounds (VOCs) 106, 111, 542
Volden, C. 271
Volvo Cars AB *93*
Volz, U. 454
von der Leyen, Ursula 512
VOSViewer software 449, 489–490, 493
VRF *see* Value Reporting Foundation

Walmart 103
Wang, B. 517–518
Wang, J. 395
Wang, M. 252
water, environmental impact 110–111
water discharge 125n10
Waterfund 104, 107, 110–111
water withdrawal 125n10
Watson, D. J. 88
Watts, E. M. 191
Watts, N. 321
WBA *see* World Benchmarking Alliance
WBCSD *see* World Business Council for Sustainable Development
Weber, O. 247
Web of Science database 448, 493
Weiss, M. 90
Welker, M. 170
well-being 150
Wellington, F. 129
Wetland Extent Trend (WET) database **368**
Wetland Extent Trend (WET) Index **367**
WICI *see* World Intellectual Capital Initiative
Willer, R. 155
willingness-to-pay (WTP) 106
wind farms, Sweden 246–247
WK_{it} 172

Wolf, J. 169
Wong, R. M. 96
Workforce Score (*WorkforceScore*) 171
World Bank 75, 223, 386, 513
World Benchmarking Alliance (WBA) 304
World Business Council for Sustainable Development (WBCSD) 23
World Database on Key Biodiversity Areas **368**
World Database on Protected Areas **368**
World Economic Forum 215
World Governance Index (*WGI*) 134
World Governance Indicator (*WGI*) 172
World Health Organization 223
World Intellectual Capital Initiative (WICI) 31
Worldscope 107
WTP *see* willingness-to-pay
Wu, M.-W. 341
Wu, Q. 552
Wu, X. 549

Xi Jinping 275

Yagil, J. 548
Yang, C. 303
Yang, M. 168

Zadek, S. 284
Zambia 219, 220
ZEBRA (Zero wastE Blade ReseArch) 382
Zerbib, O. D. 192, 197, 518
Zhang, D. 493
Zhang, Y. 250, 395, 519
Zhang, Ze 548–549
Zheng, H. 517–518
Zhou, G. 516–517
Zimmerman, B. 394
Z-Score 172